THE THEORY OF QUANTUM INFORMATION

This largely self-contained book on the theory of quantum information focuses on precise mathematical formulations and proofs of fundamental facts that form the foundation of the subject. It is intended for graduate students and researchers in mathematics, computer science, and theoretical physics seeking to develop a thorough understanding of key results, proof techniques, and methodologies that are relevant to a wide range of research topics within the theory of quantum information and computation.

The book is accessible to readers with an understanding of basic mathematics, including linear algebra, mathematical analysis, and probability theory. An introductory chapter summarizes these necessary mathematical prerequisites, and starting from this foundation the book includes clear and complete proofs of all results it presents. Each subsequent chapter includes challenging exercises intended to help readers develop their own skills for discovering proofs concerning the theory of quantum information.

JOHN WATROUS is a Professor in the School of Computer Science and a Faculty Member of the Institute for Quantum Computing at the University of Waterloo, Canada. He is also an Affiliate Member of the Perimeter Institute for Theoretical Physics and a Senior Fellow of the Canadian Institute for Advanced Research. Quantum information and computation has been his primary research focus for over 20 years.

THE THEORY OF QUANTUM INFORMATION

JOHN WATROUS

University of Waterloo, Canada

CAMBRIDGE
UNIVERSITY PRESS

CAMBRIDGE
UNIVERSITY PRESS

University Printing House, Cambridge CB2 8BS, United Kingdom

One Liberty Plaza, 20th Floor, New York, NY 10006, USA

477 Williamstown Road, Port Melbourne, VIC 3207, Australia

314–321, 3rd Floor, Plot 3, Splendor Forum, Jasola District Centre, New Delhi – 110025, India

79 Anson Road, #06–04/06, Singapore 079906

Cambridge University Press is part of the University of Cambridge.

It furthers the University's mission by disseminating knowledge in the pursuit of education, learning, and research at the highest international levels of excellence.

www.cambridge.org
Information on this title: www.cambridge.org/9781107180567
DOI: 10.1017/9781316848142

First published 2018

A catalogue record for this publication is available from the British Library.

ISBN 978-1-107-18056-7 Hardback

Contents

Preface

This is a book on the mathematical theory of quantum information, focusing on a formal presentation of definitions, theorems, and proofs. It is primarily intended for graduate students and researchers having some familiarity with quantum information and computation, such as would be covered in an introductory-level undergraduate or graduate course, or in one of several books on the subject that now exist.

Quantum information science has seen an explosive development in recent years, particularly within the past two decades. A comprehensive treatment of the subject, even if restricted to its theoretical aspects, would certainly require a series of books rather than just one. Consistent with this fact, the selection of topics covered herein is not intended to be fully representative of the subject. Quantum error correction and fault tolerance, quantum algorithms and complexity theory, quantum cryptography, and topological quantum computation are among the many interesting and fundamental topics found within the theoretical branches of quantum information science that are not covered in this book. Nevertheless, one is likely to encounter some of the core mathematical notions discussed in this book when studying these topics.

More broadly speaking, while the theory of quantum information is of course motivated both by quantum mechanics and by the potential utility of implementing quantum computing devices, these topics fall well outside of the scope of this book. The Schrödinger equation will not be found within these pages, and the difficult technological challenge of building quantum information processing devices is blissfully ignored. Indeed, no attention is paid in general to motives for studying the theory of quantum information; it is assumed that the reader has already been motivated to study this theory, and is perhaps interested in proving new theorems on quantum information of his or her own.

Some readers will find that this book deviates in some respects from the standard conventions of quantum information and computation, particularly with respect to notation and terminology. For example, the commonly used Dirac notation is not used in this book, and names and symbols associated with certain concepts differ from many other works. These differences are, however, fairly cosmetic, and those who have previously grown familiar with the notation and conventions of quantum information that are not followed in this book should not find it overly difficult to translate between the text and their own preferred notation and terminology.

Each chapter aside from the first includes a collection of exercises, some of which can reasonably be viewed as straightforward, and some of which are considerably more difficult. While the exercises may potentially be useful to course instructors, their true purpose is to be useful to students of the subject; there is no substitute for the learning experience to be found in wrestling with (and ideally solving) a difficult problem. In some cases the exercises represent the results of published research papers, and in those cases there has naturally been no attempt to disguise this fact or hide their sources, which may clearly reveal their solutions.

I thank Debbie Leung, Ashwin Nayak, Marco Piani, and Patrick Hayden for helpful discussions on some of the topics covered in this book. Over a number of years, this book has developed from a set of lecture notes, through a couple of drafts, to the present version, and during that time many people have brought mistakes to my attention and made other valuable suggestions, and I thank all of them. While the list of such people has grown quite long, and will not be included in this preface, I would be remiss if I did not gratefully acknowledge the efforts of Yuan Su and Maris Ozols, who provided extensive and detailed comments, corrections, and suggestions. Thanks are also due to Sascha Agne for assisting me with German translations.

The Institute for Quantum Computing and the School of Computer Science at the University of Waterloo have provided me both with the opportunity to write this book and with an environment in which it was possible, for which I am grateful. I also gratefully acknowledge financial support for my research program provided by the Natural Sciences and Engineering Research Council of Canada and the Canadian Institute for Advanced Research.

Finally, I thank Christiane, Anne, Liam, and Ethan, for reasons that have nothing to do with quantum information.

1

Mathematical Preliminaries

This chapter is intended to serve as a review of mathematical concepts to be used throughout this book, and also as a reference to be consulted as subsequent chapters are studied, if the need should arise. The first section focuses on linear algebra, and the second on analysis and related topics. Unlike the other chapters in this book, the present chapter does not include proofs, and is not intended to serve as a primary source for the material it reviews – a collection of references provided at the end of the chapter may be consulted by readers interested in a proper development of this material.

1.1 Linear Algebra

The theory of quantum information relies heavily on linear algebra in finite-dimensional spaces. The subsections that follow present an overview of the aspects of this subject that are most relevant within the theory of quantum information. It is assumed that the reader is already familiar with the most basic notions of linear algebra, including those of linear dependence and independence, subspaces, spanning sets, bases, and dimension.

1.1.1 Complex Euclidean Spaces

The notion of a complex Euclidean space is used throughout this book. One associates a complex Euclidean space with every discrete and finite system; and fundamental notions such as states and measurements of systems are represented in linear-algebraic terms that refer to these spaces.

Definition of Complex Euclidean Spaces

An *alphabet* is a finite and nonempty set, whose elements may be considered to be *symbols*. Alphabets will generally be denoted by capital Greek letters, including Σ, Γ, and Λ, while lower-case Roman letters near the beginning of the alphabet, including a, b, c, and d, will be used to denote symbols in alphabets. Examples of alphabets include the *binary alphabet* $\{0, 1\}$, the n-fold Cartesian product $\{0, 1\}^n$ of the binary alphabet with itself, and the alphabet $\{1, \ldots, n\}$, for n being a fixed positive integer.

For any alphabet Σ, one denotes by $\mathbb{C}^\Sigma$ the set of all functions from Σ to the complex numbers $\mathbb{C}$. The set $\mathbb{C}^\Sigma$ forms a vector space of dimension $|\Sigma|$ over the complex numbers when addition and scalar multiplication are defined in the following standard way:

1. Addition: for vectors $u, v \in \mathbb{C}^\Sigma$, the vector $u + v \in \mathbb{C}^\Sigma$ is defined by the equation $(u + v)(a) = u(a) + v(a)$ for all $a \in \Sigma$.
2. Scalar multiplication: for a vector $u \in \mathbb{C}^\Sigma$ and a scalar $\alpha \in \mathbb{C}$, the vector $\alpha u \in \mathbb{C}^\Sigma$ is defined by the equation $(\alpha u)(a) = \alpha u(a)$ for all $a \in \Sigma$.

A vector space defined in this way will be called a *complex Euclidean space*.[1] The value $u(a)$ is referred to as the *entry* of u indexed by a, for each $u \in \mathbb{C}^\Sigma$ and $a \in \Sigma$. The vector whose entries are all zero is simply denoted 0.

Complex Euclidean spaces will be denoted by scripted capital letters near the end of the alphabet, such as $\mathcal{W}$, $\mathcal{X}$, $\mathcal{Y}$, and $\mathcal{Z}$. Subsets of these spaces will also be denoted by scripted letters, and when possible this book will follow a convention to use letters such as $\mathcal{A}$, $\mathcal{B}$, and $\mathcal{C}$ near the beginning of the alphabet when these subsets are not necessarily vector spaces. Vectors will be denoted by lower-case Roman letters, again near the end of the alphabet, such as u, v, w, x, y, and z.

When n is a positive integer, one typically writes $\mathbb{C}^n$ rather than $\mathbb{C}^{\{1,\ldots,n\}}$, and it is also typical that one views a vector $u \in \mathbb{C}^n$ as an n-tuple of the form $u = (\alpha_1, \ldots, \alpha_n)$, or as a column vector of the form

$$u = \begin{pmatrix} \alpha_1 \\ \vdots \\ \alpha_n \end{pmatrix}, \tag{1.1}$$

for complex numbers $\alpha_1, \ldots, \alpha_n$.

For an arbitrary alphabet Σ, the complex Euclidean space $\mathbb{C}^\Sigma$ may be viewed as being equivalent to $\mathbb{C}^n$ for $n = |\Sigma|$; one simply fixes a bijection

$$f \colon \{1, \ldots, n\} \to \Sigma \tag{1.2}$$

and associates each vector $u \in \mathbb{C}^\Sigma$ with the vector in $\mathbb{C}^n$ whose k-th entry

---

[1] Many quantum information theorists prefer to use the term *Hilbert space*. The term *complex Euclidean space* will be preferred in this book, however, as the term *Hilbert space* refers to a more general notion that allows the possibility of infinite index sets.

is $u(f(k))$, for each $k \in \{1, \ldots, n\}$. This may be done implicitly when there is a natural or obviously preferred choice for the bijection f. For example, the elements of the alphabet $\Sigma = \{0, 1\}^2$ are naturally ordered 00, 01, 10, 11. Each vector $u \in \mathbb{C}^{\Sigma}$ may therefore be associated with the 4-tuple

$$(u(00), u(01), u(10), u(11)), \tag{1.3}$$

or with the column vector

$$\begin{pmatrix} u(00) \\ u(01) \\ u(10) \\ u(11) \end{pmatrix}, \tag{1.4}$$

when it is convenient to do this. While little or no generality would be lost in restricting one's attention to complex Euclidean spaces of the form $\mathbb{C}^n$ for this reason, it is both natural and convenient within computational and information-theoretic settings to allow complex Euclidean spaces to be indexed by arbitrary alphabets.

Inner Products and Norms of Vectors

The *inner product* $\langle u, v \rangle$ of two vectors $u, v \in \mathbb{C}^{\Sigma}$ is defined as

$$\langle u, v \rangle = \sum_{a \in \Sigma} \overline{u(a)}\, v(a). \tag{1.5}$$

It may be verified that the inner product satisfies the following properties:

1. Linearity in the second argument:

$$\langle u, \alpha v + \beta w \rangle = \alpha \langle u, v \rangle + \beta \langle u, w \rangle \tag{1.6}$$

   for all $u, v, w \in \mathbb{C}^{\Sigma}$ and $\alpha, \beta \in \mathbb{C}$.
2. Conjugate symmetry:

$$\langle u, v \rangle = \overline{\langle v, u \rangle} \tag{1.7}$$

   for all $u, v \in \mathbb{C}^{\Sigma}$.
3. Positive definiteness:

$$\langle u, u \rangle \geq 0 \tag{1.8}$$

   for all $u \in \mathbb{C}^{\Sigma}$, with equality if and only if $u = 0$.

It is typical that any function satisfying these three properties is referred to as an inner product, but this is the only inner product for vectors in complex Euclidean spaces that is considered in this book.

The *Euclidean norm* of a vector $u \in \mathbb{C}^{\Sigma}$ is defined as

$$\|u\| = \sqrt{\langle u, u \rangle} = \sqrt{\sum_{a \in \Sigma} |u(a)|^2}. \tag{1.9}$$

The Euclidean norm possesses the following properties, which define the more general notion of a norm:

1. Positive definiteness: $\|u\| \geq 0$ for all $u \in \mathbb{C}^{\Sigma}$, with $\|u\| = 0$ if and only if $u = 0$.
2. Positive scalability: $\|\alpha u\| = |\alpha| \|u\|$ for all $u \in \mathbb{C}^{\Sigma}$ and $\alpha \in \mathbb{C}$.
3. The triangle inequality: $\|u + v\| \leq \|u\| + \|v\|$ for all $u, v \in \mathbb{C}^{\Sigma}$.

The *Cauchy–Schwarz inequality* states that

$$|\langle u, v \rangle| \leq \|u\| \|v\| \tag{1.10}$$

for all $u, v \in \mathbb{C}^{\Sigma}$, with equality if and only if u and v are linearly dependent. The collection of all unit vectors in a complex Euclidean space $\mathcal{X}$ is called the *unit sphere* in that space, and is denoted

$$\mathcal{S}(\mathcal{X}) = \{u \in \mathcal{X} : \|u\| = 1\}. \tag{1.11}$$

The Euclidean norm represents the case $p = 2$ of the class of *p-norms*, defined for each $u \in \mathbb{C}^{\Sigma}$ as

$$\|u\|_p = \left(\sum_{a \in \Sigma} |u(a)|^p \right)^{\frac{1}{p}} \tag{1.12}$$

for $p < \infty$, and

$$\|u\|_\infty = \max\{|u(a)| : a \in \Sigma\}. \tag{1.13}$$

The above three norm properties (positive definiteness, positive scalability, and the triangle inequality) hold for $\|\cdot\|$ replaced by $\|\cdot\|_p$ for any choice of $p \in [1, \infty]$.

Orthogonality and Orthonormality

Two vectors $u, v \in \mathbb{C}^{\Sigma}$ are said to be *orthogonal* if $\langle u, v \rangle = 0$. The notation $u \perp v$ is also used to indicate that u and v are orthogonal. More generally, for any set $\mathcal{A} \subseteq \mathbb{C}^{\Sigma}$, the notation $u \perp \mathcal{A}$ indicates that $\langle u, v \rangle = 0$ for all vectors $v \in \mathcal{A}$.

A collection of vectors

$$\{u_a : a \in \Gamma\} \subset \mathbb{C}^{\Sigma}, \tag{1.14}$$

indexed by an alphabet Γ, is said to be an *orthogonal set* if it holds that

$\langle u_a, u_b \rangle = 0$ for all choices of $a, b \in \Gamma$ with $a \neq b$. A collection of nonzero orthogonal vectors is necessarily linearly independent.

An orthogonal set of *unit* vectors is called an *orthonormal set*, and when such a set forms a basis it is called an *orthonormal basis*. It holds that an orthonormal set of the form (1.14) is an orthonormal basis of $\mathbb{C}^\Sigma$ if and only if $|\Gamma| = |\Sigma|$. The *standard basis* of $\mathbb{C}^\Sigma$ is the orthonormal basis given by $\{e_a : a \in \Sigma\}$, where

$$e_a(b) = \begin{cases} 1 & \text{if } a = b \\ 0 & \text{if } a \neq b \end{cases} \tag{1.15}$$

for all $a, b \in \Sigma$.

Direct Sums of Complex Euclidean Spaces

The *direct sum* of n complex Euclidean spaces $\mathcal{X}_1 = \mathbb{C}^{\Sigma_1}, \ldots, \mathcal{X}_n = \mathbb{C}^{\Sigma_n}$ is the complex Euclidean space

$$\mathcal{X}_1 \oplus \cdots \oplus \mathcal{X}_n = \mathbb{C}^{\Sigma_1 \sqcup \cdots \sqcup \Sigma_n}, \tag{1.16}$$

where $\Sigma_1 \sqcup \cdots \sqcup \Sigma_n$ denotes the *disjoint union* of the alphabets $\Sigma_1, \ldots, \Sigma_n$, defined as

$$\Sigma_1 \sqcup \cdots \sqcup \Sigma_n = \bigcup_{k \in \{1,\ldots,n\}} \{(k, a) : a \in \Sigma_k\}. \tag{1.17}$$

For vectors $u_1 \in \mathcal{X}_1, \ldots, u_n \in \mathcal{X}_n$, the notation $u_1 \oplus \cdots \oplus u_n \in \mathcal{X}_1 \oplus \cdots \oplus \mathcal{X}_n$ refers to the vector for which

$$(u_1 \oplus \cdots \oplus u_n)(k, a) = u_k(a), \tag{1.18}$$

for each $k \in \{1, \ldots, n\}$ and $a \in \Sigma_k$. If each u_k is viewed as a column vector of dimension $|\Sigma_k|$, the vector $u_1 \oplus \cdots \oplus u_n$ may be viewed as a column vector

$$\begin{pmatrix} u_1 \\ \vdots \\ u_n \end{pmatrix} \tag{1.19}$$

having dimension $|\Sigma_1| + \cdots + |\Sigma_n|$.

Every element of the space $\mathcal{X}_1 \oplus \cdots \oplus \mathcal{X}_n$ can be written as $u_1 \oplus \cdots \oplus u_n$ for a unique choice of vectors $u_1, \ldots, u_n$. The following identities hold for every choice of $u_1, v_1 \in \mathcal{X}_1, \ldots, u_n, v_n \in \mathcal{X}_n$, and $\alpha \in \mathbb{C}$:

$$u_1 \oplus \cdots \oplus u_n + v_1 \oplus \cdots \oplus v_n = (u_1 + v_1) \oplus \cdots \oplus (u_n + v_n), \tag{1.20}$$

$$\alpha(u_1 \oplus \cdots \oplus u_n) = (\alpha u_1) \oplus \cdots \oplus (\alpha u_n), \tag{1.21}$$

$$\langle u_1 \oplus \cdots \oplus u_n, v_1 \oplus \cdots \oplus v_n \rangle = \langle u_1, v_1 \rangle + \cdots + \langle u_n, v_n \rangle. \tag{1.22}$$

Tensor Products of Complex Euclidean Spaces

The *tensor product* of n complex Euclidean spaces $\mathcal{X}_1 = \mathbb{C}^{\Sigma_1}, \ldots, \mathcal{X}_n = \mathbb{C}^{\Sigma_n}$ is the complex Euclidean space

$$\mathcal{X}_1 \otimes \cdots \otimes \mathcal{X}_n = \mathbb{C}^{\Sigma_1 \times \cdots \times \Sigma_n}. \tag{1.23}$$

For vectors $u_1 \in \mathcal{X}_1, \ldots, u_n \in \mathcal{X}_n$, the notation $u_1 \otimes \cdots \otimes u_n \in \mathcal{X}_1 \otimes \cdots \otimes \mathcal{X}_n$ refers to the vector for which

$$(u_1 \otimes \cdots \otimes u_n)(a_1, \ldots, a_n) = u_1(a_1) \cdots u_n(a_n). \tag{1.24}$$

Vectors of the form $u_1 \otimes \cdots \otimes u_n$ are called *elementary tensors*. They span the space $\mathcal{X}_1 \otimes \cdots \otimes \mathcal{X}_n$, but not every element of $\mathcal{X}_1 \otimes \cdots \otimes \mathcal{X}_n$ is an elementary tensor.

The following identities hold for all vectors $u_1, v_1 \in \mathcal{X}_1, \ldots, u_n, v_n \in \mathcal{X}_n$, scalars $\alpha, \beta \in \mathbb{C}$, and indices $k \in \{1, \ldots, n\}$:

$$\begin{aligned} u_1 \otimes &\cdots \otimes u_{k-1} \otimes (\alpha u_k + \beta v_k) \otimes u_{k+1} \otimes \cdots \otimes u_n \\ &= \alpha \left(u_1 \otimes \cdots \otimes u_{k-1} \otimes u_k \otimes u_{k+1} \otimes \cdots \otimes u_n \right) \\ &\quad + \beta \left(u_1 \otimes \cdots \otimes u_{k-1} \otimes v_k \otimes u_{k+1} \otimes \cdots \otimes u_n \right), \end{aligned} \tag{1.25}$$

$$\langle u_1 \otimes \cdots \otimes u_n, v_1 \otimes \cdots \otimes v_n \rangle = \langle u_1, v_1 \rangle \cdots \langle u_n, v_n \rangle. \tag{1.26}$$

Tensor products are often defined in a way that is more abstract (and more generally applicable) than the definition above, which is sometimes known more specifically as the *Kronecker product*. The following proposition is a reflection of the more abstract definition.

Proposition 1.1 *Let $\mathcal{X}_1, \ldots, \mathcal{X}_n$ and $\mathcal{Y}$ be complex Euclidean spaces and let*

$$\phi \colon \mathcal{X}_1 \times \cdots \times \mathcal{X}_n \to \mathcal{Y} \tag{1.27}$$

be a multilinear function, meaning a function for which the mapping

$$u_k \mapsto \phi(u_1, \ldots, u_n) \tag{1.28}$$

is linear for all $k \in \{1, \ldots, n\}$ and every fixed choice of vectors $u_1, \ldots, u_{k-1}$, $u_{k+1}, \ldots, u_n$. There exists a unique linear mapping

$$A\colon \mathcal{X}_1 \otimes \cdots \otimes \mathcal{X}_n \to \mathcal{Y} \tag{1.29}$$

such that

$$\phi(u_1, \ldots, u_n) = A(u_1 \otimes \cdots \otimes u_n) \tag{1.30}$$

for all choices of $u_1 \in \mathcal{X}_1, \ldots, u_n \in \mathcal{X}_n$.

If $\mathcal{X}$ is a complex Euclidean space, $u \in \mathcal{X}$ is a vector, and n is a positive integer, then the notations $\mathcal{X}^{\otimes n}$ and $u^{\otimes n}$ refer to the n-fold tensor product of either $\mathcal{X}$ or u with itself. It is often convenient to make the identification

$$\mathcal{X}^{\otimes n} = \mathcal{X}_1 \otimes \cdots \otimes \mathcal{X}_n, \tag{1.31}$$

under the assumption that $\mathcal{X}_1, \ldots, \mathcal{X}_n$ and $\mathcal{X}$ all refer to the same complex Euclidean space; this allows one to refer to the different tensor factors in $\mathcal{X}^{\otimes n}$ individually, and to express $\mathcal{X}_1 \otimes \cdots \otimes \mathcal{X}_n$ more concisely.

Remark A rigid interpretation of the definitions above suggests that tensor products of complex Euclidean spaces (or of vectors in complex Euclidean spaces) are not associative, insofar as Cartesian products are not associative. For instance, given alphabets Σ, Γ, and Λ, the alphabet $(\Sigma \times \Gamma) \times \Lambda$ contains elements of the form $((a, b), c)$, the alphabet $\Sigma \times (\Gamma \times \Lambda)$ contains elements of the form $(a, (b, c))$, and the alphabet $\Sigma \times \Gamma \times \Lambda$ contains elements of the form (a, b, c), for $a \in \Sigma$, $b \in \Gamma$, and $c \in \Lambda$. For $\mathcal{X} = \mathbb{C}^\Sigma$, $\mathcal{Y} = \mathbb{C}^\Gamma$, and $\mathcal{Z} = \mathbb{C}^\Lambda$, one may therefore view the complex Euclidean spaces $(\mathcal{X} \otimes \mathcal{Y}) \otimes \mathcal{Z}$, $\mathcal{X} \otimes (\mathcal{Y} \otimes \mathcal{Z})$, and $\mathcal{X} \otimes \mathcal{Y} \otimes \mathcal{Z}$ as being different.

However, the alphabets $(\Sigma \times \Gamma) \times \Lambda$, $\Sigma \times (\Gamma \times \Lambda)$, and $\Sigma \times \Gamma \times \Lambda$ can of course be viewed as equivalent by simply removing parentheses. For this reason, there is a natural equivalence between the complex Euclidean spaces $(\mathcal{X} \otimes \mathcal{Y}) \otimes \mathcal{Z}$, $\mathcal{X} \otimes (\mathcal{Y} \otimes \mathcal{Z})$, and $\mathcal{X} \otimes \mathcal{Y} \otimes \mathcal{Z}$. Whenever it is convenient, identifications of this sort are made implicitly throughout this book. For example, given vectors $u \in \mathcal{X} \otimes \mathcal{Y}$ and $v \in \mathcal{Z}$, the vector $u \otimes v$ may be treated as an element of $\mathcal{X} \otimes \mathcal{Y} \otimes \mathcal{Z}$ rather than $(\mathcal{X} \otimes \mathcal{Y}) \otimes \mathcal{Z}$.

Although such instances are much less common in this book, a similar convention applies to direct sums of complex Euclidean spaces.

Real Euclidean Spaces

Real Euclidean spaces are defined in a similar way to complex Euclidean spaces, except that the field of complex numbers $\mathbb{C}$ is replaced by the field of real numbers $\mathbb{R}$ in each of the definitions and concepts in which it arises.

Naturally, complex conjugation acts trivially in the real case, and therefore may be omitted.

Complex Euclidean spaces will play a more prominent role than real ones in this book. Real Euclidean spaces will, nevertheless, be important in those settings that make use of concepts from the theory of convexity. The space of Hermitian operators acting on a given complex Euclidean space is an important example of a real vector space that can be identified with a real Euclidean space, as is discussed in the subsection following this one.

1.1.2 Linear Operators

Given complex Euclidean spaces $\mathcal{X}$ and $\mathcal{Y}$, one writes $\mathrm{L}(\mathcal{X}, \mathcal{Y})$ to refer to the collection of all linear mappings of the form

$$A: \mathcal{X} \to \mathcal{Y}. \tag{1.32}$$

Such mappings will be referred to as *linear operators*, or simply *operators*, from $\mathcal{X}$ to $\mathcal{Y}$ in this book. Parentheses are omitted when expressing the action of linear operators on vectors when no confusion arises in doing so. For instance, one writes Au rather than $A(u)$ to denote the vector resulting from the application of an operator $A \in \mathrm{L}(\mathcal{X}, \mathcal{Y})$ to a vector $u \in \mathcal{X}$.

The set $\mathrm{L}(\mathcal{X}, \mathcal{Y})$ forms a complex vector space when addition and scalar multiplication are defined as follows:

1. Addition: for operators $A, B \in \mathrm{L}(\mathcal{X}, \mathcal{Y})$, the operator $A + B \in \mathrm{L}(\mathcal{X}, \mathcal{Y})$ is defined by the equation

$$(A + B)u = Au + Bu \tag{1.33}$$

   for all $u \in \mathcal{X}$.
2. Scalar multiplication: for an operator $A \in \mathrm{L}(\mathcal{X}, \mathcal{Y})$ and a scalar $\alpha \in \mathbb{C}$, the operator $\alpha A \in \mathrm{L}(\mathcal{X}, \mathcal{Y})$ is defined by the equation

$$(\alpha A)u = \alpha Au \tag{1.34}$$

   for all $u \in \mathcal{X}$.

Matrices and Their Correspondence with Operators

A *matrix* over the complex numbers is a mapping of the form

$$M : \Gamma \times \Sigma \to \mathbb{C} \tag{1.35}$$

for alphabets Σ and Γ. For $a \in \Gamma$ and $b \in \Sigma$ the value $M(a, b)$ is called the (a, b) *entry* of M, and the elements a and b are referred to as *indices* in this context: a is the *row index* and b is the *column index* of the entry $M(a, b)$. Addition and scalar multiplication of matrices are defined in a similar way to vectors in complex Euclidean spaces:

1. Addition: for matrices $M : \Gamma \times \Sigma \to \mathbb{C}$ and $N : \Gamma \times \Sigma \to \mathbb{C}$, the matrix $M + N$ is defined as

$$(M + N)(a, b) = M(a, b) + N(a, b) \qquad (1.36)$$

for all $a \in \Gamma$ and $b \in \Sigma$.

2. Scalar multiplication: for a matrix $M : \Gamma \times \Sigma \to \mathbb{C}$ and a scalar $\alpha \in \mathbb{C}$, the matrix αM is defined as

$$(\alpha M)(a, b) = \alpha M(a, b) \qquad (1.37)$$

for all $a \in \Gamma$ and $b \in \Sigma$.

In addition, one defines matrix multiplication as follows:

3. Matrix multiplication: for matrices $M : \Gamma \times \Lambda \to \mathbb{C}$ and $N : \Lambda \times \Sigma \to \mathbb{C}$, the matrix $MN : \Gamma \times \Sigma \to \mathbb{C}$ is defined as

$$(MN)(a, b) = \sum_{c \in \Lambda} M(a, c) N(c, b) \qquad (1.38)$$

for all $a \in \Gamma$ and $b \in \Sigma$.

For any choice of complex Euclidean spaces $\mathcal{X} = \mathbb{C}^\Sigma$ and $\mathcal{Y} = \mathbb{C}^\Gamma$, there is a bijective linear correspondence between the set of operators $\mathrm{L}(\mathcal{X}, \mathcal{Y})$ and the collection of all matrices taking the form $M : \Gamma \times \Sigma \to \mathbb{C}$ that is obtained as follows. With each operator $A \in \mathrm{L}(\mathcal{X}, \mathcal{Y})$, one associates the matrix M defined as

$$M(a, b) = \langle e_a, A e_b \rangle \qquad (1.39)$$

for $a \in \Gamma$ and $b \in \Sigma$. The operator A is uniquely determined by M, and may be recovered from M by the equation

$$(Au)(a) = \sum_{b \in \Sigma} M(a, b) u(b) \qquad (1.40)$$

for all $a \in \Gamma$. With respect to this correspondence, matrix multiplication is equivalent to operator composition.

Hereafter in this book, linear operators will be associated with matrices implicitly, without the introduction of names that distinguish matrices from the operators with which they are associated. With this in mind, the notation

$$A(a, b) = \langle e_a, A e_b \rangle \qquad (1.41)$$

is introduced for each $A \in L(\mathcal{X}, \mathcal{Y})$, $a \in \Gamma$, and $b \in \Sigma$ (where it is to be assumed that $\mathcal{X} = \mathbb{C}^{\Sigma}$ and $\mathcal{Y} = \mathbb{C}^{\Gamma}$, as above).

The Standard Basis of a Space of Operators

For every choice of complex Euclidean spaces $\mathcal{X} = \mathbb{C}^{\Sigma}$ and $\mathcal{Y} = \mathbb{C}^{\Gamma}$, and each choice of symbols $a \in \Gamma$ and $b \in \Sigma$, the operator $E_{a,b} \in L(\mathcal{X}, \mathcal{Y})$ is defined as

$$E_{a,b} u = u(b) e_a \tag{1.42}$$

for every $u \in \mathcal{X}$. Equivalently, $E_{a,b}$ is defined by the equation

$$E_{a,b}(c, d) = \begin{cases} 1 & \text{if } (c, d) = (a, b) \\ 0 & \text{otherwise} \end{cases} \tag{1.43}$$

holding for all $c \in \Gamma$ and $d \in \Sigma$. The collection

$$\{E_{a,b} \colon a \in \Gamma, \ b \in \Sigma\} \tag{1.44}$$

forms a basis of $L(\mathcal{X}, \mathcal{Y})$ known as the *standard basis* of this space. The number of elements in this basis is, of course, consistent with the fact that the dimension of $L(\mathcal{X}, \mathcal{Y})$ is given by $\dim(L(\mathcal{X}, \mathcal{Y})) = \dim(\mathcal{X}) \dim(\mathcal{Y})$.

The Entry-Wise Conjugate, Transpose, and Adjoint

For every operator $A \in L(\mathcal{X}, \mathcal{Y})$, for complex Euclidean spaces $\mathcal{X} = \mathbb{C}^{\Sigma}$ and $\mathcal{Y} = \mathbb{C}^{\Gamma}$, one defines three additional operators,

$$\overline{A} \in L(\mathcal{X}, \mathcal{Y}) \quad \text{and} \quad A^{\mathsf{T}}, A^* \in L(\mathcal{Y}, \mathcal{X}), \tag{1.45}$$

as follows:

1. The operator $\overline{A} \in L(\mathcal{X}, \mathcal{Y})$ is the operator whose matrix representation has entries that are complex conjugates to the matrix representation of A:

$$\overline{A}(a, b) = \overline{A(a, b)} \tag{1.46}$$

for all $a \in \Gamma$ and $b \in \Sigma$.

2. The operator $A^{\mathsf{T}} \in L(\mathcal{Y}, \mathcal{X})$ is the operator whose matrix representation is obtained by *transposing* the matrix representation of A:

$$A^{\mathsf{T}}(b, a) = A(a, b) \tag{1.47}$$

for all $a \in \Gamma$ and $b \in \Sigma$.

3. The operator $A^* \in L(\mathcal{Y}, \mathcal{X})$ is the uniquely determined operator that satisfies the equation

$$\langle v, Au \rangle = \langle A^*v, u \rangle \tag{1.48}$$

for all $u \in \mathcal{X}$ and $v \in \mathcal{Y}$. It may be obtained by performing both of the operations described in items 1 and 2:

$$A^* = \overline{A^\mathsf{T}}. \tag{1.49}$$

The operators $\overline{A}$, A^T, and A^* are called the *entry-wise conjugate, transpose,* and *adjoint* operators to A, respectively.

The mappings $A \mapsto \overline{A}$ and $A \mapsto A^*$ are conjugate linear and $A \mapsto A^\mathsf{T}$ is linear:

$$\overline{\alpha A + \beta B} = \overline{\alpha}\,\overline{A} + \overline{\beta}\,\overline{B},$$
$$(\alpha A + \beta B)^* = \overline{\alpha}A^* + \overline{\beta}B^*,$$
$$(\alpha A + \beta B)^\mathsf{T} = \alpha A^\mathsf{T} + \beta B^\mathsf{T},$$

for all $A, B \in L(\mathcal{X}, \mathcal{Y})$ and $\alpha, \beta \in \mathbb{C}$. These mappings are bijections, each being its own inverse.

Each vector $u \in \mathcal{X}$ in a complex Euclidean space $\mathcal{X}$ may be identified with the linear operator in $L(\mathbb{C}, \mathcal{X})$ defined as $\alpha \mapsto \alpha u$ for all $\alpha \in \mathbb{C}$. Through this identification, the linear mappings $\overline{u} \in L(\mathbb{C}, \mathcal{X})$ and $u^\mathsf{T}, u^* \in L(\mathcal{X}, \mathbb{C})$ are defined as above. As an element of $\mathcal{X}$, the vector $\overline{u}$ is simply the entry-wise complex conjugate of u, i.e., if $\mathcal{X} = \mathbb{C}^\Sigma$ then

$$\overline{u}(a) = \overline{u(a)} \tag{1.50}$$

for every $a \in \Sigma$. For each vector $u \in \mathcal{X}$ the mapping $u^* \in L(\mathcal{X}, \mathbb{C})$ satisfies $u^*v = \langle u, v \rangle$ for all $v \in \mathcal{X}$.

Kernel, Image, and Rank

The *kernel* of an operator $A \in L(\mathcal{X}, \mathcal{Y})$ is the subspace of $\mathcal{X}$ defined as

$$\ker(A) = \{u \in \mathcal{X} : Au = 0\}, \tag{1.51}$$

while the *image* of A is the subspace of $\mathcal{Y}$ defined as

$$\mathrm{im}(A) = \{Au : u \in \mathcal{X}\}. \tag{1.52}$$

For every operator $A \in L(\mathcal{X}, \mathcal{Y})$, one has that

$$\ker(A) = \ker(A^*A) \quad \text{and} \quad \mathrm{im}(A) = \mathrm{im}(AA^*), \tag{1.53}$$

as well as the equation

$$\dim(\ker(A)) + \dim(\mathrm{im}(A)) = \dim(\mathcal{X}). \tag{1.54}$$

The *rank* of an operator $A \in L(\mathcal{X}, \mathcal{Y})$, denoted rank$(A)$, is the dimension of the image of A:

$$\text{rank}(A) = \dim(\text{im}(A)). \tag{1.55}$$

By (1.53) and (1.54), one may conclude that

$$\text{rank}(A) = \text{rank}(AA^*) = \text{rank}(A^*A) \tag{1.56}$$

for every $A \in L(\mathcal{X}, \mathcal{Y})$.

For any choice of vectors $u \in \mathcal{X}$ and $v \in \mathcal{Y}$, the operator $vu^* \in L(\mathcal{X}, \mathcal{Y})$ satisfies

$$(vu^*)w = v(u^*w) = \langle u, w \rangle v \tag{1.57}$$

for all $w \in \mathcal{X}$. Assuming that u and v are nonzero, the operator vu^* has rank equal to one, and every rank-one operator in $L(\mathcal{X}, \mathcal{Y})$ can be expressed in this form for vectors u and v that are unique up to scalar multiples.

Operators Involving Direct Sums of Complex Euclidean Spaces

Suppose that

$$\mathcal{X}_1 = \mathbb{C}^{\Sigma_1}, \ldots, \mathcal{X}_n = \mathbb{C}^{\Sigma_n} \quad \text{and} \quad \mathcal{Y}_1 = \mathbb{C}^{\Gamma_1}, \ldots, \mathcal{Y}_m = \mathbb{C}^{\Gamma_m} \tag{1.58}$$

are complex Euclidean spaces, for alphabets $\Sigma_1, \ldots, \Sigma_n$ and $\Gamma_1, \ldots, \Gamma_m$. For a given operator

$$A \in L(\mathcal{X}_1 \oplus \cdots \oplus \mathcal{X}_n, \mathcal{Y}_1 \oplus \cdots \oplus \mathcal{Y}_m), \tag{1.59}$$

there exists a unique collection of operators

$$\{A_{j,k} \in L(\mathcal{X}_k, \mathcal{Y}_j) : 1 \leq j \leq m, \ 1 \leq k \leq n\} \tag{1.60}$$

for which the equation

$$A_{j,k}(a, b) = A((j, a), (k, b)) \tag{1.61}$$

holds for all $j \in \{1, \ldots, m\}$, $k \in \{1, \ldots, n\}$, $a \in \Gamma_j$, and $b \in \Sigma_k$. For all vectors $u_1 \in \mathcal{X}_1, \ldots, u_n \in \mathcal{X}_n$, one has that

$$A(u_1 \oplus \cdots \oplus u_n) = v_1 \oplus \cdots \oplus v_m \tag{1.62}$$

for $v_1 \in \mathcal{Y}_1, \ldots, v_m \in \mathcal{Y}_m$ being defined as

$$v_j = \sum_{k=1}^{n} A_{j,k} u_k \tag{1.63}$$

for each $j \in \{1, \ldots, m\}$. Conversely, for any collection of operators of the form (1.60), there is a unique operator A of the form (1.59) that obeys the equations (1.62) and (1.63) for all vectors $u_1 \in \mathcal{X}_1, \ldots, u_n \in \mathcal{X}_n$.

There is therefore a bijective correspondence between operators of the form (1.59) and collections of operators of the form (1.60). With respect to the matrix representations of these operators, this correspondence may be expressed succinctly as

$$A = \begin{pmatrix} A_{1,1} & \cdots & A_{1,n} \\ \vdots & \ddots & \vdots \\ A_{m,1} & \cdots & A_{m,n} \end{pmatrix}. \tag{1.64}$$

One interprets the right-hand side of (1.64) as the specification of the operator having the form (1.59) that is defined by the collection (1.60) in this way.

Tensor Products of Operators

Suppose that

$$\mathcal{X}_1 = \mathbb{C}^{\Sigma_1}, \ldots, \mathcal{X}_n = \mathbb{C}^{\Sigma_n} \quad \text{and} \quad \mathcal{Y}_1 = \mathbb{C}^{\Gamma_1}, \ldots, \mathcal{Y}_n = \mathbb{C}^{\Gamma_n} \tag{1.65}$$

are complex Euclidean spaces, for alphabets $\Sigma_1, \ldots, \Sigma_n$ and $\Gamma_1, \ldots, \Gamma_n$. For any choice of operators

$$A_1 \in \mathrm{L}(\mathcal{X}_1, \mathcal{Y}_1), \ldots, A_n \in \mathrm{L}(\mathcal{X}_n, \mathcal{Y}_n), \tag{1.66}$$

one defines the tensor product

$$A_1 \otimes \cdots \otimes A_n \in \mathrm{L}(\mathcal{X}_1 \otimes \cdots \otimes \mathcal{X}_n, \mathcal{Y}_1 \otimes \cdots \otimes \mathcal{Y}_n) \tag{1.67}$$

of these operators to be the unique operator that satisfies the equation

$$(A_1 \otimes \cdots \otimes A_n)(u_1 \otimes \cdots \otimes u_n) = (A_1 u_1) \otimes \cdots \otimes (A_n u_n) \tag{1.68}$$

for all choices of $u_1 \in \mathcal{X}_1, \ldots, u_n \in \mathcal{X}_n$. This operator may equivalently be defined in terms of its matrix representation as

$$(A_1 \otimes \cdots \otimes A_n)((a_1, \ldots, a_n), (b_1, \ldots, b_n))$$
$$= A_1(a_1, b_1) \cdots A_n(a_n, b_n) \tag{1.69}$$

for all $a_1 \in \Gamma_1, \ldots, a_n \in \Gamma_n$ and $b_1 \in \Sigma_1, \ldots, b_n \in \Sigma_n$.

For every choice of complex Euclidean spaces $\mathcal{X}_1, \ldots, \mathcal{X}_n, \mathcal{Y}_1, \ldots, \mathcal{Y}_n$, and $\mathcal{Z}_1, \ldots, \mathcal{Z}_n$, operators

$$A_1, B_1 \in \mathrm{L}(\mathcal{X}_1, \mathcal{Y}_1), \ldots, A_n, B_n \in \mathrm{L}(\mathcal{X}_n, \mathcal{Y}_n),$$
$$C_1 \in \mathrm{L}(\mathcal{Y}_1, \mathcal{Z}_1), \ldots, C_n \in \mathrm{L}(\mathcal{Y}_n, \mathcal{Z}_n), \tag{1.70}$$

and scalars $\alpha, \beta \in \mathbb{C}$, the following equations hold:

$$A_1 \otimes \cdots \otimes A_{k-1} \otimes (\alpha A_k + \beta B_k) \otimes A_{k+1} \otimes \cdots \otimes A_n$$
$$= \alpha(A_1 \otimes \cdots \otimes A_{k-1} \otimes A_k \otimes A_{k+1} \otimes \cdots \otimes A_n) \tag{1.71}$$
$$+ \beta(A_1 \otimes \cdots \otimes A_{k-1} \otimes B_k \otimes A_{k+1} \otimes \cdots \otimes A_n),$$

$$(C_1 \otimes \cdots \otimes C_n)(A_1 \otimes \cdots \otimes A_n) = (C_1 A_1) \otimes \cdots \otimes (C_n A_n), \tag{1.72}$$

$$(A_1 \otimes \cdots \otimes A_n)^\mathsf{T} = A_1^\mathsf{T} \otimes \cdots \otimes A_n^\mathsf{T}, \tag{1.73}$$

$$\overline{A_1 \otimes \cdots \otimes A_n} = \overline{A_1} \otimes \cdots \otimes \overline{A_n}, \tag{1.74}$$

$$(A_1 \otimes \cdots \otimes A_n)^* = A_1^* \otimes \cdots \otimes A_n^*. \tag{1.75}$$

Similar to vectors, for an operator A and a positive integer n, the notation $A^{\otimes n}$ refers to the n-fold tensor product of A with itself.

Square Operators

For every complex Euclidean space $\mathcal{X}$, the notation $\mathrm{L}(\mathcal{X})$ is understood to be a shorthand for $\mathrm{L}(\mathcal{X}, \mathcal{X})$. Operators in the space $\mathrm{L}(\mathcal{X})$ will be called *square operators*, due to the fact that their matrix representations are square, with rows and columns indexed by the same set.

The space $\mathrm{L}(\mathcal{X})$ is an *associative algebra*; in addition to being a vector space, the composition of square operators is associative and bilinear:

$$(XY)Z = X(YZ),$$
$$Z(\alpha X + \beta Y) = \alpha ZX + \beta ZY, \tag{1.76}$$
$$(\alpha X + \beta Y)Z = \alpha XZ + \beta YZ,$$

for every choice of $X, Y, Z \in \mathrm{L}(\mathcal{X})$ and $\alpha, \beta \in \mathbb{C}$.

The *identity operator* $\mathbb{1} \in \mathrm{L}(\mathcal{X})$ is the operator defined as $\mathbb{1} u = u$ for all $u \in \mathcal{X}$. It may also be defined by its matrix representation as

$$\mathbb{1}(a, b) = \begin{cases} 1 & \text{if } a = b \\ 0 & \text{if } a \neq b \end{cases} \tag{1.77}$$

for all $a, b \in \Sigma$, assuming $\mathcal{X} = \mathbb{C}^\Sigma$. One writes $\mathbb{1}_\mathcal{X}$ rather than $\mathbb{1}$ when it is helpful to indicate explicitly that this operator acts on $\mathcal{X}$.

For a complex Euclidean space $\mathcal{X}$, an operator $X \in \mathrm{L}(\mathcal{X})$ is *invertible* if there exists an operator $Y \in \mathrm{L}(\mathcal{X})$ such that $YX = \mathbb{1}$. When such an operator Y exists, it is necessarily unique and is denoted X^{-1}. When the inverse X^{-1} of X exists, it must also satisfy $XX^{-1} = \mathbb{1}$.

Trace and Determinant

The *diagonal* entries of a square operator $X \in L(\mathcal{X})$, for $\mathcal{X} = \mathbb{C}^{\Sigma}$, are those of the form $X(a, a)$ for $a \in \Sigma$. The *trace* of a square operator $X \in L(\mathcal{X})$ is defined as the sum of its diagonal entries:

$$\text{Tr}(X) = \sum_{a \in \Sigma} X(a, a). \tag{1.78}$$

Alternatively, the trace is the unique linear function $\text{Tr}: L(\mathcal{X}) \to \mathbb{C}$ such that, for all vectors $u, v \in \mathcal{X}$, one has

$$\text{Tr}(uv^*) = \langle v, u \rangle. \tag{1.79}$$

For every choice of complex Euclidean spaces $\mathcal{X}$ and $\mathcal{Y}$ and operators $A \in L(\mathcal{X}, \mathcal{Y})$ and $B \in L(\mathcal{Y}, \mathcal{X})$, it holds that

$$\text{Tr}(AB) = \text{Tr}(BA). \tag{1.80}$$

This property is known as the *cyclic property* of the trace.

By means of the trace, one defines an inner product on the space $L(\mathcal{X}, \mathcal{Y})$ as follows:

$$\langle A, B \rangle = \text{Tr}(A^* B) \tag{1.81}$$

for all $A, B \in L(\mathcal{X}, \mathcal{Y})$. It may be verified that this inner product satisfies the requisite properties of being an inner product:

1. Linearity in the second argument:

$$\langle A, \alpha B + \beta C \rangle = \alpha \langle A, B \rangle + \beta \langle A, C \rangle \tag{1.82}$$

for all $A, B, C \in L(\mathcal{X}, \mathcal{Y})$ and $\alpha, \beta \in \mathbb{C}$.
2. Conjugate symmetry:

$$\langle A, B \rangle = \overline{\langle B, A \rangle} \tag{1.83}$$

for all $A, B \in L(\mathcal{X}, \mathcal{Y})$.
3. Positive definiteness: $\langle A, A \rangle \geq 0$ for all $A \in L(\mathcal{X}, \mathcal{Y})$, with equality if and only if $A = 0$.

The *determinant* of a square operator $X \in L(\mathcal{X})$, for $\mathcal{X} = \mathbb{C}^{\Sigma}$, is defined by the equation

$$\text{Det}(X) = \sum_{\pi \in \text{Sym}(\Sigma)} \text{sign}(\pi) \prod_{a \in \Sigma} X(a, \pi(a)). \tag{1.84}$$

Here, the set $\text{Sym}(\Sigma)$ denotes the collection of all permutations $\pi: \Sigma \to \Sigma$, and $\text{sign}(\pi) \in \{-1, +1\}$ denotes the sign (or parity) of the permutation π. The determinant is multiplicative,

$$\text{Det}(XY) = \text{Det}(X)\text{Det}(Y) \tag{1.85}$$

for all $X, Y \in \text{L}(\mathcal{X})$, and $\text{Det}(X) \neq 0$ if and only if X is invertible.

Eigenvectors and Eigenvalues

If $X \in \text{L}(\mathcal{X})$ is an operator and $u \in \mathcal{X}$ is a nonzero vector for which it holds that

$$Xu = \lambda u \tag{1.86}$$

for some choice of $\lambda \in \mathbb{C}$, then u is said to be an *eigenvector* of X and λ is its corresponding *eigenvalue*.

For every operator $X \in \text{L}(\mathcal{X})$, one has that

$$p_X(\alpha) = \text{Det}(\alpha \mathbb{1}_{\mathcal{X}} - X) \tag{1.87}$$

is a monic polynomial in the variable α having degree $\dim(\mathcal{X})$, known as the *characteristic polynomial* of X. The *spectrum* of X, denoted $\text{spec}(X)$, is the multiset containing the roots of the polynomial p_X, where each root appears a number of times equal to its multiplicity. As p_X is monic, it holds that

$$p_X(\alpha) = \prod_{\lambda \in \text{spec}(X)} (\alpha - \lambda). \tag{1.88}$$

Each element $\lambda \in \text{spec}(X)$ is necessarily an eigenvalue of X, and every eigenvalue of X is contained in $\text{spec}(X)$.

The trace and determinant may be expressed in terms of the spectrum as follows:

$$\text{Tr}(X) = \sum_{\lambda \in \text{spec}(X)} \lambda \quad \text{and} \quad \text{Det}(X) = \prod_{\lambda \in \text{spec}(X)} \lambda \tag{1.89}$$

for every $X \in \text{L}(\mathcal{X})$. The *spectral radius* of an operator $X \in \text{L}(\mathcal{X})$ is the maximum absolute value $|\lambda|$ taken over all eigenvalues λ of X. For every choice of operators $X, Y \in \text{L}(\mathcal{X})$ it holds that

$$\text{spec}(XY) = \text{spec}(YX). \tag{1.90}$$

Lie Brackets and Commutants

A set $\mathcal{A} \subseteq \text{L}(\mathcal{X})$ is a *subalgebra* of $\text{L}(\mathcal{X})$ if it is closed under addition, scalar multiplication, and operator composition:

$$X + Y \in \mathcal{A}, \quad \alpha X \in \mathcal{A}, \quad \text{and} \quad XY \in \mathcal{A} \tag{1.91}$$

for all $X, Y \in \mathcal{A}$ and $\alpha \in \mathbb{C}$. A subalgebra $\mathcal{A}$ of $L(\mathcal{X})$ is said to be *self-adjoint* if it holds that $X^* \in \mathcal{A}$ for every $X \in \mathcal{A}$, and is said to be *unital* if it holds that $\mathbb{1} \in \mathcal{A}$.

For any pair of operators $X, Y \in L(\mathcal{X})$, the *Lie bracket* $[X, Y] \in L(\mathcal{X})$ is defined as

$$[X, Y] = XY - YX. \tag{1.92}$$

It holds that $[X, Y] = 0$ if and only if X and Y *commute*: $XY = YX$. For any subset of operators $\mathcal{A} \subseteq L(\mathcal{X})$, one defines the *commutant* of $\mathcal{A}$ as

$$\mathrm{comm}(\mathcal{A}) = \{Y \in L(\mathcal{X}) : [X, Y] = 0 \text{ for all } X \in \mathcal{A}\}. \tag{1.93}$$

The commutant of every subset of $L(\mathcal{X})$ is a unital subalgebra of $L(\mathcal{X})$.

Important Classes of Operators

The following classes of operators have particular importance in the theory of quantum information:

1. *Normal operators.* An operator $X \in L(\mathcal{X})$ is *normal* if it commutes with its adjoint: $[X, X^*] = 0$, or equivalently, $XX^* = X^*X$. The importance of this collection of operators, for the purposes of this book, is mainly derived from two facts: (i) the normal operators are those for which the spectral theorem (discussed later in Section 1.1.3) holds, and (ii) most of the special classes of operators that are discussed below are subsets of the normal operators.

2. *Hermitian operators.* An operator $X \in L(\mathcal{X})$ is *Hermitian* if $X = X^*$. The set of Hermitian operators acting on a complex Euclidean space $\mathcal{X}$ will hereafter be denoted $\mathrm{Herm}(\mathcal{X})$ in this book:

$$\mathrm{Herm}(\mathcal{X}) = \{X \in L(\mathcal{X}) : X = X^*\}. \tag{1.94}$$

   Every Hermitian operator is a normal operator.

3. *Positive semidefinite operators.* An operator $X \in L(\mathcal{X})$ is *positive semidefinite* if it holds that $X = Y^*Y$ for some operator $Y \in L(\mathcal{X})$. Positive semidefinite operators will, as a convention, often be denoted by the letters P, Q, and R in this book. The collection of positive semidefinite operators acting on $\mathcal{X}$ is denoted $\mathrm{Pos}(\mathcal{X})$, so that

$$\mathrm{Pos}(\mathcal{X}) = \{Y^*Y : Y \in L(\mathcal{X})\}. \tag{1.95}$$

   Every positive semidefinite operator is Hermitian.

4. *Positive definite operators.* A positive semidefinite operator $P \in \text{Pos}(\mathcal{X})$ is said to be *positive definite* if, in addition to being positive semidefinite, it is invertible. The notation

$$\text{Pd}(\mathcal{X}) = \{P \in \text{Pos}(\mathcal{X}): \text{Det}(P) \neq 0\} \tag{1.96}$$

will be used to denote the set of such operators for a complex Euclidean space $\mathcal{X}$.

5. *Density operators.* Positive semidefinite operators having trace equal to 1 are called *density operators.* Lower-case Greek letters, such as ρ, ξ, and σ, are conventionally used to denote density operators. The notation

$$\text{D}(\mathcal{X}) = \{\rho \in \text{Pos}(\mathcal{X}): \text{Tr}(\rho) = 1\} \tag{1.97}$$

will be used to denote the collection of density operators acting on a complex Euclidean space $\mathcal{X}$.

6. *Projection operators.* A positive semidefinite operator $\Pi \in \text{Pos}(\mathcal{X})$ is said to be a *projection operator*[2] if, in addition to being positive semidefinite, it satisfies the equation $\Pi^2 = \Pi$. Equivalently, a projection operator is a Hermitian operator whose only eigenvalues are 0 and 1. The collection of all projection operators of the form $\Pi \in \text{Pos}(\mathcal{X})$ is denoted $\text{Proj}(\mathcal{X})$. For each subspace $\mathcal{V} \subseteq \mathcal{X}$, there is a uniquely defined projection operator $\Pi \in \text{Proj}(\mathcal{X})$ satisfying $\text{im}(\Pi) = \mathcal{V}$; when it is convenient, the notation $\Pi_{\mathcal{V}}$ is used to refer to this projection operator.

7. *Isometries.* An operator $A \in \text{L}(\mathcal{X}, \mathcal{Y})$ is an *isometry* if it preserves the Euclidean norm: $\|Au\| = \|u\|$ for all $u \in \mathcal{X}$. This condition is equivalent to $A^*A = \mathbb{1}_{\mathcal{X}}$. The notation

$$\text{U}(\mathcal{X}, \mathcal{Y}) = \{A \in \text{L}(\mathcal{X}, \mathcal{Y}): A^*A = \mathbb{1}_{\mathcal{X}}\} \tag{1.98}$$

is used to denote this class of operators. In order for an isometry of the form $A \in \text{U}(\mathcal{X}, \mathcal{Y})$ to exist, it must hold that $\dim(\mathcal{Y}) \geq \dim(\mathcal{X})$. Every isometry preserves not only the Euclidean norm, but inner products as well: $\langle Au, Av \rangle = \langle u, v \rangle$ for all $u, v \in \mathcal{X}$.

8. *Unitary operators.* The set of isometries mapping a complex Euclidean space $\mathcal{X}$ to itself is denoted $\text{U}(\mathcal{X})$, and operators in this set are *unitary operators.* The letters U, V, and W will often be used to refer to unitary operators (and sometimes to isometries more generally) in this book. Every unitary operator $U \in \text{U}(\mathcal{X})$ is necessarily invertible and satisfies the equation $UU^* = U^*U = \mathbb{1}_{\mathcal{X}}$, and is therefore normal.

---

[2] Sometimes the term *projection operator* refers to an operator $X \in \text{L}(\mathcal{X})$ that satisfies the equation $X^2 = X$, but that might not be Hermitian. This is not the meaning that is associated with this term in this book.

9. *Diagonal operators.* An operator $X \in L(\mathcal{X})$, for a complex Euclidean space of the form $\mathcal{X} = \mathbb{C}^\Sigma$, is a *diagonal operator* if $X(a, b) = 0$ for all $a, b \in \Sigma$ with $a \neq b$. For a given vector $u \in \mathcal{X}$, one writes $\mathrm{Diag}(u) \in L(\mathcal{X})$ to denote the diagonal operator defined as

$$\mathrm{Diag}(u)(a, b) = \begin{cases} u(a) & \text{if } a = b \\ 0 & \text{if } a \neq b. \end{cases} \tag{1.99}$$

Further Remarks on Hermitian and Positive Semidefinite Operators

The sum of two Hermitian operators is Hermitian, as is a real scalar multiple of a Hermitian operator. The inner product of two Hermitian operators is real as well. For every choice of a complex Euclidean space $\mathcal{X}$, the space $\mathrm{Herm}(\mathcal{X})$ therefore forms a vector space over the real numbers on which an inner product is defined.

Indeed, under the assumption that $\mathcal{X} = \mathbb{C}^\Sigma$, it holds that the space $\mathrm{Herm}(\mathcal{X})$ and the real Euclidean space $\mathbb{R}^{\Sigma \times \Sigma}$ are *isometrically isomorphic*: there exists a linear bijection

$$\phi \colon \mathbb{R}^{\Sigma \times \Sigma} \to \mathrm{Herm}(\mathcal{X}) \tag{1.100}$$

with the property that

$$\langle \phi(u), \phi(v) \rangle = \langle u, v \rangle \tag{1.101}$$

for all $u, v \in \mathbb{R}^{\Sigma \times \Sigma}$. The existence of such a linear bijection allows one to directly translate many statements about real Euclidean spaces to the space of Hermitian operators acting on a complex Euclidean space.

One way to define a mapping ϕ as above is as follows. First, assume that a total ordering of Σ has been fixed, and define a collection

$$\{H_{a,b} \colon (a, b) \in \Sigma \times \Sigma\} \subset \mathrm{Herm}(\mathcal{X}) \tag{1.102}$$

as

$$H_{a,b} = \begin{cases} E_{a,a} & \text{if } a = b \\ \frac{1}{\sqrt{2}}(E_{a,b} + E_{b,a}) & \text{if } a < b \\ \frac{1}{\sqrt{2}}(iE_{a,b} - iE_{b,a}) & \text{if } a > b \end{cases} \tag{1.103}$$

for each pair $(a, b) \in \Sigma \times \Sigma$. It holds that (1.102) is an orthonormal set (with respect to the usual inner product defined on $L(\mathcal{X})$), and moreover every element of $\mathrm{Herm}(\mathcal{X})$ can be expressed uniquely as a real linear combination of the operators in this set. The mapping ϕ defined by the equation

$$\phi(e_{(a,b)}) = H_{a,b}, \tag{1.104}$$

and extended to all of $\mathbb{R}^{\Sigma \times \Sigma}$ by linearity, satisfies the requirement (1.101).

The eigenvalues of a Hermitian operator are necessarily real numbers, and can therefore be ordered from largest to smallest. For every complex Euclidean space $\mathcal{X}$ and every Hermitian operator $H \in \mathrm{Herm}(\mathcal{X})$, the vector

$$\lambda(H) = (\lambda_1(H), \lambda_2(H), \ldots, \lambda_n(H)) \in \mathbb{R}^n \qquad (1.105)$$

is defined so that

$$\mathrm{spec}(H) = \{\lambda_1(H), \lambda_2(H), \ldots, \lambda_n(H)\} \qquad (1.106)$$

and

$$\lambda_1(H) \geq \lambda_2(H) \geq \cdots \geq \lambda_n(H). \qquad (1.107)$$

The notation $\lambda_k(H)$ may also be used in isolation to refer to the k-th largest eigenvalue of a Hermitian operator H.

The eigenvalues of Hermitian operators can be characterized by a theorem known as the *Courant–Fischer theorem*, which is as follows.

Theorem 1.2 (Courant–Fischer theorem) *Let $\mathcal{X}$ be a complex Euclidean space of dimension n and let $H \in \mathrm{Herm}(\mathcal{X})$ be a Hermitian operator. For every $k \in \{1, \ldots, n\}$ it holds that*

$$
\begin{aligned}
\lambda_k(H) &= \max_{u_1,\ldots,u_{n-k} \in \mathcal{S}(\mathcal{X})} \min_{\substack{v \in \mathcal{S}(\mathcal{X}) \\ v \perp \{u_1,\ldots,u_{n-k}\}}} v^* H v \\
&= \min_{u_1,\ldots,u_{k-1} \in \mathcal{S}(\mathcal{X})} \max_{\substack{v \in \mathcal{S}(\mathcal{X}) \\ v \perp \{u_1,\ldots,u_{k-1}\}}} v^* H v.
\end{aligned}
\qquad (1.108)
$$

(It is to be interpreted that the maximum or minimum is omitted if it is to be taken over an empty set of vectors, and that $v \perp \varnothing$ holds for all $v \in \mathcal{X}$.)

There are alternative ways to describe positive semidefinite operators that are useful in different situations. In particular, the following statements are equivalent for every operator $P \in \mathrm{L}(\mathcal{X})$:

1. P is positive semidefinite.
2. $P = A^* A$ for an operator $A \in \mathrm{L}(\mathcal{X}, \mathcal{Y})$, for some choice of a complex Euclidean space $\mathcal{Y}$.
3. P is Hermitian and every eigenvalue of P is nonnegative.
4. $\langle u, Pu \rangle$ is a nonnegative real number for all $u \in \mathcal{X}$.
5. $\langle Q, P \rangle$ is a nonnegative real number for all $Q \in \mathrm{Pos}(\mathcal{X})$.
6. There exists a collection of vectors $\{u_a : a \in \Sigma\} \subset \mathcal{X}$ for which it holds that $P(a, b) = \langle u_a, u_b \rangle$ for all $a, b \in \Sigma$.

7. There exists a collection of vectors $\{u_a : a \in \Sigma\} \subset \mathcal{Y}$, for some choice of a complex Euclidean space $\mathcal{Y}$, for which it holds that $P(a, b) = \langle u_a, u_b \rangle$ for all $a, b \in \Sigma$.

Along similar lines, one has that the following statements are equivalent for every operator $P \in L(\mathcal{X})$:

1. P is positive definite.
2. P is Hermitian, and every eigenvalue of P is positive.
3. $\langle u, Pu \rangle$ is a positive real number for every nonzero $u \in \mathcal{X}$.
4. $\langle Q, P \rangle$ is a positive real number for every nonzero $Q \in \text{Pos}(\mathcal{X})$.
5. There exists a positive real number $\varepsilon > 0$ such that $P - \varepsilon \mathbb{1} \in \text{Pos}(\mathcal{X})$.

The notations $P \geq 0$ and $0 \leq P$ indicate that P is positive semidefinite, while $P > 0$ and $0 < P$ indicate that P is positive definite. More generally, for Hermitian operators X and Y, one writes either $X \geq Y$ or $Y \leq X$ to indicate that $X - Y$ is positive semidefinite, and either $X > Y$ or $Y < X$ to indicate that $X - Y$ is positive definite.

Linear Maps on Square Operators

Linear maps of the form

$$\Phi : L(\mathcal{X}) \to L(\mathcal{Y}), \tag{1.109}$$

for complex Euclidean spaces $\mathcal{X}$ and $\mathcal{Y}$, play a fundamental role in the theory of quantum information. The set of all such maps is denoted $T(\mathcal{X}, \mathcal{Y})$, and is itself a complex vector space when addition and scalar multiplication are defined in the straightforward way:

1. Addition: given two maps $\Phi, \Psi \in T(\mathcal{X}, \mathcal{Y})$, the map $\Phi + \Psi \in T(\mathcal{X}, \mathcal{Y})$ is defined as

$$(\Phi + \Psi)(X) = \Phi(X) + \Psi(X) \tag{1.110}$$

for all $X \in L(\mathcal{X})$.
2. Scalar multiplication: given a map $\Phi \in T(\mathcal{X}, \mathcal{Y})$ and a scalar $\alpha \in \mathbb{C}$, the map $\alpha \Phi \in T(\mathcal{X}, \mathcal{Y})$ is defined as

$$(\alpha \Phi)(X) = \alpha \Phi(X) \tag{1.111}$$

for all $X \in L(\mathcal{X})$.

For a given map $\Phi \in T(\mathcal{X}, \mathcal{Y})$, the *adjoint* of Φ is defined to be the unique map $\Phi^* \in T(\mathcal{Y}, \mathcal{X})$ that satisfies

$$\langle \Phi^*(Y), X \rangle = \langle Y, \Phi(X) \rangle \tag{1.112}$$

for all $X \in L(\mathcal{X})$ and $Y \in L(\mathcal{Y})$.

Tensor products of maps of the form (1.109) are defined in a similar way to tensor products of operators. More specifically, for any choice of complex Euclidean spaces $\mathcal{X}_1, \ldots, \mathcal{X}_n$ and $\mathcal{Y}_1, \ldots, \mathcal{Y}_n$ and linear maps

$$\Phi_1 \in T(\mathcal{X}_1, \mathcal{Y}_1), \quad \ldots, \quad \Phi_n \in T(\mathcal{X}_n, \mathcal{Y}_n), \tag{1.113}$$

one defines the tensor product of these maps

$$\Phi_1 \otimes \cdots \otimes \Phi_n \in T(\mathcal{X}_1 \otimes \cdots \otimes \mathcal{X}_n, \mathcal{Y}_1 \otimes \cdots \otimes \mathcal{Y}_n) \tag{1.114}$$

to be the unique linear map that satisfies the equation

$$(\Phi_1 \otimes \cdots \otimes \Phi_n)(X_1 \otimes \cdots \otimes X_n) = \Phi_1(X_1) \otimes \cdots \otimes \Phi_n(X_n) \tag{1.115}$$

for all operators $X_1 \in L(\mathcal{X}_1), \ldots, X_n \in L(\mathcal{X}_n)$. As for vectors and operators, the notation $\Phi^{\otimes n}$ denotes the n-fold tensor product of a map Φ with itself.

The notation $T(\mathcal{X})$ is understood to be a shorthand for $T(\mathcal{X}, \mathcal{X})$. The identity map $\mathbb{1}_{L(\mathcal{X})} \in T(\mathcal{X})$ is defined as

$$\mathbb{1}_{L(\mathcal{X})}(X) = X \tag{1.116}$$

for all $X \in L(\mathcal{X})$.

The trace function defined for square operators acting on $\mathcal{X}$ is a linear mapping of the form

$$\text{Tr} : L(\mathcal{X}) \to \mathbb{C}. \tag{1.117}$$

By making the identification $L(\mathbb{C}) = \mathbb{C}$, one sees that the trace function is a linear map of the form

$$\text{Tr} \in T(\mathcal{X}, \mathbb{C}). \tag{1.118}$$

For a second complex Euclidean space $\mathcal{Y}$, one may consider the map

$$\text{Tr} \otimes \mathbb{1}_{L(\mathcal{Y})} \in T(\mathcal{X} \otimes \mathcal{Y}, \mathcal{Y}). \tag{1.119}$$

By the definition of the tensor product of maps stated above, this is the unique map that satisfies the equation

$$(\text{Tr} \otimes \mathbb{1}_{L(\mathcal{Y})})(X \otimes Y) = \text{Tr}(X)Y \tag{1.120}$$

for all operators $X \in L(\mathcal{X})$ and $Y \in L(\mathcal{Y})$. This map is called the *partial trace*, and is more commonly denoted $\text{Tr}_{\mathcal{X}}$. Along similar lines, the map $\text{Tr}_{\mathcal{Y}} \in T(\mathcal{X} \otimes \mathcal{Y}, \mathcal{X})$ is defined as

$$\text{Tr}_{\mathcal{Y}} = \mathbb{1}_{L(\mathcal{X})} \otimes \text{Tr}. \tag{1.121}$$

Generalizations of these maps may also be defined for tensor products of three or more complex Euclidean spaces.

The following classes of maps of the form (1.109) are among those that are discussed in greater detail later in this book:

1. *Hermitian-preserving maps.* A map $\Phi \in T(\mathcal{X}, \mathcal{Y})$ is *Hermitian-preserving* if it holds that

$$\Phi(H) \in \text{Herm}(\mathcal{Y}) \tag{1.122}$$

   for every Hermitian operator $H \in \text{Herm}(\mathcal{X})$.
2. *Positive maps.* A map $\Phi \in T(\mathcal{X}, \mathcal{Y})$ is *positive* if it holds that

$$\Phi(P) \in \text{Pos}(\mathcal{Y}) \tag{1.123}$$

   for every positive semidefinite operator $P \in \text{Pos}(\mathcal{X})$.
3. *Completely positive maps.* A map $\Phi \in T(\mathcal{X}, \mathcal{Y})$ is *completely positive* if it holds that

$$\Phi \otimes \mathbb{1}_{L(\mathcal{Z})} \tag{1.124}$$

   is a positive map for every complex Euclidean space $\mathcal{Z}$. The set of all completely positive maps of this form is denoted $\text{CP}(\mathcal{X}, \mathcal{Y})$.
4. *Trace-preserving maps.* A map $\Phi \in T(\mathcal{X}, \mathcal{Y})$ is *trace-preserving* if it holds that

$$\text{Tr}(\Phi(X)) = \text{Tr}(X) \tag{1.125}$$

   for all $X \in L(\mathcal{X})$.
5. *Unital maps.* A map $\Phi \in T(\mathcal{X}, \mathcal{Y})$ is *unital* if

$$\Phi(\mathbb{1}_{\mathcal{X}}) = \mathbb{1}_{\mathcal{Y}}. \tag{1.126}$$

Maps of these sorts are discussed in greater detail in Chapters 2 and 4.

The Operator–Vector Correspondence

There is a correspondence between the spaces $L(\mathcal{Y}, \mathcal{X})$ and $\mathcal{X} \otimes \mathcal{Y}$, for any choice of complex Euclidean spaces $\mathcal{X} = \mathbb{C}^{\Sigma}$ and $\mathcal{Y} = \mathbb{C}^{\Gamma}$, that will be used repeatedly throughout this book. This correspondence is given by the linear mapping

$$\text{vec}: L(\mathcal{Y}, \mathcal{X}) \to \mathcal{X} \otimes \mathcal{Y}, \tag{1.127}$$

defined by the action

$$\text{vec}(E_{a,b}) = e_a \otimes e_b \tag{1.128}$$

for all $a \in \Sigma$ and $b \in \Gamma$. In other words, this mapping is the change of basis taking the standard basis of $L(\mathcal{Y}, \mathcal{X})$ to the standard basis of $\mathcal{X} \otimes \mathcal{Y}$. By linearity, it holds that

$$\text{vec}(uv^*) = u \otimes \overline{v} \tag{1.129}$$

for $u \in \mathcal{X}$ and $v \in \mathcal{Y}$. This includes the special cases

$$\mathrm{vec}(u) = u \quad \text{and} \quad \mathrm{vec}(v^*) = \overline{v}, \tag{1.130}$$

obtained by setting $v = 1$ and $u = 1$, respectively.

The vec mapping is a linear bijection, which implies that every vector $u \in \mathcal{X} \otimes \mathcal{Y}$ uniquely determines an operator $A \in \mathrm{L}(\mathcal{Y}, \mathcal{X})$ that satisfies $\mathrm{vec}(A) = u$. It is also an isometry, in the sense that

$$\langle A, B \rangle = \langle \mathrm{vec}(A), \mathrm{vec}(B) \rangle \tag{1.131}$$

for all $A, B \in \mathrm{L}(\mathcal{Y}, \mathcal{X})$.

A few specific identities concerning the vec mapping will be especially useful throughout this book. One such identity is

$$(A_0 \otimes A_1) \, \mathrm{vec}(B) = \mathrm{vec}(A_0 B A_1^{\mathsf{T}}), \tag{1.132}$$

holding for all operators $A_0 \in \mathrm{L}(\mathcal{X}_0, \mathcal{Y}_0)$, $A_1 \in \mathrm{L}(\mathcal{X}_1, \mathcal{Y}_1)$, and $B \in \mathrm{L}(\mathcal{X}_1, \mathcal{X}_0)$, over all choices of complex Euclidean spaces $\mathcal{X}_0$, $\mathcal{X}_1$, $\mathcal{Y}_0$, and $\mathcal{Y}_1$. Two more such identities are

$$\mathrm{Tr}_{\mathcal{Y}}\big(\mathrm{vec}(A)\,\mathrm{vec}(B)^*\big) = AB^*, \tag{1.133}$$
$$\mathrm{Tr}_{\mathcal{X}}\big(\mathrm{vec}(A)\,\mathrm{vec}(B)^*\big) = A^{\mathsf{T}}\overline{B}, \tag{1.134}$$

which hold for all operators $A, B \in \mathrm{L}(\mathcal{Y}, \mathcal{X})$, over all choices of complex Euclidean spaces $\mathcal{X}$ and $\mathcal{Y}$.

1.1.3 Operator Decompositions and Norms

Two decompositions of operators – the *spectral decomposition* and *singular value decomposition* – along with various related notions, are discussed in the present section. Among these related notions is a class of operator norms called *Schatten norms*, which include the trace norm, the Frobenius norm, and the spectral norm. These three norms are used frequently throughout this book.

The Spectral Theorem

The *spectral theorem* establishes that every normal operator can be expressed as a linear combination of projections onto pairwise orthogonal subspaces. A formal statement of the spectral theorem follows.

Theorem 1.3 (Spectral theorem) *Let $\mathcal{X}$ be a complex Euclidean space and let $X \in L(\mathcal{X})$ be a normal operator. There exist a positive integer m, distinct complex numbers $\lambda_1, \ldots, \lambda_m \in \mathbb{C}$, and nonzero projection operators $\Pi_1, \ldots, \Pi_m \in \mathrm{Proj}(\mathcal{X})$ satisfying $\Pi_1 + \cdots + \Pi_m = \mathbb{1}_{\mathcal{X}}$, such that*

$$X = \sum_{k=1}^{m} \lambda_k \Pi_k. \tag{1.135}$$

The scalars $\lambda_1, \ldots, \lambda_m$ and projection operators $\Pi_1, \ldots, \Pi_m$ are unique, up to their ordering: each scalar λ_k is an eigenvalue of X with multiplicity equal to the rank of Π_k, and Π_k is the projection operator onto the space spanned by the eigenvectors of X corresponding to the eigenvalue λ_k.

The expression of a normal operator X in the form of the equation (1.135) is called a *spectral decomposition* of X.

A simple corollary of the spectral theorem follows. It expresses essentially the same fact as the spectral theorem, but in a slightly different form that will sometimes be convenient to refer to later in the book.

Corollary 1.4 *Let $\mathcal{X}$ be a complex Euclidean space having dimension n, let $X \in L(\mathcal{X})$ be a normal operator, and assume that*

$$\mathrm{spec}(X) = \{\lambda_1, \ldots, \lambda_n\}. \tag{1.136}$$

There exists an orthonormal basis $\{x_1, \ldots, x_n\}$ of $\mathcal{X}$ such that

$$X = \sum_{k=1}^{n} \lambda_k x_k x_k^*. \tag{1.137}$$

It is evident from the expression (1.137), along with the requirement that the set $\{x_1, \ldots, x_n\}$ is an orthonormal basis, that each x_k is an eigenvector of X whose corresponding eigenvalue is λ_k. It is also evident that any operator X that is expressible in such a form as (1.137) is normal, implying that the condition of normality is equivalent to the existence of an orthonormal basis of eigenvectors.

On a few occasions later in the book, it will be convenient to index the eigenvectors and eigenvalues of a given normal operator $X \in L(\mathbb{C}^\Sigma)$ by symbols in the alphabet Σ rather than by integers in the set $\{1, \ldots, n\}$ for $n = |\Sigma|$. It follows immediately from Corollary 1.4 that a normal operator $X \in L(\mathbb{C}^\Sigma)$ may be expressed as

$$X = \sum_{a \in \Sigma} \lambda_a x_a x_a^* \tag{1.138}$$

for some choice of an orthonormal basis $\{x_a : a \in \Sigma\}$ of $\mathbb{C}^\Sigma$ and a collection of complex numbers $\{\lambda_a : a \in \Sigma\}$. Indeed, such an expression may be derived from (1.137) by associating symbols in the alphabet Σ with integers in the set $\{1, \ldots, n\}$ with respect to an arbitrarily chosen bijection.

It is convenient to refer to expressions of operators having either of the forms (1.137) or (1.138) as *spectral decompositions*, despite the fact that they may differ slightly from the form (1.135). Unlike the form (1.135), the forms (1.137) and (1.138) are generally not unique. Along similar lines, the term *spectral theorem* is sometimes used to refer to the statement of Corollary 1.4, as opposed to the statement of Theorem 1.3. These conventions are followed throughout this book when there is no danger of any confusion resulting from their use.

The following important theorem states that the same orthonormal basis of eigenvectors $\{x_1, \ldots, x_n\}$ may be chosen for any two normal operators under the assumption that they commute.

Theorem 1.5 *Let $\mathcal{X}$ be a complex Euclidean space having dimension n and let $X, Y \in \mathrm{L}(\mathcal{X})$ be normal operators for which $[X, Y] = 0$. There exists an orthonormal basis $\{x_1, \ldots, x_n\}$ of $\mathcal{X}$ such that*

$$X = \sum_{k=1}^{n} \alpha_k x_k x_k^* \quad and \quad Y = \sum_{k=1}^{n} \beta_k x_k x_k^*, \tag{1.139}$$

for some choice of complex numbers $\alpha_1, \ldots, \alpha_n, \beta_1, \ldots, \beta_n$ satisfying

$$\mathrm{spec}(X) = \{\alpha_1, \ldots, \alpha_n\} \quad and \quad \mathrm{spec}(Y) = \{\beta_1, \ldots, \beta_n\}. \tag{1.140}$$

Jordan–Hahn Decompositions

Every Hermitian operator is normal and has real eigenvalues. It therefore follows from the spectral theorem (Theorem 1.3) that, for every Hermitian operator $H \in \mathrm{Herm}(\mathcal{X})$, there exist a positive integer m, nonzero projection operators $\Pi_1, \ldots, \Pi_m$ satisfying

$$\Pi_1 + \cdots + \Pi_m = \mathbb{1}_{\mathcal{X}}, \tag{1.141}$$

and real numbers $\lambda_1, \ldots, \lambda_m$ such that

$$H = \sum_{k=1}^{m} \lambda_k \Pi_k. \tag{1.142}$$

By defining operators

$$P = \sum_{k=1}^{m} \max\{\lambda_k, 0\} \, \Pi_k \quad and \quad Q = \sum_{k=1}^{m} \max\{-\lambda_k, 0\} \, \Pi_k, \tag{1.143}$$

one finds that

$$H = P - Q \tag{1.144}$$

for $P, Q \in \text{Pos}(\mathcal{X})$ satisfying $PQ = 0$. The expression (1.144) of a given Hermitian operator H in this form, for positive semidefinite operators P and Q satisfying $PQ = 0$, is called a *Jordan–Hahn decomposition*. There is only one such expression for a given operator $H \in \text{Herm}(\mathcal{X})$; the operators P and Q are uniquely defined by the requirements that $P, Q \in \text{Pos}(\mathcal{X})$, $PQ = 0$, and $H = P - Q$.

Functions of Normal Operators

Every function of the form $f \colon \mathbb{C} \to \mathbb{C}$ may be extended to the set of normal operators in $\text{L}(\mathcal{X})$, for a given complex Euclidean space $\mathcal{X}$, by means of the spectral theorem (Theorem 1.3). In particular, if $X \in \text{L}(\mathcal{X})$ is normal and has the spectral decomposition (1.135), then one defines

$$f(X) = \sum_{k=1}^{m} f(\lambda_k) \Pi_k. \tag{1.145}$$

Naturally, functions defined only on subsets of $\mathbb{C}$ may be extended to normal operators whose eigenvalues are restricted accordingly.

The following examples of scalar functions extended to operators will be important later in this book:

1. For $r > 0$, the function $\lambda \mapsto \lambda^r$ is defined for all $\lambda \in [0, \infty)$. For a positive semidefinite operator $P \in \text{Pos}(\mathcal{X})$ having spectral decomposition

$$P = \sum_{k=1}^{m} \lambda_k \Pi_k, \tag{1.146}$$

for which it necessarily holds that $\lambda_k \geq 0$ for all $k \in \{1, \dots, m\}$, one defines

$$P^r = \sum_{k=1}^{m} \lambda_k^r \, \Pi_k. \tag{1.147}$$

For positive integer values of r, it is evident that P^r coincides with the usual meaning of this expression given by operator multiplication.

The case that $r = 1/2$ is particularly common, and in this case one may write $\sqrt{P}$ to denote $P^{1/2}$. The operator $\sqrt{P}$ is the unique positive semidefinite operator that satisfies the equation

$$\sqrt{P}\sqrt{P} = P. \tag{1.148}$$

2. Along similar lines to the previous example, for any real number $r \in \mathbb{R}$, the function $\lambda \mapsto \lambda^r$ is defined for all $\lambda \in (0, \infty)$. For a given positive definite operator $P \in \mathrm{Pd}(\mathcal{X})$ having a spectral decomposition of the form (1.146), for which it holds that $\lambda_k > 0$ for all $k \in \{1, \ldots, m\}$, one defines P^r in a similar way to (1.147) above.

3. The (base-2) logarithm function $\lambda \mapsto \log(\lambda)$ is defined for all $\lambda \in (0, \infty)$. For a given positive definite operator $P \in \mathrm{Pd}(\mathcal{X})$, having a spectral decomposition (1.146) as above, one defines

$$\log(P) = \sum_{k=1}^{m} \log(\lambda_k) \Pi_k. \tag{1.149}$$

The Singular Value Theorem

The *singular value theorem* has a close relationship to the spectral theorem. Unlike the spectral theorem, however, the singular value theorem holds for arbitrary (nonzero) operators, as opposed to just normal operators.

Theorem 1.6 (Singular value theorem)   *Let $A \in \mathrm{L}(\mathcal{X}, \mathcal{Y})$ be a nonzero operator having rank equal to r, for complex Euclidean spaces $\mathcal{X}$ and $\mathcal{Y}$. There exist orthonormal sets $\{x_1, \ldots, x_r\} \subset \mathcal{X}$ and $\{y_1, \ldots, y_r\} \subset \mathcal{Y}$, along with positive real numbers $s_1, \ldots, s_r$, such that*

$$A = \sum_{k=1}^{r} s_k y_k x_k^*. \tag{1.150}$$

An expression of a given operator A in the form of (1.150) is said to be a *singular value decomposition* of A. The numbers $s_1, \ldots, s_r$ are called *singular values* and the vectors $x_1, \ldots, x_r$ and $y_1, \ldots, y_r$ are called *right* and *left singular vectors*, respectively.

The singular values $s_1, \ldots, s_r$ of an operator A are uniquely determined, up to their ordering. It will be assumed hereafter that singular values are always ordered from largest to smallest: $s_1 \geq \cdots \geq s_r$. When it is necessary to indicate the dependence of these singular values on the operator A, they are denoted $s_1(A), \ldots, s_r(A)$. Although 0 is not formally considered to be a singular value of any operator, it is convenient to also define $s_k(A) = 0$ for $k > \mathrm{rank}(A)$, and to take $s_k(A) = 0$ for all $k \geq 1$ when $A = 0$. The notation $s(A)$ is used to refer to the vector of singular values

$$s(A) = (s_1(A), \ldots, s_r(A)), \tag{1.151}$$

or to an extension of this vector

$$s(A) = (s_1(A), \ldots, s_m(A)) \tag{1.152}$$

when it is convenient to view it as an element of $\mathbb{R}^m$ for $m > \text{rank}(A)$.

As suggested above, there is a close relationship between the singular value theorem and the spectral theorem. In particular, the singular value decomposition of an operator A and the spectral decompositions of the operators A^*A and AA^* are related in the following way: it holds that

$$s_k(A) = \sqrt{\lambda_k(AA^*)} = \sqrt{\lambda_k(A^*A)} \tag{1.153}$$

for $1 \leq k \leq \text{rank}(A)$, and moreover the right singular vectors of A are eigenvectors of A^*A and the left singular vectors of A are eigenvectors of AA^*. One is free, in fact, to choose the left singular vectors of A to be any orthonormal collection of eigenvectors of AA^* for which the corresponding eigenvalues are nonzero – and once this is done the right singular vectors will be uniquely determined. Alternatively, the right singular vectors of A may be chosen to be any orthonormal collection of eigenvectors of A^*A for which the corresponding eigenvalues are nonzero, which uniquely determines the left singular vectors.

In the special case that $X \in \text{L}(\mathcal{X})$ is a normal operator, one may obtain a singular value decomposition of X directly from a spectral decomposition of the form

$$X = \sum_{k=1}^{n} \lambda_k x_k x_k^*. \tag{1.154}$$

In particular, one may define $S = \{k \in \{1, \ldots, n\} : \lambda_k \neq 0\}$, and set

$$s_k = |\lambda_k| \quad \text{and} \quad y_k = \frac{\lambda_k}{|\lambda_k|} x_k \tag{1.155}$$

for each $k \in S$. The expression

$$X = \sum_{k \in S} s_k y_k x_k^* \tag{1.156}$$

then represents a singular value decomposition of X, up to a relabeling of the terms in the sum.

The following corollary represents a reformulation of the singular value theorem that is useful in some situations.

Corollary 1.7 *Let $\mathcal{X}$ and $\mathcal{Y}$ be complex Euclidean spaces, let $A \in \text{L}(\mathcal{X}, \mathcal{Y})$ be a nonzero operator, and let $r = \text{rank}(A)$. There exist a diagonal and positive definite operator $D \in \text{Pd}(\mathbb{C}^r)$ and isometries $U \in \text{U}(\mathbb{C}^r, \mathcal{X})$ and $V \in \text{U}(\mathbb{C}^r, \mathcal{Y})$ such that $A = VDU^*$.*

Polar Decompositions

For every square operator $X \in L(\mathcal{X})$, it is possible to choose a positive semidefinite operator $P \in \text{Pos}(\mathcal{X})$ and a unitary operator $W \in U(\mathcal{X})$ such that the equation

$$X = WP \tag{1.157}$$

holds; this follows from Corollary 1.7 by taking $W = VU^*$ and $P = UDU^*$. Alternatively, by similar reasoning it is possible to write

$$X = PW \tag{1.158}$$

for a (generally different) choice of operators $P \in \text{Pos}(\mathcal{X})$ and $W \in U(\mathcal{X})$. The expressions (1.157) and (1.158) are known as *polar decompositions* of X.

The Moore–Penrose Pseudo-Inverse

For a given operator $A \in L(\mathcal{X}, \mathcal{Y})$, one defines an operator $A^+ \in L(\mathcal{Y}, \mathcal{X})$, known as the *Moore–Penrose pseudo-inverse* of A, as the unique operator that possesses the following properties:

1. $AA^+A = A$,
2. $A^+AA^+ = A^+$, and
3. AA^+ and A^+A are both Hermitian.

It is evident that there is at least one such choice of A^+, for if

$$A = \sum_{k=1}^{r} s_k y_k x_k^* \tag{1.159}$$

is a singular value decomposition of a nonzero operator A, then

$$A^+ = \sum_{k=1}^{r} \frac{1}{s_k} x_k y_k^* \tag{1.160}$$

possesses the three properties listed above. One may observe that AA^+ and A^+A are projection operators, projecting onto the spaces spanned by the left singular vectors and right singular vectors of A, respectively.

The fact that A^+ is uniquely determined by the above equations may be verified as follows. Suppose that $B, C \in L(\mathcal{Y}, \mathcal{X})$ both possess the above properties:

1. $ABA = A = ACA$,
2. $BAB = B$ and $CAC = C$, and
3. AB, BA, AC, and CA are all Hermitian.

It follows that

$$
\begin{aligned}
B = BAB &= (BA)^*B = A^*B^*B = (ACA)^*B^*B \\
&= A^*C^*A^*B^*B = (CA)^*(BA)^*B = CABAB \\
&= CAB = CACAB = C(AC)^*(AB)^* = CC^*A^*B^*A^* \\
&= CC^*(ABA)^* = CC^*A^* = C(AC)^* = CAC = C,
\end{aligned} \tag{1.161}
$$

which shows that $B = C$.

Schmidt Decompositions

Let $\mathcal{X}$ and $\mathcal{Y}$ be complex Euclidean spaces, and suppose that $u \in \mathcal{X} \otimes \mathcal{Y}$ is a nonzero vector. Given that the vec mapping is a bijection, there exists a unique operator $A \in \mathrm{L}(\mathcal{Y}, \mathcal{X})$ such that $u = \mathrm{vec}(A)$. For any singular value decomposition

$$
A = \sum_{k=1}^{r} s_k x_k y_k^*, \tag{1.162}
$$

it holds that

$$
u = \mathrm{vec}(A) = \mathrm{vec}\left(\sum_{k=1}^{r} s_k x_k y_k^* \right) = \sum_{k=1}^{r} s_k x_k \otimes \overline{y_k}. \tag{1.163}
$$

The orthonormality of $\{y_1, \ldots, y_r\}$ implies that $\{\overline{y_1}, \ldots, \overline{y_r}\}$ is orthonormal as well. It follows that every nonzero vector $u \in \mathcal{X} \otimes \mathcal{Y}$ can be expressed in the form

$$
u = \sum_{k=1}^{r} s_k x_k \otimes z_k \tag{1.164}
$$

for positive real numbers $s_1, \ldots, s_r$ and orthonormal sets $\{x_1, \ldots, x_r\} \subset \mathcal{X}$ and $\{z_1, \ldots, z_r\} \subset \mathcal{Y}$. An expression of u having this form is called a *Schmidt decomposition* of u.

Norms of Operators

A *norm* on the space of operators $\mathrm{L}(\mathcal{X}, \mathcal{Y})$, for complex Euclidean spaces $\mathcal{X}$ and $\mathcal{Y}$, is a function $\|\cdot\|$ satisfying the following properties:

1. Positive definiteness: $\|A\| \geq 0$ for all $A \in \mathrm{L}(\mathcal{X}, \mathcal{Y})$, with $\|A\| = 0$ if and only if $A = 0$.
2. Positive scalability: $\|\alpha A\| = |\alpha| \|A\|$ for all $A \in \mathrm{L}(\mathcal{X}, \mathcal{Y})$ and $\alpha \in \mathbb{C}$.
3. The triangle inequality: $\|A + B\| \leq \|A\| + \|B\|$ for all $A, B \in \mathrm{L}(\mathcal{X}, \mathcal{Y})$.

Many interesting and useful norms can be defined on spaces of operators, but this book will mostly be concerned with a single family of norms called *Schatten p-norms*. This family includes the three most commonly used norms in quantum information theory: the *spectral norm*, the *Frobenius norm*, and the *trace norm*.

For any operator $A \in L(\mathcal{X}, \mathcal{Y})$ and any real number $p \geq 1$, one defines the Schatten p-norm of A as

$$\|A\|_p = \left(\operatorname{Tr}\left((A^*A)^{\frac{p}{2}} \right) \right)^{\frac{1}{p}}. \tag{1.165}$$

The Schatten ∞-norm is defined as

$$\|A\|_\infty = \max \left\{ \|Au\| : u \in \mathcal{X}, \ \|u\| \leq 1 \right\}, \tag{1.166}$$

which coincides with $\lim_{p \to \infty} \|A\|_p$, explaining why the subscript ∞ is used. The Schatten p-norm of an operator A coincides with the ordinary vector p-norm of the vector of singular values of A:

$$\|A\|_p = \|s(A)\|_p. \tag{1.167}$$

The Schatten p-norms possess a variety of properties, including the ones summarized in the following list:

1. The Schatten p-norms are non-increasing in p: for every operator A and for $1 \leq p \leq q \leq \infty$, it holds that

$$\|A\|_p \geq \|A\|_q. \tag{1.168}$$

2. For every nonzero operator A and for $1 \leq p \leq q \leq \infty$, it holds that

$$\|A\|_p \leq \operatorname{rank}(A)^{\frac{1}{p} - \frac{1}{q}} \|A\|_q. \tag{1.169}$$

   In particular, one has

$$\|A\|_1 \leq \sqrt{\operatorname{rank}(A)} \|A\|_2 \quad \text{and} \quad \|A\|_2 \leq \sqrt{\operatorname{rank}(A)} \|A\|_\infty. \tag{1.170}$$

3. For every $p \in [1, \infty]$, the Schatten p-norm is isometrically invariant (and therefore unitarily invariant): for every $A \in L(\mathcal{X}, \mathcal{Y})$, $U \in U(\mathcal{Y}, \mathcal{Z})$, and $V \in U(\mathcal{X}, \mathcal{W})$ it holds that

$$\|A\|_p = \|UAV^*\|_p. \tag{1.171}$$

4. For each $p \in [1, \infty]$, one defines $p^* \in [1, \infty]$ by the equation

$$\frac{1}{p} + \frac{1}{p^*} = 1. \tag{1.172}$$

For every operator $A \in L(\mathcal{X}, \mathcal{Y})$, it holds that the Schatten p-norm and p^*-norm are dual, in the sense that

$$\|A\|_p = \max\{|\langle B, A \rangle| : B \in L(\mathcal{X}, \mathcal{Y}), \|B\|_{p^*} \leq 1\}. \qquad (1.173)$$

One consequence of (1.173) is the inequality

$$|\langle B, A \rangle| \leq \|A\|_p \|B\|_{p^*}, \qquad (1.174)$$

which is known as the *Hölder inequality* for Schatten norms.

5. For operators $A \in L(\mathcal{Z}, \mathcal{W})$, $B \in L(\mathcal{Y}, \mathcal{Z})$, and $C \in L(\mathcal{X}, \mathcal{Y})$, and any choice of $p \in [1, \infty]$, it holds that

$$\|ABC\|_p \leq \|A\|_\infty \|B\|_p \|C\|_\infty. \qquad (1.175)$$

It follows that the Schatten p-norm is *submultiplicative*:

$$\|AB\|_p \leq \|A\|_p \|B\|_p. \qquad (1.176)$$

6. For every $p \in [1, \infty]$ and every $A \in L(\mathcal{X}, \mathcal{Y})$, it holds that

$$\|A\|_p = \|A^*\|_p = \|A^\mathsf{T}\|_p = \|\overline{A}\|_p. \qquad (1.177)$$

The Schatten 1-norm is commonly called the *trace norm*, the Schatten 2-norm is also known as the *Frobenius norm*, and the Schatten ∞-norm is called the *spectral norm* or *operator norm*. Some additional properties of these three norms are as follows:

1. *The spectral norm.* The spectral norm $\|\cdot\|_\infty$ is special in several respects. It is the operator norm *induced* by the Euclidean norm, which is its defining property (1.166). It also has the property that

$$\|A^*A\|_\infty = \|AA^*\|_\infty = \|A\|_\infty^2 \qquad (1.178)$$

for every $A \in L(\mathcal{X}, \mathcal{Y})$. Hereafter in this book, the spectral norm of an operator A will be written $\|A\|$ rather than $\|A\|_\infty$, which reflects the fundamental importance of this norm.

2. *The Frobenius norm.* Substituting $p = 2$ into the definition of $\|\cdot\|_p$, one sees that the Frobenius norm $\|\cdot\|_2$ is given by

$$\|A\|_2 = (\mathrm{Tr}(A^*A))^{\frac{1}{2}} = \sqrt{\langle A, A \rangle}, \qquad (1.179)$$

and is therefore analogous to the Euclidean norm for vectors, but defined by the inner product on $L(\mathcal{X}, \mathcal{Y})$.

In essence, the Frobenius norm corresponds to the Euclidean norm of an operator viewed as a vector:

$$\|A\|_2 = \|\mathrm{vec}(A)\| = \sqrt{\sum_{a,b} |A(a,b)|^2}, \tag{1.180}$$

where a and b range over the indices of the matrix representation of A.

3. *The trace norm.* Substituting $p = 1$ into the definition of $\|\cdot\|_p$, one has that the trace norm $\|\cdot\|_1$ is given by

$$\|A\|_1 = \mathrm{Tr}\left(\sqrt{A^*A}\right), \tag{1.181}$$

which is equal to the sum of the singular values of A. For two density operators $\rho, \sigma \in \mathrm{D}(\mathcal{X})$, the value $\|\rho - \sigma\|_1$ is typically referred to as the *trace distance* between ρ and σ.

A useful expression of $\|X\|_1$, for any square operator $X \in \mathrm{L}(\mathcal{X})$, is

$$\|X\|_1 = \max\{|\langle U, X \rangle| : U \in \mathrm{U}(\mathcal{X})\}, \tag{1.182}$$

which follows from (1.167) and the singular value theorem (Theorem 1.6). As a result, one has that the trace norm is non-increasing under the action of partial tracing: for every operator $X \in \mathrm{L}(\mathcal{X} \otimes \mathcal{Y})$, it holds that

$$\begin{aligned}
\|\mathrm{Tr}_{\mathcal{Y}}(X)\|_1 &= \max\{|\langle U \otimes \mathbb{1}_{\mathcal{Y}}, X \rangle| : U \in \mathrm{U}(\mathcal{X})\} \\
&\leq \max\{|\langle V, X \rangle| : V \in \mathrm{U}(\mathcal{X} \otimes \mathcal{Y})\} = \|X\|_1.
\end{aligned} \tag{1.183}$$

The identity

$$\|\alpha uu^* - \beta vv^*\|_1 = \sqrt{(\alpha + \beta)^2 - 4\alpha\beta|\langle u, v \rangle|^2}, \tag{1.184}$$

which holds for all unit vectors u, v and nonnegative real numbers α, β, is used multiple times in this book. It may be proved by considering the spectrum of $\alpha uu^* - \beta vv^*$; this operator is Hermitian, and has at most two nonzero eigenvalues, represented by the expression

$$\frac{\alpha - \beta}{2} \pm \frac{1}{2}\sqrt{(\alpha + \beta)^2 - 4\alpha\beta|\langle u, v \rangle|^2}. \tag{1.185}$$

In particular, for unit vectors u and v, one has

$$\|uu^* - vv^*\|_1 = 2\sqrt{1 - |\langle u, v \rangle|^2}. \tag{1.186}$$

1.2 Analysis, Convexity, and Probability Theory

Some of the proofs to be presented in this book will make use of concepts from analysis, convexity, and probability theory. The summary that follows provides an overview of these concepts, narrowly focused on the needs of this book.

1.2.1 Analysis and Convexity

In the same spirit as the previous section on linear algebra, it is assumed that the reader is familiar with the most basic notions of mathematical analysis, including the supremum and infimum of sets of real numbers, sequences and limits, and standard univariate calculus over the real numbers.

The discussion below is limited to finite-dimensional real and complex vector spaces – and the reader is cautioned that some of the stated facts rely on the assumption that one is working with finite-dimensional spaces. For the remainder of the subsection, $\mathcal{V}$ and $\mathcal{W}$ will denote finite-dimensional real or complex vector spaces upon which some norm $\|\cdot\|$ is defined. Unless it is explicitly noted otherwise, the norm may be chosen arbitrarily – so the symbol $\|\cdot\|$ may not necessarily denote the Euclidean norm or spectral norm in this section.

Open and Closed Sets

A set $\mathcal{A} \subseteq \mathcal{V}$ is *open* if, for every $u \in \mathcal{A}$, there exists $\varepsilon > 0$ such that

$$\{v \in \mathcal{V}: \|u - v\| < \varepsilon\} \subseteq \mathcal{A}. \tag{1.187}$$

A set $\mathcal{A} \subseteq \mathcal{V}$ is *closed* if the complement of $\mathcal{A}$, defined as

$$\mathcal{V}\backslash\mathcal{A} = \{v \in \mathcal{V}: v \notin \mathcal{A}\}, \tag{1.188}$$

is open. Given subsets $\mathcal{A} \subseteq \mathcal{B} \subseteq \mathcal{V}$, one defines that $\mathcal{A}$ is open or closed *relative to* $\mathcal{B}$ if $\mathcal{A}$ is the intersection of $\mathcal{B}$ with some set in $\mathcal{V}$ that is open or closed, respectively. Equivalently, $\mathcal{A}$ is open relative to $\mathcal{B}$ if, for every $u \in \mathcal{A}$, there exists a choice of $\varepsilon > 0$ such that

$$\{v \in \mathcal{B}: \|u - v\| < \varepsilon\} \subseteq \mathcal{A}; \tag{1.189}$$

and $\mathcal{A}$ is closed relative to $\mathcal{B}$ if $\mathcal{B}\backslash\mathcal{A}$ is open relative to $\mathcal{B}$.

For subsets $\mathcal{A} \subseteq \mathcal{B} \subseteq \mathcal{V}$, one defines the *closure* of $\mathcal{A}$ relative to $\mathcal{B}$ as the intersection of all subsets $\mathcal{C}$ such that $\mathcal{A} \subseteq \mathcal{C} \subseteq \mathcal{B}$ and $\mathcal{C}$ is closed relative to $\mathcal{B}$. In other words, this is the smallest set that contains $\mathcal{A}$ and is closed relative to $\mathcal{B}$. The set $\mathcal{A}$ is *dense* in $\mathcal{B}$ if the closure of $\mathcal{A}$ relative to $\mathcal{B}$ is $\mathcal{B}$ itself.

Continuous Functions

Let $f: \mathcal{A} \to \mathcal{W}$ be a function defined on some subset $\mathcal{A} \subseteq \mathcal{V}$. For any vector $u \in \mathcal{A}$, the function f is said to be *continuous* at u if the following holds: for every $\varepsilon > 0$ there exists $\delta > 0$ such that

$$\| f(v) - f(u) \| < \varepsilon \tag{1.190}$$

for all $v \in \mathcal{A}$ satisfying $\| u - v \| < \delta$. If f is continuous at every vector in $\mathcal{A}$, then one simply says that f is *continuous on* $\mathcal{A}$.

For a function $f: \mathcal{A} \to \mathcal{W}$ defined on some subset $\mathcal{A} \subseteq \mathcal{V}$, the *preimage* of a set $\mathcal{B} \subseteq \mathcal{W}$ is defined as

$$f^{-1}(\mathcal{B}) = \{ u \in \mathcal{A} : f(u) \in \mathcal{B} \}. \tag{1.191}$$

Such a function f is continuous on $\mathcal{A}$ if and only if the preimage of every open set in $\mathcal{W}$ is open relative to $\mathcal{A}$. Equivalently, f is continuous on $\mathcal{A}$ if and only if the preimage of every closed set in $\mathcal{W}$ is closed relative to $\mathcal{A}$.

For a positive real number κ, a function $f: \mathcal{A} \to \mathcal{W}$ defined on a subset $\mathcal{A} \subseteq \mathcal{V}$ is said to be a *κ-Lipschitz function* if

$$\| f(u) - f(v) \| \leq \kappa \| u - v \| \tag{1.192}$$

for all $u, v \in \mathcal{A}$. Every κ-Lipschitz function is necessarily continuous.

Compact Sets

A set $\mathcal{A} \subseteq \mathcal{V}$ is *compact* if every sequence in $\mathcal{A}$ has a subsequence that converges to a vector $u \in \mathcal{A}$. As a consequence of the fact that $\mathcal{V}$ is assumed to be finite-dimensional, one has that a set $\mathcal{A} \subseteq \mathcal{V}$ is compact if and only if it is both closed and bounded – a fact known as the *Heine–Borel theorem*.

Two properties regarding continuous functions and compact sets that are particularly noteworthy for the purposes of this book are as follows:

1. If $\mathcal{A}$ is compact and $f: \mathcal{A} \to \mathbb{R}$ is continuous on $\mathcal{A}$, then f achieves both a maximum and minimum value on $\mathcal{A}$.
2. If $\mathcal{A} \subset \mathcal{V}$ is compact and $f: \mathcal{V} \to \mathcal{W}$ is continuous on $\mathcal{A}$, then

$$f(\mathcal{A}) = \{ f(u) : u \in \mathcal{A} \} \tag{1.193}$$

is also compact. In words, continuous functions always map compact sets to compact sets.

Differentiation of Multivariate Real Functions

Basic multivariate calculus will be employed on a few occasions later in this book, and in these cases it will be sufficient to consider only real-valued functions.

Suppose n is a positive integer, $f \colon \mathbb{R}^n \to \mathbb{R}$ is a function, and $u \in \mathbb{R}^n$ is a vector. Under the assumption that the partial derivative

$$\partial_k f(u) = \lim_{\alpha \to 0} \frac{f(u + \alpha e_k) - f(u)}{\alpha} \tag{1.194}$$

exists and is finite for each $k \in \{1, \ldots, n\}$, one defines the *gradient vector* of f at u as

$$\nabla f(u) = (\partial_1 f(u), \ldots, \partial_n f(u)). \tag{1.195}$$

A function $f \colon \mathbb{R}^n \to \mathbb{R}$ is *differentiable* at a vector $u \in \mathbb{R}^n$ if there exists a vector $v \in \mathbb{R}^n$ with the following property: for every sequence $(w_1, w_2, \ldots)$ of vectors in $\mathbb{R}^n$ that converges to 0, one has that

$$\lim_{k \to \infty} \frac{|f(u + w_k) - f(u) - \langle v, w_k \rangle|}{\|w_k\|} = 0 \tag{1.196}$$

(where here $\|\cdot\|$ denotes the Euclidean norm). In this case the vector v is necessarily unique, and one writes $v = (Df)(u)$. If f is differentiable at u, then it holds that

$$(Df)(u) = \nabla f(u). \tag{1.197}$$

It may be the case that the gradient vector $\nabla f(u)$ is defined for a vector u at which f is not differentiable, but if the function $u \mapsto \nabla f(u)$ is continuous at u, then f is necessarily differentiable at u.

If a function $f \colon \mathbb{R}^n \to \mathbb{R}$ is both differentiable and κ-Lipschitz, for $\|\cdot\|$ being the Euclidean norm, then for all $u \in \mathbb{R}^n$ it must hold that

$$\|\nabla f(u)\| \leq \kappa. \tag{1.198}$$

Finally, suppose $g_1, \ldots, g_n \colon \mathbb{R} \to \mathbb{R}$ are functions that are differentiable at a real number $\alpha \in \mathbb{R}$ and $f \colon \mathbb{R}^n \to \mathbb{R}$ is a function that is differentiable at the vector $(g_1(\alpha), \ldots, g_n(\alpha))$. The *chain rule* for differentiation implies that the function $h \colon \mathbb{R} \to \mathbb{R}$ defined as

$$h(\beta) = f(g_1(\beta), \ldots, g_n(\beta)) \tag{1.199}$$

is differentiable at α, with its derivative being given by

$$h'(\alpha) = \langle \nabla f(g_1(\alpha), \ldots, g_n(\alpha)), (g_1'(\alpha), \ldots, g_n'(\alpha)) \rangle. \tag{1.200}$$

Nets

Let $\mathcal{V}$ be a real or complex vector space, let $\mathcal{A} \subseteq \mathcal{V}$ be a subset of $\mathcal{V}$, let $\|\cdot\|$ be a norm on $\mathcal{V}$, and let $\varepsilon > 0$ be a positive real number. A set of vectors $\mathcal{N} \subseteq \mathcal{A}$ is an *ε-net* for $\mathcal{A}$ if, for every vector $u \in \mathcal{A}$, there exists a vector $v \in \mathcal{N}$ such that $\|u - v\| \leq \varepsilon$. An ε-net $\mathcal{N}$ for $\mathcal{A}$ is *minimal* if $\mathcal{N}$ is finite and every ε-net of $\mathcal{A}$ contains at least $|\mathcal{N}|$ vectors.

The following theorem gives an upper bound for the number of elements in a minimal ε-net for the unit ball

$$\mathcal{B}(\mathcal{X}) = \{u \in \mathcal{X} : \|u\| \leq 1\} \tag{1.201}$$

in a complex Euclidean space, with respect to the Euclidean norm.

Theorem 1.8 (Pisier) *Let $\mathcal{X}$ be a complex Euclidean space of dimension n and let $\varepsilon > 0$ be a positive real number. With respect to the Euclidean norm on $\mathcal{X}$, there exists an ε-net $\mathcal{N} \subset \mathcal{B}(\mathcal{X})$ for the unit ball $\mathcal{B}(\mathcal{X})$ such that*

$$|\mathcal{N}| \leq \left(1 + \frac{2}{\varepsilon}\right)^{2n}. \tag{1.202}$$

The proof of this theorem does not require a complicated construction; one may take $\mathcal{N}$ to be any maximal set of vectors chosen from the unit ball for which it holds that $\|u - v\| \geq \varepsilon$ for all $u, v \in \mathcal{N}$ with $u \neq v$. Such a set is necessarily an ε-net for $\mathcal{B}(\mathcal{X})$, and the bound on $|\mathcal{N}|$ is obtained by comparing the volume of $\mathcal{B}(\mathcal{X})$ with the volume of the union of $\varepsilon/2$ balls around vectors in $\mathcal{N}$.

Borel Sets and Functions

Throughout this subsection, $\mathcal{A} \subseteq \mathcal{V}$ and $\mathcal{B} \subseteq \mathcal{W}$ will denote fixed subsets of finite-dimensional real or complex vector spaces $\mathcal{V}$ and $\mathcal{W}$.

A set $\mathcal{C} \subseteq \mathcal{A}$ is said to be a *Borel subset* of $\mathcal{A}$ if one or more of the following inductively defined properties holds:

1. $\mathcal{C}$ is an open set relative to $\mathcal{A}$.
2. $\mathcal{C}$ is the complement of a Borel subset of $\mathcal{A}$.
3. For $\{\mathcal{C}_1, \mathcal{C}_2, \ldots\}$ being a countable collection of Borel subsets of $\mathcal{A}$, it holds that $\mathcal{C}$ is equal to the union

$$\mathcal{C} = \bigcup_{k=1}^{\infty} \mathcal{C}_k. \tag{1.203}$$

The collection of all Borel subsets of $\mathcal{A}$ is denoted $\mathrm{Borel}(\mathcal{A})$.

A function $f \colon \mathcal{A} \to \mathcal{B}$ is a *Borel function* if $f^{-1}(\mathcal{C}) \in \mathrm{Borel}(\mathcal{A})$ for all $\mathcal{C} \in \mathrm{Borel}(\mathcal{B})$. That is, Borel functions are functions for which the preimage of every Borel subset is also a Borel subset. If f is a continuous function, then f is necessarily a Borel function. Another important type of Borel function is any function of the form

$$f(u) = \chi_C(u)\, v \tag{1.204}$$

for any choice of $v \in \mathcal{B}$ and

$$\chi_C(u) = \begin{cases} 1 & \text{if } u \in \mathcal{C} \\ 0 & \text{if } u \notin \mathcal{C} \end{cases} \tag{1.205}$$

being the characteristic function of a Borel subset $\mathcal{C} \in \mathrm{Borel}(\mathcal{A})$.

The collection of all Borel functions $f\colon \mathcal{A} \to \mathcal{B}$ possesses a variety of closure properties, including the following properties:

1. If $\mathcal{B}$ is a vector space, $f, g\colon \mathcal{A} \to \mathcal{B}$ are Borel functions, and α is a scalar (either real or complex, depending on whether $\mathcal{B}$ is a real or complex vector space), then the functions αf and $f + g$ are also Borel functions.
2. If $\mathcal{B}$ is a subalgebra of $\mathrm{L}(\mathcal{Z})$, for $\mathcal{Z}$ being a real or complex Euclidean space, and $f, g\colon \mathcal{A} \to \mathcal{B}$ are Borel functions, then the function $h\colon \mathcal{A} \to \mathcal{B}$ defined by

$$h(u) = f(u)g(u) \tag{1.206}$$

for all $u \in \mathcal{A}$ is also a Borel function. (This includes the special cases $f, g\colon \mathcal{A} \to \mathbb{R}$ and $f, g\colon \mathcal{A} \to \mathbb{C}$.)

Measures on Borel Sets

A *Borel measure* (or simply a *measure*) defined on $\mathrm{Borel}(\mathcal{A})$ is a function

$$\mu\colon \mathrm{Borel}(\mathcal{A}) \to [0, \infty] \tag{1.207}$$

that possesses two properties:

1. $\mu(\varnothing) = 0$.
2. For any countable collection $\{\mathcal{C}_1, \mathcal{C}_2, \ldots\} \subseteq \mathrm{Borel}(\mathcal{A})$ of pairwise disjoint Borel subsets of $\mathcal{A}$, it holds that

$$\mu\left(\bigcup_{k=1}^{\infty} \mathcal{C}_k\right) = \sum_{k=1}^{\infty} \mu(\mathcal{C}_k). \tag{1.208}$$

A measure μ defined on $\mathrm{Borel}(\mathcal{A})$ is said to be *normalized* if it holds that $\mu(\mathcal{A}) = 1$. The term *probability measure* is also used to refer to a normalized measure.

There exists a measure ν defined on Borel($\mathbb{R}$), known as the *standard Borel measure*,[3] that has the property

$$\nu([\alpha, \beta]) = \beta - \alpha \qquad (1.209)$$

for all choices of $\alpha, \beta \in \mathbb{R}$ with $\alpha \leq \beta$.

If $\mathcal{A}_1, \ldots, \mathcal{A}_n$ are subsets of (not necessarily equal) finite-dimensional real or complex vector spaces, and

$$\mu_k \colon \text{Borel}(\mathcal{A}_k) \to [0, \infty] \qquad (1.210)$$

is a measure for each $k \in \{1, \ldots, n\}$, then there is a uniquely defined *product measure*

$$\mu_1 \times \cdots \times \mu_n \colon \text{Borel}(\mathcal{A}_1 \times \cdots \times \mathcal{A}_n) \to [0, \infty] \qquad (1.211)$$

for which

$$(\mu_1 \times \cdots \times \mu_n)(\mathcal{B}_1 \times \cdots \times \mathcal{B}_n) = \mu_1(\mathcal{B}_1) \cdots \mu_n(\mathcal{B}_n) \qquad (1.212)$$

for all $\mathcal{B}_1 \in \text{Borel}(\mathcal{A}_1), \ldots, \mathcal{B}_n \in \text{Borel}(\mathcal{A}_n)$.

Integration of Borel Functions

For some (but not all) Borel functions $f \colon \mathcal{A} \to \mathcal{B}$, and for μ being a Borel measure of the form $\mu \colon \text{Borel}(\mathcal{A}) \to [0, \infty]$, one may define the integral

$$\int f(u) \, d\mu(u), \qquad (1.213)$$

which is an element of $\mathcal{B}$ when it is defined.

An understanding of the specifics of the definition through which such an integral is defined is not critical within the context of this book, but some readers may find that a high-level overview of the definition is helpful in associating an intuitive meaning to the integrals that do arise. In short, one defines what is meant by the integral of an increasingly large collection of functions, beginning with functions taking nonnegative real values, and then proceeding to vector-valued (or operator-valued) functions by taking linear combinations.

1. *Nonnegative simple functions.* A function $g \colon \mathcal{A} \to [0, \infty)$ is a *nonnegative simple function* if it may be written as

$$g(u) = \sum_{k=1}^{m} \alpha_k \chi_k(u) \qquad (1.214)$$

---

[3] The standard Borel measure agrees with the well-known *Lebesgue measure* on every Borel subset of $\mathbb{R}$. The Lebesgue measure is also defined for some subsets of $\mathbb{R}$ that are not Borel subsets, which endows it with additional properties that happen not to be relevant within the context of this book.

for a nonnegative integer m, distinct positive real numbers $\alpha_1, \ldots, \alpha_m$, and characteristic functions $\chi_1, \ldots, \chi_m$ given by

$$\chi_k(u) = \begin{cases} 1 & \text{if } u \in C_k \\ 0 & \text{if } u \notin C_k \end{cases} \tag{1.215}$$

for disjoint Borel sets $C_1, \ldots, C_m \in \text{Borel}(\mathcal{A})$. (It is to be understood that the sum is empty when $m = 0$, which corresponds to g being identically zero.)

A nonnegative simple function g of the form (1.214) is *integrable* with respect to a measure $\mu: \text{Borel}(\mathcal{A}) \to [0, \infty]$ if $\mu(C_k)$ is finite for every $k \in \{1, \ldots, m\}$, and in this case the integral of g with respect to μ is defined as

$$\int g(u) \, \mathrm{d}\mu(u) = \sum_{k=1}^{m} \alpha_k \, \mu(C_k). \tag{1.216}$$

This is a well-defined quantity, by virtue of the fact that the expression (1.214) happens to be unique for a given simple function g.

2. *Nonnegative Borel functions.* The integral of a Borel function of the form $f: \mathcal{A} \to [0, \infty)$, with respect to a given measure $\mu: \text{Borel}(\mathcal{A}) \to [0, \infty]$, is defined as

$$\int f(u) \, \mathrm{d}\mu(u) = \sup \int g(u) \, \mathrm{d}\mu(u), \tag{1.217}$$

where the supremum is taken over all nonnegative simple functions of the form $g: \mathcal{A} \to [0, \infty)$ for which it holds that $g(u) \le f(u)$ for all $u \in \mathcal{A}$. It is said that f is *integrable* if the supremum value in (1.217) is finite.

3. *Real and complex Borel functions.* A Borel function $g: \mathcal{A} \to \mathbb{R}$ is *integrable* with respect to a measure $\mu: \text{Borel}(\mathcal{A}) \to [0, \infty]$ if there exist integrable Borel functions $f_0, f_1: \mathcal{A} \to [0, \infty)$ such that $g = f_0 - f_1$, and in this case the integral of g with respect to μ is defined as

$$\int g(u) \, \mathrm{d}\mu(u) = \int f_0(u) \, \mathrm{d}\mu(u) - \int f_1(u) \, \mathrm{d}\mu(u). \tag{1.218}$$

Similarly, a Borel function $h: \mathcal{A} \to \mathbb{C}$ is *integrable* with respect to a measure $\mu: \text{Borel}(\mathcal{A}) \to [0, \infty]$ if there exist integrable Borel functions $g_0, g_1: \mathcal{A} \to \mathbb{R}$ such that $h = g_0 + ig_1$, and in this case the integral of h with respect to μ is defined as

$$\int h(u) \, \mathrm{d}\mu(u) = \int g_0(u) \, \mathrm{d}\mu(u) + i \int g_1(u) \, \mathrm{d}\mu(u). \tag{1.219}$$

4. *Arbitrary Borel functions.* An arbitrary Borel function $f\colon \mathcal{A} \to \mathcal{B}$ is *integrable* with respect to a given measure $\mu\colon \mathrm{Borel}(\mathcal{A}) \to [0,\infty]$ if there exist a finite-dimensional vector space $\mathcal{W}$ such that $\mathcal{B} \subseteq \mathcal{W}$, a basis $\{w_1,\ldots,w_m\}$ of $\mathcal{W}$, and integrable functions $g_1,\ldots,g_m\colon \mathcal{A} \to \mathbb{R}$ or $g_1,\ldots,g_m\colon \mathcal{A} \to \mathbb{C}$ (depending on whether $\mathcal{W}$ is a real or complex vector space) such that

$$f(u) = \sum_{k=1}^{m} g_k(u) w_k. \tag{1.220}$$

In this case, the integral of f with respect to μ is defined as

$$\int f(u)\, \mathrm{d}\mu(u) = \sum_{k=1}^{m} \left(\int g_k(u)\, \mathrm{d}\mu(u) \right) w_k. \tag{1.221}$$

The fact that the third and fourth items in this list lead to uniquely defined integrals of integrable functions is not immediate and requires a proof.

A selection of properties and conventions regarding integrals defined in this way, targeted to the specific needs of this book, follows.

1. *Linearity.* For integrable functions f and g, and scalar values α and β, one has

$$\int (\alpha f(u) + \beta g(u))\, \mathrm{d}\mu(u) = \alpha \int f(u)\, \mathrm{d}\mu(u) + \beta \int g(u)\, \mathrm{d}\mu(u). \tag{1.222}$$

2. *Standard Borel measure as the default.* Hereafter in this book, whenever $f\colon \mathbb{R} \to \mathbb{R}$ is an integrable function, and ν denotes the standard Borel measure on $\mathbb{R}$, the shorthand notation

$$\int f(\alpha)\, \mathrm{d}\alpha = \int f(\alpha)\, \mathrm{d}\nu(\alpha) \tag{1.223}$$

will be used. It is the case that, whenever f is an integrable function for which the commonly studied *Riemann integral* is defined, the Riemann integral will be in agreement with the integral defined as above for the standard Borel measure – so this shorthand notation is not likely to lead to confusion or ambiguity.

3. *Integration over subsets.* For an integrable function $f\colon \mathcal{A} \to \mathcal{B}$ and a Borel subset $\mathcal{C} \in \mathrm{Borel}(\mathcal{A})$, one defines

$$\int_{\mathcal{C}} f(u)\, \mathrm{d}\mu(u) = \int f(u)\chi_{\mathcal{C}}(u)\, \mathrm{d}\mu(u), \tag{1.224}$$

for χ_C being the characteristic function of C. The notation

$$\int_\beta^\gamma f(\alpha)\,d\alpha = \int_{[\beta,\gamma]} f(\alpha)\,d\alpha \tag{1.225}$$

is also used in the case that f takes the form $f\colon \mathbb{R} \to B$ and $\beta, \gamma \in \mathbb{R}$ satisfy $\beta \leq \gamma$.

4. *Order of integration.* Suppose that $\mathcal{A}_0 \subseteq \mathcal{V}_0$, $\mathcal{A}_1 \subseteq \mathcal{V}_1$, and $B \subseteq \mathcal{W}$ are subsets of finite-dimensional real or complex vector spaces, where it is to be assumed that $\mathcal{V}_0$ and $\mathcal{V}_1$ are either both real or both complex for simplicity. If $\mu_0\colon \operatorname{Borel}(\mathcal{A}_0) \to [0,\infty]$ and $\mu_1\colon \operatorname{Borel}(\mathcal{A}_1) \to [0,\infty]$ are Borel measures, $f\colon \mathcal{A}_0 \times \mathcal{A}_1 \to B$ is a Borel function, and f is integrable with respect to the product measure $\mu_0 \times \mu_1$, then it holds (by a theorem known as *Fubini's theorem*) that

$$\int \left(\int f(u,v)\,d\mu_0(u) \right) d\mu_1(v) = \int f(u,v)\,d(\mu_0 \times \mu_1)(u,v)$$
$$= \int \left(\int f(u,v)\,d\mu_1(v) \right) d\mu_0(u). \tag{1.226}$$

Convex Sets, Cones, and Functions

Let $\mathcal{V}$ be a vector space over the real or complex numbers. A subset C of $\mathcal{V}$ is *convex* if, for all vectors $u, v \in C$ and scalars $\lambda \in [0,1]$, it holds that

$$\lambda u + (1 - \lambda)v \in C. \tag{1.227}$$

Intuitively speaking, this means that, for any two distinct elements u and v of C, the line segment whose endpoints are u and v lies entirely within C. The intersection of any collection of convex sets is also convex.

If $\mathcal{V}$ and $\mathcal{W}$ are vector spaces, either both over the real numbers or both over the complex numbers, and $\mathcal{A} \subseteq \mathcal{V}$ and $\mathcal{B} \subseteq \mathcal{W}$ are convex sets, then the set

$$\{u \oplus v : u \in \mathcal{A},\, v \in \mathcal{B}\} \subseteq \mathcal{V} \oplus \mathcal{W} \tag{1.228}$$

is also convex. Moreover, if $A \in \mathrm{L}(\mathcal{V}, \mathcal{W})$ is an operator, then the set

$$\{Au : u \in \mathcal{A}\} \subseteq \mathcal{W} \tag{1.229}$$

is convex as well.

A set $\mathcal{K} \subseteq \mathcal{V}$ is a *cone* if, for all choices of $u \in \mathcal{K}$ and $\lambda \geq 0$, one has that $\lambda u \in \mathcal{K}$. The cone *generated* by a set $\mathcal{A} \subseteq \mathcal{V}$ is defined as

$$\operatorname{cone}(\mathcal{A}) = \{\lambda u : u \in \mathcal{A},\, \lambda \geq 0\}. \tag{1.230}$$

If $\mathcal{A}$ is a compact set that does not include 0, then $\mathrm{cone}(\mathcal{A})$ is necessarily a closed set. A *convex cone* is simply a cone that is also convex. A cone $\mathcal{K}$ is convex if and only if it is closed under addition, meaning that $u + v \in \mathcal{K}$ for every choice of $u, v \in \mathcal{K}$.

A function $f: \mathcal{C} \to \mathbb{R}$ defined on a convex set $\mathcal{C} \subseteq \mathcal{V}$ is a *convex function* if the inequality

$$f(\lambda u + (1 - \lambda)v) \leq \lambda f(u) + (1 - \lambda)f(v) \tag{1.231}$$

holds for all $u, v \in \mathcal{C}$ and $\lambda \in [0, 1]$. A function $f: \mathcal{C} \to \mathbb{R}$ defined on a convex set $\mathcal{C} \subseteq \mathcal{V}$ is a *midpoint convex function* if the inequality

$$f\left(\frac{u + v}{2}\right) \leq \frac{f(u) + f(v)}{2} \tag{1.232}$$

holds for all $u, v \in \mathcal{C}$. Every continuous midpoint convex function is convex.

A function $f: \mathcal{C} \to \mathbb{R}$ defined on a convex set $\mathcal{C} \subseteq \mathcal{V}$ is a *concave function* if $-f$ is convex. Equivalently, f is concave if the reverse of the inequality (1.231) holds for all $u, v \in \mathcal{C}$ and $\lambda \in [0, 1]$. Similarly, a function $f: \mathcal{C} \to \mathbb{R}$ defined on a convex set $\mathcal{C} \subseteq \mathcal{V}$ is a *midpoint concave function* if $-f$ is a midpoint convex function, and therefore every continuous midpoint concave function is concave.

Convex Hulls

For any alphabet Σ, a vector $p \in \mathbb{R}^{\Sigma}$ is said to be a *probability vector* if it holds that $p(a) \geq 0$ for all $a \in \Sigma$ and

$$\sum_{a \in \Sigma} p(a) = 1. \tag{1.233}$$

The set of all such vectors will be denoted $\mathcal{P}(\Sigma)$.

For any vector space $\mathcal{V}$ and any subset $\mathcal{A} \subseteq \mathcal{V}$, a *convex combination* of vectors in $\mathcal{A}$ is any expression of the form

$$\sum_{a \in \Sigma} p(a)u_a, \tag{1.234}$$

for some choice of an alphabet Σ, a probability vector $p \in \mathcal{P}(\Sigma)$, and a collection

$$\{u_a : a \in \Sigma\} \subseteq \mathcal{A} \tag{1.235}$$

of vectors in $\mathcal{A}$.

The *convex hull* of a set $\mathcal{A} \subseteq \mathcal{V}$, denoted $\mathrm{conv}(\mathcal{A})$, is the intersection of all convex sets containing $\mathcal{A}$. The set $\mathrm{conv}(\mathcal{A})$ is equal to the set of all vectors that may be written as a convex combination of elements of $\mathcal{A}$. (This is true even in the case that $\mathcal{A}$ is infinite.) The convex hull $\text{conv}(\mathcal{A})$ of a closed set $\mathcal{A}$ need not itself be closed. However, if $\mathcal{A}$ is compact, then so too is $\text{conv}(\mathcal{A})$.

The theorem that follows provides an upper bound on the number of elements over which one must take convex combinations in order to generate every point in the convex hull of a given set. The theorem refers to the notion of an *affine subspace*: a set $\mathcal{U} \subseteq \mathcal{V}$ is an affine subspace of $\mathcal{V}$ having dimension n if there exist a subspace $\mathcal{W} \subseteq \mathcal{V}$ of dimension n and a vector $u \in \mathcal{V}$ such that

$$\mathcal{U} = \{u + v : v \in \mathcal{W}\}. \tag{1.236}$$

Theorem 1.9 (Carathéodory's theorem) *Let $\mathcal{V}$ be a real vector space and let $\mathcal{A}$ be a subset of $\mathcal{V}$. Assume, moreover, that $\mathcal{A}$ is contained in an affine subspace of $\mathcal{V}$ having dimension n. For every vector $v \in \text{conv}(\mathcal{A})$ in the convex hull of $\mathcal{A}$, there exist $m \leq n+1$ vectors $u_1, \ldots, u_m \in \mathcal{A}$ such that $v \in \text{conv}(\{u_1, \ldots, u_m\})$.*

Extreme Points

A point $w \in \mathcal{C}$ in a convex set $\mathcal{C}$ is said to be an *extreme point* of $\mathcal{C}$ if, for every expression

$$w = \lambda u + (1 - \lambda)v \tag{1.237}$$

for which $u, v \in \mathcal{C}$ and $\lambda \in (0, 1)$, it holds that $u = v = w$. In words, the extreme points are those elements of $\mathcal{C}$ that do not lie properly between two distinct points of $\mathcal{C}$.

The following theorem states that every convex and compact subset of a finite-dimensional vector space, over the real or complex numbers, is equal to the convex hull of its extreme points.

Theorem 1.10 (Minkowski) *Let $\mathcal{V}$ be a finite-dimensional vector space over the real or complex numbers, let $\mathcal{C} \subseteq \mathcal{V}$ be a compact and convex set, and let $\mathcal{A} \subseteq \mathcal{C}$ be the set of extreme points of $\mathcal{C}$. It holds that $\mathcal{C} = \text{conv}(\mathcal{A})$.*

A few examples of convex and compact sets, along with an identification of their extreme points, follow.

1. *The spectral norm unit ball.* For any complex Euclidean space $\mathcal{X}$, the set

$$\{X \in \text{L}(\mathcal{X}) : \|X\| \leq 1\} \tag{1.238}$$

is a convex and compact set. The extreme points of this set are the unitary operators $\text{U}(\mathcal{X})$.

2. *The trace norm unit ball.* For any complex Euclidean space $\mathcal{X}$, the set

$$\{X \in L(\mathcal{X}) : \|X\|_1 \leq 1\} \tag{1.239}$$

   is a convex and compact set. The extreme points of this set are those operators of the form uv^* for $u, v \in \mathcal{S}(\mathcal{X})$ unit vectors.

3. *Density operators.* For any complex Euclidean space $\mathcal{X}$, the set $D(\mathcal{X})$ of density operators acting on $\mathcal{X}$ is convex and compact. The extreme points of $D(\mathcal{X})$ coincide with the rank-one projection operators. These are the operators of the form uu^* for $u \in \mathcal{S}(\mathcal{X})$ being a unit vector.

4. *Probability vectors.* For any alphabet Σ, the set of probability vectors $\mathcal{P}(\Sigma)$ is convex and compact. The extreme points of this set are the elements of the standard basis $\{e_a : a \in \Sigma\}$ of $\mathbb{R}^\Sigma$.

Hyperplane Separation and Min–Max Theorems

Convex sets in real Euclidean spaces possess a fundamentally important property: every vector lying outside of a given convex set in a real Euclidean space can be separated from that convex set by a *hyperplane*. That is, if the underlying real Euclidean space has dimension n, then there exist an affine subspace of that space having dimension $n-1$ that divides the entire space into two half-spaces: one contains the convex set and the other contains the chosen point lying outside of the convex set. The following theorem represents one specific formulation of this fact.

Theorem 1.11 (Hyperplane separation theorem) *Let $\mathcal{V}$ be a real Euclidean space, let $\mathcal{C} \subset \mathcal{V}$ be a closed, convex subset of $\mathcal{V}$, and let $u \in \mathcal{V}$ be a vector with $u \notin \mathcal{C}$. There exist a vector $v \in \mathcal{V}$ and a scalar $\alpha \in \mathbb{R}$ such that*

$$\langle v, u \rangle < \alpha \leq \langle v, w \rangle \tag{1.240}$$

for all $w \in \mathcal{C}$. If $\mathcal{C}$ is a cone, then v may be chosen so that (1.240) *holds for $\alpha = 0$.*

Another theorem concerning convex sets that finds uses in the theory of quantum information is the following theorem.

Theorem 1.12 (Sion's min–max theorem) *Let $\mathcal{X}$ and $\mathcal{Y}$ be real or complex Euclidean spaces, let $\mathcal{A} \subseteq \mathcal{X}$ and $\mathcal{B} \subseteq \mathcal{Y}$ be convex sets with $\mathcal{B}$ compact, and let $f : \mathcal{A} \times \mathcal{B} \to \mathbb{R}$ be a continuous function such that*

1. *$u \mapsto f(u, v)$ is a convex function on $\mathcal{A}$ for all $v \in \mathcal{B}$, and*
2. *$v \mapsto f(u, v)$ is a concave function on $\mathcal{B}$ for all $u \in \mathcal{A}$.*

It holds that

$$\inf_{u \in \mathcal{A}} \max_{v \in \mathcal{B}} f(u, v) = \max_{v \in \mathcal{B}} \inf_{u \in \mathcal{A}} f(u, v). \tag{1.241}$$

1.2.2 Probability Theory

Concepts from probability theory will play an important role throughout much of this book. Probability distributions over alphabets or other finite sets will be viewed as having fundamental importance; they arise naturally when information-theoretic tasks and settings are considered. The reader is assumed to have familiarity with basic probability theory for distributions over sets with finitely many elements. It will also be convenient to use the language of probability theory to discuss properties of Borel measures.

Random Variables Distributed With Respect to Probability Measures

Suppose $\mathcal{A}$ is a subset of a finite-dimensional real or complex vector space $\mathcal{V}$ and $\mu : \mathrm{Borel}(\mathcal{A}) \to [0, 1]$ is a probability measure (by which it is meant that μ is a normalized Borel measure). A *random variable* X distributed with respect to μ is a real-valued, integrable Borel function of the form

$$X : \mathcal{A} \to \mathbb{R}, \tag{1.242}$$

which is typically viewed as representing an outcome of a random process of some sort.

For every Borel subset $\mathcal{B} \subseteq \mathbb{R}$ of the real numbers, the probability that X takes a value in $\mathcal{B}$ is defined as

$$\mathrm{Pr}(X \in \mathcal{B}) = \mu(\{u \in \mathcal{A} : X(u) \in \mathcal{B}\}). \tag{1.243}$$

As a matter of notational convenience, one often writes expressions such as

$$\mathrm{Pr}(X \geq \beta) \quad \text{and} \quad \mathrm{Pr}(|X - \beta| \geq \varepsilon), \tag{1.244}$$

which are to be understood as meaning $\mathrm{Pr}(X \in \mathcal{B})$ for

$$\mathcal{B} = \{\alpha \in \mathbb{R} : \alpha \geq \beta\} \quad \text{and} \quad \mathcal{B} = \{\alpha \in \mathbb{R} : |\alpha - \beta| \geq \varepsilon\}, \tag{1.245}$$

respectively. Other expressions of this form are interpreted in an analogous way.

The *union bound* states, for any random variable X and arbitrary Borel subsets $\mathcal{B}_1, \ldots, \mathcal{B}_n$ of $\mathbb{R}$, that

$$\mathrm{Pr}(X \in \mathcal{B}_1 \cup \cdots \cup \mathcal{B}_n) \leq \mathrm{Pr}(X \in \mathcal{B}_1) + \cdots + \mathrm{Pr}(X \in \mathcal{B}_n). \tag{1.246}$$

The *expected value* (or *mean value*) of a random variable X, distributed with respect to a probability measure $\mu \colon \mathrm{Borel}(\mathcal{A}) \to [0, 1]$, is defined as

$$\mathrm{E}(X) = \int X(u) \, \mathrm{d}\mu(u). \tag{1.247}$$

If X is a random variable taking nonnegative real values, then it holds that

$$\mathrm{E}(X) = \int_0^\infty \Pr(X \geq \lambda) \, \mathrm{d}\lambda. \tag{1.248}$$

Random Variables for Discrete Distributions

For a given alphabet Σ and a probability vector $p \in \mathcal{P}(\Sigma)$, one may also define a random variable X, distributed with respect to p, in an analogous way to a random variable distributed with respect to a Borel measure. In particular, such a random variable is a function of the form

$$X \colon \Sigma \to \mathbb{R}, \tag{1.249}$$

and for every subset $\Gamma \subseteq \Sigma$ one writes

$$\Pr(X \in \Gamma) = \sum_{a \in \Gamma} p(a). \tag{1.250}$$

In this case, the *expected value* (or *mean value*) of X is

$$\mathrm{E}(X) = \sum_{a \in \Sigma} p(a) X(a). \tag{1.251}$$

It is, in some sense, not necessary for random variables distributed with respect to probability vectors of the form $p \in \mathcal{P}(\Sigma)$ to be viewed as being fundamentally different from random variables distributed with respect to Borel probability measures. Indeed, one may consider the set

$$\{1, \dots, n\} \subset \mathbb{R}, \tag{1.252}$$

for some choice of a positive integer n, and observe that every subset of $\{1, \dots, n\}$ is a Borel subset of this set. The Borel probability measures

$$\mu \colon \mathrm{Borel}(\{1, \dots, n\}) \to [0, 1] \tag{1.253}$$

coincide precisely with the set of all probability vectors $p \in \mathcal{P}(\{1, \dots, n\})$ through the equations

$$\mu(\mathcal{B}) = \sum_{b \in \mathcal{B}} p(b) \quad \text{and} \quad p(a) = \mu(\{a\}), \tag{1.254}$$

for every $\mathcal{B} \subseteq \{1, \dots, n\}$ and $a \in \{1, \dots, n\}$.

Thus, by associating an arbitrary alphabet Σ with the set $\{1, \ldots, n\}$, one finds that a random variable distributed with respect to a probability vector $p \in \mathcal{P}(\Sigma)$ is represented by a random variable distributed with respect to a Borel probability measure.

Vector- and Operator-Valued Random Variables

It is sometimes convenient to define random variables that take vector or operator values, rather than real number values. Random variables of this sort will always be specified explicitly in terms of ordinary random variables (i.e., ones that take real values) in this book. For example, given random variables $X_1, \ldots, X_n$ and $Y_1, \ldots, Y_n$, for some choice of a positive integer n, one may refer to the vector-valued random variables

$$(X_1, \ldots, X_n) \in \mathbb{R}^n \quad \text{and} \quad (X_1 + iY_1, \ldots, X_n + iY_n) \in \mathbb{C}^n. \tag{1.255}$$

The default meaning of the term *random variable* should be understood as referring to real-valued random variables, and the term *vector-valued random variable* or *operator-valued random variable* will be used when referring to random variables obtained in the manner just described.

Independent and Identically Distributed Random Variables

Two random variables X and Y are said to be *independent* if

$$\Pr((X, Y) \in \mathcal{A} \times \mathcal{B}) = \Pr(X \in \mathcal{A}) \Pr(Y \in \mathcal{B}) \tag{1.256}$$

for every choice of Borel subsets $\mathcal{A}, \mathcal{B} \subseteq \mathbb{R}$, and are said to be *identically distributed* if

$$\Pr(X \in \mathcal{A}) = \Pr(Y \in \mathcal{A}) \tag{1.257}$$

for every Borel subset $\mathcal{A} \subseteq \mathbb{R}$. In general, these conditions do not require that X and Y are defined with respect to the same Borel measure. In both cases, these notions may be extended to more than two random variables, as well as to vector-valued random variables, in a straightforward way.

Suppose that $\mathcal{A}$ is a subset of a finite-dimensional real or complex vector space, $\mu \colon \mathrm{Borel}(\mathcal{A}) \to [0, 1]$ is a probability measure, and $Y \colon \mathcal{A} \to \mathbb{R}$ is a random variable distributed with respect to μ. For any choice of a positive integer n, one may consider *independent and identically distributed* random variables $X_1, \ldots, X_n$, each being distributed in the same way as Y. For the purposes of this book, one may assume without loss of generality that this means that $X_1, \ldots, X_n$ are Borel functions, taking the form

$$X_k \colon \mathcal{A}^n \to \mathbb{R} \tag{1.258}$$

and being defined as

$$X_k(u_1, \ldots, u_n) = Y(u_k) \tag{1.259}$$

for each k and each $(u_1, \ldots, u_n) \in \mathcal{A}^n$. Moreover, each X_k is understood to be distributed with respect to the n-fold product measure $\mu \times \cdots \times \mu$ on $\mathcal{A}^n$. In essence, this formal specification represents the simple and intuitive notion that $X_1, \ldots, X_n$ are uncorrelated copies of the random variable Y.

A Few Fundamental Theorems

A few fundamental theorems concerning random variables will be used later in this book. While these theorems do hold for more general notions of random variables, the theorem statements that follow should be understood to apply to random variables distributed with respect to Borel probability measures (including random variables distributed with respect to probability vectors of the form $p \in \mathcal{P}(\Sigma)$ as a special case, as described above).

The first theorem to be stated in this subsection is *Markov's inequality*, which provides a sometimes coarse upper bound on the probability that a nonnegative random variable exceeds a given threshold value.

Theorem 1.13 (Markov's inequality) *Let X be a random variable taking nonnegative real values, and let $\varepsilon > 0$ be a positive real number. It holds that*

$$\Pr(X \geq \varepsilon) \leq \frac{\mathrm{E}(X)}{\varepsilon}. \tag{1.260}$$

The next theorem, known as *Jensen's inequality*, concerns the expected value of a convex function applied to a random variable.

Theorem 1.14 (Jensen's inequality) *Suppose that X is a random variable and $f \colon \mathbb{R} \to \mathbb{R}$ is a convex function. It holds that*

$$f(\mathrm{E}(X)) \leq \mathrm{E}(f(X)). \tag{1.261}$$

Two additional theorems – known as the *weak law of large numbers* and *Hoeffding's inequality* – provide bounds on the deviation of the average value of a collection of independent and identically distributed random variables from their mean value.

Theorem 1.15 (Weak law of large numbers) *Let X be a random variable and let $\alpha = \mathrm{E}(X)$. Assume, moreover, for every positive integer n, that $X_1, \ldots, X_n$ are independent random variables identically distributed to X. For every positive real number $\varepsilon > 0$, it holds that*

$$\lim_{n \to \infty} \Pr\left(\left| \frac{X_1 + \cdots + X_n}{n} - \alpha \right| \geq \varepsilon \right) = 0. \tag{1.262}$$

Theorem 1.16 (Hoeffding's inequality) *Let $X_1, \ldots, X_n$ be independent and identically distributed random variables taking values in the interval $[0, 1]$ and having mean value α. For every positive real number $\varepsilon > 0$ it holds that*

$$\Pr\left(\left| \frac{X_1 + \cdots + X_n}{n} - \alpha \right| \geq \varepsilon \right) \leq 2 \exp(-2n\varepsilon^2). \tag{1.263}$$

Gaussian Measure and Normally Distributed Random Variables

The *standard Gaussian measure* on $\mathbb{R}$ is the Borel probability measure

$$\gamma \colon \mathrm{Borel}(\mathbb{R}) \to [0, 1] \tag{1.264}$$

defined as

$$\gamma(\mathcal{A}) = \frac{1}{\sqrt{2\pi}} \int_{\mathcal{A}} \exp\left(-\frac{\alpha^2}{2}\right) d\alpha \tag{1.265}$$

for every $\mathcal{A} \in \mathrm{Borel}(\mathbb{R})$, where the integral is to be taken with respect to the standard Borel measure on $\mathbb{R}$. The fact that this is a well-defined measure follows from the observation that the function

$$\alpha \mapsto \begin{cases} \frac{1}{\sqrt{2\pi}} \exp\left(-\frac{\alpha^2}{2}\right) & \text{if } \alpha \in \mathcal{A} \\ 0 & \text{otherwise} \end{cases} \tag{1.266}$$

is an integrable Borel function for every Borel subset $\mathcal{A} \subseteq \mathbb{R}$, and the fact that it is a probability measure follows from the Gaussian integral

$$\int \exp\left(-\frac{\alpha^2}{2}\right) d\alpha = \sqrt{2\pi}. \tag{1.267}$$

A random variable X is a *standard normal random variable* if it holds that $\Pr(X \in \mathcal{A}) = \gamma(\mathcal{A})$ for every $\mathcal{A} \in \mathrm{Borel}(\mathbb{R})$. This is equivalent to saying that X is identically distributed to a random variable $Y(\alpha) = \alpha$ distributed with respect to the standard Gaussian measure γ on $\mathbb{R}$.

The following integrals are among many integrals of a similar sort that are useful when reasoning about standard normal random variables:

1. For every positive real number $\lambda > 0$ and every real number $\beta \in \mathbb{R}$ it holds that

$$\int \exp(-\lambda \alpha^2 + \beta \alpha) \, d\alpha = \sqrt{\frac{\pi}{\lambda}} \exp\left(\frac{\beta^2}{4\lambda}\right). \tag{1.268}$$

2. For every positive integer n, it holds that

$$\int_0^\infty \alpha^n \, d\gamma(\alpha) = \frac{2^{\frac{n}{2}} \Gamma\!\left(\frac{n+1}{2}\right)}{2\sqrt{\pi}}, \tag{1.269}$$

where the Γ-function may be defined at positive half-integer points as follows:

$$\Gamma\!\left(\frac{m+1}{2}\right) = \begin{cases} \sqrt{\pi} & \text{if } m = 0 \\ 1 & \text{if } m = 1 \\ \frac{m-1}{2}\Gamma\!\left(\frac{m-1}{2}\right) & \text{if } m \geq 2. \end{cases} \tag{1.270}$$

3. For every positive real number $\lambda > 0$ and every pair of real numbers $\beta_0, \beta_1 \in \mathbb{R}$ with $\beta_0 \leq \beta_1$ it holds that

$$\int_{\beta_0}^{\beta_1} \alpha \exp(-\lambda\alpha^2) \, d\alpha = \frac{1}{2\lambda} \exp(-\lambda\beta_0^2) - \frac{1}{2\lambda} \exp(-\lambda\beta_1^2). \tag{1.271}$$

This formula also holds for infinite values of β_0 and β_1, with the natural interpretation $\exp(-\infty) = 0$.

For every positive integer n, the *standard Gaussian measure* on $\mathbb{R}^n$ is the Borel probability measure

$$\gamma_n \colon \mathrm{Borel}(\mathbb{R}^n) \to [0, 1] \tag{1.272}$$

obtained by taking the n-fold product measure of γ with itself. Equivalently,

$$\gamma_n(\mathcal{A}) = (2\pi)^{-\frac{n}{2}} \int_{\mathcal{A}} \exp\!\left(-\frac{\|u\|^2}{2}\right) d\nu_n(u), \tag{1.273}$$

where ν_n denotes the n-fold product measure of the standard Borel measure ν with itself and the norm is the Euclidean norm.

The standard Gaussian measure on $\mathbb{R}^n$ is invariant under orthogonal transformations (which include rotations):

$$\gamma_n(U\mathcal{A}) = \gamma_n(\mathcal{A}) \tag{1.274}$$

for every Borel set $\mathcal{A} \subseteq \mathbb{R}^n$ and every orthogonal operator $U \in \mathrm{L}(\mathbb{R}^n)$, meaning one that satisfies $UU^{\mathsf{T}} = \mathbb{1}$. Therefore, for independent standard normal random variables $X_1, \ldots, X_n$, one has that the vector-valued random variable $(X_1, \ldots, X_n)$ is identically distributed to the vector-valued random variable $(Y_1, \ldots, Y_n)$ obtained by defining

$$Y_k = \sum_{j=1}^n U(k, j) X_j \tag{1.275}$$

for each $k \in \{1, \ldots, n\}$, for $U \in \mathrm{L}(\mathbb{R}^n)$ being any orthogonal operator. As a consequence of this fact, one has that if the standard Gaussian measure is projected onto a subspace, it is equivalent to the standard Gaussian measure on that subspace.

Proposition 1.17 *Let m and n be positive integers satisfying $m < n$ and let $V \in \mathrm{L}(\mathbb{R}^m, \mathbb{R}^n)$ satisfy $V^\mathsf{T} V = \mathbb{1}$. For every Borel set $\mathcal{A} \subseteq \mathbb{R}^m$, one has*

$$\gamma_m(\mathcal{A}) = \gamma_n(\{u \in \mathbb{R}^n : V^\mathsf{T} u \in \mathcal{A}\}). \tag{1.276}$$

It follows from this proposition that the standard Gaussian measure $\gamma_n(\mathcal{V})$ of any proper subspace $\mathcal{V}$ of $\mathbb{R}^n$ is zero.

Finally, for independent standard normal random variables $X_1, \ldots, X_n$, one may define a random variable

$$Y = \sqrt{X_1^2 + \cdots + X_n^2}. \tag{1.277}$$

The distribution of Y is known as the χ-*distribution*. The mean value of Y has the following closed-form expression:

$$\mathrm{E}(Y) = \frac{\sqrt{2}\,\Gamma\!\left(\frac{n+1}{2}\right)}{\Gamma\!\left(\frac{n}{2}\right)}. \tag{1.278}$$

From this expression, it may be proved that

$$\mathrm{E}(Y) = \upsilon_n \sqrt{n}, \tag{1.279}$$

where $(\upsilon_1, \upsilon_2, \ldots)$ is a strictly increasing sequence that begins

$$\upsilon_1 = \sqrt{\frac{2}{\pi}}, \quad \upsilon_2 = \frac{\sqrt{\pi}}{2}, \quad \upsilon_3 = \sqrt{\frac{8}{3\pi}}, \quad \cdots \tag{1.280}$$

and converges to 1 in the limit as n goes to infinity.

1.2.3 Semidefinite Programming

The paradigm of *semidefinite programming* finds numerous applications in the theory of quantum information, both analytical and computational. This section describes a formulation of semidefinite programming that is well-suited to its (primarily analytical) applications found in this book.

Definitions Associated With Semidefinite Programs

Let $\mathcal{X}$ and $\mathcal{Y}$ be complex Euclidean spaces, let $\Phi \in \mathrm{T}(\mathcal{X}, \mathcal{Y})$ be a Hermitian-preserving map, and let $A \in \mathrm{Herm}(\mathcal{X})$ and $B \in \mathrm{Herm}(\mathcal{Y})$ be Hermitian operators. A *semidefinite program* is a triple (Φ, A, B), with which the following pair of optimization problems is associated:

Primal problem	Dual problem
maximize: $\langle A, X \rangle$	minimize: $\langle B, Y \rangle$
subject to: $\Phi(X) = B$,	subject to: $\Phi^*(Y) \geq A$,
$\quad\quad\quad X \in \mathrm{Pos}(\mathcal{X})$.	$\quad\quad\quad Y \in \mathrm{Herm}(\mathcal{Y})$.

With these problems in mind, one defines the *primal feasible* set $\mathcal{A}$ and the *dual feasible* set $\mathcal{B}$ of (Φ, A, B) as follows:

$$\begin{aligned}
\mathcal{A} &= \{X \in \mathrm{Pos}(\mathcal{X}): \Phi(X) = B\}, \\
\mathcal{B} &= \{Y \in \mathrm{Herm}(\mathcal{Y}): \Phi^*(Y) \geq A\}.
\end{aligned} \tag{1.281}$$

Operators $X \in \mathcal{A}$ and $Y \in \mathcal{B}$ are also said to be *primal feasible* and *dual feasible*, respectively.

The function $X \mapsto \langle A, X \rangle$, from $\mathrm{Herm}(\mathcal{X})$ to $\mathbb{R}$, is the *primal objective function*, while the function $Y \mapsto \langle B, Y \rangle$, from $\mathrm{Herm}(\mathcal{Y})$ to $\mathbb{R}$, is the *dual objective function* of (Φ, A, B). The *optimum values* associated with the primal and dual problems are defined as

$$\alpha = \sup\{\langle A, X \rangle: X \in \mathcal{A}\} \quad \text{and} \quad \beta = \inf\{\langle B, Y \rangle: Y \in \mathcal{B}\}, \tag{1.282}$$

respectively. (If it is the case that $\mathcal{A} = \varnothing$ or $\mathcal{B} = \varnothing$, then one defines $\alpha = -\infty$ and $\beta = \infty$, respectively.)

Semidefinite Programming Duality

Semidefinite programs have associated with them a notion of *duality*, which refers to the special relationship between the primal and dual problems.

The property of *weak duality*, which holds for all semidefinite programs, is that the primal optimum can never exceed the dual optimum. In more succinct terms, it necessarily holds that $\alpha \leq \beta$. This implies that every dual feasible operator $Y \in \mathcal{B}$ provides an upper bound of $\langle B, Y \rangle$ on the value $\langle A, X \rangle$ that is achievable over all choices of a primal feasible $X \in \mathcal{A}$, and likewise every primal feasible operator $X \in \mathcal{A}$ provides a lower bound of $\langle A, X \rangle$ on the value $\langle B, Y \rangle$ that is achievable over all dual feasible operators $Y \in \mathcal{B}$.

It is not always the case that the primal optimum and dual optimum of a semidefinite program (Φ, A, B) agree, but for many semidefinite programs that arise naturally in applications, the primal optimum and dual optimum will be equal. This situation is called *strong duality*. The following theorem provides one set of conditions under which strong duality is guaranteed.

Theorem 1.18 (Slater's theorem for semidefinite programs) *Let $\mathcal{X}$ and $\mathcal{Y}$ be complex Euclidean spaces, let $\Phi \in \mathrm{T}(\mathcal{X}, \mathcal{Y})$ be a Hermitian-preserving map, and let $A \in \mathrm{Herm}(\mathcal{X})$ and $B \in \mathrm{Herm}(\mathcal{Y})$ be Hermitian operators. Letting $\mathcal{A}$, $\mathcal{B}$, α, and β be as defined above for the semidefinite program (Φ, A, B), one has the following two implications:*

1. *If α is finite and there exists a Hermitian operator $Y \in \mathrm{Herm}(\mathcal{Y})$ such that $\Phi^*(Y) > A$, then $\alpha = \beta$, and moreover there exists a primal feasible operator $X \in \mathcal{A}$ such that $\langle A, X \rangle = \alpha$.*
2. *If β is finite and there exists a positive definite operator $X \in \mathrm{Pd}(\mathcal{X})$ such that $\Phi(X) = B$, then $\alpha = \beta$, and moreover there exists a dual feasible operator $Y \in \mathcal{B}$ such that $\langle B, Y \rangle = \beta$.*

In the situation that the optimum primal and dual values are equal, and are both achieved for some choice of feasible operators, a simple relationship between these operators, known as *complementary slackness*, must hold.

Proposition 1.19 (Complementary slackness for semidefinite programs) *Let $\mathcal{X}$ and $\mathcal{Y}$ be complex Euclidean spaces, let $\Phi \in \mathrm{T}(\mathcal{X}, \mathcal{Y})$ be a Hermitian-preserving map, and let $A \in \mathrm{Herm}(\mathcal{X})$ and $B \in \mathrm{Herm}(\mathcal{Y})$ be Hermitian operators. Let $\mathcal{A}$ and $\mathcal{B}$ be the primal feasible and dual feasible sets associated with the semidefinite program (Φ, A, B), and suppose that $X \in \mathcal{A}$ and $Y \in \mathcal{B}$ are operators satisfying $\langle A, X \rangle = \langle B, Y \rangle$. It holds that*

$$\Phi^*(Y)X = AX. \tag{1.283}$$

Simplified Forms and Alternative Expressions of Semidefinite Programs

Semidefinite programs are typically presented in a way that is somewhat less formal than a precise specification of a triple (Φ, A, B), for $\Phi \in \mathrm{T}(\mathcal{X}, \mathcal{Y})$ being a Hermitian-preserving map and $A \in \mathrm{Herm}(\mathcal{X})$ and $B \in \mathrm{Herm}(\mathcal{Y})$ being Hermitian operators. Rather, the primal and dual problems are stated directly, often in a simplified form, and it is sometimes left to the reader to formulate a triple (Φ, A, B) that corresponds to the simplified problem statements.

Two examples of semidefinite programs follow, in both cases including their formal specifications and simplified forms.

Example 1.20 (Semidefinite program for the trace norm) Let $\mathcal{X}$ and $\mathcal{Y}$ be complex Euclidean spaces and let $K \in \mathrm{L}(\mathcal{X}, \mathcal{Y})$ be any operator. Define a Hermitian-preserving map $\Phi \in \mathrm{T}(\mathcal{X} \oplus \mathcal{Y})$ as

$$\Phi \begin{pmatrix} X & \cdot \\ \cdot & Y \end{pmatrix} = \begin{pmatrix} X & 0 \\ 0 & Y \end{pmatrix} \tag{1.284}$$

for all $X \in L(\mathcal{X})$ and $Y \in L(\mathcal{Y})$, where the dots represent elements of $L(\mathcal{X}, \mathcal{Y})$ and $L(\mathcal{Y}, \mathcal{X})$ that are effectively zeroed out by Φ. The map Φ is self-adjoint: $\Phi^* = \Phi$. Also define $A, B \in \text{Herm}(\mathcal{X} \oplus \mathcal{Y})$ as

$$A = \frac{1}{2} \begin{pmatrix} 0 & K^* \\ K & 0 \end{pmatrix} \quad \text{and} \quad B = \begin{pmatrix} \mathbb{1}_{\mathcal{X}} & 0 \\ 0 & \mathbb{1}_{\mathcal{Y}} \end{pmatrix}. \tag{1.285}$$

The primal and dual problems associated with the semidefinite program (Φ, A, B) may, after some simplifications, be expressed as follows:

Primal problem	Dual problem
maximize: $\frac{1}{2}\langle K, Z \rangle + \frac{1}{2}\langle K^*, Z^* \rangle$	minimize: $\frac{1}{2}\text{Tr}(X) + \frac{1}{2}\text{Tr}(Y)$
subject to: $\begin{pmatrix} \mathbb{1}_{\mathcal{X}} & Z^* \\ Z & \mathbb{1}_{\mathcal{Y}} \end{pmatrix} \geq 0,$	subject to: $\begin{pmatrix} X & -K^* \\ -K & Y \end{pmatrix} \geq 0,$
$Z \in L(\mathcal{X}, \mathcal{Y}).$	$X \in \text{Pos}(\mathcal{X}),$
	$Y \in \text{Pos}(\mathcal{Y}).$

The primal and dual optima are equal for all choices of K, and given by $\|K\|_1$. (Given a singular value decomposition of K, one can construct both a primal feasible and dual feasible solution achieving this value.)

A standard way of expressing this semidefinite program would be to list only the simplified primal and dual problems given above, letting the triple (Φ, A, B) be specified implicitly.

Example 1.21 (Semidefinite programs with inequality constraints)   Let $\mathcal{X}$, $\mathcal{Y}$, and $\mathcal{Z}$ be complex Euclidean spaces, let $\Phi \in T(\mathcal{X}, \mathcal{Y})$ and $\Psi \in T(\mathcal{X}, \mathcal{Z})$ be Hermitian-preserving maps, and let $A \in \text{Herm}(\mathcal{X})$, $B \in \text{Herm}(\mathcal{Y})$, and $C \in \text{Herm}(\mathcal{Z})$ be Hermitian operators. Define a map

$$\Xi \in T(\mathcal{X} \oplus \mathcal{Z}, \mathcal{Y} \oplus \mathcal{Z}) \tag{1.286}$$

as

$$\Xi \begin{pmatrix} X & \cdot \\ \cdot & Z \end{pmatrix} = \begin{pmatrix} \Phi(X) & 0 \\ 0 & \Psi(X) + Z \end{pmatrix} \tag{1.287}$$

for all $X \in L(\mathcal{X})$ and $Z \in L(\mathcal{Z})$. (Similar to the previous example, the dots in the argument to Ξ represent arbitrary elements of $L(\mathcal{X}, \mathcal{Z})$ and $L(\mathcal{Z}, \mathcal{X})$ upon which Ξ does not depend.) The adjoint map

$$\Xi^* \in T(\mathcal{Y} \oplus \mathcal{Z}, \mathcal{X} \oplus \mathcal{Z}) \tag{1.288}$$

to Ξ is given by

$$\Xi^* \begin{pmatrix} Y & \cdot \\ \cdot & Z \end{pmatrix} = \begin{pmatrix} \Phi^*(Y) + \Psi^*(Z) & 0 \\ 0 & Z \end{pmatrix}. \tag{1.289}$$

The primal and dual problems of the semidefinite program specified by the map Ξ, together with the Hermitian operators

$$\begin{pmatrix} A & 0 \\ 0 & 0 \end{pmatrix} \in \mathrm{Herm}(\mathcal{X} \oplus \mathcal{Z}) \quad \text{and} \quad \begin{pmatrix} B & 0 \\ 0 & C \end{pmatrix} \in \mathrm{Herm}(\mathcal{Y} \oplus \mathcal{Z}), \tag{1.290}$$

may be expressed in the following simplified form:

Primal problem	Dual problem
maximize: $\langle A, X \rangle$	minimize: $\langle B, Y \rangle + \langle C, Z \rangle$
subject to: $\Phi(X) = B,$	subject to: $\Phi^*(Y) + \Psi^*(Z) \geq A,$
$\Psi(X) \leq C,$	$Y \in \mathrm{Herm}(\mathcal{Y}),$
$X \in \mathrm{Pos}(\mathcal{X}).$	$Z \in \mathrm{Pos}(\mathcal{Z}).$

It is sometimes convenient to consider semidefinite programming problems of this form, that include both equality and inequality constraints in the primal problem, as opposed to just equality constraints.

1.3 Suggested References

Several textbooks cover the material on linear algebra summarized in this chapter; the classic books of Halmos (1978) and Hoffman and Kunze (1971) are two examples. Readers interested in a more modern development of linear algebra for finite-dimensional spaces are referred to the book of Axler (1997). The books of Horn and Johnson (1985) and Bhatia (1997) also cover much of the material on linear algebra that has been summarized in this chapter (and a great deal more, including relevant theorems to be proved in subsequent chapters of this book), with a focus on the matrix-theoretic aspects of the subject.

There are also many textbooks on mathematical analysis, including the classic texts of Rudin (1964) and Apostol (1974), as well as the books of Bartle (1966) and Halmos (1974), which focus on measure theory. The book of Rockafellar (1970) is a standard reference on convex analysis, and the two-volume collection of Feller (1968, 1971) is a standard reference on probability theory. Semidefinite programming is discussed by Wolkowicz, Saigal, and Vandenberge (2000).

2

Basic Notions of Quantum Information

This chapter introduces the most basic objects and notions of quantum information theory, including *registers, states, channels,* and *measurements,* and investigates some of their elementary properties.

2.1 Registers and States

This first section of the chapter concerns *registers* and *states*. A register is an abstraction of a physical device in which quantum information may be stored, and the state of a register represents a description of its contents at a particular instant.

2.1.1 Registers and Classical State Sets

The term *register* is intended to be suggestive of a computer component in which some finite amount of data can be stored and manipulated. While this is a reasonable picture to keep in mind, it should be understood that any physical system in which a finite amount of data may be stored, and whose state may change over time, could be modeled as a register. For example, a register could represent a medium used to transmit information from a sender to a receiver. At an intuitive level, what is most important is that registers represent mathematical abstractions of physical objects, or parts of physical objects, that store information.

Definition of Registers

The following formal definition of a register is intended to capture a basic but nevertheless important idea, which is that multiple registers may be viewed collectively as forming a single register. It is natural to choose an inductive definition for this reason.

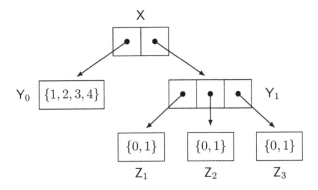

Figure 2.1 The tree associated with the registers described in Example 2.2.

Definition 2.1 A *register* X is either one of the following two objects:

1. An alphabet Σ.
2. An n-tuple $X = (Y_1, \ldots, Y_n)$, where n is a positive integer and $Y_1, \ldots, Y_n$ are registers.

Registers of the first type are called *simple registers* and registers of the second type are called *compound registers* when it is helpful to distinguish them.

In the case of a simple register $X = \Sigma$, the alphabet Σ represents the set of *classical states* that the register may store. The classical state set associated with a compound register will be specified shortly. As is suggested by the definition, registers will be denoted by capital letters in a *sans serif* font, such as X, Y, and Z. Sometimes registers will be subscripted, such as $X_1, \ldots, X_n$, when it is necessary to refer to a variable number of registers or convenient to name them in this way for some other reason.

Based on Definition 2.1, one may naturally identify a tree structure with a given register, with each leaf node corresponding to a simple register. A register Y is said to be a *subregister* of X if the tree associated with Y is a subtree of the tree associated with X.

Example 2.2 Define registers X, Y_0, Y_1, Z_1, Z_2, and Z_3, as follows:

$$X = (Y_0, Y_1), \qquad Y_0 = \{1, 2, 3, 4\}, \qquad Z_1 = \{0, 1\},$$
$$Y_1 = (Z_1, Z_2, Z_3), \qquad Z_2 = \{0, 1\}, \qquad (2.1)$$
$$Z_3 = \{0, 1\}.$$

The tree associated with the register X is illustrated in Figure 2.1. The subregisters of X include Y_0, Y_1, Z_1, Z_2, Z_3, and (trivially) X itself.

The Classical State Set of a Register

Every register has associated with it a *classical state set*, as specified by the following definition.

Definition 2.3 The *classical state set* of a register X is determined as follows:

1. If $X = \Sigma$ is a simple register, the classical state set of X is Σ.
2. If $X = (Y_1, \ldots, Y_n)$ is a compound register, the classical state set of X is the Cartesian product

$$\Sigma = \Gamma_1 \times \cdots \times \Gamma_n, \tag{2.2}$$

where Γ_k denotes the classical state set associated with the register Y_k for each $k \in \{1, \ldots, n\}$.

Elements of a register's classical state set are called *classical states* of that register.

The term *classical state* is intended to be suggestive of the classical notion of a state in computer science. Intuitively speaking, a classical state of a register can be recognized unambiguously, like the values 0 and 1 stored by a single-bit memory component. The term *classical state* should not be confused with the term *state*, which by default will mean *quantum state* rather than *classical state* throughout this book.

A register is said to be *trivial* if its classical state set contains just a single element. While trivial registers are useless from the viewpoint of information processing, it is mathematically convenient to allow for this possibility. The reader will note, however, that registers with *empty* classical state sets are disallowed by the definition. This is consistent with the idea that registers represent physical systems; while it is possible that a physical system could have just one possible classical state, it is nonsensical for a system to have no states whatsoever.

Reductions of Classical States

There is a straightforward way in which each classical state of a register uniquely determines a classical state for each of its subregisters. To be more precise, suppose that

$$X = (Y_1, \ldots, Y_n) \tag{2.3}$$

is a compound register. Let $\Gamma_1, \ldots, \Gamma_n$ denote the classical state sets of the registers $Y_1, \ldots, Y_n$, respectively, so that the classical state set of X is equal to $\Sigma = \Gamma_1 \times \cdots \times \Gamma_n$. A given classical state $a = (b_1, \ldots, b_n)$ of X then determines that the classical state of Y_k is $b_k \in \Gamma_k$, for each $k \in \{1, \ldots, n\}$. By applying this definition recursively, one defines a unique classical state of each subregister of X.

Conversely, the classical state of any register is uniquely determined by the classical states of its simple subregisters. Every classical state of a given register X therefore uniquely determines a classical state of any register whose simple subregisters form a subset of those of X. For instance, if X takes the form (2.3), then one may wish to consider a new register

$$\mathsf{Z} = (\mathsf{Y}_{k_1}, \ldots, \mathsf{Y}_{k_m}) \tag{2.4}$$

for some choice of indices $1 \leq k_1 < \cdots < k_m \leq n$. If $a = (b_1, \ldots, b_n)$ is the classical state of X at a particular moment, then the corresponding state of Z is $(b_{k_1}, \ldots, b_{k_m})$.

2.1.2 Quantum States of Registers

Quantum states, as they will be presented in this book, may be viewed as being analogous to probabilistic states, with which the reader is assumed to have some familiarity.

Probabilistic States of Registers

A *probabilistic state* of a register X refers to a probability distribution, or random mixture, over the classical states of that register. Assuming the classical state set of X is Σ, a probabilistic state of X is identified with a probability vector $p \in \mathcal{P}(\Sigma)$; the value $p(a)$ represents the probability associated with a given classical state $a \in \Sigma$. It is typical that one views a probabilistic state as being a mathematical representation of the contents of a register, or of a hypothetical individual's knowledge of the contents of a register, at a particular moment.

The difference between probabilistic states and quantum states is that, whereas probabilistic states are represented by probability vectors, quantum states are represented by *density operators* (q.v. Section 1.1.2). Unlike the notion of a probabilistic state, which has a relatively clear and intuitive meaning, the notion of a quantum state can seem non-intuitive. While it is both natural and interesting to seek an understanding of why nature appears to be well-modeled by quantum states in certain regimes, this book will not attempt to provide such an understanding: quantum states will be considered as mathematical objects and nothing more.

The Complex Euclidean Space Associated With a Register

It is helpful to introduce the following terminology to discuss quantum states in mathematical terms.

Definition 2.4 The complex Euclidean space associated with a register X is defined to be $\mathbb{C}^\Sigma$, for Σ being the classical state set of X.

The complex Euclidean space associated with a given register will be denoted by the same letter as the register itself, but with a *scripted* font rather than a *sans serif* font. For example, the complex Euclidean space associated with a register X will be denoted $\mathcal{X}$, and the spaces associated with registers $Y_1, \ldots, Y_n$ will be denoted $\mathcal{Y}_1, \ldots, \mathcal{Y}_n$.

The reader will note that the complex Euclidean space $\mathcal{X}$ associated with a compound register $X = (Y_1, \ldots, Y_n)$ is given by the tensor product

$$\mathcal{X} = \mathcal{Y}_1 \otimes \cdots \otimes \mathcal{Y}_n. \tag{2.5}$$

This fact follows directly from the definition stating that the classical state set of X is given by $\Sigma = \Gamma_1 \times \cdots \times \Gamma_n$, assuming that the classical state sets of $Y_1, \ldots, Y_n$ are $\Gamma_1, \ldots, \Gamma_n$, respectively; one has that the complex Euclidean space associated with X is

$$\mathcal{X} = \mathbb{C}^\Sigma = \mathbb{C}^{\Gamma_1 \times \cdots \times \Gamma_n} = \mathcal{Y}_1 \otimes \cdots \otimes \mathcal{Y}_n \tag{2.6}$$

for $\mathcal{Y}_1 = \mathbb{C}^{\Gamma_1}, \ldots, \mathcal{Y}_n = \mathbb{C}^{\Gamma_n}$.

Definition of Quantum States

As stated above, quantum states are represented by density operators. The following definition makes this precise.

Definition 2.5 A *quantum state* is a density operator of the form $\rho \in D(\mathcal{X})$ for some choice of a complex Euclidean space $\mathcal{X}$.

When one refers to a quantum state of a register X, it is to be understood that the state in question takes the form $\rho \in D(\mathcal{X})$ for $\mathcal{X}$ being the complex Euclidean space associated with X. It is common that the term *state* is used in place of *quantum state* in the setting of quantum information, because it is the default assumption that one is primarily concerned with quantum states (as opposed to classical states and probabilistic states) in this setting.

Convex Combinations of Quantum States

For every complex Euclidean space $\mathcal{X}$, the set $D(\mathcal{X})$ is a convex set. For any choice of an alphabet Γ, a collection

$$\{\rho_a : a \in \Gamma\} \subseteq D(\mathcal{X}) \tag{2.7}$$

of quantum states, and a probability vector $p \in \mathcal{P}(\Gamma)$, it therefore holds that the convex combination

$$\rho = \sum_{a \in \Gamma} p(a)\rho_a \tag{2.8}$$

is an element of $D(\mathcal{X})$. The state ρ defined by the equation (2.8) is said to be a *mixture* of the states $\{\rho_a : a \in \Gamma\}$ according to the probability vector p.

Suppose that X is a register whose associated complex Euclidean space is $\mathcal{X}$. It is taken as an axiom that a random selection of $a \in \Gamma$ according to the probability vector p, followed by a preparation of X in the state ρ_a, results in X being in the state ρ defined in (2.8). More succinctly, random selections of quantum states are assumed to be represented by convex combinations of density operators.

Ensembles of Quantum States

The notion of a probability distribution over a finite set of quantum states arises frequently in the theory of quantum information. A distribution of the form described above may be succinctly represented by a function

$$\eta : \Gamma \to \mathrm{Pos}(\mathcal{X}) \tag{2.9}$$

satisfying the constraint

$$\mathrm{Tr}\left(\sum_{a \in \Gamma} \eta(a)\right) = 1. \tag{2.10}$$

A function η of this sort is called an *ensemble* of states. The interpretation of an ensemble of states $\eta : \Gamma \to \mathrm{Pos}(\mathcal{X})$ is that, for each element $a \in \Gamma$, the operator $\eta(a)$ represents a state together with the probability associated with that state: the probability is $\mathrm{Tr}(\eta(a))$, while the state is

$$\rho_a = \frac{\eta(a)}{\mathrm{Tr}(\eta(a))}. \tag{2.11}$$

(The operator ρ_a is, of course, determined only when $\eta(a) \neq 0$. In the case that $\eta(a) = 0$ for some choice of a, one does not generally need to specify a specific density operator ρ_a, as it corresponds to a discrete event that occurs with probability zero.)

Pure States

A quantum state $\rho \in D(\mathcal{X})$ is said to be a *pure state* if it has rank equal to 1. Equivalently, ρ is a pure state if there exists a unit vector $u \in \mathcal{X}$ such that

$$\rho = uu^*. \tag{2.12}$$

It follows from the spectral theorem (Corollary 1.4) that every quantum state is a mixture of pure quantum states, and moreover that a state $\rho \in D(\mathcal{X})$ is pure if and only if it is an extreme point of the set $D(\mathcal{X})$.

It is common that one refers to the pure state (2.12) simply as u, rather than uu^*. There is an ambiguity that arises in following this convention: if one considers two unit vectors u and $v = \alpha u$, for any choice of $\alpha \in \mathbb{C}$ with $|\alpha| = 1$, then their corresponding pure states uu^* and vv^* are equal, as

$$vv^* = |\alpha|^2 uu^* = uu^*. \tag{2.13}$$

Fortunately, this convention does not generally cause confusion; it must simply be kept in mind that every pure state corresponds to an equivalence class of unit vectors, where u and v are equivalent if and only if $v = \alpha u$ for some choice of $\alpha \in \mathbb{C}$ with $|\alpha| = 1$, and that any particular unit vector may be viewed as being a representative of a pure state from this equivalence class.

Flat States

A quantum state $\rho \in D(\mathcal{X})$ is said to be a *flat state* if it holds that

$$\rho = \frac{\Pi}{\text{Tr}(\Pi)} \tag{2.14}$$

for a nonzero projection operator $\Pi \in \text{Proj}(\mathcal{X})$. The symbol ω will often be used to denote a flat state, and the notation

$$\omega_{\mathcal{V}} = \frac{\Pi_{\mathcal{V}}}{\text{Tr}(\Pi_{\mathcal{V}})} \tag{2.15}$$

is sometimes used to denote the flat state proportional to the projection $\Pi_{\mathcal{V}}$ onto a nonzero subspace $\mathcal{V} \subseteq \mathcal{X}$. Specific examples of flat states include pure states, which correspond to the case that Π is a rank-one projection, and the *completely mixed state*

$$\omega = \frac{\mathbb{1}_{\mathcal{X}}}{\dim(\mathcal{X})}. \tag{2.16}$$

Intuitively speaking, the completely mixed state represents the state of complete ignorance, analogous to a uniform probabilistic state.

Classical States and Probabilistic States as Quantum States

Suppose X is a register and Σ is the classical state set of X, so that the complex Euclidean space associated with X is $\mathcal{X} = \mathbb{C}^{\Sigma}$. Within the set $D(\mathcal{X})$ of states of X, one may represent the possible classical states of X in the following simple way: the operator $E_{a,a} \in D(\mathcal{X})$ is taken as a representation of the register X being in the classical state a, for each $a \in \Sigma$. Through this association, probabilistic states of registers correspond to diagonal density operators, with each probabilistic state $p \in \mathcal{P}(\Sigma)$ being represented by the density operator

$$\sum_{a \in \Sigma} p(a) E_{a,a} = \mathrm{Diag}(p). \tag{2.17}$$

In this way, the set of probabilistic states of a given register form a subset of the set of all quantum states of that register (with the containment being proper unless the register is trivial).[1]

Within some contexts, it may be necessary or appropriate to specify that one or more registers are *classical registers*. Informally speaking, a classical register is one whose states are restricted to being diagonal density operators, corresponding to classical (probabilistic) states as just described. A more formal and precise meaning of this terminology must be postponed until the section on quantum channels following this one.

Product States

Suppose $X = (Y_1, \ldots, Y_n)$ is a compound register. A state $\rho \in D(\mathcal{X})$ is said to be a *product state* of X if it takes the form

$$\rho = \sigma_1 \otimes \cdots \otimes \sigma_n \tag{2.18}$$

for $\sigma_1 \in D(\mathcal{Y}_1), \ldots, \sigma_n \in D(\mathcal{Y}_n)$ being states of $Y_1, \ldots, Y_n$, respectively. Product states represent independence among the states of registers, and when the compound register $X = (Y_1, \ldots, Y_n)$ is in a product state ρ of the form (2.18), the registers $Y_1, \ldots, Y_n$ are said to be *independent*. When it is not the case that $Y_1, \ldots, Y_n$ are independent, they are said to be *correlated*.

Example 2.6 Consider a compound register of the form $X = (Y, Z)$, for Y and Z being registers sharing the classical state set $\{0, 1\}$. (Registers having the classical state set $\{0, 1\}$ are typically called *qubits*, which is short for *quantum bits*.)

---

[1] The other basic notions of quantum information to be discussed in this chapter have a similar character of admitting analogous probabilistic notions as special cases. In general, the theory of quantum information may be seen as an extension of classical information theory, including the study of random processes, protocols, and computations.

The state $\rho \in D(\mathcal{Y} \otimes \mathcal{Z})$ defined as

$$\rho = \frac{1}{4}E_{0,0} \otimes E_{0,0} + \frac{1}{4}E_{0,0} \otimes E_{1,1} + \frac{1}{4}E_{1,1} \otimes E_{0,0} + \frac{1}{4}E_{1,1} \otimes E_{1,1} \qquad (2.19)$$

is an example of a product state, as one may write

$$\rho = \left(\frac{1}{2}E_{0,0} + \frac{1}{2}E_{1,1}\right) \otimes \left(\frac{1}{2}E_{0,0} + \frac{1}{2}E_{1,1}\right). \qquad (2.20)$$

Equivalently, in matrix form, one has

$$\rho = \begin{pmatrix} \frac{1}{4} & 0 & 0 & 0 \\ 0 & \frac{1}{4} & 0 & 0 \\ 0 & 0 & \frac{1}{4} & 0 \\ 0 & 0 & 0 & \frac{1}{4} \end{pmatrix} = \begin{pmatrix} \frac{1}{2} & 0 \\ 0 & \frac{1}{2} \end{pmatrix} \otimes \begin{pmatrix} \frac{1}{2} & 0 \\ 0 & \frac{1}{2} \end{pmatrix}. \qquad (2.21)$$

The states $\sigma, \tau \in D(\mathcal{Y} \otimes \mathcal{Z})$ defined as

$$\sigma = \frac{1}{2}E_{0,0} \otimes E_{0,0} + \frac{1}{2}E_{1,1} \otimes E_{1,1} \qquad (2.22)$$

and

$$\tau = \frac{1}{2}E_{0,0} \otimes E_{0,0} + \frac{1}{2}E_{0,1} \otimes E_{0,1} + \frac{1}{2}E_{1,0} \otimes E_{1,0} + \frac{1}{2}E_{1,1} \otimes E_{1,1} \qquad (2.23)$$

are examples of states that are not product states, as they cannot be written as tensor products, and therefore represent correlations between the registers Y and Z. In matrix form, these states are as follows:

$$\sigma = \begin{pmatrix} \frac{1}{2} & 0 & 0 & 0 \\ 0 & 0 & 0 & 0 \\ 0 & 0 & 0 & 0 \\ 0 & 0 & 0 & \frac{1}{2} \end{pmatrix} \quad \text{and} \quad \tau = \begin{pmatrix} \frac{1}{2} & 0 & 0 & \frac{1}{2} \\ 0 & 0 & 0 & 0 \\ 0 & 0 & 0 & 0 \\ \frac{1}{2} & 0 & 0 & \frac{1}{2} \end{pmatrix}. \qquad (2.24)$$

The states ρ and σ are diagonal, so they correspond to probabilistic states; ρ represents the situation in which Y and Z store independent random bits, while σ represents the situation in which Y and Z store perfectly correlated random bits. The state τ does not represent a probabilistic state, and more specifically is an example of an *entangled* state. Entanglement is a particular type of correlation having great significance in quantum information theory, and is the primary focus of Chapter 6.

Bases of Density Operators

It is an elementary fact, but nevertheless a useful one, that for every complex Euclidean space $\mathcal{X}$ there exist spanning sets of the space $L(\mathcal{X})$ consisting only of density operators. One implication of this fact is that every linear mapping of the form

$$\phi \colon \mathrm{L}(\mathcal{X}) \to \mathbb{C} \tag{2.25}$$

is uniquely determined by its action on the elements of $\mathrm{D}(\mathcal{X})$. This implies, for instance, that channels and measurements are uniquely determined by their actions on density operators. The following example describes one way of constructing such a spanning set.

Example 2.7 Let Σ be an alphabet, and assume that a total ordering has been defined on Σ. For every pair $(a, b) \in \Sigma \times \Sigma$, define a density operator $\rho_{a,b} \in \mathrm{D}(\mathbb{C}^\Sigma)$ as follows:

$$\rho_{a,b} = \begin{cases} E_{a,a} & \text{if } a = b \\ \frac{1}{2}(e_a + e_b)(e_a + e_b)^* & \text{if } a < b \\ \frac{1}{2}(e_a + ie_b)(e_a + ie_b)^* & \text{if } a > b. \end{cases} \tag{2.26}$$

For each pair $(a, b) \in \Sigma \times \Sigma$ with $a < b$, one has

$$\left(\rho_{a,b} - \frac{1}{2}\rho_{a,a} - \frac{1}{2}\rho_{b,b}\right) - i\left(\rho_{b,a} - \frac{1}{2}\rho_{a,a} - \frac{1}{2}\rho_{b,b}\right) = E_{a,b},$$
$$\left(\rho_{a,b} - \frac{1}{2}\rho_{a,a} - \frac{1}{2}\rho_{b,b}\right) + i\left(\rho_{b,a} - \frac{1}{2}\rho_{a,a} - \frac{1}{2}\rho_{b,b}\right) = E_{b,a}, \tag{2.27}$$

and from these equations it follows that

$$\mathrm{span}\{\rho_{a,b} \colon (a, b) \in \Sigma \times \Sigma\} = \mathrm{L}(\mathbb{C}^\Sigma). \tag{2.28}$$

2.1.3 Reductions and Purifications of Quantum States

One may consider a register obtained by removing one or more subregisters from a given compound register. The quantum state of any register that results from this process, viewed in isolation from the subregisters that were removed, is uniquely determined by the state of the original compound register. This section explains how such states are determined. The special case in which the original compound register is in a pure state is particularly important, and is discussed in detail.

The Partial Trace and Reductions of Quantum States

Let $\mathsf{X} = (\mathsf{Y}_1, \ldots, \mathsf{Y}_n)$ be a compound register, for $n \geq 2$. For any choice of $k \in \{1, \ldots, n\}$, one may form a new register

$$(\mathsf{Y}_1, \ldots, \mathsf{Y}_{k-1}, \mathsf{Y}_{k+1}, \ldots, \mathsf{Y}_n) \tag{2.29}$$

by removing the register Y_k from X and leaving the remaining registers untouched. For every state $\rho \in D(\mathcal{X})$ of X, the state of the register (2.29) that is determined by this process is called the *reduction* of ρ to the register (2.29), and is denoted $\rho[Y_1, \ldots, Y_{k-1}, Y_{k+1}, \ldots, Y_n]$. This state is defined as

$$\rho[Y_1, \ldots, Y_{k-1}, Y_{k+1}, \ldots, Y_n] = \mathrm{Tr}_{\mathcal{Y}_k}(\rho), \tag{2.30}$$

where

$$\mathrm{Tr}_{\mathcal{Y}_k} \in \mathrm{T}(\mathcal{Y}_1 \otimes \cdots \otimes \mathcal{Y}_n, \mathcal{Y}_1 \otimes \cdots \otimes \mathcal{Y}_{k-1} \otimes \mathcal{Y}_{k+1} \otimes \cdots \otimes \mathcal{Y}_n) \tag{2.31}$$

denotes the *partial trace* mapping (q.v. Section 1.1.2).[2] This is the unique linear mapping that satisfies the equation

$$\mathrm{Tr}_{\mathcal{Y}_k}(Y_1 \otimes \cdots \otimes Y_n) = \mathrm{Tr}(Y_k) Y_1 \otimes \cdots \otimes Y_{k-1} \otimes Y_{k+1} \otimes \cdots \otimes Y_n \tag{2.32}$$

for all operators $Y_1 \in \mathrm{L}(\mathcal{Y}_1), \ldots, Y_n \in \mathrm{L}(\mathcal{Y}_n)$. Alternatively, one may define

$$\mathrm{Tr}_{\mathcal{Y}_k} = \mathbb{1}_{\mathrm{L}(\mathcal{Y}_1)} \otimes \cdots \otimes \mathbb{1}_{\mathrm{L}(\mathcal{Y}_{k-1})} \otimes \mathrm{Tr} \otimes \mathbb{1}_{\mathrm{L}(\mathcal{Y}_{k+1})} \otimes \cdots \otimes \mathbb{1}_{\mathrm{L}(\mathcal{Y}_n)}, \tag{2.33}$$

where it is to be understood that the trace mapping on the right-hand side of this equation acts on $\mathrm{L}(\mathcal{Y}_k)$.

If the classical state sets of $Y_1, \ldots, Y_n$ are $\Gamma_1, \ldots, \Gamma_n$, respectively, one may write the $((a_1, \ldots, a_{k-1}, a_{k+1}, \ldots, a_n), (b_1, \ldots, b_{k-1}, b_{k+1}, \ldots, b_n))$ entry of the state $\rho[Y_1, \ldots, Y_{k-1}, Y_{k+1}, \ldots, Y_n]$ explicitly as

$$\sum_{c \in \Gamma_k} \rho((a_1, \ldots, a_{k-1}, c, a_{k+1}, \ldots, a_n), (b_1, \ldots, b_{k-1}, c, b_{k+1}, \ldots, b_n)) \tag{2.34}$$

for each choice of $a_j, b_j \in \Gamma_j$ and j ranging over the set $\{1, \ldots, n\} \backslash \{k\}$.

Example 2.8 Let Y and Z be registers, both having the classical state set Σ, let X = (Y, Z), and let $u \in \mathcal{X} = \mathcal{Y} \otimes \mathcal{Z}$ be defined as

$$u = \frac{1}{\sqrt{|\Sigma|}} \sum_{a \in \Sigma} e_a \otimes e_a, \tag{2.35}$$

so that

$$uu^* = \frac{1}{|\Sigma|} \sum_{a,b \in \Sigma} E_{a,b} \otimes E_{a,b}. \tag{2.36}$$

It holds that

$$(uu^*)[Y] = \frac{1}{|\Sigma|} \sum_{a,b \in \Sigma} \mathrm{Tr}(E_{a,b}) E_{a,b} = \frac{1}{|\Sigma|} \mathbb{1}_{\mathcal{Y}}. \tag{2.37}$$

---

[2] It should be noted that reductions of states are determined in this way, by means of the partial trace, by necessity – no other choice is consistent with the basic notions concerning channels and measurements to be discussed in the sections following this one.

The state uu^* is the canonical example of a *maximally entangled* state of two registers sharing the classical state set Σ.

By applying this definition iteratively, one finds that each state ρ of the register $(Y_1, \ldots, Y_n)$ uniquely determines the state of

$$(Y_{k_1}, \ldots, Y_{k_m}), \tag{2.38}$$

for $k_1, \ldots, k_m$ being any choice of indices satisfying $1 \leq k_1 < \cdots < k_m \leq n$. The state determined by this process is denoted $\rho[Y_{k_1}, \ldots, Y_{k_m}]$ and again is called the reduction of ρ to $(Y_{k_1}, \ldots, Y_{k_m})$.

The definition above may be generalized in a natural way so that it allows one to specify the states that result from removing an arbitrary collection of subregisters from a given compound register, assuming that this removal results in a valid register. For the registers described in Example 2.2, for instance, removing the subregister Z_3 from X while it is in the state ρ would leave the resulting register in the state

$$\left(\mathbb{1}_{L(\mathcal{Y}_0)} \otimes \left(\mathbb{1}_{L(\mathcal{Z}_1)} \otimes \mathbb{1}_{L(\mathcal{Z}_2)} \otimes \mathrm{Tr} \right) \right)(\rho), \tag{2.39}$$

with the understanding that the trace mapping is defined with respect to $\mathcal{Z}_3$. The pattern represented by this example, in which identity mappings and trace mappings are tensored in accordance with the structure of the register under consideration, is generalized in the most straightforward way to other examples. While it is possible to formalize this definition in complete generality, there is little point in doing so for the purposes of this book: all of the instances of state reductions to be encountered are either cases where the reductions take the form $\rho[Y_{k_1}, \ldots, Y_{k_m}]$, as discussed above, or are easily specified explicitly as in the case of the example (2.39) just mentioned.

Purifications of States and Operators

In a variety of situations that arise in quantum information theory, wherein a given register X is being considered, it is useful to assume (or simply to imagine) that X is a subregister of a compound register (X, Y), and to view a given state $\rho \in D(\mathcal{X})$ of X as having been obtained as a reduction

$$\rho = \sigma[X] = \mathrm{Tr}_{\mathcal{Y}}(\sigma) \tag{2.40}$$

of some state σ of (X, Y). Such a state σ is called an *extension* of ρ. It is particularly useful to consider the case in which σ is a pure state, and to ask what the possible states of X are that can arise from a pure state of (X, Y) in this way. This question has a simple answer to be justified shortly: a state $\rho \in D(\mathcal{X})$ of X can arise in this way if and only if the rank of ρ does not exceed the number of classical states of the register Y removed from (X, Y) to obtain X.

The following definition is representative of the situation just described. The notion of a *purification* that it defines is used extensively throughout the remainder of the book.

Definition 2.9 Let $\mathcal{X}$ and $\mathcal{Y}$ be complex Euclidean spaces, let $P \in \mathrm{Pos}(\mathcal{X})$ be a positive semidefinite operator, and let $u \in \mathcal{X} \otimes \mathcal{Y}$ be a vector. The vector u is said to be a *purification* of P if

$$\mathrm{Tr}_{\mathcal{Y}}(uu^*) = P. \tag{2.41}$$

This definition deviates slightly from the setting described above in two respects. One is that P is not required to have unit trace, and the other is that the vector u is taken to be the object that purifies P rather than the operator uu^*. Allowing P to be an arbitrary positive semidefinite operator is a useful generalization that will cause no difficulties in developing the concept of a purification (and the term *extension* is generalized in a similar way), while referring to u rather than uu^* as the purification of P is simply a matter of convenience based on the specific ways that the notion is most typically used – it is also common that the operator uu^* is the object referred to as a purification.

It is straightforward to generalize the notion of a purification. One may, for instance, consider the situation in which X is a register that is obtained by removing one or more subregisters from an arbitrary compound register Z. A purification of a given state $\rho \in \mathrm{D}(\mathcal{X})$ in this context would refer to any pure state of Z whose reduction to X is equal to ρ. The most interesting aspects of purifications are, however, represented by Definition 2.9, so the remainder of the section focuses on this specific definition of purifications for simplicity. It is to be understood, however, that the various facts concerning purifications discussed extend easily and directly to a more general notion of a purification.

Conditions for the Existence of Purifications

The vec mapping, defined in Section 1.1.2, is useful for understanding purifications. Given that this mapping is a linear bijection from $\mathrm{L}(\mathcal{Y}, \mathcal{X})$ to $\mathcal{X} \otimes \mathcal{Y}$, every vector $u \in \mathcal{X} \otimes \mathcal{Y}$ may be written as $u = \mathrm{vec}(A)$ for some choice of an operator $A \in \mathrm{L}(\mathcal{Y}, \mathcal{X})$. By the identity (1.133), it holds that

$$\mathrm{Tr}_{\mathcal{Y}}(uu^*) = \mathrm{Tr}_{\mathcal{Y}}(\mathrm{vec}(A)\,\mathrm{vec}(A)^*) = AA^*. \tag{2.42}$$

This establishes an equivalence between the following statements, for a given choice of $P \in \mathrm{Pos}(\mathcal{X})$:

1. There exists a purification $u \in \mathcal{X} \otimes \mathcal{Y}$ of P.
2. There exists an operator $A \in \mathrm{L}(\mathcal{Y}, \mathcal{X})$ such that $P = AA^*$.

The next theorem, whose proof is based on this observation, justifies the answer given above to the question on necessary and sufficient conditions for the existence of a purification of a given operator.

Theorem 2.10 *Let $\mathcal{X}$ and $\mathcal{Y}$ be complex Euclidean spaces, and let $P \in \mathrm{Pos}(\mathcal{X})$ be a positive semidefinite operator. There exists a vector $u \in \mathcal{X} \otimes \mathcal{Y}$ such that $\mathrm{Tr}_{\mathcal{Y}}(uu^*) = P$ if and only if $\dim(\mathcal{Y}) \geq \mathrm{rank}(P)$.*

Proof As observed above, the existence of a vector $u \in \mathcal{X} \otimes \mathcal{Y}$ for which $\mathrm{Tr}_{\mathcal{Y}}(uu^*) = P$ is equivalent to the existence of an operator $A \in \mathrm{L}(\mathcal{Y}, \mathcal{X})$ satisfying $P = AA^*$. Under the assumption that such an operator A exists, it must hold that $\mathrm{rank}(P) = \mathrm{rank}(A)$, and therefore $\dim(\mathcal{Y}) \geq \mathrm{rank}(P)$.

Conversely, under the assumption $\dim(\mathcal{Y}) \geq \mathrm{rank}(P)$, one may prove the existence of an operator $A \in \mathrm{L}(\mathcal{Y}, \mathcal{X})$ satisfying $P = AA^*$ as follows. Let $r = \mathrm{rank}(P)$ and use the spectral theorem (Corollary 1.4) to write

$$P = \sum_{k=1}^{r} \lambda_k(P) x_k x_k^* \tag{2.43}$$

for $\{x_1, \ldots, x_r\} \subset \mathcal{X}$ being an orthonormal set. For an arbitrary choice of an orthonormal set $\{y_1, \ldots, y_r\} \subset \mathcal{Y}$, which must exist by the assumption $\dim(\mathcal{Y}) \geq \mathrm{rank}(P)$, the operator

$$A = \sum_{k=1}^{r} \sqrt{\lambda_k(P)} x_k y_k^* \tag{2.44}$$

satisfies $AA^* = P$. $\qquad\square$

Corollary 2.11 *Let $\mathcal{X}$ and $\mathcal{Y}$ be complex Euclidean spaces satisfying $\dim(\mathcal{Y}) \geq \dim(\mathcal{X})$. For every positive semidefinite operator $P \in \mathrm{Pos}(\mathcal{X})$, there exists a vector $u \in \mathcal{X} \otimes \mathcal{Y}$ such that $\mathrm{Tr}_{\mathcal{Y}}(uu^*) = P$.*

Unitary Equivalence of Purifications

Having established a simple condition under which a purification of a given positive semidefinite operator exists, it is natural to consider the possible relationships among different purifications of a given operator. The following theorem establishes a useful relationship between purifications that must always hold.

Theorem 2.12 (Unitary equivalence of purifications)   *Let $\mathcal{X}$ and $\mathcal{Y}$ be complex Euclidean spaces, let $u, v \in \mathcal{X} \otimes \mathcal{Y}$ be vectors, and assume that*

$$\mathrm{Tr}_{\mathcal{Y}}(uu^*) = \mathrm{Tr}_{\mathcal{Y}}(vv^*). \tag{2.45}$$

There exists a unitary operator $U \in \mathrm{U}(\mathcal{Y})$ such that $v = (\mathbb{1}_{\mathcal{X}} \otimes U)u$.

Proof   Let $A, B \in \mathrm{L}(\mathcal{Y}, \mathcal{X})$ be the unique operators satisfying $u = \mathrm{vec}(A)$ and $v = \mathrm{vec}(B)$, and let $P \in \mathrm{Pos}(\mathcal{X})$ satisfy

$$\mathrm{Tr}_{\mathcal{Y}}(uu^*) = P = \mathrm{Tr}_{\mathcal{Y}}(vv^*). \tag{2.46}$$

It therefore holds that $AA^* = P = BB^*$. Letting $r = \mathrm{rank}(P)$, it follows that $\mathrm{rank}(A) = r = \mathrm{rank}(B)$.

Next, let $x_1, \ldots, x_r \in \mathcal{X}$ be any orthonormal sequence of eigenvectors of P with corresponding eigenvalues $\lambda_1(P), \ldots, \lambda_r(P)$. As $AA^* = P = BB^*$, it is possible to select singular value decompositions

$$A = \sum_{k=1}^{r} \sqrt{\lambda_k(P)} x_k y_k^* \quad \text{and} \quad B = \sum_{k=1}^{r} \sqrt{\lambda_k(P)} x_k w_k^* \tag{2.47}$$

of A and B, for some choice of orthonormal collections $\{y_1, \ldots, y_r\}$ and $\{w_1, \ldots, w_r\}$ of vectors in $\mathcal{Y}$ (as discussed in Section 1.1.3).

Finally, let $V \in \mathrm{U}(\mathcal{Y})$ be any unitary operator satisfying $Vw_k = y_k$ for every $k \in \{1, \ldots, r\}$. It follows that $AV = B$, and by taking $U = V^\mathsf{T}$ one has

$$(\mathbb{1}_{\mathcal{X}} \otimes U)u = (\mathbb{1}_{\mathcal{X}} \otimes V^\mathsf{T}) \mathrm{vec}(A) = \mathrm{vec}(AV) = \mathrm{vec}(B) = v, \tag{2.48}$$

as required. $\square$

2.2 Quantum Channels

Quantum channels represent discrete changes in states of registers that are to be considered physically realizable (in an idealized sense). For example, the steps of a quantum computation, or any other processing of quantum information, as well as the effects of errors and noise on quantum registers, are modeled as quantum channels.

2.2.1 Definitions and Basic Notions Concerning Channels

In mathematical terms, a quantum channel is a linear map, from one space of square operators to another, that satisfies the two conditions of *complete positivity* and *trace preservation*.

Definition 2.13 A *quantum channel* (or simply a *channel*, for short) is a linear map

$$\Phi \colon L(\mathcal{X}) \to L(\mathcal{Y}) \tag{2.49}$$

(i.e., an element $\Phi \in T(\mathcal{X}, \mathcal{Y})$), for some choice of complex Euclidean spaces $\mathcal{X}$ and $\mathcal{Y}$, satisfying two properties:

1. Φ is completely positive.
2. Φ is trace-preserving.

The collection of all channels of the form (2.49) is denoted $C(\mathcal{X}, \mathcal{Y})$, and one writes $C(\mathcal{X})$ as a shorthand for $C(\mathcal{X}, \mathcal{X})$.

For a given choice of registers X and Y, one may view that a channel of the form $\Phi \in C(\mathcal{X}, \mathcal{Y})$ is a transformation from X into Y. That is, when such a transformation takes place, it is to be viewed that the register X ceases to exist, with Y being formed in its place. Moreover, the state of Y is obtained by applying the map Φ to the state $\rho \in D(\mathcal{X})$ of X, yielding $\Phi(\rho) \in D(\mathcal{Y})$. When it is the case that X = Y, one may simply view that the state of the register X has been changed according to the mapping Φ.

Example 2.14 Let $\mathcal{X}$ be a complex Euclidean space and let $U \in U(\mathcal{X})$ be a unitary operator. The map $\Phi \in C(\mathcal{X})$ defined by

$$\Phi(X) = UXU^* \tag{2.50}$$

for every $X \in L(\mathcal{X})$ is an example of a channel. Channels of this form are called *unitary channels*. The *identity channel* $\mathbb{1}_{L(\mathcal{X})}$ is one example of a unitary channel, obtained by setting $U = \mathbb{1}_{\mathcal{X}}$. Intuitively speaking, this channel represents an ideal quantum communication channel or a perfect component in a quantum computer memory, which causes no change in the state of the register X it acts upon.

Example 2.15 Let $\mathcal{X}$ and $\mathcal{Y}$ be complex Euclidean spaces, and let $\sigma \in D(\mathcal{Y})$ be a density operator. The mapping $\Phi \in C(\mathcal{X}, \mathcal{Y})$ defined by

$$\Phi(X) = \text{Tr}(X)\sigma, \tag{2.51}$$

for every $X \in L(\mathcal{X})$, is a channel. It holds that $\Phi(\rho) = \sigma$ for every $\rho \in D(\mathcal{X})$; in effect, the channel Φ represents the action of discarding the register X, and replacing it with the register Y initialized to the state σ. Channels of this form will be called *replacement channels*.

The channels described in the two previous examples (along with other examples of channels) will be discussed in greater detail in Section 2.2.3. While one may prove directly that these mappings are indeed channels, these facts will follow immediately from more general results to be presented in Section 2.2.2.

Product Channels

Suppose $X_1, \ldots, X_n$ and $Y_1, \ldots, Y_n$ are registers, and recall that one denotes by $\mathcal{X}_1, \ldots, \mathcal{X}_n$ and $\mathcal{Y}_1, \ldots, \mathcal{Y}_n$ the complex Euclidean spaces associated with these registers. A channel

$$\Phi \in C(\mathcal{X}_1 \otimes \cdots \otimes \mathcal{X}_n, \mathcal{Y}_1 \otimes \cdots \otimes \mathcal{Y}_n) \qquad (2.52)$$

transforming $(X_1, \ldots, X_n)$ into $(Y_1, \ldots, Y_n)$ is called a *product channel* if

$$\Phi = \Psi_1 \otimes \cdots \otimes \Psi_n \qquad (2.53)$$

for some choice of channels $\Psi_1 \in C(\mathcal{X}_1, \mathcal{Y}_1), \ldots, \Psi_n \in C(\mathcal{X}_n, \mathcal{Y}_n)$. Product channels represent an independent application of a sequence of channels to a sequence of registers, in a similar way to product states representing independence among the states of registers.

An important special case involving independent channels is the situation in which a given channel is performed on one register, while nothing at all is done to one or more other registers under consideration. (As suggested in Example 2.14, the act of doing nothing at all to a register is equivalent to performing the identity channel on that register.)

Example 2.16 Suppose that X, Y, and Z are registers, and $\Phi \in C(\mathcal{X}, \mathcal{Y})$ is a channel that transforms X into Y. Also suppose that the compound register (X, Z) is in some particular state $\rho \in D(\mathcal{X} \otimes \mathcal{Z})$ at some instant, and the channel Φ is applied to X, transforming it into Y. The resulting state of the pair (Y, Z) is then given by

$$(\Phi \otimes \mathbb{1}_{L(\mathcal{Z})})(\rho) \in D(\mathcal{Y} \otimes \mathcal{Z}), \qquad (2.54)$$

as one views that the identity channel $\mathbb{1}_{L(\mathcal{Z})}$ has independently been applied to the register Z.

Example 2.16 illustrates the importance of the requirement that channels are completely positive. That is, it must hold that $(\Phi \otimes \mathbb{1}_{L(\mathcal{Z})})(\rho)$ is a density operator for every choice of Z and every density operator $\rho \in D(\mathcal{X} \otimes \mathcal{Z})$, which together with the linearity of Φ implies that Φ is completely positive (in addition to being trace-preserving).

State Preparations as Quantum Channels

As stated in Section 2.1.1, a register is *trivial* if its classical state set consists of a single element. The complex Euclidean space associated with a trivial register is therefore one-dimensional: it must take the form $\mathbb{C}^{\{a\}}$ for $\{a\}$ being the singleton classical state set of the register. No generality is lost in associating such a space with the field of complex numbers $\mathbb{C}$, and in making the identification $L(\mathbb{C}) = \mathbb{C}$, one finds that the scalar 1 is the only possible state for a trivial register. As is to be expected, such a register is therefore completely useless from an information processing viewpoint; the presence of a trivial register does nothing more than to tensor the scalar 1 to the state of any other registers under consideration.

It is instructive nevertheless to consider the properties of channels that involve trivial registers. Suppose, in particular, that X is a trivial register and Y is arbitrary, and consider a channel of the form $\Phi \in C(\mathcal{X}, \mathcal{Y})$ that transforms X into Y. It must hold that Φ is given by

$$\Phi(\alpha) = \alpha\rho \tag{2.55}$$

for all $\alpha \in \mathbb{C}$, for some choice of $\rho \in D(\mathcal{Y})$, as Φ must be linear and it must hold that $\Phi(1)$ is positive semidefinite and has trace equal to 1. The channel Φ defined by (2.55) may be viewed as the *preparation* of the quantum state ρ in a new register Y. The trivial register X can be considered as being essentially a placeholder for this preparation, which is to occur at whatever moment the channel Φ is performed. In this way, a state preparation may be seen as the application of this form of channel.

To see that every mapping of the form (2.55) is indeed a channel, for an arbitrary choice of a density operator $\rho \in D(\mathcal{Y})$, one may check that the conditions of complete positivity and trace preservation hold. The mapping Φ given by (2.55) is obviously trace-preserving whenever $\mathrm{Tr}(\rho) = 1$, and the complete positivity of Φ is implied by the following simple proposition.

Proposition 2.17 *Let $\mathcal{Y}$ be a complex Euclidean space and let $P \in \mathrm{Pos}(\mathcal{Y})$ be a positive semidefinite operator. The mapping $\Phi \in T(\mathbb{C}, \mathcal{Y})$ defined as $\Phi(\alpha) = \alpha P$ for all $\alpha \in \mathbb{C}$ is completely positive.*

Proof Let $\mathcal{Z}$ be any complex Euclidean space. The action of the mapping $\Phi \otimes \mathbb{1}_{L(\mathcal{Z})}$ on an operator $Z \in L(\mathcal{Z}) = L(\mathbb{C} \otimes \mathcal{Z})$ is given by

$$(\Phi \otimes \mathbb{1}_{L(\mathcal{Z})})(Z) = P \otimes Z. \tag{2.56}$$

If Z is positive semidefinite, then $P \otimes Z$ is positive semidefinite as well, and therefore Φ is completely positive. $\square$

The Trace Mapping as a Channel

Another situation in which a channel Φ involves a trivial register is when this channel transforms an arbitrary register X into a trivial register Y. By identifying the complex Euclidean space $\mathcal{Y}$ with the complex numbers $\mathbb{C}$ as before, one has that the channel Φ must take the form $\Phi \in C(\mathcal{X}, \mathbb{C})$.

The only mapping of this form that can possibly preserve trace is the trace mapping itself, and so it must hold that

$$\Phi(X) = \mathrm{Tr}(X) \tag{2.57}$$

for all $X \in L(\mathcal{X})$. To say that a register X has been transformed into a trivial register Y is tantamount to saying that X has been destroyed, discarded, or simply ignored. This channel was, in effect, introduced in Section 2.1.3 when reductions of quantum states were defined.

In order to conclude that the trace mapping is indeed a valid channel, it is necessary to verify that it is completely positive. One way to prove this simple fact is to combine the following proposition with Proposition 2.17.

Proposition 2.18 *Let $\Phi \in T(\mathcal{X}, \mathcal{Y})$ be a positive map, for $\mathcal{X}$ and $\mathcal{Y}$ being complex Euclidean spaces. It holds that Φ^* is positive.*

Proof By the positivity of Φ, it holds that $\Phi(P) \in \mathrm{Pos}(\mathcal{Y})$ for every positive semidefinite operator $P \in \mathrm{Pos}(\mathcal{X})$, which is equivalent to the condition that

$$\langle Q, \Phi(P) \rangle \geq 0 \tag{2.58}$$

for all $P \in \mathrm{Pos}(\mathcal{X})$ and $Q \in \mathrm{Pos}(\mathcal{Y})$. It follows that

$$\langle \Phi^*(Q), P \rangle = \langle Q, \Phi(P) \rangle \geq 0 \tag{2.59}$$

for all $P \in \mathrm{Pos}(\mathcal{X})$ and $Q \in \mathrm{Pos}(\mathcal{Y})$, which is equivalent to $\Phi^*(Q) \in \mathrm{Pos}(\mathcal{X})$ for every $Q \in \mathrm{Pos}(\mathcal{Y})$. The mapping Φ^* is therefore positive. $\square$

Remark Proposition 2.18 implies that if $\Phi \in CP(\mathcal{X}, \mathcal{Y})$ is a completely positive map, then the adjoint map Φ^* is also completely positive; for if Φ is completely positive, then $\Phi \otimes \mathbb{1}_{L(\mathcal{Z})}$ is positive for every complex Euclidean space $\mathcal{Z}$, and therefore $(\Phi \otimes \mathbb{1}_{L(\mathcal{Z})})^* = \Phi^* \otimes \mathbb{1}_{L(\mathcal{Z})}$ is also positive.

Corollary 2.19 *The trace mapping $\mathrm{Tr} \in T(\mathcal{X}, \mathbb{C})$, for any choice of a complex Euclidean space $\mathcal{X}$, is completely positive.*

Proof The adjoint of the trace is given by $\mathrm{Tr}^*(\alpha) = \alpha \mathbb{1}_{\mathcal{X}}$ for every $\alpha \in \mathbb{C}$. This map is completely positive by Proposition 2.17, therefore the trace map is completely positive by the remark above. $\square$

2.2.2 Representations and Characterizations of Channels

Suppose $\Phi \in C(\mathcal{X}, \mathcal{Y})$ is a channel, for $\mathcal{X}$ and $\mathcal{Y}$ being complex Euclidean spaces. It may, in some situations, be sufficient to view such a channel abstractly, as a completely positive and trace-preserving linear map of the form $\Phi \colon L(\mathcal{X}) \to L(\mathcal{Y})$ and nothing more. In other situations, it may be useful to consider a more concrete representation of such a channel.

Four specific representations of channels (and of arbitrary maps of the form $\Phi \in T(\mathcal{X}, \mathcal{Y})$, for complex Euclidean spaces $\mathcal{X}$ and $\mathcal{Y}$) are discussed in this section. These different representations reveal interesting properties of channels, and will find uses in different situations throughout this book. The simple relationships among the representations generally allow one to convert from one representation into another, and therefore to choose the representation that is best suited to a given situation.

The Natural Representation

For any choice of complex Euclidean spaces $\mathcal{X}$ and $\mathcal{Y}$, and for every linear map $\Phi \in T(\mathcal{X}, \mathcal{Y})$, it is evident that the mapping

$$\text{vec}(X) \mapsto \text{vec}(\Phi(X)) \tag{2.60}$$

is linear, as it can be represented as a composition of linear mappings. There must therefore exist a linear operator $K(\Phi) \in L(\mathcal{X} \otimes \mathcal{X}, \mathcal{Y} \otimes \mathcal{Y})$ for which it holds that

$$K(\Phi)\,\text{vec}(X) = \text{vec}(\Phi(X)) \tag{2.61}$$

for all $X \in L(\mathcal{X})$. The operator $K(\Phi)$, which is uniquely determined by the requirement that (2.61) holds for all $X \in L(\mathcal{X})$, is the *natural representation* of Φ, as it directly represents the action of Φ as a linear map (with respect to the operator–vector correspondence).

It may be noted that the mapping $K \colon T(\mathcal{X}, \mathcal{Y}) \to L(\mathcal{X} \otimes \mathcal{X}, \mathcal{Y} \otimes \mathcal{Y})$ is linear:

$$K(\alpha\Phi + \beta\Psi) = \alpha K(\Phi) + \beta K(\Psi) \tag{2.62}$$

for all choices of $\alpha, \beta \in \mathbb{C}$ and $\Phi, \Psi \in T(\mathcal{X}, \mathcal{Y})$. Moreover, K is a bijection, as the action of a given mapping Φ can be recovered from $K(\Phi)$; for each operator $X \in L(\mathcal{X})$, one has that $Y = \Phi(X)$ is the unique operator satisfying $\text{vec}(Y) = K(\Phi)\,\text{vec}(X)$.

The natural representation respects the notion of adjoints, meaning that

$$K(\Phi^*) = (K(\Phi))^* \tag{2.63}$$

for every map $\Phi \in T(\mathcal{X}, \mathcal{Y})$ (with the understanding that K refers to a mapping from $T(\mathcal{Y}, \mathcal{X})$ to $L(\mathcal{Y} \otimes \mathcal{Y}, \mathcal{X} \otimes \mathcal{X})$ on the left-hand side of this equation, obtained by reversing the roles of $\mathcal{X}$ and $\mathcal{Y}$ in the definition above).

Despite the fact that the natural representation $K(\Phi)$ of a mapping Φ is a direct representation of the action of Φ as a linear map, this representation is the one of the four representations to be discussed in this section that is the least directly connected to the properties of complete positivity and trace preservation. As such, it will turn out to be the least useful of the four representations from the viewpoint of this book. One explanation for why this is so is that the aspects of a given map Φ that relate to the operator structure of its input and output arguments is not represented by $K(\Phi)$ in a convenient or readily accessible form. The operator–vector correspondence has the effect of ignoring this structure.

The Choi Representation

For any choice of complex Euclidean spaces $\mathcal{X}$ and $\mathcal{Y}$, one may define a mapping $J \colon T(\mathcal{X}, \mathcal{Y}) \to L(\mathcal{Y} \otimes \mathcal{X})$ as

$$J(\Phi) = \left(\Phi \otimes \mathbb{1}_{L(\mathcal{X})} \right) \left(\mathrm{vec}(\mathbb{1}_{\mathcal{X}}) \, \mathrm{vec}(\mathbb{1}_{\mathcal{X}})^* \right) \tag{2.64}$$

for each $\Phi \in T(\mathcal{X}, \mathcal{Y})$. Alternatively, under the assumption that $\mathcal{X} = \mathbb{C}^\Sigma$, one may write

$$J(\Phi) = \sum_{a,b \in \Sigma} \Phi(E_{a,b}) \otimes E_{a,b}. \tag{2.65}$$

The operator $J(\Phi)$ is called the *Choi representation* (or the *Choi operator*) of Φ.

It is evident from the equation (2.65) that the mapping J is a linear bijection. An alternative way to prove that the mapping J is a bijection is to observe that the action of the mapping Φ can be recovered from the operator $J(\Phi)$ by means of the equation

$$\Phi(X) = \mathrm{Tr}_{\mathcal{X}} \left(J(\Phi)(\mathbb{1}_{\mathcal{Y}} \otimes X^{\mathsf{T}}) \right). \tag{2.66}$$

There is a close connection between the operator structure of $J(\Phi)$ and the aspects of Φ that relate to the operator structure of its input and output arguments. A central component of this connection is that a given map Φ is completely positive if and only if $J(\Phi)$ is positive semidefinite (as is established by Theorem 2.22 below).

For a given map $\Phi \in T(\mathcal{X}, \mathcal{Y})$, the rank of its Choi representation $J(\Phi)$ is called the *Choi rank* of Φ.

Kraus Representations

For any choice of complex Euclidean spaces $\mathcal{X}$ and $\mathcal{Y}$, an alphabet Σ, and collections

$$\{A_a : a \in \Sigma\} \quad \text{and} \quad \{B_a : a \in \Sigma\} \tag{2.67}$$

of operators drawn from the space $\mathrm{L}(\mathcal{X}, \mathcal{Y})$, one may define a linear map $\Phi \in \mathrm{T}(\mathcal{X}, \mathcal{Y})$ as

$$\Phi(X) = \sum_{a \in \Sigma} A_a X B_a^* \tag{2.68}$$

for every $X \in \mathrm{L}(\mathcal{X})$. The expression (2.68) is a *Kraus representation* of the map Φ. It will be established shortly that a Kraus representation exists for every map of the form $\Phi \in \mathrm{T}(\mathcal{X}, \mathcal{Y})$. Unlike the natural representation and Choi representation, however, Kraus representations are not unique.

Under the assumption that Φ is determined by the above equation (2.68), it holds that

$$\Phi^*(Y) = \sum_{a \in \Sigma} A_a^* Y B_a, \tag{2.69}$$

as follows from a calculation relying on the cyclic property of the trace:

$$\left\langle Y, \sum_{a \in \Sigma} A_a X B_a^* \right\rangle = \sum_{a \in \Sigma} \mathrm{Tr}(Y^* A_a X B_a^*)$$

$$= \sum_{a \in \Sigma} \mathrm{Tr}(B_a^* Y^* A_a X) = \left\langle \sum_{a \in \Sigma} A_a^* Y B_a, X \right\rangle \tag{2.70}$$

for every $X \in \mathrm{L}(\mathcal{X})$ and $Y \in \mathrm{L}(\mathcal{Y})$.

It is common in the theory of quantum information that one encounters Kraus representations for which $A_a = B_a$ for each $a \in \Sigma$. As is established by Theorem 2.22 below, such representations exist precisely when the map being considered is completely positive.

Stinespring Representations

Suppose $\mathcal{X}$, $\mathcal{Y}$, and $\mathcal{Z}$ are complex Euclidean spaces and $A, B \in \mathrm{L}(\mathcal{X}, \mathcal{Y} \otimes \mathcal{Z})$ are operators. One may then define a map $\Phi \in \mathrm{T}(\mathcal{X}, \mathcal{Y})$ as

$$\Phi(X) = \mathrm{Tr}_{\mathcal{Z}}(AXB^*) \tag{2.71}$$

for every $X \in \mathrm{L}(\mathcal{X})$. The expression (2.71) is a *Stinespring representation* of the map Φ. Similar to Kraus representations, Stinespring representations always exist for a given map Φ, and are not unique.

If a map $\Phi \in T(\mathcal{X}, \mathcal{Y})$ has a Stinespring representation taking the form (2.71), then it holds that

$$\Phi^*(Y) = A^*(Y \otimes \mathbb{1}_{\mathcal{Z}})B \tag{2.72}$$

for all $Y \in L(\mathcal{Y})$. This observation follows from a calculation:

$$\begin{aligned}
\langle Y, \Phi(X) \rangle &= \langle Y, \text{Tr}_{\mathcal{Z}}(AXB^*) \rangle = \langle Y \otimes \mathbb{1}_{\mathcal{Z}}, AXB^* \rangle \\
&= \text{Tr}((Y \otimes \mathbb{1}_{\mathcal{Z}})^*AXB^*) = \text{Tr}(B^*(Y \otimes \mathbb{1}_{\mathcal{Z}})^*AX) \\
&= \langle A^*(Y \otimes \mathbb{1}_{\mathcal{Z}})B, X \rangle
\end{aligned} \tag{2.73}$$

for every $X \in L(\mathcal{X})$ and $Y \in L(\mathcal{Y})$. Expressions of the form (2.72) are also sometimes referred to as Stinespring representations (in this case of the map Φ^*), although the terminology will not be used in this way in this book.

Similar to Kraus representations, it is common in quantum information theory that one encounters Stinespring representations for which $A = B$. Also similar to Kraus representations, such representations exist if and only if Φ is completely positive.

Relationships Among the Representations

The following proposition relates the four representations discussed above to one another, and (implicitly) shows how any one of the representations may be converted into any other.

Proposition 2.20 *Let $\mathcal{X}$ and $\mathcal{Y}$ be complex Euclidean spaces, let Σ be an alphabet, let $\{A_a : a \in \Sigma\}$, $\{B_a : a \in \Sigma\} \subset L(\mathcal{X}, \mathcal{Y})$ be collections of operators indexed by Σ, and let $\Phi \in T(\mathcal{X}, \mathcal{Y})$. The following four statements, which correspond as indicated to the four representations introduced above, are equivalent:*

1. *(Natural representation.) It holds that*

$$K(\Phi) = \sum_{a \in \Sigma} A_a \otimes \overline{B_a}. \tag{2.74}$$

2. *(Choi representation.) It holds that*

$$J(\Phi) = \sum_{a \in \Sigma} \text{vec}(A_a) \text{vec}(B_a)^*. \tag{2.75}$$

3. *(Kraus representations.) It holds that*

$$\Phi(X) = \sum_{a \in \Sigma} A_a X B_a^* \tag{2.76}$$

for all $X \in L(\mathcal{X})$.

4. *(Stinespring representations.)* For $\mathcal{Z} = \mathbb{C}^\Sigma$ and $A, B \in \mathrm{L}(\mathcal{X}, \mathcal{Y} \otimes \mathcal{Z})$
   defined as

$$A = \sum_{a \in \Sigma} A_a \otimes e_a \quad and \quad B = \sum_{a \in \Sigma} B_a \otimes e_a, \tag{2.77}$$

   it holds that

$$\Phi(X) = \mathrm{Tr}_{\mathcal{Z}}\left(AXB^*\right) \tag{2.78}$$

   for all $X \in \mathrm{L}(\mathcal{X})$.

Proof The equivalence between statements 3 and 4 is a straightforward calculation. The equivalence between statements 1 and 3 follows from the identity

$$\mathrm{vec}(A_a X B_a^*) = \left(A_a \otimes \overline{B_a}\right) \mathrm{vec}(X) \tag{2.79}$$

for all choices of $a \in \Sigma$ and $X \in \mathrm{L}(\mathcal{X})$. Finally, the equivalence between statements 2 and 3 follows from the equations

$$\begin{aligned}
(A_a \otimes \mathbb{1}_{\mathcal{X}}) \,\mathrm{vec}(\mathbb{1}_{\mathcal{X}}) &= \mathrm{vec}(A_a), \\
\mathrm{vec}(\mathbb{1}_{\mathcal{X}})^*(B_a^* \otimes \mathbb{1}_{\mathcal{X}}) &= \mathrm{vec}(B_a)^*,
\end{aligned} \tag{2.80}$$

which hold for every $a \in \Sigma$. $\qquad\square$

Corollary 2.21 *Let $\mathcal{X}$ and $\mathcal{Y}$ be complex Euclidean spaces, let $\Phi \in \mathrm{T}(\mathcal{X}, \mathcal{Y})$ be a nonzero linear map, and let $r = \mathrm{rank}(J(\Phi))$ be the Choi rank of Φ. The following two facts hold:*

1. *For Σ being any alphabet with $|\Sigma| = r$, there exists a Kraus representation of Φ having the form*

$$\Phi(X) = \sum_{a \in \Sigma} A_a X B_a^*, \tag{2.81}$$

   for some choice of $\{A_a : a \in \Sigma\}$, $\{B_a : a \in \Sigma\} \subset \mathrm{L}(\mathcal{X}, \mathcal{Y})$.
2. *For $\mathcal{Z}$ being any complex Euclidean space with $\dim(\mathcal{Z}) = r$, there exists a Stinespring representation of Φ having the form*

$$\Phi(X) = \mathrm{Tr}_{\mathcal{Z}}\left(AXB^*\right), \tag{2.82}$$

   for some choice of operators $A, B \in \mathrm{L}(\mathcal{X}, \mathcal{Y} \otimes \mathcal{Z})$.

Proof For Σ being any alphabet with $|\Sigma| = r$, it is possible to write

$$J(\Phi) = \sum_{a \in \Sigma} u_a v_a^* \tag{2.83}$$

for some choice of vectors

$$\{u_a : a \in \Sigma\}, \{v_a : a \in \Sigma\} \subset \mathcal{Y} \otimes \mathcal{X}. \tag{2.84}$$

In particular, one may take $\{u_a : a \in \Sigma\}$ to be any basis for the image of $J(\Phi)$, which uniquely determines a collection $\{v_a : a \in \Sigma\}$ for which (2.83) holds. Taking $\{A_a : a \in \Sigma\}$ and $\{B_a : a \in \Sigma\}$ to be operators defined by the equations

$$\text{vec}(A_a) = u_a \quad \text{and} \quad \text{vec}(B_a) = v_a \tag{2.85}$$

for every $a \in \Sigma$, it follows from Proposition 2.20 that the expression (2.81) is a Kraus representation of Φ. Moreover, it holds that the expression (2.82) is a Stinespring representation of Φ for $A, B \in L(\mathcal{X}, \mathcal{Y} \otimes \mathcal{Z})$ defined as

$$A = \sum_{a \in \Sigma} A_a \otimes e_a \quad \text{and} \quad B = \sum_{a \in \Sigma} B_a \otimes e_a, \tag{2.86}$$

which completes the proof. $\qquad\qquad\qquad\qquad\qquad\qquad\qquad\qquad$ $\square$

Characterizations of Completely Positive Maps

Characterizations of completely positive maps, based on their Choi, Kraus, and Stinespring representations, will now be presented.

Theorem 2.22 *Let $\Phi \in T(\mathcal{X}, \mathcal{Y})$ be a nonzero map, for complex Euclidean spaces $\mathcal{X}$ and $\mathcal{Y}$. The following statements are equivalent:*

1. *Φ is completely positive.*
2. *$\Phi \otimes \mathbb{1}_{L(\mathcal{X})}$ is positive.*
3. *$J(\Phi) \in \text{Pos}(\mathcal{Y} \otimes \mathcal{X})$.*
4. *There exists a collection $\{A_a : a \in \Sigma\} \subset L(\mathcal{X}, \mathcal{Y})$, for some choice of an alphabet Σ, for which*

$$\Phi(X) = \sum_{a \in \Sigma} A_a X A_a^* \tag{2.87}$$

    for all $X \in L(\mathcal{X})$.
5. *Statement 4 holds for an alphabet Σ satisfying $|\Sigma| = \text{rank}(J(\Phi))$.*
6. *There exists an operator $A \in L(\mathcal{X}, \mathcal{Y} \otimes \mathcal{Z})$, for some choice of a complex Euclidean space $\mathcal{Z}$, such that*

$$\Phi(X) = \text{Tr}_{\mathcal{Z}}(A X A^*) \tag{2.88}$$

    for all $X \in L(\mathcal{X})$.
7. *Statement 6 holds for $\mathcal{Z}$ having dimension equal to $\text{rank}(J(\Phi))$.*

Proof The theorem will be proved by establishing the following implications among the seven statements, which are sufficient to imply their equivalence:

$$(1) \Rightarrow (2) \Rightarrow (3) \Rightarrow (5) \Rightarrow (4) \Rightarrow (1)$$
$$(5) \Rightarrow (7) \Rightarrow (6) \Rightarrow (1)$$

Note that some of these implications are immediate: statement 1 implies statement 2 by the definition of complete positivity, statement 5 trivially implies statement 4, statement 7 trivially implies statement 6, and statement 5 implies statement 7 by Proposition 2.20.

Assume $\Phi \otimes \mathbb{1}_{L(\mathcal{X})}$ is positive. Because

$$\operatorname{vec}(\mathbb{1}_{\mathcal{X}}) \operatorname{vec}(\mathbb{1}_{\mathcal{X}})^* \in \operatorname{Pos}(\mathcal{X} \otimes \mathcal{X}) \tag{2.89}$$

and

$$J(\Phi) = (\Phi \otimes \mathbb{1}_{L(\mathcal{X})})(\operatorname{vec}(\mathbb{1}_{\mathcal{X}}) \operatorname{vec}(\mathbb{1}_{\mathcal{X}})^*), \tag{2.90}$$

it follows that $J(\Phi) \in \operatorname{Pos}(\mathcal{Y} \otimes \mathcal{X})$, so statement 2 implies statement 3.

Next, assume $J(\Phi) \in \operatorname{Pos}(\mathcal{Y} \otimes \mathcal{X})$. It follows by the spectral theorem (Corollary 1.4), together with the fact that every eigenvalue of a positive semidefinite operator is nonnegative, that one may write

$$J(\Phi) = \sum_{a \in \Sigma} u_a u_a^*, \tag{2.91}$$

for some choice of an alphabet Σ with $|\Sigma| = \operatorname{rank}(J(\Phi))$ and a collection

$$\{u_a : a \in \Sigma\} \subset \mathcal{Y} \otimes \mathcal{X} \tag{2.92}$$

of vectors. Taking $A_a \in L(\mathcal{X}, \mathcal{Y})$ to be the operator defined by the equation $\operatorname{vec}(A_a) = u_a$ for each $a \in \Sigma$, one has that

$$J(\Phi) = \sum_{a \in \Sigma} \operatorname{vec}(A_a) \operatorname{vec}(A_a)^*. \tag{2.93}$$

The equation (2.87) therefore holds for every $X \in L(\mathcal{X})$ by Proposition 2.20, which establishes that statement 3 implies statement 5.

Now suppose (2.87) holds for every $X \in L(\mathcal{X})$, for some alphabet Σ and a collection

$$\{A_a : a \in \Sigma\} \subset L(\mathcal{X}, \mathcal{Y}) \tag{2.94}$$

of operators. For a complex Euclidean space $\mathcal{W}$ and a positive semidefinite operator $P \in \operatorname{Pos}(\mathcal{X} \otimes \mathcal{W})$, it is evident that

$$(A_a \otimes \mathbb{1}_{\mathcal{W}})P(A_a \otimes \mathbb{1}_{\mathcal{W}})^* \in \operatorname{Pos}(\mathcal{Y} \otimes \mathcal{W}) \tag{2.95}$$

for each $a \in \Sigma$, and therefore

$$\left(\Phi \otimes \mathbb{1}_{L(W)}\right)(P) \in \text{Pos}(\mathcal{Y} \otimes \mathcal{W}) \tag{2.96}$$

by the fact that $\text{Pos}(\mathcal{Y} \otimes \mathcal{W})$ is a convex cone. It follows that Φ is completely positive, so statement 4 implies statement 1.

Finally, suppose (2.88) holds for every $X \in L(\mathcal{X})$, for some complex Euclidean space $\mathcal{Z}$ and an operator $A \in L(\mathcal{X}, \mathcal{Y} \otimes \mathcal{Z})$. For any complex Euclidean space $\mathcal{W}$ and any positive semidefinite operator $P \in \text{Pos}(\mathcal{X} \otimes \mathcal{W})$, it is again evident that

$$(A \otimes \mathbb{1}_{W})P(A \otimes \mathbb{1}_{W})^{*} \in \text{Pos}(\mathcal{Y} \otimes \mathcal{Z} \otimes \mathcal{W}), \tag{2.97}$$

so that

$$\left(\Phi \otimes \mathbb{1}_{L(W)}\right)(P) = \text{Tr}_{\mathcal{Z}}\left((A \otimes \mathbb{1}_{W})P(A \otimes \mathbb{1}_{W})^{*}\right) \in \text{Pos}(\mathcal{Y} \otimes \mathcal{W}) \tag{2.98}$$

by the complete positivity of the trace (Corollary 2.19). It therefore holds that the map Φ is completely positive, so statement 6 implies statement 1, which completes the proof. $\qquad\square$

One consequence of this theorem is the following corollary, which relates Kraus representations of a given completely positive map.

Corollary 2.23 *Let Σ be an alphabet, let $\mathcal{X}$ and $\mathcal{Y}$ be complex Euclidean spaces, and assume $\{A_a : a \in \Sigma\}$, $\{B_a : a \in \Sigma\} \subset L(\mathcal{X}, \mathcal{Y})$ are collections of operators for which*

$$\sum_{a \in \Sigma} A_a X A_a^{*} = \sum_{a \in \Sigma} B_a X B_a^{*} \tag{2.99}$$

for all $X \in L(\mathcal{X})$. There exists a unitary operator $U \in U(\mathbb{C}^{\Sigma})$ such that

$$B_a = \sum_{b \in \Sigma} U(a,b) A_b \tag{2.100}$$

for all $a \in \Sigma$.

Proof The maps

$$X \mapsto \sum_{a \in \Sigma} A_a X A_a^{*} \quad \text{and} \quad X \mapsto \sum_{a \in \Sigma} B_a X B_a^{*} \tag{2.101}$$

agree for all $X \in L(\mathcal{X})$, and therefore their Choi representations must be equal:

$$\sum_{a \in \Sigma} \text{vec}(A_a)\,\text{vec}(A_a)^{*} = \sum_{a \in \Sigma} \text{vec}(B_a)\,\text{vec}(B_a)^{*}. \tag{2.102}$$

Let $\mathcal{Z} = \mathbb{C}^\Sigma$ and define vectors $u, v \in \mathcal{Y} \otimes \mathcal{X} \otimes \mathcal{Z}$ as

$$u = \sum_{a \in \Sigma} \text{vec}(A_a) \otimes e_a \quad \text{and} \quad v = \sum_{a \in \Sigma} \text{vec}(B_a) \otimes e_a, \tag{2.103}$$

so that

$$\begin{aligned}
\text{Tr}_\mathcal{Z}(uu^*) &= \sum_{a \in \Sigma} \text{vec}(A_a)\,\text{vec}(A_a)^* \\
&= \sum_{a \in \Sigma} \text{vec}(B_a)\,\text{vec}(B_a)^* = \text{Tr}_\mathcal{Z}(vv^*).
\end{aligned} \tag{2.104}$$

By the unitary equivalence of purifications (Theorem 2.12), there must exist a unitary operator $U \in \text{U}(\mathcal{Z})$ such that

$$v = (\mathbb{1}_{\mathcal{Y} \otimes \mathcal{X}} \otimes U)u. \tag{2.105}$$

Thus, for each $a \in \Sigma$ it holds that

$$\text{vec}(B_a) = (\mathbb{1}_{\mathcal{Y} \otimes \mathcal{X}} \otimes e_a^*)v = (\mathbb{1}_{\mathcal{Y} \otimes \mathcal{X}} \otimes e_a^* U)u = \sum_{b \in \Sigma} U(a, b)\,\text{vec}(A_b), \tag{2.106}$$

which is equivalent to (2.100). $\qquad\square$

Along similar lines to the previous corollary is the following one, which concerns Stinespring representations rather than Kraus representations. As the proof reveals, the two corollaries are essentially equivalent.

Corollary 2.24 *Let $\mathcal{X}$, $\mathcal{Y}$, and $\mathcal{Z}$ be complex Euclidean spaces and let operators $A, B \in \text{L}(\mathcal{X}, \mathcal{Y} \otimes \mathcal{Z})$ satisfy the equation*

$$\text{Tr}_\mathcal{Z}(AXA^*) = \text{Tr}_\mathcal{Z}(BXB^*) \tag{2.107}$$

for every $X \in \text{L}(\mathcal{X})$. There exists a unitary operator $U \in \text{U}(\mathcal{Z})$ such that

$$B = (\mathbb{1}_\mathcal{Y} \otimes U)A. \tag{2.108}$$

Proof Let Σ be the alphabet for which $\mathcal{Z} = \mathbb{C}^\Sigma$, and define two collections $\{A_a : a \in \Sigma\}$, $\{B_a : a \in \Sigma\} \subset \text{L}(\mathcal{X}, \mathcal{Y})$ of operators as

$$A_a = (\mathbb{1}_\mathcal{Y} \otimes e_a^*)A \quad \text{and} \quad B_a = (\mathbb{1}_\mathcal{Y} \otimes e_a^*)B, \tag{2.109}$$

for each $a \in \Sigma$, so that

$$A = \sum_{a \in \Sigma} A_a \otimes e_a \quad \text{and} \quad B = \sum_{a \in \Sigma} B_a \otimes e_a. \tag{2.110}$$

The equation (2.107) is equivalent to (2.99) in Corollary 2.23. It follows from that corollary that there exists a unitary operator $U \in \text{U}(\mathcal{Z})$ such that (2.100) holds, which is equivalent to $B = (\mathbb{1}_\mathcal{Y} \otimes U)A$. $\qquad\square$

A map $\Phi \in T(\mathcal{X}, \mathcal{Y})$ is said to be *Hermitian-preserving* if it holds that $\Phi(H) \in \text{Herm}(\mathcal{Y})$ for all $H \in \text{Herm}(\mathcal{X})$. The following theorem, which provides four alternative characterizations of this class of maps, is proved through the use of Theorem 2.22.

Theorem 2.25 *Let $\Phi \in T(\mathcal{X}, \mathcal{Y})$ be a map, for complex Euclidean spaces $\mathcal{X}$ and $\mathcal{Y}$. The following statements are equivalent:*

1. *Φ is Hermitian-preserving.*
2. *It holds that $(\Phi(X))^* = \Phi(X^*)$ for every $X \in L(\mathcal{X})$.*
3. *It holds that $J(\Phi) \in \text{Herm}(\mathcal{Y} \otimes \mathcal{X})$.*
4. *There exist completely positive maps $\Phi_0, \Phi_1 \in \text{CP}(\mathcal{X}, \mathcal{Y})$ for which $\Phi = \Phi_0 - \Phi_1$.*
5. *There exist positive maps $\Phi_0, \Phi_1 \in T(\mathcal{X}, \mathcal{Y})$ for which $\Phi = \Phi_0 - \Phi_1$.*

Proof Assume first that Φ is a Hermitian-preserving map. For an arbitrary operator $X \in L(\mathcal{X})$, one may write $X = H + iK$ for $H, K \in \text{Herm}(\mathcal{X})$ being defined as

$$H = \frac{X + X^*}{2} \quad \text{and} \quad K = \frac{X - X^*}{2i}. \tag{2.111}$$

As $\Phi(H)$ and $\Phi(K)$ are both Hermitian and Φ is linear, it follows that

$$(\Phi(X))^* = (\Phi(H) + i\Phi(K))^*$$
$$= \Phi(H) - i\Phi(K) = \Phi(H - iK) = \Phi(X^*). \tag{2.112}$$

Statement 1 therefore implies statement 2.

Next, assume statement 2 holds, and let Σ be the alphabet for which $\mathcal{X} = \mathbb{C}^\Sigma$. One then has that

$$J(\Phi)^* = \sum_{a,b \in \Sigma} \Phi(E_{a,b})^* \otimes E_{a,b}^* = \sum_{a,b \in \Sigma} \Phi(E_{a,b}^*) \otimes E_{a,b}^*$$
$$= \sum_{a,b \in \Sigma} \Phi(E_{b,a}) \otimes E_{b,a} = J(\Phi). \tag{2.113}$$

It follows that $J(\Phi)$ is Hermitian, and therefore statement 3 holds.

Now assume statement 3 holds. Let $J(\Phi) = P_0 - P_1$ be the Jordan–Hahn decomposition of $J(\Phi)$, and let $\Phi_0, \Phi_1 \in \text{CP}(\mathcal{X}, \mathcal{Y})$ be the maps for which $J(\Phi_0) = P_0$ and $J(\Phi_1) = P_1$. Because P_0 and P_1 are positive semidefinite, it follows from Theorem 2.22 that Φ_0 and Φ_1 are completely positive maps. By the linearity of the mapping J associated with the Choi representation, it holds that $J(\Phi) = J(\Phi_0 - \Phi_1)$, and therefore $\Phi = \Phi_0 - \Phi_1$, implying that statement 4 holds.

Statement 4 trivially implies statement 5.

Finally, assume statement 5 holds. Let $H \in \mathrm{Herm}(\mathcal{X})$ be a Hermitian operator, and let $H = P_0 - P_1$, for $P_0, P_1 \in \mathrm{Pos}(\mathcal{X})$, be the Jordan–Hahn decomposition of H. It holds that $\Phi_a(P_b) \in \mathrm{Pos}(\mathcal{Y})$, for all $a, b \in \{0, 1\}$, by the positivity of Φ_0 and Φ_1. Therefore, one has that

$$\Phi(H) = (\Phi_0(P_0) + \Phi_1(P_1)) - (\Phi_0(P_1) + \Phi_1(P_0)) \tag{2.114}$$

is the difference between two positive semidefinite operators, and is therefore Hermitian. Thus, statement 1 holds.

As the implications $(1) \Rightarrow (2) \Rightarrow (3) \Rightarrow (4) \Rightarrow (5) \Rightarrow (1)$ among the statements have been established, the theorem is proved. $\qquad\square$

Characterizations of Trace-Preserving Maps

The next theorem provides multiple characterizations of the class of trace-preserving maps.

Theorem 2.26 *Let $\Phi \in \mathrm{T}(\mathcal{X}, \mathcal{Y})$ be a map, for complex Euclidean spaces $\mathcal{X}$ and $\mathcal{Y}$. The following statements are equivalent:*

1. *Φ is a trace-preserving map.*
2. *Φ^* is a unital map.*
3. *$\mathrm{Tr}_{\mathcal{Y}}(J(\Phi)) = \mathbb{1}_{\mathcal{X}}$.*
4. *There exist collections $\{A_a : a \in \Sigma\}$, $\{B_a : a \in \Sigma\} \subset \mathrm{L}(\mathcal{X}, \mathcal{Y})$ of operators such that*

$$\Phi(X) = \sum_{a \in \Sigma} A_a X B_a^* \tag{2.115}$$

   and

$$\sum_{a \in \Sigma} A_a^* B_a = \mathbb{1}_{\mathcal{X}}. \tag{2.116}$$

5. *For all collections $\{A_a : a \in \Sigma\}$, $\{B_a : a \in \Sigma\} \subset \mathrm{L}(\mathcal{X}, \mathcal{Y})$ of operators satisfying (2.115), the equation (2.116) must also hold.*
6. *There exist operators $A, B \in \mathrm{L}(\mathcal{X}, \mathcal{Y} \otimes \mathcal{Z})$, for some complex Euclidean space $\mathcal{Z}$, such that*

$$\Phi(X) = \mathrm{Tr}_{\mathcal{Z}}(A X B^*) \tag{2.117}$$

   and $A^* B = \mathbb{1}_{\mathcal{X}}$.
7. *For every choice of operators $A, B \in \mathrm{L}(\mathcal{X}, \mathcal{Y} \otimes \mathcal{Z})$ satisfying (2.117), it holds that $A^* B = \mathbb{1}_{\mathcal{X}}$.*

Proof Under the assumption that Φ preserves trace, it holds that

$$\langle \mathbb{1}_{\mathcal{X}}, X \rangle = \mathrm{Tr}(X) = \mathrm{Tr}(\Phi(X)) = \langle \mathbb{1}_{\mathcal{Y}}, \Phi(X) \rangle = \langle \Phi^*(\mathbb{1}_{\mathcal{Y}}), X \rangle, \qquad (2.118)$$

and therefore

$$\langle \mathbb{1}_{\mathcal{X}} - \Phi^*(\mathbb{1}_{\mathcal{Y}}), X \rangle = 0, \qquad (2.119)$$

for all $X \in \mathrm{L}(\mathcal{X})$. It follows that $\Phi^*(\mathbb{1}_{\mathcal{Y}}) = \mathbb{1}_{\mathcal{X}}$, and therefore Φ^* is unital. Along similar lines, the assumption that Φ^* is unital implies

$$\mathrm{Tr}(\Phi(X)) = \langle \mathbb{1}_{\mathcal{Y}}, \Phi(X) \rangle = \langle \Phi^*(\mathbb{1}_{\mathcal{Y}}), X \rangle = \langle \mathbb{1}_{\mathcal{X}}, X \rangle = \mathrm{Tr}(X) \qquad (2.120)$$

for every $X \in \mathrm{L}(\mathcal{X})$, and therefore Φ preserves trace. The equivalence of statements 1 and 2 has been established.

Next, assume that $\{A_a : a \in \Sigma\}$, $\{B_a : a \in \Sigma\} \subset \mathrm{L}(\mathcal{X}, \mathcal{Y})$ satisfy

$$\Phi(X) = \sum_{a \in \Sigma} A_a X B_a^* \qquad (2.121)$$

for all $X \in \mathrm{L}(\mathcal{X})$. It therefore holds that

$$\Phi^*(Y) = \sum_{a \in \Sigma} A_a^* Y B_a \qquad (2.122)$$

for every $Y \in \mathrm{L}(\mathcal{Y})$, and in particular it holds that

$$\Phi^*(\mathbb{1}_{\mathcal{Y}}) = \sum_{a \in \Sigma} A_a^* B_a. \qquad (2.123)$$

Thus, if Φ^* is a unital map, then

$$\sum_{a \in \Sigma} A_a^* B_a = \mathbb{1}_{\mathcal{X}}, \qquad (2.124)$$

and so it has been proved that statement 2 implies statement 5. On the other hand, if (2.124) holds, then it follows that $\Phi^*(\mathbb{1}_{\mathcal{Y}}) = \mathbb{1}_{\mathcal{X}}$, so that Φ^* is unital. Therefore, statement 4 implies statement 2. As statement 5 implies statement 4, by virtue of the fact that Kraus representations exist for every map, the equivalence of statements 2, 4, and 5 has been established.

Now assume that $A, B \in \mathrm{L}(\mathcal{X}, \mathcal{Y} \otimes \mathcal{Z})$ satisfy $\Phi(X) = \mathrm{Tr}_{\mathcal{Z}}(AXB^*)$ for every $X \in \mathrm{L}(\mathcal{X})$. It follows that

$$\Phi^*(Y) = A^*(Y \otimes \mathbb{1}_{\mathcal{Z}})B \qquad (2.125)$$

for all $Y \in \mathrm{L}(\mathcal{Y})$, and in particular $\Phi^*(\mathbb{1}_{\mathcal{Y}}) = A^*B$. The equivalence of statements 2, 6, and 7 follows by the same reasoning as for the case of statements 2, 4, and 5.

Finally, let Γ be the alphabet for which $\mathcal{X} = \mathbb{C}^\Gamma$, and consider the operator

$$\mathrm{Tr}_{\mathcal{Y}}(J(\Phi)) = \sum_{a,b \in \Gamma} \mathrm{Tr}(\Phi(E_{a,b})) E_{a,b}. \tag{2.126}$$

If Φ preserves trace, then it follows that

$$\mathrm{Tr}(\Phi(E_{a,b})) = \begin{cases} 1 & \text{if } a = b \\ 0 & \text{if } a \neq b, \end{cases} \tag{2.127}$$

and therefore

$$\mathrm{Tr}_{\mathcal{Y}}(J(\Phi)) = \sum_{a \in \Gamma} E_{a,a} = \mathbb{1}_{\mathcal{X}}. \tag{2.128}$$

Conversely, if $\mathrm{Tr}_{\mathcal{Y}}(J(\Phi)) = \mathbb{1}_{\mathcal{X}}$, then a consideration of the expression (2.126) reveals that (2.127) must hold. As the set $\{E_{a,b} : a, b \in \Gamma\}$ is a basis of $\mathrm{L}(\mathcal{X})$, one concludes by linearity that Φ preserves trace. Statements 1 and 3 are therefore equivalent, which completes the proof. $\quad\square$

Characterizations of Channels

Theorems 2.22 and 2.26 can be combined, providing characterizations of channels based on their Choi, Kraus, and Stinespring representations.

Corollary 2.27 *Let $\Phi \in \mathrm{T}(\mathcal{X}, \mathcal{Y})$ be a map, for complex Euclidean spaces $\mathcal{X}$ and $\mathcal{Y}$. The following statements are equivalent:*

1. *Φ is a channel.*
2. *$J(\Phi) \in \mathrm{Pos}(\mathcal{Y} \otimes \mathcal{X})$ and $\mathrm{Tr}_{\mathcal{Y}}(J(\Phi)) = \mathbb{1}_{\mathcal{X}}$.*
3. *There exist an alphabet Σ and a collection $\{A_a : a \in \Sigma\} \subset \mathrm{L}(\mathcal{X}, \mathcal{Y})$ satisfying*

$$\sum_{a \in \Sigma} A_a^* A_a = \mathbb{1}_{\mathcal{X}} \quad \text{and} \quad \Phi(X) = \sum_{a \in \Sigma} A_a X A_a^* \tag{2.129}$$

   for all $X \in \mathrm{L}(\mathcal{X})$.
4. *Statement 3 holds for $|\Sigma| = \mathrm{rank}(J(\Phi))$.*
5. *There exists an isometry $A \in \mathrm{U}(\mathcal{X}, \mathcal{Y} \otimes \mathcal{Z})$, for some choice of a complex Euclidean space $\mathcal{Z}$, such that*

$$\Phi(X) = \mathrm{Tr}_{\mathcal{Z}}(AXA^*) \tag{2.130}$$

   for all $X \in \mathrm{L}(\mathcal{X})$.
6. *Statement 5 holds under the requirement $\dim(\mathcal{Z}) = \mathrm{rank}(J(\Phi))$.*

For every choice of complex Euclidean spaces $\mathcal{X}$ and $\mathcal{Y}$, one has that the set of channels $C(\mathcal{X}, \mathcal{Y})$ is compact and convex. One way to prove this fact makes use of the previous corollary.

Proposition 2.28 *Let $\mathcal{X}$ and $\mathcal{Y}$ be complex Euclidean spaces. The set $C(\mathcal{X}, \mathcal{Y})$ is compact and convex.*

Proof The map $J: T(\mathcal{X}, \mathcal{Y}) \to L(\mathcal{Y} \otimes \mathcal{X})$ defining the Choi representation is linear and invertible. By Corollary 2.27, one has $J^{-1}(\mathcal{A}) = C(\mathcal{X}, \mathcal{Y})$ for $\mathcal{A}$ being defined as

$$\mathcal{A} = \{X \in \text{Pos}(\mathcal{Y} \otimes \mathcal{X}): \text{Tr}_{\mathcal{Y}}(X) = \mathbb{1}_{\mathcal{X}}\}. \tag{2.131}$$

It therefore suffices to prove that $\mathcal{A}$ is compact and convex. It is evident that $\mathcal{A}$ is closed and convex, as it is the intersection of the positive semidefinite cone $\text{Pos}(\mathcal{Y} \otimes \mathcal{X})$ with the affine subspace

$$\{X \in L(\mathcal{Y} \otimes \mathcal{X}): \text{Tr}_{\mathcal{Y}}(X) = \mathbb{1}_{\mathcal{X}}\}, \tag{2.132}$$

both of which are closed and convex. To complete the proof, it suffices to prove that $\mathcal{A}$ is bounded. For every $X \in \mathcal{A}$, one has

$$\|X\|_1 = \text{Tr}(X) = \text{Tr}(\text{Tr}_{\mathcal{Y}}(X)) = \text{Tr}(\mathbb{1}_{\mathcal{X}}) = \dim(\mathcal{X}), \tag{2.133}$$

and therefore $\mathcal{A}$ is bounded, as required. $\square$

Corollary 2.27 will be used frequently throughout this book, sometimes implicitly. The next proposition, which builds on the unitary equivalence of purifications (Theorem 2.12) to relate a given purification of a positive semidefinite operator to any extension of that operator, is one example of an application of this corollary.

Proposition 2.29 *Let $\mathcal{X}$, $\mathcal{Y}$, and $\mathcal{Z}$ be complex Euclidean spaces, and suppose that $u \in \mathcal{X} \otimes \mathcal{Y}$ and $P \in \text{Pos}(\mathcal{X} \otimes \mathcal{Z})$ satisfy*

$$\text{Tr}_{\mathcal{Y}}(uu^*) = \text{Tr}_{\mathcal{Z}}(P). \tag{2.134}$$

There exists a channel $\Phi \in C(\mathcal{Y}, \mathcal{Z})$ such that

$$(\mathbb{1}_{L(\mathcal{X})} \otimes \Phi)(uu^*) = P. \tag{2.135}$$

Proof Let $\mathcal{W}$ be a complex Euclidean space having dimension sufficiently large so that

$$\dim(\mathcal{W}) \geq \text{rank}(P) \quad \text{and} \quad \dim(\mathcal{Z} \otimes \mathcal{W}) \geq \dim(\mathcal{Y}), \tag{2.136}$$

and let $A \in U(\mathcal{Y}, \mathcal{Z} \otimes \mathcal{W})$ be any isometry. Also let $v \in \mathcal{X} \otimes \mathcal{Z} \otimes \mathcal{W}$ satisfy $\text{Tr}_{\mathcal{W}}(vv^*) = P$. It holds that

$$\text{Tr}_{\mathcal{Z} \otimes \mathcal{W}}((\mathbb{1}_{\mathcal{X}} \otimes A)uu^*(\mathbb{1}_{\mathcal{X}} \otimes A)^*)$$
$$= \text{Tr}_{\mathcal{Y}}(uu^*) = \text{Tr}_{\mathcal{Z}}(P) = \text{Tr}_{\mathcal{Z} \otimes \mathcal{W}}(vv^*). \tag{2.137}$$

By Theorem 2.12 there must exist a unitary operator $U \in U(\mathcal{Z} \otimes \mathcal{W})$ such that

$$(\mathbb{1}_{\mathcal{X}} \otimes UA)u = v. \tag{2.138}$$

Define $\Phi \in T(\mathcal{Y}, \mathcal{Z})$ as

$$\Phi(Y) = \text{Tr}_{\mathcal{W}}((UA)Y(UA)^*) \tag{2.139}$$

for all $Y \in L(\mathcal{Y})$. By Corollary 2.27, one has that Φ is a channel. It holds that

$$(\mathbb{1}_{L(\mathcal{X})} \otimes \Phi)(uu^*) = \text{Tr}_{\mathcal{W}}((\mathbb{1}_{\mathcal{X}} \otimes UA)uu^*(\mathbb{1}_{\mathcal{X}} \otimes UA)^*)$$
$$= \text{Tr}_{\mathcal{W}}(vv^*) = P, \tag{2.140}$$

as required. $\qquad\square$

2.2.3 Examples of Channels and Other Mappings

This section describes examples of channels, and other maps, along with their specifications according to the four types of representations discussed above. Many other examples and general classifications of channels and maps will be encountered throughout the book.

Isometric and Unitary Channels

Let $\mathcal{X}$ and $\mathcal{Y}$ be complex Euclidean spaces, let $A, B \in L(\mathcal{X}, \mathcal{Y})$ be operators, and consider the map $\Phi \in T(\mathcal{X}, \mathcal{Y})$ defined by

$$\Phi(X) = AXB^* \tag{2.141}$$

for all $X \in L(\mathcal{X})$.

In the case that $A = B$, and assuming in addition that this operator is a linear isometry from $\mathcal{X}$ to $\mathcal{Y}$, it follows from Corollary 2.27 that Φ is a channel. Such a channel is said to be an *isometric channel*. If $\mathcal{Y} = \mathcal{X}$ and $A = B$ is a unitary operator, Φ is said to be a *unitary channel*. Unitary channels, and convex combinations of unitary channels, are discussed in greater detail in Chapter 4.

The natural representation of the map Φ defined by (2.141) is

$$K(\Phi) = A \otimes \overline{B} \tag{2.142}$$

and the Choi representation of Φ is

$$J(\Phi) = \text{vec}(A)\,\text{vec}(B)^*. \tag{2.143}$$

The expression (2.141) is a Kraus representation of Φ, and may also be regarded as a trivial example of a Stinespring representation if one takes $\mathcal{Z} = \mathbb{C}$ and observes that the trace acts as the identity mapping on $\mathbb{C}$.

The identity mapping $\mathbb{1}_{\text{L}(\mathcal{X})}$ is a simple example of a unitary channel. The natural representation of this channel is the identity operator $\mathbb{1}_{\mathcal{X}} \otimes \mathbb{1}_{\mathcal{X}}$, while its Choi representation is given by the rank-one operator $\text{vec}(\mathbb{1}_{\mathcal{X}})\,\text{vec}(\mathbb{1}_{\mathcal{X}})^*$.

Replacement Channels and the Completely Depolarizing Channel

Let $\mathcal{X}$ and $\mathcal{Y}$ be complex Euclidean spaces, let $A \in \text{L}(\mathcal{X})$ and $B \in \text{L}(\mathcal{Y})$ be operators, and consider the map $\Phi \in \text{T}(\mathcal{X}, \mathcal{Y})$ defined as

$$\Phi(X) = \langle A, X \rangle\, B \tag{2.144}$$

for all $X \in \text{L}(\mathcal{X})$. The natural representation of Φ is

$$K(\Phi) = \text{vec}(B)\,\text{vec}(A)^*, \tag{2.145}$$

and the Choi representation of Φ is

$$J(\Phi) = B \otimes \overline{A}. \tag{2.146}$$

Kraus and Stinespring representations of Φ may also be constructed, although they are not necessarily enlightening in this particular case. One way to obtain a Kraus representation of Φ is to first write

$$A = \sum_{a \in \Sigma} u_a x_a^* \quad \text{and} \quad B = \sum_{b \in \Gamma} v_b y_b^*, \tag{2.147}$$

for some choice of alphabets Σ and Γ and four sets of vectors:

$$\begin{aligned} \{u_a : a \in \Sigma\},\ \{x_a : a \in \Sigma\} \subset \mathcal{X}, \\ \{v_b : b \in \Gamma\},\ \{y_b : b \in \Gamma\} \subset \mathcal{Y}. \end{aligned} \tag{2.148}$$

It then follows that one Kraus representation of Φ is given by

$$\Phi(X) = \sum_{(a,b) \in \Sigma \times \Gamma} C_{a,b} X D_{a,b}^*, \tag{2.149}$$

where $C_{a,b} = v_b u_a^*$ and $D_{a,b} = y_b x_a^*$ for each $a \in \Sigma$ and $b \in \Gamma$, and one Stinespring representation is given by

$$\Phi(X) = \mathrm{Tr}_{\mathcal{Z}}(C X D^*), \tag{2.150}$$

where

$$C = \sum_{(a,b)\in\Sigma\times\Gamma} C_{a,b} \otimes e_{(a,b)}, \quad D = \sum_{(a,b)\in\Sigma\times\Gamma} D_{a,b} \otimes e_{(a,b)}, \tag{2.151}$$

and $\mathcal{Z} = \mathbb{C}^{\Sigma\times\Gamma}$.

If A and B are positive semidefinite operators and the map $\Phi \in \mathrm{T}(\mathcal{X}, \mathcal{Y})$ is defined by (2.144) for all $X \in \mathrm{L}(\mathcal{X})$, then $J(\Phi) = B \otimes \overline{A}$ is positive semidefinite, and therefore Φ is completely positive by Theorem 2.22. In the case that $A = \mathbb{1}_{\mathcal{X}}$ and $B = \sigma$ for some density operator $\sigma \in \mathrm{D}(\mathcal{Y})$, the map Φ is also trace-preserving, and is therefore a channel. Such a channel is a *replacement channel*: it effectively discards its input, replacing it with the state σ.

The *completely depolarizing channel* $\Omega \in \mathrm{C}(\mathcal{X})$ is an important example of a replacement channel. This channel is defined as

$$\Omega(X) = \mathrm{Tr}(X)\omega \tag{2.152}$$

for all $X \in \mathrm{L}(\mathcal{X})$, where

$$\omega = \frac{\mathbb{1}_{\mathcal{X}}}{\dim(\mathcal{X})} \tag{2.153}$$

denotes the completely mixed state defined with respect to the space $\mathcal{X}$. Equivalently, Ω is the unique channel transforming every density operator into this completely mixed state: $\Omega(\rho) = \omega$ for all $\rho \in \mathrm{D}(\mathcal{X})$. From the equations (2.145) and (2.146), one has that the natural representation of the completely depolarizing channel $\Omega \in \mathrm{C}(\mathcal{X})$ is

$$K(\Omega) = \frac{\mathrm{vec}(\mathbb{1}_{\mathcal{X}})\,\mathrm{vec}(\mathbb{1}_{\mathcal{X}})^*}{\dim(\mathcal{X})}, \tag{2.154}$$

while the Choi representation of this channel is

$$J(\Omega) = \frac{\mathbb{1}_{\mathcal{X}} \otimes \mathbb{1}_{\mathcal{X}}}{\dim(\mathcal{X})}. \tag{2.155}$$

The Transpose Map

Let Σ be an alphabet, let $\mathcal{X} = \mathbb{C}^{\Sigma}$, and let $\mathrm{T} \in \mathrm{T}(\mathcal{X})$ denote the transpose map, defined as

$$\mathrm{T}(X) = X^{\mathsf{T}} \tag{2.156}$$

for all $X \in L(\mathcal{X})$. This map will play an important role in Chapter 6, due to its connections to properties of entangled states.

The natural representation $K(T)$ of T must, by definition, satisfy

$$K(T)\operatorname{vec}(X) = \operatorname{vec}(X^\mathsf{T}) \tag{2.157}$$

for all $X \in L(\mathcal{X})$. By considering those operators of the form $X = uv^\mathsf{T}$ for vectors $u, v \in \mathcal{X}$, one finds that

$$K(T)(u \otimes v) = v \otimes u. \tag{2.158}$$

It follows that $K(T) = W$, for $W \in L(\mathcal{X} \otimes \mathcal{X})$ being the *swap operator*, which is defined by the action $W(u \otimes v) = v \otimes u$ for all vectors $u, v \in \mathcal{X}$.

The Choi representation of T is also equal to the swap operator, as

$$J(T) = \sum_{a,b \in \Sigma} E_{b,a} \otimes E_{a,b} = W. \tag{2.159}$$

Under the assumption that $|\Sigma| \geq 2$, it therefore follows from Theorem 2.22 that T is not a completely positive map, as W is not a positive semidefinite operator in this case.

One example of a Kraus representation of T is

$$T(X) = \sum_{a,b \in \Sigma} E_{a,b} X E_{b,a}^* \tag{2.160}$$

for all $X \in L(\mathcal{X})$, from which it follows that $T(X) = \operatorname{Tr}_{\mathcal{Z}}(AXB^*)$ is a Stinespring representation of T for $\mathcal{Z} = \mathbb{C}^{\Sigma \times \Sigma}$,

$$A = \sum_{a,b \in \Sigma} E_{a,b} \otimes e_{(a,b)}, \quad \text{and} \quad B = \sum_{a,b \in \Sigma} E_{b,a} \otimes e_{(a,b)}. \tag{2.161}$$

The Completely Dephasing Channel

Let Σ be an alphabet and let $\mathcal{X} = \mathbb{C}^\Sigma$. The map $\Delta \in T(\mathcal{X})$ defined as

$$\Delta(X) = \sum_{a \in \Sigma} X(a,a) E_{a,a} \tag{2.162}$$

for every $X \in L(\mathcal{X})$ is an example of a channel known as the *completely dephasing channel*. This channel has the effect of replacing every off-diagonal entry of a given operator $X \in L(\mathcal{X})$ by 0 and leaving the diagonal entries unchanged.

Through the association of diagonal density operators with probabilistic states, as discussed in Section 2.1.2, one may view the channel Δ as an ideal channel for *classical communication*: it acts as the identity mapping on every diagonal density operator, so that it effectively transmits classical probabilistic states without error, while all other states are mapped to the probabilistic state given by their diagonal entries.

The natural representation of Δ must satisfy the equation

$$K(\Delta)\operatorname{vec}(E_{a,b}) = \begin{cases} \operatorname{vec}(E_{a,b}) & \text{if } a = b \\ 0 & \text{if } a \neq b, \end{cases} \tag{2.163}$$

which is equivalent to

$$K(\Delta)(e_a \otimes e_b) = \begin{cases} e_a \otimes e_b & \text{if } a = b \\ 0 & \text{if } a \neq b, \end{cases} \tag{2.164}$$

for every $a, b \in \Sigma$. It follows that

$$K(\Delta) = \sum_{a \in \Sigma} E_{a,a} \otimes E_{a,a}. \tag{2.165}$$

Similar to the transpose mapping, the Choi representation of Δ happens to coincide with its natural representation, as the calculation

$$J(\Delta) = \sum_{a,b \in \Sigma} \Delta(E_{a,b}) \otimes E_{a,b} = \sum_{a \in \Sigma} E_{a,a} \otimes E_{a,a} \tag{2.166}$$

reveals. It is evident from this expression, together with Corollary 2.27, that Δ is indeed a channel.

One example of a Kraus representation of Δ is

$$\Delta(X) = \sum_{a \in \Sigma} E_{a,a} X E_{a,a}^*, \tag{2.167}$$

and an example of a Stinespring representation of Δ is

$$\Delta(X) = \operatorname{Tr}_{\mathcal{Z}}(AXA^*) \tag{2.168}$$

for $\mathcal{Z} = \mathbb{C}^\Sigma$ and

$$A = \sum_{a \in \Sigma} (e_a \otimes e_a) e_a^*. \tag{2.169}$$

A Digression on Classical Registers

Classical probabilistic states of registers may be associated with diagonal density operators, as discussed in Section 2.1.2. The term *classical register* was mentioned in that discussion but not fully explained. It is appropriate to make this notion more precise, now that channels (and the completely dephasing channel in particular) have been introduced.

From a mathematical point of view, classical registers are not defined in a manner that is distinct from ordinary (quantum) registers. Rather, the term *classical register* will be used to refer to any register that, by the nature of the processes under consideration, would be unaffected by an application of the completely dephasing channel Δ at any moment during its existence. Every state of a classical register is necessarily a diagonal density operator, corresponding to a probabilistic state, as these are the density operators that are invariant under the action of the channel Δ. Moreover, the correlations that may exist between a classical register and one or more other registers are limited. For example, for a classical register X and an arbitrary register Y, the only states of the compound register (X, Y) that are consistent with the term *classical register* being applied to X are those taking the form

$$\sum_{a \in \Sigma} p(a) E_{a,a} \otimes \rho_a, \qquad (2.170)$$

for Σ being the classical state set of X, $\{\rho_a : a \in \Sigma\} \subseteq \mathrm{D}(\mathcal{Y})$ being an arbitrary collection of states of Y, and $p \in \mathcal{P}(\Sigma)$ being a probability vector. States of this form are commonly called *classical–quantum* states. It is both natural and convenient in some situations to associate the state (2.170) with the ensemble $\eta : \Sigma \to \mathrm{Pos}(\mathcal{Y})$ defined as $\eta(a) = p(a)\rho_a$ for each $a \in \Sigma$.

2.2.4 Extremal Channels

For any choice of complex Euclidean spaces $\mathcal{X}$ and $\mathcal{Y}$, the set of channels $\mathrm{C}(\mathcal{X}, \mathcal{Y})$ is compact and convex (by Proposition 2.28). A characterization of the extreme points of this set is given by Theorem 2.31 below. The following lemma will be used in the proof of this theorem.

Lemma 2.30 *Let $A \in \mathrm{L}(\mathcal{Y}, \mathcal{X})$ be an operator, for complex Euclidean spaces $\mathcal{X}$ and $\mathcal{Y}$. It holds that*

$$\{P \in \mathrm{Pos}(\mathcal{X}) : \mathrm{im}(P) \subseteq \mathrm{im}(A)\} = \{AQA^* : Q \in \mathrm{Pos}(\mathcal{Y})\}. \qquad (2.171)$$

Proof For every $Q \in \mathrm{Pos}(\mathcal{Y})$, it holds that AQA^* is positive semidefinite and satisfies $\mathrm{im}(AQA^*) \subseteq \mathrm{im}(A)$. The set on the right-hand side of (2.171) is therefore contained in the set on the left-hand side.

For the reverse containment, if $P \in \mathrm{Pos}(\mathcal{X})$ satisfies $\mathrm{im}(P) \subseteq \mathrm{im}(A)$, then by setting

$$Q = A^+ P (A^+)^*, \qquad (2.172)$$

for A^+ denoting the Moore–Penrose pseudo-inverse of A, one obtains

$$AQA^* = (AA^+) P (AA^+)^* = \Pi_{\mathrm{im}(A)} P \Pi_{\mathrm{im}(A)} = P, \qquad (2.173)$$

which completes the proof. $\qquad\qquad\qquad\qquad\qquad\qquad\qquad\qquad\qquad\square$

Theorem 2.31 (Choi) *Let $\mathcal{X}$ and $\mathcal{Y}$ be complex Euclidean spaces, let $\Phi \in C(\mathcal{X}, \mathcal{Y})$ be a channel, and let $\{A_a : a \in \Sigma\} \subset L(\mathcal{X}, \mathcal{Y})$ be a linearly independent set of operators satisfying*

$$\Phi(X) = \sum_{a \in \Sigma} A_a X A_a^* \tag{2.174}$$

for all $X \in L(\mathcal{X})$. The channel Φ is an extreme point of the set $C(\mathcal{X}, \mathcal{Y})$ if and only if the collection

$$\{A_b^* A_a : (a, b) \in \Sigma \times \Sigma\} \subset L(\mathcal{X}) \tag{2.175}$$

of operators is linearly independent.

Proof Let $\mathcal{Z} = \mathbb{C}^\Sigma$, define an operator $M \in L(\mathcal{Z}, \mathcal{Y} \otimes \mathcal{X})$ as

$$M = \sum_{a \in \Sigma} \mathrm{vec}(A_a) e_a^*, \tag{2.176}$$

and observe that

$$MM^* = \sum_{a \in \Sigma} \mathrm{vec}(A_a) \, \mathrm{vec}(A_a)^* = J(\Phi). \tag{2.177}$$

As $\{A_a : a \in \Sigma\}$ is a linearly independent collection of operators, it must hold that $\ker(M) = \{0\}$.

Assume first that Φ is not an extreme point of $C(\mathcal{X}, \mathcal{Y})$. It follows that there exist channels $\Psi_0, \Psi_1 \in C(\mathcal{X}, \mathcal{Y})$, with $\Psi_0 \neq \Psi_1$, along with a scalar $\lambda \in (0, 1)$, such that

$$\Phi = \lambda \Psi_0 + (1 - \lambda) \Psi_1. \tag{2.178}$$

Let $P = J(\Phi)$, $Q_0 = J(\Psi_0)$, and $Q_1 = J(\Psi_1)$, so that

$$P = \lambda Q_0 + (1 - \lambda) Q_1. \tag{2.179}$$

As Φ, Ψ_0, and Ψ_1 are channels, the operators $P, Q_0, Q_1 \in \mathrm{Pos}(\mathcal{Y} \otimes \mathcal{X})$ are positive semidefinite and satisfy

$$\mathrm{Tr}_{\mathcal{Y}}(P) = \mathrm{Tr}_{\mathcal{Y}}(Q_0) = \mathrm{Tr}_{\mathcal{Y}}(Q_1) = \mathbb{1}_{\mathcal{X}}, \tag{2.180}$$

by Corollary 2.27.

As λ is positive and the operators Q_0 and Q_1 are positive semidefinite, the equation (2.179) implies

$$\mathrm{im}(Q_0) \subseteq \mathrm{im}(P) = \mathrm{im}(M). \tag{2.181}$$

It follows by Lemma 2.30 that there exists a positive semidefinite operator $R_0 \in \mathrm{Pos}(\mathcal{Z})$ for which $Q_0 = M R_0 M^*$. By similar reasoning, there exists a positive semidefinite operator $R_1 \in \mathrm{Pos}(\mathcal{Z})$ for which $Q_1 = M R_1 M^*$.

Letting $H = R_0 - R_1$, one finds that

$$0 = \text{Tr}_{\mathcal{Y}}(Q_0) - \text{Tr}_{\mathcal{Y}}(Q_1) = \text{Tr}_{\mathcal{Y}}(MHM^*) = \sum_{a,b\in\Sigma} H(a,b)\left(A_b^* A_a\right)^{\mathsf{T}}, \quad (2.182)$$

and therefore

$$\sum_{a,b\in\Sigma} H(a,b)A_b^* A_a = 0. \quad (2.183)$$

Because $\Psi_0 \neq \Psi_1$, it holds that $Q_0 \neq Q_1$, so $R_0 \neq R_1$, and therefore $H \neq 0$. It has therefore been proved that $\{A_b^* A_a : (a,b) \in \Sigma \times \Sigma\}$ is a linearly dependent collection of operators.

Now assume the set (2.175) is linearly dependent:

$$\sum_{a,b\in\Sigma} Z(a,b)A_b^* A_a = 0 \quad (2.184)$$

for some choice of a nonzero operator $Z \in \text{L}(\mathcal{Z})$. By taking the adjoint of both sides of this equation, one finds that

$$\sum_{a,b\in\Sigma} Z^*(a,b)A_b^* A_a = 0, \quad (2.185)$$

from which it follows that

$$\sum_{a,b\in\Sigma} H(a,b)A_b^* A_a = 0 \quad (2.186)$$

for both of the Hermitian operators

$$H = \frac{Z + Z^*}{2} \quad \text{and} \quad H = \frac{Z - Z^*}{2i}. \quad (2.187)$$

At least one of these operators must be nonzero, which implies that (2.186) must hold for some choice of a nonzero Hermitian operator H. Let such a choice of H be fixed, and assume moreover that $\|H\| = 1$ (which causes no loss of generality as (2.186) still holds if H is replaced by $H/\|H\|$).

Let $\Psi_0, \Psi_1 \in \text{T}(\mathcal{X}, \mathcal{Y})$ be the mappings defined by the equations

$$J(\Psi_0) = M(\mathbb{1} + H)M^* \quad \text{and} \quad J(\Psi_1) = M(\mathbb{1} - H)M^*. \quad (2.188)$$

Because H is Hermitian and satisfies $\|H\| = 1$, one has that the operators $\mathbb{1} + H$ and $\mathbb{1} - H$ are both positive semidefinite. The operators $M(\mathbb{1}+H)M^*$ and $M(\mathbb{1} - H)M^*$ are therefore positive semidefinite as well, implying that

Ψ_0 and Ψ_1 are completely positive, by Theorem 2.22. It holds that

$$\text{Tr}_{\mathcal{Y}}\left(MHM^*\right) = \sum_{a,b \in \Sigma} H(a,b)\left(A_b^* A_a\right)^{\mathsf{T}}$$

$$= \left(\sum_{a,b \in \Sigma} H(a,b) A_b^* A_a\right)^{\mathsf{T}} = 0 \qquad (2.189)$$

and therefore the following two equations hold:

$$\begin{aligned} \text{Tr}_{\mathcal{Y}}\left(J(\Psi_0)\right) &= \text{Tr}_{\mathcal{Y}}\left(MM^*\right) + \text{Tr}_{\mathcal{Y}}\left(MHM^*\right) = \text{Tr}_{\mathcal{Y}}(J(\Phi)) = \mathbb{1}_{\mathcal{X}}, \\ \text{Tr}_{\mathcal{Y}}\left(J(\Psi_1)\right) &= \text{Tr}_{\mathcal{Y}}\left(MM^*\right) - \text{Tr}_{\mathcal{Y}}\left(MHM^*\right) = \text{Tr}_{\mathcal{Y}}(J(\Phi)) = \mathbb{1}_{\mathcal{X}}. \end{aligned} \qquad (2.190)$$

Thus, Ψ_0 and Ψ_1 are trace-preserving by Theorem 2.26, and are therefore channels.

Finally, given that $H \neq 0$ and $\ker(M) = \{0\}$, it holds that $J(\Psi_0) \neq J(\Psi_1)$, so that $\Psi_0 \neq \Psi_1$. As

$$\frac{1}{2}J(\Psi_0) + \frac{1}{2}J(\Psi_1) = MM^* = J(\Phi), \qquad (2.191)$$

one has that

$$\Phi = \frac{1}{2}\Psi_0 + \frac{1}{2}\Psi_1, \qquad (2.192)$$

which demonstrates that Φ is not an extreme point of $C(\mathcal{X}, \mathcal{Y})$. $\square$

Example 2.32 Let $\mathcal{X}$ and $\mathcal{Y}$ be complex Euclidean spaces such that $\dim(\mathcal{X}) \leq \dim(\mathcal{Y})$, let $A \in U(\mathcal{X}, \mathcal{Y})$ be an isometry, and let $\Phi \in C(\mathcal{X}, \mathcal{Y})$ be the isometric channel defined by

$$\Phi(X) = AXA^* \qquad (2.193)$$

for all $X \in L(\mathcal{X})$. The set $\{A^*A\}$ contains a single nonzero operator, and is therefore linearly independent. By Theorem 2.31, Φ is an extreme point of the set $C(\mathcal{X}, \mathcal{Y})$.

Example 2.33 Let $\Sigma = \{0,1\}$ denote the binary alphabet, and let $\mathcal{X} = \mathbb{C}^{\Sigma}$ and $\mathcal{Y} = \mathbb{C}^{\Sigma \times \Sigma}$. Also define operators $A_0, A_1 \in L(\mathcal{X}, \mathcal{Y})$ as

$$\begin{aligned} A_0 &= \frac{1}{\sqrt{6}}\left(2E_{00,0} + E_{01,1} + E_{10,1}\right), \\ A_1 &= \frac{1}{\sqrt{6}}\left(2E_{11,1} + E_{01,0} + E_{10,0}\right). \end{aligned} \qquad (2.194)$$

(Elements of the form $(a,b) \in \Sigma \times \Sigma$ have been written as ab for the sake of clarity.) Expressed as matrices (with respect to the natural orderings of Σ and $\Sigma \times \Sigma$), these operators are as follows:

$$A_0 = \frac{1}{\sqrt{6}} \begin{pmatrix} 2 & 0 \\ 0 & 1 \\ 0 & 1 \\ 0 & 0 \end{pmatrix} \quad \text{and} \quad A_1 = \frac{1}{\sqrt{6}} \begin{pmatrix} 0 & 0 \\ 1 & 0 \\ 1 & 0 \\ 0 & 2 \end{pmatrix}. \tag{2.195}$$

Now, define a channel $\Phi \in C(\mathcal{X}, \mathcal{Y})$ as

$$\Phi(X) = A_0 X A_0^* + A_1 X A_1^* \tag{2.196}$$

for every $X \in L(\mathcal{X})$. It holds that

$$A_0^* A_0 = \frac{1}{3} \begin{pmatrix} 2 & 0 \\ 0 & 1 \end{pmatrix}, \qquad A_0^* A_1 = \frac{1}{3} \begin{pmatrix} 0 & 0 \\ 1 & 0 \end{pmatrix},$$

$$A_1^* A_0 = \frac{1}{3} \begin{pmatrix} 0 & 1 \\ 0 & 0 \end{pmatrix}, \qquad A_1^* A_1 = \frac{1}{3} \begin{pmatrix} 1 & 0 \\ 0 & 2 \end{pmatrix}. \tag{2.197}$$

The set

$$\{A_0^* A_0, A_0^* A_1, A_1^* A_0, A_1^* A_1\} \tag{2.198}$$

is linearly independent, and therefore Theorem 2.31 implies that Φ is an extreme point of $C(\mathcal{X}, \mathcal{Y})$.

2.3 Measurements

Measurements provide the mechanism through which classical information may be extracted from quantum states. This section defines measurements, and various notions connected with measurements, and provides a basic mathematical development of this concept.

2.3.1 *Two Equivalent Definitions of Measurements*

When a hypothetical observer measures a register, the observer obtains a classical measurement outcome (as opposed to a description of the state of the register, for instance). In general, this measurement outcome is generated at random, according to a probability distribution that is determined by the measurement together with the state of the register immediately before the measurement was performed. In this way, measurements allow one to associate a meaning to the density operator description of quantum states, at least insofar as the density operators determine the probabilities with which different classical outcomes occur for each possible measurement.

Measurements can be defined in mathematical terms in two different, but equivalent, ways. Both ways will be described in this section, and their equivalence will be explained.

Measurements Defined by Measurement Operators

The following definition represents the first formulation of measurements to be described in this book. The precise mathematical meaning of the term *measurement* used throughout this book coincides with this definition.

Definition 2.34 A *measurement* is a function of the form

$$\mu\colon \Sigma \to \mathrm{Pos}(\mathcal{X}), \tag{2.199}$$

for some choice of an alphabet Σ and a complex Euclidean space $\mathcal{X}$, satisfying the constraint

$$\sum_{a\in\Sigma} \mu(a) = \mathbb{1}_{\mathcal{X}}. \tag{2.200}$$

The set Σ is the set of *measurement outcomes* of this measurement, and each operator $\mu(a)$ is the *measurement operator* associated with the outcome $a \in \Sigma$.

When a measurement μ is performed on a given register X, it must be assumed that μ takes the form (2.199), for some choice of an alphabet Σ and for $\mathcal{X}$ being the complex Euclidean space associated with X. Two things happen when such a measurement is performed, assuming the state of X immediately prior to the measurement is $\rho \in \mathrm{D}(\mathcal{X})$:

1. An element of Σ is selected at random. The probability distribution that describes this random selection is represented by the probability vector $p \in \mathcal{P}(\Sigma)$ defined as

$$p(a) = \langle \mu(a), \rho \rangle \tag{2.201}$$

   for each $a \in \Sigma$.
2. The register X ceases to exist, in the sense that it no longer has a defined state and cannot be considered in further calculations.

It is evident from the first item that the probabilities associated with the outcomes of a given measurement depend linearly on the state that is measured. It is also evident that the probability vector $p \in \mathcal{P}(\Sigma)$ defined by (2.201) is indeed a probability vector: as ρ and $\mu(a)$ are both positive semidefinite, their inner product $\langle \mu(a), \rho \rangle$ is nonnegative, and summing these values gives

$$\sum_{a \in \Sigma} p(a) = \sum_{a \in \Sigma} \langle \mu(a), \rho \rangle = \langle \mathbb{1}_{\mathcal{X}}, \rho \rangle = \mathrm{Tr}(\rho) = 1. \qquad (2.202)$$

The assumption that registers cease to exist after being measured is not universal within quantum information theory – an alternative definition, in which the states of registers after they are measured is specified, does not make this requirement. Measurements of this alternative type, which are called *nondestructive measurements* in this book, are discussed in greater detail in Section 2.3.2. Nondestructive measurements can, however, be described as compositions of ordinary measurements (as described above) and channels. For this reason, no generality is lost in making the assumption that registers cease to exist upon being measured.

It is sometimes convenient to specify a measurement by describing its measurement operators as a collection indexed by its set of measurement outcomes. In particular, when one refers to a measurement as a collection

$$\{P_a : a \in \Sigma\} \subset \mathrm{Pos}(\mathcal{X}), \qquad (2.203)$$

it is to be understood that the measurement is given by $\mu \colon \Sigma \to \mathrm{Pos}(\mathcal{X})$, where $\mu(a) = P_a$ for each $a \in \Sigma$.

Measurements as Channels

The second formulation of measurements, which is equivalent to the first, essentially describes measurements as channels whose outputs are stored in classical registers. The following definition of *quantum-to-classical channels* makes this notion precise.

Definition 2.35 Let $\Phi \in \mathrm{C}(\mathcal{X}, \mathcal{Y})$ be a channel, for complex Euclidean spaces $\mathcal{X}$ and $\mathcal{Y}$. It is said that Φ is a *quantum-to-classical channel* if

$$\Phi = \Delta\Phi, \qquad (2.204)$$

for $\Delta \in \mathrm{C}(\mathcal{Y})$ denoting the completely dephasing channel, defined with respect to the space $\mathcal{Y}$.

An equivalent condition for a channel $\Phi \in \mathrm{C}(\mathcal{X}, \mathcal{Y})$ to be a quantum-to-classical channel is that $\Phi(\rho)$ is a diagonal density operator for every $\rho \in \mathrm{D}(\mathcal{X})$. The following simple proposition establishes that this is so.

Proposition 2.36 Let $\Phi \in \mathrm{C}(\mathcal{X}, \mathcal{Y})$ be a channel, for complex Euclidean spaces $\mathcal{X}$ and $\mathcal{Y}$. It holds that Φ is a quantum-to-classical channel if and only if $\Phi(\rho)$ is diagonal for every $\rho \in \mathrm{D}(\mathcal{X})$.

Proof If Φ is a quantum-to-classical channel, then

$$\Phi(\rho) = \Delta(\Phi(\rho)), \tag{2.205}$$

and therefore $\Phi(\rho)$ is diagonal, for every density operator $\rho \in D(\mathcal{X})$.

Conversely, if $\Phi(\rho)$ is diagonal, then $\Phi(\rho) = \Delta(\Phi(\rho))$, and therefore

$$(\Phi - \Delta\Phi)(\rho) = 0, \tag{2.206}$$

for every $\rho \in D(\mathcal{X})$. As the density operators $D(\mathcal{X})$ span all of $L(\mathcal{X})$, it follows that $\Phi = \Delta\Phi$, and therefore Φ is a quantum-to-classical channel. $\square$

The next theorem reveals the equivalence between quantum-to-classical channels and measurements. In essence, quantum-to-classical channels of the form $\Phi \in C(\mathcal{X}, \mathcal{Y})$ represent precisely those channels that can be realized as a measurement of a register X, according to a measurement $\mu: \Sigma \to \mathrm{Pos}(\mathcal{X})$, followed by the measurement outcome being stored in a register Y having classical state set Σ.

Theorem 2.37 *Let $\mathcal{X}$ be a complex Euclidean space, let Σ be an alphabet, and let $\mathcal{Y} = \mathbb{C}^\Sigma$. The following two complementary facts hold:*

1. *For every quantum-to-classical channel $\Phi \in C(\mathcal{X}, \mathcal{Y})$, there exists a unique measurement $\mu: \Sigma \to \mathrm{Pos}(\mathcal{X})$ for which the equation*

$$\Phi(X) = \sum_{a \in \Sigma} \langle \mu(a), X \rangle E_{a,a} \tag{2.207}$$

   holds for all $X \in L(\mathcal{X})$.
2. *For every measurement $\mu: \Sigma \to \mathrm{Pos}(\mathcal{X})$, the mapping $\Phi \in T(\mathcal{X}, \mathcal{Y})$ defined by (2.207) for all $X \in L(\mathcal{X})$ is a quantum-to-classical channel.*

Proof Assume first that $\Phi \in C(\mathcal{X}, \mathcal{Y})$ is a quantum-to-classical channel. It therefore holds that

$$\Phi(X) = \Delta(\Phi(X)) = \sum_{a \in \Sigma} \langle E_{a,a}, \Phi(X) \rangle E_{a,a} = \sum_{a \in \Sigma} \langle \Phi^*(E_{a,a}), X \rangle E_{a,a} \tag{2.208}$$

for all $X \in L(\mathcal{X})$. Define a function $\mu: \Sigma \to L(\mathcal{X})$ as

$$\mu(a) = \Phi^*(E_{a,a}) \tag{2.209}$$

for each $a \in \Sigma$. As Φ is positive, so too is Φ^* (by Proposition 2.18), and therefore $\mu(a) \in \mathrm{Pos}(\mathcal{X})$ for each $a \in \Sigma$. Moreover, as Φ preserves trace, it holds (by Theorem 2.26) that Φ^* is unital, and therefore

$$\sum_{a \in \Sigma} \mu(a) = \sum_{a \in \Sigma} \Phi^*(E_{a,a}) = \Phi^*(\mathbb{1}_{\mathcal{Y}}) = \mathbb{1}_{\mathcal{X}}. \tag{2.210}$$

It follows that μ is a measurement for which (2.207) holds for all $X \in L(\mathcal{X})$.

Toward proving the uniqueness of the measurement μ satisfying (2.207) for all $X \in L(\mathcal{X})$, let $\nu \colon \Sigma \to \mathrm{Pos}(\mathcal{X})$ be an arbitrary measurement for which the equation

$$\Phi(X) = \sum_{a \in \Sigma} \langle \nu(a), X \rangle \, E_{a,a} \tag{2.211}$$

holds for all $X \in L(\mathcal{X})$. One then has that

$$\sum_{a \in \Sigma} \langle \mu(a) - \nu(a), X \rangle \, E_{a,a} = 0 \tag{2.212}$$

for all $X \in L(\mathcal{X})$, which implies that $\nu(a) = \mu(a)$ for every $a \in \Sigma$, and completes the proof of the first fact.

Now assume that $\mu \colon \Sigma \to \mathrm{Pos}(\mathcal{X})$ is a measurement, and let $\Phi \in T(\mathcal{X}, \mathcal{Y})$ be defined by (2.207). The Choi representation of this map is

$$J(\Phi) = \sum_{a \in \Sigma} E_{a,a} \otimes \overline{\mu(a)}. \tag{2.213}$$

This is a positive semidefinite operator, and it holds that

$$\mathrm{Tr}_{\mathcal{Y}}(J(\Phi)) = \sum_{a \in \Sigma} \overline{\mu(a)} = \overline{\mathbb{1}_{\mathcal{X}}} = \mathbb{1}_{\mathcal{X}}. \tag{2.214}$$

By Corollary 2.27, it holds that Φ is a channel. It is evident from inspection that $\Phi(\rho)$ is diagonal for every $\rho \in D(\mathcal{X})$, and therefore Φ is a quantum-to-classical channel by Proposition 2.36, which completes the proof of the second statement. $\qquad\square$

As the following proposition establishes, the set of quantum-to-classical channels of the form $\Phi \in C(\mathcal{X}, \mathcal{Y})$ is both compact and convex.

Proposition 2.38 *Let $\mathcal{X}$ and $\mathcal{Y}$ be complex Euclidean spaces. The set of quantum-to-classical channels having the form $\Phi \in C(\mathcal{X}, \mathcal{Y})$ is compact and convex.*

Proof It will first be observed that the set of quantum-to-classical channels of the form $\Phi \in C(\mathcal{X}, \mathcal{Y})$ is given by

$$\{\Delta\Psi \colon \Psi \in C(\mathcal{X}, \mathcal{Y})\}, \tag{2.215}$$

for $\Delta \in C(\mathcal{Y})$ being the completely dephasing channel defined with respect to the space $\mathcal{Y}$. Indeed, for every channel $\Psi \in C(\mathcal{X}, \mathcal{Y})$, it holds that $\Delta\Psi$ is a quantum-to-classical channel by virtue of the fact that the channel Δ is idempotent (i.e., $\Delta\Delta = \Delta$). On the other hand, every quantum-to-classical channel Φ satisfies $\Phi = \Delta\Phi$ by definition, and is therefore represented in the set (2.215) by taking $\Psi = \Phi$.

By Proposition 2.28, the set $C(\mathcal{X}, \mathcal{Y})$ is compact and convex. The mapping $\Psi \mapsto \Delta\Psi$ defined on $C(\mathcal{X}, \mathcal{Y})$ is continuous, and therefore it maps $C(\mathcal{X}, \mathcal{Y})$ to a compact and convex set. The image of $C(\mathcal{X}, \mathcal{Y})$ under this mapping is precisely the set (2.215), which coincides with the set of quantum-to-classical channels of the form $\Phi \in C(\mathcal{X}, \mathcal{Y})$, so the proof is complete. $\qquad\square$

2.3.2 Basic Notions Concerning Measurements

The subsections that follow introduce various notions and facts connected with measurements.

Product Measurements

Suppose $\mathsf{X} = (\mathsf{Y}_1, \ldots, \mathsf{Y}_n)$ is a compound register. One may then consider a collection of measurements

$$\mu_1 \colon \Sigma_1 \to \mathrm{Pos}(\mathcal{Y}_1)$$
$$\vdots \qquad\qquad\qquad (2.216)$$
$$\mu_n \colon \Sigma_n \to \mathrm{Pos}(\mathcal{Y}_n)$$

to be performed independently on the registers $\mathsf{Y}_1, \ldots, \mathsf{Y}_n$. Such a process may be viewed as a single measurement

$$\mu \colon \Sigma_1 \times \cdots \times \Sigma_n \to \mathrm{Pos}(\mathcal{X}) \qquad (2.217)$$

on X that is defined as

$$\mu(a_1, \ldots, a_n) = \mu_1(a_1) \otimes \cdots \otimes \mu_n(a_n) \qquad (2.218)$$

for each tuple $(a_1, \ldots, a_n) \in \Sigma_1 \times \cdots \times \Sigma_n$. A measurement μ of this sort is said to be a *product measurement* on X.

It may be verified that when a product measurement is performed on a product state, the measurement outcomes resulting from the individual measurements are independently distributed.

Partial Measurements

Suppose $\mathsf{X} = (\mathsf{Y}_1, \ldots, \mathsf{Y}_n)$ is a compound register, and a measurement

$$\mu \colon \Sigma \to \mathrm{Pos}(\mathcal{Y}_k) \qquad (2.219)$$

is performed only on the register Y_k, for a single choice of $k \in \{1, \ldots, n\}$. Such a measurement must not only produce a measurement outcome $a \in \Sigma$, but must also determine the resulting state of the register

$$(\mathsf{Y}_1, \ldots, \mathsf{Y}_{k-1}, \mathsf{Y}_{k+1}, \ldots, \mathsf{Y}_n), \tag{2.220}$$

conditioned on the measurement outcome that was obtained. For a given state $\rho \in \mathrm{D}(\mathcal{X})$ of the register X, the probability for each measurement outcome to appear, along with the corresponding post-measurement state of the register (2.220), may be calculated by considering the quantum-to-classical channel that corresponds to the measurement μ.

Let this quantum-to-classical channel be denoted by $\Phi \in \mathrm{C}(\mathcal{Y}_k, \mathcal{Z})$, for $\mathcal{Z} = \mathbb{C}^\Sigma$, so that

$$\Phi(Y) = \sum_{a \in \Sigma} \langle \mu(a), Y \rangle E_{a,a} \tag{2.221}$$

for every $Y \in \mathrm{L}(\mathcal{Y}_k)$. Consider the state of the compound register

$$(\mathsf{Z}, \mathsf{Y}_1, \ldots, \mathsf{Y}_{k-1}, \mathsf{Y}_{k+1}, \ldots, \mathsf{Y}_n) \tag{2.222}$$

obtained by applying the channel Φ to Y_k, followed by the application of a channel that performs the permutation of registers

$$(\mathsf{Y}_1, \ldots, \mathsf{Y}_{k-1}, \mathsf{Z}, \mathsf{Y}_{k+1}, \ldots, \mathsf{Y}_n) \to (\mathsf{Z}, \mathsf{Y}_1, \ldots, \mathsf{Y}_{k-1}, \mathsf{Y}_{k+1}, \ldots, \mathsf{Y}_n) \tag{2.223}$$

without changing the contents of these individual registers. The state of the register (2.222) that results may be written explicitly as

$$\sum_{a \in \Sigma} E_{a,a} \otimes \mathrm{Tr}_{\mathcal{Y}_k} \big((\mathbb{1}_{\mathcal{Y}_1 \otimes \cdots \otimes \mathcal{Y}_{k-1}} \otimes \mu(a) \otimes \mathbb{1}_{\mathcal{Y}_{k+1} \otimes \cdots \otimes \mathcal{Y}_n}) \rho \big). \tag{2.224}$$

The state (2.224) is a classical–quantum state, and is naturally associated with the ensemble

$$\eta : \Sigma \to \mathrm{Pos}(\mathcal{Y}_1 \otimes \cdots \otimes \mathcal{Y}_{k-1} \otimes \mathcal{Y}_{k+1} \otimes \cdots \otimes \mathcal{Y}_n) \tag{2.225}$$

defined as

$$\eta(a) = \mathrm{Tr}_{\mathcal{Y}_k} \big((\mathbb{1}_{\mathcal{Y}_1 \otimes \cdots \otimes \mathcal{Y}_{k-1}} \otimes \mu(a) \otimes \mathbb{1}_{\mathcal{Y}_{k+1} \otimes \cdots \otimes \mathcal{Y}_n}) \rho \big) \tag{2.226}$$

for each $a \in \Sigma$. This ensemble describes the distribution of measurement outcomes of the measurement μ and the states of the remaining registers that result. That is, each measurement outcome $a \in \Sigma$ appears with probability

$$\mathrm{Tr}(\eta(a)) = \langle \mu(a), \rho[\mathsf{Y}_k] \rangle, \tag{2.227}$$

and conditioned on an outcome $a \in \Sigma$ that appears with positive probability, the resulting state of $(\mathsf{Y}_1, \ldots, \mathsf{Y}_{k-1}, \mathsf{Y}_{k+1}, \ldots, \mathsf{Y}_n)$ becomes

$$\frac{\eta(a)}{\mathrm{Tr}(\eta(a))} = \frac{\mathrm{Tr}_{\mathcal{Y}_k} \big((\mathbb{1}_{\mathcal{Y}_1 \otimes \cdots \otimes \mathcal{Y}_{k-1}} \otimes \mu(a) \otimes \mathbb{1}_{\mathcal{Y}_{k+1} \otimes \cdots \otimes \mathcal{Y}_n}) \rho \big)}{\langle \mu(a), \rho[\mathsf{Y}_k] \rangle}. \tag{2.228}$$

Example 2.39 Let Σ be an alphabet, and let Y and Z be registers whose classical state sets are given by Σ, so that $\mathcal{Y} = \mathbb{C}^{\Sigma}$ and $\mathcal{Z} = \mathbb{C}^{\Sigma}$. Define a state $\tau \in D(\mathcal{Y} \otimes \mathcal{Z})$ as

$$\tau = \frac{1}{|\Sigma|} \sum_{b,c \in \Sigma} E_{b,c} \otimes E_{b,c}, \tag{2.229}$$

and consider an arbitrary measurement $\mu \colon \Gamma \to \mathrm{Pos}(\mathcal{Y})$. If this measurement is performed on Y when the pair (Y, Z) is in the state τ, then each outcome $a \in \Gamma$ appears with probability

$$p(a) = \langle \mu(a), \rho[\mathsf{Y}] \rangle = \frac{\mathrm{Tr}(\mu(a))}{|\Sigma|}. \tag{2.230}$$

Conditioned on the event that the measurement outcome a appears, the state of Z becomes

$$
\begin{aligned}
&\frac{1}{p(a)} \mathrm{Tr}_{\mathcal{Y}} \big((\mu(a) \otimes \mathbb{1}_{\mathcal{Z}}) \tau \big) \\
&= \frac{|\Sigma|}{\mathrm{Tr}(\mu(a))} \frac{1}{|\Sigma|} \sum_{b,c \in \Sigma} \mathrm{Tr}(\mu(a) E_{b,c}) E_{b,c} = \frac{\mu(a)^{\mathsf{T}}}{\mathrm{Tr}(\mu(a))}.
\end{aligned}
\tag{2.231}
$$

Projective Measurements and Naimark's Theorem

A measurement $\mu \colon \Sigma \to \mathrm{Pos}(\mathcal{X})$ is said to be a *projective measurement* if each of its measurement operators is a projection: $\mu(a) \in \mathrm{Proj}(\mathcal{X})$ for every $a \in \Sigma$.

The following proposition demonstrates that the measurement operators of a projective measurement must be pairwise orthogonal, and must therefore project onto orthogonal subspaces. For a projective measurement of the form $\mu \colon \Sigma \to \mathrm{Pos}(\mathcal{X})$, there can therefore be no more than $\dim(\mathcal{X})$ distinct values of $a \in \Sigma$ for which $\mu(a)$ is nonzero.

Proposition 2.40 *Let Σ be an alphabet, let $\mathcal{X}$ be a complex Euclidean space, and let $\mu \colon \Sigma \to \mathrm{Pos}(\mathcal{X})$ be a projective measurement. The set*

$$\{ \mu(a) \colon a \in \Sigma \} \tag{2.232}$$

is an orthogonal set.

Proof As μ is a measurement, it holds that

$$\sum_{a \in \Sigma} \mu(a) = \mathbb{1}_{\mathcal{X}}, \tag{2.233}$$

and therefore this sum must square to itself:

$$\sum_{a,b\in\Sigma} \mu(a)\mu(b) = \left(\sum_{a\in\Sigma}\mu(a)\right)^2 = \sum_{a\in\Sigma}\mu(a). \tag{2.234}$$

Because each operator $\mu(a)$ is a projection operator, it follows that

$$\sum_{a,b\in\Sigma} \mu(a)\mu(b) = \sum_{a\in\Sigma}\mu(a) + \sum_{\substack{a,b\in\Sigma \\ a\neq b}}\mu(a)\mu(b), \tag{2.235}$$

and therefore

$$\sum_{\substack{a,b\in\Sigma \\ a\neq b}}\mu(a)\mu(b) = 0. \tag{2.236}$$

Taking the trace of both sides of this equation yields

$$\sum_{\substack{a,b\in\Sigma \\ a\neq b}}\langle\mu(a),\mu(b)\rangle = 0. \tag{2.237}$$

The inner product of any two positive semidefinite operators is nonnegative, and therefore $\langle\mu(a),\mu(b)\rangle = 0$ for all $a,b\in\Sigma$ with $a\neq b$, which completes the proof. $\qquad\square$

For any orthonormal basis $\{x_a : a\in\Sigma\}$ of a complex Euclidean space $\mathcal{X} = \mathbb{C}^\Sigma$, the measurement $\mu\colon \Sigma\to\mathrm{Pos}(\mathcal{X})$ defined as

$$\mu(a) = x_a x_a^* \tag{2.238}$$

for each $a\in\Sigma$ is an example of a projective measurement. A measurement of this sort is known more specifically as a *complete projective measurement*. This is the measurement that is commonly referred to as the *measurement with respect to the basis* $\{x_a : a\in\Sigma\}$.

Example 2.41 Let Σ be an alphabet and let $\mathcal{X} = \mathbb{C}^\Sigma$. The *measurement with respect to the standard basis* of $\mathcal{X}$ is the measurement $\mu\colon \Sigma\to\mathrm{Pos}(\mathcal{X})$ defined as

$$\mu(a) = E_{a,a} \tag{2.239}$$

for each $a\in\Sigma$. For a given state $\rho\in\mathrm{D}(\mathcal{X})$, the probability associated with each measurement outcome $a\in\Sigma$, were this state to be measured according to μ, is equal to the corresponding diagonal entry $\rho(a,a)$. One may also observe that the quantum-to-classical channel associated with this measurement is the completely dephasing channel $\Delta\in\mathrm{C}(\mathcal{X})$.

The following theorem, known as *Naimark's theorem*, establishes a link between arbitrary measurements and projective measurements. It implies that any measurement can be viewed as a projective measurement on a compound register that includes the original register as a subregister.

Theorem 2.42 (Naimark's theorem) *Let $\mathcal{X}$ be a complex Euclidean space, let Σ be an alphabet, let $\mu\colon \Sigma \to \mathrm{Pos}(\mathcal{X})$ be a measurement, and let $\mathcal{Y} = \mathbb{C}^\Sigma$. There exists an isometry $A \in \mathrm{U}(\mathcal{X}, \mathcal{X} \otimes \mathcal{Y})$ such that*

$$\mu(a) = A^*(\mathbb{1}_\mathcal{X} \otimes E_{a,a})A \tag{2.240}$$

for every $a \in \Sigma$.

Proof Define an operator $A \in \mathrm{L}(\mathcal{X}, \mathcal{X} \otimes \mathcal{Y})$ as

$$A = \sum_{a \in \Sigma} \sqrt{\mu(a)} \otimes e_a. \tag{2.241}$$

It holds that

$$A^*A = \sum_{a \in \Sigma} \mu(a) = \mathbb{1}_\mathcal{X}, \tag{2.242}$$

and therefore A is an isometry. The required equation (2.240) holds for each $a \in \Sigma$, so the proof is complete. $\qquad\square$

Corollary 2.43 *Let $\mathcal{X}$ be a complex Euclidean space, let Σ be an alphabet, and let $\mu\colon \Sigma \to \mathrm{Pos}(\mathcal{X})$ be a measurement. Also let $\mathcal{Y} = \mathbb{C}^\Sigma$ and let $u \in \mathcal{Y}$ be a unit vector. There exists a projective measurement $\nu\colon \Sigma \to \mathrm{Pos}(\mathcal{X} \otimes \mathcal{Y})$ such that*

$$\langle \nu(a), X \otimes uu^* \rangle = \langle \mu(a), X \rangle \tag{2.243}$$

for every $X \in \mathrm{L}(\mathcal{X})$.

Proof Let $A \in \mathrm{U}(\mathcal{X}, \mathcal{X} \otimes \mathcal{Y})$ be the isometry whose existence is implied by Theorem 2.42. Choose $U \in \mathrm{U}(\mathcal{X} \otimes \mathcal{Y})$ to be any unitary operator for which the equation

$$U(\mathbb{1}_\mathcal{X} \otimes u) = A \tag{2.244}$$

is satisfied, and define $\nu\colon \Sigma \to \mathrm{Pos}(\mathcal{X} \otimes \mathcal{Y})$ as

$$\nu(a) = U^*(\mathbb{1}_\mathcal{X} \otimes E_{a,a})U \tag{2.245}$$

for each $a \in \Sigma$. It holds that ν is a projective measurement, and moreover

$$\begin{aligned}\langle \nu(a), X \otimes uu^* \rangle &= \langle (\mathbb{1}_\mathcal{X} \otimes u^*)U^*(\mathbb{1}_\mathcal{X} \otimes E_{a,a})U(\mathbb{1}_\mathcal{X} \otimes u), X \rangle \\ &= \langle A^*(\mathbb{1}_\mathcal{X} \otimes E_{a,a})A, X \rangle = \langle \mu(a), X \rangle \end{aligned} \tag{2.246}$$

for each $a \in \Sigma$, as required. $\qquad\square$

Information-Complete Measurements

States of registers are uniquely determined by the measurement statistics they generate. More precisely, the knowledge of the probability associated with every outcome of every measurement that could be performed on a given register is sufficient to obtain a description of that register's state. In fact, something stronger may be said, which is that there exist choices of measurements that uniquely determine every possible state of a register by the measurement statistics that they alone generate. Such measurements, which are known as *information-complete measurements*, are characterized by the property that their measurement operators span the entire space of operators from which they are drawn.

In more explicit terms, a measurement $\mu\colon \Sigma \to \mathrm{Pos}(\mathcal{X})$ on a complex Euclidean space $\mathcal{X}$ is said to be an *information-complete measurement* if it holds that

$$\mathrm{span}\{\mu(a)\colon a \in \Sigma\} = \mathrm{L}(\mathcal{X}). \tag{2.247}$$

For any such measurement, and for any choice of $\rho \in \mathrm{D}(\mathcal{X})$, it holds that the probability vector $p \in \mathcal{P}(\Sigma)$ defined by $p(a) = \langle \mu(a), \rho \rangle$ uniquely determines the state ρ. This fact is evident from the following proposition.

Proposition 2.44 *Let Σ be an alphabet, let $\mathcal{X}$ be a complex Euclidean space, and let $\{A_a\colon a \in \Sigma\} \subset \mathrm{L}(\mathcal{X})$ be a collection of operators for which*

$$\mathrm{span}\{A_a\colon a \in \Sigma\} = \mathrm{L}(\mathcal{X}). \tag{2.248}$$

The mapping $\phi\colon \mathrm{L}(\mathcal{X}) \to \mathbb{C}^\Sigma$ defined by

$$(\phi(X))(a) = \langle A_a, X \rangle, \tag{2.249}$$

for each $X \in \mathrm{L}(\mathcal{X})$ and $a \in \Sigma$, is an injective mapping.

Proof Let $X, Y \in \mathrm{L}(\mathcal{X})$ satisfy $\phi(X) = \phi(Y)$, so that

$$\langle A_a, X - Y \rangle = 0 \tag{2.250}$$

for every $a \in \Sigma$. As $\{A_a\colon a \in \Sigma\}$ spans $\mathrm{L}(\mathcal{X})$, it follows by the conjugate linearity of the inner product that

$$\langle Z, X - Y \rangle = 0 \tag{2.251}$$

for every $Z \in \mathrm{L}(\mathcal{X})$, and consequently $X - Y = 0$, which completes the proof. $\qquad\square$

The following example provides one way of constructing information-complete measurements, for any choice of a complex Euclidean space.

Example 2.45 Let Σ be an alphabet, let $\mathcal{X} = \mathbb{C}^{\Sigma}$, and let

$$\{\rho_{a,b} \colon (a,b) \in \Sigma \times \Sigma\} \subseteq D(\mathcal{X}) \tag{2.252}$$

be a collection of density operators that spans all of $L(\mathcal{X})$. One such set was constructed in Example 2.7. Also define

$$Q = \sum_{(a,b)\in\Sigma\times\Sigma} \rho_{a,b} \tag{2.253}$$

and observe that Q is necessarily positive definite; if this were not so, there would exist a nonzero vector $u \in \mathcal{X}$ satisfying $\langle \rho_{a,b}, uu^* \rangle = 0$ for each pair $(a,b) \in \Sigma \times \Sigma$, in contradiction with Proposition 2.44. It may be verified that the function $\mu \colon \Sigma \times \Sigma \to \mathrm{Pos}(\mathcal{X})$, defined by

$$\mu(a,b) = Q^{-\frac{1}{2}} \rho_{a,b} Q^{-\frac{1}{2}} \tag{2.254}$$

for each $(a,b) \in \Sigma \times \Sigma$, is an information-complete measurement.

Nondestructive Measurements and Instruments

It is convenient in some situations to consider an alternative definition of measurements that does not dictate that registers are destroyed upon being measured. Instead, a measured register is left in some particular state that depends both on its initial state and on the measurement outcome obtained. More generally, one may consider that the measured register is transformed into another register as a result of the measurement process.

One specific alternative definition, which is frequently taken as the definition of a measurement by other authors, describes such a process by a collection

$$\{M_a \colon a \in \Sigma\} \subset L(\mathcal{X}), \tag{2.255}$$

where Σ is the alphabet of measurement outcomes and $\mathcal{X}$ is the complex Euclidean space corresponding to the register being measured, such that the constraint

$$\sum_{a\in\Sigma} M_a^* M_a = \mathbb{1}_{\mathcal{X}} \tag{2.256}$$

is satisfied. When this form of measurement is applied to a register X in a given state $\rho \in D(\mathcal{X})$, two things happen:

1. An element of Σ is selected at random, with each outcome $a \in \Sigma$ being obtained with probability $\langle M_a^* M_a, \rho \rangle$.

2. Conditioned on the measurement outcome $a \in \Sigma$ having been obtained, the state of the register X becomes

$$\frac{M_a \rho M_a^*}{\langle M_a^* M_a, \rho \rangle}. \tag{2.257}$$

Measurements of this sort will be referred to as *nondestructive measurements* in this book.

A somewhat more general notion of a measurement is described by a collection

$$\{\Phi_a : a \in \Sigma\} \subset \mathrm{CP}(\mathcal{X}, \mathcal{Y}), \tag{2.258}$$

where Σ is the measurement outcome alphabet, $\mathcal{X}$ is the complex Euclidean space corresponding to the register that is measured, and $\mathcal{Y}$ is an arbitrary complex Euclidean space. In this case, these mappings must necessarily sum to a channel:

$$\sum_{a \in \Sigma} \Phi_a \in \mathrm{C}(\mathcal{X}, \mathcal{Y}). \tag{2.259}$$

When this form of measurement is applied to a register X in a given state $\rho \in \mathrm{D}(\mathcal{X})$, two things happen:

1. An element of Σ is selected at random, with each outcome $a \in \Sigma$ being obtained with probability $\mathrm{Tr}(\Phi_a(\rho))$.
2. Conditioned on the measurement outcome $a \in \Sigma$ having been obtained, X is transformed into a new register Y having state

$$\frac{\Phi_a(\rho)}{\mathrm{Tr}(\Phi_a(\rho))}. \tag{2.260}$$

The generalized notion of a measurement obtained in this way is called an *instrument* (or a *quantum instrument*). Nondestructive measurements of the form (2.255) may be represented by instruments of the form (2.258) by defining

$$\Phi_a(X) = M_a X M_a^* \tag{2.261}$$

for each $a \in \Sigma$.

Processes that are expressible as instruments, including nondestructive measurements, can alternatively be described as compositions of channels and (ordinary) measurements. Specifically, for a given instrument of the form (2.258), one may introduce a (classical) register Z having classical state set Σ, and define a channel $\Phi \in \mathrm{C}(\mathcal{X}, \mathcal{Z} \otimes \mathcal{Y})$ as

$$\Phi(X) = \sum_{a \in \Sigma} E_{a,a} \otimes \Phi_a(X) \tag{2.262}$$

for every $X \in \mathrm{L}(\mathcal{X})$. The fact that Φ is indeed a channel follows directly from the constraints placed on a function of the form (2.258) that must be satisfied for it to be considered an instrument: the complete positivity of the collection of mappings $\{\Phi_a : a \in \Sigma\}$ implies that Φ is completely positive, while the condition (2.259) implies that Φ preserves trace.

Now, if such a channel Φ is applied to a register X, and then the register Z is measured with respect to the standard basis of $\mathcal{Z}$, the distribution of measurement outcomes, as well as the corresponding state of Y conditioned on each possible outcome, is identical to the process associated with the instrument (2.258), as described above.

2.3.3 Extremal Measurements and Ensembles

Measurements and ensembles may be regarded as elements of convex sets in a fairly straightforward way. A characterization of the extreme points of these sets is obtained below.

Convex Combinations of Measurements

For $\mathcal{X}$ being a complex Euclidean space and Σ being an alphabet, one may take convex combinations of measurements of the form $\mu : \Sigma \to \mathrm{Pos}(\mathcal{X})$ in the following way. For an alphabet Γ, a probability vector $p \in \mathcal{P}(\Gamma)$, and a collection $\{\mu_b : b \in \Gamma\}$ of measurements taking the form $\mu_b : \Sigma \to \mathrm{Pos}(\mathcal{X})$ for each $b \in \Gamma$, one defines the measurement

$$\mu = \sum_{b \in \Gamma} p(b)\mu_b \qquad (2.263)$$

by the equation

$$\mu(a) = \sum_{b \in \Gamma} p(b)\mu_b(a) \qquad (2.264)$$

holding for all $a \in \Sigma$. Equivalently, such a convex combination is taken with respect to the most straightforward way of regarding the set of all functions of the form $\theta : \Sigma \to \mathrm{Herm}(\mathcal{X})$ as a vector space over the real numbers.

An equivalent description of this notion may be obtained through the identification of each measurement $\mu : \Sigma \to \mathrm{Pos}(\mathcal{X})$ with its corresponding quantum-to-classical channel

$$\Phi_\mu(X) = \sum_{a \in \Sigma} \langle \mu(a), X \rangle E_{a,a}. \qquad (2.265)$$

Convex combinations of measurements then correspond to ordinary convex combinations of their associated channels.

The measurement described by the convex combination (2.263) may be viewed as being equivalent to a process whereby $b \in \Gamma$ is chosen according to the probability vector p, and the measurement μ_b is performed for the chosen symbol $b \in \Gamma$. The outcome of the measurement μ_b is taken as the output of the new measurement, while the symbol $b \in \Gamma$ is discarded.

Extremal Measurements

As was established by Proposition 2.38, the set of all quantum-to-classical channels is compact and convex. A measurement is said to be an *extremal measurement* if its corresponding quantum-to-classical channel corresponds to an extreme point of this set. The definition below states this condition in concrete terms. A characterization of extremal measurements is provided by the theorem that follows.

Definition 2.46   Let Σ be an alphabet and let $\mathcal{X}$ be a complex Euclidean space. A measurement $\mu \colon \Sigma \to \mathrm{Pos}(\mathcal{X})$ is an *extremal measurement* if, for all choices of measurements $\mu_0, \mu_1 \colon \Sigma \to \mathrm{Pos}(\mathcal{X})$ satisfying $\mu = \lambda \mu_0 + (1 - \lambda)\mu_1$ for some real number $\lambda \in (0, 1)$, one has $\mu_0 = \mu_1$.

Theorem 2.47   *Let $\mathcal{X}$ be a complex Euclidean space, let Σ be an alphabet, and let $\mu \colon \Sigma \to \mathrm{Pos}(\mathcal{X})$ be a measurement. It holds that μ is an extremal measurement if and only if, for every function $\theta \colon \Sigma \to \mathrm{Herm}(\mathcal{X})$ satisfying*

$$\sum_{a \in \Sigma} \theta(a) = 0 \qquad\qquad (2.266)$$

and $\mathrm{im}(\theta(a)) \subseteq \mathrm{im}(\mu(a))$ for every $a \in \Sigma$, one necessarily has that θ is identically zero: $\theta(a) = 0$ for each $a \in \Sigma$.

Proof   The theorem will be proved in the contrapositive form. Assume first that μ is not an extremal measurement, so there exist distinct measurements $\mu_0, \mu_1 \colon \Sigma \to \mathrm{Pos}(\mathcal{X})$ and a scalar value $\lambda \in (0, 1)$ for which

$$\mu = \lambda \mu_0 + (1 - \lambda)\mu_1. \qquad\qquad (2.267)$$

It follows that distinct measurements $\nu_0, \nu_1 \colon \Sigma \to \mathrm{Pos}(\mathcal{X})$ exist for which

$$\mu = \frac{\nu_0 + \nu_1}{2}. \qquad\qquad (2.268)$$

In particular, one may set

$$\begin{aligned} \nu_0 &= 2\lambda \mu_0 + (1 - 2\lambda)\mu_1 \quad \text{and} \quad \nu_1 = \mu_1, && \text{if } \lambda \le 1/2; \\ \nu_0 &= \mu_0 \quad \text{and} \quad \nu_1 = (2\lambda - 1)\mu_0 + (2 - 2\lambda)\mu_1, && \text{if } \lambda \ge 1/2. \end{aligned} \qquad (2.269)$$

Define $\theta\colon \Sigma \to \mathrm{Herm}(\mathcal{X})$ as $\theta(a) = \nu_0(a) - \nu_1(a)$ for each $a \in \Sigma$. It holds that

$$\sum_{a\in\Sigma} \theta(a) = \sum_{a\in\Sigma} \nu_0(a) - \sum_{a\in\Sigma} \nu_1(a) = \mathbb{1}_\mathcal{X} - \mathbb{1}_\mathcal{X} = 0. \tag{2.270}$$

Moreover,

$$\mathrm{im}(\theta(a)) \subseteq \mathrm{im}(\nu_0(a)) + \mathrm{im}(\nu_1(a)) = \mathrm{im}(\mu(a)) \tag{2.271}$$

for each $a \in \Sigma$, where the equality is a consequence of the facts that $\nu_0(a)$ and $\nu_1(a)$ are positive semidefinite and $\mu(a) = (\nu_0(a) + \nu_1(a))/2$. Finally, given that ν_0 and ν_1 are distinct, it is not the case that θ is identically zero.

Now assume that $\theta\colon \Sigma \to \mathrm{Herm}(\mathcal{X})$ is a function that is not identically zero, and that satisfies

$$\sum_{a\in\Sigma} \theta(a) = 0 \tag{2.272}$$

and $\mathrm{im}(\theta(a)) \subseteq \mathrm{im}(\mu(a))$ for every $a \in \Sigma$. For each $a \in \Sigma$, there must exist a positive real number $\varepsilon_a > 0$ for which

$$\mu(a) + \varepsilon_a \theta(a) \geq 0 \quad \text{and} \quad \mu(a) - \varepsilon_a \theta(a) \geq 0, \tag{2.273}$$

by virtue of the fact that $\mu(a)$ is positive semidefinite and $\theta(a)$ is a Hermitian operator with $\mathrm{im}(\theta(a)) \subseteq \mathrm{im}(\mu(a))$. Let

$$\varepsilon = \min\{\varepsilon_a \colon a \in \Sigma\} \tag{2.274}$$

and define

$$\mu_0 = \mu - \varepsilon\theta \quad \text{and} \quad \mu_1 = \mu + \varepsilon\theta. \tag{2.275}$$

It is evident that $\mu = (\mu_0 + \mu_1)/2$. As θ is not identically zero and ε is positive, it holds that μ_0 and μ_1 are distinct. Finally, it holds that μ_0 and μ_1 are measurements: the assumption (2.272) implies that

$$\sum_{a\in\Sigma} \mu_0(a) = \sum_{a\in\Sigma} \mu_1(a) = \sum_{a\in\Sigma} \mu(a) = \mathbb{1}_\mathcal{X}, \tag{2.276}$$

while the inequalities (2.273) imply that the measurement operators $\mu_0(a)$ and $\mu_1(a)$ are positive semidefinite for each $a \in \Sigma$. It has therefore been established that μ is not an extremal measurement, which completes the proof. $\qquad\square$

Theorem 2.47 has various implications, including the corollaries below. The first corollary makes the observation that extremal measurements can have at most $\dim(\mathcal{X})^2$ nonzero measurement operators.

Corollary 2.48 *Let $\mathcal{X}$ be a complex Euclidean space, let Σ be an alphabet, and let $\mu\colon \Sigma \to \mathrm{Pos}(\mathcal{X})$ be a measurement. If μ is an extremal measurement, then*

$$|\{a \in \Sigma\colon \mu(a) \neq 0\}| \leq \dim(\mathcal{X})^2. \tag{2.277}$$

Proof The corollary will be proved in the contrapositive form. Let

$$\Gamma = \{a \in \Sigma\colon \mu(a) \neq 0\}, \tag{2.278}$$

assume that $|\Gamma| > \dim(\mathcal{X})^2$, and consider the collection of measurement operators $\{\mu(a)\colon a \in \Gamma\}$ as a subset of the real vector space $\mathrm{Herm}(\mathcal{X})$. By the assumption $|\Gamma| > \dim(\mathcal{X})^2$, it must hold that the set $\{\mu(a)\colon a \in \Gamma\}$ is linearly dependent, and therefore there exist real numbers $\{\alpha_a\colon a \in \Gamma\}$, not all of which are zero, so that

$$\sum_{a \in \Gamma} \alpha_a \mu(a) = 0. \tag{2.279}$$

Define a function $\theta\colon \Sigma \to \mathrm{Herm}(\mathcal{X})$ as

$$\theta(a) = \begin{cases} \alpha_a \mu(a) & \text{if } a \in \Gamma \\ 0 & \text{if } a \notin \Gamma. \end{cases} \tag{2.280}$$

It holds that θ is not identically zero, and satisfies

$$\sum_{a \in \Sigma} \theta(a) = 0 \tag{2.281}$$

and $\mathrm{im}(\theta(a)) \subseteq \mathrm{im}(\mu(a))$ for every $a \in \Sigma$. By Theorem 2.47, measurement μ is therefore not an extremal measurement, which completes the proof. $\square$

Corollary 2.48, together with Proposition 2.38 and Theorem 1.10, implies the following corollary.

Corollary 2.49 *Let $\mathcal{X}$ be a complex Euclidean space, let Σ be an alphabet, and let $\mu\colon \Sigma \to \mathrm{Pos}(\mathcal{X})$ be a measurement. There exists an alphabet Γ, a probability vector $p \in \mathcal{P}(\Gamma)$, and a collection of measurements $\{\mu_b\colon b \in \Gamma\}$, taking the form $\mu_b\colon \Sigma \to \mathrm{Pos}(\mathcal{X})$ and satisfying*

$$|\{a \in \Sigma\colon \mu_b(a) \neq 0\}| \leq \dim(\mathcal{X})^2 \tag{2.282}$$

for each $b \in \Gamma$, such that

$$\mu = \sum_{b \in \Gamma} p(b)\mu_b. \tag{2.283}$$

For measurements whose measurement operators all have rank equal to one, Theorem 2.47 yields a simple criterion for extremality, as represented by the following corollary.

Corollary 2.50 *Let $\mathcal{X}$ be a complex Euclidean space, let Σ be an alphabet, and let $\{x_a : a \in \Sigma\} \subset \mathcal{X}$ be a collection of nonzero vectors satisfying*

$$\sum_{a \in \Sigma} x_a x_a^* = \mathbb{1}_{\mathcal{X}}. \tag{2.284}$$

The measurement $\mu \colon \Sigma \to \mathrm{Pos}(\mathcal{X})$ defined by $\mu(a) = x_a x_a^*$ for each $a \in \Sigma$ is an extremal measurement if and only if $\{x_a x_a^* : a \in \Sigma\} \subset \mathrm{Herm}(\mathcal{X})$ is a linearly independent set.

Proof The corollary follows from Theorem 2.47, together with the fact that a Hermitian operator $H \in \mathrm{Herm}(\mathcal{X})$ and a vector $u \in \mathcal{X}$ satisfy the condition $\mathrm{im}(H) \subseteq \mathrm{im}(uu^*)$ if and only if $H = \alpha uu^*$ for some $\alpha \in \mathbb{C}$. $\qquad\square$

Another implication of Theorem 2.47 is that projective measurements are necessarily extremal.

Corollary 2.51 *Let $\mathcal{X}$ be a complex Euclidean space, let Σ be an alphabet, and let $\mu \colon \Sigma \to \mathrm{Pos}(\mathcal{X})$ be a projective measurement. It holds that μ is an extremal measurement.*

Proof Let $\theta \colon \Sigma \to \mathrm{Herm}(\mathcal{X})$ be a function satisfying

$$\sum_{a \in \Sigma} \theta(a) = 0 \tag{2.285}$$

and $\mathrm{im}(\theta(a)) \subseteq \mathrm{im}(\mu(a))$ for every $a \in \Sigma$. For each $b \in \Sigma$, it therefore holds that

$$\sum_{a \in \Sigma} \mu(b)\theta(a) = 0. \tag{2.286}$$

By Proposition 2.40, the collection $\{\mu(b) : b \in \Sigma\}$ is orthogonal. Therefore, every vector in the image of $\theta(a)$ must be orthogonal to every vector in the image of $\mu(b)$ whenever $a \neq b$, so that

$$\mu(b)\theta(a) = \begin{cases} \theta(a) & \text{if } a = b \\ 0 & \text{if } a \neq b. \end{cases} \tag{2.287}$$

It follows that $\theta(b) = 0$ for every $b \in \Sigma$, and therefore the function θ is identically zero. As this is so for every choice of θ, as described above, it follows from Theorem 2.47 that μ is an extremal measurement. $\qquad\square$

Convex Combinations of Ensembles of States

Convex combinations of ensembles of states may be defined in essentially the same way that convex combinations of measurements are defined. That is, if $\mathcal{X}$ is a complex Euclidean space, Σ and Γ are alphabets, $p \in \mathcal{P}(\Gamma)$ is a probability vector, and

$$\eta_b : \Sigma \rightarrow \mathrm{Pos}(\mathcal{X}) \tag{2.288}$$

is an ensemble of states for each $b \in \Gamma$, then the function $\eta : \Sigma \rightarrow \mathrm{Pos}(\mathcal{X})$ defined by

$$\eta(a) = \sum_{b \in \Gamma} p(b) \eta_b(a) \tag{2.289}$$

for every $a \in \Sigma$ is also an ensemble. One writes

$$\eta = \sum_{b \in \Gamma} p(b) \eta_b \tag{2.290}$$

in this situation. If a density operator $\rho_b \in \mathrm{D}(\mathcal{X})$, representing the average state of the ensemble η_b, is defined as

$$\rho_b = \sum_{a \in \Sigma} \eta_b(a) \tag{2.291}$$

for each $b \in \Gamma$, then it must hold that the average state of the ensemble η is given by

$$\sum_{a \in \Sigma} \eta(a) = \sum_{b \in \Gamma} p(b) \rho_b. \tag{2.292}$$

It is a straightforward consequence of the spectral theorem (as represented by Corollary 1.4) that the extreme points of the set of all ensembles of the form $\eta : \Sigma \rightarrow \mathrm{Pos}(\mathcal{X})$ take a simple form; they are the ensembles η that are defined as

$$\eta(a) = \begin{cases} uu^* & \text{if } a = b \\ 0 & \text{if } a \neq b, \end{cases} \tag{2.293}$$

for some choice of a unit vector $u \in \mathcal{X}$ and a symbol $b \in \Sigma$.

In some situations, however, it is appropriate to consider just the subset of ensembles of the form $\eta : \Sigma \rightarrow \mathrm{Pos}(\mathcal{X})$ that have a particular average state ρ. This set possesses essentially the same convex structure as the set of measurements of the same form. The following proposition establishes one useful fact along these lines.

Proposition 2.52 *Let $\eta\colon \Sigma \to \mathrm{Pos}(\mathcal{X})$ be an ensemble, for $\mathcal{X}$ a complex Euclidean space and Σ an alphabet, and let*

$$\rho = \sum_{a \in \Sigma} \eta(a). \tag{2.294}$$

There exist an alphabet Γ and a collection of ensembles $\{\eta_b : b \in \Gamma\}$ taking the form $\eta_b\colon \Sigma \to \mathrm{Pos}(\mathcal{X})$ so that the following properties are satisfied:

1. *For each $b \in \Gamma$, the average state of η_b is ρ:*

$$\sum_{a \in \Sigma} \eta_b(a) = \rho. \tag{2.295}$$

2. *For each $b \in \Gamma$, it holds that*

$$\left|\{a \in \Sigma : \eta_b(a) \neq 0\}\right| \leq \mathrm{rank}(\rho)^2. \tag{2.296}$$

3. *The ensemble η is a convex combination of the ensembles $\{\eta_b : b \in \Gamma\}$. Equivalently, it holds that*

$$\eta = \sum_{b \in \Gamma} p(b)\eta_b \tag{2.297}$$

for some choice of a probability vector $p \in \mathcal{P}(\Gamma)$.

Proof Let $\mathcal{Y}$ be a complex Euclidean space satisfying $\dim(\mathcal{Y}) = \mathrm{rank}(\rho)$, and let $A \in \mathrm{L}(\mathcal{Y}, \mathcal{X})$ be an operator satisfying $AA^* = \rho$. Such an operator A must necessarily satisfy $\ker(A) = \{0\}$ and $\mathrm{im}(A) = \mathrm{im}(\rho)$. For each $a \in \Sigma$, it holds that

$$\mathrm{im}(\eta(a)) \subseteq \mathrm{im}(\rho) = \mathrm{im}(A). \tag{2.298}$$

By Lemma 2.30, one may therefore conclude that there exists a positive semidefinite operator $Q_a \in \mathrm{Pos}(\mathcal{Y})$ such that

$$\eta(a) = AQ_aA^*, \tag{2.299}$$

for each $a \in \Sigma$.

Now define $\mu\colon \Sigma \to \mathrm{Pos}(\mathcal{Y})$ as $\mu(a) = Q_a$ for each $a \in \Sigma$. As

$$AA^* = \rho = \sum_{a \in \Sigma} \eta(a) = A\left(\sum_{a \in \Sigma} \mu(a)\right)A^*, \tag{2.300}$$

the fact that $\ker(A) = \{0\}$ implies that

$$\sum_{a \in \Sigma} \mu(a) = \mathbb{1}_{\mathcal{Y}}, \tag{2.301}$$

and therefore μ is a measurement.

By Corollary 2.49, there exists an alphabet Γ, a collection of measurements $\{\mu_b : b \in \Gamma\}$ taking the form $\mu_b : \Sigma \to \mathrm{Pos}(\mathcal{Y})$ and satisfying

$$|\{a \in \Sigma : \mu_b(a) \neq 0\}| \leq \dim(\mathcal{Y})^2 \tag{2.302}$$

for each $b \in \Gamma$, and a probability vector $p \in \mathcal{P}(\Gamma)$, such that

$$\mu = \sum_{b \in \Gamma} p(b)\mu_b. \tag{2.303}$$

Define a function $\eta_b : \Sigma \to \mathrm{Pos}(\mathcal{X})$ for each $b \in \Gamma$ as

$$\eta_b(a) = A\mu_b(a)A^* \tag{2.304}$$

for each $a \in \Sigma$. It is evident that each η_b is an ensemble whose average state is ρ, by virtue of the fact that each μ_b is a measurement, and the requirement (2.296) follows directly from (2.302). Finally, one has

$$\sum_{b \in \Gamma} p(b)\eta_b(a) = A\left(\sum_{b \in \Gamma} p(b)\mu_b(a)\right)A^* = A\mu(a)A^* = \eta(a) \tag{2.305}$$

for each $a \in \Sigma$, and therefore (2.297) holds, which completes the proof. $\square$

2.4 Exercises

Exercise 2.1 Let Σ be an alphabet, let $\mathcal{X}$ be a complex Euclidean space, and let $\phi : \mathrm{Herm}(\mathcal{X}) \to \mathbb{R}^{\Sigma}$ be a linear function. Prove that these two statements are equivalent:

1. It holds that $\phi(\rho) \in \mathcal{P}(\Sigma)$ for every density operator $\rho \in \mathrm{D}(\mathcal{X})$.
2. There exists a measurement $\mu : \Sigma \to \mathrm{Pos}(\mathcal{X})$ such that

$$(\phi(H))(a) = \langle \mu(a), H \rangle \tag{2.306}$$

for every $H \in \mathrm{Herm}(\mathcal{X})$ and $a \in \Sigma$.

Exercise 2.2 Let $\mathcal{X}$ and $\mathcal{Y}$ be complex Euclidean spaces, let Σ be an alphabet, and let $\eta : \Sigma \to \mathrm{Pos}(\mathcal{X})$ be an ensemble of states. Suppose further that $u \in \mathcal{X} \otimes \mathcal{Y}$ is a vector such that

$$\mathrm{Tr}_{\mathcal{Y}}(uu^*) = \sum_{a \in \Sigma} \eta(a). \tag{2.307}$$

Prove that there exists a measurement $\mu : \Sigma \to \mathrm{Pos}(\mathcal{Y})$ such that

$$\eta(a) = \mathrm{Tr}_{\mathcal{Y}}((\mathbb{1}_{\mathcal{X}} \otimes \mu(a))uu^*) \tag{2.308}$$

for all $a \in \Sigma$.

Exercise 2.3 Let $\Phi \in \mathrm{CP}(\mathcal{X}, \mathcal{Y})$ be a nonzero completely positive map, for $\mathcal{X}$ and $\mathcal{Y}$ being complex Euclidean spaces, and let $r = \mathrm{rank}(J(\Phi))$ be the Choi rank of Φ. Prove that there exists a complex Euclidean space $\mathcal{Z}$ having dimension r, along with an operator $A \in \mathrm{L}(\mathcal{X} \otimes \mathcal{Z}, \mathcal{Y})$, such that

$$\Phi(X) = A(X \otimes \mathbb{1}_{\mathcal{Z}})A^* \tag{2.309}$$

for all $X \in \mathrm{L}(\mathcal{X})$. Give a simple equation involving the operator A that is equivalent to Φ preserving trace.

Exercise 2.4 Let $\mathcal{X}$ and $\mathcal{Y}$ be complex Euclidean spaces, let $\Phi \in \mathrm{T}(\mathcal{X}, \mathcal{Y})$ be a positive map, and let $\Delta \in \mathrm{C}(\mathcal{Y})$ denote the completely dephasing channel with respect to the space $\mathcal{Y}$. Prove that $\Delta\Phi$ is completely positive.

Exercise 2.5 Let $\Phi \in \mathrm{C}(\mathcal{X} \otimes \mathcal{Z}, \mathcal{Y} \otimes \mathcal{W})$ be a channel, for complex Euclidean spaces $\mathcal{X}$, $\mathcal{Y}$, $\mathcal{Z}$, and $\mathcal{W}$. Prove that the following two statements are equivalent:

1. There exists a channel $\Psi \in \mathrm{C}(\mathcal{X}, \mathcal{Y})$ such that

$$\mathrm{Tr}_{\mathcal{W}}(J(\Phi)) = J(\Psi) \otimes \mathbb{1}_{\mathcal{Z}}. \tag{2.310}$$

2. There exists a complex Euclidean space $\mathcal{V}$ with $\dim(\mathcal{V}) \leq \dim(\mathcal{X} \otimes \mathcal{Y})$, along with channels $\Phi_0 \in \mathrm{C}(\mathcal{X}, \mathcal{Y} \otimes \mathcal{V})$ and $\Phi_1 \in \mathrm{C}(\mathcal{V} \otimes \mathcal{Z}, \mathcal{W})$, such that

$$\Phi = (\mathbb{1}_{\mathrm{L}(\mathcal{Y})} \otimes \Phi_1)(\Phi_0 \otimes \mathbb{1}_{\mathrm{L}(\mathcal{Z})}). \tag{2.311}$$

Exercise 2.6 Let $\mathcal{X}$, $\mathcal{Y}$, $\mathcal{Z}$, and $\mathcal{W}$ be complex Euclidean spaces.

(a) Prove that every operator $P \in \mathrm{Pos}(\mathcal{Y} \otimes \mathcal{X})$ satisfying the equation

$$\langle P, J(\Phi) \rangle = 1 \tag{2.312}$$

for every channel $\Phi \in \mathrm{C}(\mathcal{X}, \mathcal{Y})$ must take the form

$$P = \mathbb{1}_{\mathcal{Y}} \otimes \rho \tag{2.313}$$

for some choice of $\rho \in \mathrm{D}(\mathcal{X})$.

(b) Let $\Xi \in \mathrm{CP}(\mathcal{Y} \otimes \mathcal{X}, \mathcal{W} \otimes \mathcal{Z})$ be a completely positive map for which the following statement holds: for every channel $\Phi \in \mathrm{C}(\mathcal{X}, \mathcal{Y})$, there exists a channel $\Psi \in \mathrm{C}(\mathcal{Z}, \mathcal{W})$ such that

$$\Xi(J(\Phi)) = J(\Psi). \tag{2.314}$$

Prove that there must exist a unital map $\Lambda \in \mathrm{CP}(\mathcal{X}, \mathcal{Z})$ such that

$$\mathrm{Tr}_{\mathcal{W}}(\Xi(X)) = \Lambda(\mathrm{Tr}_{\mathcal{Y}}(X)) \tag{2.315}$$

for all $X \in \mathrm{L}(\mathcal{Y} \otimes \mathcal{X})$.

(c) Let $\Xi \in \mathrm{CP}(\mathcal{Y} \otimes \mathcal{X}, \mathcal{W} \otimes \mathcal{Z})$ be a completely positive map satisfying the same requirement as described in part (b). Prove that there exist channels $\Xi_0 \in \mathrm{C}(\mathcal{Z}, \mathcal{X} \otimes \mathcal{V})$ and $\Xi_1 \in \mathrm{C}(\mathcal{Y} \otimes \mathcal{V}, \mathcal{W})$, for some choice of a complex Euclidean space $\mathcal{V}$, for which the following property holds: for every channel $\Phi \in \mathrm{C}(\mathcal{X}, \mathcal{Y})$, the channel $\Psi \in \mathrm{C}(\mathcal{Z}, \mathcal{W})$ that is uniquely determined by (2.314) is given by

$$\Psi = \Xi_1(\Phi \otimes \mathbb{1}_{\mathrm{L}(\mathcal{V})})\Xi_0. \tag{2.316}$$

2.5 Bibliographic Remarks

The theory of quantum information represents a mathematical formulation of certain aspects of quantum physics, particularly aspects relating to the storage and processing of information in abstract physical systems. While the history of quantum physics is not within the scope of this book, it is appropriate to mention that the mathematical theory discussed in this book is rooted in the work of the many physicists who first developed that field, including Planck, Einstein, Bohr, Heisenberg, Schrödinger, Born, Dirac, and Pauli. Much of this work was placed on a firm mathematical foundation by von Neumann's (1955) *Mathematical Foundations of Quantum Mechanics*.

The description of quantum states as density operators was independently proposed by von Neumann (1927b) and Landau (1927), a notion equivalent to that of quantum channels was proposed by Haag and Kastler (1964), and the definition of measurements adopted in this book was proposed by Davies and Lewis (1970). The importance of this definition of measurements was articulated by Holevo (1972, 1973b,c,d); earlier formulations of the theory considered only projective measurements. The books of Helstrom (1976) and Kraus (1983) further refined these key foundational aspects of the theory of quantum information.

Further information on the history of quantum information can be found in the books of Peres (1993), Nielsen and Chuang (2000), and Wilde (2013), which are also indispensable references on the theory itself. Kitaev, Shen, and Vyalyi (2002) and Bengtsson and Życzkowski (2006) also describe the mathematical formalism that has been presented in this chapter, and include discussions of some specific topics connected with quantum information and computation.

The Choi representation is so-named for Choi (1975), who characterized completely positive maps (as represented by the equivalence of statements 1 and 3 in Theorem 2.22). Theorem 2.31 was proved in the same paper. A similar representation to the Choi representation was used earlier by de Pillis

(1967) and Jamiołkowski (1972), and there are arguments to be made for the claim that the representation may be considered as folklore.

Theorem 2.22 is an amalgamation of results that are generally attributed to Stinespring (1955), Kraus (1971, 1983), and Choi (1975). Stinespring and Kraus also proved more general results holding for infinite-dimensional spaces; Theorem 2.22 presents only the finite-dimensional analogues of the results they proved. (Several theorems to be presented in this book have a similar character, often having originally been proved in the setting of C*-algebras, as compared with the simpler setting of complex Euclidean spaces.) Theorems 2.25 and 2.26 include equivalences that may be derived from the work of de Pillis (1967) and Jamiołkowski (1972), respectively.

Theorem 2.42 is a simplified variant of a theorem commonly known as Naimark's theorem (or Naimark's dilation theorem). A more general form of this theorem, holding for certain infinite-dimensional spaces and measure-theoretic formulations of measurements having infinitely many outcomes, was proved by Naimark (1943), whose name is sometimes alternatively transliterated as Neumark. This theorem is now commonly viewed as being a direct consequence of the later work of Stinespring mentioned above.

The characterization of extremal measurements given by Theorem 2.47 is equivalent to one obtained by Parthasarathy (1999). Results equivalent to Corollaries 2.48, 2.50, and 2.51 were observed in the same paper. The fact that projective measurements are extremal (Corollary 2.51) was also proved earlier by Holevo (1973d).

Exercise 2.2 is representative of a fact first proved by Hughston, Jozsa, and Wootters (1993). The fact represented by Exercise 2.5 is due to Eggeling, Schlingemann, and Werner (2002), answering a question raised by Beckman, Gottesman, Nielsen, and Preskill (2001) (who credit David DiVincenzo for raising the question). Gutoski and Watrous (2007) and Chiribella, D'Ariano, and Perinotti (2009) generalized this result to quantum processes having inputs and outputs that alternate for multiple steps. Exercise 2.6 is representative of a related result of Chiribella, D'Ariano, and Perinotti (2008).

3

Similarity and Distance Among States and Channels

The main focus of this chapter is on quantifiable notions of similarity and distance between quantum states, the task of discrimination among two or more quantum state alternatives, and related notions involving channels.

There are three main sections of the chapter, the first of which discusses the task of *discrimination* between pairs of quantum states, its connection to the trace norm, and generalizations of this task to more than two states. The second section introduces the *fidelity* function and describes some of its basic properties, formulations, and connections to other concepts. The third section discusses the *completely bounded trace norm*, which is a natural analogue of the trace norm for mappings between spaces of operators, and establishes a connection between this norm and the task of discrimination between pairs of quantum channels.

3.1 Quantum State Discrimination

It is a natural question to ask how well a given collection of quantum states can be discriminated by means of a measurement. The hypothetical task of *state discrimination* serves as an abstraction through which this question may be considered.

In the simplest formulation of the state discrimination task, one of two known quantum states is selected at random, and a register prepared in that state is made available to a hypothetical individual. This individual's goal is to determine, by performing a measurement on the given register, which of the two states was selected. A theorem known as the *Holevo–Helstrom theorem* gives a closed-form expression, based on the trace norm of a weighted difference between the two possible states, for the probability that an optimally chosen measurement correctly identifies the selected state.

An explicit description of an optimal measurement may be obtained from the proof of this theorem.

State discrimination may also be considered in the situation where more than two states are to be discriminated. An analysis of this task is more difficult than the two-state case, and a simple, closed-form expression for the optimal success probability to discriminate three or more given states is not known in general. It is possible, however, to represent this optimal success probability through the use of semidefinite programming, which provides a valuable analytical tool through which state discrimination may be analyzed. Approximate solutions, together with bounds on their performance, are also considered.

3.1.1 Discriminating Between Pairs of Quantum States

The task of discriminating between two fixed quantum states $\rho_0, \rho_1 \in D(\mathcal{X})$ of a given register X is the simplest form of the state discrimination task. A key aspect of the analysis of the task that follows is that it establishes a close connection between state discrimination and the trace norm. Somewhat more generally, one finds that the trace norm provides a natural way of quantifying the "measurable difference" between two quantum states.

Discriminating Between Pairs of Probabilistic States

Before discussing the task of state discrimination between pairs of quantum states, it is appropriate to consider an analogous problem for probabilistic states. To this end, consider the following scenario involving two hypothetical individuals: Alice and Bob.

Scenario 3.1 Let X be a register with classical state set Σ and let Y be a register with classical state set $\{0,1\}$. Both X and Y are to be viewed as classical registers in this scenario. Also let $p_0, p_1 \in \mathcal{P}(\Sigma)$ be probability vectors, representing probabilistic states of X, and let $\lambda \in [0,1]$ be a real number. The vectors p_0 and p_1, as well as the number λ, are assumed to be known to both Alice and Bob.

Alice prepares the register Y in a probabilistic state, so that its value is 0 with probability λ and 1 with probability $1 - \lambda$. Conditioned on the classical state of Y, Alice performs one of the following actions:

1. If $Y = 0$, Alice prepares X in the probabilistic state p_0.
2. If $Y = 1$, Alice prepares X in the probabilistic state p_1.

The register X is then given to Bob.

Bob's goal is to correctly determine the value of the bit stored in Y, using only the information he can gather from an observation of X.

An optimal strategy in this scenario for Bob, assuming that he wishes to maximize the probability of correctly guessing the value stored in Y, may be derived from Bayes' theorem, which implies

$$\Pr(\mathsf{Y} = 0 | \mathsf{X} = b) = \frac{\lambda p_0(b)}{\lambda p_0(b) + (1 - \lambda) p_1(b)},$$

$$\Pr(\mathsf{Y} = 1 | \mathsf{X} = b) = \frac{(1 - \lambda) p_1(b)}{\lambda p_0(b) + (1 - \lambda) p_1(b)},$$

(3.1)

for each $b \in \Sigma$. Given the knowledge that $\mathsf{X} = b$, Bob should therefore choose the more likely value for Y: if it holds that $\lambda p_0(b) > (1 - \lambda) p_1(b)$, then Bob should guess that $\mathsf{Y} = 0$, while if $\lambda p_0(b) < (1 - \lambda) p_1(b)$, then Bob should guess that $\mathsf{Y} = 1$. In the case that $\lambda p_0(b) = (1 - \lambda) p_1(b)$, Bob can guess either $\mathsf{Y} = 0$ or $\mathsf{Y} = 1$ arbitrarily without affecting his probability of being correct, as the two values are equally likely in this situation.

The probability that Bob correctly identifies the value stored in Y using this strategy can be understood by first considering the probability that he is correct *minus* the probability that he is incorrect. This difference in probabilities is represented by the quantity

$$\sum_{b \in \Sigma} |\lambda p_0(b) - (1 - \lambda) p_1(b)| = \|\lambda p_0 - (1 - \lambda) p_1\|_1.$$

(3.2)

It follows that the probability that Bob is correct is given by the quantity

$$\frac{1}{2} + \frac{1}{2} \|\lambda p_0 - (1 - \lambda) p_1\|_1.$$

(3.3)

This expression makes clear the close connection between probabilistic state discrimination and the vector 1-norm.

Notice that

$$0 \leq \|\lambda p_0 - (1 - \lambda) p_1\|_1 \leq 1,$$

(3.4)

where the second inequality follows from the triangle inequality. This is consistent with the interpretation of the expression (3.3) as a probability. In an extreme case where

$$\|\lambda p_0 - (1 - \lambda) p_1\|_1 = 0,$$

(3.5)

which requires $\lambda = 1/2$ and $p_0 = p_1$, Bob is essentially reduced to guessing arbitrarily and will be correct with probability $1/2$. In the other extreme,

$$\|\lambda p_0 - (1 - \lambda) p_1\|_1 = 1,$$

(3.6)

it must hold that λp_0 and $(1-\lambda)p_1$ have disjoint supports, and thus Bob can determine the value of Y without error. Intermediate values, in which both inequalities in (3.4) hold strictly, correspond to different degrees of certainty in Bob's guess.

Discriminating Between Pairs of Quantum States

The task of discriminating between pairs of quantum states is represented by the following scenario, which is the natural quantum generalization of Scenario 3.1.

Scenario 3.2 Let X be a register and let Y be a register having classical state set $\{0, 1\}$. The register Y is to be viewed as a classical register, while X is an arbitrary register. Also let $\rho_0, \rho_1 \in D(\mathcal{X})$ be states of X, and let $\lambda \in [0, 1]$ be a real number. The states ρ_0 and ρ_1, as well as the number λ, are assumed to be known to both Alice and Bob.

Alice prepares the register Y in a probabilistic state, so that its value is 0 with probability λ and 1 with probability $1 - \lambda$. Conditioned on the classical state of Y, Alice performs one of the following actions:

1. If $Y = 0$, Alice prepares X in the state ρ_0.

2. If $Y = 1$, Alice prepares X in the state ρ_1.

The register X is then given to Bob.

Bob's goal is to correctly determine the binary value stored in Y, by means of a measurement of X.

The main goal of the discussion that follows is to establish an analogous connection between this scenario and the trace norm to the one between Scenario 3.1 and the vector 1-norm discussed above. The following lemma, which happens to concern the spectral norm rather than the trace norm, is useful for establishing this connection. The lemma is stated in greater generality than is required for the purposes of the present section, but the more general form will find uses elsewhere in this book.

Lemma 3.3 *Let $\mathcal{X}$ be a complex Euclidean space, let Σ be an alphabet, let $u \in \mathbb{C}^\Sigma$ be a vector, and let $\{P_a : a \in \Sigma\} \subset \mathrm{Pos}(\mathcal{X})$ be a collection of positive semidefinite operators. It holds that*

$$\left\| \sum_{a \in \Sigma} u(a) P_a \right\| \leq \|u\|_\infty \left\| \sum_{a \in \Sigma} P_a \right\|. \tag{3.7}$$

Proof Define an operator $A \in \mathrm{L}(\mathcal{X}, \mathcal{X} \otimes \mathbb{C}^{\Sigma})$ as

$$A = \sum_{a \in \Sigma} \sqrt{P_a} \otimes e_a. \tag{3.8}$$

The spectral norm is submultiplicative with respect to compositions and multiplicative with respect to tensor products, and therefore

$$\left\| \sum_{a \in \Sigma} u(a) P_a \right\| = \left\| \sum_{a \in \Sigma} u(a) A^* (\mathbb{1}_{\mathcal{X}} \otimes E_{a,a}) A \right\|$$

$$\leq \| A^* \| \left\| \sum_{a \in \Sigma} u(a) E_{a,a} \right\| \| A \| = \| u \|_{\infty} \| A \|^2. \tag{3.9}$$

By the spectral norm property (1.178), one has

$$\| A \|^2 = \| A^* A \| = \left\| \sum_{a \in \Sigma} P_a \right\|, \tag{3.10}$$

which completes the proof. $\qquad\square$

A direct connection between Scenario 3.2 and the trace norm can now be established. The next theorem, known as the Holevo–Helstrom theorem, expresses this connection in mathematical terms.

Theorem 3.4 (Holevo–Helstrom theorem) *Let $\mathcal{X}$ be a complex Euclidean space, let $\rho_0, \rho_1 \in \mathrm{D}(\mathcal{X})$ be density operators, and let $\lambda \in [0, 1]$. For every choice of a measurement $\mu \colon \{0, 1\} \to \mathrm{Pos}(\mathcal{X})$, it holds that*

$$\lambda \langle \mu(0), \rho_0 \rangle + (1 - \lambda) \langle \mu(1), \rho_1 \rangle \leq \frac{1}{2} + \frac{1}{2} \| \lambda \rho_0 - (1 - \lambda) \rho_1 \|_1. \tag{3.11}$$

Moreover, there exists a projective measurement $\mu \colon \{0, 1\} \to \mathrm{Pos}(\mathcal{X})$ for which equality is achieved in (3.11).

Proof Define

$$\rho = \lambda \rho_0 + (1 - \lambda) \rho_1 \quad \text{and} \quad X = \lambda \rho_0 - (1 - \lambda) \rho_1, \tag{3.12}$$

so that

$$\lambda \rho_0 = \frac{\rho + X}{2} \quad \text{and} \quad (1 - \lambda) \rho_1 = \frac{\rho - X}{2}, \tag{3.13}$$

and therefore

$$\lambda \langle \mu(0), \rho_0 \rangle + (1 - \lambda) \langle \mu(1), \rho_1 \rangle = \frac{1}{2} + \frac{1}{2} \langle \mu(0) - \mu(1), X \rangle. \tag{3.14}$$

By Lemma 3.3, together with the Hölder inequality for Schatten norms, it follows that

$$\frac{1}{2} + \frac{1}{2}\langle \mu(0) - \mu(1), X \rangle$$
$$\leq \frac{1}{2} + \frac{1}{2}\|\mu(0) - \mu(1)\| \, \|X\|_1 \leq \frac{1}{2} + \frac{1}{2}\|X\|_1. \tag{3.15}$$

Combining (3.14) and (3.15) yields (3.11).

To show that equality is achieved in (3.11) for a projective measurement $\mu: \{0,1\} \to \mathrm{Pos}(\mathcal{X})$, one may consider the Jordan–Hahn decomposition

$$X = P - Q, \tag{3.16}$$

for $P, Q \in \mathrm{Pos}(\mathcal{X})$. Define $\mu: \{0,1\} \to \mathrm{Pos}(\mathcal{X})$ as

$$\mu(0) = \Pi_{\mathrm{im}(P)} \quad \text{and} \quad \mu(1) = \mathbb{1} - \Pi_{\mathrm{im}(P)}, \tag{3.17}$$

which is a projective measurement. It holds that

$$\langle \mu(0) - \mu(1), X \rangle = \mathrm{Tr}(P) + \mathrm{Tr}(Q) = \|X\|_1, \tag{3.18}$$

and therefore

$$\lambda \langle \mu(0), \rho_0 \rangle + (1 - \lambda)\langle \mu(1), \rho_1 \rangle = \frac{1}{2} + \frac{1}{2}\|X\|_1, \tag{3.19}$$

which completes the proof. $\qquad\square$

It follows from Theorem 3.4 that an optimal choice of a measurement for Bob in Scenario 3.2 correctly determines the value of Y with probability

$$\frac{1}{2} + \frac{1}{2}\|\lambda \rho_0 - (1 - \lambda)\rho_1\|_1, \tag{3.20}$$

and this optimal probability is achieved by a projective measurement.

One might question the implicit claim that the possible strategies for Bob in Scenario 3.2 are exhausted by the consideration of measurements having 0 and 1 as the only possible outcomes. For instance, Bob could measure X using a measurement with three or more outcomes, and then base his guess for the value of Y on the measurement outcome obtained. However, no generality is introduced by this type of strategy, or any other strategy having access to the register X alone. Any process used by Bob to eventually produce a binary-valued guess for the classical state of Y must define a binary-valued measurement, and Theorem 3.4 may be applied to this measurement.

The following proposition, whose proof has some overlap with the proof of Theorem 3.4, establishes a useful relationship between the trace norm of an operator and the 1-norm of a vector obtained from that operator's inner products with the measurement operators of any measurement.

Proposition 3.5   *Let $\mathcal{X}$ be a complex Euclidean space, let Σ be an alphabet, let $\mu\colon \Sigma \to \mathrm{Pos}(\mathcal{X})$ be a measurement, and let $X \in \mathrm{L}(\mathcal{X})$ be an operator. Define a vector $v \in \mathbb{C}^{\Sigma}$ as*

$$v(a) = \langle \mu(a), X \rangle \qquad (3.21)$$

for each $a \in \Sigma$. It holds that $\|v\|_1 \leq \|X\|_1$.

Proof   One has

$$\|v\|_1 = \sum_{a\in\Sigma} |\langle \mu(a), X \rangle| = \sum_{a\in\Sigma} u(a)\langle \mu(a), X \rangle = \left\langle \sum_{a\in\Sigma} \overline{u(a)}\mu(a), X \right\rangle \qquad (3.22)$$

for some choice of a vector $u \in \mathbb{C}^{\Sigma}$ satisfying $|u(a)| = 1$ for each $a \in \Sigma$. By Lemma 3.3, together with Hölder's inequality for Schatten norms, it follows that

$$\|v\|_1 \leq \left\| \sum_{a\in\Sigma} \overline{u(a)}\mu(a) \right\| \|X\|_1 \leq \|X\|_1, \qquad (3.23)$$

as required.   □

Discriminating Between Convex Sets of Quantum States

The task of state discrimination between pairs of quantum states may be generalized to one in which two convex sets of quantum states are to be discriminated. The following scenario describes this task in more precise terms.

Scenario 3.6   Let X be a register and let Y be a register having classical state set $\{0, 1\}$. The register Y is to be viewed as a classical register, while X is an arbitrary register. Also let $\mathcal{C}_0, \mathcal{C}_1 \subseteq \mathrm{D}(\mathcal{X})$ be nonempty, convex sets of states, and let $\lambda \in [0, 1]$ be a real number. The sets $\mathcal{C}_0$ and $\mathcal{C}_1$, as well as the number λ, are assumed to be known to both Alice and Bob.

Alice prepares the register Y in a probabilistic state, so that its value is 0 with probability λ and 1 with probability $1 - \lambda$. Conditioned on the classical state of Y, Alice performs one of the following actions:

1. If $\mathsf{Y} = 0$, Alice prepares X in any state $\rho_0 \in \mathcal{C}_0$ of her choice.
2. If $\mathsf{Y} = 1$, Alice prepares X in any state $\rho_1 \in \mathcal{C}_1$ of her choice.

The register X is then given to Bob.

Bob's goal is to correctly determine the binary value stored in Y, by means of a measurement of X.

The description of Scenario 3.6 does not specify how Alice is to choose ρ_0 or ρ_1, beyond stating the requirement that $\rho_0 \in \mathcal{C}_0$ and $\rho_1 \in \mathcal{C}_1$. It could be, for instance, that Alice chooses these states randomly according to fixed distributions, or she could choose the states adversarially, even based on a knowledge of the measurement Bob intends to use. What is relevant is that Bob can make no assumptions regarding Alice's choices for ρ_0 and ρ_1, beyond the requirement that she chooses $\rho_0 \in \mathcal{C}_0$ and $\rho_1 \in \mathcal{C}_1$.

One may note that Scenario 3.2 represents a special case of Scenario 3.6 in which $\mathcal{C}_0$ and $\mathcal{C}_1$ are the singleton sets $\{\rho_0\}$ and $\{\rho_1\}$, respectively.

It follows from the Holevo–Helstrom theorem (Theorem 3.4) that Bob cannot hope to succeed in his task in Scenario 3.6 with probability higher than

$$\frac{1}{2} + \frac{1}{2}\|\lambda\rho_0 - (1-\lambda)\rho_1\|_1, \tag{3.24}$$

for whichever states $\rho_0 \in \mathcal{C}_0$ and $\rho_1 \in \mathcal{C}_1$ Alice chooses, for this is his optimal success probability when he has the additional knowledge that Alice chooses either ρ_0 or ρ_1. The following proposition implies that Bob can succeed with probability at least

$$\frac{1}{2} + \frac{1}{2}\inf_{\rho_0,\rho_1} \|\lambda\rho_0 - (1-\lambda)\rho_1\|_1, \tag{3.25}$$

where the infimum is taken over all choices of $\rho_0 \in \mathcal{C}_0$ and $\rho_1 \in \mathcal{C}_1$. In light of the limitation imposed by the Holevo–Helstrom theorem, this is necessarily the optimal probability of success in the worst case.

Theorem 3.7 *Let $\mathcal{C}_0, \mathcal{C}_1 \subseteq D(\mathcal{X})$ be nonempty, convex sets, for $\mathcal{X}$ being a complex Euclidean space, and let $\lambda \in [0,1]$. It holds that*

$$\max_{\mu} \inf_{\rho_0,\rho_1} \left(\lambda\langle\mu(0), \rho_0\rangle + (1-\lambda)\langle\mu(1), \rho_1\rangle\right)$$

$$= \inf_{\rho_0,\rho_1} \max_{\mu} \left(\lambda\langle\mu(0), \rho_0\rangle + (1-\lambda)\langle\mu(1), \rho_1\rangle\right) \tag{3.26}$$

$$= \frac{1}{2} + \frac{1}{2}\inf_{\rho_0,\rho_1} \|\lambda\rho_0 - (1-\lambda)\rho_1\|_1,$$

where the infima are over all choices of $\rho_0 \in \mathcal{C}_0$ and $\rho_1 \in \mathcal{C}_1$, and the maxima are over all choices of binary measurements $\mu\colon \{0,1\} \to \mathrm{Pos}(\mathcal{X})$.

Proof Define sets $\mathcal{A}, \mathcal{B} \subset \mathrm{Pos}(\mathcal{X} \oplus \mathcal{X})$ as

$$\mathcal{A} = \left\{ \begin{pmatrix} \rho_0 & 0 \\ 0 & \rho_1 \end{pmatrix} : \rho_0 \in \mathcal{C}_0,\ \rho_1 \in \mathcal{C}_1 \right\} \tag{3.27}$$

and

$$
\mathcal{B} = \left\{ \begin{pmatrix} \lambda P_0 & 0 \\ 0 & (1-\lambda)P_1 \end{pmatrix} : P_0, P_1 \in \mathrm{Pos}(\mathcal{X}),\ P_0 + P_1 = \mathbb{1}_{\mathcal{X}} \right\}, \qquad (3.28)
$$

as well as a function $f \colon \mathcal{A} \times \mathcal{B} \to \mathbb{R}$ as $f(A, B) = \langle A, B \rangle$. It holds that $\mathcal{A}$ and $\mathcal{B}$ are convex, $\mathcal{B}$ is compact, and f is bilinear, so that

$$
\inf_{A \in \mathcal{A}} \max_{B \in \mathcal{B}} f(A, B) = \max_{B \in \mathcal{B}} \inf_{A \in \mathcal{A}} f(A, B) \qquad (3.29)
$$

by Sion's min–max theorem (Theorem 1.12). Equation (3.29) is equivalent to the first equality of (3.26), and the second equality in (3.26) follows from Theorem 3.4. $\qquad\qquad\square$

3.1.2 Discriminating Quantum States of an Ensemble

The remaining variant of quantum state discrimination to be discussed in this chapter is similar to the one represented by Scenario 3.2, except that more than two possible states, selected from a given ensemble, are to be discriminated. The following scenario describes this task in more precise terms.

Scenario 3.8   Let X be a register, let Σ be an alphabet, and let Y be a register having classical state set Σ. The register Y is to be viewed as a classical register, while X is an arbitrary register. Also let $\eta \colon \Sigma \to \mathrm{Pos}(\mathcal{X})$ be an ensemble of states, assumed to be known to both Alice and Bob.

Alice prepares the pair (Y, X) in the classical–quantum state

$$
\sigma = \sum_{a \in \Sigma} E_{a,a} \otimes \eta(a) \qquad (3.30)
$$

determined by the ensemble η. Equivalently, the register Y takes each value $a \in \Sigma$ with probability $p(a) = \mathrm{Tr}(\eta(a))$, and conditioned on the event $\mathsf{Y} = a$ the state of X is set to

$$
\frac{\eta(a)}{\mathrm{Tr}(\eta(a))}, \qquad (3.31)
$$

for each $a \in \Sigma$. The register X is then given to Bob.

Bob's goal is to correctly determine the classical state stored in Y, using only the information he can gather from a measurement of X.

For any measurement $\mu \colon \Sigma \to \mathrm{Pos}(\mathcal{X})$ chosen by Bob, the probability that he correctly predicts the classical state of Y is given by the expression

$$
\sum_{a \in \Sigma} \langle \mu(a), \eta(a) \rangle. \qquad (3.32)
$$

It is therefore natural to consider a maximization of this quantity over all choices of the measurement μ.

More generally, one may substitute an arbitrary function of the form $\phi \colon \Sigma \to \mathrm{Herm}(\mathcal{X})$ in place of the ensemble $\eta \colon \Sigma \to \mathrm{Pos}(\mathcal{X})$, and consider a maximization of the quantity

$$\sum_{a \in \Sigma} \langle \mu(a), \phi(a) \rangle \tag{3.33}$$

over all measurements $\mu \colon \Sigma \to \mathrm{Pos}(\mathcal{X})$. One situation in which this more general optimization problem is meaningful is a variant of Scenario 3.8 in which different payoff values are associated to each pair (a, b), representing the state a of Alice's register Y and Bob's measurement outcome b. If Bob receives a payoff value of $K(a, b)$ for producing the measurement outcome b when Alice's register Y holds the symbol a, for instance, Bob's expected gain for a given measurement $\mu \colon \Sigma \to \mathrm{Pos}(\mathcal{X})$ is given by

$$\sum_{a \in \Sigma} \sum_{b \in \Sigma} K(a, b) \langle \mu(b), \eta(a) \rangle = \sum_{b \in \Sigma} \langle \mu(b), \phi(b) \rangle \tag{3.34}$$

for

$$\phi(b) = \sum_{a \in \Sigma} K(a, b)\, \eta(a). \tag{3.35}$$

This sort of hypothetical situation could be further generalized by allowing the classical state set of Alice's register Y and Bob's set of measurement outcomes to disagree.

A Semidefinite Program for Optimal Measurements

For any choice of a function $\phi \colon \Sigma \to \mathrm{Herm}(\mathcal{X})$, for a complex Euclidean space $\mathcal{X}$ and an alphabet Σ, define

$$\mathrm{opt}(\phi) = \max_{\mu} \sum_{a \in \Sigma} \langle \mu(a), \phi(a) \rangle, \tag{3.36}$$

where the maximum is over all measurements of the form $\mu \colon \Sigma \to \mathrm{Pos}(\mathcal{X})$. This optimal value is necessarily achieved for some choice of a measurement, as it is a maximization of a continuous function over a compact set, which justifies the use of the maximum rather than the supremum. It may also be said that a particular choice of a measurement μ is *optimal* for ϕ if the above expression (3.33) coincides with the value $\mathrm{opt}(\phi)$.

There is no closed-form expression that is known to represent the value $\mathrm{opt}(\phi)$ for an arbitrary choice of a function $\phi \colon \Sigma \to \mathrm{Herm}(\mathcal{X})$. However, it is possible to express the value $\mathrm{opt}(\phi)$ by a semidefinite program, providing a method by which it may be numerically calculated using a computer. A simplified description of the primal and dual problems associated with such a semidefinite program are as follows:

Primal problem (simplified)

$$\text{maximize:} \quad \sum_{a \in \Sigma} \langle \mu(a), \phi(a) \rangle$$

$$\text{subject to:} \quad \mu \colon \Sigma \to \mathrm{Pos}(\mathcal{X}),$$

$$\sum_{a \in \Sigma} \mu(a) = \mathbb{1}_{\mathcal{X}}.$$

Dual problem (simplified)

$$\text{minimize:} \quad \mathrm{Tr}(Y)$$

$$\text{subject to:} \quad Y \geq \phi(a) \quad (\text{for all } a \in \Sigma),$$

$$Y \in \mathrm{Herm}(\mathcal{X}).$$

A formal expression of this semidefinite program that conforms to the definition of semidefinite programs presented in Section 1.2.3 is given by the triple $(\Phi, A, \mathbb{1}_{\mathcal{X}})$, where the mapping $\Phi \in \mathrm{T}(\mathcal{Y} \otimes \mathcal{X}, \mathcal{X})$ is defined as the partial trace $\Phi = \mathrm{Tr}_{\mathcal{Y}}$, for $\mathcal{Y} = \mathbb{C}^{\Sigma}$, and the operator A is defined as

$$A = \sum_{a \in \Sigma} E_{a,a} \otimes \phi(a). \tag{3.37}$$

The primal and dual problems associated with the triple $(\Phi, A, \mathbb{1}_{\mathcal{X}})$ are as follows:

Primal problem (formal)

$$\text{maximize:} \quad \langle A, X \rangle$$

$$\text{subject to:} \quad \mathrm{Tr}_{\mathcal{Y}}(X) = \mathbb{1}_{\mathcal{X}},$$

$$X \in \mathrm{Pos}(\mathcal{Y} \otimes \mathcal{X}).$$

Dual problem (formal)

$$\text{minimize:} \quad \mathrm{Tr}(Y)$$

$$\text{subject to:} \quad \mathbb{1}_{\mathcal{Y}} \otimes Y \geq A,$$

$$Y \in \mathrm{Herm}(\mathcal{X}).$$

These problems are equivalent to the simplified primal and dual problems described above. In greater detail, any feasible solution μ to the simplified primal problem described above gives rise to the feasible solution

$$X = \sum_{a \in \Sigma} E_{a,a} \otimes \mu(a) \qquad (3.38)$$

to the formal primal problem, in which the same objective value

$$\langle A, X \rangle = \sum_{a \in \Sigma} \langle \mu(a), \phi(a) \rangle \qquad (3.39)$$

is achieved. While a feasible solution X to the formal primal problem need not take the form (3.38) in general, one may nevertheless obtain a feasible solution μ to the simplified primal problem from such an operator X by setting

$$\mu(a) = (e_a^* \otimes \mathbb{1}_{\mathcal{X}}) X (e_a \otimes \mathbb{1}_{\mathcal{X}}) \qquad (3.40)$$

for each $a \in \Sigma$. The equality (3.39) again holds, and therefore the two primal problems have the same optimal value. The fact that the two dual problems are equivalent is evident from the observation that the inequality

$$\mathbb{1}_{\mathcal{Y}} \otimes Y \geq \sum_{a \in \Sigma} E_{a,a} \otimes \phi(a) \qquad (3.41)$$

is equivalent to the inequality $Y \geq \phi(a)$ holding for every $a \in \Sigma$.

Strong duality holds for this semidefinite program. The operator

$$X = \frac{1}{|\Sigma|} \mathbb{1}_{\mathcal{Y}} \otimes \mathbb{1}_{\mathcal{X}} \qquad (3.42)$$

is a strictly feasible primal solution, while $Y = \gamma \mathbb{1}_{\mathcal{X}}$ is a strictly feasible dual solution for any real value $\gamma > \lambda_1(A)$. It follows from Slater's theorem for semidefinite programs (Theorem 1.18) that the optimal primal and dual values for the semidefinite program are equal, and moreover the optimum value is achieved in both the primal and dual problems.

Criteria for Measurement Optimality

It may be difficult to obtain an analytic description of a measurement $\mu \colon \Sigma \to \mathrm{Pos}(\mathcal{X})$ that is optimal for a given function $\phi \colon \Sigma \to \mathrm{Herm}(\mathcal{X})$, given the lack of a known closed-form expression for such a measurement. In contrast, it is straightforward to verify that an optimal measurement is indeed optimal by means of the following theorem.

Theorem 3.9 (Holevo–Yuen–Kennedy–Lax) *Let $\phi\colon \Sigma \to \mathrm{Herm}(\mathcal{X})$ be a function and let $\mu\colon \Sigma \to \mathrm{Pos}(\mathcal{X})$ be a measurement, for $\mathcal{X}$ being a complex Euclidean space and Σ being an alphabet. The measurement μ is optimal for the function ϕ if and only if the operator*

$$Y = \sum_{a \in \Sigma} \phi(a)\mu(a) \tag{3.43}$$

is Hermitian and satisfies $Y \geq \phi(b)$ for every $b \in \Sigma$.

Proof Let $\mathcal{Y} = \mathbb{C}^\Sigma$ and define an operator $X \in \mathrm{Herm}(\mathcal{Y} \otimes \mathcal{X})$ as

$$X = \sum_{a \in \Sigma} E_{a,a} \otimes \mu(a). \tag{3.44}$$

Suppose first that μ is an optimal measurement for ϕ, so that X is an optimal primal solution to the semidefinite program $(\Phi, A, \mathbb{1}_{\mathcal{X}})$ representing $\mathrm{opt}(\phi)$, as described previously. As the dual optimum of this semidefinite program is always achieved, one may choose $Z \in \mathrm{Herm}(\mathcal{X})$ to be such a dual optimal solution. By the property of complementary slackness for semidefinite programs (Proposition 1.19), it necessarily holds that

$$(\mathbb{1}_{\mathcal{Y}} \otimes Z)X = AX. \tag{3.45}$$

Taking the partial trace of both sides of (3.45) over $\mathcal{Y}$, one finds that

$$Z = Z \operatorname{Tr}_{\mathcal{Y}}(X) = \operatorname{Tr}_{\mathcal{Y}}(AX) = \sum_{a \in \Sigma} \phi(a)\mu(a) = Y. \tag{3.46}$$

The operator Y is therefore dual feasible, and is therefore Hermitian and satisfies $Y \geq \phi(b)$ for every $b \in \Sigma$.

To prove the reverse implication, one may observe that if Y is Hermitian and satisfies $Y \geq \phi(b)$ for every $b \in \Sigma$, then it is a dual feasible solution to the semidefinite program $(\Phi, A, \mathbb{1}_{\mathcal{X}})$ representing $\mathrm{opt}(\phi)$. Because μ is a measurement, the operator X defined in (3.44) is primal feasible for this semidefinite program. The objective values achieved by X in the primal problem and Y in the dual problem are both equal to

$$\sum_{a \in \Sigma} \langle \mu(a), \phi(a) \rangle. \tag{3.47}$$

The equality between these values implies that both are optimal by the property of weak duality of semidefinite programs. The measurement μ is therefore optimal for ϕ. □

The Pretty Good Measurement

Returning to Bob's task, as described in Scenario 3.8, suppose an ensemble $\eta \colon \Sigma \to \mathrm{Pos}(\mathcal{X})$ is given, and a measurement $\mu \colon \Sigma \to \mathrm{Pos}(\mathcal{X})$ maximizing the probability

$$\sum_{a \in \Sigma} \langle \mu(a), \eta(a) \rangle \tag{3.48}$$

of a correct determination of the state of Alice's classical register Y is sought.

In a concrete setting in which an explicit description of η is known, the semidefinite programming formulation of $\mathrm{opt}(\eta)$ allows for an efficient numerical approximation to a measurement μ that is optimal for η. This approach may, however, be unsatisfactory in more abstract settings, such as ones in which it is necessary to view η as being indeterminate. Although Theorem 3.9 allows for a verification that a given optimal measurement is indeed optimal, it does not provide a method to find a measurement that is optimal.

One alternative to searching for an optimal measurement is to consider measurements that are determined from η by closed-form expressions, but that might be sub-optimal. The so-called *pretty good measurement* is an example of such a measurement.

To define the pretty good measurement for a given ensemble η, one first considers the average state

$$\rho = \sum_{a \in \Sigma} \eta(a) \tag{3.49}$$

of η. In the case that ρ is positive definite, the pretty good measurement associated with η is the measurement $\mu \colon \Sigma \to \mathrm{Pos}(\mathcal{X})$ defined as

$$\mu(a) = \rho^{-\frac{1}{2}} \eta(a) \rho^{-\frac{1}{2}}. \tag{3.50}$$

In general, when ρ is not necessarily invertible, one may use the Moore–Penrose pseudo-inverse of ρ, in place of the inverse of ρ, to define[1] the pretty good measurement associated with η as

$$\mu(a) = \sqrt{\rho^+}\, \eta(a) \sqrt{\rho^+} + \frac{1}{|\Sigma|} \Pi_{\ker(\rho)} \tag{3.52}$$

for every $a \in \Sigma$.

---

[1] It should be noted that, although the equation (3.52) is taken here as the definition of the pretty good measurement, it is somewhat arbitrary in the case that ρ is not invertible. Any measurement $\mu \colon \Sigma \to \mathrm{Pos}(\mathcal{X})$ satisfying

$$\mu(a) \geq \sqrt{\rho^+}\, \eta(a) \sqrt{\rho^+} \tag{3.51}$$

for all $a \in \Sigma$ would be equivalent with respect to the discussion that follows.

Although the pretty good measurement will generally not be optimal for a given ensemble, it will always achieve a probability of a correct prediction that is at least the square of the optimal success probability, as the following theorem states.

Theorem 3.10 (Barnum–Knill)   *Let $\mathcal{X}$ be a complex Euclidean space, let Σ be an alphabet, let $\eta \colon \Sigma \to \mathrm{Pos}(\mathcal{X})$ be an ensemble of states, and let $\mu \colon \Sigma \to \mathrm{Pos}(\mathcal{X})$ denote the pretty good measurement associated with η. It holds that*

$$\sum_{a \in \Sigma} \langle \mu(a), \eta(a) \rangle \geq \mathrm{opt}(\eta)^2. \tag{3.53}$$

Proof   Let

$$\rho = \sum_{a \in \Sigma} \eta(a) \tag{3.54}$$

and let $\nu \colon \Sigma \to \mathrm{Pos}(\mathcal{X})$ be a measurement. For every $a \in \Sigma$ it holds that $\mathrm{im}(\eta(a)) \subseteq \mathrm{im}(\rho)$, and therefore

$$\langle \nu(a), \eta(a) \rangle = \Big\langle \rho^{\frac{1}{4}} \nu(a) \rho^{\frac{1}{4}}, (\rho^+)^{\frac{1}{4}} \eta(a) (\rho^+)^{\frac{1}{4}} \Big\rangle. \tag{3.55}$$

By the Cauchy–Schwarz inequality, it follows that

$$\langle \nu(a), \eta(a) \rangle \leq \Big\| \rho^{\frac{1}{4}} \nu(a) \rho^{\frac{1}{4}} \Big\|_2 \Big\| (\rho^+)^{\frac{1}{4}} \eta(a) (\rho^+)^{\frac{1}{4}} \Big\|_2 \tag{3.56}$$

for each $a \in \Sigma$. Applying the Cauchy–Schwarz inequality again, this time for vectors of real numbers rather than for operators, one finds that

$$\sum_{a \in \Sigma} \langle \nu(a), \eta(a) \rangle \leq \sqrt{\sum_{a \in \Sigma} \Big\| \rho^{\frac{1}{4}} \nu(a) \rho^{\frac{1}{4}} \Big\|_2^2} \sqrt{\sum_{a \in \Sigma} \Big\| (\rho^+)^{\frac{1}{4}} \eta(a) (\rho^+)^{\frac{1}{4}} \Big\|_2^2}. \tag{3.57}$$

The first factor on the right-hand side of (3.57) is at most 1. To verify that this is so, one may use the definition of the Frobenius norm to obtain the expression

$$\Big\| \rho^{\frac{1}{4}} \nu(a) \rho^{\frac{1}{4}} \Big\|_2^2 = \Big\langle \rho^{\frac{1}{4}} \nu(a) \rho^{\frac{1}{4}}, \rho^{\frac{1}{4}} \nu(a) \rho^{\frac{1}{4}} \Big\rangle = \langle \nu(a), \sqrt{\rho} \nu(a) \sqrt{\rho} \rangle \tag{3.58}$$

for each $a \in \Sigma$, from which it follows that

$$\Big\| \rho^{\frac{1}{4}} \nu(a) \rho^{\frac{1}{4}} \Big\|_2^2 \leq \mathrm{Tr}\big(\sqrt{\rho} \nu(a) \sqrt{\rho} \big), \tag{3.59}$$

by virtue of the fact that $\nu(a) \leq \mathbb{1}_{\mathcal{X}}$ and $\sqrt{\rho} \nu(a) \sqrt{\rho} \geq 0$. Summing over all $a \in \Sigma$ yields

$$\sum_{a \in \Sigma} \Big\| \rho^{\frac{1}{4}} \nu(a) \rho^{\frac{1}{4}} \Big\|_2^2 \leq \sum_{a \in \Sigma} \mathrm{Tr}\big(\sqrt{\rho} \nu(a) \sqrt{\rho} \big) = \mathrm{Tr}(\rho) = 1. \tag{3.60}$$

By the definition of the pretty good measurement, along with a similar computation to the one expressed by (3.58), one has that

$$\left\| (\rho^+)^{\frac{1}{4}} \eta(a)(\rho^+)^{\frac{1}{4}} \right\|_2^2 = \left\langle \sqrt{\rho^+}\,\eta(a)\sqrt{\rho^+}, \eta(a) \right\rangle \leq \langle \mu(a), \eta(a) \rangle \qquad (3.61)$$

for each $a \in \Sigma$, and therefore

$$\sum_{a \in \Sigma} \left\| (\rho^+)^{\frac{1}{4}} \eta(a)(\rho^+)^{\frac{1}{4}} \right\|_2^2 \leq \sum_{a \in \Sigma} \langle \mu(a), \eta(a) \rangle. \qquad (3.62)$$

By (3.57), (3.60), and (3.62) it follows that

$$\left(\sum_{a \in \Sigma} \langle \nu(a), \eta(a) \rangle \right)^2 \leq \sum_{a \in \Sigma} \langle \mu(a), \eta(a) \rangle. \qquad (3.63)$$

As this inequality holds for all measurements $\nu \colon \Sigma \to \mathrm{Pos}(\mathcal{X})$, including those measurements that are optimal for η, the proof is complete. $\qquad \square$

3.2 The Fidelity Function

This section introduces the *fidelity function*, which provides a measure of the similarity, or "overlap," between quantum states (and positive semidefinite operators more generally) that will be used extensively throughout this book. It is defined as follows.

Definition 3.11 Let $P, Q \in \mathrm{Pos}(\mathcal{X})$ be positive semidefinite operators, for $\mathcal{X}$ a complex Euclidean space. The *fidelity* $\mathrm{F}(P, Q)$ between P and Q is defined as

$$\mathrm{F}(P, Q) = \left\| \sqrt{P}\sqrt{Q} \right\|_1. \qquad (3.64)$$

The function F is called the *fidelity function*.

The fidelity function is most often considered for density operator inputs, but there is value in defining it more generally, allowing its arguments to range over arbitrary positive semidefinite operators. By expanding (3.64) according to the definition of the trace norm, an alternative expression for the fidelity function is obtained:

$$\mathrm{F}(P, Q) = \mathrm{Tr}\left(\sqrt{\sqrt{Q}P\sqrt{Q}} \right). \qquad (3.65)$$

3.2.1 Elementary Properties of the Fidelity Function

The following proposition establishes several basic properties of the fidelity function.

Proposition 3.12 *Let $P, Q \in \mathrm{Pos}(\mathcal{X})$ be positive semidefinite operators, for $\mathcal{X}$ a complex Euclidean space. The following facts hold:*

1. *The fidelity function F is continuous at (P, Q).*
2. $\mathrm{F}(P, Q) = \mathrm{F}(Q, P)$.
3. $\mathrm{F}(\lambda P, Q) = \sqrt{\lambda}\, \mathrm{F}(P, Q) = \mathrm{F}(P, \lambda Q)$ *for every real number $\lambda \geq 0$.*
4. $\mathrm{F}(P, Q) = \mathrm{F}\big(\Pi_{\mathrm{im}(Q)} P \Pi_{\mathrm{im}(Q)}, Q\big) = \mathrm{F}\big(P, \Pi_{\mathrm{im}(P)} Q \Pi_{\mathrm{im}(P)}\big)$.
5. $\mathrm{F}(P, Q) \geq 0$, *with equality if and only if $PQ = 0$.*
6. $\mathrm{F}(P, Q)^2 \leq \mathrm{Tr}(P)\,\mathrm{Tr}(Q)$, *with equality if and only if P and Q are linearly dependent.*
7. *For every complex Euclidean space $\mathcal{Y}$ with $\dim(\mathcal{Y}) \geq \dim(\mathcal{X})$ and every isometry $V \in \mathrm{U}(\mathcal{X}, \mathcal{Y})$, it holds that $\mathrm{F}(P, Q) = \mathrm{F}(VPV^*, VQV^*)$.*

Proof Statements 1, 2, and 3 follow immediately from the definition of the fidelity function (Definition 3.11): the fidelity function is a composition of continuous functions (the operator square root, operator composition, and the trace norm), and is therefore continuous at every point in its domain; it holds that $\|A\|_1 = \|A^*\|_1$ for any choice of an operator A, and therefore

$$\left\|\sqrt{P}\sqrt{Q}\right\|_1 = \left\|\left(\sqrt{P}\sqrt{Q}\right)^*\right\|_1 = \left\|\sqrt{Q}\sqrt{P}\right\|_1; \tag{3.66}$$

and by the positive scalability of the trace norm, one has

$$\left\|\sqrt{\lambda P}\sqrt{Q}\right\|_1 = \sqrt{\lambda}\left\|\sqrt{P}\sqrt{Q}\right\|_1 = \left\|\sqrt{P}\sqrt{\lambda Q}\right\|_1. \tag{3.67}$$

Moving on to the fourth statement, it follows from the observation

$$\sqrt{Q} = \sqrt{Q}\,\Pi_{\mathrm{im}(Q)} = \Pi_{\mathrm{im}(Q)}\sqrt{Q} \tag{3.68}$$

that

$$\sqrt{Q}P\sqrt{Q} = \sqrt{Q}\Pi_{\mathrm{im}(Q)}P\Pi_{\mathrm{im}(Q)}\sqrt{Q}. \tag{3.69}$$

Through the use of the expression (3.65), it follows that

$$\mathrm{F}(P, Q) = \mathrm{F}\big(\Pi_{\mathrm{im}(Q)}P\Pi_{\mathrm{im}(Q)}, Q\big). \tag{3.70}$$

This proves the first equality in statement 4, while the second equality follows through a combination of the first equality and statement 2.

Statement 5 follows from the fact that the trace norm is positive definite:

$$\left\| \sqrt{P}\sqrt{Q} \right\|_1 \geq 0, \tag{3.71}$$

with equality if and only if $\sqrt{P}\sqrt{Q} = 0$, which is equivalent to $PQ = 0$.

To prove the sixth statement, observe first that, by (1.182), there must exist a unitary operator $U \in \mathrm{U}(\mathcal{X})$ for which

$$\mathrm{F}(P,Q)^2 = \left\| \sqrt{P}\sqrt{Q} \right\|_1^2 = \left| \left\langle U, \sqrt{P}\sqrt{Q} \right\rangle \right|^2 = \left| \left\langle \sqrt{P}U, \sqrt{Q} \right\rangle \right|^2. \tag{3.72}$$

By the Cauchy–Schwarz inequality, it holds that

$$\left| \left\langle \sqrt{P}U, \sqrt{Q} \right\rangle \right|^2 \leq \left\| \sqrt{P}U \right\|_2^2 \left\| \sqrt{Q} \right\|_2^2 = \mathrm{Tr}(P)\,\mathrm{Tr}(Q), \tag{3.73}$$

which establishes the claimed inequality in statement 6. If it is the case that P and Q are linearly dependent, then it must hold that $P = \lambda Q$ or $Q = \lambda P$ for some choice of a nonnegative real number λ. In either case, it is straightforward to verify that

$$\mathrm{F}(P,Q)^2 = \mathrm{Tr}(P)\,\mathrm{Tr}(Q). \tag{3.74}$$

On the other hand, if P and Q are linearly independent, then so too are $\sqrt{P}U$ and $\sqrt{Q}$ for all unitary operators U; for if it holds that

$$\alpha\sqrt{P}U + \beta\sqrt{Q} = 0 \tag{3.75}$$

for scalars $\alpha, \beta \in \mathbb{C}$, then it follows that

$$|\alpha|^2 P = |\beta|^2 Q. \tag{3.76}$$

The assumption that P and Q are linearly independent therefore implies that a strict inequality occurs in the application of the Cauchy–Schwarz inequality in (3.73), which completes the proof of statement 6.

Finally, to prove statement 7, one may observe first that

$$\sqrt{VPV^*} = V\sqrt{P}V^* \quad \text{and} \quad \sqrt{VQV^*} = V\sqrt{Q}V^* \tag{3.77}$$

for every isometry $V \in \mathrm{U}(\mathcal{X},\mathcal{Y})$. By the isometric invariance of the trace norm, it follows that

$$\mathrm{F}(VPV^*, VQV^*) = \left\| V\sqrt{P}V^*V\sqrt{Q}V^* \right\|_1 = \left\| \sqrt{P}\sqrt{Q} \right\|_1, \tag{3.78}$$

which proves statement 7. $\qquad\square$

Statements 5 and 6 of Proposition 3.12 imply that

$$0 \leq \mathrm{F}(\rho, \sigma) \leq 1 \qquad (3.79)$$

for all density operators $\rho, \sigma \in \mathrm{D}(\mathcal{X})$. Moreover, $\mathrm{F}(\rho, \sigma) = 0$ if and only if ρ and σ have orthogonal images, and $\mathrm{F}(\rho, \sigma) = 1$ if and only if $\rho = \sigma$.

The output of the fidelity function is given by a simple formula when one of its input operators has rank equal to 1, as the next proposition states.

Proposition 3.13 *Let $\mathcal{X}$ be a complex Euclidean space, let $v \in \mathcal{X}$ be a vector, and let $P \in \mathrm{Pos}(\mathcal{X})$ be a positive semidefinite operator. It holds that*

$$\mathrm{F}(P, vv^*) = \sqrt{v^* P v}. \qquad (3.80)$$

In particular, for every choice of vectors $u, v \in \mathcal{X}$, it holds that

$$\mathrm{F}(uu^*, vv^*) = |\langle u, v \rangle|. \qquad (3.81)$$

Proof The operator

$$\sqrt{P}\, vv^* \sqrt{P} \qquad (3.82)$$

is positive semidefinite and has rank at most 1. Its largest eigenvalue is therefore

$$\lambda_1\!\left(\sqrt{P}\, vv^* \sqrt{P}\right) = \mathrm{Tr}\!\left(\sqrt{P}\, vv^* \sqrt{P}\right) = v^* P v, \qquad (3.83)$$

while its remaining eigenvalues are 0. It follows that

$$\mathrm{F}(P, vv^*) = \mathrm{Tr}\!\left(\sqrt{\sqrt{P}\, vv^* \sqrt{P}}\right) = \sqrt{\lambda_1\!\left(\sqrt{P}\, vv^* \sqrt{P}\right)} = \sqrt{v^* P v}, \quad (3.84)$$

as claimed. $\square$

The following proposition is representative of another case in which the fidelity function has a simple formula. One corollary of this proposition, known as *Winter's gentle measurement lemma*, is useful in many situations.[2]

Proposition 3.14 *Let $P, Q \in \mathrm{Pos}(\mathcal{X})$ be positive semidefinite operators, for $\mathcal{X}$ a complex Euclidean space. It holds that*

$$\mathrm{F}(P, QPQ) = \langle P, Q \rangle. \qquad (3.85)$$

---

[2] The term *gentle measurement* reflects the observation that if a measurement of a particular state yields a particular outcome with very high probability, then a nondestructive analogue of that measurement causes only a small perturbation to the state in the event that the likely outcome is obtained.

Proof It holds that

$$\sqrt{\sqrt{P}QPQ\sqrt{P}} = \sqrt{\left(\sqrt{P}Q\sqrt{P}\right)^2} = \sqrt{P}Q\sqrt{P}, \tag{3.86}$$

and therefore

$$\mathrm{F}(P, QPQ) = \mathrm{Tr}\left(\sqrt{\sqrt{P}QPQ\sqrt{P}}\right) = \mathrm{Tr}\left(\sqrt{P}Q\sqrt{P}\right) = \langle P, Q\rangle, \tag{3.87}$$

as claimed. □

Corollary 3.15 (Winter's gentle measurement lemma) *Let $\mathcal{X}$ be a complex Euclidean space, let $\rho \in \mathrm{D}(\mathcal{X})$ be a density operator, and let $P \in \mathrm{Pos}(\mathcal{X})$ be a positive semidefinite operator satisfying $P \leq \mathbb{1}_{\mathcal{X}}$ and $\langle P, \rho\rangle > 0$. It holds that*

$$\mathrm{F}\left(\rho, \frac{\sqrt{P}\rho\sqrt{P}}{\langle P, \rho\rangle}\right) \geq \sqrt{\langle P, \rho\rangle}. \tag{3.88}$$

Proof By Proposition 3.14, along with statement 3 of Proposition 3.12, one has

$$\mathrm{F}\left(\rho, \frac{\sqrt{P}\rho\sqrt{P}}{\langle P, \rho\rangle}\right) = \frac{1}{\sqrt{\langle P, \rho\rangle}}\mathrm{F}\left(\rho, \sqrt{P}\rho\sqrt{P}\right) = \frac{\langle\sqrt{P}, \rho\rangle}{\sqrt{\langle P, \rho\rangle}}. \tag{3.89}$$

Under the assumption $0 \leq P \leq \mathbb{1}$, it holds that $\sqrt{P} \geq P$, and therefore $\langle\sqrt{P}, \rho\rangle \geq \langle P, \rho\rangle$, from which the corollary follows. □

Another simple, yet very useful, property of the fidelity function is that it is multiplicative with respect to tensor products.

Proposition 3.16 *Let $P_0, Q_0 \in \mathrm{Pos}(\mathcal{X}_0)$ and $P_1, Q_1 \in \mathrm{Pos}(\mathcal{X}_1)$ be positive semidefinite operators, for complex Euclidean spaces $\mathcal{X}_0$ and $\mathcal{X}_1$. It holds that*

$$\mathrm{F}(P_0 \otimes P_1, Q_0 \otimes Q_1) = \mathrm{F}(P_0, Q_0)\,\mathrm{F}(P_1, Q_1). \tag{3.90}$$

Proof Operator square roots and compositions respect tensor products, and the trace norm is multiplicative with respect to tensor products, so

$$\mathrm{F}(P_0 \otimes P_1, Q_0 \otimes Q_1) = \left\|\sqrt{P_0 \otimes P_1}\sqrt{Q_0 \otimes Q_1}\right\|_1$$

$$= \left\|\sqrt{P_0}\sqrt{Q_0} \otimes \sqrt{P_1}\sqrt{Q_1}\right\|_1 = \left\|\sqrt{P_0}\sqrt{Q_0}\right\|_1\left\|\sqrt{P_1}\sqrt{Q_1}\right\|_1 \tag{3.91}$$

$$= \mathrm{F}(P_0, Q_0)\,\mathrm{F}(P_1, Q_1),$$

as claimed. □

3.2.2 Characterizations of the Fidelity Function

Multiple alternative characterizations of the fidelity function are known; a selection of such alternative characterizations is presented below. Some of these characterizations will allow for further properties of the fidelity function to be established, or will find other uses elsewhere in this book.

Block Operator Characterization

The first alternative characterization of the fidelity function to be presented is given by the following theorem. This characterization is particularly useful for establishing relevant properties of the fidelity function, including joint concavity in its arguments and monotonicity under the actions of channels, as will be described in the section following this one.

Theorem 3.17 *Let $\mathcal{X}$ be a complex Euclidean space and let $P, Q \in \mathrm{Pos}(\mathcal{X})$ be positive semidefinite operators. It holds that*

$$
\mathrm{F}(P,Q) = \max\left\{|\mathrm{Tr}(X)| : X \in \mathrm{L}(\mathcal{X}), \begin{pmatrix} P & X \\ X^* & Q \end{pmatrix} \in \mathrm{Pos}(\mathcal{X} \oplus \mathcal{X})\right\}. \quad (3.92)
$$

The following lemma, which will find other uses elsewhere in this book, will be used to prove Theorem 3.17. The lemma is stated in slightly greater generality than is needed in the present context, in that it does not require P and Q to act on the same space, but there is no added difficulty in proving it with this greater generality.

Lemma 3.18 *Let $\mathcal{X}$ and $\mathcal{Y}$ be complex Euclidean spaces, let $P \in \mathrm{Pos}(\mathcal{X})$ and $Q \in \mathrm{Pos}(\mathcal{Y})$ be positive semidefinite operators, and let $X \in \mathrm{L}(\mathcal{Y}, \mathcal{X})$ be an operator. It holds that*

$$
\begin{pmatrix} P & X \\ X^* & Q \end{pmatrix} \in \mathrm{Pos}(\mathcal{X} \oplus \mathcal{Y}) \quad (3.93)
$$

if and only if $X = \sqrt{P}K\sqrt{Q}$ for some choice of $K \in \mathrm{L}(\mathcal{Y}, \mathcal{X})$ satisfying $\|K\| \leq 1$.

Proof Suppose first that $X = \sqrt{P}K\sqrt{Q}$ for $K \in \mathrm{L}(\mathcal{Y}, \mathcal{X})$ being an operator for which $\|K\| \leq 1$. It follows that $KK^* \leq \mathbb{1}_{\mathcal{X}}$, and therefore

$$
0 \leq \begin{pmatrix} \sqrt{P}K \\ \sqrt{Q} \end{pmatrix}\begin{pmatrix} K^*\sqrt{P} & \sqrt{Q} \end{pmatrix} = \begin{pmatrix} \sqrt{P}KK^*\sqrt{P} & X \\ X^* & Q \end{pmatrix} \leq \begin{pmatrix} P & X \\ X^* & Q \end{pmatrix}. \quad (3.94)
$$

For the reverse implication, assume

$$\begin{pmatrix} P & X \\ X^* & Q \end{pmatrix} \in \text{Pos}(\mathcal{X} \oplus \mathcal{Y}), \tag{3.95}$$

and define

$$K = \sqrt{P^+} X \sqrt{Q^+}. \tag{3.96}$$

It will be proved that $X = \sqrt{P} K \sqrt{Q}$ and $\|K\| \leq 1$. Observe first that, for every Hermitian operator $H \in \text{Herm}(\mathcal{X})$, the block operator

$$\begin{pmatrix} H & 0 \\ 0 & \mathbb{1} \end{pmatrix} \begin{pmatrix} P & X \\ X^* & Q \end{pmatrix} \begin{pmatrix} H & 0 \\ 0 & \mathbb{1} \end{pmatrix} = \begin{pmatrix} HPH & HX \\ X^*H & Q \end{pmatrix} \tag{3.97}$$

is positive semidefinite. In particular, for $H = \Pi_{\text{ker}(P)}$ being the projection onto the kernel of P, one has that the operator

$$\begin{pmatrix} 0 & \Pi_{\text{ker}(P)} X \\ X^* \Pi_{\text{ker}(P)} & Q \end{pmatrix} \tag{3.98}$$

is positive semidefinite, which implies that $\Pi_{\text{ker}(P)} X = 0$, and therefore $\Pi_{\text{im}(P)} X = X$. Through a similar argument, one finds that $X \Pi_{\text{im}(Q)} = X$. It therefore follows that

$$\sqrt{P} K \sqrt{Q} = \Pi_{\text{im}(P)} X \Pi_{\text{im}(Q)} = X. \tag{3.99}$$

Next, note that

$$\begin{pmatrix} x^* P x & x^* X y \\ y^* X^* x & y^* Q y \end{pmatrix} = \begin{pmatrix} x^* & 0 \\ 0 & y^* \end{pmatrix} \begin{pmatrix} P & X \\ X^* & Q \end{pmatrix} \begin{pmatrix} x & 0 \\ 0 & y \end{pmatrix} \geq 0 \tag{3.100}$$

for every choice of vectors $x \in \mathcal{X}$ and $y \in \mathcal{Y}$. Setting

$$x = \sqrt{P^+} u \quad \text{and} \quad y = \sqrt{Q^+} v \tag{3.101}$$

for arbitrarily chosen unit vectors $u \in \mathcal{X}$ and $v \in \mathcal{Y}$, one finds that

$$\begin{pmatrix} 1 & u^* K v \\ v^* K^* u & 1 \end{pmatrix} \geq \begin{pmatrix} u^* \Pi_{\text{im}(P)} u & u^* K v \\ v^* K^* u & v^* \Pi_{\text{im}(Q)} v \end{pmatrix} \geq 0 \tag{3.102}$$

and therefore $|u^* K v| \leq 1$. As this inequality holds for all unit vectors u and v, it follows that $\|K\| \leq 1$, as required. $\qquad\square$

Proof of Theorem 3.17 By Lemma 3.18, the expression on the right-hand side of the equation (3.92) may be written as

$$\max \left\{ \left| \text{Tr}\left(\sqrt{P} K \sqrt{Q} \right) \right| : K \in \text{L}(\mathcal{X}), \|K\| \leq 1 \right\}, \tag{3.103}$$

which is equivalent to

$$\max\left\{\left|\langle K, \sqrt{P}\sqrt{Q}\rangle\right| : K \in L(\mathcal{X}), \|K\| \leq 1\right\}. \tag{3.104}$$

By the duality of the trace and spectral norms, as expressed by (1.173), one has

$$\max\left\{\left|\langle K, \sqrt{P}\sqrt{Q}\rangle\right| : K \in L(\mathcal{X}), \|K\| \leq 1\right\}$$
$$= \left\|\sqrt{P}\sqrt{Q}\right\|_1 = F(P, Q), \tag{3.105}$$

which completes the proof. □

Remark For any choice of operators $P, Q \in \mathrm{Pos}(\mathcal{X})$ and $X \in L(\mathcal{X})$, and a scalar $\alpha \in \mathbb{C}$ satisfying $|\alpha| = 1$, it holds that

$$\begin{pmatrix} P & X \\ X^* & Q \end{pmatrix} \in \mathrm{Pos}(\mathcal{X} \oplus \mathcal{X}) \tag{3.106}$$

if and only if

$$\begin{pmatrix} P & \alpha X \\ \overline{\alpha} X^* & Q \end{pmatrix} \in \mathrm{Pos}(\mathcal{X} \oplus \mathcal{X}). \tag{3.107}$$

This fact follows from Lemma 3.18. Alternatively, one may conclude that (3.106) implies (3.107) through the equation

$$\begin{pmatrix} \mathbb{1} & 0 \\ 0 & \alpha\mathbb{1} \end{pmatrix}^* \begin{pmatrix} P & X \\ X^* & Q \end{pmatrix} \begin{pmatrix} \mathbb{1} & 0 \\ 0 & \alpha\mathbb{1} \end{pmatrix} = \begin{pmatrix} P & \alpha X \\ \overline{\alpha} X^* & Q \end{pmatrix}, \tag{3.108}$$

while the reverse implication is obtained similarly, through the equation

$$\begin{pmatrix} \mathbb{1} & 0 \\ 0 & \alpha\mathbb{1} \end{pmatrix} \begin{pmatrix} P & \alpha X \\ \overline{\alpha} X^* & Q \end{pmatrix} \begin{pmatrix} \mathbb{1} & 0 \\ 0 & \alpha\mathbb{1} \end{pmatrix}^* = \begin{pmatrix} P & X \\ X^* & Q \end{pmatrix}. \tag{3.109}$$

For any two positive semidefinite operators $P, Q \in \mathrm{Pos}(\mathcal{X})$, it therefore holds that the fidelity $F(P, Q)$ is given by the expression

$$\max\left\{\Re(\mathrm{Tr}(X)) : X \in L(\mathcal{X}), \begin{pmatrix} P & X \\ X^* & Q \end{pmatrix} \in \mathrm{Pos}(\mathcal{X} \oplus \mathcal{X})\right\}, \tag{3.110}$$

where $\Re(\beta)$ denotes the real part of a complex number β. Moreover, there must exist an operator $X \in L(\mathcal{X})$ such that

$$\begin{pmatrix} P & X \\ X^* & Q \end{pmatrix} \in \mathrm{Pos}(\mathcal{X} \oplus \mathcal{X}) \tag{3.111}$$

and $F(P, Q) = \mathrm{Tr}(X)$.

The characterization of the fidelity function established by Theorem 3.17 provides an expression of the fidelity $F(P, Q)$ corresponding to the optimal value of a semidefinite program, as will now be explained. First, define a map $\Phi \in T(\mathcal{X} \oplus \mathcal{X})$ as

$$\Phi \begin{pmatrix} X_0 & \cdot \\ \cdot & X_1 \end{pmatrix} = \frac{1}{2} \begin{pmatrix} X_0 & 0 \\ 0 & X_1 \end{pmatrix} \tag{3.112}$$

for every $X_0, X_1 \in L(\mathcal{X})$, where the dots represent elements of $L(\mathcal{X})$ that have no influence on the output of this map. One may verify that the map Φ is self-adjoint: $\Phi = \Phi^*$. Then, for a given choice of $P, Q \in \text{Pos}(\mathcal{X})$, define Hermitian operators $A, B \in \text{Herm}(\mathcal{X} \oplus \mathcal{X})$ as

$$A = \frac{1}{2} \begin{pmatrix} 0 & \mathbb{1} \\ \mathbb{1} & 0 \end{pmatrix} \quad \text{and} \quad B = \frac{1}{2} \begin{pmatrix} P & 0 \\ 0 & Q \end{pmatrix}. \tag{3.113}$$

The primal and dual optimization problems associated with the semidefinite program (Φ, A, B), after minor simplifications, are as follows:

Primal problem	Dual problem
maximize: $\quad \frac{1}{2} \text{Tr}(X) + \frac{1}{2} \text{Tr}(X^*)$	minimize: $\quad \frac{1}{2}\langle P, Y_0\rangle + \frac{1}{2}\langle Q, Y_1\rangle$
subject to: $\begin{pmatrix} P & X \\ X^* & Q \end{pmatrix} \geq 0,$	subject to: $\begin{pmatrix} Y_0 & -\mathbb{1} \\ -\mathbb{1} & Y_1 \end{pmatrix} \geq 0,$
$X \in L(\mathcal{X}).$	$Y_0, Y_1 \in \text{Herm}(\mathcal{X}).$

The optimal primal value of this semidefinite program is equal to $F(P, Q)$, as it is in agreement with the expression (3.110).

The primal problem is evidently feasible, as one may simply take $X = 0$ to obtain a primal feasible solution. The dual problem is strictly feasible: for any choice of $Y_0 > \mathbb{1}$ and $Y_1 > \mathbb{1}$, one has that the operator

$$\begin{pmatrix} Y_0 & -\mathbb{1} \\ -\mathbb{1} & Y_1 \end{pmatrix} \tag{3.114}$$

is positive definite. Strong duality therefore follows by Slater's theorem for semidefinite programs (Theorem 1.18).

Alberti's Theorem

As the semidefinite program for the fidelity described above possesses the property of strong duality, its dual optimum must be equal to the primal optimum $F(P, Q)$. The next theorem is a consequence of this observation.

Theorem 3.19 *Let $\mathcal{X}$ be a complex Euclidean space and let $P, Q \in \mathrm{Pos}(\mathcal{X})$ be positive semidefinite operators. It holds that*

$$\mathrm{F}(P, Q) = \inf\left\{\frac{1}{2}\langle P, Y\rangle + \frac{1}{2}\langle Q, Y^{-1}\rangle : Y \in \mathrm{Pd}(\mathcal{X})\right\}. \tag{3.115}$$

Proof Through the use of Lemma 3.18, one may verify that the operator

$$\begin{pmatrix} Y_0 & -\mathbb{1} \\ -\mathbb{1} & Y_1 \end{pmatrix} \tag{3.116}$$

is positive semidefinite, for a given choice of $Y_0, Y_1 \in \mathrm{Herm}(\mathcal{X})$, if and only if both Y_0 and Y_1 are positive definite and satisfy $Y_1 \geq Y_0^{-1}$. Because Q is positive semidefinite, it holds that $\langle Q, Y_1\rangle \geq \langle Q, Y_0^{-1}\rangle$ provided $Y_0 > 0$ and $Y_1 \geq Y_0^{-1}$, so the dual problem associated to the semidefinite program (Φ, A, B) defined from P and Q as above is equivalent to a minimization of

$$\frac{1}{2}\langle P, Y\rangle + \frac{1}{2}\langle Q, Y^{-1}\rangle \tag{3.117}$$

over all positive definite operators $Y \in \mathrm{Pd}(\mathcal{X})$. As the optimum value of the dual problem is equal to $\mathrm{F}(P, Q)$, the theorem follows. $\square$

Theorem 3.19 implies the following corollary, which states a fact known as Alberti's theorem.[3]

Corollary 3.20 (Alberti's theorem) *Let $\mathcal{X}$ be a complex Euclidean space and let $P, Q \in \mathrm{Pos}(\mathcal{X})$ be positive semidefinite operators. It holds that*

$$\mathrm{F}(P, Q)^2 = \inf\left\{\langle P, Y\rangle\langle Q, Y^{-1}\rangle : Y \in \mathrm{Pd}(\mathcal{X})\right\}. \tag{3.118}$$

Proof If either of P or Q is zero, the corollary is trivial, so it may be taken as an assumption that neither P nor Q is zero for the remainder of the proof.

The arithmetic–geometric mean inequality implies that

$$\sqrt{\langle P, Y\rangle\langle Q, Y^{-1}\rangle} \leq \frac{1}{2}\langle P, Y\rangle + \frac{1}{2}\langle Q, Y^{-1}\rangle \tag{3.119}$$

for every operator $Y \in \mathrm{Pd}(\mathcal{X})$. By Theorem 3.19, one concludes that

$$\inf\left\{\langle P, Y\rangle\langle Q, Y^{-1}\rangle : Y \in \mathrm{Pd}(\mathcal{X})\right\} \leq \mathrm{F}(P, Q)^2. \tag{3.120}$$

On the other hand, for any choice of $Y \in \mathrm{Pd}(\mathcal{X})$, it holds that

$$\sqrt{\langle P, Y\rangle\langle Q, Y^{-1}\rangle} = \sqrt{\langle P, \alpha Y\rangle\langle Q, (\alpha Y)^{-1}\rangle} \tag{3.121}$$

---

[3] One may also prove that Corollary 3.20 implies Theorem 3.19, so the two facts are in fact equivalent.

for every nonzero real number $\alpha \in \mathbb{R}$. In particular, for

$$\alpha = \sqrt{\frac{\langle Q, Y^{-1} \rangle}{\langle P, Y \rangle}}, \tag{3.122}$$

which has been selected so that $\langle P, \alpha Y \rangle = \langle Q, (\alpha Y)^{-1} \rangle$, one has

$$\sqrt{\langle P, Y \rangle \langle Q, Y^{-1} \rangle} = \sqrt{\langle P, \alpha Y \rangle \langle Q, (\alpha Y)^{-1} \rangle}$$
$$= \frac{1}{2} \langle P, \alpha Y \rangle + \frac{1}{2} \langle Q, (\alpha Y)^{-1} \rangle \geq \mathrm{F}(P, Q), \tag{3.123}$$

and therefore

$$\inf \left\{ \langle P, Y \rangle \langle Q, Y^{-1} \rangle : Y \in \mathrm{Pd}(\mathcal{X}) \right\} \geq \mathrm{F}(P, Q)^2, \tag{3.124}$$

which completes the proof. $\qquad\qquad\square$

It is possible to prove Theorem 3.19 directly, without making use of semidefinite programming duality, as the following proof demonstrates.

Alternative proof of Theorem 3.19 The special case in which $P = Q$ will be considered first. In this case, one aims to prove

$$\inf \left\{ \frac{1}{2} \langle Y, P \rangle + \frac{1}{2} \langle Y^{-1}, P \rangle : Y \in \mathrm{Pd}(\mathcal{X}) \right\} = \mathrm{Tr}(P). \tag{3.125}$$

As $Y = \mathbb{1}$ is positive definite, it is evident that the infimum in (3.125) is at most $\mathrm{Tr}(P)$, so it suffices to prove

$$\frac{1}{2} \langle Y, P \rangle + \frac{1}{2} \langle Y^{-1}, P \rangle \geq \mathrm{Tr}(P) \tag{3.126}$$

for every choice of $Y \in \mathrm{Pd}(\mathcal{X})$. As the operator

$$\frac{Y + Y^{-1}}{2} - \mathbb{1} = \frac{1}{2} \left(Y^{\frac{1}{2}} - Y^{-\frac{1}{2}} \right)^2 \tag{3.127}$$

is the square of a Hermitian operator, it must be positive semidefinite, and therefore

$$\frac{1}{2} \langle Y + Y^{-1}, P \rangle \geq \langle \mathbb{1}, P \rangle = \mathrm{Tr}(P). \tag{3.128}$$

This proves that equation (3.125) holds, and therefore proves the theorem in the special case $P = Q$.

Next, one may consider the case in which P and Q are positive definite operators. Let

$$R = \sqrt{\sqrt{P} Q \sqrt{P}}, \tag{3.129}$$

and define a mapping $\Phi \in \mathrm{CP}(\mathcal{X})$ as

$$\Phi(X) = R^{-\frac{1}{2}}\sqrt{P}X\sqrt{P}R^{-\frac{1}{2}} \tag{3.130}$$

for every $X \in \mathrm{L}(\mathcal{X})$. For any choice of $Y \in \mathrm{Pd}(\mathcal{X})$, it holds that

$$\langle \Phi(Y), R \rangle = \langle Y, P \rangle \quad \text{and} \quad \langle \Phi(Y)^{-1}, R \rangle = \langle Y^{-1}, Q \rangle, \tag{3.131}$$

and therefore

$$\inf_{Y \in \mathrm{Pd}(\mathcal{X})} \frac{\langle Y, P \rangle + \langle Y^{-1}, Q \rangle}{2} = \inf_{Y \in \mathrm{Pd}(\mathcal{X})} \frac{\langle \Phi(Y), R \rangle + \langle \Phi(Y)^{-1}, R \rangle}{2}. \tag{3.132}$$

Observing that, as Y ranges over all positive definite operators, so too does $\Phi(Y)$, one has that

$$\inf_{Y \in \mathrm{Pd}(\mathcal{X})} \frac{\langle Y, P \rangle + \langle Y^{-1}, Q \rangle}{2} = \mathrm{Tr}(R) = \mathrm{F}(P, Q) \tag{3.133}$$

by the special case considered in the initial part of the proof.

Finally, in the most general case, the theorem follows from a continuity argument. In greater detail, for every positive real number $\varepsilon > 0$, one has

$$\frac{1}{2}\langle Y, P \rangle + \frac{1}{2}\langle Y^{-1}, Q \rangle \leq \frac{1}{2}\langle Y, P + \varepsilon \mathbb{1} \rangle + \frac{1}{2}\langle Y^{-1}, Q + \varepsilon \mathbb{1} \rangle \tag{3.134}$$

for every choice of $Y \in \mathrm{Pd}(\mathcal{X})$. Taking the infimum over all positive definite operators $Y \in \mathrm{Pd}(\mathcal{X})$ yields the inequality

$$\inf_{Y \in \mathrm{Pd}(\mathcal{X})} \frac{\langle Y, P \rangle + \langle Y^{-1}, Q \rangle}{2} \leq \mathrm{F}(P + \varepsilon \mathbb{1}, Q + \varepsilon \mathbb{1}), \tag{3.135}$$

which holds by virtue of the fact that $P + \varepsilon \mathbb{1}$ and $Q + \varepsilon \mathbb{1}$ are necessarily positive definite. As this inequality holds for all $\varepsilon > 0$, it follows from the continuity of the fidelity function that

$$\inf_{Y \in \mathrm{Pd}(\mathcal{X})} \frac{\langle Y, P \rangle + \langle Y^{-1}, Q \rangle}{2} \leq \mathrm{F}(P, Q). \tag{3.136}$$

On the other hand, for each choice of $Y \in \mathrm{Pd}(\mathcal{X})$, one has

$$\frac{1}{2}\langle Y, P + \varepsilon \mathbb{1} \rangle + \frac{1}{2}\langle Y^{-1}, Q + \varepsilon \mathbb{1} \rangle \geq \mathrm{F}(P + \varepsilon \mathbb{1}, Q + \varepsilon \mathbb{1}) \tag{3.137}$$

for all $\varepsilon > 0$, and therefore the inequality

$$\frac{1}{2}\langle Y, P \rangle + \frac{1}{2}\langle Y^{-1}, Q \rangle \geq \mathrm{F}(P, Q) \tag{3.138}$$

follows from the continuity of the expressions on both the left- and right-hand sides of (3.137). This is so for all $Y \in \mathrm{Pd}(\mathcal{X})$, and therefore

$$\inf_{Y \in \mathrm{Pd}(\mathcal{X})} \frac{\langle Y, P \rangle + \langle Y^{-1}, Q \rangle}{2} \geq \mathrm{F}(P, Q), \tag{3.139}$$

which completes the proof. $\qquad\square$

Uhlmann's Theorem

Uhlmann's theorem establishes a link between the fidelity function and the notion of a purification of a state (or of a positive semidefinite operator more generally), providing a characterization of the fidelity function that finds many uses in the theory of quantum information. The lemma that follows will be used to prove this theorem.

Lemma 3.21 *Let $A, B \in \mathrm{L}(\mathcal{Y}, \mathcal{X})$ be operators, for complex Euclidean spaces $\mathcal{X}$ and $\mathcal{Y}$. It holds that*

$$\mathrm{F}(AA^*, BB^*) = \|A^* B\|_1. \tag{3.140}$$

Proof Using the polar decomposition of operators, one may write

$$\begin{pmatrix} 0 & A \\ 0 & 0 \end{pmatrix} = PU \quad \text{and} \quad \begin{pmatrix} 0 & B \\ 0 & 0 \end{pmatrix} = QV, \tag{3.141}$$

for positive semidefinite operators $P, Q \in \mathrm{Pos}(\mathcal{X} \oplus \mathcal{Y})$ and unitary operators $U, V \in \mathrm{U}(\mathcal{X} \oplus \mathcal{Y})$. The following equations may be verified:

$$P^2 = \begin{pmatrix} AA^* & 0 \\ 0 & 0 \end{pmatrix}, \quad Q^2 = \begin{pmatrix} BB^* & 0 \\ 0 & 0 \end{pmatrix}, \tag{3.142}$$

and

$$U^* PQV = \begin{pmatrix} 0 & 0 \\ 0 & A^* B \end{pmatrix}. \tag{3.143}$$

By the isometric invariance of the trace norm, it follows that

$$\mathrm{F}(AA^*, BB^*) = \left\| \sqrt{AA^*} \sqrt{BB^*} \right\|_1$$
$$= \|PQ\|_1 = \|U^* PQV\|_1 = \|A^* B\|_1, \tag{3.144}$$

as required. $\qquad\square$

Theorem 3.22 (Uhlmann's theorem) *Let $\mathcal{X}$ and $\mathcal{Y}$ be complex Euclidean spaces, let $P, Q \in \mathrm{Pos}(\mathcal{X})$ be positive semidefinite operators having rank at most $\dim(\mathcal{Y})$, and let $u \in \mathcal{X} \otimes \mathcal{Y}$ satisfy $\mathrm{Tr}_{\mathcal{Y}}(uu^*) = P$. It holds that*

$$\mathrm{F}(P, Q) = \max\{|\langle u, v \rangle| : v \in \mathcal{X} \otimes \mathcal{Y}, \ \mathrm{Tr}_{\mathcal{Y}}(vv^*) = Q\}. \tag{3.145}$$

Proof Let $A \in L(\mathcal{Y}, \mathcal{X})$ be the operator for which $u = \text{vec}(A)$, let $w \in \mathcal{X} \otimes \mathcal{Y}$ be a vector satisfying $Q = \text{Tr}_{\mathcal{Y}}(ww^*)$, and let $B \in L(\mathcal{Y}, \mathcal{X})$ be the operator for which $w = \text{vec}(B)$. It follows by the unitary equivalence of purifications (Theorem 2.12) that

$$
\begin{aligned}
\max\{&|\langle u, v\rangle| : v \in \mathcal{X} \otimes \mathcal{Y}, \ \text{Tr}_{\mathcal{Y}}(vv^*) = Q\} \\
&= \max\{|\langle u, (\mathbb{1}_{\mathcal{X}} \otimes U)w\rangle| : U \in \text{U}(\mathcal{Y})\} \\
&= \max\{|\langle A, BU^{\mathsf{T}}\rangle| : U \in \text{U}(\mathcal{Y})\} \qquad (3.146) \\
&= \max\{|\langle \overline{U}, A^*B\rangle| : U \in \text{U}(\mathcal{Y})\} \\
&= \|A^*B\|_1.
\end{aligned}
$$

By Lemma 3.21, it holds that

$$
\|A^*B\|_1 = \text{F}(AA^*, BB^*) = \text{F}(P, Q), \qquad (3.147)
$$

which completes the proof. $\qquad\qquad\qquad\qquad\qquad\qquad\qquad\qquad\qquad\square$

It will be convenient later in the chapter to make use of the following corollary, which is essentially a rephrasing of Lemma 3.21.

Corollary 3.23 *Let $u, v \in \mathcal{X} \otimes \mathcal{Y}$ be vectors, for complex Euclidean spaces $\mathcal{X}$ and $\mathcal{Y}$. It holds that*

$$
\text{F}(\text{Tr}_{\mathcal{Y}}(uu^*), \text{Tr}_{\mathcal{Y}}(vv^*)) = \|\text{Tr}_{\mathcal{X}}(vu^*)\|_1. \qquad (3.148)
$$

Proof Let $A, B \in L(\mathcal{Y}, \mathcal{X})$ be the operators for which $u = \text{vec}(A)$ and $v = \text{vec}(B)$. By Lemma 3.21, one has

$$
\begin{aligned}
\text{F}(\text{Tr}_{\mathcal{Y}}(uu^*), \text{Tr}_{\mathcal{Y}}(vv^*)) &= \text{F}(AA^*, BB^*) \\
&= \|A^*B\|_1 = \|(A^*B)^{\mathsf{T}}\|_1 = \|\text{Tr}_{\mathcal{X}}(vu^*)\|_1
\end{aligned} \qquad (3.149)
$$

as required. $\qquad\qquad\qquad\qquad\qquad\qquad\qquad\qquad\qquad\qquad\qquad\square$

Bhattacharyya Coefficient Characterization

The last characterization of the fidelity function to be described in this section is based on a quantity known as the *Bhattacharyya coefficient*. For any alphabet Σ, and for vectors $u, v \in [0, \infty)^{\Sigma}$ having nonnegative real number entries, the Bhattacharyya coefficient $\text{B}(u, v)$ is defined as

$$
\text{B}(u, v) = \sum_{a \in \Sigma} \sqrt{u(a)} \sqrt{v(a)}. \qquad (3.150)
$$

The connection between the Bhattacharyya coefficient and the fidelity function concerns the measurement statistics generated from pairs of states. To explain this connection, the following notation is helpful: for positive semidefinite operators $P, Q \in \mathrm{Pos}(\mathcal{X})$ and a measurement $\mu \colon \Sigma \to \mathrm{Pos}(\mathcal{X})$, one defines

$$\mathrm{B}(P, Q \mid \mu) = \sum_{a \in \Sigma} \sqrt{\langle \mu(a), P \rangle} \sqrt{\langle \mu(a), Q \rangle}. \tag{3.151}$$

Equivalently,

$$\mathrm{B}(P, Q \mid \mu) = \mathrm{B}(u, v) \tag{3.152}$$

for $u, v \in [0, \infty)^{\Sigma}$ being the vectors defined as

$$u(a) = \langle \mu(a), P \rangle \quad \text{and} \quad v(a) = \langle \mu(a), Q \rangle \tag{3.153}$$

for each $a \in \Sigma$.

Theorem 3.24 *Let $\mathcal{X}$ be a complex Euclidean space, let Σ be an alphabet, and let $P, Q \in \mathrm{Pos}(\mathcal{X})$ be positive semidefinite operators. For every choice of a measurement $\mu \colon \Sigma \to \mathrm{Pos}(\mathcal{X})$, it holds that*

$$\mathrm{F}(P, Q) \leq \mathrm{B}(P, Q \mid \mu). \tag{3.154}$$

Moreover, if it holds that $|\Sigma| \geq \dim(\mathcal{X})$, then there exists a measurement $\mu \colon \Sigma \to \mathrm{Pos}(\mathcal{X})$ for which equality holds in (3.154).

Proof Assume first that $\mu \colon \Sigma \to \mathrm{Pos}(\mathcal{X})$ is an arbitrary measurement, and let $U \in \mathrm{U}(\mathcal{X})$ be a unitary operator satisfying

$$\mathrm{F}(P, Q) = \left\| \sqrt{P} \sqrt{Q} \right\|_1 = \left\langle U, \sqrt{P} \sqrt{Q} \right\rangle. \tag{3.155}$$

By the triangle inequality followed by the Cauchy–Schwarz inequality, one finds that

$$\mathrm{F}(P, Q) = \left\langle U, \sqrt{P} \sqrt{Q} \right\rangle = \sum_{a \in \Sigma} \left\langle U, \sqrt{P} \mu(a) \sqrt{Q} \right\rangle$$

$$\leq \sum_{a \in \Sigma} \left| \left\langle \sqrt{\mu(a)} \sqrt{P} U, \sqrt{\mu(a)} \sqrt{Q} \right\rangle \right| \tag{3.156}$$

$$\leq \sum_{a \in \Sigma} \sqrt{\langle \mu(a), P \rangle} \sqrt{\langle \mu(a), Q \rangle} = \mathrm{B}(P, Q \mid \mu).$$

Next, it will be proved, under the assumption $|\Sigma| \geq \dim(\mathcal{X})$, that there exists a measurement $\mu \colon \Sigma \to \mathrm{Pos}(\mathcal{X})$ for which $\mathrm{F}(P, Q) = \mathrm{B}(P, Q \mid \mu)$. It suffices to prove that there is a measurement

$$\mu \colon \{1, \ldots, n\} \to \mathrm{Pos}(\mathcal{X}) \tag{3.157}$$

for which $\mathrm{F}(P, Q) = \mathrm{B}(P, Q \mid \mu)$, for $n = \dim(\mathcal{X})$.

Consider first the case in which P is invertible. Define

$$R = P^{-\frac{1}{2}} \left(\sqrt{P} Q \sqrt{P} \right)^{\frac{1}{2}} P^{-\frac{1}{2}}, \qquad (3.158)$$

and assume

$$R = \sum_{k=1}^{n} \lambda_k(R) u_k u_k^* \qquad (3.159)$$

is a spectral decomposition of R. One may verify that $Q = RPR$, from which it follows that

$$
\begin{aligned}
\sum_{k=1}^{n} \sqrt{\langle u_k u_k^*, P \rangle} \sqrt{\langle u_k u_k^*, Q \rangle} &= \sum_{k=1}^{n} \sqrt{\langle u_k u_k^*, P \rangle} \sqrt{\langle u_k u_k^*, RPR \rangle} \\
&= \sum_{k=1}^{n} \lambda_k(R) \langle u_k u_k^*, P \rangle = \langle R, P \rangle = \mathrm{Tr} \left(\sqrt{\sqrt{P} Q \sqrt{P}} \right) = \mathrm{F}(P, Q).
\end{aligned}
\qquad (3.160)
$$

The measurement $\mu \colon \{1, \ldots, n\} \to \mathrm{Pos}(\mathcal{X})$ defined by

$$\mu(k) = u_k u_k^* \qquad (3.161)$$

for each $k \in \{1, \ldots, n\}$ therefore satisfies $\mathrm{F}(P, Q) = \mathrm{B}(P, Q \,|\, \mu)$.

Finally, the case in which $r = \mathrm{rank}(P) < n$ will be considered. Let $\Pi = \Pi_{\mathrm{im}(P)}$ denote the projection onto the image of P. By restricting one's attention to this subspace, the argument above may be seen to imply the existence of an orthonormal basis $\{u_1, \ldots, u_r\}$ for $\mathrm{im}(P)$ that satisfies

$$\mathrm{F}(P, \Pi Q \Pi) = \sum_{k=1}^{r} \sqrt{\langle u_k u_k^*, P \rangle} \sqrt{\langle u_k u_k^*, \Pi Q \Pi \rangle}. \qquad (3.162)$$

Let $\{u_1, \ldots, u_n\}$ be any orthonormal basis of $\mathcal{X}$ obtained by completing the orthonormal set $\{u_1, \ldots, u_r\}$. As $\langle u_k u_k^*, P \rangle = 0$ for $k > r$ and

$$\langle u_k u_k^*, \Pi Q \Pi \rangle = \langle u_k u_k^*, Q \rangle \qquad (3.163)$$

for $k \leq r$, it follows that

$$
\begin{aligned}
\sum_{k=1}^{n} \sqrt{\langle u_k u_k^*, P \rangle} \sqrt{\langle u_k u_k^*, Q \rangle} \\
= \sum_{k=1}^{r} \sqrt{\langle u_k u_k^*, P \rangle} \sqrt{\langle u_k u_k^*, \Pi Q \Pi \rangle} = \mathrm{F}(P, \Pi Q \Pi) = \mathrm{F}(P, Q),
\end{aligned}
\qquad (3.164)
$$

where the final equality holds by statement 4 of Proposition 3.12. Thus, the measurement $\mu \colon \{1, \ldots, n\} \to \mathrm{Pos}(\mathcal{X})$ defined by (3.161) for each $k \in \{1, \ldots, n\}$ satisfies $\mathrm{F}(P, Q) = \mathrm{B}(P, Q \,|\, \mu)$, which completes the proof. $\qquad \square$

3.2.3 Further Properties of the Fidelity Function

Various properties of the fidelity function can be established by means of the alternative characterizations presented in Section 3.2.2.

Joint Concavity and Monotonicity Under the Action of Channels

The next theorem will be proved using the block operator characterization of the fidelity function (Theorem 3.17). As a corollary of this theorem, one finds that the fidelity function is *jointly concave* in its arguments.

Theorem 3.25 *Let $P_0, P_1, Q_0, Q_1 \in \mathrm{Pos}(\mathcal{X})$ be positive semidefinite operators, for $\mathcal{X}$ being a complex Euclidean space. It holds that*

$$\mathrm{F}(P_0 + P_1, Q_0 + Q_1) \geq \mathrm{F}(P_0, Q_0) + \mathrm{F}(P_1, Q_1). \tag{3.165}$$

Proof By Theorem 3.17 (together with the remark that follows it), one may choose operators $X_0, X_1 \in \mathrm{L}(\mathcal{X})$ such that the block operators

$$\begin{pmatrix} P_0 & X_0 \\ X_0^* & Q_0 \end{pmatrix} \quad \text{and} \quad \begin{pmatrix} P_1 & X_1 \\ X_1^* & Q_1 \end{pmatrix} \tag{3.166}$$

are both positive semidefinite, and such that

$$\mathrm{Tr}(X_0) = \mathrm{F}(P_0, Q_0) \quad \text{and} \quad \mathrm{Tr}(X_1) = \mathrm{F}(P_1, Q_1). \tag{3.167}$$

The sum of two positive semidefinite operators is positive semidefinite, and therefore

$$\begin{pmatrix} P_0 + P_1 & X_0 + X_1 \\ (X_0 + X_1)^* & Q_0 + Q_1 \end{pmatrix} = \begin{pmatrix} P_0 & X_0 \\ X_0^* & Q_0 \end{pmatrix} + \begin{pmatrix} P_1 & X_1 \\ X_1^* & Q_1 \end{pmatrix} \tag{3.168}$$

is positive semidefinite. Applying Theorem 3.17 again, one finds that

$$\mathrm{F}(P_0 + P_1, Q_0 + Q_1) \geq |\mathrm{Tr}(X_0 + X_1)| = \mathrm{F}(P_0, Q_0) + \mathrm{F}(P_1, Q_1), \tag{3.169}$$

as required. $\qquad \square$

Corollary 3.26 (Joint concavity of fidelity) *Let $\mathcal{X}$ be a complex Euclidean space, let $\rho_0, \rho_1, \sigma_0, \sigma_1 \in \mathrm{D}(\mathcal{X})$ be density operators, and let $\lambda \in [0, 1]$. It holds that*

$$\mathrm{F}(\lambda \rho_0 + (1 - \lambda)\rho_1, \lambda \sigma_0 + (1 - \lambda)\sigma_1)$$
$$\geq \lambda \mathrm{F}(\rho_0, \sigma_0) + (1 - \lambda) \mathrm{F}(\rho_1, \sigma_1). \tag{3.170}$$

Proof By Theorem 3.25, together with statement 3 of Proposition 3.12, it holds that

$$
\begin{aligned}
F(\lambda\rho_0 + (1-\lambda)\rho_1, \lambda\sigma_0 + (1-\lambda)\sigma_1) & \\
\geq F(\lambda\rho_0, \lambda\sigma_0) + F((1-\lambda)\rho_1, (1-\lambda)\sigma_1) & \qquad (3.171)\\
= \lambda F(\rho_0, \sigma_0) + (1-\lambda) F(\rho_1, \sigma_1), &
\end{aligned}
$$

as claimed.   □

The joint concavity of the fidelity function implies that the fidelity function is concave in each of its arguments individually:

$$
F(\lambda\rho_0 + (1-\lambda)\rho_1, \sigma) \geq \lambda F(\rho_0, \sigma) + (1-\lambda) F(\rho_1, \sigma) \qquad (3.172)
$$

for all $\rho_0, \rho_1, \sigma \in D(\mathcal{X})$ and $\lambda \in [0,1]$, and similar for concavity in the second argument rather than the first.

The *monotonicity* of the fidelity function under the action of channels is another fundamental property that may be established using the block operator characterization.

Theorem 3.27 *Let $\mathcal{X}$ and $\mathcal{Y}$ be complex Euclidean spaces, let $\Phi \in C(\mathcal{X}, \mathcal{Y})$ be a channel, and let $P, Q \in \mathrm{Pos}(\mathcal{X})$ be positive semidefinite operators. It holds that*

$$
F(P, Q) \leq F(\Phi(P), \Phi(Q)). \qquad (3.173)
$$

Proof By Theorem 3.17, one may choose $X \in L(\mathcal{X})$ so that

$$
\begin{pmatrix} P & X \\ X^* & Q \end{pmatrix} \qquad (3.174)
$$

is positive semidefinite and satisfies $|\mathrm{Tr}(X)| = F(P, Q)$. By the complete positivity of Φ, the block operator

$$
\begin{pmatrix} \Phi(P) & \Phi(X) \\ \Phi(X^*) & \Phi(Q) \end{pmatrix} = \begin{pmatrix} \Phi(P) & \Phi(X) \\ \Phi(X)^* & \Phi(Q) \end{pmatrix} \qquad (3.175)
$$

is positive semidefinite as well. Invoking Theorem 3.17 again, and using the fact that Φ is trace-preserving, it follows that

$$
F(\Phi(P), \Phi(Q)) \geq |\mathrm{Tr}(\Phi(X))| = |\mathrm{Tr}(X)| = F(P, Q), \qquad (3.176)
$$

as required.   □

Fidelity Between Extensions of Operators

Suppose, for a given choice of complex Euclidean spaces $\mathcal{X}$ and $\mathcal{Y}$, that $P_0, P_1 \in \text{Pos}(\mathcal{X})$ and $Q_0 \in \text{Pos}(\mathcal{X} \otimes \mathcal{Y})$ are positive semidefinite operators such that Q_0 extends P_0, meaning that $\text{Tr}_{\mathcal{Y}}(Q_0) = P_0$. For every positive semidefinite operator $Q_1 \in \text{Pos}(\mathcal{X} \otimes \mathcal{Y})$ satisfying $\text{Tr}_{\mathcal{Y}}(Q_1) = P_1$, it follows from Theorem 3.27 that

$$\text{F}(Q_0, Q_1) \leq \text{F}(\text{Tr}_{\mathcal{Y}}(Q_0), \text{Tr}_{\mathcal{Y}}(Q_1)) = \text{F}(P_0, P_1). \tag{3.177}$$

It is natural, in some situations, to consider the maximum value that the fidelity $\text{F}(Q_0, Q_1)$ may take, over all choices of an operator $Q_1 \in \text{Pos}(\mathcal{X} \otimes \mathcal{Y})$ extending P_1. As the following theorem establishes, this maximum value is necessarily equal to $\text{F}(P_0, P_1)$, irrespective of the choice of Q_0.

Theorem 3.28 *Let $P_0, P_1 \in \text{Pos}(\mathcal{X})$ and $Q_0 \in \text{Pos}(\mathcal{X} \otimes \mathcal{Y})$ be positive semidefinite operators, for $\mathcal{X}$ and $\mathcal{Y}$ complex Euclidean spaces, and assume that $\text{Tr}_{\mathcal{Y}}(Q_0) = P_0$. It holds that*

$$\max\{\text{F}(Q_0, Q_1): Q_1 \in \text{Pos}(\mathcal{X} \otimes \mathcal{Y}), \, \text{Tr}_{\mathcal{Y}}(Q_1) = P_1\} = \text{F}(P_0, P_1). \tag{3.178}$$

Proof Let $\mathcal{Z}$ be a complex Euclidean space with $\dim(\mathcal{Z}) = \dim(\mathcal{X} \otimes \mathcal{Y})$, and choose any vector $u_0 \in \mathcal{X} \otimes \mathcal{Y} \otimes \mathcal{Z}$ satisfying

$$\text{Tr}_{\mathcal{Z}}(u_0 u_0^*) = Q_0. \tag{3.179}$$

As Q_0 is an extension of P_0, it follows that

$$\text{Tr}_{\mathcal{Y} \otimes \mathcal{Z}}(u_0 u_0^*) = P_0. \tag{3.180}$$

By Uhlmann's theorem (Theorem 3.22), there exists a vector $u_1 \in \mathcal{X} \otimes \mathcal{Y} \otimes \mathcal{Z}$ so that

$$\text{Tr}_{\mathcal{Y} \otimes \mathcal{Z}}(u_1 u_1^*) = P_1 \quad \text{and} \quad |\langle u_0, u_1 \rangle| = \text{F}(P_0, P_1). \tag{3.181}$$

By setting

$$Q_1 = \text{Tr}_{\mathcal{Z}}(u_1 u_1^*) \tag{3.182}$$

and applying Theorem 3.27 (for the channel being the partial trace over $\mathcal{Z}$), one has

$$\begin{aligned} \text{F}(Q_0, Q_1) &= \text{F}(\text{Tr}_{\mathcal{Z}}(u_0 u_0^*), \text{Tr}_{\mathcal{Z}}(u_1 u_1^*)) \\ &\geq \text{F}(u_0 u_0^*, u_1 u_1^*) = |\langle u_0, u_1 \rangle| = \text{F}(P_0, P_1). \end{aligned} \tag{3.183}$$

This demonstrates that the maximum in (3.178) is at least $\text{F}(P_0, P_1)$. The maximum is at most $\text{F}(P_0, P_1)$ by (3.177), and so the proof is complete. $\square$

A Sum-of-Squares Relationship for Fidelity

The next theorem states a useful fact relating the fidelity between two fixed states and the sum of the squared fidelities between these two states and a third.

Theorem 3.29 *Let $\rho_0, \rho_1 \in D(\mathcal{X})$ be density operators, for $\mathcal{X}$ a complex Euclidean space. It holds that*

$$\max_{\sigma \in D(\mathcal{X})} \left(F(\rho_0, \sigma)^2 + F(\rho_1, \sigma)^2 \right) = 1 + F(\rho_0, \rho_1). \qquad (3.184)$$

Proof The proof will make use of the fact that, for any two unit vectors u_0 and u_1, chosen from an arbitrary complex Euclidean space, there is a simple closed-form expression for the largest eigenvalue of the sum of the rank-one projections corresponding to these vectors:

$$\lambda_1 \left(u_0 u_0^* + u_1 u_1^* \right) = 1 + |\langle u_0, u_1 \rangle|. \qquad (3.185)$$

There are two steps of the proof, both of which combine the expression (3.185) with Uhlmann's theorem (Theorem 3.22).

The first step proves the existence of a density operator $\sigma \in D(\mathcal{X})$ such that

$$F(\rho_0, \sigma)^2 + F(\rho_1, \sigma)^2 \geq 1 + F(\rho_0, \rho_1). \qquad (3.186)$$

Let $\mathcal{Y}$ be any complex Euclidean space such that $\dim(\mathcal{Y}) = \dim(\mathcal{X})$, and let $u_0, u_1 \in \mathcal{X} \otimes \mathcal{Y}$ be vectors satisfying the following equations:

$$\begin{aligned}
\mathrm{Tr}_{\mathcal{Y}}(u_0 u_0^*) &= \rho_0, \\
\mathrm{Tr}_{\mathcal{Y}}(u_1 u_1^*) &= \rho_1, \\
|\langle u_0, u_1 \rangle| &= F(\rho_0, \rho_1).
\end{aligned} \qquad (3.187)$$

The fact that there exists such a choice of vectors follows from Uhlmann's theorem. Let $v \in \mathcal{X} \otimes \mathcal{Y}$ be a unit eigenvector of the operator $u_0 u_0^* + u_1 u_1^*$ that corresponds to its largest eigenvalue, so that

$$v^* \left(u_0 u_0^* + u_1 u_1^* \right) v = 1 + |\langle u_0, u_1 \rangle|, \qquad (3.188)$$

and let

$$\sigma = \mathrm{Tr}_{\mathcal{Y}}(v v^*). \qquad (3.189)$$

Using Uhlmann's theorem again, one has

$$F(\rho_0, \sigma) \geq |\langle u_0, v \rangle| \quad \text{and} \quad F(\rho_1, \sigma) \geq |\langle u_1, v \rangle|, \qquad (3.190)$$

so that

$$\mathrm{F}(\rho_0, \sigma)^2 + \mathrm{F}(\rho_1, \sigma)^2 \geq v^*(u_0 u_0^* + u_1 u_1^*) v$$
$$= 1 + |\langle u_0, u_1 \rangle| = 1 + \mathrm{F}(\rho_0, \rho_1), \tag{3.191}$$

which proves the required inequality.

The second step of the proof is to establish that the inequality

$$\mathrm{F}(\rho_0, \sigma)^2 + \mathrm{F}(\rho_1, \sigma)^2 \leq 1 + \mathrm{F}(\rho_0, \rho_1) \tag{3.192}$$

holds for every $\sigma \in \mathrm{D}(\mathcal{X})$. Again, let $\mathcal{Y}$ be a complex Euclidean space with $\dim(\mathcal{Y}) = \dim(\mathcal{X})$, let $\sigma \in \mathrm{D}(\mathcal{X})$ be chosen arbitrarily, and choose $v \in \mathcal{X} \otimes \mathcal{Y}$ to be any unit vector satisfying

$$\sigma = \mathrm{Tr}_{\mathcal{Y}}(vv^*). \tag{3.193}$$

Also let $u_0, u_1 \in \mathcal{X} \otimes \mathcal{Y}$ be unit vectors satisfying the following equations:

$$\begin{aligned}
\mathrm{Tr}_{\mathcal{Y}}(u_0 u_0^*) &= \rho_0, \\
\mathrm{Tr}_{\mathcal{Y}}(u_1 u_1^*) &= \rho_1, \\
|\langle u_0, v \rangle| &= \mathrm{F}(\rho_0, \sigma), \\
|\langle u_1, v \rangle| &= \mathrm{F}(\rho_1, \sigma).
\end{aligned} \tag{3.194}$$

As in the first step of the proof, the existence of such vectors is implied by Uhlmann's theorem. As v is a unit vector, it holds that

$$v^*(u_0 u_0^* + u_1 u_1^*) v \leq \lambda_1(u_0 u_0^* + u_1 u_1^*)$$
$$= 1 + |\langle u_0, u_1 \rangle| \leq 1 + \mathrm{F}(\rho_0, \rho_1), \tag{3.195}$$

where the last inequality is, once again, implied by Uhlmann's theorem. Therefore, one has

$$\mathrm{F}(\rho_0, \sigma)^2 + \mathrm{F}(\rho_1, \sigma)^2 = v^*(u_0 u_0^* + u_1 u_1^*) v \leq 1 + \mathrm{F}(\rho_0, \rho_1), \tag{3.196}$$

as required. $\qquad\square$

Fidelity Between Inputs and Outputs of Completely Positive Maps

With respect to the storage and transmission of quantum information, the identity map represents an ideal quantum channel, as this channel causes no disturbance to the quantum states it acts upon. For this reason, it may be desirable to measure the similarity between a given channel of the form $\Phi \in \mathrm{C}(\mathcal{X})$ and the identity channel $\mathbb{1}_{\mathrm{L}(\mathcal{X})}$ in some settings.

One setting in which such a comparison is made arises in connection with quantum source coding (to be discussed in Section 5.3.2). Here, one is interested in the fidelity between the input and output states of a given channel $\Phi \in \mathrm{C}(\mathcal{X})$, under the assumption that the channel acts on a state

$\sigma \in D(\mathcal{X} \otimes \mathcal{Y})$ that extends a known fixed state $\rho \in D(\mathcal{X})$. The *mapping fidelity*, which is specified by the following definition, is representative of this situation when σ is taken as a purification of the state ρ.

Definition 3.30   Let $\mathcal{X}$ be a complex Euclidean space, let $\Phi \in CP(\mathcal{X})$ be a completely positive map, and let $P \in Pos(\mathcal{X})$ be a positive semidefinite operator. The *mapping fidelity* of Φ with respect to P is defined as

$$F(\Phi, P) = F\left(uu^*, (\Phi \otimes \mathbb{1}_{L(\mathcal{X})})(uu^*)\right) \tag{3.197}$$

for $u = \mathrm{vec}(\sqrt{P})$.

The mapping fidelity is also called the *channel fidelity* when Φ is a channel and $P = \rho$ is a density operator. (It is also commonly called the *entanglement fidelity* in this case, although that terminology will not be used in this book.)

An explicit formula for the mapping fidelity $F(\Phi, P)$, from any Kraus representation of the mapping Φ, is given by the following proposition.

Proposition 3.31   *Let $\{A_a : a \in \Sigma\} \subset L(\mathcal{X})$ be a collection of operators, for $\mathcal{X}$ a complex Euclidean space and Σ an alphabet, and let $\Phi \in CP(\mathcal{X})$ be the completely positive map defined as*

$$\Phi(X) = \sum_{a \in \Sigma} A_a X A_a^* \tag{3.198}$$

for all $X \in L(\mathcal{X})$. For every operator $P \in Pos(\mathcal{X})$, it holds that

$$F(\Phi, P) = \sqrt{\sum_{a \in \Sigma} |\langle P, A_a \rangle|^2}. \tag{3.199}$$

Proof   Using Proposition 3.13, one may evaluate the expression (3.197) to obtain

$$F(\Phi, P) = \sqrt{\sum_{a \in \Sigma} \left|\mathrm{vec}(\sqrt{P})^*(A_a \otimes \mathbb{1}_{\mathcal{X}})\,\mathrm{vec}(\sqrt{P})\right|^2}$$

$$= \sqrt{\sum_{a \in \Sigma} |\langle \sqrt{P}, A_a \sqrt{P}\rangle|^2} = \sqrt{\sum_{a \in \Sigma} |\langle P, A_a \rangle|^2}, \tag{3.200}$$

as required. $\square$

As the next proposition implies, the purification $u = \mathrm{vec}(\sqrt{P})$ taken in the definition of the mapping fidelity is representative of a worst-case scenario. That is, for an arbitrary state $\sigma \in D(\mathcal{X} \otimes \mathcal{Y})$ that extends a known fixed state $\rho \in D(\mathcal{X})$, the fidelity $F\left(\sigma, (\Phi \otimes \mathbb{1}_{L(\mathcal{Y})})(\sigma)\right)$ can be no smaller than the mapping fidelity $F(\Phi, \rho)$.

Proposition 3.32 *Let $\Phi \in \mathrm{CP}(\mathcal{X})$ be a completely positive map and let $P \in \mathrm{Pos}(\mathcal{X})$ be a positive semidefinite operator, for $\mathcal{X}$ a complex Euclidean space. Suppose further that $u \in \mathcal{X} \otimes \mathcal{Y}$ is a vector satisfying $\mathrm{Tr}_{\mathcal{Y}}(uu^*) = P$ and $Q \in \mathrm{Pos}(\mathcal{X} \otimes \mathcal{Z})$ is an operator satisfying $\mathrm{Tr}_{\mathcal{Z}}(Q) = P$, for complex Euclidean spaces $\mathcal{Y}$ and $\mathcal{Z}$. It holds that*

$$\mathrm{F}(Q, (\Phi \otimes \mathbb{1}_{\mathrm{L}(\mathcal{Z})})(Q)) \geq \mathrm{F}(uu^*, (\Phi \otimes \mathbb{1}_{\mathrm{L}(\mathcal{Y})})(uu^*)). \qquad (3.201)$$

Proof By Proposition 2.29, there must exist a channel $\Psi \in \mathrm{C}(\mathcal{Y}, \mathcal{Z})$ such that

$$(\mathbb{1}_{\mathrm{L}(\mathcal{X})} \otimes \Psi)(uu^*) = Q. \qquad (3.202)$$

By Theorem 3.27, one has

$$
\begin{aligned}
\mathrm{F}\big(uu^*, &(\Phi \otimes \mathbb{1}_{\mathrm{L}(\mathcal{Y})})(uu^*)\big) \\
&\leq \mathrm{F}\big((\mathbb{1}_{\mathrm{L}(\mathcal{X})} \otimes \Psi)(uu^*), (\Phi \otimes \Psi)(uu^*)\big) \qquad (3.203) \\
&= \mathrm{F}(Q, (\Phi \otimes \mathbb{1}_{\mathrm{L}(\mathcal{Z})})(Q)),
\end{aligned}
$$

which completes the proof. $\qquad \square$

It is also evident from this proposition that taking any other purification of P in place of $u = \mathrm{vec}(\sqrt{P})$ in Definition 3.30 would yield precisely the same value.

Fuchs–van de Graaf Inequalities

The final property of the fidelity function to be established in this section concerns its connection to the trace distance between quantum states. This is an important relationship, as it allows for an approximate conversion between the more operationally motivated trace distance and the often more analytically robust fidelity function evaluated on a given pair of states.

Theorem 3.33 (Fuchs–van de Graaf inequalities) *Let $\mathcal{X}$ be a complex Euclidean space and let $\rho, \sigma \in \mathrm{D}(\mathcal{X})$ be density operators. It holds that*

$$1 - \frac{1}{2}\|\rho - \sigma\|_1 \leq \mathrm{F}(\rho, \sigma) \leq \sqrt{1 - \frac{1}{4}\|\rho - \sigma\|_1^2}. \qquad (3.204)$$

Equivalently,

$$2 - 2\,\mathrm{F}(\rho, \sigma) \leq \|\rho - \sigma\|_1 \leq 2\sqrt{1 - \mathrm{F}(\rho, \sigma)^2}. \qquad (3.205)$$

Proof The proof will establish the two inequalities in (3.205) separately, beginning with the first. By Theorem 3.24, there exists an alphabet Σ and a measurement $\mu \colon \Sigma \to \mathrm{Pos}(\mathcal{X})$ such that

$$\mathrm{F}(\rho, \sigma) = \mathrm{B}(\rho, \sigma \,|\, \mu). \qquad (3.206)$$

Fix such a measurement, and define probability vectors $p, q \in \mathcal{P}(\Sigma)$ as

$$p(a) = \langle \mu(a), \rho \rangle \quad \text{and} \quad q(a) = \langle \mu(a), \sigma \rangle \tag{3.207}$$

for each $a \in \Sigma$, so that $\mathrm{B}(p, q) = \mathrm{F}(\rho, \sigma)$. By Proposition 3.5, together with the observation that

$$\left(\sqrt{\alpha} - \sqrt{\beta} \right)^2 \leq |\alpha - \beta| \tag{3.208}$$

for every choice of nonnegative real numbers $\alpha, \beta \geq 0$, it follows that

$$\|\rho - \sigma\|_1 \geq \|p - q\|_1 = \sum_{a \in \Sigma} |p(a) - q(a)|$$

$$\geq \sum_{a \in \Sigma} \left(\sqrt{p(a)} - \sqrt{q(a)} \right)^2 = 2 - 2\,\mathrm{B}(p, q) = 2 - 2\,\mathrm{F}(\rho, \sigma). \tag{3.209}$$

The first inequality in (3.205) is therefore proved.

Next, the second inequality in (3.205) will be proved. Let $\mathcal{Y}$ be a complex Euclidean space with $\dim(\mathcal{Y}) = \dim(\mathcal{X})$. It follows by Uhlmann's theorem (Theorem 3.22) that there exists a choice of unit vectors $u, v \in \mathcal{X} \otimes \mathcal{Y}$ satisfying the equations

$$\mathrm{Tr}_{\mathcal{Y}}(uu^*) = \rho, \quad \mathrm{Tr}_{\mathcal{Y}}(vv^*) = \sigma, \quad \text{and} \quad |\langle u, v \rangle| = \mathrm{F}(\rho, \sigma). \tag{3.210}$$

By the identity (1.186), it holds that

$$\|uu^* - vv^*\|_1 = 2\sqrt{1 - |\langle u, v \rangle|^2} = 2\sqrt{1 - \mathrm{F}(\rho, \sigma)^2}. \tag{3.211}$$

Consequently, by the monotonicity of the trace norm under partial tracing (1.183), one has

$$\|\rho - \sigma\|_1 \leq \|uu^* - vv^*\|_1 = 2\sqrt{1 - \mathrm{F}(\rho, \sigma)^2}. \tag{3.212}$$

The second inequality in (3.205) has been established, which completes the proof. □

The use of the Bhattacharyya coefficient characterization of the fidelity (Theorem 3.24) in the above proof may be substituted by the following operator norm inequality, which is a useful inequality in its own right.

Lemma 3.34 *Let $\mathcal{X}$ be a complex Euclidean space and let $P_0, P_1 \in \mathrm{Pos}(\mathcal{X})$ be positive semidefinite operators. It holds that*

$$\|P_0 - P_1\|_1 \geq \left\| \sqrt{P_0} - \sqrt{P_1} \right\|_2^2. \tag{3.213}$$

Proof Let

$$\sqrt{P_0} - \sqrt{P_1} = Q_0 - Q_1, \tag{3.214}$$

for $Q_0, Q_1 \in \mathrm{Pos}(\mathcal{X})$, be the Jordan–Hahn decomposition of $\sqrt{P_0} - \sqrt{P_1}$, and let Π_0 and Π_1 be the projections onto $\mathrm{im}(Q_0)$ and $\mathrm{im}(Q_1)$, respectively. The operator $\Pi_0 - \Pi_1$ has spectral norm at most 1, and therefore

$$\| P_0 - P_1 \|_1 \geq \langle \Pi_0 - \Pi_1, P_0 - P_1 \rangle. \tag{3.215}$$

Through the use of the operator identity

$$A^2 - B^2 = \frac{1}{2}(A - B)(A + B) + \frac{1}{2}(A + B)(A - B), \tag{3.216}$$

one finds that

$$
\begin{aligned}
&\langle \Pi_0 - \Pi_1, P_0 - P_1 \rangle \\
&= \frac{1}{2}\Big\langle \Pi_0 - \Pi_1, \big(\sqrt{P_0} - \sqrt{P_1}\big)\big(\sqrt{P_0} + \sqrt{P_1}\big) \Big\rangle \\
&\quad + \frac{1}{2}\Big\langle \Pi_0 - \Pi_1, \big(\sqrt{P_0} + \sqrt{P_1}\big)\big(\sqrt{P_0} - \sqrt{P_1}\big) \Big\rangle \\
&= \frac{1}{2}\mathrm{Tr}\Big((Q_0 + Q_1)\big(\sqrt{P_0} + \sqrt{P_1}\big)\Big) \\
&\quad + \frac{1}{2}\mathrm{Tr}\Big(\big(\sqrt{P_0} + \sqrt{P_1}\big)(Q_0 + Q_1)\Big) \\
&= \Big\langle Q_0 + Q_1, \sqrt{P_0} + \sqrt{P_1} \Big\rangle.
\end{aligned}
\tag{3.217}
$$

Finally, as Q_0, Q_1, $\sqrt{P_0}$, and $\sqrt{P_1}$ are positive semidefinite, one has

$$
\begin{aligned}
&\Big\langle Q_0 + Q_1, \sqrt{P_0} + \sqrt{P_1} \Big\rangle \\
&\quad \geq \Big\langle Q_0 - Q_1, \sqrt{P_0} - \sqrt{P_1} \Big\rangle = \Big\| \sqrt{P_0} - \sqrt{P_1} \Big\|_2^2,
\end{aligned}
\tag{3.218}
$$

which completes the proof. □

Alternative proof of Theorem 3.33 For the first inequality in (3.205), one has

$$
\begin{aligned}
\| \rho - \sigma \|_1 &\geq \Big\| \sqrt{\rho} - \sqrt{\sigma} \Big\|_2^2 = \mathrm{Tr}\big(\sqrt{\rho} - \sqrt{\sigma}\big)^2 \\
&= 2 - 2\,\mathrm{Tr}\big(\sqrt{\rho}\sqrt{\sigma}\big) \geq 2 - 2\,\mathrm{F}(\rho, \sigma)
\end{aligned}
\tag{3.219}
$$

by Lemma 3.34. The second inequality in (3.205) is proved as before. □

3.3 Channel Distances and Discrimination

The trace norm induces a notion of distance between quantum states that is closely related to the task of state discrimination, as established by the Holevo–Helstrom theorem (Theorem 3.4). The present section discusses an analogous notion of distance for channels, induced by a norm known as the *completely bounded trace norm*, along with a similar connection to the task of *channel discrimination*.

3.3.1 Channel Discrimination

The task of discriminating between pairs of channels is represented by the scenario that follows.

Scenario 3.35 Let X and Y be registers, and let Z be a register having classical state set $\{0, 1\}$. The register Z is to be viewed as a classical register, while X and Y are arbitrary. Also let $\Phi_0, \Phi_1 \in C(\mathcal{X}, \mathcal{Y})$ be channels and let $\lambda \in [0, 1]$ be a real number. The channels Φ_0 and Φ_1, as well as the number λ, are assumed to be known to both Alice and Bob.

Alice prepares the register Z in a probabilistic state, so that its state is 0 with probability λ and 1 with probability $1 - \lambda$. Alice receives the register X from Bob, and conditioned on the classical state of Z, Alice performs one of two actions:

1. If $Z = 0$, Alice transforms X into Y according to the action of Φ_0.
2. If $Z = 1$, Alice transforms X into Y according to the action of Φ_1.

The register Y is then given to Bob.

Bob's goal is to determine the classical state of Z, through an interaction with Alice, as just described.

One approach Bob may choose to take in this scenario is to select a state $\sigma \in D(\mathcal{X})$ that maximizes the quantity

$$\left\| \lambda \rho_0 - (1 - \lambda)\rho_1 \right\|_1, \tag{3.220}$$

for $\rho_0 = \Phi_0(\sigma)$ and $\rho_1 = \Phi_1(\sigma)$. If he prepares the register X in the state σ and gives it to Alice, he will get back Y in either of the states ρ_0 or ρ_1, and can then measure Y using an optimal measurement for discriminating ρ_0 and ρ_1 given with probabilities λ and $1 - \lambda$, respectively.

This, however, is not the most general approach. More generally, Bob may make use of an *auxiliary* register W in the following way. First, he prepares the pair of registers (X, W) in some chosen state $\sigma \in D(\mathcal{X} \otimes \mathcal{W})$, and then he allows Alice to transform X into Y according to Φ_0 or Φ_1. This results in the pair (Y, W) being in one of the two states

$$\rho_0 = (\Phi_0 \otimes \mathbb{1}_{\mathrm{L}(W)})(\sigma) \quad \text{and} \quad \rho_1 = (\Phi_1 \otimes \mathbb{1}_{\mathrm{L}(W)})(\sigma), \tag{3.221}$$

with probabilities λ and $1 - \lambda$, respectively. Finally, he measures the pair (Y, W) in order to discriminate these two states. This more general approach can, in some cases, result in a striking improvement in the probability to correctly discriminate Φ_0 and Φ_1, as the following example illustrates.

Example 3.36 Let $n \geq 2$, let Σ be an alphabet with $|\Sigma| = n$, and let X be a register having classical state set Σ. Define two channels $\Phi_0, \Phi_1 \in C(\mathcal{X})$ as follows:

$$\Phi_0(X) = \frac{1}{n+1}((\operatorname{Tr} X)\mathbb{1} + X^{\mathsf{T}}),$$

$$\Phi_1(X) = \frac{1}{n-1}((\operatorname{Tr} X)\mathbb{1} - X^{\mathsf{T}}), \tag{3.222}$$

for all $X \in \mathrm{L}(\mathcal{X})$.

The maps Φ_0 and Φ_1, which are sometimes called the *Werner–Holevo channels*, are indeed channels. These maps are evidently trace-preserving, and the fact that they are completely positive follows from a calculation of their Choi representations:

$$J(\Phi_0) = \frac{\mathbb{1} \otimes \mathbb{1} + W}{n+1} \quad \text{and} \quad J(\Phi_1) = \frac{\mathbb{1} \otimes \mathbb{1} - W}{n-1}, \tag{3.223}$$

where $W \in \mathrm{L}(\mathcal{X} \otimes \mathcal{X})$ is the swap operator, which satisfies $W(u \otimes v) = v \otimes u$ for every $u, v \in \mathcal{X}$. As W is unitary and Hermitian, the operators $J(\Phi_0)$ and $J(\Phi_1)$ are both positive semidefinite.

Now, consider the channels Φ_0 and Φ_1, along with the scalar value

$$\lambda = \frac{n+1}{2n}, \tag{3.224}$$

in Scenario 3.35. It holds that

$$\lambda \Phi_0(X) - (1 - \lambda)\Phi_1(X) = \frac{1}{n}X^{\mathsf{T}} \tag{3.225}$$

for every $X \in \mathrm{L}(\mathcal{X})$, and therefore

$$\left\| \lambda \Phi_0(\sigma) - (1 - \lambda)\Phi_1(\sigma) \right\|_1 = \frac{1}{n} \tag{3.226}$$

for every choice of a density operator $\sigma \in \mathrm{D}(\mathcal{X})$. This quantity is relatively small when n is large, which is consistent with the observation that $\Phi_0(\sigma)$ and $\Phi_1(\sigma)$ are both close to the completely mixed state for any choice of an input $\sigma \in D(\mathcal{X})$. If Bob prepares X in some state σ, and elects not to use an auxiliary register W, his probability to correctly identify the classical state of Z is therefore at most

$$\frac{1}{2} + \frac{1}{2n}. \tag{3.227}$$

On the other hand, if Bob makes use of an auxiliary register, the situation is quite different. In particular, suppose that W is a register sharing the same classical state set Σ as X, and suppose that Bob prepares the pair (X, W) in the state $\tau \in D(\mathcal{X} \otimes \mathcal{W})$ defined as

$$\tau = \frac{1}{n} \sum_{a,b \in \Sigma} E_{a,b} \otimes E_{a,b}. \tag{3.228}$$

The actions of the channels Φ_0 and Φ_1 on this state are as follows:

$$\left(\Phi_0 \otimes \mathbb{1}_{L(\mathcal{W})}\right)(\tau) = \frac{\mathbb{1} \otimes \mathbb{1} + W}{n^2 + n},$$
$$\left(\Phi_1 \otimes \mathbb{1}_{L(\mathcal{W})}\right)(\tau) = \frac{\mathbb{1} \otimes \mathbb{1} - W}{n^2 - n}. \tag{3.229}$$

These are orthogonal density operators, following from the calculation

$$\langle \mathbb{1} \otimes \mathbb{1} + W, \mathbb{1} \otimes \mathbb{1} - W \rangle = \mathrm{Tr}(\mathbb{1} \otimes \mathbb{1} + W - W - W^2) = 0. \tag{3.230}$$

It is therefore the case that the states $\left(\Phi_0 \otimes \mathbb{1}_{L(\mathcal{W})}\right)(\tau)$ and $\left(\Phi_1 \otimes \mathbb{1}_{L(\mathcal{W})}\right)(\tau)$ can be discriminated without error: for every $\lambda \in [0, 1]$, one has

$$\left\| \lambda \left(\Phi_0 \otimes \mathbb{1}_{L(\mathcal{W})}\right)(\tau) - (1 - \lambda)\left(\Phi_1 \otimes \mathbb{1}_{L(\mathcal{W})}\right)(\tau) \right\|_1 = 1. \tag{3.231}$$

By making use of an auxiliary register W in this way, Bob can therefore correctly discriminate the channels Φ_0 and Φ_1 without error.

This example makes clear that auxiliary registers must be taken into account when considering the optimal probability with which channels can be discriminated.

3.3.2 The Completely Bounded Trace Norm

This section defines a norm on the space of mappings $T(\mathcal{X}, \mathcal{Y})$, for complex Euclidean spaces $\mathcal{X}$ and $\mathcal{Y}$, known as the *completely bounded trace norm*, and establishes some of its properties. The precise connection between this norm and the task of channel discrimination will be explained in the section following this one, but it will be evident from its definition that this norm is motivated in part by the discussion from the previous section stressing the importance of auxiliary registers in the task of channel discrimination.

The Induced Trace Norm

When introducing the completely bounded trace norm, it is appropriate to begin with the definition of a related norm known as the *induced trace norm*.

Definition 3.37 Let $\mathcal{X}$ and $\mathcal{Y}$ be complex Euclidean spaces. The *induced trace norm* of a map $\Phi \in T(\mathcal{X}, \mathcal{Y})$ is defined as

$$\|\Phi\|_1 = \max\{\|\Phi(X)\|_1 : X \in L(\mathcal{X}), \|X\|_1 \leq 1\}. \tag{3.232}$$

True to its name, this norm is an example of an *induced norm*; in general, one may consider the norm obtained by replacing the two trace norms in this definition with any other choices of norms defined on $L(\mathcal{X})$ and $L(\mathcal{Y})$. The use of the maximum, rather than the supremum, is justified in this context by the observation that the norm defined on $L(\mathcal{Y})$ is continuous and the unit ball with respect to the norm defined on $L(\mathcal{X})$ is compact.

Generally speaking, the induced trace norm fails to provide a physically well-motivated measure of distance between channels. It will, nevertheless, be useful to consider some basic properties of this norm, for many of these properties will be inherited by the completely bounded trace norm, to be defined shortly.

The first property of the induced trace norm to be observed is that the maximum in Definition 3.37 is always achieved by a rank-one operator X.

Proposition 3.38 Let $\Phi \in T(\mathcal{X}, \mathcal{Y})$ be a map, for complex Euclidean spaces $\mathcal{X}$ and $\mathcal{Y}$. It holds that

$$\|\Phi\|_1 = \max_{u,v \in \mathcal{S}(\mathcal{X})} \|\Phi(uv^*)\|_1. \tag{3.233}$$

Proof Every operator in $X \in L(\mathcal{X})$ satisfying $\|X\|_1 \leq 1$ can be written as a convex combination of operators of the form uv^*, for $u, v \in \mathcal{S}(\mathcal{X})$ being unit vectors. Equation (3.233) follows from the fact that the trace norm is a convex function. $\square$

Under the additional assumption that the mapping under consideration is positive, one has that the maximum in Definition 3.37 is achieved by a rank-one projection, as the following theorem states.

Theorem 3.39 (Russo–Dye) Let $\mathcal{X}$ and $\mathcal{Y}$ be complex Euclidean spaces and let $\Phi \in T(\mathcal{X}, \mathcal{Y})$ be a positive map. It holds that

$$\|\Phi\|_1 = \max_{u \in \mathcal{S}(\mathcal{X})} \mathrm{Tr}(\Phi(uu^*)). \tag{3.234}$$

Proof Using the duality of the trace and spectral norms, along with the identity (1.182), one finds that

$$\|\Phi\|_1 = \max_{U \in \mathrm{U}(\mathcal{Y})} \|\Phi^*(U)\|. \tag{3.235}$$

Consider an arbitrary unitary operator $U \in \mathrm{U}(\mathcal{Y})$, and let

$$U = \sum_{k=1}^{m} \lambda_k \Pi_k \tag{3.236}$$

be the spectral decomposition of U. As Φ is positive, it holds that Φ^* is also positive (by Proposition 2.18), and therefore

$$\Phi^*(\Pi_k) \in \mathrm{Pos}(\mathcal{X}) \tag{3.237}$$

for each index $k \in \{1, \ldots, m\}$. By Lemma 3.3, along with the observation that the eigenvalues $\lambda_1, \ldots, \lambda_m$ all lie on the unit circle, it follows that

$$\|\Phi^*(U)\| = \left\| \sum_{k=1}^{m} \lambda_k \Phi^*(\Pi_k) \right\| \le \left\| \sum_{k=1}^{m} \Phi^*(\Pi_k) \right\| = \|\Phi^*(\mathbb{1}_\mathcal{Y})\|. \tag{3.238}$$

Consequently, as $\mathbb{1}_\mathcal{Y}$ is itself a unitary operator, one has

$$\|\Phi\|_1 = \|\Phi^*(\mathbb{1}_\mathcal{Y})\|. \tag{3.239}$$

Finally, as $\Phi^*(\mathbb{1}_\mathcal{Y})$ is necessarily positive semidefinite, it follows that

$$\|\Phi^*(\mathbb{1}_\mathcal{Y})\| = \max_{u \in \mathcal{S}(\mathcal{X})} \langle uu^*, \Phi^*(\mathbb{1}_\mathcal{Y}) \rangle = \max_{u \in \mathcal{S}(\mathcal{X})} \mathrm{Tr}(\Phi(uu^*)), \tag{3.240}$$

which completes the proof. $\square$

Corollary 3.40 *Let $\Phi \in \mathrm{T}(\mathcal{X}, \mathcal{Y})$ be a positive and trace-preserving map, for complex Euclidean spaces $\mathcal{X}$ and $\mathcal{Y}$. It holds that $\|\Phi\|_1 = 1$.*

Remark Observe that the previous corollary establishes that the trace norm is monotonically decreasing not only under the action of all channels, but also under the action of trace-preserving positive maps more generally:

$$\|\Phi(X)\|_1 \le \|X\|_1 \tag{3.241}$$

for all $X \in \mathrm{L}(\mathcal{X})$ and all positive, trace-preserving maps $\Phi \in \mathrm{T}(\mathcal{X}, \mathcal{Y})$.

The next proposition establishes three basic properties of the induced trace norm: submultiplicativity under compositions, additivity of channel differences under compositions, and unitary invariance.

Proposition 3.41 *For every choice of complex Euclidean spaces $\mathcal{X}$, $\mathcal{Y}$, and $\mathcal{Z}$, the following facts regarding the induced trace norm hold:*

1. *For all maps $\Phi \in T(\mathcal{X}, \mathcal{Y})$ and $\Psi \in T(\mathcal{Y}, \mathcal{Z})$, it holds that*

$$\|\Psi\Phi\|_1 \leq \|\Psi\|_1 \|\Phi\|_1. \tag{3.242}$$

2. *For all channels $\Phi_0, \Psi_0 \in C(\mathcal{X}, \mathcal{Y})$ and $\Phi_1, \Psi_1 \in C(\mathcal{Y}, \mathcal{Z})$, it holds that*

$$\|\Psi_1\Psi_0 - \Phi_1\Phi_0\|_1 \leq \|\Psi_0 - \Phi_0\|_1 + \|\Psi_1 - \Phi_1\|_1. \tag{3.243}$$

3. *Let $\Phi \in T(\mathcal{X}, \mathcal{Y})$ be a map, let $U_0, V_0 \in U(\mathcal{X})$ and $U_1, V_1 \in U(\mathcal{Y})$ be unitary operators, and let $\Psi \in T(\mathcal{X}, \mathcal{Y})$ be defined as*

$$\Psi(X) = U_1 \Phi(U_0 X V_0) V_1 \tag{3.244}$$

for all $X \in L(\mathcal{X})$. It holds that $\|\Psi\|_1 = \|\Phi\|_1$.

Proof To prove the first fact, one may observe that $\|\Psi(Y)\|_1 \leq \|\Psi\|_1 \|Y\|_1$ for every $Y \in L(\mathcal{Y})$, and therefore

$$\|\Psi(\Phi(X))\|_1 \leq \|\Psi\|_1 \|\Phi(X)\|_1 \tag{3.245}$$

for every $X \in L(\mathcal{X})$. Taking the maximum over all $X \in L(\mathcal{X})$ with $\|X\|_1 \leq 1$ yields the inequality (3.242).

To prove the second fact, one may apply the triangle inequality, the inequality (3.242), and Corollary 3.40, to obtain

$$\begin{aligned}
\|\Psi_1\Psi_0 - \Phi_1\Phi_0\|_1 &\leq \|\Psi_1\Psi_0 - \Psi_1\Phi_0\|_1 + \|\Psi_1\Phi_0 - \Phi_1\Phi_0\|_1 \\
&= \|\Psi_1(\Psi_0 - \Phi_0)\|_1 + \|(\Psi_1 - \Phi_1)\Phi_0\|_1 \\
&\leq \|\Psi_1\|_1 \|\Psi_0 - \Phi_0\|_1 + \|\Psi_1 - \Phi_1\|_1 \|\Phi_0\|_1 \\
&= \|\Psi_0 - \Phi_0\|_1 + \|\Psi_1 - \Phi_1\|_1.
\end{aligned} \tag{3.246}$$

Finally, by the unitary invariance of the trace norm, it follows that

$$\begin{aligned}
\|\Psi(X)\|_1 &= \|U_1 \Phi(U_0 X V_0) V_1\|_1 = \|\Phi(U_0 X V_0)\|_1 \\
&\leq \|\Phi\|_1 \|U_0 X V_0\|_1 = \|\Phi\|_1 \|X\|_1
\end{aligned} \tag{3.247}$$

for all $X \in L(\mathcal{X})$, and therefore $\|\Psi\|_1 \leq \|\Phi\|_1$. By observing that

$$\Phi(X) = U_1^* \Psi(U_0^* X V_0^*) V_1^* \tag{3.248}$$

for all $X \in L(\mathcal{X})$, one finds that $\|\Phi\|_1 \leq \|\Psi\|_1$ through a similar argument, which proves the third fact. $\square$

One undesirable property of the induced trace norm is that it fails to be multiplicative with respect to tensor products, as the following example (which is closely related to Example 3.36) illustrates.

Example 3.42 Let $n \geq 2$, let Σ be an alphabet with $|\Sigma| = n$, let $\mathcal{X} = \mathbb{C}^{\Sigma}$, and consider the transpose map $\mathrm{T} \in \mathrm{T}(\mathcal{X})$, defined as $\mathrm{T}(X) = X^{\mathsf{T}}$ for all $X \in \mathrm{L}(\mathcal{X})$. It is evident that $\|\mathrm{T}\|_1 = 1$, as $\|X\|_1 = \|X^{\mathsf{T}}\|_1$ for every operator $X \in \mathrm{L}(\mathcal{X})$, and it holds that $\|\mathbb{1}_{\mathrm{L}(\mathcal{X})}\|_1 = 1$. On the other hand, one has

$$\left\|\mathrm{T} \otimes \mathbb{1}_{\mathrm{L}(\mathcal{X})}\right\|_1 = n. \tag{3.249}$$

To verify this claim, one may first consider the density operator

$$\tau = \frac{1}{n} \sum_{a,b \in \Sigma} E_{a,b} \otimes E_{a,b} \in \mathrm{D}(\mathcal{X} \otimes \mathcal{X}), \tag{3.250}$$

which has trace norm equal to 1. It holds that

$$\left\|(\mathrm{T} \otimes \mathbb{1}_{\mathrm{L}(\mathcal{X})})(\tau)\right\|_1 = \frac{1}{n}\|W\|_1 = n \tag{3.251}$$

for $W \in \mathrm{U}(\mathcal{X} \otimes \mathcal{X})$ denoting the swap operator, and therefore

$$\left\|\mathrm{T} \otimes \mathbb{1}_{\mathrm{L}(\mathcal{X})}\right\|_1 \geq n. \tag{3.252}$$

To prove that $\|\mathrm{T} \otimes \mathbb{1}_{\mathrm{L}(\mathcal{X})}\|_1$ is no larger than n, one may first observe that the relationship (1.169) between the trace and Frobenius norms implies

$$\left\|(\mathrm{T} \otimes \mathbb{1}_{\mathrm{L}(\mathcal{X})})(X)\right\|_1 \leq n\left\|(\mathrm{T} \otimes \mathbb{1}_{\mathrm{L}(\mathcal{X})})(X)\right\|_2 \tag{3.253}$$

for every operator $X \in \mathrm{L}(\mathcal{X} \otimes \mathcal{X})$. As the entries of the operators X and $(\mathrm{T} \otimes \mathbb{1}_{\mathrm{L}(\mathcal{X})})(X)$ are equal, up to being shuffled by the transposition mapping, one has that

$$\left\|(\mathrm{T} \otimes \mathbb{1}_{\mathrm{L}(\mathcal{X})})(X)\right\|_2 = \|X\|_2. \tag{3.254}$$

Finally, by (1.168) it holds that $\|X\|_2 \leq \|X\|_1$, from which it follows that

$$\left\|\mathrm{T} \otimes \mathbb{1}_{\mathrm{L}(\mathcal{X})}\right\|_1 \leq n. \tag{3.255}$$

Definition of the Completely Bounded Trace Norm

The *completely bounded trace norm* is defined below. In words, its value for a given map is simply the induced trace norm of that map tensored with the identity map on the same input space as the mapping itself.

Definition 3.43 For any choice of complex Euclidean spaces $\mathcal{X}$ and $\mathcal{Y}$, the *completely bounded trace norm* of a mapping $\Phi \in \mathrm{T}(\mathcal{X}, \mathcal{Y})$ is defined as

$$\|\|\Phi\|\|_1 = \left\|\Phi \otimes \mathbb{1}_{\mathrm{L}(\mathcal{X})}\right\|_1. \tag{3.256}$$

As the discussion in Section 3.3.1 has suggested, this is the more relevant norm, when compared with the induced trace norm, within the context of the channel discrimination task. In essence, the completely bounded trace norm quantifies the effect that a map may have when it acts on just one tensor factor of a tensor product space (or, in more physical terms, just one part of a compound system), as opposed to the action of that map on its input space alone. As it turns out, this definition yields not only a norm that is more relevant to the channel discrimination task, but also one possessing many interesting and desirable properties (including multiplicativity with respect to tensor products).

The specific choice to take the identity mapping on $L(\mathcal{X})$, as opposed to $L(\mathcal{Y})$, or $L(\mathcal{Z})$ for some other complex Euclidean space $\mathcal{Z}$, is explained in greater detail below. In simple terms, the space $\mathcal{X}$ is sufficiently large, and just large enough in the worst case, that the value (3.256) does not change if the identity mapping on $L(\mathcal{X})$ is replaced by the identity mapping on $L(\mathcal{Z})$, for any complex Euclidean space $\mathcal{Z}$ having dimension at least as large as the dimension of $\mathcal{X}$.

Basic Properties of the Completely Bounded Trace Norm

The proposition that follows, which is immediate from Proposition 3.38, Corollary 3.40, and the third statement of Proposition 3.41, summarizes a few basic properties that the completely bounded trace norm inherits from the induced trace norm.

Proposition 3.44 *The following facts regarding the completely bounded trace norm hold, for every choice of complex Euclidean spaces $\mathcal{X}$ and $\mathcal{Y}$:*

1. *For all maps $\Phi \in T(\mathcal{X}, \mathcal{Y})$, it holds that*

$$|||\Phi|||_1 = \max\left\{ \left\| (\Phi \otimes \mathbb{1}_{L(\mathcal{X})})(uv^*) \right\|_1 : u, v \in \mathcal{S}(\mathcal{X} \otimes \mathcal{X}) \right\}. \qquad (3.257)$$

2. *For all channels $\Phi \in C(\mathcal{X}, \mathcal{Y})$, it holds that $|||\Phi|||_1 = 1$.*

3. *Let $\Phi \in T(\mathcal{X}, \mathcal{Y})$ be a map, let $U_0, V_0 \in U(\mathcal{X})$ and $U_1, V_1 \in U(\mathcal{Y})$ be unitary operators, and let $\Psi \in T(\mathcal{X}, \mathcal{Y})$ be defined as*

$$\Psi(X) = U_1 \Phi(U_0 X V_0) V_1 \qquad (3.258)$$

for all $X \in L(\mathcal{X})$. It holds that $|||\Psi|||_1 = |||\Phi|||_1$.

The next lemma will allow further properties of the completely bounded trace norm to be established.

Lemma 3.45 *Let* $\Phi \in \mathrm{T}(\mathcal{X}, \mathcal{Y})$ *be a map, for complex Euclidean spaces* $\mathcal{X}$ *and* $\mathcal{Y}$. *For every choice of a complex Euclidean space* $\mathcal{Z}$ *and unit vectors* $x, y \in \mathcal{X} \otimes \mathcal{Z}$, *there exist unit vectors* $u, v \in \mathcal{X} \otimes \mathcal{X}$ *such that the following equalities hold:*

$$
\begin{aligned}
\left\| (\Phi \otimes \mathbb{1}_{\mathrm{L}(\mathcal{Z})})(xy^*) \right\|_1 &= \left\| (\Phi \otimes \mathbb{1}_{\mathrm{L}(\mathcal{X})})(uv^*) \right\|_1, \\
\left\| (\Phi \otimes \mathbb{1}_{\mathrm{L}(\mathcal{Z})})(xx^*) \right\|_1 &= \left\| (\Phi \otimes \mathbb{1}_{\mathrm{L}(\mathcal{X})})(uu^*) \right\|_1.
\end{aligned}
\tag{3.259}
$$

Proof In the case that $\dim(\mathcal{Z}) \leq \dim(\mathcal{X})$, the lemma is straightforward: for any choice of an isometry $U \in \mathrm{U}(\mathcal{Z}, \mathcal{X})$, the vectors $u = (\mathbb{1}_{\mathcal{X}} \otimes U)x$ and $v = (\mathbb{1}_{\mathcal{X}} \otimes U)y$ satisfy the required conditions.

If $\dim(\mathcal{Z}) > \dim(\mathcal{X})$, one may consider Schmidt decompositions

$$
x = \sum_{k=1}^{n} \sqrt{p_k}\, x_k \otimes z_k \quad \text{and} \quad y = \sum_{k=1}^{n} \sqrt{q_k}\, y_k \otimes w_k
\tag{3.260}
$$

of x and y, for $n = \dim(\mathcal{X})$, from which a suitable choice for the vectors u and v is given by

$$
u = \sum_{k=1}^{n} \sqrt{p_k}\, x_k \otimes x_k \quad \text{and} \quad v = \sum_{k=1}^{n} \sqrt{q_k}\, y_k \otimes y_k.
\tag{3.261}
$$

For linear isometries $U, V \in \mathrm{U}(\mathcal{X}, \mathcal{Z})$ defined as

$$
U = \sum_{k=1}^{n} z_k x_k^* \quad \text{and} \quad V = \sum_{k=1}^{n} w_k y_k^*,
\tag{3.262}
$$

it holds that $x = (\mathbb{1}_{\mathcal{X}} \otimes U)u$ and $y = (\mathbb{1}_{\mathcal{X}} \otimes V)v$, and therefore

$$
\begin{aligned}
\left\| (\Phi \otimes \mathbb{1}_{\mathrm{L}(\mathcal{Z})})(xy^*) \right\|_1 &= \left\| (\Phi \otimes \mathbb{1}_{\mathrm{L}(\mathcal{Z})})((\mathbb{1} \otimes U)uv^*(\mathbb{1} \otimes V^*)) \right\|_1 \\
&= \left\| (\mathbb{1} \otimes U)(\Phi \otimes \mathbb{1}_{\mathrm{L}(\mathcal{X})})(uv^*)(\mathbb{1} \otimes V^*) \right\|_1 \\
&= \left\| (\Phi \otimes \mathbb{1}_{\mathrm{L}(\mathcal{X})})(uv^*) \right\|_1,
\end{aligned}
\tag{3.263}
$$

and

$$
\begin{aligned}
\left\| (\Phi \otimes \mathbb{1}_{\mathrm{L}(\mathcal{Z})})(xx^*) \right\|_1 &= \left\| (\Phi \otimes \mathbb{1}_{\mathrm{L}(\mathcal{Z})})((\mathbb{1} \otimes U)uu^*(\mathbb{1} \otimes U^*)) \right\|_1 \\
&= \left\| (\mathbb{1} \otimes U)(\Phi \otimes \mathbb{1}_{\mathrm{L}(\mathcal{X})})(uu^*)(\mathbb{1} \otimes U^*) \right\|_1 \\
&= \left\| (\Phi \otimes \mathbb{1}_{\mathrm{L}(\mathcal{X})})(uu^*) \right\|_1,
\end{aligned}
\tag{3.264}
$$

as required. $\qquad \square$

With Lemma 3.45 in hand, the following theorem may be proved. The theorem implies a claim that was made earlier: the identity map on $\mathrm{L}(\mathcal{X})$ in Definition 3.43 can be replaced by the identity map on $\mathrm{L}(\mathcal{Z})$, for any space $\mathcal{Z}$ having dimension at least that of $\mathcal{X}$, without changing the value of the norm.

Theorem 3.46 *Let $\mathcal{X}$ and $\mathcal{Y}$ be complex Euclidean spaces, let $\Phi \in \mathrm{T}(\mathcal{X}, \mathcal{Y})$ be a map, and let $\mathcal{Z}$ be a complex Euclidean space. It holds that*

$$\left\| \Phi \otimes \mathbb{1}_{\mathrm{L}(\mathcal{Z})} \right\|_1 \leq \left\| |\Phi| \right\|_1 , \tag{3.265}$$

with equality holding under the assumption that $\dim(\mathcal{Z}) \geq \dim(\mathcal{X})$.

Proof By Proposition 3.38, there exist unit vectors $x, y \in \mathcal{X} \otimes \mathcal{Z}$ such that

$$\left\| \Phi \otimes \mathbb{1}_{\mathrm{L}(\mathcal{Z})} \right\|_1 = \left\| (\Phi \otimes \mathbb{1}_{\mathrm{L}(\mathcal{Z})})(xy^*) \right\|_1. \tag{3.266}$$

Therefore, by Lemma 3.45, there exist unit vectors $u, v \in \mathcal{X} \otimes \mathcal{X}$ such that

$$\left\| \Phi \otimes \mathbb{1}_{\mathrm{L}(\mathcal{Z})} \right\|_1 = \left\| (\Phi \otimes \mathbb{1}_{\mathrm{L}(\mathcal{X})})(uv^*) \right\|_1 , \tag{3.267}$$

which implies

$$\left\| \Phi \otimes \mathbb{1}_{\mathrm{L}(\mathcal{Z})} \right\|_1 \leq \left\| |\Phi| \right\|_1. \tag{3.268}$$

Under the assumption that $\dim(\mathcal{Z}) \geq \dim(\mathcal{X})$, there exists an isometry $V \in \mathrm{U}(\mathcal{X}, \mathcal{Z})$. For every operator $X \in \mathrm{L}(\mathcal{X} \otimes \mathcal{X})$ with $\|X\|_1 \leq 1$, the isometric invariance of the trace norm implies

$$
\begin{aligned}
\left\| (\Phi \otimes \mathbb{1}_{\mathrm{L}(\mathcal{X})})(X) \right\|_1 &= \left\| (\mathbb{1}_{\mathcal{Y}} \otimes V)(\Phi \otimes \mathbb{1}_{\mathrm{L}(\mathcal{X})})(X)(\mathbb{1}_{\mathcal{Y}} \otimes V)^* \right\|_1 \\
&= \left\| (\Phi \otimes \mathbb{1}_{\mathrm{L}(\mathcal{Z})})((\mathbb{1}_{\mathcal{X}} \otimes V)X(\mathbb{1}_{\mathcal{X}} \otimes V)^*) \right\|_1 \\
&\leq \left\| \Phi \otimes \mathbb{1}_{\mathrm{L}(\mathcal{Z})} \right\|_1 \left\| (\mathbb{1}_{\mathcal{X}} \otimes V)X(\mathbb{1}_{\mathcal{X}} \otimes V)^* \right\|_1 \quad (3.269) \\
&= \left\| \Phi \otimes \mathbb{1}_{\mathrm{L}(\mathcal{Z})} \right\|_1 \|X\|_1 \\
&\leq \left\| \Phi \otimes \mathbb{1}_{\mathrm{L}(\mathcal{Z})} \right\|_1.
\end{aligned}
$$

It therefore holds that

$$\left\| |\Phi| \right\|_1 \leq \left\| \Phi \otimes \mathbb{1}_{\mathrm{L}(\mathcal{Z})} \right\|_1 , \tag{3.270}$$

which completes the proof. $\square$

Corollary 3.47 *Let $\mathcal{X}$, $\mathcal{Y}$, and $\mathcal{Z}$ be complex Euclidean spaces and let $\Phi \in \mathrm{T}(\mathcal{X}, \mathcal{Y})$ be a map. It holds that*

$$\left\| |\Phi \otimes \mathbb{1}_{\mathrm{L}(\mathcal{Z})}| \right\|_1 = \left\| |\Phi| \right\|_1. \tag{3.271}$$

By means of Theorem 3.46, one may prove that the completely bounded trace norm possesses properties analogous to ones established for the induced trace norm by statements 1 and 2 of Proposition 3.41.

Proposition 3.48 *For every choice of complex Euclidean spaces $\mathcal{X}$, $\mathcal{Y}$, and $\mathcal{Z}$, the following facts regarding the completely bounded trace norm hold:*

1. *For all maps $\Phi \in \mathrm{T}(\mathcal{X}, \mathcal{Y})$ and $\Psi \in \mathrm{T}(\mathcal{Y}, \mathcal{Z})$, it holds that*

$$\vert\vert\vert \Psi\Phi \vert\vert\vert_1 \le \vert\vert\vert \Psi \vert\vert\vert_1 \, \vert\vert\vert \Phi \vert\vert\vert_1. \tag{3.272}$$

2. *For all channels $\Phi_0, \Psi_0 \in \mathrm{C}(\mathcal{X}, \mathcal{Y})$ and $\Phi_1, \Psi_1 \in \mathrm{C}(\mathcal{Y}, \mathcal{Z})$, it holds that*

$$\vert\vert\vert \Psi_1\Psi_0 - \Phi_1\Phi_0 \vert\vert\vert_1 \le \vert\vert\vert \Psi_0 - \Phi_0 \vert\vert\vert_1 + \vert\vert\vert \Psi_1 - \Phi_1 \vert\vert\vert_1. \tag{3.273}$$

Proof By Proposition 3.41, one concludes that

$$\vert\vert\vert \Psi\Phi \vert\vert\vert_1 = \left\Vert \Psi\Phi \otimes \mathbb{1}_{\mathrm{L}(\mathcal{X})} \right\Vert_1 \le \left\Vert \Psi \otimes \mathbb{1}_{\mathrm{L}(\mathcal{X})} \right\Vert_1 \left\Vert \Phi \otimes \mathbb{1}_{\mathrm{L}(\mathcal{X})} \right\Vert_1 \tag{3.274}$$

and

$$\begin{aligned}
\vert\vert\vert \Psi_1\Psi_0 - \Phi_1\Phi_0 \vert\vert\vert_1 &= \left\Vert \Psi_1\Psi_0 \otimes \mathbb{1}_{\mathrm{L}(\mathcal{X})} - \Phi_1\Phi_0 \otimes \mathbb{1}_{\mathrm{L}(\mathcal{X})} \right\Vert_1 \\
&\le \left\Vert \Psi_0 \otimes \mathbb{1}_{\mathrm{L}(\mathcal{X})} - \Phi_0 \otimes \mathbb{1}_{\mathrm{L}(\mathcal{X})} \right\Vert_1 + \left\Vert \Psi_1 \otimes \mathbb{1}_{\mathrm{L}(\mathcal{X})} - \Phi_1 \otimes \mathbb{1}_{\mathrm{L}(\mathcal{X})} \right\Vert_1.
\end{aligned} \tag{3.275}$$

The proposition follows by Theorem 3.46. $\square$

The fact that the completely bounded trace norm is multiplicative with respect to tensor products may also be proved.

Theorem 3.49 *Let $\Phi_0 \in \mathrm{T}(\mathcal{X}_0, \mathcal{Y}_0)$ and $\Phi_1 \in \mathrm{T}(\mathcal{X}_1, \mathcal{Y}_1)$ be maps, for $\mathcal{X}_0$, $\mathcal{X}_1$, $\mathcal{Y}_0$, and $\mathcal{Y}_1$ being complex Euclidean spaces. It holds that*

$$\vert\vert\vert \Phi_0 \otimes \Phi_1 \vert\vert\vert_1 = \vert\vert\vert \Phi_0 \vert\vert\vert_1 \, \vert\vert\vert \Phi_1 \vert\vert\vert_1. \tag{3.276}$$

Proof By Proposition 3.48 and Corollary 3.47, it follows that

$$\begin{aligned}
\vert\vert\vert \Phi_0 \otimes \Phi_1 \vert\vert\vert_1 &= \vert\vert\vert (\Phi_0 \otimes \mathbb{1}_{\mathrm{L}(\mathcal{Y}_1)})(\mathbb{1}_{\mathrm{L}(\mathcal{X}_0)} \otimes \Phi_1) \vert\vert\vert_1 \\
&\le \vert\vert\vert \Phi_0 \otimes \mathbb{1}_{\mathrm{L}(\mathcal{Y}_1)} \vert\vert\vert_1 \, \vert\vert\vert \mathbb{1}_{\mathrm{L}(\mathcal{X}_0)} \otimes \Phi_1 \vert\vert\vert_1 = \vert\vert\vert \Phi_0 \vert\vert\vert_1 \, \vert\vert\vert \Phi_1 \vert\vert\vert_1.
\end{aligned} \tag{3.277}$$

It remains to prove the reverse inequality.

First, choose operators $X_0 \in \mathrm{L}(\mathcal{X}_0 \otimes \mathcal{X}_0)$ and $X_1 \in \mathrm{L}(\mathcal{X}_1 \otimes \mathcal{X}_1)$ such that $\Vert X_0 \Vert_1 = 1$ and $\Vert X_1 \Vert_1 = 1$, and such that these equalities hold:

$$\begin{aligned}
\vert\vert\vert \Phi_0 \vert\vert\vert_1 &= \left\Vert (\Phi_0 \otimes \mathbb{1}_{\mathrm{L}(\mathcal{X}_0)})(X_0) \right\Vert_1, \\
\vert\vert\vert \Phi_1 \vert\vert\vert_1 &= \left\Vert (\Phi_1 \otimes \mathbb{1}_{\mathrm{L}(\mathcal{X}_1)})(X_1) \right\Vert_1.
\end{aligned} \tag{3.278}$$

As the trace norm is multiplicative with respect to tensor products, it follows that $\Vert X_0 \otimes X_1 \Vert_1 = 1$.

Next, observe that

$$\begin{aligned}
\vert\vert\vert \Phi_0 \otimes \Phi_1 \vert\vert\vert_1 &= \left\Vert \Phi_0 \otimes \Phi_1 \otimes \mathbb{1}_{\mathrm{L}(\mathcal{X}_0 \otimes \mathcal{X}_1)} \right\Vert_1 \\
&= \left\Vert \Phi_0 \otimes \mathbb{1}_{\mathrm{L}(\mathcal{X}_0)} \otimes \Phi_1 \otimes \mathbb{1}_{\mathrm{L}(\mathcal{X}_1)} \right\Vert_1.
\end{aligned} \tag{3.279}$$

The second equality follows from the unitary invariance of the induced trace norm (the third statement of Proposition 3.41), which implies that this norm is invariant under permuting the ordering of tensor factors of maps. Again using the multiplicativity of the trace norm with respect to tensor products, it follows that

$$
\begin{aligned}
\left\| \left\| \Phi_0 \otimes \Phi_1 \right\| \right\|_1 &\geq \left\| (\Phi_0 \otimes \mathbb{1}_{\mathrm{L}(\mathcal{X}_0)} \otimes \Phi_1 \otimes \mathbb{1}_{\mathrm{L}(\mathcal{X}_1)})(X_0 \otimes X_1) \right\|_1 \\
&= \left\| (\Phi_0 \otimes \mathbb{1}_{\mathrm{L}(\mathcal{X}_0)})(X_0) \right\|_1 \left\| (\Phi_1 \otimes \mathbb{1}_{\mathrm{L}(\mathcal{X}_1)})(X_1) \right\|_1 \qquad (3.280) \\
&= \left\| \left\| \Phi_0 \right\| \right\|_1 \left\| \left\| \Phi_1 \right\| \right\|_1 ,
\end{aligned}
$$

which completes the proof. $\qquad\square$

3.3.3 Distances Between Channels

This section explains the connection between the completely bounded trace norm and the task of channel discrimination that was alluded to above, and discusses other aspects of the notion of distance between channels induced by the completely bounded trace norm.

The Completely Bounded Trace Norm of Hermitian-Preserving Maps

For a given map $\Phi \in \mathrm{T}(\mathcal{X}, \mathcal{Y})$, one has that

$$
\left\| \left\| \Phi \right\| \right\|_1 = \left\| (\Phi \otimes \mathbb{1}_{\mathrm{L}(\mathcal{X})})(uv^*) \right\|_1 \qquad (3.281)
$$

for some choice of unit vectors $u, v \in \mathcal{X} \otimes \mathcal{X}$. The stronger condition that

$$
\left\| \left\| \Phi \right\| \right\|_1 = \left\| (\Phi \otimes \mathbb{1}_{\mathrm{L}(\mathcal{X})})(uu^*) \right\|_1 \qquad (3.282)
$$

for a single unit vector $u \in \mathcal{X} \otimes \mathcal{X}$ does not generally hold; without any restrictions on Φ, this could not reasonably be expected.

When the map Φ is Hermitian-preserving, however, there will always exist a unit vector $u \in \mathcal{X} \otimes \mathcal{X}$ for which (3.282) holds. This fact is stated as Theorem 3.51 below, whose proof makes use of the following lemma.

Lemma 3.50 *Let $\mathcal{X}$ and $\mathcal{Y}$ be complex Euclidean spaces, let $\Phi \in \mathrm{T}(\mathcal{X}, \mathcal{Y})$ be a Hermitian-preserving map, and let $\mathcal{Z}$ be any complex Euclidean space with $\dim(\mathcal{Z}) \geq 2$. There exists a unit vector $u \in \mathcal{X} \otimes \mathcal{Z}$ such that*

$$
\left\| (\Phi \otimes \mathbb{1}_{\mathrm{L}(\mathcal{Z})})(uu^*) \right\|_1 \geq \left\| \left\| \Phi \right\| \right\|_1 . \qquad (3.283)
$$

Proof Let $X \in \mathrm{L}(\mathcal{X})$ be an operator for which it holds that $\|X\|_1 = 1$ and $\|\Phi(X)\|_1 = \|\|\Phi\|\|_1$. Let $z_0, z_1 \in \mathcal{Z}$ be any two orthogonal unit vectors, define a Hermitian operator $H \in \mathrm{Herm}(\mathcal{X} \otimes \mathcal{Z})$ as

$$
H = \frac{1}{2} X \otimes z_0 z_1^* + \frac{1}{2} X^* \otimes z_1 z_0^*, \qquad (3.284)
$$

and observe that $\|H\|_1 = \|X\|_1 = 1$. Moreover, one has

$$
\begin{aligned}
(\Phi \otimes \mathbb{1}_{\mathrm{L}(\mathcal{Z})})(H) &= \frac{1}{2}\Phi(X) \otimes z_0 z_1^* + \frac{1}{2}\Phi(X^*) \otimes z_1 z_0^* \\
&= \frac{1}{2}\Phi(X) \otimes z_0 z_1^* + \frac{1}{2}\Phi(X)^* \otimes z_1 z_0^*,
\end{aligned}
\tag{3.285}
$$

where the second equality follows from Theorem 2.25, together with the assumption that Φ is a Hermitian-preserving map. It is therefore the case that

$$
\left\|(\Phi \otimes \mathbb{1}_{\mathrm{L}(\mathcal{Z})})(H)\right\|_1 = \left\|\Phi(X)\right\|_1 = \|\Phi\|_1.
\tag{3.286}
$$

Now consider a spectral decomposition

$$
H = \sum_{k=1}^{n} \lambda_k u_k u_k^*
\tag{3.287}
$$

for $n = \dim(\mathcal{X} \otimes \mathcal{Z})$. By the triangle inequality, one has

$$
\left\|(\Phi \otimes \mathbb{1}_{\mathrm{L}(\mathcal{Z})})(H)\right\|_1 \leq \sum_{k=1}^{n} |\lambda_k| \left\|(\Phi \otimes \mathbb{1}_{\mathrm{L}(\mathcal{Z})})(u_k u_k^*)\right\|_1.
\tag{3.288}
$$

As $\|H\|_1 = 1$, the expression on the right-hand side of the inequality (3.288) is a convex combination of the values

$$
\left\|(\Phi \otimes \mathbb{1}_{\mathrm{L}(\mathcal{Z})})(u_k u_k^*)\right\|_1,
\tag{3.289}
$$

ranging over $k \in \{1, \dots, n\}$. There must therefore exist $k \in \{1, \dots, n\}$ for which the inequality

$$
\left\|(\Phi \otimes \mathbb{1}_{\mathrm{L}(\mathcal{Z})})(u_k u_k^*)\right\|_1 \geq \left\|(\Phi \otimes \mathbb{1}_{\mathrm{L}(\mathcal{Z})})(H)\right\|_1 = \|\Phi\|_1
\tag{3.290}
$$

is satisfied. Setting $u = u_k$ completes the proof. $\qquad\square$

Theorem 3.51   Let $\Phi \in \mathrm{T}(\mathcal{X}, \mathcal{Y})$ be a Hermitian-preserving map, for $\mathcal{X}$ and $\mathcal{Y}$ being complex Euclidean spaces. It holds that

$$
\|\|\Phi\|\|_1 = \max_{u \in \mathcal{S}(\mathcal{X} \otimes \mathcal{X})} \left\|(\Phi \otimes \mathbb{1}_{\mathrm{L}(\mathcal{X})})(uu^*)\right\|_1.
\tag{3.291}
$$

Proof   For every unit vector $u \in \mathcal{X} \otimes \mathcal{X}$, it holds that

$$
\left\|(\Phi \otimes \mathbb{1}_{\mathrm{L}(\mathcal{X})})(uu^*)\right\|_1 \leq \left\|\Phi \otimes \mathbb{1}_{\mathrm{L}(\mathcal{X})}\right\|_1 = \|\|\Phi\|\|_1,
\tag{3.292}
$$

so it suffices to prove that there exists a unit vector $u \in \mathcal{X} \otimes \mathcal{X}$ for which

$$
\left\|(\Phi \otimes \mathbb{1}_{\mathrm{L}(\mathcal{X})})(uu^*)\right\|_1 \geq \left\|\Phi \otimes \mathbb{1}_{\mathrm{L}(\mathcal{X})}\right\|_1 = \|\|\Phi\|\|_1.
\tag{3.293}
$$

Let $\mathcal{Z} = \mathbb{C}^2$. By Lemma 3.50 there exists a unit vector $x \in \mathcal{X} \otimes \mathcal{X} \otimes \mathcal{Z}$ such that

$$\left\| (\Phi \otimes \mathbb{1}_{L(\mathcal{X})} \otimes \mathbb{1}_{L(\mathcal{Z})})(xx^*) \right\|_1 \geq \left\| \Phi \otimes \mathbb{1}_{L(\mathcal{X})} \right\|_1, \tag{3.294}$$

and by Lemma 3.45 there must exist a unit vector $u \in \mathcal{X} \otimes \mathcal{X}$ such that

$$\left\| (\Phi \otimes \mathbb{1}_{L(\mathcal{X})})(uu^*) \right\|_1 = \left\| (\Phi \otimes \mathbb{1}_{L(\mathcal{X})} \otimes \mathbb{1}_{L(\mathcal{Z})})(xx^*) \right\|_1. \tag{3.295}$$

For such a choice of u, one has (3.293), which completes the proof. $\qquad\square$

A Channel Analogue of the Holevo–Helstrom Theorem

The next theorem represents an analogue of the Holevo–Helstrom theorem (Theorem 3.4) for channels rather than states, with the completely bounded trace norm replacing the trace norm accordingly.

Theorem 3.52 *Let $\Phi_0, \Phi_1 \in C(\mathcal{X}, \mathcal{Y})$ be channels, for complex Euclidean spaces $\mathcal{X}$ and $\mathcal{Y}$, and let $\lambda \in [0, 1]$. For any choice of a complex Euclidean space $\mathcal{Z}$, a measurement $\mu \colon \{0, 1\} \to \mathrm{Pos}(\mathcal{Y} \otimes \mathcal{Z})$, and a density operator $\sigma \in \mathrm{D}(\mathcal{X} \otimes \mathcal{Z})$, it holds that*

$$\lambda \langle \mu(0), (\Phi_0 \otimes \mathbb{1}_{L(\mathcal{Z})})(\sigma) \rangle + (1 - \lambda) \langle \mu(1), (\Phi_1 \otimes \mathbb{1}_{L(\mathcal{Z})})(\sigma) \rangle$$
$$\leq \frac{1}{2} + \frac{1}{2} \left\|\left| \lambda \Phi_0 - (1 - \lambda)\Phi_1 \right|\right\|_1. \tag{3.296}$$

Moreover, for any choice of $\mathcal{Z}$ satisfying $\dim(\mathcal{Z}) \geq \dim(\mathcal{X})$, equality is achieved in (3.296) for some choice of a projective measurement μ and a pure state σ.

Proof By the Holevo–Helstrom theorem (Theorem 3.4), the quantity on the left-hand side of (3.296) is at most

$$\frac{1}{2} + \frac{1}{2} \left\| \lambda(\Phi_0 \otimes \mathbb{1}_{L(\mathcal{Z})})(\sigma) - (1 - \lambda)(\Phi_1 \otimes \mathbb{1}_{L(\mathcal{Z})})(\sigma) \right\|_1. \tag{3.297}$$

This value is upper-bounded by

$$\frac{1}{2} + \frac{1}{2} \left\| (\lambda \Phi_0 - (1 - \lambda)\Phi_1) \otimes \mathbb{1}_{L(\mathcal{Z})} \right\|_1, \tag{3.298}$$

which is at most

$$\frac{1}{2} + \frac{1}{2} \left\|\left| \lambda \Phi_0 - (1 - \lambda)\Phi_1 \right|\right\|_1 \tag{3.299}$$

by Theorem 3.46.

The mapping $\lambda\Phi_0 - (1-\lambda)\Phi_1$ is Hermitian-preserving, by virtue of the fact that Φ_0 and Φ_1 are completely positive and λ is a real number. By Theorem 3.51, there must therefore exist a unit vector $u \in \mathcal{X} \otimes \mathcal{X}$ for which

$$
\begin{aligned}
&\left\|\lambda(\Phi_0 \otimes \mathbb{1}_{\mathrm{L}(\mathcal{X})})(uu^*) - (1-\lambda)(\Phi_1 \otimes \mathbb{1}_{\mathrm{L}(\mathcal{X})})(uu^*)\right\|_1 \\
&= \left\|\left\|\lambda\Phi_0 - (1-\lambda)\Phi_1\right\|\right\|_1.
\end{aligned} \tag{3.300}
$$

Under the assumption that $\dim(\mathcal{Z}) \geq \dim(\mathcal{X})$, one therefore has

$$
\begin{aligned}
&\left\|\lambda(\Phi_0 \otimes \mathbb{1}_{\mathrm{L}(\mathcal{Z})})(\sigma) - (1-\lambda)(\Phi_1 \otimes \mathbb{1}_{\mathrm{L}(\mathcal{Z})})(\sigma)\right\|_1 \\
&= \left\|\left\|\lambda\Phi_0 - (1-\lambda)\Phi_1\right\|\right\|_1
\end{aligned} \tag{3.301}
$$

for the pure state

$$
\sigma = (\mathbb{1}_{\mathcal{X}} \otimes V)uu^*(\mathbb{1}_{\mathcal{X}} \otimes V^*), \tag{3.302}
$$

for an arbitrary choice of an isometry $V \in \mathrm{U}(\mathcal{X}, \mathcal{Z})$.

Finally, by the Holevo–Helstrom theorem (Theorem 3.4), there must exist a projective measurement $\mu\colon \{0,1\} \to \mathrm{Pos}(\mathcal{Y} \otimes \mathcal{Z})$ such that

$$
\begin{aligned}
&\lambda\langle\mu(0), (\Phi_0 \otimes \mathbb{1}_{\mathrm{L}(\mathcal{Z})})(\sigma)\rangle + (1-\lambda)\langle\mu(1), (\Phi_1 \otimes \mathbb{1}_{\mathrm{L}(\mathcal{Z})})(\sigma)\rangle \\
&= \frac{1}{2} + \frac{1}{2}\left\|\lambda(\Phi_0 \otimes \mathbb{1}_{\mathrm{L}(\mathcal{Z})})(\sigma) - (1-\lambda)(\Phi_1 \otimes \mathbb{1}_{\mathrm{L}(\mathcal{Z})})(\sigma)\right\|_1 \\
&= \frac{1}{2} + \frac{1}{2}\left\|\left\|\lambda\Phi_0 - (1-\lambda)\Phi_1\right\|\right\|_1,
\end{aligned} \tag{3.303}
$$

which completes the proof. □

Distances Between Networks of Channels

Many computations and interactions that arise in the study of quantum information and computation can be represented as *networks* of channels. Here, one supposes that a collection of channels $\Phi_1, \ldots, \Phi_N$ having varying input and output spaces are arranged in an acyclic network, as suggested by the example depicted in Figure 3.1. The completely bounded trace norm is well-suited to analyses concerning errors, inaccuracies, and noise that may occur in such networks.

By composing the channels $\Phi_1, \ldots, \Phi_N$ in a manner consistent with the network, a single channel Φ is obtained. Assuming the registers $\mathsf{X}_1, \ldots, \mathsf{X}_n$ are treated as inputs to the network and registers $\mathsf{Y}_1, \ldots, \mathsf{Y}_m$ are output, the channel Φ representing the composition of the channels $\Phi_1, \ldots, \Phi_N$ takes the form

$$
\Phi \in \mathrm{C}(\mathcal{X}_1 \otimes \cdots \otimes \mathcal{X}_n, \mathcal{Y}_1 \otimes \cdots \otimes \mathcal{Y}_m). \tag{3.304}
$$

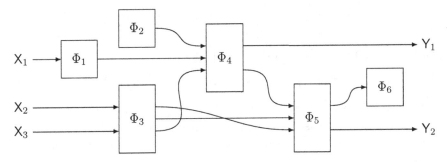

Figure 3.1 A hypothetical example of an acyclic network of channels. The arrows represent registers, and one assumes the input and output spaces of the channels (represented by rectangles) are compatible with the registers represented by the arrows. For instance, the channel Φ_1 transforms the register X_1 into some other register (not explicitly named in the figure), which is the second of three inputs to the channel Φ_4. By composing the channels $\Phi_1, \ldots, \Phi_6$ in the manner suggested by the figure, one obtains a single channel $\Phi \in C(\mathcal{X}_1 \otimes \mathcal{X}_2 \otimes \mathcal{X}_3, \mathcal{Y}_1 \otimes \mathcal{Y}_2)$.

Now suppose that $\Psi_1, \ldots, \Psi_N$ are channels whose input spaces and output spaces agree with $\Phi_1, \ldots, \Phi_N$, respectively, and that Ψ_k is substituted for Φ_k for each $k \in \{1, \ldots, N\}$. Equivalently, the channels $\Psi_1, \ldots, \Psi_N$ are composed in a manner that is consistent with the description of the network, yielding a channel

$$\Psi \in C(\mathcal{X}_1 \otimes \cdots \otimes \mathcal{X}_n, \mathcal{Y}_1 \otimes \cdots \otimes \mathcal{Y}_m) \tag{3.305}$$

in place of Φ. It could be, for instance, that $\Phi_1, \ldots, \Phi_N$ represent ideal channels that are specified by a protocol or algorithm while $\Psi_1, \ldots, \Psi_N$ represent slightly noisy or corrupted variants of $\Phi_1, \ldots, \Phi_N$.

It is natural to ask how much Φ and Ψ may differ, as a function of the differences between Φ_k and Ψ_k, for $k \in \{1, \ldots, N\}$. An upper bound on the completely bounded trace norm of the difference between Φ and Ψ is obtained by induction from Proposition 3.48 along with Corollary 3.47:

$$\vertvert\vert \Phi - \Psi \vertvert\vert_1 \leq \vertvert\vert \Phi_1 - \Psi_1 \vertvert\vert_1 + \cdots + \vertvert\vert \Phi_N - \Psi_N \vertvert\vert_1. \tag{3.306}$$

Therefore, irrespective of the properties of the network under consideration, the differences between the channels Φ_k and Ψ_k, for $k \in \{1, \ldots, N\}$, only accumulate additively when composed in a network.

Discrimination Between Pairs of Isometric Channels

As Example 3.36 illustrates, it is necessary in some instances of Scenario 3.35 for Bob to use an auxiliary register W in order to optimally discriminate a given pair of channels. One interesting case in which it is *not* necessary for Bob to make use of an auxiliary register in this scenario is when the two channels are isometric channels, defined as

$$\Phi_0(X) = V_0 X V_0^* \quad \text{and} \quad \Phi_1(X) = V_1 X V_1^* \tag{3.307}$$

for all $X \in L(\mathcal{X})$, for some choice of isometries $V_0, V_1 \in U(\mathcal{X}, \mathcal{Y})$. The fact that an auxiliary register is not needed for an optimal discrimination in this case is proved below. The proof makes use of the notion of the *numerical range* of an operator.

Definition 3.53   Let $\mathcal{X}$ be a complex Euclidean space and let $X \in L(\mathcal{X})$ be an operator. The *numerical range* of X is the set $\mathcal{N}(X) \subset \mathbb{C}$ defined as follows:

$$\mathcal{N}(X) = \{u^* X u : u \in \mathcal{S}(\mathcal{X})\}. \tag{3.308}$$

In general, every eigenvalue of a given operator X is contained in $\mathcal{N}(X)$, and one may prove that $\mathcal{N}(X)$ is equal to the convex hull of the eigenvalues of X in the case that X is normal. For non-normal operators, however, this will not generally be the case. It is, however, always the case that $\mathcal{N}(X)$ is compact and convex, which is the content of the following theorem.

Theorem 3.54 (Toeplitz–Hausdorff theorem)   *For any complex Euclidean space $\mathcal{X}$ and any operator $X \in L(\mathcal{X})$, the set $\mathcal{N}(X)$ is compact and convex.*

Proof   The function $f : \mathcal{S}(\mathcal{X}) \to \mathbb{C}$ defined by $f(u) = u^* X u$ is continuous, and the unit sphere $\mathcal{S}(\mathcal{X})$ is compact. Continuous functions map compact sets to compact sets, implying that $\mathcal{N}(X) = f(\mathcal{S}(\mathcal{X}))$ is compact.

It remains to prove that $\mathcal{N}(X)$ is convex. Fix any choice of $\alpha, \beta \in \mathcal{N}(X)$ and a real number $\lambda \in [0, 1]$. It will be proved that

$$\lambda \alpha + (1 - \lambda)\beta \in \mathcal{N}(X), \tag{3.309}$$

which suffices to prove the theorem. It will be assumed hereafter that $\alpha \neq \beta$, as the assertion is trivial in the case that $\alpha = \beta$.

By the definition of the numerical range, one may choose unit vectors $u, v \in \mathcal{S}(\mathcal{X})$ such that $u^* X u = \alpha$ and $v^* X v = \beta$. By the assumption that $\alpha \neq \beta$, one has that the vectors u and v are linearly independent. Next, define

$$Y = \frac{-\beta}{\alpha - \beta} \mathbb{1}_{\mathcal{X}} + \frac{1}{\alpha - \beta} X \tag{3.310}$$

so that $u^* Y u = 1$ and $v^* Y v = 0$. Let $H, K \in \text{Herm}(\mathcal{X})$ be defined as

$$H = \frac{Y + Y^*}{2} \quad \text{and} \quad K = \frac{Y - Y^*}{2i}, \tag{3.311}$$

so that $Y = H + iK$. It follows that

$$u^*Hu = 1, \qquad v^*Hv = 0,$$
$$u^*Ku = 0, \qquad v^*Kv = 0. \tag{3.312}$$

Without loss of generality, it may be assumed that u^*Kv is purely imaginary (i.e., has real part equal to 0), for otherwise v may be replaced by $e^{i\theta}v$ for an appropriate choice of θ without changing any of the previously observed properties.

As u and v are linearly independent, the vector $tu + (1-t)v$ is nonzero for every choice of $t \in \mathbb{R}$. Thus, for each $t \in [0,1]$, one may define a unit vector

$$z(t) = \frac{tu + (1-t)v}{\|tu + (1-t)v\|}. \tag{3.313}$$

Because $u^*Ku = v^*Kv = 0$ and u^*Kv is purely imaginary, it follows that $z(t)^*Kz(t) = 0$ for every $t \in [0,1]$, and therefore

$$z(t)^*Yz(t) = z(t)^*Hz(t) = \frac{t^2 + t(1-t)(v^*Hu + u^*Hv)}{\|tu + (1-t)v\|^2}. \tag{3.314}$$

The expression on the right-hand side of (3.314) is a continuous real-valued function mapping 0 to 0 and 1 to 1. Consequently, there must exist at least one choice of $t \in [0,1]$ such that $z(t)^*Yz(t) = \lambda$. Let $w = z(t)$ for such choice of t, so that $w^*Yw = \lambda$. It holds that w is a unit vector, and

$$w^*Xw = (\alpha - \beta)\left(\frac{\beta}{\alpha - \beta} + w^*Yw\right) = \lambda\alpha + (1-\lambda)\beta. \tag{3.315}$$

It has therefore been shown that $\lambda\alpha + (1-\lambda)\beta \in \mathcal{N}(X)$ as required. $\qquad\square$

Theorem 3.55 *Let $\mathcal{X}$ and $\mathcal{Y}$ be complex Euclidean spaces for which it holds that $\dim(\mathcal{X}) \leq \dim(\mathcal{Y})$, let $V_0, V_1 \in \mathrm{U}(\mathcal{X}, \mathcal{Y})$ be isometries, and define channels $\Phi_0, \Phi_1 \in \mathrm{C}(\mathcal{X}, \mathcal{Y})$ as*

$$\Phi_0(X) = V_0 X V_0^* \quad and \quad \Phi_1(X) = V_1 X V_1^* \tag{3.316}$$

for all $X \in \mathrm{L}(\mathcal{X})$. There exists a unit vector $u \in \mathcal{X}$ such that

$$\left\|\lambda\Phi_0(uu^*) - (1-\lambda)\Phi_1(uu^*)\right\|_1 = \left\|\!\left\|\lambda\Phi_0 - (1-\lambda)\Phi_1\right\|\!\right\|_1 \tag{3.317}$$

for every $\lambda \in [0,1]$.

Proof Using the identity (1.184), one finds that

$$\left\|\lambda\Phi_0(uu^*) - (1-\lambda)\Phi_1(uu^*)\right\|_1$$
$$= \sqrt{1 - 4\lambda(1-\lambda)\left|u^*V_0^*V_1 u\right|^2}, \tag{3.318}$$

for every unit vector $u \in \mathcal{X}$, and similarly

$$\left\| \lambda(\Phi_0 \otimes \mathbb{1}_{L(\mathcal{Z})})(vv^*) - (1-\lambda)(\Phi_1 \otimes \mathbb{1}_{L(\mathcal{Z})})(vv^*) \right\|_1$$
$$= \sqrt{1 - 4\lambda(1-\lambda) \left| v^*(V_0^* V_1 \otimes \mathbb{1}_{\mathcal{Z}})v \right|^2} \qquad (3.319)$$

for every complex Euclidean space $\mathcal{Z}$ and unit vector $v \in \mathcal{X} \otimes \mathcal{Z}$. Taking $\mathcal{Z}$ to be a complex Euclidean space with $\dim(\mathcal{Z}) = \dim(\mathcal{X})$, it follows from (3.319) together with Theorem 3.51 that there exists a unit vector $v \in \mathcal{X} \otimes \mathcal{Z}$ such that

$$\left\| \left\| \lambda\Phi_0 - (1-\lambda)\Phi_1 \right\| \right\|_1 = \sqrt{1 - 4\lambda(1-\lambda) \left| v^*(V_0^* V_1 \otimes \mathbb{1}_{\mathcal{Z}})v \right|^2}. \qquad (3.320)$$

Now, one may observe that

$$v^*(V_0^* V_1 \otimes \mathbb{1}_{\mathcal{Z}})v = \langle \rho, V_0^* V_1 \rangle \qquad (3.321)$$

for $\rho = \mathrm{Tr}_{\mathcal{Z}}(vv^*)$. By considering a spectral decomposition of ρ, one finds that the value represented by (3.321) is a convex combination of values of the form

$$w^* V_0^* V_1 w, \qquad (3.322)$$

where $w \in \mathcal{X}$ ranges over a set of unit eigenvectors of ρ. Each of these values is contained in the numerical range of $V_0^* V_1$, so by the Toeplitz–Hausdorff theorem (Theorem 3.54) there must exist a unit vector $u \in \mathcal{X}$ such that

$$u^* V_0^* V_1 u = \langle \rho, V_0^* V_1 \rangle. \qquad (3.323)$$

By (3.318), it follows that

$$\left\| \lambda\Phi_0(uu^*) - (1-\lambda)\Phi_1(uu^*) \right\|_1 = \left\| \left\| \lambda\Phi_0 - (1-\lambda)\Phi_1 \right\| \right\|_1. \qquad (3.324)$$

Observing that the vector u does not depend on λ, the proof is complete. $\square$

The Completely Bounded Trace Distance From a Channel to the Identity

Returning once again to Example 3.36, one has that the Werner–Holevo channels can be perfectly discriminated through the use of a sufficiently large auxiliary register, but are nearly indistinguishable without the use of an auxiliary register (assuming the space with respect to which the channels are defined has large dimension). The Werner–Holevo channels have another feature that is relevant to the discussion that follows, which is that they are highly noisy channels; their outputs are close to the completely mixed state for every possible input state.

One may ask if a similar phenomenon, in which an auxiliary register has a dramatic effect on the optimal probability of successfully discriminating channels, occurs when one of the channels is the identity channel. This is a natural question, as the closeness of a given channel to the identity channel may be a relevant figure of merit of that channel in some situations. The following theorem demonstrates that the phenomenon suggested above is limited in this setting. In particular, the theorem demonstrates that the potential advantage of using an auxiliary register in discriminating a given channel from the identity channel is dimension-independent.

Theorem 3.56 *Let $\mathcal{X}$ be a complex Euclidean space, let $\Phi \in C(\mathcal{X})$ be a channel, let $\varepsilon \in [0, 2]$, and suppose that*

$$\|\Phi(\rho) - \rho\|_1 \leq \varepsilon \tag{3.325}$$

for every density operator $\rho \in D(\mathcal{X})$. It holds that

$$\left\|\left\|\Phi - \mathbb{1}_{L(\mathcal{X})}\right\|\right\|_1 \leq \sqrt{2\varepsilon}. \tag{3.326}$$

Proof It is evident from the assumptions of the theorem that, for every unit vector $u \in \mathcal{X}$, one has

$$\|\Phi(uu^*) - uu^*\|_1 \leq \varepsilon, \tag{3.327}$$

and therefore

$$\left|\langle uu^*, \Phi(uu^*) - uu^* \rangle\right| \leq \frac{\varepsilon}{2}. \tag{3.328}$$

The first main step of the proof will be to establish a bound of a similar nature:

$$\left|\langle uv^*, \Phi(uv^*) - uv^* \rangle\right| \leq \frac{\varepsilon}{2}, \tag{3.329}$$

for every pair of orthogonal unit vectors $u, v \in \mathcal{X}$. Toward this goal, assume that $u, v \in \mathcal{X}$ are orthogonal unit vectors, and define a unit vector

$$w_k = \frac{u + i^k v}{\sqrt{2}} \tag{3.330}$$

for each $k \in \{0, 1, 2, 3\}$. From the observation that

$$uv^* = \frac{1}{2} \sum_{k=0}^{3} i^k w_k w_k^*, \tag{3.331}$$

it follows that

$$\Phi(uv^*) - uv^* = \frac{1}{2} \sum_{k=0}^{3} i^k \left(\Phi(w_k w_k^*) - w_k w_k^*\right). \tag{3.332}$$

Because the spectral norm of a traceless Hermitian operator is at most one-half of its trace norm, it follows that

$$\left\| \Phi(uv^*) - uv^* \right\| \leq \frac{1}{2} \sum_{k=0}^{3} \left\| \Phi(w_k w_k^*) - w_k w_k^* \right\|$$

$$\leq \frac{1}{4} \sum_{k=0}^{3} \left\| \Phi(w_k w_k^*) - w_k w_k^* \right\|_1 \leq \frac{\varepsilon}{2}. \tag{3.333}$$

This implies the desired bound (3.329).

Now, let $z \in \mathcal{X} \otimes \mathcal{X}$ be a unit vector, expressed in the form of a Schmidt decomposition

$$z = \sum_{a \in \Sigma} \sqrt{p(a)} \, x_a \otimes y_a, \tag{3.334}$$

for Σ being an alphabet, $\{x_a : a \in \Sigma\}$ and $\{y_a : a \in \Sigma\}$ being orthonormal subsets of $\mathcal{X}$, and $p \in \mathcal{P}(\Sigma)$ being a probability vector. It holds that

$$\langle zz^*, (\Phi \otimes \mathbb{1}_{\mathrm{L}(\mathcal{X})})(zz^*) \rangle = \sum_{a,b \in \Sigma} p(a)p(b) \langle x_a x_b^*, \Phi(x_a x_b^*) \rangle, \tag{3.335}$$

and therefore, by the triangle inequality and the bounds (3.328) and (3.329) from above,

$$1 - \langle zz^*, (\Phi \otimes \mathbb{1}_{\mathrm{L}(\mathcal{X})})(zz^*) \rangle = \left| \langle zz^*, (\Phi \otimes \mathbb{1}_{\mathrm{L}(\mathcal{X})})(zz^*) - zz^* \rangle \right|$$

$$\leq \sum_{a,b \in \Sigma} p(a)p(b) \left| \langle x_a x_b^*, \Phi(x_a x_b^*) - x_a x_b^* \rangle \right| \leq \frac{\varepsilon}{2}. \tag{3.336}$$

Using the expression of the fidelity function when one of its arguments has rank equal to one, as given by Proposition 3.13, it follows that

$$\mathrm{F}\big((\Phi \otimes \mathbb{1}_{\mathrm{L}(\mathcal{X})})(zz^*), zz^*\big)^2 \geq 1 - \frac{\varepsilon}{2}. \tag{3.337}$$

Therefore, by one of the Fuchs–van de Graaf inequalities (Theorem 3.33), it follows that

$$\left\| (\Phi \otimes \mathbb{1}_{\mathrm{L}(\mathcal{X})})(zz^*) - zz^* \right\|_1$$

$$\leq 2\sqrt{1 - \mathrm{F}\big((\Phi \otimes \mathbb{1}_{\mathrm{L}(\mathcal{X})})(zz^*), zz^*\big)^2} \leq \sqrt{2\varepsilon}. \tag{3.338}$$

Because $\Phi - \mathbb{1}_{\mathrm{L}(\mathcal{X})}$ is a Hermitian-preserving map, the theorem follows by Theorem 3.51. $\qquad\square$

3.3.4 Characterizations of the Completely Bounded Trace Norm

Two alternative characterizations of the completely bounded trace norm are presented below, along with a theorem concerning the completely bounded trace norm of maps having bounded Choi rank.

The Maximum Output Fidelity Between Completely Positive Maps

It is possible to characterize the completely bounded trace norm of a map in terms of the *maximum output fidelity* between two completely positive maps derived from the given map. The maximum output fidelity is defined as follows.

Definition 3.57 Let $\Psi_0, \Psi_1 \in \mathrm{CP}(\mathcal{X}, \mathcal{Y})$ be completely positive maps, for $\mathcal{X}$ and $\mathcal{Y}$ being complex Euclidean spaces. The *maximum output fidelity* between Ψ_0 and Ψ_1 is defined as

$$\mathrm{F}_{\max}(\Psi_0, \Psi_1) = \max_{\rho_0, \rho_1 \in \mathrm{D}(\mathcal{X})} \mathrm{F}(\Psi_0(\rho_0), \Psi_1(\rho_1)). \tag{3.339}$$

For any choice of vectors of the form $u, v \in \mathcal{X} \otimes \mathcal{Y}$, for $\mathcal{X}$ and $\mathcal{Y}$ being arbitrary complex Euclidean spaces, Corollary 3.23 states that

$$\left\| \mathrm{Tr}_{\mathcal{Y}}(vu^*) \right\|_1 = \mathrm{F}\big(\mathrm{Tr}_{\mathcal{X}}(uu^*), \mathrm{Tr}_{\mathcal{X}}(vv^*)\big). \tag{3.340}$$

An extension of this fact provides a link between the completely bounded trace norm and the maximum output fidelity. In considering this extension, it is convenient to isolate the fact represented by the lemma that follows.

Lemma 3.58 *Let* $A_0, A_1 \in \mathrm{L}(\mathcal{X}, \mathcal{Y} \otimes \mathcal{Z})$ *be operators, for* $\mathcal{X}$, $\mathcal{Y}$, *and* $\mathcal{Z}$ *being complex Euclidean spaces, and define maps* $\Psi_0, \Psi_1 \in \mathrm{CP}(\mathcal{X}, \mathcal{Z})$ *and* $\Phi \in \mathrm{T}(\mathcal{X}, \mathcal{Y})$ *as follows:*

$$\begin{aligned} \Psi_0(X) &= \mathrm{Tr}_{\mathcal{Y}}(A_0 X A_0^*), \\ \Psi_1(X) &= \mathrm{Tr}_{\mathcal{Y}}(A_1 X A_1^*), \\ \Phi(X) &= \mathrm{Tr}_{\mathcal{Z}}(A_0 X A_1^*), \end{aligned} \tag{3.341}$$

for every $X \in \mathrm{L}(\mathcal{X})$. *Also let* $u_0, u_1 \in \mathcal{X} \otimes \mathcal{W}$ *be vectors, for* $\mathcal{W}$ *being a complex Euclidean space. It holds that*

$$\left\| \big(\Phi \otimes \mathbb{1}_{\mathrm{L}(\mathcal{W})}\big)(u_0 u_1^*) \right\|_1 = \mathrm{F}\big(\Psi_0(\mathrm{Tr}_{\mathcal{W}}(u_0 u_0^*)), \Psi_1(\mathrm{Tr}_{\mathcal{W}}(u_1 u_1^*))\big). \tag{3.342}$$

Proof Let $W \in \mathrm{U}(\mathcal{Y} \otimes \mathcal{Z} \otimes \mathcal{W}, \mathcal{Z} \otimes \mathcal{Y} \otimes \mathcal{W})$ be the operator defined by the equation

$$W(y \otimes z \otimes w) = z \otimes y \otimes w, \tag{3.343}$$

holding for all $y \in \mathcal{Y}$, $z \in \mathcal{Z}$, and $w \in \mathcal{W}$. In other words, W represents a reordering of tensor factors, from $\mathcal{Y} \otimes \mathcal{Z} \otimes \mathcal{W}$ to $\mathcal{Z} \otimes \mathcal{Y} \otimes \mathcal{W}$. It is evident that one has

$$
\begin{aligned}
(\Phi \otimes \mathbb{1}_{\mathrm{L}(\mathcal{W})})(u_0 u_1^*) &= \mathrm{Tr}_{\mathcal{Z}}((A_0 \otimes \mathbb{1}_{\mathcal{W}}) u_0 u_1^*(A_1^* \otimes \mathbb{1}_{\mathcal{W}})) \\
&= \mathrm{Tr}_{\mathcal{Z}}(W(A_0 \otimes \mathbb{1}_{\mathcal{W}}) u_0 u_1^*(A_1^* \otimes \mathbb{1}_{\mathcal{W}}) W^*).
\end{aligned}
\tag{3.344}
$$

Applying Corollary 3.23, one has

$$
\begin{aligned}
&\left\| (\Phi \otimes \mathbb{1}_{\mathrm{L}(\mathcal{W})})(u_0 u_1^*) \right\|_1 \\
&= \mathrm{F}\Big(\mathrm{Tr}_{\mathcal{Y} \otimes \mathcal{W}}(W(A_0 \otimes \mathbb{1}_{\mathcal{W}}) u_0 u_0^*(A_0^* \otimes \mathbb{1}_{\mathcal{W}}) W^*), \\
&\qquad \mathrm{Tr}_{\mathcal{Y} \otimes \mathcal{W}}(W(A_1 \otimes \mathbb{1}_{\mathcal{W}}) u_1 u_1^*(A_1^* \otimes \mathbb{1}_{\mathcal{W}}) W^*) \Big) \\
&= \mathrm{F}\Big(\mathrm{Tr}_{\mathcal{Y}}(A_0 \, \mathrm{Tr}_{\mathcal{W}}(u_0 u_0^*) A_0^*), \mathrm{Tr}_{\mathcal{Y}}(A_1 \, \mathrm{Tr}_{\mathcal{W}}(u_1 u_1^*) A_1^*) \Big) \\
&= \mathrm{F}(\Psi_0(\mathrm{Tr}_{\mathcal{W}}(u_0 u_0^*)), \Psi_1(\mathrm{Tr}_{\mathcal{W}}(u_1 u_1^*))),
\end{aligned}
\tag{3.345}
$$

as required. $\qquad \square$

Theorem 3.59 *Let $A_0, A_1 \in \mathrm{L}(\mathcal{X}, \mathcal{Y} \otimes \mathcal{Z})$ be operators, for $\mathcal{X}$, $\mathcal{Y}$, and $\mathcal{Z}$ being complex Euclidean spaces, and define maps $\Psi_0, \Psi_1 \in \mathrm{CP}(\mathcal{X}, \mathcal{Z})$ and $\Phi \in \mathrm{T}(\mathcal{X}, \mathcal{Y})$ as follows:*

$$
\begin{aligned}
\Psi_0(X) &= \mathrm{Tr}_{\mathcal{Y}}(A_0 X A_0^*), \\
\Psi_1(X) &= \mathrm{Tr}_{\mathcal{Y}}(A_1 X A_1^*), \\
\Phi(X) &= \mathrm{Tr}_{\mathcal{Z}}(A_0 X A_1^*),
\end{aligned}
\tag{3.346}
$$

for every $X \in \mathrm{L}(\mathcal{X})$. It holds that

$$
\|\|\Phi\|\|_1 = \mathrm{F}_{\max}(\Psi_0, \Psi_1).
\tag{3.347}
$$

Proof Let $\mathcal{W}$ be a complex Euclidean space with $\dim(\mathcal{W}) = \dim(\mathcal{X})$. By Proposition 3.44 and Lemma 3.58, one has

$$
\begin{aligned}
\|\|\Phi\|\|_1 &= \max_{u_0, u_1 \in \mathcal{S}(\mathcal{X} \otimes \mathcal{W})} \left\| (\Phi \otimes \mathbb{1}_{\mathrm{L}(\mathcal{W})})(u_0 u_1^*) \right\|_1 \\
&= \max_{u_0, u_1 \in \mathcal{S}(\mathcal{X} \otimes \mathcal{W})} \mathrm{F}(\Psi_0(\mathrm{Tr}_{\mathcal{W}}(u_0 u_0^*)), \Psi_1(\mathrm{Tr}_{\mathcal{W}}(u_1 u_1^*))) \\
&= \max_{\rho_0, \rho_1 \in \mathrm{D}(\mathcal{X})} \mathrm{F}(\Psi_0(\rho_0), \Psi_1(\rho_1)) \\
&= \mathrm{F}_{\max}(\Psi_0, \Psi_1),
\end{aligned}
\tag{3.348}
$$

as required. $\qquad \square$

Remark The proof of Theorem 3.59 establishes a connection between those choices of density operators $\rho_0, \rho_1 \in D(\mathcal{X})$ achieving the maximal value in the expression

$$F_{\max}(\Psi_0, \Psi_1) = \max_{\rho_0, \rho_1 \in D(\mathcal{X})} F(\Psi_0(\rho_0), \Psi_1(\rho_1)) \qquad (3.349)$$

and the choices of vectors $u_0, u_1 \in \mathcal{S}(\mathcal{X} \otimes \mathcal{W})$ achieving the maximal value in the expression

$$\vert\vert\vert \Phi \vert\vert\vert_1 = \max_{u_0, u_1 \in \mathcal{S}(\mathcal{X} \otimes \mathcal{W})} \left\Vert (\Phi \otimes \mathbb{1}_{L(\mathcal{W})})(u_0 u_1^*) \right\Vert_1. \qquad (3.350)$$

Specifically, for any choice of unit vectors $u_0, u_1 \in \mathcal{S}(\mathcal{X} \otimes \mathcal{W})$, one may take

$$\rho_0 = \text{Tr}_{\mathcal{W}}(u_0 u_0^*) \quad \text{and} \quad \rho_1 = \text{Tr}_{\mathcal{W}}(u_1 u_1^*), \qquad (3.351)$$

and conversely, for any choice of density operators $\rho_0, \rho_1 \in D(\mathcal{X})$, one may take $u_0, u_1 \in \mathcal{S}(\mathcal{X} \otimes \mathcal{W})$ to be arbitrary purifications of ρ_0, ρ_1, respectively, with equal values being obtained in the above expressions in both cases.

By combining Theorem 3.59 with the multiplicativity of the completely bounded trace norm with respect to tensor products (Theorem 3.49), one finds that the maximum output fidelity is also multiplicative with respect to tensor products.

Corollary 3.60 *Let $\mathcal{X}_0$, $\mathcal{X}_1$, $\mathcal{Y}_0$, and $\mathcal{Y}_1$ be complex Euclidean spaces and let $\Phi_0, \Psi_0 \in CP(\mathcal{X}_0, \mathcal{Y}_0)$ and $\Phi_1, \Psi_1 \in CP(\mathcal{X}_1, \mathcal{Y}_1)$ be completely positive maps. It holds that*

$$F_{\max}(\Phi_0 \otimes \Phi_1, \Psi_0 \otimes \Psi_1) = F_{\max}(\Phi_0, \Psi_0) \, F_{\max}(\Phi_1, \Psi_1). \qquad (3.352)$$

This corollary implies a simple but not necessarily obvious fact, which is that the maximum output fidelity between two completely positive product maps is achieved for product state inputs. It may be contrasted with some other quantities of interest (such as the minimum output entropy of a quantum channel, to be discussed in Chapter 7) that fail to respect tensor products in this way.

A Semidefinite Program for Maximum Output Fidelity

It is natural to ask if the value $\vert\vert\vert \Phi \vert\vert\vert_1$ of the completely bounded trace norm of a given map $\Phi \in T(\mathcal{X}, \mathcal{Y})$ can be efficiently calculated. While there is no closed-form expression that is known to represent this value, it is equal to the optimal value of a semidefinite program that has a simple description in terms of the mapping Φ. In particular, when Theorem 3.59 is combined with the semidefinite program for the fidelity function discussed in Section 3.2.2, a semidefinite program for the completely bounded trace norm is obtained. This allows for an efficient calculation of the value $\|\|\Phi\|\|_1$ using a computer, as well as an efficient method of verification through the use of semidefinite programming duality.

In greater detail, let $\Phi \in T(\mathcal{X}, \mathcal{Y})$ be a map, for complex Euclidean spaces $\mathcal{X}$ and $\mathcal{Y}$, and assume that a Stinespring representation of Φ is known:

$$\Phi(X) = \text{Tr}_{\mathcal{Z}}(A_0 X A_1^*) \tag{3.353}$$

for all $X \in L(\mathcal{X})$, for $A_0, A_1 \in L(\mathcal{X}, \mathcal{Y} \otimes \mathcal{Z})$ being operators for some complex Euclidean space $\mathcal{Z}$. Define completely positive maps $\Psi_0, \Psi_1 \in CP(\mathcal{X}, \mathcal{Z})$ as follows:

$$\begin{aligned} \Psi_0(X) &= \text{Tr}_{\mathcal{Y}}(A_0 X A_0^*), \\ \Psi_1(X) &= \text{Tr}_{\mathcal{Y}}(A_1 X A_1^*), \end{aligned} \tag{3.354}$$

for all $X \in L(\mathcal{X})$. Next, consider the semidefinite program whose primal problem is as follows:

Primal problem

$$\text{maximize:} \quad \frac{1}{2}\text{Tr}(Y) + \frac{1}{2}\text{Tr}(Y^*)$$

$$\text{subject to:} \quad \begin{pmatrix} \Psi_0(\rho_0) & Y \\ Y^* & \Psi_1(\rho_1) \end{pmatrix} \geq 0$$

$$\rho_0, \rho_1 \in D(\mathcal{X}), \ Y \in L(\mathcal{Z}).$$

Such a semidefinite program may be expressed with greater formality, with respect to the definition of semidefinite programs presented in Section 1.2.3, in the following way.

First, one defines a Hermitian-preserving map

$$\Xi \colon L(\mathcal{X} \oplus \mathcal{X} \oplus \mathcal{Z} \oplus \mathcal{Z}) \to L(\mathbb{C} \oplus \mathbb{C} \oplus \mathcal{Z} \oplus \mathcal{Z}) \tag{3.355}$$

as

$$\begin{aligned} \Xi &\begin{pmatrix} X_0 & \cdot & \cdot & \cdot \\ \cdot & X_1 & \cdot & \cdot \\ \cdot & \cdot & Z_0 & \cdot \\ \cdot & \cdot & \cdot & Z_1 \end{pmatrix} \\ &= \frac{1}{2} \begin{pmatrix} \text{Tr}(X_0) & 0 & 0 & 0 \\ 0 & \text{Tr}(X_1) & 0 & 0 \\ 0 & 0 & Z_0 - \Psi_0(X_0) & 0 \\ 0 & 0 & 0 & Z_1 - \Psi_1(X_1) \end{pmatrix} \end{aligned} \tag{3.356}$$

for all $X_0, X_1 \in \mathrm{L}(\mathcal{X})$ and $Z_0, Z_1 \in \mathrm{L}(\mathcal{Z})$, and where the dots represent operators on appropriately chosen spaces upon which Ξ does not depend.

Next, one defines Hermitian operators $A \in \mathrm{Herm}(\mathcal{X} \oplus \mathcal{X} \oplus \mathcal{Z} \oplus \mathcal{Z})$ and $B \in \mathrm{Herm}(\mathbb{C} \oplus \mathbb{C} \oplus \mathcal{Z} \oplus \mathcal{Z})$ as

$$A = \frac{1}{2} \begin{pmatrix} 0 & 0 & 0 & 0 \\ 0 & 0 & 0 & 0 \\ 0 & 0 & 0 & 1 \\ 0 & 0 & 1 & 0 \end{pmatrix} \quad \text{and} \quad B = \frac{1}{2} \begin{pmatrix} 1 & 0 & 0 & 0 \\ 0 & 1 & 0 & 0 \\ 0 & 0 & 0 & 0 \\ 0 & 0 & 0 & 0 \end{pmatrix}. \tag{3.357}$$

It is evident that the primal problem specified above is equivalent to the maximization of the quantity $\langle A, X \rangle$ over all choices of

$$X = \begin{pmatrix} X_0 & \cdot & \cdot & \cdot \\ \cdot & X_1 & \cdot & \cdot \\ \cdot & \cdot & Z_0 & Y \\ \cdot & \cdot & Y^* & Z_1 \end{pmatrix} \in \mathrm{Pos}(\mathcal{X} \oplus \mathcal{X} \oplus \mathcal{Z} \oplus \mathcal{Z}) \tag{3.358}$$

obeying the constraint $\Xi(X) = B$.

The adjoint mapping to Ξ is given by

$$\Xi^* \begin{pmatrix} \lambda_0 & \cdot & \cdot & \cdot \\ \cdot & \lambda_1 & \cdot & \cdot \\ \cdot & \cdot & Z_0 & \cdot \\ \cdot & \cdot & \cdot & Z_1 \end{pmatrix}$$

$$= \frac{1}{2} \begin{pmatrix} \lambda_0 \mathbb{1}_{\mathcal{X}} - \Psi_0^*(Z_0) & 0 & 0 & 0 \\ 0 & \lambda_1 \mathbb{1}_{\mathcal{X}} - \Psi_1^*(Z_1) & 0 & 0 \\ 0 & 0 & Z_0 & 0 \\ 0 & 0 & 0 & Z_1 \end{pmatrix}, \tag{3.359}$$

so the dual problem corresponding to the semidefinite program (Ξ, A, B) is to minimize the quantity $(\lambda_0 + \lambda_1)/2$ subject to the conditions

$$\lambda_0 \mathbb{1}_{\mathcal{X}} \geq \Psi_0^*(Z_0) \quad \text{and} \quad \lambda_1 \mathbb{1}_{\mathcal{X}} \geq \Psi_1^*(Z_1), \tag{3.360}$$

for $Z_0, Z_1 \in \mathrm{Herm}(\mathcal{Z})$ being Hermitian operators satisfying

$$\begin{pmatrix} Z_0 & 0 \\ 0 & Z_1 \end{pmatrix} \geq \begin{pmatrix} 0 & \mathbb{1} \\ \mathbb{1} & 0 \end{pmatrix}. \tag{3.361}$$

Observing that Z_0 and Z_1 must be positive definite in order for (3.361) to be satisfied, along with the fact that Ψ_0^* and Ψ_1^* are positive, one obtains the following statement of the dual problem:

Dual problem

minimize: $\dfrac{1}{2}\|\Psi_0^*(Z_0)\| + \dfrac{1}{2}\|\Psi_1^*(Z_1)\|$

subject to: $\begin{pmatrix} Z_0 & -\mathbb{1}_{\mathcal{Z}} \\ -\mathbb{1}_{\mathcal{Z}} & Z_1 \end{pmatrix} \geq 0$

$Z_0, Z_1 \in \mathrm{Pd}(\mathcal{Z}).$

To prove that strong duality holds for this semidefinite program, one may observe that the primal problem is feasible and the dual problem is strictly feasible. In particular, with respect to the semidefinite program's formal specification, as just described, one has that the operator

$$\begin{pmatrix} \rho_0 & 0 & 0 & 0 \\ 0 & \rho_1 & 0 & 0 \\ 0 & 0 & \Psi_0(\rho_0) & 0 \\ 0 & 0 & 0 & \Psi_1(\rho_1) \end{pmatrix} \tag{3.362}$$

is primal feasible, for an arbitrary choice of density operators $\rho_0, \rho_1 \in \mathrm{D}(\mathcal{X})$. The strict feasibility of the dual problem may be verified by observing, for instance, that the operator

$$\begin{pmatrix} 2\lambda_0 & 0 & 0 & 0 \\ 0 & 2\lambda_1 & 0 & 0 \\ 0 & 0 & 2\mathbb{1}_{\mathcal{Z}} & 0 \\ 0 & 0 & 0 & 2\mathbb{1}_{\mathcal{Z}} \end{pmatrix} \tag{3.363}$$

is strictly dual feasible, provided that $\lambda_0 > \|\Psi_0^*(\mathbb{1}_{\mathcal{Z}})\|$ and $\lambda_1 > \|\Psi_1^*(\mathbb{1}_{\mathcal{Z}})\|$. It follows by Slater's theorem (Theorem 1.18) that the primal and dual optimal values are equal, and moreover the primal optimal value is achieved for some choice of a primal feasible operator.

The fact that the optimal value of the semidefinite program is in agreement with the completely bounded norm $\|\|\Phi\|\|_1$ follows from Theorem 3.59 together with Theorem 3.17.

The dual problem stated above may be further simplified as follows:

Dual problem (simplified)

minimize: $\dfrac{1}{2}\|\Psi_0^*(Z)\| + \dfrac{1}{2}\|\Psi_1^*(Z^{-1})\|$

subject to: $Z \in \mathrm{Pd}(\mathcal{Z}).$

To verify that this problem has the same optimal value as the dual problem stated above, one may first observe that the inequality (3.361) holds if and only if Z_0 and Z_1 are both positive definite and satisfy $Z_1 \geq Z_0^{-1}$. For any such choice of Z_0 and Z_1, the inequality

$$\| \Psi_1^*(Z_1) \| \geq \| \Psi_1^*(Z_0^{-1}) \| \tag{3.364}$$

holds by the positivity of Ψ_1^*, implying that no generality is lost in restricting one's attention to operators $Z_0 = Z$ and $Z_1 = Z^{-1}$ for $Z \in \mathrm{Pd}(\mathcal{Z})$. The following theorem is a consequence of this observation.

Theorem 3.61 *Let $A_0, A_1 \in \mathrm{L}(\mathcal{X}, \mathcal{Y} \otimes \mathcal{Z})$ be operators, for $\mathcal{X}$, $\mathcal{Y}$, and $\mathcal{Z}$ being complex Euclidean spaces, and define maps $\Psi_0, \Psi_1 \in \mathrm{CP}(\mathcal{X}, \mathcal{Z})$ and $\Phi \in \mathrm{T}(\mathcal{X}, \mathcal{Y})$ as follows:*

$$\begin{aligned}
\Psi_0(X) &= \mathrm{Tr}_{\mathcal{Y}}(A_0 X A_0^*), \\
\Psi_1(X) &= \mathrm{Tr}_{\mathcal{Y}}(A_1 X A_1^*), \\
\Phi(X) &= \mathrm{Tr}_{\mathcal{Z}}(A_0 X A_1^*),
\end{aligned} \tag{3.365}$$

for every $X \in \mathrm{L}(\mathcal{X})$. It holds that

$$\| |\Phi| \|_1 = \inf_{Z \in \mathrm{Pd}(\mathcal{Z})} \left(\frac{1}{2} \| \Psi_0^*(Z) \| + \frac{1}{2} \| \Psi_1^*(Z^{-1}) \| \right). \tag{3.366}$$

Spectral Norm Characterization of the Completely Bounded Trace Norm

Consider a map $\Phi \in \mathrm{T}(\mathcal{X}, \mathcal{Y})$, for complex Euclidean spaces $\mathcal{X}$ and $\mathcal{Y}$. One has, by Theorem 2.22, that a given complex Euclidean space $\mathcal{Z}$ admits a Stinespring representation

$$\Phi(X) = \mathrm{Tr}_{\mathcal{Z}}(A_0 X A_1^*) \tag{3.367}$$

of Φ, for some choice of operators $A_0, A_1 \in \mathrm{L}(\mathcal{X}, \mathcal{Y} \otimes \mathcal{Z})$, if and only if the dimension of $\mathcal{Z}$ is at least as large as the Choi rank of Φ. An equivalent condition to (3.367) holding for all operators $X \in \mathrm{L}(\mathcal{X})$ is that

$$J(\Phi) = \mathrm{Tr}_{\mathcal{Z}}(\mathrm{vec}(A_0) \, \mathrm{vec}(A_1)^*). \tag{3.368}$$

As the next theorem states, the completely bounded trace norm of Φ is equal to the infimum value of the product $\|A_0\| \|A_1\|$, ranging over all such choices of A_0 and A_1.

Theorem 3.62 (Smith) *Let $\Phi \in \mathrm{T}(\mathcal{X}, \mathcal{Y})$ be a map, for complex Euclidean spaces $\mathcal{X}$ and $\mathcal{Y}$, let $\mathcal{Z}$ be a complex Euclidean space for which it holds that $\dim(\mathcal{Z}) \geq \mathrm{rank}(J(\Phi))$, and let*

$$\begin{aligned}
\mathcal{K}_\Phi = \{ (A_0, A_1) &\in \mathrm{L}(\mathcal{X}, \mathcal{Y} \otimes \mathcal{Z}) \times \mathrm{L}(\mathcal{X}, \mathcal{Y} \otimes \mathcal{Z}): \\
J(\Phi) &= \mathrm{Tr}_{\mathcal{Z}}(\mathrm{vec}(A_0) \, \mathrm{vec}(A_1)^*) \}.
\end{aligned} \tag{3.369}$$

It holds that

$$\||\Phi\||_1 = \inf_{(A_0, A_1) \in \mathcal{K}_\Phi} \|A_0\| \|A_1\|. \tag{3.370}$$

Proof There exists a pair of unit vectors $u, v \in \mathcal{X} \otimes \mathcal{X}$ such that, for any pair of operators $(A_0, A_1) \in \mathcal{K}_\Phi$, one has

$$\||\Phi\||_1 = \left\| \text{Tr}_{\mathcal{Z}} \left((A_0 \otimes \mathbb{1}_{\mathcal{X}}) uv^* (A_1 \otimes \mathbb{1}_{\mathcal{X}})^* \right) \right\|_1. \tag{3.371}$$

By the monotonicity of the trace norm under partial tracing (1.183) and the multiplicativity of the spectral norm with respect to tensor products, it follows that

$$\begin{aligned}
\||\Phi\||_1 &\leq \left\| (A_0 \otimes \mathbb{1}_{\mathcal{X}}) uv^* (A_1 \otimes \mathbb{1}_{\mathcal{X}})^* \right\|_1 \\
&= \left\| (A_0 \otimes \mathbb{1}_{\mathcal{X}}) u \right\| \left\| (A_1 \otimes \mathbb{1}_{\mathcal{X}}) v \right\| \\
&\leq \| A_0 \otimes \mathbb{1}_{\mathcal{X}} \| \| A_1 \otimes \mathbb{1}_{\mathcal{X}} \| \\
&= \| A_0 \| \| A_1 \|.
\end{aligned} \tag{3.372}$$

As this inequality holds for every pair $(A_0, A_1) \in \mathcal{K}_\Phi$, it follows that

$$\||\Phi\||_1 \leq \inf_{(A_0, A_1) \in \mathcal{K}_\Phi} \|A_0\| \|A_1\|. \tag{3.373}$$

It remains to prove the reverse inequality. To this end, fix any pair of operators $(B_0, B_1) \in \mathcal{K}_\Phi$, and define $\Psi_0, \Psi_1 \in \text{CP}(\mathcal{X}, \mathcal{Z})$ as

$$\begin{aligned}
\Psi_0(X) &= \text{Tr}_{\mathcal{Y}}(B_0 X B_0^*), \\
\Psi_1(X) &= \text{Tr}_{\mathcal{Y}}(B_1 X B_1^*),
\end{aligned} \tag{3.374}$$

for all $X \in \text{L}(\mathcal{X})$, so that

$$\begin{aligned}
\Psi_0^*(Z) &= B_0^*(\mathbb{1}_{\mathcal{Y}} \otimes Z) B_0, \\
\Psi_1^*(Z) &= B_1^*(\mathbb{1}_{\mathcal{Y}} \otimes Z) B_1,
\end{aligned} \tag{3.375}$$

for every $Z \in \text{L}(\mathcal{Z})$. By Theorem 3.61, the expression (3.366) holds. For any choice of a positive real number $\varepsilon > 0$, there must therefore exist a positive definite operator $Z \in \text{Pd}(\mathcal{Z})$ so that

$$\frac{1}{2} \| \Psi_0^*(Z) \| + \frac{1}{2} \| \Psi_1^*(Z^{-1}) \| < \||\Phi\||_1 + \varepsilon. \tag{3.376}$$

By the arithmetic–geometric mean inequality, it follows that

$$\sqrt{\| \Psi_0^*(Z) \|} \sqrt{\| \Psi_1^*(Z^{-1}) \|} < \||\Phi\||_1 + \varepsilon. \tag{3.377}$$

Setting

$$A_0 = \left(\mathbb{1}_{\mathcal{Y}} \otimes Z^{\frac{1}{2}}\right) B_0,$$
$$A_1 = \left(\mathbb{1}_{\mathcal{Y}} \otimes Z^{-\frac{1}{2}}\right) B_1,$$

(3.378)

one has that $(A_0, A_1) \in \mathcal{K}_\Phi$ by the cyclic property of the trace. Moreover, it holds that

$$\|A_0\| \|A_1\| = \sqrt{\|A_0^* A_0\|} \sqrt{\|A_1^* A_1\|}$$
$$= \sqrt{\|\Psi_0^*(Z)\|} \sqrt{\|\Psi_1^*(Z^{-1})\|} < \||\Phi\||_1 + \varepsilon.$$

(3.379)

As it has been established that, for any choice of $\varepsilon > 0$, there exists a pair of operators $(A_0, A_1) \in \mathcal{K}_\Phi$ satisfying the inequality (3.379), it follows that

$$\inf_{(A_0, A_1) \in \mathcal{K}_\Phi} \|A_0\| \|A_1\| \leq \||\Phi\||_1,$$

(3.380)

which completes the proof. $\qquad\square$

The Completely Bounded Trace Norm of Maps With Bounded Choi Rank

For a given map $\Phi \in \mathrm{T}(\mathcal{X}, \mathcal{Y})$ and a complex Euclidean space $\mathcal{Z}$, it holds (by Theorem 3.46) that

$$\|\Phi \otimes \mathbb{1}_{\mathrm{L}(\mathcal{Z})}\|_1 \leq \||\Phi\||_1,$$

(3.381)

with equality under the condition that $\dim(\mathcal{Z}) \geq \dim(\mathcal{X})$. If it is the case that $\dim(\mathcal{Z}) < \dim(\mathcal{X})$, then equality may fail to hold. For instance, the transpose map $\mathrm{T}(X) = X^{\mathsf{T}}$ on an arbitrary complex Euclidean space $\mathcal{X}$ is such that

$$\|\mathrm{T} \otimes \mathbb{1}_{\mathrm{L}(\mathcal{Z})}\|_1 = \min\{\dim(\mathcal{X}), \dim(\mathcal{Z})\}$$

(3.382)

for every complex Euclidean space $\mathcal{Z}$.

It is the case, however, that equality holds in (3.381) under a different and generally incomparable assumption, which is that the dimension of $\mathcal{Z}$ is at least as large as the Choi rank of Φ, as the following theorem states.

Theorem 3.63 (Timoney) *Let $\mathcal{X}$, $\mathcal{Y}$, and $\mathcal{Z}$ be complex Euclidean spaces, let $\Phi \in \mathrm{T}(\mathcal{X}, \mathcal{Y})$ be a map, and assume $\dim(\mathcal{Z}) \geq \mathrm{rank}(J(\Phi))$. It holds that*

$$\||\Phi\||_1 = \|\Phi \otimes \mathbb{1}_{\mathrm{L}(\mathcal{Z})}\|_1.$$

(3.383)

The proof of Theorem 3.63 to be presented below makes use of the following lemma.

Lemma 3.64   *Let $\mathcal{X}$ and $\mathcal{Y}$ be complex Euclidean spaces, let $\Phi \in \mathrm{T}(\mathcal{X}, \mathcal{Y})$ be a positive map, and let $P \in \mathrm{Pos}(\mathcal{Y})$ be a nonzero positive semidefinite operator satisfying $P = \Phi(\rho)$ for some choice of a density operator $\rho \in \mathrm{D}(\mathcal{X})$. There exists a density operator $\sigma \in \mathrm{D}(\mathcal{X})$ with $\mathrm{rank}(\sigma) \leq \mathrm{rank}(P)$ that satisfies $P = \Phi(\sigma)$.*

Proof   Define a set

$$\mathcal{C} = \{\xi \in \mathrm{D}(\mathcal{X}) \colon \Phi(\xi) = P\}. \tag{3.384}$$

The set $\mathcal{C}$ is nonempty by the assumptions of the lemma, and it is evidently both compact and convex. There must therefore exist an extreme point of $\mathcal{C}$. Let σ be such an extreme point and let $r = \mathrm{rank}(\sigma)$. It will be proved that $r \leq \mathrm{rank}(P)$, which suffices to prove the lemma.

Let $n = \dim(\mathcal{X})$ and $m = \mathrm{rank}(P)$, and let $\Pi = \Pi_{\mathrm{im}(P)}$. Define a linear map $\Psi \colon \mathrm{Herm}(\mathcal{X}) \to \mathrm{Herm}(\mathcal{Y} \oplus \mathbb{C})$ as

$$\Psi(H) = \begin{pmatrix} \Pi\Phi(H)\Pi & 0 \\ 0 & \langle \mathbb{1}_{\mathcal{Y}} - \Pi, \Phi(H) \rangle \end{pmatrix} \tag{3.385}$$

for all $H \in \mathrm{Herm}(\mathcal{X})$. The image of Ψ has dimension at most $m^2 + 1$, and therefore the kernel of Ψ is a subspace of $\mathrm{Herm}(\mathcal{X})$ having dimension at least $n^2 - m^2 - 1$. Also define a subspace $\mathcal{W} \subseteq \mathrm{Herm}(\mathcal{X})$ as

$$\mathcal{W} = \{H \in \mathrm{Herm}(\mathcal{X}) \colon \mathrm{im}(H) \subseteq \mathrm{im}(\sigma) \text{ and } \mathrm{Tr}(H) = 0\}. \tag{3.386}$$

The dimension of $\mathcal{W}$ is equal to $r^2 - 1$.

Now consider any operator $H \in \mathrm{ker}(\Psi) \cap \mathcal{W}$. As $\mathrm{im}(H) \subseteq \mathrm{im}(\sigma)$ and σ is positive semidefinite, there must exist a positive real number $\varepsilon > 0$ for which $\sigma + \varepsilon H$ and $\sigma - \varepsilon H$ are both positive semidefinite. As H is traceless, it follow that $\sigma + \varepsilon H$ and $\sigma - \varepsilon H$ are density operators. By the assumption that $H \in \mathrm{ker}(\Psi)$, one has $\langle \mathbb{1}_{\mathcal{Y}} - \Pi, \Phi(H) \rangle = 0$, and therefore

$$\langle \mathbb{1}_{\mathcal{Y}} - \Pi, \Phi(\sigma + \varepsilon H) \rangle = \langle \mathbb{1}_{\mathcal{Y}} - \Pi, P + \varepsilon\Phi(H) \rangle = 0. \tag{3.387}$$

By the positivity of Φ, it follows that

$$\Phi(\sigma + \varepsilon H) = \Pi\Phi(\sigma + \varepsilon H)\Pi = P + \varepsilon\,\Pi\Phi(H)\Pi = P. \tag{3.388}$$

By similar reasoning, $\Phi(\sigma - \varepsilon H) = P$. It has therefore been proved that $\sigma + \varepsilon H$ and $\sigma - \varepsilon H$ are both elements of $\mathcal{C}$; but given that σ was chosen to be an extreme point of $\mathcal{C}$ and

$$\frac{1}{2}(\sigma + \varepsilon H) + \frac{1}{2}(\sigma - \varepsilon H) = \sigma, \tag{3.389}$$

it follows that $H = 0$. Consequently, the subspace $\ker(\Psi) \cap \mathcal{W}$ must have dimension 0.

Finally, given that $\mathrm{Herm}(\mathcal{X})$ has dimension n^2, $\ker(\Psi) \subseteq \mathrm{Herm}(\mathcal{X})$ has dimension at least $n^2 - m^2 - 1$, $\mathcal{W} \subseteq \mathrm{Herm}(\mathcal{X})$ has dimension $r^2 - 1$, and $\ker(\Psi) \cap \mathcal{W}$ has dimension 0, it follows that

$$\left(n^2 - m^2 - 1\right) + \left(r^2 - 1\right) \leq n^2, \tag{3.390}$$

and therefore

$$r^2 \leq m^2 + 2. \tag{3.391}$$

As r and m are positive integers, it follows that $r \leq m$, which completes the proof. $\qquad\square$

Proof of Theorem 3.63 One may choose operators $A_0, A_1 \in \mathrm{L}(\mathcal{X}, \mathcal{Y} \otimes \mathcal{Z})$ such that

$$\Phi(X) = \mathrm{Tr}_{\mathcal{Z}}(A_0 X A_1^*) \tag{3.392}$$

for all $X \in \mathrm{L}(\mathcal{X})$, by Corollary 2.21. By Theorem 3.59, it follows that

$$\|\|\Phi\|\|_1 = \mathrm{F}_{\max}(\Psi_0, \Psi_1) \tag{3.393}$$

for $\Psi_0, \Psi_1 \in \mathrm{CP}(\mathcal{X}, \mathcal{Z})$ being the completely positive maps defined by

$$\begin{aligned}
\Psi_0(X) &= \mathrm{Tr}_{\mathcal{Y}}(A_0 X A_0^*), \\
\Psi_1(X) &= \mathrm{Tr}_{\mathcal{Y}}(A_1 X A_1^*),
\end{aligned} \tag{3.394}$$

for all $X \in \mathrm{L}(\mathcal{X})$. Let $\rho_0, \rho_1 \in \mathrm{D}(\mathcal{X})$ be density operators that satisfy

$$\mathrm{F}(\Psi_0(\rho_0), \Psi_1(\rho_1)) = \mathrm{F}_{\max}(\Psi_0, \Psi_1) = \|\|\Phi\|\|_1. \tag{3.395}$$

The operators $P_0 = \Psi_0(\rho_0)$ and $P_1 = \Psi_1(\rho_1)$ are elements of $\mathrm{Pos}(\mathcal{Z})$, so their ranks cannot exceed the dimension of $\mathcal{Z}$. It follows from Lemma 3.64 that there exist density operators $\sigma_0, \sigma_1 \in \mathrm{D}(\mathcal{X})$, whose ranks also do not exceed the dimension of $\mathcal{Z}$, such that $\Psi_0(\sigma_0) = P_0$ and $\Psi_1(\sigma_1) = P_1$. Thus, one has that

$$\mathrm{F}(\Psi_0(\sigma_0), \Psi_1(\sigma_1)) = \|\|\Phi\|\|_1. \tag{3.396}$$

Because σ_0 and σ_1 have rank at most the dimension of $\mathcal{Z}$, there must exist unit vectors $u_0, u_1 \in \mathcal{X} \otimes \mathcal{Z}$ satisfying

$$\begin{aligned}
\sigma_0 &= \mathrm{Tr}_{\mathcal{Z}}(u_0 u_0^*), \\
\sigma_1 &= \mathrm{Tr}_{\mathcal{Z}}(u_1 u_1^*).
\end{aligned} \tag{3.397}$$

By Lemma 3.58, one has that

$$\left\|(\Phi \otimes \mathbb{1}_{\mathrm{L}(\mathcal{Z})})(u_0 u_1^*)\right\|_1 = \mathrm{F}(\Psi_0(\sigma_0), \Psi_1(\sigma_1)) = \|\|\Phi\|\|_1, \tag{3.398}$$

which establishes that

$$\left\| \Phi \otimes \mathbb{1}_{\mathrm{L}(\mathcal{Z})} \right\|_1 \geq \left\| |\Phi| \right\|_1. \tag{3.399}$$

As the reverse inequality holds by Theorem 3.46, the proof is complete. $\square$

Corollary 3.65 *Let* $\Phi_0, \Phi_1 \in \mathrm{C}(\mathcal{X}, \mathcal{Y})$ *be channels, for complex Euclidean spaces* $\mathcal{X}$ *and* $\mathcal{Y}$, *and let* $\mathcal{Z}$ *be any complex Euclidean space with*

$$\dim(\mathcal{Z}) \geq 2 \operatorname{rank}(J(\Phi_0 - \Phi_1)). \tag{3.400}$$

There exists a unit vector $u \in \mathcal{X} \otimes \mathcal{Z}$ *such that*

$$\left\| (\Phi_0 \otimes \mathbb{1}_{\mathrm{L}(\mathcal{Z})})(uu^*) - (\Phi_1 \otimes \mathbb{1}_{\mathrm{L}(\mathcal{Z})})(uu^*) \right\|_1 = \left\| |\Phi_0 - \Phi_1| \right\|_1. \tag{3.401}$$

Proof The theorem is vacuous when $\Phi_0 = \Phi_1$, so it will be assumed that this is not the case. Let $\mathcal{W}$ be a complex Euclidean space having dimension equal to $\operatorname{rank}(J(\Phi_0 - \Phi_1))$. By Theorem 3.63, it holds that

$$\left\| |\Phi_0 - \Phi_1| \right\|_1 = \left\| \Phi_0 \otimes \mathbb{1}_{\mathrm{L}(\mathcal{W})} - \Phi_1 \otimes \mathbb{1}_{\mathrm{L}(\mathcal{W})} \right\|_1. \tag{3.402}$$

By Lemma 3.50, it follows that there exists a unit vector $v \in \mathcal{X} \otimes \mathcal{W} \otimes \mathcal{V}$, for $\mathcal{V}$ being any complex Euclidean space with dimension equal to 2, such that

$$\left\| (\Phi_0 \otimes \mathbb{1}_{\mathrm{L}(\mathcal{W} \otimes \mathcal{V})})(vv^*) - (\Phi_1 \otimes \mathbb{1}_{\mathrm{L}(\mathcal{W} \otimes \mathcal{V})})(vv^*) \right\|_1 \geq \left\| |\Phi_0 - \Phi_1| \right\|_1. \tag{3.403}$$

Now, under the assumption that $\dim(\mathcal{Z}) \geq 2 \operatorname{rank}(J(\Phi_0 - \Phi_1))$, there must exist a linear isometry of the form $V \in \mathrm{U}(\mathcal{W} \otimes \mathcal{V}, \mathcal{Z})$. One may set

$$u = (\mathbb{1}_{\mathcal{X}} \otimes V)v \tag{3.404}$$

to obtain

$$\begin{aligned}
&\left\| (\Phi_0 \otimes \mathbb{1}_{\mathrm{L}(\mathcal{Z})})(uu^*) - (\Phi_1 \otimes \mathbb{1}_{\mathrm{L}(\mathcal{Z})})(uu^*) \right\|_1 \\
&= \left\| (\mathbb{1}_{\mathcal{Y}} \otimes V)((\Phi_0 \otimes \mathbb{1}_{\mathrm{L}(\mathcal{W} \otimes \mathcal{V})})(vv^*) \right. \\
&\quad \left. - (\Phi_1 \otimes \mathbb{1}_{\mathrm{L}(\mathcal{W} \otimes \mathcal{V})})(vv^*))(\mathbb{1}_{\mathcal{Y}} \otimes V^*) \right\|_1 \\
&= \left\| (\Phi_0 \otimes \mathbb{1}_{\mathrm{L}(\mathcal{W} \otimes \mathcal{V})})(vv^*) - (\Phi_1 \otimes \mathbb{1}_{\mathrm{L}(\mathcal{W} \otimes \mathcal{V})})(vv^*) \right\|_1 \\
&\geq \left\| |\Phi_0 - \Phi_1| \right\|_1
\end{aligned} \tag{3.405}$$

by the isometric invariance of the trace norm together with (3.403). As the reverse inequality holds for all unit vectors $u \in \mathcal{X} \otimes \mathcal{Z}$ by Theorem 3.46, the proof is complete. $\square$

3.4 Exercises

Exercise 3.1 Let $\mathcal{X}$ be a complex Euclidean space, let $\rho_0, \rho_1 \in D(\mathcal{X})$ be states, and let $\delta = F(\rho_0, \rho_1)$. Also let n be a positive integer and define two new density operators as follows:

$$\sigma_0 = \frac{1}{2^{n-1}} \sum_{\substack{a_1,\ldots,a_n \in \{0,1\} \\ a_1+\cdots+a_n \text{ even}}} \rho_{a_1} \otimes \cdots \otimes \rho_{a_n},$$

$$\sigma_1 = \frac{1}{2^{n-1}} \sum_{\substack{a_1,\ldots,a_n \in \{0,1\} \\ a_1+\cdots+a_n \text{ odd}}} \rho_{a_1} \otimes \cdots \otimes \rho_{a_n}. \tag{3.406}$$

Prove that

$$F(\sigma_0, \sigma_1) \geq 1 - \exp\left(-\frac{n\delta^2}{2}\right). \tag{3.407}$$

Exercise 3.2 Let $P, Q \in \text{Pos}(\mathcal{X})$ be positive semidefinite operators and let $\Phi \in T(\mathcal{X}, \mathcal{Y})$ be a trace-preserving and positive (but not necessarily completely positive) map, for complex Euclidean spaces $\mathcal{X}$ and $\mathcal{Y}$. Prove that

$$F(P, Q) \leq F(\Phi(P), \Phi(Q)). \tag{3.408}$$

Exercise 3.3 Find an example of two channels $\Phi_0, \Phi_1 \in C(\mathcal{X}, \mathcal{Y})$, for some choice of complex Euclidean spaces $\mathcal{X}$ and $\mathcal{Y}$, such that

$$\left\| \Phi_0(\rho) - \Phi_1(\rho) \right\|_1 < \left\| \Phi_0 - \Phi_1 \right\|_1 \tag{3.409}$$

for every density operator $\rho \in D(\mathcal{X})$.

Exercise 3.4 Let $\Phi \in T(\mathcal{X}, \mathcal{Y})$ be a map, for complex Euclidean spaces $\mathcal{X}$ and $\mathcal{Y}$. Prove that

$$\left\| \Phi \right\|_1 = \max_{\rho_0, \rho_1 \in D(\mathcal{X})} \left\| \left(\mathbb{1}_{\mathcal{Y}} \otimes \sqrt{\rho_0}\right) J(\Phi) \left(\mathbb{1}_{\mathcal{Y}} \otimes \sqrt{\rho_1}\right) \right\|_1. \tag{3.410}$$

Exercise 3.5 Let $H \in \text{Herm}(\mathcal{Y} \otimes \mathcal{X})$ be a Hermitian operator, for complex Euclidean spaces $\mathcal{X}$ and $\mathcal{Y}$, and consider the problem of maximizing the value

$$\langle H, J(\Phi) \rangle \tag{3.411}$$

over all choices of a channel $\Phi \in C(\mathcal{X}, \mathcal{Y})$. Prove that a channel $\Phi \in C(\mathcal{X}, \mathcal{Y})$ satisfies

$$\langle H, J(\Phi) \rangle = \max\{\langle H, J(\Psi) \rangle : \Psi \in C(\mathcal{X}, \mathcal{Y})\} \tag{3.412}$$

if and only if the operator $\text{Tr}_{\mathcal{Y}}(H J(\Phi))$ is Hermitian and satisfies

$$\mathbb{1}_{\mathcal{Y}} \otimes \text{Tr}_{\mathcal{Y}}(H J(\Phi)) \geq H. \tag{3.413}$$

Exercise 3.6   Let $\Phi \in T(\mathcal{X}, \mathcal{Y})$ be a map, for complex Euclidean spaces $\mathcal{X}$ and $\mathcal{Y}$, and let $n = \dim(\mathcal{X})$. Prove that

$$\|\|\Phi\|\|_1 \leq \|J(\Phi)\|_1 \leq n\|\|\Phi\|\|_1. \tag{3.414}$$

3.5 Bibliographic Remarks

The task of quantum state discrimination was evidently first formulated (in abstract terms) by Helstrom (1967), although instances of the task with respect to specific quantum physical systems had certainly been considered earlier. Theorem 3.4 was proved by Helstrom (1967) for the restricted case of projective measurements, and by Holevo (1972) for general measurements.

Theorem 3.7 was proved by Gutoski and Watrous (2005), and a slightly weaker form of the theorem (for finite sets of states) was proved by Jain (2005) around the same time, using Sion's min–max theorem. Jain's proof extends to the more general case, and this is the proof presented in this chapter.

Theorem 3.9 is attributed to Holevo (1972, 1973a) and Yuen, Kennedy, and Lax (1970, 1975). The semidefinite programming formulation that has been used in the proof of this theorem is due to Yuen, Kennedy, and Lax, although it was not recognized as a semidefinite program in their work (as their work predates much of the development of semidefinite programming). Eldar, Megretski, and Verghese (2003) recognized this optimization problem as a semidefinite program.

The pretty good measurement was so-named by Hausladen and Wootters (1994) – it is one among a family of measurements introduced earlier by Belavkin (1975) and considered in other works (such as Eldar and Forney (2001)). Theorem 3.10 is due to Barnum and Knill (2002).

The fidelity function was introduced by Uhlmann (1976), who referred to it as the *transition probability*. (Uhlmann defined the transition probability as the square of the fidelity function, as it has been defined in this book. Many authors follow the convention of referring to the square of the fidelity function as the fidelity function.) Uhlmann also proved Theorem 3.22 and observed several elementary properties of the fidelity function in the same paper. Corollary 3.20 is due to Alberti (1983), and Theorem 3.27 is due to Alberti and Uhlmann (1983). The term *fidelity* was first introduced by Jozsa (1994), who presented a simplified proof of Uhlmann's theorem.

A variant of Corollary 3.15 was proved by Winter (1999), stated in terms of the trace distance rather than the fidelity. Theorem 3.24 is due to Fuchs and Caves (1995), Theorem 3.29 is due to Spekkens and Rudolph (2001), and

Theorem 3.33 is due to Fuchs and van de Graaf (1999). Theorem 3.17 and the semidefinite program associated with that theorem were independently found by Killoran (2012) and Watrous (2013).

The channel fidelity was introduced by Schumacher (1996), who named it the entanglement fidelity and established some basic results about it, including a derivation of its expression as represented by Proposition 3.31 and the fact that it is invariant under the choice of the purification used to define it. A proof of Proposition 3.32 appears in Nielson (1998).

The relevance of the completely bounded trace norm to the theory of quantum information and computation was first realized by Kitaev (1997), who took the spectral norm characterization (Theorem 3.62) as the definition and proved its equivalence to Definition 3.43. Several basic properties of the completely bounded trace norm were established in the same paper, and in the work of Aharonov, Kitaev, and Nisan (1998). Kitaev used the notation $\|\cdot\|_\diamond$ rather than $\|\|\cdot\|\|_1$ when referring to the completely bounded trace norm, which led to it being referred to as the "diamond norm." This norm's close relationship to the completely bounded norm, which is important in the study of operator algebras, later came to be realized; in finite dimensions, the completely bounded norm of a map is equal to the completely bounded trace norm of that map's adjoint. The book of Paulsen (2002) provides an overview of the properties, uses, and history of this norm in the subject of operator algebras.

Example 3.36 appears to be somewhat of a folklore result. A variation of this example appears in Kretschmann, Schlingemann, and Werner (2008), and had been recognized by others (including this author) a couple of years earlier. A different example of a similar character, but not giving as sharp a separation, appears in Kitaev, Shen, and Vyalyi (2002). (See example 11.1 and the text immediately following in that book.) Underlying all of these examples is the observation that the transpose mapping provides a separation between the induced trace norm and the completely bounded trace norm; an equivalent example goes back (at least) to Arveson (1969).

Theorem 3.39 is equivalent to a theorem of Russo and Dye (1966). Results similar to Lemma 3.45 appear in Gilchrist, Langford, and Nielsen (2005) and Watrous (2005), and a fact equivalent to Lemma 3.50 appears in Rosgen and Watrous (2005). Theorem 3.55 is stated in Aharonov, Kitaev, and Nisan (1998) for the case of unitary channels, and an equivalent statement was proved by Childs, Preskill, and Renes (2000). A similar bound to the one in Theorem 3.56 appears in Kretschmann and Werner (2004).

Theorem 3.59 appears (as an exercise, together with a solution) in Kitaev, Shen, and Vyalyi (2002). Theorem 3.62 is due to Smith (1983). Theorem 3.63

is due to Timoney (2003), and the proof of this theorem given in this chapter is from Watrous (2008).

The completely bounded trace norm can be expressed as a semidefinite program in a few different ways, as was proved by Watrous (2009b, 2013). Ben-Aroya and Ta-Shma (2010) independently proved that the completely bounded trace norm can be efficiently computed through the use of convex programming techniques, and a similar statement was made by Gilchrist, Langford, and Nielsen (2005) concerning the slightly more restricted task of computing the completely bounded trace norm of the difference between two channels. Other computational methods for evaluating the completely bounded trace norm, but not accompanied by proofs of their computational efficiency, were devised by Zarikian (2006) and Johnston, Kribs, and Paulsen (2009).

4

Unital Channels and Majorization

This chapter studies the class of *unital channels*, together with the notion of *majorization* for Hermitian operators. The first section of the chapter introduces various subclasses of unital channels, including mixed-unitary channels, Weyl-covariant channels, and Schur channels, and the second section concerns properties of unital channels in general. The third section discusses majorization for Hermitian operators, together with an analogous notion for real vectors. The following definition of unital channels will be used throughout the chapter.

Definition 4.1 Let $\mathcal{X}$ be a complex Euclidean space. A channel $\Phi \in C(\mathcal{X})$ is a *unital channel* if $\Phi(\mathbb{1}_{\mathcal{X}}) = \mathbb{1}_{\mathcal{X}}$.

More generally, one could consider any channel of the form $\Phi \in C(\mathcal{X}, \mathcal{Y})$ meeting the condition $\Phi(\mathbb{1}_{\mathcal{X}}) = \mathbb{1}_{\mathcal{Y}}$, for some choice of complex Euclidean spaces $\mathcal{X}$ and $\mathcal{Y}$, to be a unital channel. However, as channels must preserve trace, the existence of such a channel implies $\dim(\mathcal{Y}) = \dim(\mathcal{X})$; and for this reason there is little generality lost in restricting the definition of unital channels to those of the form $\Phi \in C(\mathcal{X})$. Moreover, the requirement that unital channels take the form $\Phi \in C(\mathcal{X})$, for some choice of a complex Euclidean space $\mathcal{X}$, is both natural and convenient with respect to the topics to be discussed in this chapter.

4.1 Subclasses of Unital Channels

Three classes of unital channels are introduced in this section: *mixed-unitary channels*, *Weyl-covariant channels*, and *Schur channels*. Various properties of these classes, as well as relationships among them, and to general unital channels, are discussed.

4.1.1 Mixed-Unitary Channels

Every unitary channel is evidently unital, as is any convex combination of unitary channels. Channels of the later sort will be referred to as *mixed-unitary* channels, as the following definition makes precise.

Definition 4.2 Let $\mathcal{X}$ be a complex Euclidean space and let $\Phi \in C(\mathcal{X})$ be a channel. It is said that Φ is a *mixed-unitary channel* if there exist an alphabet Σ, a probability vector $p \in \mathcal{P}(\Sigma)$, and a collection of unitary operators $\{U_a : a \in \Sigma\} \subset U(\mathcal{X})$ such that

$$\Phi(X) = \sum_{a \in \Sigma} p(a) U_a X U_a^* \tag{4.1}$$

for every $X \in L(\mathcal{X})$. Equivalently, a mapping $\Phi \in C(\mathcal{X})$ is a mixed-unitary channel if it is a convex combination of unitary channels.

An Example of a Unital Channel That is Not Mixed-Unitary

While every mixed-unitary channel is necessarily unital, the converse of this statement does not hold, as the following example illustrates.

Example 4.3 Let $\mathcal{X} = \mathbb{C}^3$ and define $\Phi \in C(\mathcal{X})$ as

$$\Phi(X) = \frac{1}{2} \operatorname{Tr}(X)\mathbb{1} - \frac{1}{2}X^{\mathsf{T}} \tag{4.2}$$

for all $X \in L(\mathcal{X})$. Example 3.36 has established that Φ is a channel, and it is evident that Φ is unital, but it is not a mixed-unitary channel.

To verify that Φ is not a mixed-unitary channel, observe first that

$$\Phi(X) = A_1 X A_1^* + A_2 X A_2^* + A_3 X A_3^* \tag{4.3}$$

for all $X \in L(\mathcal{X})$, for

$$A_1 = \begin{pmatrix} 0 & 0 & 0 \\ 0 & 0 & \frac{1}{\sqrt{2}} \\ 0 & \frac{-1}{\sqrt{2}} & 0 \end{pmatrix}, \quad A_2 = \begin{pmatrix} 0 & 0 & \frac{1}{\sqrt{2}} \\ 0 & 0 & 0 \\ \frac{-1}{\sqrt{2}} & 0 & 0 \end{pmatrix}, \quad A_3 = \begin{pmatrix} 0 & \frac{1}{\sqrt{2}} & 0 \\ \frac{-1}{\sqrt{2}} & 0 & 0 \\ 0 & 0 & 0 \end{pmatrix}. \tag{4.4}$$

The fact that the expression (4.3) does indeed hold for all $X \in L(\mathcal{X})$ follows from the observation that the Choi representation of the map defined by the right-hand side of that equation is in agreement with $J(\Phi)$, as calculated in Example 3.36:

$$\frac{1}{2}\mathbb{1} \otimes \mathbb{1} - \frac{1}{2}W = \sum_{k=1}^{3} \operatorname{vec}(A_k) \operatorname{vec}(A_k)^*, \tag{4.5}$$

for W denoting the swap operator on $\mathcal{X} \otimes \mathcal{X}$.

Now observe that the collection $\{A_j^* A_k : 1 \leq j, k \leq 3\}$ includes the following operators:

$$A_1^* A_1 = \begin{pmatrix} 0 & 0 & 0 \\ 0 & \frac{1}{2} & 0 \\ 0 & 0 & \frac{1}{2} \end{pmatrix}, \quad A_1^* A_2 = \begin{pmatrix} 0 & 0 & 0 \\ \frac{1}{2} & 0 & 0 \\ 0 & 0 & 0 \end{pmatrix}, \quad A_1^* A_3 = \begin{pmatrix} 0 & 0 & 0 \\ 0 & 0 & 0 \\ \frac{-1}{2} & 0 & 0 \end{pmatrix},$$

$$A_2^* A_1 = \begin{pmatrix} 0 & \frac{1}{2} & 0 \\ 0 & 0 & 0 \\ 0 & 0 & 0 \end{pmatrix}, \quad A_2^* A_2 = \begin{pmatrix} \frac{1}{2} & 0 & 0 \\ 0 & 0 & 0 \\ 0 & 0 & \frac{1}{2} \end{pmatrix}, \quad A_2^* A_3 = \begin{pmatrix} 0 & 0 & 0 \\ 0 & 0 & 0 \\ 0 & \frac{1}{2} & 0 \end{pmatrix}, \quad (4.6)$$

$$A_3^* A_1 = \begin{pmatrix} 0 & 0 & \frac{-1}{2} \\ 0 & 0 & 0 \\ 0 & 0 & 0 \end{pmatrix}, \quad A_3^* A_2 = \begin{pmatrix} 0 & 0 & 0 \\ 0 & 0 & \frac{1}{2} \\ 0 & 0 & 0 \end{pmatrix}, \quad A_3^* A_3 = \begin{pmatrix} \frac{1}{2} & 0 & 0 \\ 0 & \frac{1}{2} & 0 \\ 0 & 0 & 0 \end{pmatrix}.$$

This is a linearly independent collection, as an inspection reveals. It follows from Theorem 2.31 that Φ is an extreme point of the set of channels $C(\mathcal{X})$. As Φ is not itself a unitary channel, it follows that it cannot be expressed as a convex combination of unitary channels.

Pinching Channels

Many interesting examples of mixed-unitary channels are known. One type of channel, called a *pinching channel*, provides a collection of examples.

Definition 4.4 Let $\mathcal{X}$ be a complex Euclidean space. A channel $\Phi \in C(\mathcal{X})$ is said to be a *pinching channel*, or simply a *pinching*, if there exists a collection $\{\Pi_a : a \in \Sigma\}$ of projection operators satisfying

$$\sum_{a \in \Sigma} \Pi_a = \mathbb{1}_{\mathcal{X}} \qquad (4.7)$$

(i.e., such that the set $\{\Pi_a : a \in \Sigma\}$ represents a projective measurement) for which

$$\Phi(X) = \sum_{a \in \Sigma} \Pi_a X \Pi_a \qquad (4.8)$$

for all $X \in L(\mathcal{X})$.

The action of the channel defined by (4.8) on a register X is equivalent to X being measured with respect to a nondestructive measurement defined by $\{\Pi_a : a \in \Sigma\}$, followed by the measurement outcome being discarded.

Example 4.5 The channel $\Phi \in C(\mathbb{C}^5)$ defined as

$$\Phi(X) = \Pi_0 X \Pi_0 + \Pi_1 X \Pi_1 \qquad (4.9)$$

for

$$\Pi_0 = E_{1,1} + E_{2,2} \quad \text{and} \quad \Pi_1 = E_{3,3} + E_{4,4} + E_{5,5} \tag{4.10}$$

is an example of a pinching channel. This channel has the following action on a general operator in $\mathrm{L}(\mathcal{X})$, expressed in matrix form:

$$\Phi \begin{pmatrix} \alpha_{1,1} & \alpha_{1,2} & \alpha_{1,3} & \alpha_{1,4} & \alpha_{1,5} \\ \alpha_{2,1} & \alpha_{2,2} & \alpha_{2,3} & \alpha_{2,4} & \alpha_{2,5} \\ \alpha_{3,1} & \alpha_{3,2} & \alpha_{3,3} & \alpha_{3,4} & \alpha_{3,5} \\ \alpha_{4,1} & \alpha_{4,2} & \alpha_{4,3} & \alpha_{4,4} & \alpha_{4,5} \\ \alpha_{5,1} & \alpha_{5,2} & \alpha_{5,3} & \alpha_{5,4} & \alpha_{5,5} \end{pmatrix} = \begin{pmatrix} \alpha_{1,1} & \alpha_{1,2} & 0 & 0 & 0 \\ \alpha_{2,1} & \alpha_{2,2} & 0 & 0 & 0 \\ 0 & 0 & \alpha_{3,3} & \alpha_{3,4} & \alpha_{3,5} \\ 0 & 0 & \alpha_{4,3} & \alpha_{4,4} & \alpha_{4,5} \\ 0 & 0 & \alpha_{5,3} & \alpha_{5,4} & \alpha_{5,5} \end{pmatrix}. \tag{4.11}$$

The action of this channel is suggestive of the matrix representing the input operator being "pinched," causing a certain pattern of off-diagonal entries to become 0, which explains the terminology used to describe such maps. When a pinching channel is defined by a collection of projection operators that are not diagonal in the standard basis, the term is not descriptive in this way, but it is used nevertheless.

While it is not immediate from the definition that every pinching channel is a mixed-unitary channel, it is fairly straightforward to establish that this is so, as the proof of the following proposition reveals.

Proposition 4.6 *Let $\mathcal{X}$ be a complex Euclidean space, let Σ be an alphabet, and let $\{\Pi_a : a \in \Sigma\}$ be a collection of projection operators on $\mathcal{X}$ satisfying*

$$\sum_{a \in \Sigma} \Pi_a = \mathbb{1}_{\mathcal{X}}. \tag{4.12}$$

The channel $\Phi \in \mathrm{C}(\mathcal{X})$ defined by

$$\Phi(X) = \sum_{a \in \Sigma} \Pi_a X \Pi_a \tag{4.13}$$

for all $X \in \mathrm{L}(\mathcal{X})$ is a mixed-unitary channel.

Proof Consider the collection $\{-1, 1\}^{\Sigma}$ of vectors in $\mathbb{C}^{\Sigma}$ having entries drawn from the set $\{-1, 1\}$, and define a unitary operator

$$U_w = \sum_{a \in \Sigma} w(a) \Pi_a \tag{4.14}$$

for every such vector $w \in \{-1, 1\}^{\Sigma}$. It holds that

$$\frac{1}{2^{|\Sigma|}} \sum_{w \in \{-1,1\}^{\Sigma}} U_w X U_w^* = \frac{1}{2^{|\Sigma|}} \sum_{a,b \in \Sigma} \sum_{w \in \{-1,1\}^{\Sigma}} w(a) w(b) \Pi_a X \Pi_b \tag{4.15}$$

for every $X \in L(\mathcal{X})$. To simplify this expression, one may observe that

$$\frac{1}{2^{|\Sigma|}} \sum_{w \in \{-1,1\}^{\Sigma}} w(a)w(b) = \begin{cases} 1 & \text{if } a = b \\ 0 & \text{if } a \neq b \end{cases} \tag{4.16}$$

for every choice of $a, b \in \Sigma$, and therefore

$$\frac{1}{2^{|\Sigma|}} \sum_{w \in \{-1,1\}^{\Sigma}} U_w X U_w^* = \sum_{a \in \Sigma} \Pi_a X \Pi_a = \Phi(X) \tag{4.17}$$

for every $X \in L(\mathcal{X})$. This demonstrates that Φ is a mixed-unitary channel, as required. $\qquad\square$

Example 4.7 The completely dephasing channel $\Delta \in C(\mathcal{X})$ defined on any complex Euclidean space $\mathcal{X} = \mathbb{C}^{\Sigma}$ is an example of a pinching channel, as it is defined according to Definition 4.4 by the collection of projection operators $\{E_{a,a}: a \in \Sigma\}$. By Proposition 4.6, it follows that Δ is a mixed-unitary channel.

Environment-Assisted Channel Correction

Mixed-unitary channels have an alternative characterization based on the notion of *environment-assisted channel correction*, which is as follows.

Let $\Phi \in C(\mathcal{X})$ be a channel, represented in Stinespring form as

$$\Phi(X) = \text{Tr}_{\mathcal{Z}}(AXA^*) \tag{4.18}$$

for all $X \in L(\mathcal{X})$, for some choice of a complex Euclidean space $\mathcal{Z}$ and an isometry $A \in U(\mathcal{X}, \mathcal{X} \otimes \mathcal{Z})$. Environment-assisted channel correction refers to the existence of an alphabet Σ, a collection of channels

$$\{\Psi_a: a \in \Sigma\} \subset C(\mathcal{X}), \tag{4.19}$$

and a measurement $\mu: \Sigma \to \text{Pos}(\mathcal{Z})$, for which the equation

$$X = \sum_{a \in \Sigma} \Psi_a\big(\text{Tr}_{\mathcal{Z}}((\mathbb{1}_{\mathcal{X}} \otimes \mu(a))AXA^*)\big) \tag{4.20}$$

holds for all $X \in L(\mathcal{X})$.

An interpretation of the equation (4.20) is as follows. One imagines that a register X contains a quantum state $\rho \in D(\mathcal{X})$. The action of the mapping $X \mapsto AXA^*$ has the effect of encoding this state into the state of the pair (X, Z), for Z being a second register. By discarding the register Z, the register X is left in the state $\Phi(\rho)$, which may potentially be quite different from ρ. In essence, the register Z represents an "environment," to which some part of the encoding of ρ may have escaped or leaked. The measurement μ on Z, followed by the application of Ψ_a to X (for whichever outcome $a \in \Sigma$ resulted from the measurement), is viewed as an attempt to *correct* X, so that it is transformed back into ρ. The equation (4.20) represents the situation in which a perfect correction of this sort is accomplished.

The following theorem implies that a perfect correction of the sort just described is possible if and only if Φ is a mixed-unitary channel.

Theorem 4.8 *Let $A \in \mathrm{U}(\mathcal{X}, \mathcal{X} \otimes \mathcal{Z})$ be an isometry, for complex Euclidean spaces $\mathcal{X}$ and $\mathcal{Z}$, and let $\Phi \in \mathrm{C}(\mathcal{X})$ be the channel defined by*

$$\Phi(X) = \mathrm{Tr}_{\mathcal{Z}}(AXA^*) \tag{4.21}$$

for all $X \in \mathrm{L}(\mathcal{X})$. The following two statements are equivalent:

1. *Φ is a mixed-unitary channel.*
2. *There exist an alphabet Σ, a measurement $\mu \colon \Sigma \to \mathrm{Pos}(\mathcal{Z})$, and a collection of channels $\{\Psi_a : a \in \Sigma\} \subset \mathrm{C}(\mathcal{X})$ for which*

$$X = \sum_{a \in \Sigma} \Psi_a\big(\mathrm{Tr}_{\mathcal{Z}}\big((\mathbb{1}_{\mathcal{X}} \otimes \mu(a))AXA^*\big)\big) \tag{4.22}$$

for all $X \in \mathrm{L}(\mathcal{X})$.

Proof Assume first that statement 1 holds, so that

$$\Phi(X) = \sum_{a \in \Sigma} p(a) U_a X U_a^* \tag{4.23}$$

for every $X \in \mathrm{L}(\mathcal{X})$, for some choice of an alphabet Σ, a collection of unitary operators $\{U_a : a \in \Sigma\} \subset \mathrm{U}(\mathcal{X})$, and a probability vector $p \in \mathcal{P}(\Sigma)$. There is no loss of generality in assuming $|\Sigma| \geq \dim(\mathcal{Z})$; one may add any finite number of elements to Σ, take $p(a) = 0$, and choose $U_a \in \mathrm{U}(\mathcal{X})$ arbitrarily for the added elements, maintaining the validity of the expression (4.23). By this assumption, there must exist a collection $\{v_a : a \in \Sigma\} \subset \mathcal{Z}$ of vectors for which

$$\sum_{a \in \Sigma} v_a v_a^* = \mathbb{1}_{\mathcal{Z}}. \tag{4.24}$$

Fix such a collection, and define operators $\{A_a : a \in \Sigma\} \subset \mathrm{L}(\mathcal{X})$ as

$$A_a = (\mathbb{1}_{\mathcal{X}} \otimes v_a^*)A \tag{4.25}$$

for each $a \in \Sigma$. It holds that

$$\Phi(X) = \mathrm{Tr}_{\mathcal{Z}}(AXA^*) = \sum_{a \in \Sigma} A_a X A_a^* \tag{4.26}$$

for every $X \in L(\mathcal{X})$. Therefore, by Corollary 2.23, there must exist a unitary operator $W \in U(\mathbb{C}^{\Sigma})$ such that

$$\sqrt{p(a)}U_a = \sum_{b \in \Sigma} W(a, b)A_b \tag{4.27}$$

for every $a \in \Sigma$.

For each symbol $a \in \Sigma$, define a vector $u_a \in \mathcal{Z}$ as

$$u_a = \sum_{b \in \Sigma} \overline{W(a, b)}v_b, \tag{4.28}$$

and define $\mu \colon \Sigma \to \text{Pos}(\mathcal{Z})$ as $\mu(a) = u_a u_a^*$ for each $a \in \Sigma$. Because W is a unitary operator, it holds that

$$\sum_{a \in \Sigma} \mu(a) = \sum_{a,b,c \in \Sigma} \overline{W(a, b)}W(a, c)v_b v_c^* = \sum_{b \in \Sigma} v_b v_b^* = \mathbb{1}_{\mathcal{Z}}, \tag{4.29}$$

and therefore μ is a measurement. Also define a collection $\{\Psi_a \colon a \in \Sigma\}$ of channels as

$$\Psi_a(X) = U_a^* X U_a \tag{4.30}$$

for every $X \in L(\mathcal{X})$ and $a \in \Sigma$.

Now, it holds that

$$(\mathbb{1}_{\mathcal{X}} \otimes u_a^*)A = \sum_{b \in \Sigma} W(a, b)A_b = \sqrt{p(a)}U_a, \tag{4.31}$$

and therefore

$$\text{Tr}_{\mathcal{Z}}\big((\mathbb{1}_{\mathcal{X}} \otimes \mu(a))AXA^*\big) = p(a)U_a X U_a^*, \tag{4.32}$$

for each $a \in \Sigma$. It follows that

$$\sum_{a \in \Sigma} \Psi_a\big(\text{Tr}_{\mathcal{Z}}((\mathbb{1}_{\mathcal{X}} \otimes \mu(a))AXA^*)\big) = \sum_{a \in \Sigma} p(a)U_a^* U_a X U_a^* U_a = X \tag{4.33}$$

for all $X \in L(\mathcal{X})$. Statement 1 therefore implies statement 2.

Next, assume statement 2 holds. For each $a \in \Sigma$, define $\Phi_a \in \text{CP}(\mathcal{X})$ as

$$\Phi_a(X) = \text{Tr}_{\mathcal{Z}}\big((\mathbb{1}_{\mathcal{X}} \otimes \mu(a))AXA^*\big) \tag{4.34}$$

for all $X \in L(\mathcal{X})$. Also let

$$\{A_{a,b} \colon a \in \Sigma, b \in \Gamma\} \quad \text{and} \quad \{B_{a,b} \colon a \in \Sigma, b \in \Gamma\} \tag{4.35}$$

be collections of operators in $L(\mathcal{X})$, for a suitable choice of an alphabet Γ, yielding Kraus representations

$$\Psi_a(X) = \sum_{b \in \Gamma} A_{a,b} X A_{a,b}^* \quad \text{and} \quad \Phi_a(X) = \sum_{c \in \Gamma} B_{a,c} X B_{a,c}^* \tag{4.36}$$

for all $a \in \Sigma$ and $X \in \mathrm{L}(\mathcal{X})$. (Taking a common alphabet Γ as an index set for these representations is only done to simplify notation and causes no loss of generality; one is free to include the zero operator among the Kraus operators of either map any number of times.) By the assumption that statement 2 holds, one has

$$\sum_{a \in \Sigma} \Psi_a \Phi_a = \mathbb{1}_{\mathrm{L}(\mathcal{X})}, \tag{4.37}$$

so the Choi representations of the two sides of (4.37) must agree:

$$\sum_{a \in \Sigma} \sum_{b,c \in \Gamma} \mathrm{vec}(A_{a,b} B_{a,c}) \, \mathrm{vec}(A_{a,b} B_{a,c})^* = \mathrm{vec}(\mathbb{1}_{\mathcal{X}}) \, \mathrm{vec}(\mathbb{1}_{\mathcal{X}})^*. \tag{4.38}$$

There must therefore exist a collection $\{\alpha_{a,b,c} : a \in \Sigma, \, b, c \in \Gamma\}$ of complex numbers for which the equation

$$A_{a,b} B_{a,c} = \alpha_{a,b,c} \mathbb{1}_{\mathcal{X}} \tag{4.39}$$

holds for all $a \in \Sigma$ and $b, c \in \Gamma$. This collection must also evidently satisfy the constraint

$$\sum_{a \in \Sigma} \sum_{b,c \in \Gamma} |\alpha_{a,b,c}|^2 = 1. \tag{4.40}$$

Consequently, one has

$$\sum_{b \in \Gamma} |\alpha_{a,b,c}|^2 \mathbb{1}_{\mathcal{X}} = \sum_{b \in \Gamma} B_{a,c}^* A_{a,b}^* A_{a,b} B_{a,c} = B_{a,c}^* B_{a,c} \tag{4.41}$$

for every $a \in \Sigma$ and $c \in \Gamma$, owing to the fact that each mapping Ψ_a is a channel. For every $a \in \Sigma$ and $c \in \Gamma$ it must therefore hold that

$$B_{a,c} = \beta_{a,c} U_{a,c} \tag{4.42}$$

for some choice of a unitary operator $U_{a,c} \in \mathrm{U}(\mathcal{X})$ and a complex number $\beta_{a,c} \in \mathbb{C}$ satisfying

$$|\beta_{a,c}|^2 = \sum_{b \in \Gamma} |\alpha_{a,b,c}|^2. \tag{4.43}$$

It follows that

$$\Phi(X) = \sum_{a \in \Sigma} \Phi_a(X) = \sum_{a \in \Sigma} \sum_{c \in \Gamma} p(a,c) U_{a,c} X U_{a,c}^*, \tag{4.44}$$

for $p \in \mathcal{P}(\Sigma \times \Gamma)$ being the probability vector defined as $p(a,c) = |\beta_{a,c}|^2$ for each $a \in \Sigma$ and $c \in \Gamma$. The channel Φ is therefore mixed-unitary, so it has been proved that statement 2 implies statement 1. $\qquad\square$

Mixed-Unitary Channels and Carathéodory's Theorem

Every mixed-unitary channel $\Phi \in C(\mathcal{X})$ is, by definition, an element of the convex hull of the set of unitary channels. Using Carathéodory's theorem (Theorem 1.9), one may obtain upper bounds on the number of unitary channels that must be averaged to obtain any mixed-unitary channel. The following proposition proves one bound along these lines.

Proposition 4.9 *Let $\mathcal{X}$ be a complex Euclidean space, let $n = \dim(\mathcal{X})$, and let $\Phi \in C(\mathcal{X})$ be a mixed-unitary channel. There exist a positive integer m satisfying*

$$m \leq n^4 - 2n^2 + 2, \tag{4.45}$$

a collection of unitary operators $\{U_1, \ldots, U_m\} \subset U(\mathcal{X})$, and a probability vector $(p_1, \ldots, p_m)$ such that

$$\Phi(X) = \sum_{k=1}^{m} p_k U_k X U_k^* \tag{4.46}$$

for all $X \in L(\mathcal{X})$.

Proof Consider the linear map $\Xi \colon \mathrm{Herm}(\mathcal{X} \otimes \mathcal{X}) \to \mathrm{Herm}(\mathcal{X} \oplus \mathcal{X})$ defined by the equation

$$\Xi(X \otimes Y) = \begin{pmatrix} \mathrm{Tr}(X)Y & 0 \\ 0 & \mathrm{Tr}(Y)X \end{pmatrix} \tag{4.47}$$

for all $X, Y \in \mathrm{Herm}(\mathcal{X})$, and fix any orthogonal basis $\{\mathbb{1}, H_1, \ldots, H_{n^2-1}\}$ of $\mathrm{Herm}(\mathcal{X})$ that contains the identity operator. It holds that

$$\Xi(H_j \otimes H_k) = 0 \tag{4.48}$$

for every choice of $j, k \in \{1, \ldots, n^2 - 1\}$, while the operators

$$\Xi(\mathbb{1} \otimes H_k), \quad \Xi(H_k \otimes \mathbb{1}), \quad \text{and} \quad \Xi(\mathbb{1} \otimes \mathbb{1}), \tag{4.49}$$

ranging over all choices of $k \in \{1, \ldots, n^2 - 1\}$, are all nonzero and pairwise orthogonal. The kernel of Ξ is therefore equal to the subspace spanned by the orthogonal collection

$$\{H_j \otimes H_k : 1 \leq j, k \leq n^2 - 1\}. \tag{4.50}$$

In particular, the dimension of the kernel of the mapping Ξ is

$$(n^2 - 1)^2 = n^4 - 2n^2 + 1. \tag{4.51}$$

Next, consider any unitary operator $U \in \mathrm{U}(\mathcal{X})$, and let $\Psi_U \in \mathrm{C}(\mathcal{X})$ be the unitary channel defined as $\Psi_U(X) = UXU^*$ for every $X \in \mathrm{L}(\mathcal{X})$. Evaluating the mapping Ξ defined above on the Choi representation of Ψ_U yields

$$\Xi(J(\Psi_U)) = \Xi(\mathrm{vec}(U)\,\mathrm{vec}(U)^*) = \begin{pmatrix} \mathbb{1} & 0 \\ 0 & \mathbb{1} \end{pmatrix}. \tag{4.52}$$

The Choi representation of Ψ_U is therefore drawn from an affine subspace of $\mathrm{Herm}(\mathcal{X} \otimes \mathcal{X})$ having dimension $n^4 - 2n^2 + 1$.

Because Φ is a mixed-unitary channel, the Choi representation $J(\Phi)$ of Φ is contained in the convex hull of those operators of the form $J(\Psi_U)$, for U ranging over the set of unitary operators $\mathrm{U}(\mathcal{X})$. It therefore follows from Carathéodory's theorem that

$$J(\Phi) = \sum_{k=1}^{m} p_k J(\Psi_{U_k}) \tag{4.53}$$

for some choice of a positive integer m satisfying (4.45), unitary operators $U_1, \ldots, U_m \in \mathrm{U}(\mathcal{X})$, and a probability vector $(p_1, \ldots, p_m)$. Equivalently,

$$\Phi(X) = \sum_{k=1}^{m} p_k U_k X U_k^* \tag{4.54}$$

for all $X \in \mathrm{L}(\mathcal{X})$, for the same choice of m, $U_1, \ldots, U_m$, and $(p_1, \ldots, p_m)$, which completes the proof. $\qquad\square$

A similar technique to the one used in the proof above may be used to obtain an upper bound on the number of channels, drawn from an arbitrary collection, that must be averaged to obtain a given element in the convex hull of that collection. As a corollary, one obtains a different (and often better) bound on the number of unitary channels that must be averaged to obtain a given mixed-unitary channel.

Theorem 4.10 *Let $\mathcal{X}$ and $\mathcal{Y}$ be complex Euclidean spaces, let $\mathcal{A} \subseteq \mathrm{C}(\mathcal{X}, \mathcal{Y})$ be any nonempty collection of channels, and let $\Phi \in \mathrm{conv}(\mathcal{A})$ be a channel in the convex hull of $\mathcal{A}$. There exist a positive integer*

$$m \leq \mathrm{rank}(J(\Phi))^2, \tag{4.55}$$

a probability vector $(p_1, \ldots, p_m)$, and a selection of channels $\Psi_1, \ldots, \Psi_m \in \mathcal{A}$ such that

$$\Phi = p_1 \Psi_1 + \cdots + p_m \Psi_m. \tag{4.56}$$

Proof Let $r = \mathrm{rank}(J(\Phi))$ and let Π be the projection operator onto the image of $J(\Phi)$. Define a linear map

$$\Xi: \mathrm{Herm}(\mathcal{Y} \otimes \mathcal{X}) \to \mathrm{Herm}(\mathbb{C} \oplus (\mathcal{Y} \otimes \mathcal{X}) \oplus (\mathcal{Y} \otimes \mathcal{X})) \qquad (4.57)$$

as

$$\Xi(H) = \begin{pmatrix} \mathrm{Tr}(H) & 0 & 0 \\ 0 & (\mathbb{1} - \Pi)H(\mathbb{1} - \Pi) & (\mathbb{1} - \Pi)H\Pi \\ 0 & \Pi H(\mathbb{1} - \Pi) & 0 \end{pmatrix} \qquad (4.58)$$

for each $H \in \mathrm{Herm}(\mathcal{Y} \otimes \mathcal{X})$. It holds that $\Xi(H) = 0$ for precisely those Hermitian operators H satisfying

$$H = \Pi H \Pi \quad \text{and} \quad \mathrm{Tr}(H) = 0, \qquad (4.59)$$

and therefore the kernel of Ξ has dimension $r^2 - 1$.

Let

$$\mathcal{B} = \{\Psi \in \mathcal{A}: \mathrm{im}(J(\Psi)) \subseteq \mathrm{im}(J(\Phi))\}, \qquad (4.60)$$

and observe that $\Phi \in \mathrm{conv}(\mathcal{B})$, by virtue of the fact that $\Phi \in \mathrm{conv}(\mathcal{A})$. For each channel $\Psi \in \mathcal{B}$ it holds that

$$\Xi(J(\Psi)) = \begin{pmatrix} \dim(\mathcal{X}) & 0 & 0 \\ 0 & 0 & 0 \\ 0 & 0 & 0 \end{pmatrix}. \qquad (4.61)$$

There is therefore an affine subspace of $\mathrm{Herm}(\mathcal{Y} \otimes \mathcal{X})$ of dimension $r^2 - 1$ that contains $J(\Psi)$, for every $\Psi \in \mathcal{B}$. As $J(\Phi)$ is a convex combination of operators in this affine subspace, it follows from Carathéodory's theorem that there exist an integer $m \leq (r^2 - 1) + 1 = r^2$, a selection of channels $\Psi_1, \ldots, \Psi_m \in \mathcal{B} \subseteq \mathcal{A}$, and a probability vector $(p_1, \ldots, p_m)$ such that

$$J(\Phi) = p_1 J(\Psi_1) + \cdots + p_m J(\Psi_m). \qquad (4.62)$$

The equation (4.62) is equivalent to (4.56), which completes the proof. $\square$

Corollary 4.11 *Let $\mathcal{X}$ be a complex Euclidean space and let $\Phi \in \mathrm{C}(\mathcal{X})$ be a mixed-unitary channel. There exist a positive integer $m \leq \mathrm{rank}(J(\Phi))^2$, a selection of unitary operators $U_1, \ldots, U_m \in \mathrm{U}(\mathcal{X})$, and a probability vector $(p_1, \ldots, p_m)$ such that*

$$\Phi(X) = \sum_{k=1}^{m} p_k U_k X U_k^* \qquad (4.63)$$

for all $X \in \mathrm{L}(\mathcal{X})$.

4.1.2 Weyl-Covariant Channels

This section concerns *Weyl-covariant channels*, which are a class of unital channels that relate (in multiple ways) to a collection of operators known as *discrete Weyl operators*.

Discrete Weyl Operators

For every positive integer n, the set $\mathbb{Z}_n$ is defined as

$$\mathbb{Z}_n = \{0, \ldots, n-1\}. \tag{4.64}$$

This set forms a ring, with respect to addition and multiplication modulo n, and whenever elements of $\mathbb{Z}_n$ appear in arithmetic expressions in this book, the default assumption is that the operations are to be taken modulo n.

The *discrete Weyl operators* are a collection of unitary operators acting on $\mathcal{X} = \mathbb{C}^{\mathbb{Z}_n}$, for a given positive integer n, defined in the following way.[1] One first defines a scalar value

$$\zeta = \exp\left(\frac{2\pi i}{n}\right), \tag{4.65}$$

along with unitary operators

$$U = \sum_{c \in \mathbb{Z}_n} E_{c+1,c} \quad \text{and} \quad V = \sum_{c \in \mathbb{Z}_n} \zeta^c E_{c,c}. \tag{4.66}$$

For each pair $(a, b) \in \mathbb{Z}_n \times \mathbb{Z}_n$, the discrete Weyl operator $W_{a,b} \in \mathrm{U}(\mathcal{X})$ is then defined as

$$W_{a,b} = U^a V^b, \tag{4.67}$$

or equivalently as

$$W_{a,b} = \sum_{c \in \mathbb{Z}_n} \zeta^{bc} E_{a+c,c}. \tag{4.68}$$

Example 4.12 For $n = 2$, the discrete Weyl operators (in matrix form) are given by

$$W_{0,0} = \begin{pmatrix} 1 & 0 \\ 0 & 1 \end{pmatrix}, \quad W_{0,1} = \begin{pmatrix} 1 & 0 \\ 0 & -1 \end{pmatrix},$$
$$W_{1,0} = \begin{pmatrix} 0 & 1 \\ 1 & 0 \end{pmatrix}, \quad W_{1,1} = \begin{pmatrix} 0 & -1 \\ 1 & 0 \end{pmatrix}. \tag{4.69}$$

---

[1] It is sometimes convenient to extend the definition of the discrete Weyl operators from complex Euclidean spaces of the form $\mathcal{X} = \mathbb{C}^{\mathbb{Z}_n}$ to arbitrary complex Euclidean spaces $\mathcal{X} = \mathbb{C}^{\Sigma}$, simply by placing Σ in correspondence with $\mathbb{Z}_n$, for $n = |\Sigma|$, in some fixed but otherwise arbitrary way.

Equivalently,

$$W_{0,0} = \mathbb{1}, \quad W_{0,1} = \sigma_z, \quad W_{1,0} = \sigma_x, \quad W_{1,1} = -i\sigma_y, \tag{4.70}$$

where

$$\sigma_x = \begin{pmatrix} 0 & 1 \\ 1 & 0 \end{pmatrix}, \quad \sigma_y = \begin{pmatrix} 0 & -i \\ i & 0 \end{pmatrix}, \quad \text{and} \quad \sigma_z = \begin{pmatrix} 1 & 0 \\ 0 & -1 \end{pmatrix} \tag{4.71}$$

are the *Pauli operators*.

It holds that

$$UV = \sum_{c \in \mathbb{Z}_n} \zeta^c E_{c+1,c} \quad \text{and} \quad VU = \sum_{c \in \mathbb{Z}_n} \zeta^{c+1} E_{c+1,c}, \tag{4.72}$$

from which the commutation relation

$$VU = \zeta UV \tag{4.73}$$

follows. Identities that may be derived using this relation, together with straightforward calculations, include

$$\overline{W_{a,b}} = W_{a,-b}, \quad W_{a,b}^{\mathsf{T}} = \zeta^{-ab} W_{-a,b}, \quad \text{and} \quad W_{a,b}^* = \zeta^{ab} W_{-a,-b} \tag{4.74}$$

for all $a, b \in \mathbb{Z}_n$, and

$$W_{a,b} W_{c,d} = \zeta^{bc} W_{a+c,b+d} = \zeta^{bc-ad} W_{c,d} W_{a,b} \tag{4.75}$$

for all $a, b, c, d \in \mathbb{Z}_n$.

From the equation

$$\sum_{c \in \mathbb{Z}_n} \zeta^{ac} = \begin{cases} n & \text{if } a = 0 \\ 0 & \text{if } a \in \{1, \ldots, n-1\} \end{cases} \tag{4.76}$$

it follows that

$$\mathrm{Tr}(W_{a,b}) = \begin{cases} n & \text{if } (a, b) = (0,0) \\ 0 & \text{otherwise.} \end{cases} \tag{4.77}$$

Combining this observation with (4.75) yields

$$\langle W_{a,b}, W_{c,d} \rangle = \begin{cases} n & \text{if } (a, b) = (c, d) \\ 0 & \text{if } (a, b) \neq (c, d) \end{cases} \tag{4.78}$$

for all $a, b, c, d \in \mathbb{Z}_n$. The set

$$\left\{ \frac{1}{\sqrt{n}} W_{a,b} \colon (a, b) \in \mathbb{Z}_n \times \mathbb{Z}_n \right\} \tag{4.79}$$

therefore forms an orthonormal set. Because the cardinality of this set is equal to the dimension of $L(\mathcal{X})$, it therefore forms an orthonormal basis for this space.

The *discrete Fourier transform operator* $F \in U(\mathcal{X})$, defined as

$$F = \frac{1}{\sqrt{n}} \sum_{a,b \in \mathbb{Z}_n} \zeta^{ab} E_{a,b}, \tag{4.80}$$

has a special connection with the discrete Weyl operators. The fact that F is unitary may be verified by a direct calculation:

$$F^*F = \frac{1}{n} \sum_{a,b,c \in \mathbb{Z}_n} \zeta^{a(b-c)} E_{c,b} = \sum_{b \in \mathbb{Z}_n} E_{b,b} = \mathbb{1}. \tag{4.81}$$

It may also be verified that $FU = VF$ and $FV = U^*F$, from which it follows that

$$FW_{a,b} = \zeta^{-ab} W_{-b,a} F \tag{4.82}$$

for all $a, b \in \mathbb{Z}_n$.

Weyl-Covariant Maps and Channels

A map $\Phi \in T(\mathcal{X})$, for $\mathcal{X} = \mathbb{C}^{\mathbb{Z}_n}$ as above, is a *Weyl-covariant map* if it commutes with the action of conjugation by every discrete Weyl operator, as the following definition makes precise.

Definition 4.13   Let $\mathcal{X} = \mathbb{C}^{\mathbb{Z}_n}$ for n a positive integer. A map $\Phi \in T(\mathcal{X})$ is a *Weyl-covariant map* if

$$\Phi(W_{a,b} X W_{a,b}^*) = W_{a,b} \Phi(X) W_{a,b}^* \tag{4.83}$$

for every $X \in L(\mathcal{X})$ and $(a, b) \in \mathbb{Z}_n \times \mathbb{Z}_n$. If, in addition to being a Weyl-covariant map, Φ is a channel, then Φ is said to be a *Weyl-covariant channel*.

From this definition it follows that the set of Weyl-covariant maps of the form $\Phi \in T(\mathcal{X})$ is a linear subspace of $T(\mathcal{X})$; for any two Weyl-covariant maps $\Phi, \Psi \in T(\mathcal{X})$ and scalars $\alpha, \beta \in \mathbb{C}$, the map $\alpha\Phi + \beta\Psi$ is also Weyl-covariant. It follows from this observation that the set of Weyl-covariant channels of the form $\Phi \in C(\mathcal{X})$ is a convex subset of $C(\mathcal{X})$.

The next theorem provides two alternative characterizations of Weyl-covariant maps. One characterization states that a map is Weyl-covariant if and only if each discrete Weyl operator is an eigenoperator of that map.[2] The other characterization states that a map is Weyl-covariant if and only

---

[2] The term *eigenoperator* should be interpreted in the natural way, which is an operator analogue of an eigenvector for a linear map that acts on a space of operators.

if it is a linear combination of conjugations by discrete Weyl operators. The two characterizations are related by the discrete Fourier transform operator.

Theorem 4.14 *Let $\mathcal{X} = \mathbb{C}^{\mathbb{Z}_n}$ for a positive integer n, and let $\Phi \in \mathrm{T}(\mathcal{X})$ be a map. The following statements are equivalent:*

1. *Φ is a Weyl-covariant map.*
2. *There exists an operator $A \in \mathrm{L}(\mathcal{X})$ such that*
$$\Phi(W_{a,b}) = A(a,b)W_{a,b} \tag{4.84}$$
   for all $(a,b) \in \mathbb{Z}_n \times \mathbb{Z}_n$.
3. *There exists an operator $B \in \mathrm{L}(\mathcal{X})$ such that*
$$\Phi(X) = \sum_{a,b \in \mathbb{Z}_n} B(a,b)W_{a,b}XW_{a,b}^* \tag{4.85}$$
   for all $X \in \mathrm{L}(\mathcal{X})$.

Under the assumption that these three statements hold, the operators A and B in statements 2 and 3 are related by the equation
$$A^{\mathsf{T}} = nF^*BF. \tag{4.86}$$

Proof Assume Φ is a Weyl-covariant map and consider the operator
$$W_{a,b}^*\Phi(W_{a,b}), \tag{4.87}$$

for $(a,b) \in \mathbb{Z}_n \times \mathbb{Z}_n$ chosen arbitrarily. For every choice of $(c,d) \in \mathbb{Z}_n \times \mathbb{Z}_n$, it holds that
$$\begin{aligned}
W_{a,b}^*\Phi(W_{a,b})W_{c,d}^* &= W_{a,b}^*W_{c,d}^*W_{c,d}\Phi(W_{a,b})W_{c,d}^* \\
&= W_{a,b}^*W_{c,d}^*\Phi(W_{c,d}W_{a,b}W_{c,d}^*) \\
&= W_{c,d}^*W_{a,b}^*\Phi(W_{a,b}W_{c,d}W_{c,d}^*) \\
&= W_{c,d}^*W_{a,b}^*\Phi(W_{a,b}), \tag{4.88}
\end{aligned}$$

where the second equality has used the Weyl covariance of Φ and the third equality has used the fact that
$$W_{c,d}W_{a,b} = \alpha\, W_{a,b}W_{c,d} \quad \text{and} \quad W_{a,b}^*W_{c,d}^* = \overline{\alpha}\, W_{c,d}^*W_{a,b}^* \tag{4.89}$$

for $\alpha = \zeta^{ad-bc}$. It follows that
$$[W_{a,b}^*\Phi(W_{a,b}), W_{c,d}^*] = 0 \tag{4.90}$$

for all $(c,d) \in \mathbb{Z}_n \times \mathbb{Z}_n$. As the set of all discrete Weyl operators forms a basis for $\mathrm{L}(\mathcal{X})$, it must therefore hold that $W_{a,b}^*\Phi(W_{a,b})$ commutes with all operators in $\mathrm{L}(\mathcal{X})$, and is therefore equal to a scalar multiple of the identity operator.

As this is true for every choice of $(a, b) \in \mathbb{Z}_n \times \mathbb{Z}_n$, it follows that one may choose an operator $A \in \mathrm{L}(\mathcal{X})$ so that

$$W_{a,b}^* \Phi(W_{a,b}) = A(a, b)\mathbb{1}, \tag{4.91}$$

and therefore

$$\Phi(W_{a,b}) = A(a, b)W_{a,b}, \tag{4.92}$$

for all $(a, b) \in \mathbb{Z}_n \times \mathbb{Z}_n$. Statement 1 therefore implies statement 2.

The reverse implication, that statement 2 implies statement 1, is implied by the commutation relation (4.75). In greater detail, suppose statement 2 holds, and let $(a, b) \in \mathbb{Z}_n \times \mathbb{Z}_n$. For each pair $(c, d) \in \mathbb{Z}_n \times \mathbb{Z}_n$, one has

$$\begin{aligned}
\Phi(W_{a,b}W_{c,d}W_{a,b}^*) &= \zeta^{bc-ad}\Phi(W_{c,d}) = A(c, d)\zeta^{bc-ad}W_{c,d} \\
&= A(c, d)W_{a,b}W_{c,d}W_{a,b}^* = W_{a,b}\Phi(W_{c,d})W_{a,b}^*,
\end{aligned} \tag{4.93}$$

and therefore, again using the fact that the discrete Weyl operators form a basis for $\mathrm{L}(\mathcal{X})$, one has

$$\Phi(W_{a,b}XW_{a,b}^*) = W_{a,b}\Phi(X)W_{a,b}^* \tag{4.94}$$

for all $X \in \mathrm{L}(\mathcal{X})$ by linearity.

Now assume statement 3 holds for some choice of $B \in \mathrm{L}(\mathcal{X})$. Using the commutation relation (4.75) once again, it follows that

$$\Phi(W_{c,d}) = \sum_{a,b \in \mathbb{Z}_n} B(a, b)W_{a,b}W_{c,d}W_{a,b}^* = \sum_{a,b \in \mathbb{Z}_n} \zeta^{bc-ad}B(a, b)W_{c,d} \tag{4.95}$$

for every pair $(c, d) \in \mathbb{Z}_n \times \mathbb{Z}_n$. Choosing $A \in \mathrm{L}(\mathcal{X})$ so that

$$A(c, d) = \sum_{a,b \in \mathbb{Z}_n} \zeta^{bc-ad}B(a, b) \tag{4.96}$$

for all $(c, d) \in \mathbb{Z}_n \times \mathbb{Z}_n$, which is equivalent to $A = (nF^*BF)^\mathsf{T}$, one has that

$$\Phi(W_{c,d}) = A(c, d)W_{c,d} \tag{4.97}$$

for all $(c, d) \in \mathbb{Z}_n \times \mathbb{Z}_n$. Statement 3 therefore implies statement 2, with the operators A and B being related as claimed.

Finally, assume statement 2 holds for some choice of $A \in \mathrm{L}(\mathcal{X})$, and define $B = \frac{1}{n}FA^\mathsf{T}F^*$. By a similar calculation to the one used to establish the previous implication, one has

$$\begin{aligned}
\Phi(W_{c,d}) &= A(c, d)W_{c,d} \\
&= \sum_{a,b \in \mathbb{Z}_n} \zeta^{bc-ad}B(a, b)W_{c,d} = \sum_{a,b \in \mathbb{Z}_n} B(a, b)W_{a,b}W_{c,d}W_{a,b}^*
\end{aligned} \tag{4.98}$$

for every pair $(c, d) \in \mathbb{Z}_n \times \mathbb{Z}_n$, and therefore

$$\Phi(X) = \sum_{a,b \in \mathbb{Z}_n} B(a, b) W_{a,b} X W_{a,b}^* \qquad (4.99)$$

for all $X \in L(\mathcal{X})$ by linearity. Statement 2 therefore implies statement 3, where again A and B are related as claimed. $\qquad \square$

Corollary 4.15 *Let $\mathcal{X} = \mathbb{C}^{\mathbb{Z}_n}$ for a positive integer n, and let $\Phi \in C(\mathcal{X})$ be a Weyl-covariant channel. There exists a probability vector $p \in \mathcal{P}(\mathbb{Z}_n \times \mathbb{Z}_n)$ such that*

$$\Phi(X) = \sum_{a,b \in \mathbb{Z}_n} p(a, b) W_{a,b} X W_{a,b}^* \qquad (4.100)$$

for all $X \in L(\mathcal{X})$. In particular, it holds that Φ is a mixed-unitary channel.

Proof By Theorem 4.14, there exists an operator $B \in L(\mathcal{X})$ such that

$$\Phi(X) = \sum_{a,b \in \mathbb{Z}_n} B(a, b) W_{a,b} X W_{a,b}^* \qquad (4.101)$$

for all $X \in L(\mathcal{X})$. It follows that

$$J(\Phi) = \sum_{a,b \in \mathbb{Z}_n} B(a, b) \operatorname{vec}(W_{a,b}) \operatorname{vec}(W_{a,b})^*, \qquad (4.102)$$

which is a positive semidefinite operator given the assumption that Φ is completely positive. This implies that $B(a, b)$ is nonnegative for every pair $(a, b) \in \mathbb{Z}_n \times \mathbb{Z}_n$, by virtue of the fact that the vectors

$$\{\operatorname{vec}(W_{a,b}) : a, b \in \mathbb{Z}_n\} \qquad (4.103)$$

form an orthogonal set. It holds that

$$\operatorname{Tr}(\Phi(X)) = \sum_{a,b \in \mathbb{Z}_n} B(a, b) \operatorname{Tr}(W_{a,b} X W_{a,b}^*) = \sum_{a,b \in \mathbb{Z}_n} B(a, b) \operatorname{Tr}(X) \quad (4.104)$$

for every $X \in L(\mathcal{X})$, and therefore

$$\sum_{a,b \in \mathbb{Z}_n} B(a, b) = 1 \qquad (4.105)$$

by the assumption that Φ preserves trace. Defining $p(a, b) = B(a, b)$ for every pair $(a, b) \in \mathbb{Z}_n \times \mathbb{Z}_n$, one has that p is a probability vector, which completes the proof. $\qquad \square$

Completely Depolarizing and Dephasing Channels

The *completely depolarizing channel* $\Omega \in C(\mathcal{X})$ and the *completely dephasing channel* $\Delta \in C(\mathcal{X})$ are defined, for any choice of a complex Euclidean space $\mathcal{X} = \mathbb{C}^\Sigma$, as follows:

$$\Omega(X) = \frac{\operatorname{Tr}(X)}{\dim(\mathcal{X})} \mathbb{1}_\mathcal{X} \quad \text{and} \quad \Delta(X) = \sum_{a \in \Sigma} X(a,a) E_{a,a} \tag{4.106}$$

for all $X \in L(\mathcal{X})$ (q.v. Section 2.2.3). In the case that the complex Euclidean space $\mathcal{X}$ takes the form $\mathcal{X} = \mathbb{C}^{\mathbb{Z}_n}$ for a positive integer n, these channels are both examples of Weyl-covariant channels.

The fact that the completely depolarizing channel is a Weyl-covariant channel follows from the observation that

$$\Omega(W_{a,b}) = \begin{cases} W_{a,b} & \text{if } (a,b) = (0,0) \\ 0 & \text{if } (a,b) \neq (0,0), \end{cases} \tag{4.107}$$

or equivalently $\Omega(W_{a,b}) = E_{0,0}(a,b) W_{a,b}$, for every $(a,b) \in \mathbb{Z}_n \times \mathbb{Z}_n$. Thus, by Theorem 4.14, together with the observation that

$$\frac{1}{n} F E_{0,0} F^* = \frac{1}{n^2} \sum_{a,b \in \mathbb{Z}_n} E_{a,b}, \tag{4.108}$$

one has that

$$\Omega(X) = \frac{1}{n^2} \sum_{a,b \in \mathbb{Z}_n} W_{a,b} X W_{a,b}^* \tag{4.109}$$

for all $X \in L(\mathcal{X})$. An alternative way to establish the validity of (4.109) is to observe that the Choi operator of the map defined by the right-hand side of that equation is in agreement with the Choi operator of Ω:

$$\frac{1}{n^2} \sum_{a,b \in \mathbb{Z}_n} \operatorname{vec}(W_{a,b}) \operatorname{vec}(W_{a,b})^* = \frac{1}{n} \mathbb{1}_\mathcal{X} \otimes \mathbb{1}_\mathcal{X} = J(\Omega). \tag{4.110}$$

As mentioned in the footnote on page 212, one may translate the notion of a discrete Weyl operator from a space of the form $\mathbb{C}^{\mathbb{Z}_n}$ to an arbitrary complex Euclidean space $\mathbb{C}^\Sigma$ through any fixed correspondence between the elements of Σ and $\mathbb{Z}_n$ (assuming $n = |\Sigma|$). It follows that the completely depolarizing channel $\Omega \in C(\mathcal{X})$ is a mixed-unitary channel for any choice of a complex Euclidean space $\mathcal{X} = \mathbb{C}^\Sigma$, as it is equal to the Weyl-covariant channel defined above with respect to any chosen correspondence between Σ and $\mathbb{Z}_n$.

The completely dephasing channel is a Weyl-covariant channel, as is evident from the observation that

$$\Delta(W_{a,b}) = \begin{cases} W_{a,b} & \text{if } a = 0 \\ 0 & \text{if } a \neq 0, \end{cases} \tag{4.111}$$

or equivalently $\Delta(W_{a,b}) = A(a,b)W_{a,b}$ for

$$A = \sum_{c \in \mathbb{Z}_n} E_{0,c}, \tag{4.112}$$

for all $(a,b) \in \mathbb{Z}_n \times \mathbb{Z}_n$. By Theorem 4.14, together with the observation that $FA^{\mathsf{T}}F^* = A$, it follows that

$$\Delta(X) = \frac{1}{n} \sum_{c \in \mathbb{Z}_n} W_{0,c} X W_{0,c}^* \tag{4.113}$$

for all $X \in \mathrm{L}(\mathcal{X})$.

4.1.3 Schur Channels

Schur channels, which are defined as follows, represent another interesting subclass of unital channels.

Definition 4.16 Let $\mathcal{X} = \mathbb{C}^\Sigma$ be a complex Euclidean space, for Σ an alphabet. A map $\Phi \in \mathrm{T}(\mathcal{X})$ is said to be a *Schur map* if there exists an operator $A \in \mathrm{L}(\mathcal{X})$ satisfying

$$\Phi(X) = A \odot X, \tag{4.114}$$

where $A \odot X$ denotes the entry-wise product of A and X:

$$(A \odot X)(a,b) = A(a,b)X(a,b) \tag{4.115}$$

for all $a, b \in \Sigma$. If, in addition, the map Φ is a channel, then it is said to be a *Schur channel*.

The following proposition provides a simple condition under which a given Schur map is completely positive (or, equivalently, positive).

Proposition 4.17 *Let Σ be an alphabet, let $\mathcal{X} = \mathbb{C}^\Sigma$, let $A \in \mathrm{L}(\mathcal{X})$ be an operator, and let $\Phi \in \mathrm{T}(\mathcal{X})$ be the Schur map defined as $\Phi(X) = A \odot X$ for all $X \in \mathrm{L}(\mathcal{X})$. The following statements are equivalent:*

1. *A is positive semidefinite.*
2. *Φ is positive.*
3. *Φ is completely positive.*

Proof Suppose A is positive semidefinite. It holds that

$$J(\Phi) = \sum_{a,b \in \Sigma} \Phi(E_{a,b}) \otimes E_{a,b} = \sum_{a,b \in \Sigma} A(a,b) E_{a,b} \otimes E_{a,b} = VAV^* \quad (4.116)$$

for $V \in \mathrm{U}(\mathcal{X}, \mathcal{X} \otimes \mathcal{X})$ being the isometry defined as

$$V = \sum_{a \in \Sigma} (e_a \otimes e_a) e_a^*. \quad (4.117)$$

This implies that $J(\Phi)$ is positive semidefinite, so Φ is completely positive by Theorem 2.22. It has been proved that statement 1 implies statement 3.

Statement 3 trivially implies statement 2, as every completely positive map is positive.

Finally, assume that Φ is positive. The operator $X \in \mathrm{L}(\mathcal{X})$ whose entries are all equal to 1 (i.e., $X(a,b) = 1$ for all $a, b \in \Sigma$) is positive semidefinite. By the positivity of Φ, it therefore holds that $\Phi(X) = A$ is positive semidefinite. Statement 2 therefore implies statement 1, which completes the proof. $\qquad \square$

In a similar spirit to the previous proposition, the following proposition provides a simple condition under which a given Schur map preserves trace (or, equivalently, is unital).

Proposition 4.18 *Let Σ be an alphabet, let $\mathcal{X} = \mathbb{C}^\Sigma$, let $A \in \mathrm{L}(\mathcal{X})$ be an operator, and let $\Phi \in \mathrm{T}(\mathcal{X})$ be the Schur map defined as*

$$\Phi(X) = A \odot X \quad (4.118)$$

for all $X \in \mathrm{L}(\mathcal{X})$. The following statements are equivalent:

1. *$A(a,a) = 1$ for every $a \in \Sigma$.*
2. *Φ preserves trace.*
3. *Φ is unital.*

Proof Suppose $A(a,a) = 1$ for every $a \in \Sigma$. It follows that Φ is unital, as

$$\Phi(\mathbb{1}) = A \odot \mathbb{1} = \sum_{a \in \Sigma} A(a,a) E_{a,a} = \sum_{a \in \Sigma} E_{a,a} = \mathbb{1}. \quad (4.119)$$

It also follows that Φ preserves trace, as

$$\mathrm{Tr}(\Phi(X)) = \sum_{a \in \Sigma} (A \odot X)(a,a)$$
$$= \sum_{a \in \Sigma} A(a,a) X(a,a) = \sum_{a \in \Sigma} X(a,a) = \mathrm{Tr}(X) \quad (4.120)$$

for all $X \in \mathrm{L}(\mathcal{X})$.

The assumption that Φ preserves trace implies that

$$A(a, a) = \mathrm{Tr}(A(a, a)E_{a,a}) = \mathrm{Tr}(\Phi(E_{a,a})) = \mathrm{Tr}(E_{a,a}) = 1 \qquad (4.121)$$

for all $a \in \Sigma$. Statements 1 and 2 are therefore equivalent.

Finally, the assumption that Φ is unital implies

$$\sum_{a \in \Sigma} A(a, a)E_{a,a} = \Phi(\mathbb{1}) = \mathbb{1} = \sum_{a \in \Sigma} E_{a,a}, \qquad (4.122)$$

and therefore $A(a, a) = 1$ for every $a \in \Sigma$. Statements 1 and 3 are therefore equivalent. $\qquad \square$

Completely positive Schur maps may alternatively be characterized as the class of maps having Kraus representations consisting only of equal pairs of diagonal operators, as the following theorem states.

Theorem 4.19 *Let Σ be an alphabet, let $\mathcal{X} = \mathbb{C}^{\Sigma}$ be the complex Euclidean space indexed by Σ, and let $\Phi \in \mathrm{CP}(\mathcal{X})$ be a completely positive map. The following statements are equivalent:*

1. *Φ is a Schur map.*
2. *There exists a Kraus representation of Φ having the form*

$$\Phi(X) = \sum_{a \in \Gamma} A_a X A_a^*, \qquad (4.123)$$

   for some alphabet Γ, such that $A_a \in \mathrm{L}(\mathcal{X})$ is a diagonal operator for each $a \in \Gamma$.
3. *For every Kraus representation of Φ having the form (4.123), A_a is a diagonal operator for each $a \in \Gamma$.*

Proof Suppose first that Φ is a Schur map, given by

$$\Phi(X) = P \odot X \qquad (4.124)$$

for all $X \in \mathrm{L}(\mathcal{X})$, for some operator $P \in \mathrm{L}(\mathcal{X})$. By the assumption that Φ is completely positive, Proposition 4.17 implies that P is positive semidefinite. As was computed in the proof of that proposition, the Choi representation of Φ is given by

$$J(\Phi) = V P V^* \qquad (4.125)$$

for

$$V = \sum_{b \in \Sigma} (e_b \otimes e_b) e_b^*. \qquad (4.126)$$

Consider an arbitrary Kraus representation of Φ having the form (4.123), for some alphabet Γ and a collection $\{A_a : a \in \Gamma\} \subset \mathrm{L}(\mathcal{X})$ of operators. As the Choi representation of the map defined by the right-hand side of that equation must agree with (4.125), it holds that

$$\sum_{a \in \Gamma} \mathrm{vec}(A_a) \, \mathrm{vec}(A_a)^* = VPV^*, \qquad (4.127)$$

and therefore

$$\mathrm{vec}(A_a) \in \mathrm{im}(V) = \mathrm{span}\{e_b \otimes e_b : b \in \Sigma\} \qquad (4.128)$$

for every $a \in \Gamma$. This is equivalent to the condition that A_a is diagonal for every $a \in \Gamma$, and so it has been proved that statement 1 implies statement 3.

Statement 3 trivially implies statement 2, so it remains to prove that statement 2 implies statement 1. For a Kraus representation of Φ having the form (4.123), where Γ is an alphabet and $\{A_a : a \in \Gamma\}$ is a collection of diagonal operators, let $\{v_a : a \in \Gamma\} \subset \mathcal{X}$ be the collection of vectors satisfying $A_a = \mathrm{Diag}(v_a)$ for each $a \in \Gamma$, and define

$$P = \sum_{a \in \Gamma} v_a v_a^*. \qquad (4.129)$$

A calculation reveals that

$$P \odot X = \sum_{a \in \Gamma} \sum_{b,c \in \Sigma} X(b,c) \, v_a(b) \overline{v_a(c)} \, E_{b,c} = \sum_{a \in \Gamma} A_a X A_a^* \qquad (4.130)$$

for every $X \in \mathrm{L}(\mathcal{X})$. It has therefore been proved that Φ is a Schur map, so statement 2 implies statement 1 as required. $\qquad \square$

4.2 General Properties of Unital Channels

This section proves a few basic facts holding for unital channels in general. In particular, the extreme points of the set of all unital channels defined with respect to a given space are characterized, and properties relating to fixed points and norms of unital channels are established.

4.2.1 Extreme Points of the Set of Unital Channels

Theorem 2.31 provides a criterion through which one may determine if a given channel $\Phi \in \mathrm{C}(\mathcal{X})$ is an extreme point of the set of all channels $\mathrm{C}(\mathcal{X})$. Theorem 4.21, stated below, establishes that a similar criterion holds when the set $\mathrm{C}(\mathcal{X})$ is replaced by the set of all unital channels

$$\{\Phi \in \mathrm{C}(\mathcal{X}) : \Phi(\mathbb{1}_{\mathcal{X}}) = \mathbb{1}_{\mathcal{X}}\}. \qquad (4.131)$$

Indeed, the criterion for extremal unital channels will follow directly from Theorem 2.31, together with an embedding of the set (4.131) into the set of all channels of the form $C(\mathcal{X} \oplus \mathcal{X})$.

Assume that a complex Euclidean space $\mathcal{X}$ has been fixed, and define an operator

$$V \in L(\mathcal{X} \otimes \mathcal{X}, (\mathcal{X} \oplus \mathcal{X}) \otimes (\mathcal{X} \oplus \mathcal{X})) \tag{4.132}$$

by the equation

$$V \operatorname{vec}(X) = \operatorname{vec} \begin{pmatrix} X & 0 \\ 0 & X^{\mathsf{T}} \end{pmatrix} \tag{4.133}$$

holding for all operators $X \in L(\mathcal{X})$. It may be verified that $V^*V = 2\mathbb{1}_{\mathcal{X} \otimes \mathcal{X}}$. For every map $\Phi \in T(\mathcal{X})$, define $\phi(\Phi) \in T(\mathcal{X} \oplus \mathcal{X})$ to be the unique map for which the equation

$$J(\phi(\Phi)) = V J(\Phi) V^* \tag{4.134}$$

holds, and observe that the mapping $\phi \colon T(\mathcal{X}) \to T(\mathcal{X} \oplus \mathcal{X})$ defined in this way is linear and injective. If $\Phi \in T(\mathcal{X})$ is defined by a Kraus representation

$$\Phi(X) = \sum_{a \in \Sigma} A_a X B_a^*, \tag{4.135}$$

then it holds that

$$\phi(\Phi) \begin{pmatrix} X_{0,0} & X_{0,1} \\ X_{1,0} & X_{1,1} \end{pmatrix} = \sum_{a \in \Sigma} \begin{pmatrix} A_a & 0 \\ 0 & A_a^{\mathsf{T}} \end{pmatrix} \begin{pmatrix} X_{0,0} & X_{0,1} \\ X_{1,0} & X_{1,1} \end{pmatrix} \begin{pmatrix} B_a & 0 \\ 0 & B_a^{\mathsf{T}} \end{pmatrix}^* \tag{4.136}$$

is a Kraus representation of $\phi(\Phi)$. The following observations concerning the mapping $\phi \colon T(\mathcal{X}) \to T(\mathcal{X} \oplus \mathcal{X})$ may be verified:

1. A map $\Phi \in T(\mathcal{X})$ is completely positive if and only if $\phi(\Phi) \in T(\mathcal{X} \oplus \mathcal{X})$ is completely positive.
2. A map $\Phi \in T(\mathcal{X})$ is both trace-preserving and unital if and only if $\phi(\Phi) \in T(\mathcal{X} \oplus \mathcal{X})$ is trace-preserving.

In particular, $\Phi \in C(\mathcal{X})$ is a unital channel if and only if $\phi(\Phi) \in C(\mathcal{X} \oplus \mathcal{X})$ is a channel. In this case, $\phi(\Phi)$ will also happen to be unital.

Lemma 4.20 *Let $\mathcal{X}$ be a complex Euclidean space, let $\Phi \in C(\mathcal{X})$ be a unital channel, and let $\phi(\Phi) \in C(\mathcal{X} \oplus \mathcal{X})$ be the channel defined from Φ by the equation (4.134). It holds that Φ is an extreme point of the set of all unital channels in $C(\mathcal{X})$ if and only if $\phi(\Phi)$ is an extreme point of the set of channels $C(\mathcal{X} \oplus \mathcal{X})$.*

Proof Suppose first that Φ is not an extreme point of the set of all unital channels in $C(\mathcal{X})$, so that

$$\Phi = \lambda\Psi_0 + (1 - \lambda)\Psi_1 \tag{4.137}$$

for distinct unital channels $\Psi_0, \Psi_1 \in C(\mathcal{X})$ and a scalar $\lambda \in (0, 1)$. As the mapping ϕ is linear and injective, it therefore holds that

$$\phi(\Phi) = \lambda\phi(\Psi_0) + (1 - \lambda)\phi(\Psi_1), \tag{4.138}$$

which is a proper convex combination of distinct channels. This implies that $\phi(\Phi)$ is not an extreme point of the set of channels $C(\mathcal{X} \oplus \mathcal{X})$.

Suppose, on the other hand, that $\phi(\Phi)$ is not an extreme point of the set of channels $C(\mathcal{X} \oplus \mathcal{X})$, so that

$$\phi(\Phi) = \lambda\Xi_0 + (1 - \lambda)\Xi_1 \tag{4.139}$$

for distinct channels $\Xi_0, \Xi_1 \in C(\mathcal{X} \oplus \mathcal{X})$ and a scalar $\lambda \in (0, 1)$. Taking the Choi representations of both sides of this equation yields

$$V J(\Phi) V^* = \lambda J(\Xi_0) + (1 - \lambda) J(\Xi_1). \tag{4.140}$$

It therefore follows from Lemma 2.30 that

$$J(\Xi_0) = V Q_0 V^* \quad \text{and} \quad J(\Xi_1) = V Q_1 V^* \tag{4.141}$$

for some choice of positive semidefinite operators $Q_0, Q_1 \in \text{Pos}(\mathcal{X} \otimes \mathcal{X})$. Letting $\Psi_0, \Psi_1 \in T(\mathcal{X})$ be the maps defined by

$$J(\Psi_0) = Q_0 \quad \text{and} \quad J(\Psi_1) = Q_1, \tag{4.142}$$

one has

$$\Xi_0 = \phi(\Psi_0) \quad \text{and} \quad \Xi_1 = \phi(\Psi_1). \tag{4.143}$$

As Ξ_0 and Ξ_1 are distinct channels, it follows that Ψ_0 and Ψ_1 are distinct unital channels. It holds that

$$\phi(\Phi) = \lambda\phi(\Psi_0) + (1 - \lambda)\phi(\Psi_1) \tag{4.144}$$

and therefore

$$\Phi = \lambda\Psi_0 + (1 - \lambda)\Psi_1, \tag{4.145}$$

which implies that Φ is not an extreme point of the set of all unital channels in $C(\mathcal{X})$. $\qquad\square$

Theorem 4.21 *Let $\mathcal{X}$ be a complex Euclidean space, let $\Phi \in C(\mathcal{X})$ be a unital channel, let Σ be an alphabet, and let $\{A_a : a \in \Sigma\} \subset L(\mathcal{X})$ be a linearly independent set of operators satisfying*

$$\Phi(X) = \sum_{a \in \Sigma} A_a X A_a^* \tag{4.146}$$

for all $X \in L(\mathcal{X})$. The channel Φ is an extreme point of the set of all unital channels in $C(\mathcal{X})$ if and only if the collection

$$\left\{ \begin{pmatrix} A_b^* A_a & 0 \\ 0 & A_a A_b^* \end{pmatrix} : (a, b) \in \Sigma \times \Sigma \right\} \tag{4.147}$$

of operators is linearly independent.

Proof By Lemma 4.20, the channel Φ is an extreme point of the set of unital channels in $C(\mathcal{X})$ if and only if the channel $\phi(\Phi)$ is an extreme point of the set $C(\mathcal{X} \oplus \mathcal{X})$, for $\phi : T(\mathcal{X}) \to T(\mathcal{X} \oplus \mathcal{X})$ being the mapping defined by the equation (4.134). By Theorem 2.31, it follows that $\phi(\Phi)$ is an extreme point of the set of channels $C(\mathcal{X} \oplus \mathcal{X})$ if and only if

$$\left\{ \begin{pmatrix} A_b^* A_a & 0 \\ 0 & \overline{A_b} A_a^\mathsf{T} \end{pmatrix} : (a, b) \in \Sigma \times \Sigma \right\} \tag{4.148}$$

is a linearly independent collection of operators. Taking the transpose of the lower right-hand block, which does not change whether or not the set is linearly independent, it follows that $\phi(\Phi)$ is an extreme point of the set $C(\mathcal{X} \oplus \mathcal{X})$ if and only if the set (4.147) is linearly independent. $\square$

Unital Qubit Channels Are Mixed-Unitary

There exist non-mixed-unitary unital channels, as shown in Example 4.3. The existence of such channels, however, requires that the underlying space has dimension at least 3; when Theorem 4.21 is combined with the following lemma, one concludes that every unital qubit channel is mixed-unitary.

Lemma 4.22 *Let $\mathcal{X}$ be a complex Euclidean space and let $A_0, A_1 \in L(\mathcal{X})$ be operators such that*

$$A_0^* A_0 + A_1^* A_1 = \mathbb{1}_{\mathcal{X}} = A_0 A_0^* + A_1 A_1^*. \tag{4.149}$$

There exist unitary operators $U, V \in U(\mathcal{X})$ such that $V A_0 U^*$ and $V A_1 U^*$ are diagonal operators.

Proof It suffices to prove that there exists a unitary operator $W \in U(\mathcal{X})$ such that the operators $W A_0$ and $W A_1$ are both normal and satisfy

$$[W A_0, W A_1] = 0, \tag{4.150}$$

for then it follows by Theorem 1.5 that one may choose U so that $U W A_0 U^*$ and $U W A_1 U^*$ are diagonal, and then take $V = U W$.

Let $U_0, U_1 \in U(\mathcal{X})$ and $P_0, P_1 \in \text{Pos}(\mathcal{X})$ be operators providing the polar decompositions $A_0 = U_0 P_0$ and $A_1 = U_1 P_1$, and let $W = U_0^*$. It holds that $W A_0 = P_0$, which is positive semidefinite and therefore normal. To verify that $W A_1$ is normal, observe that the assumption (4.149) implies

$$U_1 P_1^2 U_1^* = \mathbb{1} - U_0 P_0^2 U_0^* \quad \text{and} \quad P_1^2 = \mathbb{1} - P_0^2, \tag{4.151}$$

and therefore

$$(W A_1)(W A_1)^* = U_0^* U_1 P_1^2 U_1^* U_0 = U_0^* (\mathbb{1} - U_0 P_0^2 U_0^*) U_0$$
$$= \mathbb{1} - P_0^2 = P_1^2 = P_1 U_1^* U_0 U_0^* U_1 P_1 = (W A_1)^* (W A_1). \tag{4.152}$$

It remains to prove that the operators $W A_0$ and $W A_1$ commute. It follows from the equation $P_1^2 = \mathbb{1} - P_0^2$ that P_0^2 and P_1^2 commute. As P_0^2 and P_1^2 are commuting positive semidefinite operators, it therefore holds that P_0 and P_1 commute. Substituting $P_1^2 = \mathbb{1} - P_0^2$ into the equation

$$U_1 P_1^2 U_1^* = \mathbb{1} - U_0 P_0^2 U_0^*, \tag{4.153}$$

one finds that

$$U_0 P_0^2 U_0^* = U_1 P_0^2 U_1^*, \tag{4.154}$$

and therefore, by taking the square root of both sides of this equation,

$$U_0 P_0 U_0^* = U_1 P_0 U_1^*. \tag{4.155}$$

This implies that

$$P_0 U_0^* U_1 = U_0^* U_1 P_0, \tag{4.156}$$

and therefore P_0 and $U_0^* U_1$ commute. It follows that

$$(W A_0)(W A_1) = P_0 U_0^* U_1 P_1 = U_0^* U_1 P_1 P_0 = (W A_1)(W A_0), \tag{4.157}$$

and so $W A_0$ and $W A_1$ commute, as required. $\qquad\square$

Theorem 4.23 *Let $\mathcal{X}$ be a complex Euclidean space with $\dim(\mathcal{X}) = 2$. Every unital channel $\Phi \in C(\mathcal{X})$ is a mixed-unitary channel.*

Proof The set

$$\{\Phi \in C(\mathcal{X}): \Phi(\mathbb{1}_\mathcal{X}) = \mathbb{1}_\mathcal{X}\} \tag{4.158}$$

of unital channels, defined with respect to the space $\mathcal{X}$, is both compact and convex; both of these properties are consequences of the fact that this set is equal to the intersection of the compact and convex set $C(\mathcal{X})$ with the (closed) affine subspace of all maps $\Phi \in T(\mathcal{X})$ satisfying $\Phi(\mathbb{1}_\mathcal{X}) = \mathbb{1}_\mathcal{X}$. As this set is compact and convex, Theorem 1.10 implies that it is equal to the convex hull of its extreme points. To complete the proof, it therefore suffices to establish that every unital channel $\Phi \in C(\mathcal{X})$ that is not a unitary channel is not an extreme point of the set (4.158).

Toward this goal, let $\Phi \in C(\mathcal{X})$ be an arbitrary unital channel, and let $\{A_a : a \in \Sigma\} \subset L(\mathcal{X})$ be a linearly independent collection of operators satisfying

$$\Phi(X) = \sum_{a \in \Sigma} A_a X A_a^* \tag{4.159}$$

for all $X \in L(\mathcal{X})$. One has that Φ is a unitary channel if and only if $|\Sigma| = 1$, so it suffices to prove that Φ is not an extreme point of the set (4.158) whenever $|\Sigma| \geq 2$.

By Theorem 4.21, the channel Φ is an extreme point of the set (4.158) if and only if

$$\left\{ \begin{pmatrix} A_b^* A_a & 0 \\ 0 & A_a A_b^* \end{pmatrix} : (a,b) \in \Sigma \times \Sigma \right\} \subset L(\mathcal{X} \oplus \mathcal{X}) \tag{4.160}$$

is a linearly independent collection of operators. There are two cases that must be considered: the first case is that $|\Sigma| \geq 3$ and the second case is that $|\Sigma| = 2$.

For the first case, one has that the collection (4.160) includes at least nine operators drawn from the eight-dimensional subspace

$$\left\{ \begin{pmatrix} X & 0 \\ 0 & Y \end{pmatrix} : X, Y \in L(\mathcal{X}) \right\}. \tag{4.161}$$

Thus, if $|\Sigma| \geq 3$, then the collection (4.160) cannot be linearly independent, and therefore Φ is not an extreme point of the set (4.158).

It remains to consider the case $|\Sigma| = 2$. There is no loss of generality in assuming $\Sigma = \{0,1\}$ and $\mathcal{X} = \mathbb{C}^\Sigma$. By the assumption that Φ is unital and preserves trace, it holds that

$$A_0^* A_0 + A_1^* A_1 = \mathbb{1}_\mathcal{X} = A_0 A_0^* + A_1 A_1^*. \tag{4.162}$$

By Lemma 4.22, there must exist unitary operators $U, V \in \mathrm{U}(\mathcal{X})$ such that $V A_0 U^*$ and $V A_1 U^*$ are diagonal operators:

$$V A_0 U^* = \alpha_0 E_{0,0} + \beta_0 E_{1,1},$$
$$V A_1 U^* = \alpha_1 E_{0,0} + \beta_1 E_{1,1}. \tag{4.163}$$

The following equations therefore hold for every choice of $a, b \in \Sigma$:

$$A_b^* A_a = \alpha_a \overline{\alpha_b} U^* E_{0,0} U + \beta_a \overline{\beta_b} U^* E_{1,1} U,$$
$$A_a A_b^* = \alpha_a \overline{\alpha_b} V^* E_{0,0} V + \beta_a \overline{\beta_b} V^* E_{1,1} V. \tag{4.164}$$

The set (4.160) is therefore contained in the subspace spanned by the set of operators

$$\left\{ \begin{pmatrix} U^* E_{0,0} U & 0 \\ 0 & V^* E_{0,0} V \end{pmatrix}, \begin{pmatrix} U^* E_{1,1} U & 0 \\ 0 & V^* E_{1,1} V \end{pmatrix} \right\}. \tag{4.165}$$

The collection (4.160) contains four operators drawn from a two-dimensional space, and therefore cannot be linearly independent. This implies that the channel Φ is not an extreme point of the set (4.158), which completes the proof. $\qquad\square$

4.2.2 Fixed Points, Spectra, and Norms of Unital Channels

Every channel of the form $\Phi \in \mathrm{C}(\mathcal{X})$ must have at least one density operator fixed point, meaning a density operator $\rho \in \mathrm{D}(\mathcal{X})$ satisfying

$$\Phi(\rho) = \rho. \tag{4.166}$$

One may see this fact as a consequence of the Brouwer fixed-point theorem, which states that every continuous function mapping a compact, convex set in a Euclidean space to itself must have a fixed point. The full power of the Brouwer fixed-point theorem is, however, really not needed in this case; the fact that channels are linear maps allows for a simpler proof. The following theorem establishes this fact in slightly greater generality, for any positive and trace-preserving map $\Phi \in \mathrm{T}(\mathcal{X})$.

Theorem 4.24 *Let $\mathcal{X}$ be a complex Euclidean space and let $\Phi \in \mathrm{T}(\mathcal{X})$ be a positive and trace-preserving map. There exists a density operator $\rho \in \mathrm{D}(\mathcal{X})$ such that $\Phi(\rho) = \rho$.*

Proof For each nonnegative integer n, define a map $\Psi_n \in \mathrm{T}(\mathcal{X})$ as

$$\Psi_n(X) = \frac{1}{2^n} \sum_{k=0}^{2^n - 1} \Phi^k(X) \tag{4.167}$$

for each $X \in L(\mathcal{X})$, and define a set

$$\mathcal{C}_n = \{\Psi_n(\rho) : \rho \in D(\mathcal{X})\}. \tag{4.168}$$

As Φ is linear, positive, and trace-preserving, the same is true of Ψ_n, and so it follows that $\mathcal{C}_n$ is a compact and convex subset of $D(\mathcal{X})$. By the convexity of the set $\mathcal{C}_n$, it holds that

$$\Psi_{n+1}(\rho) = \frac{1}{2}\Psi_n(\rho) + \frac{1}{2}\Psi_n\left(\Phi^{2^n}(\rho)\right) \in \mathcal{C}_n \tag{4.169}$$

for every $\rho \in D(\mathcal{X})$, and therefore $\mathcal{C}_{n+1} \subseteq \mathcal{C}_n$, for every n. As each $\mathcal{C}_n$ is compact and $\mathcal{C}_{n+1} \subseteq \mathcal{C}_n$ for all n, it follows that there must exist an element

$$\rho \in \mathcal{C}_0 \cap \mathcal{C}_1 \cap \cdots \tag{4.170}$$

contained in the intersection of all of these sets.

Now, fix any choice of ρ satisfying (4.170). For an arbitrary nonnegative integer n, it holds that $\rho = \Psi_n(\sigma)$ for some choice of $\sigma \in D(\mathcal{X})$, and therefore

$$\Phi(\rho) - \rho = \Phi(\Psi_n(\sigma)) - \Psi_n(\sigma) = \frac{\Phi^{2^n}(\sigma) - \sigma}{2^n}. \tag{4.171}$$

As the trace distance between two density operators cannot exceed 2, it follows that

$$\|\Phi(\rho) - \rho\|_1 \leq \frac{1}{2^{n-1}}. \tag{4.172}$$

This bound holds for every n, which implies $\|\Phi(\rho) - \rho\|_1 = 0$, and therefore $\Phi(\rho) = \rho$ as required. $\qquad\square$

There is, of course, no difficulty in proving the existence of a density operator fixed point of a unital channel: if $\Phi \in C(\mathcal{X})$ is a unital channel, then $\omega = \mathbb{1}_{\mathcal{X}}/\dim(\mathcal{X})$ is a density operator fixed point of Φ. What is more interesting is the fact that the collection of all operators $X \in L(\mathcal{X})$ satisfying $\Phi(X) = X$ forms a unital subalgebra of $L(\mathcal{X})$, as the following theorem implies.

Theorem 4.25 *Let $\mathcal{X}$ be a complex Euclidean space and let $\Phi \in C(\mathcal{X})$ be a unital channel. Also let Σ be an alphabet and let $\{A_a : a \in \Sigma\} \subset L(\mathcal{X})$ be a collection of operators satisfying*

$$\Phi(X) = \sum_{a \in \Sigma} A_a X A_a^* \tag{4.173}$$

for all $X \in L(\mathcal{X})$. For every $X \in L(\mathcal{X})$ it holds that $\Phi(X) = X$ if and only if $[X, A_a] = 0$ for every $a \in \Sigma$.

Proof If $X \in L(\mathcal{X})$ is an operator for which $[X, A_a] = 0$ for every $a \in \Sigma$, then

$$\Phi(X) = \sum_{a \in \Sigma} A_a X A_a^* = \sum_{a \in \Sigma} X A_a A_a^* = X\Phi(\mathbb{1}) = X, \qquad (4.174)$$

where the last equality follows from the assumption that Φ is unital.

Now suppose that $X \in L(\mathcal{X})$ is an operator for which $\Phi(X) = X$, and consider the positive semidefinite operator

$$\sum_{a \in \Sigma} [X, A_a] [X, A_a]^*. \qquad (4.175)$$

Expanding this operator and using the assumptions that Φ is unital and $\Phi(X) = X$ (and therefore $\Phi(X^*) = \Phi(X)^* = X^*$, as Φ must be Hermitian-preserving), one has

$$\sum_{a \in \Sigma} [X, A_a] [X, A_a]^*$$

$$= \sum_{a \in \Sigma} (X A_a - A_a X)(A_a^* X^* - X^* A_a^*)$$

$$= \sum_{a \in \Sigma} (X A_a A_a^* X^* - A_a X A_a^* X^* - X A_a X^* A_a^* + A_a X X^* A_a^*) \qquad (4.176)$$

$$= X X^* - \Phi(X) X^* - X \Phi(X^*) + \Phi(X X^*)$$

$$= \Phi(X X^*) - X X^*.$$

As Φ is a channel, and is therefore trace-preserving, it holds that the trace of the operator represented by the previous equation is zero. The only traceless positive semidefinite operator is the zero operator, and therefore

$$\sum_{a \in \Sigma} [X, A_a] [X, A_a]^* = 0. \qquad (4.177)$$

This implies that each of the terms $[X, A_a] [X, A_a]^*$ is zero, and therefore each operator $[X, A_a]$ is zero. $\qquad \square$

For any channel of the form $\Phi \in C(\mathcal{X})$, for $\mathcal{X}$ being a complex Euclidean space, one has that the natural representation of Φ is a square operator of the form $K(\Phi) \in L(\mathcal{X} \otimes \mathcal{X})$. The following proposition establishes that the spectral radius of $K(\Phi)$ is necessarily equal to 1.

Proposition 4.26 *Let $\mathcal{X}$ be a complex Euclidean space and let $\Phi \in T(\mathcal{X})$ be a positive and trace-preserving map. The spectral radius of $K(\Phi)$ is equal to 1.*

Proof By Theorem 4.24, there must exist a density operator $\rho \in D(\mathcal{X})$ such that $\Phi(\rho) = \rho$, which implies that $K(\Phi)$ has an eigenvalue equal to 1.

It remains to prove that every eigenvalue of $K(\Phi)$ is at most 1 in absolute value, which is equivalent to the statement that $|\lambda| \leq 1$ for every choice of a nonzero operator $X \in L(\mathcal{X})$ and a complex number $\lambda \in \mathbb{C}$ satisfying

$$\Phi(X) = \lambda X. \tag{4.178}$$

Suppose that $X \in L(\mathcal{X})$ is a nonzero operator and $\lambda \in \mathbb{C}$ is a scalar satisfying (4.178). By Corollary 3.40, it holds that $\|\Phi\|_1 = 1$, and therefore

$$1 \geq \frac{\|\Phi(X)\|_1}{\|X\|_1} = \frac{\|\lambda X\|_1}{\|X\|_1} = |\lambda|. \tag{4.179}$$

The required bound on λ holds, which completes the proof. $\square$

While the spectral radius of the natural representation $K(\Phi)$ of every channel $\Phi \in C(\mathcal{X})$ must equal 1, the spectral norm of $K(\Phi)$ will not generally be 1. As the following theorem establishes, this happens if and only if Φ is a unital channel. Similar to Theorem 4.24 and Proposition 4.26, the property of complete positivity is not needed in the proof of this fact, and so it holds not only for channels, but also for all positive and trace-preserving maps.

Theorem 4.27 *Let $\mathcal{X}$ be a complex Euclidean space and let $\Phi \in T(\mathcal{X})$ be a positive and trace-preserving map. It holds that Φ is unital if and only if $\|K(\Phi)\| = 1$.*

Proof Assume first that Φ is a unital map. It is evident that $\|K(\Phi)\| \geq 1$, as Proposition 4.26 has established that the spectral radius of $K(\Phi)$ is 1, and the spectral norm of any square operator is at least as large as its spectral radius. It therefore suffices to prove that $\|K(\Phi)\| \leq 1$, which is equivalent to the condition that

$$\|\Phi(X)\|_2 \leq \|X\|_2 \tag{4.180}$$

for all $X \in L(\mathcal{X})$.

Consider first an arbitrary Hermitian operator $H \in \text{Herm}(\mathcal{X})$. Let

$$H = \sum_{k=1}^{n} \lambda_k x_k x_k^* \tag{4.181}$$

be a spectral decomposition of H, for $n = \dim(\mathcal{X})$, and let

$$\rho_k = \Phi(x_k x_k^*) \tag{4.182}$$

for each $k \in \{1, \ldots, n\}$. One has that $\rho_1, \ldots, \rho_n$ are density operators, as a consequence of the fact that Φ is positive and preserves trace. Moreover, as Φ is unital, it follows that $\rho_1 + \cdots + \rho_n = \mathbb{1}$. It holds that

$$\left\| \Phi(H) \right\|_2^2 = \left\| \lambda_1 \rho_1 + \cdots + \lambda_n \rho_n \right\|_2^2 = \sum_{1 \le j,k \le n} \lambda_j \lambda_k \langle \rho_j, \rho_k \rangle. \tag{4.183}$$

The Cauchy–Schwarz inequality implies that

$$\sum_{1 \le j,k \le n} \lambda_j \lambda_k \langle \rho_j, \rho_k \rangle$$

$$\le \sqrt{\sum_{1 \le j,k \le n} \lambda_j^2 \langle \rho_j, \rho_k \rangle} \sqrt{\sum_{1 \le j,k \le n} \lambda_k^2 \langle \rho_j, \rho_k \rangle} = \sum_{k=1}^{n} \lambda_k^2 = \left\| H \right\|_2^2, \tag{4.184}$$

where the first equality has followed from the fact that $\rho_1 + \cdots + \rho_n = \mathbb{1}$. It has therefore been established that $\| \Phi(H) \|_2 \le \| H \|_2$ for all Hermitian operators $H \in \mathrm{Herm}(\mathcal{X})$.

Now consider any operator $X \in \mathrm{L}(\mathcal{X})$, written as $X = H + iK$ for

$$H = \frac{X + X^*}{2} \quad \text{and} \quad K = \frac{X - X^*}{2i} \tag{4.185}$$

being Hermitian operators, and observe that

$$\left\| X \right\|_2^2 = \left\| H \right\|_2^2 + \left\| K \right\|_2^2. \tag{4.186}$$

As Φ is necessarily Hermitian-preserving, one finds that

$$\left\| \Phi(X) \right\|_2^2 = \left\| \Phi(H) + i\Phi(K) \right\|_2^2 = \left\| \Phi(H) \right\|_2^2 + \left\| \Phi(K) \right\|_2^2. \tag{4.187}$$

Therefore

$$\left\| \Phi(X) \right\|_2^2 = \left\| \Phi(H) \right\|_2^2 + \left\| \Phi(K) \right\|_2^2 \le \left\| H \right\|_2^2 + \left\| K \right\|_2^2 = \left\| X \right\|_2^2, \tag{4.188}$$

so $\| \Phi(X) \|_2 \le \| X \|_2$. It has therefore been proved that, if Φ is unital, then $\| K(\Phi) \| = 1$.

Now suppose that $\| K(\Phi) \| = 1$, which is equivalent to the condition that $\| \Phi(X) \|_2 \le \| X \|_2$ for every $X \in \mathrm{L}(\mathcal{X})$. In particular, it must hold that

$$\left\| \Phi(\mathbb{1}) \right\|_2 \le \left\| \mathbb{1} \right\|_2 = \sqrt{n}, \tag{4.189}$$

for $n = \dim(\mathcal{X})$. As Φ is positive and preserves trace, one has that $\Phi(\mathbb{1})$ is positive semidefinite and has trace equal to n. When these observations are combined with the Cauchy–Schwarz inequality, one finds that

$$n = \mathrm{Tr}\big(\Phi(\mathbb{1})\big) = \langle \mathbb{1}, \Phi(\mathbb{1}) \rangle \le \left\| \mathbb{1} \right\|_2 \left\| \Phi(\mathbb{1}) \right\|_2 \le n. \tag{4.190}$$

Equality is therefore obtained in the Cauchy–Schwarz inequality, implying that $\Phi(\mathbb{1})$ and $\mathbb{1}$ are linearly dependent. As $\mathrm{Tr}(\mathbb{1}) = \mathrm{Tr}(\Phi(\mathbb{1}))$, it follows that $\Phi(\mathbb{1})$ and $\mathbb{1}$ must in fact be equal, and therefore Φ is unital. $\qquad\square$

4.3 Majorization

This section introduces the *majorization* relation for Hermitian operators, which is a generalization of a similar concept for real vectors. Intuitively speaking, the majorization relation formalizes the notion of one object being obtained from another through a certain sort of "random mixing process."

One may formalize the majorization relation, both for real vectors and for Hermitian operators, in multiple, equivalent ways. Once formalized, it is a very useful mathematical concept. In the theory of quantum information, majorization has a particularly striking application in the form of Nielsen's theorem (Theorem 6.33 in Chapter 6), which gives a precise characterization of the possible transformations between bipartite pure states that may be performed by two individuals whose communications with one another are restricted to classical information transmissions.

4.3.1 Majorization for Real Vectors

The definition of the majorization relation for real vectors to be presented in this book is based on the class of *doubly stochastic* operators. A discussion of such operators follows, after which the majorization relation for real vectors is defined.

Doubly Stochastic Operators

Let Σ be an alphabet, and consider the real Euclidean space $\mathbb{R}^\Sigma$. An operator $A \in \mathrm{L}(\mathbb{R}^\Sigma)$ acting on this vector space is said to be *stochastic* if

1. $A(a, b) \geq 0$ for all $a, b \in \Sigma$, and
2. $\sum_{a \in \Sigma} A(a, b) = 1$ for all $b \in \Sigma$.

This condition is equivalent to $A e_b$ being a probability vector for each $b \in \Sigma$, or equivalently, to the fact that A maps probability vectors to probability vectors.

An operator $A \in \mathrm{L}(\mathbb{R}^\Sigma)$ is said to be *doubly stochastic* if

1. $A(a, b) \geq 0$ for all $a, b \in \Sigma$,
2. $\sum_{a \in \Sigma} A(a, b) = 1$ for all $b \in \Sigma$, and
3. $\sum_{b \in \Sigma} A(a, b) = 1$ for all $a \in \Sigma$.

That is, an operator A is doubly stochastic if and only if both A and A^T (or, equivalently, both A and A^*) are stochastic, which is equivalent to the condition that every row and every column of the matrix representation of A forms a probability vector.

Doubly stochastic operators have a close relationship to *permutation operators*. For each permutation $\pi \in \mathrm{Sym}(\Sigma)$, one defines the permutation operator $V_\pi \in \mathrm{L}(\mathbb{R}^\Sigma)$ as

$$V_\pi(a, b) = \begin{cases} 1 & \text{if } a = \pi(b) \\ 0 & \text{otherwise} \end{cases} \tag{4.191}$$

for every $(a, b) \in \Sigma \times \Sigma$. Equivalently, V_π is the unique operator satisfying the equation $V_\pi e_b = e_{\pi(b)}$ for each $b \in \Sigma$. It is evident that permutation operators are doubly stochastic. The next theorem establishes that the set of all doubly stochastic operators is, in fact, equal to the convex hull of the permutation operators.

Theorem 4.28 (Birkhoff–von Neumann theorem) *Let Σ be an alphabet and let $A \in \mathrm{L}(\mathbb{R}^\Sigma)$ be an operator. It holds that A is doubly stochastic if and only if there exists a probability vector $p \in \mathcal{P}(\mathrm{Sym}(\Sigma))$ such that*

$$A = \sum_{\pi \in \mathrm{Sym}(\Sigma)} p(\pi) V_\pi. \tag{4.192}$$

Proof The set of all doubly stochastic operators acting on $\mathbb{R}^\Sigma$ is convex and compact, and is therefore equal to the convex hull of its extreme points by Theorem 1.10. The theorem will therefore follow from the demonstration that every extreme point of this set is a permutation operator. With this fact in mind, let A be a doubly stochastic operator that is not a permutation operator. It will be proved that A is not an extreme point of the set of doubly stochastic operators, which is sufficient to complete the proof.

Given that A is doubly stochastic but not a permutation operator, there must exist at least one pair $(a_1, b_1) \in \Sigma \times \Sigma$ such that $A(a_1, b_1) \in (0, 1)$. As $\sum_b A(a_1, b) = 1$ and $A(a_1, b_1) \in (0, 1)$, one may conclude that there exists an index $b_2 \neq b_1$ such that $A(a_1, b_2) \in (0, 1)$. Applying similar reasoning, but to the first index rather than the second, it follows that there must exist an index $a_2 \neq a_1$ such that $A(a_2, b_2) \in (0, 1)$. Repeating this argument, one may eventually find a closed loop of even length among the entries of A that are contained in the interval $(0, 1)$, alternating between the first and second indices (i.e., between rows and columns). A loop must eventually be formed, given that there are only finitely many entries in the matrix A; and an odd-length loop can be avoided by an appropriate choice for the entry that closes the loop. This process is illustrated in Figure 4.1.

Let $\varepsilon \in (0, 1)$ be equal to the minimum value over the entries in a closed loop of the form just described, and define B to be the operator obtained by setting each entry in the closed loop to be $\pm\varepsilon$, alternating sign among the

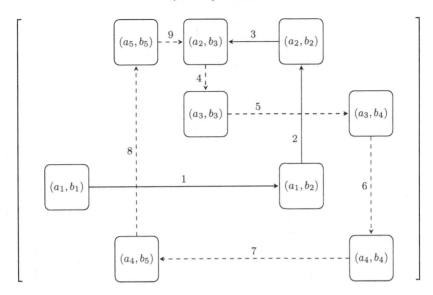

Figure 4.1 An example of a closed loop consisting of entries of A that are contained in the interval $(0,1)$. The loop is indicated by the dashed lines.

entries as suggested in Figure 4.2. All of the other entries in B are set to 0. Finally, consider the operators $A + B$ and $A - B$. As A is doubly stochastic and the row and column sums of B are all 0, it holds that both $A + B$ and $A - B$ also have row and column sums equal to 1. As ε was chosen to be no larger than the smallest entry within the chosen closed loop, none of the entries of $A + B$ or $A - B$ are negative, and therefore $A - B$ and $A + B$ are doubly stochastic. As B is nonzero, it holds that $A + B$ and $A - B$ are distinct. Thus,

$$A = \frac{1}{2}(A + B) + \frac{1}{2}(A - B) \tag{4.193}$$

is a proper convex combination of doubly stochastic operators, and therefore not an extreme point of the set of doubly stochastic operators. □

Definition and Characterizations of Majorization for Real Vectors

A definition of the majorization relation for vectors of real numbers, based on the actions of doubly stochastic operators, is as follows.

Definition 4.29 Let Σ be an alphabet and let $u, v \in \mathbb{R}^{\Sigma}$ be vectors. It is said that u *majorizes* v, written $v \prec u$, if there exists a doubly stochastic operator $A \in \mathrm{L}(\mathbb{R}^{\Sigma})$ for which $v = Au$.

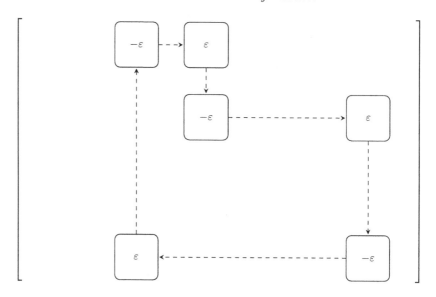

Figure 4.2 The operator B. All entries besides those indicated are 0.

By the Birkhoff–von Neumann theorem (Theorem 4.28), one may view this definition as formalizing the sort of "random mixing process" suggested at the beginning of the current section. An operator A is doubly stochastic if and only if it is equal to a convex combination of permutation operators, so the relation $v \prec u$ holds precisely when v can be obtained by randomly choosing a permutation $\pi \in \mathrm{Sym}(\Sigma)$, with respect to a chosen distribution $p \in \mathcal{P}(\mathrm{Sym}(\Sigma))$, shuffling the entries of u in accordance with the chosen permutation π, and then averaging the resulting vectors with respect to p.

The following theorem provides two alternative characterizations of the majorization relation for real vectors. The statement of the theorem makes use of the following notation: for every vector $u \in \mathbb{R}^{\Sigma}$ and for $n = |\Sigma|$, one writes

$$r(u) = (r_1(u), \dots, r_n(u)) \tag{4.194}$$

to denote the vector obtained by *sorting* the entries of u in decreasing order. In other words, one has

$$\{u(a) : a \in \Sigma\} = \{r_1(u), \dots, r_n(u)\}, \tag{4.195}$$

where the equality considers the two sides of the equation to be multisets, and moreover $r_1(u) \geq \cdots \geq r_n(u)$.

Theorem 4.30 *Let Σ be an alphabet and let $u, v \in \mathbb{R}^\Sigma$. The following statements are equivalent:*

1. $v \prec u$.
2. *For $n = |\Sigma|$, one has*

$$r_1(u) + \cdots + r_m(u) \geq r_1(v) + \cdots + r_m(v) \qquad (4.196)$$

for every choice of $m \in \{1, \ldots, n-1\}$, as well as

$$r_1(u) + \cdots + r_n(u) = r_1(v) + \cdots + r_n(v). \qquad (4.197)$$

3. *There exists a unitary operator $U \in \mathrm{U}(\mathbb{C}^\Sigma)$ such that, for the doubly stochastic operator $A \in \mathrm{L}(\mathbb{R}^\Sigma)$ defined as*

$$A(a, b) = |U(a, b)|^2 \qquad (4.198)$$

for all $a, b \in \Sigma$, one has $v = Au$.

Proof Assume first that statement 1 holds, so that there exists a doubly stochastic operator $A \in \mathrm{L}(\mathbb{R}^\Sigma)$ such that $Au = v$. It will be proved that

$$\sum_{a \in \Sigma} u(a) = \sum_{a \in \Sigma} v(a), \qquad (4.199)$$

and that, for every subset $S \subseteq \Sigma$, there exists a subset $T \subseteq \Sigma$ such that $|S| = |T|$ and

$$\sum_{a \in T} u(a) \geq \sum_{a \in S} v(a). \qquad (4.200)$$

This will imply statement 2; the condition (4.199) is equivalent to (4.197), while (4.200) implies (4.196) when one considers the case that S comprises the indices of the m largest entries of v, for each $m \in \{1, \ldots, n-1\}$. The first condition (4.199) is immediate from the assumption that A is stochastic:

$$\sum_{a \in \Sigma} v(a) = \sum_{a \in \Sigma} (Au)(a) = \sum_{a, b \in \Sigma} A(a, b)u(b) = \sum_{b \in \Sigma} u(b). \qquad (4.201)$$

To prove the second condition, observe first that the Birkhoff–von Neumann theorem (Theorem 4.28) implies that

$$A = \sum_{\pi \in \mathrm{Sym}(\Sigma)} p(\pi) V_\pi \qquad (4.202)$$

for some choice of a probability vector $p \in \mathcal{P}(\mathrm{Sym}(\Sigma))$. For an arbitrary choice of a subset $S \subseteq \Sigma$, the expression (4.202) implies that

$$\sum_{a \in S} v(a) = \sum_{a \in S} (Au)(a) = \sum_{\pi \in \mathrm{Sym}(\Sigma)} p(\pi) \sum_{b \in \pi^{-1}(S)} u(b). \qquad (4.203)$$

A convex combination of a collection of real numbers cannot exceed the maximal element in that set, and therefore there must exist a permutation $\pi \in \mathrm{Sym}(\Sigma)$ such that

$$\sum_{b \in \pi^{-1}(S)} u(b) \geq \sum_{a \in S} v(a). \tag{4.204}$$

As $|\pi^{-1}(S)| = |S|$, the inequality (4.200) has been proved for a suitable choice of an index set T. It has therefore been proved that statement 1 implies statement 2.

Next it will be proved that statement 2 implies statement 3, which is the most difficult implication of the proof. The implication will be proved by induction on $n = |\Sigma|$, for which the base case $n = 1$ is trivial. It will therefore be assumed that $n \geq 2$ for the remainder of the proof. As the majorization relationship is invariant under renaming and independently reordering the indices of the vectors under consideration, there is no loss of generality in assuming that $\Sigma = \{1, \ldots, n\}$, that $u = (u_1, \ldots, u_n)$ satisfies $u_1 \geq \cdots \geq u_n$, and that $v = (v_1, \ldots, v_n)$ satisfies $v_1 \geq \cdots \geq v_n$.

Under the assumption that statement 2 holds, it must be the case that $u_1 \geq v_1 \geq u_k$ for some choice of $k \in \{1, \ldots, n\}$. Fix k to be minimal among all such indices. There are two cases: $k = 1$ and $k > 1$.

If it is the case that $k = 1$, then $u_1 = v_1$, from which it follows that

$$u_2 + \cdots + u_m \geq v_2 + \cdots + v_m \tag{4.205}$$

for every $m \in \{2, \ldots, n-1\}$, as well as

$$u_2 + \cdots + u_n = v_2 + \cdots + v_n. \tag{4.206}$$

Define vectors $x = (u_2, \ldots, u_n)$ and $y = (v_2, \ldots, v_n)$. By the hypothesis of induction, there must therefore exist a unitary operator V, whose entries are indexed by the set $\{2, \ldots, n\}$, having the property that the doubly stochastic operator B defined by

$$B(a, b) = |V(a, b)|^2 \tag{4.207}$$

for all $a, b \in \{2, \ldots, n\}$ satisfies $y = Bx$. Taking U to be the unitary operator

$$U = \begin{pmatrix} 1 & 0 \\ 0 & V \end{pmatrix} \tag{4.208}$$

and letting A be defined by

$$A(a, b) = |U(a, b)|^2 \tag{4.209}$$

for all $a, b \in \{1, \ldots, n\}$, one has that $v = Au$, as required.

If it is the case that $k > 1$, then $u_1 > v_1 \geq u_k$, and so there must exist a real number $\lambda \in [0, 1)$ such that $v_1 = \lambda u_1 + (1 - \lambda)u_k$. Define vectors $x = (x_2, \ldots, x_n)$ and $y = (y_2, \ldots, y_n)$ as

$$x = (u_2, \ldots, u_{k-1}, (1 - \lambda)u_1 + \lambda u_k, u_{k+1}, \ldots, u_n),$$
$$y = (v_2, \ldots, v_n).$$

(4.210)

For $m \in \{2, \ldots, k-1\}$ it holds that

$$x_2 + \cdots + x_m = u_2 + \cdots + u_m > (m-1)v_1 \geq v_2 + \cdots + v_m, \quad (4.211)$$

by virtue of the fact that k is the minimal index for which $v_1 \geq u_k$. For $m \in \{k, \ldots, n\}$ it holds that

$$x_2 + \cdots + x_m$$

$$= (1 - \lambda)u_1 + u_2 + \cdots + u_{k-1} + \lambda u_k + u_{k+1} + \cdots + u_m \quad (4.212)$$

$$= u_1 + \cdots + u_m - v_1 \geq v_1 + \cdots + v_m - v_1 = v_2 + \cdots + v_m,$$

with equality when $m = n$. By the hypothesis of induction, there must therefore exist a unitary operator V, whose entries are indexed by the set $\{2, \ldots, n\}$, having the property that the doubly stochastic operator B defined by

$$B(a, b) = |V(a, b)|^2 \quad (4.213)$$

for every $a, b \in \{2, \ldots, n\}$ satisfies $y = Bx$. Let W be the unitary operator defined by

$$W e_1 = \sqrt{\lambda} e_1 - \sqrt{1 - \lambda} e_k,$$
$$W e_k = \sqrt{1 - \lambda} e_1 + \sqrt{\lambda} e_k,$$

(4.214)

and $W e_a = e_a$ for $a \in \{2, \ldots, n\}\backslash\{k\}$, and let

$$U = \begin{pmatrix} 1 & 0 \\ 0 & V \end{pmatrix} W. \quad (4.215)$$

The entries of U may be calculated explicitly:

$$
\begin{array}{ll}
U(1,1) = \sqrt{\lambda} & U(a, 1) = -\sqrt{1 - \lambda}V(a, k) \\
U(1, k) = \sqrt{1 - \lambda} & U(a, k) = \sqrt{\lambda}V(a, k) \\
U(1, b) = 0 & U(a, b) = V(a, b)
\end{array}
\quad (4.216)
$$

for $a \in \{2, \ldots, n\}$ and $b \in \{2, \ldots, n\}\backslash\{k\}$. Letting A be the doubly stochastic operator defined by

$$A(a, b) = |U(a, b)|^2 \quad (4.217)$$

for every $a, b \in \{1, \ldots, n\}$, one obtains an operator whose entries are given by

$$
\begin{aligned}
A(1, 1) &= \lambda & A(a, 1) &= (1 - \lambda)B(a, k) \\
A(1, k) &= 1 - \lambda & A(a, k) &= \lambda B(a, k) \\
A(1, b) &= 0 & A(a, b) &= B(a, b)
\end{aligned}
\tag{4.218}
$$

for $a \in \{2, \ldots, n\}$ and $b \in \{2, \ldots, n\} \setminus \{k\}$. Equivalently,

$$
A = \begin{pmatrix} 1 & 0 \\ 0 & B \end{pmatrix} D,
\tag{4.219}
$$

for D being the doubly stochastic operator defined by

$$
\begin{aligned}
De_1 &= \lambda e_1 + (1 - \lambda)e_k, \\
De_k &= (1 - \lambda)e_1 + \lambda e_k,
\end{aligned}
\tag{4.220}
$$

and $De_a = e_a$ for $a \in \{2, \ldots, n\} \setminus \{k\}$. It holds that

$$
Du = \begin{pmatrix} v_1 \\ x \end{pmatrix}
\tag{4.221}
$$

and therefore

$$
Au = \begin{pmatrix} v_1 \\ Bx \end{pmatrix} = v.
\tag{4.222}
$$

It has therefore been proved that statement 2 implies statement 3.

The final step is to observe that statement 3 implies statement 1, which is trivial, as the operator A determined by statement 3 must be doubly stochastic. $\qquad \square$

Remark In light of the equivalence between the first and third statements in Theorem 4.30, it is natural to ask if every doubly stochastic operator $A \in \mathrm{L}(\mathbb{R}^\Sigma)$ is given by $A(a, b) = |U(a, b)|^2$ for some choice of a unitary operator $U \in \mathrm{U}(\mathbb{C}^\Sigma)$. This is not the case: the operator

$$
A = \frac{1}{2} \begin{pmatrix} 0 & 1 & 1 \\ 1 & 0 & 1 \\ 1 & 1 & 0 \end{pmatrix}
\tag{4.223}
$$

in $\mathrm{L}(\mathbb{R}^3)$ is an example of a doubly stochastic operator that cannot be derived from a unitary operator in this fashion. Indeed, if A is to be derived from a unitary operator $U \in \mathrm{U}(\mathbb{C}^3)$, then U must take the form

$$
U = \frac{1}{\sqrt{2}} \begin{pmatrix} 0 & \alpha_2 & \alpha_1 \\ \alpha_3 & 0 & \beta_1 \\ \beta_3 & \beta_2 & 0 \end{pmatrix}
\tag{4.224}
$$

for $\alpha_1, \alpha_2, \alpha_3, \beta_1, \beta_2$, and β_3 complex numbers on the unit circle. However, if U is unitary, then it must hold that

$$\mathbb{1} = UU^* = \frac{1}{2} \begin{pmatrix} |\alpha_1|^2 + |\alpha_2|^2 & \alpha_1 \overline{\beta_1} & \alpha_2 \overline{\beta_2} \\ \overline{\alpha_1} \beta_1 & |\alpha_3|^2 + |\beta_1|^2 & \alpha_3 \overline{\beta_3} \\ \overline{\alpha_2} \beta_2 & \overline{\alpha_3} \beta_3 & |\beta_2|^2 + |\beta_3|^2 \end{pmatrix}. \qquad (4.225)$$

This is impossible, as none of the off-diagonal entries of the operator on the right-hand side of (4.225) can equal zero for $\alpha_1, \alpha_2, \alpha_3, \beta_1, \beta_2$, and β_3 being complex numbers on the unit circle.

4.3.2 Majorization for Hermitian Operators

The majorization relation for Hermitian operators will now be defined. This relation inherits the essential characteristics of its real vector analogue; and similar to its real vector analogue, it may be characterized in multiple ways. After a discussion of its alternative characterizations, two applications of majorization for Hermitian operators will be presented.

Definition and Characterizations of Majorization for Hermitian Operators

In analogy to the intuitive description of the majorization relation for real vectors suggested previously, one may view that one Hermitian operator X majorizes another Hermitian operator Y if it is the case that Y can be obtained from X through a "random mixing" process. One natural way to formalize the notion of "random mixing" for Hermitian operators is to consider mixed-unitary channels to be representative of such processes. The following definition adopts this viewpoint.

Definition 4.31   Let $X, Y \in \mathrm{Herm}(\mathcal{X})$ be Hermitian operators, for $\mathcal{X}$ a complex Euclidean space. It is said that X *majorizes* Y, written $Y \prec X$, if there exists a mixed-unitary channel $\Phi \in \mathrm{C}(\mathcal{X})$ for which $\Phi(X) = Y$.

There is, *a priori*, no reason to prefer Definition 4.31 over one possible alternative, in which the condition that Φ is mixed-unitary is replaced by the condition that Φ is a unital channel. This is indeed a natural alternative because unital channels are, in some sense, analogous to doubly stochastic operators acting on real Euclidean spaces, while mixed-unitary channels are analogous to convex combinations of permutation operators. The failure of a direct quantum analogue to the Birkhoff–von Neumann theorem to hold is responsible for this apparent difference between two possible definitions of majorization for Hermitian operators.

The following theorem demonstrates that these two alternatives are, in fact, equivalent. The theorem also provides two additional characterizations of the majorization relation for Hermitian operators.

Theorem 4.32 (Uhlmann)   *Let $X, Y \in \mathrm{Herm}(\mathcal{X})$ be Hermitian operators, for $\mathcal{X}$ a complex Euclidean space. The following statements are equivalent:*

1. *$Y \prec X$.*
2. *There exists a unital channel $\Phi \in \mathrm{C}(\mathcal{X})$ such that $Y = \Phi(X)$.*
3. *There exists a positive, trace-preserving, and unital map $\Phi \in \mathrm{T}(\mathcal{X})$ such that $Y = \Phi(X)$.*
4. *$\lambda(Y) \prec \lambda(X)$.*

Proof   Under the assumption that statement 1 holds, there exists a mixed-unitary channel $\Phi \in \mathrm{C}(\mathcal{X})$ such that $Y = \Phi(X)$. Such a channel is necessarily unital, and therefore statement 1 trivially implies statement 2. As every unital channel is positive, trace-preserving, and unital, statement 2 trivially implies statement 3.

Now assume that statement 3 holds. Let $n = \dim(\mathcal{X})$, and let

$$X = \sum_{j=1}^{n} \lambda_j(X)\, x_j x_j^* \quad \text{and} \quad Y = \sum_{k=1}^{n} \lambda_k(Y)\, y_k y_k^* \qquad (4.226)$$

be spectral decompositions of X and Y, respectively. As $\Phi(X) = Y$, one concludes that

$$\lambda_k(Y) = \sum_{j=1}^{n} \lambda_j(X)\, y_k^* \Phi(x_j x_j^*) y_k \qquad (4.227)$$

for each $k \in \{1, \dots, n\}$. Equivalently, $\lambda(Y) = A\lambda(X)$ for $A \in \mathrm{L}(\mathbb{R}^n)$ being the operator defined as

$$A(k, j) = y_k^* \Phi(x_j x_j^*) y_k \qquad (4.228)$$

for every $j, k \in \{1, \dots, n\}$. Each entry of A is nonnegative by the positivity of Φ; by the fact that Φ preserves trace, it holds that

$$\sum_{k=1}^{n} A(k, j) = 1 \qquad (4.229)$$

for each $j \in \{1, \dots, n\}$; and by the fact that Φ is unital, it holds that

$$\sum_{j=1}^{n} A(k, j) = 1 \qquad (4.230)$$

for each $k \in \{1, \dots, n\}$. The operator A is therefore doubly stochastic, so that $\lambda(Y) \prec \lambda(X)$. It has therefore been proved that statement 3 implies statement 4.

Finally, assume $\lambda(Y) \prec \lambda(X)$. Again consider spectral decompositions of X and Y as in (4.226). One may conclude from Theorem 4.28 that there exists a probability vector $p \in \mathcal{P}(S_n)$ such that

$$\lambda(Y) = \sum_{\pi \in S_n} p(\pi) V_\pi \lambda(X). \tag{4.231}$$

By defining a unitary operator

$$U_\pi = \sum_{j=1}^{n} y_{\pi(j)} x_j^* \tag{4.232}$$

for each permutation $\pi \in S_n = \mathrm{Sym}(\{1, \ldots, n\})$, one has that

$$\sum_{\pi \in S_n} p(\pi) U_\pi X U_\pi^*$$
$$= \sum_{j=1}^{n} \sum_{\pi \in S_n} p(\pi) \lambda_j(X) y_{\pi(j)} y_{\pi(j)}^* = \sum_{k=1}^{n} \lambda_k(Y) y_k y_k^* = Y. \tag{4.233}$$

It therefore holds that $Y \prec X$, and so statement 4 implies statement 1, which completes the proof. $\qquad\square$

Two Applications of Hermitian Operator Majorization

The theorems that follow offer a sample of the applications of majorization for Hermitian operators. The first theorem, whose proof makes essential use of Theorem 4.32, provides a precise characterization of those real vectors that may be obtained as the diagonal entries of a given Hermitian operator with respect to an arbitrary choice of an orthonormal basis.

Theorem 4.33 (Schur–Horn theorem) *Let $\mathcal{X}$ be a complex Euclidean space, let $n = \dim(\mathcal{X})$, and let $X \in \mathrm{Herm}(\mathcal{X})$ be a Hermitian operator. The following two implications, which are converse to one another, hold:*

1. *For every orthonormal basis $\{x_1, \ldots, x_n\}$ of $\mathcal{X}$, the vector $v \in \mathbb{R}^n$ defined by $v(k) = x_k^* X x_k$ for each $k \in \{1, \ldots, n\}$ satisfies $v \prec \lambda(X)$.*
2. *For every vector $v \in \mathbb{R}^n$ satisfying $v \prec \lambda(X)$, there exists an orthonormal basis $\{x_1, \ldots, x_n\}$ of $\mathcal{X}$ for which $v(k) = x_k^* X x_k$ for each $k \in \{1, \ldots, n\}$.*

Proof Suppose $\{x_1, \ldots, x_n\}$ is an orthonormal basis of $\mathcal{X}$ and $v \in \mathbb{R}^n$ is defined as $v(k) = x_k^* X x_k$ for each $k \in \{1, \ldots, n\}$. Define a map $\Phi \in \mathrm{T}(\mathcal{X})$ as

$$\Phi(Y) = \sum_{k=1}^{n} x_k x_k^* Y x_k x_k^* \tag{4.234}$$

for every operator $Y \in L(\mathcal{X})$, and observe that Φ is a pinching channel. By Proposition 4.6, it follows that Φ is a mixed-unitary channel. One therefore has $\Phi(X) \prec X$, which implies $\lambda(\Phi(X)) \prec \lambda(X)$ by Theorem 4.32. As

$$\Phi(X) = \sum_{k=1}^{n} v(k) x_k x_k^*, \tag{4.235}$$

it is evident that

$$\mathrm{spec}(\Phi(X)) = \{v(1), \ldots, v(n)\}, \tag{4.236}$$

or equivalently that

$$\lambda(\Phi(X)) = V_\pi v \tag{4.237}$$

for a permutation operator V_π that has the effect of ordering the entries of v from largest to smallest:

$$(V_\pi v)(1) \geq \cdots \geq (V_\pi v)(n). \tag{4.238}$$

It follows that $v \prec \lambda(X)$, as is required to establish the first implication.

Now suppose $v \in \mathbb{R}^n$ is a vector satisfying $v \prec \lambda(X)$, and let

$$X = \sum_{k=1}^{n} \lambda_k(X) u_k u_k^* \tag{4.239}$$

be a spectral decomposition of X. By Theorem 4.30, the assumption that $v \prec \lambda(X)$ implies that there exists a unitary operator $U \in U(\mathbb{C}^n)$ such that, for $A \in L(\mathbb{R}^n)$ defined by

$$A(j, k) = |U(j, k)|^2 \tag{4.240}$$

for $j, k \in \{1, \ldots, n\}$, one has $v = A\lambda(X)$. Define $V \in U(\mathcal{X}, \mathbb{C}^n)$ as

$$V = \sum_{k=1}^{n} e_k u_k^* \tag{4.241}$$

and let

$$x_k = V^* U^* V u_k \tag{4.242}$$

for each $k \in \{1, \ldots, n\}$. The operator $V^* U^* V \in U(\mathcal{X})$ is a unitary operator, implying that $\{x_1, \ldots, x_n\}$ is an orthonormal basis of $\mathcal{X}$. It holds that

$$x_k^* X x_k = \sum_{j=1}^{n} |U(k, j)|^2 \lambda_j(X) = (A\lambda(X))(k) = v(k), \tag{4.243}$$

which establishes the second implication. $\qquad \square$

The next theorem, representing a second application of majorization for Hermitian operators, characterizes the collection of probability vectors that are consistent with the representation of a given density operator as a mixture of pure states.

Theorem 4.34 *Let $\mathcal{X}$ be a complex Euclidean space, let $\rho \in D(\mathcal{X})$ be a density operator, let $n = \dim(\mathcal{X})$, and let $p = (p_1, \ldots, p_n)$ be a probability vector. There exists a collection of (not necessarily orthogonal) unit vectors $\{u_1, \ldots, u_n\} \subset \mathcal{X}$ such that*

$$\rho = \sum_{k=1}^{n} p_k u_k u_k^* \tag{4.244}$$

if and only if $p \prec \lambda(\rho)$.

Proof Assume first that

$$\rho = \sum_{k=1}^{n} p_k u_k u_k^* \tag{4.245}$$

for a collection $\{u_1, \ldots, u_n\} \subset \mathcal{X}$ of unit vectors. Define $A \in L(\mathbb{C}^n, \mathcal{X})$ as

$$A = \sum_{k=1}^{n} \sqrt{p_k}\, u_k e_k^*, \tag{4.246}$$

and observe that $AA^* = \rho$. It holds that

$$A^*A = \sum_{j=1}^{n} \sum_{k=1}^{n} \sqrt{p_j p_k} \langle u_k, u_j \rangle E_{k,j}, \tag{4.247}$$

and therefore

$$e_k^* A^* A e_k = p_k \tag{4.248}$$

for every $k \in \{1, \ldots, n\}$. By Theorem 4.33, this implies $p \prec \lambda(A^*A)$. As

$$\lambda(A^*A) = \lambda(AA^*) = \lambda(\rho), \tag{4.249}$$

it follows that $p \prec \lambda(\rho)$. One of the required implications of the theorem has therefore been proved.

Now assume that $p \prec \lambda(\rho)$. By Theorem 4.33, there exists an orthonormal basis $\{x_1, \ldots, x_n\}$ of $\mathcal{X}$ with the property that

$$p_k = x_k^* \rho x_k \tag{4.250}$$

for each $k \in \{1, \ldots, n\}$. Let

$$y_k = \sqrt{\rho}\, x_k \tag{4.251}$$

and define

$$
u_k = \begin{cases} \frac{y_k}{\|y_k\|} & \text{if } y_k \neq 0 \\ z & \text{if } y_k = 0 \end{cases} \tag{4.252}
$$

for each $k \in \{1, \dots, n\}$, where $z \in \mathcal{X}$ is an arbitrarily chosen unit vector. One has that

$$
\|y_k\|^2 = \langle \sqrt{\rho} x_k, \sqrt{\rho} x_k \rangle = x_k^* \rho x_k = p_k, \tag{4.253}
$$

for each $k \in \{1, \dots, n\}$, and therefore

$$
\sum_{k=1}^{n} p_k u_k u_k^* = \sum_{k=1}^{n} y_k y_k^* = \sum_{k=1}^{n} \sqrt{\rho} x_k x_k^* \sqrt{\rho} = \rho. \tag{4.254}
$$

This proves the other required implication of the theorem. $\square$

4.4 Exercises

Exercise 4.1   Let $\mathcal{X}$ be a complex Euclidean space with $\dim(\mathcal{X}) = 3$ and let $\Phi \in C(\mathcal{X})$ be a Schur channel. Prove that Φ is a mixed-unitary channel.

Exercise 4.2   For every positive integer $n \geq 2$, define a unital channel $\Phi_n \in C(\mathbb{C}^n)$ as

$$
\Phi_n(X) = \frac{\text{Tr}(X)\mathbb{1}_n - X^\mathsf{T}}{n - 1} \tag{4.255}
$$

for every $X \in L(\mathbb{C}^n)$, where $\mathbb{1}_n$ denotes the identity operator on $\mathbb{C}^n$. Prove that Φ_n is not mixed-unitary when n is odd.

A correct solution to this exercise generalizes Example 4.3, but a different argument will be needed than the one in that example when $n \geq 5$.

Exercise 4.3   Let n be a positive integer, let $\mathcal{X} = \mathbb{C}^{\mathbb{Z}_n}$, let

$$
\{W_{a,b} : a, b \in \mathbb{Z}_n\} \subset U(\mathcal{X}) \tag{4.256}
$$

be the set of discrete Weyl operators acting on $\mathcal{X}$, and let $\Phi \in C(\mathcal{X})$ be a channel. Prove that the following two statements are equivalent:

1. Φ is both a Schur channel and a Weyl-covariant channel.
2. There exists a probability vector $p \in \mathcal{P}(\mathbb{Z}_n)$ such that

$$
\Phi(X) = \sum_{a \in \mathbb{Z}_n} p(a) W_{0,a} X W_{0,a}^* \tag{4.257}
$$

for all $X \in L(\mathcal{X})$.

Exercise 4.4 Let $\mathcal{X}$ be a complex Euclidean space and let $\Phi \in T(\mathcal{X})$ be a Hermitian-preserving map. Prove that the following two statements are equivalent:

1. Φ is positive, trace-preserving, and unital.
2. $\Phi(H) \prec H$ for every Hermitian operator $H \in \mathrm{Herm}(\mathcal{X})$.

Exercise 4.5 Let $\mathcal{X}$ be a complex Euclidean space, let $\rho \in D(\mathcal{X})$ be a density operator, let $p = (p_1, \ldots, p_m)$ be a probability vector, and assume $p_1 \geq p_2 \geq \cdots \geq p_m$. Prove that there exist unit vectors $u_1, \ldots, u_m \in \mathcal{X}$ satisfying

$$\rho = \sum_{k=1}^{m} p_k u_k u_k^* \tag{4.258}$$

if and only if

$$p_1 + \cdots + p_k \leq \lambda_1(\rho) + \cdots + \lambda_k(\rho) \tag{4.259}$$

for all k satisfying $1 \leq k \leq \mathrm{rank}(\rho)$.

A correct solution to this problem generalizes Theorem 4.34, as m need not coincide with the dimension of $\mathcal{X}$.

Exercise 4.6 Let $\mathcal{X}$ be a complex Euclidean space, let $n = \dim(\mathcal{X})$, and let $\Phi \in C(\mathcal{X})$ be a unital channel. Following the conventions discussed in Section 1.1.3 of Chapter 1, let $s_1(Y) \geq \cdots \geq s_n(Y)$ denote the singular values of a given operator $Y \in L(\mathcal{X})$, ordered from largest to smallest, and taking $s_k(Y) = 0$ when $k > \mathrm{rank}(Y)$. Prove that, for every operator $X \in L(\mathcal{X})$, it holds that

$$s_1(X) + \cdots + s_m(X) \geq s_1(\Phi(X)) + \cdots + s_m(\Phi(X)) \tag{4.260}$$

for every $m \in \{1, \ldots, n\}$.

4.5 Bibliographic Remarks

Unital channels are sometimes referred to as *doubly stochastic* maps in the mathematics literature, although that term has also been used in reference to positive (but not necessarily completely positive), trace-preserving, and unital maps. The extreme points of sets of unital channels were studied by Landau and Streater (1993); the facts represented by Theorem 4.21, Example 4.3, and Theorem 4.23 appear in that paper. Related results for positive, trace-preserving, and unital maps had previously been discovered by Tregub (1986), who also gave a different example of a unital (Schur) channel that is not mixed-unitary. Another class of examples of this type appear in the work of Kümmerer and Maassen (1987).

Mixed-unitary channels have often been called *random unitary* channels, as in the case of Audenaert and Scheel (2008). The notion of environment-assisted channel correction was suggested by Alber, Beth, Charnes, Delgado, Grassl, and Mussinger (2001). Theorem 4.8, which characterizes mixed-unitary channels based on this notion, follows from a slightly more general result due to Gregoratti and Werner (2003). Corollary 4.11 is due to Buscemi (2006), who proved it through the use of the characterization represented by Theorem 4.8.

The discrete Weyl operators appear in Weyl's work on group-theoretic aspects of quantum mechanics (see, for instance, sections 14 and 15 in chapter IV of Weyl (1950)). The notion of covariance applies not only to the discrete Weyl operators and quantum channels, but also to other collections of unitary operators and algebraic objects. There is some discussion of this notion in Weyl (1950), and it was considered more explicitly for quantum instruments by Davies (1970). Channel covariance with respect to the discrete Weyl operators was considered by Holevo (1993, 1996), and the facts represented by Theorem 4.14 may be derived from that work.

Schur (1911) proved that the positive semidefinite cone is closed under entry-wise products – a fact now referred to as the *Schur product theorem*. The entry-wise product of operators is called the *Schur product*, and Schur maps are so named for this reason. The term *Hadamard product* is also used sometimes to refer to the entry-wise product, and correspondingly Schur maps are sometimes referred to as *Hadamard maps*. Schur maps are also referred to as *diagonal maps* by some authors, as they correspond to maps with diagonal Kraus operators (as is stated in Theorem 4.19).

Theorem 4.25 is due to Kribs (2003), whose proof made use of arguments that can be found in the paper of Lindblad (1999). Fixed points of quantum channels, unital channels, and other classes of completely positive maps have also been studied by other researchers, including Bratteli, Jorgensen, Kishimoto, and Werner (2000), Arias, Gheondea, and Gutter (2002), and others. Theorem 4.27 is a special case of a theorem due to Pérez-García, Wolf, Petz, and Ruskai (2006). (The theorem holds for a more general class of norms, not just the spectral norm.)

The notion of majorization for real vectors was developed in the first half of the twentieth century by mathematicians including Hardy, Littlewood, Pólya, Schur, Radó, and Horn. Details on the history of majorization may be found in Marshall, Olkin, and Arnold (2011). The extension of this notion to Hermitian operators is due to Uhlmann (1971, 1972, 1973), as is Theorem 4.32. (See also the book of Alberti and Uhlmann (1982).) The two implications of Theorem 4.33 were proved by Schur (1923) and Horn (1954), respectively, and Theorem 4.34 is due to Nielsen (2000).

5

Quantum Entropy and Source Coding

The *von Neumann entropy* of a quantum state is an information-theoretic measure of the amount of randomness or uncertainty that is inherent to that state, and the *quantum relative entropy* of one quantum state with respect to another is a related measure of the degree to which the first state differs from the second. This chapter defines these functions, establishes some of their fundamental properties, and explains their connections to the task of *source coding*.

5.1 Classical Entropy

The von Neumann entropy and quantum relative entropy functions are quantum analogues of classical information-theoretic notions: the Shannon entropy and (classical) relative entropy functions. It is appropriate to begin the chapter with a discussion of these classical notions, as an investigation of the mathematical properties of the von Neumann entropy and quantum relative entropy functions builds naturally on their classical counterparts.

5.1.1 Definitions of Classical Entropic Functions

With respect to the definition that follows, the Shannon entropy is specified for every vector with nonnegative entries, over any real Euclidean space. Although it is most common that this function is considered in the case that its argument is a probability vector, it is convenient nevertheless to extend its domain in this way.

Definition 5.1 Let Σ be an alphabet and let $u \in [0, \infty)^{\Sigma}$ be a vector of nonnegative real numbers indexed by Σ. One defines the *Shannon entropy* of the vector u as

$$H(u) = -\sum_{\substack{a \in \Sigma \\ u(a)>0}} u(a) \log(u(a)). \qquad (5.1)$$

(Here, and throughout this book, $\log(\alpha)$ refers to the base-2 logarithm of α. The natural logarithm of α is written $\ln(\alpha)$.)

The Shannon entropy $H(p)$ of a probability vector $p \in \mathcal{P}(\Sigma)$ is often described as the amount of randomness, measured in bits, inherent to the distribution represented by p. Alternatively, $H(p)$ may be described as the number of bits of uncertainty one has regarding the outcome of a random process described by p before the outcome is learned, or as the number of bits of information one gains as a result of learning which element $a \in \Sigma$ has been produced by such a process.

In the simple case that $\Sigma = \{0, 1\}$ and $p(0) = p(1) = 1/2$, for instance, it holds that $H(p) = 1$. This is natural, as one would expect that the amount of uncertainty of a uniformly generated random bit, measured in bits, would be 1 bit of uncertainty. In contrast, for a deterministic process, meaning one in which p is an elementary unit vector, there is no randomness or uncertainty, and no information gain when the selection is learned. Correspondingly, one has that the entropy $H(p)$ is zero in this case.

It is important to recognize, however, that intuitive descriptions of the Shannon entropy, as a measure of randomness, uncertainty, or information gain, must be viewed as representing expectations rather than absolute or definitive measures. The following example illustrates this point.

Example 5.2 Let m be a positive integer, let

$$\Sigma = \left\{0, 1, \ldots, 2^{m^2}\right\}, \qquad (5.2)$$

and define a probability vector $p \in \mathcal{P}(\Sigma)$ as follows:

$$p(a) = \begin{cases} 1 - \frac{1}{m} & \text{if } a = 0 \\ \frac{1}{m}2^{-m^2} & \text{if } 1 \leq a \leq 2^{m^2}. \end{cases} \qquad (5.3)$$

A calculation reveals that $H(p) > m$, and yet the outcome 0 appears with probability $1 - 1/m$ in a random selection described by p. So, as m grows, one becomes more and more "certain" that the outcome will be 0, and yet the "uncertainty" (as measured by the entropy) increases.

This example does not represent a paradox or suggest that the Shannon entropy is not reasonably viewed as a measure of uncertainty. If one considers an experiment in which a very large number of elements of Σ are selected independently, each according to the probability vector p, then the value $H(p)$ indeed does correspond more intuitively to the average or expected amount of uncertainty of each random selection.

Sometimes one speaks of the Shannon entropy of a classical register X, with the notation $H(X)$ being used for this purpose. This is a convenient shorthand to be interpreted as meaning $H(p)$, for the probability vector p describing the probabilistic state of X at the moment under consideration. Notations such as $H(X, Y)$ and $H(X_1, \ldots, X_n)$ are used in place of $H((X, Y))$ and $H((X_1, \ldots, X_n))$ when referring to the Shannon entropy of compound registers. Along similar lines, the notation $H(\alpha_1, \ldots, \alpha_n)$ will be used in place of $H((\alpha_1, \ldots, \alpha_n))$ when it is convenient to refer to the entropy of a vector written as $(\alpha_1, \ldots, \alpha_n)$.

The *relative entropy* function, which is also known as the *Kullback–Leibler divergence*, is closely related to the Shannon entropy. For the purposes of this book, the primary motivation for its introduction is that it serves as a useful analytic tool for reasoning about the Shannon entropy.

Definition 5.3 Let Σ be an alphabet and let $u, v \in [0, \infty)^\Sigma$ be vectors of nonnegative real numbers indexed by Σ. The *relative entropy* $D(u \| v)$ of u with respect to v is defined as follows. If it is the case that the support of u is contained in the support of v (i.e., $u(a) > 0$ implies $v(a) > 0$ for all $a \in \Sigma$), then $D(u \| v)$ is defined as

$$
D(u \| v) = \sum_{\substack{a \in \Sigma \\ u(a) > 0}} u(a) \log\left(\frac{u(a)}{v(a)}\right). \tag{5.4}
$$

For all other choices of u and v, one defines $D(u \| v) = \infty$.

Like the Shannon entropy function, the relative entropy is most typically considered in cases where its arguments are probability vectors, but again it is convenient to extend its domain to arbitrary nonnegative real vectors.

For a given pair of probability vectors $p, q \in \mathcal{P}(\Sigma)$, the relative entropy $D(p \| q)$ may be viewed as a measure of how much p differs from q in a certain information-theoretic sense. Analytically speaking, it fails to satisfy the requirements of being a true metric: it is not symmetric, it takes infinite values for some pairs of inputs, and it does not satisfy the triangle inequality. When extended to arbitrary vectors of the form $u, v \in [0, \infty)^\Sigma$, it may also take negative values. Despite these apparent shortcomings, the relative entropy is an indispensable information-theoretic tool.

Two additional functions derived from the Shannon entropy function are the *conditional Shannon entropy* and the *mutual information*. Both concern correlations between two classical registers X and Y, and are functions of the joint probabilistic state of the pair (X, Y). The conditional Shannon entropy of X given Y is defined as

$$H(\mathsf{X} \,|\, \mathsf{Y}) = H(\mathsf{X}, \mathsf{Y}) - H(\mathsf{Y}). \tag{5.5}$$

Intuitively speaking, this quantity is a measure of the expected uncertainty regarding the classical state of X one would have upon learning the classical state of Y. The *mutual information* between X and Y is defined as

$$I(\mathsf{X} : \mathsf{Y}) = H(\mathsf{X}) + H(\mathsf{Y}) - H(\mathsf{X}, \mathsf{Y}). \tag{5.6}$$

This quantity can alternatively be expressed as

$$I(\mathsf{X} : \mathsf{Y}) = H(\mathsf{Y}) - H(\mathsf{Y}|\mathsf{X}) = H(\mathsf{X}) - H(\mathsf{X}|\mathsf{Y}). \tag{5.7}$$

One typically views this quantity as representing the expected amount of information about X that one gains by learning the classical state of Y, or (equivalently) that one gains about Y by learning the classical state of X.

5.1.2 Properties of Classical Entropic Functions

The Shannon and relative entropy functions possess a variety of useful and interesting properties. This section establishes several basic properties of these functions.

Scalar Analogues of Shannon Entropy and Relative Entropy

For the purposes of establishing basic analytic properties of the Shannon and relative entropy functions, it is helpful to define functions representing scalar analogues of these functions. These scalar functions are to be defined with respect to the natural logarithm rather than the base-2 logarithm, as this will simplify some of the calculations to follow, particularly when they make use of differential calculus.

The first function $\eta \colon [0, \infty) \to \mathbb{R}$, which represents a scalar analogue of the Shannon entropy, is defined as follows:

$$\eta(\alpha) = \begin{cases} -\alpha \ln(\alpha) & \alpha > 0 \\ 0 & \alpha = 0. \end{cases} \tag{5.8}$$

The function η is continuous everywhere on its domain, and derivatives of η of all orders exist for all positive real numbers. In particular,

$$\eta'(\alpha) = -(1 + \ln(\alpha)) \tag{5.9}$$

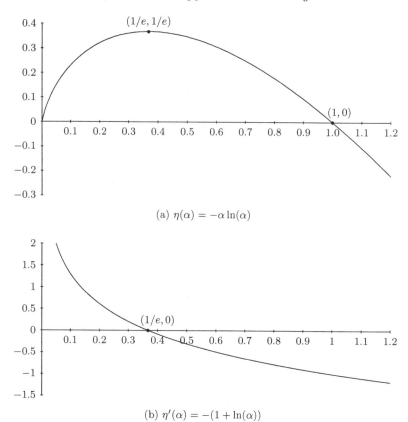

(a) $\eta(\alpha) = -\alpha \ln(\alpha)$

(b) $\eta'(\alpha) = -(1 + \ln(\alpha))$

Figure 5.1 Plots of the functions η and η'.

and

$$\eta^{(n+1)}(\alpha) = \frac{(-1)^n (n-1)!}{\alpha^n} \tag{5.10}$$

for $n \geq 1$, for all $\alpha > 0$. Plots of the function η and its first derivative η' are shown in Figure 5.1. As the second derivative of η is negative for all $\alpha > 0$, one has that η is a concave function:

$$\eta(\lambda \alpha + (1 - \lambda)\beta) \geq \lambda \eta(\alpha) + (1 - \lambda)\eta(\beta) \tag{5.11}$$

for all $\alpha, \beta \geq 0$ and $\lambda \in [0, 1]$.

The second function $\theta : [0, \infty)^2 \to (-\infty, \infty]$, which represents a scalar analogue of the relative entropy, is defined as follows:

$$\theta(\alpha, \beta) = \begin{cases} 0 & \text{if } \alpha = 0 \\ \infty & \text{if } \alpha > 0 \text{ and } \beta = 0 \\ \alpha \ln(\alpha/\beta) & \text{if } \alpha > 0 \text{ and } \beta > 0. \end{cases} \tag{5.12}$$

It is evident from this definition that, when restricted to positive real number arguments $\alpha, \beta > 0$, the value $\theta(\alpha, \beta)$ is negative when $\alpha < \beta$, zero when $\alpha = \beta$, and positive when $\alpha > \beta$.

It is useful to note that the functions θ and η are related by the identity

$$\theta(\alpha, \beta) = -\beta\,\eta\left(\frac{\alpha}{\beta}\right), \tag{5.13}$$

which holds for all $\alpha \in [0, \infty)$ and $\beta \in (0, \infty)$. The function θ is continuous at every point (α, β) for which $\beta > 0$. It is not continuous at any point $(\alpha, 0)$, however, as every neighborhood of such a point contains both finite and infinite values.

The following useful lemma regarding the function θ is equivalent to a fact commonly known as the *log-sum inequality*.

Lemma 5.4 *Let $\alpha_0, \alpha_1, \beta_0, \beta_1 \in [0, \infty)$ be nonnegative real numbers. It holds that*

$$\theta(\alpha_0 + \alpha_1, \beta_0 + \beta_1) \leq \theta(\alpha_0, \beta_0) + \theta(\alpha_1, \beta_1). \tag{5.14}$$

Proof If either of β_0 or β_1 is zero, the inequality is straightforward. More specifically, if $\beta_0 = 0$ and $\alpha_0 = 0$, the inequality is equivalent to

$$\theta(\alpha_1, \beta_1) \leq \theta(\alpha_1, \beta_1), \tag{5.15}$$

which is trivial, while if $\beta_0 = 0$ and $\alpha_0 > 0$, the right-hand side of (5.14) is infinite. A similar argument holds when $\beta_1 = 0$ by symmetry.

In the case that both β_0 and β_1 are positive, the inequality may be proved by combining the identity (5.13) with the concavity of η:

$$
\begin{aligned}
\theta(\alpha_0, \beta_0) &+ \theta(\alpha_1, \beta_1) \\
&= -(\beta_0 + \beta_1)\left[\frac{\beta_0}{\beta_0 + \beta_1}\,\eta\left(\frac{\alpha_0}{\beta_0}\right) + \frac{\beta_1}{\beta_0 + \beta_1}\,\eta\left(\frac{\alpha_1}{\beta_1}\right)\right] \\
&\geq -(\beta_0 + \beta_1)\,\eta\left(\frac{\alpha_0 + \alpha_1}{\beta_0 + \beta_1}\right) \\
&= \theta(\alpha_0 + \alpha_1, \beta_0 + \beta_1),
\end{aligned}
\tag{5.16}
$$

as claimed. $\square$

Elementary Properties of Shannon Entropy and Relative Entropy

The Shannon entropy function may be expressed in terms of the η-function as follows:

$$H(u) = \frac{1}{\ln(2)} \sum_{a \in \Sigma} \eta(u(a)), \tag{5.17}$$

for every choice of an alphabet Σ and a vector $u \in [0, \infty)^{\Sigma}$. As the function η is continuous everywhere on its domain, the Shannon entropy function is continuous everywhere on its domain as well. The concavity of η implies the concavity of the Shannon entropy, as the following proposition states.

Proposition 5.5 (Concavity of Shannon entropy)   *Let Σ be an alphabet, let $u, v \in [0, \infty)^\Sigma$ be vectors, and let $\lambda \in [0, 1]$. It holds that*

$$H(\lambda u + (1 - \lambda)v) \geq \lambda H(u) + (1 - \lambda) H(v). \tag{5.18}$$

Proof   By the concavity of the function η, one has

$$H(\lambda u + (1 - \lambda)v) = \frac{1}{\ln(2)} \sum_{a \in \Sigma} \eta(\lambda u(a) + (1 - \lambda)v(a))$$

$$\geq \frac{\lambda}{\ln(2)} \sum_{a \in \Sigma} \eta(u(a)) + \frac{1 - \lambda}{\ln(2)} \sum_{a \in \Sigma} \eta(v(a)) \tag{5.19}$$

$$= \lambda H(u) + (1 - \lambda) H(v),$$

as required. $\square$

The next proposition states two identities that involve the Shannon entropy of direct sums and tensor products of vectors. Both identities may be verified through direct calculations.

Proposition 5.6   *Let $u \in [0, \infty)^\Sigma$ and $v \in [0, \infty)^\Gamma$ be vectors, for alphabets Σ and Γ. It holds that*

$$H(u \oplus v) = H(u) + H(v) \tag{5.20}$$

and

$$H(u \otimes v) = H(u) \sum_{b \in \Gamma} v(b) + H(v) \sum_{a \in \Sigma} u(a). \tag{5.21}$$

One may observe that, for any choice of probability vectors $p \in \mathcal{P}(\Sigma)$ and $q \in \mathcal{P}(\Gamma)$, the identity (5.21) implies that

$$H(p \otimes q) = H(p) + H(q). \tag{5.22}$$

As a special case of the same identity, one finds that

$$H(\alpha p) = \alpha H(p) - \alpha \log(\alpha) \tag{5.23}$$

for every scalar $\alpha > 0$ and every probability vector $p \in \mathcal{P}(\Sigma)$.

The relative entropy function may be expressed using the θ-function as follows:

$$D(u \| v) = \frac{1}{\ln(2)} \sum_{a \in \Sigma} \theta(u(a), v(a)), \tag{5.24}$$

for every choice of an alphabet Σ and vectors $u, v \in [0, \infty)^\Sigma$. It therefore holds that the relative entropy function is continuous when its domain is restricted to choices of v having only positive entries, but is not continuous at any point (u, v) for which v has one or more zero entries.

The next proposition, which implies that the relative entropy between any two probability vectors is nonnegative, represents one application of Lemma 5.4.

Proposition 5.7 *Let Σ be an alphabet, let $u, v \in [0, \infty)^{\Sigma}$ be vectors, and assume that*

$$\sum_{a \in \Sigma} u(a) \geq \sum_{a \in \Sigma} v(a). \tag{5.25}$$

It holds that $\mathrm{D}(u \| v) \geq 0$. In particular, $\mathrm{D}(p \| q) \geq 0$ for all choices of probability vectors $p, q \in \mathcal{P}(\Sigma)$.

Proof By Lemma 5.4, it holds that

$$\mathrm{D}(u \| v) = \frac{1}{\ln(2)} \sum_{a \in \Sigma} \theta(u(a), v(a)) \geq \frac{1}{\ln(2)} \theta\left(\sum_{a \in \Sigma} u(a), \sum_{a \in \Sigma} v(a)\right). \tag{5.26}$$

The proposition follows from the fact that $\theta(\alpha, \beta) \geq 0$ for every choice of nonnegative real numbers $\alpha, \beta \in [0, \infty)$ satisfying $\alpha \geq \beta$. $\qquad\square$

Remark Theorem 5.15, proved later in the present chapter, establishes a quantitative lower bound on the relative entropy $\mathrm{D}(p \| q)$ in terms of the 1-norm distance $\| p - q \|_1$ between any two probability vectors p and q.

Proposition 5.7 may be used to prove upper and lower bounds on the Shannon entropy, as in the proof of the following proposition.

Proposition 5.8 *Let Σ be an alphabet, let $u \in [0, \infty)^{\Sigma}$ be a nonzero vector, and let*

$$\alpha = \sum_{a \in \Sigma} u(a). \tag{5.27}$$

It holds that

$$0 \leq \mathrm{H}(u) + \alpha \log(\alpha) \leq \alpha \log(|\Sigma|). \tag{5.28}$$

In particular, it holds that $0 \leq \mathrm{H}(p) \leq \log(|\Sigma|)$ for every probability vector $p \in \mathcal{P}(\Sigma)$.

Proof First, suppose $p \in \mathcal{P}(\Sigma)$ is a probability vector. The Shannon entropy $\mathrm{H}(p)$ may be written as

$$\mathrm{H}(p) = \sum_{\substack{a \in \Sigma \\ p(a) > 0}} p(a) \log\left(\frac{1}{p(a)}\right), \tag{5.29}$$

which is a convex combination of nonnegative real numbers, by virtue of the fact that $p(a) \leq 1$ for each $a \in \Sigma$. It follows that $\mathrm{H}(p) \geq 0$.

Next, let $q \in \mathcal{P}(\Sigma)$ be the probability vector defined by $q(a) = 1/|\Sigma|$ for each $a \in \Sigma$. One may evaluate the relative entropy $\mathrm{D}(p\|q)$ directly from its definition, obtaining

$$\mathrm{D}(p\|q) = -\,\mathrm{H}(p) + \log(|\Sigma|). \tag{5.30}$$

As p and q are probability vectors, Proposition 5.7 implies that the relative entropy $\mathrm{D}(p\|q)$ is nonnegative, and therefore $\mathrm{H}(p) \leq \log(|\Sigma|)$.

Now consider $u \in [0,\infty)^{\Sigma}$ and α, as in the statement of the proposition. Let $p \in \mathcal{P}(\Sigma)$ be the probability vector defined by the equation $\alpha p = u$. By (5.23), one has

$$\mathrm{H}(u) = \mathrm{H}(\alpha p) = \alpha\,\mathrm{H}(p) - \alpha \log(\alpha). \tag{5.31}$$

Given that $0 \leq \mathrm{H}(p) \leq \log(|\Sigma|)$, it follows that

$$-\,\alpha \log(\alpha) \leq \mathrm{H}(u) \leq \alpha \log(|\Sigma|) - \alpha \log(\alpha), \tag{5.32}$$

which completes the proof. $\qquad\square$

Remark Proposition 5.8 assumes that u is a nonzero vector, which implies that $\alpha > 0$. The inequalities stated by the proposition are trivially satisfied for $u = 0$, provided one makes the interpretation $0 \log(0) = 0$.

Proposition 5.7 may also be used to prove that the Shannon entropy is subadditive, in the sense described by the next proposition. Intuitively speaking, this property reflects the idea that the amount of uncertainty one has about a compound register cannot be greater than the total uncertainty one has about its individual registers.

Proposition 5.9 (Subadditivity of Shannon entropy) *Let X and Y be classical registers. With respect to an arbitrary probabilistic state of these registers, it holds that*

$$\mathrm{H}(\mathsf{X},\mathsf{Y}) \leq \mathrm{H}(\mathsf{X}) + \mathrm{H}(\mathsf{Y}). \tag{5.33}$$

Proof Let $p \in \mathcal{P}(\Sigma \times \Gamma)$ denote an arbitrary probabilistic state of the pair (X,Y), for Σ and Γ being the classical state sets of X and Y, respectively. A calculation based on the definition of the relative entropy and elementary properties of logarithms reveals the equality

$$\mathrm{D}(p\|p[\mathsf{X}] \otimes p[\mathsf{Y}]) = \mathrm{H}(\mathsf{X}) + \mathrm{H}(\mathsf{Y}) - \mathrm{H}(\mathsf{X},\mathsf{Y}). \tag{5.34}$$

As the relative entropy of one probability vector with respect to another is nonnegative by Proposition 5.7, the required inequality follows. $\qquad\square$

One may observe that Proposition 5.9 is equivalent to the statement that the mutual information $I(X:Y)$ between two registers is necessarily nonnegative, or equivalently that the conditional Shannon entropy $H(Y|X)$ of one register Y given another register X is no larger than the (unconditional) Shannon entropy $H(Y)$ of the register Y alone: $H(Y|X) \leq H(Y)$.

The next proposition establishes a related fact: the Shannon entropy of a pair of classical registers (X, Y) cannot be less than the Shannon entropy of either of the registers viewed in isolation. Equivalently, the conditional Shannon entropy $H(X|Y)$ is nonnegative for all probabilistic states of the pair (X, Y).

Proposition 5.10 *Let* X *and* Y *be classical registers. With respect to an arbitrary probabilistic state of these registers, it holds that*

$$H(X) \leq H(X, Y). \tag{5.35}$$

Proof Let Σ and Γ denote the classical state sets of X and Y, respectively, and let $p \in \mathcal{P}(\Sigma \times \Gamma)$ be an arbitrary probabilistic state of (X, Y). The logarithm is an increasing function, and therefore

$$\log(p(a, b)) \leq \log\left(\sum_{c \in \Gamma} p(a, c)\right) \tag{5.36}$$

for every pair $(a, b) \in \Sigma \times \Gamma$. Assuming one adopts the interpretation $0 \log(0) = 0$, it follows that

$$H(X, Y) = -\sum_{a \in \Sigma} \sum_{b \in \Gamma} p(a, b) \log(p(a, b))$$

$$\geq -\sum_{a \in \Sigma} \left(\sum_{b \in \Gamma} p(a, b)\right) \log\left(\sum_{c \in \Gamma} p(a, c)\right) = H(X), \tag{5.37}$$

as required. $\qquad\square$

Remark It should be noted that Proposition 5.10 does not carry over to the von Neumann entropy of quantum states (cf. Theorem 5.25).

The next theorem represents a direct and straightforward application of Lemma 5.4. A quantum analogue of this theorem, which is stated and proved in Section 5.2.3, is not known to have nearly so straightforward a proof.

Theorem 5.11 *Let* Σ *be an alphabet and let* $u_0, u_1, v_0, v_1 \in [0, \infty)^{\Sigma}$ *be vectors of nonnegative real numbers indexed by* Σ. *It holds that*

$$D(u_0 + u_1 \| v_0 + v_1) \leq D(u_0 \| v_0) + D(u_1 \| v_1). \tag{5.38}$$

Proof By Lemma 5.4 it holds that

$$
\begin{aligned}
\mathrm{D}&(u_0 + u_1 \| v_0 + v_1) \\
&= \frac{1}{\ln(2)} \sum_{a \in \Sigma} \theta(u_0(a) + u_1(a), v_0(a) + v_1(a)) \\
&\leq \frac{1}{\ln(2)} \sum_{a \in \Sigma} \left(\theta(u_0(a), v_0(a)) + \theta(u_1(a), v_1(a)) \right) \\
&= \mathrm{D}(u_0 \| v_0) + \mathrm{D}(u_1 \| v_1),
\end{aligned} \tag{5.39}
$$

as claimed. $\qquad\square$

For all vectors $u, v \in [0, \infty)^\Sigma$ and scalars $\alpha, \beta \in [0, \infty)$ it holds that

$$
\mathrm{D}(\alpha u \| \beta v) = \alpha \, \mathrm{D}(u \| v) + \frac{1}{\ln(2)} \theta(\alpha, \beta) \sum_{a \in \Sigma} u(a), \tag{5.40}
$$

provided one makes the interpretation $0 \cdot \infty = 0$ in the case that $\alpha = 0$ and $\mathrm{D}(u \| v) = \infty$, or in the case that $\theta(\alpha, \beta) = \infty$ and $u = 0$. This can be verified through a direct calculation. As $\theta(\alpha, \alpha) = 0$ for all $\alpha \in [0, \infty)$, one obtains the identity

$$
\mathrm{D}(\alpha u \| \alpha v) = \alpha \, \mathrm{D}(u \| v), \tag{5.41}
$$

where again it is to be interpreted that $0 \cdot \infty = 0$. Alternatively, one may verify that this identity holds by observing that

$$
\theta(\alpha \beta, \alpha \gamma) = \alpha \, \theta(\beta, \gamma) \tag{5.42}
$$

for all nonnegative real numbers $\alpha, \beta, \gamma \in [0, \infty)$. Through this identity, one obtains the following corollary to Theorem 5.11.

Corollary 5.12 (Joint convexity of relative entropy)   *Let Σ be an alphabet, let $u_0, u_1, v_0, v_1 \in [0, \infty)^\Sigma$ be vectors of nonnegative real numbers indexed by Σ, and let $\lambda \in [0, 1]$. It holds that*

$$
\begin{aligned}
\mathrm{D}&(\lambda u_0 + (1 - \lambda)u_1 \| \lambda v_0 + (1 - \lambda)v_1) \\
&\leq \lambda \, \mathrm{D}(u_0 \| v_0) + (1 - \lambda) \, \mathrm{D}(u_1 \| v_1).
\end{aligned} \tag{5.43}
$$

Through a similar argument, one may prove that the relative entropy of one vector with respect to another cannot increase under the action of any stochastic operation performed simultaneously on the two vectors.

Theorem 5.13   *Let Σ and Γ be alphabets, let $u, v \in [0, \infty)^\Sigma$ be vectors, and let $A \in \mathrm{L}(\mathbb{R}^\Sigma, \mathbb{R}^\Gamma)$ be a stochastic operator. It holds that*

$$
\mathrm{D}(Au \| Av) \leq \mathrm{D}(u \| v). \tag{5.44}
$$

Proof By Lemma 5.4 along with the identity (5.42), it holds that

$$D(Au\|Av) = \frac{1}{\ln(2)} \sum_{a\in\Gamma} \theta\left(\sum_{b\in\Sigma} A(a,b)u(b), \sum_{b\in\Sigma} A(a,b)v(b)\right)$$

$$\leq \frac{1}{\ln(2)} \sum_{a\in\Gamma}\sum_{b\in\Sigma} A(a,b)\,\theta(u(b),v(b)) \qquad (5.45)$$

$$= \frac{1}{\ln(2)} \sum_{b\in\Sigma} \theta(u(b),v(b))$$

$$= D(u\|v),$$

as required. $\qquad\square$

Quantitative Bounds on Shannon Entropy and Relative Entropy

Two bounds, one concerning the Shannon entropy and one concerning the relative entropy, will now be proved. The first bound is a quantitative form of the statement that the Shannon entropy function is continuous on the set of all probability vectors.

Theorem 5.14 (Audenaert) *Let $p_0, p_1 \in \mathcal{P}(\Sigma)$ be probability vectors, for Σ being an alphabet with $|\Sigma| \geq 2$. It holds that*

$$|H(p_0) - H(p_1)| \leq \lambda \log(|\Sigma| - 1) + H(\lambda, 1 - \lambda) \qquad (5.46)$$

for $\lambda = \frac{1}{2}\|p_0 - p_1\|_1$.

Proof The theorem holds trivially when $p_0 = p_1$, so it will be assumed that this is not the case. Let $\Sigma_0, \Sigma_1 \subset \Sigma$ be disjoint sets defined as

$$\Sigma_0 = \{a \in \Sigma : p_0(a) > p_1(a)\},$$
$$\Sigma_1 = \{a \in \Sigma : p_0(a) < p_1(a)\}, \qquad (5.47)$$

and let vectors $u_0, u_1 \in [0,1]^\Sigma$ be defined as

$$u_0(a) = \begin{cases} p_0(a) - p_1(a) & \text{if } a \in \Sigma_0 \\ 0 & \text{otherwise,} \end{cases} \qquad (5.48)$$

$$u_1(a) = \begin{cases} p_1(a) - p_0(a) & \text{if } a \in \Sigma_1 \\ 0 & \text{otherwise,} \end{cases} \qquad (5.49)$$

for every $a \in \Sigma$. It holds that $p_0 - p_1 = u_0 - u_1$ and $u_0(a)u_1(a) = 0$ for all $a \in \Sigma$, and moreover

$$\sum_{a\in\Sigma} u_0(a) = \lambda = \sum_{a\in\Sigma} u_1(a). \qquad (5.50)$$

Taking $w \in [0,1]^\Sigma$ to be defined as

$$w(a) = \min\{p_0(a), p_1(a)\} \tag{5.51}$$

for every $a \in \Sigma$, one finds that $p_0 = u_0 + w$, $p_1 = u_1 + w$, and

$$\sum_{a \in \Sigma} w(a) = 1 - \lambda. \tag{5.52}$$

Next, observe that the identity

$$(\alpha + \beta) \log(\alpha + \beta) - \alpha \log(\alpha) - \beta \log(\beta)$$
$$= (\alpha + \beta) \operatorname{H}\left(\frac{\alpha}{\alpha + \beta}, \frac{\beta}{\alpha + \beta}\right) \tag{5.53}$$

holds for every choice of nonnegative real numbers α and β, assuming at least one of them is positive (and, as is to be expected, interpreting $0 \log(0)$ as 0 if either α or β is 0). Through this identity, the following two expressions are obtained:

$$\operatorname{H}(u_0) + \operatorname{H}(w) - \operatorname{H}(p_0) = \sum_{a \in \Sigma_0} p_0(a) \operatorname{H}\left(\frac{u_0(a)}{p_0(a)}, \frac{w(a)}{p_0(a)}\right), \tag{5.54}$$

$$\operatorname{H}(u_1) + \operatorname{H}(w) - \operatorname{H}(p_1) = \sum_{a \in \Sigma_1} p_1(a) \operatorname{H}\left(\frac{u_1(a)}{p_1(a)}, \frac{w(a)}{p_1(a)}\right). \tag{5.55}$$

In both cases, the restriction of the sums to the sets Σ_0 and Σ_1 reflects the exclusion of 0 summands. Both sums include only nonnegative summands, and therefore

$$\operatorname{H}(p_0) \leq \operatorname{H}(u_0) + \operatorname{H}(w) \quad \text{and} \quad \operatorname{H}(p_1) \leq \operatorname{H}(u_1) + \operatorname{H}(w). \tag{5.56}$$

By setting

$$\alpha_0 = \sum_{a \in \Sigma_0} p_0(a) \quad \text{and} \quad \alpha_1 = \sum_{a \in \Sigma_1} p_1(a), \tag{5.57}$$

one has that

$$\sum_{a \in \Sigma_0} w(a) = \alpha_0 - \lambda \quad \text{and} \quad \sum_{a \in \Sigma_1} w(a) = \alpha_1 - \lambda, \tag{5.58}$$

which implies that $\alpha_0, \alpha_1 \in [\lambda, 1]$. By the concavity of the Shannon entropy (Proposition 5.5), the following two inequalities are obtained:

$$\operatorname{H}(u_0) + \operatorname{H}(w) - \operatorname{H}(p_0) \leq \alpha_0 \operatorname{H}\left(\frac{\lambda}{\alpha_0}, 1 - \frac{\lambda}{\alpha_0}\right), \tag{5.59}$$

$$\operatorname{H}(u_1) + \operatorname{H}(w) - \operatorname{H}(p_1) \leq \alpha_1 \operatorname{H}\left(\frac{\lambda}{\alpha_1}, 1 - \frac{\lambda}{\alpha_1}\right). \tag{5.60}$$

Given that the function

$$f_\lambda(\alpha) = \alpha \, \mathrm{H}\left(\frac{\lambda}{\alpha}, 1 - \frac{\lambda}{\alpha}\right) \tag{5.61}$$

is strictly increasing on the interval $[\lambda, 1]$, it follows that

$$\begin{aligned} 0 \leq \mathrm{H}(u_0) + \mathrm{H}(w) - \mathrm{H}(p_0) \leq \mathrm{H}(\lambda, 1 - \lambda), \\ 0 \leq \mathrm{H}(u_1) + \mathrm{H}(w) - \mathrm{H}(p_1) \leq \mathrm{H}(\lambda, 1 - \lambda). \end{aligned} \tag{5.62}$$

By the triangle inequality together with (5.62), one may therefore conclude that

$$\begin{aligned} |\mathrm{H}(p_0) &- \mathrm{H}(p_1)| - |\mathrm{H}(u_0) - \mathrm{H}(u_1)| \\ &\leq |(\mathrm{H}(p_0) - \mathrm{H}(u_0) - \mathrm{H}(w)) - (\mathrm{H}(p_1) - \mathrm{H}(u_1) - \mathrm{H}(w))| \\ &\leq \mathrm{H}(\lambda, 1 - \lambda). \end{aligned} \tag{5.63}$$

To complete the proof, it suffices to prove

$$|\mathrm{H}(u_0) - \mathrm{H}(u_1)| \leq \lambda \log(|\Sigma| - 1). \tag{5.64}$$

For any alphabet Γ and any vector $v \in [0, \infty)^\Gamma$ with

$$\sum_{b \in \Gamma} v(b) = \lambda, \tag{5.65}$$

it holds that

$$-\lambda \log(\lambda) \leq \mathrm{H}(v) \leq \lambda \log(|\Gamma|) - \lambda \log(\lambda), \tag{5.66}$$

as was demonstrated in Proposition 5.8. Given that u_0 and u_1 are supported on disjoint subsets of Σ and have entries summing to the same value λ, it follows that

$$|\mathrm{H}(u_0) - \mathrm{H}(u_1)| \leq \lambda \log(|\Gamma|), \tag{5.67}$$

for Γ being a proper subset of Σ. The largest value obtained for the upper bound occurs when Γ has one fewer element than Σ, yielding the required inequality (5.64), which completes the proof. $\square$

The second bound, which concerns the relative entropy function, is a quantitative form of Proposition 5.7. It lower-bounds the relative entropy $\mathrm{D}(p_0 \| p_1)$, for probability vectors p_0 and p_1, by a quantity determined by their 1-norm distance $\|p_0 - p_1\|_1$.

Theorem 5.15 (Pinsker's inequality) *Let $p_0, p_1 \in \mathcal{P}(\Sigma)$ be probability vectors, for Σ being an alphabet. It holds that*

$$\mathrm{D}(p_0 \| p_1) \geq \frac{1}{2 \ln(2)} \|p_0 - p_1\|_1^2. \tag{5.68}$$

The proof of Theorem 5.15 will make use of the following lemma, which is equivalent to a special case of the theorem in which $|\Sigma| = 2$.

Lemma 5.16 *For all choices of real numbers $\alpha, \beta \in [0,1]$ it holds that*

$$\theta(\alpha, \beta) + \theta(1 - \alpha, 1 - \beta) \geq 2(\alpha - \beta)^2. \tag{5.69}$$

Proof The inequality in the statement of the lemma is immediate in the case that $\beta \in \{0, 1\}$. In the case that $\alpha \in \{0, 1\}$ and $\beta \in (0, 1)$, the inequality in the statement of the lemma is equivalent to

$$- \ln(\beta) \geq 2(1 - \beta)^2, \tag{5.70}$$

which can be verified using elementary calculus. It remains to consider the case where $\alpha, \beta \in (0, 1)$. Under this assumption it may be verified that

$$
\begin{aligned}
\theta(\alpha, \beta) &+ \theta(1 - \alpha, 1 - \beta) \\
&= (\eta(\beta) + \eta(1 - \beta)) - (\eta(\alpha) + \eta(1 - \alpha)) \\
&\quad + (\alpha - \beta)(\eta'(\beta) - \eta'(1 - \beta)) \\
&= f(\beta) - f(\alpha) + (\alpha - \beta)f'(\beta)
\end{aligned} \tag{5.71}
$$

for $f \colon [0,1] \to \mathbb{R}$ defined as $f(\gamma) = \eta(\gamma) + \eta(1 - \gamma)$ for all $\gamma \in [0,1]$. By Taylor's theorem it holds that

$$f(\alpha) = f(\beta) + (\alpha - \beta)f'(\beta) + \frac{1}{2}(\alpha - \beta)^2 f''(\gamma) \tag{5.72}$$

for some choice of γ being a convex combination of α and β. Equation (5.72) therefore holds for some choice of $\gamma \in (0, 1)$. Evaluating the second derivative of f yields

$$f''(\gamma) = -\left(\frac{1}{\gamma} + \frac{1}{1 - \gamma}\right), \tag{5.73}$$

whereby it follows that $f''(\gamma) \leq -4$ for all $\gamma \in (0, 1)$. This implies the inequality (5.69), which completes the proof. □

Proof of Theorem 5.15 Define disjoint sets $\Sigma_0, \Sigma_1, \Gamma \subseteq \Sigma$ as

$$\Sigma_0 = \{a \in \Sigma : p_0(a) > p_1(a)\}, \tag{5.74}$$
$$\Sigma_1 = \{a \in \Sigma : p_0(a) < p_1(a)\}, \tag{5.75}$$
$$\Gamma = \{a \in \Sigma : p_0(a) = p_1(a)\}, \tag{5.76}$$

and define a stochastic operator $A \in \mathrm{L}(\mathbb{R}^\Sigma, \mathbb{R}^{\{0,1\}})$ as

$$A = \sum_{a \in \Sigma_0} E_{0,a} + \sum_{a \in \Sigma_1} E_{1,a} + \frac{1}{2}\sum_{a \in \Gamma}(E_{0,a} + E_{1,a}). \tag{5.77}$$

Let

$$\alpha = (Ap_0)(0) \quad \text{and} \quad \beta = (Ap_1)(0), \tag{5.78}$$

and note that

$$(Ap_0)(1) = 1 - \alpha \quad \text{and} \quad (Ap_1)(1) = 1 - \beta, \tag{5.79}$$

as p_0 and p_1 are probability vectors and A is stochastic. It holds that

$$\alpha - \beta = \sum_{a \in \Sigma_0} (p_0(a) - p_1(a)) = \sum_{a \in \Sigma_1} (p_1(a) - p_0(a)) = \frac{1}{2} \| p_0 - p_1 \|_1. \tag{5.80}$$

By Theorem 5.13 and Lemma 5.16, one finds that

$$\mathrm{D}(p_0 \| p_1) \geq \mathrm{D}(Ap_0 \| Ap_1) = \frac{1}{\ln(2)} \left(\theta(\alpha, \beta) + \theta(1 - \alpha, 1 - \beta) \right)$$

$$\geq \frac{2}{\ln(2)} (\alpha - \beta)^2 = \frac{1}{2\ln(2)} \| p_0 - p_1 \|_1^2, \tag{5.81}$$

as required. $\qquad\qquad\qquad\qquad\qquad\qquad\qquad\qquad\qquad\qquad\qquad\square$

5.2 Quantum Entropy

The von Neumann entropy and quantum relative entropy functions, which may be viewed as extensions of the Shannon entropy and relative entropy functions from nonnegative vectors to positive semidefinite operators, are defined in this section. Fundamental properties of these functions, including the key properties of joint convexity of the quantum relative entropy and strong subadditivity of the von Neumann entropy, are established.

5.2.1 Definitions of Quantum Entropic Functions

The von Neumann entropy function represents a natural extension of the Shannon entropy function from nonnegative vectors to positive semidefinite operators; as the following definition states, the von Neumann entropy is defined as the Shannon entropy of a given positive semidefinite operator's vector of eigenvalues.

Definition 5.17 Let $P \in \mathrm{Pos}(\mathcal{X})$ be a positive semidefinite operator, for $\mathcal{X}$ a complex Euclidean space. The *von Neumann entropy* of P is defined as

$$\mathrm{H}(P) = \mathrm{H}(\lambda(P)), \tag{5.82}$$

for $\lambda(P)$ being the vector of eigenvalues of P.

The von Neumann entropy may also be expressed as

$$H(P) = -\operatorname{Tr}(P\log(P)). \tag{5.83}$$

Formally speaking, this expression assumes that the operator $P\log(P)$ is defined for all positive semidefinite operators $P \in \operatorname{Pos}(\mathcal{X})$, despite the fact that $\log(P)$ is only defined for positive definite operators P. The natural interpretation is that $P\log(P)$ refers to the operator obtained by extending the scalar function

$$\alpha \mapsto \begin{cases} \alpha\log(\alpha) & \text{if } \alpha > 0 \\ 0 & \text{if } \alpha = 0 \end{cases} \tag{5.84}$$

to positive semidefinite operators in the usual way (q.v. Section 1.1.3).

Similar to the Shannon entropy usually being considered for probability vectors, it is most common that one considers the von Neumann entropy function on density operator inputs. Also similar to the Shannon entropy, it is convenient to speak of the von Neumann entropy $H(X)$ of a register X, which means the quantity $H(\rho)$ for $\rho \in D(\mathcal{X})$ representing the state of X at the moment being considered. Once again, the notation $H(X, Y)$ is taken to mean $H((X, Y))$, and likewise for other forms of compound registers.

The study of the von Neumann entropy is aided by the consideration of the *quantum relative entropy*, which is an extension of the ordinary relative entropy from vectors to positive semidefinite operators.

Definition 5.18 Let $P, Q \in \operatorname{Pos}(\mathcal{X})$ be positive semidefinite operators, for a complex Euclidean space $\mathcal{X}$. The *quantum relative entropy* of P with respect to Q is defined as

$$D(P\|Q) = \begin{cases} \operatorname{Tr}(P\log(P)) - \operatorname{Tr}(P\log(Q)) & \text{if } \operatorname{im}(P) \subseteq \operatorname{im}(Q) \\ \infty & \text{otherwise.} \end{cases} \tag{5.85}$$

This definition is deserving of a short explanation because, as before, the logarithm is really only defined for positive definite operators. However, the operator $P\log(Q)$ has a natural interpretation for positive semidefinite operators P and Q that satisfy $\operatorname{im}(P) \subseteq \operatorname{im}(Q)$. The action of this operator on the subspace $\operatorname{im}(Q)$ is well-defined, as Q is a positive definite operator when restricted to this subspace, while its action on the subspace $\ker(Q)$ is taken to be the zero operator. This interpretation is equivalent to identifying $0\log(0)$ with 0, as the condition $\operatorname{im}(P) \subseteq \operatorname{im}(Q)$ implies that P acts as the zero operator on $\ker(Q)$. The operator $P\log(P)$ is defined for all positive semidefinite operators P, as was discussed previously.

It will be convenient to make note of a concrete expression for the value $D(P\|Q)$, assuming $\mathrm{im}(P) \subseteq \mathrm{im}(Q)$. Let $n = \dim(\mathcal{X})$ and suppose that

$$P = \sum_{j=1}^{n} \lambda_j(P)\, x_j x_j^* \quad \text{and} \quad Q = \sum_{k=1}^{n} \lambda_k(Q)\, y_k y_k^* \tag{5.86}$$

are spectral decompositions of P and Q. Let $r = \mathrm{rank}(P)$ and $s = \mathrm{rank}(Q)$, and observe that the expressions of P and Q in (5.86) may be truncated to r and s terms, respectively. It then holds that

$$D(P\|Q) = \sum_{j=1}^{r}\sum_{k=1}^{s} |\langle x_j, y_k\rangle|^2\, \lambda_j(P)\big(\log(\lambda_j(P)) - \log(\lambda_k(Q))\big). \tag{5.87}$$

The omission of the indices $j \in \{r+1, \ldots, n\}$ and $k \in \{s+1, \ldots, n\}$ in the sums is consistent with the identification $0\log(0) = 0$ suggested above. In particular, if k is such that $\lambda_k(Q) = 0$, then it must hold that

$$|\langle x_j, y_k\rangle|^2 \lambda_j(P) = 0 \tag{5.88}$$

for all $j \in \{1, \ldots, n\}$ by the assumption $\mathrm{im}(P) \subseteq \mathrm{im}(Q)$. An alternative expression for the quantum relative entropy $D(P\|Q)$, for P and Q having spectral decompositions (5.86), which is valid for all choices of P and Q, is given by

$$D(P\|Q) = \frac{1}{\ln(2)} \sum_{j=1}^{n}\sum_{k=1}^{n} \theta\big(|\langle x_j, y_k\rangle|^2\lambda_j(P), |\langle x_j, y_k\rangle|^2\lambda_k(Q)\big). \tag{5.89}$$

The *conditional von Neumann entropy* and *quantum mutual information* are defined in an analogous manner to the conditional Shannon entropy and mutual information. More precisely, for two registers X and Y in a given state of interest, one defines the conditional von Neumann entropy of X given Y as

$$H(\mathsf{X}|\mathsf{Y}) = H(\mathsf{X}, \mathsf{Y}) - H(\mathsf{Y}), \tag{5.90}$$

and one defines the quantum mutual information between X and Y as

$$I(\mathsf{X}:\mathsf{Y}) = H(\mathsf{X}) + H(\mathsf{Y}) - H(\mathsf{X}, \mathsf{Y}). \tag{5.91}$$

5.2.2 Elementary Properties of Quantum Entropic Functions

This section discusses elementary properties of the von Neumann entropy and quantum relative entropy functions. Specifically, these are properties that may be established without making essential use of the joint convexity of the quantum relative entropy, which is proved in the section following this one, or other equivalent statements.

Continuity of the von Neumann Entropy

The von Neumann entropy function is continuous, owing to the fact that it is a composition of continuous functions: the Shannon entropy function is continuous at every point in its domain, as is the function

$$\lambda\colon \operatorname{Herm}(\mathcal{X}) \to \mathbb{R}^n, \tag{5.92}$$

for $n = \dim(\mathcal{X})$.

Simple Identities Concerning Quantum Entropy

The three propositions that follow are stated as propositions for the sake of convenience. They may be verified directly through the definitions of the von Neumann entropy and quantum relative entropy functions.

Proposition 5.19 *Let $\mathcal{X}$ and $\mathcal{Y}$ be complex Euclidean spaces for which it holds that $\dim(\mathcal{X}) \leq \dim(\mathcal{Y})$, let $P, Q \in \operatorname{Pos}(\mathcal{X})$ be positive semidefinite operators, and let $V \in \operatorname{U}(\mathcal{X}, \mathcal{Y})$ be an isometry. It holds that*

$$\operatorname{H}(VPV^*) = \operatorname{H}(P) \quad and \quad \operatorname{D}(VPV^* \| VQV^*) = \operatorname{D}(P \| Q). \tag{5.93}$$

Proposition 5.20 *Let $\mathcal{X}$ and $\mathcal{Y}$ be complex Euclidean spaces and let $P \in \operatorname{Pos}(\mathcal{X})$ and $Q \in \operatorname{Pos}(\mathcal{Y})$ be positive semidefinite operators. It holds that*

$$\operatorname{H}\left(\begin{pmatrix} P & 0 \\ 0 & Q \end{pmatrix} \right) = \operatorname{H}(P) + \operatorname{H}(Q) \tag{5.94}$$

and

$$\operatorname{H}(P \otimes Q) = \operatorname{Tr}(Q)\operatorname{H}(P) + \operatorname{Tr}(P)\operatorname{H}(Q). \tag{5.95}$$

In particular, it holds that

$$\operatorname{H}(\rho \otimes \sigma) = \operatorname{H}(\rho) + \operatorname{H}(\sigma) \tag{5.96}$$

for all choices of density operators $\rho \in \operatorname{D}(\mathcal{X})$ and $\sigma \in \operatorname{D}(\mathcal{Y})$.

Proposition 5.21 *Let $P_0, Q_0 \in \operatorname{Pos}(\mathcal{X})$ and $P_1, Q_1 \in \operatorname{Pos}(\mathcal{Y})$ be positive semidefinite operators, for complex Euclidean spaces $\mathcal{X}$ and $\mathcal{Y}$, and assume that P_0 and P_1 are nonzero. It holds that*

$$\operatorname{D}(P_0 \otimes P_1 \| Q_0 \otimes Q_1) = \operatorname{Tr}(P_1)\operatorname{D}(P_0 \| Q_0) + \operatorname{Tr}(P_0)\operatorname{D}(P_1 \| Q_1). \tag{5.97}$$

As a consequence of the tensor product identities in the second and third of these propositions, one finds that the following two identities hold for all choices of a complex Euclidean space $\mathcal{X}$, positive semidefinite operators $P, Q \in \text{Pos}(\mathcal{X})$, and scalars $\alpha, \beta \in (0, \infty)$:

$$\text{H}(\alpha P) = \alpha \, \text{H}(P) - \alpha \log(\alpha) \, \text{Tr}(P), \tag{5.98}$$

$$\text{D}(\alpha P \| \beta Q) = \alpha \, \text{D}(P \| Q) + \alpha \log(\alpha/\beta) \, \text{Tr}(P). \tag{5.99}$$

Klein's Inequality

An analogous statement to Proposition 5.7 in the quantum setting is known as *Klein's inequality*. It implies that the quantum relative entropy function is nonnegative for density operator inputs.

Proposition 5.22 (Klein's inequality) *Let $\mathcal{X}$ be a complex Euclidean space, let $P, Q \in \text{Pos}(\mathcal{X})$ be positive semidefinite operators, and assume that $\text{Tr}(P) \geq \text{Tr}(Q)$. It holds that $\text{D}(P \| Q) \geq 0$. In particular, it holds that $\text{D}(\rho \| \sigma) \geq 0$ for every choice of density operators $\rho, \sigma \in \text{D}(\mathcal{X})$.*

Proof Let $n = \dim(\mathcal{X})$ and let

$$P = \sum_{j=1}^{n} \lambda_j(P) \, x_j x_j^* \quad \text{and} \quad Q = \sum_{k=1}^{n} \lambda_k(Q) \, y_k y_k^* \tag{5.100}$$

be spectral decompositions of P and Q. By Lemma 5.4, it holds that

$$\begin{aligned}
\text{D}(P \| Q) &= \frac{1}{\ln(2)} \sum_{j,k} \theta\Big(|\langle x_j, y_k \rangle|^2 \lambda_j(P), \, |\langle x_j, y_k \rangle|^2 \lambda_k(Q) \Big) \\
&\geq \frac{1}{\ln(2)} \theta\Big(\sum_{j,k} |\langle x_j, y_k \rangle|^2 \lambda_j(P), \sum_{j,k} |\langle x_j, y_k \rangle|^2 \lambda_k(Q) \Big) \tag{5.101} \\
&= \frac{1}{\ln(2)} \theta(\text{Tr}(P), \text{Tr}(Q)),
\end{aligned}$$

where the sums are over all $j, k \in \{1, \ldots, n\}$. By the assumption that $\text{Tr}(P) \geq \text{Tr}(Q)$, one concludes that $\theta(\text{Tr}(P), \text{Tr}(Q)) \geq 0$, which completes the proof. $\qquad \square$

Concavity and Subadditivity of von Neumann Entropy

Similar to the Shannon entropy, the von Neumann entropy is concave and subadditive, as the following two theorems establish.

Theorem 5.23 (Concavity of von Neumann entropy) *Let $\mathcal{X}$ be a complex Euclidean space, let $P, Q \in \text{Pos}(\mathcal{X})$ be positive semidefinite operators, and let $\lambda \in [0, 1]$. It holds that*

$$\text{H}(\lambda P + (1 - \lambda)Q) \geq \lambda \, \text{H}(P) + (1 - \lambda) \, \text{H}(Q). \tag{5.102}$$

Proof A straightforward computation reveals that

$$D\left(\begin{pmatrix} P & 0 \\ 0 & Q \end{pmatrix} \middle\| \begin{pmatrix} \frac{P+Q}{2} & 0 \\ 0 & \frac{P+Q}{2} \end{pmatrix}\right) = 2\,\mathrm{H}\left(\frac{P+Q}{2}\right) - \mathrm{H}(P) - \mathrm{H}(Q). \quad (5.103)$$

As the operators

$$\begin{pmatrix} P & 0 \\ 0 & Q \end{pmatrix} \quad \text{and} \quad \begin{pmatrix} \frac{P+Q}{2} & 0 \\ 0 & \frac{P+Q}{2} \end{pmatrix} \qquad (5.104)$$

have the same trace, the quantity represented by (5.103) is nonnegative by Klein's inequality (Proposition 5.22). It therefore holds that

$$\mathrm{H}\left(\frac{P+Q}{2}\right) \geq \frac{1}{2}\,\mathrm{H}(P) + \frac{1}{2}\,\mathrm{H}(Q), \qquad (5.105)$$

which implies that the von Neumann entropy is midpoint concave on the domain $\mathrm{Pos}(\mathcal{X})$. As the von Neumann entropy function is continuous on all of $\mathrm{Pos}(\mathcal{X})$, it follows that it is in fact a concave function on this domain, which completes the proof. □

Theorem 5.24 (Subadditivity of von Neumann entropy) *Let* X *and* Y *be registers. For every state of the register* (X, Y), *it holds that*

$$\mathrm{H}(\mathsf{X}, \mathsf{Y}) \leq \mathrm{H}(\mathsf{X}) + \mathrm{H}(\mathsf{Y}). \qquad (5.106)$$

Proof The inequality in the statement of the proposition may equivalently be written

$$\mathrm{H}(\rho) \leq \mathrm{H}(\rho[\mathsf{X}]) + \mathrm{H}(\rho[\mathsf{Y}]) \qquad (5.107)$$

for $\rho \in \mathrm{D}(\mathcal{X} \otimes \mathcal{Y})$ denoting an arbitrary state of the pair (X, Y). Using the formula

$$\log(P \otimes Q) = \log(P) \otimes \mathbb{1} + \mathbb{1} \otimes \log(Q), \qquad (5.108)$$

together with the fact that

$$\mathrm{im}(\rho) \subseteq \mathrm{im}(\rho[\mathsf{X}] \otimes \rho[\mathsf{Y}]), \qquad (5.109)$$

it may be observed that

$$D(\rho \| \rho[\mathsf{X}] \otimes \rho[\mathsf{Y}]) = -\mathrm{H}(\rho) + \mathrm{H}(\rho[\mathsf{X}]) + \mathrm{H}(\rho[\mathsf{Y}]). \qquad (5.110)$$

It holds that (5.110) is nonnegative by Klein's inequality (Proposition 5.22), and therefore the inequality (5.107) follows. □

Von Neumann Entropy and Purifications

Let X and Y be registers, and assume the compound register (X, Y) is in a pure state uu^*, for $u \in \mathcal{X} \otimes \mathcal{Y}$ being a unit vector. By means of the Schmidt decomposition, one may write

$$u = \sum_{a \in \Sigma} \sqrt{p(a)} \, x_a \otimes y_a \tag{5.111}$$

for some alphabet Σ, a probability vector $p \in \mathcal{P}(\Sigma)$, and orthonormal sets $\{x_a : a \in \Sigma\} \subset \mathcal{X}$ and $\{y_a : a \in \Sigma\} \subset \mathcal{Y}$. It holds that

$$(uu^*)[X] = \sum_{a \in \Sigma} p(a) x_a x_a^* \quad \text{and} \quad (uu^*)[Y] = \sum_{a \in \Sigma} p(a) y_a y_a^*, \tag{5.112}$$

and therefore

$$H(X) = H(p) = H(Y). \tag{5.113}$$

This simple observation, when combined with the notion of purifications of states, provides a useful tool for reasoning about the von Neumann entropy of collections of registers. The proof of the following theorem offers one example along these lines.

Theorem 5.25 *Let* X *and* Y *be registers. For every state of the register* (X, Y)*, it holds that*

$$H(X) \leq H(Y) + H(X, Y). \tag{5.114}$$

Proof Let $\rho \in D(\mathcal{X} \otimes \mathcal{Y})$ be a state of the pair (X, Y), and introduce a new register Z whose associated complex Euclidean space $\mathcal{Z}$ has dimension at least $\mathrm{rank}(\rho)$. By Theorem 2.10, there must exist a unit vector $u \in \mathcal{X} \otimes \mathcal{Y} \otimes \mathcal{Z}$ such that

$$\rho = \mathrm{Tr}_{\mathcal{Z}}(uu^*). \tag{5.115}$$

Now, consider the situation in which the compound register (X, Y, Z) is in the pure state uu^*, which is consistent with the state of (X, Y) being ρ by the requirement (5.115). By the argument suggested above, one finds that

$$H(X) = H(Y, Z) \quad \text{and} \quad H(X, Y) = H(Z). \tag{5.116}$$

By the subadditivity of the von Neumann entropy (Theorem 5.24), one has

$$H(Y, Z) \leq H(Y) + H(Z), \tag{5.117}$$

and therefore (5.114) holds. The required inequality has been established for all choices of the state ρ, which completes the proof. $\square$

The Fannes–Audenaert Inequality

The next theorem establishes an upper bound on the difference between the values of the von Neumann entropy function of two density operators. It may be seen as a quantitative form of the statement that the von Neumann entropy is continuous, restricted to density operator inputs. It is essentially a quantum generalization of Theorem 5.14, and its proof is based on that theorem.

Theorem 5.26 (Fannes–Audenaert inequality) *Let $\rho_0, \rho_1 \in D(\mathcal{X})$ be density operators, for $\mathcal{X}$ a complex Euclidean space of dimension $n \geq 2$, and let*

$$\delta = \frac{1}{2}\|\rho_0 - \rho_1\|_1. \tag{5.118}$$

It holds that

$$|\mathrm{H}(\rho_0) - \mathrm{H}(\rho_1)| \leq \delta \log(n-1) + \mathrm{H}(\delta, 1-\delta). \tag{5.119}$$

The following lemma relating the trace distance between two Hermitian operators to the 1-norm distance between vectors of their eigenvalues is used to reduce Theorem 5.26 to Theorem 5.14.

Lemma 5.27 *Let $X, Y \in \mathrm{Herm}(\mathcal{X})$ be Hermitian operators, for $\mathcal{X}$ being a complex Euclidean space of dimension n. It holds that*

$$\sum_{k=1}^{n}|\lambda_k(X) - \lambda_k(Y)| \leq \|X - Y\|_1 \leq \sum_{k=1}^{n}|\lambda_k(X) - \lambda_{n-k+1}(Y)|. \tag{5.120}$$

Proof Consider first a Jordan–Hahn decomposition of $X - Y$. Explicitly, let $P, Q \in \mathrm{Pos}(\mathcal{X})$ be orthogonal positive semidefinite operators such that

$$X - Y = P - Q. \tag{5.121}$$

Also let $Z = P + Y$, which is equivalent to $Z = Q + X$. As $Z \geq X$, it follows from the Courant–Fischer theorem (Theorem 1.2) that $\lambda_k(Z) \geq \lambda_k(X)$ for all $k \in \{1, \ldots, n\}$. Thus,

$$\begin{aligned}
\lambda_k(X) - \lambda_k(Y) &\leq (\lambda_k(X) - \lambda_k(Y)) + 2(\lambda_k(Z) - \lambda_k(X)) \\
&= 2\lambda_k(Z) - (\lambda_k(X) + \lambda_k(Y)).
\end{aligned} \tag{5.122}$$

By similar reasoning it follows that

$$\lambda_k(Y) - \lambda_k(X) \leq 2\lambda_k(Z) - (\lambda_k(X) + \lambda_k(Y)), \tag{5.123}$$

and therefore

$$|\lambda_k(X) - \lambda_k(Y)| \leq 2\lambda_k(Z) - (\lambda_k(X) + \lambda_k(Y)). \tag{5.124}$$

Consequently, one has

$$\sum_{k=1}^{n} |\lambda_k(X) - \lambda_k(Y)| \leq \sum_{k=1}^{n} (2\lambda_k(Z) - (\lambda_k(X) + \lambda_k(Y))) \tag{5.125}$$

$$= 2\operatorname{Tr}(Z) - \operatorname{Tr}(X) - \operatorname{Tr}(Y) = \operatorname{Tr}(P) + \operatorname{Tr}(Q) = \|X - Y\|_1.$$

This proves the first inequality.

To prove the second inequality, observe that

$$\|X - Y\|_1 = \langle 2\Pi - \mathbb{1}, X - Y \rangle \tag{5.126}$$

for some choice of a projection operator Π, owing to the fact that $X - Y$ is Hermitian. Let $r = \operatorname{rank}(\Pi)$, and note the following two inequalities:

$$\begin{aligned} \langle \Pi, X \rangle &\leq \lambda_1(X) + \cdots + \lambda_r(X), \\ \langle \Pi, Y \rangle &\geq \lambda_{n-r+1}(Y) + \cdots + \lambda_n(Y). \end{aligned} \tag{5.127}$$

It follows that

$$\begin{aligned} &\|X - Y\|_1 \\ &\leq 2\big(\lambda_1(X) + \cdots + \lambda_r(X)\big) - 2\big(\lambda_{n-r+1}(Y) + \cdots + \lambda_n(Y)\big) \\ &\quad - \operatorname{Tr}(X) + \operatorname{Tr}(Y) \\ &= \sum_{k=1}^{r} (\lambda_k(X) - \lambda_{n-k+1}(Y)) + \sum_{k=r+1}^{n} (\lambda_{n-k+1}(Y) - \lambda_k(X)) \\ &\leq \sum_{k=1}^{n} |\lambda_k(X) - \lambda_{n-k+1}(Y)|, \end{aligned} \tag{5.128}$$

as required. $\qquad\square$

Proof of Theorem 5.26 Define $\delta_0, \delta_1 \in [0, 1]$ as follows:

$$\begin{aligned} \delta_0 &= \frac{1}{2} \sum_{k=1}^{n} |\lambda_k(\rho_0) - \lambda_k(\rho_1)|, \\ \delta_1 &= \frac{1}{2} \sum_{k=1}^{n} |\lambda_k(\rho_0) - \lambda_{n-k+1}(\rho_1)|. \end{aligned} \tag{5.129}$$

By Lemma 5.27 it holds that $\delta_0 \leq \delta \leq \delta_1$, and therefore $\delta = \alpha\delta_0 + (1-\alpha)\delta_1$ for some choice of $\alpha \in [0, 1]$. By Theorem 5.14 it holds that

$$\begin{aligned} &|\mathrm{H}(\rho_0) - \mathrm{H}(\rho_1)| \\ &= |\mathrm{H}(\lambda_1(\rho_0), \ldots, \lambda_n(\rho_0)) - \mathrm{H}(\lambda_1(\rho_1), \ldots, \lambda_n(\rho_1))| \\ &\leq \delta_0 \log(n-1) + \mathrm{H}(\delta_0, 1-\delta_0) \end{aligned} \tag{5.130}$$

and

$$|H(\rho_0) - H(\rho_1)|$$
$$= |H(\lambda_1(\rho_0), \dots, \lambda_n(\rho_0)) - H(\lambda_n(\rho_1), \dots, \lambda_1(\rho_1))| \qquad (5.131)$$
$$\leq \delta_1 \log(n-1) + H(\delta_1, 1 - \delta_1).$$

Thus, by the concavity of the Shannon entropy function (Proposition 5.5), it follows that

$$|H(\rho_0) - H(\rho_1)| \leq (\alpha\delta_0 + (1-\alpha)\delta_1) \log(n-1)$$
$$+ \alpha\, H(\delta_0, 1 - \delta_0) + (1-\alpha)\, H(\delta_1, 1 - \delta_1) \qquad (5.132)$$
$$\leq \delta \log(n-1) + H(\delta, 1 - \delta),$$

as required.   □

The Fannes–Audenaert inequality is saturated for all values of $\delta \in [0,1]$ and $n \geq 2$. For instance, for any choice of $n \geq 2$ and $\Sigma = \{1, \dots, n\}$, one may consider the density operators

$$\rho_0 = E_{1,1} \quad \text{and} \quad \rho_1 = (1-\delta)E_{1,1} + \frac{\delta}{n-1} \sum_{k=2}^{n} E_{k,k}. \qquad (5.133)$$

It holds that

$$\delta = \frac{1}{2}\|\rho_0 - \rho_1\|_1 \qquad (5.134)$$

and

$$|H(\rho_0) - H(\rho_1)| = H(\rho_1) = H(\delta, 1 - \delta) + \delta \log(n-1). \qquad (5.135)$$

The Quantum Relative Entropy as a Limit of Difference Quotients

As the following proposition states, the quantum relative entropy can be expressed as the limit of a simple expression of its arguments. This fact will be useful in Section 5.2.3, for the task of proving that the quantum relative entropy is jointly convex.

Proposition 5.28 *Let $P, Q \in \mathrm{Pos}(\mathcal{X})$ be positive semidefinite operators, for $\mathcal{X}$ a complex Euclidean space. It holds that*

$$D(P\|Q) = \frac{1}{\ln(2)} \lim_{\varepsilon \downarrow 0} \frac{\mathrm{Tr}(P) - \langle P^{1-\varepsilon}, Q^{\varepsilon} \rangle}{\varepsilon}. \qquad (5.136)$$

Proof The proposition is immediate in the case that $\mathrm{im}(P) \not\subseteq \mathrm{im}(Q)$, for in this case

$$\lim_{\varepsilon \downarrow 0} \left(\mathrm{Tr}(P) - \langle P^{1-\varepsilon}, Q^{\varepsilon} \rangle \right) = \langle P, \mathbb{1} - \Pi_{\mathrm{im}(Q)} \rangle \qquad (5.137)$$

is a positive real number. This implies that the limit in (5.136) evaluates to positive infinity, which is in agreement with the quantum relative entropy. The proposition is also immediate when $P = 0$. It therefore remains to consider the case that P is a nonzero operator and $\mathrm{im}(P) \subseteq \mathrm{im}(Q)$, which is taken as an assumption for the remainder of the proof.

Let $r = \mathrm{rank}(P)$ and $s = \mathrm{rank}(Q)$. By the spectral theorem (as stated by Corollary 1.4), one may write

$$P = \sum_{j=1}^{r} \lambda_j(P) \, x_j x_j^* \quad \text{and} \quad Q = \sum_{k=1}^{s} \lambda_k(Q) \, y_k y_k^* \tag{5.138}$$

for orthonormal collections of vectors $\{x_1, \ldots, x_r\}$ and $\{y_1, \ldots, y_s\}$. Define a function $f : \mathbb{R} \to \mathbb{R}$ as

$$f(\alpha) = \sum_{j=1}^{r} \sum_{k=1}^{s} |\langle x_j, y_k \rangle|^2 \, \lambda_j(P)^{1-\alpha} \, \lambda_k(Q)^\alpha \tag{5.139}$$

for all $\alpha \in \mathbb{R}$. This function is differentiable at every point $\alpha \in \mathbb{R}$, with its derivative given by

$$f'(\alpha) = - \sum_{j=1}^{r} \sum_{k=1}^{s} |\langle x_j, y_k \rangle|^2 \, \lambda_j(P)^{1-\alpha} \, \lambda_k(Q)^\alpha \ln\left(\frac{\lambda_j(P)}{\lambda_k(Q)}\right). \tag{5.140}$$

Now, it holds that

$$f(\alpha) = \langle P^{1-\alpha}, Q^\alpha \rangle \tag{5.141}$$

for every $\alpha \in (0, 1)$, while

$$f(0) = \langle P, \Pi_{\mathrm{im}(Q)} \rangle = \mathrm{Tr}(P). \tag{5.142}$$

Evaluating the derivative of f at 0 yields

$$f'(0) = - \ln(2) \, \mathrm{D}(P \| Q), \tag{5.143}$$

while the definition of the derivative, as the limit of difference quotients, yields

$$f'(0) = \lim_{\varepsilon \downarrow 0} \frac{f(\varepsilon) - f(0)}{\varepsilon} = \lim_{\varepsilon \downarrow 0} \frac{\langle P^{1-\varepsilon}, Q^\varepsilon \rangle - \mathrm{Tr}(P)}{\varepsilon}. \tag{5.144}$$

The proposition follows by combining equations (5.144) and (5.143). $\square$

5.2.3 Joint Convexity of Quantum Relative Entropy

This section contains a proof of a fundamental fact concerning the quantum relative entropy, which is that it is a jointly convex function. By making use of this key fact, one may prove that several other important properties of the von Neumann entropy and quantum relative entropy functions hold.

Proof of the Joint Convexity of the Quantum Relative Entropy

Multiple proofs of the joint convexity of the quantum relative entropy are known. The proof to be presented below will make use of the following technical lemma relating the diagonal and off-diagonal blocks of any 2-by-2 positive semidefinite block operator, under the assumption that the blocks are Hermitian and the diagonal blocks commute.

Lemma 5.29 *Let $\mathcal{X}$ be a complex Euclidean space, let $P, Q \in \mathrm{Pos}(\mathcal{X})$ be positive semidefinite operators such that $[P, Q] = 0$, and let $H \in \mathrm{Herm}(\mathcal{X})$ be a Hermitian operator for which*

$$\begin{pmatrix} P & H \\ H & Q \end{pmatrix} \in \mathrm{Pos}(\mathcal{X} \oplus \mathcal{X}). \tag{5.145}$$

It holds that $H \leq \sqrt{P}\sqrt{Q}$.

Proof The lemma will first be proved for P and Q being positive definite operators. By Lemma 3.18 it follows that

$$\left\| P^{-\frac{1}{2}} H Q^{-\frac{1}{2}} \right\| \leq 1, \tag{5.146}$$

which implies that every eigenvalue of the operator $P^{-\frac{1}{2}} H Q^{-\frac{1}{2}}$ is bounded by 1 in absolute value. As P and Q commute, it holds that the eigenvalues of $P^{-\frac{1}{4}} Q^{-\frac{1}{4}} H Q^{-\frac{1}{4}} P^{-\frac{1}{4}}$ agree with those of $P^{-\frac{1}{2}} H Q^{-\frac{1}{2}}$, and therefore

$$\lambda_1\left(P^{-\frac{1}{4}} Q^{-\frac{1}{4}} H Q^{-\frac{1}{4}} P^{-\frac{1}{4}}\right) \leq 1. \tag{5.147}$$

The inequality (5.147) is equivalent to

$$P^{-\frac{1}{4}} Q^{-\frac{1}{4}} H Q^{-\frac{1}{4}} P^{-\frac{1}{4}} \leq \mathbb{1}, \tag{5.148}$$

which, again by the commutativity of P and Q, implies $H \leq \sqrt{P}\sqrt{Q}$.

In the general case where P and Q are not necessarily positive definite, the argument above may be applied to $P + \varepsilon \mathbb{1}$ and $Q + \varepsilon \mathbb{1}$ in place of P and Q, respectively, to obtain

$$H \leq \sqrt{P + \varepsilon \mathbb{1}}\sqrt{Q + \varepsilon \mathbb{1}} \tag{5.149}$$

for all $\varepsilon > 0$. The function $\varepsilon \mapsto \sqrt{P + \varepsilon \mathbb{1}}\sqrt{Q + \varepsilon \mathbb{1}} - H$ is continuous on the domain $[0, \infty)$, and so the preimage of the closed set $\mathrm{Pos}(\mathcal{X})$ under this function is closed. Given that every $\varepsilon > 0$ is contained in this preimage, it follows that 0 is contained in the preimage as well: $\sqrt{P}\sqrt{Q} - H$ is positive semidefinite, which proves the lemma. $\qquad \square$

The next step toward the joint convexity of the quantum relative entropy is to prove the following theorem. It is one formulation of a fact known as *Lieb's concavity theorem*.

Theorem 5.30 (Lieb's concavity theorem) *Let $A_0, A_1 \in \mathrm{Pos}(\mathcal{X})$ and $B_0, B_1 \in \mathrm{Pos}(\mathcal{Y})$ be positive semidefinite operators, for complex Euclidean spaces $\mathcal{X}$ and $\mathcal{Y}$. For every choice of a real number $\alpha \in [0, 1]$ it holds that*

$$(A_0 + A_1)^\alpha \otimes (B_0 + B_1)^{1-\alpha} \geq A_0^\alpha \otimes B_0^{1-\alpha} + A_1^\alpha \otimes B_1^{1-\alpha}. \tag{5.150}$$

Remark Within the context of this theorem and its proof, one should make the interpretation $P^0 = \Pi_{\mathrm{im}(P)}$ for every positive semidefinite operator P.

Proof of Theorem 5.30 For every real number $\alpha \in [0, 1]$, define operators as follows:

$$\begin{aligned} X(\alpha) &= A_0^\alpha \otimes B_0^{1-\alpha}, \\ Y(\alpha) &= A_1^\alpha \otimes B_1^{1-\alpha}, \\ Z(\alpha) &= (A_0 + A_1)^\alpha \otimes (B_0 + B_1)^{1-\alpha}. \end{aligned} \tag{5.151}$$

The operators within these three individual collections commute, meaning

$$[X(\alpha), X(\beta)] = 0, \quad [Y(\alpha), Y(\beta)] = 0, \quad \text{and} \quad [Z(\alpha), Z(\beta)] = 0 \tag{5.152}$$

for every choice of $\alpha, \beta \in [0, 1]$, and moreover it holds that

$$\sqrt{X(\alpha)}\sqrt{X(\beta)} = X\left(\frac{\alpha + \beta}{2}\right), \tag{5.153}$$

$$\sqrt{Y(\alpha)}\sqrt{Y(\beta)} = Y\left(\frac{\alpha + \beta}{2}\right), \tag{5.154}$$

$$\sqrt{Z(\alpha)}\sqrt{Z(\beta)} = Z\left(\frac{\alpha + \beta}{2}\right). \tag{5.155}$$

With respect to these operators, the statement of the theorem is equivalent to the claim that

$$Z(\alpha) \geq X(\alpha) + Y(\alpha) \tag{5.156}$$

for every $\alpha \in [0, 1]$. The function

$$\alpha \mapsto Z(\alpha) - (X(\alpha) + Y(\alpha)) \tag{5.157}$$

defined on the interval $[0, 1]$ is continuous, and therefore the preimage of the closed set $\mathrm{Pos}(\mathcal{X} \otimes \mathcal{Y})$ under this function is closed. It therefore suffices to prove that the set of all $\alpha \in [0, 1]$ for which (5.156) holds is dense in $[0, 1]$.

Now, suppose it has been proved that

$$Z(\alpha) \geq X(\alpha) + Y(\alpha) \quad \text{and} \quad Z(\beta) \geq X(\beta) + Y(\beta) \tag{5.158}$$

for some particular choice of real numbers $\alpha, \beta \in [0, 1]$. It holds that

$$\begin{pmatrix} \sqrt{X(\alpha)} \\ \sqrt{X(\beta)} \end{pmatrix} \begin{pmatrix} \sqrt{X(\alpha)} & \sqrt{X(\beta)} \end{pmatrix} = \begin{pmatrix} X(\alpha) & X\left(\frac{\alpha+\beta}{2}\right) \\ X\left(\frac{\alpha+\beta}{2}\right) & X(\beta) \end{pmatrix} \tag{5.159}$$

is positive semidefinite, and likewise

$$\begin{pmatrix} \sqrt{Y(\alpha)} \\ \sqrt{Y(\beta)} \end{pmatrix} \begin{pmatrix} \sqrt{Y(\alpha)} & \sqrt{Y(\beta)} \end{pmatrix} = \begin{pmatrix} Y(\alpha) & Y\left(\frac{\alpha+\beta}{2}\right) \\ Y\left(\frac{\alpha+\beta}{2}\right) & Y(\beta) \end{pmatrix} \tag{5.160}$$

is positive semidefinite. The sum of these two matrices is therefore positive semidefinite, and given the inequalities (5.158) it therefore follows that

$$\begin{pmatrix} Z(\alpha) & X\left(\frac{\alpha+\beta}{2}\right) + Y\left(\frac{\alpha+\beta}{2}\right) \\ X\left(\frac{\alpha+\beta}{2}\right) + Y\left(\frac{\alpha+\beta}{2}\right) & Z(\beta) \end{pmatrix} \tag{5.161}$$

is positive semidefinite. Invoking Lemma 5.29, one finds that

$$X\left(\frac{\alpha+\beta}{2}\right) + Y\left(\frac{\alpha+\beta}{2}\right) \leq \sqrt{Z(\alpha)}\sqrt{Z(\beta)} = Z\left(\frac{\alpha+\beta}{2}\right). \tag{5.162}$$

It trivially holds that $Z(0) \geq X(0) + Y(0)$ and $Z(1) \geq X(1) + Y(1)$. For any choice of $\alpha, \beta \in [0, 1]$, one has that the inequalities (5.158) together imply that

$$Z\left(\frac{\alpha+\beta}{2}\right) \geq X\left(\frac{\alpha+\beta}{2}\right) + Y\left(\frac{\alpha+\beta}{2}\right). \tag{5.163}$$

The inequality (5.156) must therefore hold for every $\alpha \in [0, 1]$ taking the form $\alpha = k/2^n$ for nonnegative integers k and n with $k \leq 2^n$. The set of all such α is dense in $[0, 1]$, so the theorem is proved. $\qquad \square$

Corollary 5.31   *Let $P_0, P_1, Q_0, Q_1 \in \mathrm{Pos}(\mathcal{X})$ be positive semidefinite operators, for $\mathcal{X}$ a complex Euclidean space. It holds that*

$$\langle (P_0 + P_1)^\alpha, (Q_0 + Q_1)^{1-\alpha} \rangle \geq \langle P_0^\alpha, Q_0^{1-\alpha} \rangle + \langle P_1^\alpha, Q_1^{1-\alpha} \rangle \tag{5.164}$$

for every $\alpha \in [0, 1]$.

Proof By making the substitution $A_0 = P_0$, $A_1 = P_1$, $B_0 = Q_0^{\mathsf{T}}$, and $B_1 = Q_1^{\mathsf{T}}$ in Theorem 5.30, one finds that

$$(P_0 + P_1)^{\alpha} \otimes (Q_0^{\mathsf{T}} + Q_1^{\mathsf{T}})^{1-\alpha} \geq P_0^{\alpha} \otimes (Q_0^{\mathsf{T}})^{1-\alpha} + P_1^{\alpha} \otimes (Q_1^{\mathsf{T}})^{1-\alpha}, \quad (5.165)$$

and therefore

$$\begin{aligned}
&\text{vec}(\mathbb{1}_{\mathcal{X}})^* \big((P_0 + P_1)^{\alpha} \otimes (Q_0^{\mathsf{T}} + Q_1^{\mathsf{T}})^{1-\alpha}\big) \text{vec}(\mathbb{1}_{\mathcal{X}}) \\
&\quad \geq \text{vec}(\mathbb{1}_{\mathcal{X}})^* \big(P_0^{\alpha} \otimes (Q_0^{\mathsf{T}})^{1-\alpha} + P_1^{\alpha} \otimes (Q_1^{\mathsf{T}})^{1-\alpha}\big) \text{vec}(\mathbb{1}_{\mathcal{X}}).
\end{aligned} \quad (5.166)$$

Simplifying the two sides of this inequality yields (5.164), as required. $\qquad\square$

The joint convexity of the quantum relative entropy now follows from a combination of Corollary 5.31 with Proposition 5.28.

Theorem 5.32 *Let $\mathcal{X}$ be a complex Euclidean space and let P_0, P_1, Q_0, $Q_1 \in \text{Pos}(\mathcal{X})$ be positive semidefinite operators. It holds that*

$$D(P_0 + P_1 \| Q_0 + Q_1) \leq D(P_0 \| Q_0) + D(P_1 \| Q_1). \quad (5.167)$$

Proof By Proposition 5.28 together with Corollary 5.31 it holds that

$$\begin{aligned}
&D(P_0 + P_1 \| Q_0 + Q_1) \\
&= \frac{1}{\ln(2)} \lim_{\varepsilon \downarrow 0} \frac{\text{Tr}(P_0 + P_1) - \langle (P_0 + P_1)^{1-\varepsilon}, (Q_0 + Q_1)^{\varepsilon} \rangle}{\varepsilon} \\
&\leq \frac{1}{\ln(2)} \left(\lim_{\varepsilon \downarrow 0} \frac{\text{Tr}(P_0) - \langle P_0^{1-\varepsilon}, Q_0^{\varepsilon} \rangle}{\varepsilon} + \lim_{\varepsilon \downarrow 0} \frac{\text{Tr}(P_1) - \langle P_1^{1-\varepsilon}, Q_1^{\varepsilon} \rangle}{\varepsilon} \right) \\
&= D(P_0 \| Q_0) + D(P_1 \| Q_1),
\end{aligned} \quad (5.168)$$

which proves the theorem. $\qquad\square$

Corollary 5.33 (Joint convexity of quantum relative entropy) *Let $\mathcal{X}$ be a complex Euclidean space, let P_0, P_1, Q_0, $Q_1 \in \text{Pos}(\mathcal{X})$ be positive semidefinite operators, and let $\lambda \in [0,1]$. It holds that*

$$\begin{aligned}
&D(\lambda P_0 + (1-\lambda)P_1 \| \lambda Q_0 + (1-\lambda)Q_1) \\
&\quad \leq \lambda \, D(P_0 \| Q_0) + (1-\lambda) \, D(P_1 \| Q_1).
\end{aligned} \quad (5.169)$$

Proof The corollary is trivial in case $\lambda = 0$ or $\lambda = 1$. Otherwise, combining Theorem 5.32 with the identity (5.99) yields

$$\begin{aligned}
&D(\lambda P_0 + (1-\lambda)P_1 \| \lambda Q_0 + (1-\lambda)Q_1) \\
&\quad \leq D(\lambda P_0 \| \lambda Q_0) + D((1-\lambda)P_1 \| (1-\lambda)Q_1) \\
&\quad = \lambda \, D(P_0 \| Q_0) + (1-\lambda) \, D(P_1 \| Q_1),
\end{aligned} \quad (5.170)$$

as required. $\qquad\square$

Monotonicity of Quantum Relative Entropy

As was suggested above, the fact that the quantum relative entropy function is jointly convex has several interesting implications. One such implication is that the quantum relative entropy function is monotonically decreasing under the action of any channel. The next proposition establishes that this is so for mixed-unitary channels, and the theorem that follows establishes that the same is true for all channels.

Proposition 5.34 *Let $\mathcal{X}$ be a complex Euclidean space, let $\Phi \in C(\mathcal{X})$ be a mixed-unitary channel, and let $P, Q \in \mathrm{Pos}(\mathcal{X})$ be positive semidefinite operators. It holds that*

$$\mathrm{D}(\Phi(P) \| \Phi(Q)) \leq \mathrm{D}(P \| Q). \tag{5.171}$$

Proof As Φ is a mixed-unitary channel, there must exist an alphabet Σ, a collection of unitary operators $\{U_a : a \in \Sigma\} \subset \mathrm{U}(\mathcal{X})$, and a probability vector $p \in \mathcal{P}(\Sigma)$, such that

$$\Phi(X) = \sum_{a \in \Sigma} p(a) U_a X U_a^* \tag{5.172}$$

for all $X \in \mathrm{L}(\mathcal{X})$. Applying Corollary 5.33, along with Proposition 5.19, one has

$$
\begin{aligned}
\mathrm{D}(\Phi(P) \| \Phi(Q)) &= \mathrm{D}\left(\sum_{a \in \Sigma} p(a) U_a P U_a^* \,\Big\|\, \sum_{a \in \Sigma} p(a) U_a Q U_a^* \right) \\
&\leq \sum_{a \in \Sigma} p(a)\, \mathrm{D}(U_a P U_a^* \| U_a Q U_a^*) = \sum_{a \in \Sigma} p(a)\, \mathrm{D}(P \| Q) = \mathrm{D}(P \| Q),
\end{aligned} \tag{5.173}
$$

as required. $\qquad\square$

Theorem 5.35 (Monotonicity of quantum relative entropy) *Let $\mathcal{X}$ and $\mathcal{Y}$ be complex Euclidean spaces, let $P, Q \in \mathrm{Pos}(\mathcal{X})$ be positive semidefinite operators, and let $\Phi \in C(\mathcal{X}, \mathcal{Y})$ be a channel. It holds that*

$$\mathrm{D}(\Phi(P) \| \Phi(Q)) \leq \mathrm{D}(P \| Q). \tag{5.174}$$

Proof By Corollary 2.27 there must exist a complex Euclidean space $\mathcal{Z}$ and a linear isometry $A \in \mathrm{U}(\mathcal{X}, \mathcal{Y} \otimes \mathcal{Z})$ for which

$$\Phi(X) = \mathrm{Tr}_{\mathcal{Z}}(A X A^*) \tag{5.175}$$

for all $X \in \mathrm{L}(\mathcal{X})$. Let $\Omega \in C(\mathcal{Z})$ denote the completely depolarizing channel, defined by $\Omega(Z) = \mathrm{Tr}(Z) \omega$ for all $Z \in \mathrm{L}(\mathcal{Z})$, where

$$\omega = \frac{\mathbb{1}_{\mathcal{Z}}}{\dim(\mathcal{Z})} \tag{5.176}$$

denotes the completely mixed state with respect to the space $\mathcal{Z}$. As was demonstrated in Section 4.1.2, the channel Ω is a mixed-unitary channel, from which it follows that $\mathbb{1}_{\mathrm{L}(\mathcal{Y})} \otimes \Omega$ is also a mixed-unitary channel. By Proposition 5.34, together with Proposition 5.19, it therefore holds that

$$
\begin{aligned}
\mathrm{D}((\mathbb{1}_{\mathrm{L}(\mathcal{Y})} &\otimes \Omega)(APA^*) \| (\mathbb{1}_{\mathrm{L}(\mathcal{Y})} \otimes \Omega)(AQA^*)) \\
&\leq \mathrm{D}(APA^* \| AQA^*) = \mathrm{D}(P \| Q).
\end{aligned}
\tag{5.177}
$$

As

$$
(\mathbb{1}_{\mathrm{L}(\mathcal{Y})} \otimes \Omega)(AXA^*) = \mathrm{Tr}_{\mathcal{Z}}(AXA^*) \otimes \omega = \Phi(X) \otimes \omega
\tag{5.178}
$$

for all $X \in \mathrm{L}(\mathcal{X})$, it follows by Proposition 5.21 that

$$
\mathrm{D}(\Phi(P) \| \Phi(Q)) = \mathrm{D}(\Phi(P) \otimes \omega \| \Phi(Q) \otimes \omega) \leq \mathrm{D}(P \| Q),
\tag{5.179}
$$

which completes the proof. $\qquad\square$

Strong Subadditivity of von Neumann Entropy

Another implication of the joint convexity of quantum relative entropy is the following theorem, stating that the von Neumann entropy possesses a property known as *strong subadditivity*.

Theorem 5.36 (Strong subadditivity of von Neumann entropy) *Let* X, Y, *and* Z *be registers. For every state of the register* (X, Y, Z) *it holds that*

$$
\mathrm{H}(\mathsf{X}, \mathsf{Y}, \mathsf{Z}) + \mathrm{H}(\mathsf{Z}) \leq \mathrm{H}(\mathsf{X}, \mathsf{Z}) + \mathrm{H}(\mathsf{Y}, \mathsf{Z}).
\tag{5.180}
$$

Proof Let $\rho \in \mathrm{D}(\mathcal{X} \otimes \mathcal{Y} \otimes \mathcal{Z})$ be chosen arbitrarily and let

$$
\omega = \frac{\mathbb{1}_{\mathcal{X}}}{\dim(\mathcal{X})}
\tag{5.181}
$$

denote the completely mixed state with respect to the space $\mathcal{X}$. The following two equalities may be verified directly:

$$
\begin{aligned}
\mathrm{D}(\rho[\mathsf{X}, \mathsf{Y}, \mathsf{Z}] &\| \omega \otimes \rho[\mathsf{Y}, \mathsf{Z}]) \\
&= -\mathrm{H}(\rho[\mathsf{X}, \mathsf{Y}, \mathsf{Z}]) + \mathrm{H}(\rho[\mathsf{Y}, \mathsf{Z}]) + \log(\dim(\mathcal{X}))
\end{aligned}
\tag{5.182}
$$

and

$$
\begin{aligned}
\mathrm{D}(\rho[\mathsf{X}, \mathsf{Z}] &\| \omega \otimes \rho[\mathsf{Z}]) \\
&= -\mathrm{H}(\rho[\mathsf{X}, \mathsf{Z}]) + \mathrm{H}(\rho[\mathsf{Z}]) + \log(\dim(\mathcal{X})).
\end{aligned}
\tag{5.183}
$$

Taking the channel $\Phi \in \mathrm{C}(\mathcal{X} \otimes \mathcal{Y} \otimes \mathcal{Z}, \mathcal{X} \otimes \mathcal{Z})$ to be the partial trace over $\mathcal{Y}$ in Theorem 5.35, one finds that

$$
\mathrm{D}(\rho[\mathsf{X}, \mathsf{Z}] \| \omega \otimes \rho[\mathsf{Z}]) \leq \mathrm{D}(\rho[\mathsf{X}, \mathsf{Y}, \mathsf{Z}] \| \omega \otimes \rho[\mathsf{Y}, \mathsf{Z}]),
\tag{5.184}
$$

and therefore

$$H(\rho[X, Y, Z]) + H(\rho[Z]) \leq H(\rho[X, Z]) + H(\rho[Y, Z]), \tag{5.185}$$

which proves the theorem. $\qquad\qquad\square$

The corollary that follows gives an equivalent statement to the strong subadditivity of von Neumann entropy, stated in terms of the quantum mutual information.

Corollary 5.37 *Let* X, Y, *and* Z *be registers. For every state of the register* (X, Y, Z) *it holds that*

$$I(X : Z) \leq I(X : Y, Z). \tag{5.186}$$

Proof By Theorem 5.36 it holds that

$$H(X, Y, Z) + H(Z) \leq H(X, Z) + H(Y, Z), \tag{5.187}$$

which is equivalent to

$$H(Z) - H(X, Z) \leq H(Y, Z) - H(X, Y, Z). \tag{5.188}$$

Adding $H(X)$ to both sides gives

$$H(X) + H(Z) - H(X, Z) \leq H(X) + H(Y, Z) - H(X, Y, Z). \tag{5.189}$$

This inequality is equivalent to (5.186), which completes the proof. $\qquad\square$

The Quantum Pinsker Inequality

The final implication of the joint convexity of quantum relative entropy to be presented in this section is a quantum analogue of Theorem 5.15 that establishes a lower bound on the quantum relative entropy between two density operators in terms of their trace distance.

Theorem 5.38 (Quantum Pinsker inequality) *Let* $\rho_0, \rho_1 \in D(\mathcal{X})$ *be density operators, for* $\mathcal{X}$ *a complex Euclidean space. It holds that*

$$D(\rho_0 \| \rho_1) \geq \frac{1}{2 \ln(2)} \| \rho_0 - \rho_1 \|_1^2. \tag{5.190}$$

Proof Let $\Sigma = \{0, 1\}$ and let $\mu : \Sigma \to \text{Pos}(\mathcal{X})$ be a measurement that optimally discriminates between the states ρ_0 and ρ_1, assuming they are given with equal probability, as discussed in Section 3.1.1. For probability vectors $p_0, p_1 \in \mathcal{P}(\Sigma)$ defined as $p_0(a) = \langle \mu(a), \rho_0 \rangle$ and $p_1(a) = \langle \mu(a), \rho_1 \rangle$ for each $a \in \Sigma$, one concludes that

$$\| p_0 - p_1 \|_1 = \| \rho_0 - \rho_1 \|_1. \tag{5.191}$$

Now let $\Phi \in C(\mathcal{X}, \mathbb{C}^\Sigma)$ be the quantum-to-classical channel associated with μ, which satisfies

$$\Phi(X) = \langle\mu(0), X\rangle E_{0,0} + \langle\mu(1), X\rangle E_{1,1} \qquad (5.192)$$

for each $X \in L(\mathcal{X})$. By Theorem 5.35, it holds that

$$D(\rho_0 \| \rho_1) \geq D(\Phi(\rho_0) \| \Phi(\rho_1)) = D(p_0 \| p_1), \qquad (5.193)$$

and by Theorem 5.15 it holds that

$$D(p_0 \| p_1) \geq \frac{1}{2\ln(2)} \|p_0 - p_1\|_1^2. \qquad (5.194)$$

The theorem follows from (5.191), (5.193), and (5.194). $\qquad\qquad\square$

5.3 Source Coding

This section discusses the notion of *source coding*, as it relates to quantum information, and to the von Neumann entropy function in particular. The term *source coding*, as it is interpreted here, refers to the process of encoding information produced by a given source in such a way that it may later be decoded. One natural goal of such a process is to compress the information produced by the source, in order to reduce costs of storage or transmission. Three principal variants of source coding will be discussed.

The first is a purely classical variant in which information from a given classical source is encoded into a fixed-length binary string in such a way that the information produced by the source can be decoded with high probability. *Shannon's source coding theorem* establishes asymptotic bounds on compression rates that are achievable for this task, given a standard assumption on the source.

The second variant of source coding to be discussed is a quantum analogue to the first; a source produces quantum information that is to be encoded into a sequence of qubits and then decoded. A theorem due to Schumacher, representing a quantum analogue of Shannon's source coding theorem, establishes asymptotic bounds on the rates of compression that are achievable for this task.

The third variant of source coding to be considered is one in which a source produces classical information, which is encoded into the quantum state of a collection of registers, and then decoded through a measurement performed on these registers. Theorems due to Holevo and Nayak establish fundamental limitations on two specific formulations of this task.

5.3.1 Classical Source Coding

In the first variant of source coding to be considered in the present section, a classical source produces a sequence of symbols, chosen independently from a known probability distribution. This sequence is to be encoded into a binary string in such a way that it may later be decoded, revealing the original sequence produced by the source with high probability.

The main purpose of this discussion, as it pertains to this book, is to introduce basic concepts and techniques regarding classical source coding that will carry over to the analogous quantum variant of this task. With this purpose in mind, the discussion is limited to *fixed-length* coding schemes. These are schemes in which the length of each encoding is determined only by the number of symbols produced by the source, and not by the symbols themselves. A typical goal when designing such a scheme is to minimize the length of the binary string encodings while allowing for a recovery of the original sequence with high probability.

Shannon's source coding theorem[1] establishes a fundamental connection between the rates of compression that can be achieved by such schemes and the Shannon entropy of the probability vector describing the source.

Coding Schemes and the Statement of Shannon's Source Coding Theorem

Let Σ be an alphabet, let $p \in \mathcal{P}(\Sigma)$ be a probability vector, and let $\Gamma = \{0, 1\}$ denote the binary alphabet. For any choice of a positive integer n and real numbers $\alpha > 0$ and $\delta \in (0, 1)$, and for $m = \lfloor \alpha n \rfloor$, a pair of mappings

$$f : \Sigma^n \to \Gamma^m,$$
$$g : \Gamma^m \to \Sigma^n$$

(5.195)

is said to be an (n, α, δ)-*coding scheme* for p if it holds that

$$\sum_{a_1 \cdots a_n \in G} p(a_1) \cdots p(a_n) > 1 - \delta,$$

(5.196)

for

$$G = \{a_1 \cdots a_n \in \Sigma^n : g(f(a_1 \cdots a_n)) = a_1 \cdots a_n\}.$$

(5.197)

(Here, and throughout the remainder of this chapter, elements of sets of the form Σ^n are written as strings $a_1 \cdots a_n$ rather than n-tuples $(a_1, \ldots, a_n)$, and likewise for Cartesian products of other alphabets.)

---

[1] It is a fixed-length coding scheme variant of this theorem that is presented in this chapter, as this variant translates more directly to the quantum setting. Shannon's source coding theorem is often stated in terms of *variable-length* coding schemes, with which one aims for a perfect recovery of the symbols produced by the source while minimizing the expected length of the binary string encodings.

The expression on the left-hand side of (5.196) represents the probability that a random choice of symbols $a_1, \ldots, a_n \in \Sigma$, with each symbol chosen independently according to the probability vector p, results in a sequence satisfying

$$g(f(a_1 \cdots a_n)) = a_1 \cdots a_n. \tag{5.198}$$

The following scenario describes an abstract setting in which such coding schemes may be considered.

Scenario 5.39 Alice has a device (the source) that sequentially generates symbols chosen at random from an alphabet Σ. Each randomly generated symbol is independently distributed according to a probability vector p. Alice allows the device to produce a string of n symbols $a_1 \cdots a_n$, and aims to communicate this string to Bob using as few bits of communication as possible.

To do this, Alice and Bob will use a coding scheme taking the form (5.195), which is assumed to have been agreed upon before the random generation of the symbols $a_1 \cdots a_n$. Alice *encodes* $a_1 \cdots a_n$ into a string of $m = \lfloor \alpha n \rfloor$ bits by computing $f(a_1 \cdots a_n)$, and sends the resulting string $f(a_1 \cdots a_n)$ to Bob. Bob *decodes* the string by applying the function g, obtaining $g(f(a_1 \cdots a_n))$. The coding scheme is said to be *correct* in the event that (5.198) holds, which is equivalent to $a_1 \cdots a_n \in G$, for then Bob will have obtained the correct string $a_1 \cdots a_n$.

If it is the case that the pair (f, g) is an (n, α, δ)-coding scheme for p, then the number δ is an upper bound on the probability that the coding scheme fails to be correct, so that Bob does not recover the string Alice obtained from the source, while α represents the average number of bits (as the value of n increases) needed to encode each symbol.

For a given probability vector p, it is evident that an (n, α, δ)-coding scheme will exist for some choices of the parameters n, α, and δ, and not others. The range of values of α for which coding schemes exist is closely related to the Shannon entropy $\mathrm{H}(p)$, as the following theorem establishes.

Theorem 5.40 (Shannon's source coding theorem) *Let Σ be an alphabet, let $p \in \mathcal{P}(\Sigma)$ be a probability vector, and let $\alpha > 0$ and $\delta \in (0, 1)$ be real numbers. The following statements hold:*

1. *If $\alpha > \mathrm{H}(p)$, then there exists an (n, α, δ)-coding scheme for p for all but finitely many positive integers n.*
2. *If $\alpha < \mathrm{H}(p)$, then there exists an (n, α, δ)-coding scheme for p for at most finitely many positive integers n.*

A proof of this theorem is presented below, following a discussion of the notion of a *typical string*, which is central to the proof. The general notion of typicality, which can be formalized in various specific ways, will also play a major role in Chapter 8, which is devoted to the topic of quantum channel capacities.

Typical Strings

The notion of a typical string, for a given distribution of symbols, a string length, and an error parameter, is defined as follows.

Definition 5.41   Let Σ be an alphabet, let $p \in \mathcal{P}(\Sigma)$ be a probability vector, let n be a positive integer, and let $\varepsilon > 0$ be a positive real number. A string $a_1 \cdots a_n \in \Sigma^n$ is said to be ε-*typical with respect to* p if

$$2^{-n(\mathrm{H}(p)+\varepsilon)} < p(a_1) \cdots p(a_n) < 2^{-n(\mathrm{H}(p)-\varepsilon)}. \tag{5.199}$$

The notation $T_{n,\varepsilon}(p)$ refers to the set of all strings $a_1 \cdots a_n \in \Sigma^n$ for which the inequalities (5.199) hold, and when the probability vector p can safely be taken as being implicit, one may write $T_{n,\varepsilon}$ rather than $T_{n,\varepsilon}(p)$.

A random selection of a string $a_1 \cdots a_n \in \Sigma^n$, with each symbol being independently distributed according to $p \in \mathcal{P}(\Sigma)$, is increasingly likely to be ε-typical as n grows, as the following proposition demonstrates.

Proposition 5.42   *Let Σ be an alphabet, let $p \in \mathcal{P}(\Sigma)$ be a probability vector, and let $\varepsilon > 0$. It holds that*

$$\lim_{n \to \infty} \sum_{a_1 \cdots a_n \in T_{n,\varepsilon}(p)} p(a_1) \cdots p(a_n) = 1. \tag{5.200}$$

Proof   Define a random variable $X : \Sigma \to [0, \infty)$ as

$$X(a) = \begin{cases} -\log(p(a)) & \text{if } p(a) > 0 \\ 0 & \text{if } p(a) = 0 \end{cases} \tag{5.201}$$

and distributed according to the probability vector p. The expected value of this random variable is given by $\mathrm{E}(X) = \mathrm{H}(p)$.

Now, for any positive integer n, and for $X_1, \ldots, X_n$ being independent random variables, each identically distributed to X, one has

$$\Pr\left(\left| \frac{X_1 + \cdots + X_n}{n} - \mathrm{H}(p) \right| < \varepsilon \right) = \sum_{a_1 \cdots a_n \in T_{n,\varepsilon}(p)} p(a_1) \cdots p(a_n). \tag{5.202}$$

The conclusion of the proposition therefore follows from the weak law of large numbers (Theorem 1.15). $\square$

The proposition that follows establishes an upper bound on the number of ε-typical strings of a given length.

Proposition 5.43 *Let Σ be an alphabet, let $p \in \mathcal{P}(\Sigma)$ be a probability vector, let $\varepsilon > 0$ be a positive real number, and let n be a positive integer. It holds that*

$$|T_{n,\varepsilon}(p)| < 2^{n(\mathrm{H}(p)+\varepsilon)}. \tag{5.203}$$

Proof By the definition of ε-typicality, one has

$$1 \geq \sum_{a_1 \cdots a_n \in T_{n,\varepsilon}(p)} p(a_1) \cdots p(a_n) > 2^{-n(\mathrm{H}(p)+\varepsilon)} \, |T_{n,\varepsilon}(p)|, \tag{5.204}$$

and therefore $|T_{n,\varepsilon}(p)| < 2^{n(\mathrm{H}(p)+\varepsilon)}$. $\qquad\square$

Proof of Shannon's Source Coding Theorem

Shannon's source coding theorem (Theorem 5.40) can be proved through a conceptually simple argument: a suitable coding scheme may be obtained for sufficiently large values of n by assigning a unique binary string to each typical string, with every other string encoded arbitrarily; and conversely, any coding scheme that fails to account for a large fraction of the typical strings can be shown to fail with high probability.

Proof of Theorem 5.40 Assume first that $\alpha > \mathrm{H}(p)$, and choose $\varepsilon > 0$ so that $\alpha > \mathrm{H}(p) + 2\varepsilon$. A coding scheme of the form

$$\begin{aligned} f_n &: \Sigma^n \to \Gamma^m, \\ g_n &: \Gamma^m \to \Sigma^n, \end{aligned} \tag{5.205}$$

for $m = \lfloor \alpha n \rfloor$, will be defined for every integer n satisfying $n > 1/\varepsilon$. Observe, for each $n > 1/\varepsilon$, that the assumption $\alpha > \mathrm{H}(p) + 2\varepsilon$ implies that

$$m = \lfloor \alpha n \rfloor > n(\mathrm{H}(p) + \varepsilon). \tag{5.206}$$

By Proposition 5.43 it holds that

$$|T_{n,\varepsilon}| < 2^{n(\mathrm{H}(p)+\varepsilon)} < 2^m, \tag{5.207}$$

and one may therefore define a function $f_n : \Sigma^n \to \Gamma^m$ that is injective when restricted to $T_{n,\varepsilon}$, together with a function $g_n : \Gamma^m \to \Sigma^n$ that is chosen so that

$$g_n(f_n(a_1 \cdots a_n)) = a_1 \cdots a_n \tag{5.208}$$

for every $a_1 \cdots a_n \in T_{n,\varepsilon}$. Thus, for

$$G_n = \{a_1 \cdots a_n \in \Sigma^n : g_n(f_n(a_1 \cdots a_n)) = a_1 \cdots a_n\}, \tag{5.209}$$

it holds that $T_{n,\varepsilon} \subseteq G_n$, and therefore

$$\sum_{a_1 \cdots a_n \in G_n} p(a_1) \cdots p(a_n) \geq \sum_{a_1 \cdots a_n \in T_{n,\varepsilon}} p(a_1) \cdots p(a_n). \tag{5.210}$$

It follows by Proposition 5.42 that the quantity on the right-hand side of (5.210) is greater than $1 - \delta$ for sufficiently large values of n. Therefore, for sufficiently large values of n it holds that the coding scheme (f_n, g_n) is an (n, α, δ)-coding scheme, which proves the first statement of the theorem.

Now assume that $\alpha < \mathrm{H}(p)$, let a coding scheme of the form (5.205) be fixed for each n, and let $G_n \subseteq \Sigma^n$ be as defined in (5.209). It must hold that

$$|G_n| \leq 2^m = 2^{\lfloor \alpha n \rfloor} \tag{5.211}$$

for each n, as the coding scheme cannot be correct for two or more distinct strings that map to the same encoding. To complete the proof, it suffices to prove that

$$\lim_{n \to \infty} \sum_{a_1 \cdots a_n \in G_n} p(a_1) \cdots p(a_n) = 0. \tag{5.212}$$

Toward this goal, observe that for every positive integer n and real number $\varepsilon > 0$ it holds that

$$G_n \subseteq (\Sigma^n \backslash T_{n,\varepsilon}) \cup (G_n \cap T_{n,\varepsilon}), \tag{5.213}$$

and therefore

$$\begin{aligned}
&\sum_{a_1 \cdots a_n \in G_n} p(a_1) \cdots p(a_n) \\
&\leq \left(1 - \sum_{a_1 \cdots a_n \in T_{n,\varepsilon}} p(a_1) \cdots p(a_n) \right) + 2^{-n(\mathrm{H}(p) - \varepsilon)} |G_n|.
\end{aligned} \tag{5.214}$$

Choosing $\varepsilon > 0$ so that $\alpha < \mathrm{H}(p) - \varepsilon$, one has

$$\lim_{n \to \infty} 2^{-n(\mathrm{H}(p) - \varepsilon)} |G_n| = 0. \tag{5.215}$$

As Proposition 5.42 implies that

$$\lim_{n \to \infty} \sum_{a_1 \cdots a_n \in T_{n,\varepsilon}} p(a_1) \cdots p(a_n) = 1, \tag{5.216}$$

it follows that (5.212) holds, which completes the proof. $\qquad\square$

5.3.2 Quantum Source Coding

There is a natural way to formulate a quantum analogue of classical source coding, which is as follows. It is assumed that a source produces a sequence of registers $X_1, \ldots, X_n$, for some choice of a positive integer n, with all of these registers sharing the same classical state set Σ. The complex Euclidean spaces associated with these registers are therefore given by $\mathcal{X}_k = \mathbb{C}^\Sigma$, for $k = 1, \ldots, n$, and one may therefore make the identification

$$\mathcal{X}^{\otimes n} = \mathcal{X}_1 \otimes \cdots \otimes \mathcal{X}_n \tag{5.217}$$

for $\mathcal{X} = \mathbb{C}^\Sigma$. The state of the compound register $(X_1, \ldots, X_n)$ produced by the source is assumed to be given by $\rho^{\otimes n}$. That is, for some choice of a state $\rho \in \mathrm{D}(\mathcal{X})$, the registers $X_1, \ldots, X_n$ are independent, and each in the state ρ. The quantum information stored in these registers is to be encoded and decoded in a similar way to the classical setting, through the use of quantum channels rather than deterministic encoding and decoding functions.

Quantum Coding Schemes

A *quantum coding scheme* consists of a pair of channels (Φ, Ψ); the channel Φ represents the encoding process and Ψ represents the decoding process. The encoding channel Φ transforms $(X_1, \ldots, X_n)$ into $(Y_1, \ldots, Y_m)$, for some choice of an integer m, where $Y_1, \ldots, Y_m$ are registers having classical sets equal to the binary alphabet $\Gamma = \{0, 1\}$. In other words, each register Y_k represents a qubit. The decoding channel Ψ transforms $(Y_1, \ldots, Y_m)$ back into $(X_1, \ldots, X_n)$.

The desired property of such a scheme is for the composition $\Psi\Phi$ to act trivially, or nearly trivially, on the compound register $(X_1, \ldots, X_n)$, under the assumption that the registers $X_1, \ldots, X_n$ are independent and each in the state ρ as suggested above. It must be stressed that it is not sufficient to require that the state of $(X_1, \ldots, X_n)$ be close to $\rho^{\otimes n}$ after the decoding channel is applied – this would be a trivial requirement failing to recognize that there might initially be correlations among $X_1, \ldots, X_n$ and one or more other registers that must be respected by the coding process. Indeed, for any complex Euclidean space $\mathcal{Z}$ and a state $\sigma \in \mathrm{D}(\mathcal{X}_1 \otimes \cdots \otimes \mathcal{X}_n \otimes \mathcal{Z})$ satisfying

$$\sigma[X_1, \ldots, X_n] = \rho^{\otimes n}, \tag{5.218}$$

it is required of a good coding scheme that the state $(\Psi\Phi \otimes \mathbb{1}_{\mathrm{L}(\mathcal{Z})})(\sigma)$ is approximately equal to σ.

The particular notion of approximate equality that will be considered is based on the fidelity function. This is a convenient choice, as it allows for the utilization of the closed-form expression of the channel fidelity given by Proposition 3.31. One could alternatively use the trace distance in place of the fidelity function, but this would not change the asymptotic behavior of the sorts of quantum coding schemes considered in this section, as the Fuchs–van de Graaf inequalities (Theorem 3.33) directly imply.

In accordance with the discussion above, quantum coding schemes are to be defined more precisely as follows. Let Σ be an alphabet, let $\rho \in \mathrm{D}(\mathcal{X})$ be a density operator, for $\mathcal{X} = \mathbb{C}^{\Sigma}$, and let n be a positive integer. Also let $\Gamma = \{0,1\}$ denote the binary alphabet, let $\mathcal{Y} = \mathbb{C}^{\Gamma}$, let $\alpha > 0$ and $\delta \in (0,1)$ be real numbers, and let $m = \lfloor \alpha n \rfloor$. A pair of channels

$$\Phi \in \mathrm{C}(\mathcal{X}^{\otimes n}, \mathcal{Y}^{\otimes m}) \quad \text{and} \quad \Psi \in \mathrm{C}(\mathcal{Y}^{\otimes m}, \mathcal{X}^{\otimes n}) \tag{5.219}$$

is an (n, α, δ)-*quantum coding scheme* for ρ if it holds that

$$\mathrm{F}(\Psi\Phi, \rho^{\otimes n}) > 1 - \delta, \tag{5.220}$$

for $\mathrm{F}(\Psi\Phi, \rho^{\otimes n})$ denoting the channel fidelity of $\Psi\Phi$ with respect to $\rho^{\otimes n}$ (q.v. Section 3.2.3).

Schumacher's Quantum Source Coding Theorem

The following theorem is a quantum analogue to Shannon's source coding theorem (Theorem 5.40), establishing conditions under which quantum coding schemes exist.

Theorem 5.44 (Schumacher)   *Let Σ be an alphabet, let $\rho \in \mathrm{D}(\mathbb{C}^{\Sigma})$ be a density operator, and let $\alpha > 0$ and $\delta \in (0,1)$ be real numbers. The following statements hold:*

1. *If $\alpha > \mathrm{H}(\rho)$, then there exists an (n, α, δ)-quantum coding scheme for ρ for all but finitely many positive integers n.*
2. *If $\alpha < \mathrm{H}(\rho)$, then there exists an (n, α, δ)-quantum coding scheme for ρ for at most finitely many positive integers n.*

Proof   By the spectral theorem (as stated by Corollary 1.4), one may write

$$\rho = \sum_{a \in \Sigma} p(a) u_a u_a^*, \tag{5.221}$$

for some choice of a probability vector $p \in \mathcal{P}(\Sigma)$ and an orthonormal basis $\{u_a : a \in \Sigma\}$ of $\mathbb{C}^{\Sigma}$. The association of the eigenvectors and eigenvalues of ρ with the elements of Σ may be chosen arbitrarily, and is assumed to be fixed for the remainder of the proof. By the definition of the von Neumann entropy, it holds that $\mathrm{H}(\rho) = \mathrm{H}(p)$.

Assume first that $\alpha > H(\rho)$, and choose $\varepsilon > 0$ to be sufficiently small so that $\alpha > H(\rho) + 2\varepsilon$. Along similar lines to the proof of Theorem 5.40, a quantum coding scheme (Φ_n, Ψ_n) of the form

$$\Phi_n \in C(\mathcal{X}^{\otimes n}, \mathcal{Y}^{\otimes m}) \quad \text{and} \quad \Psi_n \in C(\mathcal{Y}^{\otimes m}, \mathcal{X}^{\otimes n}) \tag{5.222}$$

will be defined for every $n > 1/\varepsilon$, where $m = \lfloor \alpha n \rfloor$. It will then be shown that (Φ_n, Ψ_n) is an (n, α, δ)-quantum coding scheme for sufficiently large values of n.

For a given choice of $n > 1/\varepsilon$, the quantum coding scheme (Φ_n, Ψ_n) is defined as follows. First, consider the set of ε-typical strings

$$T_{n,\varepsilon} = T_{n,\varepsilon}(p) \subseteq \Sigma^n \tag{5.223}$$

associated with the probability vector p, and define a projection operator $\Pi_{n,\varepsilon} \in \text{Proj}(\mathcal{X}^{\otimes n})$ as follows:

$$\Pi_{n,\varepsilon} = \sum_{a_1 \cdots a_n \in T_{n,\varepsilon}} u_{a_1} u_{a_1}^* \otimes \cdots \otimes u_{a_n} u_{a_n}^*. \tag{5.224}$$

The subspace upon which this operator projects is the ε-*typical subspace* of $\mathcal{X}^{\otimes n}$ with respect to ρ. Notice that

$$\langle \Pi_{n,\varepsilon}, \rho^{\otimes n} \rangle = \sum_{a_1 \cdots a_n \in T_{n,\varepsilon}} p(a_1) \cdots p(a_n). \tag{5.225}$$

Now, by Shannon's source coding theorem (or, to be more precise, the proof of that theorem given in the previous subsection), there exists a classical coding scheme (f_n, g_n) for p that satisfies

$$g_n(f_n(a_1 \cdots a_n)) = a_1 \cdots a_n \tag{5.226}$$

for every ε-typical string $a_1 \cdots a_n \in T_{n,\varepsilon}$. Define a linear operator of the form

$$A_n \in L(\mathcal{X}^{\otimes n}, \mathcal{Y}^{\otimes m}) \tag{5.227}$$

as follows:

$$A_n = \sum_{a_1 \cdots a_n \in T_{n,\varepsilon}} e_{f_n(a_1 \cdots a_n)} (u_{a_1} \otimes \cdots \otimes u_{a_n})^*. \tag{5.228}$$

Finally, define channels Φ_n and Ψ_n of the form (5.222) as

$$\Phi_n(X) = A_n X A_n^* + \langle \mathbb{1} - A_n^* A_n, X \rangle \sigma, \tag{5.229}$$

$$\Psi_n(Y) = A_n^* Y A_n + \langle \mathbb{1} - A_n A_n^*, Y \rangle \xi \tag{5.230}$$

for all $X \in L(\mathcal{X}^{\otimes n})$ and $Y \in L(\mathcal{Y}^{\otimes m})$, for density operators $\sigma \in D(\mathcal{Y}^{\otimes m})$ and $\xi \in D(\mathcal{X}^{\otimes n})$ chosen arbitrarily.

It remains to prove that (Φ_n, Ψ_n) is an (n, α, δ)-quantum coding scheme for sufficiently large values of n. From the expressions (5.229) and (5.230) it follows that there must exist a Kraus representation of the channel $\Psi_n \Phi_n$ having the form

$$(\Psi_n \Phi_n)(X) = (A_n^* A_n) X (A_n^* A_n)^* + \sum_{k=1}^{N} C_{n,k} X C_{n,k}^* \tag{5.231}$$

for some choice of an integer N and a collection of operators $C_{n,1}, \ldots, C_{n,N}$, which will have no effect on the analysis that follows. By Proposition 3.31, it therefore holds that

$$\mathrm{F}(\Psi_n \Phi_n, \rho^{\otimes n}) \geq \langle \rho^{\otimes n}, A_n^* A_n \rangle = \langle \rho^{\otimes n}, \Pi_{n,\varepsilon} \rangle. \tag{5.232}$$

As

$$\lim_{n \to \infty} \langle \Pi_{n,\varepsilon}, \rho^{\otimes n} \rangle = 1, \tag{5.233}$$

it follows that (Φ_n, Ψ_n) is an (n, α, δ)-quantum coding scheme for all sufficiently large n, which proves the first statement in the theorem.

Now assume that $\alpha < \mathrm{H}(\rho)$, and suppose that Φ_n and Ψ_n are arbitrary channels of the form (5.222) for each positive integer n. It will be proved that, for any choice of $\delta \in (0, 1)$, the pair (Φ_n, Ψ_n) fails to be an (n, α, δ)-quantum coding scheme for all sufficiently large values of n.

Fix any choice of a positive integer n, and let

$$\Phi_n(X) = \sum_{k=1}^{N} A_k X A_k^* \quad \text{and} \quad \Psi_n(Y) = \sum_{k=1}^{N} B_k Y B_k^* \tag{5.234}$$

be Kraus representations of Φ_n and Ψ_n, where

$$\begin{aligned} A_1, \ldots, A_N &\in \mathrm{L}(\mathcal{X}^{\otimes n}, \mathcal{Y}^{\otimes m}), \\ B_1, \ldots, B_N &\in \mathrm{L}(\mathcal{Y}^{\otimes m}, \mathcal{X}^{\otimes n}). \end{aligned} \tag{5.235}$$

(The assumption that both representations have the same number of Kraus operators is made only for notational convenience. This assumption causes no loss of generality; one may include the zero operator as a Kraus operator for either channel any desired number of times.) It follows that

$$(\Psi_n \Phi_n)(X) = \sum_{1 \leq j, k \leq N} (B_k A_j) X (B_k A_j)^* \tag{5.236}$$

is a Kraus representation of the composition $\Psi_n \Phi_n$. For the purposes of this analysis, the key aspect of this Kraus representation is that

$$\mathrm{rank}(B_k A_j) \leq \dim(\mathcal{Y}^{\otimes m}) = 2^m \tag{5.237}$$

for all choices of $j, k \in \{1, \ldots, N\}$. Indeed, for each $k \in \{1, \ldots, N\}$, one may choose a projection operator $\Pi_k \in \mathrm{Proj}(\mathcal{X}^{\otimes n})$ with $\mathrm{rank}(\Pi_k) \leq 2^m$ such that $\Pi_k B_k = B_k$. Therefore,

$$
\begin{aligned}
\mathrm{F}(\Psi_n \Phi_n, \rho^{\otimes n})^2 &= \sum_{1 \leq j, k \leq N} \left| \langle B_k A_j, \rho^{\otimes n} \rangle \right|^2 \\
&= \sum_{1 \leq j, k \leq N} \left| \langle \Pi_k B_k A_j, \rho^{\otimes n} \rangle \right|^2 \\
&= \sum_{1 \leq j, k \leq N} \left| \left\langle B_k A_j \sqrt{\rho^{\otimes n}}, \Pi_k \sqrt{\rho^{\otimes n}} \right\rangle \right|^2 \\
&\leq \sum_{1 \leq j, k \leq N} \mathrm{Tr}\left(B_k A_j \rho^{\otimes n} A_j^* B_k^* \right) \langle \Pi_k, \rho^{\otimes n} \rangle,
\end{aligned}
\tag{5.238}
$$

where the inequality follows from the Cauchy–Schwarz inequality. As each Π_k has rank bounded by 2^m, it follows that

$$
\langle \Pi_k, \rho^{\otimes n} \rangle \leq \sum_{i=1}^{2^m} \lambda_i(\rho^{\otimes n}) = \sum_{a_1 \cdots a_n \in G_n} p(a_1) \cdots p(a_n)
\tag{5.239}
$$

for some subset $G_n \subseteq \Sigma^n$ having size at most 2^m. As the channel $\Psi_n \Phi_n$ is trace-preserving, it holds that

$$
\sum_{1 \leq j, k \leq N} \mathrm{Tr}\left(B_k A_j \rho^{\otimes n} A_j^* B_k^* \right) = 1,
\tag{5.240}
$$

and, moreover, one has that each term in this sum is nonnegative. The final expression of (5.238) is therefore equal to a convex combination of values, each of which is bounded as in (5.239), which implies that

$$
\mathrm{F}(\Psi_n \Phi_n, \rho^{\otimes n})^2 \leq \sum_{a_1 \cdots a_n \in G_n} p(a_1) \cdots p(a_n).
\tag{5.241}
$$

Finally, reasoning precisely as in the proof of Theorem 5.40, one has that the assumption $\alpha < \mathrm{H}(\rho) = \mathrm{H}(p)$ implies that

$$
\lim_{n \to \infty} \sum_{a_1 \cdots a_n \in G_n} p(a_1) \cdots p(a_n) = 0
\tag{5.242}
$$

by the fact that G_n has size bounded by 2^m. This implies that, for any fixed choice of $\delta \in (0, 1)$, the pair (Φ_n, Ψ_n) fails to be an (n, α, δ)-quantum coding scheme for all but finitely many values of n. $\qquad \square$

5.3.3 Encoding Classical Information Into Quantum States

The final type of source coding to be discussed in this section is one in which classical information is encoded into a quantum state, and then decoded by means of a measurement. The following scenario represents one abstraction of this task.

Scenario 5.45   Let X and Z be classical registers having classical state sets Σ and Γ, respectively, and let Y be a register. Also let $p \in \mathcal{P}(\Sigma)$ be a probability vector, let

$$\{\rho_a : a \in \Sigma\} \subset D(\mathcal{Y}) \tag{5.243}$$

be a collection of states, and let $\mu \colon \Gamma \to \mathrm{Pos}(\mathcal{Y})$ be a measurement.

Alice obtains an element $a \in \Sigma$, stored in the register X, that has been randomly generated by a source according to the probability vector p. She prepares Y in the state ρ_a and sends Y to Bob. Bob measures Y with respect to the measurement μ, and stores the outcome of this measurement in the classical register Z. This measurement outcome represents information that Bob has obtained regarding the classical state of X.

It is natural to consider the situation in which $\Gamma = \Sigma$ in this scenario, and to imagine that Bob aims to recover the symbol stored in Alice's register X; this is essentially the state discrimination problem discussed in Section 3.1.2. In the discussion that follows, however, it will not be taken as an assumption that this is necessarily Bob's strategy.

Assuming that Alice and Bob operate as described in Scenario 5.45, the pair (X, Z) will be left in the probabilistic state $q \in \mathcal{P}(\Sigma \times \Gamma)$ defined by

$$q(a, b) = p(a)\langle \mu(b), \rho_a \rangle \tag{5.244}$$

for every pair $(a, b) \in \Sigma \times \Gamma$. For an ensemble $\eta \colon \Sigma \to \mathrm{Pos}(\mathcal{Y})$ defined as

$$\eta(a) = p(a)\,\rho_a \tag{5.245}$$

for each $a \in \Sigma$, the probability vector q may equivalently be expressed as

$$q(a, b) = \langle \mu(b), \eta(a) \rangle \tag{5.246}$$

for each $(a, b) \in \Sigma \times \Gamma$.

A fundamental question regarding this scenario is the following: How much information can Bob's register Z contain about the state of Alice's register X? A theorem known as *Holevo's theorem* establishes an upper bound on this amount of information, as represented by the mutual information between Alice's register X and Bob's register Z. Holevo's theorem is phrased in terms of two functions of the ensemble η, the *accessible information* and the *Holevo information*, which are introduced below.

Accessible Information

With Scenario 5.45 and the discussion above in mind, let $\eta\colon \Sigma \to \mathrm{Pos}(\mathcal{Y})$ be an ensemble, let $\mu\colon \Gamma \to \mathrm{Pos}(\mathcal{Y})$ be a measurement, and let $q \in \mathcal{P}(\Sigma \times \Gamma)$ be the probability vector defined as in (5.246), representing a probabilistic state of the pair of classical registers (X, Z). The notation $\mathrm{I}_\mu(\eta)$ will denote the mutual information between X and Z, with respect to a probabilistic state defined in this way, so that

$$\mathrm{I}_\mu(\eta) = \mathrm{H}(q[\mathsf{X}]) + \mathrm{H}(q[\mathsf{Z}]) - \mathrm{H}(q) = \mathrm{D}(q \| q[\mathsf{X}] \otimes q[\mathsf{Z}]). \tag{5.247}$$

Now assume the ensemble η is fixed, while no constraints are placed on the measurement μ. The *accessible information* $\mathrm{I}_{\mathrm{acc}}(\eta)$ of the ensemble η is defined as the supremum value, ranging over all possible choices of a measurement μ, that may be obtained in this way. That is,

$$\mathrm{I}_{\mathrm{acc}}(\eta) = \sup_\mu \mathrm{I}_\mu(\eta), \tag{5.248}$$

where the supremum is over all choices of an alphabet Γ and a measurement $\mu\colon \Gamma \to \mathrm{Pos}(\mathcal{Y})$.

Although it is not necessarily apparent from its definition, the accessible information $\mathrm{I}_{\mathrm{acc}}(\eta)$ of an ensemble $\eta\colon \Sigma \to \mathrm{Pos}(\mathcal{Y})$ is indeed achieved by some choice of an alphabet Γ and a measurement $\mu\colon \Gamma \to \mathrm{Pos}(\mathcal{Y})$. The following lemma is useful for establishing this fact.

Lemma 5.46 *Let Σ and Γ be alphabets, let $\mathcal{Y}$ be a complex Euclidean space, and let $\eta\colon \Sigma \to \mathrm{Pos}(\mathcal{Y})$ be an ensemble of states. Also let $\mu_0, \mu_1\colon \Gamma \to \mathrm{Pos}(\mathcal{Y})$ be measurements and let $\lambda \in [0,1]$ be a real number. It holds that*

$$\mathrm{I}_{\lambda\mu_0 + (1-\lambda)\mu_1}(\eta) \leq \lambda \mathrm{I}_{\mu_0}(\eta) + (1-\lambda) \mathrm{I}_{\mu_1}(\eta). \tag{5.249}$$

Proof Let X and Z be classical registers having classical state sets Σ and Γ, respectively. Define a probability vector $p \in \mathcal{P}(\Sigma)$ as

$$p(a) = \mathrm{Tr}(\eta(a)) \tag{5.250}$$

for all $a \in \Sigma$. Also define probability vectors $q_0, q_1 \in \mathcal{P}(\Sigma \times \Gamma)$, representing probabilistic states of the pair (X, Z), as

$$q_0(a,b) = \langle \mu_0(b), \eta(a) \rangle \quad \text{and} \quad q_1(a,b) = \langle \mu_1(b), \eta(a) \rangle \tag{5.251}$$

for all $(a,b) \in \Sigma \times \Gamma$. By the joint convexity of the relative entropy function, it holds that

$$
\begin{aligned}
I_{\lambda\mu_0+(1-\lambda)\mu_1}&(\eta) \\
&= D(\lambda q_0 + (1-\lambda)q_1 \| p \otimes (\lambda q_0[\mathsf{Z}] + (1-\lambda)q_1[\mathsf{Z}])) \\
&\leq \lambda D(q_0 \| p \otimes q_0[\mathsf{Z}]) + (1-\lambda) D(q_1 \| p \otimes q_1[\mathsf{Z}]) \\
&= \lambda I_{\mu_0}(\eta) + (1-\lambda) I_{\mu_1}(\eta),
\end{aligned}
\tag{5.252}
$$

as required.   □

Theorem 5.47 *Let Σ be an alphabet, let $\mathcal{Y}$ be a complex Euclidean space, and let $\eta\colon \Sigma \to \mathrm{Pos}(\mathcal{Y})$ be an ensemble of states. There exists an alphabet Γ with $|\Gamma| \leq \dim(\mathcal{Y})^2$ and a measurement $\mu\colon \Gamma \to \mathrm{Pos}(\mathcal{Y})$ such that*

$$
I_\mu(\eta) = I_{\mathrm{acc}}(\eta).
\tag{5.253}
$$

Proof Let $\nu\colon \Lambda \to \mathrm{Pos}(\mathcal{Y})$ be a measurement, for an arbitrary choice of an alphabet Λ. By Lemma 5.46, the function

$$
\mu \mapsto I_\mu(\eta)
\tag{5.254}
$$

is convex on the set of all measurements of the form $\mu\colon \Lambda \to \mathrm{Pos}(\mathcal{Y})$. As every measurement of this form can be written as a convex combination of extremal measurements of the same form, one has that there must exist an extremal measurement $\mu\colon \Lambda \to \mathrm{Pos}(\mathcal{Y})$ satisfying $I_\mu(\eta) \geq I_\nu(\eta)$. By Corollary 2.48, the assumption that $\mu\colon \Lambda \to \mathrm{Pos}(\mathcal{Y})$ is extremal implies that

$$
|\{a \in \Lambda \colon \mu(a) \neq 0\}| \leq \dim(\mathcal{Y})^2.
\tag{5.255}
$$

The value $I_\mu(\eta)$ does not change if μ is restricted to the alphabet

$$
\Gamma = \{a \in \Lambda \colon \mu(a) \neq 0\},
\tag{5.256}
$$

and therefore one has that there must exist a measurement $\mu\colon \Gamma \to \mathrm{Pos}(\mathcal{Y})$, for Γ satisfying $|\Gamma| \leq \dim(\mathcal{Y})^2$, such that $I_\mu(\eta) \geq I_\nu(\eta)$.

It follows that $I_{\mathrm{acc}}(\eta)$ is equal to the supremum value of $I_\mu(\eta)$, ranging over all measurements μ having at most $\dim(\mathcal{Y})^2$ measurement outcomes. The quantity $I_\mu(\eta)$ is invariant under renaming the measurement outcomes of μ, so there is no loss of generality in restricting this supremum to the set of measurements having a single set Γ of measurement outcomes satisfying $|\Gamma| = \dim(\mathcal{Y})^2$. The supremum is therefore taken over a compact set, from which it follows that there exists a measurement $\mu\colon \Gamma \to \mathrm{Pos}(\mathcal{Y})$ for which the supremum value is achieved, which completes the proof.   □

The Holevo Information

Again with Scenario 5.45 in mind, let X be a classical register, let Σ be the classical state set of X, let Y be a register, and let $\eta\colon \Sigma \to \mathrm{Pos}(\mathcal{Y})$ be an ensemble. As described in Section 2.2.3, one associates the classical–quantum state

$$\sigma = \sum_{a \in \Sigma} E_{a,a} \otimes \eta(a) \tag{5.257}$$

of the pair (X, Y) with the ensemble η. The *Holevo information* (also called the *Holevo χ-quantity*) of the ensemble η, which is denoted $\chi(\eta)$, is defined as the quantum mutual information $\mathrm{I}(\mathsf{X} : \mathsf{Y})$ between the registers X and Y with respect to the state σ.

Under the assumption that the ensemble η is written as

$$\eta(a) = p(a)\,\rho_a \tag{5.258}$$

for each $a \in \Sigma$, for a probability vector $p \in \mathcal{P}(\Sigma)$ and a collection

$$\{\rho_a : a \in \Sigma\} \subseteq \mathrm{D}(\mathcal{Y}) \tag{5.259}$$

of states, the Holevo information of η may be calculated as follows:

$$
\begin{aligned}
\chi(\eta) &= \mathrm{I}(\mathsf{X} : \mathsf{Y}) \\
&= \mathrm{H}(\mathsf{X}) + \mathrm{H}(\mathsf{Y}) - \mathrm{H}(\mathsf{X}, \mathsf{Y}) \\
&= \mathrm{H}(p) + \mathrm{H}\!\left(\sum_{a \in \Sigma} p(a)\,\rho_a\right) - \mathrm{H}\!\left(\sum_{a \in \Sigma} p(a)\, E_{a,a} \otimes \rho_a\right) \\
&= \mathrm{H}\!\left(\sum_{a \in \Sigma} p(a)\,\rho_a\right) - \sum_{a \in \Sigma} p(a)\,\mathrm{H}(\rho_a),
\end{aligned}
\tag{5.260}
$$

where the last equality has made use of the identity (5.98). Alternatively, one may write

$$\chi(\eta) = \mathrm{H}\!\left(\sum_{a \in \Sigma} \eta(a)\right) - \sum_{\substack{a \in \Sigma \\ \eta(a) \neq 0}} \mathrm{Tr}(\eta(a))\,\mathrm{H}\!\left(\frac{\eta(a)}{\mathrm{Tr}(\eta(a))}\right), \tag{5.261}$$

or, equivalently,

$$\chi(\eta) = \mathrm{H}\!\left(\sum_{a \in \Sigma} \eta(a)\right) - \sum_{a \in \Sigma} \mathrm{H}(\eta(a)) + \mathrm{H}(p). \tag{5.262}$$

It follows from the concavity of the von Neumann entropy (Theorem 5.23), or by the subadditivity of the von Neumann entropy (Theorem 5.24), that the Holevo information $\chi(\eta)$ is nonnegative for every ensemble η.

At an intuitive level, the Holevo information may be interpreted in the following way. When the pair of registers (X, Y) is in the classical–quantum state σ as described above, and the register Y is considered in isolation, its von Neumann entropy is given by

$$H(Y) = H\left(\sum_{a \in \Sigma} p(a)\rho_a\right). \tag{5.263}$$

If one learns the classical state $a \in \Sigma$ of X, then from their perspective the von Neumann entropy of Y drops to $H(\rho_a)$. The Holevo information $\chi(\eta)$ may therefore be viewed as representing the average decrease in the von Neumann entropy of Y that is expected when one learns the classical state of X.

It cannot be said that the Holevo information is convex in general, but the following proposition provides two conditions under which it is. The proof follows a similar argument to the proof of Lemma 5.46.

Proposition 5.48 *Let $\eta_0 \colon \Sigma \to \mathrm{Pos}(\mathcal{Y})$ and $\eta_1 \colon \Sigma \to \mathrm{Pos}(\mathcal{Y})$ be ensembles of states, for $\mathcal{Y}$ a complex Euclidean space and Σ an alphabet, and suppose further that at least one of the following two conditions is satisfied:*

1. *The ensembles η_0 and η_1 have the same average state:*

$$\sum_{a \in \Sigma} \eta_0(a) = \rho = \sum_{a \in \Sigma} \eta_1(a), \tag{5.264}$$

   for some choice of $\rho \in \mathrm{D}(\mathcal{Y})$.
2. *The ensembles η_0 and η_1 correspond to the same probability distribution, over possibly different states:*

$$\mathrm{Tr}(\eta_0(a)) = p(a) = \mathrm{Tr}(\eta_1(a)) \tag{5.265}$$

   for each $a \in \Sigma$, for some choice of a probability vector $p \in \mathcal{P}(\Sigma)$.

For every real number $\lambda \in [0, 1]$, it holds that

$$\chi(\lambda\eta_0 + (1 - \lambda)\eta_1) \le \lambda\chi(\eta_0) + (1 - \lambda)\chi(\eta_1). \tag{5.266}$$

Proof Let $\mathcal{X} = \mathbb{C}^\Sigma$, let X and Y be registers corresponding to the spaces $\mathcal{X}$ and $\mathcal{Y}$, and define classical–quantum states $\sigma_0, \sigma_1 \in \mathrm{D}(\mathcal{X} \otimes \mathcal{Y})$ as

$$\sigma_0 = \sum_{a \in \Sigma} E_{a,a} \otimes \eta_0(a) \quad \text{and} \quad \sigma_1 = \sum_{a \in \Sigma} E_{a,a} \otimes \eta_1(a). \tag{5.267}$$

For a given choice of $\lambda \in [0, 1]$, define $\sigma = \lambda\sigma_0 + (1 - \lambda)\sigma_1$. The Holevo information of the ensembles η_0, η_1, and $\lambda\eta_0 + (1 - \lambda)\eta_1$ may be expressed as follows:

$$\begin{aligned} \chi(\eta_0) &= D(\sigma_0 \| \sigma_0[\mathsf{X}] \otimes \sigma_0[\mathsf{Y}]), \\ \chi(\eta_1) &= D(\sigma_1 \| \sigma_1[\mathsf{X}] \otimes \sigma_1[\mathsf{Y}]), \end{aligned} \tag{5.268}$$

and

$$\chi(\lambda\eta_0 + (1 - \lambda)\eta_1) = D(\sigma \| \sigma[\mathsf{X}] \otimes \sigma[\mathsf{Y}]). \tag{5.269}$$

Under the first condition in the statement of the proposition, it holds that $\sigma_0[\mathsf{Y}] = \sigma_1[\mathsf{Y}] = \sigma[\mathsf{Y}] = \rho$. In this case, the inequality (5.266) is equivalent to

$$D(\sigma \| \sigma[\mathsf{X}] \otimes \rho) \leq \lambda\, D(\sigma_0 \| \sigma_0[\mathsf{X}] \otimes \rho) + (1 - \lambda)\, D(\sigma_1 \| \sigma_1[\mathsf{X}] \otimes \rho), \tag{5.270}$$

which holds by the joint convexity of the quantum relative entropy function (Corollary 5.33).

Under the second condition in the statement of the proposition, one has $\sigma_0[\mathsf{X}] = \sigma_1[\mathsf{X}] = \sigma[\mathsf{X}] = \mathrm{Diag}(p)$. Exchanging the roles of X and Y from the first condition, one has that the proof follows by similar reasoning. $\qquad \square$

Holevo's Theorem

The next theorem, known as *Holevo's theorem*, establishes that the accessible information is upper-bounded by the Holevo information, for all ensembles of states.

Theorem 5.49 (Holevo's theorem) *Let $\eta\colon \Sigma \to \mathrm{Pos}(\mathcal{Y})$ be an ensemble of states, for Σ an alphabet and $\mathcal{Y}$ a complex Euclidean space. It holds that $\mathrm{I}_{\mathrm{acc}}(\eta) \leq \chi(\eta)$.*

Proof Let X be a classical register having classical state set Σ and let Y be a register whose associated complex Euclidean space is $\mathcal{Y}$. Define a state $\sigma \in D(\mathcal{X} \otimes \mathcal{Y})$ as

$$\sigma = \sum_{a \in \Sigma} E_{a,a} \otimes \eta(a), \tag{5.271}$$

and suppose that the pair (X, Y) is in the state σ. It holds that

$$\chi(\eta) = D(\sigma \| \sigma[\mathsf{X}] \otimes \sigma[\mathsf{Y}]). \tag{5.272}$$

Next, let Γ be an alphabet, let Z be a classical register having classical state set Γ, and let $\mu\colon \Gamma \to \mathrm{Pos}(\mathcal{Y})$ be a measurement. Define a channel $\Phi \in C(\mathcal{Y}, \mathcal{Z})$ as

$$\Phi(Y) = \sum_{b \in \Gamma} \langle \mu(b), Y \rangle E_{b,b} \tag{5.273}$$

for all $Y \in L(\mathcal{Y})$, which is the quantum-to-classical channel associated with the measurement μ, and consider the situation in which Y is transformed into Z by means of Φ. One has that

$$(\mathbb{1}_{L(\mathcal{X})} \otimes \Phi)(\sigma) = \sum_{a \in \Sigma} \sum_{b \in \Gamma} \langle \mu(b), \eta(a) \rangle E_{a,a} \otimes E_{b,b} = \mathrm{Diag}(q), \qquad (5.274)$$

for $q \in \mathcal{P}(\Sigma \times \Gamma)$ being the probability vector defined as

$$q(a, b) = \langle \mu(b), \eta(a) \rangle \qquad (5.275)$$

for all $a \in \Sigma$ and $b \in \Gamma$. It follows that

$$\begin{aligned} \mathrm{I}_\mu(\eta) &= \mathrm{D}(q \| q[\mathsf{X}] \otimes q[\mathsf{Z}]) \\ &= \mathrm{D}((\mathbb{1}_{L(\mathcal{X})} \otimes \Phi)(\sigma) \| (\mathbb{1}_{L(\mathcal{X})} \otimes \Phi)(\sigma[\mathsf{X}] \otimes \sigma[\mathsf{Y}])), \end{aligned} \qquad (5.276)$$

and therefore $\mathrm{I}_\mu(\eta) \leq \chi(\eta)$, as the quantum relative entropy does not increase under the action of a channel (by Theorem 5.35). As this bound holds for all measurements μ, the theorem follows. $\qquad \square$

For every collection of density operators $\{\rho_a : a \in \Sigma\} \subseteq \mathrm{D}(\mathcal{Y})$ and every probability vector $p \in \mathcal{P}(\Sigma)$, it holds that

$$\begin{aligned} \mathrm{H}\left(\sum_{a \in \Sigma} p(a)\rho_a\right) &- \sum_{a \in \Sigma} p(a)\,\mathrm{H}(\rho_a) \\ &\leq \mathrm{H}\left(\sum_{a \in \Sigma} p(a)\rho_a\right) \leq \log(\dim(\mathcal{Y})), \end{aligned} \qquad (5.277)$$

and therefore the Holevo information of every ensemble $\eta: \Sigma \to \mathrm{Pos}(\mathcal{Y})$ is upper-bounded by $\log(\dim(\mathcal{Y}))$. The following corollary of Theorem 5.49 is a consequence of this observation.

Corollary 5.50   *Let Σ be an alphabet, let $\mathcal{Y}$ be a complex Euclidean space, and let $\eta: \Sigma \to \mathrm{Pos}(\mathcal{Y})$ be an ensemble of states. It holds that*

$$\mathrm{I}_{\mathrm{acc}}(\eta) \leq \log(\dim(\mathcal{Y})). \qquad (5.278)$$

Although this is indeed a simple corollary to Theorem 5.49, it nevertheless establishes the following conceptually important fact: if two individuals share no prior correlations or shared resources, and one individual sends the other a quantum register of a given dimension n, then no more than $\log(n)$ bits of classical information will have been transmitted through this process.

Quantum Random Access Codes

An interesting variation of source coding involves the notion of a *quantum random access code*. This is a coding scheme in which a sequence of classical symbols is encoded into a quantum state in such a way that one may obtain information about just one of the encoded symbols, chosen arbitrarily by the individual performing the decoding operation. The following scenario provides an abstraction of this type of scheme.

Scenario 5.51 Let Σ and Γ be alphabets, let n be a positive integer, let $X_1, \ldots, X_n$ be classical registers, each having classical state set Σ, let Z be a classical register having classical state set Γ, and let Y be a register. Also let $p \in \mathcal{P}(\Sigma)$ be a probability vector, let

$$\{\rho_{a_1 \cdots a_n} : a_1 \cdots a_n \in \Sigma^n\} \subseteq D(\mathcal{Y}) \tag{5.279}$$

be a collection of states indexed by Σ^n, and let $\mu_1, \ldots, \mu_n : \Gamma \to \mathrm{Pos}(\mathcal{Y})$ be measurements.

Alice obtains the registers $X_1, \ldots, X_n$, which have been independently prepared by a source, with p being the probabilistic state of each of these registers. She observes the classical state $a_1 \cdots a_n \in \Sigma^n$ of $(X_1, \ldots, X_n)$, and prepares the register Y in the state $\rho_{a_1 \cdots a_n}$, which is then sent to Bob. Bob selects an index $k \in \{1, \ldots, n\}$ of his choice, measures Y with respect to the measurement μ_k, and stores the outcome in the classical register Z. The classical state of Z represents the information Bob has obtained regarding the classical state of X_k.

The following example describes an instance of this scenario in which Alice encodes two classical bits into one qubit in such a way that Bob can recover the encoded bit of his choice with a reasonably high probability of success.

Example 5.52 Let $\Sigma = \{0, 1\}$ denote the binary alphabet. For every real number θ, define a density operator $\sigma(\theta) \in D(\mathbb{C}^\Sigma)$ as

$$\sigma(\theta) = \begin{pmatrix} \cos^2(\theta) & \cos(\theta)\sin(\theta) \\ \cos(\theta)\sin(\theta) & \sin^2(\theta) \end{pmatrix}, \tag{5.280}$$

and observe that each of these operators is a rank-one projection.

Alice obtains two classical registers X_1 and X_2, both having classical state set Σ. It is to be assumed that the probabilistic states of these registers are independent and uniformly distributed. She encodes the classical state $(a_1, a_2) \in \Sigma \times \Sigma$ of the pair (X_1, X_2) into the quantum state $\rho_{a_1 a_2} \in D(\mathbb{C}^\Sigma)$

defined as

$$\rho_{00} = \sigma(\pi/8), \qquad \rho_{10} = \sigma(3\pi/8),$$
$$\rho_{01} = \sigma(7\pi/8), \qquad \rho_{11} = \sigma(5\pi/8). \tag{5.281}$$

Bob receives the qubit $\rho_{a_1 a_2}$ from Alice, and decides whether he wishes to learn the classical state a_1 of X_1 or the classical state a_2 of X_2. If Bob wishes to learn a_1, he measures the qubit with respect to the measurement μ_1 defined as

$$\mu_1(0) = \sigma(0) \quad \text{and} \quad \mu_1(1) = \sigma(\pi/2). \tag{5.282}$$

If instead Bob wishes to learn a_2, he measures the qubit with respect to the measurement μ_2 defined as

$$\mu_2(0) = \sigma(\pi/4) \quad \text{and} \quad \mu_2(1) = \sigma(3\pi/4). \tag{5.283}$$

Using the formula

$$\langle \sigma(\phi), \sigma(\theta) \rangle = \cos^2(\phi - \theta), \tag{5.284}$$

one concludes from a case analysis that, if Bob measures $\rho_{a_1 a_2}$ with respect to the measurement μ_k, he will obtain the measurement outcome a_k with probability $\cos^2(\pi/8) \approx 0.85$ in all cases.

With Scenario 5.51 in mind, one may define a *quantum random access code* for a given choice of a positive integer n and a probability vector $p \in \mathcal{P}(\Sigma)$ as consisting of two objects: the first is the collection of density operators

$$\{\rho_{a_1 \cdots a_n} : a_1 \cdots a_n \in \Sigma^n\} \subseteq \mathrm{D}(\mathcal{Y}) \tag{5.285}$$

representing the encodings of the possible sequences $a_1 \cdots a_n \in \Sigma^n$, and the second is the sequence of measurements

$$\mu_1, \ldots, \mu_n : \Gamma \to \mathrm{Pos}(\mathcal{Y}) \tag{5.286}$$

that reveal information concerning one of the initial registers $X_1, \ldots, X_n$.

The amount of information revealed by such a quantum random access code may be represented by a vector $(\alpha_1, \ldots, \alpha_n)$, where α_k represents the mutual information between X_k and Z, conditioned on the measurement μ_k having been performed and the outcome of that measurement stored in Z. The vector $(\alpha_1, \ldots, \alpha_n)$ may be defined in more precise terms as follows. First, one defines an ensemble $\eta : \Sigma^n \to \mathrm{Pos}(\mathcal{Y})$ as

$$\eta(a_1 \cdots a_n) = p(a_1) \cdots p(a_n) \, \rho_{a_1 \cdots a_n} \tag{5.287}$$

for each $a_1 \cdots a_n \in \Sigma^n$. Then, for each $k \in \{1, \ldots, n\}$, one defines

$$\alpha_k = \mathrm{I}(X_k : Z), \tag{5.288}$$

where the mutual information is defined with respect to the probabilistic state $q_k \in \mathcal{P}(\Sigma^n \times \Gamma)$ of the compound register $(\mathsf{X}_1, \ldots, \mathsf{X}_n, \mathsf{Z})$ given by

$$q_k(a_1 \cdots a_n, b) = \langle \mu_k(b), \eta(a_1 \cdots a_n) \rangle \tag{5.289}$$

for each $a_1 \cdots a_n \in \Sigma^n$ and $b \in \Gamma$.

Nayak's Theorem

Although Example 5.52 suggests a potential for quantum random access codes to provide significant advantages over classical coding schemes, it is a false impression. The following theorem demonstrates that quantum random access codes are strongly limited in their capabilities.

Theorem 5.53 (Nayak's theorem) *Let Σ be an alphabet, let $p \in \mathcal{P}(\Sigma)$ be a probability vector, and let n be a positive integer. Also let $\mathcal{Y}$ be a complex Euclidean space, let Γ be an alphabet, and let*

$$\{\rho_{a_1 \cdots a_n} : a_1 \cdots a_n \in \Sigma^n\} \subseteq \mathrm{D}(\mathcal{Y}) \quad \text{and} \quad \mu_1, \ldots, \mu_n : \Gamma \to \mathrm{Pos}(\mathcal{Y}) \tag{5.290}$$

be a quantum random access code for p. Assuming that $(\alpha_1, \ldots, \alpha_n)$ is a vector representing the amount of information revealed by this code for the distribution p, in the manner defined above, it must hold that

$$\sum_{k=1}^{n} \alpha_k \leq \chi(\eta) \tag{5.291}$$

for $\eta : \Sigma^n \to \mathrm{Pos}(\mathcal{Y})$ being the ensemble defined by

$$\eta(a_1 \cdots a_n) = p(a_1) \cdots p(a_n) \rho_{a_1 \cdots a_n} \tag{5.292}$$

for each $a_1 \cdots a_n \in \Sigma^n$.

Proof Let $\mathsf{X}_1, \ldots, \mathsf{X}_n$ be classical registers, each having classical state set Σ, and let Y be a register whose associated complex Euclidean space is $\mathcal{Y}$ (as in Scenario 5.51). Let

$$\sigma = \sum_{a_1 \cdots a_n \in \Sigma^n} p(a_1) \cdots p(a_n) E_{a_1, a_1} \otimes \cdots \otimes E_{a_n, a_n} \otimes \rho_{a_1 \cdots a_n} \tag{5.293}$$

be the classical–quantum state of the compound register $(\mathsf{X}_1, \ldots, \mathsf{X}_n, \mathsf{Y})$ corresponding to the ensemble η. With respect to the state σ, one has that

$$\mathrm{I}(\mathsf{X}_1, \ldots, \mathsf{X}_n : \mathsf{Y}) = \chi(\eta). \tag{5.294}$$

Now, it holds that

$$\begin{aligned}
&\mathrm{I}(\mathsf{X}_1, \ldots, \mathsf{X}_n : \mathsf{Y}) \\
&= \mathrm{I}(\mathsf{X}_n : \mathsf{Y}) + \mathrm{I}(\mathsf{X}_1, \ldots, \mathsf{X}_{n-1} : \mathsf{X}_n, \mathsf{Y}) - \mathrm{I}(\mathsf{X}_1, \ldots, \mathsf{X}_{n-1} : \mathsf{X}_n).
\end{aligned} \tag{5.295}$$

This identity (which is equivalent to an identity commonly known as the *chain rule* for quantum mutual information) holds independent of the state of these registers, and may be verified by expanding the definition of the quantum mutual information. In the particular case of the state σ, one has that

$$I(X_1, \ldots, X_{n-1} : X_n) = 0, \tag{5.296}$$

as the registers $X_1, \ldots, X_n$ are independent with respect to this state. Thus,

$$\begin{aligned} I(X_1, \ldots, X_n : Y) &= I(X_n : Y) + I(X_1, \ldots, X_{n-1} : X_n, Y) \\ &\geq I(X_n : Y) + I(X_1, \ldots, X_{n-1} : Y), \end{aligned} \tag{5.297}$$

where the inequality holds by Corollary 5.37. By applying this inequality recursively, one finds that

$$I(X_1, \ldots, X_n : Y) \geq \sum_{k=1}^{n} I(X_k : Y). \tag{5.298}$$

Finally, one may observe that $\alpha_k \leq I(X_k : Y)$ for each $k \in \{1, \ldots, n\}$, as a consequence of Holevo's theorem (Theorem 5.49). Thus,

$$\sum_{k=1}^{n} \alpha_k \leq I(X_1, \ldots, X_n : Y) = \chi(\eta), \tag{5.299}$$

as required. ☐

One interesting type of quantum random access code, which includes the code suggested by Example 5.52, is one in which Σ and Γ are equal to the binary alphabet, and one aims for the classical state of the register Z to agree with X_k for whichever index $k \in \{1, \ldots, n\}$ was measured. Theorem 5.53 implies a strong limitation on schemes of this sort. The following lemma, which is a special case of an inequality known as *Fano's inequality*, is useful for analyzing this special case.

Lemma 5.54 *Let X and Y be classical registers sharing the same classical state set $\Sigma = \{0, 1\}$, and assume the pair (X, Y) is in a probabilistic state $q \in \mathcal{P}(\Sigma \times \Sigma)$ for which $q[X](0) = q[X](1) = 1/2$ and*

$$q(0,0) + q(1,1) = \lambda \tag{5.300}$$

for $\lambda \in [0, 1]$. (In words, the state of X is uniformly distributed and Y and X agree with probability λ.) It holds that $I(X : Y) \geq 1 - H(\lambda, 1 - \lambda)$.

Proof Define Z to be a classical register having classical state set Σ, and let $p \in \mathcal{P}(\Sigma \times \Sigma \times \Sigma)$ be the probability vector defined as

$$p(a, b, c) = \begin{cases} q(a, b) & \text{if } c = a \oplus b \\ 0 & \text{otherwise,} \end{cases} \tag{5.301}$$

where $a \oplus b$ denotes the exclusive-OR of the binary values a and b. In words, p describes the probabilistic state of (X, Y, Z) for which (X, Y) is distributed according to q and Z is set to the exclusive-OR of X and Y. With respect to this state, one has

$$H(Z) = H(\lambda, 1 - \lambda). \tag{5.302}$$

Moreover, it holds that

$$H(X|Y) = H(Z|Y), \tag{5.303}$$

as the classical states of X and Z uniquely determine one another for each fixed classical state of Y. Finally, by the subadditivity of Shannon entropy (Proposition 5.9), one has that

$$H(Z|Y) \leq H(Z). \tag{5.304}$$

Consequently,

$$\begin{aligned} I(X : Y) = H(X) - H(X|Y) &= 1 - H(Z|Y) \\ &\geq 1 - H(Z) = 1 - H(\lambda, 1 - \lambda), \end{aligned} \tag{5.305}$$

as required. $\qquad\square$

Corollary 5.55 *Let $\Sigma = \{0, 1\}$ denote the binary alphabet, let n be a positive integer, let $\mathcal{Y}$ be a complex Euclidean space, and let $\lambda \in [1/2, 1]$ be a real number. Also let*

$$\{\rho_{a_1 \cdots a_n} : a_1 \cdots a_n \in \Sigma^n\} \subseteq D(\mathcal{Y}) \tag{5.306}$$

be a collection of density operators, and let

$$\mu_1, \ldots, \mu_n : \Sigma \to \mathrm{Pos}(\mathcal{Y}) \tag{5.307}$$

be measurements. If it holds that

$$\langle \mu_k(a_k), \rho_{a_1 \cdots a_n} \rangle \geq \lambda \tag{5.308}$$

for every choice of $k \in \{1, \ldots, n\}$ and $a_1 \ldots a_n \in \Sigma^n$, then

$$\log(\dim(\mathcal{Y})) \geq (1 - H(\lambda, 1 - \lambda))n. \tag{5.309}$$

Proof Let $p \in P(\Sigma)$ be the uniform distribution and define an ensemble $\eta \colon \Sigma^n \to \mathrm{Pos}(\mathcal{Y})$ as

$$\eta(a_1 \cdots a_n) = p(a_1) \cdots p(a_n) \rho_{a_1 \cdots a_n} = \frac{1}{2^n} \rho_{a_1 \cdots a_n} \tag{5.310}$$

for each string $a_1 \cdots a_n \in \Sigma^n$. Let $(\alpha_1, \ldots, \alpha_n)$ be the vector representing the amount of information revealed by the quantum random access code defined by the collection $\{\rho_{a_1 \cdots a_n} \colon a_1 \cdots a_n \in \Sigma^n\}$ and the measurements $\mu_1, \ldots, \mu_n$ for the distribution p. By combining Lemma 5.54 with the fact that $\mathrm{H}(\alpha, 1 - \alpha)$ is a decreasing function of α on the interval $[1/2, 1]$, one finds that

$$\alpha_k \geq 1 - \mathrm{H}(\lambda, 1 - \lambda) \tag{5.311}$$

for every $k \in \{1, \ldots, n\}$. Therefore, by Theorem 5.53, it holds that

$$\chi(\eta) \geq (1 - \mathrm{H}(\lambda, 1 - \lambda))n. \tag{5.312}$$

As the Holevo information of η is upper-bounded by $\log(\dim(\mathcal{Y}))$, the proof is complete. $\qquad\square$

Thus, for the special type of random access code under consideration, the number of qubits required to encode a binary string of length n is linear in n, with the constant of proportionality tending to 1 as the error tolerance decreases.

5.4 Exercises

Exercise 5.1 Let X, Y and Z be registers. Prove that the following two inequalities hold for all states $\rho \in \mathrm{D}(\mathcal{X} \otimes \mathcal{Y} \otimes \mathcal{Z})$ of these registers:

(a) $\mathrm{I}(\mathsf{X}, \mathsf{Y} : \mathsf{Z}) + \mathrm{I}(\mathsf{Y} : \mathsf{Z}) \geq \mathrm{I}(\mathsf{X} : \mathsf{Z})$,
(b) $\mathrm{H}(\mathsf{X}, \mathsf{Y}|\mathsf{Z}) + \mathrm{H}(\mathsf{Y}|\mathsf{Z}) \geq \mathrm{H}(\mathsf{X}|\mathsf{Z}) - 2\,\mathrm{H}(\mathsf{Z})$.

Exercise 5.2 Let Σ be an alphabet, let $\mathcal{X}$, $\mathcal{Y}$, and $\mathcal{Z}$ be complex Euclidean spaces, let $\rho \in \mathrm{D}(\mathcal{X} \otimes \mathcal{Z})$ be a density operator, let $p \in P(\Sigma)$ be a probability vector, and let $\{\Phi_a \colon a \in \Sigma\} \subseteq C(\mathcal{X}, \mathcal{Y})$ be a collection of channels. Define an ensemble $\eta \colon \Sigma \to \mathrm{Pos}(\mathcal{Y} \otimes \mathcal{Z})$ as

$$\eta(a) = p(a)\big(\Phi_a \otimes \mathbb{1}_{\mathrm{L}(\mathcal{Z})}\big)(\rho) \tag{5.313}$$

for each $a \in \Sigma$. Prove that

$$\chi(\eta) \leq \mathrm{H}\!\left(\sum_{a \in \Sigma} p(a)\Phi_a\big(\mathrm{Tr}_{\mathcal{Z}}(\rho)\big)\right) + \sum_{a \in \Sigma} p(a)\,\mathrm{H}(\Phi_a(\mathrm{Tr}_{\mathcal{Z}}(\rho))). \tag{5.314}$$

Exercise 5.3 Let X, Y, and Z be registers.

(a) Prove that, for every state $\rho \in D(\mathcal{X} \otimes \mathcal{Y} \otimes \mathcal{Z})$ of these registers, it holds that

$$I(X, Y : Z) \leq I(Y : X, Z) + 2\,H(X). \tag{5.315}$$

(b) Let Σ be the classical state set of X, let $\{\sigma_a : a \in \Sigma\} \subseteq D(\mathcal{Y} \otimes \mathcal{Z})$ be a collection of density operators, let $p \in \mathcal{P}(\Sigma)$ be a probability vector, and let

$$\rho = \sum_{a \in \Sigma} p(a) E_{a,a} \otimes \sigma_a \tag{5.316}$$

be a state of (X, Y, Z). Prove that, with respect to the state ρ, one has

$$I(X, Y : Z) \leq I(Y : X, Z) + H(X). \tag{5.317}$$

Exercise 5.4 Let Σ be an alphabet and let $\mathcal{X}$ and $\mathcal{Y}$ be complex Euclidean spaces. Also let $\Phi \in C(\mathcal{X}, \mathcal{Y})$ be a channel, let $\eta : \Sigma \to \mathrm{Pos}(\mathcal{X})$ be an ensemble, and define an ensemble $\Phi(\eta) : \Sigma \to \mathrm{Pos}(\mathcal{Y})$ as

$$(\Phi(\eta))(a) = \Phi(\eta(a)) \tag{5.318}$$

for each $a \in \Sigma$. Prove that $\chi(\Phi(\eta)) \leq \chi(\eta)$.

Exercise 5.5 Let X and Y be registers and let $\rho_0, \rho_1 \in D(\mathcal{X} \otimes \mathcal{Y})$ be states of these registers. Prove that, for every choice of $\lambda \in [0, 1]$, it holds that

$$\begin{aligned} H(\lambda\rho_0 + (1 - \lambda)\rho_1) &- H(\lambda\rho_0[Y] + (1 - \lambda)\rho_1[Y]) \\ &\geq \lambda(H(\rho_0) - H(\rho_0[Y])) + (1 - \lambda)(H(\rho_1) - H(\rho_1[Y])). \end{aligned} \tag{5.319}$$

(Equivalently, prove that the conditional von Neumann entropy of X given Y is a concave function of the state of these registers.)

Exercise 5.6 Let X and Y be registers and let $\rho \in D(\mathcal{X} \otimes \mathcal{Y})$ be a state of these registers for which it holds that

$$\rho = \sum_{a \in \Sigma} p(a) \sigma_a \otimes \xi_a,$$

for some choice of an alphabet Σ, a probability vector $p \in \mathcal{P}(\Sigma)$, and two collections of states $\{\sigma_a : a \in \Sigma\} \subseteq D(\mathcal{X})$ and $\{\xi_a : a \in \Sigma\} \subseteq D(\mathcal{Y})$.

(a) Prove that, with respect to the state ρ, it holds that $I(X : Y) \leq H(p)$.

(b) Prove that

$$H(\rho) \geq \sum_{a \in \Sigma} p(a)\,H(\sigma_a) + H\left(\sum_{a \in \Sigma} p(a)\xi_a\right). \tag{5.320}$$

5.5 Bibliographic Remarks

The Shannon entropy was defined in Shannon's paper (Shannon, 1948), which is generally viewed as representing the birth of information theory. Several fundamental facts were proved in that paper, including Shannon's source coding theorem (of which Theorem 5.40 is a variant) and Shannon's channel coding theorem. Shannon also defined the conditional entropy in the same paper, considered the mutual information (although not under that name), and proved that the entropy function now bearing his name is the unique function of a probability vector, up to a normalization, satisfying a few simple axioms that a measure of information and uncertainty should naturally possess. Shannon observed the similarity in form of his entropy function to the notion of entropy in statistical mechanics in his 1948 paper, and was later quoted as saying that he used the name "entropy" on the advice of von Neumann (Tribus and McIrvine, 1971). More substantive connections between these different notions of entropy have been considered by several researchers (see, for instance, Rosenkrantz (1989)).

The relative entropy function was defined by Kullback and Leibler (1951). Theorem 5.14 is due to Audenaert (2007). A variant of Pinsker's inequality (Theorem 5.15, but with a smaller constant factor) was proved by Pinsker (1964) and later refined by others, including Csiszár and Kullback. Further information on classical information theory can be found in books on the subject, including the books of Ash (1990) and Cover and Thomas (2006), among many others.

The von Neumann entropy was first defined by von Neumann in a paper (von Neumann, 1927a) and then investigated in greater detail in his 1932 book (for later translation in English, see von Neumann (1955)), in both cases within the context of quantum statistical mechanics. Despite Shannon's reported discussion with von Neumann regarding the Shannon entropy, there is no evidence known to suggest that von Neumann ever considered the information-theoretic aspects of the von Neumann entropy function.

The quantum relative entropy was defined by Umegaki (1962). A fact from which Klein's inequality (as stated in Proposition 5.22) may be derived was proved many years earlier by Klein (1931). Theorem 5.25 was proved by Araki and Lieb (1970), who also introduced the purification method through which it is proved in the same paper. A weaker version of the Fannes–Audenaert inequality (Theorem 5.26) was proved by Fannes (1973), and was later strengthened by Audenaert (2007) (through a reduction to the classical result stated in Theorem 5.14, which was proved in the same paper).

Lieb's concavity theorem was proved by Lieb (1973). The statement of this theorem represented by Theorem 5.30 is due to Ando (1979). Multiple proofs of this theorem are known; the proof presented in this book is an adaptation of one appearing in the book of Simon (1979) with simplifications inspired by Ando's methodology (Ando, 1979). Simon attributes the central idea of his proof to Uhlmann (1977). The strong subadditivity of von Neumann entropy was first conjectured by Lanford and Robinson (1968) and proved by Lieb and Ruskai (1973) using Lieb's concavity theorem. Lindblad (1974) proved the joint convexity of quantum relative entropy, also using Lieb's concavity theorem. The quantum Pinsker inequality (Theorem 5.38) appears in a paper of Hiai, Ohya, and Tsukada (1981), and may be obtained as a special case of a more general theorem due to Uhlmann (1977).

Theorem 5.44 was proved by Schumacher (1995). Holevo (1973a) proved his eponymous theorem (Theorem 5.49) through a different proof than the one presented in this chapter – Holevo's proof did not make use of the strong subadditivity of von Neumann entropy or Lieb's concavity theorem.

Quantum random access codes were proposed by Ambainis, Nayak, Ta-Shma, and Vazirani (1999); they proved a somewhat weaker limitation on quantum random access codes than what is established by Corollary 5.55, which was proved by Nayak (1999b) a short time later. (The two previously referenced papers appeared in conference proceedings, and were consolidated as a journal paper (Ambainis, Nayak, Ta-Shma, and Vazirani 2002).) Nayak's theorem, as stated in Theorem 5.53, follows from the proof of a closely related theorem that appears in Nayak's Ph.D. thesis (Nayak, 1999a).

6

Bipartite Entanglement

Entanglement is a fundamental concept in quantum information theory, considered by many to be a quintessential characteristic that distinguishes quantum systems from their classical counterparts. Informally speaking, a state of a collection of registers $X_1, \ldots, X_n$ is said to be *entangled* when it is not possible to specify the correlations that exist among the registers in classical terms. When it is possible to describe these correlations in classical terms, the registers are said to be in a *separable* state. Entanglement among two or more registers is therefore synonymous with a lack of separability.

This chapter introduces notions associated with bipartite entanglement, in which correlations between precisely two registers (or two collections of registers) are considered. Topics to be discussed include the property of separability, which is applicable not only to states but also to channels and measurements; aspects of entanglement manipulation and quantification; and a discussion of operational phenomena associated with entanglement, including teleportation, dense coding, and nonclassical correlations among measurements on separated systems.

6.1 Separability

This section introduces the notion of separability, which is applicable to states, channels, and measurements on bipartite systems. It is possible to define a multipartite variant of this concept, but only bipartite separability is considered in this book.

6.1.1 Separable Operators and States

The property of separability for operators acting on bipartite tensor product spaces is defined as follows.

Definition 6.1 For any choice of complex Euclidean spaces $\mathcal{X}$ and $\mathcal{Y}$, the set $\mathrm{Sep}(\mathcal{X} : \mathcal{Y})$ is defined as the set containing all positive semidefinite operators $R \in \mathrm{Pos}(\mathcal{X} \otimes \mathcal{Y})$ for which there exists an alphabet Σ and two collections of positive semidefinite operators,

$$\{P_a : a \in \Sigma\} \subset \mathrm{Pos}(\mathcal{X}) \quad \text{and} \quad \{Q_a : a \in \Sigma\} \subset \mathrm{Pos}(\mathcal{Y}), \qquad (6.1)$$

such that

$$R = \sum_{a \in \Sigma} P_a \otimes Q_a. \qquad (6.2)$$

Elements of the set $\mathrm{Sep}(\mathcal{X} : \mathcal{Y})$ are called *separable operators*.

Remark It must be stressed that separability is defined with respect to a particular tensor product structure of the underlying complex Euclidean space of a given operator, as the previous definition reflects. When the term *separable operator* is used, one must therefore make this tensor product structure known (if it is not implicit). An operator $R \in \mathrm{Pos}(\mathcal{X} \otimes \mathcal{Y} \otimes \mathcal{Z})$ may, for instance, be an element of $\mathrm{Sep}(\mathcal{X} : \mathcal{Y} \otimes \mathcal{Z})$ but not $\mathrm{Sep}(\mathcal{X} \otimes \mathcal{Y} : \mathcal{Z})$.

By restricting the definition above to density operators, one obtains a definition of *separable states*.

Definition 6.2 Let $\mathcal{X}$ and $\mathcal{Y}$ be complex Euclidean spaces. One defines

$$\mathrm{SepD}(\mathcal{X} : \mathcal{Y}) = \mathrm{Sep}(\mathcal{X} : \mathcal{Y}) \cap \mathrm{D}(\mathcal{X} \otimes \mathcal{Y}). \qquad (6.3)$$

Elements of the set $\mathrm{SepD}(\mathcal{X} : \mathcal{Y})$ are called *separable states* (or *separable density operators*).

Convex Properties of Separable Operators and States

The sets $\mathrm{Sep}(\mathcal{X} : \mathcal{Y})$ and $\mathrm{SepD}(\mathcal{X} : \mathcal{Y})$ possess various properties relating to convexity, a few of which will now be observed.

Proposition 6.3 *For every choice of complex Euclidean spaces $\mathcal{X}$ and $\mathcal{Y}$, the set $\mathrm{SepD}(\mathcal{X} : \mathcal{Y})$ is convex, and the set $\mathrm{Sep}(\mathcal{X} : \mathcal{Y})$ is a convex cone.*

Proof It will first be proved that $\mathrm{Sep}(\mathcal{X} : \mathcal{Y})$ is a convex cone. It suffices to prove that $\mathrm{Sep}(\mathcal{X} : \mathcal{Y})$ is closed under addition as well as multiplication by any nonnegative real number. To this end, assume that $R_0, R_1 \in \mathrm{Sep}(\mathcal{X} : \mathcal{Y})$ are separable operators and $\lambda \geq 0$ is a nonnegative real number. One may write

$$R_0 = \sum_{a \in \Sigma_0} P_a \otimes Q_a \quad \text{and} \quad R_1 = \sum_{a \in \Sigma_1} P_a \otimes Q_a \qquad (6.4)$$

for disjoint alphabets, Σ_0 and Σ_1, and two collections of positive semidefinite operators,

$$\begin{aligned}\{P_a : a \in \Sigma_0 \cup \Sigma_1\} &\subset \mathrm{Pos}(\mathcal{X}), \\ \{Q_a : a \in \Sigma_0 \cup \Sigma_1\} &\subset \mathrm{Pos}(\mathcal{Y}).\end{aligned} \tag{6.5}$$

It holds that

$$R_0 + R_1 = \sum_{a \in \Sigma_0 \cup \Sigma_1} P_a \otimes Q_a, \tag{6.6}$$

and therefore $R_0 + R_1 \in \mathrm{Sep}(\mathcal{X} : \mathcal{Y})$. Moreover, it holds that

$$\lambda R_0 = \sum_{a \in \Sigma_0} (\lambda P_a) \otimes Q_a. \tag{6.7}$$

As $\lambda P \in \mathrm{Pos}(\mathcal{X})$ for every positive semidefinite operator $P \in \mathrm{Pos}(\mathcal{X})$, it follows that $\lambda R_0 \in \mathrm{Sep}(\mathcal{X} : \mathcal{Y})$.

The fact that $\mathrm{SepD}(\mathcal{X} : \mathcal{Y})$ is convex follows from the fact that it is equal to the intersection of two convex sets, $\mathrm{Sep}(\mathcal{X} : \mathcal{Y})$ and $\mathrm{D}(\mathcal{X} \otimes \mathcal{Y})$. □

The next proposition, when combined with the previous one, implies that $\mathrm{Sep}(\mathcal{X} : \mathcal{Y})$ is equal to the cone generated by $\mathrm{SepD}(\mathcal{X} : \mathcal{Y})$.

Proposition 6.4 *Let $\mathcal{Z}$ be a complex Euclidean space, let $\mathcal{A} \subseteq \mathrm{Pos}(\mathcal{Z})$ be a cone, and assume that $\mathcal{B} = \mathcal{A} \cap \mathrm{D}(\mathcal{Z})$ is nonempty. It holds that*

$$\mathcal{A} = \mathrm{cone}(\mathcal{B}). \tag{6.8}$$

Proof Suppose first that $\rho \in \mathcal{B}$ and $\lambda \geq 0$. It follows that $\lambda \rho \in \mathcal{A}$ by virtue of the fact that $\mathcal{B} \subseteq \mathcal{A}$ and $\mathcal{A}$ is a cone, and therefore

$$\mathrm{cone}(\mathcal{B}) \subseteq \mathcal{A}. \tag{6.9}$$

Now suppose that $P \in \mathcal{A}$. If $P = 0$, then one has that $P = \lambda \rho$ for $\lambda = 0$ and $\rho \in \mathcal{B}$ being chosen arbitrarily. If $P \neq 0$, then consider the density operator $\rho = P / \mathrm{Tr}(P)$. It holds that $\rho \in \mathcal{A}$ because $1/\mathrm{Tr}(P) > 0$ and $\mathcal{A}$ is a cone, and therefore $\rho \in \mathcal{B}$. As $P = \lambda \rho$ for $\lambda = \mathrm{Tr}(P) > 0$, it follows that $P \in \mathrm{cone}(\mathcal{B})$. Therefore,

$$\mathcal{A} \subseteq \mathrm{cone}(\mathcal{B}), \tag{6.10}$$

which completes the proof. □

Two equivalent ways of specifying separable states are provided by the next proposition, which is a straightforward consequence of the spectral theorem.

Proposition 6.5 *Let $\xi \in D(\mathcal{X} \otimes \mathcal{Y})$ be a density operator, for complex Euclidean spaces $\mathcal{X}$ and $\mathcal{Y}$. The following statements are equivalent:*

1. *$\xi \in \text{SepD}(\mathcal{X} : \mathcal{Y})$.*
2. *There exist an alphabet Σ, collections of states $\{\rho_a : a \in \Sigma\} \subseteq D(\mathcal{X})$ and $\{\sigma_a : a \in \Sigma\} \subseteq D(\mathcal{Y})$, and a probability vector $p \in \mathcal{P}(\Sigma)$, such that*

$$\xi = \sum_{a \in \Sigma} p(a)\, \rho_a \otimes \sigma_a. \tag{6.11}$$

3. *There exist an alphabet Σ, collections of unit vectors $\{x_a : a \in \Sigma\} \subset \mathcal{X}$ and $\{y_a : a \in \Sigma\} \subset \mathcal{Y}$, and a probability vector $p \in \mathcal{P}(\Sigma)$, such that*

$$\xi = \sum_{a \in \Sigma} p(a)\, x_a x_a^* \otimes y_a y_a^*. \tag{6.12}$$

Proof The third statement trivially implies the second, and it is immediate that the second statement implies the first, as $\text{SepD}(\mathcal{X} : \mathcal{Y})$ is convex and $\rho_a \otimes \sigma_a \in \text{SepD}(\mathcal{X} : \mathcal{Y})$ for each $a \in \Sigma$. It remains to prove that the first statement implies the third.

Let $\xi \in \text{SepD}(\mathcal{X} : \mathcal{Y})$. As $\xi \in \text{Sep}(\mathcal{X} : \mathcal{Y})$, one may write

$$\xi = \sum_{b \in \Gamma} P_b \otimes Q_b \tag{6.13}$$

for some choice of an alphabet Γ and collections $\{P_b : b \in \Gamma\} \subset \text{Pos}(\mathcal{X})$ and $\{Q_b : b \in \Gamma\} \subset \text{Pos}(\mathcal{Y})$ of positive semidefinite operators. Let $n = \dim(\mathcal{X})$, let $m = \dim(\mathcal{Y})$, and consider spectral decompositions of these operators as follows:

$$P_b = \sum_{j=1}^{n} \lambda_j(P_b) u_{b,j} u_{b,j}^* \quad \text{and} \quad Q_b = \sum_{k=1}^{m} \lambda_k(Q_b) v_{b,k} v_{b,k}^*, \tag{6.14}$$

for each $b \in \Gamma$. Define $\Sigma = \Gamma \times \{1, \ldots, n\} \times \{1, \ldots, m\}$, and define

$$\begin{aligned} p((b,j,k)) &= \lambda_j(P_b)\lambda_k(Q_b), \\ x_{(b,j,k)} &= u_{b,j}, \\ y_{(b,j,k)} &= v_{b,k}, \end{aligned} \tag{6.15}$$

for every $(b, j, k) \in \Sigma$. A straightforward computation reveals that

$$\sum_{a \in \Sigma} p(a)\, x_a x_a^* \otimes y_a y_a^* = \sum_{b \in \Gamma} P_b \otimes Q_b = \xi. \tag{6.16}$$

Moreover, each value $p(a)$ is nonnegative, and because

$$\sum_{a \in \Sigma} p(a) = \text{Tr}(\xi) = 1, \tag{6.17}$$

it follows that p is a probability vector. It has therefore been proved that statement 1 implies statement 3. $\qquad\square$

By the equivalence of the first and second statements in the previous proposition, it holds that a given separable state $\xi \in \mathrm{SepD}(\mathcal{X}:\mathcal{Y})$ represents a classical probability distribution over independent quantum states of a pair of registers (X,Y); and in this sense the possible states of the registers X and Y, when considered in isolation, are classically correlated.

For a separable state $\xi \in \mathrm{SepD}(\mathcal{X}:\mathcal{Y})$, the expression (6.12) is generally not unique – there may be many inequivalent ways that ξ can be expressed in this form. It is important to observe that an expression of this form cannot necessarily be obtained directly from a spectral decomposition of ξ. Indeed, for some choices of $\xi \in \mathrm{SepD}(\mathcal{X}:\mathcal{Y})$ it may hold that every expression of ξ in the form (6.12) requires that Σ has cardinality strictly larger than $\mathrm{rank}(\xi)$. An upper bound on the size of the alphabet Σ required for an expression of the form (6.12) to exist may, however, be obtained from Carathéodory's theorem (Theorem 1.9).

Proposition 6.6 *Let $\xi \in \mathrm{SepD}(\mathcal{X}:\mathcal{Y})$ be a separable state, for $\mathcal{X}$ and $\mathcal{Y}$ being complex Euclidean spaces. There exist an alphabet Σ such that $|\Sigma| \leq \mathrm{rank}(\xi)^2$, two collections of unit vectors $\{x_a : a \in \Sigma\} \subset \mathcal{X}$ and $\{y_a : a \in \Sigma\} \subset \mathcal{Y}$, and a probability vector $p \in \mathcal{P}(\Sigma)$ such that*

$$\xi = \sum_{a \in \Sigma} p(a)\, x_a x_a^* \otimes y_a y_a^*. \tag{6.18}$$

Proof By Proposition 6.5 it holds that

$$\mathrm{SepD}(\mathcal{X}:\mathcal{Y}) = \mathrm{conv}\{xx^* \otimes yy^* : x \in \mathcal{S}(\mathcal{X}),\, y \in \mathcal{S}(\mathcal{Y})\}, \tag{6.19}$$

from which it follows that ξ is contained in the set

$$\mathrm{conv}\{xx^* \otimes yy^* : x \in \mathcal{S}(\mathcal{X}),\, y \in \mathcal{S}(\mathcal{Y}),\, \mathrm{im}(xx^* \otimes yy^*) \subseteq \mathrm{im}(\xi)\}. \tag{6.20}$$

Every density operator $\rho \in \mathrm{D}(\mathcal{X} \otimes \mathcal{Y})$ satisfying $\mathrm{im}(\rho) \subseteq \mathrm{im}(\xi)$ is contained in the real affine subspace

$$\{H \in \mathrm{Herm}(\mathcal{X} \otimes \mathcal{Y}) : \mathrm{im}(H) \subseteq \mathrm{im}(\xi),\, \mathrm{Tr}(H) = 1\} \tag{6.21}$$

of dimension $\mathrm{rank}(\xi)^2 - 1$, and therefore the proposition follows directly from Carathéodory's theorem. $\qquad\square$

By combining the previous proposition with Proposition 6.4, one obtains the following corollary.

Corollary 6.7 *Let $R \in \mathrm{Sep}(\mathcal{X} : \mathcal{Y})$ be a nonzero separable operator, for complex Euclidean spaces $\mathcal{X}$ and $\mathcal{Y}$. There exist an alphabet Σ such that $|\Sigma| \leq \mathrm{rank}(R)^2$, along with two collections of vectors $\{x_a : a \in \Sigma\} \subset \mathcal{X}$ and $\{y_a : a \in \Sigma\} \subset \mathcal{Y}$, such that*

$$R = \sum_{a \in \Sigma} x_a x_a^* \otimes y_a y_a^*. \tag{6.22}$$

The last observation to be made about separable operators and states in this subsection is the following proposition, which establishes a basic topological property of the sets $\mathrm{Sep}(\mathcal{X} : \mathcal{Y})$ and $\mathrm{SepD}(\mathcal{X} : \mathcal{Y})$.

Proposition 6.8 *For every choice of complex Euclidean spaces $\mathcal{X}$ and $\mathcal{Y}$, the set $\mathrm{SepD}(\mathcal{X} : \mathcal{Y})$ is compact and the set $\mathrm{Sep}(\mathcal{X} : \mathcal{Y})$ is closed.*

Proof The unit spheres $\mathcal{S}(\mathcal{X})$ and $\mathcal{S}(\mathcal{Y})$ are compact, which implies that their Cartesian product $\mathcal{S}(\mathcal{X}) \times \mathcal{S}(\mathcal{Y})$ is also compact. The function

$$\phi : \mathcal{S}(\mathcal{X}) \times \mathcal{S}(\mathcal{Y}) \to \mathrm{Pos}(\mathcal{X} \otimes \mathcal{Y}) : (x, y) \mapsto xx^* \otimes yy^* \tag{6.23}$$

is continuous, and therefore the set

$$\phi(\mathcal{S}(\mathcal{X}) \times \mathcal{S}(\mathcal{Y})) = \{xx^* \otimes yy^* : x \in \mathcal{S}(\mathcal{X}), \, y \in \mathcal{S}(\mathcal{Y})\} \tag{6.24}$$

is compact. Because the convex hull of a compact set is necessarily compact, it follows that $\mathrm{SepD}(\mathcal{X} : \mathcal{Y})$ is compact.

As $\mathrm{SepD}(\mathcal{X} : \mathcal{Y})$ is compact, and does not include 0, the cone it generates is closed, and therefore $\mathrm{Sep}(\mathcal{X} : \mathcal{Y})$ is closed. $\qquad\square$

The Horodecki Criterion

The next theorem provides an alternative characterization of separability, demonstrating that the property of separability for operators has a close connection with the property of positivity for maps.

Theorem 6.9 (Horodecki criterion) *Let $\mathcal{X}$ and $\mathcal{Y}$ be complex Euclidean spaces and let $R \in \mathrm{Pos}(\mathcal{X} \otimes \mathcal{Y})$ be a positive semidefinite operator. The following three statements are equivalent:*

1. *$R \in \mathrm{Sep}(\mathcal{X} : \mathcal{Y})$.*
2. *For every choice of a complex Euclidean space $\mathcal{Z}$ and a positive map $\Phi \in \mathrm{T}(\mathcal{X}, \mathcal{Z})$ it holds that*

$$(\Phi \otimes \mathbb{1}_{\mathrm{L}(\mathcal{Y})})(R) \in \mathrm{Pos}(\mathcal{Z} \otimes \mathcal{Y}). \tag{6.25}$$

3. *For every positive and unital map $\Phi \in \mathrm{T}(\mathcal{X}, \mathcal{Y})$, it holds that*

$$(\Phi \otimes \mathbb{1}_{\mathrm{L}(\mathcal{Y})})(R) \in \mathrm{Pos}(\mathcal{Y} \otimes \mathcal{Y}). \tag{6.26}$$

Proof Suppose first that $R \in \mathrm{Sep}(\mathcal{X} : \mathcal{Y})$, so that

$$R = \sum_{a \in \Sigma} P_a \otimes Q_a \tag{6.27}$$

for some choice of an alphabet Σ and collections $\{P_a : a \in \Sigma\} \subset \mathrm{Pos}(\mathcal{X})$ and $\{Q_a : a \in \Sigma\} \subset \mathrm{Pos}(\mathcal{Y})$. For every complex Euclidean space $\mathcal{Z}$ and every positive map $\Phi \in \mathrm{T}(\mathcal{X}, \mathcal{Z})$ it holds that

$$\left(\Phi \otimes \mathbb{1}_{\mathrm{L}(\mathcal{Y})}\right)(R) = \sum_{a \in \Sigma} \Phi(P_a) \otimes Q_a \in \mathrm{Pos}(\mathcal{Z} \otimes \mathcal{Y}), \tag{6.28}$$

by virtue of the fact that $\Phi(P_a)$ is a positive semidefinite operator for each $a \in \Sigma$. Statement 1 therefore implies statement 2.

Statement 2 trivially implies statement 3.

Finally, the fact that statement 3 implies statement 1 will be proved in the contrapositive form. To this end, assume $R \in \mathrm{Pos}(\mathcal{X} \otimes \mathcal{Y})$ is not a separable operator. As $\mathrm{Sep}(\mathcal{X} : \mathcal{Y})$ is a closed, convex cone within the real vector space $\mathrm{Herm}(\mathcal{X} \otimes \mathcal{Y})$, the hyperplane separation theorem (Theorem 1.11) implies that there must exist a Hermitian operator $H \in \mathrm{Herm}(\mathcal{X} \otimes \mathcal{Y})$ such that $\langle H, R \rangle < 0$ and $\langle H, S \rangle \geq 0$ for every $S \in \mathrm{Sep}(\mathcal{X} : \mathcal{Y})$. The operator H will be used to define a positive and unital map $\Phi \in \mathrm{T}(\mathcal{X}, \mathcal{Y})$ for which

$$\left(\Phi \otimes \mathbb{1}_{\mathrm{L}(\mathcal{Y})}\right)(R) \notin \mathrm{Pos}(\mathcal{Y} \otimes \mathcal{Y}). \tag{6.29}$$

First, let $\Psi \in \mathrm{T}(\mathcal{Y}, \mathcal{X})$ be the unique map for which $J(\Psi) = H$, choose $\varepsilon > 0$ to be a sufficiently small positive real number so that the inequality

$$\langle H, R \rangle + \varepsilon \, \mathrm{Tr}(R) < 0 \tag{6.30}$$

is satisfied, and define $\Xi \in \mathrm{T}(\mathcal{X}, \mathcal{Y})$ as

$$\Xi(X) = \Psi^*(X) + \varepsilon \, \mathrm{Tr}(X)\mathbb{1}_{\mathcal{Y}} \tag{6.31}$$

for every $X \in \mathrm{L}(\mathcal{X})$. For arbitrarily chosen positive semidefinite operators $P \in \mathrm{Pos}(\mathcal{X})$ and $Q \in \mathrm{Pos}(\mathcal{Y})$, it is the case that

$$P \otimes \overline{Q} \in \mathrm{Sep}(\mathcal{X} : \mathcal{Y}), \tag{6.32}$$

and therefore

$$0 \leq \langle H, P \otimes \overline{Q} \rangle = \langle P \otimes \overline{Q}, J(\Psi) \rangle = \langle P, \Psi(Q) \rangle. \tag{6.33}$$

The fact that this inequality holds for every choice of $P \in \mathrm{Pos}(\mathcal{X})$ and $Q \in \mathrm{Pos}(\mathcal{Y})$ implies that $\Psi(Q) \in \mathrm{Pos}(\mathcal{X})$ for every choice of $Q \in \mathrm{Pos}(\mathcal{Y})$, and therefore Ψ is a positive map. It follows from Proposition 2.18 that Ψ^* is a positive map as well. For every nonzero positive semidefinite operator

$P \in \mathrm{Pos}(\mathcal{X})$, the operator $\Xi(P)$ is therefore equal to a positive semidefinite operator $\Psi^*(P)$ plus a positive multiple of the identity operator.

Now let $A = \Xi(\mathbb{1}_{\mathcal{X}})$, which is necessarily a positive definite operator, and define $\Phi \in \mathrm{T}(\mathcal{X}, \mathcal{Y})$ as

$$\Phi(X) = A^{-\frac{1}{2}}\Xi(X)A^{-\frac{1}{2}} \tag{6.34}$$

for every $X \in \mathrm{L}(\mathcal{X})$. It remains to verify that Φ is a positive and unital map for which (6.29) holds. The positivity of Φ follows from the fact that Ξ is positive, and it holds that

$$\Phi(\mathbb{1}_{\mathcal{X}}) = A^{-\frac{1}{2}}\Xi(\mathbb{1}_{\mathcal{X}})A^{-\frac{1}{2}} = A^{-\frac{1}{2}}AA^{-\frac{1}{2}} = \mathbb{1}_{\mathcal{Y}}, \tag{6.35}$$

establishing that Φ is unital. Finally, through the following computation, one may verify that the operator $(\Phi \otimes \mathbb{1}_{\mathrm{L}(\mathcal{Y})})(R)$ is not positive semidefinite:

$$\begin{aligned}
\Big\langle \mathrm{vec}\big(\sqrt{A}\big)\,\mathrm{vec}\big(\sqrt{A}\big)^*, (\Phi \otimes \mathbb{1}_{\mathrm{L}(\mathcal{Y})})(R)\Big\rangle & \\
= \Big\langle \mathrm{vec}(\mathbb{1}_{\mathcal{Y}})\,\mathrm{vec}(\mathbb{1}_{\mathcal{Y}})^*, (\Xi \otimes \mathbb{1}_{\mathrm{L}(\mathcal{Y})})(R)\Big\rangle & \\
= \langle J(\Xi^*), R\rangle & \tag{6.36} \\
= \langle J(\Psi) + \varepsilon \mathbb{1}_{\mathcal{X}} \otimes \mathbb{1}_{\mathcal{Y}}, R\rangle & \\
= \langle H, R\rangle + \varepsilon \,\mathrm{Tr}(R) & \\
< 0. &
\end{aligned}$$

This completes the proof. $\qquad\square$

One immediate application of Theorem 6.9 is that it provides a method for proving that certain positive semidefinite operators are not separable. The following example demonstrates this method for two families of states known as *Werner states* and *isotropic states*.

Example 6.10 Let Σ be an alphabet, and let $\mathcal{X}$ and $\mathcal{Y}$ be complex Euclidean spaces of the form $\mathcal{X} = \mathbb{C}^{\Sigma}$ and $\mathcal{Y} = \mathbb{C}^{\Sigma}$. The *swap operator* $W \in \mathrm{L}(\mathcal{X} \otimes \mathcal{Y})$ is the unique operator satisfying

$$W(x \otimes y) = y \otimes x \tag{6.37}$$

for all vectors $x, y \in \mathbb{C}^{\Sigma}$. Equivalently, this operator is given by

$$W = \sum_{a,b \in \Sigma} E_{a,b} \otimes E_{b,a}. \tag{6.38}$$

The operator W is both unitary and Hermitian, with eigenvalues 1 and -1.

The eigenspace of W corresponding to the eigenvalue 1 is spanned by the orthonormal collection

$$\left\{ \frac{e_a \otimes e_b + e_b \otimes e_a}{\sqrt{2}} : a, b \in \Sigma, \ a < b \right\} \cup \{ e_a \otimes e_a : a \in \Sigma \}, \qquad (6.39)$$

where it has been assumed that a total ordering of the alphabet Σ has been fixed, while the eigenspace corresponding to the eigenvalue -1 is spanned by the orthonormal collection

$$\left\{ \frac{e_a \otimes e_b - e_b \otimes e_a}{\sqrt{2}} : a, b \in \Sigma, \ a < b \right\}. \qquad (6.40)$$

Let $n = |\Sigma|$, and define projection operators $\Delta_0, \Delta_1, \Pi_0, \Pi_1 \in \mathrm{Proj}(\mathcal{X} \otimes \mathcal{Y})$ as follows:

$$\Delta_0 = \frac{1}{n} \sum_{a,b \in \Sigma} E_{a,b} \otimes E_{a,b}, \qquad \Pi_0 = \frac{1}{2} \mathbb{1} \otimes \mathbb{1} + \frac{1}{2} W, \qquad (6.41)$$

$$\Delta_1 = \mathbb{1} \otimes \mathbb{1} - \Delta_0, \qquad \Pi_1 = \mathbb{1} \otimes \mathbb{1} - \Pi_0. \qquad (6.42)$$

That these operators are indeed projection operators follows from the fact that they are Hermitian and square to themselves. Alternatively, one may observe that $\Delta_0 = uu^*$ is the projection onto the one-dimensional subspace of $\mathcal{X} \otimes \mathcal{Y}$ spanned by the unit vector

$$u = \frac{1}{\sqrt{n}} \sum_{a \in \Sigma} e_a \otimes e_a, \qquad (6.43)$$

Δ_1 is the projection onto the orthogonal complement of this subspace, and Π_0 and Π_1 are the projection operators onto the subspaces spanned by the collections (6.39) and (6.40), respectively. (The images of Π_0 and Π_1 are also known as the *symmetric* and *anti-symmetric* subspaces of $\mathbb{C}^\Sigma \otimes \mathbb{C}^\Sigma$, and are considered in greater detail and generality in Chapter 7.) It holds that

$$\mathrm{rank}(\Delta_0) = 1, \qquad \mathrm{rank}(\Pi_0) = \binom{n+1}{2},$$

$$\mathrm{rank}(\Delta_1) = n^2 - 1, \qquad \mathrm{rank}(\Pi_1) = \binom{n}{2}. \qquad (6.44)$$

States of the form

$$\lambda \Delta_0 + (1 - \lambda) \frac{\Delta_1}{n^2 - 1} \qquad (6.45)$$

are known as *isotropic states*, and states of the form

$$\lambda\frac{\Pi_0}{\binom{n+1}{2}} + (1 - \lambda)\frac{\Pi_1}{\binom{n}{2}} \tag{6.46}$$

are known as *Werner states* (for $\lambda \in [0, 1]$ in both cases).

Now, let $T \in T(\mathcal{X})$ denote the transpose mapping, defined by the action $T(X) = X^{\mathsf{T}}$ for all $X \in L(\mathcal{X})$. The mapping T is a positive map. Using the observation that

$$(T \otimes \mathbb{1}_{L(\mathcal{Y})})(\Delta_0) = \frac{1}{n}W, \tag{6.47}$$

which may be verified directly, as well as $T(\mathbb{1}_{\mathcal{X}}) = \mathbb{1}_{\mathcal{X}}$ and $T^2 = \mathbb{1}_{L(\mathcal{X})}$, the following relations may be obtained:

$$(T \otimes \mathbb{1}_{L(\mathcal{Y})})(\Delta_0) = \frac{1}{n}\Pi_0 - \frac{1}{n}\Pi_1, \tag{6.48}$$

$$(T \otimes \mathbb{1}_{L(\mathcal{Y})})(\Delta_1) = \frac{n-1}{n}\Pi_0 + \frac{n+1}{n}\Pi_1, \tag{6.49}$$

$$(T \otimes \mathbb{1}_{L(\mathcal{Y})})(\Pi_0) = \frac{n+1}{2}\Delta_0 + \frac{1}{2}\Delta_1, \tag{6.50}$$

$$(T \otimes \mathbb{1}_{L(\mathcal{Y})})(\Pi_1) = -\frac{n-1}{2}\Delta_0 + \frac{1}{2}\Delta_1. \tag{6.51}$$

For $\lambda \in [0, 1]$, the equations

$$(T \otimes \mathbb{1}_{L(\mathcal{Y})})\left(\lambda\Delta_0 + (1 - \lambda)\frac{\Delta_1}{n^2 - 1}\right)$$
$$= \left(\frac{1 + \lambda n}{2}\right)\frac{\Pi_0}{\binom{n+1}{2}} + \left(\frac{1 - \lambda n}{2}\right)\frac{\Pi_1}{\binom{n}{2}} \tag{6.52}$$

and

$$(T \otimes \mathbb{1}_{L(\mathcal{Y})})\left(\lambda\frac{\Pi_0}{\binom{n+1}{2}} + (1 - \lambda)\frac{\Pi_1}{\binom{n}{2}}\right)$$
$$= \left(\frac{2\lambda - 1}{n}\right)\Delta_0 + \left(1 - \frac{2\lambda - 1}{n}\right)\frac{\Delta_1}{n^2 - 1} \tag{6.53}$$

are implied. It therefore holds that the isotropic state (6.45) is entangled (i.e., not separable) for $\lambda \in (1/n, 1]$, while the Werner state (6.46) is entangled for $\lambda \in [0, 1/2)$.[1]

---

[1] It does indeed hold that the isotropic state (6.45) is separable for $\lambda \in [0, 1/n]$ and the Werner state (6.46) is separable for $\lambda \in [1/2, 1]$. These facts are proved in Chapter 7 (q.v. Example 7.25).

A Separable Neighborhood of the Identity Operator

By means of the Horodecki criterion (Theorem 6.9), it may be proved that there exists a neighborhood of the identity operator $\mathbb{1}_{\mathcal{X}} \otimes \mathbb{1}_{\mathcal{Y}}$, for any choice of complex Euclidean spaces $\mathcal{X}$ and $\mathcal{Y}$, in which *every* positive semidefinite operator is separable. Consequently, every density operator $D(\mathcal{X} \otimes \mathcal{Y})$ that is sufficiently close to the completely mixed state is separable. In order to prove this fact, which is stated in more precise terms in Theorem 6.13 below, the following lemma will be used.

Lemma 6.11 *Let Σ be an alphabet, let $\mathcal{X}$ be a complex Euclidean space, let $\{X_{a,b} : a, b \in \Sigma\} \subset \mathrm{L}(\mathcal{X})$ be a collection of operators, and let $\mathcal{Y} = \mathbb{C}^{\Sigma}$. The operator*

$$X = \sum_{a,b \in \Sigma} X_{a,b} \otimes E_{a,b} \in \mathrm{L}(\mathcal{X} \otimes \mathcal{Y}) \tag{6.54}$$

satisfies

$$\|X\|^2 \leq \sum_{a,b \in \Sigma} \|X_{a,b}\|^2. \tag{6.55}$$

Proof For each $a \in \Sigma$, define an operator $Y_a \in \mathrm{L}(\mathcal{X} \otimes \mathcal{Y})$ as

$$Y_a = \sum_{b \in \Sigma} X_{a,b} \otimes E_{a,b}. \tag{6.56}$$

By expanding the product $Y_a Y_a^*$ and applying the triangle inequality, the multiplicativity of the spectral norm under tensor products, and the spectral norm identity (1.178), one finds that

$$\|Y_a Y_a^*\| = \left\| \sum_{b \in \Sigma} X_{a,b} X_{a,b}^* \otimes E_{a,a} \right\| \leq \sum_{b \in \Sigma} \|X_{a,b} X_{a,b}^*\| = \sum_{b \in \Sigma} \|X_{a,b}\|^2. \tag{6.57}$$

Also observe that

$$X^* X = \sum_{a \in \Sigma} Y_a^* Y_a. \tag{6.58}$$

Therefore, by (6.57) together with the triangle inequality and the spectral norm identity (1.178), it holds that

$$\|X\|^2 = \|X^* X\| \leq \sum_{a \in \Sigma} \|Y_a^* Y_a\| \leq \sum_{a,b \in \Sigma} \|X_{a,b}\|^2, \tag{6.59}$$

as required. $\qquad\square$

In addition, the following theorem (which is equivalent to Theorem 3.39) will be needed.

Theorem 6.12 *Let $\Phi \in T(\mathcal{X}, \mathcal{Y})$ be a positive and unital map, for complex Euclidean spaces $\mathcal{X}$ and $\mathcal{Y}$. It holds that*

$$\|\Phi(X)\| \leq \|X\| \tag{6.60}$$

for every operator $X \in L(\mathcal{X})$.

Proof By the assumption that Φ is positive and unital, Proposition 2.18 and Theorem 2.26 imply that Φ^* is positive and trace-preserving. For operators $X \in L(\mathcal{X})$ and $Y \in L(\mathcal{Y})$, one therefore has

$$\begin{aligned} |\langle Y, \Phi(X) \rangle| = |\langle \Phi^*(Y), X \rangle| &\leq \|X\| \|\Phi^*(Y)\|_1 \\ &\leq \|X\| \|Y\|_1 \|\Phi^*\|_1 = \|X\| \|Y\|_1, \end{aligned} \tag{6.61}$$

where the final equality follows by Corollary 3.40 (to Theorem 3.39). By maximizing over all operators $Y \in L(\mathcal{Y})$ that satisfy $\|Y\|_1 \leq 1$, one finds that $\|\Phi(X)\| \leq \|X\|$ for every $X \in L(\mathcal{X})$, as required. $\qquad\square$

Theorem 6.13 *Let $H \in \mathrm{Herm}(\mathcal{X} \otimes \mathcal{Y})$ be a Hermitian operator satisfying $\|H\|_2 \leq 1$, for complex Euclidean spaces $\mathcal{X}$ and $\mathcal{Y}$. It holds that*

$$\mathbb{1}_{\mathcal{X}} \otimes \mathbb{1}_{\mathcal{Y}} - H \in \mathrm{Sep}(\mathcal{X} : \mathcal{Y}). \tag{6.62}$$

Proof Let $\Phi \in T(\mathcal{X}, \mathcal{Y})$ be an arbitrarily chosen positive and unital map. Let Σ be the alphabet for which $\mathcal{Y} = \mathbb{C}^\Sigma$, and write

$$H = \sum_{a,b \in \Sigma} H_{a,b} \otimes E_{a,b}. \tag{6.63}$$

It holds that

$$(\Phi \otimes \mathbb{1}_{L(\mathcal{Y})})(H) = \sum_{a,b \in \Sigma} \Phi(H_{a,b}) \otimes E_{a,b}, \tag{6.64}$$

and therefore

$$\left\| (\Phi \otimes \mathbb{1}_{L(\mathcal{Y})})(H) \right\|^2 \leq \sum_{a,b \in \Sigma} \|\Phi(H_{a,b})\|^2$$

$$\leq \sum_{a,b \in \Sigma} \|H_{a,b}\|^2 \leq \sum_{a,b \in \Sigma} \|H_{a,b}\|_2^2 = \|H\|_2^2 \leq 1. \tag{6.65}$$

(The first inequality is implied by Lemma 6.11, and the second inequality is implied by Theorem 6.12.) The positivity of Φ implies that $(\Phi \otimes \mathbb{1}_{L(\mathcal{Y})})(H)$ is Hermitian, and therefore $(\Phi \otimes \mathbb{1}_{L(\mathcal{Y})})(H) \leq \mathbb{1}_{\mathcal{X}} \otimes \mathbb{1}_{\mathcal{Y}}$. It follows that

$$(\Phi \otimes \mathbb{1}_{L(\mathcal{Y})})(\mathbb{1}_{\mathcal{X}} \otimes \mathbb{1}_{\mathcal{Y}} - H) = \mathbb{1}_{\mathcal{X}} \otimes \mathbb{1}_{\mathcal{Y}} - (\Phi \otimes \mathbb{1}_{L(\mathcal{Y})})(H) \geq 0. \tag{6.66}$$

Because (6.66) holds for all positive and unital maps Φ, one concludes from Theorem 6.9 that $\mathbb{1}_{\mathcal{X}} \otimes \mathbb{1}_{\mathcal{Y}} - H$ is separable. $\qquad\square$

Bipartite Operator Entanglement Rank

Let $\mathcal{X}$ and $\mathcal{Y}$ be complex Euclidean spaces, and consider the collection of all positive semidefinite operators $R \in \mathrm{Pos}(\mathcal{X} \otimes \mathcal{Y})$ for which there exists an alphabet Σ and a collection of operators $\{A_a : a \in \Sigma\} \subset \mathrm{L}(\mathcal{Y}, \mathcal{X})$ such that

$$R = \sum_{a \in \Sigma} \mathrm{vec}(A_a)\,\mathrm{vec}(A_a)^* \tag{6.67}$$

and $\mathrm{rank}(A_a) \leq 1$ for each $a \in \Sigma$. An operator $A \in \mathrm{L}(\mathcal{Y}, \mathcal{X})$ has rank at most 1 if and only if there exist vectors $u \in \mathcal{X}$ and $v \in \mathcal{Y}$ such that $\mathrm{vec}(A) = u \otimes v$, and from this observation it follows that the collection of operators R just described coincides with $\mathrm{Sep}(\mathcal{X} : \mathcal{Y})$.

It is useful to generalize this notion, allowing for arbitrary upper bounds on the rank of the operators $\{A_a : a \in \Sigma\}$, along the lines of the following definition.

Definition 6.14   Let $\mathcal{X}$ and $\mathcal{Y}$ be complex Euclidean spaces and let $r \geq 1$ be a positive integer. The set $\mathrm{Ent}_r(\mathcal{X} : \mathcal{Y})$ is defined to be the set of all operators $R \in \mathrm{Pos}(\mathcal{X} \otimes \mathcal{Y})$ for which there exists an alphabet Σ and a collection of operators

$$\{A_a : a \in \Sigma\} \subset \mathrm{L}(\mathcal{Y}, \mathcal{X}) \tag{6.68}$$

satisfying $\mathrm{rank}(A_a) \leq r$ for each $a \in \Sigma$, such that

$$R = \sum_{a \in \Sigma} \mathrm{vec}(A_a)\,\mathrm{vec}(A_a)^*. \tag{6.69}$$

An element $R \in \mathrm{Ent}_r(\mathcal{X}:\mathcal{Y})$ is said to have *entanglement rank* bounded by r. The *entanglement rank* of $R \in \mathrm{Pos}(\mathcal{X} \otimes \mathcal{Y})$, with respect to the bipartition between $\mathcal{X}$ and $\mathcal{Y}$, is the minimum value of $r \geq 1$ such that $R \in \mathrm{Ent}_r(\mathcal{X}:\mathcal{Y})$.

As indicated above, it holds that

$$\mathrm{Sep}(\mathcal{X} : \mathcal{Y}) = \mathrm{Ent}_1(\mathcal{X} : \mathcal{Y}), \tag{6.70}$$

and from Definition 6.14 it is immediate that

$$\mathrm{Ent}_{r-1}(\mathcal{X} : \mathcal{Y}) \subseteq \mathrm{Ent}_r(\mathcal{X} : \mathcal{Y}) \tag{6.71}$$

for every integer $r \geq 2$.

The containment (6.71) is proper, provided $r \leq \min\{\dim(\mathcal{X}), \dim(\mathcal{Y})\}$. To see that this is so, consider any operator $B \in \mathrm{L}(\mathcal{Y}, \mathcal{X})$ having rank equal to r, and suppose that

$$\mathrm{vec}(B)\,\mathrm{vec}(B)^* = \sum_{a \in \Sigma} \mathrm{vec}(A_a)\,\mathrm{vec}(A_a)^* \tag{6.72}$$

for some collection of operators $\{A_a : a \in \Sigma\} \subset \mathrm{L}(\mathcal{Y}, \mathcal{X})$. As the operator represented by this equation has rank equal to 1, it must hold that $A_a = \alpha_a B$ for each $a \in \Sigma$, for $\{\alpha_a : a \in \Sigma\}$ being a collection of complex numbers satisfying

$$\sum_{a \in \Sigma} |\alpha_a|^2 = 1. \tag{6.73}$$

It is therefore not possible that (6.72) holds when each operator A_a has rank strictly smaller than r, and therefore

$$\mathrm{vec}(B)\,\mathrm{vec}(B)^* \notin \mathrm{Ent}_{r-1}(\mathcal{X} : \mathcal{Y}). \tag{6.74}$$

It is immediate, on the other hand, that $\mathrm{vec}(B)\,\mathrm{vec}(B)^* \in \mathrm{Ent}_r(\mathcal{X} : \mathcal{Y})$.

Finally, one may observe that

$$\mathrm{Ent}_n(\mathcal{X} : \mathcal{Y}) = \mathrm{Pos}(\mathcal{X} \otimes \mathcal{Y}) \tag{6.75}$$

for $n \geq \min\{\dim(\mathcal{X}), \dim(\mathcal{Y})\}$, as every operator $A \in \mathrm{L}(\mathcal{Y}, \mathcal{X})$ has rank bounded by n in this case.

The following simple proposition concerning entanglement rank will be useful in subsequent sections of this chapter.

Proposition 6.15 *Let $B \in \mathrm{L}(\mathcal{Y}, \mathcal{X})$ be an operator, for complex Euclidean spaces $\mathcal{X}$ and $\mathcal{Y}$, and assume that $\|B\| \leq 1$. For every positive integer r and every operator*

$$P \in \mathrm{Ent}_r(\mathcal{X} : \mathcal{Y}) \tag{6.76}$$

having entanglement rank bounded by r, it holds that

$$\langle \mathrm{vec}(B)\,\mathrm{vec}(B)^*, P \rangle \leq r \,\mathrm{Tr}(P). \tag{6.77}$$

Proof Under the assumption that P has entanglement rank bounded by r, one may write

$$P = \sum_{a \in \Sigma} \mathrm{vec}(A_a)\,\mathrm{vec}(A_a)^* \tag{6.78}$$

for an alphabet Σ and a collection of operators $\{A_a : a \in \Sigma\} \subset \mathrm{L}(\mathcal{Y}, \mathcal{X})$ for which $\mathrm{rank}(A_a) \leq r$ for every $a \in \Sigma$. For every operator $A \in \mathrm{L}(\mathcal{Y}, \mathcal{X})$, one has

$$|\langle B, A \rangle|^2 \leq \|A\|_1^2 \leq \mathrm{rank}(A)\,\|A\|_2^2, \tag{6.79}$$

so that evaluating the inner product in the statement of the proposition yields

$$\langle \mathrm{vec}(B)\,\mathrm{vec}(B)^*, P \rangle = \sum_{a \in \Sigma} |\langle B, A_a \rangle|^2$$

$$\leq \sum_{a \in \Sigma} \mathrm{rank}(A_a) \|A_a\|_2^2 \leq r \sum_{a \in \Sigma} \|A_a\|_2^2 = r\,\mathrm{Tr}(P), \tag{6.80}$$

as required.   □

Example 6.16 Let Σ be an alphabet, let $n = |\Sigma|$, let $\mathcal{X} = \mathbb{C}^\Sigma$ and $\mathcal{Y} = \mathbb{C}^\Sigma$, and define a density operator $\tau \in \mathrm{D}(\mathcal{X} \otimes \mathcal{Y})$ as

$$\tau = \frac{1}{n} \sum_{a,b \in \Sigma} E_{a,b} \otimes E_{a,b}. \tag{6.81}$$

The density operator τ, which coincides with the isotropic state Δ_0 defined in Example 6.10, is the canonical example of a maximally entangled state with respect to the spaces $\mathcal{X}$ and $\mathcal{Y}$. One may observe that

$$\tau = \frac{1}{n}\,\mathrm{vec}(\mathbb{1})\,\mathrm{vec}(\mathbb{1})^* \tag{6.82}$$

for $\mathbb{1}$ denoting the identity operator on $\mathbb{C}^\Sigma$, which may be viewed as an element of the set $\mathrm{L}(\mathcal{Y}, \mathcal{X})$ in the most straightforward way.

For every positive integer r and every density operator

$$\rho \in \mathrm{D}(\mathcal{X} \otimes \mathcal{Y}) \cap \mathrm{Ent}_r(\mathcal{X} : \mathcal{Y}) \tag{6.83}$$

having entanglement rank bounded by r, Proposition 6.15 implies that

$$\langle \tau, \rho \rangle = \frac{1}{n} \langle \mathrm{vec}(\mathbb{1})\,\mathrm{vec}(\mathbb{1})^*, \rho \rangle \leq \frac{r}{n}. \tag{6.84}$$

One therefore has that every state of bounded entanglement rank must have a proportionately small inner product with the state τ.

6.1.2 Separable Maps and the LOCC Paradigm

Separable maps are defined in an analogous way to separable operators, reflecting the natural correspondence between completely positive maps and positive semidefinite operators. The resulting notion of separability for maps, including channels, is algebraic in nature; and it cannot be said that it is directly motivated from a physical or operational viewpoint.

This notion of separability for channels is, however, closely connected to the more operationally motivated notion of channels implementable by *local operations and classical communication*, or *LOCC* for short. An LOCC channel is a channel that can be implemented by two individuals whose local actions are unrestricted (corresponding to arbitrary measurements or channels), but whose communications with one another are restricted to be classical. This paradigm provides a foundation from which properties of entanglement are commonly studied, particularly in settings in which entanglement is viewed as a resource for information processing.

Separable Map and Channels

As suggested above, the notion of separability for maps is defined in an analogous way to separability for operators. The following definition states this in more precise terms.

Definition 6.17 Let $\mathcal{X}$, $\mathcal{Y}$, $\mathcal{Z}$, and $\mathcal{W}$ be complex Euclidean spaces. The set $\mathrm{SepCP}(\mathcal{X}, \mathcal{Z} : \mathcal{Y}, \mathcal{W})$ is defined as the set of all completely positive maps of the form

$$\Xi \in \mathrm{CP}(\mathcal{X} \otimes \mathcal{Y}, \mathcal{Z} \otimes \mathcal{W}) \tag{6.85}$$

for which there exist an alphabet Σ and collections of completely positive maps $\{\Phi_a : a \in \Sigma\} \subset \mathrm{CP}(\mathcal{X}, \mathcal{Z})$ and $\{\Psi_a : a \in \Sigma\} \subset \mathrm{CP}(\mathcal{Y}, \mathcal{W})$ such that

$$\Xi = \sum_{a \in \Sigma} \Phi_a \otimes \Psi_a. \tag{6.86}$$

Elements of the set $\mathrm{SepCP}(\mathcal{X}, \mathcal{Z} : \mathcal{Y}, \mathcal{W})$ are called *separable maps*.

As the following simple proposition states, separable maps are precisely those completely positive maps having Kraus representations for which the individual Kraus operators are tensor products of operators. A direct proof of this proposition is obtained by considering Kraus representations of the maps Φ_a and Ψ_a in Definition 6.17, along the same lines as the proof of Proposition 6.5.

Proposition 6.18 *Let $\mathcal{X}$, $\mathcal{Y}$, $\mathcal{Z}$, and $\mathcal{W}$ be complex Euclidean spaces and let $\Xi \in \mathrm{CP}(\mathcal{X} \otimes \mathcal{Y}, \mathcal{Z} \otimes \mathcal{W})$ be a completely positive map. It holds that*

$$\Phi \in \mathrm{SepCP}(\mathcal{X}, \mathcal{Z} : \mathcal{Y}, \mathcal{W}) \tag{6.87}$$

if and only if there exists an alphabet Σ and collections of operators

$$\{A_a : a \in \Sigma\} \subset \mathrm{L}(\mathcal{X}, \mathcal{Z}) \quad and \quad \{B_a : a \in \Sigma\} \subset \mathrm{L}(\mathcal{Y}, \mathcal{W}) \tag{6.88}$$

such that

$$\Xi(X) = \sum_{a \in \Sigma} (A_a \otimes B_a) X (A_a \otimes B_a)^* \tag{6.89}$$

for every operator $X \in \mathrm{L}(\mathcal{X} \otimes \mathcal{Y})$.

Another straightforward proposition regarding separable maps follows, and, like the previous proposition, it may be verified directly. It implies that the set of all separable maps is closed under composition.

Proposition 6.19 *Let $\mathcal{X}, \mathcal{Y}, \mathcal{Z}, \mathcal{W}, \mathcal{U}$, and $\mathcal{V}$ be complex Euclidean spaces, and suppose that Φ and Ψ are separable maps of the form*

$$\Phi \in \mathrm{SepCP}(\mathcal{X}, \mathcal{U} : \mathcal{Y}, \mathcal{V}) \quad \text{and} \quad \Psi \in \mathrm{SepCP}(\mathcal{U}, \mathcal{Z} : \mathcal{V}, \mathcal{W}). \tag{6.90}$$

It holds that the composition $\Psi\Phi$ is separable:

$$\Psi\Phi \in \mathrm{SepCP}(\mathcal{X}, \mathcal{Z} : \mathcal{Y}, \mathcal{W}). \tag{6.91}$$

Similar to the analogous case for states, one defines the set of separable channels by simply restricting the definition of separability for completely positive maps to channels.

Definition 6.20 For complex Euclidean spaces $\mathcal{X}, \mathcal{Y}, \mathcal{Z}$, and $\mathcal{W}$, one defines

$$\begin{aligned}
\mathrm{SepC}(\mathcal{X}, \mathcal{Z} : \mathcal{Y}, \mathcal{W}) & \\
= \mathrm{SepCP}(\mathcal{X}, \mathcal{Z} : \mathcal{Y}, \mathcal{W}) &\cap \mathrm{C}(\mathcal{X} \otimes \mathcal{Y}, \mathcal{Z} \otimes \mathcal{W}).
\end{aligned} \tag{6.92}$$

Elements of the set $\mathrm{SepC}(\mathcal{X}, \mathcal{Z} : \mathcal{Y}, \mathcal{W})$ are referred to as *separable channels*.

It should be noted that, unlike the analogous case of states, separable channels need not be equal to convex combinations of product channels, as the following example illustrates.

Example 6.21 Let $\Sigma = \{0, 1\}$ denote the binary alphabet, let $\mathcal{X}, \mathcal{Y}, \mathcal{Z}$, and $\mathcal{W}$ all be equal to $\mathbb{C}^\Sigma$, and define a channel $\Xi \in \mathrm{C}(\mathcal{X} \otimes \mathcal{Y}, \mathcal{Z} \otimes \mathcal{W})$ by the equation

$$\Xi(E_{a,b} \otimes E_{c,d}) = \begin{cases} E_{a,a} \otimes E_{a,a} & \text{if } a = b \text{ and } c = d \\ 0 & \text{if } a \neq b \text{ or } c \neq d, \end{cases} \tag{6.93}$$

holding for all $a, b, c, d \in \Sigma$. It is the case that Ξ is a separable channel, meaning that $\Xi \in \mathrm{SepC}(\mathcal{X}, \mathcal{Z} : \mathcal{Y}, \mathcal{W})$. Indeed, one may write

$$\Xi = \Phi_0 \otimes \Psi_0 + \Phi_1 \otimes \Psi_1 \tag{6.94}$$

for completely positive maps defined as follows:

$$\begin{aligned}
\Phi_0(X) &= \langle E_{0,0}, X \rangle E_{0,0}, \quad \Psi_0(X) = \mathrm{Tr}(X) E_{0,0}, \\
\Phi_1(X) &= \langle E_{1,1}, X \rangle E_{1,1}, \quad \Psi_1(X) = \mathrm{Tr}(X) E_{1,1},
\end{aligned} \tag{6.95}$$

for every $X \in \mathrm{L}(\mathbb{C}^\Sigma)$.

It is not possible, however, to express the channel Ξ in the form

$$\Xi = \sum_{a \in \Gamma} p(a) \Phi_a \otimes \Psi_a \qquad (6.96)$$

for any choice of an alphabet Γ, a probability vector $p \in \mathrm{P}(\Gamma)$, and two collections of channels

$$\{\Phi_a : a \in \Gamma\} \subset \mathrm{C}(\mathcal{X}, \mathcal{Z}) \quad \text{and} \quad \{\Psi_a : a \in \Gamma\} \subset \mathrm{C}(\mathcal{Y}, \mathcal{W}). \qquad (6.97)$$

To verify this claim, consider the fact that

$$\Xi(E_{0,0} \otimes \rho) = E_{0,0} \otimes E_{0,0} \quad \text{and} \quad \Xi(E_{1,1} \otimes \rho) = E_{1,1} \otimes E_{1,1} \qquad (6.98)$$

for every density operator $\rho \in \mathrm{D}(\mathcal{Y})$. If it were the case that (6.96) were true for each Φ_a and Ψ_a being a channel, then one would necessarily have

$$\sum_{a \in \Gamma} p(a) \Phi_a(E_{0,0}) \otimes \Psi_a(\rho) = E_{0,0} \otimes E_{0,0}, \qquad (6.99)$$

and therefore, by tracing over the space $\mathcal{Z}$,

$$\sum_{a \in \Sigma} p(a) \Psi_a(\rho) = E_{0,0} \qquad (6.100)$$

for every $\rho \in \mathrm{D}(\mathcal{Y})$. By similar reasoning, it would simultaneously hold that

$$\sum_{a \in \Sigma} p(a) \Phi_a(E_{1,1}) \otimes \Psi_a(\rho) = E_{1,1} \otimes E_{1,1}, \qquad (6.101)$$

and therefore

$$\sum_{a \in \Sigma} p(a) \Psi_a(\rho) = E_{1,1} \qquad (6.102)$$

for every $\rho \in \mathrm{D}(\mathcal{Y})$. The equations (6.100) and (6.102) are in contradiction, implying that Ξ is not equal to a convex combination of product channels.

Intuitively speaking, the situation represented by the previous example is quite simple. Channels that can be expressed as a convex combination of product channels correspond to transformations that may be implemented by means of *local operations and shared randomness* – no communication is needed to implement them, and such channels do not allow for a direct causal relationship to hold among the input and output systems across the bipartition with respect to which separability is considered. The channel Ξ, on the other hand, induces a direct causal relationship of this form.

As the following proposition states, a given completely positive map is separable if and only if its Choi representation is separable, with respect to the natural bipartition of the tensor product space over which it is defined.

Proposition 6.22　*Let $\Xi \in \mathrm{CP}(\mathcal{X} \otimes \mathcal{Y}, \mathcal{Z} \otimes \mathcal{W})$ be a completely positive map, for complex Euclidean spaces $\mathcal{X}$, $\mathcal{Y}$, $\mathcal{Z}$, and $\mathcal{W}$, and define an isometry*

$$V \in \mathrm{U}(\mathcal{Z} \otimes \mathcal{W} \otimes \mathcal{X} \otimes \mathcal{Y}, \mathcal{Z} \otimes \mathcal{X} \otimes \mathcal{W} \otimes \mathcal{Y}) \tag{6.103}$$

by the equation

$$V \operatorname{vec}(A \otimes B) = \operatorname{vec}(A) \otimes \operatorname{vec}(B) \tag{6.104}$$

holding for all operators $A \in \mathrm{L}(\mathcal{X}, \mathcal{Z})$ and $B \in \mathrm{L}(\mathcal{Y}, \mathcal{W})$. It holds that

$$\Xi \in \mathrm{SepCP}(\mathcal{X}, \mathcal{Z} : \mathcal{Y}, \mathcal{W}) \tag{6.105}$$

if and only if

$$V J(\Xi) V^* \in \mathrm{Sep}(\mathcal{Z} \otimes \mathcal{X} : \mathcal{W} \otimes \mathcal{Y}). \tag{6.106}$$

Proof　Assume first that Ξ is a separable map. By Proposition 6.18, there must exist an alphabet Σ and two collections of operators,

$$\{A_a : a \in \Sigma\} \subset \mathrm{L}(\mathcal{X}, \mathcal{Z}) \quad \text{and} \quad \{B_a : a \in \Sigma\} \subset \mathrm{L}(\mathcal{Y}, \mathcal{W}), \tag{6.107}$$

such that

$$\Xi(X) = \sum_{a \in \Sigma} (A_a \otimes B_a) X (A_a \otimes B_a)^* \tag{6.108}$$

for every operator $X \in \mathrm{L}(\mathcal{X} \otimes \mathcal{Y})$. The Choi representation of Ξ is therefore given by

$$J(\Xi) = \sum_{a \in \Sigma} \operatorname{vec}(A_a \otimes B_a) \operatorname{vec}(A_a \otimes B_a)^*, \tag{6.109}$$

so that

$$V J(\Xi) V^* = \sum_{a \in \Sigma} \operatorname{vec}(A_a) \operatorname{vec}(A_a)^* \otimes \operatorname{vec}(B_a) \operatorname{vec}(B_a)^*, \tag{6.110}$$

which is evidently contained in $\mathrm{Sep}(\mathcal{Z} \otimes \mathcal{X} : \mathcal{W} \otimes \mathcal{Y})$.

Conversely, if $V J(\Xi) V^*$ is separable, then it must be possible to express this operator in the form (6.110) for some choice of an alphabet Σ and two collections of operators as in (6.107). It therefore follows that (6.109) is a Choi representation of Ξ, so that (6.108) holds for all $X \in \mathrm{L}(\mathcal{X} \otimes \mathcal{Y})$. The map Ξ is therefore separable, which completes the proof.　□

Remark　The isometry V defined in Proposition 6.22 may alternatively be defined by the action

$$V(z \otimes w \otimes x \otimes y) = z \otimes x \otimes w \otimes y, \tag{6.111}$$

for every choice of vectors $x \in \mathcal{X}$, $y \in \mathcal{Y}$, $z \in \mathcal{Z}$, and $w \in \mathcal{W}$. In words, this isometry represents a permutation of tensor factors, allowing a relationship concerning separability with respect to a particular bipartition to be stated precisely.

It is not uncommon in the theory of quantum information literature that statements of this nature are made without an explicit mention of such an isometry. This can sometimes simplify expressions and generally does not lead to any confusion – the isometry can usually be taken as being implicit, particularly in cases when the underlying complex Euclidean spaces have distinct names. In the interest of clarity and formality, however, this book will always represent such permutations of tensor factors explicitly.

Separable channels are not capable of creating entanglement: a separable channel applied to a separable state yields another separable state. More generally, separable maps cannot cause an increase in entanglement rank, as the following theorem establishes.

Theorem 6.23 *Let $\mathcal{X}$, $\mathcal{Y}$, $\mathcal{Z}$, and $\mathcal{W}$ be complex Euclidean spaces and let $\Xi \in \mathrm{SepCP}(\mathcal{X}, \mathcal{Z} : \mathcal{Y}, \mathcal{W})$ be a separable map. For every positive integer r and every operator $P \in \mathrm{Ent}_r(\mathcal{X} : \mathcal{Y})$, it holds that $\Xi(P) \in \mathrm{Ent}_r(\mathcal{Z} : \mathcal{W})$.*

Proof For an operator $P \in \mathrm{Ent}_r(\mathcal{X} : \mathcal{Y})$ having entanglement rank bounded by r, there must exist an alphabet Γ and a collection of operators

$$\{X_b : b \in \Gamma\} \subset \mathrm{L}(\mathcal{Y}, \mathcal{X}), \tag{6.112}$$

satisfying $\mathrm{rank}(X_b) \leq r$ for every $b \in \Gamma$, such that

$$P = \sum_{b \in \Gamma} \mathrm{vec}(X_b) \, \mathrm{vec}(X_b)^*. \tag{6.113}$$

By Proposition 6.18, it follows that

$$\begin{aligned} \Xi(P) &= \sum_{a \in \Sigma} \sum_{b \in \Gamma} (A_a \otimes B_a) \, \mathrm{vec}(X_b) \, \mathrm{vec}(X_b)^* (A_a \otimes B_a)^* \\ &= \sum_{a \in \Sigma} \sum_{b \in \Gamma} \mathrm{vec}(A_a X_b B_a^{\mathsf{T}}) \, \mathrm{vec}(A_a X_b B_a^{\mathsf{T}})^* \end{aligned} \tag{6.114}$$

for some choice of an alphabet Σ and two collections of operators

$$\{A_a : a \in \Sigma\} \subset \mathrm{L}(\mathcal{X}, \mathcal{Z}) \quad \text{and} \quad \{B_a : a \in \Sigma\} \subset \mathrm{L}(\mathcal{Y}, \mathcal{W}). \tag{6.115}$$

For every $a \in \Sigma$ and $b \in \Gamma$, it holds that

$$\mathrm{rank}(A_a X_b B_a^{\mathsf{T}}) \leq \mathrm{rank}(X_b) \leq r, \tag{6.116}$$

and therefore $\Xi(P) \in \mathrm{Ent}_r(\mathcal{Z} : \mathcal{W})$, as required. $\qquad\square$

Corollary 6.24 *Let* $\Xi \in \mathrm{SepCP}(\mathcal{X}, \mathcal{Z} : \mathcal{Y}, \mathcal{W})$ *be a separable map, for complex Euclidean spaces* $\mathcal{X}$, $\mathcal{Y}$, $\mathcal{Z}$, *and* $\mathcal{W}$. *For every separable operator* $P \in \mathrm{Sep}(\mathcal{X} : \mathcal{Y})$, *it holds that* $\Xi(P)$ *is also separable:* $\Xi(P) \in \mathrm{Sep}(\mathcal{Z} : \mathcal{W})$.

LOCC Channels

As was stated at the beginning of the present subsection, LOCC channels represent transformations of quantum states that may be implemented by two individuals that communicate with one another classically and perform quantum channels and measurements on registers they hold locally.

For instance, one individual may apply a combination of channels and measurements to a collection of registers in their possession and then transmit the measurement outcomes to the other individual. Upon receiving this transmission, the other individual may apply a combination of channels and measurements, possibly depending on the communicated measurement outcomes, to a collection of registers in their possession. In general, LOCC channels represent the cumulative effect of composing any finite number of transformations of this sort.[2]

The following definition formalizes this notion. Naturally, it is possible to generalize this definition to three or more individuals, although this will not be done in this book.

Definition 6.25 Let $\mathcal{X}$, $\mathcal{Y}$, $\mathcal{Z}$, and $\mathcal{W}$ be complex Euclidean spaces and let $\Xi \in \mathrm{C}(\mathcal{X} \otimes \mathcal{Y}, \mathcal{Z} \otimes \mathcal{W})$ be a channel. The channel Ξ is an *LOCC channel* under these conditions:

1. If there exists an alphabet Σ and a collection

$$\{\Phi_a : a \in \Sigma\} \subset \mathrm{CP}(\mathcal{X}, \mathcal{Z}) \tag{6.117}$$

of completely positive maps satisfying

$$\sum_{a \in \Sigma} \Phi_a \in \mathrm{C}(\mathcal{X}, \mathcal{Z}), \tag{6.118}$$

along with a collection

$$\{\Psi_a : a \in \Sigma\} \subseteq \mathrm{C}(\mathcal{Y}, \mathcal{W}) \tag{6.119}$$

of channels, such that

$$\Xi = \sum_{a \in \Sigma} \Phi_a \otimes \Psi_a, \tag{6.120}$$

then Ξ is a *one-way right LOCC channel*.

---

[2] One may consider variants of the definition that allow for an unbounded number of classical transmissions that terminate with probability 1 according to a chosen stopping rule. Only the finite case is considered in this book for simplicity.

2. If there exists an alphabet Σ and a collection

$$\{\Psi_a : a \in \Sigma\} \subset \mathrm{CP}(\mathcal{Y}, \mathcal{W}) \tag{6.121}$$

of completely positive maps satisfying

$$\sum_{a \in \Sigma} \Psi_a \in \mathrm{C}(\mathcal{Y}, \mathcal{W}), \tag{6.122}$$

along with a collection

$$\{\Phi_a : a \in \Sigma\} \subseteq \mathrm{C}(\mathcal{X}, \mathcal{Z}) \tag{6.123}$$

of channels, such that (6.120) holds, then Ξ is a *one-way left LOCC channel*.

3. The channel Ξ is an *LOCC channel* if it is equal to a finite composition of one-way left and one-way right LOCC channels. That is, either Ξ is a one-way left LOCC channel, a one-way right LOCC channel, or there exists an integer $m \geq 2$, complex Euclidean spaces $\mathcal{U}_1, \ldots, \mathcal{U}_{m-1}$ and $\mathcal{V}_1, \ldots, \mathcal{V}_{m-1}$, and channels

$$\begin{aligned}
\Xi_1 &\in \mathrm{C}(\mathcal{X} \otimes \mathcal{Y}, \mathcal{U}_1 \otimes \mathcal{V}_1), \\
\Xi_2 &\in \mathrm{C}(\mathcal{U}_1 \otimes \mathcal{V}_1, \mathcal{U}_2 \otimes \mathcal{V}_2), \\
&\vdots \\
\Xi_m &\in \mathrm{C}(\mathcal{U}_{m-1} \otimes \mathcal{V}_{m-1}, \mathcal{Z} \otimes \mathcal{W}),
\end{aligned} \tag{6.124}$$

each of which is either a one-way left LOCC channel or a one-way right LOCC channel, such that Ξ is equal to the composition $\Xi = \Xi_m \cdots \Xi_1$.

The collection of all such LOCC channels is denoted $\mathrm{LOCC}(\mathcal{X}, \mathcal{Z} : \mathcal{Y}, \mathcal{W})$.

Remark In the definition above, one-way left and one-way right LOCC channels represent channels that can be implemented by local operations and one-way classical communication. In both cases, the channel Ξ may be viewed as having resulted from actions performed by two individuals, Alice and Bob. Alice begins with a register X and Bob begins with Y, and as a result of their actions these registers are transformed into Z and W, respectively.

In the case of a one-way right LOCC channel Ξ, the communication is from Alice to Bob (moving to the *right*, assuming Alice is on the left and Bob is on the right), with the alphabet Σ representing the set of possible classical messages that may be transmitted. Alice's actions are described by a collection of completely positive maps

$$\{\Phi_a : a \in \Sigma\} \subset \mathrm{CP}(\mathcal{X}, \mathcal{Z}) \tag{6.125}$$

that satisfies the constraint

$$\sum_{a \in \Sigma} \Phi_a \in C(\mathcal{X}, \mathcal{Z}). \tag{6.126}$$

In essence, this collection specifies an instrument (q.v. Section 2.3.2). Assuming the classical communication is represented by a classical register V having associated complex Euclidean space $\mathcal{V} = \mathbb{C}^\Sigma$, Alice's action would be described by the channel $\Phi \in C(\mathcal{X}, \mathcal{Z} \otimes \mathcal{V})$ defined by

$$\Phi(X) = \sum_{a \in \Sigma} \Phi_a(X) \otimes E_{a,a} \tag{6.127}$$

for all $X \in L(\mathcal{X})$. The register V is sent to Bob, who observes its classical state (or, equivalently, measures V with respect to the standard basis) and transforms his register Y into W according to the channel $\Psi_a \in C(\mathcal{Y}, \mathcal{W})$, for $a \in \Sigma$ being the classical state of V that was observed. Assuming that the register V is discarded after Bob applies the appropriate channel, the combined actions of Alice and Bob are described by Ξ.

For a one-way left LOCC channel Ξ, the situation is similar, with the roles of Alice and Bob switched.

It is apparent from Definition 6.25, together with the fact that separable channels are closed under composition (Proposition 6.19), that every LOCC channel is a separable channel.

Proposition 6.26 *For every choice of complex Euclidean spaces $\mathcal{X}$, $\mathcal{Y}$, $\mathcal{Z}$, and $\mathcal{W}$, it holds that*

$$\mathrm{LOCC}(\mathcal{X}, \mathcal{Z} : \mathcal{Y}, \mathcal{W}) \subseteq \mathrm{SepC}(\mathcal{X}, \mathcal{Z} : \mathcal{Y}, \mathcal{W}). \tag{6.128}$$

6.1.3 Separable and LOCC Measurements

As was explained in Section 2.3.1, one may associate a quantum-to-classical channel with each measurement, with the classical output of the channel representing the outcome of the measurement. Through an identification of this sort, the notions of separable and LOCC channels may be extended to measurements.

Definitions of Separable and LOCC Measurements

The following definition of separable and LOCC measurements refers to an association of quantum-to-classical channels with measurements that has been adapted to a bipartite setting.

Definition 6.27 Let Σ be an alphabet, let $\mathcal{X}$ and $\mathcal{Y}$ be complex Euclidean spaces, and let $\mu\colon \Sigma \to \mathrm{Pos}(\mathcal{X} \otimes \mathcal{Y})$ be a measurement. Define complex Euclidean spaces $\mathcal{Z} = \mathbb{C}^{\Sigma}$ and $\mathcal{W} = \mathbb{C}^{\Sigma}$, and define a channel

$$\Phi_{\mu} \in \mathrm{C}(\mathcal{X} \otimes \mathcal{Y}, \mathcal{Z} \otimes \mathcal{W}) \tag{6.129}$$

as

$$\Phi_{\mu}(X) = \sum_{a \in \Sigma} \langle \mu(a), X \rangle \, E_{a,a} \otimes E_{a,a} \tag{6.130}$$

for every $X \in \mathrm{L}(\mathcal{X} \otimes \mathcal{Y})$. The measurement μ is a *separable measurement* if

$$\Phi_{\mu} \in \mathrm{SepC}(\mathcal{X}, \mathcal{Z} : \mathcal{Y}, \mathcal{W}), \tag{6.131}$$

and μ is an *LOCC measurement* if

$$\Phi_{\mu} \in \mathrm{LOCC}(\mathcal{X}, \mathcal{Z} : \mathcal{Y}, \mathcal{W}). \tag{6.132}$$

For a given measurement μ, the channel Φ_{μ} specified in Definition 6.27 is similar to the quantum-to-classical channel one would normally associate with μ, except that two copies of the measurement outcome are produced rather than one. In a bipartite setting, this is a natural way of associating a quantum-to-classical channel with a measurement. If this measurement is performed on a pair of registers (X, Y) by two individuals, Alice and Bob, where it is assumed that Alice holds X and Bob holds Y, the channel Φ_{μ} represents the measurement μ under the assumption that both individuals learn the measurement outcome after the measurement is performed.

One alternative to Definition 6.27 is to replace the channel Φ_{μ} by the quantum-to-classical channel that would ordinarily be associated with the measurement μ, along with a specification of which side of the bipartition the measurement outcome is to fall (requiring this channel to be separable or LOCC, as in the stated definition). In essence, with respect to a situation in which Alice and Bob are performing the measurement μ as suggested above, such a definition specifies which of the individuals obtains the measurement outcome. This alternative creates an asymmetry in the definition, but is equivalent to Definition 6.27.

With respect to Definition 6.27, the separability of a given measurement is equivalent to the constraint that each measurement operator is separable, as the following proposition states.

Proposition 6.28 *Let $\mathcal{X}$ and $\mathcal{Y}$ be complex Euclidean spaces, let Σ be an alphabet, and let μ be a measurement of the form $\mu\colon \Sigma \to \mathrm{Pos}(\mathcal{X} \otimes \mathcal{Y})$. It holds that μ is a separable measurement if and only if $\mu(a) \in \mathrm{Sep}(\mathcal{X} : \mathcal{Y})$ for every $a \in \Sigma$.*

Proof Consider the Choi representation of the mapping Φ_μ, as specified in Definition 6.27, which is given by

$$J(\Phi_\mu) = \sum_{a \in \Sigma} E_{a,a} \otimes E_{a,a} \otimes \overline{\mu(a)}. \tag{6.133}$$

Along similar lines to the statement of Proposition 6.22, let

$$V \in U(\mathcal{Z} \otimes \mathcal{W} \otimes \mathcal{X} \otimes \mathcal{Y}, \mathcal{Z} \otimes \mathcal{X} \otimes \mathcal{W} \otimes \mathcal{Y}) \tag{6.134}$$

be the isometry defined by the equation

$$V \operatorname{vec}(A \otimes B) = \operatorname{vec}(A) \otimes \operatorname{vec}(B) \tag{6.135}$$

holding for all operators $A \in L(\mathcal{X}, \mathcal{Z})$ and $B \in L(\mathcal{Y}, \mathcal{W})$. If it is the case that $\mu(a) \in \operatorname{Sep}(\mathcal{X} : \mathcal{Y})$ for every $a \in \Sigma$, then it follows directly that

$$V J(\Phi_\mu) V^* \in \operatorname{Sep}(\mathcal{Z} \otimes \mathcal{X} : \mathcal{W} \otimes \mathcal{Y}), \tag{6.136}$$

which implies that μ is a separable measurement by Proposition 6.22.

Now suppose that μ is a separable measurement, so that (6.136) holds. Define a mapping

$$\Xi_a \in T(\mathcal{Z} \otimes \mathcal{X} \otimes \mathcal{W} \otimes \mathcal{Y}, \mathcal{X} \otimes \mathcal{Y}), \tag{6.137}$$

for each $a \in \Sigma$, as

$$\Xi_a(X) = ((e_a^* \otimes \mathbb{1}_\mathcal{X}) \otimes (e_a^* \otimes \mathbb{1}_\mathcal{Y})) X ((e_a \otimes \mathbb{1}_\mathcal{X}) \otimes (e_a \otimes \mathbb{1}_\mathcal{Y})) \tag{6.138}$$

for all $X \in L(\mathcal{Z} \otimes \mathcal{X} \otimes \mathcal{W} \otimes \mathcal{Y})$. It is evident from this definition that Ξ_a is a separable mapping for each $a \in \Sigma$, meaning

$$\Xi_a \in \operatorname{SepCP}(\mathcal{Z} \otimes \mathcal{X}, \mathcal{X} : \mathcal{W} \otimes \mathcal{Y}, \mathcal{Y}). \tag{6.139}$$

It holds that

$$\overline{\mu(a)} = \Xi_a(V J(\Phi_\mu) V^*) \tag{6.140}$$

for each $a \in \Sigma$, from which it follows that

$$\overline{\mu(a)} \in \operatorname{Sep}(\mathcal{X} : \mathcal{Y}) \tag{6.141}$$

by Corollary 6.24. This is equivalent to $\mu(a) \in \operatorname{Sep}(\mathcal{X} : \mathcal{Y})$ for each $a \in \Sigma$, as the entry-wise complex conjugate of every separable operator is evidently separable, which completes the proof. $\qquad\square$

For two complex Euclidean spaces $\mathcal{X}$ and $\mathcal{Y}$, along with an alphabet Σ, it is the case that the set of all separable measurements of the form

$$\mu : \Sigma \to \operatorname{Pos}(\mathcal{X} \otimes \mathcal{Y}) \tag{6.142}$$

is a proper subset of the set of all measurements of the same form (aside from the trivial cases in which one of $\dim(\mathcal{X})$, $\dim(\mathcal{Y})$, or $|\Sigma|$ equals 1). As every LOCC channel is separable, it follows that every LOCC measurement is a separable measurement.

One-Way LOCC Measurements

An interesting restricted type of LOCC measurement is one in which only *one-way communication* is permitted. The following definition formalizes this type of measurement.

Definition 6.29 Let $\mathcal{X}$ and $\mathcal{Y}$ be complex Euclidean spaces, let Σ be an alphabet, and let

$$\mu: \Sigma \to \mathrm{Pos}(\mathcal{X} \otimes \mathcal{Y}) \tag{6.143}$$

be a measurement. The measurement μ is a *one-way LOCC measurement* if either of the following two conditions is met:

1. There exists an alphabet Γ and a measurement $\nu: \Gamma \to \mathrm{Pos}(\mathcal{X})$, along with a measurement $\pi_b: \Sigma \to \mathrm{Pos}(\mathcal{Y})$ for each $b \in \Gamma$, such that the equation

$$\mu(a) = \sum_{b \in \Gamma} \nu(b) \otimes \pi_b(a) \tag{6.144}$$

   holds for every $a \in \Sigma$. In this case the measurement μ is said to be a *one-way right LOCC measurement.*

2. There exists an alphabet Γ and a measurement $\nu: \Gamma \to \mathrm{Pos}(\mathcal{Y})$, along with a measurement $\pi_b: \Sigma \to \mathrm{Pos}(\mathcal{X})$ for each $b \in \Gamma$, such that the equation

$$\mu(a) = \sum_{b \in \Gamma} \pi_b(a) \otimes \nu(b) \tag{6.145}$$

   holds for every $a \in \Sigma$. In this case the measurement μ is said to be a *one-way left LOCC measurement.*

Limitations on State Discrimination by Separable Measurements

One may consider the problem of state discrimination, as was discussed in Chapter 3, in which measurements are restricted to be separable or LOCC measurements. Many examples of sets of orthogonal pure states are known that cannot be discriminated by separable or LOCC measurements without error. The following theorem provides one class of examples, and implies that there exist relatively small sets of orthogonal pure states having this characteristic.

Theorem 6.30 *Let $\mathcal{X}$ and $\mathcal{Y}$ be complex Euclidean spaces, let $n = \dim(\mathcal{Y})$, and assume $n \leq \dim(\mathcal{X})$. Also let*

$$\{U_1, \ldots, U_m\} \in \mathrm{U}(\mathcal{Y}, \mathcal{X}) \tag{6.146}$$

be an orthogonal collection of isometries, and let $u_k \in \mathcal{X} \otimes \mathcal{Y}$ be the unit vector defined as

$$u_k = \frac{1}{\sqrt{n}} \operatorname{vec}(U_k) \tag{6.147}$$

for each $k \in \{1, \ldots, m\}$. For every separable measurement of the form

$$\mu \colon \{1, \ldots, m\} \to \operatorname{Sep}(\mathcal{X} : \mathcal{Y}) \tag{6.148}$$

it holds that

$$\sum_{k=1}^{m} \langle \mu(k), u_k u_k^* \rangle \leq \dim(\mathcal{X}). \tag{6.149}$$

Proof   Under the assumption that μ is a separable measurement, one may write

$$\mu(k) = \sum_{a \in \Sigma} P_{k,a} \otimes Q_{k,a} \tag{6.150}$$

for each $k \in \{1, \ldots, m\}$, for some choice of an alphabet Σ and collections of positive semidefinite operators as follows:

$$\begin{aligned} \{P_{k,a} : k \in \{1, \ldots, m\}, \, a \in \Sigma\} &\subset \operatorname{Pos}(\mathcal{X}), \\ \{Q_{k,a} : k \in \{1, \ldots, m\}, \, a \in \Sigma\} &\subset \operatorname{Pos}(\mathcal{Y}). \end{aligned} \tag{6.151}$$

(No generality is lost in using the same alphabet Σ in the expressions (6.150) for each choice of k, as one is free to choose Σ to be as large as is needed, and to set $P_{k,a} = 0$ or $Q_{k,a} = 0$ for some choices of k and a as necessary.) It holds that

$$\begin{aligned} \langle \mu(k), \operatorname{vec}(U_k) \operatorname{vec}(U_k)^* \rangle &= \sum_{a \in \Sigma} \operatorname{Tr}(U_k^* P_{k,a} U_k Q_{k,a}^{\mathsf{T}}) \\ &\leq \sum_{a \in \Sigma} \|U_k^* P_{k,a} U_k\|_2 \|Q_{k,a}\|_2 \leq \sum_{a \in \Sigma} \|P_{k,a}\|_1 \|Q_{k,a}\|_1 \\ &= \sum_{a \in \Sigma} \operatorname{Tr}(P_{k,a}) \operatorname{Tr}(Q_{k,a}) = \operatorname{Tr}(\mu(k)), \end{aligned} \tag{6.152}$$

and therefore

$$\sum_{k=1}^{m} \langle \mu(k), \operatorname{vec}(U_k) \operatorname{vec}(U_k)^* \rangle \leq \sum_{k=1}^{m} \operatorname{Tr}(\mu(k)) = n \dim(\mathcal{X}). \tag{6.153}$$

The theorem follows by dividing both sides of this inequality by n. $\square$

For any set of unit vectors $\{u_1, \ldots, u_m\}$ as described by this theorem, for which $m > \dim(\mathcal{X})$, one therefore has that

$$\frac{1}{m} \sum_{k=1}^{m} \langle \mu(k), u_k u_k^* \rangle \leq \frac{\dim(\mathcal{X})}{m} < 1. \tag{6.154}$$

Consequently, for one of the m pure states associated with these vectors being selected uniformly at random, any separable measurement that aims to discriminate these states must err with probability strictly greater than 0.

LOCC Discrimination of Any Pair of Orthogonal Pure States

Although Theorem 6.30 establishes that there exist relatively small sets of orthogonal pure states that cannot be perfectly discriminated by separable measurements, the same cannot be said about *pairs* of orthogonal pure states. Indeed, every pair of orthogonal pure states can be discriminated without error by a one-way LOCC measurement. The following lemma is used to prove this fact.

Lemma 6.31 *Let $\mathcal{X}$ be a complex Euclidean space of dimension n and let $X \in \mathrm{L}(\mathcal{X})$ be an operator satisfying $\mathrm{Tr}(X) = 0$. There exists an orthonormal basis $\{x_1, \ldots, x_n\}$ of $\mathcal{X}$ such that $x_k^* X x_k = 0$ for all $k \in \{1, \ldots, n\}$.*

Proof The proof is by induction on n. The base case $n = 1$ is immediate, so it will be assumed that $n \geq 2$ for the rest of the proof. It will also be assumed that $\mathcal{X} = \mathbb{C}^n$, which causes no loss of generality.

For every integer $k \in \{1, \ldots, n\}$, it holds that $\lambda_k(X) \in \mathcal{N}(X)$, where $\mathcal{N}(X)$ denotes the numerical range of X. By the Toeplitz–Hausdorff theorem (Theorem 3.54), the numerical range is convex, and therefore

$$0 = \frac{1}{n} \mathrm{Tr}(X) = \frac{1}{n} \sum_{k=1}^{n} \lambda_k(X) \in \mathcal{N}(X). \tag{6.155}$$

By the definition of the numerical range, there must therefore exist a unit vector $x_n \in \mathcal{X}$ such that $x_n^* X x_n = 0$.

Let $V \in \mathrm{U}(\mathbb{C}^{n-1}, \mathbb{C}^n)$ be any isometry that satisfies $x_n \perp \mathrm{im}(V)$, which is equivalent to

$$VV^* = \mathbb{1} - x_n x_n^*. \tag{6.156}$$

It holds that

$$\mathrm{Tr}(V^* X V) = \mathrm{Tr}((\mathbb{1} - x_n x_n^*)X) = \mathrm{Tr}(X) - x_n^* X x_n = 0. \tag{6.157}$$

As $V^* X V \in \mathrm{L}(\mathbb{C}^{n-1})$, the hypothesis of induction implies that there exists an orthonormal basis $\{u_1, \ldots, u_{n-1}\}$ of $\mathbb{C}^{n-1}$ such that

$$u_k^*(V^*XV)u_k = 0 \tag{6.158}$$

for all $k \in \{1, \ldots, n-1\}$. Define $x_k = Vu_k$ for each $k \in \{1, \ldots, n-1\}$, and observe that $\{x_1, \ldots, x_{n-1}\}$ is an orthonormal set, with each element x_k of this set satisfying $x_k^*Xx_k = 0$. As V is an isometry and $x_n \perp \mathrm{im}(X)$, it follows that $\{x_1, \ldots, x_n\}$ is an orthonormal basis of $\mathcal{X}$ having the property stated by the lemma. $\qquad \square$

Theorem 6.32 *Let $u_0, u_1 \in \mathcal{X} \otimes \mathcal{Y}$ be orthogonal unit vectors, for $\mathcal{X}$ and $\mathcal{Y}$ being complex Euclidean spaces. There exists a one-way LOCC measurement*

$$\mu \colon \{0, 1\} \to \mathrm{Pos}(\mathcal{X} \otimes \mathcal{Y}) \tag{6.159}$$

such that

$$\langle \mu(0), u_0 u_0^* \rangle = 1 = \langle \mu(1), u_1 u_1^* \rangle. \tag{6.160}$$

Proof Let $n = \dim(\mathcal{Y})$ and let $A_0, A_1 \in \mathrm{L}(\mathcal{Y}, \mathcal{X})$ be the unique operators satisfying $u_0 = \mathrm{vec}(A_0)$ and $u_1 = \mathrm{vec}(A_1)$. The orthogonality of the vectors u_0 and u_1 is equivalent to the condition $\mathrm{Tr}(A_0^*A_1) = 0$. By Lemma 6.31, there exists an orthonormal basis $\{x_1, \ldots, x_n\}$ of $\mathcal{Y}$ with the property that $x_k^*A_0^*A_1x_k = 0$, which is equivalent to the condition that

$$\langle A_0 x_k x_k^* A_0^*, A_1 x_k x_k^* A_1^* \rangle = 0, \tag{6.161}$$

for every $k \in \{1, \ldots, n\}$.

Define a measurement $\nu \colon \{1, \ldots, n\} \to \mathrm{Pos}(\mathcal{Y})$ as

$$\nu(k) = \overline{x_k} x_k^{\mathsf{T}} \tag{6.162}$$

for each $k \in \{1, \ldots, n\}$. By the equation (6.161), one has that there must exist a measurement $\pi_k \colon \{0, 1\} \to \mathrm{Pos}(\mathcal{X})$, for each $k \in \{1, \ldots, n\}$, such that

$$\langle \pi_k(0), A_1 x_k x_k^* A_1^* \rangle = 0 = \langle \pi_k(1), A_0 x_k x_k^* A_0^* \rangle. \tag{6.163}$$

Finally, define $\mu \colon \{0, 1\} \to \mathrm{Pos}(\mathcal{X} \otimes \mathcal{Y})$ as

$$\mu(a) = \sum_{k=1}^{n} \pi_k(a) \otimes \nu(k) \tag{6.164}$$

for each $a \in \{0, 1\}$, which is a one-way measurement with respect to the second condition of Definition 6.29. It holds that

$$\langle \mu(0), u_1 u_1^* \rangle = \sum_{k=1}^{n} \langle \pi_k(0), (\mathbb{1} \otimes x_k^\mathsf{T}) \operatorname{vec}(A_1) \operatorname{vec}(A_1)^* (\mathbb{1} \otimes \overline{x_k}) \rangle$$

$$= \sum_{k=1}^{n} \langle \pi_k(0), A_1 x_k x_k^* A_1^* \rangle = 0,$$

(6.165)

and through a similar calculation one finds that $\langle \mu(1), u_0 u_0^* \rangle = 0$, which completes the proof. $\qquad\square$

Remark The preceding proof may be adapted in a straightforward way to prove that there exists a one-way LOCC measurement respecting the first condition of Definition 6.29, as opposed to the second, that satisfies the requirements of the theorem.

6.2 Manipulation of Entanglement

As presented in the previous section, entanglement is defined as a lack of separability: for two complex Euclidean spaces $\mathcal{X}$ and $\mathcal{Y}$, a bipartite state $\rho \in \mathrm{D}(\mathcal{X} \otimes \mathcal{Y})$ that is not contained in the set $\mathrm{SepD}(\mathcal{X} : \mathcal{Y})$ is entangled with respect to the bipartition between $\mathcal{X}$ and $\mathcal{Y}$. This definition is qualitative, in the sense that it does not provide a measure of how much entanglement is present in a given state or suggest how two entangled states might relate to one another. The present section discusses such notions, and develops basic concepts and techniques relating to quantitative aspects of entanglement.

6.2.1 Entanglement Transformation

The next theorem establishes a necessary and sufficient condition under which two individuals may transform one pure state into another by means of local operations and classical communication. The condition concerns the reductions of the initial and final pure states to one of the two individuals, requiring that the reduction of the initial state is majorized by the reduction of the final state. This condition is not only equivalent to the existence of an LOCC (or even a separable) channel transforming the initial state to the final state, but also implies that the transformation can be accomplished with one-way classical communication, from either of the two individuals to the other. The theorem offers a tool through which two fundamental ways of quantifying how much entanglement exists in a given state, called the *entanglement cost* and the *distillable entanglement*, may be analyzed for pure states.

Theorem 6.33 (Nielsen's theorem)   *Let $\mathcal{X}$ and $\mathcal{Y}$ be complex Euclidean spaces and let $u, v \in \mathcal{X} \otimes \mathcal{Y}$ be unit vectors. The following statements are equivalent:*

1. $\mathrm{Tr}_{\mathcal{Y}}(uu^*) \prec \mathrm{Tr}_{\mathcal{Y}}(vv^*)$.
2. *There exist an alphabet Σ and collections of operators*

$$\{U_a : a \in \Sigma\} \subset \mathrm{U}(\mathcal{X}) \quad and \quad \{B_a : a \in \Sigma\} \subset \mathrm{L}(\mathcal{Y}) \tag{6.166}$$

   satisfying

$$\sum_{a \in \Sigma} B_a^* B_a = \mathbb{1}_{\mathcal{Y}} \tag{6.167}$$

   and

$$vv^* = \sum_{a \in \Sigma} (U_a \otimes B_a) uu^* (U_a \otimes B_a)^*. \tag{6.168}$$

3. *There exist an alphabet Σ and collections of operators*

$$\{A_a : a \in \Sigma\} \subset \mathrm{L}(\mathcal{X}) \quad and \quad \{V_a : a \in \Sigma\} \subset \mathrm{U}(\mathcal{Y}) \tag{6.169}$$

   satisfying

$$\sum_{a \in \Sigma} A_a^* A_a = \mathbb{1}_{\mathcal{X}} \tag{6.170}$$

   and

$$vv^* = \sum_{a \in \Sigma} (A_a \otimes V_a) uu^* (A_a \otimes V_a)^*. \tag{6.171}$$

4. *There exists a separable channel[3] $\Phi \in \mathrm{SepC}(\mathcal{X} : \mathcal{Y})$ such that*

$$vv^* = \Phi(uu^*). \tag{6.172}$$

Proof   Let $X, Y \in \mathrm{L}(\mathcal{Y}, \mathcal{X})$ be the unique operators for which $u = \mathrm{vec}(X)$ and $v = \mathrm{vec}(Y)$, and let

$$X = \sum_{k=1}^{r} s_k x_k y_k^* \tag{6.173}$$

be a singular value decomposition of X, for $r = \mathrm{rank}(X)$.

Assume first that statement 1 holds, which is equivalent to $XX^* \prec YY^*$. There must therefore exist an alphabet Σ, a probability vector $p \in \mathcal{P}(\Sigma)$, and a collection of unitary operators $\{W_a : a \in \Sigma\} \subset \mathrm{U}(\mathcal{X})$ such that

$$XX^* = \sum_{a \in \Sigma} p(a) W_a YY^* W_a^*. \tag{6.174}$$

---

[3] As one may expect, the notation $\mathrm{SepC}(\mathcal{X} : \mathcal{Y})$ is a shorthand for $\mathrm{SepC}(\mathcal{X}, \mathcal{X} : \mathcal{Y}, \mathcal{Y})$.

Let $\mathcal{Z} = \mathbb{C}^\Sigma$ and define an operator $Z \in \mathrm{L}(\mathcal{Y} \otimes \mathcal{Z}, \mathcal{X})$ as

$$Z = \sum_{a \in \Sigma} \sqrt{p(a)} W_a Y \otimes e_a^*. \tag{6.175}$$

It holds that

$$ZZ^* = \sum_{a \in \Sigma} p(a) W_a YY^* W_a^* = XX^*, \tag{6.176}$$

and therefore Z and X agree on their singular values, and on the possible choices for their left singular vectors. It follows that one may write

$$Z = \sum_{k=1}^{r} s_k x_k w_k^* \tag{6.177}$$

for $\{w_1, \ldots, w_r\} \subset \mathcal{Y} \otimes \mathcal{Z}$ being an orthonormal collection of vectors. Let $V \in \mathrm{U}(\mathcal{Y}, \mathcal{Y} \otimes \mathcal{Z})$ be an isometry for which $V y_k = w_k$ for all $k \in \{1, \ldots, r\}$, so that $XV^* = Z$.

Now, define operators

$$U_a = W_a^* \quad \text{and} \quad B_a = (\mathbb{1}_\mathcal{Y} \otimes e_a^*)\overline{V} \tag{6.178}$$

for each $a \in \Sigma$. As V is an isometry, so too is $\overline{V}$, and therefore

$$\sum_{a \in \Sigma} B_a^* B_a = \sum_{a \in \Sigma} V^\mathsf{T}(\mathbb{1}_\mathcal{Y} \otimes E_{a,a})\overline{V} = V^\mathsf{T}\overline{V} = \mathbb{1}_\mathcal{Y}. \tag{6.179}$$

It holds that

$$W_a^* X B_a^\mathsf{T} = W_a^* XV^*(\mathbb{1}_\mathcal{Y} \otimes e_a) = W_a^* Z(\mathbb{1}_\mathcal{Y} \otimes e_a) = \sqrt{p(a)}Y \tag{6.180}$$

for each $a \in \Sigma$, and therefore

$$\begin{aligned}
\sum_{a \in \Sigma} &(U_a \otimes B_a)uu^*(U_a \otimes B_a)^* \\
&= \sum_{a \in \Sigma} \mathrm{vec}(W_a^* X B_a^\mathsf{T}) \, \mathrm{vec}(W_a^* X B_a^\mathsf{T})^* \\
&= \sum_{a \in \Sigma} p(a) \, \mathrm{vec}(Y) \, \mathrm{vec}(Y)^* \\
&= vv^*.
\end{aligned} \tag{6.181}$$

It has been established that statement 1 implies statement 2.

The fact that statement 1 implies statement 3 is established by a similar argument with the roles of $\mathcal{X}$ and $\mathcal{Y}$ exchanged, along with the observation that $\mathrm{Tr}_\mathcal{Y}(uu^*) \prec \mathrm{Tr}_\mathcal{Y}(vv^*)$ is equivalent to $\mathrm{Tr}_\mathcal{X}(uu^*) \prec \mathrm{Tr}_\mathcal{X}(vv^*)$.

Statements 2 and 3 each imply statement 4 directly, as the mappings defined by the actions

$$uu^* \mapsto \sum_{a \in \Sigma} (U_a \otimes B_a) uu^* (U_a \otimes B_a)^*,$$
$$uu^* \mapsto \sum_{a \in \Sigma} (A_a \otimes V_a) uu^* (A_a \otimes V_a)^* \tag{6.182}$$

are both separable channels.

Finally, assume statement 4 holds, letting $\Phi \in \mathrm{SepC}(\mathcal{X} : \mathcal{Y})$ be a fixed separable channel for which $\Phi(uu^*) = vv^*$. It will be proved that

$$\lambda(XX^*) \prec \lambda(YY^*); \tag{6.183}$$

by Theorem 4.32, this relation is equivalent to $XX^* \prec YY^*$, which in turn is equivalent to statement 1. Let $n = \dim(\mathcal{X})$, and observe that

$$\sum_{k=1}^{n} \lambda_k(XX^*) = \mathrm{Tr}(XX^*) = 1 = \mathrm{Tr}(YY^*) = \sum_{k=1}^{n} \lambda_k(YY^*), \tag{6.184}$$

by the assumption that u and v are unit vectors. By Theorem 4.30, one finds that the relation (6.183) will therefore follow from the inequality

$$\sum_{k=m}^{n} \lambda_k(YY^*) \leq \sum_{k=m}^{n} \lambda_k(XX^*) \tag{6.185}$$

holding for every choice of $m \in \{1, \dots, n\}$.

By the separability of the channel Φ, there must exist an alphabet Σ and two collections of operators

$$\{A_a : a \in \Sigma\} \subset \mathrm{L}(\mathcal{X}) \quad \text{and} \quad \{B_a : a \in \Sigma\} \subset \mathrm{L}(\mathcal{Y}), \tag{6.186}$$

with $\{A_a \otimes B_a : a \in \Sigma\}$ being a set of Kraus operators of Φ, for which

$$vv^* = \sum_{a \in \Sigma} (A_a \otimes B_a) uu^* (A_a \otimes B_a)^*. \tag{6.187}$$

As vv^* is a rank-one operator, it follows that there must exist a probability vector $p \in \mathcal{P}(\Sigma)$ such that

$$(A_a \otimes B_a) uu^* (A_a \otimes B_a)^* = p(a) vv^*, \tag{6.188}$$

which is equivalent to

$$\mathrm{vec}(A_a X B_a^{\mathsf{T}}) \, \mathrm{vec}(A_a X B_a^{\mathsf{T}})^* = p(a) \, \mathrm{vec}(Y) \, \mathrm{vec}(Y)^*, \tag{6.189}$$

for each $a \in \Sigma$. By taking the partial trace over $\mathcal{Y}$, it follows that

$$A_a X B_a^{\mathsf{T}} \overline{B_a} X^* A_a^* = p(a) YY^* \tag{6.190}$$

for each $a \in \Sigma$, and therefore

$$\sum_{k=m}^{n} \lambda_k(YY^*) = \sum_{k=m}^{n} \sum_{a \in \Sigma} \lambda_k \Big(A_a X B_a^\mathsf{T} \overline{B_a} X^* A_a^* \Big) \qquad (6.191)$$

for each $m \in \{1, \ldots, n\}$.

Next, for each choice of $a \in \Sigma$ and $m \in \{1, \ldots, n\}$, let $\Pi_{a,m} \in \mathrm{Proj}(\mathcal{X})$ be the projection operator onto the orthogonal complement of the subspace of $\mathcal{X}$ spanned by the set $\{A_a x_1, \ldots, A_a x_{m-1}\}$, where one is to assume $x_k = 0$ for $k > r$. By the definition of these projection operators, it is evident that

$$\big\langle \Pi_{a,m}, A_a X B_a^\mathsf{T} \overline{B_a} X^* A_a^* \big\rangle = \big\langle \Pi_{a,m}, A_a X_m B_a^\mathsf{T} \overline{B_a} X_m^* A_a^* \big\rangle \qquad (6.192)$$

for every $a \in \Sigma$ and $m \in \{1, \ldots, n\}$, where

$$X_m = \sum_{k=m}^{r} s_k x_k y_k^*, \qquad (6.193)$$

and one is to interpret that $X_m = 0$ for $m > r$. Because each operator $\Pi_{a,m}$ is a projection, and the operator $A_a X_m B_a^\mathsf{T} \overline{B_a} X_m^* A_a^*$ is positive semidefinite, it follows that

$$\big\langle \Pi_{a,m}, A_a X_m B_a^\mathsf{T} \overline{B_a} X_m^* A_a^* \big\rangle \leq \mathrm{Tr}\Big(A_a X_m B_a^\mathsf{T} \overline{B_a} X_m^* A_a^* \Big). \qquad (6.194)$$

Using the fact that Φ is a channel, and therefore preserves trace, one finds that

$$\sum_{a \in \Sigma} \mathrm{Tr}\Big(A_a X_m B_a^\mathsf{T} \overline{B_a} X_m^* A_a^* \Big) = \mathrm{Tr}\big(\Phi(\mathrm{vec}(X_m)\,\mathrm{vec}(X_m)^*) \big)$$

$$\qquad (6.195)$$

$$= \mathrm{Tr}\big(\mathrm{vec}(X_m)\,\mathrm{vec}(X_m)^* \big) = \mathrm{Tr}(X_m X_m^*) = \sum_{k=m}^{n} \lambda_k(XX^*)$$

for each $m \in \{1, \ldots, n\}$.

Finally, as it necessarily holds that $\mathrm{rank}(\Pi_{a,m}) \geq n - m + 1$ for every $a \in \Sigma$ and $m \in \{1, \ldots, n\}$, it follows that

$$\big\langle \Pi_{a,m}, A_a X B_a^\mathsf{T} \overline{B_a} X^* A_a^* \big\rangle \geq \sum_{k=m}^{n} \lambda_k \Big(A_a X B_a^\mathsf{T} \overline{B_a} X^* A_a^* \Big). \qquad (6.196)$$

By combining (6.191), (6.192), (6.194), (6.195), and (6.196), one finds that

$$\sum_{k=m}^{n} \lambda_k(YY^*) \leq \sum_{k=m}^{n} \lambda_k(XX^*), \qquad (6.197)$$

which establishes (6.183), and therefore completes the proof. $\qquad \square$

Theorem 6.33 implies the following corollary, which characterizes the pure state transformations, possibly involving different complex Euclidean spaces, that may be realized by LOCC channels.

Corollary 6.34 *Let $\mathcal{X}$, $\mathcal{Y}$, $\mathcal{Z}$, and $\mathcal{W}$ be complex Euclidean spaces and let $x \in \mathcal{X} \otimes \mathcal{Y}$ and $y \in \mathcal{Z} \otimes \mathcal{W}$ be unit vectors. The following statements are equivalent:*

1. *For $\rho = \operatorname{Tr}_{\mathcal{Y}}(xx^*)$, $\sigma = \operatorname{Tr}_{\mathcal{W}}(yy^*)$, and $r = \min\{\operatorname{rank}(\rho), \operatorname{rank}(\sigma)\}$, it holds that*

$$\lambda_1(\rho) + \cdots + \lambda_m(\rho) \leq \lambda_1(\sigma) + \cdots + \lambda_m(\sigma) \tag{6.198}$$

for every $m \in \{1, \ldots, r\}$.
2. *There exists a one-way right LOCC channel $\Phi \in \operatorname{LOCC}(\mathcal{X}, \mathcal{Z} : \mathcal{Y}, \mathcal{W})$ for which it holds that $\Phi(xx^*) = yy^*$.*
3. *There exists a one-way left LOCC channel $\Phi \in \operatorname{LOCC}(\mathcal{X}, \mathcal{Z} : \mathcal{Y}, \mathcal{W})$ for which it holds that $\Phi(xx^*) = yy^*$.*
4. *There exists a separable channel $\Phi \in \operatorname{SepC}(\mathcal{X}, \mathcal{Z} : \mathcal{Y}, \mathcal{W})$ for which it holds that $\Phi(xx^*) = yy^*$.*

Proof Define four isometries, $A_0 \in \operatorname{U}(\mathcal{X}, \mathcal{X} \oplus \mathcal{Z})$, $B_0 \in \operatorname{U}(\mathcal{Y}, \mathcal{Y} \oplus \mathcal{W})$, $A_1 \in \operatorname{U}(\mathcal{Z}, \mathcal{X} \oplus \mathcal{Z})$, and $B_1 \in \operatorname{U}(\mathcal{W}, \mathcal{Y} \oplus \mathcal{W})$, as follows:

$$
\begin{aligned}
A_0 x &= x \oplus 0, & A_1 z &= 0 \oplus z, \\
B_0 y &= y \oplus 0, & B_1 w &= 0 \oplus w,
\end{aligned}
\tag{6.199}
$$

for every choice of vectors $x \in \mathcal{X}$, $y \in \mathcal{Y}$, $z \in \mathcal{Z}$, and $w \in \mathcal{W}$. Also define four channels, $\Psi_0 \in \operatorname{C}(\mathcal{X} \oplus \mathcal{Z}, \mathcal{X})$, $\Lambda_0 \in \operatorname{C}(\mathcal{Y} \oplus \mathcal{W}, \mathcal{Y})$, $\Psi_1 \in \operatorname{C}(\mathcal{X} \oplus \mathcal{Z}, \mathcal{Z})$, and $\Lambda_1 \in \operatorname{C}(\mathcal{Y} \oplus \mathcal{W}, \mathcal{W})$, as

$$
\begin{aligned}
\Psi_0(X) &= A_0^* X A_0 + \langle \mathbb{1}_{\mathcal{X} \oplus \mathcal{Z}} - A_0 A_0^*, X \rangle \tau_0, \\
\Lambda_0(Y) &= B_0^* Y B_0 + \langle \mathbb{1}_{\mathcal{Y} \oplus \mathcal{W}} - B_0 B_0^*, Y \rangle \xi_0, \\
\Psi_1(X) &= A_1^* X A_1 + \langle \mathbb{1}_{\mathcal{X} \oplus \mathcal{Z}} - A_1 A_1^*, X \rangle \tau_1, \\
\Lambda_1(Y) &= B_1^* Y B_1 + \langle \mathbb{1}_{\mathcal{Y} \oplus \mathcal{W}} - B_1 B_1^*, Y \rangle \xi_1,
\end{aligned}
\tag{6.200}
$$

for all $X \in \operatorname{L}(\mathcal{X} \oplus \mathcal{Z})$ and $Y \in \operatorname{L}(\mathcal{Y} \oplus \mathcal{W})$, where $\tau_0 \in \operatorname{D}(\mathcal{X})$, $\xi_0 \in \operatorname{D}(\mathcal{Y})$, $\tau_1 \in \operatorname{D}(\mathcal{Z})$, and $\xi_1 \in \operatorname{D}(\mathcal{W})$ are fixed, but otherwise arbitrarily selected, density operators.

Assume first that statement 1 holds. One concludes that

$$A_0 \rho A_0^* \prec A_1 \sigma A_1^*, \tag{6.201}$$

and therefore the four equivalent statements of Theorem 6.33 hold for the vectors

$$u = (A_0 \otimes B_0)x \quad \text{and} \quad v = (A_1 \otimes B_1)y. \tag{6.202}$$

There must therefore exist a one-way right LOCC channel Ξ, of the form specified in the statement of Theorem 6.33, such that $\Xi(uu^*) = vv^*$. Define $\Phi \in C(\mathcal{X} \otimes \mathcal{Y}, \mathcal{Z} \otimes \mathcal{W})$ as

$$\Phi(X) = ((\Psi_1 \otimes \Lambda_1)\Xi)((A_0 \otimes B_0)X(A_0 \otimes B_0)^*) \tag{6.203}$$

for every $X \in L(\mathcal{X} \otimes \mathcal{Y})$. It holds that Φ is a one-way right LOCC channel satisfying $\Phi(xx^*) = yy^*$, and therefore statement 1 implies statement 2. The fact that statement 1 implies statement 3 is similar.

Statements 2 and 3 trivially imply that statement 4 holds.

Finally, assume statement 4 holds. Define a channel Ξ as

$$\Xi(X) = (A_1 \otimes B_1)(\Phi(\Psi_0 \otimes \Lambda_0))(X)(A_1 \otimes B_1)^* \tag{6.204}$$

for all $X \in L((\mathcal{X} \oplus \mathcal{Z}) \otimes (\mathcal{Y} \oplus \mathcal{W}))$. The channel Ξ is separable and satisfies

$$\Xi(uu^*) = vv^* \tag{6.205}$$

for vectors u and v as in (6.202). The four equivalent statements listed in Theorem 6.33 therefore hold for u and v, which implies

$$\begin{aligned} \text{Tr}_{\mathcal{Y} \oplus \mathcal{W}}&((A_0 \otimes B_0)xx^*(A_0 \otimes B_0)^*) \\ &\prec \text{Tr}_{\mathcal{Y} \oplus \mathcal{W}}((A_1 \otimes B_1)yy^*(A_1 \otimes B_1)^*). \end{aligned} \tag{6.206}$$

This relation is equivalent to (6.201), which implies that statement 1 holds, and completes the proof. $\qquad\square$

6.2.2 Distillable Entanglement and Entanglement Cost

Let $\rho \in D(\mathcal{X} \otimes \mathcal{Y})$ be a state, for complex Euclidean spaces $\mathcal{X}$ and $\mathcal{Y}$. There are various ways in which one may quantify the amount of entanglement that is present in ρ, with respect to the bipartition between $\mathcal{X}$ and $\mathcal{Y}$. The *distillable entanglement* and *entanglement cost* represent two such measures. The distillable entanglement concerns the rate at which copies of the state ρ can be converted into copies of the maximally entangled two-qubit state

$$\tau = \frac{1}{2} \sum_{a,b \in \{0,1\}} E_{a,b} \otimes E_{a,b} \tag{6.207}$$

with high accuracy by means of an LOCC channel. The entanglement cost refers to the reverse process; it is the rate at which approximate copies of ρ

may be produced from copies of τ by an LOCC channel. In both cases, it is the asymptotic behavior of these processes, as the number of copies of each state grows, that is taken as the measure of entanglement.

For every bipartite state, the distillable entanglement is upper-bounded by the entanglement cost, with the two measures coinciding for pure states. In general, however, the two quantities may differ, with the entanglement cost being strictly larger than the distillable entanglement in some cases.

Notation Related to Distillable Entanglement and Entanglement Cost

The following notation will be useful when discussing both the distillable entanglement and entanglement cost of a bipartite state $\rho \in D(\mathcal{X} \otimes \mathcal{Y})$.

First, for a given positive integer n, representing the number of copies of the state ρ to be manipulated for either the distillable entanglement or entanglement cost, one may define an isometry

$$U_n \in U((\mathcal{X} \otimes \mathcal{Y})^{\otimes n}, \mathcal{X}^{\otimes n} \otimes \mathcal{Y}^{\otimes n}) \tag{6.208}$$

by the action

$$U_n(\mathrm{vec}(A_1) \otimes \cdots \otimes \mathrm{vec}(A_n)) = \mathrm{vec}(A_1 \otimes \cdots \otimes A_n) \tag{6.209}$$

for all operators $A_1, \ldots, A_n \in L(\mathcal{Y}, \mathcal{X})$. Equivalently, U_n is defined by the action

$$\begin{aligned} U_n((x_1 \otimes y_1) \otimes \cdots \otimes (x_n \otimes y_n)) \\ = (x_1 \otimes \cdots \otimes x_n) \otimes (y_1 \otimes \cdots \otimes y_n) \end{aligned} \tag{6.210}$$

for all vectors $x_1, \ldots, x_n \in \mathcal{X}$ and $y_1, \ldots, y_n \in \mathcal{Y}$. This isometry has the effect of reordering the tensor factors of the space $(\mathcal{X} \otimes \mathcal{Y})^{\otimes n}$ so that it takes the form of a bipartite tensor product space $\mathcal{X}^{\otimes n} \otimes \mathcal{Y}^{\otimes n}$ that allows for notions concerning entanglement and separability to be conveniently stated.

Next, the binary alphabet will be denoted $\Gamma = \{0, 1\}$, and the state

$$\tau = \frac{1}{2} \sum_{a,b \in \{0,1\}} E_{a,b} \otimes E_{a,b} \tag{6.211}$$

is to be considered as an element of the set $D(\mathcal{Z} \otimes \mathcal{W})$, for $\mathcal{Z} = \mathbb{C}^\Gamma$ and $\mathcal{W} = \mathbb{C}^\Gamma$. Similar to above, one may define an isometry

$$V_m \in U((\mathcal{Z} \otimes \mathcal{W})^{\otimes m}, \mathcal{Z}^{\otimes m} \otimes \mathcal{W}^{\otimes m}) \tag{6.212}$$

playing an analogous role to the isometry U_n, but for the spaces $\mathcal{Z}$ and $\mathcal{W}$ in place of $\mathcal{X}$ and $\mathcal{Y}$. This isometry is defined by the action

$$V_m(\mathrm{vec}(B_1) \otimes \cdots \otimes \mathrm{vec}(B_m)) = \mathrm{vec}(B_1 \otimes \cdots \otimes B_m) \tag{6.213}$$

for all operators $B_1, \ldots, B_m \in L(\mathcal{W}, \mathcal{Z})$. Equivalently, V_m is defined by the action

$$
\begin{aligned}
V_m\big((z_1 \otimes w_1) \otimes \cdots \otimes (z_m \otimes w_m)\big) \\
= (z_1 \otimes \cdots \otimes z_m) \otimes (w_1 \otimes \cdots \otimes w_m)
\end{aligned}
\tag{6.214}
$$

for all vectors $z_1, \ldots, z_m \in \mathcal{Z}$ and $w_1, \ldots, w_m \in \mathcal{W}$.

Definitions of Distillable Entanglement and Entanglement Cost

With respect to the notation introduced above, the *distillable entanglement* and *entanglement cost* are defined as follows.

Definition 6.35 Let X and Y be registers and let $\rho \in D(\mathcal{X} \otimes \mathcal{Y})$ be a state of (X, Y). With respect to the state ρ, the *distillable entanglement* $E_D(\mathsf{X} : \mathsf{Y})$ of the pair (X, Y) is the supremum value of all nonnegative real numbers $\alpha \geq 0$ for which the following statement holds: there exists a sequence of LOCC channels $(\Psi_1, \Psi_2, \ldots)$, where

$$
\Psi_n \in \mathrm{LOCC}(\mathcal{X}^{\otimes n}, \mathcal{Z}^{\otimes m} : \mathcal{Y}^{\otimes n}, \mathcal{W}^{\otimes m})
\tag{6.215}
$$

for $m = \lfloor \alpha n \rfloor$, such that

$$
\lim_{n \to \infty} \mathrm{F}\Big(V_m \tau^{\otimes m} V_m^*, \, \Psi_n(U_n \rho^{\otimes n} U_n^*)\Big) = 1.
\tag{6.216}
$$

Definition 6.36 Let X and Y be registers and let $\rho \in D(\mathcal{X} \otimes \mathcal{Y})$ be a state of (X, Y). With respect to the state ρ, the *entanglement cost* $E_c(\mathsf{X} : \mathsf{Y})$ of the pair (X, Y) is the infimum value of all nonnegative real numbers $\alpha \geq 0$ for which the following statement holds: there exists a sequence of LOCC channels $(\Phi_1, \Phi_2, \ldots)$, where

$$
\Phi_n \in \mathrm{LOCC}(\mathcal{Z}^{\otimes m}, \mathcal{X}^{\otimes n} : \mathcal{W}^{\otimes m}, \mathcal{Y}^{\otimes n})
\tag{6.217}
$$

for $m = \lfloor \alpha n \rfloor$, such that

$$
\lim_{n \to \infty} \mathrm{F}\Big(U_n \rho^{\otimes n} U_n^*, \, \Phi_n(V_m \tau^{\otimes m} V_m^*)\Big) = 1.
\tag{6.218}
$$

It is intuitive that the entanglement cost should be at least as large as the distillable entanglement, for any choice of $\rho \in D(\mathcal{X} \otimes \mathcal{Y})$, for otherwise one could repeatedly distill copies of the state τ from copies of a given state ρ, use them to produce more copies of ρ, and repeat this process indefinitely, eventually producing any desired number of copies of τ from a finite number of copies of ρ. Such an "entanglement factory" must surely not be possible through local operations and classical communication alone. The following proposition confirms this intuition.

Proposition 6.37 *Let* X *and* Y *be registers. With respect to every state of the pair* (X, Y) *it holds that* $\mathrm{E}_{\mathrm{D}}(\mathsf{X} : \mathsf{Y}) \leq \mathrm{E}_{\mathrm{C}}(\mathsf{X} : \mathsf{Y})$.

Proof Suppose that n, m, and k are nonnegative integers, and

$$\begin{aligned}
\Phi_n &\in \mathrm{LOCC}(\mathcal{Z}^{\otimes m}, \mathcal{X}^{\otimes n} : \mathcal{W}^{\otimes m}, \mathcal{Y}^{\otimes n}), \\
\Psi_n &\in \mathrm{LOCC}(\mathcal{X}^{\otimes n}, \mathcal{Z}^{\otimes k} : \mathcal{Y}^{\otimes n}, \mathcal{W}^{\otimes k})
\end{aligned} \tag{6.219}$$

are LOCC channels. The composition $\Psi_n \Phi_n$ is an LOCC, and therefore separable, channel. It holds that

$$V_m \tau^{\otimes m} V_m^* \in \mathrm{Ent}_{2^m}(\mathcal{Z}^{\otimes m} : \mathcal{W}^{\otimes m}), \tag{6.220}$$

and Theorem 6.23 implies that

$$(\Psi_n \Phi_n)(V_m \tau^{\otimes m} V_m^*) \in \mathrm{Ent}_{2^m}(\mathcal{Z}^{\otimes k} : \mathcal{W}^{\otimes k}). \tag{6.221}$$

By Proposition 6.15, one finds that

$$\begin{aligned}
&\mathrm{F}\!\left((\Psi_n \Phi_n)(V_m \tau^{\otimes m} V_m^*), V_k \tau^{\otimes k} V_k^*\right)^2 \\
&= \left\langle (\Psi_n \Phi_n)(V_m \tau^{\otimes m} V_m^*), V_k \tau^{\otimes k} V_k^* \right\rangle \leq 2^{m-k}.
\end{aligned} \tag{6.222}$$

Now, let $\rho \in \mathrm{D}(\mathcal{X} \otimes \mathcal{Y})$ be any state of the pair (X, Y), and suppose α and β are nonnegative real numbers satisfying the requirements of the definitions of entanglement cost and distillable entanglement, respectively, for the state ρ. For all $\varepsilon > 0$, there must therefore exist a sufficiently large positive integer n such that, for $m = \lfloor \alpha n \rfloor$ and $k = \lfloor \beta n \rfloor$, there exist LOCC channels of the form (6.219) for which the following bounds hold:

$$\begin{aligned}
\mathrm{F}\!\left(\Phi_n(V_m \tau^{\otimes m} V_m^*), U_n \rho^{\otimes n} U_n^*\right) &> 1 - \varepsilon, \\
\mathrm{F}\!\left(\Psi_n(U_n \rho^{\otimes n} V_n^*), V_k \tau^{\otimes k} V_k^*\right) &> 1 - \varepsilon.
\end{aligned} \tag{6.223}$$

Therefore, by Theorem 3.29, together with the monotonicity of the fidelity function under the action of channels (Theorem 3.27), one may conclude that

$$\mathrm{F}\!\left((\Psi_n \Phi_n)(V_m \tau^{\otimes m} V_m^*), V_k \tau^{\otimes k} V_k^*\right) > 1 - 4\varepsilon. \tag{6.224}$$

Taking $\varepsilon < 1/16$, one concludes that

$$\mathrm{F}\!\left((\Psi_n \Phi_n)(V_m \tau^{\otimes m} V_m^*), V_k \tau^{\otimes k} V_k^*\right)^2 > \frac{1}{2}, \tag{6.225}$$

and therefore $m \geq k$ by (6.222). As this is so for all sufficiently large n, it follows that $\beta \leq \alpha$. One concludes that $\mathrm{E}_{\mathrm{D}}(\mathsf{X} : \mathsf{Y}) \leq \mathrm{E}_{\mathrm{C}}(\mathsf{X} : \mathsf{Y})$. $\qquad\square$

Pure State Entanglement

The next theorem demonstrates that the entanglement cost and distillable entanglement are equal for bipartite pure states; in both cases, the value of these measures agrees with the von Neumann entropy of the states obtained by restricting the given pure state to either part of its bipartition.

Theorem 6.38 *Let* X *and* Y *be registers. With respect to every pure state of the pair* (X, Y), *one has*

$$E_D(X : Y) = H(X) = H(Y) = E_C(X : Y). \tag{6.226}$$

Proof Let $u \in \mathcal{X} \otimes \mathcal{Y}$ be a unit vector, and consider the pure state uu^* of the pair (X, Y). The equality $H(X) = H(Y)$ was discussed in Section 5.1.2. Specifically, by means of the Schmidt decomposition, one may write

$$u = \sum_{a \in \Sigma} \sqrt{p(a)}\, x_a \otimes y_a \tag{6.227}$$

for some choice of an alphabet Σ, a probability vector $p \in \mathcal{P}(\Sigma)$, and two orthonormal collections $\{x_a : a \in \Sigma\} \subset \mathcal{X}$ and $\{y_a : a \in \Sigma\} \subset \mathcal{Y}$. It holds that

$$\mathrm{Tr}_{\mathcal{Y}}(uu^*) = \sum_{a \in \Sigma} p(a) x_a x_a^* \quad \text{and} \quad \mathrm{Tr}_{\mathcal{X}}(uu^*) = \sum_{a \in \Sigma} p(a) y_a y_a^*, \tag{6.228}$$

which implies that $H(X) = H(p) = H(Y)$.

Next, recall that, for every positive integer n and positive real number $\varepsilon > 0$, the set of ε-typical strings $T_{n,\varepsilon}$ with respect to p contains those strings $a_1 \cdots a_n \in \Sigma^n$ for which

$$2^{-n(H(p)+\varepsilon)} < p(a_1) \cdots p(a_n) < 2^{-n(H(p)-\varepsilon)}. \tag{6.229}$$

With this set in mind, one may define a vector $v_{n,\varepsilon} \in \mathcal{X}^{\otimes n} \otimes \mathcal{Y}^{\otimes n}$, for every positive integer n and positive real number $\varepsilon > 0$, as

$$v_{n,\varepsilon} = \sum_{a_1 \cdots a_n \in T_{n,\varepsilon}} \sqrt{p(a_1) \cdots p(a_n)}\, x_{a_1 \cdots a_n} \otimes y_{a_1 \cdots a_n}, \tag{6.230}$$

where the shorthand notations

$$x_{a_1 \cdots a_n} = x_{a_1} \otimes \cdots \otimes x_{a_n} \quad \text{and} \quad y_{a_1 \cdots a_n} = y_{a_1} \otimes \cdots \otimes y_{a_n} \tag{6.231}$$

have been used for the sake of brevity. Also define a normalized version of the vector $v_{n,\varepsilon}$ as

$$w_{n,\varepsilon} = \frac{v_{n,\varepsilon}}{\|v_{n,\varepsilon}\|}. \tag{6.232}$$

Observe that

$$2^{-n(\mathrm{H}(p)+\varepsilon)} < \lambda_k \left(\mathrm{Tr}_{\mathcal{Y}^{\otimes n}} \left(v_{n,\varepsilon} v_{n,\varepsilon}^* \right) \right) < 2^{-n(\mathrm{H}(p)-\varepsilon)}, \tag{6.233}$$

and therefore

$$\frac{2^{-n(\mathrm{H}(p)+\varepsilon)}}{\|v_{n,\varepsilon}\|^2} < \lambda_k \left(\mathrm{Tr}_{\mathcal{Y}^{\otimes n}} \left(w_{n,\varepsilon} w_{n,\varepsilon}^* \right) \right) < \frac{2^{-n(\mathrm{H}(p)-\varepsilon)}}{\|v_{n,\varepsilon}\|^2}, \tag{6.234}$$

for $k = 1, \ldots, |T_{n,\varepsilon}|$, while the remaining eigenvalues are zero in both cases.

Now, consider the entanglement cost of the pair (X, Y) with respect to the state uu^*. Let α be any real number such that $\alpha > \mathrm{H}(p)$, let $\varepsilon > 0$ be sufficiently small so that $\alpha > \mathrm{H}(p) + 2\varepsilon$, and consider any choice of $n > 1/\varepsilon$. For $m = \lfloor \alpha n \rfloor$, it holds that $m \geq n(\mathrm{H}(p) + \varepsilon)$, and moreover

$$\lambda_k \left(\mathrm{Tr}_{\mathcal{W}^{\otimes m}} \left(V_m \tau^{\otimes m} V_m^* \right) \right) = 2^{-m} \tag{6.235}$$

for $k = 1, \ldots, 2^m$. As

$$2^{-m} \leq 2^{-n(\mathrm{H}(p)+\varepsilon)} \leq \frac{2^{-n(\mathrm{H}(p)+\varepsilon)}}{\|v_{n,\varepsilon}\|^2}, \tag{6.236}$$

it follows that

$$\sum_{j=1}^{k} \lambda_j \left(\mathrm{Tr}_{\mathcal{W}^{\otimes m}} \left(V_m \tau^{\otimes m} V_m^* \right) \right) \leq \sum_{j=1}^{k} \lambda_j \left(\mathrm{Tr}_{\mathcal{Y}^{\otimes n}} \left(w_{n,\varepsilon} w_{n,\varepsilon}^* \right) \right) \tag{6.237}$$

for every $k \in \{1, \ldots, 2^m\}$. It follows by Corollary 6.34 to Nielsen's theorem (Theorem 6.33) that there exists an LOCC channel

$$\Phi_n \in \mathrm{LOCC}(\mathcal{Z}^{\otimes m}, \mathcal{X}^{\otimes n} : \mathcal{W}^{\otimes m}, \mathcal{Y}^{\otimes n}) \tag{6.238}$$

such that

$$\Phi_n(V_m \tau^{\otimes m} V_m^*) = w_{n,\varepsilon} w_{n,\varepsilon}^*. \tag{6.239}$$

As

$$\mathrm{F}\left(U_n (uu^*)^{\otimes n} U_n^*, w_{n,\varepsilon} w_{n,\varepsilon}^* \right)^2 = \sum_{a_1 \cdots a_n \in T_{n,\varepsilon}} p(a_1) \cdots p(a_n), \tag{6.240}$$

which approaches 1 in the limit as n approaches infinity, it follows that $\mathrm{E}_{\mathrm{c}}(\mathsf{X}:\mathsf{Y}) \leq \alpha$. As this is so for all $\alpha > \mathrm{H}(p)$, the inequality $\mathrm{E}_{\mathrm{c}}(\mathsf{X}:\mathsf{Y}) \leq \mathrm{H}(p)$ follows.

Next, consider the distillable entanglement of (X, Y) with respect to the state uu^*. If $\mathrm{H}(p) = 0$, then there is nothing to prove, as the distillable entanglement is trivially nonnegative, so it will be assumed hereafter that $\mathrm{H}(p) > 0$. Let α be a real number such that $\alpha < \mathrm{H}(p)$, and let $\varepsilon \in (0, 1)$ be sufficiently small so that $\alpha < \mathrm{H}(p) - 2\varepsilon$. Consider any choice of a positive integer $n \geq -\log(1-\varepsilon)/\varepsilon$, and let $m = \lfloor \alpha n \rfloor$. It holds that

$$m \leq n(\mathrm{H}(p) - \varepsilon) + \log(1 - \varepsilon), \tag{6.241}$$

and therefore

$$\frac{2^{-n(\mathrm{H}(p)-\varepsilon)}}{1-\varepsilon} \leq 2^{-m}. \tag{6.242}$$

As the quantity

$$\|v_{n,\varepsilon}\|^2 = \sum_{a_1\cdots a_n \in T_{n,\varepsilon}} p(a_1)\cdots p(a_n) \tag{6.243}$$

approaches 1 in the limit as n approaches infinity, it follows that

$$\frac{2^{-n(\mathrm{H}(p)-\varepsilon)}}{\|v_{n,\varepsilon}\|^2} \leq 2^{-m} \tag{6.244}$$

for all but finitely many positive integers n.

Now, consider any choice of n for which (6.244) holds (where $m = \lfloor \alpha n \rfloor$ as before). One therefore has

$$\sum_{j=1}^{k} \lambda_j \left(\mathrm{Tr}_{\mathcal{Y}^{\otimes n}}\left(w_{n,\varepsilon} w_{n,\varepsilon}^*\right) \right) \leq \sum_{j=1}^{k} \lambda_j \left(\mathrm{Tr}_{\mathcal{W}^{\otimes m}}\left(V_m \tau^{\otimes m} V_m^*\right) \right) \tag{6.245}$$

for every $k \in \{1, \ldots, 2^m\}$. Again using Corollary 6.34, one has that there must exist an LOCC channel

$$\Phi_n \in \mathrm{LOCC}(\mathcal{X}^{\otimes n}, \mathcal{Z}^{\otimes m} : \mathcal{Y}^{\otimes n}, \mathcal{W}^{\otimes m}) \tag{6.246}$$

such that

$$\Phi_n(w_{n,\varepsilon} w_{n,\varepsilon}^*) = V_m \tau^{\otimes m} V_m^*. \tag{6.247}$$

Making use of the monotonicity of the fidelity function under the action of any channel (Theorem 3.27), one finds that

$$\begin{aligned}
\mathrm{F}&\left(\Phi_n(U_n(uu^*)^{\otimes n} U_n^*), V_m \tau^{\otimes m} V_m^*\right)^2 \\
&= \mathrm{F}\left(\Phi_n(U_n(uu^*)^{\otimes n} U_n^*), \Phi_n(w_{n,\varepsilon} w_{n,\varepsilon}^*)\right)^2 \\
&\geq \mathrm{F}\left(U_n(uu^*)^{\otimes n} U_n^*, w_{n,\varepsilon} w_{n,\varepsilon}^*\right)^2 \\
&= \sum_{a_1\cdots a_n \in T_{n,\varepsilon}} p(a_1)\cdots p(a_n).
\end{aligned} \tag{6.248}$$

The quantity on the right-hand side of this inequality approaches 1 in the limit as n approaches infinity, from which it follows that $\mathrm{E_D}(\mathsf{X}:\mathsf{Y}) \geq \alpha$. As this is so for all $\alpha < \mathrm{H}(p)$, one concludes that $\mathrm{E_D}(\mathsf{X}:\mathsf{Y}) \geq \mathrm{H}(p)$.

It has been proved that

$$\mathrm{E_C}(\mathsf{X}:\mathsf{Y}) \leq \mathrm{H}(p) \leq \mathrm{E_D}(\mathsf{X}:\mathsf{Y}). \tag{6.249}$$

The inequality $\mathrm{E_D}(\mathsf{X}:\mathsf{Y}) \leq \mathrm{E_C}(\mathsf{X}:\mathsf{Y})$ holds by Proposition 6.37, so the proof is complete. $\qquad\qquad\qquad\qquad\qquad\qquad\qquad\qquad\qquad\qquad\quad\Box$

Remark For a given unit vector $u \in \mathcal{X} \otimes \mathcal{Y}$, for complex Euclidean spaces $\mathcal{X}$ and $\mathcal{Y}$, the quantity in (6.226) is known as the *entanglement entropy* of the pure state uu^*.

6.2.3 Bound Entanglement and Partial Transposition

Informally speaking, Theorem 6.38 implies that all pure state entanglement is equivalent in the bipartite setting. A bipartite pure state is entangled if and only if it has positive entanglement entropy. Moreover, given any two entangled pure states, one necessarily has that an approximate conversion between a large number of copies of the first state and the second state is possible through the use of an LOCC channel, at a rate determined by the ratio of the entanglement entropies of the two states.

The situation is more complex for mixed states. One respect in which this is so is that there exist entangled states having no distillable entanglement. The entanglement in such states, which is referred to as *bound entanglement*, can never be converted into pure state entanglement through the use of an LOCC channel. The fact that states of this sort exist may be proved through the use of properties of the transpose mapping.

The Partial Transpose and Separability

For any complex Euclidean space $\mathcal{X}$, the transpose mapping $\mathrm{T} \in \mathrm{T}(\mathcal{X})$ is defined as

$$\mathrm{T}(X) = X^{\mathsf{T}} \tag{6.250}$$

for all $X \in \mathrm{L}(\mathcal{X})$. As this is a positive map, it follows by the Horodecki criterion (Theorem 6.9) that

$$(\mathrm{T} \otimes \mathbb{1}_{\mathrm{L}(\mathcal{Y})})(R) \in \mathrm{Pos}(\mathcal{X} \otimes \mathcal{Y}) \tag{6.251}$$

for every separable operator $R \in \mathrm{Sep}(\mathcal{X}:\mathcal{Y})$. If $P \in \mathrm{Pos}(\mathcal{X} \otimes \mathcal{Y})$ is a positive semidefinite operator for which

$$(\mathrm{T} \otimes \mathbb{1}_{\mathrm{L}(\mathcal{Y})})(P) \notin \mathrm{Pos}(\mathcal{X} \otimes \mathcal{Y}), \tag{6.252}$$

then one may therefore conclude that P is not separable.

The converse of this statement does not hold in general. Given a positive semidefinite operator $P \in \mathrm{Pos}(\mathcal{X} \otimes \mathcal{Y})$ for which

$$(\mathrm{T} \otimes \mathbb{1}_{\mathrm{L}(\mathcal{Y})})(P) \in \mathrm{Pos}(\mathcal{X} \otimes \mathcal{Y}), \tag{6.253}$$

one may not conclude that P is separable; an example of a nonseparable operator possessing the property (6.253) is described below.

It is the case, however, that an operator $P \in \mathrm{Pos}(\mathcal{X} \otimes \mathcal{Y})$ satisfying the condition (6.253) is highly constrained, in some sense, with respect to the way it is entangled. With this idea in mind, one defines the sets of PPT operators and PPT states (short for *positive partial transpose* operators and states) as follows.

Definition 6.39 For any choice of complex Euclidean spaces $\mathcal{X}$ and $\mathcal{Y}$, the set $\mathrm{PPT}(\mathcal{X} : \mathcal{Y})$ is defined as the set of all operators $P \in \mathrm{Pos}(\mathcal{X} \otimes \mathcal{Y})$ that satisfy

$$(\mathrm{T} \otimes \mathbb{1}_{\mathrm{L}(\mathcal{Y})})(P) \in \mathrm{Pos}(\mathcal{X} \otimes \mathcal{Y}). \tag{6.254}$$

Elements of the set $\mathrm{PPT}(\mathcal{X} : \mathcal{Y})$ are called *PPT operators*, while elements of the set $\mathrm{PPT}(\mathcal{X} : \mathcal{Y}) \cap \mathrm{D}(\mathcal{X} \otimes \mathcal{Y})$ are called *PPT states*.

Unextendable Product Sets and Nonseparable PPT Operators

One method by which nonseparable PPT operators may be constructed involves the notion of an *unextendable product set*. For complex Euclidean spaces $\mathcal{X}$ and $\mathcal{Y}$, an orthonormal collection of vectors of the form

$$\mathcal{A} = \{u_1 \otimes v_1, \ldots, u_m \otimes v_m\}, \tag{6.255}$$

for unit vectors $u_1, \ldots, u_m \in \mathcal{X}$ and $v_1, \ldots, v_m \in \mathcal{Y}$, is an *unextendable product set* if two properties hold:

1. $\mathcal{A}$ spans a proper subspace of $\mathcal{X} \otimes \mathcal{Y}$. (Equivalently, $m < \dim(\mathcal{X} \otimes \mathcal{Y})$.)
2. For every choice of vectors $x \in \mathcal{X}$ and $y \in \mathcal{Y}$ satisfying $x \otimes y \perp \mathcal{A}$, it must hold that $x \otimes y = 0$.

Example 6.40 Define unit vectors $u_1, \ldots, u_5 \in \mathcal{X}$ and $v_1, \ldots, v_5 \in \mathcal{Y}$, for $\mathcal{X} = \mathbb{C}^3$ and $\mathcal{Y} = \mathbb{C}^3$, as follows:

$$
\begin{aligned}
u_1 &= e_1, & v_1 &= \frac{1}{\sqrt{2}}(e_1 - e_2), \\
u_2 &= e_3, & v_2 &= \frac{1}{\sqrt{2}}(e_2 - e_3), \\
u_3 &= \frac{1}{\sqrt{2}}(e_1 - e_2), & v_3 &= e_3, \\
u_4 &= \frac{1}{\sqrt{2}}(e_2 - e_3), & v_4 &= e_1, \\
u_5 &= \frac{1}{\sqrt{3}}(e_1 + e_2 + e_3), & v_5 &= \frac{1}{\sqrt{3}}(e_1 + e_2 + e_3).
\end{aligned}
\tag{6.256}
$$

It therefore holds, for each $k \in \{1, \ldots, 5\}$, that $u_k \otimes v_k = \mathrm{vec}(A_k)$ for

$$
A_1 = \frac{1}{\sqrt{2}} \begin{pmatrix} 1 & -1 & 0 \\ 0 & 0 & 0 \\ 0 & 0 & 0 \end{pmatrix}, \quad A_2 = \frac{1}{\sqrt{2}} \begin{pmatrix} 0 & 0 & 0 \\ 0 & 0 & 0 \\ 0 & 1 & -1 \end{pmatrix},
$$

$$
A_3 = \frac{1}{\sqrt{2}} \begin{pmatrix} 0 & 0 & 1 \\ 0 & 0 & -1 \\ 0 & 0 & 0 \end{pmatrix}, \quad A_4 = \frac{1}{\sqrt{2}} \begin{pmatrix} 0 & 0 & 0 \\ 1 & 0 & 0 \\ -1 & 0 & 0 \end{pmatrix},
\tag{6.257}
$$

$$
A_5 = \frac{1}{3} \begin{pmatrix} 1 & 1 & 1 \\ 1 & 1 & 1 \\ 1 & 1 & 1 \end{pmatrix}.
$$

The set

$$
\mathcal{A} = \{u_1 \otimes v_1, \ldots, u_5 \otimes v_5\}
\tag{6.258}
$$

is orthonormal by inspection. If $x \in \mathcal{X}$ and $y \in \mathcal{Y}$ satisfy

$$
\langle x \otimes y, u_k \otimes v_k \rangle = \langle x, u_k \rangle \langle y, v_k \rangle = 0
\tag{6.259}
$$

for $k = 1, \ldots, 5$, then one must have $\langle x, u_k \rangle = 0$ for at least three distinct choices of $k \in \{1, \ldots, 5\}$ or $\langle y, v_k \rangle = 0$ for at least three distinct choices of $k \in \{1, \ldots, 5\}$. As every three distinct choices of u_k span all of $\mathcal{X}$ and every three distinct choices of v_k span all of $\mathcal{Y}$, it follows that $x \otimes y = 0$. The set $\mathcal{A}$ is therefore an unextendable product set.

The projection onto the subspace orthogonal to an unextendable product set must be both PPT and entangled, as the following theorem states.

Theorem 6.41 *Let $\mathcal{X}$ and $\mathcal{Y}$ be complex Euclidean spaces, let*

$$\mathcal{A} = \{u_1 \otimes v_1, \ldots, u_m \otimes v_m\} \tag{6.260}$$

be an unextendable product set in $\mathcal{X} \otimes \mathcal{Y}$, and define

$$\Pi = \sum_{k=1}^{m} u_k u_k^* \otimes v_k v_k^*. \tag{6.261}$$

It holds that

$$\mathbb{1}_{\mathcal{X}} \otimes \mathbb{1}_{\mathcal{Y}} - \Pi \in \mathrm{PPT}(\mathcal{X} : \mathcal{Y}) \setminus \mathrm{Sep}(\mathcal{X} : \mathcal{Y}). \tag{6.262}$$

Proof From the assumption that $\mathcal{A}$ is an orthonormal set, one may conclude that $\{\overline{u_1} \otimes v_1, \ldots, \overline{u_k} \otimes v_k\}$ is an orthonormal set as well. It follows that

$$(\mathrm{T} \otimes \mathbb{1}_{\mathrm{L}(\mathcal{Y})})(\Pi) = \sum_{k=1}^{m} \overline{u_k} u_k^{\mathsf{T}} \otimes v_k v_k^* \tag{6.263}$$

is a projection operator, and therefore

$$(\mathrm{T} \otimes \mathbb{1}_{\mathrm{L}(\mathcal{Y})})(\Pi) \le \mathbb{1}_{\mathcal{X}} \otimes \mathbb{1}_{\mathcal{Y}}. \tag{6.264}$$

As

$$(\mathrm{T} \otimes \mathbb{1}_{\mathrm{L}(\mathcal{Y})})(\mathbb{1}_{\mathcal{X}} \otimes \mathbb{1}_{\mathcal{Y}}) = \mathbb{1}_{\mathcal{X}} \otimes \mathbb{1}_{\mathcal{Y}}, \tag{6.265}$$

one obtains the inclusion

$$(\mathrm{T} \otimes \mathbb{1}_{\mathrm{L}(\mathcal{Y})})(\mathbb{1}_{\mathcal{X}} \otimes \mathbb{1}_{\mathcal{Y}} - \Pi) \in \mathrm{Pos}(\mathcal{X} \otimes \mathcal{Y}). \tag{6.266}$$

It therefore holds that

$$\mathbb{1}_{\mathcal{X}} \otimes \mathbb{1}_{\mathcal{Y}} - \Pi \in \mathrm{PPT}(\mathcal{X} : \mathcal{Y}). \tag{6.267}$$

Now, toward a contradiction, assume that

$$\mathbb{1}_{\mathcal{X}} \otimes \mathbb{1}_{\mathcal{Y}} - \Pi \in \mathrm{Sep}(\mathcal{X} : \mathcal{Y}), \tag{6.268}$$

which implies that

$$\mathbb{1}_{\mathcal{X}} \otimes \mathbb{1}_{\mathcal{Y}} - \Pi = \sum_{a \in \Sigma} x_a x_a^* \otimes y_a y_a^* \tag{6.269}$$

for some choice of an alphabet Σ and collections $\{x_a : a \in \Sigma\} \subset \mathcal{X}$ and $\{y_a : a \in \Sigma\} \subset \mathcal{Y}$. It holds that

$$\sum_{k=1}^{m} \sum_{a \in \Sigma} |\langle x_a \otimes y_a, u_k \otimes v_k \rangle|^2$$
$$= \sum_{k=1}^{m} (u_k \otimes v_k)^* (\mathbb{1}_{\mathcal{X}} \otimes \mathbb{1}_{\mathcal{Y}} - \Pi)(u_k \otimes v_k) = 0, \tag{6.270}$$

and therefore

$$\langle x_a \otimes y_a, u_k \otimes v_k \rangle = 0 \tag{6.271}$$

for every $a \in \Sigma$ and $k \in \{1, \ldots, m\}$. As $\mathcal{A}$ is an unextendable product set, it follows that $x_a \otimes y_a = 0$ for every $a \in \Sigma$, and therefore

$$\mathbb{1}_{\mathcal{X}} \otimes \mathbb{1}_{\mathcal{Y}} - \Pi = 0. \tag{6.272}$$

This, however, is in contradiction with the assumption $m < \dim(\mathcal{X} \otimes \mathcal{Y})$. It follows that

$$\mathbb{1}_{\mathcal{X}} \otimes \mathbb{1}_{\mathcal{Y}} - \Pi \notin \mathrm{Sep}(\mathcal{X} : \mathcal{Y}), \tag{6.273}$$

which completes the proof. $\qquad\qquad\qquad\qquad\qquad\qquad\qquad\qquad\qquad\qquad\square$

PPT States Have No Distillable Entanglement

PPT states may not always be separable, but they exhibit similar properties to separable states in some respects. One such respect is that their overlap with every maximally entangled state is small. The next proposition, which is reminiscent of Proposition 6.15, is representative of this fact.

Proposition 6.42 *Let $A \in \mathrm{L}(\mathcal{Y}, \mathcal{X})$ be an operator satisfying $\|A\| \leq 1$, for $\mathcal{X}$ and $\mathcal{Y}$ being complex Euclidean spaces. For every $P \in \mathrm{PPT}(\mathcal{X} : \mathcal{Y})$ it holds that*

$$\langle \mathrm{vec}(A) \mathrm{vec}(A)^*, P \rangle \leq \mathrm{Tr}(P). \tag{6.274}$$

Proof The transpose mapping is its own adjoint and inverse, and therefore

$$\begin{aligned} &\langle \mathrm{vec}(A) \mathrm{vec}(A)^*, P \rangle \\ &= \langle (\mathrm{T} \otimes \mathbb{1}_{\mathrm{L}(\mathcal{Y})})(\mathrm{vec}(A) \mathrm{vec}(A)^*), (\mathrm{T} \otimes \mathbb{1}_{\mathrm{L}(\mathcal{Y})})(P) \rangle. \end{aligned} \tag{6.275}$$

It holds that

$$\mathrm{vec}(A) = (\mathbb{1}_{\mathcal{X}} \otimes A^{\mathsf{T}}) \mathrm{vec}(\mathbb{1}_{\mathcal{X}}), \tag{6.276}$$

which implies that

$$(\mathrm{T} \otimes \mathbb{1}_{\mathrm{L}(\mathcal{Y})})(\mathrm{vec}(A) \mathrm{vec}(A)^*) = (\mathbb{1}_{\mathcal{X}} \otimes A^{\mathsf{T}}) W (\mathbb{1}_{\mathcal{X}} \otimes \overline{A}) \tag{6.277}$$

for $W \in \mathrm{U}(\mathcal{X} \otimes \mathcal{X})$ denoting the swap operator on $\mathcal{X} \otimes \mathcal{X}$. The operator represented by (6.277) has spectral norm at most 1, and therefore

$$\begin{aligned} &\langle (\mathrm{T} \otimes \mathbb{1}_{\mathrm{L}(\mathcal{Y})})(\mathrm{vec}(A) \mathrm{vec}(A)^*), (\mathrm{T} \otimes \mathbb{1}_{\mathrm{L}(\mathcal{Y})})(P) \rangle \\ &\qquad \leq \|(\mathrm{T} \otimes \mathbb{1}_{\mathrm{L}(\mathcal{Y})})(P)\|_1. \end{aligned} \tag{6.278}$$

Finally, because $P \in \mathrm{PPT}(\mathcal{X} : \mathcal{Y})$, together with the observation that the transpose mapping preserves trace, one has

$$\left\| (\mathrm{T} \otimes \mathbb{1}_{\mathrm{L}(\mathcal{Y})})(P) \right\|_1 = \mathrm{Tr}(P). \tag{6.279}$$

The proposition follows from (6.275), (6.278), and (6.279). □

Example 6.43 Similar to Example 6.16, let Σ be an alphabet, let $n = |\Sigma|$, and let $\mathcal{X} = \mathbb{C}^\Sigma$ and $\mathcal{Y} = \mathbb{C}^\Sigma$. Define a density operator $\tau \in \mathrm{D}(\mathcal{X} \otimes \mathcal{Y})$ as

$$\tau = \frac{1}{n} \sum_{a,b \in \Sigma} E_{a,b} \otimes E_{a,b} = \frac{1}{n} \mathrm{vec}(\mathbb{1}) \, \mathrm{vec}(\mathbb{1})^*, \tag{6.280}$$

where $\mathbb{1}$ denotes the identity operator on $\mathbb{C}^\Sigma$, which may be viewed as an element of the set $\mathrm{L}(\mathcal{Y}, \mathcal{X})$. For every PPT state

$$\rho \in \mathrm{D}(\mathcal{X} \otimes \mathcal{Y}) \cap \mathrm{PPT}(\mathcal{X} : \mathcal{Y}), \tag{6.281}$$

it holds that

$$\langle \tau, \rho \rangle = \frac{1}{n} \langle \mathrm{vec}(\mathbb{1}) \, \mathrm{vec}(\mathbb{1})^*, \rho \rangle \leq \frac{1}{n} \tag{6.282}$$

by Proposition 6.42. Thus, with respect to their overlap with the maximally entangled state τ, one has that PPT operators are bounded in a similar way to separable operators.

Proposition 6.42, when combined with the next proposition stating that separable maps (and therefore LOCC channels) map PPT operators to PPT operators, leads to a proof that PPT states have distillable entanglement equal to zero.

Proposition 6.44 *Let $\mathcal{X}$, $\mathcal{Y}$, $\mathcal{Z}$, and $\mathcal{W}$ be complex Euclidean spaces, let $P \in \mathrm{PPT}(\mathcal{X} : \mathcal{Y})$ be a PPT operator, and let $\Phi \in \mathrm{SepCP}(\mathcal{X}, \mathcal{Z} : \mathcal{Y}, \mathcal{W})$ be a separable map. It holds that $\Phi(P) \in \mathrm{PPT}(\mathcal{Z} : \mathcal{W})$.*

Proof For any choice of operators $A \in \mathrm{L}(\mathcal{X}, \mathcal{Z})$ and $B \in \mathrm{L}(\mathcal{Y}, \mathcal{W})$, the assumption $P \in \mathrm{PPT}(\mathcal{X} : \mathcal{Y})$ implies that

$$\begin{aligned} &(\mathrm{T} \otimes \mathbb{1}_{\mathrm{L}(\mathcal{W})})\big((A \otimes B) P (A \otimes B)^*\big) \\ &= (\overline{A} \otimes B)(\mathrm{T} \otimes \mathbb{1}_{\mathrm{L}(\mathcal{Y})})(P)(\overline{A} \otimes B)^* \in \mathrm{Pos}(\mathcal{Z} \otimes \mathcal{W}). \end{aligned} \tag{6.283}$$

(In this equation, T refers to the transpose mapping on $\mathcal{Z}$ or $\mathcal{X}$, as the context dictates.) As Φ is separable, one has

$$\Phi(X) = \sum_{a \in \Sigma} (A_a \otimes B_a) X (A_a \otimes B_a)^* \tag{6.284}$$

for all $X \in \mathrm{L}(\mathcal{X} \otimes \mathcal{Y})$, for some choice of an alphabet Σ and collections of operators $\{A_a : a \in \Sigma\} \subset L(\mathcal{X}, \mathcal{Z})$ and $\{B_a : a \in \Sigma\} \subset L(\mathcal{Y}, \mathcal{W})$. Consequently, one has that

$$(\mathrm{T} \otimes \mathbb{1}_{\mathrm{L}(\mathcal{W})})(\Phi(P)) = \sum_{a \in \Sigma} (\overline{A_a} \otimes B_a)(\mathrm{T} \otimes \mathbb{1}_{\mathrm{L}(\mathcal{Y})})(P)(\overline{A_a} \otimes B_a)^* \quad (6.285)$$

is positive semidefinite, and therefore $\Phi(P) \in \mathrm{PPT}(\mathcal{Z} : \mathcal{W})$, as required. $\square$

Theorem 6.45 *Let* X *and* Y *be registers and consider a PPT state*

$$\rho \in \mathrm{PPT}(\mathcal{X} : \mathcal{Y}) \cap \mathrm{D}(\mathcal{X} \otimes \mathcal{Y}) \qquad (6.286)$$

of the pair (X, Y). *With respect to the state* ρ, *it holds that* $\mathrm{E}_{\mathrm{D}}(\mathsf{X} : \mathsf{Y}) = 0$.

Proof Let $\Gamma = \{0, 1\}$, let $\mathcal{Z} = \mathbb{C}^\Gamma$ and $\mathcal{W} = \mathbb{C}^\Gamma$, and let $\tau \in \mathrm{D}(\mathcal{Z} \otimes \mathcal{W})$ be defined as

$$\tau = \frac{1}{2} \sum_{a,b \in \Gamma} E_{a,b} \otimes E_{a,b}. \qquad (6.287)$$

Suppose $\alpha > 0$, let n be any positive integer for which $m = \lfloor \alpha n \rfloor \geq 1$, and consider any LOCC channel $\Phi \in \mathrm{LOCC}(\mathcal{X}^{\otimes n}, \mathcal{Z}^{\otimes m} : \mathcal{Y}^{\otimes n}, \mathcal{W}^{\otimes m})$. Recall the operators U_n and V_m as defined by (6.210) and (6.213). It holds that

$$U_n \rho^{\otimes n} U_n^* \in \mathrm{PPT}(\mathcal{X}^{\otimes n} : \mathcal{Y}^{\otimes n}), \qquad (6.288)$$

and therefore

$$\Phi(U_n \rho^{\otimes n} U_n^*) \in \mathrm{PPT}(\mathcal{Z}^{\otimes m} : \mathcal{W}^{\otimes m}) \qquad (6.289)$$

by Proposition 6.44. One may therefore conclude from Proposition 6.42 that

$$\mathrm{F}\left(V_m \tau^{\otimes m} V_m^*, \Phi(U_n \rho^{\otimes n} U_n^*)\right) \leq 2^{-\frac{m}{2}} \leq \frac{1}{\sqrt{2}}. \qquad (6.290)$$

The number α therefore fails to satisfy the requirements of Definition 6.35. It follows that $\mathrm{E}_{\mathrm{D}}(\mathsf{X} : \mathsf{Y}) = 0$. $\square$

6.3 Phenomena Associated With Entanglement

This section discusses a few notions generally associated with entanglement: teleportation, dense coding, and nonclassical correlations. These notions serve as representatives of the sorts of operational effects that entanglement may induce.

6.3.1 Teleportation and Dense Coding

In quantum information theory, *teleportation* has traditionally referred to a protocol by which a single-qubit quantum channel is implemented through the use of a maximally entangled pair of qubits along with two classical bits of communication. Informally speaking, teleportation suggests the following transformation:

> one pair of maximally entangled qubits
> + two bits of classical communication
>
> $\rightarrow$ one qubit of quantum communication.

The *dense coding* protocol offers a trade-off of resources that is, in some sense, complementary to teleportation. Again, traditionally speaking, it is a protocol by which a two-bit classical channel is implemented through the use of a maximally entangled pair of qubits and a single-qubit quantum channel. In this case, the suggested transformation is as follows:

> one pair of maximally entangled qubits
> + one qubit of quantum communication
>
> $\rightarrow$ two bits of classical communication.

In both cases, the maximally entangled pair of qubits is consumed by the conversion between two classical bits and one qubit of communication; in essence, the entangled pair of qubits functions as a resource allowing for this conversion.

In the discussion that follows, teleportation and dense coding will be considered in greater generality. The traditional protocols suggested above will emerge as specific instances of more general classes of protocols.

Teleportation

Consider the following scenario in which two individuals, Alice and Bob, aim to implement an ideal quantum channel through the combined use of entanglement and classical communication.

Scenario 6.46 (Teleportation)   Alice holds a register X and Bob holds Y. Both registers have the same classical state set Σ, and the state of the pair (X, Y) is given by the maximally entangled state

$$\tau = \frac{1}{|\Sigma|} \sum_{b,c \in \Sigma} E_{b,c} \otimes E_{b,c}. \tag{6.291}$$

Alice obtains a new register Z, whose classical state set is also Σ, and she wishes to transmit Z to Bob. Alice and Bob attempt to accomplish this task using classical communication together with the shared entangled state τ, by means of a protocol as follows:

1. Alice performs a measurement $\mu \colon \Gamma \to \mathrm{Pos}(\mathcal{Z} \otimes \mathcal{X})$ on the pair (Z, X), where Γ is an arbitrarily chosen alphabet, and sends the outcome $a \in \Gamma$ of this measurement to Bob.
2. For $\{\Psi_a : a \in \Gamma\} \subseteq \mathrm{C}(\mathcal{Y}, \mathcal{Z})$ being a collection of channels indexed by Γ, Bob applies the channel Ψ_a to Y, for whichever symbol $a \in \Gamma$ was sent to him by Alice, transforming this register into a new register Z.

An analysis will reveal that this protocol accomplishes the task at hand for a suitable choice for Alice's measurement and Bob's collection of channels.

Remark One may consider more general scenarios along similar lines to Scenario 6.46. For instance, X, Y, and Z might not share the same classical state set, the initial state of the pair (X, Y) might be initialized to a different state than τ, and Alice and Bob might aim to implement a channel different from the identity channel. The discussion that follows, however, will focus on the setting described in Scenario 6.46 in the interest of simplicity.

For any choice of Alice's measurement μ and Bob's collection of channels $\{\Psi_a : a \in \Gamma\}$, the channel $\Phi \in \mathrm{C}(\mathcal{Z})$ that is implemented by the protocol described in Scenario 6.46 may be expressed as

$$\Phi(Z) = \frac{1}{|\Sigma|} \sum_{a \in \Gamma} \sum_{b,c \in \Sigma} \langle \mu(a), Z \otimes E_{b,c} \rangle \Psi_a(E_{b,c}) \tag{6.292}$$

for all $Z \in \mathrm{L}(\mathcal{Z})$.

The following theorem provides a characterization of those measurements and collections of channels for which the channel Φ is equal to the identity channel, which represents an ideal transmission of quantum information from Alice to Bob. (The statement of the theorem refers to a single complex Euclidean space $\mathcal{X}$, rather than $\mathcal{X}$, $\mathcal{Y}$, and $\mathcal{Z}$, and includes the assumption that none of the measurement operators of μ are identically zero, as this allows for a simpler statement and proof of the characterization.)

Theorem 6.47 *Let Σ and Γ be alphabets and let $\mathcal{X} = \mathbb{C}^{\Sigma}$ be a complex Euclidean space. Also let*

$$\mu \colon \Gamma \to \mathrm{Pos}(\mathcal{X} \otimes \mathcal{X}) \tag{6.293}$$

be a measurement such that $\mu(a) \neq 0$ for every $a \in \Gamma$, and let

$$\{\Psi_a : a \in \Gamma\} \subseteq \mathrm{C}(\mathcal{X}) \tag{6.294}$$

be a collection of channels. The following two statements are equivalent:

1. *It holds that*

$$X = \frac{1}{|\Sigma|} \sum_{a \in \Gamma} \sum_{b,c \in \Sigma} \langle \mu(a), X \otimes E_{b,c} \rangle \Psi_a(E_{b,c}) \qquad (6.295)$$

for every $X \in L(\mathcal{X})$.

2. *There exists a collection $\{U_a : a \in \Gamma\} \subset U(\mathcal{X})$ of unitary operators and a probability vector $p \in \mathcal{P}(\Gamma)$ such that*

$$\mu(a) = p(a)|\Sigma| \operatorname{vec}(U_a) \operatorname{vec}(U_a)^* \quad and \quad \Psi_a(X) = U_a X U_a^* \qquad (6.296)$$

for every choice of $a \in \Gamma$ and $X \in L(\mathcal{X})$.

The proof of Theorem 6.47 will make use of the following proposition, which establishes that a channel of the form $\Phi \in C(\mathcal{X})$, for any complex Euclidean space $\mathcal{X}$, can be the inverse of a completely positive map only if it is a unitary channel.

Proposition 6.48 *Let $\mathcal{X}$ be a complex Euclidean space, let $\Phi \in C(\mathcal{X})$ be a channel, and let $\Psi \in CP(\mathcal{X})$ be a completely positive map for which $\Phi\Psi = \mathbb{1}_{L(\mathcal{X})}$. There exists a unitary operator $U \in U(\mathcal{X})$ such that*

$$\Phi(X) = U^* X U \quad and \quad \Psi(X) = U X U^* \qquad (6.297)$$

for all $X \in L(\mathcal{X})$.

Proof   As Ψ is completely positive, and evidently nonzero, its Choi operator $J(\Psi)$ is a nonzero positive semidefinite operator. By the spectral theorem (Corollary 1.4), it is therefore possible to write

$$J(\Psi) = \sum_{k=1}^{r} \operatorname{vec}(A_k) \operatorname{vec}(A_k)^* \qquad (6.298)$$

for $r = \operatorname{rank}(J(\Psi))$ and $\{A_1, \dots, A_r\} \subset L(\mathcal{X})$ being an orthogonal collection of nonzero operators. Consequently, one has

$$\sum_{k=1}^{r} (\Phi \otimes \mathbb{1}_{L(\mathcal{X})})(\operatorname{vec}(A_k) \operatorname{vec}(A_k)^*) \qquad (6.299)$$
$$= (\Phi \otimes \mathbb{1}_{L(\mathcal{X})})(J(\Psi)) = J(\Phi\Psi) = \operatorname{vec}(\mathbb{1}_{\mathcal{X}}) \operatorname{vec}(\mathbb{1}_{\mathcal{X}})^*.$$

As $\operatorname{vec}(\mathbb{1}_{\mathcal{X}}) \operatorname{vec}(\mathbb{1}_{\mathcal{X}})^*$ has rank equal to one, and each operator

$$(\Phi \otimes \mathbb{1}_{L(\mathcal{X})})(\operatorname{vec}(A_k) \operatorname{vec}(A_k)^*) \qquad (6.300)$$

is positive semidefinite (by the complete positivity of Φ), it follows that there must exist a probability vector $(p_1, \dots, p_r)$ such that

$$(\Phi \otimes \mathbb{1}_{L(\mathcal{X})})(\operatorname{vec}(A_k) \operatorname{vec}(A_k)^*) = p_k \operatorname{vec}(\mathbb{1}_{\mathcal{X}}) \operatorname{vec}(\mathbb{1}_{\mathcal{X}})^* \qquad (6.301)$$

for each $k \in \{1, \ldots, r\}$. Because Φ preserves trace, it follows that

$$(A_k^* A_k)^{\mathsf{T}} = (\mathrm{Tr} \otimes \mathbb{1}_{\mathrm{L}(\mathcal{X})})(\mathrm{vec}(A_k) \, \mathrm{vec}(A_k)^*) = p_k \mathbb{1}_{\mathcal{X}}, \tag{6.302}$$

and therefore $A_k = \sqrt{p_k} U_k$ for some choice of a unitary operator $U_k \in \mathrm{U}(\mathcal{X})$, for each $k \in \{1, \ldots, r\}$. This implies that

$$\begin{aligned}
(\mathbb{1}_{\mathcal{X}} \otimes U_k^{\mathsf{T}}) J(\Phi) (\mathbb{1}_{\mathcal{X}} \otimes U_k^{\mathsf{T}})^* &= (\Phi \otimes \mathbb{1}_{\mathrm{L}(\mathcal{X})})(\mathrm{vec}(U_k) \, \mathrm{vec}(U_k)^*) \\
&= \mathrm{vec}(\mathbb{1}_{\mathcal{X}}) \, \mathrm{vec}(\mathbb{1}_{\mathcal{X}})^*,
\end{aligned} \tag{6.303}$$

and therefore

$$J(\Phi) = \mathrm{vec}(U_k^*) \, \mathrm{vec}(U_k^*)^*, \tag{6.304}$$

again for each $k \in \{1, \ldots, r\}$. As $\{A_1, \ldots, A_r\}$ is a collection of nonzero, orthogonal operators, and is therefore linearly independent, one concludes that $r = 1$ and $p_1 = 1$; and by setting $U = U_1$ the proposition is proved. $\square$

Proof of Theorem 6.47 Assume that statement 1 holds. For each $a \in \Gamma$, define a map $\Xi_a \in \mathrm{T}(\mathcal{X})$ as

$$\Xi_a(X) = \frac{1}{|\Sigma|} \sum_{b,c \in \Sigma} \langle \mu(a), X \otimes E_{b,c} \rangle E_{b,c} \tag{6.305}$$

for all $X \in \mathrm{L}(\mathcal{X})$. The Choi operator of Ξ_a is given by

$$J(\Xi_a) = \frac{1}{|\Sigma|} W \overline{\mu(a)} W, \tag{6.306}$$

for $W \in \mathrm{U}(\mathcal{X} \otimes \mathcal{X})$ denoting the swap operator. As $J(\Xi_a) \in \mathrm{Pos}(\mathcal{X} \otimes \mathcal{X})$ for each $a \in \Gamma$, it follows that Ξ_a is completely positive, and moreover is nonzero by the assumption that $\mu(a)$ is nonzero. Statement 1 may now be expressed as

$$\sum_{a \in \Gamma} \Psi_a \Xi_a = \mathbb{1}_{\mathrm{L}(\mathcal{X})}, \tag{6.307}$$

which is equivalent to

$$\sum_{a \in \Gamma} J(\Psi_a \Xi_a) = \mathrm{vec}(\mathbb{1}_{\mathcal{X}}) \, \mathrm{vec}(\mathbb{1}_{\mathcal{X}})^*. \tag{6.308}$$

As the composition $\Psi_a \Xi_a$ is necessarily completely positive and nonzero for each $a \in \Gamma$, and the operator $\mathrm{vec}(\mathbb{1}_{\mathcal{X}}) \, \mathrm{vec}(\mathbb{1}_{\mathcal{X}})^*$ has rank equal to 1, it follows that there must exist a probability vector $p \in \mathcal{P}(\Gamma)$ such that

$$J(\Psi_a \Xi_a) = p(a) \, \mathrm{vec}(\mathbb{1}_{\mathcal{X}}) \, \mathrm{vec}(\mathbb{1}_{\mathcal{X}})^* \tag{6.309}$$

for each $a \in \Gamma$. Consequently,

$$\frac{(\Psi_a \Xi_a)(X)}{p(a)} = X \tag{6.310}$$

for every $X \in L(\mathcal{X})$. By Proposition 6.48, there must exist a collection of unitary operators $\{U_a : a \in \Gamma\} \subset U(\mathcal{X})$ such that

$$\Psi_a(X) = U_a X U_a^* \quad \text{and} \quad \frac{1}{p(a)} \Xi_a(X) = U_a^* X U_a \tag{6.311}$$

for every $a \in \Gamma$ and $X \in L(\mathcal{X})$. Thus,

$$\frac{1}{|\Sigma|} W \overline{\mu(a)} W = J(\Xi_a) = p(a) \operatorname{vec}(U_a^*) \operatorname{vec}(U_a^*)^*, \tag{6.312}$$

and because $W \operatorname{vec}(Y) = \operatorname{vec}(Y^\mathsf{T})$ for every $Y \in L(\mathcal{X})$, one therefore has

$$\mu(a) = p(a)|\Sigma| \operatorname{vec}(U_a) \operatorname{vec}(U_a)^* \tag{6.313}$$

for each $a \in \Gamma$. Statement 1 therefore implies statement 2.

Now assume statement 2 holds. As μ is assumed to be a measurement, it must be the case that

$$\sum_{a \in \Gamma} p(a) \operatorname{vec}(U_a) \operatorname{vec}(U_a)^* = \frac{1}{|\Sigma|} \mathbb{1}_{\mathcal{X}} \otimes \mathbb{1}_{\mathcal{X}}. \tag{6.314}$$

The operator represented by the equation (6.314) coincides with the Choi operator $J(\Omega)$ of the completely depolarizing channel $\Omega \in C(\mathcal{X})$. It follows that one may write

$$\Omega(X) = \sum_{a \in \Gamma} p(a) U_a X U_a^* \tag{6.315}$$

for every $X \in L(\mathcal{X})$. Because the natural representation of the completely depolarizing channel is given by

$$K(\Omega) = \frac{1}{|\Sigma|} \sum_{b,c \in \Sigma} E_{b,c} \otimes E_{b,c}, \tag{6.316}$$

one finds that

$$\sum_{a \in \Gamma} p(a) \overline{U_a} \otimes U_a = \overline{K(\Omega)} = \frac{1}{|\Sigma|} \sum_{b,c \in \Sigma} E_{b,c} \otimes E_{b,c} \tag{6.317}$$

by Proposition 2.20.

Now consider the channel $\Phi \in C(\mathcal{X})$ defined by

$$\Phi(X) = \frac{1}{|\Sigma|} \sum_{a \in \Gamma} \sum_{b,c \in \Sigma} \langle \mu(a), X \otimes E_{b,c} \rangle \Psi_a(E_{b,c}) \tag{6.318}$$

for every $X \in L(\mathcal{X})$. Making use of the expression (6.317), one may write

$$\Phi(X) = \sum_{a,b \in \Gamma} p(b) \langle \mu(a), X \otimes \overline{U_b} \rangle \Psi_a(U_b) \qquad (6.319)$$

for every $X \in L(\mathcal{X})$. By substituting according to (6.296), one obtains

$$
\begin{aligned}
\Phi(X) &= |\Sigma| \sum_{a,b \in \Gamma} p(a)p(b) \, \mathrm{vec}(U_a)^* (X \otimes \overline{U_b}) \, \mathrm{vec}(U_a) U_a U_b U_a^* \\
&= |\Sigma| \sum_{a,b \in \Gamma} p(a)p(b) \langle U_a U_b U_a^*, X \rangle U_a U_b U_a^*.
\end{aligned}
\qquad (6.320)
$$

The natural representation $K(\Phi)$ of the channel Φ is therefore given by

$$
\begin{aligned}
&|\Sigma| \sum_{a,b \in \Gamma} p(a)p(b) \, \mathrm{vec}(U_a U_b U_a^*) \, \mathrm{vec}(U_a U_b U_a^*)^* \\
&= \sum_{a \in \Gamma} p(a)(U_a \otimes \overline{U_a}) \left(|\Sigma| \sum_{b \in \Gamma} p(b) \, \mathrm{vec}(U_b) \, \mathrm{vec}(U_b)^* \right) (U_a \otimes \overline{U_a})^* \quad (6.321) \\
&= \mathbb{1}_{\mathcal{X}} \otimes \mathbb{1}_{\mathcal{X}},
\end{aligned}
$$

where the last equality has made use of (6.314). It follows that Φ is equal to the identity channel, and therefore statement 2 implies statement 1. $\square$

Theorem 6.47 implies that every mixed-unitary representation of the completely depolarizing channel gives rise to a teleportation protocol, as the following corollary makes precise.

Corollary 6.49 *Let Σ and Γ be alphabets, let $\mathcal{X} = \mathbb{C}^{\Sigma}$, let*

$$\{U_a : a \in \Gamma\} \subset U(\mathcal{X}) \qquad (6.322)$$

be a collection of unitary operators, let $p \in \mathcal{P}(\Gamma)$ be a probability vector, and assume that

$$\Omega(X) = \sum_{a \in \Gamma} p(a) U_a X U_a^* \qquad (6.323)$$

for every $X \in L(\mathcal{X})$, where $\Omega \in C(\mathcal{X})$ denotes the completely depolarizing channel with respect to the space $\mathcal{X}$. For $\mu: \Gamma \to \mathrm{Pos}(\mathcal{X} \otimes \mathcal{X})$ defined as

$$\mu(a) = p(a) |\Sigma| \, \mathrm{vec}(U_a) \, \mathrm{vec}(U_a)^* \qquad (6.324)$$

for each $a \in \Gamma$, one has that μ is a measurement, and moreover

$$X = \frac{1}{|\Sigma|} \sum_{a \in \Gamma} \sum_{b,c \in \Sigma} \langle \mu(a), X \otimes E_{b,c} \rangle U_a E_{b,c} U_a^* \qquad (6.325)$$

for all $X \in L(\mathcal{X})$.

Proof There is no loss of generality in assuming that $p(a) \neq 0$ for every $a \in \Gamma$, for otherwise one could define an alphabet $\Gamma_0 = \{a \in \Gamma : p(a) \neq 0\}$, verify that the corollary holds in this case, and observe that the statement of the corollary is equivalent when Γ is replaced by Γ_0 in this way.

It is evident that μ is a measurement, as each $\mu(a)$ is positive semidefinite and it holds that

$$\sum_{a \in \Gamma} \mu(a) = \sum_{a \in \Gamma} p(a)|\Sigma| \operatorname{vec}(U_a) \operatorname{vec}(U_a)^* = |\Sigma| J(\Omega) = \mathbb{1}_{\mathcal{X}} \otimes \mathbb{1}_{\mathcal{X}}. \quad (6.326)$$

By defining $\Psi_a(X) = U_a X U_a^*$ for every $X \in \mathrm{L}(\mathcal{X})$ and $a \in \Gamma$, one has that statement 2 of Theorem 6.47 is satisfied. This implies that statement 1 of that theorem holds, which is equivalent to (6.325), and therefore completes the proof. $\qquad \square$

Example 6.50 Let $\Gamma = \Sigma \times \Sigma$, for $\Sigma = \{0, 1\}$ denoting the binary alphabet. Elements of Γ will be viewed as binary strings of length 2 for convenience. Define $p \in \mathcal{P}(\Gamma)$ as

$$p(00) = p(01) = p(10) = p(11) = \frac{1}{4} \quad (6.327)$$

and define unitary operators $U_{00}, U_{01}, U_{10}, U_{11} \in \mathrm{U}(\mathbb{C}^\Sigma)$ as follows:

$$U_{00} = \begin{pmatrix} 1 & 0 \\ 0 & 1 \end{pmatrix}, \quad U_{01} = \begin{pmatrix} 1 & 0 \\ 0 & -1 \end{pmatrix},$$

$$U_{10} = \begin{pmatrix} 0 & 1 \\ 1 & 0 \end{pmatrix}, \quad U_{11} = \begin{pmatrix} 0 & -1 \\ 1 & 0 \end{pmatrix}. \quad (6.328)$$

The operators $U_{00}, U_{01}, U_{10}, U_{11}$ coincide with the discrete Weyl operators acting on the space $\mathbb{C}^\Sigma$, and (as explained in Section 4.1.2) provide a mixed-unitary realization of the completely depolarizing channel $\Omega \in \mathrm{C}(\mathbb{C}^\Sigma)$:

$$\frac{1}{4} \sum_{a,b \in \Sigma} U_{ab} X U_{ab}^* = \frac{\operatorname{Tr}(X)}{2} \mathbb{1} \quad (6.329)$$

for every $X \in \mathrm{L}(\mathbb{C}^\Sigma)$. Consequently, by taking $\mu : \Gamma \to \mathrm{Pos}(\mathbb{C}^\Sigma \otimes \mathbb{C}^\Sigma)$ to be the measurement defined as

$$\mu(00) = \frac{\operatorname{vec}(U_{00}) \operatorname{vec}(U_{00})^*}{2}, \quad \mu(01) = \frac{\operatorname{vec}(U_{01}) \operatorname{vec}(U_{01})^*}{2},$$

$$\mu(10) = \frac{\operatorname{vec}(U_{10}) \operatorname{vec}(U_{10})^*}{2}, \quad \mu(11) = \frac{\operatorname{vec}(U_{11}) \operatorname{vec}(U_{11})^*}{2}, \quad (6.330)$$

or equivalently $\mu(ab) = u_{ab}u_{ab}^*$ for

$$u_{00} = \frac{e_{00} + e_{11}}{\sqrt{2}}, \qquad u_{01} = \frac{e_{00} - e_{11}}{\sqrt{2}},$$

$$u_{10} = \frac{e_{01} + e_{10}}{\sqrt{2}}, \qquad u_{11} = \frac{e_{01} - e_{10}}{\sqrt{2}},$$

(6.331)

and setting $\Psi_{ab}(X) = U_{ab}XU_{ab}^*$ for each $X \in L(\mathbb{C}^\Sigma)$ and $a, b \in \Sigma$, one obtains a teleportation protocol as described in Scenario 6.46. Indeed, the resulting protocol is equivalent to the traditional notion of teleportation in which an ideal single-qubit channel is implemented using a maximally entangled pair of qubits along with two classical bits of communication. The set $\{u_{00}, u_{01}, u_{10}, u_{11}\}$ is typically called the *Bell basis*, and μ represents a measurement with respect to this basis.

Example 6.51 The previous example may be generalized as follows. Let $\Sigma = \mathbb{Z}_n$ for any positive integer n, let $\Gamma = \Sigma \times \Sigma$, and let the collection $\{U_{ab} : a, b \in \Sigma\} \subset U(\mathbb{C}^\Sigma)$ of unitary operators be in correspondence with the discrete Weyl operators acting on $\mathbb{C}^\Sigma$. By taking $\mu : \Gamma \to \mathrm{Pos}(\mathbb{C}^\Sigma \otimes \mathbb{C}^\Sigma)$ to be the measurement defined as

$$\mu(ab) = \frac{\mathrm{vec}(U_{ab}) \, \mathrm{vec}(U_{ab})^*}{n}$$

(6.332)

for each $a, b \in \Sigma$, and setting $\Psi_{ab}(X) = U_{ab}XU_{ab}^*$ for each $X \in L(\mathbb{C}^\Sigma)$, one again obtains a teleportation protocol as described in Scenario 6.46.

In the teleportation protocols described in the previous two examples, the number of distinct classical symbols that must be transmitted is equal to the square of the number of classical states in the quantum system that is teleported. This is optimal, as the following corollary states.

Corollary 6.52 *Let Σ and Γ be alphabets, let $\mu : \Gamma \to \mathrm{Pos}(\mathbb{C}^\Sigma \otimes \mathbb{C}^\Sigma)$ be a measurement, and let $\{\Psi_a : a \in \Gamma\} \subseteq C(\mathbb{C}^\Sigma)$ be a collection of channels such that*

$$X = \frac{1}{|\Sigma|} \sum_{a \in \Gamma} \sum_{b,c \in \Sigma} \langle \mu(a), X \otimes E_{b,c} \rangle \Psi_a(E_{b,c})$$

(6.333)

for every $X \in L(\mathbb{C}^\Sigma)$. It holds that $|\Gamma| \geq |\Sigma|^2$.

Proof By Theorem 6.47, it follows that

$$\mu(a) = p(a)|\Sigma| \, \mathrm{vec}(U_a) \, \mathrm{vec}(U_a)^*$$

(6.334)

for each $a \in \Gamma$, for some choice of a probability vector $p \in \mathcal{P}(\Gamma)$ and a collection of unitary operators $\{U_a : a \in \Gamma\} \subset \mathrm{U}(\mathbb{C}^\Sigma)$. Each operator $\mu(a)$ has rank at most one, while

$$\sum_{a \in \Gamma} \mu(a) = \mathbb{1}_\Sigma \otimes \mathbb{1}_\Sigma \tag{6.335}$$

has rank $|\Sigma|^2$. It follows that $|\Gamma| \geq |\Sigma|^2$ as required. $\qquad\square$

Dense Coding

Along similar lines to the discussion of teleportation above, a scenario in which Alice and Bob aim to implement an ideal classical channel through shared entanglement and quantum communication may be considered.

Scenario 6.53 (Dense coding) Alice holds a register X and Bob holds Y. Both registers have the same classical state set Σ, and the state of the pair (X, Y) is given by the maximally entangled state

$$\tau = \frac{1}{|\Sigma|} \sum_{b,c \in \Sigma} E_{b,c} \otimes E_{b,c}. \tag{6.336}$$

Alice obtains a classical register Z having classical state set Γ. She wishes to transmit the classical state Z to Bob by means of a protocol as follows:

1. Alice applies one of a collection of channels

$$\{\Psi_a : a \in \Gamma\} \subseteq \mathrm{C}(\mathcal{X}) \tag{6.337}$$

   to X, with the channel applied being indexed by the classical state $a \in \Gamma$ of Z. The register X is then sent to Bob.
2. Bob performs a measurement

$$\mu : \Gamma \to \mathrm{Pos}(\mathcal{X} \otimes \mathcal{Y}) \tag{6.338}$$

   on the pair (X, Y). The outcome $b \in \Gamma$ is interpreted as the result of the transmission from Alice.

It is not surprising that protocols of this sort exist that function as desired, meaning that Bob's measurement outcome $b \in \Gamma$ corresponds precisely to the classical state $a \in \Gamma$ of Alice's register Z. Indeed, when Γ is no larger than Σ, the task is trivially accomplished. What is more interesting is that there are protocols of this form that work perfectly in the case that Γ is as large as $\Sigma \times \Sigma$.

The following proposition establishes that a dense coding protocol may be derived from an arbitrary mixed-unitary realization of the completely depolarizing channel, provided the unitary operators are drawn uniformly from a set indexed by $\Sigma \times \Sigma$.

Proposition 6.54 *Let Σ be an alphabet, let $\mathcal{X} = \mathbb{C}^\Sigma$, and let*

$$\tau = \frac{1}{|\Sigma|} \sum_{c,d \in \Sigma} E_{c,d} \otimes E_{c,d}. \tag{6.339}$$

Assume $\{U_{ab} : ab \in \Sigma \times \Sigma\} \subset \mathrm{U}(\mathcal{X})$ is a collection of unitary operators such that

$$\Omega(X) = \frac{1}{|\Sigma|^2} \sum_{ab \in \Sigma \times \Sigma} U_{ab} X U_{ab}^* \tag{6.340}$$

for all $X \in \mathrm{L}(\mathcal{X})$, where $\Omega \in \mathrm{C}(\mathcal{X})$ is the completely depolarizing channel with respect to the space $\mathcal{X}$. For $\{\Psi_{ab} : ab \in \Sigma \times \Sigma\} \subseteq \mathrm{C}(\mathcal{X})$ being a collection of channels defined as

$$\Psi_{ab}(X) = U_{ab} X U_{ab}^* \tag{6.341}$$

for each $ab \in \Sigma \times \Sigma$ and $X \in \mathrm{L}(\mathcal{X})$, and for $\mu : \Sigma \times \Sigma \to \mathrm{Pos}(\mathcal{X} \otimes \mathcal{X})$ being defined as

$$\mu(ab) = \frac{\mathrm{vec}(U_{ab}) \, \mathrm{vec}(U_{ab})^*}{|\Sigma|} \tag{6.342}$$

for each $ab \in \Sigma \times \Sigma$, it holds that μ is a measurement and

$$\langle \mu(cd), (\Psi_{ab} \otimes \mathbb{1}_{\mathrm{L}(\mathcal{X})})(\tau) \rangle = \begin{cases} 1 & \text{if } ab = cd \\ 0 & \text{if } ab \neq cd \end{cases} \tag{6.343}$$

for all $a, b, c, d \in \Sigma$.

Proof It holds that

$$\sum_{ab \in \Sigma \times \Sigma} \mu(ab) = |\Sigma| J(\Omega) = \mathbb{1}_{\mathcal{X}} \otimes \mathbb{1}_{\mathcal{X}}. \tag{6.344}$$

As each operator $\mu(ab)$ is evidently positive semidefinite, it follows that μ is a measurement. For each $ab \in \Sigma \times \Sigma$, one has

$$\begin{aligned} &\langle \mu(ab), (\Psi_{ab} \otimes \mathbb{1}_{\mathrm{L}(\mathcal{X})})(\tau) \rangle \\ &= \frac{1}{|\Sigma|^2} \langle \mathrm{vec}(U_{ab}) \, \mathrm{vec}(U_{ab})^*, \mathrm{vec}(U_{ab}) \, \mathrm{vec}(U_{ab})^* \rangle = 1. \end{aligned} \tag{6.345}$$

Because $(\Psi_{ab} \otimes \mathbb{1}_{\mathrm{L}(\mathcal{X})})(\tau)$ is a density operator for each $ab \in \Sigma \times \Sigma$, it follows that

$$\langle \mu(cd), (\Psi_{ab} \otimes \mathbb{1}_{\mathrm{L}(\mathcal{X})})(\tau) \rangle = 0 \tag{6.346}$$

for $cd \neq ab$, which completes the proof. $\qquad \square$

Example 6.55 As in Example 6.50, let $\Sigma = \{0,1\}$ and define unitary operators $U_{00}, U_{01}, U_{10}, U_{11} \in U(\mathbb{C}^\Sigma)$ as follows:

$$U_{00} = \begin{pmatrix} 1 & 0 \\ 0 & 1 \end{pmatrix}, \quad U_{01} = \begin{pmatrix} 1 & 0 \\ 0 & -1 \end{pmatrix},$$

$$U_{10} = \begin{pmatrix} 0 & 1 \\ 1 & 0 \end{pmatrix}, \quad U_{11} = \begin{pmatrix} 0 & -1 \\ 1 & 0 \end{pmatrix}. \tag{6.347}$$

As the operators $U_{00}, U_{01}, U_{10}, U_{11}$ provide a mixed-unitary realization of the completely depolarizing channel, by taking $\mu \colon \Sigma \times \Sigma \to \mathrm{Pos}(\mathbb{C}^\Sigma \otimes \mathbb{C}^\Sigma)$ to be the measurement defined as

$$\mu(00) = \frac{\mathrm{vec}(U_{00})\,\mathrm{vec}(U_{00})^*}{2}, \quad \mu(01) = \frac{\mathrm{vec}(U_{01})\,\mathrm{vec}(U_{01})^*}{2},$$

$$\mu(10) = \frac{\mathrm{vec}(U_{10})\,\mathrm{vec}(U_{10})^*}{2}, \quad \mu(11) = \frac{\mathrm{vec}(U_{11})\,\mathrm{vec}(U_{11})^*}{2}, \tag{6.348}$$

and setting $\Psi_{ab}(X) = U_{ab}XU_{ab}^*$ for each $X \in L(\mathbb{C}^\Sigma)$, as in Example 6.50, one obtains a dense coding protocol as described in Scenario 6.53. The resulting protocol is equivalent to the traditional notion of dense coding in which an ideal two-bit classical channel is implemented using a maximally entangled pair of qubits along with one qubit of quantum communication.

In analogy to the more general type of teleportation protocol described previously, one may consider the capabilities of dense coding protocols for arbitrary choices of an alphabet Γ, as opposed to $\Gamma = \Sigma \times \Sigma$. In particular, suppose Alice's channels are given by the collection

$$\{\Psi_a : a \in \Gamma\} \subseteq C(\mathcal{X}), \tag{6.349}$$

for an arbitrary alphabet Γ, and that the symbol $a \in \Gamma$ Alice wishes to send to Bob is randomly selected according to a probability vector $p \in \mathcal{P}(\Gamma)$. The state of the pair (X, Y) prior to Bob's measurement is described by the ensemble $\eta \colon \Gamma \to \mathrm{Pos}(\mathcal{X} \otimes \mathcal{X})$ defined as

$$\eta(a) = \frac{p(a)}{|\Sigma|} \sum_{b,c \in \Sigma} \Psi_a(E_{b,c}) \otimes E_{b,c} \tag{6.350}$$

for all $a \in \Gamma$. The following theorem provides a characterization of when the Holevo information $\chi(\eta)$ of this ensemble attains its maximum possible value, which is $2\log(|\Sigma|)$.

Theorem 6.56 *Let Σ and Γ be alphabets, let $p \in \mathcal{P}(\Gamma)$ be a probability vector such that $p(a) \neq 0$ for all $a \in \Gamma$, and let*

$$\{\Psi_a : a \in \Gamma\} \subseteq C(\mathbb{C}^\Sigma) \tag{6.351}$$

be a collection of channels. The following two statements are equivalent:

1. *For the ensemble $\eta : \Gamma \to \mathrm{Pos}(\mathbb{C}^\Sigma \otimes \mathbb{C}^\Sigma)$ defined as*

$$\eta(a) = \frac{p(a)}{|\Sigma|} \sum_{b,c \in \Sigma} \Psi_a(E_{b,c}) \otimes E_{b,c} \tag{6.352}$$

for all $a \in \Gamma$, one has that $\chi(\eta) = 2 \log(|\Sigma|)$.

2. *There exists a collection $\{U_a : a \in \Gamma\} \subset \mathrm{U}(\mathbb{C}^\Sigma)$ of unitary operators such that*

$$\Psi_a(X) = U_a X U_a^* \tag{6.353}$$

for every choice of $a \in \Gamma$ and $X \in \mathrm{L}(\mathbb{C}^\Sigma)$, and moreover it holds that

$$\Omega(X) = \sum_{a \in \Gamma} p(a) U_a X U_a^* \tag{6.354}$$

for all $X \in \mathrm{L}(\mathbb{C}^\Sigma)$, where $\Omega \in C(\mathbb{C}^\Sigma)$ denotes the completely depolarizing channel defined with respect to the space $\mathbb{C}^\Sigma$.

Proof The Holevo information of the ensemble η defined by (6.352) is

$$\chi(\eta) = \mathrm{H}\left(\sum_{a \in \Gamma} \frac{p(a)}{|\Sigma|} \sum_{b,c \in \Sigma} \Psi_a(E_{b,c}) \otimes E_{b,c}\right)$$
$$- \sum_{a \in \Gamma} p(a) \, \mathrm{H}\left(\frac{1}{|\Sigma|} \sum_{b,c \in \Sigma} \Psi_a(E_{b,c}) \otimes E_{b,c}\right), \tag{6.355}$$

which may alternatively be written as

$$\chi(\eta) = \mathrm{H}\left(\sum_{a \in \Gamma} p(a) \frac{J(\Psi_a)}{|\Sigma|}\right) - \sum_{a \in \Gamma} p(a) \, \mathrm{H}\left(\frac{J(\Psi_a)}{|\Sigma|}\right). \tag{6.356}$$

Under the assumption that $\chi(\eta) = 2 \log(|\Sigma|)$, it must hold that

$$\mathrm{H}\left(\sum_{a \in \Gamma} p(a) \frac{J(\Psi_a)}{|\Sigma|}\right) = 2\log(|\Sigma|) \quad \text{and} \quad \mathrm{H}\left(\frac{J(\Psi_a)}{|\Sigma|}\right) = 0 \tag{6.357}$$

for each $a \in \Gamma$. The rank of $J(\Psi_a)$ is therefore equal to 1 for each $a \in \Gamma$, and as each Ψ_a is a channel it follows that there must exist a collection of unitary operators

$$\{U_a : a \in \Gamma\} \subset \mathrm{U}(\mathbb{C}^\Sigma) \tag{6.358}$$

such that (6.353) holds for each $X \in L(\mathbb{C}^{\Sigma})$ and each $a \in \Gamma$. The first equation of (6.357) is equivalent to

$$\sum_{a \in \Gamma} p(a) \frac{J(\Psi_a)}{|\Sigma|} = \frac{\mathbb{1} \otimes \mathbb{1}}{|\Sigma|^2}, \tag{6.359}$$

which implies

$$\sum_{a \in \Gamma} p(a) \operatorname{vec}(U_a) \operatorname{vec}(U_a)^* = \frac{\mathbb{1} \otimes \mathbb{1}}{|\Sigma|} = J(\Omega), \tag{6.360}$$

and therefore

$$\sum_{a \in \Gamma} p(a) U_a X U_a^* = \Omega(X) \tag{6.361}$$

for all $X \in L(\mathbb{C}^{\Sigma})$. Statement 1 therefore implies statement 2.

Under the assumption that statement 2 holds, the Holevo information of η may be calculated directly:

$$
\begin{aligned}
\chi(\eta) &= H\!\left(\sum_{a \in \Gamma} \frac{p(a)}{|\Sigma|} \sum_{b,c \in \Sigma} \Psi_a(E_{b,c}) \otimes E_{b,c} \right) \\
&\quad - \sum_{a \in \Gamma} p(a) \, H\!\left(\frac{1}{|\Sigma|} \sum_{b,c \in \Sigma} \Psi_a(E_{b,c}) \otimes E_{b,c} \right) \\
&= H\!\left(\frac{\mathbb{1} \otimes \mathbb{1}}{|\Sigma|^2} \right) - \sum_{a \in \Gamma} p(a) \, H\!\left(\frac{\operatorname{vec}(U_a) \operatorname{vec}(U_a)^*}{|\Sigma|} \right) \\
&= 2 \log(|\Sigma|).
\end{aligned}
\tag{6.362}
$$

Statement 2 therefore implies statement 1, which completes the proof. $\qquad\square$

6.3.2 Nonclassical Correlations

The definition of entanglement, as the absence of separability, is not directly related to an observable physical phenomenon. Entanglement is, however, fundamentally connected with the correlations that may exist among the outcomes of measurements performed on two or more separate parts of a physical system. To describe this connection, it is helpful to consider the following scenario.

Scenario 6.57 Two individuals, Alice and Bob, share a compound register (X, Y), with Alice holding X and Bob holding Y. Two events occur:

1. Alice receives an input symbol, drawn from a fixed alphabet Σ_{A}, and she must produce an output symbol from a fixed alphabet Γ_{A}.

2. Bob receives an input symbol, drawn from a fixed alphabet Σ_B, and he must produce an output symbol from a fixed alphabet Γ_B.

Alice and Bob cannot communicate with one another at any point after they have received their input symbols. The output symbols they produce may, in general, be probabilistic, possibly resulting from measurements made on whichever one of the registers X or Y is in the possession of the individual performing the measurement.

The discussion that follows is primarily concerned with the collections of output distributions that may be produced by Alice and Bob, as described in the scenario above, through measurements on a shared entangled state, as compared with the correlations that may result from the initial state of (X, Y) being separable.

Correlation Operators

The output distributions produced by Alice and Bob in a particular instance of Scenario 6.57, ranging over all pairs of input symbols, may collectively be described by a single operator

$$C \in \mathrm{L}\left(\mathbb{R}^{\Sigma_\mathrm{B} \times \Gamma_\mathrm{B}}, \mathbb{R}^{\Sigma_\mathrm{A} \times \Gamma_\mathrm{A}}\right), \tag{6.363}$$

defined so that $C((a,c),(b,d))$ is the probability that Alice and Bob output $(c,d) \in \Gamma_\mathrm{A} \times \Gamma_\mathrm{B}$, assuming they are given the input pair $(a,b) \in \Sigma_\mathrm{A} \times \Sigma_\mathrm{B}$. Such an operator must satisfy certain constraints. For instance, to carry the interpretation that C represents a collection of probability distributions, each entry must be a nonnegative real number, and it must hold that

$$\sum_{(c,d) \in \Gamma_\mathrm{A} \times \Gamma_\mathrm{B}} C((a,c),(b,d)) = 1 \tag{6.364}$$

for every pair $(a,b) \in \Sigma_\mathrm{A} \times \Sigma_\mathrm{B}$. Additional constraints are imposed by the assumption that Alice and Bob are separated and cannot communicate.

Definition 6.58 Let Σ_A, Σ_B, Γ_A, and Γ_B be alphabets, and let

$$C \in \mathrm{L}\left(\mathbb{R}^{\Sigma_\mathrm{B} \times \Gamma_\mathrm{B}}, \mathbb{R}^{\Sigma_\mathrm{A} \times \Gamma_\mathrm{A}}\right) \tag{6.365}$$

be an operator.

1. The operator C is a *deterministic correlation operator* if

$$C = \sum_{(a,b) \in \Sigma_\mathrm{A} \times \Sigma_\mathrm{B}} E_{a,b} \otimes E_{f(a),g(b)}, \tag{6.366}$$

or equivalently

$$C((a,c),(b,d)) = \begin{cases} 1 & \text{if } c = f(a) \text{ and } d = g(b) \\ 0 & \text{otherwise,} \end{cases} \tag{6.367}$$

for some choice of functions $f \colon \Sigma_A \to \Gamma_A$ and $g \colon \Sigma_B \to \Gamma_B$. It is said that C is a *probabilistic correlation operator* if C is equal to a convex combination of deterministic correlation operators.

2. The operator C is a *quantum correlation operator* if there exist complex Euclidean spaces $\mathcal{X}$ and $\mathcal{Y}$, a state $\rho \in D(\mathcal{X} \otimes \mathcal{Y})$, and two collections of measurements $\{\mu_a \colon a \in \Sigma_A\}$ and $\{\nu_b \colon b \in \Sigma_B\}$, taking the form

$$\mu_a \colon \Gamma_A \to \text{Pos}(\mathcal{X}) \quad \text{and} \quad \nu_b \colon \Gamma_B \to \text{Pos}(\mathcal{Y}), \tag{6.368}$$

such that

$$C((a,c),(b,d)) = \langle \mu_a(c) \otimes \nu_b(d), \rho \rangle \tag{6.369}$$

for every $a \in \Sigma_A$, $b \in \Sigma_B$, $c \in \Gamma_A$, and $d \in \Gamma_B$.

Example 6.59 Let Σ_A, Σ_B, Γ_A, and Γ_B all be equal to the binary alphabet $\Sigma = \{0,1\}$, let $\mathcal{X} = \mathbb{C}^\Sigma$ and $\mathcal{Y} = \mathbb{C}^\Sigma$, define $\tau \in D(\mathcal{X} \otimes \mathcal{Y})$ to be the maximally entangled state

$$\tau = \frac{1}{2} \sum_{a,b \in \Sigma} E_{a,b} \otimes E_{a,b}, \tag{6.370}$$

and define measurements $\mu_0, \mu_1 \colon \Gamma_A \to \text{Pos}(\mathcal{X})$ and $\nu_0, \nu_1 \colon \Gamma_B \to \text{Pos}(\mathcal{Y})$ as

$$\begin{aligned} \mu_0(0) &= \Pi_0, & \mu_0(1) &= \Pi_{\pi/2}, \\ \mu_1(0) &= \Pi_{\pi/4}, & \mu_1(1) &= \Pi_{3\pi/4}, \\ \nu_0(0) &= \Pi_{\pi/8}, & \nu_0(1) &= \Pi_{5\pi/8}, \\ \nu_1(0) &= \Pi_{7\pi/8}, & \nu_1(1) &= \Pi_{3\pi/8}, \end{aligned} \tag{6.371}$$

for

$$\Pi_\theta = \begin{pmatrix} \cos^2(\theta) & \cos(\theta)\sin(\theta) \\ \cos(\theta)\sin(\theta) & \sin^2(\theta) \end{pmatrix}. \tag{6.372}$$

Equivalently, these measurement operators are as described in Figure 6.1.

For this choice of τ, and because each of the measurement operators above have real number entries, it holds that

$$\langle \mu_a(c) \otimes \nu_b(d), \tau \rangle = \frac{1}{2} \langle \mu_a(c), \nu_b(d) \rangle \tag{6.373}$$

$$\mu_0(0) = \begin{pmatrix} 1 & 0 \\ 0 & 0 \end{pmatrix}, \qquad\qquad \mu_0(1) = \begin{pmatrix} 0 & 0 \\ 0 & 1 \end{pmatrix},$$

$$\mu_1(0) = \begin{pmatrix} \frac{1}{2} & \frac{1}{2} \\ \frac{1}{2} & \frac{1}{2} \end{pmatrix}, \qquad\qquad \mu_1(1) = \begin{pmatrix} \frac{1}{2} & -\frac{1}{2} \\ -\frac{1}{2} & \frac{1}{2} \end{pmatrix},$$

$$\nu_0(0) = \begin{pmatrix} \frac{2+\sqrt{2}}{4} & \frac{\sqrt{2}}{4} \\ \frac{\sqrt{2}}{4} & \frac{2-\sqrt{2}}{4} \end{pmatrix}, \qquad \nu_0(1) = \begin{pmatrix} \frac{2-\sqrt{2}}{4} & -\frac{\sqrt{2}}{4} \\ -\frac{\sqrt{2}}{4} & \frac{2+\sqrt{2}}{4} \end{pmatrix},$$

$$\nu_1(0) = \begin{pmatrix} \frac{2+\sqrt{2}}{4} & -\frac{\sqrt{2}}{4} \\ -\frac{\sqrt{2}}{4} & \frac{2-\sqrt{2}}{4} \end{pmatrix}, \qquad \nu_1(1) = \begin{pmatrix} \frac{2-\sqrt{2}}{4} & \frac{\sqrt{2}}{4} \\ \frac{\sqrt{2}}{4} & \frac{2+\sqrt{2}}{4} \end{pmatrix}.$$

Figure 6.1 Matrix representations of the measurement operators described in Example 6.59.

for each $a \in \Sigma_A$, $b \in \Sigma_B$, $c \in \Gamma_A$, and $d \in \Gamma_B$. A calculation reveals that the quantum correlation operator defined by (6.369) is given by

$$C = \begin{pmatrix} \frac{2+\sqrt{2}}{8} & \frac{2-\sqrt{2}}{8} & \frac{2+\sqrt{2}}{8} & \frac{2-\sqrt{2}}{8} \\ \frac{2-\sqrt{2}}{8} & \frac{2+\sqrt{2}}{8} & \frac{2-\sqrt{2}}{8} & \frac{2+\sqrt{2}}{8} \\ \frac{2+\sqrt{2}}{8} & \frac{2-\sqrt{2}}{8} & \frac{2-\sqrt{2}}{8} & \frac{2+\sqrt{2}}{8} \\ \frac{2-\sqrt{2}}{8} & \frac{2+\sqrt{2}}{8} & \frac{2+\sqrt{2}}{8} & \frac{2-\sqrt{2}}{8} \end{pmatrix}. \tag{6.374}$$

It will be demonstrated shortly that the operator C is not a probabilistic correlation operator.

Example 6.60 Let Σ_A, Σ_B, Γ_A, and Γ_B all be equal to the binary alphabet $\Sigma = \{0, 1\}$. There are 16 deterministic correlation operators, which are in correspondence with the 16 possible pairs of functions (f, g) having the form $f \colon \Sigma_A \to \Gamma_A$ and $g \colon \Sigma_B \to \Gamma_B$. As matrices, these operators are as described in Figure 6.2.

Bell Inequalities

By its definition, the set of all probabilistic correlation operators of the form

$$C \in \mathrm{L}\big(\mathbb{R}^{\Sigma_B \times \Gamma_B}, \mathbb{R}^{\Sigma_A \times \Gamma_A}\big) \tag{6.375}$$

is convex. Indeed, this set is given by the convex hull of a finite set, as there are finitely many deterministic correlation operators of the same form. From this fact it follows that the set of all probabilistic correlation operators of the form (6.375) is compact. Therefore, by the separating hyperplane theorem

$$
\begin{pmatrix} 1 & 0 & 1 & 0 \\ 0 & 0 & 0 & 0 \\ 1 & 0 & 1 & 0 \\ 0 & 0 & 0 & 0 \end{pmatrix},
\begin{pmatrix} 1 & 0 & 0 & 1 \\ 0 & 0 & 0 & 0 \\ 1 & 0 & 0 & 1 \\ 0 & 0 & 0 & 0 \end{pmatrix},
\begin{pmatrix} 0 & 1 & 1 & 0 \\ 0 & 0 & 0 & 0 \\ 0 & 1 & 1 & 0 \\ 0 & 0 & 0 & 0 \end{pmatrix},
\begin{pmatrix} 0 & 1 & 0 & 1 \\ 0 & 0 & 0 & 0 \\ 0 & 1 & 0 & 1 \\ 0 & 0 & 0 & 0 \end{pmatrix},
$$

$$
\begin{pmatrix} 1 & 0 & 1 & 0 \\ 0 & 0 & 0 & 0 \\ 0 & 0 & 0 & 0 \\ 1 & 0 & 1 & 0 \end{pmatrix},
\begin{pmatrix} 1 & 0 & 0 & 1 \\ 0 & 0 & 0 & 0 \\ 0 & 0 & 0 & 0 \\ 1 & 0 & 0 & 1 \end{pmatrix},
\begin{pmatrix} 0 & 1 & 1 & 0 \\ 0 & 0 & 0 & 0 \\ 0 & 0 & 0 & 0 \\ 0 & 1 & 1 & 0 \end{pmatrix},
\begin{pmatrix} 0 & 1 & 0 & 1 \\ 0 & 0 & 0 & 0 \\ 0 & 0 & 0 & 0 \\ 0 & 1 & 0 & 1 \end{pmatrix},
$$

$$
\begin{pmatrix} 0 & 0 & 0 & 0 \\ 1 & 0 & 1 & 0 \\ 1 & 0 & 1 & 0 \\ 0 & 0 & 0 & 0 \end{pmatrix},
\begin{pmatrix} 0 & 0 & 0 & 0 \\ 1 & 0 & 0 & 1 \\ 1 & 0 & 0 & 1 \\ 0 & 0 & 0 & 0 \end{pmatrix},
\begin{pmatrix} 0 & 0 & 0 & 0 \\ 0 & 1 & 1 & 0 \\ 0 & 1 & 1 & 0 \\ 0 & 0 & 0 & 0 \end{pmatrix},
\begin{pmatrix} 0 & 0 & 0 & 0 \\ 0 & 1 & 0 & 1 \\ 0 & 1 & 0 & 1 \\ 0 & 0 & 0 & 0 \end{pmatrix},
$$

$$
\begin{pmatrix} 0 & 0 & 0 & 0 \\ 1 & 0 & 1 & 0 \\ 0 & 0 & 0 & 0 \\ 1 & 0 & 1 & 0 \end{pmatrix},
\begin{pmatrix} 0 & 0 & 0 & 0 \\ 1 & 0 & 0 & 1 \\ 0 & 0 & 0 & 0 \\ 1 & 0 & 0 & 1 \end{pmatrix},
\begin{pmatrix} 0 & 0 & 0 & 0 \\ 0 & 1 & 1 & 0 \\ 0 & 0 & 0 & 0 \\ 0 & 1 & 1 & 0 \end{pmatrix},
\begin{pmatrix} 0 & 0 & 0 & 0 \\ 0 & 1 & 0 & 1 \\ 0 & 0 & 0 & 0 \\ 0 & 1 & 0 & 1 \end{pmatrix}.
$$

Figure 6.2 Matrix representations of the correlation operators described in Example 6.60.

(Theorem 1.11), if an operator

$$
D \in L\big(\mathbb{R}^{\Sigma_B \times \Gamma_B}, \mathbb{R}^{\Sigma_A \times \Gamma_A}\big) \tag{6.376}
$$

is not a probabilistic correlation operator, there must exist an operator

$$
K \in L\big(\mathbb{R}^{\Sigma_B \times \Gamma_B}, \mathbb{R}^{\Sigma_A \times \Gamma_A}\big) \tag{6.377}
$$

and a real number α such that

$$
\langle K, D \rangle > \alpha \quad \text{and} \quad \langle K, C \rangle \leq \alpha \tag{6.378}
$$

for all probabilistic correlation operators C of the form (6.375).

For a fixed choice of an operator K and a real number α, the inequality $\langle K, C \rangle \leq \alpha$ is traditionally called a *Bell inequality*, assuming it is satisfied for every probabilistic correlation operator C of the form (6.375). When this is the case, the inequality $\langle K, D \rangle > \alpha$ is called a *Bell inequality violation* if it holds for some choice of a quantum correlation operator D.

The illustration of a Bell inequality violation can provide a convenient way to demonstrate that certain correlation operators are not probabilistic, as the following example illustrates.

Example 6.61 (Clauser–Horn–Shimony–Holt inequality)   Let Σ_{A}, Σ_{B}, Γ_{A}, and Γ_{B} all be equal to the binary alphabet $\Sigma = \{0, 1\}$, and define

$$K \in \mathrm{L}\big(\mathbb{R}^{\Sigma_{\mathrm{B}} \times \Gamma_{\mathrm{B}}}, \mathbb{R}^{\Sigma_{\mathrm{A}} \times \Gamma_{\mathrm{A}}}\big) \tag{6.379}$$

as

$$K = \begin{pmatrix} 1 & -1 & 1 & -1 \\ -1 & 1 & -1 & 1 \\ 1 & -1 & -1 & 1 \\ -1 & 1 & 1 & -1 \end{pmatrix}. \tag{6.380}$$

For every deterministic correlation operator

$$C \in \mathrm{L}\big(\mathbb{R}^{\Sigma_{\mathrm{B}} \times \Gamma_{\mathrm{B}}}, \mathbb{R}^{\Sigma_{\mathrm{A}} \times \Gamma_{\mathrm{A}}}\big) \tag{6.381}$$

it holds that

$$\langle K, C \rangle \leq 2, \tag{6.382}$$

which may be verified by an inspection of the 16 deterministic correlation operators in Example 6.60. It follows by convexity that the same inequality holds for C being any probabilistic correlation operator. On the other hand, the quantum correlation operator

$$D = \begin{pmatrix} \frac{2+\sqrt{2}}{8} & \frac{2-\sqrt{2}}{8} & \frac{2+\sqrt{2}}{8} & \frac{2-\sqrt{2}}{8} \\ \frac{2-\sqrt{2}}{8} & \frac{2+\sqrt{2}}{8} & \frac{2-\sqrt{2}}{8} & \frac{2+\sqrt{2}}{8} \\ \frac{2+\sqrt{2}}{8} & \frac{2-\sqrt{2}}{8} & \frac{2-\sqrt{2}}{8} & \frac{2+\sqrt{2}}{8} \\ \frac{2-\sqrt{2}}{8} & \frac{2+\sqrt{2}}{8} & \frac{2+\sqrt{2}}{8} & \frac{2-\sqrt{2}}{8} \end{pmatrix} \tag{6.383}$$

described in Example 6.59 satisfies

$$\langle K, D \rangle = 2\sqrt{2}. \tag{6.384}$$

This demonstrates that D is not a probabilistic correlation operator.

Correlations Among Binary-Valued Measurements

For a given choice of alphabets Σ_{A}, Σ_{B}, Γ_{A}, and Γ_{B}, and an operator

$$K \in \mathrm{L}\big(\mathbb{R}^{\Sigma_{\mathrm{B}} \times \Gamma_{\mathrm{B}}}, \mathbb{R}^{\Sigma_{\mathrm{A}} \times \Gamma_{\mathrm{A}}}\big), \tag{6.385}$$

it may be quite difficult in some cases to determine the supremum value of $\langle K, C \rangle$, optimized over all quantum correlation operators of the form

$$C \in \mathrm{L}\big(\mathbb{R}^{\Sigma_{\mathrm{B}} \times \Gamma_{\mathrm{B}}}, \mathbb{R}^{\Sigma_{\mathrm{A}} \times \Gamma_{\mathrm{A}}}\big). \tag{6.386}$$

There is, however, an interesting class of operators K for which this problem is solvable. This is the class for which the output alphabets Γ_A and Γ_B are both equal to the binary alphabet $\Sigma = \{0, 1\}$, and furthermore the operator K takes the form

$$K = M \otimes \begin{pmatrix} 1 & -1 \\ -1 & 1 \end{pmatrix} \tag{6.387}$$

for some choice of an operator

$$M \in L(\mathbb{R}^{\Sigma_B}, \mathbb{R}^{\Sigma_A}). \tag{6.388}$$

Operators of the form (6.387) have a simple interpretation when considered in the context of Bell inequalities and violations – they effectively assign the value $M(a, b)$ to the event that Alice and Bob output equal binary-valued answers, and the value $-M(a, b)$ to the event that their outputs differ, for each possible input pair (a, b).

The following theorem, known as Tsirelson's theorem, provides the basis for a solution to the problem under consideration.

Theorem 6.62 (Tsirelson's theorem) *Let Σ_A and Σ_B be alphabets and let $X \in L(\mathbb{R}^{\Sigma_B}, \mathbb{R}^{\Sigma_A})$ be an operator. The following statements are equivalent:*

1. *There exist complex Euclidean spaces $\mathcal{X}$ and $\mathcal{Y}$, a state $\rho \in D(\mathcal{X} \otimes \mathcal{Y})$, and two collections*

    $$\{A_a : a \in \Sigma_A\} \subset \mathrm{Herm}(\mathcal{X}) \quad and \quad \{B_b : b \in \Sigma_B\} \subset \mathrm{Herm}(\mathcal{Y}) \tag{6.389}$$

    of operators satisfying $\|A_a\| \leq 1$, $\|B_b\| \leq 1$, and

    $$X(a, b) = \langle A_a \otimes B_b, \rho \rangle \tag{6.390}$$

    for every $a \in \Sigma_A$ and $b \in \Sigma_B$.
2. *Statement 1 holds under the additional requirement that, for some choice of an alphabet Γ, one has $\mathcal{X} = \mathbb{C}^\Gamma$, $\mathcal{Y} = \mathbb{C}^\Gamma$, and*

    $$\rho = \frac{1}{|\Gamma|} \sum_{c,d \in \Gamma} E_{c,d} \otimes E_{c,d}, \tag{6.391}$$

    and furthermore that the operators in the collections

    $$\{A_a : a \in \Sigma_A\} \quad and \quad \{B_b : b \in \Sigma_B\} \tag{6.392}$$

    are unitary (in addition to being Hermitian).
3. *There exist operators*

    $$P \in \mathrm{Pos}(\mathbb{C}^{\Sigma_A}) \quad and \quad Q \in \mathrm{Pos}(\mathbb{C}^{\Sigma_B}), \tag{6.393}$$

with $P(a, a) = 1$ and $Q(b, b) = 1$ for every $a \in \Sigma_A$ and $b \in \Sigma_B$, such that

$$\begin{pmatrix} P & X \\ X^* & Q \end{pmatrix} \in \mathrm{Pos}(\mathbb{C}^{\Sigma_A} \oplus \mathbb{C}^{\Sigma_B}). \tag{6.394}$$

4. *There exist two collections*

$$\{u_a : a \in \Sigma_A\},\ \{v_b : b \in \Sigma_B\} \subset \mathbb{R}^{\Sigma_A} \oplus \mathbb{R}^{\Sigma_B} \tag{6.395}$$

of unit vectors such that

$$X(a, b) = \langle u_a, v_b \rangle \tag{6.396}$$

for every $a \in \Sigma_A$ and $b \in \Sigma_B$.

The proof of this theorem will make use of a collection of unitary and Hermitian operators known as *Weyl–Brauer operators*.

Definition 6.63   Let m be a positive integer, let $\Gamma = \{0, 1\}$, and let $\mathcal{Z} = \mathbb{C}^\Gamma$. The *Weyl–Brauer operators*

$$V_0, \ldots, V_{2m} \in \mathrm{L}(\mathcal{Z}^{\otimes m}) \tag{6.397}$$

of order m are defined as follows: $V_0 = \sigma_z^{\otimes m}$ and

$$\begin{aligned} V_{2k-1} &= \sigma_z^{\otimes (k-1)} \otimes \sigma_x \otimes \mathbb{1}^{\otimes (m-k)}, \\ V_{2k} &= \sigma_z^{\otimes (k-1)} \otimes \sigma_y \otimes \mathbb{1}^{\otimes (m-k)}, \end{aligned} \tag{6.398}$$

for $k = 1, \ldots, m$, where $\mathbb{1}$ denotes the identity operator on $\mathcal{Z}$ and σ_x, σ_y, and σ_z are given by the Pauli operators. In matrix form, these operators are as follows:

$$\mathbb{1} = \begin{pmatrix} 1 & 0 \\ 0 & 1 \end{pmatrix},\quad \sigma_x = \begin{pmatrix} 0 & 1 \\ 1 & 0 \end{pmatrix},\quad \sigma_y = \begin{pmatrix} 0 & -i \\ i & 0 \end{pmatrix},\quad \sigma_z = \begin{pmatrix} 1 & 0 \\ 0 & -1 \end{pmatrix}. \tag{6.399}$$

Example 6.64   In the case $m = 3$, the Weyl–Brauer operators $V_0, \ldots, V_6$ are

$$\begin{aligned} V_0 &= \sigma_z \otimes \sigma_z \otimes \sigma_z, \\ V_1 &= \sigma_x \otimes \mathbb{1} \otimes \mathbb{1}, \\ V_2 &= \sigma_y \otimes \mathbb{1} \otimes \mathbb{1}, \\ V_3 &= \sigma_z \otimes \sigma_x \otimes \mathbb{1}, \\ V_4 &= \sigma_z \otimes \sigma_y \otimes \mathbb{1}, \\ V_5 &= \sigma_z \otimes \sigma_z \otimes \sigma_x, \\ V_6 &= \sigma_z \otimes \sigma_z \otimes \sigma_y. \end{aligned} \tag{6.400}$$

A proposition summarizing the properties of the Weyl–Brauer operators that are relevant to the proof of Tsirelson's theorem follows.

Proposition 6.65 *Let m be a positive integer, let $V_0, \ldots, V_{2m}$ denote the Weyl–Brauer operators of order m, and let*

$$(\alpha_0, \ldots, \alpha_{2m}), (\beta_0, \ldots, \beta_{2m}) \in \mathbb{R}^{2m+1} \tag{6.401}$$

be vectors of real numbers. It holds that

$$\left(\sum_{k=0}^{2m} \alpha_k V_k \right)^2 = \left(\sum_{k=0}^{2m} \alpha_k^2 \right) \mathbb{1}^{\otimes m} \tag{6.402}$$

and

$$\frac{1}{2^m} \left\langle \sum_{j=0}^{2m} \alpha_j V_j, \sum_{k=0}^{2m} \beta_k V_k \right\rangle = \sum_{k=0}^{2m} \alpha_k \beta_k. \tag{6.403}$$

Proof The Pauli operators anti-commute in pairs:

$$\sigma_x \sigma_y = -\sigma_y \sigma_x, \quad \sigma_x \sigma_z = -\sigma_z \sigma_x, \quad \text{and} \quad \sigma_y \sigma_z = -\sigma_z \sigma_y. \tag{6.404}$$

By an inspection of the definition of the Weyl–Brauer operators, it follows that $V_0, \ldots, V_{2m}$ also anti-commute in pairs:

$$V_j V_k = -V_k V_j \tag{6.405}$$

for distinct choices of $j, k \in \{0, \ldots, 2m\}$. Moreover, each V_k is both unitary and Hermitian, and therefore $V_k^2 = \mathbb{1}^{\otimes m}$. It follows that

$$\left(\sum_{k=0}^{2m} \alpha_k V_k \right)^2 = \sum_{k=0}^{2m} \alpha_k^2 V_k^2 + \sum_{0 \le j < k \le 2m} \alpha_j \alpha_k (V_j V_k + V_k V_j)$$

$$= \left(\sum_{k=0}^{2m} \alpha_k^2 \right) \mathbb{1}^{\otimes m}. \tag{6.406}$$

Moreover,

$$\langle V_j, V_k \rangle = \begin{cases} 2^m & \text{if } j = k \\ 0 & \text{if } j \ne k, \end{cases} \tag{6.407}$$

and therefore

$$\frac{1}{2^m} \left\langle \sum_{j=0}^{2m} \alpha_j V_j, \sum_{k=0}^{2m} \beta_k V_k \right\rangle = \frac{1}{2^m} \sum_{j=0}^{2m} \sum_{k=0}^{2m} \alpha_j \beta_k \langle V_j, V_k \rangle = \sum_{k=0}^{2m} \alpha_k \beta_k, \tag{6.408}$$

as required. $\qquad\square$

Proof of Theorem 6.62   The following implications among the statements will suffice to prove the theorem:

$$(2) \Rightarrow (1) \Rightarrow (3) \Rightarrow (4) \Rightarrow (2). \tag{6.409}$$

The first implication, that statement 2 implies statement 1, is trivial.

Assume statement 1 holds, define an operator

$$K = \sum_{a \in \Sigma_A} e_a \, \mathrm{vec}\big((A_a \otimes \mathbb{1})\sqrt{\rho}\big)^* + \sum_{b \in \Sigma_B} e_b \, \mathrm{vec}\big((\mathbb{1} \otimes B_b)\sqrt{\rho}\big)^*, \tag{6.410}$$

and consider the operator $KK^* \in \mathrm{Pos}(\mathbb{C}^{\Sigma_A \sqcup \Sigma_B})$, which may be written in a block form as

$$KK^* = \begin{pmatrix} P & Y \\ Y^* & Q \end{pmatrix} \tag{6.411}$$

for $P \in \mathrm{Pos}(\mathbb{C}^{\Sigma_A})$, $Q \in \mathrm{Pos}(\mathbb{C}^{\Sigma_B})$, and $Y \in \mathrm{L}(\mathbb{C}^{\Sigma_B}, \mathbb{C}^{\Sigma_A})$. It holds that

$$Y(a,b) = \langle (A_a \otimes \mathbb{1})\sqrt{\rho}, (\mathbb{1} \otimes B_b)\sqrt{\rho} \rangle = \langle A_a \otimes B_b, \rho \rangle = X(a,b) \tag{6.412}$$

for every $a \in \Sigma_A$ and $b \in \Sigma_B$, and therefore $Y = X$. Moreover, for each $a \in \Sigma_A$ one has

$$P(a,a) = \langle (A_a \otimes \mathbb{1})\sqrt{\rho}, (A_a \otimes \mathbb{1})\sqrt{\rho} \rangle = \langle A_a^2 \otimes \mathbb{1}, \rho \rangle, \tag{6.413}$$

which is necessarily a nonnegative real number in the interval $[0,1]$; and through a similar calculation, one finds that $Q(b,b)$ is also a nonnegative integer in the interval $[0,1]$ for each $b \in \Sigma_B$. A nonnegative real number may be added to each diagonal entry of this operator to yield another positive semidefinite operator, so one has that statement 3 holds. It has therefore been proved that statement 1 implies statement 3.

Next, assume statement 3 holds, and observe that

$$\frac{1}{2}\begin{pmatrix} P & X \\ X^* & Q \end{pmatrix} + \frac{1}{2}\begin{pmatrix} P & X \\ X^* & Q \end{pmatrix}^{\mathsf{T}} = \begin{pmatrix} \frac{P + \overline{P}}{2} & X \\ X^* & \frac{Q + \overline{Q}}{2} \end{pmatrix} \tag{6.414}$$

is a positive semidefinite operator having real number entries, and all of its diagonal entries are equal to 1. Define

$$u_a = \begin{pmatrix} \frac{P + \overline{P}}{2} & X \\ X^* & \frac{Q + \overline{Q}}{2} \end{pmatrix}^{\frac{1}{2}} \begin{pmatrix} e_a \\ 0 \end{pmatrix} \quad \text{and} \quad v_b = \begin{pmatrix} \frac{P + \overline{P}}{2} & X \\ X^* & \frac{Q + \overline{Q}}{2} \end{pmatrix}^{\frac{1}{2}} \begin{pmatrix} 0 \\ e_b \end{pmatrix} \tag{6.415}$$

for each $a \in \Sigma_A$ and $b \in \Sigma_B$. As the square root of a positive semidefinite operator having real number entries also has real number entries, one has that u_a and v_b are unit vectors with real number entries, and moreover it holds that

$$\langle u_a, v_b \rangle = X(a, b) \tag{6.416}$$

for all $a \in \Sigma_A$ and $b \in \Sigma_B$. It has therefore been proved that statement 3 implies statement 4.

Finally, assume statement 4 holds. Let

$$m = \left\lceil \frac{|\Sigma_A| + |\Sigma_B| - 1}{2} \right\rceil, \tag{6.417}$$

so that $2m+1 \geq |\Sigma_A|+|\Sigma_B|$, and let $f \colon \Sigma_A \sqcup \Sigma_B \to \{0, \ldots, 2m\}$ be a fixed but otherwise arbitrarily chosen injective function. Let $\Gamma = \{0, 1\}$, let $\mathcal{Z} = \mathbb{C}^\Gamma$, and define

$$A_a = \sum_{c \in \Sigma_A \sqcup \Sigma_B} u_a(c) V_{f(c)} \quad \text{and} \quad B_b = \sum_{c \in \Sigma_A \sqcup \Sigma_B} v_b(c) V_{f(c)}^{\mathsf{T}} \tag{6.418}$$

for each $a \in \Sigma_A$ and $b \in \Sigma_B$, for $V_0, \ldots, V_{2m}$ being the Weyl–Brauer operators of order m, regarded as elements of $\mathrm{L}(\mathcal{Z}^{\otimes m})$. As the vectors $\{u_a \colon a \in \Sigma_A\}$ and $\{v_b \colon b \in \Sigma_B\}$ are unit vectors having real number entries, it follows from Proposition 6.65 that the operators $\{A_a \colon a \in \Sigma_A\}$ and $\{B_b \colon b \in \Sigma_B\}$ are unitary, and it is evident that they are Hermitian as well. Define

$$\tau = \frac{1}{2^m} \operatorname{vec}(\mathbb{1}_{\mathcal{Z}}^{\otimes m}) \operatorname{vec}(\mathbb{1}_{\mathcal{Z}}^{\otimes m})^*. \tag{6.419}$$

For each choice of $a \in \Sigma_A$ and $b \in \Sigma_B$ it holds that

$$\begin{aligned}
\langle A_a \otimes B_b, \tau \rangle &= \frac{1}{2^m} \operatorname{Tr}(A_a B_b^{\mathsf{T}}) \\
&= \frac{1}{2^m} \sum_{c,d \in \Sigma_A \sqcup \Sigma_B} \langle u_a(c) V_{f(c)}, v_b(d) V_{f(d)} \rangle = \langle u_a, v_b \rangle,
\end{aligned} \tag{6.420}$$

again by Proposition 6.65. This is equivalent to statement 2 (taking Γ^m in place of Γ). It has therefore been proved that statement 4 implies statement 2, which completes the proof. $\qquad \square$

As a consequence of Tsirelson's theorem (Theorem 6.62), there exists a semidefinite program for the supremum value of the inner product $\langle K, C \rangle$, for K taking the form (6.387) and for C ranging over all quantum correlation operators of the form

$$C \in \mathrm{L}(\mathbb{R}^{\Sigma_B \times \Gamma_B}, \mathbb{R}^{\Sigma_A \times \Gamma_A}), \tag{6.421}$$

for Σ_A and Σ_B being arbitrary alphabets and Γ_A and Γ_B both being equal to the binary alphabet $\Gamma = \{0, 1\}$.

To understand why this is so, consider an arbitrary quantum correlation operator C, which must be given by

$$C((a,c),(b,d)) = \langle \mu_a(c) \otimes \nu_b(d), \rho \rangle \tag{6.422}$$

for every $a \in \Sigma_A$, $b \in \Sigma_B$, and $c, d \in \Gamma$, for some choice of complex Euclidean spaces $\mathcal{X}$ and $\mathcal{Y}$, a state $\rho \in D(\mathcal{X} \otimes \mathcal{Y})$, and two collections of measurements $\{\mu_a : a \in \Sigma_A\}$ and $\{\nu_b : b \in \Sigma_B\}$ whose elements take the form

$$\mu_a : \Gamma \to \mathrm{Pos}(\mathcal{X}) \quad \text{and} \quad \nu_b : \Gamma \to \mathrm{Pos}(\mathcal{Y}). \tag{6.423}$$

For an operator K of the form (6.387) for some choice of $M \in \mathrm{L}(\mathbb{R}^{\Sigma_B}, \mathbb{R}^{\Sigma_A})$, one has that the value of the inner product $\langle K, C \rangle$ is given by

$$\sum_{(a,b) \in \Sigma_A \times \Sigma_B} M(a,b) \langle (\mu_a(0) - \mu_a(1)) \otimes (\nu_b(0) - \nu_b(1)), \rho \rangle. \tag{6.424}$$

Now, an operator H, acting on an arbitrary complex Euclidean space, may be written as

$$H = \mu(0) - \mu(1) \tag{6.425}$$

for some binary-valued measurement μ if and only if H is Hermitian and satisfies $\|H\| \leq 1$. Thus, an optimization of the expression (6.424) over all choices of the measurements $\{\mu_a : a \in \Sigma_A\}$ and $\{\nu_b : b \in \Sigma_B\}$ is equivalent to an optimization of the expression

$$\sum_{(a,b) \in \Sigma_A \times \Sigma_B} M(a,b) \langle A_a \otimes B_b, \rho \rangle \tag{6.426}$$

over all collections

$$\{A_a : a \in \Sigma_A\} \subset \mathrm{Herm}(\mathcal{X}) \quad \text{and} \quad \{B_b : b \in \Sigma_B\} \subset \mathrm{Herm}(\mathcal{Y}) \tag{6.427}$$

of Hermitian operators satisfying $\|A_a\| \leq 1$ and $\|B_b\| \leq 1$, for every $a \in \Sigma_A$ and $b \in \Sigma_B$, respectively.

By optimizing over all complex Euclidean spaces $\mathcal{X}$ and $\mathcal{Y}$ and density operators $\rho \in D(\mathcal{X} \otimes \mathcal{Y})$, one finds (by Theorem 6.62) that the supremum value of $\langle K, C \rangle$ over all quantum correlation operators C is equal to the supremum value of the inner product $\langle M, X \rangle$ over all choices of operators $X \in \mathrm{L}(\mathbb{R}^{\Sigma_B}, \mathbb{R}^{\Sigma_A})$ for which it holds that

$$\begin{pmatrix} P & X \\ X^* & Q \end{pmatrix} \in \mathrm{Pos}(\mathbb{C}^{\Sigma_A} \oplus \mathbb{C}^{\Sigma_B}), \tag{6.428}$$

for $P \in \mathrm{Pos}(\mathbb{C}^{\Sigma_A})$ and $Q \in \mathrm{Pos}(\mathbb{C}^{\Sigma_B})$ satisfying $P(a,a) = 1$ and $Q(b,b) = 1$ for every $a \in \Sigma_A$ and $b \in \Sigma_B$. Such an optimization corresponds directly to the following primal problem of a semidefinite program:

Primal problem

maximize: $\quad \dfrac{1}{2}\langle M, X\rangle + \dfrac{1}{2}\langle M^*, X^*\rangle$

subject to: $\quad \begin{pmatrix} P & X \\ X^* & Q \end{pmatrix} \geq 0,$

$$\Delta(P) = \mathbb{1}, \ \Delta(Q) = \mathbb{1},$$
$$P \in \mathrm{Pos}(\mathbb{C}^{\Sigma_A}), \ Q \in \mathrm{Pos}(\mathbb{C}^{\Sigma_B}),$$
$$X \in \mathrm{L}(\mathbb{C}^{\Sigma_B}, \mathbb{C}^{\Sigma_A}).$$

In this problem, Δ refers to the completely dephasing channel, defined with respect to either $\mathbb{C}^{\Sigma_A}$ or $\mathbb{C}^{\Sigma_B}$, and $\mathbb{1}$ denotes the identity operator on either of these spaces, as the context dictates without ambiguity.

The dual problem of this semidefinite program is as follows:

Dual problem

minimize: $\quad \dfrac{1}{2}\mathrm{Tr}(Y) + \dfrac{1}{2}\mathrm{Tr}(Z)$

subject to: $\quad \begin{pmatrix} \Delta(Y) & -M \\ -M^* & \Delta(Z) \end{pmatrix} \geq 0,$

$$Y \in \mathrm{Herm}(\mathbb{C}^{\Sigma_A}),$$
$$Z \in \mathrm{Herm}(\mathbb{C}^{\Sigma_B}).$$

It follows from Slater's theorem (Theorem 1.18) that strong duality holds for this semidefinite program – strict feasibility holds for both the primal and dual problems.

Example 6.66 (Tsirelson's bound) Consider the operator

$$K = \begin{pmatrix} 1 & -1 & 1 & -1 \\ -1 & 1 & -1 & 1 \\ 1 & -1 & -1 & 1 \\ -1 & 1 & 1 & -1 \end{pmatrix} = M \otimes \begin{pmatrix} 1 & -1 \\ -1 & 1 \end{pmatrix} \tag{6.429}$$

for

$$M = \begin{pmatrix} 1 & 1 \\ 1 & -1 \end{pmatrix}, \tag{6.430}$$

which was examined in Example 6.61. One has $\|M\| = \sqrt{2}$, so that

$$\begin{pmatrix} \sqrt{2}\,\mathbb{1} & -M \\ -M^* & \sqrt{2}\,\mathbb{1} \end{pmatrix} \geq 0. \tag{6.431}$$

By taking $Y = \sqrt{2}\mathbb{1}$ and $Z = \sqrt{2}\mathbb{1}$ in the dual problem above, a feasible dual solution achieving the objective value $2\sqrt{2}$ is obtained. Therefore,

$$\langle K, C \rangle \leq 2\sqrt{2} \tag{6.432}$$

for every quantum correlation operator C. The Bell inequality violation exhibited in Example 6.61 is therefore optimal for this choice of K.

6.4 Exercises

Exercise 6.1 Let $\Phi \in C(\mathcal{X}, \mathcal{Y})$ be a channel, for complex Euclidean spaces $\mathcal{X}$ and $\mathcal{Y}$. Prove that the following three statements are equivalent:

1. For every complex Euclidean space $\mathcal{Z}$ and every state $\rho \in D(\mathcal{X} \otimes \mathcal{Z})$, it holds that

$$(\Phi \otimes \mathbb{1}_{L(\mathcal{Z})})(\rho) \in \mathrm{SepD}(\mathcal{Y} : \mathcal{Z}). \tag{6.433}$$

2. $J(\Phi) \in \mathrm{Sep}(\mathcal{Y} : \mathcal{X})$.
3. There exist an alphabet Σ, a measurement $\mu \colon \Sigma \to \mathrm{Pos}(\mathcal{X})$, and a collection of states $\{\sigma_a \colon a \in \Sigma\} \subseteq D(\mathcal{Y})$ such that

$$\Phi(X) = \sum_{a \in \Sigma} \langle \mu(a), X \rangle \sigma_a \tag{6.434}$$

for all $X \in L(\mathcal{X})$.

Channels for which these statements hold are called *entanglement-breaking* channels.

Exercise 6.2 Let $\mathcal{X}$ and $\mathcal{Y}$ be complex Euclidean spaces, let $n = \dim(\mathcal{Y})$, and assume $n \leq \dim(\mathcal{X})$. Also let $\{U_1, \ldots, U_m\} \in U(\mathcal{Y}, \mathcal{X})$ be an orthogonal collection of isometries, and let $u_k \in \mathcal{X} \otimes \mathcal{Y}$ be the unit vector defined as

$$u_k = \frac{1}{\sqrt{n}} \mathrm{vec}(U_k) \tag{6.435}$$

for each $k \in \{1, \ldots, m\}$. Prove that if $\mu \colon \{1, \ldots, m\} \to \mathrm{Pos}(\mathcal{X} \otimes \mathcal{Y})$ is a measurement satisfying $\mu(k) \in \mathrm{PPT}(\mathcal{X} : \mathcal{Y})$ for every $k \in \{1, \ldots, m\}$, then

$$\sum_{k=1}^{m} \langle \mu(k), u_k u_k^* \rangle \leq \dim(\mathcal{X}). \tag{6.436}$$

(Observe that a correct solution to this exercise generalizes Theorem 6.30.)

Exercise 6.3 Let X and Y be registers and let $\rho \in D(\mathcal{X} \otimes \mathcal{Y})$ be a state of the pair (X, Y). With respect to ρ, one defines the *entanglement of formation* between X and Y as

$$E_F(X : Y) = \inf \left\{ \sum_{a \in \Sigma} p(a) \, H(\text{Tr}_{\mathcal{Y}}(u_a u_a^*)) : \sum_{a \in \Sigma} p(a) u_a u_a^* = \rho \right\}, \quad (6.437)$$

where the infimum is over all choices of an alphabet Σ, a probability vector $p \in \mathcal{P}(\Sigma)$, and a collection of unit vectors $\{u_a : a \in \Sigma\} \subset \mathcal{X} \otimes \mathcal{Y}$ for which it holds that

$$\sum_{a \in \Sigma} p(a) u_a u_a^* = \rho. \quad (6.438)$$

(a) Prove that the infimum in (6.437) is achieved for some choice of Σ, p, and $\{u_a : a \in \Sigma\}$ for which $|\Sigma| \leq \dim(\mathcal{X} \otimes \mathcal{Y})^2$.

(b) Suppose that Z and W are registers and $\Phi \in \text{LOCC}(\mathcal{X}, \mathcal{Z} : \mathcal{Y}, \mathcal{W})$ is an LOCC channel. Prove that

$$E_F(Z : W)_\sigma \leq E_F(X : Y)_\rho \quad (6.439)$$

where $\sigma = \Phi(\rho)$ and $E_F(X:Y)_\rho$ and $E_F(Z:W)_\sigma$ denote the entanglement of formation of the pairs (X, Y) and (Z, W) with respect to the states ρ and σ, respectively.

(c) Prove a more general statement than the one required of a solution to part (b), holding not only for all LOCC channels, but for all separable channels of the form $\Phi \in \text{SepC}(\mathcal{X}, \mathcal{Z} : \mathcal{Y}, \mathcal{W})$.

Exercise 6.4 Let $\mathcal{X}$ and $\mathcal{Y}$ be complex Euclidean spaces, and assume that both spaces have dimension at least 2. Prove that there exist entanglement-breaking channels $\Phi_0, \Phi_1 \in C(\mathcal{X}, \mathcal{Y})$, as defined in Exercise 6.1, such that

$$\||\Phi_0 - \Phi_1\||_1 > \|\Phi_0(\rho) - \Phi_1(\rho)\|_1 \quad (6.440)$$

for every $\rho \in D(\mathcal{X})$. Such channels have the seemingly strange property that they destroy entanglement, and yet evaluating them on an entangled state helps to discriminate between them.

Exercise 6.5 Let Σ be an alphabet, let $\mathcal{X}$ and $\mathcal{Y}$ be complex Euclidean spaces of the form $\mathcal{X} = \mathbb{C}^\Sigma$ and $\mathcal{Y} = \mathbb{C}^\Sigma$, let $n = |\Sigma|$, and consider the projections $\Delta_0, \Delta_1, \Pi_0$, and Π_1 defined in Example 6.10. Also define

$$\rho_0 = \frac{\Pi_0}{\binom{n+1}{2}}, \quad \rho_1 = \frac{\Pi_1}{\binom{n}{2}}, \quad \sigma_0 = \Delta_0, \quad \text{and} \quad \sigma_1 = \frac{\Delta_1}{n^2 - 1}. \quad (6.441)$$

The states ρ_0 and ρ_1 are therefore Werner states, while σ_0 and σ_1 are isotropic states.

(a) Prove that if $\mu \colon \{0,1\} \to \mathrm{Pos}(\mathcal{X} \otimes \mathcal{Y})$ is a measurement satisfying $\mu(0), \mu(1) \in \mathrm{PPT}(\mathcal{X} : \mathcal{Y})$, then

$$\frac{1}{2}\langle \mu(0), \rho_0 \rangle + \frac{1}{2}\langle \mu(1), \rho_1 \rangle \leq \frac{1}{2} + \frac{1}{n+1}. \tag{6.442}$$

Prove that there exists an LOCC measurement μ for which (6.442) holds with equality.

(b) Prove that if $\nu \colon \{0,1\} \to \mathrm{Pos}(\mathcal{X} \otimes \mathcal{Y})$ is a measurement satisfying $\nu(0), \nu(1) \in \mathrm{PPT}(\mathcal{X} : \mathcal{Y})$, then

$$\frac{1}{2}\langle \nu(0), \sigma_0 \rangle + \frac{1}{2}\langle \nu(1), \sigma_1 \rangle \leq 1 - \frac{1}{2n+2}. \tag{6.443}$$

Prove that there exists an LOCC measurement ν for which (6.443) holds with equality.

Exercise 6.6 Let N and m be positive integers, and assume that there exist unitary and Hermitian operators $U_0, \ldots, U_{2m} \in \mathrm{L}(\mathbb{C}^N)$ that anticommute in pairs: $U_j U_k = -U_k U_j$ for distinct choices of $j, k \in \{0, \ldots, 2m\}$. Prove that the collection

$$\left\{ U_0^{a_0} \cdots U_{2m}^{a_{2m}} : a_0, \ldots, a_{2m} \in \{0,1\},\ a_0 + \cdots + a_{2m} \text{ is even} \right\} \tag{6.444}$$

is an orthogonal collection, and conclude that $N \geq 2^m$. (Observe that a correct solution to this exercise implies that the Weyl–Brauer operators have the minimum possible dimension required to possess the properties mentioned above.)

6.5 Bibliographic Remarks

Although it was not formally defined or called entanglement therein, the phenomenon of entanglement was first recognized by Einstein, Podolsky, and Rosen (1935). Einstein, Podolsky, and Rosen's work inspired Schrödinger to investigate the phenomenon of entanglement, and to give it its name; he published a three-part paper in German (Schrödinger, 1935a,b,c), as well as two related English-language papers (Schrödinger, 1935d, 1936) discussing entanglement and other issues, as they pertained to the nature of quantum physics at that time. (An English translation of Schrödinger's three-part paper in German was published later (Trimmer, 1980).) The identification of entanglement with a lack of separability is due to Werner (1989), who used the terms *classically correlated* and *EPR (Einstein–Podolsky–Rosen) correlated* rather than *separable* and *entangled*.

The equivalence of the first two statements in Theorem 6.9 was proved by M. Horodecki, P. Horodecki, and R. Horodecki (1996), and Proposition 6.6 was proved by P. Horodecki (1997). Several elementary analytic facts about the set of separable states that have been discussed in Section 6.1.1 were also observed in the papers proving these facts. The equivalence of the third statement in Theorem 6.9 to the first two was proved a few years later by P. Horodecki (2001). In general, it is likely to be a computationally difficult task to test a bipartite density operator for separability, as suggested by the computational hardness result proved by Gurvits (2003).

The fact that any operator sufficiently close to the identity operator in a bipartite tensor product space is separable was first proved by Życzkowski, P. Horodecki, Sanpera, and Lewenstein (1998). Theorem 6.13 is due to Gurvits and Barnum (2002).

The local operations and classical communication paradigm, also called the *distant labs* paradigm, arose naturally in quantum information theory as various quantum information processing tasks were considered. Among the first researchers to consider this paradigm were Peres and Wootters (1991), who compared the capabilities of LOCC measurements to general measurements in a setting in which information is encoded into bipartite product states. The teleportation procedure of Bennett, Brassard, Crépeau, Jozsa, Peres, and Wootters (1993) followed shortly after.

There are natural extensions of the definition of LOCC channels that have not been discussed in this chapter. In particular, the definition of LOCC channels in the present chapter requires an LOCC channel to be a finite composition of one-way LOCC channels, corresponding to a fixed number of classical message transmissions between two individuals implementing the channel, but one may also consider channels implemented by a potentially unbounded number of message transmissions. It is known that the set of LOCC channels, as they have been defined in this chapter, is generally not closed for a fixed choice of spaces; this was proved (for bipartite channels) by Chitambar, Leung, Mančinska, Ozols, and Winter (2014). The definition of LOCC channels presented in this chapter is based on one of the definitions considered by these authors.

The class of separable channels was identified by Vedral, Plenio, Rippin, and Knight (1997), although they did not raise the possibility (first suggested by Rains (1997)) that some separable channels might not be LOCC channels. The existence of separable measurements that are not LOCC measurements (and, in fact, not even approached by a sequence of LOCC measurements in the limit) was proved by Bennett, DiVincenzo, Fuchs, Mor, Rains, Shor, Smolin, and Wootters (1999b). Childs, Leung, Mančinska, and Ozols (2013) give a simplified proof of this fact, along with some generalizations of it.

The distillable entanglement and entanglement cost measures were defined by Bennett, Bernstein, Popescu, and Schumacher (1996a). They used the term *entanglement of formation* rather than entanglement cost – but that terminology has since come to refer to the measure of entanglement described in Exercise 6.3. Theorem 6.38 was proved in the same paper through the design and analysis of LOCC channels for entanglement distillation and its reverse for pure states.

Entanglement distillation for general quantum states was considered by Bennett, Brassard, Popescu, Schumacher, Smolin, and Wootters (1996c) and Bennett, DiVincenzo, Smolin, and Wootters (1996b) around the same time. It is known that the entanglement cost of every bipartite entangled state is nonzero (Yang, M. Horodecki, R. Horodecki, and Synak-Radtke, 2005).

The entanglement rank was first defined by Terhal and P. Horodecki (2000), who referred to it as the *Schmidt number* of a density operator (as it generalizes the number of nonzero terms in a Schmidt decomposition of the vector representation of a given pure state). They also proved that the entanglement rank of a state cannot increase under the action of an LOCC channel, based on related observations by Lo and Popescu (2001) regarding pure states, and that it is generally not multiplicative with respect to tensor products.

Theorem 6.30 was proved by Nathanson (2005), and Theorem 6.32 was proved by Walgate, Short, Hardy, and Vedral (2000).

The equivalence of statements 1, 2, and 3 in Theorem 6.33, as well as statement 4 for LOCC channels rather than separable channels, was proved by Nielsen (1999). Nielsen's proof used the fact that every bipartite pure state transformation induced by an LOCC channel is also induced by a one-way LOCC channel, which was proved earlier by Lo and Popescu (2001). The proof of Theorem 6.38 concerning entanglement distillation and cost for pure states also appears in the same paper of Nielsen. The equivalence of statement 4 of Nielsen's theorem with the first three statements was proved by Gheorghiu and Griffiths (2008).

Peres (1996) proposed the computationally efficient partial transpose test for separability of bipartite density operators; he observed that separable states are necessarily PPT, and that interesting families of entangled states were revealed to be entangled through this test. By the Horodecki criterion (Theorem 6.9) proved shortly after, it follows that the partial transpose test correctly identifies all entangled states in a tensor product of two complex

Euclidean spaces, both of dimension 2 or one of dimension 2 and one of dimension 3, based on work of Størmer (1963) and Woronowicz (1976), but that entangled PPT states in higher dimensions must exist (M. Horodecki, P. Horodecki, and R. Horodecki, 1996). The first explicit examples of entangled PPT states were given by P. Horodecki (1997); the unextendable product set construction of such states is due to Bennett, DiVincenzo, Mor, Shor, Smolin, and Terhal (1999c), who introduced the notion of an unextendable product set as well as the specific example given in this chapter. Proposition 6.44 and Theorem 6.45 were proved by M. Horodecki, P. Horodecki, and R. Horodecki (1998).

As was already mentioned above, the teleportation procedure described in Example 6.50 is due to Bennett, Brassard, Crépeau, Jozsa, Peres, and Wootters (1993). The dense coding procedure described in Example 6.55 is due to Bennett and Wiesner (1992). These procedures have been generalized in various ways. The general presentation of teleportation and dense coding in this chapter is based on work of Werner (2001).

The fact that entangled states may induce nonclassical correlations was discovered by Bell in a highly influential paper (Bell, 1964). The Bell inequality described in Example 6.61 is due to Clauser, Horne, Shimony, and Holt (1969). Some entangled states fail to induce nonclassical correlations – this was demonstrated for the special case in which projective measurements are made on the two parts of a bipartite state by Werner (1989), and for the general case (allowing arbitrary measurements) by Barrett (2002). The entangled states constructed by Werner that have this property are among those described in Example 6.10. Theorem 6.62 is due to Tsirel'son (1987).

This chapter has presented just a small part of an extensive body of work on entanglement. Readers interested in learning more about this topic are referred to the survey of R. Horodecki, P. Horodecki, M. Horodecki, and K. Horodecki (2009).

7

Permutation Invariance and Unitarily Invariant Measures

This chapter introduces two notions – *permutation invariance* and *unitarily invariant measures* – having interesting applications in quantum information theory. A state of a collection of identical registers is said to be permutation-invariant if it is unchanged under arbitrary permutations of the contents of the registers. Unitarily invariant measures are Borel measures, defined for sets of vectors or operators, that are unchanged by the action of all unitary operators acting on the underlying space. The two notions are distinct but nevertheless linked, with the interplay between them offering a useful tool for performing calculations in both settings.

7.1 Permutation-Invariant Vectors and Operators

This section of the chapter discusses properties of permutation-invariant states of collections of identical registers. Somewhat more generally, one may consider permutation-invariant positive semidefinite operators, as well as permutation-invariant vectors.

It is to be assumed for the entirety of the section that an alphabet Σ and a positive integer $n \geq 2$ have been fixed, and that $\mathsf{X}_1, \ldots, \mathsf{X}_n$ is a sequence of registers, all sharing the same classical state set Σ. The assumption that the registers $\mathsf{X}_1, \ldots, \mathsf{X}_n$ share the same classical state set Σ allows one to identify the complex Euclidean spaces $\mathcal{X}_1, \ldots, \mathcal{X}_n$ associated with these registers with a single space $\mathcal{X} = \mathbb{C}^\Sigma$, and to write

$$\mathcal{X}^{\otimes n} = \mathcal{X}_1 \otimes \cdots \otimes \mathcal{X}_n \tag{7.1}$$

for the sake of brevity.

Algebraic properties of states of the compound register $(\mathsf{X}_1, \ldots, \mathsf{X}_n)$ that relate to permutations and symmetries among the individual registers will be a primary focus of the section.

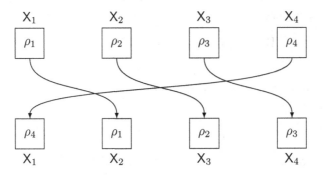

Figure 7.1 The action of the operator W_π on a register $(\mathsf{X}_1, \mathsf{X}_2, \mathsf{X}_3, \mathsf{X}_4)$ when $\pi = (1\ 2\ 3\ 4)$. If the register $(\mathsf{X}_1, \mathsf{X}_2, \mathsf{X}_3, \mathsf{X}_4)$ was initially in the product state $\rho = \rho_1 \otimes \rho_2 \otimes \rho_3 \otimes \rho_4$, and the contents of these registers were permuted according to π as illustrated, the resulting state would then be given by $W_\pi \rho W_\pi^* = \rho_4 \otimes \rho_1 \otimes \rho_2 \otimes \rho_3$. For non-product states, the action of W_π is determined by linearity.

7.1.1 The Subspace of Permutation-Invariant Vectors

Within the tensor product space

$$\mathcal{X}^{\otimes n} = \mathcal{X}_1 \otimes \cdots \otimes \mathcal{X}_n, \tag{7.2}$$

some vectors are unchanged under all permutations of the tensor factors $\mathcal{X}_1, \ldots, \mathcal{X}_n$. The set of all such vectors forms a subspace that is known as the *symmetric subspace*. A more formal description of this subspace will be given shortly, following a short discussion of those operators that represent permutations among the tensor factors of the space (7.2).

Permutations of Tensor Factors

Define a unitary operator $W_\pi \in \mathrm{U}(\mathcal{X}^{\otimes n})$, for each permutation $\pi \in S_n$, by the action

$$W_\pi(x_1 \otimes \cdots \otimes x_n) = x_{\pi^{-1}(1)} \otimes \cdots \otimes x_{\pi^{-1}(n)} \tag{7.3}$$

for every choice of vectors $x_1, \ldots, x_n \in \mathcal{X}$. The action of the operator W_π, when considered as a channel acting on a state ρ as

$$\rho \mapsto W_\pi \rho W_\pi^*, \tag{7.4}$$

corresponds to permuting the contents of the registers $\mathsf{X}_1, \ldots, \mathsf{X}_n$ in the manner described by π. Figure 7.1 depicts an example of this action.

One may observe that

$$W_\pi W_\sigma = W_{\pi\sigma} \quad \text{and} \quad W_\pi^{-1} = W_\pi^* = W_{\pi^{-1}} \tag{7.5}$$

for all permutations $\pi, \sigma \in S_n$. Each operator W_π is a permutation operator, in the sense that it is a unitary operator with entries drawn from the set $\{0, 1\}$, and therefore one has

$$\overline{W_\pi} = W_\pi \quad \text{and} \quad W_\pi^\mathsf{T} = W_\pi^* \tag{7.6}$$

for every $\pi \in S_n$.

The Symmetric Subspace

As suggested above, some vectors in $\mathcal{X}^{\otimes n}$ are invariant under the action of W_π for every choice of $\pi \in S_n$, and it holds that the set of all such vectors forms a subspace known as the *symmetric subspace*. This subspace will be denoted $\mathcal{X}^{\otimes n}$, which is defined in more precise terms as

$$\mathcal{X}^{\textcircled{\otimes} n} = \{x \in \mathcal{X}^{\otimes n} : x = W_\pi x \text{ for every } \pi \in S_n\}. \tag{7.7}$$

This space may alternatively be denoted $\mathcal{X}_1 \textcircled{\otimes} \cdots \textcircled{\otimes} \mathcal{X}_n$ when it is useful to do so. (The use of this notation naturally assumes that $\mathcal{X}_1, \ldots, \mathcal{X}_n$ have been identified with a single complex Euclidean space $\mathcal{X}$.)

The following proposition serves as a convenient starting point from which other facts regarding the symmetric subspace may be derived.

Proposition 7.1 *Let $\mathcal{X}$ be a complex Euclidean space and n a positive integer. The projection onto the symmetric subspace $\mathcal{X}^{\textcircled{\otimes} n}$ is given by*

$$\Pi_{\mathcal{X}^{\textcircled{\otimes} n}} = \frac{1}{n!} \sum_{\pi \in S_n} W_\pi. \tag{7.8}$$

Proof   Using the equations (7.5), one may verify directly that the operator

$$\Pi = \frac{1}{n!} \sum_{\pi \in S_n} W_\pi \tag{7.9}$$

is Hermitian and squares to itself, implying that it is a projection operator. It holds that $W_\pi \Pi = \Pi$ for every $\pi \in S_n$, implying that

$$\operatorname{im}(\Pi) \subseteq \mathcal{X}^{\textcircled{\otimes} n}. \tag{7.10}$$

On the other hand, for every $x \in \mathcal{X}^{\textcircled{\otimes} n}$, it is evident that $\Pi x = x$, implying

$$\mathcal{X}^{\textcircled{\otimes} n} \subseteq \operatorname{im}(\Pi). \tag{7.11}$$

As Π is a projection operator that satisfies $\operatorname{im}(\Pi) = \mathcal{X}^{\textcircled{\otimes} n}$, the proposition is proved. $\square$

An orthonormal basis for the symmetric subspace $\mathcal{X}^{\otimes n}$ will be identified next, and in the process the dimension of this space will be determined. It is helpful to make use of basic combinatorial concepts for this purpose.

First, for every alphabet Σ and every positive integer n, one defines the set $\mathrm{Bag}(n, \Sigma)$ to be the collection of all functions of the form $\phi \colon \Sigma \to \mathbb{N}$ (where $\mathbb{N} = \{0, 1, 2, \ldots\}$) possessing the property

$$\sum_{a \in \Sigma} \phi(a) = n. \tag{7.12}$$

Each function $\phi \in \mathrm{Bag}(n, \Sigma)$ may be viewed as describing a *bag* containing a total of n objects, each labeled by a symbol from the alphabet Σ. For each $a \in \Sigma$, the value $\phi(a)$ specifies the number of objects in the bag that are labeled by a. The objects are not considered to be ordered within the bag – it is only the number of objects having each possible label that is indicated by the function ϕ. Equivalently, a function $\phi \in \mathrm{Bag}(n, \Sigma)$ may be interpreted as a description of a multiset of size exactly n with elements drawn from Σ.

An n-tuple $(a_1, \ldots, a_n) \in \Sigma^n$ is *consistent* with a function $\phi \in \mathrm{Bag}(n, \Sigma)$ if and only if

$$\phi(a) = |\{k \in \{1, \ldots, n\} : a = a_k\}| \tag{7.13}$$

for every $a \in \Sigma$. In words, $(a_1, \ldots, a_n)$ is consistent with ϕ if and only if $(a_1, \ldots, a_n)$ represents one possible ordering of the elements in the multiset specified by ϕ. For each $\phi \in \mathrm{Bag}(n, \Sigma)$, the set Σ_ϕ^n is defined as the subset of Σ^n containing those elements $(a_1, \ldots, a_n) \in \Sigma^n$ that are consistent with ϕ. This yields a partition of Σ^n, as each n-tuple $(a_1, \ldots, a_n) \in \Sigma^n$ is consistent with precisely one function $\phi \in \mathrm{Bag}(n, \Sigma)$. For any two n-tuples

$$(a_1, \ldots, a_n), (b_1, \ldots, b_n) \in \Sigma_\phi^n \tag{7.14}$$

that are consistent with the same function $\phi \in \mathrm{Bag}(n, \Sigma)$, there must exist at least one permutation $\pi \in S_n$ for which

$$(a_1, \ldots, a_n) = (b_{\pi(1)}, \ldots, b_{\pi(n)}). \tag{7.15}$$

The number of distinct functions $\phi \in \mathrm{Bag}(n, \Sigma)$ is given by the formula

$$|\mathrm{Bag}(n, \Sigma)| = \binom{|\Sigma| + n - 1}{|\Sigma| - 1}, \tag{7.16}$$

and for each $\phi \in \mathrm{Bag}(n, \Sigma)$ the number of distinct n-tuples within the subset Σ_ϕ^n is given by

$$|\Sigma_\phi^n| = \frac{n!}{\prod_{a \in \Sigma}(\phi(a)!)}. \tag{7.17}$$

As the following proposition establishes, an orthonormal basis for the symmetric subspace $\mathcal{X}^{\otimes n}$ may be obtained through the notions that were just introduced.

Proposition 7.2 *Let Σ be an alphabet, let n be a positive integer, and let $\mathcal{X} = \mathbb{C}^{\Sigma}$. Define a vector $u_{\phi} \in \mathcal{X}^{\otimes n}$ for each $\phi \in \mathrm{Bag}(n, \Sigma)$ as*

$$u_{\phi} = |\Sigma_{\phi}^{n}|^{-\frac{1}{2}} \sum_{(a_1, \ldots, a_n) \in \Sigma_{\phi}^{n}} e_{a_1} \otimes \cdots \otimes e_{a_n}. \tag{7.18}$$

The collection

$$\{u_{\phi} : \phi \in \mathrm{Bag}(n, \Sigma)\} \tag{7.19}$$

is an orthonormal basis for $\mathcal{X}^{\otimes n}$.

Proof It is evident that each vector u_{ϕ} is a unit vector. Moreover, for each choice of $\phi, \psi \in \mathrm{Bag}(n, \Sigma)$ with $\phi \neq \psi$, it holds that

$$\Sigma_{\phi}^{n} \cap \Sigma_{\psi}^{n} = \varnothing, \tag{7.20}$$

and therefore $\langle u_{\phi}, u_{\psi} \rangle = 0$, as each element $(a_1, \ldots, a_n) \in \Sigma^{n}$ is consistent with precisely one element of $\mathrm{Bag}(n, \Sigma)$. It therefore holds that (7.19) is an orthonormal set. As each vector u_{ϕ} is invariant under the action of W_{π} for every $\pi \in S_n$, it holds that

$$u_{\phi} \in \mathcal{X}^{\otimes n} \tag{7.21}$$

for every $\phi \in \mathrm{Bag}(n, \Sigma)$.

To complete the proof, it remains to prove that the set

$$\{u_{\phi} : \phi \in \mathrm{Bag}(n, \Sigma)\} \tag{7.22}$$

spans all of $\mathcal{X}^{\otimes n}$. This fact follows from the observation that, for every n-tuple $(a_1, \ldots, a_n) \in \Sigma^{n}$, it holds that

$$\Pi_{\mathcal{X}^{\otimes n}}(e_{a_1} \otimes \cdots \otimes e_{a_n})$$
$$= \frac{1}{n!} \sum_{\pi \in \mathcal{S}_n} W_{\pi}(e_{a_1} \otimes \cdots \otimes e_{a_n}) = |\Sigma_{\phi}^{n}|^{-\frac{1}{2}} u_{\phi}, \tag{7.23}$$

for the unique element $\phi \in \mathrm{Bag}(n, \Sigma)$ with which the n-tuple $(a_1, \ldots, a_n)$ is consistent. $\square$

Corollary 7.3 *Let $\mathcal{X}$ be a complex Euclidean space and let n be a positive integer. It holds that*

$$\dim(\mathcal{X}^{\textcircled{s}n}) = \binom{\dim(\mathcal{X}) + n - 1}{\dim(\mathcal{X}) - 1} = \binom{\dim(\mathcal{X}) + n - 1}{n}. \tag{7.24}$$

Example 7.4 Suppose $\Sigma = \{0, 1\}$, $\mathcal{X} = \mathbb{C}^{\Sigma}$, and $n = 3$. The following four vectors form an orthonormal basis of $\mathcal{X}^{\textcircled{s}3}$:

$$
\begin{aligned}
u_0 &= e_0 \otimes e_0 \otimes e_0, \\
u_1 &= \frac{1}{\sqrt{3}}(e_0 \otimes e_0 \otimes e_1 + e_0 \otimes e_1 \otimes e_0 + e_1 \otimes e_0 \otimes e_0), \\
u_2 &= \frac{1}{\sqrt{3}}(e_0 \otimes e_1 \otimes e_1 + e_1 \otimes e_0 \otimes e_1 + e_1 \otimes e_1 \otimes e_0), \\
u_3 &= e_1 \otimes e_1 \otimes e_1.
\end{aligned}
\tag{7.25}
$$

Tensor Power Spanning Sets for the Symmetric Subspace

It is evident that the inclusion

$$v^{\otimes n} \in \mathcal{X}^{\textcircled{s}n} \tag{7.26}$$

holds for every vector $v \in \mathcal{X}$. The following theorem demonstrates that the symmetric subspace $\mathcal{X}^{\textcircled{s}n}$ is, in fact, spanned by the set of all vectors having this form. This fact remains true when the entries of v are restricted to finite subsets of $\mathbb{C}$, provided that those sets are sufficiently large.

Theorem 7.5 *Let Σ be an alphabet, let n be a positive integer, and let $\mathcal{X} = \mathbb{C}^{\Sigma}$. For any set $\mathcal{A} \subseteq \mathbb{C}$ satisfying $|\mathcal{A}| \geq n + 1$ it holds that*

$$\mathrm{span}\left\{v^{\otimes n} : v \in \mathcal{A}^{\Sigma}\right\} = \mathcal{X}^{\textcircled{s}n}. \tag{7.27}$$

Theorem 7.5 can be proved in multiple ways. One proof makes use of the following elementary fact concerning multivariate polynomials.

Lemma 7.6 (Schwartz–Zippel) *Let P be a multivariate polynomial, with variables $Z_1, \ldots, Z_m$ and complex number coefficients, that is not identically zero and has total degree at most n, and let $\mathcal{A} \subset \mathbb{C}$ be a nonempty, finite set of complex numbers. It holds that*

$$\left|\left\{(\alpha_1, \ldots, \alpha_m) \in \mathcal{A}^m : P(\alpha_1, \ldots, \alpha_m) = 0\right\}\right| \leq n|\mathcal{A}|^{m-1}. \tag{7.28}$$

Proof The lemma is trivial in the case that $|\mathcal{A}| \leq n$, so it will be assumed that $|\mathcal{A}| \geq n + 1$ for the remainder of the proof, which is by induction on m. When $m = 1$, the lemma follows from the fact that a nonzero, univariate polynomial with degree at most n can have at most n roots.

Under the assumption that $m \geq 2$, one may write

$$P(Z_1, \ldots, Z_m) = \sum_{k=0}^{n} Q_k(Z_1, \ldots, Z_{m-1}) Z_m^k, \qquad (7.29)$$

for $Q_0, \ldots, Q_n$ being complex polynomials in variables $Z_1, \ldots, Z_{m-1}$, and with the total degree of Q_k being at most $n - k$ for each $k \in \{0, \ldots, n\}$. Fix k to be the largest value in the set $\{0, \ldots, n\}$ for which Q_k is nonzero. Given that P is nonzero, there must exist such a choice of k.

As Q_k has total degree at most $n - k$, it follows from the hypothesis of induction that

$$\left| \{ (\alpha_1, \ldots, \alpha_{m-1}) \in \mathcal{A}^{m-1} : Q_k(\alpha_1, \ldots, \alpha_{m-1}) \neq 0 \} \right|$$
$$\geq |\mathcal{A}|^{m-1} - (n-k)|\mathcal{A}|^{m-2}. \qquad (7.30)$$

For each choice of $(\alpha_1, \ldots, \alpha_{m-1}) \in \mathcal{A}^{m-1}$ for which $Q_k(\alpha_1, \ldots, \alpha_{m-1}) \neq 0$, it holds that

$$P(\alpha_1, \ldots, \alpha_{m-1}, Z_m) = \sum_{j=0}^{k} Q_j(\alpha_1, \ldots, \alpha_{m-1}) Z_m^j \qquad (7.31)$$

is a univariate polynomial of degree k in the variable Z_m, implying that there must exist at least $|\mathcal{A}| - k$ choices of $\alpha_m \in \mathcal{A}$ for which

$$P(\alpha_1, \ldots, \alpha_m) \neq 0. \qquad (7.32)$$

It follows that there are at least

$$\left(|\mathcal{A}|^{m-1} - (n-k)|\mathcal{A}|^{m-2} \right) \left(|\mathcal{A}| - k \right) \geq |\mathcal{A}|^m - n|\mathcal{A}|^{m-1} \qquad (7.33)$$

distinct m-tuples $(\alpha_1, \ldots, \alpha_m) \in \mathcal{A}^m$ for which $P(\alpha_1, \ldots, \alpha_m) \neq 0$, which completes the proof of the lemma. □

Remark   Although it is irrelevant to its use in proving Theorem 7.5, one may observe that Lemma 7.6 holds for P being a multivariate polynomial over any field, not just the field of complex numbers. This fact is established by the proof above, which has not used properties of the complex numbers that do not hold for arbitrary fields.

Proof of Theorem 7.5   For every choice of a permutation $\pi \in S_n$ and a vector $v \in \mathbb{C}^{\Sigma}$, it holds that

$$W_\pi v^{\otimes n} = v^{\otimes n}. \qquad (7.34)$$

It follows that $v^{\otimes n} \in \mathcal{X}^{\otimes n}$, and therefore

$$\text{span}\left\{ v^{\otimes n} : v \in \mathcal{A}^{\Sigma} \right\} \subseteq \mathcal{X}^{\otimes n}. \qquad (7.35)$$

To prove the reverse inclusion, let $w \in \mathcal{X}^{\otimes n}$ be any nonzero vector, and write

$$w = \sum_{\phi \in \mathrm{Bag}(n,\Sigma)} \alpha_\phi u_\phi, \tag{7.36}$$

for some collection of complex number coefficients $\{\alpha_\phi : \phi \in \mathrm{Bag}(n,\Sigma)\}$, with each vector u_ϕ being defined as in (7.18). It will be proved that

$$\langle w, v^{\otimes n} \rangle \neq 0 \tag{7.37}$$

for at least one choice of a vector $v \in \mathcal{A}^\Sigma$. The required inclusion follows from this fact, for if the containment (7.35) were proper, it would be possible to choose $w \in \mathcal{X}^{\otimes n}$ that is orthogonal to $v^{\otimes n}$ for every $v \in \mathcal{A}^\Sigma$.

For the remainder of the proof it will be assumed that $\mathcal{A}$ is a finite set, which causes no loss of generality, for if $\mathcal{A}$ were infinite, one could restrict their attention to an arbitrary finite subset of $\mathcal{A}$ having size at least $n + 1$, yielding the desired inclusion.

Define a multivariate polynomial

$$Q = \sum_{\phi \in \mathrm{Bag}(n,\Sigma)} \overline{\alpha_\phi} \sqrt{|\Sigma_\phi^n|} \prod_{a \in \Sigma} Z_a^{\phi(a)} \tag{7.38}$$

in a collection of variables $\{Z_a : a \in \Sigma\}$. As the monomials

$$\prod_{a \in \Sigma} Z_a^{\phi(a)} \tag{7.39}$$

are distinct as ϕ ranges over the elements of $\mathrm{Bag}(n,\Sigma)$, with each monomial having total degree n, it follows that Q is a nonzero polynomial with total degree n. A calculation reveals that

$$Q(v) = \langle w, v^{\otimes n} \rangle \tag{7.40}$$

for every vector $v \in \mathbb{C}^\Sigma$, where $Q(v)$ refers to the complex number obtained by the substitution of the value $v(a)$ for the variable Z_a in Q for each $a \in \Sigma$. As Q is a nonzero multivariate polynomial with total degree n, it follows from the Schwartz–Zippel lemma (Lemma 7.6) that $Q(v) = 0$ for at most

$$n|\mathcal{A}|^{|\Sigma|-1} < |\mathcal{A}|^{|\Sigma|} \tag{7.41}$$

choices of vectors $v \in \mathcal{A}^\Sigma$, implying that there exists at least one vector $v \in \mathcal{A}^\Sigma$ for which $\langle w, v^{\otimes n} \rangle \neq 0$, completing the proof. $\qquad\square$

The Anti-Symmetric Subspace

Along similar lines to the symmetric subspace $\mathcal{X}^{\oplus n}$ of the tensor product space $\mathcal{X}^{\otimes n}$, one may define the *anti-symmetric subspace* of the same tensor product space as

$$\mathcal{X}^{\oplus n} = \{x \in \mathcal{X}^{\otimes n} : W_\pi x = \operatorname{sign}(\pi) x \text{ for every } \pi \in S_n\}. \tag{7.42}$$

The short discussion on the anti-symmetric subspace that follows may, for the most part, be considered as an aside; with the exception of the case in which $n = 2$, the anti-symmetric subspace does not play a significant role elsewhere in this book. It is, nevertheless, natural to consider this subspace alongside of the symmetric subspace. The following propositions establish a few basic facts about the anti-symmetric subspace.

Proposition 7.7 *Let $\mathcal{X}$ be a complex Euclidean space and n a positive integer. The projection onto the anti-symmetric subspace $\mathcal{X}^{\oplus n}$ is given by*

$$\Pi_{\mathcal{X}^{\oplus n}} = \frac{1}{n!} \sum_{\pi \in S_n} \operatorname{sign}(\pi) W_\pi. \tag{7.43}$$

Proof The proof is similar to the proof of Proposition 7.1. Using (7.5), along with the fact that $\operatorname{sign}(\pi)\operatorname{sign}(\sigma) = \operatorname{sign}(\pi\sigma)$ for every choice of $\pi, \sigma \in S_n$, it may be verified that the operator

$$\Pi = \frac{1}{n!} \sum_{\pi \in S_n} \operatorname{sign}(\pi) W_\pi \tag{7.44}$$

is Hermitian and squares to itself, implying that it is a projection operator. For every $\pi \in S_n$ it holds that

$$W_\pi \Pi = \operatorname{sign}(\pi) \Pi, \tag{7.45}$$

from which it follows that

$$\operatorname{im}(\Pi) \subseteq \mathcal{X}^{\oplus n}. \tag{7.46}$$

For every vector $x \in \mathcal{X}^{\oplus n}$, it holds that $\Pi x = x$, implying that

$$\mathcal{X}^{\oplus n} \subseteq \operatorname{im}(\Pi). \tag{7.47}$$

As Π is a projection operator satisfying $\operatorname{im}(\Pi) = \mathcal{X}^{\oplus n}$, the proposition is proved. $\qquad\square$

When constructing an orthonormal basis of the anti-symmetric subspace $\mathcal{X}^{\otimes n}$, for $\mathcal{X} = \mathbb{C}^\Sigma$, it is convenient to assume that a total ordering of Σ has been fixed. For every n-tuple $(a_1, \ldots, a_n) \in \Sigma^n$ for which $a_1 < \cdots < a_n$, define a vector

$$u_{a_1, \ldots, a_n} = \frac{1}{\sqrt{n!}} \sum_{\pi \in S_n} \mathrm{sign}(\pi) W_\pi (e_{a_1} \otimes \cdots \otimes e_{a_n}). \tag{7.48}$$

Proposition 7.8 *Let Σ be an alphabet, let $n \geq 2$ be a positive integer, let $\mathcal{X} = \mathbb{C}^\Sigma$, and define $u_{a_1, \ldots, a_n} \in \mathcal{X}^{\otimes n}$ for each n-tuple $(a_1, \ldots, a_n) \in \Sigma^n$ satisfying $a_1 < \cdots < a_n$ as in (7.48). The collection*

$$\{u_{a_1, \ldots, a_n} : (a_1, \ldots, a_n) \in \Sigma^n, \ a_1 < \cdots < a_n\} \tag{7.49}$$

is an orthonormal basis for $\mathcal{X}^{\otimes n}$.

Proof Each vector $u_{a_1, \ldots, a_n}$ is evidently a unit vector, and is contained in the space $\mathcal{X}^{\otimes n}$. For distinct n-tuples $(a_1, \ldots, a_n)$ and $(b_1, \ldots, b_n)$ with $a_1 < \cdots < a_n$ and $b_1 < \cdots < b_n$ it holds that

$$\langle u_{a_1, \ldots, a_n}, u_{b_1, \ldots, b_n} \rangle = 0, \tag{7.50}$$

as these vectors are linear combinations of disjoint sets of standard basis vectors. It therefore remains to prove that the collection (7.49) spans $\mathcal{X}^{\otimes n}$.

For any choice of distinct indices $j, k \in \{1, \ldots, n\}$, and for $(j\ k) \in S_n$ being the permutation that swaps j and k, leaving all other elements of $\{1, \ldots, n\}$ fixed, one has

$$W_{(j\ k)} \Pi_{\mathcal{X}^{\otimes n}} = -\Pi_{\mathcal{X}^{\otimes n}} = \Pi_{\mathcal{X}^{\otimes n}} W_{(j\ k)}. \tag{7.51}$$

Consequently, for any choice of an n-tuple $(a_1, \ldots, a_n) \in \Sigma^n$ for which there exist distinct indices $j, k \in \{1, \ldots, n\}$ for which $a_j = a_k$, it holds that

$$\begin{aligned}
\Pi_{\mathcal{X}^{\otimes n}} (e_{a_1} \otimes \cdots \otimes e_{a_n}) &= \Pi_{\mathcal{X}^{\otimes n}} W_{(j\ k)} (e_{a_1} \otimes \cdots \otimes e_{a_n}) \\
&= -\Pi_{\mathcal{X}^{\otimes n}} (e_{a_1} \otimes \cdots \otimes e_{a_n}),
\end{aligned} \tag{7.52}$$

and therefore

$$\Pi_{\mathcal{X}^{\otimes n}} (e_{a_1} \otimes \cdots \otimes e_{a_n}) = 0. \tag{7.53}$$

On the other hand, if $(a_1, \ldots, a_n) \in \Sigma^n$ is an n-tuple for which $a_1, \ldots, a_n$ are distinct elements of Σ, it must hold that

$$(a_{\pi(1)}, \ldots, a_{\pi(n)}) = (b_1, \ldots, b_n) \tag{7.54}$$

for some choice of a permutation $\pi \in S_n$ and an n-tuple $(b_1, \ldots, b_n) \in \Sigma^n$

satisfying $b_1 < \cdots < b_n$. One therefore has

$$\Pi_{\mathcal{X}^{\otimes n}}(e_{a_1} \otimes \cdots \otimes e_{a_n}) = \Pi_{\mathcal{X}^{\otimes n}} W_\pi(e_{b_1} \otimes \cdots \otimes e_{b_n})$$

$$= \text{sign}(\pi)\Pi_{\mathcal{X}^{\otimes n}}(e_{b_1} \otimes \cdots \otimes e_{b_n}) = \frac{\text{sign}(\pi)}{\sqrt{n!}} u_{b_1,\dots,b_n}. \tag{7.55}$$

It therefore holds that

$$\text{im}(\Pi_{\mathcal{X}^{\otimes n}}) \subseteq \text{span}\{u_{a_1,\dots,a_n} : (a_1,\dots,a_n) \in \Sigma^n, \ a_1 < \cdots < a_n\}, \tag{7.56}$$

which completes the proof. $\qquad\qquad\qquad\qquad\qquad\qquad\qquad\qquad\qquad\square$

By the previous proposition, one has that the dimension of the anti-symmetric subspace is equal to the number of n-tuples $(a_1,\dots,a_n) \in \Sigma^n$ satisfying $a_1 < \cdots < a_n$. This number is equal to the number of subsets of Σ having n elements.

Corollary 7.9 *Let $\mathcal{X}$ be a complex Euclidean space and let n be a positive integer. It holds that*

$$\dim(\mathcal{X}^{\otimes n}) = \binom{\dim(\mathcal{X})}{n}. \tag{7.57}$$

7.1.2 The Algebra of Permutation-Invariant Operators

By its definition, the symmetric subspace $\mathcal{X}^{\otimes n}$ includes all vectors $x \in \mathcal{X}^{\otimes n}$ that are invariant under the action of W_π for each $\pi \in S_n$. One may consider a similar notion for operators, with the action $x \mapsto W_\pi x$ being replaced by the action

$$X \mapsto W_\pi X W_\pi^* \tag{7.58}$$

for each $X \in \mathrm{L}(\mathcal{X}^{\otimes n})$. The notation $\mathrm{L}(\mathcal{X})^{\otimes n}$ will be used to denote the set of operators X that are invariant under this action:

$$\mathrm{L}(\mathcal{X})^{\otimes n} = \{X \in \mathrm{L}(\mathcal{X}^{\otimes n}) : X = W_\pi X W_\pi^* \text{ for all } \pi \in S_n\}. \tag{7.59}$$

Similar to the analogous notion for vectors, one may denote this set as $\mathrm{L}(\mathcal{X}_1) \otimes \cdots \otimes \mathrm{L}(\mathcal{X}_n)$ when it is convenient to do this, under the assumption that the spaces $\mathcal{X}_1,\dots,\mathcal{X}_n$ have been identified with a single space $\mathcal{X}$.

Assuming that $\mathsf{X}_1,\dots,\mathsf{X}_n$ are registers sharing the same classical state set Σ, and identifying each of the spaces $\mathcal{X}_1,\dots,\mathcal{X}_n$ with $\mathcal{X} = \mathbb{C}^\Sigma$, one observes that the density operator elements of the set $\mathrm{L}(\mathcal{X})^{\otimes n}$ represent states of the compound register $(\mathsf{X}_1,\dots,\mathsf{X}_n)$ that are invariant under all permutations of the registers $\mathsf{X}_1,\dots,\mathsf{X}_n$. Such states are said to be *exchangeable*.

Algebraic properties of the set $L(\mathcal{X})^{\otimes n}$, along with a relationship between exchangeable states and permutation-invariant vectors, are described in the subsections that follow.

Vector Space Structure of the Permutation-Invariant Operators

The notation $L(\mathcal{X})^{\otimes n}$ is a natural choice for the space of all permutation-invariant operators; if one regards $L(\mathcal{X})$ as a vector space, then $L(\mathcal{X})^{\otimes n}$ indeed coincides with the symmetric subspace of the tensor product space $L(\mathcal{X})^{\otimes n}$. The next proposition formalizes this connection and states some immediate consequences of the results of the previous section.

Proposition 7.10 *Let $\mathcal{X}$ be a complex Euclidean space, let n be a positive integer, and let $X \in L(\mathcal{X}^{\otimes n})$. The following statements are equivalent:*

1. $X \in L(\mathcal{X})^{\otimes n}$.
2. *For $V \in U(\mathcal{X}^{\otimes n} \otimes \mathcal{X}^{\otimes n}, (\mathcal{X} \otimes \mathcal{X})^{\otimes n})$ being the isometry defined by the equation*

$$V \operatorname{vec}(Y_1 \otimes \cdots \otimes Y_n) = \operatorname{vec}(Y_1) \otimes \cdots \otimes \operatorname{vec}(Y_n) \qquad (7.60)$$

holding for all $Y_1, \ldots, Y_n \in L(\mathcal{X})$, one has that

$$V \operatorname{vec}(X) \in (\mathcal{X} \otimes \mathcal{X})^{\otimes n}. \qquad (7.61)$$

3. $X \in \operatorname{span}\{Y^{\otimes n} : Y \in L(\mathcal{X})\}$.

Proof For each permutation $\pi \in S_n$, let

$$U_\pi \in U((\mathcal{X} \otimes \mathcal{X})^{\otimes n}) \qquad (7.62)$$

be the unitary operator defined by the equation

$$U_\pi(w_1 \otimes \cdots \otimes w_n) = w_{\pi^{-1}(1)} \otimes \cdots \otimes w_{\pi^{-1}(n)} \qquad (7.63)$$

holding for all vectors $w_1, \ldots, w_n \in \mathcal{X} \otimes \mathcal{X}$. Each operator U_π is analogous to W_π, as defined in (7.3), but with the space $\mathcal{X}$ replaced by $\mathcal{X} \otimes \mathcal{X}$. It holds that

$$U_\pi = V(W_\pi \otimes W_\pi)V^* \qquad (7.64)$$

for every $\pi \in S_n$, from which one may conclude that the first and second statements are equivalent.

Theorem 7.5 implies that

$$V \operatorname{vec}(X) \in (\mathcal{X} \otimes \mathcal{X})^{\otimes n} \qquad (7.65)$$

if and only if

$$V \operatorname{vec}(X) \in \operatorname{span}\{\operatorname{vec}(Y)^{\otimes n} : Y \in \mathrm{L}(\mathcal{X})\}. \qquad (7.66)$$

The containment (7.66) is equivalent to

$$\operatorname{vec}(X) \in \operatorname{span}\{\operatorname{vec}(Y^{\otimes n}) : Y \in \mathrm{L}(\mathcal{X})\}, \qquad (7.67)$$

which in turn is equivalent to

$$X \in \operatorname{span}\{Y^{\otimes n} : Y \in \mathrm{L}(\mathcal{X})\}. \qquad (7.68)$$

The second and third statements are therefore equivalent. $\qquad \square$

Theorem 7.11 *Let $\mathcal{X}$ be a complex Euclidean space and let n be a positive integer. It holds that*

$$\mathrm{L}(\mathcal{X})^{\otimes n} = \operatorname{span}\{U^{\otimes n} : U \in \mathrm{U}(\mathcal{X})\}. \qquad (7.69)$$

Proof Let Σ be the alphabet for which $\mathcal{X} = \mathbb{C}^{\Sigma}$, and let

$$D = \operatorname{Diag}(u) \qquad (7.70)$$

be a diagonal operator, for an arbitrary choice of $u \in \mathcal{X}$. It holds that $u^{\otimes n} \in \mathcal{X}^{\otimes n}$, so by Theorem 7.5 one has that

$$u^{\otimes n} \in \operatorname{span}\{v^{\otimes n} : v \in \mathbb{T}^{\Sigma}\}, \qquad (7.71)$$

for $\mathbb{T} = \{\alpha \in \mathbb{C} : |\alpha| = 1\}$ denoting the set of complex units. It is therefore possible to write

$$u^{\otimes n} = \sum_{b \in \Gamma} \beta_b v_b^{\otimes n} \qquad (7.72)$$

for some choice of an alphabet Γ, vectors $\{v_b : b \in \Gamma\} \subset \mathbb{T}^{\Sigma}$, and complex numbers $\{\beta_b : b \in \Gamma\} \subset \mathbb{C}$. It follows that

$$D^{\otimes n} = \sum_{b \in \Gamma} \beta_b U_b^{\otimes n} \qquad (7.73)$$

for $U_b \in \mathrm{U}(\mathcal{X})$ being the unitary operator defined as

$$U_b = \operatorname{Diag}(v_b) \qquad (7.74)$$

for each $b \in \Gamma$.

Now, for an arbitrary operator $A \in \mathrm{L}(\mathcal{X})$, one may write $A = VDW$ for $V, W \in \mathrm{U}(\mathcal{X})$ being unitary operators and $D \in \mathrm{L}(\mathcal{X})$ being a diagonal operator, by Corollary 1.7 (to the singular value theorem). Invoking the argument above, one may assume that (7.73) holds, and therefore

$$A^{\otimes n} = \sum_{b \in \Gamma} \beta_b (VU_bW)^{\otimes n}, \qquad (7.75)$$

for some choice of an alphabet Γ, complex numbers $\{\beta_b : b \in \Gamma\} \subset \mathbb{C}$, and diagonal unitary operators $\{U_b : b \in \Gamma\}$. As VU_bW is unitary for each $b \in \Gamma$, one has

$$A^{\otimes n} \in \text{span}\{U^{\otimes n} : U \in \text{U}(\mathcal{X})\}, \tag{7.76}$$

so by Proposition 7.10 it follows that

$$\text{L}(\mathcal{X})^{\mathbb{Q}n} \subseteq \text{span}\{U^{\otimes n} : U \in \text{U}(\mathcal{X})\}. \tag{7.77}$$

The reverse containment is immediate, so the theorem is proved. $\quad\square$

Symmetric Purifications of Exchangeable Density Operators

A density operator $\rho \in \text{D}(\mathcal{X}^{\otimes n})$ is exchangeable if and only if $\rho \in \text{L}(\mathcal{X})^{\mathbb{Q}n}$, which is equivalent to

$$\rho = W_\pi \rho W_\pi^* \tag{7.78}$$

for every permutation $\pi \in S_n$. In operational terms, an exchangeable state ρ of a compound register $(\mathsf{X}_1, \ldots, \mathsf{X}_n)$, for n identical registers $\mathsf{X}_1, \ldots, \mathsf{X}_n$, is one that does not change if the contents of these n registers are permuted in an arbitrary way.

For every symmetric unit vector $u \in \mathcal{X}^{\mathbb{Q}n}$, one has that the pure state uu^* is exchangeable, and naturally any convex combination of such states must be exchangeable as well. In general, this does not exhaust all possible exchangeable states. For instance, the completely mixed state in $\text{D}(\mathcal{X}^{\otimes n})$ is exchangeable, but the image of the density operator corresponding to this state is generally not contained within the symmetric subspace.

There is, nevertheless, an interesting relationship between exchangeable states and symmetric pure states, which is that every exchangeable state can be purified in such a way that its purification lies within a larger symmetric subspace, in the sense described by the following theorem.

Theorem 7.12 *Let Σ and Γ be alphabets with $|\Gamma| \geq |\Sigma|$ and let n be a positive integer. Also let $\mathsf{X}_1, \ldots, \mathsf{X}_n$ be registers, each having classical state set Σ, let $\mathsf{Y}_1, \ldots, \mathsf{Y}_n$ be registers, each having classical state set Γ, and let $\rho \in \text{D}(\mathcal{X}_1 \otimes \cdots \otimes \mathcal{X}_n)$ be an exchangeable density operator. There exists a unit vector*

$$u \in (\mathcal{X}_1 \otimes \mathcal{Y}_1) \mathbb{Q} \cdots \mathbb{Q} (\mathcal{X}_n \otimes \mathcal{Y}_n) \tag{7.79}$$

such that

$$(uu^*)[\mathsf{X}_1, \ldots, \mathsf{X}_n] = \rho. \tag{7.80}$$

Proof Let $A \in U(\mathbb{C}^{\Sigma}, \mathbb{C}^{\Gamma})$ be an arbitrarily chosen isometry, which one may regard as an element of $U(\mathcal{X}_k, \mathcal{Y}_k)$ for any choice of $k \in \{1, \dots, n\}$. Also let

$$V \in U((\mathcal{X}_1 \otimes \cdots \otimes \mathcal{X}_n) \otimes (\mathcal{Y}_1 \otimes \cdots \otimes \mathcal{Y}_n),$$
$$(\mathcal{X}_1 \otimes \mathcal{Y}_1) \otimes \cdots \otimes (\mathcal{X}_n \otimes \mathcal{Y}_n)) \tag{7.81}$$

be the isometry defined by the equation

$$V \operatorname{vec}(B_1 \otimes \cdots \otimes B_n) = \operatorname{vec}(B_1) \otimes \cdots \otimes \operatorname{vec}(B_n), \tag{7.82}$$

holding for all choices of $B_1 \in L(\mathcal{Y}_1, \mathcal{X}_1), \dots, B_n \in L(\mathcal{Y}_n, \mathcal{X}_n)$. Equivalently, this isometry is defined by the equation

$$V((x_1 \otimes \cdots \otimes x_n) \otimes (y_1 \otimes \cdots \otimes y_n))$$
$$= (x_1 \otimes y_1) \otimes \cdots \otimes (x_n \otimes y_n), \tag{7.83}$$

holding for all vectors $x_1 \in \mathcal{X}_1, \dots, x_n \in \mathcal{X}_n$ and $y_1 \in \mathcal{Y}_1, \dots, y_n \in \mathcal{Y}_n$.
Consider the vector

$$u = V \operatorname{vec}(\sqrt{\rho}(A^* \otimes \cdots \otimes A^*)) \in (\mathcal{X}_1 \otimes \mathcal{Y}_1) \otimes \cdots \otimes (\mathcal{X}_n \otimes \mathcal{Y}_n). \tag{7.84}$$

A calculation reveals that

$$(uu^*)[\mathsf{X}_1, \dots, \mathsf{X}_n] = \rho, \tag{7.85}$$

and so it remains to prove that u is symmetric. Because ρ is exchangeable, one has

$$(W_\pi \sqrt{\rho} W_\pi^*)^2 = W_\pi \rho W_\pi^* = \rho \tag{7.86}$$

for every permutation $\pi \in \mathcal{S}_n$, and therefore

$$W_\pi \sqrt{\rho} W_\pi^* = \sqrt{\rho} \tag{7.87}$$

by the uniqueness of the square root. By Proposition 7.10, it therefore holds that

$$\sqrt{\rho} \in \operatorname{span}\{Y^{\otimes n} : Y \in L(\mathbb{C}^{\Sigma})\}. \tag{7.88}$$

Consequently, one has

$$u \in \operatorname{span}\left\{V \operatorname{vec}\left((YA^*)^{\otimes n}\right) : Y \in L(\mathbb{C}^{\Sigma})\right\}, \tag{7.89}$$

and therefore

$$u \in \operatorname{span}\left\{\operatorname{vec}(YA^*)^{\otimes n} : Y \in L(\mathbb{C}^{\Sigma})\right\}. \tag{7.90}$$

From this containment it is evident that

$$u \in (\mathcal{X}_1 \otimes \mathcal{Y}_1) \varoslash \cdots \varoslash (\mathcal{X}_n \otimes \mathcal{Y}_n), \tag{7.91}$$

which completes the proof. □

Von Neumann's Double Commutant Theorem

To establish further properties of the set $L(\mathcal{X})^{\otimes n}$, particularly ones relating to the operator structure of its elements, it is convenient to make use of a theorem known as *von Neumann's double commutant theorem*. (See equation (1.93) on page 17 for the definition of the commutant of a set of operators.) This theorem is stated below, and its proof will make use of the following lemma.

Lemma 7.13 *Let $\mathcal{X}$ be a complex Euclidean space, let $\mathcal{V} \subseteq \mathcal{X}$ be a subspace of $\mathcal{X}$, and let $A \in L(\mathcal{X})$ be an operator. The following two statements are equivalent:*

1. *It holds that both $A\mathcal{V} \subseteq \mathcal{V}$ and $A^*\mathcal{V} \subseteq \mathcal{V}$.*
2. *It holds that $[A, \Pi_\mathcal{V}] = 0$.*

Proof Assume first that statement 2 holds. If two operators commute, then their adjoints must also commute, and so one has the following for every vector $v \in \mathcal{V}$:

$$\begin{aligned} Av &= A\Pi_\mathcal{V} v = \Pi_\mathcal{V} Av \in \mathcal{V}, \\ A^*v &= A^*\Pi_\mathcal{V} v = \Pi_\mathcal{V} A^* v \in \mathcal{V}. \end{aligned} \tag{7.92}$$

It has been proved that statement 2 implies statement 1.

Now assume statement 1 holds. For every $v \in \mathcal{V}$, one has

$$\Pi_\mathcal{V} Av = Av = A\Pi_\mathcal{V} v, \tag{7.93}$$

by virtue of the fact that $Av \in \mathcal{V}$. For every $w \in \mathcal{X}$ with $w \perp \mathcal{V}$, it must hold that

$$\langle v, Aw \rangle = \langle A^* v, w \rangle = 0 \tag{7.94}$$

for every $v \in \mathcal{V}$, following from the assumption $A^*v \in \mathcal{V}$, and therefore $Aw \perp \mathcal{V}$. Consequently,

$$\Pi_\mathcal{V} Aw = 0 = A\Pi_\mathcal{V} w. \tag{7.95}$$

As every vector $u \in \mathcal{X}$ may be written as $u = v + w$ for some choice of $v \in \mathcal{V}$ and $w \in \mathcal{X}$ with $w \perp \mathcal{V}$, equations (7.93) and (7.95) imply

$$\Pi_\mathcal{V} Au = A\Pi_\mathcal{V} u \tag{7.96}$$

for every vector $u \in \mathcal{X}$, and therefore $\Pi_\mathcal{V} A = A\Pi_\mathcal{V}$. It has been proved that statement 1 implies statement 2, which completes the proof. $\square$

Theorem 7.14 (Von Neumann's double commutant theorem) *Let $\mathcal{A}$ be a self-adjoint, unital subalgebra of $L(\mathcal{X})$, for $\mathcal{X}$ being a complex Euclidean space. It holds that*

$$\mathrm{comm}(\mathrm{comm}(\mathcal{A})) = \mathcal{A}. \tag{7.97}$$

Proof It is immediate from the definition of the commutant that

$$\mathcal{A} \subseteq \mathrm{comm}(\mathrm{comm}(\mathcal{A})), \tag{7.98}$$

and so it remains to prove the reverse inclusion.

The key idea of the proof will be to consider the algebra $\mathrm{L}(\mathcal{X} \otimes \mathcal{X})$, and to make use of its relationships with $\mathrm{L}(\mathcal{X})$. Define $\mathcal{B} \subseteq \mathrm{L}(\mathcal{X} \otimes \mathcal{X})$ as

$$\mathcal{B} = \{X \otimes \mathbb{1} : X \in \mathcal{A}\}, \tag{7.99}$$

and let Σ be the alphabet for which $\mathcal{X} = \mathbb{C}^{\Sigma}$. Every operator $Y \in \mathrm{L}(\mathcal{X} \otimes \mathcal{X})$ may be written as

$$Y = \sum_{a,b \in \Sigma} Y_{a,b} \otimes E_{a,b} \tag{7.100}$$

for a unique choice of operators $\{Y_{a,b} : a, b \in \Sigma\} \subset \mathrm{L}(\mathcal{X})$. The condition

$$Y(X \otimes \mathbb{1}) = (X \otimes \mathbb{1})Y, \tag{7.101}$$

for any operator $X \in \mathrm{L}(\mathcal{X})$ and any operator Y having the form (7.100), is equivalent to $[Y_{a,b}, X] = 0$ for every choice of $a, b \in \Sigma$, and so it follows that

$$\mathrm{comm}(\mathcal{B}) = \left\{ \sum_{a,b \in \Sigma} Y_{a,b} \otimes E_{a,b} : \{Y_{a,b} : a, b \in \Sigma\} \subset \mathrm{comm}(\mathcal{A}) \right\}. \tag{7.102}$$

For a given operator $X \in \mathrm{comm}(\mathrm{comm}(\mathcal{A}))$, it is therefore evident that

$$X \otimes \mathbb{1} \in \mathrm{comm}(\mathrm{comm}(\mathcal{B})). \tag{7.103}$$

Now, define a subspace $\mathcal{V} \subseteq \mathcal{X} \otimes \mathcal{X}$ as

$$\mathcal{V} = \{\mathrm{vec}(X) : X \in \mathcal{A}\}, \tag{7.104}$$

and let $X \in \mathcal{A}$ be chosen arbitrarily. It holds that

$$(X \otimes \mathbb{1})\mathcal{V} \subseteq \mathcal{V}, \tag{7.105}$$

owing to the fact that $\mathcal{A}$ is an algebra. As $\mathcal{A}$ is self-adjoint, it follows that $X^* \in \mathcal{A}$, and therefore

$$(X^* \otimes \mathbb{1})\mathcal{V} \subseteq \mathcal{V}. \tag{7.106}$$

Lemma 7.13 therefore implies that

$$[X \otimes \mathbb{1}, \Pi_{\mathcal{V}}] = 0. \tag{7.107}$$

As $X \in \mathcal{A}$ was chosen arbitrarily, it follows that $\Pi_{\mathcal{V}} \in \mathrm{comm}(\mathcal{B})$.

Finally, let $X \in \mathrm{comm}(\mathrm{comm}(\mathcal{A}))$ be chosen arbitrarily. As was argued above, the inclusion (7.103) therefore holds, from which the commutation relation (7.107) follows. The reverse implication of Lemma 7.13 implies the containment (7.105). In particular, given that the subalgebra $\mathcal{A}$ is unital, one has $\mathrm{vec}(\mathbb{1}) \in \mathcal{V}$, and therefore

$$\mathrm{vec}(X) = (X \otimes \mathbb{1})\,\mathrm{vec}(\mathbb{1}) \in \mathcal{V}, \tag{7.108}$$

which implies $X \in \mathcal{A}$. The containment

$$\mathrm{comm}(\mathrm{comm}(\mathcal{A})) \subseteq \mathcal{A} \tag{7.109}$$

has therefore been proved, which completes the proof. $\qquad\square$

Operator Structure of the Permutation-Invariant Operators

With von Neumann's double commutant theorem in hand, one is prepared to prove the following fundamental theorem, which concerns the operator structure of the set $\mathrm{L}(\mathcal{X})^{\otimes n}$.

Theorem 7.15 *Let $\mathcal{X}$ be a complex Euclidean space, let n be a positive integer, and let $X \in \mathrm{L}(\mathcal{X}^{\otimes n})$ be an operator. The following statements are equivalent:*

1. *It holds that $[X, Y^{\otimes n}] = 0$ for all $Y \in \mathrm{L}(\mathcal{X})$.*
2. *It holds that $[X, U^{\otimes n}] = 0$ for all $U \in \mathrm{U}(\mathcal{X})$.*
3. *It holds that*

$$X = \sum_{\pi \in S_n} u(\pi) W_\pi \tag{7.110}$$

for some choice of a vector $u \in \mathbb{C}^{S_n}$.

Proof By Proposition 7.10 and Theorem 7.11, together with the bilinearity of the Lie bracket, the first and second statements are equivalent to the inclusion

$$X \in \mathrm{comm}\left(\mathrm{L}(\mathcal{X})^{\otimes n}\right). \tag{7.111}$$

For the set $\mathcal{A} \subseteq \mathrm{L}(\mathcal{X}^{\otimes n})$ defined as

$$\mathcal{A} = \left\{ \sum_{\pi \in S_n} u(\pi) W_\pi : u \in \mathbb{C}^{S_n} \right\}, \tag{7.112}$$

one has that the third statement is equivalent to the inclusion $X \in \mathcal{A}$. To prove the theorem, it therefore suffices to demonstrate that

$$\mathcal{A} = \mathrm{comm}\left(\mathrm{L}(\mathcal{X})^{\otimes n}\right). \tag{7.113}$$

For any operator $Z \in \mathrm{L}(\mathcal{X}^{\otimes n})$, it is evident from an inspection of (7.59) that $Z \in L(\mathcal{X})^{\otimes n}$ if and only if $[Z, W_\pi] = 0$ for each $\pi \in S_n$. Again using the bilinearity of the Lie bracket, it follows that

$$L(\mathcal{X})^{\otimes n} = \text{comm}(\mathcal{A}). \tag{7.114}$$

Finally, one observes that the set $\mathcal{A}$ forms a self-adjoint, unital subalgebra of $L(\mathcal{X}^{\otimes n})$. By Theorem 7.14, one has

$$\text{comm}(L(\mathcal{X})^{\otimes n}) = \text{comm}(\text{comm}(\mathcal{A})) = \mathcal{A}, \tag{7.115}$$

which establishes the relation (7.113), and therefore completes the proof. $\square$

7.2 Unitarily Invariant Probability Measures

Two probability measures having fundamental importance in the theory of quantum information are introduced in the present section: the *uniform spherical measure*, defined on the unit sphere $\mathcal{S}(\mathcal{X})$, and the *Haar measure*, defined on the set of unitary operators $U(\mathcal{X})$, for every complex Euclidean space $\mathcal{X}$. These measures are closely connected, and may both be defined in simple and concrete terms based on the standard Gaussian measure on the real line (q.v. Section 1.2.1).

7.2.1 Uniform Spherical Measure and Haar Measure

Definitions and basic properties of the uniform spherical measure and Haar measure are discussed below, starting with the uniform spherical measure.

Uniform Spherical Measure

Intuitively speaking, the uniform spherical measure provides a formalism through which one may consider a probability distribution over vectors in a complex Euclidean space that is uniform over the unit sphere. In more precise terms, the uniform spherical measure is a probability measure μ, defined on the Borel subsets of the unit sphere $\mathcal{S}(\mathcal{X})$ of a complex Euclidean space $\mathcal{X}$, that is invariant under the action of every unitary operator:

$$\mu(\mathcal{A}) = \mu(U\mathcal{A}) \tag{7.116}$$

for every $\mathcal{A} \in \text{Borel}(\mathcal{S}(\mathcal{X}))$ and $U \in U(\mathcal{X})$.[1] One concrete way of defining such a measure is as follows.

---

[1] Indeed, the measure μ is uniquely determined by these requirements. The fact that this is so will be verified through the use of the Haar measure, which is introduced below.

Definition 7.16 Let Σ be an alphabet, let $\{X_a : a \in \Sigma\} \cup \{Y_a : a \in \Sigma\}$ be a collection of independent and identically distributed standard normal random variables, and let $\mathcal{X} = \mathbb{C}^\Sigma$. Define a vector-valued random variable Z, taking values in $\mathcal{X}$, as

$$Z = \sum_{a \in \Sigma} (X_a + iY_a)e_a. \tag{7.117}$$

The *uniform spherical measure* μ on $\mathcal{S}(\mathcal{X})$ is the Borel probability measure

$$\mu : \mathrm{Borel}(\mathcal{S}(\mathcal{X})) \to [0,1] \tag{7.118}$$

defined as

$$\mu(\mathcal{A}) = \mathrm{Pr}(\alpha Z \in \mathcal{A} \text{ for some } \alpha > 0) \tag{7.119}$$

for every $\mathcal{A} \in \mathrm{Borel}(\mathcal{S}(\mathcal{X}))$.

The fact that the uniform spherical measure μ is a well-defined Borel probability measure follows from three observations. First, one has that

$$\{x \in \mathcal{X} : \alpha x \in \mathcal{A} \text{ for some } \alpha > 0\} = \mathrm{cone}(\mathcal{A}) \backslash \{0\} \tag{7.120}$$

is a Borel subset of $\mathcal{X}$ for every Borel subset $\mathcal{A}$ of $\mathcal{S}(\mathcal{X})$, which implies that μ is a well-defined function. Second, if $\mathcal{A}$ and $\mathcal{B}$ are disjoint Borel subsets of $\mathcal{S}(\mathcal{X})$, then $\mathrm{cone}(\mathcal{A}) \backslash \{0\}$ and $\mathrm{cone}(\mathcal{B}) \backslash \{0\}$ are also disjoint, from which it follows that μ is a measure. Finally, it holds that

$$\mu(\mathcal{S}(\mathcal{X})) = \mathrm{Pr}(Z \neq 0) = 1, \tag{7.121}$$

and therefore μ is a probability measure.

It is evident that this definition is independent of how one might choose to order the elements of the alphabet Σ. For this reason, the fundamentally interesting properties of the uniform spherical measure defined on $\mathcal{S}(\mathcal{X})$ will follow from the same properties of the uniform spherical measure on $\mathcal{S}(\mathbb{C}^n)$. In some cases, restricting one's attention to complex Euclidean spaces of the form $\mathbb{C}^n$ will offer conveniences, mostly concerning notational simplicity, that will therefore cause no loss of generality.

The unitary invariance of the uniform spherical measure follows directly from the rotational invariance of the standard Gaussian measure, as the proof of the following proposition reveals.

Proposition 7.17 *For every complex Euclidean space $\mathcal{X}$, the uniform spherical measure μ on $\mathcal{S}(\mathcal{X})$ is unitarily invariant:*

$$\mu(U\mathcal{A}) = \mu(\mathcal{A}) \tag{7.122}$$

for every $\mathcal{A} \in \mathrm{Borel}(\mathcal{S}(\mathcal{X}))$ and $U \in \mathrm{U}(\mathcal{X})$.

Proof   Assume that Σ is the alphabet for which $\mathcal{X} = \mathbb{C}^\Sigma$, and let

$$\{X_a : a \in \Sigma\} \cup \{Y_a : a \in \Sigma\} \tag{7.123}$$

be a collection of independent and identically distributed standard normal random variables. Define vector-valued random variables X and Y, taking values in $\mathbb{R}^\Sigma$, as

$$X = \sum_{a \in \Sigma} X_a e_a \quad \text{and} \quad Y = \sum_{a \in \Sigma} Y_a e_a, \tag{7.124}$$

so that the vector-valued random variable Z referred to in Definition 7.16 may be expressed as $Z = X + iY$. To prove the proposition, it suffices to observe that Z and UZ are identically distributed for every unitary operator $U \in \mathrm{U}(\mathcal{X})$, for then one has that

$$\mu(U^{-1}\mathcal{A}) = \mathrm{Pr}(\alpha U Z \in \mathcal{A} \text{ for some } \alpha > 0)$$
$$= \mathrm{Pr}(\alpha Z \in \mathcal{A} \text{ for some } \alpha > 0) = \mu(\mathcal{A}) \tag{7.125}$$

for every Borel subset $\mathcal{A}$ of $\mathcal{S}(\mathcal{X})$.

To verify that Z and UZ are identically distributed, for any choice of a unitary operator $U \in \mathrm{U}(\mathcal{X})$, note that

$$\begin{pmatrix} \Re(UZ) \\ \Im(UZ) \end{pmatrix} = \begin{pmatrix} \Re(U) & -\Im(U) \\ \Im(U) & \Re(U) \end{pmatrix} \begin{pmatrix} \Re(Z) \\ \Im(Z) \end{pmatrix}$$
$$= \begin{pmatrix} \Re(U) & -\Im(U) \\ \Im(U) & \Re(U) \end{pmatrix} \begin{pmatrix} X \\ Y \end{pmatrix}, \tag{7.126}$$

where $\Re(\cdot)$ and $\Im(\cdot)$ denote the entry-wise real and imaginary parts of operators and vectors, as a calculation reveals. The operator

$$\begin{pmatrix} \Re(U) & -\Im(U) \\ \Im(U) & \Re(U) \end{pmatrix} \tag{7.127}$$

is an orthogonal operator, while the vector-valued random variable $X \oplus Y$ is distributed with respect to the standard Gaussian measure on $\mathbb{R}^\Sigma \oplus \mathbb{R}^\Sigma$, and is therefore invariant under orthogonal transformations. It therefore follows that

$$X \oplus Y \quad \text{and} \quad \Re(UZ) \oplus \Im(UZ) \tag{7.128}$$

are identically distributed, which implies that Z and UZ are also identically distributed. $\square$

Haar Measure

Along similar lines to the uniform spherical measure, a unitarily invariant
Borel probability measure η, known as the *Haar measure*,[2] may be defined
on the set of unitary operators $U(\mathcal{X})$ acting on a given complex Euclidean
space $\mathcal{X}$. More specifically, this measure is invariant with respect to both
left and right multiplication by every unitary operator:

$$\eta(U\mathcal{A}) = \eta(\mathcal{A}) = \eta(\mathcal{A}U) \tag{7.129}$$

for every choice of $\mathcal{A} \in \text{Borel}(U(\mathcal{X}))$ and $U \in U(\mathcal{X})$.

Definition 7.18 Let Σ be an alphabet, let $\mathcal{X} = \mathbb{C}^\Sigma$, and let

$$\{X_{a,b} : a, b \in \Sigma\} \cup \{Y_{a,b} : a, b \in \Sigma\} \tag{7.130}$$

be a collection of independent and identically distributed standard normal
random variables. Define an operator-valued random variable Z, taking
values in $\text{L}(\mathcal{X})$, as

$$Z = \sum_{a,b \in \Sigma} (X_{a,b} + iY_{a,b}) E_{a,b}. \tag{7.131}$$

The *Haar measure* η on $U(\mathcal{X})$ is the Borel probability measure

$$\eta : \text{Borel}(U(\mathcal{X})) \to [0, 1] \tag{7.132}$$

defined as

$$\eta(\mathcal{A}) = \Pr(PZ \in \mathcal{A} \text{ for some } P \in \text{Pd}(\mathcal{X})) \tag{7.133}$$

for every $\mathcal{A} \in \text{Borel}(U(\mathcal{X}))$.

As the following theorem states, the Haar measure, as just defined, is
indeed a Borel probability measure.

Theorem 7.19 *Let $\eta : \text{Borel}(U(\mathcal{X})) \to [0, 1]$ be as in Definition 7.18,
for any choice of a complex Euclidean space $\mathcal{X}$. It holds that η is a Borel
probability measure.*

Proof For every $\mathcal{A} \in \text{Borel}(U(\mathcal{X}))$, define a set $\mathcal{R}(\mathcal{A}) \subseteq \text{L}(\mathcal{X})$ as

$$\mathcal{R}(\mathcal{A}) = \{QU : Q \in \text{Pd}(\mathcal{X}), U \in \mathcal{A}\}. \tag{7.134}$$

For any operator $X \in \text{L}(\mathcal{X})$, one has that $PX \in \mathcal{A}$ for some $P \in \text{Pd}(\mathcal{X})$ if
and only if $X \in \mathcal{R}(\mathcal{A})$. To prove that η is a Borel measure, it therefore suffices

---

[2] The term *Haar measure* often refers to a more general notion, which is that of a measure
defined on a certain class of groups that is invariant under the action of the group on which it
is defined. The definition presented here is a restriction of this notion to the group of unitary
operators acting on a given complex Euclidean space.

to prove that $\mathcal{R}(\mathcal{A})$ is a Borel subset of $\mathrm{L}(\mathcal{X})$ for every $\mathcal{A} \in \mathrm{Borel}(\mathrm{U}(\mathcal{X}))$, and that $\mathcal{R}(\mathcal{A})$ and $\mathcal{R}(\mathcal{B})$ are disjoint provided that $\mathcal{A}$ and $\mathcal{B}$ are disjoint.

The first of these requirements follows from the observation that the set $\mathrm{Pd}(\mathcal{X}) \times \mathcal{A}$ is a Borel subset of $\mathrm{Pd}(\mathcal{X}) \times \mathrm{U}(\mathcal{X})$, with respect to the product topology on the Cartesian product of these sets, together with the fact that operator multiplication is a continuous mapping.

For the second requirement, one observes that if

$$Q_0 U_0 = Q_1 U_1 \tag{7.135}$$

for some choice of $Q_0, Q_1 \in \mathrm{Pd}(\mathcal{X})$ and $U_0, U_1 \in \mathrm{U}(\mathcal{X})$, then it must hold that $Q_0 = Q_1 V$ for V being unitary. Therefore

$$Q_0^2 = Q_1 V V^* Q_1 = Q_1^2, \tag{7.136}$$

which implies that $Q_0 = Q_1$ by the fact that positive semidefinite operators have unique square roots. It therefore holds that $U_0 = U_1$. Consequently, if $\mathcal{R}(\mathcal{A}) \cap \mathcal{R}(\mathcal{B})$ is nonempty, then the same is true of $\mathcal{A} \cap \mathcal{B}$.

It remains to prove that η is a probability measure. Assume that Σ is the alphabet for which $\mathcal{X} = \mathbb{C}^{\Sigma}$, let

$$\{X_{a,b} : a, b \in \Sigma\} \cup \{Y_{a,b} : a, b \in \Sigma\} \tag{7.137}$$

be a collection of independent and identically distributed standard normal random variables, and define an operator-valued random variable

$$Z = \sum_{a,b \in \Sigma} (X_{a,b} + i Y_{a,b}) E_{a,b}, \tag{7.138}$$

as in Definition 7.18. It holds that $PZ \in \mathrm{U}(\mathcal{X})$ for some positive definite operator $P \in \mathrm{Pd}(\mathcal{X})$ if and only if Z is nonsingular, and therefore

$$\eta(\mathrm{U}(\mathcal{X})) = \mathrm{Pr}(\mathrm{Det}(Z) \neq 0). \tag{7.139}$$

An operator is singular if and only if its column vectors form a linearly dependent set, and therefore $\mathrm{Det}(Z) = 0$ if and only if there exists a symbol $b \in \Sigma$ such that

$$\sum_{a \in \Sigma} (X_{a,b} + i Y_{a,b}) e_a \in \mathrm{span}\left\{ \sum_{a \in \Sigma} (X_{a,c} + i Y_{a,c}) e_a : c \in \Sigma \backslash \{b\} \right\}. \tag{7.140}$$

The subspace referred to in this equation is necessarily a proper subspace of $\mathcal{X}$, because its dimension is at most $|\Sigma| - 1$, and therefore the event (7.140) occurs with probability zero. By the union bound, one has that $\mathrm{Det}(Z) = 0$ with probability zero, as is implied by Proposition 1.17, and therefore $\eta(\mathrm{U}(\mathcal{X})) = 1$. $\square$

The following proposition establishes that the Haar measure is unitarily invariant, in the sense specified by (7.129).

Proposition 7.20 *Let $\mathcal{X}$ be a complex Euclidean space. The Haar measure η on $\mathrm{U}(\mathcal{X})$ satisfies*

$$\eta(U\mathcal{A}) = \eta(\mathcal{A}) = \eta(\mathcal{A}U) \tag{7.141}$$

for every $\mathcal{A} \in \mathrm{Borel}(\mathrm{U}(\mathcal{X}))$ and $U \in \mathrm{U}(\mathcal{X})$.

Proof Assume that Σ is the alphabet for which $\mathcal{X} = \mathbb{C}^{\Sigma}$, let

$$\{X_{a,b} \colon a, b \in \Sigma\} \cup \{Y_{a,b} \colon a, b \in \Sigma\} \tag{7.142}$$

be a collection of independent and identically distributed standard normal random variables, and let

$$Z = \sum_{a,b \in \Sigma} (X_{a,b} + iY_{a,b}) E_{a,b}, \tag{7.143}$$

as in Definition 7.18.

Suppose that $\mathcal{A}$ is a Borel subset of $\mathrm{U}(\mathcal{X})$ and $U \in \mathrm{U}(\mathcal{X})$ is any unitary operator. To prove the left unitary invariance of η, it suffices to prove that Z and UZ are identically distributed, and to prove the right unitary invariance of η, it suffices to prove that Z and ZU are identically distributed, for then one has

$$\begin{aligned} \eta(U\mathcal{A}) &= \mathrm{Pr}(U^{-1}PZ \in \mathcal{A} \text{ for some } P \in \mathrm{Pd}(\mathcal{X})) \\ &= \mathrm{Pr}((U^{-1}PU)Z \in \mathcal{A} \text{ for some } P \in \mathrm{Pd}(\mathcal{X})) = \eta(\mathcal{A}) \end{aligned} \tag{7.144}$$

and

$$\begin{aligned} \eta(\mathcal{A}U) &= \mathrm{Pr}(PZU^{-1} \in \mathcal{A} \text{ for some } P \in \mathrm{Pd}(\mathcal{X})) \\ &= \mathrm{Pr}(PZ \in \mathcal{A} \text{ for some } P \in \mathrm{Pd}(\mathcal{X})) = \eta(\mathcal{A}). \end{aligned} \tag{7.145}$$

The fact that UZ, Z, and ZU are identically distributed follows, through essentially the same argument as the one used to prove Proposition 7.17, from the invariance of the standard Gaussian measure under orthogonal transformations. $\square$

For every complex Euclidean space, one has that the Haar measure η on $\mathrm{U}(\mathcal{X})$ is the unique Borel probability measure that is both left and right unitarily invariant. Indeed, any Borel probability measure on $\mathrm{U}(\mathcal{X})$ that is either left unitarily invariant or right unitarily invariant must necessarily be equal to the Haar measure, as the following theorem reveals.

Theorem 7.21   *Let $\mathcal{X}$ be a complex Euclidean space and let*

$$\nu: \mathrm{Borel}(\mathrm{U}(\mathcal{X})) \to [0, 1] \tag{7.146}$$

be a Borel probability measure that possesses either of the following two properties:

1. *Left unitary invariance: $\nu(U\mathcal{A}) = \nu(\mathcal{A})$ for all Borel subsets $\mathcal{A} \subseteq \mathrm{U}(\mathcal{X})$ and all unitary operators $U \in \mathrm{U}(\mathcal{X})$.*
2. *Right unitary invariance: $\nu(\mathcal{A}U) = \nu(\mathcal{A})$ for all Borel subsets $\mathcal{A} \subseteq \mathrm{U}(\mathcal{X})$ and all unitary operators $U \in \mathrm{U}(\mathcal{X})$.*

It holds that ν is equal to the Haar measure $\eta: \mathrm{Borel}(\mathrm{U}(\mathcal{X})) \to [0, 1]$.

Proof   It will be assumed that ν is left unitarily invariant; the case in which ν is right unitarily invariant is proved through a similar argument. Let $\mathcal{A}$ be an arbitrary Borel subset of $\mathrm{U}(\mathcal{X})$, and let f denote the characteristic function of $\mathcal{A}$:

$$f(U) = \begin{cases} 1 & \text{if } U \in \mathcal{A} \\ 0 & \text{if } U \notin \mathcal{A} \end{cases} \tag{7.147}$$

for every $U \in \mathrm{U}(\mathcal{X})$. One has that

$$\nu(\mathcal{A}) = \int f(U)\,\mathrm{d}\nu(U) = \int f(VU)\,\mathrm{d}\nu(U) \tag{7.148}$$

for every unitary operator $V \in \mathrm{U}(\mathcal{X})$ by the left unitary invariance of ν. Integrating over all unitary operators V with respect to the Haar measure η yields

$$\nu(\mathcal{A}) = \iint f(VU)\,\mathrm{d}\nu(U)\,\mathrm{d}\eta(V) = \iint f(VU)\,\mathrm{d}\eta(V)\,\mathrm{d}\nu(U), \tag{7.149}$$

where the change in the order of integration is made possible by Fubini's theorem. By the right unitary invariance of the Haar measure, it follows that

$$\nu(\mathcal{A}) = \iint f(V)\,\mathrm{d}\eta(V)\,\mathrm{d}\nu(U) = \int f(V)\,\mathrm{d}\eta(V) = \eta(\mathcal{A}). \tag{7.150}$$

As $\mathcal{A}$ was chosen arbitrarily, it follows that $\nu = \eta$, as required. $\square$

The Haar measure and uniform spherical measure are closely related, as the following theorem indicates. The proof uses the same methodology as the proof of the previous theorem.

Theorem 7.22 *Let $\mathcal{X}$ be a complex Euclidean space, let μ denote the uniform spherical measure on $\mathcal{S}(\mathcal{X})$, and let η denote the Haar measure on $\mathrm{U}(\mathcal{X})$. For every $\mathcal{A} \in \mathrm{Borel}(\mathcal{S}(\mathcal{X}))$ and $x \in \mathcal{S}(\mathcal{X})$, it holds that*

$$\mu(\mathcal{A}) = \eta(\{U \in \mathrm{U}(\mathcal{X}): Ux \in \mathcal{A}\}). \tag{7.151}$$

Proof Let $\mathcal{A}$ be any Borel subset of $\mathcal{S}(\mathcal{X})$ and let f denote the characteristic function of $\mathcal{A}$:

$$f(y) = \begin{cases} 1 & \text{if } y \in \mathcal{A} \\ 0 & \text{if } y \notin \mathcal{A} \end{cases} \tag{7.152}$$

for every $y \in \mathcal{S}(\mathcal{X})$. It holds that

$$\mu(\mathcal{A}) = \int f(y) \, \mathrm{d}\mu(y) = \int f(Uy) \, \mathrm{d}\mu(y) \tag{7.153}$$

for every $U \in \mathrm{U}(\mathcal{X})$, by the unitary invariance of the uniform spherical measure. Integrating over all $U \in \mathrm{U}(\mathcal{X})$ with respect to the Haar measure and changing the order of integration by means of Fubini's theorem yields

$$\mu(\mathcal{A}) = \iint f(Uy) \, \mathrm{d}\mu(y) \, \mathrm{d}\eta(U) = \iint f(Uy) \, \mathrm{d}\eta(U) \, \mathrm{d}\mu(y). \tag{7.154}$$

Now, for any fixed choice of unit vectors $x, y \in \mathcal{S}(\mathcal{X})$, one may choose a unitary operator $V \in \mathrm{U}(\mathcal{X})$ for which it holds that $Vy = x$. By the right unitary invariance of the Haar measure, one has

$$\int f(Uy) \, \mathrm{d}\eta(U) = \int f(UVy) \, \mathrm{d}\eta(U) = \int f(Ux) \, \mathrm{d}\eta(U). \tag{7.155}$$

Consequently,

$$\begin{aligned} \mu(\mathcal{A}) &= \iint f(Uy) \, \mathrm{d}\eta(U) \, \mathrm{d}\mu(y) = \iint f(Ux) \, \mathrm{d}\eta(U) \, \mathrm{d}\mu(y) \\ &= \int f(Ux) \, \mathrm{d}\eta(U) = \eta(\{U \in \mathrm{U}(\mathcal{X}): Ux \in \mathcal{A}\}), \end{aligned} \tag{7.156}$$

as required. $\qquad\square$

Noting that the proof of the previous theorem has not made use of any properties of the measure μ aside from the fact that it is normalized and unitarily invariant, one obtains the following corollary.

Corollary 7.23 *Let $\mathcal{X}$ be a complex Euclidean space and let*

$$\nu: \mathrm{Borel}(\mathcal{S}(\mathcal{X})) \to [0, 1] \tag{7.157}$$

be a Borel probability measure that is unitarily invariant: $\nu(U\mathcal{A}) = \nu(\mathcal{A})$ for every Borel subset $\mathcal{A} \subseteq \mathcal{S}(\mathcal{X})$. It holds that ν is equal to the uniform spherical measure $\mu: \mathrm{Borel}(\mathcal{S}(\mathcal{X})) \to [0, 1]$.

Evaluating Integrals by Means of Symmetries

Some integrals defined with respect to the uniform spherical measure or Haar measure may be evaluated by considering the symmetries present in those integrals. For example, for Σ being any alphabet and μ denoting the uniform spherical measure on $\mathcal{S}(\mathbb{C}^\Sigma)$, one has that

$$\int uu^* \, d\mu(u) = \frac{\mathbb{1}}{|\Sigma|}. \tag{7.158}$$

This is so because the operator represented by the integral is necessarily positive semidefinite, has unit trace, and is invariant under conjugation by every unitary operator; $\mathbb{1}/|\Sigma|$ is the only operator having these properties.

The following lemma establishes a generalization of this fact, providing an alternative description of the projection onto the symmetric subspace defined in Section 7.1.1.

Lemma 7.24 *Let $\mathcal{X}$ be a complex Euclidean space, let n be a positive integer, and let μ denote the uniform spherical measure on $\mathcal{S}(\mathcal{X})$. It holds that*

$$\Pi_{\mathcal{X}^{\otimes n}} = \dim(\mathcal{X}^{\otimes n}) \int (uu^*)^{\otimes n} \, d\mu(u). \tag{7.159}$$

Proof Let

$$P = \dim(\mathcal{X}^{\otimes n}) \int (uu^*)^{\otimes n} \, d\mu(u), \tag{7.160}$$

and note first that

$$\mathrm{Tr}(P) = \dim(\mathcal{X}^{\otimes n}), \tag{7.161}$$

as μ is a normalized measure.

Next, by the unitary invariance of the uniform spherical measure, one has that $[P, U^{\otimes n}] = 0$ for every $U \in \mathrm{U}(\mathcal{X})$. By Theorem 7.15, it follows that

$$P = \sum_{\pi \in S_n} v(\pi) W_\pi \tag{7.162}$$

for some choice of a vector $v \in \mathbb{C}^{S_n}$. Using the fact that $u^{\otimes n} \in \mathcal{X}^{\otimes n}$ for every unit vector $u \in \mathbb{C}^\Sigma$, one necessarily has that

$$\Pi_{\mathcal{X}^{\otimes n}} P = P, \tag{7.163}$$

which implies

$$
P = \frac{1}{n!} \sum_{\sigma \in S_n} W_\sigma \sum_{\pi \in S_n} v(\pi) W_\pi = \frac{1}{n!} \sum_{\pi \in S_n} \sum_{\sigma \in S_n} v(\sigma^{-1}\pi) W_\pi
$$

$$
= \frac{1}{n!} \sum_{\sigma \in S_n} v(\sigma) \sum_{\pi \in S_n} W_\pi = \sum_{\sigma \in S_n} v(\sigma) \Pi_{\mathcal{X}^{\otimes n}}
$$

(7.164)

by Proposition 7.1. By (7.161), one has

$$
\sum_{\sigma \in S_n} v(\sigma) = 1,
$$

(7.165)

and therefore $P = \Pi_{\mathcal{X}^{\otimes n}}$, as required. $\qquad\square$

The following example represents a continuation of Example 6.10. Two channels that have a close connection to the classes of Werner states and isotropic states are analyzed based on properties of their symmetries.

Example 7.25 As in Example 6.10, let Σ be an alphabet, let $n = |\Sigma|$, and let $\mathcal{X} = \mathbb{C}^\Sigma$, and recall the four projection operators[3]

$$
\Delta_0, \Delta_1, \Pi_0, \Pi_1 \in \operatorname{Proj}(\mathcal{X} \otimes \mathcal{X})
$$

(7.166)

defined in that example:

$$
\Delta_0 = \frac{1}{n} \sum_{a,b \in \Sigma} E_{a,b} \otimes E_{a,b},
$$

(7.167)

$$
\Delta_1 = \mathbb{1} \otimes \mathbb{1} - \frac{1}{n} \sum_{a,b \in \Sigma} E_{a,b} \otimes E_{a,b},
$$

(7.168)

$$
\Pi_0 = \frac{1}{2} \mathbb{1} \otimes \mathbb{1} + \frac{1}{2} \sum_{a,b \in \Sigma} E_{a,b} \otimes E_{b,a},
$$

(7.169)

$$
\Pi_1 = \frac{1}{2} \mathbb{1} \otimes \mathbb{1} - \frac{1}{2} \sum_{a,b \in \Sigma} E_{a,b} \otimes E_{b,a}.
$$

(7.170)

Equivalently, one may write

$$
\Delta_0 = \frac{1}{n}(\mathrm{T} \otimes \mathbb{1}_{\mathrm{L}(\mathcal{X})})(W), \qquad\qquad \Pi_0 = \frac{1}{2}\mathbb{1} \otimes \mathbb{1} + \frac{1}{2}W,
$$

(7.171)

$$
\Delta_1 = \mathbb{1} \otimes \mathbb{1} - \frac{1}{n}(\mathrm{T} \otimes \mathbb{1}_{\mathrm{L}(\mathcal{X})})(W), \quad \Pi_1 = \frac{1}{2}\mathbb{1} \otimes \mathbb{1} - \frac{1}{2}W,
$$

(7.172)

---

[3] Using the notation introduced in Section 7.1.1, one may alternatively write $\Pi_0 = \Pi_{\mathcal{X} \otimes \mathcal{X}}$ and $\Pi_1 = \Pi_{\mathcal{X} \otimes \mathcal{X}}$. The notations Π_0 and Π_1 will be used within this example to maintain consistency with Example 6.10.

for $T(X) = X^{\mathsf{T}}$ denoting the transpose mapping on $L(\mathcal{X})$ and

$$W = \sum_{a,b \in \Sigma} E_{a,b} \otimes E_{b,a}, \tag{7.173}$$

which is the swap operator on $\mathcal{X} \otimes \mathcal{X}$. States of the form

$$\lambda \Delta_0 + (1-\lambda)\frac{\Delta_1}{n^2 - 1} \quad \text{and} \quad \lambda \frac{\Pi_0}{\binom{n+1}{2}} + (1-\lambda)\frac{\Pi_1}{\binom{n}{2}}, \tag{7.174}$$

for $\lambda \in [0, 1]$, were introduced in Example 6.10 as *isotropic states* and *Werner states*, respectively.

Now, consider the channel $\Xi \in C(\mathcal{X} \otimes \mathcal{X})$ defined as

$$\Xi(X) = \int (U \otimes U) X (U \otimes U)^* \, d\eta(U) \tag{7.175}$$

for all $X \in L(\mathcal{X} \otimes \mathcal{X})$, for η denoting the Haar measure on $U(\mathcal{X})$. By the unitary invariance of the Haar measure, one has that $[\Xi(X), U \otimes U] = 0$ for every $X \in L(\mathcal{X} \otimes \mathcal{X})$ and $U \in U(\mathcal{X})$. By Theorem 7.15 it holds that

$$\Xi(X) \in \mathrm{span}\{\mathbb{1} \otimes \mathbb{1}, W\} = \mathrm{span}\{\Pi_0, \Pi_1\}, \tag{7.176}$$

and it must therefore hold that

$$\Xi(X) = \alpha(X)\,\Pi_0 + \beta(X)\,\Pi_1 \tag{7.177}$$

for $\alpha(X), \beta(X) \in \mathbb{C}$ being complex numbers depending linearly on X. The channel Ξ is self-adjoint and satisfies $\Xi(\mathbb{1} \otimes \mathbb{1}) = \mathbb{1} \otimes \mathbb{1}$ and $\Xi(W) = W$, so that $\Xi(\Pi_0) = \Pi_0$ and $\Xi(\Pi_1) = \Pi_1$. The following two equations hold:

$$\begin{aligned}
\alpha(X) &= \frac{1}{\binom{n+1}{2}}\langle \Pi_0, \Xi(X) \rangle = \frac{1}{\binom{n+1}{2}}\langle \Xi(\Pi_0), X \rangle = \frac{1}{\binom{n+1}{2}}\langle \Pi_0, X \rangle, \\
\beta(X) &= \frac{1}{\binom{n}{2}}\langle \Pi_1, \Xi(X) \rangle = \frac{1}{\binom{n}{2}}\langle \Xi(\Pi_1), X \rangle = \frac{1}{\binom{n}{2}}\langle \Pi_1, X \rangle.
\end{aligned} \tag{7.178}$$

It therefore follows that

$$\Xi(X) = \frac{1}{\binom{n+1}{2}}\langle \Pi_0, X \rangle \Pi_0 + \frac{1}{\binom{n}{2}}\langle \Pi_1, X \rangle \Pi_1. \tag{7.179}$$

It is evident from this expression that, on any density operator input, the output of Ξ is a Werner state, and moreover every Werner state is fixed by this channel. The channel Ξ is sometimes called a *Werner twirling channel*.

A different but closely related channel $\Lambda \in C(\mathcal{X} \otimes \mathcal{X})$ is defined as

$$\Lambda(X) = \int (U \otimes \overline{U}) X (U \otimes \overline{U})^* \, d\eta(U) \tag{7.180}$$

for all $X \in L(\mathcal{X} \otimes \mathcal{X})$, where η again denotes the Haar measure on $U(\mathcal{X})$.

An alternative expression of this channel may be obtained by making use of the analysis of the channel Ξ presented above. The first step of this process is to observe that Λ may be obtained by composing the channel Ξ with the partial transpose in the following way:

$$\Lambda = (\mathbb{1}_{\mathrm{L}(\mathcal{X})} \otimes \mathrm{T}) \, \Xi \, (\mathbb{1}_{\mathrm{L}(\mathcal{X})} \otimes \mathrm{T}). \tag{7.181}$$

Then, using the identities

$$(\mathbb{1}_{\mathrm{L}(\mathcal{X})} \otimes \mathrm{T})(\Pi_0) = \frac{n+1}{2}\Delta_0 + \frac{1}{2}\Delta_1,$$

$$(\mathbb{1}_{\mathrm{L}(\mathcal{X})} \otimes \mathrm{T})(\Pi_1) = -\frac{n-1}{2}\Delta_0 + \frac{1}{2}\Delta_1, \tag{7.182}$$

one finds that

$$\Lambda(X) = \langle \Delta_0, X \rangle \Delta_0 + \frac{1}{n^2 - 1} \langle \Delta_1, X \rangle \Delta_1. \tag{7.183}$$

On any density operator input, the output of the channel Λ is an isotropic state, and moreover every isotropic state is fixed by Λ. The channel Λ is sometimes called an *isotropic twirling channel*.

It is evident from the specification of the channels Ξ and Λ that one has the following expressions, in which Φ_U denotes the unitary channel defined by $\Phi_U(X) = UXU^*$ for each $X \in \mathrm{L}(\mathcal{X})$:

$$\Xi \in \mathrm{conv}\{\Phi_U \otimes \Phi_U : U \in \mathrm{U}(\mathcal{X})\},$$

$$\Lambda \in \mathrm{conv}\{\Phi_U \otimes \Phi_{\overline{U}} : U \in \mathrm{U}(\mathcal{X})\}. \tag{7.184}$$

It follows that Ξ and Λ are mixed-unitary channels, and LOCC channels as well. Indeed, both channels can be implemented without communication – local operations and shared randomness are sufficient.

Finally, for any choice of orthogonal unit vectors $u, v \in \mathcal{X}$, the following equalities may be observed:

$$\langle \Pi_0, uu^* \otimes vv^* \rangle = \frac{1}{2}, \quad \langle \Pi_1, uu^* \otimes vv^* \rangle = \frac{1}{2},$$

$$\langle \Pi_0, uu^* \otimes uu^* \rangle = 1, \quad \langle \Pi_1, uu^* \otimes uu^* \rangle = 0. \tag{7.185}$$

Therefore, for every choice of $\alpha \in [0, 1]$, one has

$$\Xi(uu^* \otimes (\alpha uu^* + (1 - \alpha)vv^*)) = \frac{1+\alpha}{2} \frac{\Pi_0}{\binom{n+1}{2}} + \frac{1-\alpha}{2} \frac{\Pi_1}{\binom{n}{2}}. \tag{7.186}$$

As Ξ is a separable channel and

$$uu^* \otimes (\alpha uu^* + (1 - \alpha)vv^*) \in \mathrm{SepD}(\mathcal{X} : \mathcal{X}) \tag{7.187}$$

is a separable state, for every $\alpha \in [0, 1]$, it follows that the state (7.186) is also separable. Equivalently, the Werner state

$$\lambda \frac{\Pi_0}{\binom{n+1}{2}} + (1 - \lambda) \frac{\Pi_1}{\binom{n}{2}} \tag{7.188}$$

is separable for all $\lambda \in [1/2, 1]$. The partial transpose of the state (7.188) is

$$\frac{2\lambda - 1}{n} \Delta_0 + \left(1 - \frac{2\lambda - 1}{n}\right) \frac{\Delta_1}{n^2 - 1}. \tag{7.189}$$

Assuming $\lambda \in [1/2, 1]$, the state (7.188) is separable, and therefore its partial transpose is also separable. It follows that the isotropic state

$$\lambda \Delta_0 + (1 - \lambda) \frac{\Delta_1}{n^2 - 1} \tag{7.190}$$

is separable for all $\lambda \in [0, 1/n]$.

7.2.2 Applications of Unitarily Invariant Measures

There are many applications of integration with respect to the uniform spherical measure and Haar measure in quantum information theory. Three examples are presented below, and some additional examples involving the phenomenon of *measure concentration* are presented in Section 7.3.2.

The Quantum de Finetti Theorem

Intuitively speaking, the quantum de Finetti theorem states that if the state of a collection of identical registers is exchangeable, then the reduced state of any comparatively small number of these registers must be close to a convex combination of identical product states. This theorem will first be stated and proved for symmetric pure states, and from this theorem a more general statement for arbitrary exchangeable states may be derived using Theorem 7.12.

Theorem 7.26   *Let Σ be an alphabet, let n be a positive integer, and let $\mathsf{X}_1, \ldots, \mathsf{X}_n$ be registers, each having classical state set Σ. Also let*

$$v \in \mathcal{X}_1 \otimes \cdots \otimes \mathcal{X}_n \tag{7.191}$$

be a symmetric unit vector and let $k \in \{1, \ldots, n\}$. There exists a state

$$\tau \in \mathrm{conv}\left\{ (uu^*)^{\otimes k} : u \in \mathcal{S}(\mathbb{C}^\Sigma) \right\} \tag{7.192}$$

such that

$$\left\| (vv^*)[\mathsf{X}_1, \ldots, \mathsf{X}_k] - \tau \right\|_1 \leq \frac{4k(|\Sigma| - 1)}{n + 1}. \tag{7.193}$$

Proof It will be proved that the requirements of the theorem are satisfied by the operator

$$\tau = \binom{n + |\Sigma| - 1}{|\Sigma| - 1} \int \langle (uu^*)^{\otimes n}, vv^* \rangle (uu^*)^{\otimes k} \, d\mu(u), \qquad (7.194)$$

for μ denoting the uniform spherical measure on $\mathcal{S}(\mathbb{C}^\Sigma)$. The fact that τ is positive semidefinite is evident from its definition; and by Lemma 7.24, together with the assumption $v \in \mathcal{X}_1 \oslash \cdots \oslash \mathcal{X}_n$, one has that $\mathrm{Tr}(\tau) = 1$.

For the sake of establishing the bound (7.193), it is convenient to define

$$N_m = \binom{m + |\Sigma| - 1}{|\Sigma| - 1} \qquad (7.195)$$

for every nonnegative integer m. The following bounds on the ratio between N_{n-k} and N_n hold:

$$1 \geq \frac{N_{n-k}}{N_n} = \frac{n - k + |\Sigma| - 1}{n + |\Sigma| - 1} \cdots \frac{n - k + 1}{n + 1}$$

$$\geq \left(\frac{n - k + 1}{n + 1} \right)^{|\Sigma| - 1} \geq 1 - \frac{k(|\Sigma| - 1)}{n + 1}. \qquad (7.196)$$

For every unit vector $u \in \mathcal{S}(\mathbb{C}^\Sigma)$ and every positive integer m, define a projection operator

$$\Delta_{m,u} = (uu^*)^{\otimes m}, \qquad (7.197)$$

and also define an operator $P_u \in \mathrm{Pos}(\mathcal{X}_1 \otimes \cdots \otimes \mathcal{X}_k)$ as

$$P_u = \mathrm{Tr}_{\mathcal{X}_{k+1} \otimes \cdots \otimes \mathcal{X}_n} \left((\mathbb{1}_{\mathcal{X}_1 \otimes \cdots \otimes \mathcal{X}_k} \otimes \Delta_{n-k,u}) vv^* \right). \qquad (7.198)$$

By Lemma 7.24, together with the assumption $v \in \mathcal{X}_1 \oslash \cdots \oslash \mathcal{X}_n$, one has that

$$vv^* = N_{n-k} \int (\mathbb{1}_{\mathcal{X}_1 \otimes \cdots \otimes \mathcal{X}_k} \otimes \Delta_{n-k,u}) vv^* \, d\mu(u), \qquad (7.199)$$

and therefore

$$(vv^*)[\mathsf{X}_1, \ldots, \mathsf{X}_k] = N_{n-k} \int P_u \, d\mu(u). \qquad (7.200)$$

This density operator is to be compared with τ, which may be expressed as

$$\tau = N_n \int \Delta_{k,u} P_u \Delta_{k,u} \, d\mu(u). \qquad (7.201)$$

The primary goal of the remainder of the proof is to bound the trace norm of the operator

$$\frac{1}{N_{n-k}}(vv^*)[X_1,\ldots,X_k] - \frac{1}{N_n}\tau = \int\left(P_u - \Delta_{k,u}P_u\Delta_{k,u}\right)d\mu(u), \quad (7.202)$$

as such a bound will lead directly to a bound on the trace norm of

$$(vv^*)[X_1,\ldots,X_k] - \tau. \quad (7.203)$$

The operator identity

$$A - BAB = A(\mathbb{1} - B) + (\mathbb{1} - B)A - (\mathbb{1} - B)A(\mathbb{1} - B), \quad (7.204)$$

which holds for any two square operators A and B acting on a given space, will be useful for this purpose. It holds that

$$\int \Delta_{k,u}P_u\,d\mu(u) = \int \text{Tr}_{\mathcal{X}_{k+1}\otimes\cdots\otimes\mathcal{X}_n}\left(\Delta_{n,u}vv^*\right)d\mu(u)$$

$$= \frac{1}{N_n}(vv^*)[X_1,\ldots,X_k], \quad (7.205)$$

and therefore

$$\int(\mathbb{1} - \Delta_{k,u})P_u\,d\mu(u) = \left(\frac{1}{N_{n-k}} - \frac{1}{N_n}\right)(vv^*)[X_1,\ldots,X_k], \quad (7.206)$$

which implies

$$\left\|\int(\mathbb{1} - \Delta_{k,u})P_u\,d\mu(u)\right\|_1 = \left(\frac{1}{N_{n-k}} - \frac{1}{N_n}\right). \quad (7.207)$$

By similar reasoning, one finds that

$$\left\|\int P_u(\mathbb{1} - \Delta_{k,u})\,d\mu(u)\right\|_1 = \left(\frac{1}{N_{n-k}} - \frac{1}{N_n}\right). \quad (7.208)$$

Moreover, one has

$$\left\|\int(\mathbb{1} - \Delta_{k,u})P_u(\mathbb{1} - \Delta_{k,u})\,d\mu(u)\right\|_1$$

$$= \text{Tr}\left(\int(\mathbb{1} - \Delta_{k,u})P_u(\mathbb{1} - \Delta_{k,u})\,d\mu(u)\right) \quad (7.209)$$

$$= \text{Tr}\left(\int(\mathbb{1} - \Delta_{k,u})P_u\,d\mu(u)\right) = \left(\frac{1}{N_{n-k}} - \frac{1}{N_n}\right),$$

and therefore, by the triangle inequality together with the identity (7.204), it follows that

$$\left\|\frac{1}{N_{n-k}}(vv^*)[X_1,\ldots,X_k] - \frac{1}{N_n}\tau\right\|_1 \leq 3\left(\frac{1}{N_{n-k}} - \frac{1}{N_n}\right). \quad (7.210)$$

Having established a bound on the trace norm of the operator (7.202), the theorem follows:

$$\left\| (vv^*)[X_1, \ldots, X_k] - \tau \right\|_1$$

$$\leq N_{n-k} \left\| \frac{1}{N_{n-k}} (vv^*)[X_1, \ldots, X_k] - \frac{1}{N_n} \tau \right\|_1$$

$$+ N_{n-k} \left\| \frac{1}{N_n} \tau - \frac{1}{N_{n-k}} \tau \right\|_1 \qquad (7.211)$$

$$\leq 4 \left(1 - \frac{N_{n-k}}{N_n} \right)$$

$$\leq \frac{4k(|\Sigma| - 1)}{n + 1},$$

as required. $\qquad\qquad\square$

Corollary 7.27 (Quantum de Finetti theorem) *Let Σ be an alphabet, let n be a positive integer, and let $X_1, \ldots, X_n$ be registers sharing the same classical state set Σ. For every exchangeable density operator $\rho \in D(\mathcal{X}_1 \otimes \cdots \otimes \mathcal{X}_n)$ and every positive integer $k \in \{1, \ldots, n\}$, there exists a density operator*

$$\tau \in \text{conv}\{\sigma^{\otimes k} : \sigma \in D(\mathbb{C}^\Sigma)\} \qquad (7.212)$$

such that

$$\left\| \rho[X_1, \ldots, X_k] - \tau \right\|_1 \leq \frac{4k(|\Sigma|^2 - 1)}{n + 1}. \qquad (7.213)$$

Proof Let $Y_1, \ldots, Y_n$ be registers, all sharing the classical state set Σ. By Theorem 7.12, there exists a symmetric unit vector

$$v \in (\mathcal{X}_1 \otimes \mathcal{Y}_1) \otimes \cdots \otimes (\mathcal{X}_n \otimes \mathcal{Y}_n), \qquad (7.214)$$

representing a pure state of the compound register $((X_1, Y_1), \ldots, (X_n, Y_n))$, with the property that

$$(vv^*)[X_1, \ldots, X_n] = \rho. \qquad (7.215)$$

By Theorem 7.26, there exists a density operator

$$\xi \in \text{conv}\{(uu^*)^{\otimes k} : u \in \mathcal{S}(\mathbb{C}^\Sigma \otimes \mathbb{C}^\Sigma)\}, \qquad (7.216)$$

representing a state of the compound register $((X_1, Y_1), \ldots, (X_k, Y_k))$, such that

$$\left\| (vv^*)[(X_1, Y_1), \ldots, (X_k, Y_k)] - \xi \right\|_1 \leq \frac{4k(|\Sigma|^2 - 1)}{n + 1}. \qquad (7.217)$$

Taking $\tau = \xi[X_1, \ldots, X_k]$, one has that

$$\tau \in \mathrm{conv}\{\sigma^{\otimes k} : \sigma \in \mathrm{D}(\mathbb{C}^{\Sigma})\}, \qquad (7.218)$$

and the required bound

$$\|\rho[X_1, \ldots, X_k] - \tau\|_1 \leq \|(vv^*)[(X_1, Y_1), \ldots, (X_k, Y_k)] - \xi\|_1$$
$$\leq \frac{4k(|\Sigma|^2 - 1)}{n+1} \qquad (7.219)$$

follows by the monotonicity of the trace norm under partial tracing. $\square$

Optimal Cloning of Pure Quantum States

Let Σ be an alphabet, let n and m be positive integers with $n \leq m$, and let $X_1, \ldots, X_m$ be registers, all sharing the same classical state Σ. In the task of *cloning*, one assumes that the state of $(X_1, \ldots, X_n)$ is given by

$$\rho^{\otimes n} \in \mathrm{D}(\mathcal{X}_1 \otimes \cdots \otimes \mathcal{X}_n), \qquad (7.220)$$

for some choice of $\rho \in \mathrm{D}(\mathbb{C}^{\Sigma})$, and the goal is to transform $(X_1, \ldots, X_n)$ into $(X_1, \ldots, X_m)$ in such a way that the resulting state of this register is as close as possible to

$$\rho^{\otimes m} \in \mathrm{D}(\mathcal{X}_1 \otimes \cdots \otimes \mathcal{X}_m). \qquad (7.221)$$

One may consider the quality with which a given channel

$$\Phi \in \mathrm{C}(\mathcal{X}_1 \otimes \cdots \otimes \mathcal{X}_n, \mathcal{X}_1 \otimes \cdots \otimes \mathcal{X}_m) \qquad (7.222)$$

performs this task in a variety of specific ways. For example, one might measure the closeness of $\Phi(\rho^n)$ to ρ^m with respect to the trace norm, some other norm, or the fidelity function; and one might consider the average closeness over some distribution on the possible choices of ρ, or consider the worst case over all ρ or over some subset of possible choices for ρ. It is most typical that one assumes ρ is a pure state – the mixed state case is more complicated and has very different characteristics from the pure state case.

The specific variant of the cloning task that will be considered here is that one aims to choose a channel of the form (7.222) so as to maximize the minimum fidelity

$$\alpha(\Phi) = \inf_{u \in \mathcal{S}(\mathbb{C}^{\Sigma})} \mathrm{F}\big(\Phi((uu^*)^{\otimes n}), (uu^*)^{\otimes m}\big) \qquad (7.223)$$

over all pure states $\rho = uu^*$. The following theorem establishes an upper bound on this quantity, and states that this bound is achieved for some choice of a channel Φ.

Theorem 7.28 (Werner) *Let $\mathcal{X}$ be a complex Euclidean space and let n and m be positive integers with $n \leq m$. For every channel*

$$\Phi \in C(\mathcal{X}^{\otimes n}, \mathcal{X}^{\otimes m}) \tag{7.224}$$

it holds that

$$\inf_{u \in \mathcal{S}(\mathcal{X})} \langle \Phi((uu^*)^{\otimes n}), (uu^*)^{\otimes m} \rangle \leq \frac{N_n}{N_m}, \tag{7.225}$$

where

$$N_k = \binom{k + \dim(\mathcal{X}) - 1}{\dim(\mathcal{X}) - 1} \tag{7.226}$$

for each positive integer k. Moreover, there exists a channel Φ of the above form for which equality is achieved in (7.225).

Remark In the case that $n = 1$ and $m = 2$, one has

$$\frac{N_1}{N_2} = \frac{2}{\dim(\mathcal{X}) + 1}, \tag{7.227}$$

which is strictly less than 1 if $\dim(\mathcal{X}) \geq 2$. Theorem 7.28 therefore provides a quantitative form of the *no-cloning theorem*, which states that it is not possible to create a perfect copy of an unknown quantum state (aside from the trivial case of one-dimensional systems).

Proof of Theorem 7.28 The infimum on the left-hand side of (7.225) can be no larger than the average with respect to the uniform spherical measure on $\mathcal{S}(\mathcal{X})$:

$$\inf_{u \in \mathcal{S}(\mathcal{X})} \langle \Phi((uu^*)^{\otimes n}), (uu^*)^{\otimes m} \rangle$$
$$\leq \int \langle \Phi((uu^*)^{\otimes n}), (uu^*)^{\otimes m} \rangle \, d\mu(u). \tag{7.228}$$

As $(uu^*)^{\otimes n} \leq \Pi_{\mathcal{X}^{\otimes n}}$ for every $u \in \mathcal{S}(\mathcal{X})$, it follows that

$$\int \langle \Phi((uu^*)^{\otimes n}), (uu^*)^{\otimes m} \rangle \, d\mu(u) \leq \int \langle \Phi(\Pi_{\mathcal{X}^{\otimes n}}), (uu^*)^{\otimes m} \rangle \, d\mu(u)$$
$$= \frac{1}{N_m} \langle \Phi(\Pi_{\mathcal{X}^{\otimes n}}), \Pi_{\mathcal{X}^{\otimes m}} \rangle \leq \frac{1}{N_m} \operatorname{Tr}(\Phi(\Pi_{\mathcal{X}^{\otimes n}})) = \frac{N_n}{N_m}. \tag{7.229}$$

This establishes the required bound (7.225).

It remains to prove that there exists a channel

$$\Phi \in C(\mathcal{X}^{\otimes n}, \mathcal{X}^{\otimes m}) \tag{7.230}$$

for which equality is achieved in (7.225). Define

$$\Phi(X) = \frac{N_n}{N_m} \Pi_{\mathcal{X}^{\otimes m}} \left(X \otimes 1_{\mathcal{X}}^{\otimes(m-n)}\right)\Pi_{\mathcal{X}^{\otimes m}} + \left\langle 1_{\mathcal{X}}^{\otimes n} - \Pi_{\mathcal{X}^{\otimes n}}, X\right\rangle \sigma \tag{7.231}$$

for all $X \in L(\mathcal{X}^{\otimes n})$, where $\sigma \in D(\mathcal{X}^{\otimes m})$ is an arbitrary density operator. It is evident that Φ is completely positive, and the fact that Φ preserves trace follows from the observation

$$\left(1_{L(\mathcal{X})}^{\otimes n} \otimes \mathrm{Tr}_{\mathcal{X}}^{\otimes(m-n)}\right)(\Pi_{\mathcal{X}^{\otimes m}}) = \frac{N_m}{N_n}\Pi_{\mathcal{X}^{\otimes n}}. \tag{7.232}$$

A direct calculation reveals that

$$\left\langle (uu^*)^{\otimes m}, \Phi((uu^*)^{\otimes n})\right\rangle = \frac{N_n}{N_m} \tag{7.233}$$

for every unit vector $u \in \mathcal{S}(\mathcal{X})$, which completes the proof. $\square$

Example 7.29   The channel described in Example 2.33 is an optimal cloning channel, achieving equality in (7.225) for the case $\mathcal{X} = \mathbb{C}^2$, $n = 1$, and $m = 2$.

Unital Channels Near the Completely Depolarizing Channel

The final example of an application of unitarily invariant measures in the theory of quantum information to be presented in this section demonstrates that all unital channels sufficiently close to the completely depolarizing channel must be mixed-unitary channels. The following lemma will be used to demonstrate this fact.

Lemma 7.30   *Let $\mathcal{X}$ be a complex Euclidean space having dimension $n \geq 2$, let η denote the Haar measure on $U(\mathcal{X})$, and let $\Omega \in C(\mathcal{X})$ denote the completely depolarizing channel defined with respect to the space $\mathcal{X}$. The map $\Xi \in CP(\mathcal{X} \otimes \mathcal{X})$ defined as*

$$\Xi(X) = \int \left\langle \mathrm{vec}(U)\,\mathrm{vec}(U)^*, X\right\rangle \mathrm{vec}(U)\,\mathrm{vec}(U)^*\, d\eta(U) \tag{7.234}$$

for every $X \in L(\mathcal{X} \otimes \mathcal{X})$ is given by

$$\Xi = \frac{1}{n^2 - 1}\left(1_{L(\mathcal{X})} \otimes 1_{L(\mathcal{X})} - \Omega \otimes 1_{L(\mathcal{X})} - 1_{L(\mathcal{X})} \otimes \Omega + n^2 \Omega \otimes \Omega\right). \tag{7.235}$$

Proof Let $V \in U(\mathcal{X} \otimes \mathcal{X} \otimes \mathcal{X} \otimes \mathcal{X})$ be the permutation operator defined by the equation

$$V \operatorname{vec}(Y \otimes Z) = \operatorname{vec}(Y) \otimes \operatorname{vec}(Z), \tag{7.236}$$

holding for all $Y, Z \in L(\mathcal{X})$. Alternatively, this operator may be defined by the equation

$$V(x_1 \otimes x_2 \otimes x_3 \otimes x_4) = x_1 \otimes x_3 \otimes x_2 \otimes x_4 \tag{7.237}$$

holding for all $x_1, x_2, x_3, x_4 \in \mathcal{X}$. As V is its own inverse, one has

$$V(\operatorname{vec}(Y) \otimes \operatorname{vec}(Z)) = \operatorname{vec}(Y \otimes Z) \tag{7.238}$$

for all $Y, Z \in L(\mathcal{X})$. For every choice of maps $\Phi_0, \Phi_1 \in T(\mathcal{X})$, it holds that

$$V J(\Phi_0 \otimes \Phi_1) V^* = J(\Phi_0) \otimes J(\Phi_1). \tag{7.239}$$

Now, the Choi representation of Ξ is given by

$$J(\Xi) = \int \operatorname{vec}(U) \operatorname{vec}(U)^* \otimes \operatorname{vec}(\overline{U}) \operatorname{vec}(\overline{U})^* \, d\eta(U), \tag{7.240}$$

and therefore

$$V J(\Xi) V^* = \int \operatorname{vec}(U \otimes \overline{U}) \operatorname{vec}(U \otimes \overline{U})^* \, d\eta(U). \tag{7.241}$$

This operator is the Choi representation of the isotropic twirling channel

$$\Lambda(X) = \int (U \otimes \overline{U}) X (U \otimes \overline{U})^* \, d\eta(U) \tag{7.242}$$

defined in Example 7.25. From the analysis presented in that example, it follows that

$$V J(\Xi) V^* = \frac{1}{n^2} J(\mathbb{1}_{L(\mathcal{X})}) \otimes J(\mathbb{1}_{L(\mathcal{X})})$$
$$+ \frac{1}{n^2 - 1} \left(n J(\Omega) - \frac{1}{n} J(\mathbb{1}_{L(\mathcal{X})}) \right) \otimes \left(n J(\Omega) - \frac{1}{n} J(\mathbb{1}_{L(\mathcal{X})}) \right). \tag{7.243}$$

By expanding the expression (7.243) and making use of the identity (7.239), one obtains (7.235), as required. $\qquad \square$

Theorem 7.31 *Let $\mathcal{X}$ be a complex Euclidean space with dimension $n \geq 2$, let $\Omega \in C(\mathcal{X})$ denote the completely depolarizing channel defined with respect to the space $\mathcal{X}$, and let $\Phi \in C(\mathcal{X})$ be a unital channel. The channel*

$$\frac{n^2 - 2}{n^2 - 1} \Omega + \frac{1}{n^2 - 1} \Phi \tag{7.244}$$

is a mixed-unitary channel.

Proof Let $\Psi \in \mathrm{CP}(\mathcal{X})$ be the map defined as

$$\Psi(X) = \int \langle \mathrm{vec}(U)\,\mathrm{vec}(U)^*, J(\Phi)\rangle\, U X U^*\, d\eta(U), \qquad (7.245)$$

for η being the Haar measure on $\mathrm{U}(\mathcal{X})$. It holds that

$$\int \mathrm{vec}(U)\,\mathrm{vec}(U)^*\, d\eta(U) = \frac{1}{n}\mathbb{1}_{\mathcal{X}\otimes\mathcal{X}}, \qquad (7.246)$$

and therefore

$$\int \langle \mathrm{vec}(U)\,\mathrm{vec}(U)^*, J(\Phi)\rangle\, d\eta(U) = \frac{1}{n}\mathrm{Tr}(J(\Phi)) = 1. \qquad (7.247)$$

It follows that the mapping Ψ is a mixed-unitary channel.

By Lemma 7.30, one has $J(\Psi) = \Xi(J(\Phi))$ for $\Xi \in \mathrm{CP}(\mathcal{X}\otimes\mathcal{X})$ being defined as

$$\Xi = \frac{1}{n^2-1}\big(\mathbb{1}_{\mathrm{L}(\mathcal{X})}\otimes\mathbb{1}_{\mathrm{L}(\mathcal{X})} - \Omega\otimes\mathbb{1}_{\mathrm{L}(\mathcal{X})} - \mathbb{1}_{\mathrm{L}(\mathcal{X})}\otimes\Omega + n^2\Omega\otimes\Omega\big). \qquad (7.248)$$

By the assumption that Φ is a unital channel, one has

$$(\Omega\otimes\mathbb{1}_{\mathrm{L}(\mathcal{X})})(J(\Phi)) = (\mathbb{1}_{\mathrm{L}(\mathcal{X})}\otimes\Omega)(J(\Phi))$$
$$= (\Omega\otimes\Omega)(J(\Phi)) = \frac{\mathbb{1}_{\mathcal{X}}\otimes\mathbb{1}_{\mathcal{X}}}{n}, \qquad (7.249)$$

and therefore

$$J(\Psi) = \frac{1}{n^2-1}J(\Phi) + \frac{n^2-2}{n(n^2-1)}\mathbb{1}_{\mathcal{X}}\otimes\mathbb{1}_{\mathcal{X}}. \qquad (7.250)$$

This is equivalent to Ψ being equal to (7.244), and therefore completes the proof. $\qquad\square$

Corollary 7.32 *Let $\mathcal{X}$ be a complex Euclidean space having dimension $n \geq 2$, let $\Omega \in \mathrm{C}(\mathcal{X})$ denote the completely depolarizing channel defined with respect to the space $\mathcal{X}$, and let $\Phi \in \mathrm{T}(\mathcal{X})$ be a Hermitian-preserving, trace-preserving, and unital map satisfying*

$$\|J(\Omega) - J(\Phi)\| \leq \frac{1}{n(n^2-1)}. \qquad (7.251)$$

It holds that Φ is a mixed-unitary channel.

Proof Define a map $\Psi \in \mathrm{T}(\mathcal{X})$ as

$$\Psi = (n^2-1)\Phi - (n^2-2)\Omega. \qquad (7.252)$$

It holds that Ψ is trace-preserving and unital. Moreover, one has

$$
\begin{aligned}
J(\Psi) &= (n^2 - 1)(J(\Phi) - J(\Omega)) + J(\Omega) \\
&= (n^2 - 1)(J(\Phi) - J(\Omega)) + \frac{1}{n}\mathbb{1}_{\mathcal{X}\otimes\mathcal{X}},
\end{aligned}
\tag{7.253}
$$

which, by the assumptions of the corollary, implies that Ψ is completely positive. By Theorem 7.31 it follows that

$$
\frac{n^2 - 2}{n^2 - 1}\Omega + \frac{1}{n^2 - 1}\Psi = \Phi
\tag{7.254}
$$

is a mixed-unitary channel, which completes the proof. $\qquad\square$

7.3 Measure Concentration and Its Applications

The unitarily invariant measures introduced in the previous section exhibit a phenomenon known as *measure concentration*.[4] For the uniform spherical measure μ defined on the unit sphere of a complex Euclidean space $\mathcal{X}$, this phenomenon is reflected by the fact that, for every Lipschitz continuous function $f\colon \mathcal{S}(\mathcal{X}) \to \mathbb{R}$, the subset of $\mathcal{S}(\mathcal{X})$ on which f differs significantly from its average value (or, alternatively, any of its median values) must have relatively small measure. This phenomenon becomes more and more pronounced as the dimension of $\mathcal{X}$ grows.

Measure concentration is particularly useful in the theory of quantum information when used in the context of the *probabilistic method*. Various objects of interest, such as channels possessing certain properties, may be shown to exist by considering random choices of these objects (typically based on the uniform spherical measure or Haar measure), followed by an analysis that demonstrates that the randomly chosen object possesses the property of interest with a nonzero probability. This method has been used successfully to demonstrate the existence of several interesting classes of objects for which explicit constructions are not known.

The present section explains this methodology, with its primary goal being to prove that the minimum output entropy of quantum channels is non-additive. Toward this goal, concentration bounds are established for uniform spherical measures, leading to an asymptotically strong form of a theorem known as *Dvoretzky's theorem*.

---

[4] Measure concentration is not limited to the measures introduced in the previous section – it is a more general phenomenon. For the purposes of this book, however, it will suffice to consider measure concentration with respect to those particular measures.

7.3.1 Lévy's Lemma and Dvoretzky's Theorem

This subsection establishes facts concerning the concentration of measure phenomenon mentioned previously, for the measures defined in the previous section. A selection of bounds will be presented, mainly targeted toward a proof of Dvoretzky's theorem, which concerns the existence of a relatively large subspace V of a given complex Euclidean space X on which a given Lipschitz function $f \colon S(X) \to \mathbb{R}$ does not deviate significantly from its mean or median values with respect to the uniform spherical measure.

Concentration Bounds for Gaussian Measure

In order to prove concentration bounds for the uniform spherical measure, with respect to a given complex Euclidean space X, it is helpful to begin by proving an analogous result for the standard Gaussian measure on $\mathbb{R}^n$. Theorem 7.33, which is stated and proved below, establishes a result of this form that serves as a starting point for the concentration bounds to follow.

In the statements of the theorems representing concentration bounds to be presented below, including Theorem 7.33, it will be necessary to refer to certain universal real number constants. Such constants will, as a general convention, be denoted δ, δ_1, δ_2, etc., and must be chosen to be sufficiently small for the various theorems to hold. Although the optimization of these absolute constants should not be seen as being necessarily uninteresting or unimportant, this goal will be considered as being secondary in this book. Suitable values for these constants will be given in each case, but in some cases these values have been selected to simplify expressions and proofs rather than to optimize their values.

Theorem 7.33   *There exists a positive real number $\delta_1 > 0$ for which the following holds. For every choice of a positive integer n, independent and identically distributed standard normal random variables $X_1, \ldots, X_n$, a κ-Lipschitz function $f \colon \mathbb{R}^n \to \mathbb{R}$, and a positive real number $\varepsilon > 0$, it holds that*

$$\Pr\big(f(X_1, \ldots, X_n) - \mathrm{E}(f(X_1, \ldots, X_n)) \geq \varepsilon\big) \leq \exp\left(-\frac{\delta_1 \varepsilon^2}{\kappa^2}\right). \quad (7.255)$$

Remark   One may take $\delta_1 = 2/\pi^2$.

The proof of Theorem 7.33 will make use of the two lemmas that follow. The first lemma is a fairly standard smoothing argument that will allow for basic multivariate calculus to be applied in the proof of the theorem.

Lemma 7.34 *Let n be a positive integer, let $f \colon \mathbb{R}^n \to \mathbb{R}$ be a κ-Lipschitz function, and let $\varepsilon > 0$ be a positive real number. There exists a differentiable κ-Lipschitz function $g \colon \mathbb{R}^n \to \mathbb{R}$ such that $|f(x) - g(x)| \le \varepsilon$ for every $x \in \mathbb{R}^n$.*

Proof For every $\delta > 0$, define a function $g_\delta \colon \mathbb{R}^n \to \mathbb{R}$ as

$$g_\delta(x) = \int f(x + \delta z)\, \mathrm{d}\gamma_n(z) \qquad (7.256)$$

for all $x \in \mathbb{R}^n$, where γ_n denotes the standard Gaussian measure on $\mathbb{R}^n$. It will be proved that setting $g = g_\delta$ for a suitable choice of δ satisfies the requirements of the lemma.

First, by the assumption that f is κ-Lipschitz, it holds that

$$|f(x) - g_\delta(x)| \le \int |f(x) - f(x + \delta z)|\, \mathrm{d}\gamma_n(z)$$
$$\le \delta\kappa \int \|z\|\, \mathrm{d}\gamma_n(z) \le \delta\kappa\sqrt{n} \qquad (7.257)$$

for all $x \in \mathbb{R}^n$ and $\delta > 0$. The last inequality in (7.257) makes use of (1.279) in Chapter 1. At this point, one may fix

$$\delta = \frac{\varepsilon}{\kappa\sqrt{n}} \qquad (7.258)$$

and $g = g_\delta$, so that $|f(x) - g(x)| \le \varepsilon$ for every $x \in \mathbb{R}^n$.

Next, it holds that g is κ-Lipschitz, as the following calculation shows:

$$|g(x) - g(y)| \le \int |f(x + \delta z) - f(y + \delta z)|\, \mathrm{d}\gamma_n(z)$$
$$\le \int \kappa\|x - y\|\, \mathrm{d}\gamma_n(z) = \kappa\|x - y\|, \qquad (7.259)$$

for every $x, y \in \mathbb{R}^n$.

It remains to prove that g is differentiable. Using the definition of the standard Gaussian measure, one may calculate that the gradient of g at an arbitrary point $x \in \mathbb{R}^n$ is given by

$$\nabla g(x) = \frac{1}{\delta} \int f(x + \delta z) z\, \mathrm{d}\gamma_n(z). \qquad (7.260)$$

The fact that the integral on the right-hand side of (7.260) exists follows from the inequality

$$\int \|f(x + \delta z)z\|\, \mathrm{d}\gamma_n(z)$$
$$\le \int \|f(x + \delta z)z - f(x)z\|\, \mathrm{d}\gamma_n(z) + \int \|f(x)z\|\, \mathrm{d}\gamma_n(z) \qquad (7.261)$$
$$\le \kappa\delta \int \|z\|^2\, \mathrm{d}\gamma_n(z) + |f(x)| \int \|z\|\, \mathrm{d}\gamma_n(z) \le \kappa\delta n + |f(x)|\sqrt{n}.$$

Moreover, it holds that $\nabla g(x)$ is a continuous function of x (and in fact is Lipschitz continuous), as

$$\|\nabla g(x) - \nabla g(y)\| \leq \frac{1}{\delta} \int |f(x + \delta z) - f(y + \delta z)| \|z\| \, d\gamma_n(z)$$

$$\leq \frac{\kappa}{\delta} \|x - y\| \sqrt{n}. \tag{7.262}$$

As $\nabla g(x)$ is a continuous function of x, it follows that g is differentiable, which completes the proof. □

The second lemma establishes that the random variable $f(X_1, \ldots, X_n)$, for independent and normally distributed random variables $X_1, \ldots, X_n$ and a differentiable κ-Lipschitz function f, does not deviate too much from an independent copy of itself.

Lemma 7.35 *Let n be a positive integer, let $f \colon \mathbb{R}^n \to \mathbb{R}$ be a differentiable function satisfying $\|\nabla f(x)\| \leq \kappa$ for every $x \in \mathbb{R}^n$, let $X_1, \ldots, X_n$ and $Y_1, \ldots, Y_n$ be independent and identically distributed standard normal random variables, and define vector-valued random variables*

$$X = (X_1, \ldots, X_n) \quad and \quad Y = (Y_1, \ldots, Y_n). \tag{7.263}$$

For every real number $\lambda \in \mathbb{R}$, it holds that

$$\mathrm{E}(\exp(\lambda f(X) - \lambda f(Y))) \leq \exp\left(\frac{\lambda^2 \pi^2 \kappa^2}{8}\right). \tag{7.264}$$

Proof First, define a function $g_{x,y} \colon \mathbb{R} \to \mathbb{R}$, for every choice of vectors $x, y \in \mathbb{R}^n$, as follows:

$$g_{x,y}(\theta) = f(\sin(\theta)x + \cos(\theta)y). \tag{7.265}$$

Applying the chain rule for differentiation, one finds that

$$g'_{x,y}(\theta) = \langle \nabla f(\sin(\theta)x + \cos(\theta)y), \cos(\theta)x - \sin(\theta)y \rangle \tag{7.266}$$

for every $x, y \in \mathbb{R}^n$ and $\theta \in \mathbb{R}$. By the fundamental theorem of calculus, it therefore follows that

$$f(x) - f(y) = g_{x,y}(\pi/2) - g_{x,y}(0) = \int_0^{\frac{\pi}{2}} g'_{x,y}(\theta) \, d\theta$$

$$= \int_0^{\frac{\pi}{2}} \langle \nabla f(\sin(\theta)x + \cos(\theta)y), \cos(\theta)x - \sin(\theta)y \rangle \, d\theta. \tag{7.267}$$

Next, define a random variable Z_θ, for each $\theta \in [0, \pi/2]$, as

$$Z_\theta = \langle \nabla f(\sin(\theta)X + \cos(\theta)Y), \cos(\theta)X - \sin(\theta)Y \rangle. \tag{7.268}$$

By (7.267), it follows that

$$E(\exp(\lambda f(X) - \lambda f(Y))) = E\left(\exp\left(\lambda \int_0^{\frac{\pi}{2}} Z_\theta \, d\theta\right)\right). \tag{7.269}$$

By Jensen's inequality, one has

$$E\left(\exp\left(\lambda \int_0^{\frac{\pi}{2}} Z_\theta \, d\theta\right)\right) \leq \frac{2}{\pi} \int_0^{\frac{\pi}{2}} E\left(\exp\left(\frac{\pi\lambda}{2} Z_\theta\right)\right) d\theta. \tag{7.270}$$

Finally, one arrives at a key step of the proof: the observation that each of the random variables Z_θ is identically distributed, as a consequence of the invariance of Gaussian measure under orthogonal transformations. That is, one has the following equality of vector-valued random variables:

$$\begin{pmatrix} \sin(\theta)X + \cos(\theta)Y \\ \cos(\theta)X - \sin(\theta)Y \end{pmatrix} = \begin{pmatrix} \sin(\theta)\mathbb{1} & \cos(\theta)\mathbb{1} \\ \cos(\theta)\mathbb{1} & -\sin(\theta)\mathbb{1} \end{pmatrix} \begin{pmatrix} X \\ Y \end{pmatrix}. \tag{7.271}$$

As the distribution of $(X, Y) = (X_1, \ldots, X_n, Y_1, \ldots, Y_n)$ is invariant under orthogonal transformations, it follows that the distribution of Z_θ does not depend on θ. Consequently,

$$\frac{2}{\pi} \int_0^{\frac{\pi}{2}} E\left(\exp\left(\frac{\pi\lambda}{2} Z_\theta\right)\right) d\theta = E\left(\exp\left(\frac{\pi\lambda}{2} Z_0\right)\right). \tag{7.272}$$

This quantity can be evaluated using the Gaussian integral equation (1.268), yielding

$$E\left(\exp\left(\frac{\pi\lambda}{2} Z_0\right)\right) = E\left(\exp\left(\frac{\pi^2\lambda^2}{8} \|\nabla f(Y)\|^2\right)\right). \tag{7.273}$$

As it is to be assumed that $\|\nabla f(x)\| \leq \kappa$ for all $x \in \mathbb{R}^n$, the required bound is obtained as a result of (7.269), (7.270), (7.272), and (7.273). $\quad\square$

Proof of Theorem 7.33 Let X be a vector-valued random variable, defined as $X = (X_1, \ldots, X_n)$, and let $\lambda > 0$ be a positive real number to be specified shortly. By Markov's inequality, one has

$$\begin{aligned} \Pr(f(X) - E(f(X)) \geq \varepsilon) \\ = \Pr(\exp(\lambda f(X) - \lambda E(f(X))) \geq \exp(\lambda\varepsilon)) \\ \leq \exp(-\lambda\varepsilon) E(\exp(\lambda f(X) - \lambda E(f(X)))). \end{aligned} \tag{7.274}$$

By introducing a new random variable $Y = (Y_1, \ldots, Y_n)$, which is to be independent and identically distributed to X, one finds that

$$E(\exp(\lambda f(X) - \lambda E(f(X)))) \leq E(\exp(\lambda f(X) - \lambda f(Y))) \tag{7.275}$$

by Jensen's inequality. Combining the two previous inequalities yields

$$\Pr(f(X) - \mathrm{E}(f(X)) \geq \varepsilon) \leq \exp(-\lambda\varepsilon)\,\mathrm{E}(\exp(\lambda f(X) - \lambda f(Y))). \quad (7.276)$$

Assume first that f is differentiable, so that $\|\nabla f(x)\| \leq \kappa$ for all $x \in \mathbb{R}^n$ by the assumption that f is κ-Lipschitz. By Lemma 7.35, it follows that

$$\exp(-\lambda\varepsilon)\,\mathrm{E}(\exp(\lambda f(X) - \lambda f(Y))) \leq \exp\left(-\lambda\varepsilon + \frac{\lambda^2 \pi^2 \kappa^2}{8}\right). \quad (7.277)$$

Setting $\lambda = 4\varepsilon/(\pi^2\kappa^2)$, and combining (7.276) with (7.277), yields

$$\Pr(f(X) - \mathrm{E}(f(X)) \geq \varepsilon) \leq \exp\left(-\frac{2\varepsilon^2}{\pi^2\kappa^2}\right), \quad (7.278)$$

which is the bound claimed in the statement of the theorem (for $\delta_1 = 2/\pi^2$).

Finally, suppose that f is κ-Lipschitz, but not necessarily differentiable. By Lemma 7.34, for every $\zeta \in (0, \varepsilon/2)$ there exists a differentiable κ-Lipschitz function $g\colon \mathbb{R}^n \to \mathbb{R}$ satisfying $|f(x) - g(x)| \leq \zeta$ for every $x \in \mathbb{R}^n$, and therefore

$$\Pr(f(X) - \mathrm{E}(f(X)) \geq \varepsilon) \leq \Pr(g(X) - \mathrm{E}(g(X)) \geq \varepsilon - 2\zeta). \quad (7.279)$$

Applying the above analysis to g in place of f therefore yields

$$\Pr(f(X) - \mathrm{E}(f(X)) \geq \varepsilon) \leq \exp\left(-\frac{2(\varepsilon - 2\zeta)^2}{\pi^2\kappa^2}\right). \quad (7.280)$$

As this inequality holds for every $\zeta \in (0, \varepsilon/2)$, the theorem follows. $\qquad\square$

The following example illustrates the application of Theorem 7.33 to the Euclidean norm. The analysis to be presented in this example is relevant to the discussion of the uniform spherical measure to be discussed shortly.

Example 7.36   Let n be a positive integer and define $f(x) = \|x\|$ for each $x \in \mathbb{R}^n$. It is an immediate consequence of the triangle inequality that f is 1-Lipschitz:

$$|f(x) - f(y)| = |\|x\| - \|y\|| \leq \|x - y\| \quad (7.281)$$

for all $x, y \in \mathbb{R}^n$. The mean value of $f(X_1, \ldots, X_n)$, for $X_1, \ldots, X_n$ being independent and identically distributed standard normal random variables, has the following closed-form expression (q.v. Section 1.2.2):

$$\mathrm{E}(f(X_1, \ldots, X_n)) = \frac{\sqrt{2}\,\Gamma\left(\frac{n+1}{2}\right)}{\Gamma\left(\frac{n}{2}\right)}. \quad (7.282)$$

From this expression, an analysis reveals that

$$\mathrm{E}(f(X_1, \ldots, X_n)) = \upsilon_n \sqrt{n}, \tag{7.283}$$

where $\upsilon_1, \upsilon_2, \upsilon_3, \ldots$ is a strictly increasing sequence that begins

$$\upsilon_1 = \sqrt{\frac{2}{\pi}}, \quad \upsilon_2 = \frac{\sqrt{\pi}}{2}, \quad \upsilon_3 = \sqrt{\frac{8}{3\pi}}, \quad \ldots \tag{7.284}$$

and converges to 1 in the limit as n goes to infinity.

For any positive real number $\varepsilon > 0$, one may conclude the following two bounds from Theorem 7.33:

$$\begin{aligned}
\Pr(\|(X_1, \ldots, X_n)\| \leq (\upsilon_n - \varepsilon)\sqrt{n}) &\leq \exp(-\delta_1 \varepsilon^2 n), \\
\Pr(\|(X_1, \ldots, X_n)\| \geq (\upsilon_n + \varepsilon)\sqrt{n}) &\leq \exp(-\delta_1 \varepsilon^2 n).
\end{aligned} \tag{7.285}$$

Consequently, one has

$$\Pr(\big|\|(X_1, \ldots, X_n)\| - \upsilon_n \sqrt{n}\big| \geq \varepsilon\sqrt{n}) \leq 2\exp(-\delta_1 \varepsilon^2 n). \tag{7.286}$$

This bound illustrates that the Euclidean norm of a Gaussian-random vector $x \in \mathbb{R}^n$ is tightly concentrated around its mean value $\upsilon_n \sqrt{n}$.

Concentration Bounds for Uniform Spherical Measure

The uniform spherical measure may be derived from the standard Gaussian measure, as described in Section 7.2.1, so it is not unreasonable to expect that Theorem 7.33 might lead to an analogous fact holding for the uniform spherical measure. Indeed this is the case, as the theorems below establish.

The first theorem concerns the deviation of a Lipschitz random variable, defined with respect to the uniform spherical measure, from its mean value.

Theorem 7.37 (Lévy's lemma, mean value form)   *There exists a positive real number $\delta_2 > 0$ for which the following holds. For every κ-Lipschitz random variable $X \colon \mathcal{S}(\mathcal{X}) \to \mathbb{R}$, distributed with respect to the uniform spherical measure μ on $\mathcal{S}(\mathcal{X})$ for a given complex Euclidean space $\mathcal{X}$, and every positive real number $\varepsilon > 0$, it holds that*

$$\begin{aligned}
\Pr(X - \mathrm{E}(X) \geq \varepsilon) &\leq 2\exp\left(-\frac{\delta_2 \varepsilon^2 n}{\kappa^2}\right), \\
\Pr(X - \mathrm{E}(X) \leq -\varepsilon) &\leq 2\exp\left(-\frac{\delta_2 \varepsilon^2 n}{\kappa^2}\right),
\end{aligned} \tag{7.287}$$

and

$$\Pr(|X - \mathrm{E}(X)| \geq \varepsilon) \leq 3\exp\left(-\frac{\delta_2 \varepsilon^2 n}{\kappa^2}\right), \tag{7.288}$$

where $n = \dim(\mathcal{X})$.

Remark   One may take $\delta_2 = 1/(25\pi)$.

The proof of Lemma 7.37 will make use of the following lemma, which provides a simple mechanism for extending a Lipschitz function defined on the unit sphere of $\mathbb{C}^n$ to a Lipschitz function defined on all of $\mathbb{R}^{2n}$.

Lemma 7.38   *Let n be a positive integer and let $f \colon \mathcal{S}(\mathbb{C}^n) \to \mathbb{R}$ be a κ-Lipschitz function that is neither strictly positive nor strictly negative. Define a function $g \colon \mathbb{R}^{2n} \to \mathbb{R}$ as*

$$g(x \oplus y) = \begin{cases} \|x + iy\| f\left(\frac{x+iy}{\|x+iy\|}\right) & \text{if } x + iy \neq 0 \\ 0 & \text{if } x + iy = 0 \end{cases} \qquad (7.289)$$

for all $x, y \in \mathbb{R}^n$. It holds that g is a (3κ)-Lipschitz function.

Proof   By the assumption that f is neither strictly positive nor strictly negative, one has that for every unit vector $u \in \mathbb{C}^n$, there must exist a unit vector $v \in \mathbb{C}^n$ such that $f(u)f(v) \leq 0$. This in turn implies

$$|f(u)| \leq |f(u) - f(v)| \leq \kappa \|u - v\| \leq 2\kappa, \qquad (7.290)$$

by the assumption that f is κ-Lipschitz.

Now suppose that $x_0, y_0, x_1, y_1 \in \mathbb{R}^n$ are vectors. If it is the case that $x_0 + iy_0 = 0$ and $x_1 + iy_1 = 0$, then it is immediate that

$$|g(x_0 \oplus y_0) - g(x_1 \oplus y_1)| = 0. \qquad (7.291)$$

If it holds that $x_0 + iy_0 \neq 0$ and $x_1 + iy_1 = 0$, then (7.290) implies

$$|g(x_0 \oplus y_0) - g(x_1 \oplus y_1)| = |g(x_0 \oplus y_0)| \leq 2\kappa \|x_0 + iy_0\| = 2\kappa \|x_0 \oplus y_0\|. \quad (7.292)$$

A similar bound holds for the case in which $x_0 + iy_0 = 0$ and $x_1 + iy_1 \neq 0$.

Finally, suppose that $x_0 + iy_0$ and $x_1 + iy_1$ are both nonzero. Write

$$z_0 = x_0 + iy_0 \quad \text{and} \quad z_1 = x_1 + iy_1, \qquad (7.293)$$

and set

$$\alpha_0 = \frac{1}{\|z_0\|} \quad \text{and} \quad \alpha_1 = \frac{1}{\|z_1\|}. \qquad (7.294)$$

This implies that both $\alpha_0 z_0$ and $\alpha_1 z_1$ are unit vectors. There is no loss of generality in assuming $\alpha_0 \leq \alpha_1$; the case in which $\alpha_1 \leq \alpha_0$ is handled in a symmetric manner. By the triangle inequality, one has

$$\begin{aligned} |g(x_0 \oplus y_0) - g(x_1 \oplus y_1)| &= \big|\|z_0\| f(\alpha_0 z_0) - \|z_1\| f(\alpha_1 z_1)\big| \\ &\leq |f(\alpha_0 z_0)| \, \|z_0 - z_1\| + \|z_1\| \, |f(\alpha_0 z_0) - f(\alpha_1 z_1)|. \end{aligned} \qquad (7.295)$$

Using (7.290), one finds that the first term in the final expression of (7.295) is bounded as follows:

$$|f(\alpha_0 z_0)|\,\|z_0 - z_1\| \leq 2\kappa\|z_0 - z_1\| = 2\kappa\|x_0 \oplus y_0 - x_1 \oplus y_1\|. \qquad (7.296)$$

To bound the second term, it may first be noted that

$$\|z_1\|\,|f(\alpha_0 z_0) - f(\alpha_1 z_1)| \leq \kappa\|z_1\|\,\|\alpha_0 z_0 - \alpha_1 z_1\|, \qquad (7.297)$$

again by the assumption that f is κ-Lipschitz. Given that $0 < \alpha_0 \leq \alpha_1$, together with the fact that $\alpha_0 z_0$ and $\alpha_1 z_1$ are unit vectors, one finds that

$$\|\alpha_0 z_0 - \alpha_1 z_1\| \leq \|\alpha_1 z_0 - \alpha_1 z_1\| = \frac{\|z_0 - z_1\|}{\|z_1\|}, \qquad (7.298)$$

and therefore

$$\kappa\|z_1\|\,\|\alpha_0 z_0 - \alpha_1 z_1\| \leq \kappa\|z_0 - z_1\| = \kappa\|x_0 \oplus y_0 - x_1 \oplus y_1\|. \qquad (7.299)$$

It follows that

$$|g(x_0 \oplus y_0) - g(x_1 \oplus y_1)| \leq 3\kappa\|x_0 \oplus y_0 - x_1 \oplus y_1\|. \qquad (7.300)$$

It has therefore been established that g is (3κ)-Lipschitz, as required. $\qquad\square$

Proof of Theorem 7.37 The random variable $X - \mathrm{E}(X)$ has mean value 0, and is therefore neither strictly positive nor strictly negative. As X is κ-Lipschitz, so too is $X - \mathrm{E}(X)$, and so it follows that

$$|X - \mathrm{E}(X)| \leq 2\kappa, \qquad (7.301)$$

as argued in the first paragraph of the proof of Lemma 7.38. The inequalities (7.287) and (7.288) therefore hold trivially when $\varepsilon > 2\kappa$. For this reason it will be assumed that $\varepsilon \leq 2\kappa$ for the remainder of the proof. It will also be assumed that $\mathcal{X} = \mathbb{C}^n$, for n being an arbitrary positive integer, which will simplify the notation used throughout the proof, and which causes no loss of generality.

Define a function $g \colon \mathbb{R}^{2n} \to \mathbb{R}$ as

$$g(y \oplus z) = \begin{cases} \|y + iz\|\left(X\left(\frac{y+iz}{\|y+iz\|}\right) - \mathrm{E}(X)\right) & \text{if } y + iz \neq 0 \\ 0 & \text{if } y + iz = 0 \end{cases} \qquad (7.302)$$

for all $y, z \in \mathbb{R}^n$, which is a (3κ)-Lipschitz function by Lemma 7.38. Let $Y = (Y_1, \ldots, Y_n)$ and $Z = (Z_1, \ldots, Z_n)$ be vector-valued random variables, for $Y_1, \ldots, Y_n$ and $Z_1, \ldots, Z_n$ being independent and identically distributed standard normal random variables, and define a random variable

$$W = g(Y \oplus Z). \qquad (7.303)$$

As $X - \mathrm{E}(X)$ has mean value 0, it is evident that $\mathrm{E}(W) = 0$ as well. Finally, by considering the definition of the uniform spherical measure, one finds that

$$\Pr(X - \mathrm{E}(X) \geq \varepsilon) = \Pr(W \geq \varepsilon \|Y + iZ\|). \tag{7.304}$$

The probability (7.304) may be upper-bounded through the use of the union bound:

$$\Pr(X - \mathrm{E}(X) \geq \varepsilon) \leq \Pr\left(W \geq \varepsilon\lambda\sqrt{2n}\right) + \Pr\left(\|Y + iZ\| \leq \lambda\sqrt{2n}\right) \tag{7.305}$$

for every choice of $\lambda > 0$. By Theorem 7.33 it holds that

$$\Pr\left(W \geq \varepsilon\lambda\sqrt{2n}\right) \leq \exp\left(-\frac{2\delta_1\varepsilon^2\lambda^2 n}{9\kappa^2}\right), \tag{7.306}$$

and, as established in Example 7.36, it holds that

$$\Pr\left(\|Y + iZ\| \leq \lambda\sqrt{2n}\right) \leq \exp\left(-2\delta_1(v_{2n} - \lambda)^2 n\right). \tag{7.307}$$

Setting

$$\lambda = \frac{3\kappa v_{2n}}{3\kappa + \varepsilon} \tag{7.308}$$

yields

$$\Pr(X \geq \mathrm{E}(X) + \varepsilon) \leq 2\exp\left(-\frac{2\delta_1\varepsilon^2 v_{2n}^2 n}{(3\kappa + \varepsilon)^2}\right) \leq 2\exp\left(-\frac{\delta_1\pi\varepsilon^2 n}{50\kappa^2}\right), \tag{7.309}$$

where the second inequality makes use of the assumption $\varepsilon \leq 2\kappa$, along with the observation that $v_{2n} \geq v_2 = \sqrt{\pi}/2$. As one may take $\delta_1 = 2/\pi^2$ in Theorem 7.33, the first inequality is therefore proved for $\delta_2 = 1/(25\pi)$.

The second and third inequalities may be proved in essentially the same manner. In particular, one has

$$\begin{aligned}\Pr(X - \mathrm{E}(X) &\leq -\varepsilon) \\ &\leq \Pr\left(W \leq -\varepsilon\lambda\sqrt{2n}\right) + \Pr\left(\|Y + iZ\| \leq \lambda\sqrt{2n}\right)\end{aligned} \tag{7.310}$$

and

$$\begin{aligned}\Pr(|X - \mathrm{E}(X)| &\geq \varepsilon) \\ &\leq \Pr\left(W \geq \varepsilon\lambda\sqrt{2n}\right) + \Pr\left(W \leq -\varepsilon\lambda\sqrt{2n}\right) \\ &\quad + \Pr\left(\|Y + iZ\| \leq \lambda\sqrt{2n}\right),\end{aligned} \tag{7.311}$$

and again setting $\lambda = 3\kappa v_{2n}/(3\kappa + \varepsilon)$ yields the required bounds. $\square$

The second theorem on measure concentration for the uniform spherical measure, stated and proved below, is similar in spirit to Theorem 7.37, but it is concerned with the deviation of a Lipschitz random variable from its *median value* – or, more generally, from any of its *central values* – rather than its mean value. The next definition makes precise the notions of a median value and a central value of a random variable, after which the theorem is stated and proved.

Definition 7.39 Let X be a random variable and let β be a real number. It is said that β is a *median value* of X if

$$\Pr(X \geq \beta) \geq \frac{1}{2} \quad \text{and} \quad \Pr(X \leq \beta) \geq \frac{1}{2}, \tag{7.312}$$

and it is said that β is a *central value* of X if

$$\Pr(X \geq \beta) \geq \frac{1}{4} \quad \text{and} \quad \Pr(X \leq \beta) \geq \frac{1}{4}. \tag{7.313}$$

Theorem 7.40 (Lévy's lemma, central value form) *There exists a positive real number $\delta_3 > 0$ for which the following holds. For every complex Euclidean space $\mathcal{X}$, every κ-Lipschitz random variable*

$$X : \mathcal{S}(\mathcal{X}) \to \mathbb{R}, \tag{7.314}$$

distributed with respect to the uniform spherical measure μ on $\mathcal{S}(\mathcal{X})$, every central value β of X, and every positive real number $\varepsilon > 0$, it holds that

$$\Pr(|X - \beta| \geq \varepsilon) \leq 8 \exp\left(-\frac{\delta_3 \varepsilon^2 n}{\kappa^2}\right), \tag{7.315}$$

where $n = \dim(\mathcal{X})$.

Remark One may take $\delta_3 = 1/(100\pi)$.

Proof Let

$$\zeta = \sqrt{\frac{\ln(8)\kappa^2}{\delta_2 n}}, \tag{7.316}$$

for δ_2 being any positive real number for which Theorem 7.37 holds. By that theorem, one may conclude that the following two inequalities hold for every positive real number $\alpha > 0$:

$$\Pr(X - \mathrm{E}(X) \geq \zeta + \alpha) \leq 2 \exp\left(-\frac{\delta_2(\zeta + \alpha)^2 n}{\kappa^2}\right) < \frac{1}{4}, \tag{7.317}$$

$$\Pr(X - \mathrm{E}(X) \leq -(\zeta + \alpha)) \leq 2 \exp\left(-\frac{\delta_2(\zeta + \alpha)^2 n}{\kappa^2}\right) < \frac{1}{4}. \tag{7.318}$$

From these inequalities, one concludes that $|\mathrm{E}(X) - \beta| \leq \zeta$.

Now suppose that ε is a given positive real number. If it is the case that $\varepsilon \geq 2\zeta$, then Theorem 7.37 implies

$$\Pr(|X - \beta| \geq \varepsilon) \leq \Pr(|X - \mathrm{E}(X)| \geq \varepsilon - \zeta)$$

$$\leq \Pr\left(|X - \mathrm{E}(X)| \geq \frac{\varepsilon}{2}\right) \leq 3 \exp\left(-\frac{\delta_2 \varepsilon^2 n}{4\kappa^2}\right). \tag{7.319}$$

On the other hand, if $\varepsilon < 2\zeta$, then one has

$$\exp\left(-\frac{\delta_2 \varepsilon^2 n}{4\kappa^2}\right) > \exp\left(-\frac{\delta_2 \zeta^2 n}{\kappa^2}\right) = \frac{1}{8}, \tag{7.320}$$

so it must trivially hold that

$$\Pr(|X - \beta| \geq \varepsilon) \leq 8 \exp\left(-\frac{\delta_2 \varepsilon^2 n}{4\kappa^2}\right). \tag{7.321}$$

The required bound (7.315) therefore holds in both cases, provided one takes $\delta_3 \leq \delta_2/4$. As Theorem 7.37 holds for $\delta_2 = 1/(25\pi)$, the bound (7.315) holds for $\delta_3 = 1/(100\pi)$. □

Dvoretzky's Theorem

Dvoretzky's theorem, which plays a key role in the section following this one, establishes that a Lipschitz random variable, defined with respect to the uniform spherical measure for a given complex Euclidean space $\mathcal{X}$, must remain close to its central values everywhere on the unit sphere $\mathcal{S}(\mathcal{V})$, for some choice of a subspace $\mathcal{V} \subseteq \mathcal{X}$ having relatively large dimension. There are, in fact, multiple variants and generalizations of Dvoretzky's theorem; the variant to be considered in this book is specific to the unitarily invariant measures defined previously in the present chapter, and is applicable to *phase-invariant* functions, which are defined as follows.

Definition 7.41   Let $f: \mathcal{S}(\mathcal{X}) \to \mathbb{R}$ be a function, for a complex Euclidean space $\mathcal{X}$. The function f is said to be a *phase-invariant* function if it holds that $f(x) = f(e^{i\theta}x)$ for all $x \in \mathcal{S}(\mathcal{X})$ and $\theta \in \mathbb{R}$.

Theorem 7.42 (Dvoretzky's theorem)   *There exists a positive real number $\delta > 0$ for which the following holds. Let $X: \mathcal{S}(\mathcal{X}) \to \mathbb{R}$ be a κ-Lipschitz, phase-invariant random variable, distributed with respect to the uniform spherical measure μ on $\mathcal{S}(\mathcal{X})$ for a given complex Euclidean space $\mathcal{X}$ of dimension n, let β be a central value of X, let $\varepsilon > 0$ and $\zeta > 0$ be positive real numbers, and let $\mathcal{V} \subseteq \mathcal{X}$ be a subspace with*

$$1 \leq \dim(\mathcal{V}) \leq \frac{\delta \varepsilon^2 \zeta^2 n}{\kappa^2}. \tag{7.322}$$

For each unit vector $v \in V$, define a random variable $Y_v \colon \mathrm{U}(\mathcal{X}) \to \mathbb{R}$, distributed with respect to the Haar measure on $\mathrm{U}(\mathcal{X})$, as

$$Y_v(U) = X(Uv) \tag{7.323}$$

for every $U \in \mathrm{U}(\mathcal{X})$. It holds that

$$\Pr\big(|Y_v - \beta| \le \varepsilon \text{ for every } v \in \mathcal{S}(V)\big) \ge 1 - \zeta. \tag{7.324}$$

Remark One may take $\delta = 1/(160000\pi)$.

The proof of Theorem 7.42 will make use of the two lemmas that follow.

Lemma 7.43 *Let $\mathcal{X}$ be a complex Euclidean space of dimension $n \ge 2$ and let $f \colon \mathcal{S}(\mathcal{X}) \to \mathbb{R}$ be a κ-Lipschitz, phase-invariant function. For every unit vector $u \in \mathcal{S}(\mathcal{X})$, define a random variable $X_u \colon \mathrm{U}(\mathcal{X}) \to \mathbb{R}$, distributed with respect to the Haar measure η on $\mathrm{U}(\mathcal{X})$, as*

$$X_u(U) = f(Uu) \tag{7.325}$$

for all $U \in \mathrm{U}(\mathcal{X})$. For any pair of linearly independent unit vectors $u, v \in \mathcal{X}$ and every positive real number $\varepsilon > 0$, it holds that

$$\Pr\big(|X_u - X_v| \ge \varepsilon\big) \le 3 \exp\!\left(-\frac{\delta_2 \varepsilon^2 (n-1)}{\kappa^2 \|u - v\|^2}\right), \tag{7.326}$$

for any positive real number δ_2 satisfying the requirements of Theorem 7.37.

Proof The lemma will first be proved in the special case in which $\langle u, v \rangle$ is a nonnegative real number. First, define

$$\lambda = \frac{1 + \langle u, v \rangle}{2}, \tag{7.327}$$

which satisfies $1/2 \le \lambda < 1$ by the assumption that $\langle u, v \rangle$ is nonnegative and u and v are linearly independent. Set

$$x = \frac{u + v}{2\sqrt{\lambda}} \quad \text{and} \quad y = \frac{u - v}{2\sqrt{1 - \lambda}}, \tag{7.328}$$

so that x and y are orthonormal unit vectors for which

$$\begin{aligned} u &= \sqrt{\lambda}\,x + \sqrt{1 - \lambda}\,y, \\ v &= \sqrt{\lambda}\,x - \sqrt{1 - \lambda}\,y. \end{aligned} \tag{7.329}$$

Next, let $\mathcal{Y}$ be any complex Euclidean space having dimension $n-1$ and let $V \in \mathrm{U}(\mathcal{Y}, \mathcal{X})$ be any isometry for which $x \perp \mathrm{im}(V)$. For every $U \in \mathrm{U}(\mathcal{X})$, define a random variable $Y_U \colon \mathcal{S}(\mathcal{Y}) \to \mathbb{R}$, distributed with respect to the uniform spherical measure μ on $\mathcal{S}(\mathcal{Y})$, as

$$Y_U(w) = f\Big(U\big(\sqrt{\lambda}x + \sqrt{1-\lambda}Vw\big)\Big) - f\Big(U\big(\sqrt{\lambda}x - \sqrt{1-\lambda}Vw\big)\Big) \quad (7.330)$$

for every $w \in \mathcal{S}(\mathcal{Y})$. Using the triangle inequality, along with the fact that

$$\|u - v\| = 2\sqrt{1 - \lambda}, \tag{7.331}$$

one may verify that each Y_U is $(\kappa\|u-v\|)$-Lipschitz and satisfies $\mathrm{E}(Y_U) = 0$. By Lévy's lemma (Theorem 7.37), it therefore holds that

$$\Pr(|Y_U| \geq \varepsilon) \leq 3\exp\Big(-\frac{\delta_2\varepsilon^2(n-1)}{\kappa^2\|u-v\|^2}\Big), \tag{7.332}$$

for every $U \in \mathrm{U}(\mathcal{X})$ and every $\varepsilon > 0$.

Finally, define a random variable $Z \colon \mathrm{U}(\mathcal{X}) \times \mathcal{S}(\mathcal{Y}) \to \mathbb{R}$, distributed with respect to the product measure $\eta \times \mu$, as

$$Z(U, w) = Y_U(w) \tag{7.333}$$

for all $U \in \mathrm{U}(\mathcal{X})$ and $w \in \mathcal{S}(\mathcal{Y})$. Because the uniform spherical measure and Haar measure are both unitarily invariant, it follows that Z and $X_u - X_v$ are identically distributed. It therefore holds that

$$\begin{aligned}
\Pr(|X_u - X_v| \geq \varepsilon) &= \Pr(|Z| \geq \varepsilon) \\
&= \int \Pr(|Y_U| \geq \varepsilon)\, d\eta(U) \leq 3\exp\Big(-\frac{\delta_2\varepsilon^2(n-1)}{\kappa^2\|u-v\|^2}\Big),
\end{aligned} \tag{7.334}$$

which proves the lemma in the case that $\langle u, v \rangle$ is a nonnegative real number.

In the situation in which $\langle u, v \rangle$ is not a nonnegative real number, one may choose $\alpha \in \mathbb{C}$ with $|\alpha| = 1$ so that $\langle u, \alpha v \rangle$ is a nonnegative real number. By the assumption that f is phase-invariant, it holds that $X_v = X_{\alpha v}$, and therefore

$$\begin{aligned}
\Pr(|X_u - X_v| \geq \varepsilon) &= \Pr(|X_u - X_{\alpha v}| \geq \varepsilon) \\
&\leq 3\exp\Big(-\frac{\delta_2\varepsilon^2(n-1)}{\kappa^2\|u-\alpha v\|^2}\Big),
\end{aligned} \tag{7.335}$$

by the analysis above. As it necessarily holds that $\|u - \alpha v\| \leq \|u - v\|$, it follows that

$$\Pr(|X_u - X_v| \geq \varepsilon) \leq 3\exp\Big(-\frac{\delta_2\varepsilon^2(n-1)}{\kappa^2\|u-v\|^2}\Big) \tag{7.336}$$

for every $\varepsilon > 0$, which completes the proof. $\qquad\square$

The next lemma bounds the mean value of the maximum of a collection of nonnegative random variables satisfying a property reminiscent of the bounds obtained for the concentration results presented above.

Lemma 7.44 *Let $N \geq 2$ be a positive integer, let K and θ be positive real numbers, and let $Y_1, \ldots, Y_N$ be nonnegative random variables for which*

$$\Pr(Y_k \geq \lambda) \leq K \exp(-\theta\lambda^2) \tag{7.337}$$

for every $k \in \{1, \ldots, N\}$ and every $\lambda \geq 0$. It holds that

$$\mathrm{E}(\max\{Y_1, \ldots, Y_N\}) \leq \sqrt{\frac{\ln(N)}{\theta}} + \frac{K}{\sqrt{2\theta}}. \tag{7.338}$$

Proof As the random variables $Y_1, \ldots, Y_N$ take only nonnegative values, one may write

$$\mathrm{E}(\max\{Y_1, \ldots, Y_N\}) = \int_0^\infty \Pr(\max\{Y_1, \ldots, Y_N\} \geq \lambda)\, d\lambda. \tag{7.339}$$

Splitting the integral into two parts, and making use of the fact that the probability of any event is at most 1, yields

$$\mathrm{E}(\max\{Y_1, \ldots, Y_N\})$$
$$\leq \sqrt{\frac{\ln(N)}{\theta}} + \int_{\sqrt{\frac{\ln(N)}{\theta}}}^\infty \Pr(\max\{Y_1, \ldots, Y_N\} \geq \lambda)\, d\lambda. \tag{7.340}$$

By the union bound, together with the assumption (7.337) on $Y_1, \ldots, Y_N$, one has

$$\int_{\sqrt{\frac{\ln(N)}{\theta}}}^\infty \Pr(\max\{Y_1, \ldots, Y_N\} \geq \lambda)\, d\lambda \leq KN \int_{\sqrt{\frac{\ln(N)}{\theta}}}^\infty \exp(-\theta\lambda^2)\, d\lambda. \tag{7.341}$$

As $\ln(2) > 1/2$, it holds that $\lambda\sqrt{2\theta} > 1$ for every choice of λ satisfying

$$\lambda \geq \sqrt{\frac{\ln(N)}{\theta}}, \tag{7.342}$$

and therefore

$$\int_{\sqrt{\frac{\ln(N)}{\theta}}}^\infty \exp(-\theta\lambda^2)\, d\lambda \leq \int_{\sqrt{\frac{\ln(N)}{\theta}}}^\infty \lambda\sqrt{2\theta} \exp(-\theta\lambda^2)\, d\lambda = \frac{1}{N\sqrt{2\theta}}. \tag{7.343}$$

The required inequality now follows from (7.340), (7.341), and (7.343). $\square$

Proof of Theorem 7.42 It will be proved that any choice of $\delta > 0$ satisfying

$$\delta \leq \left(\frac{8}{\sqrt{\delta_3}} + \frac{64}{\sqrt{\delta_2}} \right)^{-2}, \tag{7.344}$$

for δ_2 and δ_3 being positive real numbers that satisfy the requirements of Theorem 7.37 and Theorem 7.40, respectively, fulfills the requirements of the theorem. Taking $\delta_2 = 1/(25\pi)$ and $\delta_3 = 1/(100\pi)$, one has that

$$\delta = \frac{1}{160000\pi} \tag{7.345}$$

satisfies the requirement (7.344). The theorem is trivial in the case $n = 1$, as the phase invariance of X implies that X is constant in this case, and for this reason it will be assumed that $n \geq 2$ for the remainder of the proof.

By Markov's inequality, one has

$$\Pr(\sup\{|Y_v - \beta| : v \in \mathcal{S}(\mathcal{V})\} \leq \varepsilon)$$
$$\geq 1 - \frac{\mathrm{E}(\sup\{|Y_v - \beta| : v \in \mathcal{S}(\mathcal{V})\})}{\varepsilon}, \tag{7.346}$$

so the theorem will follow from a demonstration that

$$\mathrm{E}(\sup\{|Y_v - \beta| : v \in \mathcal{S}(\mathcal{V})\}) \leq \zeta\varepsilon. \tag{7.347}$$

Let $m = \dim(\mathcal{V})$, and for each nonnegative integer $k \in \mathbb{N}$, let $\mathcal{N}_k$ be a minimal (2^{-k+1})-net for $\mathcal{S}(\mathcal{V})$. It is evident that $|\mathcal{N}_0| = 1$, and for every $k \in \mathbb{N}$ it holds that

$$|\mathcal{N}_k| \leq (1 + 2^k)^{2m} \leq 4^{(k+1)m} \tag{7.348}$$

by Theorem 1.8. For each $v \in \mathcal{S}(\mathcal{V})$ and $k \in \mathbb{N}$, fix $z_k(v) \in \mathcal{N}_k$ to be any element of the set $\mathcal{N}_k$ for which the distance to v is minimized, which implies that

$$\|v - z_k(v)\| \leq 2^{-k+1}. \tag{7.349}$$

One may observe that $z_0 = z_0(v)$ is independent of v, as there is a single element in the set $\mathcal{N}_0$, and also that

$$\lim_{k \to \infty} z_k(v) = v \tag{7.350}$$

for every $v \in \mathcal{S}(\mathcal{V})$.

Next, observe that

$$X(Uv) = X(Uz_0) + \sum_{k=0}^{\infty} \Big(X(Uz_{k+1}(v)) - X(Uz_k(v)) \Big), \tag{7.351}$$

for every $v \in \mathcal{S}(\mathcal{V})$ and $U \in \mathrm{U}(\mathcal{X})$; this fact may be verified by telescoping the sum and making use of (7.350), along with the continuity of X. It follows that

$$Y_v = Y_{z_0} + \sum_{k=0}^{\infty} (Y_{z_{k+1}(v)} - Y_{z_k(v)}) \tag{7.352}$$

for every $v \in S(\mathcal{V})$. By the triangle inequality, one therefore has

$$\sup\{|Y_v - \beta| : v \in S(\mathcal{V})\}$$
$$\leq |Y_{z_0} - \beta| + \sup\left\{\sum_{k=0}^{\infty} |Y_{z_{k+1}(v)} - Y_{z_k(v)}| : v \in S(\mathcal{V})\right\}. \tag{7.353}$$

The expected value of the two terms on the right-hand side of this inequality will be bounded separately.

The expected value of the first term $|Y_{z_0} - \beta|$ will be considered first. The random variable Y_{z_0} is identically distributed to X, so it follows by Theorem 7.40 that

$$\Pr(|Y_{z_0} - \beta| \geq \lambda) = \Pr(|X - \beta| \geq \lambda) \leq 8 \exp\left(-\frac{\delta_3 \lambda^2 n}{\kappa^2}\right) \tag{7.354}$$

for every $\lambda \geq 0$. This implies that

$$\mathrm{E}(|Y_{z_0} - \beta|) = \int_0^{\infty} \Pr(|Y_{z_0} - \beta| \geq \lambda) \, d\lambda$$
$$\leq 8 \int_0^{\infty} \exp\left(-\frac{\delta_3 \lambda^2 n}{\kappa^2}\right) d\lambda = 4\sqrt{\frac{\pi\kappa^2}{\delta_3 n}} < \frac{8\kappa}{\sqrt{\delta_3 n}}. \tag{7.355}$$

It remains to bound the expected value of the second term on the right-hand side of (7.353). It holds that

$$\|z_{k+1}(v) - z_k(v)\| \leq \|z_{k+1}(v) - v\| + \|v - z_k(v)\| < 2^{-k+2} \tag{7.356}$$

for all $v \in S(\mathcal{V})$ and all $k \in \mathbb{N}$, and therefore

$$\sup\left\{\sum_{k=0}^{\infty} |Y_{z_{k+1}(v)} - Y_{z_k(v)}| : v \in S(\mathcal{V})\right\}$$
$$\leq \sum_{k=0}^{\infty} \max\left\{|Y_x - Y_y| : (x, y) \in \mathcal{M}_k\right\} \tag{7.357}$$

where

$$\mathcal{M}_k = \left\{(x, y) \in \mathcal{N}_{k+1} \times \mathcal{N}_k, \|x - y\| < 2^{-k+2}\right\}. \tag{7.358}$$

By Lemma 7.43, it holds that

$$\Pr\left(|Y_x - Y_y| \geq \varepsilon\right) \leq 3\exp\left(-\frac{\delta_2 \varepsilon^2 (n-1)}{\kappa^2 \|x - y\|^2}\right) \tag{7.359}$$

for every pair of linearly independent vectors $x, y \in \mathcal{S}(\mathcal{V})$, for δ_2 being any positive real number for which Theorem 7.37 holds. (By the assumption that X is phase-invariant, one has $Y_x = Y_y$ if $x, y \in \mathcal{S}(\mathcal{V})$ are linearly dependent.) For each choice of $k \in \mathbb{N}$, it therefore follows from Lemma 7.44 that

$$\mathrm{E}\left(\max\left\{|Y_x - Y_y| : (x, y) \in \mathcal{M}_k\right\}\right) \leq \sqrt{\frac{\ln(N)}{\theta}} + \frac{3}{\sqrt{2\theta}} \tag{7.360}$$

for

$$\theta = \frac{4^k \delta_2 (n-1)}{16\kappa^2} \quad \text{and} \quad N = |\mathcal{M}_k| < 16^{(k+2)m}. \tag{7.361}$$

The remainder of the proof consists of routine calculations showing that the required bound is achieved. Using the bound

$$\sqrt{\ln(N)} \leq \sqrt{\log(N)} < 2\sqrt{(k+2)m}, \tag{7.362}$$

summing over all $k \in \mathbb{N}$, and making use of the summations

$$\sum_{k=0}^{\infty} 2^{-k}\sqrt{k+2} < \frac{7}{2} \quad \text{and} \quad \sum_{k=0}^{\infty} 2^{-k} = 2, \tag{7.363}$$

one concludes that

$$\sum_{k=0}^{\infty} \mathrm{E}\left(\max\left\{|Y_x - Y_y| : (x, y) \in \mathcal{M}_k\right\}\right) < \frac{64\kappa}{\sqrt{\delta_2}}\sqrt{\frac{m}{n}}. \tag{7.364}$$

By (7.353), (7.355), and (7.364), it follows that

$$\mathrm{E}(\sup\{|Y_v - \beta| : v \in \mathcal{S}(\mathcal{V})\}) < \left(\frac{8}{\sqrt{\delta_3}} + \frac{64}{\sqrt{\delta_2}}\right)\kappa\sqrt{\frac{m}{n}}. \tag{7.365}$$

Under the assumption that

$$m \leq \frac{\delta \varepsilon^2 \zeta^2 n}{\kappa^2}, \tag{7.366}$$

for δ satisfying (7.344), it therefore holds that

$$\mathrm{E}(\sup\{|Y_v - \beta| : v \in \mathcal{S}(\mathcal{V})\}) < \zeta\varepsilon, \tag{7.367}$$

which completes the proof. $\qquad\qquad\square$

7.3.2 Applications of Measure Concentration

Two applications of the results on measure concentration discussed in the previous subsection will now be presented. The first is a demonstration that most pure states of a pair of registers are highly entangled, and the second is a proof that the minimum output entropy of channels is non-additive in general. The two applications are related, with the second depending on the first.

Most Pure States Are Highly Entangled

Suppose that $\mathcal{X}$ and $\mathcal{Y}$ are complex Euclidean spaces, and suppose further that the dimensions $n = \dim(\mathcal{X})$ and $m = \dim(\mathcal{Y})$ of these spaces satisfy $n \leq m$. For some choices of a unit vector $u \in \mathcal{X} \otimes \mathcal{Y}$, it holds that

$$\text{Tr}_{\mathcal{Y}}(uu^*) = \omega, \tag{7.368}$$

for $\omega = \mathbb{1}/n$ denoting the completely mixed state with respect to $\mathcal{X}$. Of course, not every unit vector $u \in \mathcal{X} \otimes \mathcal{Y}$ satisfies this equation (unless $n = 1$); but as n grows, the equation holds approximately for an increasingly large portion of the set $\mathcal{S}(\mathcal{X} \otimes \mathcal{Y})$.

The following lemma establishes one specific fact along these lines, in which an approximation with respect to the 2-norm distance between states is considered. The proof makes use of Lévy's lemma (Theorem 7.37), along with calculations of integrals involving the uniform spherical measure.

Lemma 7.45 *There exists a positive real number K_0 with the following property. For complex Euclidean spaces $\mathcal{X}$ and $\mathcal{Y}$ of dimensions $n = \dim(\mathcal{X})$ and $m = \dim(\mathcal{Y})$, and for*

$$X : \mathcal{S}(\mathcal{X} \otimes \mathcal{Y}) \rightarrow \mathbb{R} \tag{7.369}$$

being a random variable, distributed with respect to the uniform spherical measure on $\mathcal{S}(\mathcal{X} \otimes \mathcal{Y})$ and defined as

$$X(u) = \left\| \text{Tr}_{\mathcal{Y}}(uu^*) - \omega \right\|_2 \tag{7.370}$$

for $\omega = \mathbb{1}/n$, it holds that

$$\Pr\left(X \geq \frac{K_0}{\sqrt{m}} \right) < 4^{-n}. \tag{7.371}$$

Proof It will be proved that the lemma holds for $K_0 = \sqrt{12/\delta_2} + 1$, for δ_2 being any positive real number satisfying the requirements of the mean value form of Lévy's lemma (Theorem 7.37).

The random variable X may alternatively be defined as

$$X(\text{vec}(A)) = \|AA^* - \omega\|_2 \tag{7.372}$$

for every operator $A \in \text{L}(\mathcal{Y}, \mathcal{X})$ satisfying $\|A\|_2 = 1$. The triangle inequality implies that

$$|X(\text{vec}(A)) - X(\text{vec}(B))| \leq \|AA^* - BB^*\|_2. \tag{7.373}$$

Again using the triangle inequality, along with the fact that the 2-norm is submultiplicative, one has

$$\|AA^* - BB^*\|_2 \leq \|AA^* - AB^*\|_2 + \|AB^* - BB^*\|_2$$
$$\leq (\|A\|_2 + \|B\|_2)\|A - B\|_2 \leq 2\|A - B\|_2, \tag{7.374}$$

for all $A, B \in \text{L}(\mathcal{Y}, \mathcal{X})$ with $\|A\|_2 = \|B\|_2 = 1$. It therefore holds that X is 2-Lipschitz.

Next, it will be proved that

$$\text{E}(X) \leq \frac{1}{\sqrt{m}}. \tag{7.375}$$

This bound follows from Jensen's inequality,

$$(\text{E}(X))^2 \leq \text{E}(X^2), \tag{7.376}$$

along with an evaluation of $\text{E}(X^2)$. To evaluate this expectation, observe first that

$$\|\text{Tr}_{\mathcal{Y}}(uu^*) - \omega\|_2^2 = \text{Tr}\left(\left(\text{Tr}_{\mathcal{Y}}(uu^*)\right)^2\right) - \frac{1}{n}. \tag{7.377}$$

For every vector $u \in \mathcal{X} \otimes \mathcal{Y}$, it holds that

$$\text{Tr}\left(\left(\text{Tr}_{\mathcal{Y}}(uu^*)\right)^2\right) = \langle V, uu^* \otimes uu^* \rangle, \tag{7.378}$$

for $V \in \text{L}(\mathcal{X} \otimes \mathcal{Y} \otimes \mathcal{X} \otimes \mathcal{Y})$ being the operator defined as

$$V(x_0 \otimes y_0 \otimes x_1 \otimes y_1) = x_1 \otimes y_0 \otimes x_0 \otimes y_1 \tag{7.379}$$

for all vectors $x_0, x_1 \in \mathcal{X}$ and $y_0, y_1 \in \mathcal{Y}$. Equivalently, for Σ and Γ denoting the alphabets for which $\mathcal{X} = \mathbb{C}^\Sigma$ and $\mathcal{Y} = \mathbb{C}^\Gamma$, one may write

$$V = \sum_{\substack{a,b \in \Sigma \\ c,d \in \Gamma}} E_{a,b} \otimes E_{c,c} \otimes E_{b,a} \otimes E_{d,d}. \tag{7.380}$$

Integrating with respect to the uniform spherical measure yields

$$\mathrm{E}(X^2) = \int \langle V, uu^* \otimes uu^* \rangle \, d\mu(u) - \frac{1}{n}$$

$$= \frac{1}{\binom{nm+1}{2}} \langle V, \Pi_{(\mathcal{X} \otimes \mathcal{Y}) \otimes (\mathcal{X} \otimes \mathcal{Y})} \rangle - \frac{1}{n}. \tag{7.381}$$

A case analysis reveals that

$$\langle E_{a,b} \otimes E_{c,c} \otimes E_{b,a} \otimes E_{d,d}, \Pi_{(\mathcal{X} \otimes \mathcal{Y}) \otimes (\mathcal{X} \otimes \mathcal{Y})} \rangle$$

$$= \begin{cases} 1 & \text{if } a = b \text{ and } c = d \\ \frac{1}{2} & \text{if } (a = b \text{ and } c \neq d) \text{ or } (a \neq b \text{ and } c = d) \\ 0 & \text{if } a \neq b \text{ and } c \neq d. \end{cases} \tag{7.382}$$

Performing the required arithmetic yields

$$\mathrm{E}(X^2) = \frac{n+m}{nm+1} - \frac{1}{n} < \frac{1}{m}, \tag{7.383}$$

and therefore (7.375) has been established.

Finally, by the mean value form of Lévy's lemma (Theorem 7.37), one has

$$\Pr\left(X \geq \frac{K_0}{\sqrt{m}}\right) \leq 2 \exp\left(-\frac{\delta_2 (K_0 - 1)^2 n}{4}\right). \tag{7.384}$$

For $K_0 = \sqrt{12/\delta_2} + 1$, one has

$$2 \exp\left(-\frac{\delta_2 (K_0 - 1)^2 n}{4}\right) = 2 \exp(-3n) < 4^{-n}, \tag{7.385}$$

which completes the proof. $\qquad\square$

If $\mathrm{Tr}_{\mathcal{Y}}(uu^*)$ is approximately equal to the completely mixed state ω, for a given unit vector $u \in \mathcal{X} \otimes \mathcal{Y}$, then it is reasonable to expect that the entanglement entropy $\mathrm{H}(\mathrm{Tr}_{\mathcal{Y}}(uu^*))$ of the pure state represented by u will be approximately equal to its maximum possible value $\log(\dim(\mathcal{X}))$, depending on the particular notions of approximate equality under consideration. The following lemma establishes a lower bound on the von Neumann entropy that allows a precise implication along these lines to be made when combined with Lemma 7.45.

Lemma 7.46 *Let $\mathcal{X}$ be a complex Euclidean space and let $n = \dim(\mathcal{X})$. For every density operator $\rho \in \mathrm{D}(\mathcal{X})$ it holds that*

$$\mathrm{H}(\rho) \geq \log(n) - \frac{n}{\ln(2)} \|\rho - \omega\|_2^2, \tag{7.386}$$

where $\omega = \mathbb{1}/n$ denotes the completely mixed state with respect to $\mathcal{X}$.

Proof It holds that $\ln(\alpha) \leq \alpha - 1$ for all $\alpha > 0$, and therefore

$$\frac{n}{\ln(2)}\|\rho - \omega\|_2^2 = \frac{n\operatorname{Tr}(\rho^2) - 1}{\ln(2)} \tag{7.387}$$

$$\geq \log(n\operatorname{Tr}(\rho^2)) = \log(n) + \log(\operatorname{Tr}(\rho^2)).$$

The logarithm function is concave, and therefore one has

$$-\operatorname{H}(p) = \sum_{a \in \Sigma} p(a)\log(p(a)) \leq \log\left(\sum_{a \in \Sigma} p(a)^2\right) \tag{7.388}$$

for every alphabet Σ and every probability vector $p \in \mathcal{P}(\Sigma)$. Consequently,

$$-\operatorname{H}(\rho) \leq \log(\operatorname{Tr}(\rho^2)), \tag{7.389}$$

and therefore

$$\frac{n}{\ln(2)}\|\rho - \omega\|_2^2 \geq \log(n) - \operatorname{H}(\rho), \tag{7.390}$$

which is equivalent to the required inequality. $\qquad\square$

As a consequence of Lemmas 7.45 and 7.46, it follows that most bipartite pure states have an entanglement entropy that is close to this quantity's maximum possible value.

Theorem 7.47 *There exists a positive real number K with the following property. For every choice of complex Euclidean spaces $\mathcal{X}$ and $\mathcal{Y}$, and for $X : \mathcal{S}(\mathcal{X} \otimes \mathcal{Y}) \to \mathbb{R}$ being a random variable, distributed with respect to the uniform spherical measure on $\mathcal{S}(\mathcal{X} \otimes \mathcal{Y})$ and defined as*

$$X(u) = \operatorname{H}(\operatorname{Tr}_{\mathcal{Y}}(uu^*)) \tag{7.391}$$

for every $u \in \mathcal{S}(\mathcal{X} \otimes \mathcal{Y})$, it holds that

$$\Pr\left(X \leq \log(n) - \frac{Kn}{m}\right) < 4^{-n}, \tag{7.392}$$

for $n = \dim(\mathcal{X})$ and $m = \dim(\mathcal{Y})$.

Proof It will be proved that the theorem holds for $K = K_0^2/\ln(2)$, where K_0 is any positive real number that satisfies the requirements of Lemma 7.45.

Define a random variable $Y : \mathcal{S}(\mathcal{X} \otimes \mathcal{Y}) \to \mathbb{R}$, distributed with respect to the uniform spherical measure, as

$$Y(u) = \|\operatorname{Tr}_{\mathcal{Y}}(uu^*) - \omega\|_2 \tag{7.393}$$

for every $u \in \mathcal{S}(\mathcal{X} \otimes \mathcal{Y})$. If a given unit vector $u \in \mathcal{X} \otimes \mathcal{Y}$ satisfies

$$Y(u) < \frac{K_0}{\sqrt{m}}, \tag{7.394}$$

then

$$X(u) > \log(n) - \frac{n}{\ln(2)}\frac{K_0^2}{m} = \log(n) - \frac{Kn}{m} \qquad (7.395)$$

by Lemma 7.46. One therefore has that

$$\Pr\left(X > \log(n) - \frac{Kn}{m}\right) \ge \Pr\left(Y < \frac{K_0}{\sqrt{m}}\right) > 1 - 4^{-n} \qquad (7.396)$$

by Lemma 7.45. This bound is equivalent to (7.392), which completes the proof. $\qquad \square$

Counter-Example to the Additivity of Minimum Output Entropy

The minimum output entropy of a channel is, as the following definition states explicitly, the minimum value of the von Neumann entropy that can be obtained by evaluating that channel on a quantum state input.

Definition 7.48 Let $\Phi \in C(\mathcal{X}, \mathcal{Y})$ be a channel, for complex Euclidean spaces $\mathcal{X}$ and $\mathcal{Y}$. The *minimum output entropy* of Φ is defined as

$$\mathrm{H_{min}}(\Phi) = \min\{\mathrm{H}(\Phi(\rho)) : \rho \in D(\mathcal{X})\}. \qquad (7.397)$$

It follows from the concavity of the von Neumann entropy function that the minimum output entropy $\mathrm{H_{min}}(\Phi)$ of a given channel $\Phi \in C(\mathcal{X}, \mathcal{Y})$ is achieved by a pure state:

$$\mathrm{H_{min}}(\Phi) = \min\{\mathrm{H}(\Phi(uu^*)) : u \in S(\mathcal{X})\}. \qquad (7.398)$$

It was a long-standing conjecture that the minimum output entropy is additive with respect to tensor products of channels. The following theorem demonstrates that this is, in fact, not the case.

Theorem 7.49 (Hastings) *There exist complex Euclidean spaces $\mathcal{X}$ and $\mathcal{Y}$ and channels $\Phi, \Psi \in C(\mathcal{X}, \mathcal{Y})$ such that*

$$\mathrm{H_{min}}(\Phi \otimes \Psi) < \mathrm{H_{min}}(\Phi) + \mathrm{H_{min}}(\Psi). \qquad (7.399)$$

A high-level overview of the proof of Theorem 7.49 is as follows. For each choice of a positive integer n, one may consider complex Euclidean spaces $\mathcal{X}$, $\mathcal{Y}$, and $\mathcal{Z}$ with

$$\dim(\mathcal{X}) = n^2, \quad \dim(\mathcal{Y}) = n, \quad \text{and} \quad \dim(\mathcal{Z}) = n^2. \qquad (7.400)$$

It will be proved, for a sufficiently large choice of n, that there exists an isometry $V \in U(\mathcal{X}, \mathcal{Y} \otimes \mathcal{Z})$ for which the channels $\Phi, \Psi \in C(\mathcal{X}, \mathcal{Y})$ defined as

$$\Phi(X) = \mathrm{Tr}_{\mathcal{Z}}(VXV^*) \quad \text{and} \quad \Psi(X) = \mathrm{Tr}_{\mathcal{Z}}(\overline{V}XV^{\mathsf{T}}) \qquad (7.401)$$

for all $X \in \mathrm{L}(\mathcal{X})$ yield the strict inequality (7.399). The existence of a suitable isometry V is proved using the probabilistic method: for any fixed isometry $V_0 \in \mathrm{U}(\mathcal{X}, \mathcal{Y} \otimes \mathcal{Z})$, the set of all unitary operators $U \in \mathrm{U}(\mathcal{Y} \otimes \mathcal{Z})$ for which the isometry $V = U V_0$ possesses the required property will be shown to have positive measure, with respect to the Haar measure on $\mathrm{U}(\mathcal{Y} \otimes \mathcal{Z})$.

The proof of Theorem 7.49 will make use of the lemmas that follow. The first lemma provides an upper bound on the minimum output entropy of the tensor product $\Phi \otimes \Psi$ for two channels Φ and Ψ defined as in (7.401).

Lemma 7.50 *Let n be a positive integer and let $\mathcal{X}$, $\mathcal{Y}$, and $\mathcal{Z}$ be complex Euclidean spaces with $\dim(\mathcal{X}) = n^2$, $\dim(\mathcal{Y}) = n$, and $\dim(\mathcal{Z}) = n^2$. Let $V \in \mathrm{U}(\mathcal{X}, \mathcal{Y} \otimes \mathcal{Z})$ be an isometry, and define channels $\Phi, \Psi \in \mathrm{C}(\mathcal{X}, \mathcal{Y})$ as*

$$\Phi(X) = \mathrm{Tr}_{\mathcal{Z}}(V X V^*) \quad and \quad \Psi(X) = \mathrm{Tr}_{\mathcal{Z}}(\overline{V} X V^{\mathsf{T}}) \tag{7.402}$$

for all $X \in \mathrm{L}(\mathcal{X})$. It holds that

$$\mathrm{H}_{\min}(\Phi \otimes \Psi) \leq 2 \log(n) - \frac{\log(n) - 2}{n}. \tag{7.403}$$

Proof Define pure states $\tau \in \mathrm{D}(\mathcal{X} \otimes \mathcal{X})$ and $\sigma \in \mathrm{D}(\mathcal{Y} \otimes \mathcal{Y})$ as follows:

$$\tau = \frac{\mathrm{vec}(\mathbb{1}_{\mathcal{X}}) \mathrm{vec}(\mathbb{1}_{\mathcal{X}})^*}{n^2} \quad and \quad \sigma = \frac{\mathrm{vec}(\mathbb{1}_{\mathcal{Y}}) \mathrm{vec}(\mathbb{1}_{\mathcal{Y}})^*}{n}. \tag{7.404}$$

A calculation reveals that

$$\langle \sigma, (\Phi \otimes \Psi)(\tau) \rangle = \frac{1}{n^3} \| \mathrm{Tr}_{\mathcal{Y}}(V V^*) \|_2^2. \tag{7.405}$$

In greater detail, supposing that $\mathcal{Y} = \mathbb{C}^{\Sigma}$, one has

$$
\begin{aligned}
&\langle \sigma, (\Phi \otimes \Psi)(\tau) \rangle \\
&= \frac{1}{n} \sum_{a,b \in \Sigma} \left\langle V^*(E_{a,b} \otimes \mathbb{1}_{\mathcal{Z}}) V \otimes V^{\mathsf{T}}(E_{a,b} \otimes \mathbb{1}_{\mathcal{Z}}) \overline{V}, \tau \right\rangle \\
&= \frac{1}{n^3} \sum_{a,b \in \Sigma} \mathrm{Tr}\left((V^*(E_{b,a} \otimes \mathbb{1}_{\mathcal{Z}}) V)(V^*(E_{a,b} \otimes \mathbb{1}_{\mathcal{Z}}) V) \right) \\
&= \frac{1}{n^3} \| \mathrm{Tr}_{\mathcal{Y}}(V V^*) \|_2^2.
\end{aligned}
\tag{7.406}
$$

The operator $\mathrm{Tr}_{\mathcal{Y}}(V V^*)$ is positive semidefinite, and has trace equal to n^2 and rank at most n^2, so it follows that its 2-norm squared must be at least n^2. Consequently, one has

$$\lambda_1((\Phi \otimes \Psi)(\tau)) \geq \langle \sigma, (\Phi \otimes \Psi)(\tau) \rangle \geq \frac{1}{n}. \tag{7.407}$$

Now, under the constraint that a given density operator $\rho \in D(\mathcal{Y} \otimes \mathcal{Y})$ has largest eigenvalue at least $1/n$, it holds that the von Neumann entropy $H(\rho)$ is maximized when this largest eigenvalue is equal to $1/n$ and all other eigenvalues are equal:

$$H(\rho) \leq \left(1 - \frac{1}{n}\right) \log(n^2 - 1) + H\left(\frac{1}{n}, 1 - \frac{1}{n}\right). \tag{7.408}$$

Because $\ln(\alpha) \geq 1 - 1/\alpha$ for all positive α, one finds that

$$H(\lambda, 1 - \lambda) \leq -\lambda \log(\lambda) + \frac{\lambda}{\ln(2)} \leq -\lambda \log(\lambda) + 2\lambda \tag{7.409}$$

for all $\lambda \in [0, 1]$, and therefore

$$H(\rho) \leq 2\log(n) - \frac{\log(n) - 2}{n}. \tag{7.410}$$

As this inequality holds for $\rho = (\Phi \otimes \Psi)(\tau)$, the proof is complete. $\qquad\square$

The remaining lemmas required for the proof of Theorem 7.49 are used to establish a lower bound on the quantity $H_{\min}(\Phi) + H_{\min}(\Psi)$, for some choice of channels Φ and Ψ taking the form (7.401). The first lemma is concerned with the modification of a random variable that is Lipschitz on a compact subset of its domain, yielding one that is Lipschitz everywhere.

Lemma 7.51 *Let $\mathcal{X}$ be a complex Euclidean space, let $X : S(\mathcal{X}) \to \mathbb{R}$ be a continuous random variable, distributed with respect to the uniform spherical measure μ on $S(\mathcal{X})$, and let $\mathcal{A} \subseteq S(\mathcal{X})$ be a compact subset of $S(\mathcal{X})$ satisfying $\mu(\mathcal{A}) \geq 3/4$. Let κ be a positive real number such that*

$$|X(x) - X(y)| \leq \kappa \|x - y\| \tag{7.411}$$

for all $x, y \in \mathcal{A}$, and define a new random variable $Y : S(\mathcal{X}) \to \mathbb{R}$, distributed with respect to μ, as

$$Y(x) = \min_{y \in \mathcal{A}}(X(y) + \kappa \|x - y\|) \tag{7.412}$$

for all $x \in S(\mathcal{X})$. The following statements hold:

1. *Y is κ-Lipschitz.*
2. *For every $x \in \mathcal{A}$, one has that $X(x) = Y(x)$.*
3. *Every median value of Y is a central value of X.*

Proof The first statement holds regardless of the behavior of X on points in $\mathcal{A}$. Consider any two vectors $x_0, x_1 \in S(\mathcal{X})$, and let $y_0, y_1 \in \mathcal{A}$ satisfy

$$Y(x_0) = X(y_0) + \kappa \|x_0 - y_0\| \quad \text{and} \quad Y(x_1) = X(y_1) + \kappa \|x_1 - y_1\|. \tag{7.413}$$

That is, y_0 and y_1 achieve the minimum values that define the function Y on x_0 and x_1, respectively. It must therefore hold that

$$X(y_0) + \kappa \|x_0 - y_0\| \leq X(y_1) + \kappa \|x_0 - y_1\|, \tag{7.414}$$

which implies

$$Y(x_0) - Y(x_1) \leq \kappa \|x_0 - y_1\| - \kappa \|x_1 - y_1\| \leq \kappa \|x_0 - x_1\|. \tag{7.415}$$

The inequality

$$Y(x_1) - Y(x_0) \leq \kappa \|x_0 - x_1\| \tag{7.416}$$

is proved through the same argument by exchanging the indices 0 and 1. It therefore holds that

$$|Y(x_0) - Y(x_1)| \leq \kappa \|x_0 - x_1\|, \tag{7.417}$$

so Y is κ-Lipschitz.

Next, consider any vector $x \in \mathcal{A}$. By the assumptions of the lemma, one has

$$|X(x) - X(y)| \leq \kappa \|x - y\| \tag{7.418}$$

for every $y \in \mathcal{A}$, and therefore

$$Y(x) - X(x) = \min_{y \in \mathcal{A}} \Big(X(y) - X(x) + \kappa \|x - y\| \Big) \geq 0. \tag{7.419}$$

On the other hand, because one may choose $y = x$ when considering the minimum, it holds that $Y(x) \leq X(x)$. It follows that $X(x) = Y(x)$, which establishes the second statement.

Finally, let $\alpha \in \mathbb{R}$ be a median value of Y, so that

$$\Pr(Y \geq \alpha) \geq \frac{1}{2} \quad \text{and} \quad \Pr(Y \leq \alpha) \geq \frac{1}{2}. \tag{7.420}$$

Define a random variable $Z \colon \mathcal{S}(\mathcal{X}) \to [0,1]$, again distributed with respect to μ, as

$$Z(x) = \begin{cases} 1 & \text{if } x \in \mathcal{A} \\ 0 & \text{if } x \notin \mathcal{A}, \end{cases} \tag{7.421}$$

so that $\Pr(Z = 0) \leq 1/4$. By the union bound, one has

$$\Pr(Y < \alpha \text{ or } Z = 0) \leq \frac{3}{4}, \tag{7.422}$$

and therefore

$$\Pr(X \geq \alpha) \geq \Pr(Y \geq \alpha \text{ and } Z = 1) \geq \frac{1}{4}. \tag{7.423}$$

By similar reasoning,

$$\Pr(X \le \alpha) \ge \Pr(Y \le \alpha \text{ and } Z = 1) \ge \frac{1}{4}. \tag{7.424}$$

This implies that α is a central value of X, which completes the proof. □

The next lemma is, in some sense, the heart of the proof of Theorem 7.49. It establishes the existence of an isometry $V \in U(\mathcal{X}, \mathcal{Y} \otimes \mathcal{Z})$ that may be taken in the definition (7.401) of the channels Φ and Ψ to obtain the inequality (7.399) for a sufficiently large value of n. It is proved through the use of Dvoretzky's theorem.

Lemma 7.52 *There exists a real number $K > 0$ for which the following statement holds. For every choice of a positive integer n, and for $\mathcal{X}$, $\mathcal{Y}$, and $\mathcal{Z}$ being complex Euclidean spaces with*

$$\dim(\mathcal{X}) = n^2, \quad \dim(\mathcal{Y}) = n, \quad and \quad \dim(\mathcal{Z}) = n^2, \tag{7.425}$$

there exists an isometry $V \in U(\mathcal{X}, \mathcal{Y} \otimes \mathcal{Z})$ such that

$$\left\| \mathrm{Tr}_{\mathcal{Z}}(V x x^* V^*) - \omega \right\|_2 \le \frac{K}{n} \tag{7.426}$$

for every unit vector $x \in \mathcal{S}(\mathcal{X})$, where $\omega = \mathbb{1}/n$ denotes the completely mixed state with respect to $\mathcal{Y}$.

Proof Let δ be a positive real number that satisfies the requirements of Dvoretzky's theorem (Theorem 7.42) and let K_0 be a positive real number satisfying the requirements of Lemma 7.45. It will be proved that the lemma holds for

$$K = K_0 + 6 \sqrt{\frac{K_0 + 1}{\delta}} + \frac{18}{\delta}. \tag{7.427}$$

Assume, for the remainder of the proof, that a positive integer n and complex Euclidean spaces $\mathcal{X}$, $\mathcal{Y}$, and $\mathcal{Z}$ satisfying (7.425) have been fixed. Let $\mathcal{V}$ be an arbitrary subspace of $\mathcal{Y} \otimes \mathcal{Z}$ having dimension n^2. Throughout the proof, μ will denote the uniform spherical measure on $\mathcal{S}(\mathcal{Y} \otimes \mathcal{Z})$, and η will denote the Haar measure on $U(\mathcal{Y} \otimes \mathcal{Z})$.

The first step of the proof is the specification of a collection of random variables; an analysis of these random variables follows their specification. First, let

$$X, Y \colon \mathcal{S}(\mathcal{Y} \otimes \mathcal{Z}) \to \mathbb{R} \tag{7.428}$$

be random variables, distributed with respect to the uniform spherical measure μ and defined as follows:

$$X(u) = \sqrt{\|\operatorname{Tr}_{\mathcal{Z}}(uu^*)\|} \quad \text{and} \quad Y(u) = \|\operatorname{Tr}_{\mathcal{Z}}(uu^*) - \omega\|_2 \qquad (7.429)$$

for all $u \in \mathcal{S}(\mathcal{Y} \otimes \mathcal{Z})$. Next, let

$$K_1 = \sqrt{K_0 + 1} + \frac{3}{\sqrt{\delta}} \quad \text{and} \quad \kappa = \frac{2K_1}{\sqrt{n}}, \qquad (7.430)$$

define a set

$$\mathcal{A} = \left\{ u \in \mathcal{S}(\mathcal{Y} \otimes \mathcal{Z}) : X(u) \leq \frac{K_1}{\sqrt{n}} \right\}, \qquad (7.431)$$

and define a random variable $Z: \mathcal{S}(\mathcal{Y} \otimes \mathcal{Z}) \to \mathbb{R}$, also distributed with respect to the uniform spherical measure μ, as

$$Z(u) = \min_{v \in \mathcal{A}} (Y(v) + \kappa \|u - v\|) \qquad (7.432)$$

for every $u \in \mathcal{S}(\mathcal{Y} \otimes \mathcal{Z})$. It is evident from their specifications that X, Y, and Z are phase-invariant random variables. Finally, for each unit vector $v \in \mathcal{S}(\mathcal{V})$, define random variables

$$P_v, Q_v, R_v: \mathrm{U}(\mathcal{Y} \otimes \mathcal{Z}) \to \mathbb{R}, \qquad (7.433)$$

distributed with respect to the Haar measure η on $\mathrm{U}(\mathcal{Y} \otimes \mathcal{Z})$, as

$$P_v(U) = X(Uv), \quad Q_v(U) = Y(Uv), \quad \text{and} \quad R_v(U) = Z(Uv), \qquad (7.434)$$

for every $U \in \mathrm{U}(\mathcal{Y} \otimes \mathcal{Z})$.

When analyzing the random variables that have just been defined, it is helpful to begin with the observation that

$$X(\operatorname{vec}(A)) = \|A\| \quad \text{and} \quad Y(\operatorname{vec}(A)) = \|AA^* - \omega\|_2 \qquad (7.435)$$

for every operator $A \in \mathrm{L}(\mathcal{Z}, \mathcal{Y})$ satisfying $\|A\|_2 = 1$. It is immediate from the first of these expressions, along with the inequality $\|A\| \leq \|A\|_2$, that X is 1-Lipschitz. Also, given that

$$\|A\|^2 = \|AA^*\| \leq \|AA^* - \omega\| + \|\omega\| \leq \|AA^* - \omega\|_2 + \frac{1}{n} \qquad (7.436)$$

for every operator $A \in \mathrm{L}(\mathcal{Z}, \mathcal{Y})$, one necessarily has that

$$X^2 \leq Y + \frac{1}{n}. \qquad (7.437)$$

By Lemma 7.45, one may therefore conclude that

$$\Pr\left(X \leq \sqrt{\frac{K_0 + 1}{n}}\right) \geq \Pr\left(Y \leq \frac{K_0}{n}\right) > \frac{3}{4}. \qquad (7.438)$$

Dvoretzky's theorem (Theorem 7.42) will be applied twice in the proof, with the first application concerning the random variables X and P_v for each $v \in \mathcal{S}(\mathcal{V})$. By (7.438), it follows that every central value of X is at most

$$\sqrt{\frac{K_0 + 1}{n}}. \tag{7.439}$$

Setting

$$\varepsilon = \frac{3}{\sqrt{\delta n}} \quad \text{and} \quad \zeta = \frac{1}{3} \tag{7.440}$$

in Dvoretzky's theorem yields

$$\mathrm{Pr}\left(P_v \leq \frac{K_1}{\sqrt{n}} \text{ for every } v \in \mathcal{S}(\mathcal{V})\right) \geq \frac{2}{3}, \tag{7.441}$$

by virtue of the fact that $\dim(\mathcal{V}) = \delta \varepsilon^2 \zeta^2 \dim(\mathcal{Y} \otimes \mathcal{Z})$.

The second application of Dvoretzky's theorem concerns Z and R_v for each $v \in \mathcal{S}(\mathcal{V})$. Before applying Dvoretzky's theorem, however, the implications of Lemma 7.51 to the random variables Y and Z will be considered. First, note that

$$\mu(\mathcal{A}) = \mathrm{Pr}\left(X \leq \frac{K_1}{\sqrt{n}}\right) \geq \mathrm{Pr}\left(X \leq \sqrt{\frac{K_0 + 1}{n}}\right) > \frac{3}{4}. \tag{7.442}$$

Second, for any choice of vectors $u, v \in \mathcal{A}$, one may write $u = \mathrm{vec}(A)$ and $v = \mathrm{vec}(B)$ for $A, B \in \mathrm{L}(\mathcal{Z}, \mathcal{Y})$ satisfying $\|A\|_2 = \|B\|_2 = 1$, so that

$$\|A\| = X(\mathrm{vec}(A)) \leq \frac{K_1}{\sqrt{n}} \quad \text{and} \quad \|B\| = X(\mathrm{vec}(B)) \leq \frac{K_1}{\sqrt{n}}. \tag{7.443}$$

This implies that

$$\begin{aligned}|Y(u) - Y(v)| &= \left|\|AA^* - \omega\|_2 - \|BB^* - \omega\|_2\right| \\ &\leq \|AA^* - BB^*\|_2 \leq (\|A\| + \|B\|)\|A - B\|_2 \leq \kappa\|u - v\|.\end{aligned} \tag{7.444}$$

It therefore follows from Lemma 7.51 that Z is κ-Lipschitz, Z and Y agree everywhere on $\mathcal{A}$, and every median value of Z is a central value of Y. By (7.438), every central value of Y is at most K_0/n, and therefore the same upper bound applies to every median value of Z. Setting

$$\varepsilon = \frac{3\kappa}{\sqrt{\delta n}} \quad \text{and} \quad \zeta = \frac{1}{3} \tag{7.445}$$

and applying Dvoretzky's theorem therefore yields

$$\mathrm{Pr}\left(R_v \leq \frac{K}{n} \text{ for all } v \in \mathcal{S}(\mathcal{V})\right) \geq \frac{2}{3}, \tag{7.446}$$

by virtue of the fact that

$$\dim(\mathcal{V}) = \frac{\delta\varepsilon^2\zeta^2}{\kappa^2} \dim(\mathcal{Y} \otimes \mathcal{Z}).$$ (7.447)

Finally, consider the random variables Y and Q_v for each $v \in \mathcal{S}(\mathcal{V})$. For every vector $u \in \mathcal{S}(\mathcal{Y} \otimes \mathcal{Z})$, one has either $u \in \mathcal{A}$ or $u \notin \mathcal{A}$; and if it holds that $u \in \mathcal{A}$, then $Y(u) = Z(u)$. Consequently, if it holds that $Y(u) > K/n$ for a given choice of $u \in \mathcal{S}(\mathcal{Y} \otimes \mathcal{Z})$, then it must hold that

$$Z(u) > \frac{K}{n} \quad \text{or} \quad X(u) > \frac{K_1}{\sqrt{n}}$$ (7.448)

(or both). By the union bound, one concludes that

$$\Pr\left(Q_v > \frac{K}{n} \text{ for some } v \in \mathcal{S}(\mathcal{V})\right)$$

$$\leq \Pr\left(R_v > \frac{K}{n} \text{ for some } v \in \mathcal{S}(\mathcal{V})\right)$$ (7.449)

$$+ \Pr\left(P_v > \frac{K_1}{\sqrt{n}} \text{ for some } v \in \mathcal{S}(\mathcal{V})\right).$$

By (7.441) and (7.446), it follows that

$$\Pr\left(Q_v \leq \frac{K}{n} \text{ for all } v \in \mathcal{S}(\mathcal{V})\right) \geq \frac{1}{3} > 0.$$ (7.450)

By (7.450), one concludes that there exists a unitary operator U for which $Q_v(U) \leq K/n$ for all $v \in \mathcal{S}(\mathcal{V})$. Taking $V_0 \in U(\mathcal{X}, \mathcal{Y} \otimes \mathcal{Z})$ to be any linear isometry for which $\text{im}(V_0) = \mathcal{V}$, one therefore has

$$\left\|\text{Tr}_{\mathcal{Z}}(UV_0 xx^* V_0^* U^*) - \omega\right\|_2 \leq \frac{K}{n}$$ (7.451)

for every unit vector $x \in \mathcal{S}(\mathcal{X})$. Taking $V = UV_0$, the lemma is proved. $\quad\square$

Finally, a proof of Theorem 7.49 is to be presented. The proof is made quite straightforward through the use of Lemmas 7.50 and 7.52.

Proof of Theorem 7.49   Let $K > 0$ be a real number for which Lemma 7.52 holds, and choose n to be a positive integer satisfying

$$\log(n) > \frac{2K^2}{\ln(2)} + 2.$$ (7.452)

For $\mathcal{X}$, $\mathcal{Y}$, and $\mathcal{Z}$ being complex Euclidean spaces with $\dim(\mathcal{X}) = n^2$, $\dim(\mathcal{Y}) = n$, and $\dim(\mathcal{Z}) = n^2$, it follows (by Lemma 7.52) that there exists an isometry $V \in \mathrm{U}(\mathcal{X}, \mathcal{Y} \otimes \mathcal{Z})$ such that

$$\left\| \mathrm{Tr}_{\mathcal{Z}}(V x x^* V^*) - \frac{\mathbb{1}_{\mathcal{Y}}}{n} \right\|_2 \leq \frac{K}{n} \tag{7.453}$$

for every unit vector $x \in \mathcal{S}(\mathcal{X})$. By Lemma 7.46, one therefore has that

$$\mathrm{H}(\mathrm{Tr}_{\mathcal{Z}}(V x x^* V^*)) \geq \log(n) - \frac{K^2}{n \ln(2)} \tag{7.454}$$

for every $x \in \mathcal{S}(\mathcal{X})$. Replacing V by the entry-wise complex conjugate of V results in the same bound:

$$\mathrm{H}(\mathrm{Tr}_{\mathcal{Z}}(\overline{V} x x^* V^{\mathsf{T}})) \geq \log(n) - \frac{K^2}{n \ln(2)} \tag{7.455}$$

for every $x \in \mathcal{S}(\mathcal{X})$.

Now, define channels $\Phi, \Psi \in \mathrm{C}(\mathcal{X}, \mathcal{Y})$ as

$$\Phi(X) = \mathrm{Tr}_{\mathcal{Z}}(V X V^*) \quad \text{and} \quad \Psi(X) = \mathrm{Tr}_{\mathcal{Z}}(\overline{V} X V^{\mathsf{T}}) \tag{7.456}$$

for all $X \in \mathrm{L}(\mathcal{X})$. One has that

$$\mathrm{H}_{\min}(\Phi) = \mathrm{H}_{\min}(\Psi) \geq \log(n) - \frac{K^2}{n \ln(2)}, \tag{7.457}$$

and therefore

$$\mathrm{H}_{\min}(\Phi) + \mathrm{H}_{\min}(\Psi) \geq 2\log(n) - \frac{2K^2}{n \ln(2)}. \tag{7.458}$$

On the other hand, Lemma 7.50 implies that

$$\mathrm{H}_{\min}(\Phi \otimes \Psi) \leq 2\log(n) - \frac{\log(n) - 2}{n}. \tag{7.459}$$

Consequently,

$$\mathrm{H}_{\min}(\Phi \otimes \Psi) - (\mathrm{H}_{\min}(\Phi) + \mathrm{H}_{\min}(\Psi))$$
$$= \frac{2K^2}{n \ln(2)} - \frac{\log(n) - 2}{n} < 0, \tag{7.460}$$

which completes the proof. $\qquad\qquad\qquad\qquad\qquad\qquad\qquad\qquad\square$

7.4 Exercises

Exercise 7.1 For every positive integer $n \geq 2$, define a unital channel $\Phi_n \in \mathrm{C}(\mathbb{C}^n)$ as

$$\Phi_n(X) = \frac{1}{n-1} \mathrm{Tr}(X) \mathbb{1}_n - \frac{1}{n-1} X^{\mathsf{T}} \tag{7.461}$$

for every $X \in \mathrm{L}(\mathbb{C}^n)$, where $\mathbb{1}_n$ denotes the identity operator on $\mathbb{C}^n$. Prove that Φ_n is a mixed-unitary channel when n is even. (Observe that this exercise is complementary to Exercise 4.2.)

Exercise 7.2 Let n and m be positive integers with $n < m$, and consider the set $\mathrm{U}(\mathbb{C}^n, \mathbb{C}^m)$ of all isometries from $\mathbb{C}^n$ to $\mathbb{C}^m$.

(a) Prove that there exists a Borel probability measure

$$\nu \colon \mathrm{Borel}(\mathrm{U}(\mathbb{C}^n, \mathbb{C}^m)) \to [0, 1] \tag{7.462}$$

for which it holds that

$$\nu(\mathcal{A}) = \nu(U\mathcal{A}V) \tag{7.463}$$

for every choice of a Borel subset $\mathcal{A} \in \mathrm{Borel}(\mathrm{U}(\mathbb{C}^n, \mathbb{C}^m))$ and unitary operators $U \in \mathrm{U}(\mathbb{C}^m)$ and $V \in \mathrm{U}(\mathbb{C}^n)$.

(b) Prove that if

$$\mu \colon \mathrm{Borel}(\mathrm{U}(\mathbb{C}^n, \mathbb{C}^m)) \to [0, 1] \tag{7.464}$$

is a Borel probability measure on $\mathrm{U}(\mathbb{C}^n, \mathbb{C}^m)$ satisfying

$$\mu(\mathcal{A}) = \mu(U\mathcal{A}) \tag{7.465}$$

for every choice of a Borel subset $\mathcal{A} \in \mathrm{Borel}(\mathrm{U}(\mathbb{C}^n, \mathbb{C}^m))$ and a unitary operator $U \in \mathrm{U}(\mathbb{C}^m)$, then it must hold that $\mu = \nu$, where ν is the measure defined by a correct solution to part (a).

Exercise 7.3 Let $\mathcal{X}$ be a complex Euclidean space, let $n = \dim(\mathcal{X})$, and define a mapping $\Phi \in \mathrm{CP}(\mathcal{X})$ as

$$\Phi(X) = n \int \langle uu^*, X \rangle uu^* \, d\mu(u) \tag{7.466}$$

for all $X \in \mathrm{L}(\mathcal{X})$, where μ denotes the uniform spherical measure on $\mathcal{S}(\mathcal{X})$. Give a simple, closed-form expression for Φ.

Exercise 7.4 Let $\mathcal{X}$ be a complex Euclidean space, let $n = \dim(\mathcal{X})$, and define a channel $\Phi \in C(\mathcal{X}, \mathcal{X} \otimes \mathcal{X})$ as

$$\Phi(X) = n \int \langle uu^*, X \rangle uu^* \otimes uu^* \, d\mu(u) \qquad (7.467)$$

for all $X \in L(\mathcal{X})$, where μ denotes the uniform spherical measure on $\mathcal{S}(\mathcal{X})$. Give a closed-form expression for the minimum cloning fidelity

$$\alpha(\Phi) = \inf_{v \in \mathcal{S}(\mathcal{X})} F(\Phi(vv^*), vv^* \otimes vv^*) \qquad (7.468)$$

obtained through the use of Φ. (Observe that Φ is a sub-optimal cloning channel, in the sense of Theorem 7.28, aside from the trivial case in which $\dim(\mathcal{X}) = 1$.)

Exercise 7.5 Prove that there exists a positive real number K with the following property. For every positive integer n and every nonnegative κ-Lipschitz random variable

$$X : \mathcal{S}(\mathbb{C}^n) \to [0, \infty), \qquad (7.469)$$

distributed with respect to the uniform spherical measure on $\mathcal{S}(\mathbb{C}^n)$, one has that

$$E(X^2) - E(X)^2 \leq \frac{K\kappa^2}{n}. \qquad (7.470)$$

Exercise 7.6 Prove that there exist positive real numbers $K, \delta > 0$ for which the following statement holds. For every choice of a complex Euclidean space $\mathcal{X}$, a κ-Lipschitz nonnegative random variable

$$X : \mathcal{S}(\mathcal{X}) \to [0, \infty), \qquad (7.471)$$

distributed with respect to the uniform spherical measure μ on $\mathcal{S}(\mathcal{X})$, and every positive real number $\varepsilon > 0$, it holds that

$$\Pr\left(\left| X - \sqrt{E(X^2)} \right| \geq \varepsilon \right) \leq K \exp\left(-\frac{\delta \varepsilon^2 n}{\kappa^2} \right). \qquad (7.472)$$

The fact established by a correct solution to Exercise 7.5 is useful for proving this result. (Observe that a correct solution to this problem establishes a variant of Lévy's lemma in which concentration occurs around the root-mean-squared value of a nonnegative random variable, as opposed to its mean or central values.)

7.5 Bibliographic Remarks

Permutation-invariant vectors and operators are commonly studied objects in multilinear algebra, which is the subject of the books of Greub (1978) and Marcus (1973, 1975), among others. These concepts and generalizations of them are also relevant to the subject of representation theory, as explained in the book of Goodman and Wallach (1998), for instance. Theorem 7.14 is a finite-dimensional form of the double commutant theorem, also known as the bicommutant theorem, proved by von Neumann (1930).

The existence of unitarily invariant measures on both the unit sphere and the set of unitary operators in a complex Euclidean space is implied by a much more general construction due to Haar (1933). Von Neumann (1933) proved the uniqueness of the measures constructed by Haar, with their two papers appearing consecutively in the same journal. This work was further generalized by Weil (1979) and others. Owing to the generality of these notions, many books that include a discussion of Haar measure do not consider the specialized definitions of uniform spherical measure or the Haar measure (for unitary operators in finite dimensions) of the sort that has been presented in this chapter. Definitions of this type are, however, fairly standard in random matrix theory. These definitions are rooted in the work of Dyson (1962a,b,c) and Diaconis and Shahshahani (1987), and a more broad overview of random matrix theory may be found in the book of Mehta (2004).

The Werner twirling channel, defined in Example 7.25, was introduced by Werner (1989) in the same paper, mentioned in the previous chapter, that introduced the states now known as Werner states. Theorem 7.28 on optimal cloning of pure states is also due to Werner (1998). The original no-cloning theorem is generally attributed to Wootters and Zurek (1982) and Deiks (1982), although an equivalent statement and proof appear in an earlier paper of Park (1970). Although not published until 1983, a paper of Wiesner (1983) proposing a scheme for unforgeable money based on quantum information, relying implicitly on the assumption that quantum states cannot be cloned, was allegedly written in the late 1960s.

Multiple versions of the quantum de Finetti theorem are known. These theorems are so-named because they generalize theorems in combinatorics and probability theory originally found in the work of de Finetti (1937). A quantum information-theoretic variant of de Finetti's eponymous theorem was first proved by Hudson and Moody (1976). Caves, Fuchs, and Schack (2002) later gave a simpler proof of this theorem. Like the original de Finetti theorem, this was a qualitative result regarding the behavior of an infinite number of identical systems. A finite quantum formulation of de Finetti's theorem, closer in spirit to classical results due to Diaconis and Freedman (1980), was proved by König and Renner (2005). Theorems 7.12 and 7.26 and Corollary 7.27 were proved by Christandl, König, Mitchison, and Renner (2007), who improved on the error bounds and generalized the results obtained by König and Renner.

Theorem 7.31 and Corollary 7.32 are due to Watrous (2009a).

Readers interested in learning more about the phenomenon of measure concentration are referred to the books of Ledoux (2001) and Milman and Schechtman (1986). Theorems 7.37 and 7.40 are variants of a theorem due to Lévy (1951). The proofs of these theorems appearing in this chapter have mostly followed those in appendix V of Milman and Schechtman's book (which are partially based on a technique due to Maurey and Pisier (1976)). Multiple formulations of Dvoretzky's theorem are known, with the original having been proved by Dvoretzky around 1960 (Dvoretzky, 1961). Mil'man (1971) gave a proof of Dvoretzky's theorem based on the measure concentration phenomenon, which he was the first to explicitly identify.

To prove Theorem 7.49 on the non-additivity of the minimum output entropy, a particularly sharp version of Dvoretzky's theorem (as stated in Theorem 7.42) is evidently required. The proof of this theorem, as well as its application to Theorem 7.49, is due to Aubrun, Szarek, and Werner (2011). The proof makes essential use of the *chaining method* of Talagrand (2006).

There are several known applications of the concentration of measure phenomenon to quantum information theory, the first of which were due to Hayden, Leung, Shor, and Winter (2004), Bennett, Hayden, Leung, Shor, and Winter (2005), and Harrow, Hayden, and Leung (2004). Theorem 7.47 is a variant of a theorem due to Hayden, Leung, and Winter (2006).

Theorem 7.49 was proved by Hastings (2009), based in part on Hayden and Winter's disproof of the so-called *maximal p-norm multiplicativity conjecture* shortly before (Hayden and Winter, 2008). As suggested above, the proof of Theorem 7.49 that has been presented in this chapter is due to Aubrun, Szarek, and Werner (2011). The implications of Hastings' discovery to the study of channel capacities is discussed in the next chapter.

8
Quantum Channel Capacities

This chapter is focused on *capacities* of quantum channels for transmitting information. The notion of a channel capacity has multiple, inequivalent formulations in the quantum setting. For example, one may consider the capacity with which classical or quantum information can be transmitted through a channel, and different resources may be available to assist with the information transmission, such as entanglement shared between a sender and receiver before the information transmission takes place.

Three fundamental theorems are presented, characterizing the capacities of quantum channels to transmit either classical or quantum information, both with and without the assistance of prior shared entanglement. When prior shared entanglement between the sender and receiver is not available, these characterizations have a somewhat undesirable property: they require a *regularization* – or an averaging over an increasingly large number of uses of a given channel – and fail to provide capacity formulas that are either explicit or efficiently computable for this reason. The apparent need for such regularizations is discussed in the last section of the chapter, along with the related phenomenon of *super-activation* of quantum capacity.

8.1 Classical Information Over Quantum Channels

The general scenario to be considered throughout this chapter involves two hypothetical individuals: a *sender* and a *receiver*. The sender attempts to transmit information, either classical or quantum, to the receiver through multiple, independent uses of a given channel Φ. Schemes are considered in which the sender prepares an input to these channel uses and the receiver processes the output in such a way that information is transmitted with a high degree of accuracy. As is standard in information theory, the chapter mainly deals with the asymptotic regime, making use of entropic notions to analyze rates of information transmission in the limit of an increasingly large number of independent channel uses.

The subject of the present section is the capacity of quantum channels to transmit *classical* information, including both the case in which the sender and receiver share prior entanglement and in which they do not. The first subsection below introduces notions and terminology concerning channel capacities that will be needed throughout the section, as well as in later parts of the chapter. The second subsection is devoted to a proof of the *Holevo–Schumacher–Westmoreland theorem*, which characterizes the capacity of a channel to transmit classical information without the use of prior shared entanglement. The final subsection proves the *entanglement-assisted capacity theorem*, which characterizes the capacity of a channel to transmit classical information with the assistance of prior shared entanglement.

8.1.1 Classical Capacities of Quantum Channels

Five quantities that relate to the information-transmitting capabilities of channels are defined below. The first two quantities – the *classical capacity* and the *entanglement-assisted classical capacity* – are fundamental within the subject of quantum channel capacities. The remaining three quantities are the *Holevo capacity*, the *entanglement-assisted Holevo capacity*, and the *coherent information*, all of which play important roles in the main results to be presented.

The Classical Capacity of a Channel

Intuitively (and somewhat informally) speaking, the classical capacity of a channel describes the average number of classical bits of information that can be transmitted, with a high degree of accuracy, through each use of that channel. As is typical for information-theoretic notions, channel capacities are more formally defined in terms of asymptotic behaviors, where the limit of an increasing number of channel uses is considered.

When stating a precise mathematical definition of classical capacity, it is convenient to refer to the *emulation* of one channel by another.

Definition 8.1 Let $\Phi \in C(\mathcal{X}, \mathcal{Y})$ and $\Psi \in C(\mathcal{Z})$ be channels, for $\mathcal{X}$, $\mathcal{Y}$, and $\mathcal{Z}$ being complex Euclidean spaces. It is said that the channel Φ *emulates* Ψ if there exist channels $\Xi_E \in C(\mathcal{Z}, \mathcal{X})$ and $\Xi_D \in C(\mathcal{Y}, \mathcal{Z})$ such that

$$\Psi = \Xi_D \Phi \Xi_E. \tag{8.1}$$

When this relationship holds, the channel Ξ_E is called an *encoding channel* and Ξ_D is called a *decoding channel*.

It is also convenient to refer to an *approximation* of a given channel by another. In this chapter, such an approximation is always assumed to be defined with respect to the completely bounded trace norm.

Definition 8.2 Let $\Psi_0, \Psi_1 \in C(\mathcal{Z})$ be channels, for $\mathcal{Z}$ being a complex Euclidean space, and let $\varepsilon > 0$ be a positive real number. The channel Ψ_0 is an *ε-approximation* to Ψ_1 (equivalently, Ψ_1 is an *ε-approximation* to Ψ_0) if

$$\left\|\left\| \Psi_0 - \Psi_1 \right\|\right\|_1 < \varepsilon. \tag{8.2}$$

The definition of the classical capacity of a channel, which makes use of the previous two definitions, is as follows.

Definition 8.3 (Classical capacity of a channel) Let $\mathcal{X}$ and $\mathcal{Y}$ be complex Euclidean spaces and let $\Phi \in C(\mathcal{X}, \mathcal{Y})$ be a channel. Let $\Gamma = \{0, 1\}$ denote the binary alphabet, let $\mathcal{Z} = \mathbb{C}^{\Gamma}$, and let $\Delta \in C(\mathcal{Z})$ denote the completely dephasing channel defined with respect to the space $\mathcal{Z}$.

1. A value $\alpha \geq 0$ is an *achievable rate* for classical information transmission through Φ if (i) $\alpha = 0$, or (ii) $\alpha > 0$ and the following holds for every positive real number $\varepsilon > 0$: for all but finitely many positive integers n, and for $m = \lfloor \alpha n \rfloor$, the channel $\Phi^{\otimes n}$ emulates an ε-approximation to the channel $\Delta^{\otimes m}$.

2. The *classical capacity* of Φ, denoted $C(\Phi)$, is the supremum value of all achievable rates for classical information transmission through Φ.

In the context of Definition 8.3, the completely dephasing channel Δ is to be viewed as an ideal channel for transmitting a single bit of classical information. When considering an emulation of the m-fold tensor product $\Delta^{\otimes m}$ of this ideal classical channel by the channel $\Phi^{\otimes n}$, no generality is lost in restricting one's attention to classical-to-quantum encoding channels Ξ_{E} and quantum-to-classical decoding channels Ξ_{D}. That is, one may assume

$$\Xi_{\mathrm{E}} = \Xi_{\mathrm{E}} \Delta^{\otimes m} \quad \text{and} \quad \Xi_{\mathrm{D}} = \Delta^{\otimes m} \Xi_{\mathrm{D}}. \tag{8.3}$$

This assumption causes no loss of generality because

$$\begin{aligned}
&\left\|\left\| (\Delta^{\otimes m} \Xi_{\mathrm{D}}) \Phi^{\otimes n} (\Xi_{\mathrm{E}} \Delta^{\otimes m}) - \Delta^{\otimes m} \right\|\right\|_1 \\
&= \left\|\left\| \Delta^{\otimes m} (\Xi_{\mathrm{D}} \Phi^{\otimes n} \Xi_{\mathrm{E}} - \Delta^{\otimes m}) \Delta^{\otimes m} \right\|\right\|_1 \\
&\leq \left\|\left\| \Xi_{\mathrm{D}} \Phi^{\otimes n} \Xi_{\mathrm{E}} - \Delta^{\otimes m} \right\|\right\|_1;
\end{aligned} \tag{8.4}$$

replacing a given choice of Ξ_{E} and Ξ_{D} by $\Xi_{\mathrm{E}} \Delta^{\otimes m}$ and $\Delta^{\otimes m} \Xi_{\mathrm{D}}$ will never decrease the quality of the emulation achieved.

In light of this observation, the implicit use of the completely bounded trace norm in Definition 8.3 may appear to be somewhat heavy-handed; an equivalent definition is obtained by requiring that $\Phi^{\otimes n}$ emulates some channel $\Psi \in C(\mathcal{Z}^{\otimes m})$ satisfying

$$\left\| (\Delta^{\otimes m}\Psi)(E_{a_1\cdots a_m, a_1\cdots a_m}) - E_{a_1\cdots a_m, a_1\cdots a_m} \right\|_1 < \varepsilon, \tag{8.5}$$

which is equivalent to

$$\langle E_{a_1\cdots a_m, a_1\cdots a_m}, \Psi(E_{a_1\cdots a_m, a_1\cdots a_m}) \rangle > 1 - \frac{\varepsilon}{2}, \tag{8.6}$$

for all $a_1\cdots a_m \in \Gamma^m$. An interpretation of this requirement is that every string $a_1\cdots a_m \in \Gamma^m$ is transmitted by Ψ with a probability of error smaller than $\varepsilon/2$.

There is, on the other hand, one benefit to using the stronger notion of channel approximation defined by the completely bounded trace norm in Definition 8.3, which is that it allows the quantum capacity (discussed later in Section 8.2) to be defined in an analogous manner to the classical capacity, simply replacing the dephasing channel Δ by the identity channel $\mathbb{1}_{L(\mathcal{Z})}$. (For the quantum capacity, the completely bounded trace norm provides the most natural notion of channel approximation.)

The following proposition is, perhaps, self-evident, but it is nevertheless worth stating explicitly. The same argument used to prove it may be applied to other notions of capacity as well; there is nothing specific to the classical capacity that is required by the proof.

Proposition 8.4 *Let $\Phi \in C(\mathcal{X}, \mathcal{Y})$ be a channel, for complex Euclidean spaces $\mathcal{X}$ and $\mathcal{Y}$, and let k be a positive integer. It holds that*

$$C(\Phi^{\otimes k}) = k\, C(\Phi). \tag{8.7}$$

Proof If it is the case that α is an achievable rate for classical information transmission through Φ, then it follows trivially that αk is an achievable rate for classical information transmission through $\Phi^{\otimes k}$. It therefore holds that

$$C(\Phi^{\otimes k}) \geq k\, C(\Phi). \tag{8.8}$$

Now assume that $\alpha > 0$ is an achievable rate for classical information transmission through $\Phi^{\otimes k}$. For any $\varepsilon > 0$ and all but finitely many positive integers n, the channel $\Phi^{\otimes k\lfloor n/k \rfloor}$ therefore emulates an ε-approximation to $\Delta^{\otimes m}$ for $m = \lfloor \alpha \lfloor n/k \rfloor \rfloor$. It will be proved that $\alpha/k - \delta$ is an achievable rate for classical information transmission through Φ for all $\delta \in (0, \alpha/k)$. For any integer $n \geq k$, the channel $\Phi^{\otimes n}$ trivially emulates any channel emulated by $\Phi^{\otimes k\lfloor n/k \rfloor}$, and for $\delta \in (0, \alpha/k)$, one has that $\alpha\lfloor n/k \rfloor \geq (\alpha/k - \delta)n$ for all but finitely many positive integers n. It therefore holds, for any $\varepsilon > 0$, and all but finitely many positive integers n, that the channel $\Phi^{\otimes n}$ emulates an ε-approximation to $\Delta^{\otimes m}$ for $m = \lfloor (\alpha/k - \delta)n \rfloor$, implying that $\alpha/k - \delta$ is an achievable rate for classical information transmission through Φ. In the case that $\alpha = 0$, one has that α/k is trivially an achievable rate for classical information transmission through Φ. Taking the supremum over all achievable rates, one finds that

$$C(\Phi) \geq \frac{1}{k} C(\Phi^{\otimes k}), \tag{8.9}$$

which completes the proof. $\qquad\square$

The Entanglement-Assisted Classical Capacity of a Channel

The entanglement-assisted classical capacity of a channel is defined in a similar way to the classical capacity, except that one assumes the sender and receiver may share any state of their choosing prior to the transmission of information through the channel. (As separable states provide no advantage in this setting, the shared state is generally assumed to be entangled.) The ability of the sender and receiver to share entanglement, as compared with the situation in which they do not, can result in a significant increase in the classical capacity of a quantum channel. For instance, shared entanglement doubles the classical capacity of the identity channel through the use of dense coding (discussed in Section 6.3.1), and an arbitrary (constant-factor) increase is possible for other choices of channels.

A formal definition for the entanglement-assisted classical capacity of a channel requires only a minor change to the definition of the ordinary classical capacity: the definition of an emulation of one channel by another is modified to allow for the existence of a shared state as follows.

Definition 8.5 Let $\Phi \in C(\mathcal{X}, \mathcal{Y})$ and $\Psi \in C(\mathcal{Z})$ be channels, for $\mathcal{X}$, $\mathcal{Y}$, and $\mathcal{Z}$ being complex Euclidean spaces. The channel Φ *emulates* Ψ *with the assistance of entanglement* if there exist a state $\xi \in D(\mathcal{V} \otimes \mathcal{W})$ and channels $\Xi_{\mathrm{E}} \in C(\mathcal{Z} \otimes \mathcal{V}, \mathcal{X})$ and $\Xi_{\mathrm{D}} \in C(\mathcal{Y} \otimes \mathcal{W}, \mathcal{Z})$, for complex Euclidean spaces $\mathcal{V}$ and $\mathcal{W}$, such that

$$\Psi(Z) = (\Xi_{\mathrm{D}}(\Phi\Xi_{\mathrm{E}} \otimes \mathbb{1}_{\mathrm{L}(\mathcal{W})}))(Z \otimes \xi) \tag{8.10}$$

for all $Z \in L(\mathcal{Z})$. (See Figure 8.1 for an illustration of the channel represented by the right-hand side of this equation.) When this relationship holds, the channel Ξ_{E} is called an *encoding channel*, Ξ_{D} is called a *decoding channel*, and ξ is referred to as the *shared state* that assists this emulation.

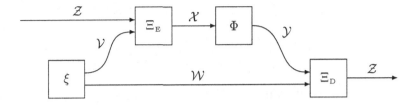

Figure 8.1 An illustration of the map $Z \mapsto \left(\Xi_{\mathrm{D}}\left(\Phi\Xi_{\mathrm{E}} \otimes \mathbb{1}_{\mathrm{L}(\mathcal{W})}\right)\right)(Z \otimes \xi)$ referred to in Definition 8.5.

Aside from the modification represented by the previous definition, the entanglement-assisted classical capacity is defined in an analogous way to the ordinary classical capacity.

Definition 8.6 (Entanglement-assisted classical capacity of a channel) Let $\Phi \in \mathrm{C}(\mathcal{X}, \mathcal{Y})$ be a channel, for complex Euclidean spaces $\mathcal{X}$ and $\mathcal{Y}$, let $\Gamma = \{0, 1\}$ denote the binary alphabet, let $\mathcal{Z} = \mathbb{C}^{\Gamma}$, and let $\Delta \in \mathrm{C}(\mathcal{Z})$ denote the completely dephasing channel defined with respect to the space $\mathcal{Z}$.

1. A value $\alpha \geq 0$ is an *achievable rate* for entanglement-assisted classical information transmission through Φ if (i) $\alpha = 0$, or (ii) $\alpha > 0$ and the following holds for every positive real number $\varepsilon > 0$: for all but finitely many positive integers n, and for $m = \lfloor \alpha n \rfloor$, the channel $\Phi^{\otimes n}$ emulates an ε-approximation to $\Delta^{\otimes m}$ with the assistance of entanglement.

2. The *entanglement-assisted classical capacity* of Φ, denoted $\mathrm{C}_{\mathrm{E}}(\Phi)$, is the supremum over all achievable rates for entanglement-assisted classical information transmission through Φ.

Through the same argument used to prove Proposition 8.4, one has that the following simple proposition holds.

Proposition 8.7 *Let $\Phi \in \mathrm{C}(\mathcal{X}, \mathcal{Y})$ be a channel, for complex Euclidean spaces $\mathcal{X}$ and $\mathcal{Y}$, and let k be a positive integer. It holds that*

$$\mathrm{C}_{\mathrm{E}}(\Phi^{\otimes k}) = k\mathrm{C}_{\mathrm{E}}(\Phi). \tag{8.11}$$

The Holevo Capacity of a Channel

Suppose that $\mathcal{X}$ is a complex Euclidean space, Σ is an alphabet, $p \in \mathcal{P}(\Sigma)$ is a probability vector, and $\{\rho_a : a \in \Sigma\} \subseteq \mathrm{D}(\mathcal{X})$ is a collection of states. Letting $\eta : \Sigma \to \mathrm{Pos}(\mathcal{X})$ be the ensemble defined as

$$\eta(a) = p(a)\rho_a \tag{8.12}$$

for each $a \in \Sigma$, one has that the Holevo information of η is given by

$$\chi(\eta) = \mathrm{H}\left(\sum_{a \in \Sigma} p(a)\rho_a\right) - \sum_{a \in \Sigma} p(a)\,\mathrm{H}(\rho_a). \tag{8.13}$$

Based on this quantity, one may define the *Holevo capacity* of a channel in the manner specified by Definition 8.8 below. This definition will make use of the following notation: for any ensemble $\eta\colon \Sigma \to \mathrm{Pos}(\mathcal{X})$ and any channel $\Phi \in \mathrm{C}(\mathcal{X}, \mathcal{Y})$, one defines the ensemble $\Phi(\eta)\colon \Sigma \to \mathrm{Pos}(\mathcal{Y})$ as

$$(\Phi(\eta))(a) = \Phi(\eta(a)) \tag{8.14}$$

for each $a \in \Sigma$. That is, $\Phi(\eta)$ is the ensemble obtained by evaluating Φ on the ensemble η in the most natural way.

Definition 8.8 Let $\Phi \in \mathrm{C}(\mathcal{X}, \mathcal{Y})$ be a channel, for $\mathcal{X}$ and $\mathcal{Y}$ being complex Euclidean spaces. The *Holevo capacity* of Φ is defined as

$$\chi(\Phi) = \sup_{\eta} \chi(\Phi(\eta)), \tag{8.15}$$

where the supremum is over all choices of an alphabet Σ and an ensemble of the form $\eta\colon \Sigma \to \mathrm{Pos}(\mathcal{X})$.

  Two restrictions may be placed on the supremum (8.15) in Definition 8.8 without decreasing the value that is defined for a given channel. The first restriction is that the supremum may be replaced by a maximum over all ensembles of the form $\eta\colon \Sigma \to \mathrm{Pos}(\mathcal{X})$, for Σ being an alphabet of size

$$|\Sigma| = \dim(\mathcal{X})^2. \tag{8.16}$$

Second, the ensembles may be restricted to ones for which $\mathrm{rank}(\eta(a)) \leq 1$ for each $a \in \Sigma$. The following proposition is useful for proving that this is so.

Proposition 8.9 *Let $\Phi \in \mathrm{C}(\mathcal{X}, \mathcal{Y})$ be a channel, for complex Euclidean spaces $\mathcal{X}$ and $\mathcal{Y}$, let Σ be an alphabet, and let $\eta\colon \Sigma \to \mathrm{Pos}(\mathcal{X})$ be an ensemble. There exist an alphabet Γ and an ensemble $\theta\colon \Gamma \to \mathrm{Pos}(\mathcal{X})$ such that*

1. $\mathrm{rank}(\theta(b)) \leq 1$ for each $b \in \Gamma$, and
2. $\chi(\Phi(\eta)) \leq \chi(\Phi(\theta))$.

Proof Assume that Λ is the alphabet for which $\mathcal{X} = \mathbb{C}^{\Lambda}$, and let

$$\eta(a) = \sum_{b \in \Lambda} \lambda_{a,b} x_{a,b} x_{a,b}^* \tag{8.17}$$

be a spectral decomposition of $\eta(a)$ for each $a \in \Sigma$. The requirements of the proposition hold for the ensemble $\theta \colon \Sigma \times \Lambda \to \mathrm{Pos}(\mathcal{X})$ defined by

$$\theta(a,b) = \lambda_{a,b} x_{a,b} x_{a,b}^{*} \tag{8.18}$$

for each $(a,b) \in \Sigma \times \Lambda$. It is evident that the first property holds, so it remains to verify the second.

Define $\mathcal{Z} = \mathbb{C}^{\Sigma}$ and $\mathcal{W} = \mathbb{C}^{\Lambda}$, and consider three registers Y, Z, and W corresponding to the spaces $\mathcal{Y}$, $\mathcal{Z}$, and $\mathcal{W}$, respectively. For the density operator $\rho \in \mathrm{D}(\mathcal{Y} \otimes \mathcal{Z} \otimes \mathcal{W})$ defined as

$$\rho = \sum_{(a,b)\in\Sigma\times\Lambda} \lambda_{a,b} \Phi\big(x_{a,b} x_{a,b}^{*}\big) \otimes E_{a,a} \otimes E_{b,b}, \tag{8.19}$$

one has that the following two equalities hold:

$$\begin{aligned} \chi(\Phi(\theta)) &= \mathrm{D}\big(\rho[\mathsf{Y},\mathsf{Z},\mathsf{W}] \,\|\, \rho[\mathsf{Y}] \otimes \rho[\mathsf{Z},\mathsf{W}]\big), \\ \chi(\Phi(\eta)) &= \mathrm{D}\big(\rho[\mathsf{Y},\mathsf{Z}] \,\|\, \rho[\mathsf{Y}] \otimes \rho[\mathsf{Z}]\big). \end{aligned} \tag{8.20}$$

The inequality $\chi(\Phi(\eta)) \leq \chi(\Phi(\theta))$ follows from the monotonicity of the quantum relative entropy function under partial tracing (which represents a special case of Theorem 5.35). $\qquad\square$

Theorem 8.10 *Let $\mathcal{X}$ and $\mathcal{Y}$ be complex Euclidean spaces, let $\Phi \in \mathrm{C}(\mathcal{X},\mathcal{Y})$ be a channel, and let Σ be an alphabet having size $|\Sigma| = \dim(\mathcal{X})^2$. There exists an ensemble $\eta \colon \Sigma \to \mathrm{Pos}(\mathcal{X})$ such that*

$$\chi(\Phi(\eta)) = \chi(\Phi). \tag{8.21}$$

One may assume, in addition, that $\mathrm{rank}(\eta(a)) \leq 1$ for each $a \in \Sigma$.

Proof Consider an arbitrary ensemble of the form $\theta \colon \Gamma \to \mathrm{Pos}(\mathcal{X})$, for Γ being any alphabet, and let

$$\sigma = \sum_{a\in\Gamma} \theta(a) \tag{8.22}$$

denote the average state of the ensemble θ. Through Proposition 2.52, one finds that there must exist an alphabet Λ, a probability vector $p \in \mathcal{P}(\Lambda)$, and a collection of ensembles $\{\theta_b : b \in \Lambda\}$ taking the form $\theta_b \colon \Gamma \to \mathrm{Pos}(\mathcal{X})$, each satisfying the constraint

$$\sum_{a\in\Gamma} \theta_b(a) = \sigma \tag{8.23}$$

and possessing the property

$$\big|\{a \in \Gamma : \theta_b(a) \neq 0\}\big| \leq \dim(\mathcal{X})^2, \tag{8.24}$$

so that θ is given by the convex combination

$$\theta = \sum_{b \in \Lambda} p(b)\theta_b. \tag{8.25}$$

By Proposition 5.48 it follows that

$$\chi(\Phi(\theta)) \leq \sum_{b \in \Lambda} p(b)\chi(\Phi(\theta_b)), \tag{8.26}$$

and so there must exist at least one choice of a symbol $b \in \Lambda$ for which $p(b) > 0$ and

$$\chi(\Phi(\theta)) \leq \chi(\Phi(\theta_b)). \tag{8.27}$$

Fix any such choice of $b \in \Lambda$, and let

$$\Gamma_0 = \{a \in \Gamma : \theta_b(a) \neq 0\}. \tag{8.28}$$

For an arbitrarily chosen injective mapping $f : \Gamma_0 \rightarrow \Sigma$, one obtains an ensemble $\eta : \Sigma \rightarrow \text{Pos}(\mathcal{X})$ such that

$$\chi(\Phi(\eta)) \geq \chi(\Phi(\theta)) \tag{8.29}$$

by setting $\eta(f(a)) = \theta_b(a)$ for every $a \in \Gamma_0$ and $\eta(c) = 0$ for $c \notin f(\Gamma_0)$.

Because the argument just presented holds for an arbitrary choice of an ensemble θ, it follows that

$$\chi(\Phi) = \sup_{\eta} \chi(\Phi(\eta)), \tag{8.30}$$

where the supremum is over all ensembles of the form $\eta : \Sigma \rightarrow \text{Pos}(\mathcal{X})$. As the set of all such ensembles is compact, there must exist an ensemble of the same form for which the equality (8.21) holds.

The additional restriction that $\text{rank}(\eta(a)) \leq 1$ for each $a \in \Sigma$ may be assumed by first using Proposition 8.9 to replace a given ensemble θ by one satisfying the restriction $\text{rank}(\theta(a)) \leq 1$ for each $a \in \Gamma$, and then proceeding with the argument above. This results in an ensemble $\eta : \Sigma \rightarrow \text{Pos}(\mathcal{X})$ with $\text{rank}(\eta(a)) \leq 1$ for each $a \in \Sigma$, and such that (8.21) holds, which completes the proof. $\qquad\square$

The Entanglement-Assisted Holevo Capacity of a Channel

Along similar lines to the entanglement-assisted classical capacity, which mirrors the definition of the classical capacity in a setting where the sender and receiver initially share a state of their choosing, one may define the entanglement-assisted Holevo capacity of a channel. The following definition is helpful when formalizing this notion.

Definition 8.11 Let Σ be an alphabet, let $\mathcal{X}$ and $\mathcal{Y}$ be complex Euclidean spaces, let $\eta\colon \Sigma \to \mathrm{Pos}(\mathcal{X} \otimes \mathcal{Y})$ be an ensemble, and let

$$\rho = \sum_{a \in \Sigma} \eta(a) \tag{8.31}$$

denote the average state of η. It is said that η is *homogeneous on* $\mathcal{Y}$ if it holds that

$$\mathrm{Tr}_{\mathcal{X}}(\eta(a)) = \mathrm{Tr}(\eta(a)) \, \mathrm{Tr}_{\mathcal{X}}(\rho) \tag{8.32}$$

for every $a \in \Sigma$.

A simple operational characterization of ensembles homogeneous on a given complex Euclidean space is provided by the following proposition. In essence, it states that this sort of ensemble is one obtained by applying a randomly selected channel to the opposite subsystem of a fixed bipartite state.

Proposition 8.12 *Let Σ be an alphabet, let $\mathcal{X}$ and $\mathcal{Y}$ be complex Euclidean spaces, and let $\eta\colon \Sigma \to \mathrm{Pos}(\mathcal{X} \otimes \mathcal{Y})$ be an ensemble. The following three statements are equivalent:*

1. *The ensemble η is homogeneous on $\mathcal{Y}$.*
2. *There exist a complex Euclidean space $\mathcal{Z}$, a state $\sigma \in \mathrm{D}(\mathcal{Z} \otimes \mathcal{Y})$, a collection of channels $\{\Phi_a : a \in \Sigma\} \subseteq \mathrm{C}(\mathcal{Z}, \mathcal{X})$, and a probability vector $p \in \mathcal{P}(\Sigma)$, such that*

$$\eta(a) = p(a)\big(\Phi_a \otimes \mathbb{1}_{\mathrm{L}(\mathcal{Y})}\big)(\sigma) \tag{8.33}$$

   for every $a \in \Sigma$.
3. *Statement 2 holds under the additional assumption that $\sigma = uu^*$ for some choice of a unit vector $u \in \mathcal{Z} \otimes \mathcal{Y}$.*

Proof The fact that the second statement implies the first is immediate, and the third statement trivially implies the second. It therefore remains to prove that the first statement implies the third.

To this end, assume that η is homogeneous on $\mathcal{Y}$, let ρ denote the average state of the ensemble η, and let

$$\xi = \mathrm{Tr}_{\mathcal{X}}(\rho). \tag{8.34}$$

Let $\mathcal{Z}$ be a complex Euclidean space of dimension $\mathrm{rank}(\xi)$, and let $u \in \mathcal{Z} \otimes \mathcal{Y}$ be a unit vector that purifies ξ:

$$\mathrm{Tr}_{\mathcal{Z}}(uu^*) = \xi. \tag{8.35}$$

As η is homogeneous on $\mathcal{Y}$, it therefore holds that

$$\mathrm{Tr}(\eta(a))\,\mathrm{Tr}_{\mathcal{Z}}(uu^*) = \mathrm{Tr}_{\mathcal{X}}(\eta(a)) \tag{8.36}$$

for every $a \in \Sigma$. By Proposition 2.29, one concludes that there must exist a channel $\Phi_a \in \mathrm{C}(\mathcal{Z},\mathcal{X})$ such that

$$\eta(a) = \mathrm{Tr}(\eta(a))(\Phi_a \otimes \mathbb{1}_{\mathrm{L}(\mathcal{Y})})(uu^*) \tag{8.37}$$

for every $a \in \Sigma$. Setting $\sigma = uu^*$ and $p(a) = \mathrm{Tr}(\eta(a))$ for each $a \in \Sigma$ completes the proof. $\square$

Definition 8.13   Let $\Phi \in \mathrm{C}(\mathcal{X},\mathcal{Y})$ be a channel, for complex Euclidean spaces $\mathcal{X}$ and $\mathcal{Y}$. The *entanglement-assisted Holevo capacity* of Φ is the quantity $\chi_{\mathrm{E}}(\Phi)$ defined as

$$\chi_{\mathrm{E}}(\Phi) = \sup_{\eta} \chi\big((\Phi \otimes \mathbb{1}_{\mathrm{L}(\mathcal{W})})(\eta)\big), \tag{8.38}$$

where the supremum is over all choices of a complex Euclidean space $\mathcal{W}$, an alphabet Σ, and an ensemble $\eta\colon \Sigma \to \mathrm{Pos}(\mathcal{X} \otimes \mathcal{W})$ homogeneous on $\mathcal{W}$.

The relationship between the entanglement-assisted classical capacity and the entanglement-assisted Holevo capacity is discussed in Section 8.1.3. In this context, for a given ensemble that is homogeneous on $\mathcal{W}$, the bipartite state whose existence is implied by Proposition 8.12 may be seen as being representative of a state shared between a sender and receiver that facilitates information transmission.

The Coherent Information

The final quantity, associated with a given channel, that is to be defined in the present subsection is the *coherent information*.

Definition 8.14   Let $\Phi \in \mathrm{C}(\mathcal{X},\mathcal{Y})$ be a channel and let $\sigma \in \mathrm{D}(\mathcal{X})$ be a state, for complex Euclidean spaces $\mathcal{X}$ and $\mathcal{Y}$. The *coherent information* of σ through Φ is the quantity $\mathrm{I}_{\mathrm{c}}(\sigma;\Phi)$ defined as

$$\mathrm{I}_{\mathrm{c}}(\sigma;\Phi) = \mathrm{H}(\Phi(\sigma)) - \mathrm{H}\big((\Phi \otimes \mathbb{1}_{\mathrm{L}(\mathcal{X})})\big(\mathrm{vec}(\sqrt{\sigma})\,\mathrm{vec}(\sqrt{\sigma})^*\big)\big). \tag{8.39}$$

The *maximum coherent information* of Φ is the quantity

$$\mathrm{I}_{\mathrm{c}}(\Phi) = \max_{\sigma \in \mathrm{D}(\mathcal{X})} \mathrm{I}_{\mathrm{c}}(\sigma;\Phi). \tag{8.40}$$

In general terms, the coherent information of a state σ through a channel Φ quantifies the correlations that exist after Φ is applied to a purification of σ. The definition implicitly takes this purification to be $\mathrm{vec}(\sqrt{\sigma})$ for the sake of simplicity and concreteness; any other purification would result in the same quantity.

Consider the state

$$\rho = (\Phi \otimes \mathbb{1}_{L(\mathcal{X})}) \left(\text{vec}(\sqrt{\sigma}) \, \text{vec}(\sqrt{\sigma})^* \right) \in D(\mathcal{Y} \otimes \mathcal{X}) \qquad (8.41)$$

of a pair of registers (Y, X), corresponding to the spaces $\mathcal{Y}$ and $\mathcal{X}$, as suggested by the definition above. One has that the coherent information $I_c(\sigma; \Phi)$ of σ through Φ is equal to $H(\mathsf{Y}) - H(\mathsf{Y}, \mathsf{X})$. The quantum mutual information between Y and X is therefore given by

$$I(\mathsf{Y} : \mathsf{X}) = I_c(\sigma; \Phi) + H(\sigma). \qquad (8.42)$$

While it is not immediately clear that the coherent information is relevant to the notion of channel capacity, it will be proved later in the chapter that this quantity is fundamentally important with respect to the entanglement-assisted classical capacity and the quantum capacity (to be defined later in Section 8.2).

The following proposition establishes an intuitive fact: with respect to an arbitrary choice of an input state, feeding the output of one channel into a second channel cannot lead to an increase in coherent information.

Proposition 8.15 *Let $\Phi \in C(\mathcal{X}, \mathcal{Y})$ and $\Psi \in C(\mathcal{Y}, \mathcal{Z})$ be channels and let $\sigma \in D(\mathcal{X})$ be a state, for complex Euclidean spaces $\mathcal{X}$, $\mathcal{Y}$, and $\mathcal{Z}$. It holds that*

$$I_c(\sigma; \Psi\Phi) \leq I_c(\sigma; \Phi). \qquad (8.43)$$

Proof Choose complex Euclidean spaces $\mathcal{W}$ and $\mathcal{V}$, along with isometries $A \in U(\mathcal{X}, \mathcal{Y} \otimes \mathcal{W})$ and $B \in U(\mathcal{Y}, \mathcal{Z} \otimes \mathcal{V})$, so that Stinespring representations of Φ and Ψ are obtained:

$$\Phi(X) = \text{Tr}_{\mathcal{W}}(AXA^*) \quad \text{and} \quad \Psi(Y) = \text{Tr}_{\mathcal{V}}(BYB^*) \qquad (8.44)$$

for all $X \in L(\mathcal{X})$ and $Y \in L(\mathcal{Y})$. Define a unit vector $u \in \mathcal{Z} \otimes \mathcal{V} \otimes \mathcal{W} \otimes \mathcal{X}$ as

$$u = (B \otimes \mathbb{1}_{\mathcal{W}} \otimes \mathbb{1}_{\mathcal{X}})(A \otimes \mathbb{1}_{\mathcal{X}}) \text{vec}(\sqrt{\sigma}). \qquad (8.45)$$

Now, consider four registers Z, V, W, and X, corresponding to the spaces $\mathcal{Z}$, $\mathcal{V}$, $\mathcal{W}$, and $\mathcal{X}$, respectively. Assuming the compound register $(\mathsf{Z}, \mathsf{V}, \mathsf{W}, \mathsf{X})$ is in the pure state uu^*, one has the following expressions:

$$\begin{aligned} I_c(\sigma; \Phi) &= H(\mathsf{Z}, \mathsf{V}) - H(\mathsf{Z}, \mathsf{V}, \mathsf{X}), \\ I_c(\sigma; \Psi\Phi) &= H(\mathsf{Z}) - H(\mathsf{Z}, \mathsf{X}). \end{aligned} \qquad (8.46)$$

The proposition follows from the strong subadditivity of the von Neumann entropy (Theorem 5.36). $\qquad\qquad\square$

It is convenient to refer to the notion of *complementary channels* in some of the proofs to be found in the present chapter. This notion is defined as follows.

Definition 8.16 Let $\Phi \in C(\mathcal{X}, \mathcal{Y})$ and $\Psi \in C(\mathcal{X}, \mathcal{Z})$ be channels, for $\mathcal{X}$, $\mathcal{Y}$, and $\mathcal{Z}$ being complex Euclidean spaces. It is said that Φ and Ψ are *complementary* if there exists an isometry $A \in U(\mathcal{X}, \mathcal{Y} \otimes \mathcal{Z})$ for which it holds that

$$\Phi(X) = \operatorname{Tr}_{\mathcal{Z}}(AXA^*) \quad \text{and} \quad \Psi(X) = \operatorname{Tr}_{\mathcal{Y}}(AXA^*) \tag{8.47}$$

for every $X \in L(\mathcal{X})$.

It is immediate from Corollary 2.27 that, for every channel $\Phi \in C(\mathcal{X}, \mathcal{Y})$, there must exist a complex Euclidean space $\mathcal{Z}$ and a channel $\Psi \in C(\mathcal{X}, \mathcal{Z})$ that is complementary to Φ; such a channel Ψ is obtained from any choice of a Stinespring representation of Φ.

Proposition 8.17 *Let $\Phi \in C(\mathcal{X}, \mathcal{Y})$ and $\Psi \in C(\mathcal{X}, \mathcal{Z})$ be complementary channels and let $\sigma \in D(\mathcal{X})$ be a state, for complex Euclidean spaces $\mathcal{X}$, $\mathcal{Y}$, and $\mathcal{Z}$. It holds that*

$$I_c(\sigma; \Phi) = H(\Phi(\sigma)) - H(\Psi(\sigma)). \tag{8.48}$$

Proof By the assumption that Φ and Ψ are complementary, there must exist an isometry $A \in U(\mathcal{X}, \mathcal{Y} \otimes \mathcal{Z})$ such that the equations (8.47) hold for every $X \in L(\mathcal{X})$. Let X, Y, and Z be registers corresponding to the spaces $\mathcal{X}$, $\mathcal{Y}$, and $\mathcal{Z}$, and define a unit vector $u \in \mathcal{Y} \otimes \mathcal{Z} \otimes \mathcal{X}$ as

$$u = (A \otimes \mathbb{1}_{\mathcal{X}}) \operatorname{vec}(\sqrt{\sigma}). \tag{8.49}$$

With respect to the pure state uu^* of the compound register $(\mathsf{Y}, \mathsf{Z}, \mathsf{X})$, it holds that $H(\mathsf{Z}) = H(\mathsf{Y}, \mathsf{X})$, and therefore

$$H\left((\Phi \otimes \mathbb{1}_{L(\mathcal{X})}) \left(\operatorname{vec}(\sqrt{\sigma}) \operatorname{vec}(\sqrt{\sigma})^* \right) \right) = H(\Psi(\sigma)), \tag{8.50}$$

from which the proposition follows. □

8.1.2 The Holevo–Schumacher–Westmoreland Theorem

The *Holevo–Schumacher–Westmoreland theorem*, which is stated and proved in the present section, establishes that the classical capacity of a quantum channel is lower-bounded by its Holevo capacity, and that by regularizing the Holevo capacity one obtains a characterization of the classical capacity. The notion of a *classical-to-quantum product state channel code*, along with a few mathematical results that are useful for analyzing these codes, will be introduced prior to the statement and proof of the Holevo–Schumacher–Westmoreland theorem.

Classical-to-Quantum Product State Channel Codes

When studying the classical capacity of quantum channels, it is instructive to consider a related but somewhat more basic task of encoding classical information using fixed sets of quantum states. When this task is connected with the notion of the classical capacity of a channel, a link must be made between the particular set of states used to encode classical information and the given channel – but it is reasonable to begin by examining the task of encoding classical information into quantum states in isolation.

Throughout the discussion that follows, $\Gamma = \{0, 1\}$ will denote the binary alphabet and

$$\{\sigma_a : a \in \Sigma\} \subseteq D(\mathcal{X}) \tag{8.51}$$

will denote a fixed collection of states, for $\mathcal{X}$ being a complex Euclidean space and Σ being an alphabet.[1] The situation to be considered is that binary strings, representing classical information, are to be encoded into tensor products of quantum states drawn from the collection (8.51) in such a way that each binary string can be recovered from its encoding with high probability.

In more precise terms, it is to be assumed that positive integers n and m have been selected, and that every binary string $b_1 \cdots b_m \in \Gamma^m$ of length m is to be *encoded* by a product state having the form

$$\sigma_{a_1} \otimes \cdots \otimes \sigma_{a_n} \in D(\mathcal{X}^{\otimes n}), \tag{8.52}$$

for some choice of a string $a_1 \cdots a_n \in \Sigma^n$. That is, a function $f \colon \Gamma^m \to \Sigma^n$ is to be selected, and each string $b_1 \cdots b_m \in \Gamma^m$ is to be encoded by the state (8.52) for $a_1 \cdots a_n = f(b_1 \cdots b_m)$. When discussing this sort of code, it is convenient to make use of the shorthand notation

$$\sigma_{a_1 \cdots a_n} = \sigma_{a_1} \otimes \cdots \otimes \sigma_{a_n} \tag{8.53}$$

for each string $a_1 \cdots a_n \in \Sigma^n$, and with respect to this notation one has that

$$\sigma_{f(b_1 \cdots b_m)} \in D(\mathcal{X}^{\otimes n}) \tag{8.54}$$

denotes the state that encodes the string $b_1 \cdots b_m \in \Gamma^m$.

---

[1] The entire discussion could be generalized to allow for arbitrary alphabets Γ in place of the binary alphabet. As there is little gain in doing this from the perspective of this book, the assumption that $\Gamma = \{0, 1\}$ is made in the interest of simplicity.

From the encoding of a given binary string, one may hope to *decode* this string by means of a measurement. Such a measurement takes the form $\mu\colon \Gamma^m \to \mathrm{Pos}(\mathcal{X}^{\otimes n})$, and succeeds in successfully recovering a particular string $b_1 \cdots b_m$ from its encoding with probability

$$\langle \mu(b_1 \cdots b_m), \sigma_{f(b_1 \cdots b_m)} \rangle. \tag{8.55}$$

As a general guideline, one is typically interested in coding schemes for which the probability of a successful decoding is close to 1 and the ratio m/n, which represents the rate at which classical information is effectively transmitted, is as large as possible. The following definition summarizes these notions.

Definition 8.18   Let Σ be an alphabet, let $\mathcal{X}$ be a complex Euclidean space, let

$$\{\sigma_a \colon a \in \Sigma\} \subseteq \mathrm{D}(\mathcal{X}) \tag{8.56}$$

be a collection of states, let $\Gamma = \{0, 1\}$ denote the binary alphabet, and let n and m be positive integers. A *classical-to-quantum product state channel code* for the collection of states (8.56) is a pair (f, μ) consisting of a function and a measurement of the forms

$$f \colon \Gamma^m \to \Sigma^n \quad \text{and} \quad \mu \colon \Gamma^m \to \mathrm{Pos}(\mathcal{X}^{\otimes n}). \tag{8.57}$$

The *rate* of such a code is equal to the ratio m/n, and the code is said to have *error bounded by* δ if it holds that

$$\langle \mu(b_1 \cdots b_m), \sigma_{f(b_1 \cdots b_m)} \rangle > 1 - \delta \tag{8.58}$$

for every string $b_1 \cdots b_m \in \Gamma^m$.

Remark   The term *channel code* is used in this definition to distinguish this type of code from a *source code*, as discussed in Chapter 5. The two notions are, in some sense, complementary. A channel code represents the situation in which information is encoded into a state that possesses some degree of randomness, while a source code represents the situation in which information produced by a random source is encoded into a chosen state.

It is evident that some choices of sets $\{\sigma_a \colon a \in \Sigma\}$ are better suited to the construction of classical-to-quantum product state channel codes than others, assuming one wishes to maximize the rate and minimize the error of such a code. For the most part, the analysis that follows will be focused on the situation in which a set of states has been fixed, and one is interested in understanding the capabilities of this particular set, with respect to classical-to-quantum product state channel codes.

Typicality for Ensembles of States

The notion of *typicality* is central to the proofs of multiple theorems to be presented in the current chapter, including a fundamental theorem on the existence of classical-to-quantum product state channel codes possessing certain rates and error bounds.

A standard definition of typicality was introduced in Section 5.3.1 – but it is an extension of this definition to ensembles of states that will be used in the context of channel coding. The following definition is a starting point for a discussion of this concept, providing a notion of typicality for joint probability distributions.

Definition 8.19 Let $p \in \mathcal{P}(\Sigma \times \Gamma)$ be a probability vector, for alphabets Σ and Γ, and let $q \in \mathcal{P}(\Sigma)$ be the marginal probability vector defined as

$$q(a) = \sum_{b \in \Gamma} p(a, b) \tag{8.59}$$

for each $a \in \Sigma$. For every choice of a positive real number $\varepsilon > 0$, a positive integer n, and a string $a_1 \cdots a_n \in \Sigma^n$ satisfying $q(a_1) \cdots q(a_n) > 0$, a string $b_1 \cdots b_n \in \Gamma^n$ is said to be ε-*typical conditioned on* $a_1 \cdots a_n \in \Sigma^n$ if

$$2^{-n(\mathrm{H}(p)-\mathrm{H}(q)+\varepsilon)} < \frac{p(a_1, b_1) \cdots p(a_n, b_n)}{q(a_1) \cdots q(a_n)} < 2^{-n(\mathrm{H}(p)-\mathrm{H}(q)-\varepsilon)}. \tag{8.60}$$

One writes $K_{a_1 \cdots a_n, \varepsilon}(p)$ to denote the set of all such strings $b_1 \cdots b_n \in \Gamma^n$.

It is also convenient to define $K_{a_1 \cdots a_n, \varepsilon}(p) = \varnothing$ for any string $a_1 \cdots a_n \in \Sigma^n$ for which $q(a_1) \cdots q(a_n) = 0$. When a probability vector $p \in \mathcal{P}(\Sigma \times \Gamma)$ is fixed, or can safely be taken as being implicit, the notation $K_{a_1 \cdots a_n, \varepsilon}$ may be used in place of $K_{a_1 \cdots a_n, \varepsilon}(p)$.

Intuitively speaking, if one were to select strings $a_1 \cdots a_n \in \Sigma^n$ and $b_1 \cdots b_n \in \Gamma^n$ by independently choosing $(a_1, b_1), \ldots, (a_n, b_n)$ at random, according to a given probability vector $p \in \mathcal{P}(\Sigma \times \Gamma)$, then it would be reasonable to expect $b_1 \cdots b_n$ to be contained in $K_{a_1 \cdots a_n, \varepsilon}(p)$, with this event becoming increasingly likely as n becomes large. This fact is established by the following proposition, which is based on the weak law of large numbers (Theorem 1.15) – the methodology is essentially the same as the analogous fact (Proposition 5.42) that was proved in regard to the standard definition of typicality discussed in Section 5.3.1.

Proposition 8.20 *Let* $p \in \mathcal{P}(\Sigma \times \Gamma)$ *be a probability vector, for alphabets* Σ *and* Γ. *For every* $\varepsilon > 0$ *it holds that*

$$\lim_{n \to \infty} \sum_{a_1 \cdots a_n \in \Sigma^n} \sum_{b_1 \cdots b_n \in K_{a_1 \cdots a_n, \varepsilon}} p(a_1, b_1) \cdots p(a_n, b_n) = 1. \tag{8.61}$$

Proof Let $q \in \mathcal{P}(\Sigma)$ be the marginal probability vector defined as

$$q(a) = \sum_{b \in \Gamma} p(a, b) \tag{8.62}$$

for each $a \in \Sigma$, and define a random variable $X : \Sigma \times \Gamma \to [0, \infty)$ as

$$X(a, b) = \begin{cases} -\log(p(a, b)) + \log(q(a)) & \text{if } p(a, b) > 0 \\ 0 & \text{if } p(a, b) = 0 \end{cases} \tag{8.63}$$

and distributed according to the probability vector p. The expected value of this random variable is given by

$$\mathrm{E}(X) = \mathrm{H}(p) - \mathrm{H}(q). \tag{8.64}$$

Now, for any positive integer n, and for $X_1, \dots, X_n$ being independent random variables, each identically distributed to X, one has

$$\Pr\left(\left| \frac{X_1 + \cdots + X_n}{n} - (\mathrm{H}(p) - \mathrm{H}(q)) \right| < \varepsilon \right)$$

$$= \sum_{a_1 \cdots a_n \in \Sigma^n} \sum_{b_1 \cdots b_n \in K_{a_1 \cdots a_n, \varepsilon}} p(a_1, b_1) \cdots p(a_n, b_n). \tag{8.65}$$

The conclusion of the proposition therefore follows from the weak law of large numbers (Theorem 1.15). $\qquad \square$

The next proposition places an upper bound on the expected size of the set $K_{a_1 \cdots a_n, \varepsilon}$. It is analogous to Proposition 5.43 for the standard definition of typicality.

Proposition 8.21 *Let $p \in \mathcal{P}(\Sigma \times \Gamma)$ be a probability vector, for alphabets Σ and Γ, and let $q \in \mathcal{P}(\Sigma)$ be the marginal probability vector defined as*

$$q(a) = \sum_{b \in \Gamma} p(a, b) \tag{8.66}$$

for each $a \in \Sigma$. For every positive integer n and every positive real number $\varepsilon > 0$, it holds that

$$\sum_{a_1 \cdots a_n \in \Sigma^n} q(a_1) \cdots q(a_n) |K_{a_1 \cdots a_n, \varepsilon}(p)| < 2^{n(\mathrm{H}(p) - \mathrm{H}(q) + \varepsilon)}. \tag{8.67}$$

Proof For each string $a_1 \cdots a_n \in \Sigma^n$ satisfying $q(a_1) \cdots q(a_n) > 0$ and each string $b_1 \cdots b_n \in K_{a_1 \cdots a_n, \varepsilon}(p)$, one has

$$2^{-n(\mathrm{H}(p) - \mathrm{H}(q) + \varepsilon)} < \frac{p(a_1, b_1) \cdots p(a_n, b_n)}{q(a_1) \cdots q(a_n)}, \tag{8.68}$$

and therefore

$$2^{-n(\mathrm{H}(p)-\mathrm{H}(q)+\varepsilon)} \sum_{a_1 \cdots a_n \in \Sigma^n} q(a_1) \cdots q(a_n) |K_{a_1 \cdots a_n,\varepsilon}(p)|$$

$$= \sum_{a_1 \cdots a_n \in \Sigma^n} \sum_{b_1 \cdots b_n \in K_{a_1 \cdots a_n,\varepsilon}(p)} q(a_1) \cdots q(a_n) 2^{-n(\mathrm{H}(p)-\mathrm{H}(q)+\varepsilon)} \qquad (8.69)$$

$$< \sum_{a_1 \cdots a_n \in \Sigma^n} \sum_{b_1 \cdots b_n \in K_{a_1 \cdots a_n,\varepsilon}} p(a_1, b_1) \cdots p(a_n, b_n) \leq 1,$$

from which the proposition follows. $\qquad \square$

The notion of typicality for joint probability distributions established by Definition 8.19 may be extended to ensembles of quantum states in a fairly straightforward fashion, by referring to spectral decompositions of the states in an ensemble.

Definition 8.22 Let $\eta\colon \Sigma \to \mathrm{Pos}(\mathcal{X})$ be an ensemble of states, for $\mathcal{X}$ a complex Euclidean space and Σ an alphabet, and let Γ be an alphabet such that $|\Gamma| = \dim(\mathcal{X})$. By the spectral theorem (as stated by Corollary 1.4), it follows that one may write

$$\eta(a) = \sum_{b \in \Gamma} p(a,b) u_{a,b} u_{a,b}^* \qquad (8.70)$$

for some choice of a probability vector $p \in \mathcal{P}(\Sigma \times \Gamma)$ and an orthonormal basis $\{u_{a,b} : b \in \Gamma\}$ of $\mathcal{X}$ for each $a \in \Sigma$. With respect to the ensemble η, and for each positive real number $\varepsilon > 0$, each positive integer n, and each string $a_1 \cdots a_n \in \Sigma^n$, the *projection onto the ε-typical subspace of $\mathcal{X}^{\otimes n}$ conditioned on $a_1 \cdots a_n$* is defined as

$$\Lambda_{a_1 \cdots a_n,\varepsilon} = \sum_{b_1 \cdots b_n \in K_{a_1 \cdots a_n,\varepsilon}(p)} u_{a_1,b_1} u_{a_1,b_1}^* \otimes \cdots \otimes u_{a_n,b_n} u_{a_n,b_n}^*. \qquad (8.71)$$

Remark For a fixed choice of a string $a_1 \cdots a_n \in \Sigma^n$, one has that the inclusion of each string $b_1 \cdots b_n$ in $K_{a_1 \cdots a_n,\varepsilon}(p)$ is determined by the multiset of values $\{p(a_1,b_1),\ldots,p(a_n,b_n)\}$ alone. Thus, the same is true regarding the inclusion of each rank-one projection in the summation (8.71). It follows that the projection $\Lambda_{a_1 \cdots a_n,\varepsilon}$ specified by Definition 8.22 is uniquely defined by the ensemble η, and is independent of the particular choices of the spectral decompositions (8.70).

Facts analogous to the previous two propositions, holding for ensembles rather than joint probability distributions, follow directly.

Proposition 8.23 *Let $\eta: \Sigma \to \mathrm{Pos}(\mathcal{X})$ be an ensemble of states, for $\mathcal{X}$ a complex Euclidean space and Σ an alphabet. For every $\varepsilon > 0$, it holds that*

$$\lim_{n\to\infty} \sum_{a_1\cdots a_n \in \Sigma^n} \langle \Lambda_{a_1\cdots a_n,\varepsilon}, \eta(a_1) \otimes \cdots \otimes \eta(a_n) \rangle = 1, \tag{8.72}$$

where, for each positive integer n, and each string $a_1 \cdots a_n \in \Sigma^n$, $\Lambda_{a_1\cdots a_n,\varepsilon}$ is the projection onto the ε-typical subspace of $\mathcal{X}^{\otimes n}$ conditioned on $a_1 \cdots a_n$, with respect to the ensemble η. Moreover, one has

$$\sum_{a_1\cdots a_n \in \Sigma^n} \mathrm{Tr}(\eta(a_1)) \cdots \mathrm{Tr}(\eta(a_n)) \, \mathrm{Tr}(\Lambda_{a_1\cdots a_n,\varepsilon}) < 2^{n(\beta+\varepsilon)} \tag{8.73}$$

for

$$\beta = \sum_{\substack{a\in\Sigma \\ \eta(a)\neq 0}} \mathrm{Tr}(\eta(a)) \, \mathrm{H}\!\left(\frac{\eta(a)}{\mathrm{Tr}(\eta(a))}\right). \tag{8.74}$$

Proof For each $a \in \Sigma$, let

$$\eta(a) = \sum_{b\in\Gamma} p(a,b) u_{a,b} u_{a,b}^* \tag{8.75}$$

be a spectral decomposition of $\eta(a)$, as described in Definition 8.22, and define $q \in \mathcal{P}(\Sigma)$ as

$$q(a) = \sum_{b\in\Gamma} p(a,b) \tag{8.76}$$

(which is equivalent to $q(a) = \mathrm{Tr}(\eta(a))$). For each positive integer n, each positive real number $\varepsilon > 0$, and each string $a_1 \cdots a_n \in \Sigma^n$, one has

$$\begin{aligned}
&\langle \Lambda_{a_1\cdots a_n,\varepsilon}, \eta(a_1) \otimes \cdots \otimes \eta(a_n) \rangle \\
&\qquad = \sum_{b_1\cdots b_n \in K_{a_1\cdots a_n,\varepsilon}} p(a_1,b_1) \cdots p(a_n,b_n),
\end{aligned} \tag{8.77}$$

and moreover

$$\beta = \mathrm{H}(p) - \mathrm{H}(q) \quad \text{and} \quad \mathrm{Tr}(\Lambda_{a_1\cdots a_n,\varepsilon}) = |K_{a_1\cdots a_n,\varepsilon}|. \tag{8.78}$$

The proposition therefore follows from Propositions 8.20 and 8.21. $\square$

A Useful Operator Inequality

It is helpful to make use of an operator inequality, stated as Lemma 8.25 below, when analyzing the performance of classical-to-quantum product state channel codes. The proof of this inequality makes use of the following fact regarding square roots of positive semidefinite operators.

Lemma 8.24 (Operator monotonicity of the square root function) *Let $\mathcal{X}$ be a complex Euclidean space and let $P, Q \in \mathrm{Pos}(\mathcal{X})$ be positive semidefinite operators. It holds that*

$$\sqrt{P} \leq \sqrt{P + Q}. \tag{8.79}$$

Proof The block operator

$$\begin{pmatrix} P & \sqrt{P} \\ \sqrt{P} & \mathbb{1} \end{pmatrix} + \begin{pmatrix} Q & 0 \\ 0 & 0 \end{pmatrix} = \begin{pmatrix} P + Q & \sqrt{P} \\ \sqrt{P} & \mathbb{1} \end{pmatrix} \tag{8.80}$$

is positive semidefinite. As $[P + Q, \mathbb{1}] = 0$ and $\sqrt{P}$ is Hermitian, it follows by Lemma 5.29 that

$$\sqrt{P} \leq \sqrt{P + Q}\sqrt{\mathbb{1}} = \sqrt{P + Q}, \tag{8.81}$$

as required. $\qquad\qquad\qquad\qquad\qquad\qquad\qquad\qquad\qquad\qquad\qquad\square$

Remark It is not difficult to prove Lemma 8.24 directly, without relying on Lemma 5.29, by using spectral properties of operators that were also employed in the proof of that lemma.

Lemma 8.25 (Hayashi–Nagaoka) *Let $\mathcal{X}$ be a complex Euclidean space, let $P, Q \in \mathrm{Pos}(\mathcal{X})$ be positive semidefinite operators, and assume $P \leq \mathbb{1}$. It holds that*

$$\mathbb{1} - \sqrt{(P + Q)^+}\, P\, \sqrt{(P + Q)^+} \leq 2(\mathbb{1} - P) + 4Q. \tag{8.82}$$

Proof For every choice of operators $A, B \in \mathrm{L}(\mathcal{X})$, one has

$$0 \leq (A - B)(A - B)^* = AA^* + BB^* - (AB^* + BA^*), \tag{8.83}$$

and therefore $AB^* + BA^* \leq AA^* + BB^*$. Setting

$$A = X\sqrt{Q} \quad \text{and} \quad B = (\mathbb{1} - X)\sqrt{Q}, \tag{8.84}$$

for a given operator $X \in \mathrm{L}(\mathcal{X})$, yields

$$XQ(\mathbb{1} - X)^* + (\mathbb{1} - X)QX^* \leq XQX^* + (\mathbb{1} - X)Q(\mathbb{1} - X)^*, \tag{8.85}$$

and therefore

$$\begin{aligned} Q &= XQX^* + XQ(\mathbb{1} - X)^* + (\mathbb{1} - X)QX^* + (\mathbb{1} - X)Q(\mathbb{1} - X)^* \\ &\leq 2XQX^* + 2(\mathbb{1} - X)Q(\mathbb{1} - X)^*. \end{aligned} \tag{8.86}$$

For the specific choice $X = \sqrt{P + Q}$, one obtains

$$Q \leq 2\sqrt{P + Q}\, Q\sqrt{P + Q} + 2\left(\mathbb{1} - \sqrt{P + Q}\right) Q \left(\mathbb{1} - \sqrt{P + Q}\right), \tag{8.87}$$

and from the observation that $Q \leq P + Q$ it follows that

$$
\begin{aligned}
Q &\leq 2\sqrt{P+Q}\, Q\sqrt{P+Q} \\
&\quad + 2\left(\mathbb{1} - \sqrt{P+Q}\right)(P+Q)\left(\mathbb{1} - \sqrt{P+Q}\right) \\
&= \sqrt{P+Q}\left(2\mathbb{1} + 4Q - 4\sqrt{P+Q} + 2P\right)\sqrt{P+Q}.
\end{aligned}
\tag{8.88}
$$

Using the fact that $P \leq \mathbb{1}$ together with Lemma 8.24, one has

$$
P \leq \sqrt{P} \leq \sqrt{P+Q},
\tag{8.89}
$$

and therefore

$$
Q \leq \sqrt{P+Q}\left(2\mathbb{1} - 2P + 4Q\right)\sqrt{P+Q}.
\tag{8.90}
$$

Conjugating both sides of this inequality by the Moore–Penrose pseudo-inverse of $\sqrt{P+Q}$ yields

$$
\sqrt{(P+Q)^+}\, Q\,\sqrt{(P+Q)^+} \leq 2\Pi_{\mathrm{im}(P+Q)} - 2P + 4Q.
\tag{8.91}
$$

It follows that

$$
\begin{aligned}
\mathbb{1} &- \sqrt{(P+Q)^+}\, P\,\sqrt{(P+Q)^+} \\
&= \mathbb{1} - \Pi_{\mathrm{im}(P+Q)} + \sqrt{(P+Q)^+}\, Q\,\sqrt{(P+Q)^+} \\
&\leq \mathbb{1} + \Pi_{\mathrm{im}(P+Q)} - 2P + 4Q \\
&\leq 2(\mathbb{1} - P) + 4Q,
\end{aligned}
\tag{8.92}
$$

as required. $\qquad\square$

An Existence Proof for Classical-to-Quantum Product State Channel Codes

Returning to the discussion of classical-to-quantum product state channel codes, assume as before that an alphabet Σ, a complex Euclidean space $\mathcal{X}$, and a collection of states

$$
\{\sigma_a : a \in \Sigma\} \subseteq \mathrm{D}(\mathcal{X})
\tag{8.93}
$$

have been fixed, and let $\Gamma = \{0, 1\}$ denote the binary alphabet. It is natural to ask, for any choice of a positive real number $\delta > 0$ and positive integers m and n, whether or not there exists a classical-to-quantum product state channel code (f, μ) for this collection, taking the form

$$
f : \Gamma^m \to \Sigma^n \quad \text{and} \quad \mu : \Gamma^m \to \mathrm{Pos}(\mathcal{X}^{\otimes n})
\tag{8.94}
$$

and having error bounded by δ.

In general, one may expect that making such a determination is not tractable from a computational point of view. It is possible, however, to prove the existence of reasonably good classical-to-quantum product state channel codes through the probabilistic method: for suitable choices of n, m, and δ, a *random* choice of a function $f: \Gamma^m \to \Sigma^n$ and a well-chosen measurement $\mu: \Gamma^m \to \mathrm{Pos}(\mathcal{X}^{\otimes n})$ are considered, and a coding scheme with error bounded by δ is obtained with a nonzero probability. The theorem that follows gives a precise statement regarding the parameters n, m, and δ through which this methodology proves the existence of classical-to-quantum product state channel codes.

Theorem 8.26 *Let Σ be an alphabet, let $\mathcal{X}$ be a complex Euclidean space, let*

$$\{\sigma_a: a \in \Sigma\} \subseteq \mathrm{D}(\mathcal{X}) \tag{8.95}$$

be a collection of states, and let $\Gamma = \{0, 1\}$ denote the binary alphabet. Also let $p \in \mathcal{P}(\Sigma)$ be a probability vector, let $\eta: \Sigma \to \mathrm{Pos}(\mathcal{X})$ be the ensemble defined as

$$\eta(a) = p(a)\sigma_a \tag{8.96}$$

for each $a \in \Sigma$, assume α is a positive real number satisfying $\alpha < \chi(\eta)$, and let $\delta > 0$ be a positive real number. For all but finitely many positive integers n, and for $m = \lfloor \alpha n \rfloor$, there exists a function $f: \Gamma^m \to \Sigma^n$ and a measurement $\mu: \Gamma^m \to \mathrm{Pos}(\mathcal{X}^{\otimes n})$ such that

$$\langle \mu(b_1 \cdots b_m), \sigma_{f(b_1 \cdots b_m)} \rangle > 1 - \delta \tag{8.97}$$

for every $b_1 \cdots b_m \in \Gamma^m$.

Proof It will first be assumed that n and m are arbitrary positive integers. As suggested previously, the proof makes use of the probabilistic method: a random function $g: \Gamma^{m+1} \to \Sigma^n$ is chosen from a particular probability distribution, a decoding measurement μ is defined for each possible choice of g, and the expected probability of a decoding error for the pair (g, μ) is analyzed. As is to be explained later in the proof, this analysis implies the existence of a channel coding scheme (f, μ), where $f: \Gamma^m \to \Sigma^n$ is derived from g, satisfying the requirements of the theorem for all but finitely many n and for $m = \lfloor \alpha n \rfloor$.

The particular distribution from which g is to be chosen is one in which each individual output symbol of g is selected independently according to the probability vector p. Equivalently, for a random selection of g according to the distribution being described, one has that

$$\Pr(g(b_1 \cdots b_{m+1}) = a_1 \cdots a_n) = p(a_1) \cdots p(a_n) \tag{8.98}$$

for every choice of $b_1 \cdots b_{m+1} \in \Gamma^{m+1}$ and $a_1 \cdots a_n \in \Sigma^n$, and moreover the outputs of a randomly chosen g on distinct choices of the input string $b_1 \cdots b_{m+1}$ are uncorrelated.

The specification of the decoding measurement μ that is to be associated with a given g is not chosen randomly; a unique measurement is defined for each g in a way that is dependent upon the ensemble η. First, let $\varepsilon > 0$ be a sufficiently small positive real number such that the inequality

$$\alpha < \chi(\eta) - 3\varepsilon \tag{8.99}$$

holds. For each string $a_1 \cdots a_n \in \Sigma^n$, let $\Lambda_{a_1 \cdots a_n}$ denote the projection onto the ε-typical subspace of $\mathcal{X}^{\otimes n}$ conditioned on $a_1 \cdots a_n$, with respect to the ensemble η, and let Π_n be the projection onto the ε-typical subspace of $\mathcal{X}^{\otimes n}$ with respect to the average state

$$\sigma = \sum_{a \in \Sigma} p(a)\sigma_a \tag{8.100}$$

of the ensemble η. (As ε has been fixed, the dependence of $\Lambda_{a_1 \cdots a_n}$ and Π_n on ε is not written explicitly, allowing for slightly less cluttered equations.) Next, for a given choice of a function $g \colon \Gamma^{m+1} \to \Sigma^n$, define an operator

$$Q = \sum_{b_1 \cdots b_{m+1} \in \Gamma^{m+1}} \Pi_n \Lambda_{g(b_1 \cdots b_{m+1})} \Pi_n , \tag{8.101}$$

and, for each binary string $b_1 \cdots b_{m+1} \in \Gamma^{m+1}$, define an operator

$$Q_{b_1 \cdots b_{m+1}} = \sqrt{Q^+} \, \Pi_n \Lambda_{g(b_1 \cdots b_{m+1})} \Pi_n \sqrt{Q^+}. \tag{8.102}$$

Each operator $Q_{b_1 \cdots b_{m+1}}$ is positive semidefinite, and moreover

$$\sum_{b_1 \cdots b_{m+1} \in \Gamma^{m+1}} Q_{b_1 \cdots b_{m+1}} = \Pi_{\mathrm{im}(Q)}. \tag{8.103}$$

Finally, the measurement $\mu \colon \Gamma^{m+1} \to \mathrm{Pos}(\mathcal{X}^{\otimes n})$ to be associated with g is defined as

$$\mu(b_1 \cdots b_{m+1}) = Q_{b_1 \cdots b_{m+1}} + \frac{1}{2^{m+1}}(\mathbb{1} - \Pi_{\mathrm{im}(Q)}) \tag{8.104}$$

for each $b_1 \cdots b_{m+1} \in \Gamma^{m+1}$.

For each choice of g, the probability that the measurement μ associated with g errs in recovering a string $b_1 \cdots b_{m+1} \in \Gamma^{m+1}$ from its encoding is equal to

$$\langle \mathbb{1} - \mu(b_1 \cdots b_{m+1}), \sigma_{g(b_1 \cdots b_{m+1})} \rangle. \tag{8.105}$$

The next phase of the proof establishes an upper bound on the average error probability

$$\frac{1}{2^{m+1}} \sum_{b_1 \cdots b_{m+1} \in \Gamma^{m+1}} \langle \mathbb{1} - \mu(b_1 \cdots b_{m+1}), \sigma_{g(b_1 \cdots b_{m+1})} \rangle, \tag{8.106}$$

for a uniformly chosen string $b_1 \cdots b_{m+1} \in \Gamma^{m+1}$. To bound this average probability of error, one may first observe that Lemma 8.25 implies that

$$\begin{aligned} &\mathbb{1} - Q_{b_1 \cdots b_{m+1}} \\ &\le 2\big(\mathbb{1} - \Pi_n \Lambda_{g(b_1 \cdots b_{m+1})} \Pi_n\big) + 4\big(Q - \Pi_n \Lambda_{g(b_1 \cdots b_{m+1})} \Pi_n\big) \end{aligned} \tag{8.107}$$

for each $b_1 \cdots b_{m+1} \in \Gamma^{m+1}$. For a fixed choice of g, the probability of an error in recovering a given string $b_1 \cdots b_{m+1}$ is therefore upper-bounded by

$$\begin{aligned} &2\langle \mathbb{1} - \Pi_n \Lambda_{g(b_1 \cdots b_{m+1})} \Pi_n, \sigma_{g(b_1 \cdots b_{m+1})} \rangle \\ &+ 4\langle Q - \Pi_n \Lambda_{g(b_1 \cdots b_{m+1})} \Pi_n, \sigma_{g(b_1 \cdots b_{m+1})} \rangle. \end{aligned} \tag{8.108}$$

The expected value of this expression will be shown to be small, under the additional assumption that $m = \lfloor \alpha n \rfloor$, when $b_1 \cdots b_{m+1} \in \Gamma^{m+1}$ is chosen uniformly and g is chosen according to the distribution described above.

The first term in the expression (8.108) will be considered first. To prove an upper bound on the expected value of this quantity, it is convenient to make use of the operator identity

$$ABA = AB + BA - B + (\mathbb{1} - A)B(\mathbb{1} - A). \tag{8.109}$$

In particular, for any choice of a string $a_1 \cdots a_n \in \Sigma^n$, this identity implies

$$\begin{aligned} &\langle \Pi_n \Lambda_{a_1 \cdots a_n} \Pi_n, \sigma_{a_1 \cdots a_n} \rangle \\ &= \langle \Pi_n \Lambda_{a_1 \cdots a_n}, \sigma_{a_1 \cdots a_n} \rangle + \langle \Lambda_{a_1 \cdots a_n} \Pi_n, \sigma_{a_1 \cdots a_n} \rangle - \langle \Lambda_{a_1 \cdots a_n}, \sigma_{a_1 \cdots a_n} \rangle \\ &\quad + \langle (\mathbb{1} - \Pi_n) \Lambda_{a_1 \cdots a_n} (\mathbb{1} - \Pi_n), \sigma_{a_1 \cdots a_n} \rangle \\ &\ge \langle \Pi_n \Lambda_{a_1 \cdots a_n}, \sigma_{a_1 \cdots a_n} \rangle + \langle \Lambda_{a_1 \cdots a_n} \Pi_n, \sigma_{a_1 \cdots a_n} \rangle - \langle \Lambda_{a_1 \cdots a_n}, \sigma_{a_1 \cdots a_n} \rangle. \end{aligned} \tag{8.110}$$

As $\Lambda_{a_1 \cdots a_n}$ is a projection operator and commutes with $\sigma_{a_1 \cdots a_n}$, it follows that

$$
\begin{aligned}
&\langle \Pi_n \Lambda_{a_1 \cdots a_n}, \sigma_{a_1 \cdots a_n} \rangle + \langle \Lambda_{a_1 \cdots a_n} \Pi_n, \sigma_{a_1 \cdots a_n} \rangle - \langle \Lambda_{a_1 \cdots a_n}, \sigma_{a_1 \cdots a_n} \rangle \\
&= \langle 2\Pi_n - \mathbb{1}, \Lambda_{a_1 \cdots a_n} \sigma_{a_1 \cdots a_n} \rangle \\
&= \langle 2\Pi_n - \mathbb{1}, \sigma_{a_1 \cdots a_n} \rangle + \langle \mathbb{1} - 2\Pi_n, (\mathbb{1} - \Lambda_{a_1 \cdots a_n}) \sigma_{a_1 \cdots a_n} \rangle \qquad (8.111) \\
&\geq \langle 2\Pi_n - \mathbb{1}, \sigma_{a_1 \cdots a_n} \rangle - \langle \mathbb{1} - \Lambda_{a_1 \cdots a_n}, \sigma_{a_1 \cdots a_n} \rangle \\
&= 2\langle \Pi_n, \sigma_{a_1 \cdots a_n} \rangle + \langle \Lambda_{a_1 \cdots a_n}, \sigma_{a_1 \cdots a_n} \rangle - 2.
\end{aligned}
$$

By combining the inequalities (8.110) and (8.111), and averaging over all choices of $a_1 \cdots a_n \in \Sigma^n$, with each a_k selected independently according to the probability vector p, one finds that

$$
\sum_{a_1 \cdots a_n \in \Sigma^n} p(a_1) \cdots p(a_n) \langle \Pi_n \Lambda_{a_1 \cdots a_n} \Pi_n, \sigma_{a_1 \cdots a_n} \rangle
$$
$$
\geq 2\langle \Pi_n, \sigma^{\otimes n} \rangle + \sum_{a_1 \cdots a_n \in \Sigma^n} p(a_1) \cdots p(a_n) \langle \Lambda_{a_1 \cdots a_n}, \sigma_{a_1 \cdots a_n} \rangle - 2. \qquad (8.112)
$$

The right-hand side of the expression (8.112) approaches 1 in the limit as n goes to infinity by Propositions 5.42 and 8.23, from which it follows that

$$
\sum_{a_1 \cdots a_n \in \Sigma^n} p(a_1) \cdots p(a_n) \langle \mathbb{1} - \Pi_n \Lambda_{a_1 \cdots a_n} \Pi_n, \sigma_{a_1 \cdots a_n} \rangle < \frac{\delta}{8} \qquad (8.113)
$$

for all but finitely many choices of a positive integer n. For any n for which the inequality (8.113) holds, and for a random selection of $g \colon \Gamma^{m+1} \to \Sigma^n$ as described above, it therefore holds that the expected value of the expression

$$
2\langle \mathbb{1} - \Pi_n \Lambda_{g(b_1 \cdots b_{m+1})} \Pi_n, \sigma_{g(b_1 \cdots b_{m+1})} \rangle \qquad (8.114)
$$

is at most $\delta/4$ for an arbitrary choice of $b_1 \cdots b_{m+1}$, and therefore the same bound holds for a uniformly selected binary string $b_1 \cdots b_{m+1} \in \Gamma^{m+1}$.

The second term in the expression (8.108) will be considered next. It may first be observed that

$$
Q - \Pi_n \Lambda_{g(b_1 \cdots b_{m+1})} \Pi_n = \sum_{\substack{c_1 \cdots c_{m+1} \in \Gamma^{m+1} \\ c_1 \cdots c_{m+1} \neq b_1 \cdots b_{m+1}}} \Pi_n \Lambda_{g(c_1 \cdots c_{m+1})} \Pi_n, \qquad (8.115)
$$

so that

$$
\begin{aligned}
&\langle Q - \Pi_n \Lambda_{g(b_1 \cdots b_{m+1})} \Pi_n, \sigma_{g(b_1 \cdots b_{m+1})} \rangle \\
&= \sum_{\substack{c_1 \cdots c_{m+1} \in \Gamma^{m+1} \\ c_1 \cdots c_{m+1} \neq b_1 \cdots b_{m+1}}} \langle \Pi_n \Lambda_{g(c_1 \cdots c_{m+1})} \Pi_n, \sigma_{g(b_1 \cdots b_{m+1})} \rangle. \qquad (8.116)
\end{aligned}
$$

The value of the function g on each input string is chosen independently according to the probability vector $p^{\otimes n}$, so there is no correlation between $g(b_1 \cdots b_{m+1})$ and $g(c_1 \cdots c_{m+1})$ for $b_1 \cdots b_{m+1} \neq c_1 \cdots c_{m+1}$. It follows that the expected value of the above expression is given by

$$(2^{m+1} - 1) \sum_{a_1 \cdots a_n \in \Sigma^n} p(a_1) \cdots p(a_n) \langle \Lambda_{a_1 \cdots a_n}, \Pi_n \sigma^{\otimes n} \Pi_n \rangle. \tag{8.117}$$

By Proposition 8.23 it holds that

$$\sum_{a_1 \cdots a_n \in \Sigma^n} p(a_1) \cdots p(a_n) \operatorname{Tr}(\Lambda_{a_1 \cdots a_n}) \leq 2^{n(\beta + \varepsilon)} \tag{8.118}$$

for

$$\beta = \sum_{a \in \Sigma} p(a) \operatorname{H}(\sigma_a), \tag{8.119}$$

and by the definition of Π_n one has that

$$\lambda_1 (\Pi_n \sigma^{\otimes n} \Pi_n) \leq 2^{-n(\operatorname{H}(\sigma) - \varepsilon)}. \tag{8.120}$$

It follows that

$$(2^{m+1} - 1) \sum_{a_1 \cdots a_n \in \Sigma^n} p(a_1) \cdots p(a_n) \langle \Lambda_{a_1 \cdots a_n}, \Pi_n \sigma^{\otimes n} \Pi_n \rangle$$
$$\leq 2^{m+1 - n(\chi(\eta) - 2\varepsilon)}, \tag{8.121}$$

so that the expected value of the second term in the expression (8.108) is upper-bounded by

$$2^{m - n(\chi(\eta) - 2\varepsilon) + 3}. \tag{8.122}$$

Now assume that $m = \lfloor \alpha n \rfloor$. For $g : \Gamma^{m+1} \to \Sigma^n$ chosen according to the distribution specified earlier and $b_1 \cdots b_{m+1} \in \Gamma^{m+1}$ chosen uniformly, one has that the expected value of the error probability (8.106) is at most

$$\frac{\delta}{4} + 2^{\alpha n - n(\chi(\eta) - 2\varepsilon) + 3} \leq \frac{\delta}{4} + 2^{-\varepsilon n + 3} \tag{8.123}$$

for all but finitely many choices of n. As

$$2^{-\varepsilon n} < \frac{\delta}{32} \tag{8.124}$$

for all sufficiently large n, it follows that the expected value of the error probability (8.106) is smaller than $\delta/2$ for all but finitely many choices of n. For all but finitely many choices of n, there must therefore exist at least one choice of a function $g\colon \Gamma^{m+1} \to \Sigma^n$ such that, for μ being the measurement associated with g, it holds that

$$\frac{1}{2^{m+1}} \sum_{b_1 \cdots b_{m+1} \in \Gamma^{m+1}} \langle \mathbb{1} - \mu(b_1 \cdots b_{m+1}), \sigma_{g(b_1 \cdots b_{m+1})} \rangle < \frac{\delta}{2}. \qquad (8.125)$$

Finally, for a given choice of n, $m = \lfloor \alpha n \rfloor$, g, and μ for which the bound (8.125) holds, consider the set

$$B = \left\{ b_1 \cdots b_{m+1} \in \Gamma^{m+1} \colon \langle \mathbb{1} - \mu(b_1 \cdots b_{m+1}), \sigma_{g(b_1 \cdots b_{m+1})} \rangle \geq \delta \right\} \qquad (8.126)$$

of all strings whose encodings incur a decoding error with probability at least δ. It holds that

$$\frac{\delta |B|}{2^{m+1}} < \frac{\delta}{2}, \qquad (8.127)$$

and therefore $|B| \leq 2^m$. By defining a function $f\colon \Gamma^m \to \Sigma^n$ as $f = gh$, for an arbitrarily chosen injection $h\colon \Gamma^m \to \Gamma^{m+1} \backslash B$, one has that

$$\langle \mu(b_1 \cdots b_m), \sigma_{f(b_1 \cdots b_m)} \rangle > 1 - \delta \qquad (8.128)$$

for every choice of $b_1 \cdots b_m \in \Gamma^m$, which completes the proof. $\qquad \square$

Statement and Proof of the Holevo–Schumacher–Westmoreland Theorem

The Holevo–Schumacher–Westmoreland theorem will now be stated, and proved through the use of Theorem 8.26.

Theorem 8.27 (Holevo–Schumacher–Westmoreland theorem) *Let $\mathcal{X}$ and $\mathcal{Y}$ be complex Euclidean spaces and let $\Phi \in \mathrm{C}(\mathcal{X}, \mathcal{Y})$ be a channel. The classical capacity of Φ is equal to its regularized Holevo capacity:*

$$\mathrm{C}(\Phi) = \lim_{n \to \infty} \frac{\chi(\Phi^{\otimes n})}{n}. \qquad (8.129)$$

Proof The first main step of the proof is to establish the inequality

$$\chi(\Phi) \leq \mathrm{C}(\Phi) \qquad (8.130)$$

through the use of Theorem 8.26. This inequality holds trivially if $\chi(\Phi) = 0$, so it will be assumed that $\chi(\Phi)$ is positive.

Consider an ensemble $\eta\colon \Sigma \to \mathrm{Pos}(\mathcal{X})$, for any alphabet Σ, expressed as $\eta(a) = p(a)\rho_a$ for each $a \in \Sigma$, where

$$\{\rho_a \colon a \in \Sigma\} \subseteq \mathrm{D}(\mathcal{X}) \qquad (8.131)$$

is a collection of states and $p \in \mathcal{P}(\Sigma)$ is a probability vector. Assume that $\chi(\Phi(\eta))$ is positive and fix a positive real number $\alpha < \chi(\Phi(\eta))$. Also define

$\sigma_a = \Phi(\rho_a)$ for each $a \in \Sigma$, let $\varepsilon > 0$ be a positive real number, let $\Gamma = \{0, 1\}$ denote the binary alphabet, and define $\mathcal{Z} = \mathbb{C}^{\Gamma}$.

By Theorem 8.26, for all but finitely many choices of a positive integer n, and for $m = \lfloor \alpha n \rfloor$, there exists a classical-to-quantum product state channel code (f, μ) of the form

$$f: \Gamma^m \to \Sigma^n \quad \text{and} \quad \mu: \Gamma^m \to \text{Pos}(\mathcal{Y}^{\otimes n}) \tag{8.132}$$

for the collection

$$\{\sigma_a : a \in \Sigma\} \subseteq D(\mathcal{Y}) \tag{8.133}$$

that errs with probability strictly less than $\varepsilon/2$ on every binary string of length m. Assume that such a choice of n, m, and a code (f, μ) have been fixed, and define encoding and decoding channels

$$\Xi_{\text{E}} \in C(\mathcal{Z}^{\otimes m}, \mathcal{X}^{\otimes n}) \quad \text{and} \quad \Xi_{\text{D}} \in C(\mathcal{Y}^{\otimes n}, \mathcal{Z}^{\otimes m}) \tag{8.134}$$

as follows:

$$\begin{aligned}
\Xi_{\text{E}}(Z) &= \sum_{b_1 \cdots b_m \in \Gamma^m} \langle E_{b_1 \cdots b_m, b_1 \cdots b_m}, Z \rangle \rho_{f(b_1 \cdots b_m)}, \\
\Xi_{\text{D}}(Y) &= \sum_{b_1 \cdots b_m \in \Gamma^m} \langle \mu(b_1 \cdots b_m), Y \rangle E_{b_1 \cdots b_m, b_1 \cdots b_m},
\end{aligned} \tag{8.135}$$

for all $Z \in L(\mathcal{Z}^{\otimes m})$ and $Y \in L(\mathcal{Y}^{\otimes n})$. It follows from the properties of the code (f, μ) suggested above that

$$\langle E_{b_1 \cdots b_m, b_1 \cdots b_m}, (\Xi_{\text{D}} \Phi^{\otimes n} \Xi_{\text{E}})(E_{b_1 \cdots b_m, b_1 \cdots b_m}) \rangle > 1 - \frac{\varepsilon}{2} \tag{8.136}$$

for every $b_1 \cdots b_m \in \Gamma^m$. As Ξ_{E} is a classical-to-quantum channel and Ξ_{D} is quantum-to-classical, one finds that $\Xi_{\text{D}} \Phi^{\otimes n} \Xi_{\text{E}}$ is an ε-approximation to the completely dephasing channel $\Delta^{\otimes m} \in C(\mathcal{Z}^{\otimes m})$.

It has been proved that, for any choice of positive real numbers $\alpha < \chi(\Phi)$ and $\varepsilon > 0$, the channel $\Phi^{\otimes n}$ emulates an ε-approximation to the completely dephasing channel $\Delta^{\otimes m}$ for all but finitely many positive integers n and for $m = \lfloor \alpha n \rfloor$. From this fact the inequality (8.130) follows. One may apply the same reasoning to the channel $\Phi^{\otimes n}$ in place of Φ, for any positive integer n, to obtain

$$\frac{\chi(\Phi^{\otimes n})}{n} \leq \frac{C(\Phi^{\otimes n})}{n} = C(\Phi). \tag{8.137}$$

The second main step of the proof establishes that the regularized Holevo capacity is an upper bound on the classical capacity of Φ. When combined with the inequality (8.137), one finds that the limit in (8.129) indeed exists and that the equality holds. There is nothing to prove if $C(\Phi) = 0$, so it will be assumed hereafter that $C(\Phi) > 0$.

Let $\alpha > 0$ be an achievable rate for classical information transmission through Φ, and let $\varepsilon > 0$ be chosen arbitrarily. It must therefore hold, for all but finitely many positive integers n, and for $m = \lfloor \alpha n \rfloor$, that $\Phi^{\otimes n}$ emulates an ε-approximation to the completely dephasing channel $\Delta^{\otimes m} \in C(\mathcal{Z}^{\otimes m})$. Let n be any positive integer for which this property holds and for which $m = \lfloor \alpha n \rfloor \geq 2$. The situation in which a sender generates a binary string of length m, uniformly at random, and transmits this string through the ε-approximation to $\Delta^{\otimes m}$ emulated by $\Phi^{\otimes n}$ will be considered.

Let X and Z be classical registers both having state set Γ^m; the register X corresponds to the randomly generated string selected by the sender and Z corresponds to the string obtained by the receiver when a copy of the string stored in X is transmitted through the ε-approximation to $\Delta^{\otimes m}$ emulated by $\Phi^{\otimes n}$. As $\Phi^{\otimes n}$ emulates an ε-approximation to $\Delta^{\otimes m}$, there must exist a collection of states

$$\{ \rho_{b_1 \cdots b_m} : b_1 \cdots b_m \in \Gamma^m \} \subseteq D(\mathcal{X}^{\otimes n}), \tag{8.138}$$

along with a measurement $\mu \colon \Gamma^m \to \mathrm{Pos}(\mathcal{Y}^{\otimes n})$, such that

$$\langle \mu(b_1 \cdots b_m), \Phi^{\otimes n}(\rho_{b_1 \cdots b_m}) \rangle > 1 - \frac{\varepsilon}{2} \tag{8.139}$$

for every binary string $b_1 \cdots b_m \in \Gamma^m$. With respect to the probability vector $p \in \mathcal{P}(\Gamma^m \times \Gamma^m)$ defined as

$$p(b_1 \cdots b_m, c_1 \cdots c_m) = \frac{1}{2^m} \langle \mu(c_1 \cdots c_m), \Phi^{\otimes n}(\rho_{b_1 \cdots b_m}) \rangle, \tag{8.140}$$

which represents the probabilistic state of (X, Z) suggested above, it follows from Holevo's theorem (Theorem 5.49) that

$$I(X : Z) \leq \chi(\Phi^{\otimes n}(\eta)), \tag{8.141}$$

where $\eta \colon \Gamma^m \to \mathrm{Pos}(\mathcal{X}^{\otimes n})$ is the ensemble defined as

$$\eta(b_1 \cdots b_m) = \frac{1}{2^m} \rho_{b_1 \cdots b_m} \tag{8.142}$$

for each $b_1 \cdots b_m \in \Gamma^m$.

A lower bound on the mutual information $I(X : Z)$ will now be derived. The distribution represented by the marginal probability vector $p[X]$ is uniform, and therefore $H(p[X]) = m$. By (8.139), each entry of the probability vector $p[Z]$ is lower-bounded by $(1 - \varepsilon/2)2^{-m}$. It is therefore possible to write

$$p[Z] = \left(1 - \frac{\varepsilon}{2} \right) r + \frac{\varepsilon}{2} q \tag{8.143}$$

for $q \in \mathcal{P}(\Gamma^m)$ being some choice of a probability vector and $r \in \mathcal{P}(\Gamma^m)$ denoting the uniform probability vector, defined as $r(b_1 \cdots b_m) = 2^{-m}$ for every $b_1 \cdots b_m \in \Gamma^m$. The inequality

$$H(p[Z]) \geq \left(1 - \frac{\varepsilon}{2}\right) H(r) + \frac{\varepsilon}{2} H(q) \geq \left(1 - \frac{\varepsilon}{2}\right) m \qquad (8.144)$$

follows by the concavity of the Shannon entropy function (Proposition 5.5). On the other hand, because the probability vector p satisfies

$$p(b_1 \cdots b_m, b_1 \cdots b_m) \geq \left(1 - \frac{\varepsilon}{2}\right) 2^{-m} \qquad (8.145)$$

for every $b_1 \cdots b_m \in \Gamma^m$, it must hold that

$$H(p) \leq -\left(1 - \frac{\varepsilon}{2}\right) \log\left(\frac{1 - \varepsilon/2}{2^m}\right) - \frac{\varepsilon}{2} \log\left(\frac{\varepsilon/2}{2^{2m} - 2^m}\right) \qquad (8.146)$$

$$< \left(1 + \frac{\varepsilon}{2}\right) m + H\left(1 - \frac{\varepsilon}{2}, \frac{\varepsilon}{2}\right) \leq \left(1 + \frac{\varepsilon}{2}\right) m + 1;$$

the first inequality is a consequence of the fact that the entropy of p subject to the constraint (8.145) is maximized when p is defined as follows:

$$p(b_1 \cdots b_m, c_1 \cdots c_m) = \begin{cases} \frac{1 - \varepsilon/2}{2^m} & b_1 \cdots b_m = c_1 \cdots c_m \\ \frac{\varepsilon/2}{2^m (2^m - 1)} & b_1 \cdots b_m \neq c_1 \cdots c_m. \end{cases} \qquad (8.147)$$

It therefore follows that

$$\chi(\Phi^{\otimes n}) \geq I(X : Z) = H(p[X]) + H(p[Z]) - H(p)$$

$$\geq (1 - \varepsilon) m - 1 \geq (1 - \varepsilon) \alpha n - 2, \qquad (8.148)$$

and consequently

$$\frac{\chi(\Phi^{\otimes n})}{n} \geq (1 - \varepsilon) \alpha - \frac{2}{n}. \qquad (8.149)$$

It has been proved, for any achievable rate $\alpha > 0$ for classical information transmission through Φ, and for any $\varepsilon > 0$, that the inequality (8.149) holds for all but finitely many positive integers n. Because the supremum over all achievable rates α for classical information transmission through Φ is equal to $C(\Phi)$, this inequality may be combined with (8.137) to obtain the required equality (8.129). $\qquad \Box$

8.1.3 The Entanglement-Assisted Classical Capacity Theorem

This section focuses on the *entanglement-assisted classical capacity theorem*, which characterizes the entanglement-assisted classical capacity of a given channel. It stands out among the capacity theorems presented in the present chapter, as no regularization is required by the characterization it provides.

Holevo–Schumacher–Westmoreland Theorem With Entanglement Assistance

A preliminary step toward the proof of the entanglement-assisted classical capacity theorem is the observation that, when the classical capacity and Holevo capacity are replaced by their entanglement-assisted formulations, a statement analogous to the Holevo–Schumacher–Westmoreland theorem holds.

Theorem 8.28 *Let $\Phi \in C(\mathcal{X}, \mathcal{Y})$ be a channel, for complex Euclidean spaces $\mathcal{X}$ and $\mathcal{Y}$. The entanglement-assisted classical capacity of Φ equals the regularized entanglement-assisted Holevo capacity of Φ:*

$$C_{\mathrm{E}}(\Phi) = \lim_{n \to \infty} \frac{\chi_{\mathrm{E}}(\Phi^{\otimes n})}{n}. \tag{8.150}$$

Proof The theorem is proved in essentially the same way as the Holevo–Schumacher–Westmoreland theorem (Theorem 8.27), with each step being modified to allow for the possibility of entanglement assistance.

In greater detail, let Σ be an alphabet, let $\mathcal{W}$ be a complex Euclidean space, let η be an ensemble of the form $\eta \colon \Sigma \to \mathrm{Pos}(\mathcal{X} \otimes \mathcal{W})$ that is homogeneous on $\mathcal{W}$, assume $\chi((\Phi \otimes \mathbb{1}_{\mathrm{L}(\mathcal{W})})(\eta))$ is positive, and let α be a positive real number satisfying

$$\alpha < \chi((\Phi \otimes \mathbb{1}_{\mathrm{L}(\mathcal{W})})(\eta)). \tag{8.151}$$

By Proposition 8.12, one may choose a complex Euclidean space $\mathcal{V}$, a state $\xi \in \mathrm{D}(\mathcal{V} \otimes \mathcal{W})$, a probability vector $p \in \mathcal{P}(\Sigma)$, and a collection of channels

$$\{\Psi_a \colon a \in \Sigma\} \subseteq C(\mathcal{V}, \mathcal{X}) \tag{8.152}$$

such that

$$\eta(a) = p(a)(\Psi_a \otimes \mathbb{1}_{\mathrm{L}(\mathcal{W})})(\xi) \tag{8.153}$$

for every $a \in \Sigma$. For each $a \in \Sigma$ let

$$\sigma_a = (\Phi\Psi_a \otimes \mathbb{1}_{\mathrm{L}(\mathcal{W})})(\xi), \tag{8.154}$$

and also let $\varepsilon > 0$ be an arbitrarily chosen positive real number.

By Theorem 8.26, for all but finitely many choices of a positive integer n, and for $m = \lfloor \alpha n \rfloor$, there exists a classical-to-quantum product state channel code (f, μ) of the form

$$f \colon \Gamma^m \to \Sigma^n \quad \text{and} \quad \mu \colon \Gamma^m \to \mathrm{Pos}((\mathcal{Y} \otimes \mathcal{W})^{\otimes n}) \tag{8.155}$$

for the collection $\{\sigma_a \colon a \in \Sigma\} \subseteq \mathrm{D}(\mathcal{Y} \otimes \mathcal{W})$ that errs with probability strictly less than $\varepsilon/2$ on every binary string of length m. Assume that such a choice of n, m, and a code (f, μ) have been fixed.

It will now be proved that the channel $\Phi^{\otimes n}$ emulates an ε-approximation to the completely dephasing channel $\Delta^{\otimes m} \in C(\mathcal{Z}^{\otimes m})$ with the assistance of entanglement. The entangled state to be used to assist this emulation is

$$V \xi^{\otimes n} V^* \in D(\mathcal{V}^{\otimes n} \otimes \mathcal{W}^{\otimes n}), \tag{8.156}$$

where $V \in U((\mathcal{V} \otimes \mathcal{W})^{\otimes n}, \mathcal{V}^{\otimes n} \otimes \mathcal{W}^{\otimes n})$ represents a permutation of tensor factors:

$$\begin{aligned}
V((v_1 \otimes w_1) \otimes \cdots \otimes (v_n \otimes w_n)) \\
= (v_1 \otimes \cdots \otimes v_n) \otimes (w_1 \otimes \cdots \otimes w_n)
\end{aligned} \tag{8.157}$$

for all vectors $v_1, \ldots, v_n \in \mathcal{V}$ and $w_1, \ldots, w_n \in \mathcal{W}$.

The encoding channel $\Xi_E \in C(\mathcal{Z}^{\otimes m} \otimes \mathcal{V}^{\otimes n}, \mathcal{X}^{\otimes n})$ used to perform this emulation is defined as

$$\Xi_E = \sum_{b_1 \cdots b_m \in \Gamma^m} \Theta_{b_1 \cdots b_m} \otimes \Psi_{f(b_1 \cdots b_m)}, \tag{8.158}$$

where

$$\Psi_{a_1 \cdots a_n} = \Psi_{a_1} \otimes \cdots \otimes \Psi_{a_n} \tag{8.159}$$

for each $a_1 \cdots a_n \in \Sigma^n$, and where $\Theta_{b_1 \cdots b_m} \in CP(\mathcal{Z}^{\otimes m}, \mathbb{C})$ is given by

$$\Theta_{b_1 \cdots b_m}(Z) = Z(b_1 \cdots b_m, b_1 \cdots b_m) \tag{8.160}$$

for every $Z \in L(\mathcal{Z}^{\otimes m})$. Described in words, the encoding map Ξ_E takes as input a compound register $(\mathsf{Z}_1, \ldots, \mathsf{Z}_m, \mathsf{V}_1, \ldots, \mathsf{V}_n)$, measures $(\mathsf{Z}_1, \ldots, \mathsf{Z}_m)$ with respect to the standard basis measurement, and applies the channel $\Psi_{f(b_1 \cdots b_m)}$ to $(\mathsf{V}_1, \ldots, \mathsf{V}_n)$, for $b_1 \cdots b_m$ being the string obtained from the standard basis measurement on $(\mathsf{Z}_1, \ldots, \mathsf{Z}_m)$.

The decoding channel $\Xi_D \in C(\mathcal{Y}^{\otimes n} \otimes \mathcal{W}^{\otimes n}, \mathcal{Z}^{\otimes m})$ used to perform the emulation is defined as

$$\Xi_D(Y) = \sum_{b_1 \cdots b_m \in \Gamma^m} \langle W\mu(b_1 \cdots b_m)W^*, Y \rangle E_{b_1 \cdots b_m, b_1 \cdots b_m} \tag{8.161}$$

for all $Y \in L(\mathcal{Y}^{\otimes n} \otimes \mathcal{W}^{\otimes n})$, where $W \in U((\mathcal{Y} \otimes \mathcal{W})^{\otimes n}, \mathcal{Y}^{\otimes n} \otimes \mathcal{W}^{\otimes n})$ is an isometry representing a permutation of tensor factors that is similar to V, but with $\mathcal{V}$ replaced by $\mathcal{Y}$:

$$\begin{aligned}
W((y_1 \otimes w_1) \otimes \cdots \otimes (y_n \otimes w_n)) \\
= (y_1 \otimes \cdots \otimes y_n) \otimes (w_1 \otimes \cdots \otimes w_n)
\end{aligned} \tag{8.162}$$

for all choices of vectors $y_1, \ldots, y_n \in \mathcal{Y}$ and $w_1, \ldots, w_n \in \mathcal{W}$.

Now, let $\Psi \in C(\mathcal{Z}^{\otimes m})$ denote the channel that has been emulated with the assistance of entanglement by the above construction; this channel may be expressed as

$$\Psi(Z) = \left(\Xi_{\mathrm{D}}\left(\Phi^{\otimes n}\Xi_{\mathrm{E}} \otimes \mathbb{1}_{\mathrm{L}(\mathcal{W})}^{\otimes n}\right)\right)\left(Z \otimes V\xi^{\otimes n}V^*\right) \qquad (8.163)$$

for every $Z \in \mathrm{L}(\mathcal{Z}^{\otimes m})$, and it may be observed that $\Psi = \Delta^{\otimes m}\Psi\Delta^{\otimes m}$. For every string $b_1 \cdots b_m \in \Gamma^m$ it holds that

$$\left(\Phi^{\otimes n}\Xi_{\mathrm{E}} \otimes \mathbb{1}_{\mathrm{L}(\mathcal{W})}^{\otimes n}\right)\left(E_{b_1\cdots b_m, b_1\cdots b_m} \otimes V\xi^{\otimes n}V^*\right) = W\sigma_{f(b_1\cdots b_m)}W^*, \qquad (8.164)$$

and therefore

$$\left\langle E_{b_1\cdots b_m, b_1\cdots b_m}, \Psi(E_{b_1\cdots b_m, b_1\cdots b_m})\right\rangle > 1 - \frac{\varepsilon}{2}. \qquad (8.165)$$

It follows that Ψ is an ε-approximation to $\Delta^{\otimes m}$, as claimed.

In summary, for any choice of positive real numbers $\alpha < \chi_{\mathrm{E}}(\Phi)$ and $\varepsilon > 0$, it holds that $\Phi^{\otimes n}$ emulates an ε-approximation to the completely dephasing channel $\Delta^{\otimes m}$ with the assistance of entanglement, for all but finitely many positive integers n and for $m = \lfloor \alpha n \rfloor$. From this fact one concludes that $\chi_{\mathrm{E}}(\Phi) \leq \mathrm{C}_{\mathrm{E}}(\Phi)$. Applying the same argument to the channel $\Phi^{\otimes n}$ in place of Φ, for any choice of a positive integer n, yields

$$\frac{\chi_{\mathrm{E}}(\Phi^{\otimes n})}{n} \leq \frac{\mathrm{C}_{\mathrm{E}}(\Phi^{\otimes n})}{n} = \mathrm{C}_{\mathrm{E}}(\Phi). \qquad (8.166)$$

Next it will be proved that the entanglement-assisted classical capacity of Φ cannot exceed its regularized entanglement-assisted Holevo capacity. As in the proof of Theorem 8.27, it may be assumed that $\mathrm{C}_{\mathrm{E}}(\Phi) > 0$, and it suffices to consider the situation in which a sender transmits a uniformly generated binary string of length m to a receiver.

Suppose $\alpha > 0$ is an achievable rate for entanglement-assisted classical information transmission through Φ, and let $\varepsilon > 0$ be chosen arbitrarily. It must therefore hold, for all but finitely many positive integers n, and for $m = \lfloor \alpha n \rfloor$, that $\Phi^{\otimes n}$ emulates an ε-approximation to the completely dephasing channel $\Delta^{\otimes m}$ with the assistance of entanglement. Let n be an arbitrarily chosen positive integer for which this property holds and for which $m = \lfloor \alpha n \rfloor \geq 2$.

As before, let X and Z be classical registers both having state set Γ^m; X stores the randomly generated string selected by the sender and Z represents the string obtained by the receiver when a copy of the string stored in X is transmitted through the ε-approximation to $\Delta^{\otimes m}$ emulated by $\Phi^{\otimes n}$ with the assistance of entanglement. By the assumption that $\Phi^{\otimes n}$ emulates an ε-approximation to $\Delta^{\otimes m}$ with the assistance of entanglement, one may conclude that there exist a choice of complex Euclidean spaces $\mathcal{V}$ and $\mathcal{W}$, a state $\xi \in D(\mathcal{V} \otimes \mathcal{W})$, a collection of channels

$$\{\Psi_{b_1 \cdots b_m} : b_1 \cdots b_m \in \Gamma^m\} \subseteq C(\mathcal{V}, \mathcal{X}^{\otimes n}), \tag{8.167}$$

and a measurement $\mu \colon \Gamma^m \to \text{Pos}(\mathcal{Y}^{\otimes n} \otimes \mathcal{W})$, such that

$$\left\langle \mu(b_1 \cdots b_m), \left(\Phi^{\otimes n} \Psi_{b_1 \cdots b_m} \otimes \mathbb{1}_{L(\mathcal{W})}\right)(\xi)\right\rangle > 1 - \frac{\varepsilon}{2} \tag{8.168}$$

for every string $b_1 \cdots b_m \in \Gamma^m$. With respect to $p \in \mathcal{P}(\Gamma^m \times \Gamma^m)$ defined as

$$
\begin{aligned}
&p(b_1 \cdots b_m, c_1 \cdots c_m) \\
&= \frac{1}{2^m} \left\langle \mu(c_1 \cdots c_m), \left(\Phi^{\otimes n} \Psi_{b_1 \cdots b_m} \otimes \mathbb{1}_{L(\mathcal{W})}\right)(\xi)\right\rangle,
\end{aligned}
\tag{8.169}
$$

which represents the probabilistic state of (X, Z) suggested above, it follows from Holevo's theorem (Theorem 5.49) that

$$\mathrm{I}(\mathsf{X} : \mathsf{Z}) \leq \chi\left((\Phi^{\otimes n} \otimes \mathbb{1}_{L(\mathcal{W})})(\eta)\right), \tag{8.170}$$

for $\eta \colon \Gamma^m \to \text{Pos}(\mathcal{X}^{\otimes n} \otimes \mathcal{W})$ being the ensemble defined as

$$\eta(b_1 \cdots b_m) = \frac{1}{2^m}\left(\Psi_{b_1 \cdots b_m} \otimes \mathbb{1}_{L(\mathcal{W})}\right)(\xi) \tag{8.171}$$

for each $b_1 \cdots b_m \in \Gamma^m$.

The same lower bound on the quantity $\mathrm{I}(\mathsf{X} : \mathsf{Z})$ derived in the proof of Theorem 8.27 holds in the present case, from which it follows that

$$\chi_{\mathrm{E}}(\Phi^{\otimes n}) \geq \mathrm{I}(\mathsf{X} : \mathsf{Z}) \geq (1 - \varepsilon)\alpha n - 2, \tag{8.172}$$

and therefore

$$\frac{\chi_{\mathrm{E}}(\Phi^{\otimes n})}{n} \geq (1 - \varepsilon)\alpha - \frac{2}{n}. \tag{8.173}$$

Thus, for any achievable rate $\alpha > 0$ for entanglement-assisted classical information transmission through Φ, and for any positive real number $\varepsilon > 0$, the inequality (8.173) holds for all but finitely many positive integers n. Because the supremum over all achievable rates α for entanglement-assisted classical information transmission through Φ is equal to $C_{\mathrm{E}}(\Phi)$, one may combine this inequality with the upper bound (8.166) to obtain the required equality (8.150). $\qquad\square$

Strongly Typical Strings and Projections

The proof of the entanglement-assisted classical capacity theorem that is presented in this book will make use of a notion of typicality, known as *strong typicality*, that differs from the standard notion discussed previously in Section 5.3.1. True to its name, strong typicality is the more restrictive of the two notions; every strongly typical string will necessarily be a typical string, up to a simple change of parameters, while some typical strings are not strongly typical.

Similar to the standard notion of typicality, one may define an ε-*strongly typical subspace* with respect to a spectral decomposition of a given state. Unlike the standard typical subspace, however, the strongly typical subspace is not always uniquely determined by a given state; it can depend on the particular choice of a spectral decomposition (in the sense of Corollary 1.4) with respect to which it is defined. Despite this apparent drawback, the notion of an ε-strongly typical subspace will be a useful tool when proving the entanglement-assisted classical capacity theorem.

The definition of strong typicality below uses the following notation, for which it is to be assumed that Σ is an alphabet and n is a positive integer. For every string $a_1 \cdots a_n \in \Sigma^n$ and symbol $a \in \Sigma$, one writes

$$N(a \,|\, a_1 \cdots a_n) = |\{k \in \{1, \ldots, n\} : a_k = a\}|, \qquad (8.174)$$

which is the number of times the symbol a occurs in the string $a_1 \cdots a_n$.

Definition 8.29 Let Σ be an alphabet, let $p \in \mathcal{P}(\Sigma)$ be a probability vector, let n be a positive integer, and let $\varepsilon > 0$ be a positive real number. A string $a_1 \cdots a_n \in \Sigma^n$ is said to be ε-*strongly typical with respect to* p if

$$\left| \frac{N(a \,|\, a_1 \cdots a_n)}{n} - p(a) \right| \leq p(a)\varepsilon \qquad (8.175)$$

for every $a \in \Sigma$. The set of all ε-strongly typical strings of length n with respect to p is denoted $S_{n,\varepsilon}(p)$ (or by $S_{n,\varepsilon}$ when p is implicit and can safely be omitted).

The average behavior of a nonnegative real-valued function defined on the individual symbols of a strongly typical string may be analyzed using the following elementary proposition.

Proposition 8.30 *Let Σ be an alphabet, let $p \in \mathcal{P}(\Sigma)$ be a probability vector, let n be a positive integer, let $\varepsilon > 0$ be a positive real number, let $a_1 \cdots a_n \in S_{n,\varepsilon}(p)$ be an ε-strongly typical string with respect to p, and let $\phi : \Sigma \to [0, \infty)$ be a nonnegative real-valued function. It holds that*

$$\left| \frac{\phi(a_1) + \cdots + \phi(a_n)}{n} - \sum_{a \in \Sigma} p(a)\phi(a) \right| \leq \varepsilon \sum_{a \in \Sigma} p(a)\phi(a). \qquad (8.176)$$

Proof The inequality (8.176) follows from the definition of strong typicality together with the triangle inequality:

$$\left| \frac{\phi(a_1) + \cdots + \phi(a_n)}{n} - \sum_{a \in \Sigma} p(a)\phi(a) \right|$$

$$= \left| \sum_{a \in \Sigma} \left(\frac{N(a \mid a_1 \cdots a_n)\phi(a)}{n} - p(a)\phi(a) \right) \right| \tag{8.177}$$

$$\leq \sum_{a \in \Sigma} \phi(a) \left| \frac{N(a \mid a_1 \cdots a_n)}{n} - p(a) \right| \leq \varepsilon \sum_{a \in \Sigma} p(a)\phi(a),$$

as required. $\qquad\square$

As a corollary to Proposition 8.30, one has that every ε-strongly typical string, with respect to a given probability vector p, is necessarily δ-typical for every choice of $\delta > \varepsilon \, H(p)$.

Corollary 8.31 *Let Σ be an alphabet, let $p \in \mathcal{P}(\Sigma)$ be a probability vector, let n be a positive integer, let $\varepsilon > 0$ be a positive real number, and let $a_1 \cdots a_n \in S_{n,\varepsilon}(p)$ be an ε-strongly typical string with respect to p. It holds that*

$$2^{-n(1+\varepsilon) \, H(p)} \leq p(a_1) \cdots p(a_n) \leq 2^{-n(1-\varepsilon) \, H(p)}. \tag{8.178}$$

Proof Define a function $\phi \colon \Sigma \to [0, \infty)$ as

$$\phi(a) = \begin{cases} -\log(p(a)) & \text{if } p(a) > 0 \\ 0 & \text{if } p(a) = 0. \end{cases} \tag{8.179}$$

With respect to this function, the implication provided by Proposition 8.30 is equivalent to (8.178). $\qquad\square$

Strings that are obtained by independently selecting symbols at random according to a given probability vector are likely to be not only typical, but strongly typical, with the probability of strong typicality increasing with string length. The following lemma establishes a quantitative bound on this probability.

Lemma 8.32 *Let Σ be an alphabet, let $p \in \mathcal{P}(\Sigma)$ be a probability vector, let n be a positive integer, and let $\varepsilon > 0$ be a positive real number. It holds that*

$$\sum_{a_1 \cdots a_n \in S_{n,\varepsilon}(p)} p(a_1) \cdots p(a_n) \geq 1 - \zeta_{n,\varepsilon}(p) \tag{8.180}$$

for

$$\zeta_{n,\varepsilon}(p) = 2 \sum_{\substack{a \in \Sigma \\ p(a) > 0}} \exp(-2n\varepsilon^2 p(a)^2). \tag{8.181}$$

Proof Suppose first that $a \in \Sigma$ is fixed, and consider the probability that a string $a_1 \cdots a_n \in \Sigma^n$, randomly selected according to the probability vector $p^{\otimes n}$, satisfies

$$\left| \frac{N(a \,|\, a_1 \cdots a_n)}{n} - p(a) \right| > p(a)\varepsilon. \tag{8.182}$$

To bound this probability, one may define $X_1, \ldots, X_n$ to be independent and identically distributed random variables, taking value 1 with probability $p(a)$ and value 0 otherwise, so that the probability of the event (8.182) is equal to

$$\Pr\left(\left| \frac{X_1 + \cdots + X_n}{n} - p(a) \right| > p(a)\varepsilon \right). \tag{8.183}$$

If it is the case that $p(a) > 0$, then Hoeffding's inequality (Theorem 1.16) implies that

$$\Pr\left(\left| \frac{X_1 + \cdots + X_n}{n} - p(a) \right| > p(a)\varepsilon \right) \leq 2\exp(-2n\varepsilon^2 p(a)^2), \tag{8.184}$$

while it holds that

$$\Pr\left(\left| \frac{X_1 + \cdots + X_n}{n} - p(a) \right| > p(a)\varepsilon \right) = 0 \tag{8.185}$$

in case $p(a) = 0$. The lemma follows from the union bound. $\qquad\square$

The next proposition establishes upper and lower bounds on the number of strings in an ε-strongly typical set for a given length.

Proposition 8.33 *Let Σ be an alphabet, let $p \in \mathcal{P}(\Sigma)$ be a probability vector, let n be a positive integer, and let $\varepsilon > 0$ be a positive real number. It holds that*

$$(1 - \zeta_{n,\varepsilon}(p))\, 2^{n(1-\varepsilon)\,\mathrm{H}(p)} \leq |S_{n,\varepsilon}(p)| \leq 2^{n(1+\varepsilon)\,\mathrm{H}(p)}, \tag{8.186}$$

for $\zeta_{n,\varepsilon}(p)$ as defined in Lemma 8.32.

Proof By Corollary 8.31, one has

$$p(a_1) \cdots p(a_n) \geq 2^{-n(1+\varepsilon)\,\mathrm{H}(p)} \tag{8.187}$$

for every string $a_1 \cdots a_n \in S_{n,\varepsilon}(p)$. Consequently,

$$1 \geq \sum_{a_1 \cdots a_n \in S_{n,\varepsilon}(p)} p(a_1) \cdots p(a_n) \geq |S_{n,\varepsilon}(p)| 2^{-n(1+\varepsilon)\,\mathrm{H}(p)}, \tag{8.188}$$

and therefore

$$|S_{n,\varepsilon}(p)| \leq 2^{n(1+\varepsilon)\,\mathrm{H}(p)}. \tag{8.189}$$

Along similar lines, one has

$$p(a_1) \cdots p(a_n) \leq 2^{-n(1-\varepsilon)\,\mathrm{H}(p)} \tag{8.190}$$

for every string $a_1 \cdots a_n \in S_{n,\varepsilon}(p)$. By Lemma 8.32, it follows that

$$1 - \zeta_{n,\varepsilon}(p) \leq \sum_{a_1 \cdots a_n \in S_{n,\varepsilon}(p)} p(a_1) \cdots p(a_n) \leq |S_{n,\varepsilon}(p)| \, 2^{-n(1-\varepsilon)\,\mathrm{H}(p)}, \tag{8.191}$$

and therefore

$$|S_{n,\varepsilon}(p)| \geq (1 - \zeta_{n,\varepsilon}(p)) \, 2^{n(1-\varepsilon)\,\mathrm{H}(p)}, \tag{8.192}$$

as required. $\qquad\square$

The ε-strongly typical subspaces associated with a given density operator are defined as follows.

Definition 8.34 Let $\mathcal{X}$ be a complex Euclidean space, let $\rho \in \mathrm{D}(\mathcal{X})$ be a density operator, let $\varepsilon > 0$ be a positive real number, and let n be a positive integer. Also let

$$\rho = \sum_{a \in \Sigma} p(a) x_a x_a^* \tag{8.193}$$

be a spectral decomposition of ρ, for Σ being an alphabet, $p \in \mathcal{P}(\Sigma)$ being a probability vector, and $\{x_a : a \in \Sigma\} \subset \mathcal{X}$ being an orthonormal set of vectors. The *projection operator onto the ε-strongly typical subspace of $\mathcal{X}^{\otimes n}$* with respect to the spectral decomposition (8.193) is defined as

$$\Lambda = \sum_{a_1 \cdots a_n \in S_{n,\varepsilon}(p)} x_{a_1} x_{a_1}^* \otimes \cdots \otimes x_{a_n} x_{a_n}^*. \tag{8.194}$$

With respect to the decomposition (8.193), the *ε-strongly typical subspace of $\mathcal{X}^{\otimes n}$* is defined as the image of Λ.

Example 8.35 Let $\Sigma = \{0,1\}$, let $\mathcal{X} = \mathbb{C}^\Sigma$, and let $\rho = \mathbb{1}/2 \in \mathrm{D}(\mathcal{X})$. With respect to the spectral decomposition

$$\rho = \frac{1}{2} e_0 e_0^* + \frac{1}{2} e_1 e_1^*, \tag{8.195}$$

for $n = 2$, and for any choice of $\varepsilon \in (0,1)$, one has that the corresponding projection operator onto the ε-strongly typical subspace is given by

$$\Lambda_0 = E_{0,0} \otimes E_{1,1} + E_{1,1} \otimes E_{0,0}. \tag{8.196}$$

Replacing the spectral decomposition by

$$\rho = \frac{1}{2} x_0 x_0^* + \frac{1}{2} x_1 x_1^*, \tag{8.197}$$

for

$$x_0 = \frac{e_0 + e_1}{\sqrt{2}} \quad \text{and} \quad x_1 = \frac{e_0 - e_1}{\sqrt{2}}, \tag{8.198}$$

one obtains the corresponding projection operator

$$\Lambda_1 = x_0 x_0^* \otimes x_1 x_1^* + x_1 x_1^* \otimes x_0 x_0^* \neq \Lambda_0. \tag{8.199}$$

Two Lemmas on the Output Entropy of Channels

The proof of the entanglement-assisted classical capacity theorem appearing at the end of the present section will make use of multiple lemmas. The two lemmas that follow concern the output entropy of channels. The first of these two lemmas will also be used in the next section of the chapter, to prove that the coherent information lower-bounds the quantum capacity of a channel.

Lemma 8.36 *Let $\mathcal{X}$ and $\mathcal{Y}$ be complex Euclidean spaces, let $\Phi \in C(\mathcal{X}, \mathcal{Y})$ be a channel, let $\rho \in D(\mathcal{X})$ be a density operator, let $\varepsilon > 0$ be a positive real number, and let n be a positive integer. Also let*

$$\rho = \sum_{a \in \Sigma} p(a) x_a x_a^* \tag{8.200}$$

be a spectral decomposition of ρ, for Σ being an alphabet, $\{x_a : a \in \Sigma\} \subset \mathcal{X}$ being an orthonormal set, and $p \in \mathcal{P}(\Sigma)$ being a probability vector, let $\Lambda_{n,\varepsilon}$ denote the projection operator onto the ε-strongly typical subspace of $\mathcal{X}^{\otimes n}$ with respect to the decomposition (8.200), and let

$$\omega_{n,\varepsilon} = \frac{\Lambda_{n,\varepsilon}}{\operatorname{Tr}(\Lambda_{n,\varepsilon})}. \tag{8.201}$$

It holds that

$$\left| \frac{H(\Phi^{\otimes n}(\omega_{n,\varepsilon}))}{n} - H(\Phi(\rho)) \right|$$

$$\leq 2\varepsilon\, H(\rho) + \varepsilon\, H(\Phi(\rho)) - \frac{\log(1 - \zeta_{n,\varepsilon}(p))}{n}, \tag{8.202}$$

for $\zeta_{n,\varepsilon}(p)$ being the quantity defined in Lemma 8.32.

Proof It may be verified that the equation

$$H(\Phi(\rho)) - \frac{1}{n}H(\Phi^{\otimes n}(\omega_{n,\varepsilon}))$$

$$= \frac{1}{n}D(\Phi^{\otimes n}(\omega_{n,\varepsilon}) \| \Phi^{\otimes n}(\rho^{\otimes n})) \tag{8.203}$$

$$+ \frac{1}{n}\text{Tr}((\Phi^{\otimes n}(\omega_{n,\varepsilon}) - \Phi(\rho)^{\otimes n})\log(\Phi(\rho)^{\otimes n}))$$

holds for every positive integer n. Bounds on the absolute values of the two terms on the right-hand side of this equation will be established separately.

The first term on the right-hand side of (8.203) is nonnegative, and an upper bound on it may be obtained from the monotonicity of the quantum relative entropy under the action of channels (Theorem 5.35). Specifically, one has

$$\frac{1}{n}D(\Phi^{\otimes n}(\omega_{n,\varepsilon}) \| \Phi^{\otimes n}(\rho^{\otimes n})) \leq \frac{1}{n}D(\omega_{n,\varepsilon} \| \rho^{\otimes n})$$

$$= -\frac{1}{n}\log(|S_{n,\varepsilon}|) - \frac{1}{n|S_{n,\varepsilon}|}\sum_{a_1 \cdots a_n \in S_{n,\varepsilon}}\log(p(a_1)\cdots p(a_n)), \tag{8.204}$$

where $S_{n,\varepsilon}$ denotes the set of ε-strongly typical strings of length n with respect to p. By Corollary 8.31 it holds that

$$-\frac{1}{n|S_{n,\varepsilon}|}\sum_{a_1 \cdots a_n \in S_{n,\varepsilon}}\log(p(a_1)\cdots p(a_n)) \leq (1+\varepsilon)H(\rho), \tag{8.205}$$

and by Proposition 8.33, one has

$$\frac{1}{n}\log(|S_{n,\varepsilon}|) \geq \frac{\log(1 - \zeta_{n,\varepsilon}(p))}{n} + (1-\varepsilon)H(\rho). \tag{8.206}$$

It therefore holds that

$$\frac{1}{n}D(\Phi^{\otimes n}(\omega_{n,\varepsilon}) \| \Phi^{\otimes n}(\rho^{\otimes n})) \leq 2\varepsilon H(\rho) - \frac{\log(1 - \zeta_{n,\varepsilon}(p))}{n}. \tag{8.207}$$

To bound the absolute value of the second term on the right-hand side of (8.203), one may first define a function $\phi \colon \Sigma \to [0, \infty)$ as

$$\phi(a) = \begin{cases} -\text{Tr}(\Phi(x_a x_a^*)\log(\Phi(\rho))) & \text{if } p(a) > 0 \\ 0 & \text{if } p(a) = 0 \end{cases} \tag{8.208}$$

for each $a \in \Sigma$. It is evident from its specification that $\phi(a)$ is nonnegative for each $a \in \Sigma$, and is finite by virtue of the fact that

$$\text{im}(\Phi(x_a x_a^*)) \subseteq \text{im}(\Phi(\rho)) \tag{8.209}$$

for each $a \in \Sigma$ with $p(a) > 0$. Using the identity

$$\log(P^{\otimes n}) = \sum_{k=1}^{n} \mathbb{1}^{\otimes(k-1)} \otimes \log(P) \otimes \mathbb{1}^{\otimes(n-k)}, \tag{8.210}$$

it may be verified that

$$\operatorname{Tr}\big(\Phi^{\otimes n}(\omega_{n,\varepsilon}) \log(\Phi(\rho)^{\otimes n})\big)$$
$$= -\frac{1}{|S_{n,\varepsilon}|} \sum_{a_1 \cdots a_n \in S_{n,\varepsilon}} (\phi(a_1) + \cdots + \phi(a_n)). \tag{8.211}$$

By combining Proposition 8.30 with the observation that

$$\operatorname{H}(\Phi(\rho)) = \sum_{a \in \Sigma} p(a)\,\phi(a), \tag{8.212}$$

one finds that

$$\left| \frac{1}{n} \operatorname{Tr}\big(\big(\Phi^{\otimes n}(\omega_{n,\varepsilon}) - \Phi(\rho)^{\otimes n}\big) \log(\Phi(\rho)^{\otimes n})\big) \right|$$

$$\leq \frac{1}{|S_{n,\varepsilon}|} \sum_{a_1 \cdots a_n \in S_{n,\varepsilon}} \left| \operatorname{H}(\Phi(\rho)) - \frac{\phi(a_1) + \cdots + \phi(a_n)}{n} \right| \tag{8.213}$$

$$\leq \varepsilon \operatorname{H}(\Phi(\rho)).$$

The inequalities (8.207) and (8.213) together imply the required inequality (8.202), which completes the proof. $\qquad\square$

Lemma 8.37 *Let $\Phi \in \mathrm{C}(\mathcal{X}, \mathcal{Y})$ be a channel, for complex Euclidean spaces $\mathcal{X}$ and $\mathcal{Y}$. The function $f\colon \mathrm{D}(\mathcal{X}) \to \mathbb{R}$ defined by*

$$f(\rho) = \operatorname{H}(\rho) - \operatorname{H}(\Phi(\rho)) \tag{8.214}$$

is concave.

Proof Let $\mathcal{Z}$ be an arbitrary complex Euclidean space, and consider first the function $g\colon \mathrm{D}(\mathcal{Y} \otimes \mathcal{Z}) \to \mathbb{R}$ defined as

$$g(\sigma) = \operatorname{H}(\sigma) - \operatorname{H}(\operatorname{Tr}_{\mathcal{Z}}(\sigma)) \tag{8.215}$$

for every $\sigma \in \mathrm{D}(\mathcal{Y} \otimes \mathcal{Z})$. An alternative expression for g is

$$g(\sigma) = -\operatorname{D}(\sigma \,\|\, \operatorname{Tr}_{\mathcal{Z}}(\sigma) \otimes \mathbb{1}_{\mathcal{Z}}), \tag{8.216}$$

and the concavity of g therefore follows from the joint convexity of quantum relative entropy (Corollary 5.33).

For a suitable choice of a complex Euclidean space $\mathcal{Z}$, let $A \in U(\mathcal{X}, \mathcal{Y} \otimes \mathcal{Z})$ be an isometry that yields a Stinespring representation of Φ:

$$\Phi(X) = \text{Tr}_{\mathcal{Z}}(AXA^*) \tag{8.217}$$

for every $X \in L(\mathcal{X})$. The function f is given by $f(\rho) = g(A\rho A^*)$ for every $\rho \in D(\mathcal{X})$, and therefore the concavity of g implies that f is concave as well. $\qquad\square$

An Additivity Lemma Concerning the Coherent Information

Another lemma that will be used in the proof of the entanglement-assisted capacity theorem is proved below. It states that the quantity

$$\max_{\sigma \in D(\mathcal{X})} (\text{H}(\sigma) + \text{I}_c(\sigma; \Phi)), \tag{8.218}$$

defined for each channel $\Phi \in C(\mathcal{X}, \mathcal{Y})$, is additive with respect to tensor products. It is precisely this quantity that the entanglement-assisted classical capacity theorem establishes is equal to the entanglement-assisted classical capacity of the channel Φ.

Lemma 8.38 (Adami–Cerf)   *Let $\Phi_0 \in C(\mathcal{X}_0, \mathcal{Y}_0)$ and $\Phi_1 \in C(\mathcal{X}_1, \mathcal{Y}_1)$ be channels, for complex Euclidean spaces $\mathcal{X}_0$, $\mathcal{X}_1$, $\mathcal{Y}_0$, and $\mathcal{Y}_1$. It holds that*

$$\max_{\sigma \in D(\mathcal{X}_0 \otimes \mathcal{X}_1)} (\text{H}(\sigma) + \text{I}_c(\sigma; \Phi_0 \otimes \Phi_1))$$
$$= \max_{\sigma_0 \in D(\mathcal{X}_0)} (\text{H}(\sigma_0) + \text{I}_c(\sigma_0; \Phi_0)) + \max_{\sigma_1 \in D(\mathcal{X}_1)} (\text{H}(\sigma_1) + \text{I}_c(\sigma_1; \Phi_1)). \tag{8.219}$$

Proof   Choose isometries $A_0 \in U(\mathcal{X}_0, \mathcal{Y}_0 \otimes \mathcal{Z}_0)$ and $A_1 \in U(\mathcal{X}_1, \mathcal{Y}_1 \otimes \mathcal{Z}_1)$, for an appropriate choice of complex Euclidean spaces $\mathcal{Z}_0$ and $\mathcal{Z}_1$, so that Stinespring representations of Φ_0 and Φ_1 are obtained:

$$\Phi_0(X_0) = \text{Tr}_{\mathcal{Z}_0}(A_0 X_0 A_0^*) \quad \text{and} \quad \Phi_1(X_1) = \text{Tr}_{\mathcal{Z}_1}(A_1 X_1 A_1^*) \tag{8.220}$$

for all $X_0 \in L(\mathcal{X}_0)$ and $X_1 \in L(\mathcal{X}_1)$. The channels $\Psi_0 \in C(\mathcal{X}_0, \mathcal{Z}_0)$ and $\Psi_1 \in C(\mathcal{X}_1, \mathcal{Z}_1)$ defined as

$$\Psi_0(X_0) = \text{Tr}_{\mathcal{Y}_0}(A_0 X_0 A_0^*) \quad \text{and} \quad \Psi_1(X_1) = \text{Tr}_{\mathcal{Y}_1}(A_1 X_1 A_1^*) \tag{8.221}$$

for all $X_0 \in L(\mathcal{X}_0)$ and $X_1 \in L(\mathcal{X}_1)$ are therefore complementary to Φ_0 and Φ_1, respectively.

Now, consider registers X_0, X_1, Y_0, Y_1, Z_0, and Z_1 corresponding to the spaces $\mathcal{X}_0$, $\mathcal{X}_1$, $\mathcal{Y}_0$, $\mathcal{Y}_1$, $\mathcal{Z}_0$, and $\mathcal{Z}_1$, respectively. Let $\sigma \in D(\mathcal{X}_0 \otimes \mathcal{X}_1)$ be an arbitrary density operator. With respect to the state

$$(A_0 \otimes A_1)\sigma(A_0 \otimes A_1)^* \in D(\mathcal{Y}_0 \otimes \mathcal{Z}_0 \otimes \mathcal{Y}_1 \otimes \mathcal{Z}_1) \tag{8.222}$$

of $(\mathsf{Y}_0, \mathsf{Z}_0, \mathsf{Y}_1, \mathsf{Z}_1)$, one has that

$$
\begin{aligned}
\mathrm{H}(\sigma) &+ \mathrm{I_c}(\sigma; \Phi_0 \otimes \Phi_1) \\
&= \mathrm{H}(\mathsf{Y}_0, \mathsf{Z}_0, \mathsf{Y}_1, \mathsf{Z}_1) + \mathrm{H}(\mathsf{Y}_0, \mathsf{Y}_1) - \mathrm{H}(\mathsf{Z}_0, \mathsf{Z}_1).
\end{aligned}
\tag{8.223}
$$

For every state of $(\mathsf{Y}_0, \mathsf{Z}_0, \mathsf{Y}_1, \mathsf{Z}_1)$, including the state (8.222), it holds that

$$
\begin{aligned}
\mathrm{H}(\mathsf{Y}_0, \mathsf{Z}_0, \mathsf{Y}_1, \mathsf{Z}_1) &\leq \mathrm{H}(\mathsf{Z}_0, \mathsf{Y}_1, \mathsf{Z}_1) + \mathrm{H}(\mathsf{Y}_0, \mathsf{Z}_0) - \mathrm{H}(\mathsf{Z}_0) \\
&\leq \mathrm{H}(\mathsf{Z}_0, \mathsf{Z}_1) + \mathrm{H}(\mathsf{Y}_1, \mathsf{Z}_1) - \mathrm{H}(\mathsf{Z}_1) + \mathrm{H}(\mathsf{Y}_0, \mathsf{Z}_0) - \mathrm{H}(\mathsf{Z}_0);
\end{aligned}
\tag{8.224}
$$

both inequalities follow from the strong subadditivity of the von Neumann entropy (Theorem 5.36). The subadditivity of the von Neumann entropy (Theorem 5.24) implies $\mathrm{H}(\mathsf{Y}_0, \mathsf{Y}_1) \leq \mathrm{H}(\mathsf{Y}_0) + \mathrm{H}(\mathsf{Y}_1)$, and therefore

$$
\begin{aligned}
\mathrm{H}(\mathsf{Y}_0, \mathsf{Z}_0, \mathsf{Y}_1, \mathsf{Z}_1) &+ \mathrm{H}(\mathsf{Y}_0, \mathsf{Y}_1) - \mathrm{H}(\mathsf{Z}_0, \mathsf{Z}_1) \\
&\leq (\mathrm{H}(\mathsf{Y}_0, \mathsf{Z}_0) + \mathrm{H}(\mathsf{Y}_0) - \mathrm{H}(\mathsf{Z}_0)) \\
&\quad + (\mathrm{H}(\mathsf{Y}_1, \mathsf{Z}_1) + \mathrm{H}(\mathsf{Y}_1) - \mathrm{H}(\mathsf{Z}_1)).
\end{aligned}
\tag{8.225}
$$

For $\sigma_0 = \sigma[\mathsf{X}_0]$ and $\sigma_1 = \sigma[\mathsf{X}_1]$, one has the equations

$$
\begin{aligned}
\mathrm{H}(\mathsf{Y}_0, \mathsf{Z}_0) + \mathrm{H}(\mathsf{Y}_0) - \mathrm{H}(\mathsf{Z}_0) &= \mathrm{H}(\sigma_0) + \mathrm{I_c}(\sigma_0; \Phi_0), \\
\mathrm{H}(\mathsf{Y}_1, \mathsf{Z}_1) + \mathrm{H}(\mathsf{Y}_1) - \mathrm{H}(\mathsf{Z}_1) &= \mathrm{H}(\sigma_1) + \mathrm{I_c}(\sigma_1; \Phi_1).
\end{aligned}
\tag{8.226}
$$

It follows that

$$
\begin{aligned}
\mathrm{H}(\sigma) &+ \mathrm{I_c}(\sigma; \Phi_0 \otimes \Phi_1) \\
&\leq (\mathrm{H}(\sigma_0) + \mathrm{I_c}(\sigma_0; \Phi_0)) + (\mathrm{H}(\sigma_1) + \mathrm{I_c}(\sigma_1; \Phi_1)).
\end{aligned}
\tag{8.227}
$$

Maximizing over all $\sigma \in \mathrm{D}(\mathcal{X}_0 \otimes \mathcal{X}_1)$, one obtains the inequality

$$
\begin{aligned}
&\max_{\sigma \in \mathrm{D}(\mathcal{X}_0 \otimes \mathcal{X}_1)} (\mathrm{H}(\sigma) + \mathrm{I_c}(\sigma; \Phi_0 \otimes \Phi_1)) \\
&\leq \max_{\sigma_0 \in \mathrm{D}(\mathcal{X}_0)} (\mathrm{H}(\sigma_0) + \mathrm{I_c}(\sigma_0; \Phi_0)) + \max_{\sigma_1 \in \mathrm{D}(\mathcal{X}_1)} (\mathrm{H}(\sigma_1) + \mathrm{I_c}(\sigma_1; \Phi_1)).
\end{aligned}
\tag{8.228}
$$

For the reverse inequality, it suffices to observe that

$$
\begin{aligned}
\mathrm{H}(\sigma_0 \otimes \sigma_1) &+ \mathrm{I_c}(\sigma_0 \otimes \sigma_1; \Phi_0 \otimes \Phi_1) \\
&= \mathrm{H}(\sigma_0) + \mathrm{I_c}(\sigma_0; \Phi_0) + \mathrm{H}(\sigma_1) + \mathrm{I_c}(\sigma_1; \Phi_1)
\end{aligned}
\tag{8.229}
$$

for every choice of $\sigma_0 \in \mathrm{D}(\mathcal{X}_0)$ and $\sigma_1 \in \mathrm{D}(\mathcal{X}_1)$, and therefore

$$
\begin{aligned}
&\max_{\sigma \in \mathrm{D}(\mathcal{X}_0 \otimes \mathcal{X}_1)} (\mathrm{H}(\sigma) + \mathrm{I_c}(\sigma; \Phi_0 \otimes \Phi_1)) \\
&\geq \max_{\sigma_0 \in \mathrm{D}(\mathcal{X}_0)} (\mathrm{H}(\sigma_0) + \mathrm{I_c}(\sigma_0; \Phi_0)) + \max_{\sigma_1 \in \mathrm{D}(\mathcal{X}_1)} (\mathrm{H}(\sigma_1) + \mathrm{I_c}(\sigma_1; \Phi_1)),
\end{aligned}
\tag{8.230}
$$

which completes the proof. $\qquad\square$

A Lower Bound on the Holevo Capacity for Flat States by Dense Coding

Next in the sequence of lemmas needed to prove the entanglement-assisted classical capacity theorem is the following lemma, which establishes a lower bound on the entanglement-assisted Holevo capacity of a given channel. Its proof may be viewed as an application of dense coding (q.v. Section 6.3.1).

Lemma 8.39 *Let $\mathcal{X}$ and $\mathcal{Y}$ be complex Euclidean spaces, let $\Phi \in C(\mathcal{X}, \mathcal{Y})$ be a channel, let $\Pi \in \text{Proj}(\mathcal{X})$ be a nonzero projection operator, and let $\omega = \Pi/\text{Tr}(\Pi)$. It holds that*

$$\chi_{\text{E}}(\Phi) \geq H(\omega) + I_{\text{C}}(\omega; \Phi). \tag{8.231}$$

Proof Let $m = \text{rank}(\Pi)$, let $\mathcal{W} = \mathbb{C}^{\mathbb{Z}_m}$, let $V \in U(\mathcal{W}, \mathcal{X})$ be any isometry satisfying $VV^* = \Pi$, and let

$$\tau = \frac{1}{m}\,\text{vec}(V)\,\text{vec}(V)^* \in D(\mathcal{X} \otimes \mathcal{W}). \tag{8.232}$$

Recall the collection of discrete Weyl operators

$$\{W_{a,b} : a, b \in \mathbb{Z}_m\} \subset U(\mathcal{W}), \tag{8.233}$$

as defined in Section 4.1.2 of Chapter 4, and define a collection of unitary channels

$$\{\Psi_{a,b} : a, b \in \mathbb{Z}_m\} \subseteq C(\mathcal{W}) \tag{8.234}$$

in correspondence with these operators:

$$\Psi_{a,b}(Y) = W_{a,b} Y W_{a,b}^* \tag{8.235}$$

for each $Y \in L(\mathcal{W})$. Finally, consider the ensemble

$$\eta : \mathbb{Z}_m \times \mathbb{Z}_m \to \text{Pos}(\mathcal{X} \otimes \mathcal{W}) \tag{8.236}$$

defined as

$$\eta(a, b) = \frac{1}{m^2}\,(\mathbb{1}_{L(\mathcal{X})} \otimes \Psi_{a,b})(\tau), \tag{8.237}$$

for all $(a, b) \in \mathbb{Z}_m \times \mathbb{Z}_m$.

It holds that

$$H\left(\frac{1}{m^2} \sum_{a,b \in \mathbb{Z}_m} (\Phi \otimes \Psi_{a,b})(\tau)\right)$$

$$= H\left(\Phi(\omega) \otimes \frac{\mathbb{1}_{\mathcal{W}}}{m}\right) = H(\Phi(\omega)) + H(\omega) \tag{8.238}$$

and

$$\frac{1}{m^2} \sum_{a,b \in \mathbb{Z}_n} H((\Phi \otimes \Psi_{a,b})(\tau)) = H((\Phi \otimes \mathbb{1}_{L(\mathcal{W})})(\tau))$$

$$= H\left((\Phi \otimes \mathbb{1}_{L(\mathcal{X})})\left(\text{vec}(\sqrt{\omega})\,\text{vec}(\sqrt{\omega})^*\right)\right),$$

(8.239)

from which it follows that

$$\chi((\Phi \otimes \mathbb{1}_{L(\mathcal{W})})(\eta)) = H(\omega) + I_c(\omega; \Phi). \tag{8.240}$$

Moreover, η is homogeneous on $\mathcal{W}$, as is evident from the fact that

$$\text{Tr}_{\mathcal{X}}(\eta(a,b)) = \frac{1}{m^3}\mathbb{1}_{\mathcal{W}} \tag{8.241}$$

for each choice of $(a,b) \in \mathbb{Z}_m \times \mathbb{Z}_m$. It therefore holds that

$$\chi_{\mathrm{E}}(\Phi) \geq \chi((\Phi \otimes \mathbb{1}_{L(\mathcal{W})})(\eta)) = H(\omega) + I_c(\omega; \Phi), \tag{8.242}$$

which completes the proof. □

An Upper Bound on the Holevo Capacity

The final lemma needed for the proof of the entanglement-assisted classical capacity theorem establishes an upper bound on the entanglement-assisted Holevo capacity of a channel.

Lemma 8.40 *Let $\Phi \in C(\mathcal{X}, \mathcal{Y})$ be a channel, for complex Euclidean spaces $\mathcal{X}$ and $\mathcal{Y}$. Also let $\mathcal{W}$ be a complex Euclidean space, let Σ be an alphabet, let $\eta: \Sigma \to \text{Pos}(\mathcal{X} \otimes \mathcal{W})$ be an ensemble that is homogeneous on $\mathcal{W}$, and let*

$$\sigma = \sum_{a \in \Sigma} \text{Tr}_{\mathcal{W}}(\eta(a)). \tag{8.243}$$

It holds that

$$\chi((\Phi \otimes \mathbb{1}_{L(\mathcal{W})})(\eta)) \leq H(\sigma) + I_c(\sigma; \Phi). \tag{8.244}$$

Proof Assume that $\mathcal{Z}$ is a complex Euclidean space and $A \in U(\mathcal{X}, \mathcal{Y} \otimes \mathcal{Z})$ is an isometry for which

$$\Phi(X) = \text{Tr}_{\mathcal{Z}}(AXA^*) \tag{8.245}$$

for all $X \in L(\mathcal{X})$. The channel $\Psi \in C(\mathcal{X}, \mathcal{Z})$ defined by

$$\Psi(X) = \text{Tr}_{\mathcal{Y}}(AXA^*) \tag{8.246}$$

for all $X \in L(\mathcal{X})$ is therefore complementary to Φ, so that

$$I_c(\sigma; \Phi) = H(\Phi(\sigma)) - H(\Psi(\sigma)). \tag{8.247}$$

It therefore suffices to prove that

$$\chi\big((\Phi \otimes \mathbb{1}_{\mathrm{L}(\mathcal{W})})(\eta)\big) \leq \mathrm{H}(\sigma) + \mathrm{H}(\Phi(\sigma)) - \mathrm{H}(\Psi(\sigma)). \tag{8.248}$$

By the assumption that η is homogeneous on $\mathcal{W}$, Proposition 8.12 implies that there must exist a complex Euclidean space $\mathcal{V}$, a collection of channels

$$\{\Xi_a : a \in \Sigma\} \subseteq \mathrm{C}(\mathcal{V}, \mathcal{X}), \tag{8.249}$$

a unit vector $u \in \mathcal{V} \otimes \mathcal{W}$, and a probability vector $p \in \mathcal{P}(\Sigma)$ such that

$$\eta(a) = p(a)\big(\Xi_a \otimes \mathbb{1}_{\mathrm{L}(\mathcal{W})}\big)(uu^*) \tag{8.250}$$

for every $a \in \Sigma$. Assume hereafter that such a choice for these objects has been fixed, and define states $\tau \in \mathrm{D}(\mathcal{W})$ and $\xi \in \mathrm{D}(\mathcal{V})$ as

$$\tau = \mathrm{Tr}_{\mathcal{V}}(uu^*) \quad \text{and} \quad \xi = \mathrm{Tr}_{\mathcal{W}}(uu^*). \tag{8.251}$$

It may be noted that

$$\sigma = \sum_{a \in \Sigma} p(a)\Xi_a(\xi). \tag{8.252}$$

Let $\mathcal{U}$ be a complex Euclidean space such that $\dim(\mathcal{U}) = \dim(\mathcal{V} \otimes \mathcal{X})$, and select a collection of isometries $\{B_a : a \in \Sigma\} \subset \mathrm{U}(\mathcal{V}, \mathcal{X} \otimes \mathcal{U})$ satisfying

$$\Xi_a(V) = \mathrm{Tr}_{\mathcal{U}}(B_a V B_a^*) \tag{8.253}$$

for every $V \in \mathrm{L}(\mathcal{V})$.

Assume momentarily that $a \in \Sigma$ has been fixed, and define a unit vector

$$v_a = (A \otimes \mathbb{1}_{\mathcal{U}} \otimes \mathbb{1}_{\mathcal{W}})(B_a \otimes \mathbb{1}_{\mathcal{W}})u \in \mathcal{Y} \otimes \mathcal{Z} \otimes \mathcal{U} \otimes \mathcal{W}. \tag{8.254}$$

Let Y, Z, U, and W be registers having corresponding complex Euclidean spaces $\mathcal{Y}, \mathcal{Z}, \mathcal{U}$, and $\mathcal{W}$, and consider the situation in which the compound register $(\mathsf{Y}, \mathsf{Z}, \mathsf{U}, \mathsf{W})$ is in the pure state $v_a v_a^*$. The following equalities may be verified:

$$\begin{aligned} \mathrm{H}(\mathsf{W}) &= \mathrm{H}(\tau), \\ \mathrm{H}(\mathsf{Y}, \mathsf{W}) &= \mathrm{H}\big((\Phi\Xi_a \otimes \mathbb{1}_{\mathrm{L}(\mathcal{W})})(uu^*)\big), \\ \mathrm{H}(\mathsf{U}, \mathsf{W}) &= \mathrm{H}(\mathsf{Y}, \mathsf{Z}) = \mathrm{H}(\Xi_a(\xi)), \\ \mathrm{H}(\mathsf{Y}, \mathsf{U}, \mathsf{W}) &= \mathrm{H}(\mathsf{Z}) = \mathrm{H}\big((\Psi\Xi_a)(\xi)\big). \end{aligned} \tag{8.255}$$

By the strong subadditivity of the von Neumann entropy (Theorem 5.36), it holds that

$$\mathrm{H}(\mathsf{W}) - \mathrm{H}(\mathsf{Y}, \mathsf{W}) \leq \mathrm{H}(\mathsf{U}, \mathsf{W}) - \mathrm{H}(\mathsf{Y}, \mathsf{U}, \mathsf{W}), \tag{8.256}$$

and therefore

$$H(\tau) - H((\Phi\Xi_a \otimes \mathbb{1}_{L(\mathcal{W})})(uu^*)) \leq H(\Xi_a(\xi)) - H((\Psi\Xi_a)(\xi)). \quad (8.257)$$

Finally, in accordance with the probability vector p, one may average the two sides of (8.257) over all $a \in \Sigma$ and apply Lemma 8.37, obtaining

$$H(\tau) - \sum_{a \in \Sigma} p(a) H((\Phi\Xi_a \otimes \mathbb{1}_{L(\mathcal{W})})(uu^*))$$
$$\leq \sum_{a \in \Sigma} p(a)(H(\Xi_a(\xi)) - H((\Psi\Xi_a)(\xi))) \leq H(\sigma) - H(\Psi(\sigma)). \quad (8.258)$$

By the subadditivity of the von Neumann entropy (Proposition 5.9) one has

$$H\left(\sum_{a \in \Sigma} p(a)(\Phi\Xi_a \otimes \mathbb{1}_{L(\mathcal{W})})(uu^*)\right) \leq H(\Phi(\sigma)) + H(\tau). \quad (8.259)$$

The inequality (8.248) follows from (8.258) and (8.259), which completes the proof. □

The Entanglement-Assisted Classical Capacity Theorem

Finally, the entanglement-assisted classical capacity theorem will be stated, and proved through the use of the lemmas presented above.

Theorem 8.41 (Entanglement-assisted classical capacity theorem) *Let $\mathcal{X}$ and $\mathcal{Y}$ be complex Euclidean spaces and let $\Phi \in C(\mathcal{X}, \mathcal{Y})$ be a channel. It holds that*

$$C_E(\Phi) = \max_{\sigma \in D(\mathcal{X})} (H(\sigma) + I_c(\sigma; \Phi)). \quad (8.260)$$

Proof By applying Lemma 8.40, followed by Lemma 8.38, one may conclude that

$$\chi_E(\Phi^{\otimes n}) \leq \max_{\sigma \in D(\mathcal{X}^{\otimes n})} (H(\sigma) + I_c(\sigma; \Phi^{\otimes n}))$$
$$= n \max_{\sigma \in D(\mathcal{X})} (H(\sigma) + I_c(\sigma; \Phi)) \quad (8.261)$$

for every positive integer n. By Theorem 8.28, it therefore follows that

$$C_E(\Phi) = \lim_{n \to \infty} \frac{\chi_E(\Phi^{\otimes n})}{n} \leq \max_{\sigma \in D(\mathcal{X})} (H(\sigma) + I_c(\sigma; \Phi)). \quad (8.262)$$

For the reverse inequality, one may first choose a complex Euclidean space $\mathcal{Z}$ and an isometry $A \in U(\mathcal{X}, \mathcal{Y} \otimes \mathcal{Z})$ such that

$$\Phi(X) = \text{Tr}_{\mathcal{Z}}(AXA^*) \quad (8.263)$$

for all $X \in \mathrm{L}(\mathcal{X})$. It holds that the channel $\Psi \in \mathrm{C}(\mathcal{X}, \mathcal{Z})$, defined by

$$\Psi(X) = \mathrm{Tr}_{\mathcal{Y}}(AXA^*) \tag{8.264}$$

for all $X \in \mathrm{L}(\mathcal{X})$, is complementary to Φ, so that Proposition 8.17 implies

$$\mathrm{I_c}(\sigma; \Phi) = \mathrm{H}(\Phi(\sigma)) - \mathrm{H}(\Psi(\sigma)) \tag{8.265}$$

for all $\sigma \in \mathrm{D}(\mathcal{X})$.

Next, let $\sigma \in \mathrm{D}(\mathcal{X})$ be any density operator, let $\delta > 0$ be chosen arbitrarily, and choose $\varepsilon > 0$ to be sufficiently small so that

$$(7\,\mathrm{H}(\sigma) + \mathrm{H}(\Phi(\sigma)) + \mathrm{H}(\Psi(\sigma)))\varepsilon < \delta. \tag{8.266}$$

Also let

$$\omega_{n,\varepsilon} = \frac{\Lambda_{n,\varepsilon}}{\mathrm{Tr}(\Lambda_{n,\varepsilon})} \tag{8.267}$$

for $\Lambda_{n,\varepsilon}$ denoting the ε-strongly typical projection with respect to any fixed spectral decomposition of σ, for each positive integer n.

By Lemma 8.36, one may conclude that the following three inequalities hold simultaneously for all but finitely many positive integers n:

$$\mathrm{H}(\sigma) - \frac{\mathrm{H}(\omega_{n,\varepsilon})}{n} \leq 3\,\mathrm{H}(\sigma)\varepsilon + \delta,$$

$$\mathrm{H}(\Phi(\sigma)) - \frac{\mathrm{H}(\Phi^{\otimes n}(\omega_{n,\varepsilon}))}{n} \leq (2\,\mathrm{H}(\sigma) + \mathrm{H}(\Phi(\sigma)))\varepsilon + \delta, \tag{8.268}$$

$$\frac{\mathrm{H}(\Phi^{\otimes n}(\omega_{n,\varepsilon}))}{n} - \mathrm{H}(\Psi(\sigma)) \leq (2\,\mathrm{H}(\sigma) + \mathrm{H}(\Psi(\sigma)))\varepsilon + \delta.$$

By Lemma 8.39, it therefore holds that

$$\frac{\chi_{\mathrm{E}}(\Phi^{\otimes n})}{n} \geq \frac{1}{n}\Big(\mathrm{H}(\omega_{n,\varepsilon}) + \mathrm{H}(\Phi^{\otimes n}(\omega_{n,\varepsilon})) - \mathrm{H}(\Psi^{\otimes n}(\omega_{n,\varepsilon}))\Big)$$

$$\geq \mathrm{H}(\sigma) + \mathrm{H}(\Phi(\sigma)) - \mathrm{H}(\Psi(\sigma)) - 4\delta \tag{8.269}$$

for all but finitely many positive integers n, and consequently

$$\mathrm{C_E}(\Phi) = \lim_{n\to\infty} \frac{\chi_{\mathrm{E}}(\Phi^{\otimes n})}{n} \geq \mathrm{H}(\sigma) + \mathrm{H}(\Phi(\sigma)) - \mathrm{H}(\Psi(\sigma)) - 4\delta. \tag{8.270}$$

As this inequality holds for all $\delta > 0$, one has

$$\mathrm{C_E}(\Phi) \geq \mathrm{H}(\sigma) + \mathrm{H}(\Phi(\sigma)) - \mathrm{H}(\Psi(\sigma)) = \mathrm{H}(\sigma) + \mathrm{I_c}(\sigma; \Phi), \tag{8.271}$$

and maximizing over all $\sigma \in \mathrm{D}(\mathcal{X})$ completes the proof. $\square$

8.2 Quantum Information Over Quantum Channels

This section is concerned with the capacity of quantum channels to transmit quantum information from a sender to a receiver. Along similar lines to the classical capacities considered in the previous section, one may consider the quantum capacity of a channel both when the sender and receiver share prior entanglement, used to assist with the information transmission, and when they do not.

As it turns out, the capacity of a channel to transmit quantum information with the assistance of entanglement is, in all cases, equal to one-half of the entanglement-assisted classical capacity of the same channel. This fact is proved below through a combination of the teleportation and dense coding protocols discussed in Section 6.3.1. As the entanglement-assisted classical capacity has already been characterized by Theorem 8.41, a characterization of the capacity of a quantum channel to transmit quantum information with the assistance of entanglement follows directly. For this reason, the primary focus of the section is on an analysis of the capacity of quantum channels to transmit quantum information without the assistance of entanglement.

The first subsection below presents a definition of the quantum capacity of a channel, together with the closely related notion of a channel's capacity to generate shared entanglement. The second subsection presents a proof of the quantum capacity theorem, which characterizes the capacity of a given channel to transmit quantum information.

8.2.1 Definitions of Quantum Capacity and Related Notions

Definitions of the *quantum capacity* and *entanglement generation capacity* of a channel are presented below, and it is proved that the two quantities coincide. The *entanglement-assisted quantum capacity* of a channel is also defined, and its simple relationship to the entanglement-assisted classical capacity of a channel is clarified.

The Quantum Capacity of a Channel

Informally speaking, the quantum capacity of a channel is the number of qubits, on average, that can be accurately transmitted with each use of that channel. Like the capacities discussed in the previous section, the quantum capacity of a channel is defined in information-theoretic terms, referring to a situation in which an asymptotically large number of channel uses, acting on a collection of possibly entangled registers, is made available.

The definition of quantum capacity that follows makes use of the same notions of an emulation of one channel by another (Definition 8.1) and of an ε-approximation of one channel by another (Definition 8.2) that were used in the previous section.

Definition 8.42 (Quantum capacity of a channel)   Let $\Phi \in C(\mathcal{X}, \mathcal{Y})$ be a channel, for complex Euclidean spaces $\mathcal{X}$ and $\mathcal{Y}$, and also let $\mathcal{Z} = \mathbb{C}^\Gamma$ for $\Gamma = \{0, 1\}$ denoting the binary alphabet.

1. A value $\alpha \geq 0$ is an *achievable rate* for the transmission of quantum information through Φ if (i) $\alpha = 0$, or (ii) $\alpha > 0$ and the following holds for every choice of a positive real number $\varepsilon > 0$: for all but finitely many positive integers n, and for $m = \lfloor \alpha n \rfloor$, the channel $\Phi^{\otimes n}$ emulates an ε-approximation to the identity channel $\mathbb{1}_{L(\mathcal{Z})}^{\otimes m}$.
2. The *quantum capacity* of Φ, which is denoted $Q(\Phi)$, is defined as the supremum of all achievable rates for quantum information transmission through Φ.

The argument through which Proposition 8.4 in the previous section was proved yields the following analogous proposition for the quantum capacity.

Proposition 8.43   Let $\Phi \in C(\mathcal{X}, \mathcal{Y})$ be a channel, for complex Euclidean spaces $\mathcal{X}$ and $\mathcal{Y}$. It holds that $Q(\Phi^{\otimes k}) = k\, Q(\Phi)$ for every positive integer k.

The Entanglement Generation Capacity of a Channel

The *entanglement generation capacity* of a channel is defined in a similar way to the quantum capacity, except that the associated task is more narrowly focused: by means of multiple, independent uses of a channel, a sender and receiver aim to establish a state, shared between them, having high fidelity with a maximally entangled state.

Definition 8.44 (Entanglement generation capacity of a channel)   Let $\mathcal{X}$ and $\mathcal{Y}$ be complex Euclidean spaces, let $\Phi \in C(\mathcal{X}, \mathcal{Y})$ be a channel, and let $\mathcal{Z} = \mathbb{C}^\Gamma$ for $\Gamma = \{0, 1\}$ denoting the binary alphabet.

1. A value $\alpha \geq 0$ is an *achievable rate* for entanglement generation through Φ if (i) $\alpha = 0$, or (ii) $\alpha > 0$ and the following holds for every positive real number $\varepsilon > 0$: for all but finitely many positive integers n, and for $m = \lfloor \alpha n \rfloor$, there exist a state $\rho \in D(\mathcal{X}^{\otimes n} \otimes \mathcal{Z}^{\otimes m})$ and a channel $\Xi \in C(\mathcal{Y}^{\otimes n}, \mathcal{Z}^{\otimes m})$ such that

$$ F\!\left(2^{-m} \operatorname{vec}(\mathbb{1}_{\mathcal{Z}}^{\otimes m}) \operatorname{vec}(\mathbb{1}_{\mathcal{Z}}^{\otimes m})^*, (\Xi\Phi^{\otimes n} \otimes \mathbb{1}_{L(\mathcal{Z})}^{\otimes m})(\rho) \right) \geq 1 - \varepsilon. \qquad (8.272) $$

2. The *entanglement generation capacity* of Φ, denoted $Q_{EG}(\Phi)$, is defined as the supremum of all achievable rates for entanglement generation through Φ.

Remark For any choice of complex Euclidean spaces $\mathcal{X}$ and $\mathcal{Y}$, a unit vector $y \in \mathcal{Y}$, and a channel $\Psi \in C(\mathcal{X}, \mathcal{Y})$, the maximum value for the fidelity $F(yy^*, \Psi(\rho))$ over $\rho \in D(\mathcal{X})$ is achieved when ρ is a pure state. It follows from this observation that the quantity $Q_{EG}(\Phi)$ would not change if the states $\rho \in D(\mathcal{X}^{\otimes n} \otimes \mathcal{Z}^{\otimes m})$ considered in the specification of achievable rates in Definition 8.44 are constrained to be pure states.

Equivalence of Quantum Capacity and Entanglement Generation Capacity

The task associated with entanglement generation capacity would seem to be more specialized than the one associated with quantum capacity. That is, the emulation of a close approximation to an identity channel evidently allows a sender and receiver to generate a shared state having high fidelity with a maximally entangled state, but it is not immediate that the ability of a channel to generate near-maximally entangled states should allow it to accurately transmit quantum information at a similar rate. One may note, in particular, that the teleportation protocol discussed in Section 6.3.1 is not immediately applicable in this situation, as the protocol requires classical communication that must be considered in the calculation of transmission rates. Nevertheless, the relationship between entanglement generation and identity channel emulation provided by the following theorem allows one to prove that the quantum capacity and entanglement generation capacity of any given channel do indeed coincide.

Theorem 8.45 *Let $\mathcal{X}$ and $\mathcal{Y}$ be complex Euclidean spaces, let $\Phi \in C(\mathcal{X}, \mathcal{Y})$ be a channel, and let $u \in \mathcal{X} \otimes \mathcal{Y}$ be a unit vector. Also let $n = \dim(\mathcal{Y})$ and let $\delta \geq 0$ be a nonnegative real number such that*

$$F\left(\frac{1}{n} \text{vec}(\mathbb{1}_{\mathcal{Y}}) \text{vec}(\mathbb{1}_{\mathcal{Y}})^*, (\Phi \otimes \mathbb{1}_{L(\mathcal{Y})})(uu^*)\right) \geq 1 - \delta. \tag{8.273}$$

For any complex Euclidean space $\mathcal{Z}$ satisfying $\dim(\mathcal{Z}) \leq n/2$, it holds that Φ emulates an ε-approximation to the identity channel $\mathbb{1}_{L(\mathcal{Z})}$ for $\varepsilon = 4\delta^{\frac{1}{4}}$.

Proof Let $A \in L(\mathcal{Y}, \mathcal{X})$ be the operator defined by the equation $\text{vec}(A) = u$, let $r = \text{rank}(A)$, and let

$$A = \sum_{k=1}^{r} \sqrt{p_k} x_k y_k^* \tag{8.274}$$

be a singular value decomposition of A, so that $(p_1, \ldots, p_r)$ is a probability vector and $\{x_1, \ldots, x_r\} \subset \mathcal{X}$ and $\{y_1, \ldots, y_r\} \subset \mathcal{Y}$ are orthonormal sets. Also define $W \in \mathrm{L}(\mathcal{Y}, \mathcal{X})$ as

$$W = \sum_{k=1}^{r} x_k y_k^*, \tag{8.275}$$

and define a unit vector $v \in \mathcal{X} \otimes \mathcal{Y}$ as

$$v = \frac{1}{\sqrt{r}} \operatorname{vec}(W). \tag{8.276}$$

By the monotonicity of the fidelity function under partial tracing, one has

$$\frac{1}{\sqrt{n}} \sum_{k=1}^{r} \sqrt{p_k} = \mathrm{F}\left(\frac{1}{n} \mathbb{1}_{\mathcal{Y}}, \mathrm{Tr}_{\mathcal{X}}(uu^*)\right)$$

$$\geq \mathrm{F}\left(\frac{1}{n} \operatorname{vec}(\mathbb{1}_{\mathcal{Y}}) \operatorname{vec}(\mathbb{1}_{\mathcal{Y}})^*, (\Phi \otimes \mathbb{1}_{\mathrm{L}(\mathcal{Y})})(uu^*)\right) \geq 1 - \delta, \tag{8.277}$$

and therefore

$$\mathrm{F}(uu^*, vv^*) = \frac{1}{\sqrt{r}} \sum_{k=1}^{r} \sqrt{p_k} \geq \frac{1}{\sqrt{n}} \sum_{k=1}^{r} \sqrt{p_k} \geq 1 - \delta. \tag{8.278}$$

Consequently, by Theorems 3.27 and 3.29, one has

$$\mathrm{F}\left(\frac{1}{n} \operatorname{vec}(\mathbb{1}_{\mathcal{Y}}) \operatorname{vec}(\mathbb{1}_{\mathcal{Y}})^*, (\Phi \otimes \mathbb{1}_{\mathrm{L}(\mathcal{Y})})(vv^*)\right) + 1$$

$$\geq \mathrm{F}\left(\frac{1}{n} \operatorname{vec}(\mathbb{1}_{\mathcal{Y}}) \operatorname{vec}(\mathbb{1}_{\mathcal{Y}})^*, (\Phi \otimes \mathbb{1}_{\mathrm{L}(\mathcal{Y})})(uu^*)\right)^2 + \mathrm{F}(vv^*, uu^*)^2 \tag{8.279}$$

$$\geq 2(1 - \delta)^2,$$

and therefore

$$\mathrm{F}\left(\frac{1}{n} \operatorname{vec}(\mathbb{1}_{\mathcal{Y}}) \operatorname{vec}(\mathbb{1}_{\mathcal{Y}})^*, (\Phi \otimes \mathbb{1}_{\mathrm{L}(\mathcal{Y})})(vv^*)\right) \geq 1 - 4\delta. \tag{8.280}$$

Next, define a projection operator $\Pi_r = W^*W \in \mathrm{Proj}(\mathcal{Y})$ and define $\mathcal{V}_r = \mathrm{im}(\Pi_r)$. For each choice of k beginning with r and decreasing to 1, choose $w_k \in \mathcal{V}_k$ to be a unit vector that minimizes the quantity

$$\alpha_k = \langle w_k w_k^*, \Phi(W w_k w_k^* W^*) \rangle, \tag{8.281}$$

and define

$$\mathcal{V}_{k-1} = \{z \in \mathcal{V}_k : \langle w_k, z \rangle = 0\}. \tag{8.282}$$

Observe that $\alpha_1 \geq \alpha_2 \geq \cdots \geq \alpha_r$ and that $\{w_1, \ldots, w_k\}$ is an orthonormal basis for $\mathcal{V}_k$, for each $k \in \{1, \ldots, r\}$. In particular, it holds that

$$v = \frac{1}{\sqrt{r}}(W \otimes \mathbb{1}_{\mathcal{Y}}) \operatorname{vec}(\Pi_r) = \frac{1}{\sqrt{r}} \sum_{k=1}^{r} W w_k \otimes \overline{w_k}. \tag{8.283}$$

At this point, a calculation reveals that

$$\mathrm{F}\left(\frac{1}{n}\operatorname{vec}(\mathbb{1}_{\mathcal{Y}})\operatorname{vec}(\mathbb{1}_{\mathcal{Y}})^*, (\Phi \otimes \mathbb{1}_{\mathrm{L}(\mathcal{Y})})(vv^*)\right)^2$$

$$= \frac{1}{nr} \sum_{j,k\in\{1,\ldots,r\}} \langle w_j w_k^*, \Phi(W w_j w_k^* W^*)\rangle. \tag{8.284}$$

By the complete positivity of Φ, one may conclude that

$$|\langle w_j w_k^*, \Phi(W w_j w_k^* W^*)\rangle|$$
$$\leq \sqrt{\langle w_j w_j^*, \Phi(W w_j w_j^* W^*)\rangle}\sqrt{\langle w_k w_k^*, \Phi(W w_k w_k^* W^*)\rangle} \tag{8.285}$$
$$= \sqrt{\alpha_j \alpha_k},$$

for each choice of $j, k \in \{1, \ldots, r\}$. Therefore, by the triangle inequality, it holds that

$$\mathrm{F}\left(\frac{1}{n}\operatorname{vec}(\mathbb{1}_{\mathcal{Y}})\operatorname{vec}(\mathbb{1}_{\mathcal{Y}})^*, (\Phi \otimes \mathbb{1}_{\mathrm{L}(\mathcal{Y})})(vv^*)\right) \leq \frac{1}{\sqrt{nr}} \sum_{k=1}^{r} \sqrt{\alpha_k}. \tag{8.286}$$

Applying the Cauchy–Schwarz inequality, one obtains

$$\frac{1}{\sqrt{nr}} \sum_{k=1}^{r} \sqrt{\alpha_k} \leq \sqrt{\frac{1}{n} \sum_{k=1}^{r} \alpha_k}, \tag{8.287}$$

and therefore

$$\frac{1}{n} \sum_{k=1}^{r} \alpha_k \geq (1 - 4\delta)^2 \geq 1 - 8\delta. \tag{8.288}$$

Now let

$$m = \max\{k \in \{1, \ldots, r\} : \alpha_k \geq 1 - 16\delta\}. \tag{8.289}$$

It follows from (8.288) that

$$1 - 8\delta \leq \frac{m}{n} + \frac{n-m}{n}(1 - 16\delta), \tag{8.290}$$

and therefore $m \geq n/2$. By the definition of the values $\alpha_1, \ldots, \alpha_r$, one may conclude that

$$\langle ww^*, \Phi(W ww^* W^*)\rangle \geq 1 - 16\delta \tag{8.291}$$

for every unit vector $w \in \mathcal{V}_m$.

Finally, let $V \in \mathrm{U}(\mathcal{Z}, \mathcal{Y})$ be any isometry for which $\mathrm{im}(V) \subseteq \mathcal{V}_m$. Such an isometry exists by the assumption that $\dim(\mathcal{Z}) \leq n/2$ together with the fact that $n/2 \leq m = \dim(\mathcal{V}_m)$. Let $\Xi_{\mathrm{E}} \in \mathrm{C}(\mathcal{Z}, \mathcal{X})$ and $\Xi_{\mathrm{D}} \in \mathrm{C}(\mathcal{Y}, \mathcal{Z})$ be channels of the form

$$\begin{aligned} \Xi_{\mathrm{E}}(Z) &= WVZV^*W^* + \Psi_{\mathrm{E}}(Z), \\ \Xi_{\mathrm{D}}(Y) &= V^*YV + \Psi_{\mathrm{D}}(Y), \end{aligned} \tag{8.292}$$

for all $Z \in \mathrm{L}(\mathcal{Z})$ and $Y \in \mathrm{L}(\mathcal{Y})$, where $\Psi_{\mathrm{E}} \in \mathrm{CP}(\mathcal{Z}, \mathcal{X})$ and $\Psi_{\mathrm{D}} \in \mathrm{CP}(\mathcal{Y}, \mathcal{Z})$ are completely positive maps that cause Ξ_{E} and Ξ_{D} to be trace-preserving. For every unit vector $z \in \mathcal{Z}$ it holds that

$$\begin{aligned} \langle zz^*, (\Xi_{\mathrm{D}}\Phi\Xi_{\mathrm{E}})(zz^*)\rangle & \\ &\geq \langle Vzz^*V^*, \Phi(WVzz^*V^*W^*)\rangle \geq 1 - 16\delta, \end{aligned} \tag{8.293}$$

and therefore

$$\left\| zz^* - (\Xi_{\mathrm{D}}\Phi\Xi_{\mathrm{E}})(zz^*) \right\|_1 \leq 8\sqrt{\delta} \tag{8.294}$$

by one of the Fuchs–van de Graaf inequalities (Theorem 3.33). Applying Theorem 3.56, one therefore finds that

$$\left\| \Xi_{\mathrm{D}}\Phi\Xi_{\mathrm{E}} - \mathbb{1}_{\mathrm{L}(\mathcal{Z})} \right\|_1 \leq 4\delta^{\frac{1}{4}}, \tag{8.295}$$

which completes the proof. $\qquad\square$

Theorem 8.46 *Let $\Phi \in \mathrm{C}(\mathcal{X}, \mathcal{Y})$ be a channel, for complex Euclidean spaces $\mathcal{X}$ and $\mathcal{Y}$. The entanglement generation capacity and the quantum capacity of Φ are equal: $\mathrm{Q}(\Phi) = \mathrm{Q}_{\mathrm{EG}}(\Phi)$.*

Proof It will first be proved that $\mathrm{Q}(\Phi) \leq \mathrm{Q}_{\mathrm{EG}}(\Phi)$, which is straightforward. If the quantum capacity of Φ is zero, there is nothing to prove, so it will be assumed that $\mathrm{Q}(\Phi) > 0$. Let $\alpha > 0$ be an achievable rate for quantum information transmission through Φ, and let $\varepsilon > 0$ be chosen arbitrarily.

Setting $\Gamma = \{0, 1\}$ and $\mathcal{Z} = \mathbb{C}^\Gamma$, one therefore has that the channel $\Phi^{\otimes n}$ emulates an ε-approximation to the identity channel $\mathbb{1}_{\mathrm{L}(\mathcal{Z})}^{\otimes m}$ for all but finitely many positive integers n and for $m = \lfloor \alpha n \rfloor$. That is, for all but finitely many positive integers n, and for $m = \lfloor \alpha n \rfloor$, there must exist channels $\Xi_{\mathrm{E}} \in \mathrm{C}(\mathcal{Z}^{\otimes m}, \mathcal{X}^{\otimes n})$ and $\Xi_{\mathrm{D}} \in \mathrm{C}(\mathcal{Y}^{\otimes n}, \mathcal{Z}^{\otimes m})$ such that

$$\left\| \Xi_{\mathrm{D}}\Phi^{\otimes n}\Xi_{\mathrm{E}} - \mathbb{1}_{\mathrm{L}(\mathcal{Z})}^{\otimes m} \right\|_1 < \varepsilon. \tag{8.296}$$

Supposing that n and m are positive integers for which such channels exist, one may consider the density operators

$$\tau = 2^{-m} \operatorname{vec}(1_{\mathcal{Z}}^{\otimes m}) \operatorname{vec}(1_{\mathcal{Z}}^{\otimes m})^* \quad \text{and} \quad \rho = (\Xi_{\mathrm{E}} \otimes 1_{\mathrm{L}(\mathcal{Z})}^{\otimes m})(\tau), \qquad (8.297)$$

along with the channel $\Xi = \Xi_{\mathrm{D}}$. One of the Fuchs–van de Graaf inequalities (Theorem 3.33) implies that

$$
\begin{aligned}
\mathrm{F}\Big(\tau, (\Xi \Phi^{\otimes n} \otimes 1_{\mathrm{L}(\mathcal{Z})}^{\otimes m})(\rho)\Big) &= \mathrm{F}\Big(\tau, (\Xi_{\mathrm{D}} \Phi^{\otimes n} \Xi_{\mathrm{E}} \otimes 1_{\mathrm{L}(\mathcal{Z})}^{\otimes m})(\tau)\Big) \\
&\geq 1 - \frac{1}{2}\big\|(\Xi_{\mathrm{D}} \Phi^{\otimes n} \Xi_{\mathrm{E}} \otimes 1_{\mathrm{L}(\mathcal{Z})}^{\otimes m})(\tau) - \tau\big\|_1 > 1 - \frac{\varepsilon}{2}.
\end{aligned}
\qquad (8.298)
$$

Because this is so for all but finitely many positive integers n and for $m = \lfloor \alpha n \rfloor$, it holds that α is an achievable rate for entanglement generation through Φ. Taking the supremum over all achievable rates α for quantum communication through Φ, one obtains $\mathrm{Q}(\Phi) \leq \mathrm{Q}_{\mathrm{EG}}(\Phi)$.

It remains to prove that $\mathrm{Q}_{\mathrm{EG}}(\Phi) \leq \mathrm{Q}(\Phi)$. As for the reverse inequality just proved, there is nothing to prove if $\mathrm{Q}_{\mathrm{EG}}(\Phi) = 0$, so it will be assumed that $\mathrm{Q}_{\mathrm{EG}}(\Phi) > 0$. Let $\alpha > 0$ be an achievable rate for entanglement generation through Φ and let $\beta \in (0, \alpha)$ be chosen arbitrarily. It will be proved that β is an achievable rate for quantum communication through Φ. The required relation $\mathrm{Q}_{\mathrm{EG}}(\Phi) \leq \mathrm{Q}(\Phi)$ follows by taking the supremum over all achievable rates α for entanglement generation through Φ and over all $\beta \in (0, \alpha)$.

Let $\varepsilon > 0$ be chosen arbitrarily and let $\delta = \varepsilon^4/256$, so that $\varepsilon = 4\delta^{\frac{1}{4}}$. For all but finitely many positive integers n, and for $m = \lfloor \alpha n \rfloor$, there exists a state $\rho \in \mathrm{D}(\mathcal{X}^{\otimes n} \otimes \mathcal{Z}^{\otimes m})$ and a channel $\Xi \in \mathrm{C}(\mathcal{Y}^{\otimes n}, \mathcal{Z}^{\otimes m})$ such that

$$\mathrm{F}\big(2^{-m} \operatorname{vec}(1_{\mathcal{Z}}^{\otimes m}) \operatorname{vec}(1_{\mathcal{Z}}^{\otimes m})^*, (\Xi \Phi^{\otimes n} \otimes 1_{\mathrm{L}(\mathcal{Z})}^{\otimes m})(\rho)\big) \geq 1 - \delta. \qquad (8.299)$$

Note that the existence of a state ρ for which (8.299) holds implies the existence of a pure state $\rho = uu^*$ for which the same inequality holds, by virtue of the fact that the function

$$
\begin{aligned}
\rho \mapsto {}& \mathrm{F}\big(2^{-m} \operatorname{vec}(1_{\mathcal{Z}}^{\otimes m}) \operatorname{vec}(1_{\mathcal{Z}}^{\otimes m})^*, (\Xi \Phi^{\otimes n} \otimes 1_{\mathrm{L}(\mathcal{Z})}^{\otimes m})(\rho)\big)^2 \\
&= \big\langle 2^{-m} \operatorname{vec}(1_{\mathcal{Z}}^{\otimes m}) \operatorname{vec}(1_{\mathcal{Z}}^{\otimes m})^*, (\Xi \Phi^{\otimes n} \otimes 1_{\mathrm{L}(\mathcal{Z})}^{\otimes m})(\rho)\big\rangle
\end{aligned}
\qquad (8.300)
$$

must achieve its maximum value (over all density operators) on a pure state. By Theorem 8.45, it follows that $\Phi^{\otimes n}$ emulates an ε-approximation to the identity channel $1_{\mathrm{L}(\mathcal{Z})}^{\otimes k}$ for $k = m - 1$.

Under the assumption $n \geq 1/(\alpha - \beta)$, one has that $\beta n \leq \alpha n - 1$. Thus, for all but finitely many positive integers n and for $k = \lfloor \beta n \rfloor$, it holds that $\Phi^{\otimes n}$ emulates an ε-approximation to the identity channel $1_{\mathrm{L}(\mathcal{Z})}^{\otimes k}$. As $\varepsilon > 0$ has been chosen arbitrarily, it follows that β is an achievable rate for quantum communication through Φ, which completes the proof. $\qquad \square$

The Entanglement-Assisted Quantum Capacity of a Channel

The entanglement-assisted quantum capacity of a channel, which will be proved is equal to one-half of its entanglement-assisted classical capacity, may be formally defined as follows.

Definition 8.47 (Entanglement-assisited quantum capacity of a channel) Let $\mathcal{X}$ and $\mathcal{Y}$ be complex Euclidean spaces and let $\Phi \in C(\mathcal{X}, \mathcal{Y})$ be a channel. Also let $\Gamma = \{0, 1\}$ denote the binary alphabet, and let $\mathcal{Z} = \mathbb{C}^{\Gamma}$.

1. A value $\alpha \geq 0$ is an *achievable rate* for entanglement-assisted quantum information transmission through Φ if (i) $\alpha = 0$, or (ii) $\alpha > 0$ and the following holds for every choice of a positive real number $\varepsilon > 0$: for all but finitely many positive integers n, and for $m = \lfloor \alpha n \rfloor$, the channel $\Phi^{\otimes n}$ emulates an ε-approximation to the identity channel $\mathbb{1}_{L(\mathcal{Z})}^{\otimes m}$ with the assistance of entanglement.

2. The *entanglement-assisted quantum capacity* of Φ, denoted $Q_E(\Phi)$, is the supremum of all achievable rates for entanglement-assisted quantum information transmission through Φ.

Proposition 8.48 *Let $\Phi \in C(\mathcal{X}, \mathcal{Y})$ be a channel, for complex Euclidean spaces $\mathcal{X}$ and $\mathcal{Y}$. It holds that*

$$Q_E(\Phi) = \frac{C_E(\Phi)}{2}. \tag{8.301}$$

Proof Assume α is an achievable rate for entanglement-assisted classical communication through Φ. It will be proved that $\alpha/2$ is an achievable rate for entanglement-assisted quantum information transmission through Φ. Taking the supremum over all achievable rates α for entanglement-assisted classical communication through Φ, one obtains

$$Q_E(\Phi) \geq \frac{C_E(\Phi)}{2}. \tag{8.302}$$

As the case $\alpha = 0$ is trivial, it will be assumed that $\alpha > 0$.

Suppose n and $m = \lfloor \alpha n \rfloor$ are positive integers and $\varepsilon > 0$ is a positive real number such that $\Phi^{\otimes n}$ emulates an ε-approximation to the channel $\Delta^{\otimes m}$, where $\Delta \in C(\mathcal{Z})$ denotes the completely dephasing channel as usual. Let $k = \lfloor m/2 \rfloor$, and consider the maximally entangled state

$$\tau = 2^{-k} \operatorname{vec}(\mathbb{1}_{\mathcal{Z}}^{\otimes k}) \operatorname{vec}(\mathbb{1}_{\mathcal{Z}}^{\otimes k})^*. \tag{8.303}$$

By tensoring τ with the state ξ used for the emulation of an ε-approximation to $\Delta^{\otimes m}$ by $\Phi^{\otimes n}$, one may define a new channel $\Psi \in C(\mathcal{Z}^{\otimes k})$ through the use of the traditional teleportation protocol (q.v. Example 6.50 in Section 6.3.1), but where the classical communication channel required for teleportation is replaced by the ε-approximation to the channel $\Delta^{\otimes m}$ emulated by $\Phi^{\otimes n}$. It holds that Ψ is an ε-approximation to the identity channel $\mathbb{1}_{L(\mathcal{Z})}^{\otimes k}$.

One therefore has that, for all $\varepsilon > 0$, for all but finitely many positive integers n, and for

$$k = \left\lfloor \frac{\lfloor \alpha n \rfloor}{2} \right\rfloor = \left\lfloor \frac{\alpha n}{2} \right\rfloor, \tag{8.304}$$

the channel $\Phi^{\otimes n}$ emulates an ε-approximation to the identity channel $\mathbb{1}_{L(\mathcal{Z})}^{\otimes k}$ through the assistance of entanglement. It is therefore the case that $\alpha/2$ is an achievable rate for entanglement-assisted quantum communication through Φ, as required.

Now assume α is an achievable rate for entanglement-assisted quantum communication through Φ. It will be proved that 2α is an achievable rate for entanglement-assisted classical communication through Φ. This statement is trivial in the case $\alpha = 0$, so it will be assumed that $\alpha > 0$. The proof is essentially the same as the reverse direction just considered, with dense coding replacing teleportation.

Suppose that n and $m = \lfloor \alpha n \rfloor$ are positive integers and $\varepsilon > 0$ is a positive real number such that $\Phi^{\otimes n}$ emulates an ε-approximation to $\mathbb{1}_{L(\mathcal{Z})}^{\otimes m}$. Using the maximally entangled state

$$\tau = 2^{-m} \operatorname{vec}(\mathbb{1}_{\mathcal{Z}}^{\otimes m}) \operatorname{vec}(\mathbb{1}_{\mathcal{Z}}^{\otimes m})^*, \tag{8.305}$$

tensored with the state ξ used for the emulation of $\mathbb{1}_{L(\mathcal{Z})}^{\otimes m}$ by $\Phi^{\otimes n}$, one may define a new channel $\Psi \in C(\mathcal{Z}^{\otimes 2m})$ through the traditional dense coding protocol (q.v. Example 6.55 in Section 6.3.1), where the quantum channel required for dense coding is replaced by the ε-approximation to the channel $\mathbb{1}_{L(\mathcal{Z})}^{\otimes m}$ emulated by $\Phi^{\otimes n}$. It holds that Ψ is an ε-approximation to $\Delta^{\otimes 2m}$.

It therefore holds, for all $\varepsilon > 0$, for all but finitely many values of n, and for $m = \lfloor \alpha n \rfloor$, that $\Phi^{\otimes n}$ emulates an ε-approximation to the channel $\Delta^{\otimes 2m}$, which implies that 2α is an achievable rate for entanglement-assisted classical communication through Φ. The inequality

$$C_{E}(\Phi) \geq 2Q_{E}(\Phi) \tag{8.306}$$

is obtained when one takes the supremum over all achievable rates α for entanglement-assisted quantum communication through Φ.

The equality (8.301) therefore holds, which completes the proof. □

8.2.2 The Quantum Capacity Theorem

The purpose of the present subsection is to state and prove the quantum capacity theorem, which yields an expression for the quantum capacity of a given channel. Similar to the Holevo–Schumacher–Westmoreland theorem (Theorem 8.27), the expression that is obtained from the quantum capacity theorem includes a regularization over an increasing number of uses of a given channel.

The subsections that follow include statements and proofs of lemmas that will be used to prove the quantum capacity theorem, as well as the statement and proof of the theorem itself.

A Decoupling Lemma

The first of several lemmas that will be used to prove the quantum capacity theorem concerns a phenomenon known as *decoupling*. Informally speaking, this is the phenomenon whereby the action of a sufficiently noisy channel on a randomly chosen subspace of its input space can be expected not only to destroy entanglement with a secondary system, but also to destroy classical correlations as well. The lemma that follows proves a fact along these lines that is specialized to the task at hand.

Lemma 8.49 Let $\mathcal{X}$, $\mathcal{Y}$, $\mathcal{W}$, and $\mathcal{Z}$ be complex Euclidean spaces such that $\dim(\mathcal{Z}) \leq \dim(\mathcal{X}) \leq \dim(\mathcal{Y} \otimes \mathcal{W})$, and let $A \in \mathrm{U}(\mathcal{X}, \mathcal{Y} \otimes \mathcal{W})$ and $V \in \mathrm{U}(\mathcal{Z}, \mathcal{X})$ be isometries. Define a state $\xi \in \mathrm{D}(\mathcal{W} \otimes \mathcal{X})$ as

$$\xi = \frac{1}{n} \mathrm{Tr}_{\mathcal{Y}}\big(\mathrm{vec}(A)\,\mathrm{vec}(A)^*\big), \tag{8.307}$$

and for each unitary operator $U \in \mathrm{U}(\mathcal{X})$ define a state $\rho_U \in \mathrm{D}(\mathcal{W} \otimes \mathcal{Z})$ as

$$\rho_U = \frac{1}{m} \mathrm{Tr}_{\mathcal{Y}}\big(\mathrm{vec}(AUV)\,\mathrm{vec}(AUV)^*\big), \tag{8.308}$$

where $n = \dim(\mathcal{X})$ and $m = \dim(\mathcal{Z})$. It holds that

$$\int \big\|\rho_U - \mathrm{Tr}_{\mathcal{Z}}(\rho_U) \otimes \omega\big\|_2^2 \, d\eta(U) \leq \mathrm{Tr}(\xi^2), \tag{8.309}$$

for $\omega = \mathbb{1}_{\mathcal{Z}}/m$ and η denoting the Haar measure on $\mathrm{U}(\mathcal{X})$.

Proof Observe first that

$$\big\|\rho_U - \mathrm{Tr}_{\mathcal{Z}}(\rho_U) \otimes \omega\big\|_2^2 = \mathrm{Tr}(\rho_U^2) - \frac{1}{m}\mathrm{Tr}\Big(\big(\mathrm{Tr}_{\mathcal{Z}}(\rho_U)\big)^2\Big). \tag{8.310}$$

The lemma requires a bound on the integral of the expression represented by (8.310) over all U, and toward this goal the two terms on the right-hand side of that equation will be integrated separately.

To integrate the first term on the right-hand side of (8.310), let Γ be the alphabet for which $\mathcal{Y} = \mathbb{C}^\Gamma$, define $B_a = (e_a^* \otimes \mathbb{1}_\mathcal{W})A$ for each $a \in \Gamma$, and observe that

$$\rho_U = \frac{1}{m} \sum_{a \in \Gamma} \operatorname{vec}(B_a UV) \operatorname{vec}(B_a UV)^*. \tag{8.311}$$

It therefore holds that

$$\begin{aligned}
\operatorname{Tr}(\rho_U^2) &= \frac{1}{m^2} \sum_{a,b \in \Gamma} \left| \operatorname{Tr}(V^* U^* B_a^* B_b UV) \right|^2 \\
&= \frac{1}{m^2} \sum_{a,b \in \Gamma} \operatorname{Tr}(V^* U^* B_a^* B_b UV \otimes V^* U^* B_b^* B_a UV) \\
&= \left\langle UVV^* U^* \otimes UVV^* U^*, \frac{1}{m^2} \sum_{a,b \in \Gamma} B_a^* B_b \otimes B_b^* B_a \right\rangle.
\end{aligned} \tag{8.312}$$

Integrating over all $U \in \mathrm{U}(\mathcal{X})$ yields

$$\int \operatorname{Tr}(\rho_U^2) \, d\eta(U) = \left\langle \Xi(VV^* \otimes VV^*), \frac{1}{m^2} \sum_{a,b \in \Gamma} B_a^* B_b \otimes B_b^* B_a \right\rangle, \tag{8.313}$$

for $\Xi \in \mathrm{C}(\mathcal{X} \otimes \mathcal{X})$ denoting the Werner twirling channel (q.v. Example 7.25 in the previous chapter). Making use of the expression

$$\Xi(X) = \frac{2}{n(n+1)} \langle \Pi_{\mathcal{X} \otimes \mathcal{X}}, X \rangle \Pi_{\mathcal{X} \otimes \mathcal{X}} + \frac{2}{n(n-1)} \langle \Pi_{\mathcal{X} \otimes \mathcal{X}}, X \rangle \Pi_{\mathcal{X} \otimes \mathcal{X}}, \tag{8.314}$$

which holds for every $X \in \mathrm{L}(\mathcal{X} \otimes \mathcal{X})$, and observing the equations

$$\langle \Pi_{\mathcal{X} \otimes \mathcal{X}}, VV^* \otimes VV^* \rangle = \frac{m(m+1)}{2}, \tag{8.315}$$

$$\langle \Pi_{\mathcal{X} \otimes \mathcal{X}}, VV^* \otimes VV^* \rangle = \frac{m(m-1)}{2}, \tag{8.316}$$

it follows that

$$\begin{aligned}
&\int \operatorname{Tr}(\rho_U^2) \, d\eta(U) \\
&= \frac{1}{nm} \left\langle \frac{m+1}{n+1} \Pi_{\mathcal{X} \otimes \mathcal{X}} + \frac{m-1}{n-1} \Pi_{\mathcal{X} \otimes \mathcal{X}}, \sum_{a,b \in \Gamma} B_a^* B_b \otimes B_b^* B_a \right\rangle.
\end{aligned} \tag{8.317}$$

A similar methodology can be used to integrate the second term on the right-hand side of (8.310). In particular, one has

$$\operatorname{Tr}_\mathcal{Z}(\rho_U) = \frac{1}{m} \sum_{a \in \Gamma} B_a UVV^* U^* B_a^*, \tag{8.318}$$

and therefore

$$\mathrm{Tr}\Big(\big(\mathrm{Tr}_{\mathcal{Z}}(\rho_U)\big)^2\Big)$$

$$= \frac{1}{m^2} \sum_{a,b\in\Gamma} \mathrm{Tr}(V^*U^*B_a^*B_bUVV^*U^*B_b^*B_aUV)$$

$$= \left\langle W_{\mathcal{Z}}, \frac{1}{m^2} \sum_{a,b\in\Gamma} V^*U^*B_a^*B_bUV \otimes V^*U^*B_b^*B_aUV \right\rangle \qquad (8.319)$$

$$= \left\langle (UV \otimes UV)W_{\mathcal{Z}}(UV \otimes UV)^*, \frac{1}{m^2} \sum_{a,b\in\Gamma} B_a^*B_b \otimes B_b^*B_a \right\rangle,$$

where $W_{\mathcal{Z}} \in \mathrm{U}(\mathcal{Z} \otimes \mathcal{Z})$ denotes the swap operator on $\mathcal{Z} \otimes \mathcal{Z}$, and the second equality has used the identity $\langle W_{\mathcal{Z}}, X \otimes Y \rangle = \mathrm{Tr}(XY)$. Integrating over all $U \in \mathrm{U}(\mathcal{X})$ yields

$$\int \mathrm{Tr}\Big(\big(\mathrm{Tr}_{\mathcal{Z}}(\rho_U)\big)^2\Big)\,d\eta(U)$$

$$= \left\langle \Xi\big((V \otimes V)W_{\mathcal{Z}}(V \otimes V)^*\big), \frac{1}{m^2} \sum_{a,b\in\Gamma} B_a^*B_b \otimes B_b^*B_a \right\rangle. \qquad (8.320)$$

By making use of the equations

$$\langle \Pi_{\mathcal{X}\varoslash\mathcal{X}}, (V \otimes V)W_{\mathcal{Z}}(V \otimes V)^* \rangle = \frac{m(m+1)}{2},$$

$$\langle \Pi_{\mathcal{X}\varogreaterslash\mathcal{X}}, (V \otimes V)W_{\mathcal{Z}}(V \otimes V)^* \rangle = -\frac{m(m-1)}{2}, \qquad (8.321)$$

and performing a similar calculation to the one above, one finds that

$$\int \mathrm{Tr}\Big(\big(\mathrm{Tr}_{\mathcal{Z}}(\rho_U)\big)^2\Big)\,d\eta(U)$$

$$= \frac{1}{nm} \left\langle \frac{m+1}{n+1}\Pi_{\mathcal{X}\varoslash\mathcal{X}} - \frac{m-1}{n-1}\Pi_{\mathcal{X}\varogreaterslash\mathcal{X}}, \sum_{a,b\in\Gamma} B_a^*B_b \otimes B_b^*B_a \right\rangle. \qquad (8.322)$$

Combining (8.310), (8.317), and (8.322), together with some algebra, it follows that

$$\int \big\| \rho_U - \mathrm{Tr}_{\mathcal{Z}}(\rho_U) \otimes \omega \big\|_2^2 \, d\eta(U)$$

$$= \frac{m^2-1}{m^2(n^2-1)} \left\langle \mathbb{1}_{\mathcal{X}} \otimes \mathbb{1}_{\mathcal{X}} - \frac{1}{n}W_{\mathcal{X}}, \sum_{a,b\in\Gamma} B_a^*B_b \otimes B_b^*B_a \right\rangle, \qquad (8.323)$$

where $W_{\mathcal{X}}$ denotes the swap operator on $\mathcal{X} \otimes \mathcal{X}$. By similar calculations to

(8.312) and (8.319) above, but replacing U and V by $\mathbb{1}_{\mathcal{X}}$, it may be verified that

$$\mathrm{Tr}(\xi^2) = \frac{1}{n^2} \mathrm{Tr}\left(\sum_{a,b \in \Gamma} B_a^* B_b \otimes B_b^* B_a \right) \tag{8.324}$$

and

$$\mathrm{Tr}\left((\mathrm{Tr}_{\mathcal{X}}(\xi))^2 \right) = \frac{1}{n^2} \left\langle W_{\mathcal{X}}, \sum_{a,b \in \Gamma} B_a^* B_b \otimes B_b^* B_a \right\rangle. \tag{8.325}$$

Consequently,

$$\int \left\| \rho_U - \mathrm{Tr}_{\mathcal{Z}}(\rho_U) \otimes \omega \right\|_2^2 d\eta(U)$$
$$= \frac{1 - m^{-2}}{1 - n^{-2}} \left(\mathrm{Tr}(\xi^2) - \frac{1}{n} \mathrm{Tr}\left((\mathrm{Tr}_{\mathcal{X}}(\xi))^2 \right) \right) \le \mathrm{Tr}(\xi^2), \tag{8.326}$$

as required. $\square$

A Lower Bound on Entanglement Generation Decoding Fidelity

The next lemma is used, within the proof of the quantum capacity theorem, to infer the existence of a decoding channel for the task of entanglement generation. This inference is based on a calculation involving a Stinespring representation of the channel through which entanglement generation is to be considered.

Lemma 8.50 *Let $\mathcal{X}$, $\mathcal{Y}$, $\mathcal{W}$, and $\mathcal{Z}$ be complex Euclidean spaces such that $\dim(\mathcal{Z}) \le \dim(\mathcal{X}) \le \dim(\mathcal{Y} \otimes \mathcal{W})$, and let $A \in \mathrm{U}(\mathcal{X}, \mathcal{Y} \otimes \mathcal{W})$ and $W \in \mathrm{U}(\mathcal{Z}, \mathcal{X})$ be isometries. Define a channel $\Phi \in \mathrm{C}(\mathcal{X}, \mathcal{Y})$ as*

$$\Phi(X) = \mathrm{Tr}_{\mathcal{W}}(AXA^*) \tag{8.327}$$

for all $X \in \mathrm{L}(\mathcal{X})$, and define a state $\rho \in \mathrm{D}(\mathcal{W} \otimes \mathcal{Z})$ as

$$\rho = \frac{1}{m} \mathrm{Tr}_{\mathcal{Y}}\left(\mathrm{vec}(AW) \, \mathrm{vec}(AW)^* \right), \tag{8.328}$$

where $m = \dim(\mathcal{Z})$. There exists a channel $\Xi \in \mathrm{C}(\mathcal{Y}, \mathcal{Z})$ such that

$$\mathrm{F}\left(\frac{1}{m} \mathrm{vec}(\mathbb{1}_{\mathcal{Z}}) \, \mathrm{vec}(\mathbb{1}_{\mathcal{Z}})^*, \frac{1}{m}(\Xi\Phi \otimes \mathbb{1}_{\mathrm{L}(\mathcal{Z})})(\mathrm{vec}(W) \, \mathrm{vec}(W)^*) \right)$$
$$\ge \mathrm{F}(\rho, \mathrm{Tr}_{\mathcal{Z}}(\rho) \otimes \omega), \tag{8.329}$$

where $\omega = \mathbb{1}_{\mathcal{Z}}/m$.

Proof Let $\mathcal{V}$ be a complex Euclidean space of sufficiently large dimension that the inequalities $\dim(\mathcal{V}) \geq \dim(\mathcal{W})$ and $\dim(\mathcal{V} \otimes \mathcal{Z}) \geq \dim(\mathcal{Y})$ hold, and let $B \in \mathrm{L}(\mathcal{W}, \mathcal{V})$ be an operator such that $\mathrm{Tr}_{\mathcal{V}}(\mathrm{vec}(B)\,\mathrm{vec}(B)^*) = \mathrm{Tr}_{\mathcal{Z}}(\rho)$. For the vector

$$u = \frac{1}{\sqrt{m}}\,\mathrm{vec}(B \otimes \mathbb{1}_{\mathcal{Z}}) \in (\mathcal{V} \otimes \mathcal{Z}) \otimes (\mathcal{W} \otimes \mathcal{Z}), \qquad (8.330)$$

one has that $\mathrm{Tr}_{\mathcal{V} \otimes \mathcal{Z}}(uu^*) = \mathrm{Tr}_{\mathcal{Z}}(\rho) \otimes \omega$. It is evident that the vector

$$v = \frac{1}{\sqrt{m}}\,\mathrm{vec}(AW) \in \mathcal{Y} \otimes \mathcal{W} \otimes \mathcal{Z} \qquad (8.331)$$

satisfies $\mathrm{Tr}_{\mathcal{Y}}(vv^*) = \rho$, so it follows by Uhlmann's theorem (Theorem 3.22) that there exists an isometry $V \in \mathrm{U}(\mathcal{Y}, \mathcal{V} \otimes \mathcal{Z})$ such that

$$\mathrm{F}(\rho, \mathrm{Tr}_{\mathcal{Z}}(\rho) \otimes \omega) = \mathrm{F}(uu^*, (V \otimes \mathbb{1}_{\mathcal{W} \otimes \mathcal{Z}})vv^*(V \otimes \mathbb{1}_{\mathcal{W} \otimes \mathcal{Z}})^*). \qquad (8.332)$$

Define a channel $\Xi \in \mathrm{C}(\mathcal{Y}, \mathcal{Z})$ as

$$\Xi(Y) = \mathrm{Tr}_{\mathcal{V}}(VYV^*) \qquad (8.333)$$

for every $Y \in \mathrm{L}(\mathcal{Y})$. It holds that

$$\mathrm{Tr}_{\mathcal{V}}(\mathrm{Tr}_{\mathcal{W}}(uu^*)) = \frac{1}{m}\,\mathrm{vec}(\mathbb{1}_{\mathcal{Z}})\,\mathrm{vec}(\mathbb{1}_{\mathcal{Z}})^* \qquad (8.334)$$

and

$$\mathrm{Tr}_{\mathcal{V}}(\mathrm{Tr}_{\mathcal{W}}((V \otimes \mathbb{1}_{\mathcal{W} \otimes \mathcal{Z}})vv^*(V \otimes \mathbb{1}_{\mathcal{W} \otimes \mathcal{Z}})^*))$$
$$= \frac{1}{m}(\Xi\Phi \otimes \mathbb{1}_{\mathrm{L}(\mathcal{Z})})(\mathrm{vec}(W)\,\mathrm{vec}(W)^*), \qquad (8.335)$$

and therefore

$$\mathrm{F}(uu^*, (V \otimes \mathbb{1}_{\mathcal{W} \otimes \mathcal{Z}})vv^*(V \otimes \mathbb{1}_{\mathcal{W} \otimes \mathcal{Z}})^*)$$
$$\leq \mathrm{F}\!\left(\frac{1}{m}\,\mathrm{vec}(\mathbb{1}_{\mathcal{Z}})\,\mathrm{vec}(\mathbb{1}_{\mathcal{Z}})^*, \frac{1}{m}(\Xi\Phi \otimes \mathbb{1}_{\mathrm{L}(\mathcal{Z})})(\mathrm{vec}(W)\,\mathrm{vec}(W)^*)\right) \qquad (8.336)$$

by the monotonicity of the fidelity under partial tracing (which is a special case of Theorem 3.27). The channel Ξ therefore satisfies the requirement of the lemma. $\square$

Two Additional Lemmas Needed for the Quantum Capacity Theorem

The two lemmas that follow represent technical facts that will be utilized in the proof of the quantum capacity theorem. The first lemma concerns the approximation of one isometry by another isometry that meets certain spectral requirements, and the second lemma is a general fact regarding the Haar measure.

Lemma 8.51 *Let $\mathcal{X}$, $\mathcal{Y}$, and $\mathcal{W}$ be complex Euclidean spaces such that* $\dim(\mathcal{X}) \leq \dim(\mathcal{Y} \otimes \mathcal{W})$, *let* $A \in \mathrm{U}(\mathcal{X}, \mathcal{Y} \otimes \mathcal{W})$ *be an isometry, let* $\Lambda \in \mathrm{Proj}(\mathcal{Y})$ *and* $\Pi \in \mathrm{Proj}(\mathcal{W})$ *be projection operators, and let* $\varepsilon \in (0, 1/4)$ *be a positive real number. Also let* $n = \dim(\mathcal{X})$, *and assume that the constraints*

$$\langle \Lambda \otimes \Pi, AA^* \rangle \geq (1 - \varepsilon)n \tag{8.337}$$

and

$$2\,\mathrm{rank}(\Pi) \leq \dim(\mathcal{W}) \tag{8.338}$$

are satisfied. There exists an isometry $B \in \mathrm{U}(\mathcal{X}, \mathcal{Y} \otimes \mathcal{W})$ *such that*

1. $\|A - B\|_2 < 3\varepsilon^{1/4}\sqrt{n}$,
2. $\mathrm{Tr}_{\mathcal{W}}(BB^*) \leq 4\Lambda\,\mathrm{Tr}_{\mathcal{W}}(AA^*)\Lambda$, *and*
3. $\mathrm{rank}(\mathrm{Tr}_{\mathcal{Y}}(BB^*)) \leq 2\,\mathrm{rank}(\Pi)$.

Proof   By means of the singular value theorem, one may write

$$(\Lambda \otimes \Pi)A = \sum_{k=1}^{n} s_k u_k x_k^* \tag{8.339}$$

for an orthonormal basis $\{x_1, \ldots, x_n\}$ of $\mathcal{X}$, an orthonormal set $\{u_1, \ldots, u_n\}$ of vectors in $\mathcal{Y} \otimes \mathcal{W}$, and a collection $\{s_1, \ldots, s_n\} \subset [0,1]$ of nonnegative real numbers. It holds that

$$\sum_{k=1}^{n} s_k^2 = \langle \Lambda \otimes \Pi, AA^* \rangle \geq (1 - \varepsilon)n. \tag{8.340}$$

Define $\Gamma \subseteq \{1, \ldots, n\}$ as

$$\Gamma = \left\{ k \in \{1, \ldots, n\} : s_k^2 \geq 1 - \sqrt{\varepsilon} \right\}, \tag{8.341}$$

and observe the inequality

$$\sum_{k=1}^{n} s_k^2 \leq |\Gamma| + (n - |\Gamma|)(1 - \sqrt{\varepsilon}). \tag{8.342}$$

From (8.340) and (8.342) it follows that

$$|\Gamma| \geq (1 - \sqrt{\varepsilon})n > \frac{n}{2}. \tag{8.343}$$

There must therefore exist an injective function $f \colon \{1, \ldots, n\}\backslash\Gamma \to \Gamma$; this function may be chosen arbitrarily, but will be fixed for the remainder of the proof.

Next, let $W \in \mathrm{U}(\mathcal{W})$ be any unitary operator satisfying $\Pi W \Pi = 0$. The assumption that $2 \operatorname{rank}(\Pi) \leq \dim(\mathcal{W})$ guarantees the existence of such an operator W. As for the function f, the unitary operator W may be chosen arbitrarily, subject to the condition $\Pi W \Pi = 0$, but is understood to be fixed for the remainder of the proof.

Finally, define an isometry $B \in \mathrm{U}(\mathcal{X}, \mathcal{Y} \otimes \mathcal{W})$ as follows:

$$B = \sum_{k \in \Gamma} u_k x_k^* + \sum_{k \in \{1,\ldots,n\}\backslash\Gamma} (\mathbb{1}_{\mathcal{Y}} \otimes W) u_{f(k)} x_k^*. \tag{8.344}$$

It remains to prove that B has the properties required by the statement of the lemma.

First, it will be verified that B is indeed an isometry. The set $\{u_k : k \in \Gamma\}$ is evidently orthonormal, as is the set

$$\{(\mathbb{1}_{\mathcal{Y}} \otimes W) u_{f(k)} : k \in \{1, \ldots, n\}\backslash\Gamma\}. \tag{8.345}$$

For every choice of $k \in \{1, \ldots, n\}$ one has

$$s_k u_k \in \operatorname{im}((\Lambda \otimes \Pi)A) \subseteq \operatorname{im}(\mathbb{1}_{\mathcal{Y}} \otimes \Pi), \tag{8.346}$$

and therefore $s_k u_k = s_k (\mathbb{1}_{\mathcal{Y}} \otimes \Pi) u_k$. It follows that

$$\begin{aligned} s_j s_k \langle u_j, (\mathbb{1}_{\mathcal{Y}} \otimes W) u_k \rangle &= s_j s_k \langle (\mathbb{1}_{\mathcal{Y}} \otimes \Pi) u_j, (\mathbb{1}_{\mathcal{Y}} \otimes \Pi W) u_k \rangle \\ &= s_j s_k \langle u_j, (\mathbb{1}_{\mathcal{Y}} \otimes \Pi W \Pi) u_k \rangle = 0 \end{aligned} \tag{8.347}$$

for every choice of $j, k \in \{1, \ldots, n\}$, by virtue of the fact that $\Pi W \Pi = 0$. For $j, k \in \Gamma$, it must hold that $s_j s_k > 0$, and therefore $u_j \perp (\mathbb{1}_{\mathcal{Y}} \otimes W) u_k$. This implies that the set

$$\{u_k : k \in \Gamma\} \cup \{(\mathbb{1}_{\mathcal{Y}} \otimes W) u_{f(k)} : k \in \{1, \ldots, n\}\backslash\Gamma\} \tag{8.348}$$

is orthonormal, and therefore B is an isometry.

Next, observe that

$$\|A - B\|_2 \leq \|A - (\Lambda \otimes \Pi)A\|_2 + \|(\Lambda \otimes \Pi)A - B\|_2. \tag{8.349}$$

The first term in this expression is bounded as

$$\|A - (\Lambda \otimes \Pi)A\|_2 = \sqrt{\langle \mathbb{1} - \Lambda \otimes \Pi, AA^* \rangle} \leq \sqrt{\varepsilon n}. \tag{8.350}$$

For the second term, it holds that

$$\begin{aligned} \|(\Lambda \otimes \Pi)A - B\|_2^2 &= \sum_{k \in \Gamma} (s_k - 1)^2 + \sum_{k \in \{1,\ldots,n\}\backslash\Gamma} (s_k^2 + 1) \\ &= n + \sum_{k=1}^{n} s_k^2 - 2 \sum_{k \in \Gamma} s_k \leq 2n - 2|\Gamma|(1 - \sqrt{\varepsilon})^{\frac{1}{2}}. \end{aligned} \tag{8.351}$$

To obtain the first equality in the previous equation, it is helpful to observe that

$$s_k u_k \perp (\mathbb{1}_{\mathcal{Y}} \otimes W) u_{f(k)} \tag{8.352}$$

for $k \in \{1, \ldots, n\} \backslash \Gamma$, which makes use of the equation (8.347) along with the inclusion $f(k) \in \Gamma$. By the inequality (8.343) it therefore holds that

$$\left\| (\Lambda \otimes \Pi) A - B \right\|_2^2 \leq 2n - 2(1 - \sqrt{\varepsilon})^{\frac{3}{2}} n < 3n\sqrt{\varepsilon}, \tag{8.353}$$

from which it follows that

$$\| A - B \|_2 < 3\varepsilon^{1/4} \sqrt{n}. \tag{8.354}$$

The first requirement on B listed in the statement of the lemma is therefore fulfilled.

The second requirement on B may be verified as follows:

$$\begin{aligned} \operatorname{Tr}_{\mathcal{W}}(BB^*) &\leq 2 \sum_{k \in \Gamma} \operatorname{Tr}_{\mathcal{W}}(u_k u_k^*) \\ &\leq \frac{2}{1 - \sqrt{\varepsilon}} \operatorname{Tr}_{\mathcal{W}}((\Lambda \otimes \Pi) AA^* (\Lambda \otimes \Pi)) \leq 4\Lambda \operatorname{Tr}_{\mathcal{W}}(AA^*)\Lambda. \end{aligned} \tag{8.355}$$

Finally, to verify that the third requirement on B is satisfied, one may again use the observation that $(\mathbb{1} \otimes \Pi) u_k = u_k$, which implies that

$$\operatorname{im}(\operatorname{Tr}_{\mathcal{Y}}(u_k u_k^*)) \subseteq \operatorname{im}(\Pi), \tag{8.356}$$

for each $k \in \Gamma$. As

$$\operatorname{Tr}_{\mathcal{Y}}(BB^*) = \sum_{k \in \Gamma} \operatorname{Tr}_{\mathcal{Y}}(u_k u_k^*) + \sum_{k \in \{1, \ldots, n\} \backslash \Gamma} W(\operatorname{Tr}_{\mathcal{Y}}(u_{f(k)} u_{f(k)}^*))W^*, \tag{8.357}$$

it follows that

$$\operatorname{im}(\operatorname{Tr}_{\mathcal{Y}}(BB^*)) \subseteq \operatorname{im}(\Pi) + \operatorname{im}(W\Pi) \tag{8.358}$$

and therefore

$$\operatorname{rank}(\operatorname{Tr}_{\mathcal{Y}}(BB^*)) \leq 2 \operatorname{rank}(\Pi), \tag{8.359}$$

as required. $\qquad \square$

Lemma 8.52 *Let $\mathcal{X}$, $\mathcal{W}$, and $\mathcal{Z}$ be complex Euclidean spaces such that $\dim(\mathcal{Z}) \leq \dim(\mathcal{X})$, let $V \in \mathrm{U}(\mathcal{Z}, \mathcal{X})$ be an isometry, and let $Z \in \mathrm{L}(\mathcal{W} \otimes \mathcal{X})$ be an operator. It holds that*

$$\int \left\| (\mathbb{1}_{\mathcal{W}} \otimes V^* U^*) Z (\mathbb{1}_{\mathcal{W}} \otimes UV) \right\|_1 \, \mathrm{d}\eta(U) \leq \frac{m}{n} \| Z \|_1 \tag{8.360}$$

where $m = \dim(\mathcal{Z})$, $n = \dim(\mathcal{X})$, and η denotes the Haar measure on $\mathrm{U}(\mathcal{X})$.

Proof Let $\{W_1, \ldots, W_{n^2}\} \subset \mathrm{U}(\mathcal{X})$ be an orthogonal collection of unitary operators. (The discrete Weyl operators, defined in Section 4.1.2, provide an explicit choice for such a collection.) It therefore holds that the completely depolarizing channel $\Omega \in \mathrm{C}(\mathcal{X})$ may be expressed as

$$\Omega(X) = \frac{1}{n^2} \sum_{k=1}^{n^2} W_k X W_k^* \tag{8.361}$$

for all $X \in \mathrm{L}(\mathcal{X})$. Define $\mathcal{Y} = \mathbb{C}^{n^2}$, and define a channel $\Phi \in \mathrm{C}(\mathcal{X}, \mathcal{Z} \otimes \mathcal{Y})$ as

$$\Phi(X) = \frac{1}{nm} \sum_{k=1}^{n^2} V^* W_k^* X W_k V \otimes E_{k,k} \tag{8.362}$$

for every $X \in \mathrm{L}(\mathcal{X})$. The fact that Φ is a channel follows from Corollary 2.27 together with the calculation

$$\frac{1}{nm} \sum_{k=1}^{n^2} W_k V V^* W_k^* = \frac{n}{m} \Omega(VV^*) = \mathbb{1}_{\mathcal{X}}. \tag{8.363}$$

Next, by the right unitary invariance of the Haar measure, it holds that

$$\int \left\| (\mathbb{1}_{\mathcal{W}} \otimes V^* U^*) Z (\mathbb{1}_{\mathcal{W}} \otimes UV) \right\|_1 \, d\eta(U)$$
$$= \int \left\| (\mathbb{1}_{\mathcal{W}} \otimes V^* W_k^* U^*) Z (\mathbb{1}_{\mathcal{W}} \otimes UW_k V) \right\|_1 \, d\eta(U) \tag{8.364}$$

for every choice of $k \in \{1, \ldots, n^2\}$, and therefore

$$\int \left\| (\mathbb{1}_{\mathcal{W}} \otimes UV)^* Z (\mathbb{1}_{\mathcal{W}} \otimes UV) \right\|_1 \, d\eta(U)$$
$$= \frac{1}{n^2} \sum_{k=1}^{n^2} \int \left\| (\mathbb{1}_{\mathcal{W}} \otimes UW_k V)^* Z (\mathbb{1}_{\mathcal{W}} \otimes UW_k V) \right\|_1 \, d\eta(U)$$
$$= \frac{1}{n^2} \int \left\| \sum_{k=1}^{n^2} (\mathbb{1}_{\mathcal{W}} \otimes UW_k V)^* Z (\mathbb{1}_{\mathcal{W}} \otimes UW_k V) \otimes E_{k,k} \right\|_1 \, d\eta(U) \tag{8.365}$$
$$= \frac{m}{n} \int \left\| (\mathbb{1}_{\mathrm{L}(\mathcal{W})} \otimes \Phi)((\mathbb{1}_{\mathcal{W}} \otimes U^*) Z (\mathbb{1}_{\mathcal{W}} \otimes U)) \right\|_1 \, d\eta(U).$$

As the trace norm is non-increasing under the action of channels, as well as unitarily invariant, it follows that

$$\frac{m}{n} \int \left\| (\mathbb{1}_{\mathrm{L}(\mathcal{W})} \otimes \Phi)((\mathbb{1}_{\mathcal{W}} \otimes U^*) Z (\mathbb{1}_{\mathcal{W}} \otimes U)) \right\|_1 \, d\eta(U)$$
$$\leq \frac{m}{n} \int \left\| (\mathbb{1}_{\mathcal{W}} \otimes U^*) Z (\mathbb{1}_{\mathcal{W}} \otimes U) \right\|_1 \, d\eta(U) = \frac{m}{n} \|Z\|_1, \tag{8.366}$$

which completes the proof. $\qquad\qquad\square$

The Quantum Capacity Theorem

As the following theorem establishes, the entanglement generation capacity of a given channel is always at least as large as the coherent information of the completely mixed state through that channel. This fact, which will be generalized to arbitrary states in place of the completely mixed state in a corollary to the theorem, lies at the heart of the proof of the quantum capacity theorem.

Theorem 8.53 Let $\Phi \in C(\mathcal{X}, \mathcal{Y})$ be a channel, for complex Euclidean spaces $\mathcal{X}$ and $\mathcal{Y}$. The entanglement generation capacity of Φ is at least the coherent information of the completely mixed state $\omega \in D(\mathcal{X})$ through Φ:

$$I_c(\omega; \Phi) \leq Q_{\mathrm{EG}}(\Phi). \tag{8.367}$$

Proof Let $\mathcal{W}$ be a complex Euclidean space such that

$$\dim(\mathcal{W}) = 2 \dim(\mathcal{X} \otimes \mathcal{Y}), \tag{8.368}$$

and let $A \in U(\mathcal{X}, \mathcal{Y} \otimes \mathcal{W})$ be an isometry for which

$$\Phi(X) = \mathrm{Tr}_{\mathcal{W}}(A X A^*) \tag{8.369}$$

for all $X \in L(\mathcal{X})$. The somewhat unusual factor of 2 on the right-hand side of (8.368) will guarantee that the assumptions required by Lemma 8.51 are met, as is mentioned later in the proof. Define a channel $\Psi \in C(\mathcal{X}, \mathcal{W})$ as

$$\Psi(X) = \mathrm{Tr}_{\mathcal{Y}}(A X A^*) \tag{8.370}$$

for all $X \in L(\mathcal{X})$, so that Ψ is complementary to Φ. It therefore holds that

$$I_c(\omega; \Phi) = H(\Phi(\omega)) - H(\Psi(\omega)). \tag{8.371}$$

The theorem is vacuous in the case that $I_c(\omega; \Phi) \leq 0$, so hereafter it will be assumed that $I_c(\omega; \Phi)$ is positive. To prove the theorem, it suffices to demonstrate that every positive real number smaller than $I_c(\omega; \Phi)$ is an achievable rate for entanglement generation through Φ. Toward this goal, assume that an arbitrary positive real number α satisfying $\alpha < I_c(\omega; \Phi)$ has been fixed, and that $\varepsilon > 0$ is a positive real number chosen to be sufficiently small so that the inequality

$$\alpha < I_c(\omega; \Phi) - 2\varepsilon \left(H(\Phi(\omega)) + H(\Psi(\omega))\right) \tag{8.372}$$

is satisfied. The remainder of the proof is devoted to proving that α is an achievable rate for entanglement generation through Φ.

Consider an arbitrary positive integer $n \geq 1/\alpha$, and let $m = \lfloor \alpha n \rfloor$. Also let $\Gamma = \{0, 1\}$ denote the binary alphabet, and let $\mathcal{Z} = \mathbb{C}^{\Gamma}$. The task in which a state having high fidelity with the maximally entangled state

$$2^{-m} \operatorname{vec}(\mathbb{1}_{\mathcal{Z}}^{\otimes m}) \operatorname{vec}(\mathbb{1}_{\mathcal{Z}}^{\otimes m})^* \tag{8.373}$$

is established between a sender and receiver through the channel $\Phi^{\otimes n}$ is to be considered. Note that the quantity $\mathrm{I_c}(\omega; \Phi)$ is at most $\log(\dim(\mathcal{X}))$, and therefore $\alpha < \log(\dim(\mathcal{X}))$, and this implies $\dim(\mathcal{Z}^{\otimes m}) \leq \dim(\mathcal{X}^{\otimes n})$. For any isometry $W \in \mathrm{U}(\mathcal{Z}^{\otimes m}, \mathcal{X}^{\otimes n})$ and a channel $\Xi \in \mathrm{C}(\mathcal{Y}^{\otimes n}, \mathcal{Z}^{\otimes m})$, the state

$$2^{-m} (\Xi \Phi^{\otimes n} \otimes \mathbb{1}_{\mathrm{L}(\mathcal{Z})}^{\otimes m}) (\operatorname{vec}(W) \operatorname{vec}(W)^*) \tag{8.374}$$

may be established through the channel $\Phi^{\otimes n}$, so one may aim to prove that there exists a choice of Ξ and W for which the fidelity between the states (8.373) and (8.374) is high.

It is helpful at this point to let $A_n \in \mathrm{U}(\mathcal{X}^{\otimes n}, \mathcal{Y}^{\otimes n} \otimes \mathcal{W}^{\otimes n})$ be the isometry defined by the equation

$$\langle y_1 \otimes \cdots \otimes y_n \otimes w_1 \otimes \cdots \otimes w_n, A_n(x_1 \otimes \cdots \otimes x_n) \rangle$$
$$= \langle y_1 \otimes w_1, Ax_1 \rangle \cdots \langle y_n \otimes w_n, Ax_n \rangle \tag{8.375}$$

holding for every choice of vectors $x_1, \ldots, x_n \in \mathcal{X}$, $y_1, \ldots, y_n \in \mathcal{Y}$, and $w_1, \ldots, w_n \in \mathcal{W}$. In effect, A_n is equivalent to $A^{\otimes n}$, except that the tensor factors in its output space have been permuted, so that the output space becomes $\mathcal{Y}^{\otimes n} \otimes \mathcal{W}^{\otimes n}$ rather than $(\mathcal{Y} \otimes \mathcal{W})^{\otimes n}$. It may be noted that

$$\Phi^{\otimes n}(X) = \operatorname{Tr}_{\mathcal{W}^{\otimes n}}(A_n X A_n^*) \quad \text{and} \quad \Psi^{\otimes n}(X) = \operatorname{Tr}_{\mathcal{Y}^{\otimes n}}(A_n X A_n^*) \tag{8.376}$$

for every $X \in \mathrm{L}(\mathcal{X}^{\otimes n})$.

Now, under the assumption that the decoding channel $\Xi \in \mathrm{C}(\mathcal{Y}^{\otimes n}, \mathcal{Z}^{\otimes m})$ has been selected optimally, Lemma 8.50 implies that the fidelity between the states (8.373) and (8.374) is lower-bounded by

$$\mathrm{F}(\rho, \operatorname{Tr}_{\mathcal{Z}^{\otimes m}}(\rho) \otimes \omega_{\mathcal{Z}}^{\otimes m}) \tag{8.377}$$

for $\rho \in \mathrm{D}(\mathcal{W}^{\otimes n} \otimes \mathcal{Z}^{\otimes m})$ defined as

$$\rho = 2^{-m} \operatorname{Tr}_{\mathcal{Y}^{\otimes n}}(\operatorname{vec}(A_n W) \operatorname{vec}(A_n W)^*) \tag{8.378}$$

and for $\omega_{\mathcal{Z}} \in \mathrm{D}(\mathcal{Z})$ denoting the completely mixed state on $\mathcal{Z}$.

The probabilistic method will be employed to prove the existence of an isometry W for which the expression (8.377) is close to 1, provided that n is sufficiently large. In particular, one may fix $V \in \mathrm{U}(\mathcal{Z}^{\otimes m}, \mathcal{X}^{\otimes n})$ to be an arbitrary isometry, and let $W = UV$ for U chosen at random with respect to the Haar measure on $\mathrm{U}(\mathcal{X}^{\otimes n})$. The analysis that follows demonstrates that, for an operator W chosen in this way, one expects the quantity (8.377) to be close to 1, for sufficiently large n, which proves the existence of a choice of W for which this is true.

Let $k = \dim(\mathcal{X})$ and define $\xi \in \mathrm{D}(\mathcal{W}^{\otimes n} \otimes \mathcal{X}^{\otimes n})$ as

$$\xi = \frac{1}{k^n} \operatorname{Tr}_{\mathcal{Y}^{\otimes n}} \left(\operatorname{vec}(A_n) \operatorname{vec}(A_n)^* \right). \tag{8.379}$$

Also define $\rho_U \in \mathrm{D}(\mathcal{W}^{\otimes n} \otimes \mathcal{Z}^{\otimes m})$ as

$$\rho_U = \frac{1}{2^m} \operatorname{Tr}_{\mathcal{Y}^{\otimes n}} \left(\operatorname{vec}(A_n UV) \operatorname{vec}(A_n UV)^* \right), \tag{8.380}$$

for each unitary operator $U \in \mathrm{U}(\mathcal{X}^{\otimes n})$, and observe that

$$\rho_U = \frac{k^n}{2^m} \left(\mathbb{1}_{\mathcal{W}}^{\otimes n} \otimes V^{\mathsf{T}} U^{\mathsf{T}} \right) \xi \left(\mathbb{1}_{\mathcal{W}}^{\otimes n} \otimes V^{\mathsf{T}} U^{\mathsf{T}} \right)^*. \tag{8.381}$$

For the isometry $W = UV$, the fidelity between the states (8.373) and (8.374) is lower-bounded by

$$\mathrm{F}\left(\rho_U, \operatorname{Tr}_{\mathcal{Z}^{\otimes m}}(\rho_U) \otimes \omega_{\mathcal{Z}}^{\otimes m} \right), \tag{8.382}$$

for a suitable choice of the decoding channel Ξ.

Let $\Lambda_{n,\varepsilon} \in \mathrm{Proj}(\mathcal{Y}^{\otimes n})$ and $\Pi_{n,\varepsilon} \in \mathrm{Proj}(\mathcal{W}^{\otimes n})$ be the projection operators onto the ε-strongly typical subspaces of $\mathcal{Y}^{\otimes n}$ and $\mathcal{W}^{\otimes n}$, with respect to any fixed choice of spectral decompositions of $\Phi(\omega)$ and $\Psi(\omega)$, respectively. One may observe that because $\varepsilon > 0$ and $\mathrm{rank}(\Psi(\omega)) \leq \dim(\mathcal{X} \otimes \mathcal{Y})$, it holds that

$$\mathrm{rank}(\Pi_{n,\varepsilon}) \leq \frac{1}{2^n} \dim(\mathcal{W}^{\otimes n}) \leq \frac{1}{2} \dim(\mathcal{W}^{\otimes n}). \tag{8.383}$$

This is a very coarse bound that will nevertheless be required in order to utilize Lemma 8.51, and explains the factor of 2 in (8.368).

By Lemma 8.32, there must exist positive real numbers K and δ, both independent of n and ε, and both assumed to be fixed for the remainder of the proof, such that for

$$\zeta_{n,\varepsilon} = K \exp(-\delta n \varepsilon^2) \tag{8.384}$$

one has these inequalities:

$$\frac{1}{k^n}\langle \Lambda_{n,\varepsilon} \otimes \mathbb{1}_{\mathcal{W}}^{\otimes n} \otimes \mathbb{1}_{\mathcal{X}}^{\otimes n}, \mathrm{vec}(A_n)\,\mathrm{vec}(A_n)^* \rangle$$
$$= \langle \Lambda_{n,\varepsilon}, (\Phi(\omega))^{\otimes n} \rangle \geq 1 - \frac{\zeta_{n,\varepsilon}}{2},$$
$$\frac{1}{k^n}\langle \mathbb{1}_{\mathcal{Y}}^{\otimes n} \otimes \Pi_{n,\varepsilon} \otimes \mathbb{1}_{\mathcal{X}}^{\otimes n}, \mathrm{vec}(A_n)\,\mathrm{vec}(A_n)^* \rangle$$
$$= \langle \Pi_{n,\varepsilon}, (\Psi(\omega))^{\otimes n} \rangle \geq 1 - \frac{\zeta_{n,\varepsilon}}{2}. \tag{8.385}$$

It follows that

$$\frac{1}{k^n}\langle \Lambda_{n,\varepsilon} \otimes \Pi_{n,\varepsilon} \otimes \mathbb{1}_{\mathcal{X}}^{\otimes n}, \mathrm{vec}(A_n)\,\mathrm{vec}(A_n)^* \rangle \geq 1 - \zeta_{n,\varepsilon}, \tag{8.386}$$

which is equivalent to

$$\langle \Lambda_{n,\varepsilon} \otimes \Pi_{n,\varepsilon}, A_n A_n^* \rangle \geq (1 - \zeta_{n,\varepsilon})\,k^n. \tag{8.387}$$

If n is sufficiently large so that $\zeta_{n,\varepsilon} < 1/4$, it follows by Lemma 8.51 that there exists an isometry $B_n \in \mathrm{U}(\mathcal{X}^{\otimes n}, \mathcal{Y}^{\otimes n} \otimes \mathcal{W}^{\otimes n})$ satisfying these three conditions:

$$\begin{aligned} \|A_n - B_n\|_2 &\leq 3\,\zeta_{n,\varepsilon}^{1/4}\,k^{n/2}, \\ \mathrm{Tr}_{\mathcal{W}^{\otimes n}}(B_n B_n^*) &\leq 4\Lambda_{n,\varepsilon}\,\mathrm{Tr}_{\mathcal{W}^{\otimes n}}(A_n A_n^*)\Lambda_{n,\varepsilon}, \\ \mathrm{rank}(\mathrm{Tr}_{\mathcal{Y}^{\otimes n}}(B_n B_n^*)) &\leq 2\,\mathrm{rank}(\Pi_{n,\varepsilon}). \end{aligned} \tag{8.388}$$

By Proposition 8.33, the third condition implies that

$$\mathrm{rank}(\mathrm{Tr}_{\mathcal{Y}^{\otimes n}}(B_n B_n^*)) \leq 2^{n(1+\varepsilon)\,\mathrm{H}(\Psi(\omega))+1}. \tag{8.389}$$

Using the second condition, together with Corollary 8.31 and the inequality $\mathrm{Tr}(P^2) \leq \lambda_1(P)\,\mathrm{Tr}(P)$, which holds for all $P \geq 0$, one obtains

$$\mathrm{Tr}\!\left(\left(\frac{1}{k^n}\,\mathrm{Tr}_{\mathcal{W}^{\otimes n}}(B_n B_n^*)\right)^2\right)$$
$$\leq \mathrm{Tr}\!\left(\left(\frac{4}{k^n}\Lambda_{n,\varepsilon}\,\mathrm{Tr}_{\mathcal{W}^{\otimes n}}(A_n A_n^*)\Lambda_{n,\varepsilon}\right)^2\right) \tag{8.390}$$
$$= 16\,\mathrm{Tr}\!\left((\Lambda_{n,\varepsilon}\Phi(\omega)^{\otimes n}\Lambda_{n,\varepsilon})^2\right)$$
$$\leq 2^{-n(1-\varepsilon)\,\mathrm{H}(\Phi(\omega))+4}.$$

Finally, define

$$\sigma = \frac{1}{k^n}\,\mathrm{Tr}_{\mathcal{Y}^{\otimes n}}(\mathrm{vec}(B_n)\,\mathrm{vec}(B_n)^*), \tag{8.391}$$

and also define

$$
\begin{aligned}
\tau_U &= \frac{1}{2^m} \operatorname{Tr}_{\mathcal{Y}^{\otimes n}} \left(\operatorname{vec}(B_n U V) \operatorname{vec}(B_n U V)^* \right) \\
&= \frac{k^n}{2^m} \left(1_{\mathcal{W}}^{\otimes n} \otimes V^{\mathsf{T}} U^{\mathsf{T}} \right) \sigma \left(1_{\mathcal{W}}^{\otimes n} \otimes V^{\mathsf{T}} U^{\mathsf{T}} \right)^*
\end{aligned}
\tag{8.392}
$$

for each $U \in \mathrm{U}(\mathcal{X}^{\otimes n})$. It holds that

$$
\begin{aligned}
&\left\| \rho_U - \operatorname{Tr}_{\mathcal{Z}^{\otimes m}} (\rho_U) \otimes \omega_{\mathcal{Z}}^{\otimes m} \right\|_1 \\
&\qquad \leq \left\| \rho_U - \tau_U \right\|_1 + \left\| \tau_U - \operatorname{Tr}_{\mathcal{Z}^{\otimes m}} (\tau_U) \otimes \omega_{\mathcal{Z}}^{\otimes m} \right\|_1 \\
&\qquad\quad + \left\| \left(\operatorname{Tr}_{\mathcal{Z}^{\otimes m}} (\tau_U) - \operatorname{Tr}_{\mathcal{Z}^{\otimes m}} (\rho_U) \right) \otimes \omega_{\mathcal{Z}}^{\otimes m} \right\|_1 \\
&\qquad \leq \left\| \tau_U - \operatorname{Tr}_{\mathcal{Z}^{\otimes m}} (\tau_U) \otimes \omega_{\mathcal{Z}}^{\otimes m} \right\|_1 + 2 \left\| \rho_U - \tau_U \right\|_1,
\end{aligned}
\tag{8.393}
$$

and so it remains to consider the average value of the two terms in the final expression of this inequality. When considering the first term in the final expression of (8.393), it may be noted that

$$
\operatorname{im}(\tau_U) \subseteq \operatorname{im}\left(\operatorname{Tr}_{\mathcal{Z}^{\otimes m}} (\tau_U) \otimes \omega_{\mathcal{Z}}^{\otimes m} \right)
\tag{8.394}
$$

and therefore

$$
\begin{aligned}
\operatorname{rank}\left(\tau_U - \operatorname{Tr}_{\mathcal{Z}^{\otimes m}} (\tau_U) \otimes \omega_{\mathcal{Z}}^{\otimes m} \right) &\leq \operatorname{rank}\left(\operatorname{Tr}_{\mathcal{Z}^{\otimes m}} (\tau_U) \otimes \omega_{\mathcal{Z}}^{\otimes m} \right) \\
&\leq 2^m \operatorname{rank}(\operatorname{Tr}_{\mathcal{Y}^{\otimes n}} (B_n B_n^*)) \leq 2^{n(1+\varepsilon) \operatorname{H}(\Psi(\omega)) + m + 1}.
\end{aligned}
\tag{8.395}
$$

In addition, one has

$$
\operatorname{Tr}(\sigma^2) = \operatorname{Tr}\left(\left(\frac{1}{k^n} \operatorname{Tr}_{\mathcal{W}^{\otimes n}} (B_n B_n^*) \right)^2 \right) \leq 2^{-n(1-\varepsilon) \operatorname{H}(\Phi(\omega)) + 4}.
\tag{8.396}
$$

Making use of Lemma 8.49, it therefore follows that

$$
\begin{aligned}
&\int \left\| \tau_U - \operatorname{Tr}_{\mathcal{Z}^{\otimes m}} (\tau_U) \otimes \omega_{\mathcal{Z}}^{\otimes m} \right\|_1^2 d\eta(U) \\
&\qquad \leq 2^{n(1+\varepsilon) \operatorname{H}(\Psi(\omega)) + m + 1} \int \left\| \tau_U - \operatorname{Tr}_{\mathcal{Z}^{\otimes m}} (\tau_U) \otimes \omega_{\mathcal{Z}}^{\otimes m} \right\|_2^2 d\eta(U) \\
&\qquad \leq 2^{n((1+\varepsilon) \operatorname{H}(\Psi(\omega)) - (1-\varepsilon) \operatorname{H}(\Phi(\omega))) + m + 5} \\
&\qquad = 2^{-n(\operatorname{I}_c(\omega; \Phi) - 2\varepsilon(\operatorname{H}(\Phi(\omega)) + \operatorname{H}(\Psi(\omega)))) + m + 5}.
\end{aligned}
\tag{8.397}
$$

By the assumption (8.372), and using the fact that $m = \lfloor \alpha n \rfloor$, one has that this quantity approaches 0 in the limit as n approaches infinity. It therefore holds (by Jensen's inequality) that the quantity

$$\int \left\| \tau_U - \mathrm{Tr}_{\mathcal{Z}^{\otimes m}}(\tau_U) \otimes \omega_{\mathcal{Z}}^{\otimes m} \right\|_1 d\eta(U) \tag{8.398}$$

also approaches 0 in the limit as n approaches infinity. The average value of the second term in the final expression of (8.393) may be upper-bounded as

$$\begin{aligned}
&\int \left\| \rho_U - \tau_U \right\|_1 d\eta(U) \\
&= \frac{k^n}{2^m} \int \left\| (\mathbb{1}_{\mathcal{W}^{\otimes n}} \otimes V^{\mathsf{T}} U^{\mathsf{T}})(\xi - \sigma)(\mathbb{1}_{\mathcal{W}^{\otimes n}} \otimes V^{\mathsf{T}} U^{\mathsf{T}})^* \right\|_1 d\eta(U) \\
&\leq \left\| \xi - \sigma \right\|_1 \leq \frac{1}{k^n} \left\| \mathrm{vec}(A_n)\,\mathrm{vec}(A_n)^* - \mathrm{vec}(B_n)\,\mathrm{vec}(B_n)^* \right\|_1 \\
&\leq \frac{2}{k^{n/2}} \left\| A_n - B_n \right\|_2 \leq 6\,\zeta_{n,\varepsilon}^{1/4}
\end{aligned} \tag{8.399}$$

by Lemma 8.52. Once again, this quantity approaches 0 in the limit as n approaches infinity. It follows that the entanglement generation capacity of Φ is at least α, which completes the proof. $\qquad\square$

Corollary 8.54 *Let $\mathcal{X}$ and $\mathcal{Y}$ be complex Euclidean spaces, let $\Phi \in \mathrm{C}(\mathcal{X}, \mathcal{Y})$ be a channel, and let $\sigma \in \mathrm{D}(\mathcal{X})$ be a density operator. The quantum capacity of Φ is lower-bounded by the coherent information of σ through Φ:*

$$\mathrm{I}_{\mathrm{c}}(\sigma; \Phi) \leq \mathrm{Q}(\Phi). \tag{8.400}$$

Proof Observe first that it is a consequence of Theorem 8.53 that

$$\mathrm{I}_{\mathrm{c}}(\omega_{\mathcal{V}}; \Phi) \leq \mathrm{Q}(\Phi) \tag{8.401}$$

for every nontrivial subspace $\mathcal{V} \subseteq \mathcal{X}$, where

$$\omega_{\mathcal{V}} = \frac{\Pi_{\mathcal{V}}}{\dim(\mathcal{V})} \tag{8.402}$$

is the flat state corresponding to the subspace $\mathcal{V}$. To verify that this is so, let $\mathcal{Z}$ be any complex Euclidean space with $\dim(\mathcal{Z}) = \dim(\mathcal{V})$, let $V \in \mathrm{U}(\mathcal{Z}, \mathcal{X})$ be an isometry such that $VV^* = \Pi_{\mathcal{V}}$, and define a channel $\Xi \in \mathrm{C}(\mathcal{Z}, \mathcal{Y})$ as

$$\Xi(Z) = \Phi(VZV^*) \tag{8.403}$$

for all $Z \in \mathrm{L}(\mathcal{Z})$. It is evident that $\mathrm{Q}(\Xi) \leq \mathrm{Q}(\Phi)$; the channel Φ emulates Ξ, so for every positive integer n it holds that $\Phi^{\otimes n}$ emulates every channel that can be emulated by $\Xi^{\otimes n}$. It follows that

$$\begin{aligned}
\mathrm{Q}(\Phi) &\geq \mathrm{Q}(\Xi) = \mathrm{Q}_{\mathrm{EG}}(\Xi) \geq \mathrm{I}_{\mathrm{c}}(\omega_{\mathcal{Z}}; \Xi) \\
&= \mathrm{I}_{\mathrm{c}}(V\omega_{\mathcal{Z}}V^*; \Phi) = \mathrm{I}_{\mathrm{c}}(\omega_{\mathcal{V}}; \Phi),
\end{aligned} \tag{8.404}$$

as claimed.

Now, let $A \in U(\mathcal{X}, \mathcal{Y} \otimes \mathcal{W})$ be an isometry such that

$$\Phi(X) = \operatorname{Tr}_{\mathcal{W}}(AXA^*) \tag{8.405}$$

for all $X \in L(\mathcal{X})$, for a suitable choice of a complex Euclidean space $\mathcal{W}$, and define a channel $\Psi \in C(\mathcal{X}, \mathcal{W})$ as

$$\Psi(X) = \operatorname{Tr}_{\mathcal{Y}}(AXA^*) \tag{8.406}$$

for all $X \in L(\mathcal{X})$. It therefore holds that Ψ is complementary to Φ, so that

$$I_{c}(\sigma; \Phi) = H(\Phi(\sigma)) - H(\Psi(\sigma)). \tag{8.407}$$

Let

$$\sigma = \sum_{a \in \Sigma} p(a) x_a x_a^* \tag{8.408}$$

be a spectral decomposition of σ, and let

$$\omega_{n,\varepsilon} = \frac{\Lambda_{n,\varepsilon}}{\operatorname{Tr}(\Lambda_{n,\varepsilon})} \in D(\mathcal{X}^{\otimes n}) \tag{8.409}$$

for each positive integer n and each positive real number $\varepsilon > 0$, for $\Lambda_{n,\varepsilon}$ denoting the projection onto the ε-strongly typical subspace of $\mathcal{X}^{\otimes n}$, with respect to the spectral decomposition (8.408).

Next, let $\varepsilon > 0$ be a positive real number, to be chosen arbitrarily. By Lemma 8.36, it follows that there must exist a positive integer n_0 such that, for all $n \geq n_0$, one has

$$\left| \frac{1}{n} H(\Phi^{\otimes n}(\omega_{n,\varepsilon})) - H(\Phi(\sigma)) \right| \leq (2 H(\sigma) + H(\Phi(\sigma)) + 1)\varepsilon. \tag{8.410}$$

Along similar lines, there must exist a positive integer n_1 such that, for all $n \geq n_1$, one has

$$\left| \frac{1}{n} H(\Psi^{\otimes n}(\omega_{n,\varepsilon})) - H(\Psi(\sigma)) \right| \leq (2 H(\sigma) + H(\Psi(\sigma)) + 1)\varepsilon. \tag{8.411}$$

There must therefore exist a positive integer n such that

$$\left| \frac{1}{n} I_{c}(\omega_{n,\varepsilon}; \Phi^{\otimes n}) - I_{c}(\sigma; \Phi) \right| \tag{8.412}$$
$$\leq (4 H(\sigma) + H(\Phi(\sigma)) + H(\Psi(\sigma)) + 2)\varepsilon.$$

By the argument presented at the beginning of the proof, it holds that

$$\frac{I_{c}(\omega_{n,\varepsilon}; \Phi^{\otimes n})}{n} \leq \frac{Q(\Phi^{\otimes n})}{n} = Q(\Phi), \tag{8.413}$$

and therefore

$$Q(\Phi) \geq I_c(\sigma; \Phi) - (4\,H(\sigma) + H(\Phi(\sigma)) + H(\Psi(\sigma)) + 2)\varepsilon. \qquad (8.414)$$

As ε has been chosen to be an arbitrary positive real number, it follows that

$$Q(\Phi) \geq I_c(\sigma; \Phi), \qquad (8.415)$$

which completes the proof. $\qquad\qquad\qquad\qquad\qquad\qquad\qquad\qquad\qquad\qquad\square$

Finally, the quantum capacity theorem may be stated and proved.

Theorem 8.55 (Quantum capacity theorem) *Let $\mathcal{X}$ and $\mathcal{Y}$ be complex Euclidean spaces and let $\Phi \in C(\mathcal{X}, \mathcal{Y})$ be a channel. It holds that*

$$Q(\Phi) = \lim_{n\to\infty} \frac{I_c(\Phi^{\otimes n})}{n}. \qquad (8.416)$$

Proof For every positive integer n and every density operator $\sigma \in D(\mathcal{X}^{\otimes n})$, one has

$$I_c(\sigma; \Phi^{\otimes n}) \leq Q(\Phi^{\otimes n}) = n\,Q(\Phi) \qquad (8.417)$$

by Corollary 8.54, and therefore

$$\frac{I_c(\Phi^{\otimes n})}{n} \leq Q(\Phi). \qquad (8.418)$$

If it holds that $Q(\Phi) = 0$, then the theorem evidently follows, so it will be assumed that $Q(\Phi) > 0$ for the remainder of the proof.

Suppose that $\alpha > 0$ is an achievable rate for entanglement generation through Φ, let $\delta \in (0,1)$ be chosen arbitrarily, and set $\varepsilon = \delta^2/2$. Also let $\Gamma = \{0,1\}$ and $\mathcal{Z} = \mathbb{C}^\Gamma$. As α is an achievable rate for entanglement generation through Φ, it holds, for all but finitely many positive integers n and for $m = \lfloor \alpha n \rfloor$, that there must exist a unit vector $u \in \mathcal{X}^{\otimes n} \otimes \mathcal{Z}^{\otimes m}$ and a channel $\Xi \in C(\mathcal{Y}^{\otimes n}, \mathcal{Z}^{\otimes m})$ such that

$$F\Big(2^{-m} \mathrm{vec}(\mathbb{1}_{\mathcal{Z}}^{\otimes m}) \mathrm{vec}(\mathbb{1}_{\mathcal{Z}}^{\otimes m})^*, (\Xi\Phi^{\otimes n} \otimes \mathbb{1}_{L(\mathcal{Z})}^{\otimes m})(uu^*)\Big) > 1 - \varepsilon, \qquad (8.419)$$

and therefore

$$\Big\| 2^{-m} \mathrm{vec}(\mathbb{1}_{\mathcal{Z}}^{\otimes m}) \mathrm{vec}(\mathbb{1}_{\mathcal{Z}}^{\otimes m})^* - (\Xi\Phi^{\otimes n} \otimes \mathbb{1}_{L(\mathcal{Z})}^{\otimes m})(uu^*) \Big\|_1 < 2\delta \qquad (8.420)$$

by one of the Fuchs–van de Graaf inequalities (Theorem 3.33). For any unit vector $u \in \mathcal{X}^{\otimes n} \otimes \mathcal{Z}^{\otimes m}$ for which the inequality (8.420) holds, one concludes from the Fannes–Audenaert inequality (Theorem 5.26) that for

$$\rho = \mathrm{Tr}_{\mathcal{Z}^{\otimes m}}(uu^*) \qquad (8.421)$$

the inequalities

$$H\big((\Xi\Phi^{\otimes n} \otimes \mathbb{1}_{L(\mathcal{Z})}^{\otimes m})(uu^*)\big) \leq 2\delta m + 1 \tag{8.422}$$

and

$$m - H\big(\Xi\Phi^{\otimes n}(\rho)\big) \leq \delta m + 1 \tag{8.423}$$

are satisfied. Together with Proposition 8.15, these inequalities imply that

$$I_c\big(\rho; \Phi^{\otimes n}\big) \geq I_c\big(\rho; \Xi\Phi^{\otimes n}\big) \geq (1 - 3\delta)m - 2. \tag{8.424}$$

As $m = \lfloor \alpha n \rfloor \geq \alpha n - 1$, it follows that

$$\frac{I_c\big(\rho; \Phi^{\otimes n}\big)}{n} \geq (1 - 3\delta)\alpha - \frac{3}{n}. \tag{8.425}$$

It has been proved, for any achievable rate $\alpha > 0$ for entanglement generation through Φ, and for any $\delta > 0$, that

$$(1 - 3\delta)\alpha - \frac{3}{n} \leq \frac{I_c\big(\rho; \Phi^{\otimes n}\big)}{n} \leq Q(\Phi) \tag{8.426}$$

for all but finitely many positive integers n. Because $Q(\Phi)$ is equal to the supremum value of all achievable rates for entanglement generation through Φ, and $\delta > 0$ may be chosen to be arbitrarily small, the required equality (8.416) follows. $\qquad\square$

8.3 Non-Additivity and Super-Activation

Expressions for the classical and quantum capacities of a quantum channel are given by regularizations of the Holevo capacity and maximum coherent information,

$$C(\Phi) = \lim_{n\to\infty} \frac{\chi(\Phi^{\otimes n})}{n} \quad \text{and} \quad Q(\Psi) = \lim_{n\to\infty} \frac{I_c(\Psi^{\otimes n})}{n}, \tag{8.427}$$

as has been established by the Holevo–Schumacher–Westmoreland theorem and quantum capacity theorem (Theorems 8.27 and 8.55). Non-regularized analogues of these formulas do not, in general, hold. In particular, the strict inequalities

$$\chi(\Phi \otimes \Phi) > 2\chi(\Phi) \quad \text{and} \quad I_c(\Psi \otimes \Psi) > 2I_c(\Psi) \tag{8.428}$$

hold for a suitable choice of channels Φ and Ψ, as is demonstrated in the subsections that follow. These examples reveal that the Holevo capacity does not coincide directly with the classical capacity, and likewise for the maximum coherent information and quantum capacity.

With respect to the Holevo capacity, the fact that a strict inequality may hold for some channels Φ in (8.428) will be demonstrated in Section 8.3.1, through the use of Theorem 7.49 from the previous chapter. The existence of such channels is far from obvious, and no explicit examples are known at the time of this book's writing – it is only the existence of such channels that is known. The now falsified conjecture that the equality

$$\chi(\Phi_0 \otimes \Phi_1) = \chi(\Phi_0) + \chi(\Phi_1) \tag{8.429}$$

should hold for all choices of channels Φ_0 and Φ_1 was known for some time as the *additivity conjecture*.

In contrast, it is not difficult to find an example of a channel Ψ for which a strict inequality in (8.428) holds. There are, in fact, very striking examples of channels that go beyond the demonstration of non-additivity of maximum coherent information. In particular, one may find channels Ψ_0 and Ψ_1 such that both Ψ_0 and Ψ_1 have zero quantum capacity, and therefore

$$I_c(\Psi_0) = I_c(\Psi_1) = 0, \tag{8.430}$$

but for which

$$I_c(\Psi_0 \otimes \Psi_1) > 0, \tag{8.431}$$

and therefore $\Psi_0 \otimes \Psi_1$ has nonzero quantum capacity. This phenomenon is known as *super-activation*, and is discussed in Section 8.3.2. From such a choice of channels Ψ_0 and Ψ_1, the construction of a channel Ψ for which the strict inequality (8.428) holds is possible.

8.3.1 Non-Additivity of the Holevo Capacity

The fact that there exists a channel Φ for which

$$\chi(\Phi \otimes \Phi) > 2\chi(\Phi) \tag{8.432}$$

is demonstrated below. The proof makes use of Theorem 7.49, together with two basic ideas: one concerns the *direct sum* of two channels, and the other is a construction that relates the minimum output entropy of a given channel to the Holevo capacity of a channel constructed from the one given.

Direct Sums of Channels and Their Minimum Output Entropy

The direct sum of two maps is defined as follows. (One may also consider direct sums of more than two maps, but it is sufficient for the needs of the present section to consider the case of just two maps.)

Definition 8.56   Let $\mathcal{X}_0$, $\mathcal{X}_1$, $\mathcal{Y}_0$, and $\mathcal{Y}_1$ be complex Euclidean spaces and let $\Phi_0 \in \mathrm{T}(\mathcal{X}_0, \mathcal{Y}_0)$ and $\Phi_1 \in \mathrm{T}(\mathcal{X}_1, \mathcal{Y}_1)$ be maps. The direct sum of Φ_0 and Φ_1 is the map $\Phi_0 \oplus \Phi_1 \in \mathrm{T}(\mathcal{X}_0 \oplus \mathcal{X}_1, \mathcal{Y}_0 \oplus \mathcal{Y}_1)$ defined as

$$(\Phi_0 \oplus \Phi_1)\begin{pmatrix} X_0 & \cdot \\ \cdot & X_1 \end{pmatrix} = \begin{pmatrix} \Phi_0(X_0) & 0 \\ 0 & \Phi_1(X_1) \end{pmatrix} \qquad (8.433)$$

for every $X_0 \in \mathrm{L}(\mathcal{X}_0)$ and $X_1 \in \mathrm{L}(\mathcal{X}_1)$. The dots in (8.433) indicate arbitrary operators in $\mathrm{L}(\mathcal{X}_1, \mathcal{X}_0)$ and $\mathrm{L}(\mathcal{X}_0, \mathcal{X}_1)$ that have no influence on the output of the map $\Phi_0 \oplus \Phi_1$.

The direct sum of two channels is also a channel, as is established by the following straightforward proposition.

Proposition 8.57   *Let $\mathcal{X}_0$, $\mathcal{X}_1$, $\mathcal{Y}_0$, and $\mathcal{Y}_1$ be complex Euclidean spaces and let $\Phi_0 \in \mathrm{C}(\mathcal{X}_0, \mathcal{Y}_0)$ and $\Phi_1 \in \mathrm{C}(\mathcal{X}_1, \mathcal{Y}_1)$ be channels. The direct sum of Φ_0 and Φ_1 is a channel: $\Phi_0 \oplus \Phi_1 \in \mathrm{C}(\mathcal{X}_0 \oplus \mathcal{X}_1, \mathcal{Y}_0 \oplus \mathcal{Y}_1)$.*

Proof   It is immediate from the definition of the direct sum of Φ_0 and Φ_1 that $\Phi_0 \oplus \Phi_1$ is trace-preserving, so it suffices to prove that $\Phi_0 \oplus \Phi_1$ is completely positive. Because Φ_0 and Φ_1 are completely positive, Kraus representations of the form

$$\Phi_0(X_0) = \sum_{a \in \Sigma} A_a X_0 A_a^* \quad \text{and} \quad \Phi_1(X_1) = \sum_{b \in \Gamma} B_b X_1 B_b^* \qquad (8.434)$$

of these maps must exist. Through a direct computation, one may verify that

$$\begin{aligned} (\Phi_0 \oplus \Phi_1)(X) &= \sum_{a \in \Sigma} \begin{pmatrix} A_a & 0 \\ 0 & 0 \end{pmatrix} X \begin{pmatrix} A_a & 0 \\ 0 & 0 \end{pmatrix}^* \\ &\quad + \sum_{b \in \Gamma} \begin{pmatrix} 0 & 0 \\ 0 & B_b \end{pmatrix} X \begin{pmatrix} 0 & 0 \\ 0 & B_b \end{pmatrix}^* \end{aligned} \qquad (8.435)$$

for all $X \in \mathrm{L}(\mathcal{X}_0 \oplus \mathcal{X}_1)$. It follows that $\Phi_0 \oplus \Phi_1$ is completely positive, as required. $\square$

By Theorem 7.49, there exist channels Φ_0 and Φ_1 such that

$$\mathrm{H}_{\min}(\Phi_0 \otimes \Phi_1) < \mathrm{H}_{\min}(\Phi_0) + \mathrm{H}_{\min}(\Phi_1). \qquad (8.436)$$

It is possible to obtain, from this fact, an example of a single channel Φ such that

$$\mathrm{H}_{\min}(\Phi \otimes \Phi) < 2\,\mathrm{H}_{\min}(\Phi). \qquad (8.437)$$

The following corollary (to Theorem 7.49) establishes that this is so.

Corollary 8.58 *There exists a channel* $\Phi \in C(\mathcal{X}, \mathcal{Y})$, *for some choice of complex Euclidean spaces* $\mathcal{X}$ *and* $\mathcal{Y}$, *such that*

$$H_{\min}(\Phi \otimes \Phi) < 2\, H_{\min}(\Phi). \tag{8.438}$$

Proof By Theorem 7.49, there exist complex Euclidean spaces $\mathcal{Z}$ and $\mathcal{W}$ and channels $\Psi_0, \Psi_1 \in C(\mathcal{Z}, \mathcal{W})$ such that

$$H_{\min}(\Psi_0 \otimes \Psi_1) < H_{\min}(\Psi_0) + H_{\min}(\Psi_1). \tag{8.439}$$

Assume that such a choice of channels has been fixed for the remainder of the proof.

Let $\sigma_0, \sigma_1 \in D(\mathcal{Z})$ be density operators satisfying

$$H(\Psi_0(\sigma_0)) = H_{\min}(\Psi_0) \quad \text{and} \quad H(\Psi_1(\sigma_1)) = H_{\min}(\Psi_1), \tag{8.440}$$

and define channels $\Phi_0, \Phi_1 \in C(\mathcal{Z}, \mathcal{W} \otimes \mathcal{W})$ as

$$\Phi_0(Z) = \Psi_0(Z) \otimes \Psi_1(\sigma_1) \quad \text{and} \quad \Phi_1(Z) = \Psi_0(\sigma_0) \otimes \Psi_1(Z) \tag{8.441}$$

for all $Z \in L(\mathcal{Z})$. Observe that

$$H_{\min}(\Phi_0) = H_{\min}(\Psi_0) + H_{\min}(\Psi_1) = H_{\min}(\Phi_1) \tag{8.442}$$

and

$$\begin{aligned} H_{\min}(\Phi_0 \otimes \Phi_1) &= H_{\min}(\Psi_0 \otimes \Psi_1) + H_{\min}(\Psi_0) + H_{\min}(\Psi_1) \\ &< 2\, H_{\min}(\Psi_0) + 2\, H_{\min}(\Psi_0) = H_{\min}(\Phi_0) + H_{\min}(\Phi_1). \end{aligned} \tag{8.443}$$

Finally, let $\mathcal{X} = \mathcal{Z} \oplus \mathcal{Z}$ and $\mathcal{Y} = (\mathcal{W} \otimes \mathcal{W}) \oplus (\mathcal{W} \otimes \mathcal{W})$, and define $\Phi \in C(\mathcal{X}, \mathcal{Y})$ as

$$\Phi = \Phi_0 \oplus \Phi_1. \tag{8.444}$$

It remains to verify that $H_{\min}(\Phi \otimes \Phi) < 2\, H_{\min}(\Phi)$.

For any state $\rho \in D(\mathcal{Z} \oplus \mathcal{Z})$, one may write

$$\rho = \begin{pmatrix} \lambda \rho_0 & Z \\ Z^* & (1-\lambda)\rho_1 \end{pmatrix} \tag{8.445}$$

for some choice of $\lambda \in [0, 1]$, $\rho_0, \rho_1 \in D(\mathcal{Z})$, and $Z \in L(\mathcal{Z})$. Evaluating Φ on such a state ρ yields

$$\Phi(\rho) = \begin{pmatrix} \lambda \Phi_0(\rho_0) & 0 \\ 0 & (1-\lambda)\Phi_1(\rho_1) \end{pmatrix}, \tag{8.446}$$

so that

$$H(\Phi(\rho)) = \lambda\, H(\Phi_0(\rho_0)) + (1-\lambda)\, H(\Phi_1(\rho_1)) + H(\lambda, 1-\lambda). \tag{8.447}$$

One concludes that

$$H_{\min}(\Phi) = H_{\min}(\Phi_0) = H_{\min}(\Phi_1). \tag{8.448}$$

Finally, define an isometry $V \in U(\mathcal{Z} \otimes \mathcal{Z}, (\mathcal{Z} \oplus \mathcal{Z}) \otimes (\mathcal{Z} \oplus \mathcal{Z}))$ by the equation

$$V(z_0 \otimes z_1) = (z_0 \oplus 0) \otimes (0 \oplus z_1) \tag{8.449}$$

holding for all $z_0, z_1 \in \mathcal{Z}$. For every choice of operators $Z_0, Z_1 \in L(\mathcal{Z})$ it therefore holds that

$$V(Z_0 \otimes Z_1)V^* = \begin{pmatrix} Z_0 & 0 \\ 0 & 0 \end{pmatrix} \otimes \begin{pmatrix} 0 & 0 \\ 0 & Z_1 \end{pmatrix}, \tag{8.450}$$

so that

$$(\Phi \otimes \Phi)(V(Z_0 \otimes Z_1)V^*) = \begin{pmatrix} \Phi_0(Z_0) & 0 \\ 0 & 0 \end{pmatrix} \otimes \begin{pmatrix} 0 & 0 \\ 0 & \Phi_1(Z_1) \end{pmatrix}. \tag{8.451}$$

One concludes that

$$H((\Phi \otimes \Phi)(V\xi V^*)) = H((\Phi_0 \otimes \Phi_1)(\xi)) \tag{8.452}$$

for every density operator $\xi \in D(\mathcal{Z} \otimes \mathcal{Z})$, and therefore

$$H_{\min}(\Phi \otimes \Phi) \leq H_{\min}(\Phi_0 \otimes \Phi_1) < H_{\min}(\Phi_0) + H_{\min}(\Phi_1) = 2\,H_{\min}(\Phi), \tag{8.453}$$

as required. $\square$

From Low Minimum Output Entropy to High Holevo Capacity

The construction to be described below allows one to conclude that there exists a channel Ψ for which the Holevo capacity is super-additive, meaning that

$$\chi(\Psi \otimes \Psi) > 2\chi(\Psi), \tag{8.454}$$

by means of Corollary 8.58.

Suppose that $\mathcal{X}$ and $\mathcal{Y}$ are complex Euclidean spaces and $\Phi \in C(\mathcal{X}, \mathcal{Y})$ is an arbitrary channel. Suppose further that Σ is an alphabet and

$$\{U_a : a \in \Sigma\} \subset U(\mathcal{Y}) \tag{8.455}$$

is a collection of unitary operators with the property that the completely depolarizing channel $\Omega \in C(\mathcal{Y})$ is given by

$$\Omega(Y) = \frac{1}{|\Sigma|} \sum_{a \in \Sigma} U_a Y U_a^* \tag{8.456}$$

for all $Y \in L(\mathcal{Y})$. (Such a collection may, for instance, be derived from the discrete Weyl operators defined in Section 4.1.2.) Let $\mathcal{Z} = \mathbb{C}^\Sigma$ and define a new channel $\Psi \in C(\mathcal{Z} \otimes \mathcal{X}, \mathcal{Y})$ by the equation

$$\Psi(E_{a,b} \otimes X) = \begin{cases} U_a \Phi(X) U_a^* & \text{if } a = b \\ 0 & \text{otherwises} \end{cases} \tag{8.457}$$

holding for all $a, b \in \Sigma$ and $X \in L(\mathcal{X})$.

The action of the channel Ψ may alternatively be described as follows. A pair of registers (Z, X) is taken as input, and a measurement of the register Z with respect to the standard basis of $\mathcal{Z}$ is made, yielding a symbol $a \in \Sigma$. The channel Φ is applied to X, resulting in a register Y, and the unitary channel described by U_a is applied to Y. The measurement outcome a is discarded and Y is taken to be the output of the channel.

As the following proposition shows, the Holevo capacity of the channel Ψ constructed in this way is determined by the minimum output entropy of the channel Φ.

Proposition 8.59 *Let $\Phi \in C(\mathcal{X}, \mathcal{Y})$ be a channel, for complex Euclidean spaces $\mathcal{X}$ and $\mathcal{Y}$, let Σ be an alphabet, let $\{U_a : a \in \Sigma\} \subset U(\mathcal{Y})$ be a collection of unitary operators for which the equation (8.456) holds for all $Y \in L(\mathcal{Y})$, let $\mathcal{Z} = \mathbb{C}^\Sigma$, and let $\Psi \in C(\mathcal{Z} \otimes \mathcal{X}, \mathcal{Y})$ be a channel defined by the equation (8.457) holding for all $a, b \in \Sigma$ and $X \in L(\mathcal{X})$. It holds that*

$$\chi(\Psi) = \log(\dim(\mathcal{Y})) - H_{\min}(\Phi). \tag{8.458}$$

Proof Consider first the ensemble $\eta : \Sigma \to \text{Pos}(\mathcal{Z} \otimes \mathcal{X})$ defined as

$$\eta(a) = \frac{1}{|\Sigma|} E_{a,a} \otimes \rho \tag{8.459}$$

for all $a \in \Sigma$, where $\rho \in D(\mathcal{X})$ is any state for which

$$H_{\min}(\Phi) = H(\Phi(\rho)). \tag{8.460}$$

One has

$$\chi(\Psi(\eta)) = H\left(\frac{1}{|\Sigma|} \sum_{a \in \Sigma} U_a \Phi(\rho) U_a^*\right) - \frac{1}{|\Sigma|} \sum_{a \in \Sigma} H(U_a \Phi(\rho) U_a^*)$$

$$= H(\Omega(\rho)) - H(\Phi(\rho))$$

$$= \log(\dim(\mathcal{Y})) - H_{\min}(\Phi). \tag{8.461}$$

It therefore holds that

$$\chi(\Psi) \geq \log(\dim(\mathcal{Y})) - H_{\min}(\Phi). \tag{8.462}$$

Next, consider an arbitrary state $\sigma \in D(\mathcal{Z} \otimes \mathcal{X})$. For $\Delta \in C(\mathcal{Z})$ denoting the completely dephasing channel, one may write

$$(\Delta \otimes \mathbb{1}_{L(\mathcal{X})})(\sigma) = \sum_{a \in \Sigma} q(a) E_{a,a} \otimes \xi_a, \tag{8.463}$$

for some choice of a probability vector $q \in \mathcal{P}(\Sigma)$ and a collection of states

$$\{\xi_a : a \in \Sigma\} \subseteq D(\mathcal{X}). \tag{8.464}$$

It holds that

$$\Psi(\sigma) = \sum_{a \in \Sigma} q(a) U_a \Phi(\xi_a) U_a^*, \tag{8.465}$$

and therefore

$$H(\Psi(\sigma)) \geq \sum_{a \in \Sigma} q(a) H(\Phi(\xi_a)) \geq H_{\min}(\Phi) \tag{8.466}$$

by the concavity of the von Neumann entropy function (Theorem 5.23).

Finally, consider an arbitrary ensemble $\eta : \Gamma \to \text{Pos}(\mathcal{Z} \otimes \mathcal{X})$, written as

$$\eta(b) = p(b) \sigma_b \tag{8.467}$$

for each $b \in \Gamma$, for $p \in \mathcal{P}(\Gamma)$ being a probability vector and

$$\{\sigma_b : b \in \Gamma\} \subseteq D(\mathcal{Z} \otimes \mathcal{X}) \tag{8.468}$$

being a collection of states. It holds that

$$\chi(\Psi(\eta)) = H\left(\sum_{b \in \Gamma} p(b) \Psi(\sigma_b)\right) - \sum_{b \in \Gamma} p(b) H(\Psi(\sigma_b)) \\ \leq \log(\dim(\mathcal{Y})) - H_{\min}(\Phi). \tag{8.469}$$

The ensemble η was chosen arbitrarily, and therefore

$$\chi(\Psi) \leq \log(\dim(\mathcal{Y})) - H_{\min}(\Phi), \tag{8.470}$$

which completes the proof. $\qquad\square$

Theorem 8.60 *There exists a channel $\Psi \in C(\mathcal{W}, \mathcal{Y})$, for some choice of complex Euclidean spaces $\mathcal{W}$ and $\mathcal{Y}$, such that*

$$\chi(\Psi \otimes \Psi) > 2\chi(\Psi). \tag{8.471}$$

Proof By Corollary 8.58 there exist complex Euclidean spaces $\mathcal{X}$ and $\mathcal{Y}$ and a channel $\Phi \in C(\mathcal{X}, \mathcal{Y})$ for which the inequality

$$H_{\min}(\Phi \otimes \Phi) < 2 H_{\min}(\Phi) \tag{8.472}$$

holds. Let Σ be an alphabet and let

$$\{U_a : a \in \Sigma\} \subset \mathrm{U}(\mathcal{Y}) \tag{8.473}$$

be a collection of unitary operators for which

$$\Omega(Y) = \frac{1}{|\Sigma|} \sum_{a \in \Sigma} U_a Y U_a^* \tag{8.474}$$

for all $Y \in \mathrm{L}(\mathcal{Y})$. Also let $\mathcal{Z} = \mathbb{C}^\Sigma$ and let $\Psi \in \mathrm{C}(\mathcal{Z} \otimes \mathcal{X}, \mathcal{Y})$ be the channel defined by the equation (8.457) above for all $a, b \in \Sigma$ and $X \in \mathrm{L}(\mathcal{X})$.

Up to a permutation of the tensor factors of its input space, $\Psi \otimes \Psi$ is equivalent to the channel $\Xi \in \mathrm{C}((\mathcal{Z} \otimes \mathcal{Z}) \otimes (\mathcal{X} \otimes \mathcal{X}), \mathcal{Y} \otimes \mathcal{Y})$ that would be obtained from the channel $\Phi \otimes \Phi$ by means of a similar construction, using the collection of unitary operators

$$\{U_a \otimes U_b : (a, b) \in \Sigma \times \Sigma\} \subset \mathrm{U}(\mathcal{Y} \otimes \mathcal{Y}). \tag{8.475}$$

It therefore follows from Proposition 8.59 that

$$\chi(\Psi) = \log(\dim(\mathcal{Y})) - \mathrm{H}_{\min}(\Phi) \tag{8.476}$$

while

$$\chi(\Psi \otimes \Psi) = \log(\dim(\mathcal{Y} \otimes \mathcal{Y})) - \mathrm{H}_{\min}(\Phi \otimes \Phi) > 2\chi(\Psi). \tag{8.477}$$

Taking $\mathcal{W} = \mathcal{Z} \otimes \mathcal{X}$, the theorem is therefore proved. $\qquad\square$

One consequence of this theorem is that an analogous statement to the Holevo–Schumacher–Westmoreland theorem (Theorem 8.27), but without a regularization, does not hold in general. That is, because

$$\mathrm{C}(\Phi) \geq \frac{\chi(\Phi \otimes \Phi)}{2}, \tag{8.478}$$

it is the case that $\mathrm{C}(\Phi) > \chi(\Phi)$ for some choices of a channel Φ.

8.3.2 Super-Activation of Quantum Channel Capacity

The purpose of the present subsection is to demonstrate the phenomenon of *super-activation*, in which the tensor product of two zero-capacity channels have positive quantum capacity. As a byproduct, one obtains an example of a channel Ψ satisfying $\mathrm{I}_c(\Psi \otimes \Psi) > 2\mathrm{I}_c(\Psi)$.

Two Classes of Zero-Capacity Channels

It is possible to prove that certain classes of channels have zero quantum capacity. Self-complementary channels and channels whose Choi operators are PPT fall into this category. (See Section 6.2.3 for more on PPT operators and states.) The following proposition establishes that channels whose Choi operators are PPT must have zero capacity.

Proposition 8.61 *Let $\Phi \in C(\mathcal{X}, \mathcal{Y})$ be a channel, for complex Euclidean spaces $\mathcal{X}$ and $\mathcal{Y}$, such that $J(\Phi) \in \mathrm{PPT}(\mathcal{Y} : \mathcal{X})$. It holds that $\mathrm{Q}(\Phi) = 0$.*

Proof The first step of the proof is to establish that, for every choice of a complex Euclidean space $\mathcal{W}$ and a state $\rho \in D(\mathcal{X} \otimes \mathcal{W})$, one has

$$\left(\Phi \otimes \mathbb{1}_{L(\mathcal{W})}\right)(\rho) \in \mathrm{PPT}(\mathcal{Y} : \mathcal{W}). \tag{8.479}$$

Toward this goal, observe that for any choice of a complex Euclidean space $\mathcal{W}$ and a positive semidefinite operator $P \in \mathrm{Pos}(\mathcal{X} \otimes \mathcal{W})$, there must exist a completely positive map $\Psi_P \in \mathrm{CP}(\mathcal{X}, \mathcal{W})$ satisfying

$$P = \left(\mathbb{1}_{L(\mathcal{X})} \otimes \Psi_P\right)\left(\mathrm{vec}(\mathbb{1}_{\mathcal{X}}) \mathrm{vec}(\mathbb{1}_{\mathcal{X}})^*\right). \tag{8.480}$$

The map Ψ_P is, in fact, uniquely defined by this requirement; one may obtain its Choi representation by swapping the tensor factors of P. It follows that, for any complex Euclidean space $\mathcal{W}$ and any state $\rho \in D(\mathcal{X} \otimes \mathcal{W})$, one must have

$$
\begin{aligned}
&\left(\mathrm{T} \otimes \mathbb{1}_{L(\mathcal{W})}\right)\left(\left(\Phi \otimes \mathbb{1}_{L(\mathcal{W})}\right)(\rho)\right) \\
&= \left(\mathbb{1}_{L(\mathcal{Y})} \otimes \Psi_\rho\right)\left(\left(\mathrm{T} \otimes \mathbb{1}_{L(\mathcal{X})}\right)(J(\Phi))\right) \in \mathrm{Pos}(\mathcal{Y} : \mathcal{W})
\end{aligned}
\tag{8.481}
$$

by virtue of the fact that Ψ_ρ is completely positive and $J(\Phi) \in \mathrm{PPT}(\mathcal{Y} : \mathcal{X})$, which establishes (8.479).

As $J(\Phi) \in \mathrm{PPT}(\mathcal{Y} : \mathcal{X})$, it follows that

$$J(\Phi^{\otimes n}) \in \mathrm{PPT}(\mathcal{Y}^{\otimes n} : \mathcal{X}^{\otimes n}) \tag{8.482}$$

for every positive integer n. For every choice of positive integers n and m, for $\mathcal{Z} = \mathbb{C}^\Gamma$ for $\Gamma = \{0, 1\}$, and for any channel $\Xi \in C(\mathcal{Y}^{\otimes n}, \mathcal{Z}^{\otimes m})$, it therefore holds that

$$\left(\Xi \Phi^{\otimes n} \otimes \mathbb{1}_{L(\mathcal{Z})}^{\otimes m}\right)(\rho) \in \mathrm{PPT}(\mathcal{Z}^{\otimes m} : \mathcal{Z}^{\otimes m}) \tag{8.483}$$

for every state $\rho \in D(\mathcal{X}^{\otimes n} \otimes \mathcal{Z}^{\otimes m})$. By Proposition 6.42, one therefore has

$$\mathrm{F}\left(2^{-m} \mathrm{vec}(\mathbb{1}_{\mathcal{Z}}^{\otimes m}) \mathrm{vec}(\mathbb{1}_{\mathcal{Z}}^{\otimes m})^*, \left(\Xi \Phi^{\otimes n} \otimes \mathbb{1}_{L(\mathcal{Z})}^{\otimes m}\right)(\rho)\right) \leq 2^{-m/2}. \tag{8.484}$$

For every choice of a positive real number $\alpha > 0$, it must therefore be the case that α fails to be an achievable rate for entanglement generation through Φ. Consequently, Φ has zero capacity for entanglement generation, which implies $Q(\Phi) = 0$ by Theorem 8.46. $\qquad\square$

The second category of channels mentioned above having zero quantum capacity are *self-complementary* channels. These are channels $\Phi \in C(\mathcal{X}, \mathcal{Y})$ such that there exists an isometry $A \in U(\mathcal{X}, \mathcal{Y} \otimes \mathcal{Y})$ such that

$$\Phi(X) = (\mathbb{1}_{L(\mathcal{Y})} \otimes \mathrm{Tr})(AXA^*) = (\mathrm{Tr} \otimes \mathbb{1}_{L(\mathcal{Y})})(AXA^*) \qquad (8.485)$$

for every $X \in L(\mathcal{X})$. By Proposition 8.17, the coherent information of every state $\sigma \in D(\mathcal{X})$ through a self-complementary channel Φ must be zero:

$$I_c(\sigma; \Phi) = H(\Phi(\sigma)) - H(\Phi(\sigma)) = 0. \qquad (8.486)$$

As every tensor power of a self-complementary channel is necessarily self-complementary, the quantum capacity theorem (Theorem 8.55) implies that self-complementary channels have zero quantum capacity. The following proposition states a more general variant of this observation.

Proposition 8.62 *Let $\Phi \in C(\mathcal{X}, \mathcal{Y})$ and $\Psi \in C(\mathcal{X}, \mathcal{Z})$ be complementary channels, for complex Euclidean spaces $\mathcal{X}$, $\mathcal{Y}$, and $\mathcal{Z}$, and suppose that there exists a channel $\Xi \in C(\mathcal{Z}, \mathcal{Y})$ such that $\Phi = \Xi\Psi$. It holds that Φ has zero quantum capacity: $Q(\Phi) = 0$.*

Proof Let n be a positive integer and let $\sigma \in D(\mathcal{X}^{\otimes n})$ be a state. One has

$$I_c(\sigma; \Phi^{\otimes n}) = I_c(\sigma; \Xi^{\otimes n}\Psi^{\otimes n}) \leq I_c(\sigma; \Psi^{\otimes n}) \qquad (8.487)$$

by Proposition 8.15. Because Ψ is complementary to Φ, it holds that $\Psi^{\otimes n}$ is complementary to $\Phi^{\otimes n}$, and therefore

$$\begin{aligned} I_c(\sigma; \Phi^{\otimes n}) &= H(\Phi^{\otimes n}(\sigma)) - H(\Psi^{\otimes n}(\sigma)) \\ &= -I_c(\sigma; \Psi^{\otimes n}) \leq -I_c(\sigma; \Phi^{\otimes n}), \end{aligned} \qquad (8.488)$$

which implies

$$I_c(\sigma; \Phi^{\otimes n}) \leq 0. \qquad (8.489)$$

As this is so for every choice of n and every state $\sigma \in D(\mathcal{X}^{\otimes n})$, it follows that $Q(\Phi) = 0$ by Theorem 8.55. $\qquad\square$

Remark Channels of the form $\Phi \in C(\mathcal{X}, \mathcal{Y})$ for which there exist a channel $\Psi \in C(\mathcal{X}, \mathcal{Z})$ complementary to Φ, as well as a channel $\Xi \in C(\mathcal{Z}, \mathcal{Y})$ for which $\Phi = \Xi\Psi$, are known as *anti-degradable channels*.

50%-Erasure Channels

A *50%-erasure channel* is a simple type of self-complementary channel that plays a special role in the example of super-activation to be presented below. For any choice of a complex Euclidean space $\mathcal{X}$, the 50%-erasure channel defined with respect to $\mathcal{X}$ is the channel $\Xi \in C(\mathcal{X}, \mathbb{C} \oplus \mathcal{X})$ defined for each $X \in L(\mathcal{X})$ as

$$\Xi(X) = \frac{1}{2} \begin{pmatrix} \mathrm{Tr}(X) & 0 \\ 0 & X \end{pmatrix}. \tag{8.490}$$

Intuitively speaking, a 50%-erasure channel acts as the identity channel with probability $1/2$, and otherwise its input is erased. Under the assumption that $\mathcal{X} = \mathbb{C}^\Sigma$, for Σ being a given alphabet, one may associate the complex Euclidean space $\mathbb{C} \oplus \mathcal{X}$ with $\mathbb{C}^{\{\#\} \cup \Sigma}$, for $\#$ being a special *blank symbol* that is not contained in Σ. With this interpretation, the event that the input is erased may be associated with the blank symbol $\#$ being produced, so that

$$\Xi(X) = \frac{1}{2} X + \frac{1}{2} \mathrm{Tr}(X) E_{\#,\#} \tag{8.491}$$

for every $X \in L(\mathcal{X})$.

For every choice of $\mathcal{X}$, the 50%-erasure channel $\Xi \in C(\mathcal{X}, \mathbb{C} \oplus \mathcal{X})$ is self-complementary: one has

$$\Xi(X) = (\mathrm{Tr} \otimes \mathbb{1})(AXA^*) = (\mathbb{1} \otimes \mathrm{Tr})(AXA^*) \tag{8.492}$$

for $A \in U(\mathcal{X}, (\mathbb{C} \oplus \mathcal{X}) \otimes (\mathbb{C} \oplus \mathcal{X}))$ being the isometry defined as

$$Ax = \frac{1}{\sqrt{2}}(0 \oplus x) \otimes (1 \oplus 0) + \frac{1}{\sqrt{2}}(1 \oplus 0) \otimes (0 \oplus x) \tag{8.493}$$

for every $x \in \mathcal{X}$. It follows that $Q(\Xi) = 0$.

A Theorem of Smith and Yard

The following theorem allows one to prove lower bounds on the maximum coherent information of a channel tensored with a 50%-erasure channel on a sufficiently large space. For a suitable choice of a zero-capacity channel tensored with a 50%-erasure channel, the theorem leads to a demonstration of the super-activation phenomenon.

Theorem 8.63 (Smith–Yard) *Let $\mathcal{X}$, $\mathcal{Y}$, and $\mathcal{Z}$ be complex Euclidean spaces, let $A \in U(\mathcal{X}, \mathcal{Y} \otimes \mathcal{Z})$ be an isometry, and let $\Phi \in C(\mathcal{X}, \mathcal{Y})$ and $\Psi \in C(\mathcal{X}, \mathcal{Z})$ be complementary channels defined as*

$$\Phi(X) = \mathrm{Tr}_{\mathcal{Z}}(AXA^*) \quad and \quad \Psi(X) = \mathrm{Tr}_{\mathcal{Y}}(AXA^*) \tag{8.494}$$

for every $X \in L(\mathcal{X})$. Also let Σ be an alphabet, let $\eta: \Sigma \to \text{Pos}(\mathcal{X})$ be an ensemble of states, let $\mathcal{W}$ be a complex Euclidean space satisfying

$$\dim(\mathcal{W}) \geq \sum_{a \in \Sigma} \text{rank}(\eta(a)), \tag{8.495}$$

and let $\Xi \in C(\mathcal{W}, \mathbb{C} \oplus \mathcal{W})$ denote the 50%-erasure channel on $\mathcal{W}$. There exists a density operator $\rho \in D(\mathcal{X} \otimes \mathcal{W})$ such that

$$I_c(\rho; \Phi \otimes \Xi) = \frac{1}{2}\chi(\Phi(\eta)) - \frac{1}{2}\chi(\Psi(\eta)). \tag{8.496}$$

Proof By the assumption

$$\dim(\mathcal{W}) \geq \sum_{a \in \Sigma} \text{rank}(\eta(a)), \tag{8.497}$$

one may choose a collection of vectors $\{u_a: a \in \Sigma\} \subset \mathcal{X} \otimes \mathcal{W}$ for which it holds that

$$\text{Tr}_{\mathcal{W}}(u_a u_a^*) = \eta(a) \tag{8.498}$$

for each $a \in \Sigma$, and for which

$$\{\text{Tr}_{\mathcal{X}}(u_a u_a^*): a \in \Sigma\} \tag{8.499}$$

is an orthogonal set of operators. Let $\mathcal{V} = \mathbb{C}^{\Sigma}$, define a unit vector

$$u = \sum_{a \in \Sigma} e_a \otimes u_a \in \mathcal{V} \otimes \mathcal{X} \otimes \mathcal{W}, \tag{8.500}$$

and let $\rho = \text{Tr}_{\mathcal{V}}(uu^*)$. One may observe that, by virtue of the fact that (8.499) is an orthogonal set, it holds that

$$\text{Tr}_{\mathcal{W}}(uu^*) = \sum_{a \in \Sigma} E_{a,a} \otimes \eta(a). \tag{8.501}$$

For the unit vector $v \in \mathcal{V} \otimes \mathcal{Y} \otimes \mathcal{Z} \otimes \mathcal{W}$ defined as $v = (\mathbb{1}_{\mathcal{V}} \otimes A \otimes \mathbb{1}_{\mathcal{W}})u$, it therefore holds that

$$\text{Tr}_{\mathcal{W}}(vv^*) = \sum_{a \in \Sigma} E_{a,a} \otimes A\eta(a)A^*. \tag{8.502}$$

The 50%-erasure channel Ξ has the property that

$$H((\Phi \otimes \Xi)(\rho)) = \frac{1}{2}H((\Phi \otimes \mathbb{1}_{L(\mathcal{W})})(\rho)) + \frac{1}{2}H(\Phi(\text{Tr}_{\mathcal{W}}(\rho))) + 1, \tag{8.503}$$

and likewise for the channel Ψ in place of Φ. As Ψ is complementary to Φ

and Ξ is self-complementary, it follows that

$$
\begin{aligned}
\mathrm{I_c}(\rho; \Phi \otimes \Xi) &= \mathrm{H}((\Phi \otimes \Xi)(\rho)) - \mathrm{H}((\Psi \otimes \Xi)(\rho)) \\
&= \frac{1}{2}\mathrm{H}((\Phi \otimes \mathbb{1}_{\mathrm{L}(\mathcal{W})})(\rho)) - \frac{1}{2}\mathrm{H}((\Psi \otimes \mathbb{1}_{\mathrm{L}(\mathcal{W})})(\rho)) \\
&\quad + \frac{1}{2}\mathrm{H}(\Phi(\mathrm{Tr}_{\mathcal{W}}(\rho))) - \frac{1}{2}\mathrm{H}(\Psi(\mathrm{Tr}_{\mathcal{W}}(\rho))).
\end{aligned}
\tag{8.504}
$$

Now, let V, Y, Z, and W be registers corresponding to the spaces $\mathcal{V}$, $\mathcal{Y}$, $\mathcal{Z}$, and $\mathcal{W}$, respectively, and consider the situation in which the compound register $(\mathsf{V}, \mathsf{Y}, \mathsf{Z}, \mathsf{W})$ is in the pure state vv^*. It holds that

$$
\begin{aligned}
\mathrm{H}((\Phi \otimes \mathbb{1}_{\mathrm{L}(\mathcal{W})})(\rho)) &= \mathrm{H}(\mathsf{Y}, \mathsf{W}) = \mathrm{H}(\mathsf{V}, \mathsf{Z}), \\
\mathrm{H}((\Psi \otimes \mathbb{1}_{\mathrm{L}(\mathcal{W})})(\rho)) &= \mathrm{H}(\mathsf{Z}, \mathsf{W}) = \mathrm{H}(\mathsf{V}, \mathsf{Y}), \\
\mathrm{H}(\Phi(\mathrm{Tr}_{\mathcal{W}}(\rho))) &= \mathrm{H}(\mathsf{Y}), \\
\mathrm{H}(\Psi(\mathrm{Tr}_{\mathcal{W}}(\rho))) &= \mathrm{H}(\mathsf{Z}),
\end{aligned}
\tag{8.505}
$$

and therefore

$$
\mathrm{I_c}(\rho; \Phi \otimes \Xi) = \frac{1}{2}\mathrm{I}(\mathsf{V} : \mathsf{Y}) - \frac{1}{2}\mathrm{I}(\mathsf{V} : \mathsf{Z}) = \frac{1}{2}\chi(\Phi(\eta)) - \frac{1}{2}\chi(\Psi(\eta)),
\tag{8.506}
$$

as required. $\qquad\square$

An Explicit Example of Super-Activation

An example of the super-activation phenomenon, based on Theorem 8.63, will now be described. The first step is to define a zero-capacity channel Φ as follows. Let

$$
A_1 = \begin{pmatrix} 0 & 0 & \alpha & 0 \\ 0 & 0 & 0 & 0 \\ \gamma & 0 & 0 & 0 \\ 0 & \gamma & 0 & 0 \end{pmatrix}, \quad
A_2 = \begin{pmatrix} 0 & 0 & 0 & 0 \\ 0 & 0 & 0 & \alpha \\ -\gamma & 0 & 0 & 0 \\ 0 & \gamma & 0 & 0 \end{pmatrix},
$$

$$
A_3 = \begin{pmatrix} \beta & 0 & 0 & 0 \\ 0 & 0 & 0 & 0 \\ 0 & 0 & \beta & 0 \\ 0 & 0 & 0 & 0 \end{pmatrix}, \quad
A_4 = \begin{pmatrix} 0 & 0 & 0 & 0 \\ \beta & 0 & 0 & 0 \\ 0 & 0 & 0 & \beta \\ 0 & 0 & 0 & 0 \end{pmatrix}, \tag{8.507}
$$

$$
A_5 = \begin{pmatrix} 0 & 0 & 0 & 0 \\ 0 & \beta & 0 & 0 \\ 0 & 0 & 0 & 0 \\ 0 & 0 & 0 & -\beta \end{pmatrix}, \quad
A_6 = \begin{pmatrix} 0 & \beta & 0 & 0 \\ 0 & 0 & 0 & 0 \\ 0 & 0 & 0 & 0 \\ 0 & 0 & \beta & 0 \end{pmatrix},
$$

where

$$\alpha = \sqrt{\sqrt{2} - 1}, \quad \beta = \sqrt{1 - \frac{1}{\sqrt{2}}}, \quad \text{and} \quad \gamma = \sqrt{\frac{1}{\sqrt{2}} - \frac{1}{2}}, \tag{8.508}$$

and define $\Phi \in C(\mathbb{C}^4)$ as

$$\Phi(X) = \sum_{k=1}^{6} A_k X A_k^* \tag{8.509}$$

for every $X \in L(\mathbb{C}^4)$.

The fact that Φ is a zero-capacity channel follows from the fact that the Choi representation of Φ is a PPT operator. One way to verify this claim is to check that

$$(T \otimes \mathbb{1}_{L(\mathbb{C}^4)})(J(\Phi)) = J(\Theta) \tag{8.510}$$

for $\Theta \in C(\mathbb{C}^4)$ being the channel defined as

$$\Theta(X) = \sum_{k=1}^{6} B_k X B_k^* \tag{8.511}$$

for every $X \in L(\mathbb{C}^4)$, where

$$B_1 = \begin{pmatrix} 0 & 0 & \alpha & 0 \\ 0 & 0 & 0 & 0 \\ \gamma & 0 & 0 & 0 \\ 0 & \gamma & 0 & 0 \end{pmatrix}, \quad B_2 = \begin{pmatrix} 0 & 0 & 0 & 0 \\ 0 & 0 & 0 & \alpha \\ \gamma & 0 & 0 & 0 \\ 0 & -\gamma & 0 & 0 \end{pmatrix},$$

$$B_3 = \begin{pmatrix} \beta & 0 & 0 & 0 \\ 0 & 0 & 0 & 0 \\ 0 & 0 & \beta & 0 \\ 0 & 0 & 0 & 0 \end{pmatrix}, \quad B_4 = \begin{pmatrix} 0 & 0 & 0 & 0 \\ \beta & 0 & 0 & 0 \\ 0 & 0 & 0 & -\beta \\ 0 & 0 & 0 & 0 \end{pmatrix}, \tag{8.512}$$

$$B_5 = \begin{pmatrix} 0 & 0 & 0 & 0 \\ 0 & \beta & 0 & 0 \\ 0 & 0 & 0 & 0 \\ 0 & 0 & 0 & \beta \end{pmatrix}, \quad B_6 = \begin{pmatrix} 0 & \beta & 0 & 0 \\ 0 & 0 & 0 & 0 \\ 0 & 0 & 0 & 0 \\ 0 & 0 & \beta & 0 \end{pmatrix}.$$

It therefore follows from Proposition 8.61 that Φ has zero quantum capacity. A channel complementary to Φ is given by $\Psi \in C(\mathbb{C}^4, \mathbb{C}^6)$ defined as

$$\Psi(X) = \sum_{k=1}^{4} C_k X C_k^* \tag{8.513}$$

for every $X \in L(\mathbb{C}^4)$, where

$$
C_1 = \begin{pmatrix} 0 & 0 & \alpha & 0 \\ 0 & 0 & 0 & 0 \\ \beta & 0 & 0 & 0 \\ 0 & 0 & 0 & 0 \\ 0 & 0 & 0 & 0 \\ 0 & \beta & 0 & 0 \end{pmatrix}, \quad
C_2 = \begin{pmatrix} 0 & 0 & 0 & 0 \\ 0 & 0 & 0 & \alpha \\ 0 & 0 & 0 & 0 \\ \beta & 0 & 0 & 0 \\ 0 & \beta & 0 & 0 \\ 0 & 0 & 0 & 0 \end{pmatrix},
$$

$$
\tag{8.514}
$$

$$
C_3 = \begin{pmatrix} \gamma & 0 & 0 & 0 \\ -\gamma & 0 & 0 & 0 \\ 0 & 0 & \beta & 0 \\ 0 & 0 & 0 & \beta \\ 0 & 0 & 0 & 0 \\ 0 & 0 & 0 & 0 \end{pmatrix}, \quad
C_4 = \begin{pmatrix} 0 & \gamma & 0 & 0 \\ 0 & \gamma & 0 & 0 \\ 0 & 0 & 0 & 0 \\ 0 & 0 & 0 & 0 \\ 0 & 0 & 0 & -\beta \\ 0 & 0 & \beta & 0 \end{pmatrix}.
$$

Finally, define density operators

$$
\sigma_0 = \begin{pmatrix} \tfrac{1}{2} & 0 & 0 & 0 \\ 0 & \tfrac{1}{2} & 0 & 0 \\ 0 & 0 & 0 & 0 \\ 0 & 0 & 0 & 0 \end{pmatrix} \quad \text{and} \quad
\sigma_1 = \begin{pmatrix} 0 & 0 & 0 & 0 \\ 0 & 0 & 0 & 0 \\ 0 & 0 & \tfrac{1}{2} & 0 \\ 0 & 0 & 0 & \tfrac{1}{2} \end{pmatrix},
\tag{8.515}
$$

and define an ensemble $\eta \colon \{0,1\} \to \mathrm{Pos}(\mathbb{C}^4)$ as

$$
\eta(0) = \frac{1}{2}\sigma_0 \quad \text{and} \quad \eta(1) = \frac{1}{2}\sigma_1.
\tag{8.516}
$$

It holds that

$$
\Phi(\sigma_0) = \begin{pmatrix} \frac{2-\sqrt{2}}{2} & 0 & 0 & 0 \\ 0 & \frac{2-\sqrt{2}}{2} & 0 & 0 \\ 0 & 0 & \frac{\sqrt{2}-1}{2} & 0 \\ 0 & 0 & 0 & \frac{\sqrt{2}-1}{2} \end{pmatrix}
\tag{8.517}
$$

and

$$
\Phi(\sigma_1) = \begin{pmatrix} \frac{\sqrt{2}-1}{2} & 0 & 0 & 0 \\ 0 & \frac{\sqrt{2}-1}{2} & 0 & 0 \\ 0 & 0 & \frac{2-\sqrt{2}}{2} & 0 \\ 0 & 0 & 0 & \frac{2-\sqrt{2}}{2} \end{pmatrix},
\tag{8.518}
$$

while

$$\Psi(\sigma_0) = \Psi(\sigma_1) = \begin{pmatrix} \frac{\sqrt{2}-1}{2} & 0 & 0 & 0 & 0 & 0 \\ 0 & \frac{\sqrt{2}-1}{2} & 0 & 0 & 0 & 0 \\ 0 & 0 & \frac{2-\sqrt{2}}{4} & 0 & 0 & 0 \\ 0 & 0 & 0 & \frac{2-\sqrt{2}}{4} & 0 & 0 \\ 0 & 0 & 0 & 0 & \frac{2-\sqrt{2}}{4} & 0 \\ 0 & 0 & 0 & 0 & 0 & \frac{2-\sqrt{2}}{4} \end{pmatrix}. \tag{8.519}$$

One therefore has that

$$\chi(\Phi(\eta)) = H\Big(\tfrac{1}{4}, \tfrac{1}{4}, \tfrac{1}{4}, \tfrac{1}{4}\Big) - H\Big(\tfrac{2-\sqrt{2}}{2}, \tfrac{2-\sqrt{2}}{2}, \tfrac{\sqrt{2}-1}{2}, \tfrac{\sqrt{2}-1}{2}\Big) > \tfrac{1}{50}, \tag{8.520}$$

while $\chi(\Psi(\eta)) = 0$. By Theorem 8.63, there must exist a density operator $\rho \in D(\mathbb{C}^4 \otimes \mathbb{C}^4)$ such that

$$I_c(\rho; \Phi \otimes \Xi) > \frac{1}{100}, \tag{8.521}$$

for $\Xi \in C(\mathbb{C}^4, \mathbb{C} \oplus \mathbb{C}^4)$ being a 50%-erasure channel. One therefore has that $Q(\Phi) = Q(\Xi) = 0$, while $Q(\Phi \otimes \Xi) > 0$.

The Need for a Regularization in the Quantum Capacity Theorem

The super-activation example described above illustrates that the maximum coherent information is not additive; one has

$$I_c(\Phi \otimes \Xi) > I_c(\Phi) + I_c(\Xi) \tag{8.522}$$

for the channels Φ and Ξ specified in that example. As these channels are different, it does not follow immediately that a strict inequality of the form

$$I_c(\Psi^{\otimes n}) > n I_c(\Psi) \tag{8.523}$$

holds for any choice of a channel Ψ and a positive integer n. It is possible, however, to conclude that such an inequality does hold (for $n = 2$) using a direct sum construction along similar lines to the one used in the context of the Holevo capacity and minimum output entropy. The following three propositions that concern direct sums of channels will be used to reach this conclusion.

Proposition 8.64 *Let $\mathcal{X}_0$, $\mathcal{X}_1$, $\mathcal{Y}_0$, $\mathcal{Y}_1$, $\mathcal{Z}_0$, and $\mathcal{Z}_1$ be complex Euclidean spaces, and let $\Phi_0 \in C(\mathcal{X}_0, \mathcal{Y}_0)$, $\Phi_1 \in C(\mathcal{X}_1, \mathcal{Y}_1)$, $\Psi_0 \in C(\mathcal{X}_0, \mathcal{Z}_0)$, and $\Psi_1 \in C(\mathcal{X}_1, \mathcal{Z}_1)$ be channels such that Ψ_0 is complementary to Φ_0 and Ψ_1 is complementary to Φ_1. The channel $\Psi_0 \oplus \Psi_1$ is complementary to $\Phi_0 \oplus \Phi_1$.*

Proof Let $A_0 \in \mathrm{U}(\mathcal{X}_0, \mathcal{Y}_0 \otimes \mathcal{Z}_0)$ and $A_1 \in \mathrm{U}(\mathcal{X}_1, \mathcal{Y}_1 \otimes \mathcal{Z}_1)$ be isometries such that the following equations hold for all $X_0 \in \mathrm{L}(\mathcal{X}_0)$ and $X_1 \in \mathrm{L}(\mathcal{X}_1)$:

$$
\begin{aligned}
\Phi_0(X_0) = \mathrm{Tr}_{\mathcal{Z}_0}(A_0 X_0 A_0^*), \qquad \Psi_0(X_0) = \mathrm{Tr}_{\mathcal{Y}_0}(A_0 X_0 A_0^*), \\
\Phi_1(X_1) = \mathrm{Tr}_{\mathcal{Z}_1}(A_1 X_1 A_1^*), \qquad \Psi_1(X_1) = \mathrm{Tr}_{\mathcal{Y}_1}(A_1 X_1 A_1^*).
\end{aligned}
\tag{8.524}
$$

Let $W \in \mathrm{U}((\mathcal{Y}_0 \otimes \mathcal{Z}_0) \oplus (\mathcal{Y}_1 \otimes \mathcal{Z}_1), (\mathcal{Y}_0 \oplus \mathcal{Y}_1) \otimes (\mathcal{Z}_0 \oplus \mathcal{Z}_1))$ be the isometry defined by the equation

$$
\begin{aligned}
W((y_0 \otimes z_0) &\oplus (y_1 \otimes z_1)) \\
&= (y_0 \oplus 0) \otimes (z_0 \oplus 0) + (0 \oplus y_1) \otimes (0 \oplus z_1)
\end{aligned}
\tag{8.525}
$$

for every $y_0 \in \mathcal{Y}_0$, $y_1 \in \mathcal{Y}_1$, $z_0 \in \mathcal{Z}_0$, and $z_1 \in \mathcal{Z}_1$. The equations

$$
\begin{aligned}
(\Phi_0 \oplus \Phi_1)(X) = \mathrm{Tr}_{\mathcal{Z}_0 \oplus \mathcal{Z}_1}\left(W \begin{pmatrix} A_0 & 0 \\ 0 & A_1 \end{pmatrix} X \begin{pmatrix} A_0^* & 0 \\ 0 & A_1^* \end{pmatrix} W^* \right), \\
(\Psi_0 \oplus \Psi_1)(X) = \mathrm{Tr}_{\mathcal{Y}_0 \oplus \mathcal{Y}_1}\left(W \begin{pmatrix} A_0 & 0 \\ 0 & A_1 \end{pmatrix} X \begin{pmatrix} A_0^* & 0 \\ 0 & A_1^* \end{pmatrix} W^* \right)
\end{aligned}
\tag{8.526}
$$

hold for all $X \in \mathrm{L}(\mathcal{X}_0 \oplus \mathcal{X}_1)$, which implies that $\Psi_0 \oplus \Psi_1$ is complementary to $\Phi_0 \oplus \Phi_1$, as required. $\qquad\square$

Proposition 8.65 *Let $\Phi_0 \in \mathrm{C}(\mathcal{X}_0, \mathcal{Y}_0)$ and $\Phi_1 \in \mathrm{C}(\mathcal{X}_1, \mathcal{Y}_1)$ be channels, for $\mathcal{X}_0$, $\mathcal{X}_1$, $\mathcal{Y}_0$, and $\mathcal{Y}_1$ being complex Euclidean spaces, and let $\sigma \in \mathrm{D}(\mathcal{X}_0 \oplus \mathcal{X}_1)$ be an arbitrary state, written as*

$$
\sigma = \begin{pmatrix} \lambda \sigma_0 & X \\ X^* & (1-\lambda)\sigma_1 \end{pmatrix}
\tag{8.527}
$$

for $\lambda \in [0, 1]$, $\sigma_0 \in \mathrm{D}(\mathcal{X}_0)$, $\sigma_1 \in \mathrm{D}(\mathcal{X}_1)$, and $X \in \mathrm{L}(\mathcal{X}_1, \mathcal{X}_0)$. It holds that

$$
\mathrm{I}_c(\sigma; \Phi_0 \oplus \Phi_1) = \lambda \mathrm{I}_c(\sigma_0; \Phi_0) + (1-\lambda) \mathrm{I}_c(\sigma_1; \Phi_1).
\tag{8.528}
$$

Proof Observe first that

$$
\begin{aligned}
\mathrm{H}((\Phi_0 \oplus \Phi_1)(\sigma)) &= \mathrm{H}\begin{pmatrix} \lambda \Phi_0(\sigma_0) & 0 \\ 0 & (1-\lambda)\Phi_1(\sigma_1) \end{pmatrix} \\
&= \lambda \mathrm{H}(\Phi_0(\sigma_0)) + (1-\lambda)\mathrm{H}(\Phi_1(\sigma_1)) + \mathrm{H}(\lambda, 1-\lambda).
\end{aligned}
\tag{8.529}
$$

Assuming that $\mathcal{Z}_0$ and $\mathcal{Z}_1$ are complex Euclidean spaces and $\Psi_0 \in \mathrm{C}(\mathcal{X}_0, \mathcal{Z}_0)$ and $\Psi_1 \in \mathrm{C}(\mathcal{X}_1, \mathcal{Z}_1)$ are channels complementary to Φ_0 and Φ_1, respectively, one has that

$$
\begin{aligned}
\mathrm{H}((\Psi_0 \oplus \Psi_1)(\sigma)) \\
= \lambda \mathrm{H}(\Psi_0(\sigma_0)) + (1-\lambda)\mathrm{H}(\Psi_1(\sigma_1)) + \mathrm{H}(\lambda, 1-\lambda)
\end{aligned}
\tag{8.530}
$$

by a similar calculation to (8.529). As $\Psi_0 \oplus \Psi_1$ is complementary to $\Phi_0 \oplus \Phi_1$, as established in Proposition 8.64, it follows that

$$
\begin{aligned}
I_c(\sigma; \Phi_0 \oplus \Phi_1) &= H((\Phi_0 \oplus \Phi_1)(\sigma)) - H((\Psi_0 \oplus \Psi_1)(\sigma)) \\
&= \lambda(H(\Phi_0(\sigma_0)) - H(\Psi_0(\sigma_0))) \\
&\quad + (1 - \lambda)(H(\Phi_1(\sigma_1)) - H(\Psi_1(\sigma_1))) \\
&= \lambda I_c(\sigma_0; \Phi_0) + (1 - \lambda)I_c(\sigma_1; \Phi_1)
\end{aligned}
\tag{8.531}
$$

as required. $\qquad\square$

Proposition 8.66 *Let $\mathcal{X}_0$, $\mathcal{X}_1$, $\mathcal{Y}_0$, and $\mathcal{Y}_1$ be complex Euclidean spaces and let $\Phi_0 \in C(\mathcal{X}_0, \mathcal{Y}_0)$ and $\Phi_1 \in C(\mathcal{X}_1, \mathcal{Y}_1)$ be channels. It holds that*

$$
I_c((\Phi_0 \oplus \Phi_1) \otimes (\Phi_0 \oplus \Phi_1)) \geq I_c(\Phi_0 \otimes \Phi_1).
\tag{8.532}
$$

Proof Define an isometry $W \in U(\mathcal{X}_0 \otimes \mathcal{X}_1, (\mathcal{X}_0 \oplus \mathcal{X}_1) \otimes (\mathcal{X}_0 \oplus \mathcal{X}_1))$ by the equation

$$
W(x_0 \otimes x_1) = (x_0 \oplus 0) \otimes (0 \oplus x_1)
\tag{8.533}
$$

holding for all $x_0 \in \mathcal{X}_0$ and $x_1 \in \mathcal{X}_1$, and along similar lines, define an isometry $V \in U(\mathcal{Y}_0 \otimes \mathcal{Y}_1, (\mathcal{Y}_0 \oplus \mathcal{Y}_1) \otimes (\mathcal{Y}_0 \oplus \mathcal{Y}_1))$ by the equation

$$
V(y_0 \otimes y_1) = (y_0 \oplus 0) \otimes (0 \oplus y_1)
\tag{8.534}
$$

for all $y_0 \in \mathcal{Y}_0$ and $y_1 \in \mathcal{Y}_1$. One has that

$$
\begin{aligned}
&((\Phi_0 \oplus \Phi_1) \otimes (\Phi_0 \oplus \Phi_1))(W(X_0 \otimes X_1)W^*) \\
&\quad = \begin{pmatrix} \Phi_0(X_0) & 0 \\ 0 & 0 \end{pmatrix} \otimes \begin{pmatrix} 0 & 0 \\ 0 & \Phi_1(X_1) \end{pmatrix} \\
&\quad = V(\Phi_0(X_0) \otimes \Phi_1(X_1))V^*
\end{aligned}
\tag{8.535}
$$

for all $X_0 \in L(\mathcal{X}_0)$ and $X_1 \in L(\mathcal{X}_1)$.

For every choice of a density operator $\sigma \in D(\mathcal{X}_0 \otimes \mathcal{X}_1)$, it follows that

$$
I_c(W\sigma W^*; (\Phi_0 \oplus \Phi_1) \otimes (\Phi_0 \oplus \Phi_1)) = I_c(\sigma; \Phi_0 \otimes \Phi_1),
\tag{8.536}
$$

which implies the proposition. $\qquad\square$

Finally, consider the channel $\Psi = \Phi \oplus \Xi$, for Φ and Ξ as in the example of super-activation described above. By Proposition 8.65, one may conclude that $I_c(\Phi \oplus \Xi) = 0$, while Proposition 8.66 implies

$$
I_c((\Phi \oplus \Xi) \otimes (\Phi \oplus \Xi)) \geq I_c(\Phi \otimes \Xi) > 0.
\tag{8.537}
$$

It therefore holds that the channel $\Psi = \Phi \oplus \Xi$ satisfies the strict inequality (8.523) for $n = 2$.

As a consequence of this fact, one has that the quantum capacity and maximum coherent information differ for some channels. In this sense, the regularization in the quantum capacity theorem (Theorem 8.55) is similar to the one in the Holevo–Schumacher–Westmoreland theorem (Theorem 8.27) in that it cannot generally be removed.

8.4 Exercises

Exercise 8.1 Let $\Phi_0 \in C(\mathcal{X}_0, \mathcal{Y}_0)$ and $\Phi_1 \in C(\mathcal{X}_1, \mathcal{Y}_1)$ be channels, for an arbitrary choice of complex Euclidean spaces $\mathcal{X}_0$, $\mathcal{X}_1$, $\mathcal{Y}_0$, and $\mathcal{Y}_1$.

(a) Prove that

$$I_c(\Phi_0 \oplus \Phi_1) = \max\{I_c(\Phi_0), I_c(\Phi_1)\}. \tag{8.538}$$

(b) Prove that

$$\chi(\Phi_0 \oplus \Phi_1) = \max_{\lambda \in [0,1]} \Big(\lambda\chi(\Phi_0) + (1 - \lambda)\chi(\Phi_1) + H(\lambda, 1 - \lambda)\Big). \tag{8.539}$$

Exercise 8.2 Let $\mathcal{X}$, $\mathcal{Y}$, $\mathcal{Z}$, and $\mathcal{W}$ be complex Euclidean spaces, let $\Phi \in C(\mathcal{X}, \mathcal{Y})$ and $\Psi \in C(\mathcal{Z}, \mathcal{W})$ be channels, and assume that Φ is an entanglement-breaking channel (q.v. Exercise 6.1). Prove that the following identities hold:

(a) $H_{\min}(\Phi \otimes \Psi) = H_{\min}(\Phi) + H_{\min}(\Psi)$.
(b) $\chi(\Phi \otimes \Psi) = \chi(\Phi) + \chi(\Psi)$.
(c) $I_c(\Phi \otimes \Psi) = I_c(\Psi)$.

Exercise 8.3 Let $\Phi \in C(\mathcal{X}, \mathcal{Y})$ be a channel, for complex Euclidean spaces $\mathcal{X}$ and $\mathcal{Y}$. It is said that Φ is *degradable* if there exists a complex Euclidean space $\mathcal{Z}$ and a channel $\Psi \in C(\mathcal{Y}, \mathcal{Z})$ such that $\Psi\Phi$ is complementary to Φ.

(a) Prove that, for any choice of a degradable channel $\Phi \in C(\mathcal{X}, \mathcal{Y})$, states $\sigma_0, \sigma_1 \in D(\mathcal{X})$, and a real number $\lambda \in [0, 1]$, the following inequality holds:

$$I_c(\lambda\sigma_0 + (1 - \lambda)\sigma_1; \Phi) \geq \lambda I_c(\sigma_0; \Phi) + (1 - \lambda)I_c(\sigma_1; \Phi). \tag{8.540}$$

(Equivalently, the function $\sigma \mapsto I_c(\sigma; \Phi)$ defined on $D(\mathcal{X})$ is concave.)
(b) Prove that, for any choice of complex Euclidean spaces $\mathcal{X}$, $\mathcal{Y}$, $\mathcal{Z}$, and $\mathcal{W}$ and degradable channels $\Phi \in C(\mathcal{X}, \mathcal{Y})$ and $\Psi \in C(\mathcal{Z}, \mathcal{W})$, it holds that

$$I_c(\Phi \otimes \Psi) = I_c(\Phi) + I_c(\Psi). \tag{8.541}$$

Exercise 8.4 Let $\mathcal{X}$ be a complex Euclidean space, let $\lambda \in [0,1]$, and define a channel $\Xi \in C(\mathcal{X}, \mathbb{C} \oplus \mathcal{X})$ as

$$\Xi(X) = \begin{pmatrix} \lambda \operatorname{Tr}(X) & 0 \\ 0 & (1-\lambda)X \end{pmatrix} \tag{8.542}$$

for all $X \in L(\mathcal{X})$.

(a) Give a closed-form expression for the coherent information $I_c(\sigma; \Xi)$ of an arbitrary state $\sigma \in D(\mathcal{X})$ through Ξ.

(b) Give a closed-form expression for the entanglement-assisted classical capacity $C_E(\Xi)$ of Ξ.

(c) Give a closed-form expression for the quantum capacity $Q(\Xi)$ of Ξ.

The closed-form expressions for parts (b) and (c) should be functions of λ and $n = \dim(\mathcal{X})$ alone.

Exercise 8.5 Let n be a positive integer, let $\mathcal{X} = \mathbb{C}^{\mathbb{Z}_n}$, and let

$$\{W_{a,b} : a, b \in \mathbb{Z}_n\} \tag{8.543}$$

denote the set of discrete Weyl operators acting on $\mathcal{X}$ (q.v. Section 4.1.2 of Chapter 4). Also let $p \in P(\mathbb{Z}_n)$ be a probability vector, and define a channel $\Phi \in C(\mathcal{X})$ as

$$\Phi(X) = \sum_{a \in \mathbb{Z}_n} p(a) W_{0,a} X W_{0,a}^* \tag{8.544}$$

for all $X \in L(\mathcal{X})$. Prove that

$$I_c(\Phi) = \log(n) - H(p). \tag{8.545}$$

Exercise 8.6 For every positive integer n and every real number $\varepsilon \in [0,1]$, define a channel $\Phi_{n,\varepsilon} \in C(\mathbb{C}^n)$ as

$$\Phi_{n,\varepsilon} = \varepsilon \mathbb{1}_n + (1-\varepsilon)\Omega_n, \tag{8.546}$$

where $\mathbb{1}_n \in C(\mathbb{C}^n)$ and $\Omega_n \in C(\mathbb{C}^n)$ denote the identity and completely depolarizing channels defined with respect to the space $\mathbb{C}^n$.

(a) Prove that, for every choice of a positive real number K, there exists a choice of n and ε for which

$$C_E(\Phi_{n,\varepsilon}) \geq K\chi(\Phi_{n,\varepsilon}) > 0. \tag{8.547}$$

(b) Prove that the fact established by a correct answer to part (a) remains true when $\chi(\Phi_{n,\varepsilon})$ is replaced by $C(\Phi_{n,\varepsilon})$.

8.5 Bibliographic Remarks

The study of quantum channel capacities is, perhaps obviously, motivated in large part by Shannon's channel coding theorem (Shannon, 1948), and the goal of obtaining analogous statements for quantum channels. It was, however, realized early in the study of quantum information theory that there would not be a single capacity of a quantum channel, but rather several inequivalent but nevertheless fundamentally interesting capacities. The survey of Bennett and Shor (1998) provides a summary of what was known about channel capacities at a relatively early point in their study.

Holevo (1998) and Schumacher and Westmoreland (1997) independently proved the Holevo–Schumacher–Westmoreland theorem (Theorem 8.27), in both cases building on Hausladen, Jozsa, Schumacher, Westmoreland, and Wootters (1996). The definition of what is now called the Holevo capacity (or the *Holevo information* of a channel) originates with the work of Holevo and Schumacher and Westmoreland. Lemma 8.25 was proved by Hayashi and Nagaoka (2003), who used it in the analysis of generalizations of the Holevo–Schumacher–Westmoreland theorem.

The entanglement-assisted classical capacity theorem (Theorem 8.41) was proved by Bennett, Shor, Smolin, and Thapliyal (1999a). The proof of this theorem presented in this chapter is due to Holevo (2002). Lemma 8.38 is due to Adami and Cerf (1997).

Tasks that involve quantum information transmission through quantum channels, along with fundamental definitions connected with such tasks, were investigated by Schumacher (1996), Schumacher and Nielsen (1996), Adami and Cerf (1997), and Barnum, Nielsen, and Schumacher (1998), among others. The entanglement generation capacity of a channel was defined by Devetak (2005), and Theorems 8.45 and 8.46 follow from results proved by Barnum, Knill, and Nielsen (2000).

The coherent information of a state through a channel was defined by Schumacher and Nielsen (1996). Lloyd (1997) recognized the fundamental connection between the maximum coherent information of a channel and its quantum capacity, and provided a heuristic argument in support of the quantum capacity theorem (Theorem 8.55). The first rigorous proof of the quantum capacity theorem to be published was due to Devetak (2005). Shor reported a different proof of this theorem prior to Devetak's proof, although it was not published. A proof appearing in a subsequent paper of Hayden, Shor, and Winter (2008b) resembles Shor's original proof.

The proof of the quantum capacity theorem presented in this chapter is due to Hayden, M. Horodecki, Winter, and Yard (2008a), incorporating some simplifying ideas due to Klesse (2008), who independently proved the same theorem based on similar techniques. The phenomenon of decoupling (as represented by Lemma 8.49) provides a key step in this proof; this basic technique was used by Devetak (2005), and was identified explicitly by M. Horodecki, Oppenheim, and Winter (2007) and Abeyesinghe, Devetak, Hayden, and Winter (2009). Further information on decoupling can be found in the Ph.D. thesis of Dupuis (2009).

Shor (2004) proved that the non-additivity of Holevo capacity follows from the non-additivity of minimum output entropy. In the same paper, Shor also proved the converse implication, which naturally had greater relevance prior to Hastings' proof that the minimum output entropy is non-additive (Hastings, 2009), along with the equivalence of these two non-additivity statements with two other statements concerning the entanglement of formation. The direct sum construction of channels and its implications to the additivity of channel capacities was investigated by Fukuda and Wolf (2007).

The fact that the coherent information is not additive in general was first proved by DiVincenzo, Shor, and Smolin (1998). Various properties of quantum erasure channels were established by Bennett, DiVincenzo, and Smolin (1997). Theorem 8.63, along with the realization that it gives an example of the super-activation phenomenon, is due to Smith and Yard (2008). The channel Φ described in the chapter giving rise to an example of super-activation, which appears in Smith and Yard's paper as well, was identified by K. Horodecki, Pankowski, M. Horodecki, and P. Horodecki (2008), as it relates to a different capacity known as the *private capacity* of a channel.

References

Abeyesinghe, A., Devetak, I., Hayden, P., and Winter, A. 2009. The mother of all protocols: restructuring quantum information's family tree. *Proceedings of the Royal Society A*, **465**(2108), 2537–2563.

Adami, C., and Cerf, N. 1997. Von Neumann capacity of noisy quantum channels. *Physical Review A*, **56**(5), 3470–3483.

Aharonov, D., Kitaev, A., and Nisan, N. 1998. Quantum circuits with mixed states. Pages 20–30 of: *Proceedings of the 30th Annual ACM Symposium on Theory of Computing*.

Alber, G., Beth, T., Charnes, C., Delgado, A., Grassl, M., and Mussinger, M. 2001. Stabilizing distinguishable qubits against spontaneous decay by detected-jump correcting quantum codes. *Physical Review Letters*, **86**(19), 4402–4405.

Alberti, P. 1983. A note on the transition probability over C*-algebras. *Letters in Mathematical Physics*, **7**(1), 25–32.

Alberti, P., and Uhlmann, A. 1982. *Stochasticity and Partial Order*. Mathematics and Its Applications, vol. 9. D. Reidel.

Alberti, P., and Uhlmann, A. 1983. Stochastic linear maps and transition probability. *Letters in Mathematical Physics*, **7**(2), 107–112.

Ambainis, A., Nayak, A., Ta-Shma, A., and Vazirani, U. 1999. Dense quantum coding and a lower bound for 1-way quantum automata. Pages 376–383 of: *Proceedings of the Thirty-First Annual ACM Symposium on Theory of Computing*.

Ambainis, A., Nayak, A., Ta-Shma, A., and Vazirani, U. 2002. Dense quantum coding and quantum finite automata. *Journal of the ACM*, **49**(4), 496–511.

Ando, T. 1979. Concavity of certain maps on positive definite matrices and applications to Haramard products. *Linear Algebra and Its Applications*, **26**, 203–241.

Apostol, T. 1974. *Mathematical Analysis*, 2nd edn. Addison-Wesley.

Araki, H., and Lieb, E. 1970. Entropy inequalities. *Communications in Mathematical Physics*, **18**(2), 160–170.

Arias, A., Gheondea, A., and Gudder, S. 2002. Fixed points of quantum operations. *Journal of Mathematical Physics*, **43**(12), 5872–5881.

Arveson, W. 1969. Subalgebras of C*-algebras. *Acta Mathematica*, **123**(1), 141–224.

Ash, R. 1990. *Information Theory*. Dover. Originally published in 1965 by Interscience.

Aubrun, G., Szarek, S., and Werner, E. 2011. Hastings' additivity counterexample via Dvoretzky's theorem. *Communications in Mathematical Physics*, **305**(1), 85–97.

Audenaert, K. 2007. A sharp Fannes-type inequality for the von Neumann entropy. *Journal of Physics A: Mathematical and Theoretical*, **40**(28), 8127–8136.

Audenaert, K., and Scheel, S. 2008. On random unitary channels. *New Journal of Physics*, **10**, 023011.

Axler, S. 1997. *Linear Algebra Done Right*, 2nd edn. Springer.

Barnum, H., and Knill, E. 2002. Reversing quantum dynamics with near-optimal quantum and classical fidelity. *Journal of Mathematical Physics*, **43**(5), 2097–2106.

Barnum, H., Nielsen, M., and Schumacher, B. 1998. Information transmission through a noisy quantum channel. *Physical Review A*, **57**(6), 4153–4175.

Barnum, H., Knill, E., and Nielsen, M. 2000. On quantum fidelities and channel capacities. *IEEE Transactions on Information Theory*, **46**(4), 1317–1329.

Barrett, J. 2002. Nonsequential positive-operator-valued measurements on entangled mixed states do not always violate a Bell inequality. *Physical Review A*, **65**(4), 042302.

Bartle, R. 1966. *The Elements of Integration*. John Wiley & Sons.

Beckman, D., Gottesman, D., Nielsen, M., and Preskill, J. 2001. Causal and localizable quantum operations. *Physical Review A*, **64**(5), 52309.

Belavkin, V. 1975. Optimal multiple quantum statistical hypothesis testing. *Stochastics*, **1**, 315–345.

Bell, J. 1964. On the Einstein Podolsky Rosen paradox. *Physics*, **1**(3), 195–200.

Ben-Aroya, A., and Ta-Shma, A. 2010. On the complexity of approximating the diamond norm. *Quantum Information and Computation*, **10**(1), 77–86.

Bengtsson, I., and Życzkowski, K. 2006. *Geometry of Quantum States*. Cambridge University Press.

Bennett, C., and Shor, P. 1998. Quantum information theory. *IEEE Transactions on Information Theory*, **44**(6), 2724–2742.

Bennett, C., and Wiesner, S. 1992. Communication via one- and two-particle operators on Einstein–Podolsky–Rosen states. *Physical Review Letters*, **69**(20), 2881–2884.

Bennett, C., Brassard, G., Crépeau, C., Jozsa, R., Peres, A., and Wootters, W. 1993. Teleporting an unknown quantum state via dual classical and EPR channels. *Physical Review Letters*, **70**(12), 1895–1899.

Bennett, C., Bernstein, H., Popescu, S., and Schumacher, B. 1996a. Concentrating partial entanglement by local operations. *Physical Review A*, **53**(4), 2046–2052.

Bennett, C., DiVincenzo, D., Smolin, J., and Wootters, W. 1996b. Mixed-state entanglement and quantum error correction. *Physical Review A*, **54**(5), 3824–3851.

Bennett, C., Brassard, G., Popescu, S., Schumacher, B., Smolin, J., and Wootters, W. 1996c. Purification of noisy entanglement and faithful teleportation via noisy channels. *Physical Review Letters*, **76**(5), 722–725.

Bennett, C., DiVincenzo, D., and Smolin, J. 1997. Capacities of quantum erasure channels. *Physical Review Letters*, **78**(16), 3217–3220.

Bennett, C., Shor, P., Smolin, J., and Thapliyal, A. 1999a. Entanglement-assisted classical capacity of noisy quantum channels. *Physical Review Letters*, **83**(15), 3081–3084.

Bennett, C., DiVincenzo, D., Fuchs, C., Mor, T., Rains, E., Shor, P., Smolin, J., and Wootters, W. 1999b. Quantum nonlocality without entanglement. *Physical Review A*, **59**, 1070–1091.

Bennett, C., DiVincenzo, D., Mor, T., Shor, P., Smolin, J., and Terhal, B. 1999c. Unextendible product bases and bound entanglement. *Physical Review Letters*, **82**(26), 5385–5388.

Bennett, C., Hayden, P., Leung, D., Shor, P., and Winter, A. 2005. Remote preparation of quantum states. *IEEE Transactions on Information Theory*, **51**(1), 56–74.

Bhatia, R. 1997. *Matrix Analysis*. Springer.

Bratteli, O., Jorgensen, P., Kishimoto, A., and Werner, R. 2000. Pure states on $\mathcal{O}_d$. *Journal of Operator Theory*, **43**(1), 97–143.

Buscemi, F. 2006. On the minimum number of unitaries needed to describe a random-unitary channel. *Physics Letters A*, **360**(2), 256–258.

Caves, C., Fuchs, C., and Schack, R. 2002. Unknown quantum states: the quantum de Finetti representation. *Journal of Mathematical Physics*, **43**(9), 4537–4559.

Childs, A., Preskill, J., and Renes, J. 2000. Quantum information and precision measurement. *Journal of Modern Optics*, **47**(2–3), 155–176.

Childs, A., Leung, D., Mančinska, L., and Ozols, M. 2013. A framework for bounding nonlocality of state discrimination. *Communications in Mathematical Physics*, **323**(3), 1121–1153.

Chiribella, G., D'Ariano, G., and Perinotti, P. 2008. Transforming quantum operations: quantum supermaps. *Europhysics Letters*, **83**(3), 30004.

Chiribella, G., D'Ariano, G., and Perinotti, P. 2009. Theoretical framework for quantum networks. *Physical Review A*, **80**(2), 022339.

Chitambar, E., Leung, D., Mančinska, L., Ozols, M., and Winter, A. 2014. Everything you always wanted to know about LOCC (but were afraid to ask). *Communications in Mathematical Physics*, **328**(1), 303–326.

Choi, M.-D. 1975. Completely positive linear maps on complex matrices. *Linear Algebra and Its Applications*, **10**(3), 285–290.

Christandl, M., König, R., Mitchison, G., and Renner, R. 2007. One-and-a-half quantum de Finetti theorems. *Communications in Mathematical Physics*, **273**(2), 473–498.

Clauser, J., Horne, M., Shimony, A., and Holt, R. 1969. Proposed experiment to test local hidden-variable theories. *Physical Review Letters*, **23**(15), 880–884.

Cover, T., and Thomas, J. 2006. *Elements of Information Theory*, 2nd edn. Wiley Interscience.

Davies, E. 1970. On the repeated measurement of continuous observables in quantum mechanics. *Journal of Functional Analysis*, **6**(2), 318–346.

Davies, E., and Lewis, J. 1970. An operational approach to quantum probability. *Communications in Mathematical Physics*, **17**, 239–260.

de Finetti, B. 1937. La prévision : ses lois logiques, ses sources subjectives. *Annales de l'Institut Henri Poincaré*, **7**(1), 1–68.

de Pillis, J. 1967. Linear transformations which preserve Hermitian and positive semidefinite operators. *Pacific Journal of Mathematics*, **23**(1), 129–137.

Deiks, D. 1982. Communication by EPR devices. *Physical Letters A*, **92**(6), 271–272.

Devetak, I. 2005. The private classical capacity and quantum capacity of a quantum channel. *IEEE Transactions on Information Theory*, **51**(1), 44–55.

Diaconis, P., and Freedman, D. 1980. Finite exchangeable sequences. *Annals of Probability*, **8**(4), 745–764.

Diaconis, P., and Shahshahani, M. 1987. The subgroup algorithm for generating uniform random variables. *Probability in the Engineering and Informational Sciences*, **1**(1), 15–32.

DiVincenzo, D., Shor, P., and Smolin, J. 1998. Quantum-channel capacity of very noisy channels. *Physical Review A*, **57**(2), 830–839.

Dupuis, F. 2009. *The Decoupling Approach to Quantum Information Theory*. Ph.D. thesis, Université de Montréal.

Dvoretzky, A. 1961. Some results on convex bodies and Banach spaces. Pages 123–160 of: *Proceedings of the International Symposium on Linear Spaces (Held at the Hebrew University of Jerusalem, July 1960)*.

Dyson, F. 1962a. Statistical theory of the energy levels of complex systems. I. *Journal of Mathematical Physics*, **3**(1), 140–156.

Dyson, F. 1962b. Statistical theory of the energy levels of complex systems. II. *Journal of Mathematical Physics*, **3**(1), 157–165.

Dyson, F. 1962c. Statistical theory of the energy levels of complex systems. III. *Journal of Mathematical Physics*, **3**(1), 166–175.

Eggeling, T., Schlingemann, D., and Werner, R. 2002. Semicausal operations are semilocalizable. *Europhysics Letters*, **57**(6), 782–788.

Einstein, A., Podolsky, B., and Rosen, N. 1935. Can quantum-mechanical description of physical reality be considered complete? *Physical Review*, **47**(10), 777–780.

Eldar, Y., and Forney, D. 2001. On quantum detection and the square-root measurement. *IEEE Transactions on Information Theory*, **47**(3), 858–872.

Eldar, Y., Megretski, A., and Verghese, G. 2003. Designing optimal quantum detectors via semidefinite programming. *IEEE Transactions on Information Theory*, **49**(4), 1007–1012.

Fannes, M. 1973. A continuity property of the entropy density for spin lattice systems. *Communications in Mathematical Physics*, **31**(4), 291–294.

Feller, W. 1968. *An Introduction to Probability Theory and Its Applications*, 3rd edn, vol. I. John Wiley & Sons.

Feller, W. 1971. *An Introduction to Probability Theory and Its Applications*, 2nd edn, vol. II. John Wiley & Sons.

Fuchs, C., and Caves, C. 1995. Mathematical techniques for quantum communication theory. *Open Systems & Information Dynamics*, **3**(3), 345–356.

Fuchs, C., and van de Graaf, J. 1999. Cryptographic distinguishability measures for quantum-mechanical states. *IEEE Transactions on Information Theory*, **45**(4), 1216–1227.

Fukuda, M., and Wolf, M. 2007. Simplifying additivity problems using direct sum constructions. *Journal of Mathematical Physics*, **48**(7), 072101.

Gheorghiu, V., and Griffiths, R. 2008. Separable operations of pure states. *Physical Review A*, **78**(2), 020304.

Gilchrist, A., Langford, N., and Nielsen, M. 2005. Distance measures to compare real and ideal quantum processes. *Physical Review A*, **71**(6), 062310.

Goodman, R., and Wallach, N. 1998. *Representations and Invariants of the Classical Groups*. Encyclopedia of Mathematics and Its Applications, vol. 68. Cambridge University Press.

Gregoratti, M., and Werner, R. 2003. Quantum lost and found. *Journal of Modern Optics*, **50**(67), 915–933.

Greub, W. 1978. *Multilinear Algebra*, 2nd edn. Springer.

Gurvits, L. 2003. Classical deterministic complexity of Edmonds' problem and quantum entanglement. Pages 10–19 of: *Proceedings of the Thirty-Fifth Annual ACM Symposium on Theory of Computing*.

Gurvits, L., and Barnum, H. 2002. Largest separable balls around the maximally mixed bipartite quantum state. *Physical Review A*, **66**(6), 062311.

Gutoski, G., and Watrous, J. 2005. Quantum interactive proofs with competing provers. Pages 605–616 of: *Proceedings of the 22nd Symposium on Theoretical Aspects of Computer Science*. Lecture Notes in Computer Science, vol. 3404. Springer.

Gutoski, G., and Watrous, J. 2007. Toward a general theory of quantum games. Pages 565–574 of: *Proceedings of the 39th Annual ACM Symposium on Theory of Computing*.

Haag, R., and Kastler, D. 1964. An algebraic approach to quantum field theory. *Journal of Mathematical Physics*, **5**(7), 848–861.

Haar, A. 1933. Der Massbegriff in der Theorie der kontinuierlichen Gruppen. *Annals of Mathematics (Second Series)*, **34**(1), 147–169.

Halmos, P. 1974. *Measure Theory*. Springer. Originally published in 1950 by Litton Educational.

Halmos, P. 1978. *Finite-Dimensional Vector Spaces*. Springer. Originally published in 1942 by Princeton University Press.

Harrow, A., Hayden, P., and Leung, D. 2004. Superdense coding of quantum states. *Physical Review Letters*, **92**(18), 187901.

Hastings, M. 2009. Superadditivity of communication capacity using entangled inputs. *Nature Physics*, **5**(4), 255–257.

Hausladen, P., and Wootters, W. 1994. A "pretty good" measurement for distinguishing quantum states. *Journal of Modern Optics*, **41**(12), 2385–2390.

Hausladen, P., Jozsa, R., Schumacher, B., Westmoreland, M., and Wootters, W. 1996. Classical information capacity of a quantum channel. *Physical Review A*, **54**(3), 1869–1876.

Hayashi, M., and Nagaoka, H. 2003. General formulas for capacity of classical–quantum channels. *IEEE Transactions on Information Theory*, **49**(7), 1753–1768.

Hayden, P., and Winter, A. 2008. Counterexamples to the maximal p-norm multiplicativity conjecture for all $p > 1$. *Communications in Mathematical Physics*, **284**(1), 263–280.

Hayden, P., Leung, D., Shor, P., and Winter, A. 2004. Randomizing quantum states: constructions and applications. *Communications in Mathematical Physics*, **250**(2), 371–391.

Hayden, P., Leung, D., and Winter, A. 2006. Aspects of generic entanglement. *Communications in Mathematical Physics*, **265**(1), 95–117.

Hayden, P., Horodecki, M., Winter, A., and Yard, J. 2008a. A decoupling approach to the quantum capacity. *Open Systems & Information Dynamics*, **15**(1), 7–19.

Hayden, P., Shor, P., and Winter, A. 2008b. Random quantum codes from Gaussian ensembles and an uncertainty relation. *Open Systems & Information Dynamics*, **15**(1), 71–89.

Helstrom, C. 1967. Detection theory and quantum mechanics. *Information and Control*, **10**, 254–291.

Helstrom, C. 1976. *Quantum Detection and Estimation Theory*. Academic Press.

Hiai, F., Ohya, M., and Tsukada, M. 1981. Sufficiency, KMS condition and relative entropy in von Neumann algebras. *Pacific Journal of Mathematics*, **96**(1), 99–109.

Hoffman, K., and Kunze, R. 1971. *Linear Algebra*, 2nd edn. Prentice-Hall.

Holevo, A. 1972. An analogue of statistical decision theory and noncommutative probability theory. *Trudy Moskovskogo Matematicheskogo Obshchestva*, **26**, 133–149.

Holevo, A. 1973a. Bounds for the quantity of information transmitted by a quantum communication channel. *Problemy Peredachi Informatsii*, **9**(3), 3–11.

Holevo, A. 1973b. Information-theoretical aspects of quantum measurement. *Problemy Peredachi Informatsii*, **9**(2), 31–42.

Holevo, A. 1973c. Statistical decision theory for quantum systems. *Journal of Multivariate Analysis*, **3**, 337–394.

Holevo, A. 1973d. Statistical problems in quantum physics. Pages 104–119 of: *Proceedings of the Second Japan–USSR Symposium on Probability Theory*. Lecture Notes in Mathematics, vol. 330. Springer.

Holevo, A. 1993. A note on covariant dynamical semigroups. *Reports on Mathematical Physics*, **32**(2), 211–216.

Holevo, A. 1996. Covariant quantum Markovian evolutions. *Journal of Mathematical Physics*, **37**(4), 1812–1832.

Holevo, A. 1998. The capacity of the quantum channel with general signal states. *IEEE Transactions on Information Theory*, **44**(1), 269–273.

Holevo, A. 2002. On entanglement-assisted classical capacity. *Journal of Mathematical Physics*, **43**(9), 4326–4333.

Horn, A. 1954. Doubly stochastic matrices and the diagonal of a rotation matrix. *American Journal of Mathematics*, **76**(3), 620–630.

Horn, R., and Johnson, C. 1985. *Matrix Analysis*. Cambridge University Press.

Horodecki, K., Pankowski, L., Horodecki, M., and Horodecki, P. 2008. Low-dimensional bound entanglement with one-way distillable cryptographic key. *IEEE Transactions on Information Theory*, **54**(6), 2621–2625.

Horodecki, M., Horodecki, P., and Horodecki, R. 1996. Separability of mixed states: necessary and sufficient conditions. *Physics Letters A*, **223**(1), 1–8.

Horodecki, M., Horodecki, P., and Horodecki, R. 1998. Mixed-state entanglement and distillation: is there a "bound" entanglement in nature? *Physical Review Letters*, **80**(24), 5239–5242.

Horodecki, M., Oppenheim, J., and Winter, A. 2007. Quantum state merging and negative information. *Communications in Mathematical Physics*, **269**(1), 107–136.

Horodecki, P. 1997. Separability criterion and inseparable mixed states with positive partial transposition. *Physics Letters A*, **232**(5), 333–339.

Horodecki, P. 2001. From entanglement witnesses to positive maps: towards optimal characterisation of separability. Pages 299–307 of: Gonis, A., and Turchi, P. (eds), *Decoherence and Its Implications in Quantum Computing and Information Transfer*. NATO Science Series III: Computer and System Sciences, vol. 182. IOS Press.

Horodecki, R., Horodecki, P., Horodecki, M., and Horodecki, K. 2009. Quantum entanglement. *Reviews of Modern Physics*, **81**(865), 865–942.

Hudson, R., and Moody, G. 1976. Locally normal symmetric states and an analogue of de Finetti's theorem. *Zeitschrift für Wahrscheinlichkeitstheorie und Verwandte Gebiete*, **33**(4), 343–351.

Hughston, L., Jozsa, R., and Wootters, W. 1993. A complete classification of quantum ensembles having a given density matrix. *Physics Letters A*, **183**(1), 14–18.

Jain, R. 2005. Distinguishing sets of quantum states. Unpublished manuscript. Available as arXiv.org e-Print quant-ph/0506205.

Jamiołkowski, A. 1972. Linear transformations which preserve trace and positive semidefiniteness of operators. *Reports on Mathematical Physics*, **3**(4), 275–278.

Johnston, N., Kribs, D., and Paulsen, V. 2009. Computing stabilized norms for quantum operations. *Quantum Information and Computation*, **9**(1), 16–35.

Jozsa, R. 1994. Fidelity for mixed quantum states. *Journal of Modern Optics*, **41**(12), 2315–2323.

Killoran, N. 2012. *Entanglement Quantification and Quantum Benchmarking of Optical Communication Devices*. Ph.D. thesis, University of Waterloo.

Kitaev, A. 1997. Quantum computations: algorithms and error correction. *Russian Mathematical Surveys*, **52**(6), 1191–1249.

Kitaev, A., Shen, A., and Vyalyi, M. 2002. *Classical and Quantum Computation*. Graduate Studies in Mathematics, vol. 47. American Mathematical Society.

Klein, O. 1931. Zur quantenmechanischen Begründung des zweiten Hauptsatzes der Wärmelehre. *Zeitschrift für Physik*, **72**(11–12), 767–775.

Klesse, R. 2008. A random coding based proof for the quantum coding theorem. *Open Systems & Information Dynamics*, **15**(1), 21–45.

König, R., and Renner, R. 2005. A de Finetti representation for finite symmetric quantum states. *Journal of Mathematical Physics*, **46**(12), 122108.

Kraus, K. 1971. General state changes in quantum theory. *Annals of Physics*, **64**, 311–335.

Kraus, K. 1983. *States, Effects, and Operations: Fundamental Notions of Quantum Theory*. Springer.

Kretschmann, D., and Werner, R. 2004. *Tema con variazioni*: quantum channel capacity. *New Journal of Physics*, **6**(1), 26.

Kretschmann, D., Schlingemann, D., and Werner, R. 2008. The information–disturbance tradeoff and the continuity of Stinespring's representation. *IEEE Transactions on Information Theory*, **54**(4), 1708–1717.

Kribs, D. 2003. Quantum channels, wavelets, dilations and representations of $\mathcal{O}_n$. *Proceedings of the Edinburgh Mathematical Society (Series 2)*, **46**, 421–433.

Kullback, S., and Leibler, R. 1951. On information and sufficiency. *Annals of Mathematical Statistics*, **22**(1), 79–86.

Kümmerer, B., and Maassen, H. 1987. The essentially commutative dilations of dynamical semigroups on M_n. *Communications in Mathematical Physics*, **109**(1), 1–22.

Landau, L. 1927. Das Dämpfungsproblem in der Wellenmechanik. *Zeitschrift für Physik*, **45**, 430–441.

Landau, L., and Streater, R. 1993. On Birkhoff's theorem for doubly stochastic completely positive maps of matrix algebras. *Linear Algebra and Its Applications*, **193**, 107–127.

Lanford, O., and Robinson, D. 1968. Mean entropy of states in quantum-statistical mechanics. *Journal of Mathematical Physics*, **9**(7), 1120–1125.

Ledoux, M. 2001. *The Concentration of Measure Phenomenon*. Mathematical Surveys and Monographs, vol. 89. American Mathematical Society.

Lévy, P. 1951. *Problémes Concrets d'Analyse Fonctionelle*. Gauthier-Villars.

Lieb, E. 1973. Convex trace functions and the Wigner–Yanase–Dyson conjecture. *Advances in Mathematics*, **11**(3), 267–288.

Lieb, E., and Ruskai, M. 1973. Proof of the strong subadditivity of quantum-mechanical entropy. *Journal of Mathematical Physics*, **14**(12), 1938–1941.

Lindblad, G. 1974. Expectation and entropy inequalities for finite quantum systems. *Communications in Mathematical Physics*, **39**(2), 111–119.

Lindblad, G. 1999. A general no-cloning theorem. *Letters in Mathematical Physics*, **47**(2), 189–196.

Lloyd, S. 1997. Capacity of the noisy quantum channel. *Physical Review A*, **55**(3), 1613–1622.

Lo, H.-K., and Popescu, S. 2001. Concentrating entanglement by local actions: beyond mean values. *Physical Review A*, **63**(2), 022301.

Marcus, M. 1973. *Finite Dimensional Multilinear Algebra*, vol. 1. Marcel Dekker.

Marcus, M. 1975. *Finite Dimensional Multilinear Algebra*, vol. 2. Marcel Dekker.

Marshall, A., Olkin, I., and Arnold, B. 2011. *Inequalities: Theory of Majorization and Its Applications*, 2nd edn. Springer.

Maurey, B., and Pisier, G. 1976. Séries de variables aléatoires vectorielles indépendantes et propriétés géométriques des espaces de Banach. *Studia Mathematica*, **58**(1), 45–90.

Mehta, M. 2004. *Random Matrices*. Elsevier.

Mil'man, V. 1971. New proof of the theorem of A. Dvoretzky on intersections of convex bodies. *Functional Analysis and Its Applications*, **5**(4), 288–295.

Milman, V., and Schechtman, G. 1986. *Asymptotic Theory of Finite Dimensional Normed Spaces*. Lecture Notes in Mathematics, vol. 1200. Springer.

Naimark, M. 1943. On a representation of additive operator set functions. *Doklady Akademii Nauk SSSR*, **41**, 359–361.

Nathanson, M. 2005. Distinguishing bipartitite orthogonal states using LOCC: best and worst cases. *Journal of Mathematical Physics*, **46**(6), 062103.

Nayak, A. 1999a. *Lower Bounds for Quantum Computation and Communication*. Ph.D. thesis, University of California, Berkeley.

Nayak, A. 1999b. Optimal lower bounds for quantum automata and random access codes. Pages 369–376 of: *40th Annual IEEE Symposium on Foundations of Computer Science*.

Nielsen, M. 1999. Conditions for a class of entanglement transformations. *Physical Review Letters*, **83**(2), 436–439.

Nielsen, M. 2000. Probability distributions consistent with a mixed state. *Physical Review A*, **62**(5), 052308.

Nielsen, M., and Chuang, I. 2000. *Quantum Computation and Quantum Information*. Cambridge University Press.

Nielson, M. 1998. *Quantum Information Theory*. Ph.D. thesis, University of New Mexico.

Park, J. 1970. The concept of transition in quantum mechanics. *Foundations of Physics*, **1**(1), 23–33.

Parthasarathy, K. 1999. Extremal decision rules in quantum hypothesis testing. *Infinite Dimensional Analysis, Quantum Probability and Related Topics*, **2**(4), 557–568.

Paulsen, V. 2002. *Completely Bounded Maps and Operator Algebras*. Cambridge Studies in Advanced Mathematics. Cambridge University Press.

Peres, A. 1993. *Quantum Theory: Concepts and Methods*. Kluwer Academic.

Peres, A. 1996. Separability criterion for density matrices. *Physical Review Letters*, **77**(8), 1413–1415.

Peres, A., and Wootters, W. 1991. Optimal detection of quantum information. *Physical Review Letters*, **66**(9), 1119–1122.

Pérez-García, D., Wolf, M., Petz, D., and Ruskai, M. 2006. Contractivity of positive and trace-preserving maps under L_p norms. *Journal of Mathematical Physics*, **47**(8), 083506.

Pinsker, M. 1964. *Information and Information Stability of Random Variables and Processes*. Holden-Day.

Rains, E. 1997. Entanglement purification via separable superoperators. Unpublished manuscript. Available as arXiv.org e-Print quant-ph/9707002.

Rockafellar, R. 1970. *Convex Analysis*. Princeton University Press.

Rosenkrantz, R. (ed). 1989. *E. T. Jaynes: Papers on Probability, Statistics and Statistical Physics*. Kluwer Academic.

Rosgen, B., and Watrous, J. 2005. On the hardness of distinguishing mixed-state quantum computations. Pages 344–354 of: *Proceedings of the 20th Annual Conference on Computational Complexity*.

Rudin, W. 1964. *Principles of Mathematical Analysis*. McGraw–Hill.

Russo, B., and Dye, H. 1966. A note on unitary operators in C*-algebras. *Duke Mathematical Journal*, **33**(2), 413–416.

Schrödinger, E. 1935a. Die gegenwärtige Situation in der Quantenmechanik. *Naturwissenschaften*, **23**(48), 807–812.

Schrödinger, E. 1935b. Die gegenwärtige Situation in der Quantenmechanik. *Naturwissenschaften*, **23**(49), 823–828.

Schrödinger, E. 1935c. Die gegenwärtige Situation in der Quantenmechanik. *Naturwissenschaften*, **23**(50), 844–849.

Schrödinger, E. 1935d. Discussion of probability relations between separated systems. *Mathematical Proceedings of the Cambridge Philosophical Society*, **31**(4), 555–563.

Schrödinger, E. 1936. Probability relations between separated systems. *Mathematical Proceedings of the Cambridge Philosophical Society*, **32**(3), 446–452.

Schumacher, B. 1995. Quantum coding. *Physical Review A*, **51**(4), 2738–2747.

Schumacher, B. 1996. Sending entanglement through noisy quantum channels. *Physical Review A*, **54**(4), 2614–2628.

Schumacher, B., and Nielsen, M. 1996. Quantum data processing and error correction. *Physical Review A*, **54**(4), 2629–2635.

Schumacher, B., and Westmoreland, M. 1997. Sending classical information via noisy quantum channels. *Physical Review A*, **56**(1), 131–138.

Schur, I. 1923. Über eine Klasse von Mittelbildungen mit Anwendungen auf die Determinantentheorie. *Sitzungsberichte der Berliner Mathematischen Gesellschaft*, **22**, 9–20.

Schur, J. 1911. Bemerkungen zur Theorie der beschränkten Bilinearformen mit unendlich vielen Veränderlichen. *Journal für die reine und angewandte Mathematik*, **140**, 1–28.

Shannon, C. 1948. A mathematical theory of communication. *Bell System Technical Journal*, **27**, 379–423.

Shor, P. 2004. Equivalence of additivity questions in quantum information theory. *Communications in Mathematical Physics*, **246**(3), 453–472.

Simon, B. 1979. *Trace Ideals and Their Applications*. London Mathematical Society Lecture Note Series, vol. 35. Cambridge University Press.

Smith, G., and Yard, J. 2008. Quantum communication with zero-capacity channels. *Science*, **321**(5897), 1812–1815.

Smith, R. 1983. Completely bounded maps between C^*-algebras. *Journal of the London Mathematical Society*, **2**(1), 157–166.

Spekkens, R., and Rudolph, T. 2001. Degrees of concealment and bindingness in quantum bit commitment protocols. *Physical Review A*, **65**(1), 012310.

Stinespring, W. 1955. Positive functions on C^*-algebras. *Proceedings of the American Mathematical Society*, **6**(2), 211–216.

Størmer, E. 1963. Positive linear maps of operator algebras. *Acta Mathematica*, **110**(1), 233–278.

Talagrand, M. 2006. *The Generic Chaining: Upper and Lower Bounds of Stochastic Processes*. Springer.

Terhal, B., and Horodecki, P. 2000. Schmidt number for density matrices. *Physical Review A*, **61**(4), 040301.

Timoney, R. 2003. Computing the norms of elementary operators. *Illinois Journal of Mathematics*, **47**(4), 1207–1226.

Tregub, S. 1986. Bistochastic operators on finite-dimensional von Neumann algebras. *Izvestiya Vysshikh Uchebnykh Zavedenii Matematika*, **30**(3), 75–77.

Tribus, M., and McIrvine, E. 1971. Energy and information. *Scientific American*, **225**(3), 179–188.

Trimmer, J. 1980. The present situation in quantum mechanics: a translation of Schrödinger's "cat paradox" paper. *Proceedings of the American Philosophical Society*, **124**(5), 323–338.

Tsirel'son, B. 1987. Quantum analogues of the Bell inequalities. The case of two spatially separated domains. *Journal of Soviet Mathematics*, **36**, 557–570.

Uhlmann, A. 1971. Sätze über Dichtematrizen. *Wissenschaftliche Zeitschrift der Karl-Marx-Universitat Leipzig. Mathematisch-naturwissenschaftliche Reihe*, **20**(4/5), 633–653.

Uhlmann, A. 1972. Endlich-dimensionale Dichtematrizen I. *Wissenschaftliche Zeitschrift der Karl-Marx-Universitat Leipzig. Mathematisch-naturwissenschaftliche Reihe*, **21**(4), 421–452.

Uhlmann, A. 1973. Endlich-dimensionale Dichtematrizen II. *Wissenschaftliche Zeitschrift der Karl-Marx-Universitat Leipzig. Mathematisch-naturwissenschaftliche Reihe*, **22**(2), 139–177.

Uhlmann, A. 1976. The "transition probability" in the state space of a $*$-algebra. *Reports on Mathematical Physics*, **9**(2), 273–279.

Uhlmann, A. 1977. Relative entropy and the Wigner–Yanase–Dyson–Lieb concavity in an interpolation theory. *Communications in Mathematical Physics*, **54**(1), 21–32.

Umegaki, H. 1962. Conditional expectations in an operator algebra IV (entropy and information). *Kodai Mathematical Seminar Reports*, **14**(2), 59–85.

Vedral, V., Plenio, M., Rippin, M., and Knight, P. 1997. Quantifying entanglement. *Physical Review Letters*, **78**(12), 2275–2278.

von Neumann, J. 1927a. Thermodynamik quantenmechanischer Gesamtheiten. *Nachrichten von der Gesellschaft der Wissenschaften zu Göttingen*, **1**(11), 273–291.

von Neumann, J. 1927b. Wahrscheinlichkeitstheoretischer aufbau der Mechanik. *Nachrichten von der Gesellschaft der Wissenschaften zu Göttingen*, **1**(11), 245–272.

von Neumann, J. 1930. Zur Algebra der Funktionaloperationen und Theorie der normalen Operatoren. *Mathematische Annalen*, **102**(1), 370–427.

von Neumann, J. 1933. Die Einfuhrung analytischer Parameter in topologischen Gruppen. *Annals of Mathematics (Second Series)*, **34**(1), 170–179.

von Neumann, J. 1955. *Mathematical Foundations of Quantum Mechanics*. Princeton University Press. Originally published in German in 1932 as *Mathematische Grundlagen der Quantenmechanik*.

Walgate, J., Short, A., Hardy, L., and Vedral, V. 2000. Local distinguishability of multipartite orthogonal quantum states. *Physical Review Letters*, **85**(23), 4972–4975.

Watrous, J. 2005. Notes on super-operator norms induced by Schatten norms. *Quantum Information and Computation*, **5**(1), 58–68.

Watrous, J. 2008. Distinguishing quantum operations having few Kraus operators. *Quantum Information and Computation*, **8**(9), 819–833.

Watrous, J. 2009a. Mixing doubly stochastic quantum channels with the completely depolarizing channel. *Quantum Information and Computation*, **9**(5/6), 406–413.

Watrous, J. 2009b. Semidefinite programs for completely bounded norms. *Theory of Computing*, **5** (art. 11), 217–238.

Watrous, J. 2013. Simpler semidefinite programs for completely bounded norms. *Chicago Journal of Theoretical Computer Science*, **2013** (art. 8), 1–19.

Weil, A. 1979. *L'Intégration dans les Groupes Topologiques et ses Applications*, 2nd edn. Hermann. Originally published in 1940.

Werner, R. 1989. Quantum states with Einstein–Podolsky–Rosen correlations admitting a hidden-variable model. *Physical Review A*, **40**(8), 4277–4281.

Werner, R. 1998. Optimal cloning of pure states. *Physical Review A*, **58**(3), 1827–1832.

Werner, R. 2001. All teleportation and dense coding schemes. *Journal of Physics A: Mathematical and General*, **34**(35), 7081–7094.

Weyl, H. 1950. *The Theory of Groups and Quantum Mechanics*. Dover. Originally published in German in 1929.

Wiesner, S. 1983. Conjugate coding. *SIGACT News*, **15**(1), 78–88.

Wilde, M. 2013. *Quantum Information Theory*. Cambridge University Press.

Winter, A. 1999. Coding theorem and strong converse for quantum channels. *IEEE Transactions on Information Theory*, **45**(7), 2481–2485.

Wolkowicz, H., Saigal, R., and Vandenberge, L. (eds). 2000. *Handbook of Semidefinite Programming: Theory, Algorithms, and Applications*. Kluwer Academic.

Wootters, W., and Zurek, W. 1982. A single quantum cannot be cloned. *Nature*, **299**, 802–803.

Woronowicz, S. 1976. Positive maps of low dimensional matrix algebras. *Reports on Mathematical Physics*, **10**(2), 165–183.

Yang, D., Horodecki, M., Horodecki, R., and Synak-Radtke, B. 2005. Irreversibility for all bound entangled states. *Physical Review Letters*, **95**(19), 190501.

Yuen, H., Kennedy, R., and Lax, M. 1970. On optimal quantum receivers for digital signal detection. *Proceedings of the IEEE*, **58**(10), 1770–1773.

Yuen, H., Kennedy, R., and Lax, M. 1975. Optimum testing of multiple hypotheses in quantum detection theory. *IEEE Transactions on Information Theory*, **21**(2), 125–134.

Zarikian, V. 2006. Alternating-projection algorithms for operator-theoretic calculation. *Linear Algebra and Its Applications*, **419**(2–3), 710–734.

Życzkowski, K., Horodecki, P., Sanpera, A., and Lewenstein, M. 1998. Volume of the set of separable states. *Physical Review A*, **58**(2), 883–892.

Index of Symbols

$A_1 \otimes \cdots \otimes A_n$	The tensor product of operators $A_1, \ldots, A_n$.	13
$A^{\otimes n}$	The n-fold tensor product of an operator A with itself.	14
$\mathrm{L}(\mathcal{X})$	Space of linear operators mapping a complex Euclidean space $\mathcal{X}$ to itself.	14
$\mathbb{1}$	The identity operator; denoted $\mathbb{1}_{\mathcal{X}}$ when it is helpful to indicate that it acts on a complex Euclidean space $\mathcal{X}$.	14
X^{-1}	The inverse of an invertible square operator X.	14
$\mathrm{Tr}(X)$	The trace of a square operator X.	15
$\langle A, B \rangle$	The inner product of operators A and B.	15
$\mathrm{Det}(X)$	The determinant of a square operator X.	15
$\mathrm{Sym}(\Sigma)$	The set of permutations, or bijective functions, of the form $\pi : \Sigma \to \Sigma$.	15
$\mathrm{sign}(\pi)$	The sign, or parity, of a permutation π.	15
$\mathrm{spec}(X)$	The spectrum of a square operator X.	16
$[X, Y]$	The Lie bracket of square operators X and Y.	17
$\mathrm{comm}(\mathcal{A})$	The commutant of a set $\mathcal{A}$ of square operators.	17
$\mathrm{Herm}(\mathcal{X})$	The set of Hermitian operators acting on a complex Euclidean space $\mathcal{X}$.	17
$\mathrm{Pos}(\mathcal{X})$	The set of positive semidefinite operators acting on a complex Euclidean space $\mathcal{X}$.	17
$\mathrm{Pd}(\mathcal{X})$	The set of positive definite operators acting on a complex Euclidean space $\mathcal{X}$.	18

$\mathrm{Tr}_{\mathcal{X}}$	The partial trace over a complex Euclidean space $\mathcal{X}$.	22
$\mathrm{CP}(\mathcal{X}, \mathcal{Y})$	The set of completely positive maps of the form $\Phi \in \mathrm{T}(\mathcal{X}, \mathcal{Y})$.	23
$\mathrm{vec}(A)$	The vec mapping applied to an operator A.	23
$\sqrt{P}$	The square root of a positive semidefinite operator P.	27
$s(A)$	The vector of singular values of an operator A.	28
$s_k(A)$	The k-th largest singular value of an operator A.	28
A^+	The Moore–Penrose pseudo-inverse of an operator A.	30
$\|A\|_p, \|A\|_\infty$	The Schatten p-norm or ∞-norm of an operator A.	32
$\|A\|$	The spectral norm of an operator A. Equivalent to the Schatten ∞-norm of A.	33
$\|A\|_2$	The Frobenius norm of an operator A. Equivalent to the Schatten 2-norm of A.	33
$\|A\|_1$	The trace norm of an operator A. Equivalent to the Schatten 1-norm of A.	34
$\nabla f(x)$	The gradient vector of a function $f : \mathbb{R}^n \to \mathbb{R}$ at a vector $x \in \mathbb{R}^n$.	37
$(Df)(x)$	The derivative of a (differentiable) function $f : \mathbb{R}^n \to \mathbb{R}$ at a vector $x \in \mathbb{R}^n$.	37
$\mathcal{B}(\mathcal{X})$	The unit ball in a complex Euclidean space $\mathcal{X}$.	38
$\mathrm{Borel}(\mathcal{A})$	The collection of all Borel subsets of a subset $\mathcal{A}$ of a real or complex vector space.	38

$r(u)$	The vector obtained by sorting the entries of a real vector u from largest to smallest.	236
$r_k(u)$	The k-th largest entry of a real vector u.	236
$Y \prec X$	Indicates that X majorizes Y, for Hermitian operators X and Y.	241
S_n	The symmetric group on n symbols. Equivalent to $\mathrm{Sym}(\{1, \ldots, n\})$.	243
$\mathrm{H}(u)$	The Shannon entropy of a vector u with nonnegative real number entries.	251
$\mathrm{H}(\mathsf{X})$	The Shannon entropy of the probabilistic state of a classical register X, or the von Neumann entropy of the quantum state of a register X.	252, 266
$\mathrm{H}(\mathsf{X}_1, \ldots, \mathsf{X}_n)$	Refers to the Shannon entropy or von Neumann entropy of the compound register $(\mathsf{X}_1, \ldots, \mathsf{X}_n)$.	252, 266
$\mathrm{D}(u\|v)$	The relative entropy of u with respect to v, for vectors u and v with nonnegative real number entries.	252
$\mathrm{H}(\mathsf{X}|\mathsf{Y})$	The conditional Shannon entropy or von Neumann entropy of a register X with respect to a register Y.	252, 267
$\mathrm{I}(\mathsf{X} : \mathsf{Y})$	The mutual information or quantum mutual information between registers X and Y.	253, 267
$\mathrm{H}(P)$	The von Neumann entropy of a positive semidefinite operator P.	265
$\mathrm{D}(P\|Q)$	The quantum relative entropy of P with respect to Q, for positive semidefinite operators P and Q.	266

Index

Printed in the United States
By Bookmasters